ELEMENTS OF *Literature* PROGRAM

INTRODUCTORY COURSE

FIRST COURSE

SECOND COURSE

THIRD COURSE

FOURTH COURSE

FIFTH COURSE
Literature of the United States
***with* Literature of the Americas**

SIXTH COURSE
Literature of Britain
***with* World Classics**

When you set out for Ithaca,
pray that your road's a long one,
full of adventure, full of discovery.

— *from* "Ithaca," by C. P. Cavafy

ELEMENTS OF Literature

THIRD COURSE

HOLT, RINEHART AND **WINSTON**

Harcourt Brace & Company

Austin • New York • Orlando • Atlanta • San Francisco • Boston • Dallas • Toronto • London

CREDITS

EDITORIAL

Project Director: Kathleen Daniel
Managing Editor: Richard Sime
Senior Book Editor: Catherine Goodridge
Editorial Staff: Phyllis Goldenberg, Linda Bosson, Robert Hoyt, Karen Kolar, Jason Tougaw
Editorial Support: Isabell Coffey, Mark Koenig, Loretto Muir, Gail Neil
Editorial Permissions: Tamara Blanken, Carrie Jones

Research and Development: Joan Burditt

PRODUCTION, DESIGN, AND PHOTO RESEARCH

Director: Athena Blackorby
Program Design: Kirchoff/Wohlberg, Inc.
Design and Electronic Files: Bill Smith Studio
Production: Dolores Keller
Photo Research: Photosearch, Inc.
Photo Resources Coordinator: Mary Monaco
Cover: Compendium Design International, Inc.

COVER

Design: Caroline Abbott, Compendium Designs, Inc.
Photo credits: compass (front and back cover), The Granger Collection, New York; sky, Darryl Torckler/Tony Stone Images; ocean waves, Kim Westerskov/Tony Stone Images; rocks, © 1993 Christopher Talbot Frank; Dionysus' ship (front and back cover), photograph by Eric Lessing/Art Resource, New York.
Quotation: from "Ithaca" by C. P. Cavafy, translated by Edmund Keeley and Philip Sherrard, courtesy of Princeton University Press. For the complete poem, see text page 946.

Requests for permission to make copies of any part of the work should be mailed to: Permissions Department, Holt, Rinehart and Winston, 6277 Sea Harbor Drive, Orlando, Florida 32887–6777.

Material from earlier editions: copyright © by Holt, Rinehart and Winston. All rights reserved.

Acknowledgments appear on pages 1046–1049, which are an extension of the copyright page.

Printed in the United States of America
ISBN 0-03-096831-3

5 6 041 99 98

PROGRAM AUTHORS

Robert Anderson, John Malcolm Brinnin, and John Leggett established the literary framework of the Elements of Literature program and developed instructional materials for the elements of drama, poetry, and fiction, respectively. Robert Probst established the pedagogical focus for the 1997 edition, and he developed and evaluated preselection and postselection material. Judith L. Irvin established the conceptual basis for the vocabulary and reading strands in the pupil's editions for grades 6–8 and in the teacher's editions for grades 6–12.

Robert Probst is Professor of English Education at Georgia State University in Atlanta. For several years he was an English teacher—in both junior and senior high school—in Maryland and Supervisor of English for the Norfolk, Virginia, Public Schools. He is the author of *Response and Analysis: Teaching Literature in Junior and Senior High School.* He has also contributed chapters to such books as *Literature Instruction: A Focus on Student Response; Reader Response in the Classroom: Evoking and Interpreting Meaning in Literature; Handbook of Research on Teaching the English Language Arts; Transactions with Literature: A Fifty-Year Perspective;* and *For Louise M. Rosenblatt.* Dr. Probst has published articles in *English Journal, Journal of Reading, Educational Leadership, Revue des Langues Vivantes, The Clearing House,* and other publications. He is a member of the National Council of Teachers of English and has worked on the Council's Committee on Research, the Commission on Reading, and the Commission on Curriculum. Dr. Probst has also served on the Board of Directors of the Adolescent Literature Assembly. He is a colleague and faculty member of the Creative Education Foundation and a member of the National Conference on Language and Literacy.

Robert Anderson is a playwright, novelist, screenwriter, and teacher. His plays include *Tea and Sympathy; Silent Night, Lonely Night; You Know I Can't Hear You When the Water's Running;* and *I Never Sang for My Father.* His screenplays include *The Nun's Story* and *The Sand Pebbles.* Mr. Anderson has taught at The Writers' Workshop at the University of Iowa, the American Theater Wing Professional Training Program, and the Salzburg Seminar in American Studies. He is a past president of the Dramatists' Guild, vice president of the Authors' League of America, and a member of the Theater Hall of Fame. He lives in Connecticut and New York.

John Malcolm Brinnin, author of six volumes of poetry that have received many prizes and awards, is a member of the American Academy and Institute of Arts and Letters. He is also a critic of poetry and a biographer of poets and was for a number of years director of New York's famous Poetry Center. His teaching career, begun at Vassar College, included long terms at the University of Connecticut and Boston University, where he succeeded Robert Lowell as Professor of Creative Writing and Contemporary Letters. Mr. Brinnin has written *Dylan Thomas in America: An Intimate Journal* and *Sextet: T. S. Eliot & Truman Capote & Others.* His home is in Key West, Florida.

John Leggett is a novelist, a biographer, and a teacher. He went to The Writers' Workshop at the University of Iowa in the spring of 1969, expecting to work there for a single semester. In 1970, he assumed temporary charge of the program, and for the next seventeen years he was its director. Mr. Leggett's novels include *Wilder Stone, The Gloucester Branch, Who Took the Gold Away?, Gulliver House,* and *Making Believe.* He is also the author of the highly acclaimed biography *Ross and Tom: Two American Tragedies* and of the biography of William Saroyan called *A Daring Young Man.* A native of New York City, Mr. Leggett now lives in California's Napa Valley.

Judith L. Irvin teaches courses in curriculum, middle school education, and educational leadership at Florida State University. Dr. Irvin is Chair of the Research Committee of the National Middle School Association and was the editor of *Research in Middle Level Education* for five years. She taught middle school for eight years before seeking her doctorate in Reading–Language Arts. Dr. Irvin writes a column, "What Research Says to the Middle Level Practitioner," for the *Middle School Journal.* Her many books include *Transforming Middle Level Education: Prospectives and Possibilities* and *Reading and the Middle School Student: Strategies to Enhance Literacy.*

SPECIAL CONTRIBUTORS

The special contributors wrote essays for various collections of the text. Their essays are signed.

Janet Burroway is a novelist and teacher who has also written children's books and a popular textbook called *Writing Fiction*. Burroway has taught at the University of Sussex, England; the University of Illinois; and the Writer's Workshop at the University of Iowa. She is currently Robert O. Lawton Distinguished Professor at Florida State University in Tallahassee. Her novels include *The Buzzards* (nominated for the Pulitzer Prize), *Raw Silk* (nominated for the National Book Award), *Opening Nights,* and *Cutting Stone*. Burroway reviews regularly for *The New York Times Book Review*.

David Adams Leeming was for many years a Professor of English and Comparative Literature at the University of Connecticut. He is the author of several books on mythology, including *Mythology: The Voyage of the Hero; The World of Myth;* and *Encyclopedia of Creation Myths*. For several years he taught English at Robert College in Istanbul, Turkey. He also served as secretary and assistant to the writer James Baldwin in New York and Istanbul. In 1994, his biography of Baldwin was published. Leeming now lives in Albuquerque, New Mexico.

WRITERS

The writers prepared instructional materials for the text under the supervision of Dr. Probst and the editorial staff.

Phyllis Goldenberg
Educational writer and editor
Miami, Florida

Carl Morse
Educational writer and editor
New York, New York

Carroll Moulton
Former teacher
Educational writer and editor
Southampton, New York

Sandra Riggs
Former teacher
Educational writer and editor
Amherst, Massachusetts

Diane Tasca
Educational writer and editor
Palo Alto, California

REVIEWERS AND CONSULTANTS

The reviewers evaluated selections for use in the text and all instructional materials. Consultants assisted the editorial staff in securing student active-reading models and provided advice on current pedagogy.

Sonja Boland
Fridley High School
Fridley, Minnesota

Marilyn Rogers Brunoehler
Center Grove High School
Greenwood, Indiana

Charlene Couvillon
Teacher / Department
Chairperson
Fort Walton Beach High School
Fort Walton Beach, Florida

Beverly A. Davenport
Boone High School
Orlando, Florida

Sharon Davis
Provo High School
Provo, Utah

Brenda Doucey
Jack Robey Junior High School
Pine Bluff, Arkansas

Ann W. Ennis
South Rowan High School
China Grove, North Carolina

Raemi L. Evans
Salisbury High School
Salisbury, North Carolina

Ann Freelove
Oakmont High School
Roseville, California

Hannah Goolsby
Bowie High School
Arlington, Texas

Faith Greenfield
Miami Edison Senior High School
Miami, Florida

Connie Guida
Fort Zumwalt North High School
O'Fallon, Missouri

Louise Jones
Central High School
San Angelo, Texas

Katherine Kelly-Garris
Penn-Trafford High School
Harrison City, Pennsylvania

Dona Langhals
Gahanna Lincoln High School
Gahanna, Ohio

Nancy Light
Clarence High School
Clarence, New York

Karen Littlejohn
Harrison High School
Colorado Springs, Colorado

Margaret Oberender
Westwood High School
Austin, Texas

Kay Price-Hawkins
Region 14 Education Service
Center
Abilene, Texas

Linda Sanders
Jenks High School
Jenks, Oklahoma

Janet Scarboro
Southeast High School
Bradenton, Florida

Reba E. Scott
Forest Brook High School
Houston, Texas

Lana Taylor
West Center for International
Learning
Colorado Springs, Colorado

Joanne M. Walen
Formerly of Washoe County
School District
Reno, Nevada

Annette Wallace
MacArthur High School
Irving, Texas

Denise Walsh
Warren High School
Downey, California

Lois Willett
Johnston High School
Austin, Texas

Ramona Wood
Cy Creek High School
Houston, Texas

Field-Test Participants

The following teachers participated in field-testing of prepublication materials for the series.

Janet Blackburn-Lewis
Western Guilford High School
Greensboro, North Carolina

Dana E. Bull
F. J. Turner High School
Beloit, Wisconsin

Maura Casey
Skyline High School
Oakland, California

Deborah N. Dean
Warner Robins Middle School
Warner Robins, Georgia

Gloria J. Dolesh
Friendly High School
Fort Washington, Maryland

Christina Donnelly
Parkdale High School
Riverdale, Maryland

Kay T. Dunlap
Norview High School
Norfolk, Virginia

Joseph Fitzgibbon
West Linn High School
West Linn, Oregon

Paul Garro
Taft High School
San Antonio, Texas

Suzanne Haffamier
Agoura High School
Agoura, California

Robert K. Jordan
Land O' Lakes High School
Land O' Lakes, Florida

Terry Juhl
Bella Vista High School
Fair Oaks, California

Elizabeth Keister
Blair Middle School
Norfolk, Virginia

Jane S. Kilgore
Warner Robins High School
Warner Robins, Georgia

Janet S. King
Reading High School
Reading, Pennsylvania

Cheryl L. Lambert
Milford Mill Academy
Baltimore, Maryland

Sarah A. Long
Robert Goddard Middle School
Seabrook, Maryland

Margaret E. McKinnon
Roger L. Putnam Vocational-
Technical High School
Springfield, Massachusetts

Donna J. Magrum
Rogers High School
Toledo, Ohio

Nancy Maheras
Western High School
Las Vegas, Nevada

Mara Malone
Central High School
Baton Rouge, Louisiana

Lourdes J. Medina
Pat Neff Middle School
San Antonio, Texas

Joan Mohon
Todd County Central High
School
Elkton, Kentucky

Terrence R. Moore
John Muir High School
Pasadena, California

Gayle C. Morey
Countryside High School
Clearwater, Florida

Beverly Mudd
Western High School
Las Vegas, Nevada

Jan Nichols
Apollo High School
Glendale, Arizona

Jeffrey S. Norton
Lewis and Clark High School
Spokane, Washington

Barbara Powell
Todd County Central High
School
Elkton, Kentucky

Gloria S. Pridmore
Morrow High School
Morrow, Georgia

Dee Richardson
Moore High School
Moore, Oklahoma

Carole A. Scala
Southwest Middle School
Orlando, Florida

Barbara A. Slaughter
Lewis and Clark High School
Spokane, Washington

Barbara B. Smith
Dr. Phillips 9th-Grade Center
Orlando, Florida

Sister Eileen Stephens, CSJ
Cathedral Preparatory Seminary
Elmhurst, New York

Sally Thompson
Andrew Jackson Middle School
Suitland, Maryland

Blanca M. Valledor
G. Holmes Braddock Senior High
School
Miami, Florida

Charla J. Walton
John C. Fremont Junior High
School
Las Vegas, Nevada

William Ward
Roger L. Putnam Vocational-
Technical High School
Springfield, Massachusetts

Lynn White
Tascosa High School
Amarillo, Texas

Noretta M. Willig
Baldwin High School
Pittsburgh, Pennsylvania

Deborah K. Woelflein
Merrimack High School
Merrimack, New Hampshire

Student Contributors

The following students wrote annotations for the Reader's Log models.

Erika Cole
Southeast High School
Bradenton, Florida

Wendy Forrest
Westwood High School
Austin, Texas

Janelle Jones
Southeast High School
Bradenton, Florida

CONTENTS

The Short-Story Collections

There have been great societies that did not use the wheel, but there have been no societies that did not tell stories.

—Ursula LeGuin

COLLECTION 1

FACING MONSTERS

The harder the conflict, the more glorious the triumph.

—Thomas Paine

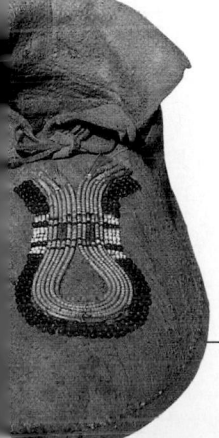

The Nonfiction Collections

*If you believe in the power of words, you can
bring about physical changes in the universe.*

—N. Scott Momaday

COLLECTION 5

WE REMEMBER

*Some memories are realities and are better than
anything that can ever happen to one again.*

—Willa Cather

COLLECTION *6*

A PLACE CALLED HOME

Home is where one starts from.

—T. S. Eliot

COLLECTION 7

WHAT I THINK

How can I know what I think till I see what I say?

—A little girl, on being told to think before she speaks

The Poetry Collections

*A word is dead
When it is said,
Some say.
I say it just
Begins to live
That day.*

—Emily Dickinson

COLLECTION *8*

SEE THE MIRACLES

*To me every hour of the light and dark is a miracle,
Every cubic inch of space is a miracle.*

—Walt Whitman

IMAGINE

*Think with your body
And dance with your mind.*

—Victor Hernandez Cruz

THE WAYS WE ARE

*Each of us inevitable;
Each of us limitless—each of us with his or her right upon the earth . . .
Each of us here as divinely as any is here.*

—Walt Whitman

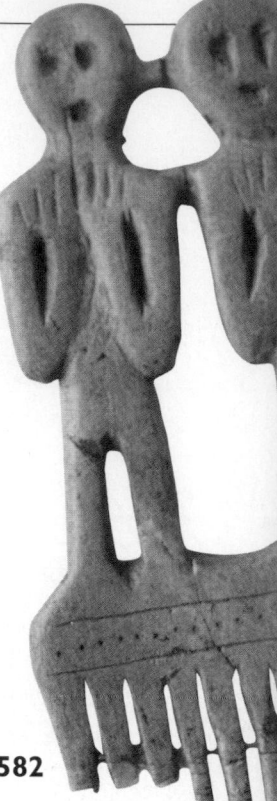

COLLECTION *11*	# SAY IT!

*Whatever we have dared to think
That dared we also say.*

—James Russell Lowell

Modern Drama

*What does theater give us that nothing else can
—not so intensely anyway, or so pleasurably?
It gives us human beings in three dimensions:
bodies that live in front of us, that move, speak,
change shape, create tension, or bestow peace.*

—Margo Jefferson

COLLECTION *12*

OPENING DOORS

A journey of a thousand miles must begin with a single step.

—Laotzu

William Shakespeare

All the world's a stage....
—*As You Like It*
(Act II, Scene 7)

THE DESTRUCTION OF INNOCENCE

COLLECTION 13

Whoever loved that loved not at first sight?
—Christopher Marlowe

The Epic

An epic is an encyclopedia of the manners, customs, and values that bind a whole civilization together.

—W. T. Jewkes

THE PERILOUS JOURNEY

If we are fortunate, if the gods and muses are smiling, about every generation someone comes along to inspire the imagination for the journey each of us takes.

—Bill Moyers

RESOURCE CENTER

The Short-Story Collections

The Journey (1991) by Mel Rosas. Oil on wood.
Courtesy Maxwell Davidson Gallery, New York.

> There have been great societies that did not use the wheel, but there have been no societies that did not tell stories.
>
> —Ursula LeGuin

1

A Writer on Storytelling

A CONVERSATION WITH ISAAC BASHEVIS SINGER

As you work through this book, you will be both a reader and a writer. Before you begin, read this interview to see what Isaac Bashevis Singer, a writer whose work is a reflection of his own life, has to say about stories and their meanings. A memoir by Singer about a character from his childhood is on page 188.

Q: What are your "rules" when you write a short story?

Singer: It must be short. A number of writers make their short stories unusually long. Chekhov and Maupassant never did this. Their short stories were really short. Of course, it should have suspense from beginning to end. With bad writers the suspense begins to diminish almost immediately and then evaporates altogether. As for the process itself, first I get the idea or the emotion. Then I need a plot, a story with a beginning, a middle, and an end. . . .

A story to me must have some surprise. The plot should be such that when you read the first page, you don't know what the second will be. When you read the second page, you don't know what the third will be, because this is how life is, full of little surprises.

The second condition is that I must have a passion to write the story. Sometimes I have a very good plot, but somehow the passion to write this story is missing. If this is the case, I would not write it.

And the third condition is the most important. I must be convinced, or at least have the illusion, that I am the only one who could write this particular story or this particular novel.

Now, for a plot you need characters. So instead of inventing characters, I contemplate the people whom I have met in my life who could fit into this story. I sometimes combine two characters and from them make one. I may take a person whom I met in this country and put him in Poland or vice versa. But just the same, I must have a model.

I don't invent characters, because the Almighty has already invented millions and billions of them. Humanity may become a million years old and I'm sure that in all this time there will not be two people who are really alike. Experts at fingerprints do not create fingerprints. They learn how to read them. In the same way the writer reads human characters.

Q: What do you suppose it is that gives readers a sense of enjoyment?

Singer: When people come together—let's say they come to a little party or gathering—you always hear them discuss character. They will say, "This one is a fool, this one is a miser." Gossip makes the conversation. It seems that the analysis of character is the highest human entertainment. And literature does it, unlike gossip, without mentioning specific names—and so it is less malicious. We always love to discuss and reveal character because human character is to us the greatest puzzle. No matter how much you know a human being, you don't know him enough.

BECOMING A STRATEGIC READER

Making Meanings

As readers, we make meaning. What a story means to us depends, at least in part, on who we are. Because you and I have had different experiences, lived in different places, known different people, we will see things differently. The meaning each of us creates from a text is therefore going to be our own. Take some time to think about what happens as we read.

1. **We connect with the text.** "This reminds me of my sister." "I had an experience like this."

2. **We ask questions.** We ask about situations or statements that puzzle us. We ask about motives. We try to figure out the meanings of unfamiliar words.

3. **We make predictions.** We wonder, "Is this what is going to happen next?" We test our predictions against the text.

4. **We interpret.** We decide what the story means as a whole and how its parts work together.

5. **We extend the text.** We reflect on the meaning of the text and think about its larger significance. We think about how the text can extend to some universal aspect of human life.

6. **We challenge the text.** We might say: "This couldn't possibly happen in real life." "This character seems too good." "I wish the story had a different ending."

HOW TO OWN A WORD

Learning from Context

When you come across an unfamiliar word, you have two resources available: what's already in your head and what's in the text— that is, all the words that surround the un- known word can sometimes give you clues to its meaning.

In the following story, one lone man, with a rifle, lies watching and waiting. He is a sniper. Suppose you are not sure what a sniper is. Here is how you can use context clues to guess at what the word means.

What exactly is a sniper?

On a rooftop near O'Connell Bridge, a Republican sniper lay watching. Beside him lay his rifle and over his shoulders was slung a pair of field glasses. His face was the face of a student, thin and ascetic, but his eyes had the cold gleam of the fanatic.

He is in a hidden position.

He is prepared to kill someone.

He's looking for something far away?

He's deadly, dangerous. "Fanatic" suggests he has a cause.

Extending Your Store of Words

What other words does *sniper* make you think of? Is it connected with taking a "snipe" at people or insulting them? Is it related to *snip,* like cutting with scissors? Is it connected with the birds at the shore called *snipes?*

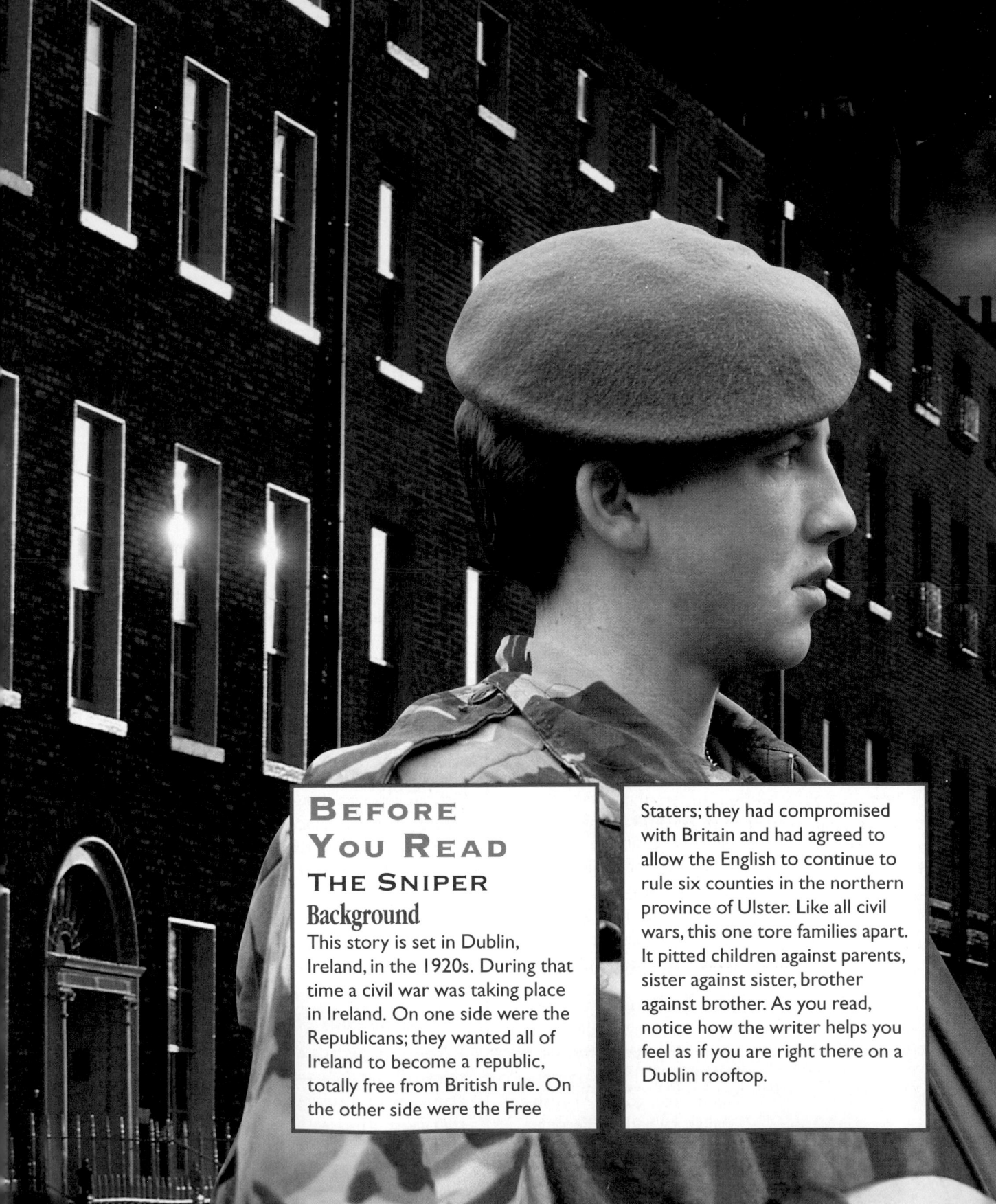

BEFORE YOU READ

THE SNIPER

Background

This story is set in Dublin, Ireland, in the 1920s. During that time a civil war was taking place in Ireland. On one side were the Republicans; they wanted all of Ireland to become a republic, totally free from British rule. On the other side were the Free Staters; they had compromised with Britain and had agreed to allow the English to continue to rule six counties in the northern province of Ulster. Like all civil wars, this one tore families apart. It pitted children against parents, sister against sister, brother against brother. As you read, notice how the writer helps you feel as if you are right there on a Dublin rooftop.

*His eyes had the cold gleam
of the fanatic.*

The Sniper

Liam O'Flaherty

The notes that follow show the thoughts of one reader as she read this short story for the first time. You might read the story yourself first, covering up her responses. Track your own responses in your Reader's Log and then compare your reading with Wendy's.

The long June twilight faded into night. Dublin lay enveloped in darkness but for the dim light of the moon that shone through fleecy clouds, casting a pale light as of approaching dawn over the streets and the dark waters of the Liffey.[1] Around the beleaguered Four Courts[2] the heavy guns roared. Here and there through the city, machine guns and rifles broke the silence of the night, spasmodically, like dogs barking on lone farms. Republicans and Free Staters were waging civil war.

This captures summer's essence beautifully.

The paragraph contains a huge contrast—between peaceful summer and violent war.

On a rooftop near O'Connell Bridge, a Republican sniper lay watching. Beside him lay his rifle and over his shoulders was slung a pair of field glasses. His face was the face of a student, thin and ascetic,[3] but his eyes had the cold gleam of the fanatic. They were deep and thoughtful, the eyes of a man who is used to looking at death.

The rooftop of a house?

Wouldn't the eyes of a man used to looking at death be cold and empty? Cold eyes and deep thoughtful eyes disagree with each other.

1. **Liffey:** river that runs through Dublin.
2. **beleaguered** (bē·lē′gərd) **Four Courts:** government buildings in Dublin that were surrounded and under attack.
3. **ascetic** (ə·set′ik): extremely self-disciplined and severe.

READER'S LOG

How can a sniper be watching silently and eating hungrily at the same time?

This guy has never done this job before. He acts carelessly.

This part made me laugh because I knew what would happen if he lit a cigarette.

What does an armored car look like? It reminds me of the vans that pick up money from businesses.

It seems that this guy just wants to shoot at something. Anything.

Wonder how the old woman knew where the sniper was.

He was eating a sandwich hungrily. He had eaten nothing since morning. He had been too excited to eat. He finished the sandwich, and, taking a flask of whiskey from his pocket, he took a short draft. Then he returned the flask to his pocket. He paused for a moment, considering whether he should risk a smoke. It was dangerous. The flash might be seen in the darkness, and there were enemies watching. He decided to take the risk.

Placing a cigarette between his lips, he struck a match, inhaled the smoke hurriedly, and put out the light. Almost immediately, a bullet flattened itself against the parapet[4] of the roof. The sniper took another whiff and put out the cigarette. Then he swore softly and crawled away to the left.

Cautiously he raised himself and peered over the parapet. There was a flash and a bullet whizzed over his head. He dropped immediately. He had seen the flash. It came from the opposite side of the street.

He rolled over the roof to a chimney stack in the rear and slowly drew himself up behind it, until his eyes were level with the top of the parapet. There was nothing to be seen— just the dim outline of the opposite housetop against the blue sky. His enemy was under cover.

Just then an armored car came across the bridge and advanced slowly up the street. It stopped on the opposite side of the street, fifty yards ahead. The sniper could hear the dull panting of the motor. His heart beat faster. It was an enemy car. He wanted to fire, but he knew it was useless. His bullets would never pierce the steel that covered the gray monster.

Then round the corner of a side street came an old woman, her head covered by a tattered shawl. She began to talk to the man in the turret of the car. She was pointing to the roof where the sniper lay. An informer.

4. **parapet** (par′ə·pet′): low wall or railing.

The turret opened. A man's head and shoulders appeared, looking toward the sniper. The sniper raised his rifle and fired. The head fell heavily on the turret wall. The woman darted toward the side street. The sniper fired again. The woman whirled round and fell with a shriek into the gutter.

Suddenly from the opposite roof a shot rang out and the sniper dropped his rifle with a curse. The rifle clattered to the roof. The sniper thought the noise would wake the dead. He stooped to pick the rifle up. He couldn't lift it. His forearm was dead. "I'm hit," he muttered.

Dropping flat onto the roof, he crawled back to the parapet. With his left hand he felt the injured right forearm. The blood was oozing through the sleeve of his coat. There was no pain—just a deadened sensation, as if the arm had been cut off.

Quickly he drew his knife from his pocket, opened it on the breastwork[5] of the parapet, and ripped open the sleeve. There was a small hole where the bullet had entered. On the other side there was no hole. The bullet had lodged in the bone. It must have fractured it. He bent the arm below the wound. The arm bent back easily. He ground his teeth to overcome the pain.

Then taking out his field dressing, he ripped open the packet with his knife. He broke the neck of the iodine bottle and let the bitter fluid drip into the wound. A paroxysm[6] of pain swept through him. He placed the cotton wadding over the wound and wrapped the dressing over it. He tied the ends with his teeth.

Then he lay still against the parapet, and, closing his eyes, he made an effort of will to overcome the pain.

In the street beneath all was still. The armored car had

5. **breastwork:** low wall put up as a military defense.
6. **paroxysm** (par'əks·iz'əm): sudden attack; fit.

READER'S LOG

The turret of what? The car? How can a car have a turret?

Nice action scene.

All of this makes me cringe! The author's description is so real that I can almost feel the character's pain.

I think I understand what happened earlier now.

retired speedily over the bridge, with the machine gunner's head hanging lifeless over the turret. The woman's corpse lay still in the gutter.

The sniper lay still for a long time nursing his wounded arm and planning escape. Morning must not find him wounded on the roof. The enemy on the opposite roof covered his escape. He must kill that enemy and he could not use his rifle. He had only a revolver to do it. Then he thought of a plan.

Taking off his cap, he placed it over the muzzle of his rifle. Then he pushed the rifle slowly upward over the parapet, until the cap was visible from the opposite side of the street. Almost immediately there was a report, and a bullet pierced the center of the cap. The sniper slanted the rifle forward. The cap slipped down into the street. Then, catching the rifle in the middle, the sniper dropped his left hand over the roof and let it hang, lifelessly. After a few moments he let the rifle drop to the street. Then he sank to the roof, dragging his hand with him.

Crawling quickly to the left, he peered up at the corner of the roof. His ruse had succeeded. The other sniper,

POBLACHT NA H EIREANN.

THE PROVISIONAL GOVERNMENT

OF THE

IRISH REPUBLIC

TO THE PEOPLE OF IRELAND.

IRISHMEN AND IRISHWOMEN: In the name of God and of the dead generations from which she receives her old tradition of nationhood, Ireland, through us, summons her children to her flag and strikes for her freedom.

Having organised and trained her manhood through her secret revolutionary organisation, the Irish Republican Brotherhood, and through her open military organisations, the Irish Volunteers and the Irish Citizen Army, having patiently perfected her discipline, having resolutely waited for the right moment to reveal itself, she now seizes that moment, and, supported by her exiled children in America and by gallant allies in Europe, but relying in the first on her own strength, she strikes in full confidence of victory.

We declare the right of the people of Ireland to the ownership of Ireland, and to the unfettered control of Irish destinies, to be sovereign and indefeasible. The long usurpation of that right by a foreign people and government has not extinguished the right, nor can it ever be extinguished except by the destruction of the Irish people. In every generation the Irish people have asserted their right to national freedom and sovereignty; six times during the past three hundred years they have asserted it in arms. Standing on that fundamental right and again asserting it in arms in the face of the world, we hereby proclaim the Irish Republic as a Sovereign Independent State, and we pledge our lives and the lives of our comrades-in-arms to the cause of its freedom, of its welfare, and of its exaltation among the nations.

The Irish Republic is entitled to, and hereby claims, the allegiance of every Irishman and Irishwoman. The Republic guarantees religious and civil liberty, equal rights and equal opportunities to all its citizens, and declares its resolve to pursue the happiness and prosperity of the whole nation and of all its parts, cherishing all the children of the nation equally, and oblivious of the differences carefully fostered by an alien government, which have divided a minority from the majority in the past.

Until our arms have brought the opportune moment for the establishment of a permanent National Government, representative of the whole people of Ireland and elected by the suffrages of all her men and women, the Provisional Government, hereby constituted, will administer the civil and military affairs of the Republic in trust for the people.

We place the cause of the Irish Republic under the protection of the Most High God, Whose blessing we invoke upon our arms, and we pray that no one who serves that cause will dishonour it by cowardice, inhumanity, or rapine. In this supreme hour the Irish nation must, by its valour and discipline and by the readiness of its children to sacrifice themselves for the common good, prove itself worthy of the august destiny to which it is called.

Signed on Behalf of the Provisional Government.

THOMAS J. CLARKE.
SEAN Mac DIARMADA. THOMAS MacDONAGH.
P. H. PEARSE. EAMONN CEANNT.
JAMES CONNOLLY. JOSEPH PLUNKETT.

Escape from what? The roof?

Suspenseful here, and more interesting.

This is risky. He might need it. Where was he before?

seeing the cap and rifle fall, thought that he had killed his man. He was now standing before a row of chimney pots, looking across, with his head clearly silhouetted against the western sky.

The Republican sniper smiled and lifted his revolver above the edge of the parapet. The distance was about fifty yards—a hard shot in the dim light, and his right arm was paining him like a thousand devils. He took a steady aim. His hand trembled with eagerness. Pressing his lips together, he took a deep breath through his nostrils and fired. He was almost deafened with the report and his arm shook with the recoil.

Then when the smoke cleared he peered across and uttered a cry of joy. His enemy had been hit. He was reeling over the parapet in his death agony. He struggled to keep his feet, but he was slowly falling forward, as if in a dream. The rifle fell from his grasp, hit the parapet, fell over, bounded off the pole of a barber's shop beneath, and then clattered on the pavement.

Then the dying man on the roof crumpled up and fell forward. The body turned over and over in space and hit the ground with a dull thud. Then it lay still.

The sniper looked at his enemy falling and he shuddered. The lust of battle died in him. He became bitten by remorse. The sweat stood out in beads on his forehead. Weakened by his wound and the long summer day of fasting and watching on the roof, he revolted from the sight of the shattered mass of his dead enemy. His teeth chattered, he began to gibber to himself, cursing the war, cursing himself, cursing everybody.

He looked at the smoking revolver in his hand, and with an oath he hurled it to the roof at his feet. The revolver went off with the concussion and the bullet whizzed past the sniper's head. He was frightened back to his senses by the shock. His nerves steadied. The cloud of fear scattered from his mind and he laughed.

Isn't the other sniper watching him?

I like this author's style. It is descriptive while being concise and suspenseful.

I thought that this man was used to death.

Wasn't it the night and early morning?

War is making this man a little crazy and irrational.

Something else will happen soon. Things are too perfect.

This is a wonderfully shocking surprise ending!

This illustrates the senseless tragedy of war, especially civil war.

Wendy Forest

—Wendy Forrest
  Westwood High School
  Austin, Texas

Taking the whiskey flask from his pocket, he emptied it at a draft. He felt reckless under the influence of the spirit. He decided to leave the roof now and look for his company commander, to report. Everywhere around was quiet. There was not much danger in going through the streets. He picked up his revolver and put it in his pocket. Then he crawled down through the skylight to the house underneath.

When the sniper reached the laneway on the street level, he felt a sudden curiosity as to the identity of the enemy sniper whom he had killed. He decided that he was a good shot, whoever he was. He wondered did he know him. Perhaps he had been in his own company before the split in the army. He decided to risk going over to have a look at him. He peered around the corner into O'Connell Street. In the upper part of the street there was heavy firing, but around here all was quiet.

The sniper darted across the street. A machine gun tore up the ground around him with a hail of bullets, but he escaped. He threw himself face downward beside the corpse. The machine gun stopped.

Then the sniper turned over the dead body and looked into his brother's face.

FACING MONSTERS

The oldest of all our stories are about conflicts between people and the monsters—real and imaginary—that threaten them. We can imagine people in prehistoric times huddled around small fires in their dark caves, telling one another stories about terrifying conflicts with monsters that got more and more fantastic as the stories were told and retold. Conflict is still the basic ingredient in our stories. Today, the monsters have disappeared in realistic stories and characters face more believable problems—floods, bullies at the corner, clashes with friends, viruses in the computer. But perhaps more common today are stories of people who struggle with problems that come from within: anger, prejudice, selfishness, fear. Why is it that so many of our stories deal with conflict? Maybe it's because stories help us absorb the courage, the strength, and the wisdom we need to confront the conflicts we face in our own passage through life.

The harder the conflict, the more glorious the triumph.

—Thomas Paine

Writer's Notebook

WORK IN PROGRESS

Think for a few minutes of all the times in life when you or someone you know struggled with something— something outside, like a hurricane, or something inside, like fear of a big exam or a tough decision. List as many of these conflicts as you can. Write freely; right now you just need to get your ideas down. Keep your notes. You'll return to them for the narrative you'll write for the Writer's Workshop on page 112.

BEFORE YOU READ
THE MOST DANGEROUS GAME

Reading Focus

The Chase

The most basic kind of conflict in storytelling pits one person against someone or something else. In movies today this conflict is often played out in hair-raising chases in which the hero or heroine is pursued by the villain over rooftops, across rivers, through sewers, down city streets. If the story is told well, we are hooked by the close calls—we keep wanting to know: "What happens next? Will he (or she) escape this time?"

A Dialogue with the Text

Before you start this famous chase story, jot down in your Reader's Log what you think its title might mean. What do you predict the conflict will be? Then, as you read, keep a double-entry journal, like the one shown here. On the left write down comments made by the characters that seem important or controversial. On the right, record your responses to the statements.

Comment	My Response
The world is made up of two classes—the hunters and the huntees. (page 14)	I'm not a huntee or hunter. This is a really cynical idea.

Elements of Literature

Conflict Makes a Story Go

A character's physical and mental struggles are **conflicts**. If a person is struggling against something outside himself or herself, the conflict is **external**. If the person is fighting to control some inner problem—such as fear, anger, or homesickness—the conflict is **internal**. Pure action stories usually hook us with violent external conflicts. Whatever kind of conflict a story is built on, it must be strong enough to keep us turning those pages—or glued to our seats.

Conflict is a struggle against some outside enemy or some internal problem.

For more on Conflict, see pages 32–33 and the Handbook of Literary Terms.

THE MOST DANGEROUS GAME

Sailors have a curious dread of the place.

Richard Connell

"Off there to the right—somewhere—is a large island," said Whitney. "It's rather a mystery——"

"What island is it?" Rainsford asked.

"The old charts call it Ship-Trap Island," Whitney replied. "A suggestive name, isn't it? Sailors have a curious dread of the place. I don't know why. Some superstition——"

"Can't see it," remarked Rainsford, trying to peer through the dank tropical night that was palpable as it pressed its thick warm blackness in upon the yacht.

"You've good eyes," said Whitney, with a laugh, "and I've seen you pick off a moose moving in the brown fall bush at four hundred yards, but even you can't see four miles or so through a moonless Caribbean night."

"Nor four yards," admitted Rainsford. "Ugh! It's like moist black velvet."

"It will be light in Rio," promised Whitney. "We should make it in a few days. I hope the jaguar guns have come from

---

WORDS TO OWN
palpable (pal′pə·bəl) *adj.:* easily felt or touched.

THE MOST DANGEROUS GAME 13

Purdey's.[1] We should have some good hunting up the Amazon. Great sport, hunting."

"The best sport in the world," agreed Rainsford.

"For the hunter," amended Whitney. "Not for the jaguar."

"Don't talk rot, Whitney," said Rainsford. "You're a big-game hunter, not a philosopher. Who cares how a jaguar feels?"

"Perhaps the jaguar does," observed Whitney.

"Bah! They've no understanding."

"Even so, I rather think they understand one thing—fear. The fear of pain and the fear of death."

"Nonsense," laughed Rainsford. "This hot weather is making you soft, Whitney. Be a realist. The world is made up of two classes—the hunters and the huntees. Luckily, you and I are the hunters. Do you think we've passed that island yet?"

"I can't tell in the dark. I hope so."

"Why?" asked Rainsford.

"The place has a reputation—a bad one."

"Cannibals?" suggested Rainsford.

"Hardly. Even cannibals wouldn't live in such a Godforsaken place. But it's gotten into sailor lore, somehow. Didn't you notice that the crew's nerves seemed a bit jumpy today?"

"They were a bit strange, now you mention it. Even Captain Nielsen——"

"Yes, even that tough-minded old Swede, who'd go up to the devil himself and ask him for a light. Those fishy blue eyes held a look I never saw there before. All I could get out of him was: 'This place has an evil name among seafaring men, sir.' Then he said to me, very gravely: 'Don't you feel anything?'—as if the air about us was actually poisonous. Now, you mustn't laugh when I tell you this—I did feel something like a sudden chill.

"There was no breeze. The sea was as flat as a plate-glass window. We were drawing near the island then. What I felt was a—a mental chill; a sort of sudden dread."

"Pure imagination," said Rainsford. "One superstitious sailor can taint the whole ship's company with his fear."

"Maybe. But sometimes I think sailors have an extra sense that tells them when they are in danger. Sometimes I think evil is a tangible thing—with wavelengths, just as sound and light have. An evil place can, so to speak, broadcast vibrations of evil. Anyhow, I'm glad we're getting out of this zone. Well, I think I'll turn in now, Rainsford."

"I'm not sleepy," said Rainsford. "I'm going to smoke another pipe on the afterdeck."

"Good night, then, Rainsford. See you at breakfast."

"Right. Good night, Whitney."

There was no sound in the night as Rainsford sat there but the muffled throb of the engine that drove the yacht swiftly through the darkness, and the swish and ripple of the wash of the propeller.

Rainsford, reclining in a steamer chair, indolently puffed on his favorite brier.[2] The sensuous drowsiness of the night was on him. "It's so dark," he thought, "that I could sleep without closing my eyes; the night would be my eyelids——"

An abrupt sound startled him. Off to the right he heard it, and his ears, expert in such matters, could not be mistaken. Again he heard the sound, and again. Somewhere, off in the blackness, someone had fired a gun three times.

Rainsford sprang up and moved quickly to the rail, mystified. He strained his eyes in the direction from which the reports had come, but it was like trying to see through a blanket. He leaped upon the rail and balanced himself there, to get greater elevation; his pipe, striking a rope, was knocked from his mouth. He lunged for it; a short, hoarse cry came from his lips as he realized he had reached too far and had lost his balance. The cry was pinched off short as the blood-warm waters of the Caribbean Sea closed over his head.

2. **brier** (brī′ər): tobacco pipe made from the root of a brier bush or tree.

----

1. **Purdey's:** British manufacturer of hunting equipment.

WORDS TO OWN
indolently (in′də·lənt·lē) *adv.*: lazily.

He struggled up to the surface and tried to cry out, but the wash from the speeding yacht slapped him in the face and the salt water in his open mouth made him gag and strangle. Desperately he struck out with strong strokes after the receding lights of the yacht, but he stopped before he had swum fifty feet. A certain coolheadedness had come to him; it was not the first time he had been in a tight place. There was a chance that his cries could be heard by someone aboard the yacht, but that chance was slender and grew more slender as the yacht raced on. He wrestled himself out of his clothes and shouted with all his power. The lights of the yacht became faint and ever-vanishing fireflies; then they were blotted out entirely by the night.

Rainsford remembered the shots. They had come from the right, and doggedly he swam in that direction, swimming with slow, deliberate strokes, conserving his strength. For a seemingly endless time he fought the sea. He began to count his strokes; he could do possibly a hundred more and then——

Rainsford heard a sound. It came out of the darkness, a high screaming sound, the sound of an animal in an extremity of anguish and terror.

He did not recognize the animal that made the sound; he did not try to; with fresh vitality he swam toward the sound. He heard it again; then it was cut short by another noise, crisp, staccato.

"Pistol shot," muttered Rainsford, swimming on.

Ten minutes of determined effort brought another sound to his ears—the most welcome he had ever heard—the muttering and growling of the sea breaking on a rocky shore. He was almost on the rocks before he saw them; on a night less calm he would have been shattered against them. With his remaining strength he dragged himself from the swirling waters. Jagged crags appeared to jut into the opaqueness.[3]

He forced himself upward, hand over hand. Gasping, his hands raw, he reached a flat place at the top. Dense jungle came down to the very edge of the cliffs. What perils that tangle of trees and underbrush might hold for him did not concern Rainsford just then. All he knew was that he was safe from his enemy, the sea,

3. **opaqueness** (ō·pāk'nis): here, darkness. Something opaque does not let light pass through. Milk is an opaque liquid; water is not.

and that utter weariness was on him. He flung himself down at the jungle edge and tumbled headlong into the deepest sleep of his life.

When he opened his eyes he knew from the position of the sun that it was late in the afternoon. Sleep had given him new vigor; a sharp hunger was picking at him. He looked about him, almost cheerfully.

"Where there are pistol shots, there are men. Where there are men, there is food," he thought. But what kind of men, he wondered, in so forbidding a place? An unbroken front of snarled and ragged jungle fringed the shore.

He saw no sign of a trail through the closely knit web of weeds and trees; it was easier to go along the shore, and Rainsford floundered along by the water. Not far from where he had landed, he stopped.

Some wounded thing, by the evidence a large animal, had thrashed about in the underbrush; the jungle weeds were crushed down and the moss was lacerated; one patch of weeds was stained crimson. A small, glittering object not far away caught Rainsford's eye and he picked it up. It was an empty cartridge.

"A twenty-two," he remarked. "That's odd. It must have been a fairly large animal too. The hunter had his nerve with him to tackle it with a light gun. It's clear that the brute put up a fight. I suppose the first three shots I heard was when the hunter flushed his quarry[4] and wounded it. The last shot was when he trailed it here and finished it."

He examined the ground closely and found what he had hoped to find—the print of hunting boots. They pointed along the cliff in the direction he had been going. Eagerly he hurried along, now slipping on a rotten log or a loose stone, but making headway; night was beginning to settle down on the island.

Bleak darkness was blacking out the sea and jungle when Rainsford sighted the lights. He came upon them as he turned a crook in the coastline, and his first thought was that he had come upon a village, for there were many lights. But as he forged along he saw to his great astonishment that all the lights were in one enormous building—a lofty structure with pointed towers plunging upward into the gloom. His eyes made out the shadowy outlines of a palatial château;[5] it was set on a high bluff, and on three sides of it cliffs dived down to where the sea licked greedy lips in the shadows.

"Mirage," thought Rainsford. But it was no mirage, he found, when he opened the tall spiked iron gate. The stone steps were real enough; the massive door with a leering gargoyle for a knocker was real enough; yet about it all hung an air of unreality.

He lifted the knocker, and it creaked up stiffly, as if it had never before been used. He let it fall, and it startled him with its booming loudness. He thought he heard steps within; the door remained closed. Again Rainsford lifted the heavy knocker and let it fall. The door opened then, opened as suddenly as if it were on a spring, and Rainsford stood blinking in the river of glaring gold light that poured out. The first thing Rainsford's eyes discerned was the largest man Rainsford had ever seen—a gigantic creature, solidly made and blackbearded to the waist. In his hand the man held a long-barreled revolver, and he was pointing it straight at Rainsford's heart.

Out of the snarl of beard two small eyes regarded Rainsford.

"Don't be alarmed," said Rainsford, with a smile which he hoped was <u>disarming</u>. "I'm no robber. I fell off a yacht. My name is Sanger Rainsford of New York City."

The menacing look in the eyes did not change. The revolver pointed as rigidly as if the giant were a statue. He gave no sign that he understood Rainsford's words or that he had even heard them. He was dressed in uniform, a black uniform trimmed with gray astrakhan.[6]

"I'm Sanger Rainsford of New York," Rainsford began again. "I fell off a yacht. I am hungry."

---

5. **château** (sha·tō′): large country house.
6. **astrakhan** (as′trə·kən): curly fur of very young lambs.

WORDS TO OWN

disarming (dis·ärm′iŋ) *adj.:* removing or lessening suspicions or fears.

---

4. **flushed his quarry:** drove the animal he was hunting out of its shelter or hiding place.

The man's only answer was to raise with his thumb the hammer of his revolver. Then Rainsford saw the man's free hand go to his forehead in a military salute, and he saw him click his heels together and stand at attention. Another man was coming down the broad marble steps, an erect, slender man in evening clothes. He advanced to Rainsford and held out his hand.

In a cultivated voice marked by a slight accent that gave it added precision and deliberateness, he said: "It is a very great pleasure and honor to welcome Mr. Sanger Rainsford, the celebrated hunter, to my home."

Automatically Rainsford shook the man's hand.

"I've read your book about hunting snow leopards in Tibet, you see," explained the man. "I am General Zaroff."

Rainsford's first impression was that the man was singularly handsome; his second was that there was an original, almost bizarre quality about the general's face. He was a tall man past middle age, for his hair was a vivid white; but his thick eyebrows and pointed military moustache were as black as the night from which Rainsford had come. His eyes, too, were black and very bright. He had high cheekbones, a sharp-cut nose, a spare, dark face, the face of a man used to giving orders, the face of an aristocrat. Turning to the giant in uniform, the general made a sign. The giant put away his pistol, saluted, withdrew.

"Ivan is an incredibly strong fellow," remarked the general, "but he has the misfortune to be deaf and dumb. A simple fellow, but, I'm afraid, like all his race, a bit of a savage."

"Is he Russian?"

"He is a Cossack,"[7] said the general, and his smile showed red lips and pointed teeth. "So am I."

"Come," he said, "we shouldn't be chatting here. We can talk later. Now you want clothes, food, rest. You shall have them. This is a most restful spot."

The menacing look in the eyes did not change.

Ivan had reappeared, and the general spoke to him with lips that moved but gave forth no sound.

"Follow Ivan, if you please, Mr. Rainsford," said the general. "I was about to have my dinner when you came. I'll wait for you. You'll find that my clothes will fit you, I think."

It was to a huge, beam-ceilinged bedroom with a canopied bed big enough for six men that Rainsford followed the silent giant. Ivan laid out an evening suit, and Rainsford, as he put it on, noticed that it came from a London tailor who ordinarily cut and sewed for none below the rank of duke.

The dining room to which Ivan conducted him was in many ways remarkable. There was a medieval magnificence about it; it suggested a baronial hall of feudal times, with its oaken panels, its high ceiling, its vast refectory table[8] where two-score men could sit down to eat. About the hall were the mounted heads of many animals—lions, tigers, elephants, moose, bears; larger or more perfect specimens Rainsford had never seen. At the great table the general was sitting, alone.

"You'll have a cocktail, Mr. Rainsford," he suggested. The cocktail was surpassingly good; and, Rainsford noted, the table appointments were of the finest—the linen, the crystal, the silver, the china.

They were eating borscht, the rich red soup with sour cream so dear to Russian palates. Half apologetically General Zaroff said: "We do our best to preserve the amenities of civilization here. Please forgive any lapses. We are well off the beaten track, you know. Do you think the champagne has suffered from its long ocean trip?"

---

8. refectory table: long, narrow table, like those used in a monastery or college dining hall.

WORDS TO OWN

amenities (ə·men′ə·tēz) *n.:* comforts and conveniences.

---

7. Cossack (käs′ak′): member of a group from Ukraine, many of whom served as horsemen to the Russian czars and were famed for their fierceness in battle.

"Not in the least," declared Rainsford. He was finding the general a most thoughtful and affable host, a true cosmopolite.[9] But there was one small trait of the general's that made Rainsford uncomfortable. Whenever he looked up from his plate he found the general studying him, appraising him narrowly.

"Perhaps," said General Zaroff, "you were surprised that I recognized your name. You see, I read all books on hunting published in English, French, and Russian. I have but one passion in my life, Mr. Rainsford, and it is the hunt."

"You have some wonderful heads here," said Rainsford as he ate a particularly well-cooked filet mignon. "That Cape buffalo is the largest I ever saw."

"Oh, that fellow. Yes, he was a monster."

"Did he charge you?"

"Hurled me against a tree," said the general. "Fractured my skull. But I got the brute."

"I've always thought," said Rainsford, "that the Cape buffalo is the most dangerous of all big game."

For a moment the general did not reply; he was smiling his curious red-lipped smile. Then he said slowly: "No. You are wrong, sir. The Cape buffalo is not the most dangerous big game." He sipped his wine. "Here in my preserve on this island," he said in the same

9. **cosmopolite** (käz·mäp′ə·līt′): knowledgeable citizen of the world.

cigarette with a silver tip; it was perfumed and gave off a smell like incense.

"We will have some capital hunting, you and I," said the general. "I shall be most glad to have your society."

"But what game——" began Rainsford.

"I'll tell you," said the general. "You will be amused, I know. I think I may say, in all modesty, that I have done a rare thing. I have invented a new sensation. May I pour you another glass of port, Mr. Rainsford?"

"Thank you, general."

The general filled both glasses and said: "God makes some men poets. Some He makes kings, some beggars. Me He made a hunter. My hand was made for the trigger, my father said. He was a very rich man, with a quarter of a million acres in the Crimea,[10] and he was an ardent sportsman. When I was only five years old, he gave me a little gun, specially made in Moscow for me, to shoot sparrows with. When I shot some of his prize turkeys with it, he did not punish me; he complimented me on my marksmanship. I killed my first bear in the Caucasus[11] when I was ten. My whole life has been one prolonged hunt. I went into the army—it was expected of noblemen's sons—and for a time commanded a division of Cossack cavalry, but my real interest was always the hunt. I have hunted every kind of game in every land. It would be impossible for me to tell you how many animals I have killed."

The general puffed at his cigarette.

"After the debacle in Russia[12] I left the country, for it was <u>imprudent</u> for an officer of the czar to stay there. Many noble Russians lost everything. I, luckily, had invested heavily in American

slow tone, "I hunt more dangerous game."

Rainsford expressed his surprise. "Is there big game on this island?"

The general nodded. "The biggest."

"Really?"

"Oh, it isn't here naturally, of course. I have to stock the island."

"What have you imported, general?" Rainsford asked. "Tigers?"

The general smiled. "No," he said. "Hunting tigers ceased to interest me some years ago. I exhausted their possibilities, you see. No thrill left in tigers, no real danger. I live for danger, Mr. Rainsford."

The general took from his pocket a gold cigarette case and offered his guest a long black

---

10. **Crimea** (krī·mē′ə): area in Ukraine bordering the Black Sea.
11. **Caucasus** (kô′kə·səs): mountainous region between southeastern Europe and western Asia.
12. **debacle** (di·bä′kəl) **in Russia:** A debacle is an overwhelming defeat. Zaroff is referring to the Russian Revolution of 1917, in which the czar and his government were overthrown.

WORDS TO OWN

imprudent (im·prōod′'nt) *adj.*: unwise.

securities, so I shall never have to open a tearoom in Monte Carlo[13] or drive a taxi in Paris. Naturally, I continued to hunt—grizzlies in your Rockies, crocodiles in the Ganges,[14] rhinoceroses in East Africa. It was in Africa that the Cape buffalo hit me and laid me up for six months. As soon as I recovered I started for the Amazon to hunt jaguars, for I had heard they were unusually cunning. They weren't." The Cossack sighed. "They were no match at all for a hunter with his wits about him and a high-powered rifle. I was bitterly disappointed. I was lying in my tent with a splitting headache one night when a terrible thought pushed its way into my mind. Hunting was beginning to bore me! And hunting, remember, had been my life. I have heard that in America businessmen often go to pieces when they give up the business that has been their life."

"Yes, that's so," said Rainsford.

The general smiled. "I had no wish to go to pieces," he said. "I must do something. Now, mine is an analytical mind, Mr. Rainsford. Doubtless that is why I enjoy the problems of the chase."

"No doubt, General Zaroff."

"So," continued the general, "I asked myself why the hunt no longer fascinated me. You are much younger than I am, Mr. Rainsford, and have not hunted as much, but you perhaps can guess the answer."

"What was it?"

"Simply this: Hunting had ceased to be what you call a sporting proposition. It had become too easy. I always got my quarry. Always. There is no greater bore than perfection."

The general lit a fresh cigarette.

"No animal had a chance with me anymore. That is no boast; it is a mathematical certainty. The animal had nothing but his legs and his instinct. Instinct is no match for reason. When I

But no animal can reason.

thought of this, it was a tragic moment for me, I can tell you."

Rainsford leaned across the table, absorbed in what his host was saying.

"It came to me as an inspiration what I must do," the general went on.

"And that was?"

The general smiled the quiet smile of one who has faced an obstacle and surmounted it with success. "I had to invent a new animal to hunt," he said.

"A new animal? You're joking."

"Not at all," said the general. "I never joke about hunting. I needed a new animal. I found one. So I bought this island, built this house, and here I do my hunting. The island is perfect for my purposes— there are jungles with a maze of trails in them, hills, swamps——"

"But the animal, General Zaroff?"

"Oh," said the general, "it supplies me with the most exciting hunting in the world. No other hunting compares with it for an instant. Every day I hunt, and I never grow bored now, for I have a quarry with which I can match my wits."

Rainsford's bewilderment showed in his face.

"I wanted the ideal animal to hunt," explained the general. "So I said: 'What are the attributes of an ideal quarry?' And the answer was, of course: 'It must have courage, cunning, and, above all, it must be able to reason.'"

"But no animal can reason," objected Rainsford.

"My dear fellow," said the general, "there is one that can."

"But you can't mean——" gasped Rainsford.

"And why not?"

"I can't believe you are serious, General Zaroff. This is a grisly joke."

"Why should I not be serious? I am speaking of hunting."

"Hunting? Good God, General Zaroff, what you speak of is murder."

The general laughed with entire good nature.

13. **Monte Carlo** (mänt′ə kär′lō): gambling resort in Monaco, a country on the Mediterranean Sea.
14. **Ganges** (gan′jēz): river in northern India and Bangladesh.

He regarded Rainsford quizzically. "I refuse to believe that so modern and civilized a young man as you seem to be harbors romantic ideas about the value of human life. Surely your experiences in the war——"

"Did not make me condone coldblooded murder," finished Rainsford stiffly.

Laughter shook the general. "How extraordinarily droll you are!" he said. "One does not expect nowadays to find a young man of the educated class, even in America, with such a naive, and, if I may say so, mid-Victorian point of view. It's like finding a snuffbox in a limousine. Ah, well, doubtless you had Puritan ancestors. So many Americans appear to have had. I'll wager you'll forget your notions when you go hunting with me. You've a genuine new thrill in store for you, Mr. Rainsford."

"Thank you, I'm a hunter, not a murderer."

"Dear me," said the general, quite unruffled, "again that unpleasant word. But I think I can show you that your scruples are quite ill-founded."

"Yes?"

"Life is for the strong, to be lived by the strong, and if need be, taken by the strong. The weak of the world were put here to give the strong pleasure. I am strong. Why should I not use my gift? If I wish to hunt, why should I not? I hunt the scum of the earth—sailors from tramp ships—lascars,[15] blacks, Chinese, whites, mongrels—a thoroughbred horse or hound is worth more than a score of them."

"But they are men," said Rainsford hotly.

"Precisely," said the general. "That is why I use them. It gives me pleasure. They can reason, after a fashion. So they are dangerous."

"But where do you get them?"

The general's left eyelid fluttered down in a wink. "This island is called Ship-Trap," he answered. "Sometimes an angry god of the high seas sends them to me. Sometimes, when Providence is not so kind, I help Providence a bit. Come to the window with me."

Rainsford went to the window and looked out toward the sea.

---

15. **lascars** (las′kərz): East Indian sailors employed on European ships.

"Watch! Out there!" exclaimed the general, pointing into the night. Rainsford's eyes saw only blackness, and then, as the general pressed a button, far out to sea Rainsford saw the flash of lights.

The general chuckled. "They indicate a channel," he said, "where there's none; giant rocks with razor edges crouch like a sea monster with wide-open jaws. They can crush a ship as easily as I crush this nut." He dropped a walnut on the hardwood floor and brought his heel grinding down on it. "Oh, yes," he said, casually, as if in answer to a question, "I have electricity. We try to be civilized here."

"Civilized? And you shoot down men?"

A trace of anger was in the general's black eyes, but it was there for but a second, and he said, in his most pleasant manner: "Dear me, what a righteous young man you are! I assure you I do not do the thing you suggest. That would be barbarous. I treat these visitors with every consideration. They get plenty of good food and exercise. They get into splendid physical condition. You shall see for yourself tomorrow."

"What do you mean?"

"We'll visit my training school," smiled the general. "It's in the cellar. I have about a dozen pupils down there now. They're from the Spanish bark *San Lucar* that had the bad luck to go on the rocks out there. A very inferior lot, I regret to say. Poor specimens and more accustomed to the deck than to the jungle."

He raised his hand, and Ivan, who served as waiter, brought thick Turkish coffee. Rainsford, with an effort, held his tongue in check.

"It's a game, you see," pursued the general blandly. "I suggest to one of them that we go hunting. I give him a supply of food and an excellent hunting knife. I give him three hours' start. I am to follow, armed only with a pistol of the smallest caliber and range. If my quarry eludes me for three whole days, he wins the game. If I find him"—the general smiled—"he loses."

WORDS TO OWN

scruples (skrōō′pəlz) *n.*: feelings of doubt or guilt about a suggested action.

"Suppose he refuses to be hunted?"

"Oh," said the general, "I give him his option, of course. He need not play that game if he doesn't wish to. If he does not wish to hunt, I turn him over to Ivan. Ivan once had the honor of serving as official knouter[16] to the Great White Czar, and he has his own ideas of sport. Invariably, Mr. Rainsford, invariably they choose the hunt."

"And if they win?"

The smile on the general's face widened. "To date I have not lost," he said.

Then he added, hastily: "I don't wish you to think me a braggart, Mr. Rainsford. Many of them afford only the most elementary sort of problem. Occasionally I strike a tartar.[17] One almost did win. I eventually had to use the dogs."

"The dogs?"

"This way, please. I'll show you."

The general steered Rainsford to a window. The lights from the windows sent a flickering illumination that made grotesque patterns on the courtyard below, and Rainsford could see moving about there a dozen or so huge black shapes; as they turned toward him, their eyes glittered greenly.

"A rather good lot, I think," observed the general. "They are let out at seven every night. If anyone should try to get into my house—or out of it—something extremely regrettable would occur to him." He hummed a snatch of song from the Folies-Bergère.[18]

"And now," said the general, "I want to show you my new collection of heads. Will you come with me to the library?"

"I hope," said Rainsford, "that you will excuse me tonight, General Zaroff. I'm really not feeling at all well."

"If he does not wish to hunt, I turn him over to Ivan."

"Ah, indeed?" the general inquired <u>solicitously</u>. "Well, I suppose that's only natural, after your long swim. You need a good, restful night's sleep. Tomorrow you'll feel like a new man, I'll wager. Then we'll hunt, eh? I've one rather promising prospect——"

Rainsford was hurrying from the room.

"Sorry you can't go with me tonight," called the general. "I expect rather fair sport—a big, strong black. He looks resourceful—— Well, good night, Mr. Rainsford; I hope you have a good night's rest."

The bed was good and the pajamas of the softest silk, and he was tired in every fiber of his being, but nevertheless Rainsford could not quiet his brain with the <u>opiate</u> of sleep. He lay, eyes wide open. Once he thought he heard stealthy steps in the corridor outside his room. He sought to throw open the door; it would not open. He went to the window and looked out. His room was high up in one of the towers. The lights of the château were out now, and it was dark and silent, but there was a fragment of sallow moon, and by its wan light he could see, dimly, the courtyard; there, weaving in and out in the pattern of shadow, were black, noiseless forms; the hounds heard him at the window and looked up, expectantly, with their green eyes. Rainsford went back to the bed and lay down. By many methods he tried to put himself to sleep. He had achieved a doze when, just as morning began to come, he heard, far off in the jungle, the faint report of a pistol.

General Zaroff did not appear until luncheon. He was dressed faultlessly in the tweeds of a

16. **knouter** (nout′ər): person who beats criminals with a knout, a kind of leather whip.
17. **strike a tartar:** get more than one bargained for. A tartar is a violent, unmanageable person.
18. **Folies-Bergère** (fô′lē ber·zher′): famous nightclub in Paris.

WORDS TO OWN

solicitously (sə·lis′ə·təs·lē) *adv.*: in a concerned manner.

opiate (ō′pē·it) *n.*: anything that tends to soothe or calm someone. An opiate may also be a medicine containing opium or a related drug used to relieve pain.

country squire. He was solicitous about the state of Rainsford's health.

"As for me," sighed the general, "I do not feel so well. I am worried, Mr. Rainsford. Last night I detected traces of my old complaint."

To Rainsford's questioning glance the general said: "Ennui. Boredom."

Then, taking a second helping of crêpes suzette,[19] the general explained: "The hunting was not good last night. The fellow lost his head. He made a straight trail that offered no problems at all. That's the trouble with these sailors; they have dull brains to begin with, and they do not know how to get about in the woods. They do excessively stupid and obvious things. It's most annoying. Will you have another glass of Chablis, Mr. Rainsford?"

"General," said Rainsford firmly, "I wish to leave this island at once."

The general raised his thickets of eyebrows; he seemed hurt. "But, my dear fellow," the general protested, "you've only just come. You've had no hunting——"

"I wish to go today," said Rainsford. He saw the dead black eyes of the general on him, studying him. General Zaroff's face suddenly brightened.

He filled Rainsford's glass with venerable Chablis from a dusty bottle.

"Tonight," said the general, "we will hunt—you and I."

Rainsford shook his head. "No, general," he said. "I will not hunt."

The general shrugged his shoulders and delicately ate a hothouse grape. "As you wish, my friend," he said. "The choice rests entirely with you. But may I not venture to suggest that you will find my idea of sport more diverting than Ivan's?"

He nodded toward the corner where the giant stood, scowling, his thick arms crossed on his hogshead of chest.

"You don't mean——" cried Rainsford.

"My dear fellow," said the general, "have I not told you I always mean what I say about hunting? This is really an inspiration. I drink to a

foeman worthy of my steel—at last."

The general raised his glass, but Rainsford sat staring at him.

"You'll find this game worth playing," the general said enthusiastically. "Your brain against mine. Your woodcraft against mine. Your strength and stamina against mine. Outdoor chess! And the stake is not without value, eh?"

"And if I win——" began Rainsford huskily.

"I'll cheerfully acknowledge myself defeated if I do not find you by midnight of the third day," said General Zaroff. "My sloop will place you on the mainland near a town."

The general read what Rainsford was thinking.

"Oh, you can trust me," said the Cossack. "I will give you my word as a gentleman and a sportsman. Of course you, in turn, must agree to say nothing of your visit here."

"I'll agree to nothing of the kind," said Rainsford.

"Oh," said the general, "in that case—— But why discuss that now? Three days hence we can discuss it over a bottle of Veuve Clicquot,[20] unless——"

The general sipped his wine.

Then a businesslike air animated him. "Ivan," he said to Rainsford, "will supply you with hunting clothes, food, a knife. I suggest you wear moccasins; they leave a poorer trail. I suggest too that you avoid the big swamp in the southeast corner of the island. We call it Death Swamp. There's quicksand there. One foolish fellow tried it. The <u>deplorable</u> part of it was that Lazarus followed him. You can imagine my feelings, Mr. Rainsford. I loved Lazarus; he was the finest hound in my pack. Well, I must beg you to excuse me now. I always take a siesta after lunch. You'll hardly have time for a nap, I fear. You'll want to start, no doubt. I shall not follow till dusk. Hunting at night is so much more exciting than by day, don't you think? Au revoir, Mr. Rainsford, au revoir."

20. **Veuve Clicquot** (vöv klē·kô′): brand of fine champagne.

19. **crêpes suzette** (krăp soo·zet′): thin pancakes folded in a hot orange-flavored sauce and served in flaming brandy.

WORDS TO OWN

deplorable (dē·plôr′ə·bəl) adj.: regrettable; very bad.

General Zaroff, with a deep, courtly bow, strolled from the room.

From another door came Ivan. Under one arm he carried khaki hunting clothes, a haversack of food, a leather sheath containing a long-bladed hunting knife; his right hand rested on a cocked revolver thrust in the crimson sash about his waist. . . .

Rainsford had fought his way through the bush for two hours. "I must keep my nerve. I must keep my nerve," he said through tight teeth.

He had not been entirely clearheaded when the château gates snapped shut behind him. His whole idea at first was to put distance between himself and General Zaroff, and, to this end, he had plunged along, spurred on by the sharp rowels[21] of something very like panic. Now he had got a grip on himself, had stopped, and was taking stock of himself and the situation.

He saw that straight flight was futile; inevitably it would bring him face to face with the sea. He was in a picture with a frame of water, and his operations, clearly, must take place within that frame.

"I'll give him a trail to follow," muttered Rainsford, and he struck off from the rude paths he had been following into the trackless wilderness. He executed a series of intricate loops; he doubled on his trail again and again, recalling all the lore of the fox hunt and all the dodges of the fox. Night found him leg-weary, with hands and face lashed by the branches, on a thickly wooded ridge. He knew it would be insane to blunder on through the dark, even if he had the strength. His need for rest was imperative and he thought: "I have played the fox; now I must play the cat of the fable." A big tree with a thick trunk and outspread branches was nearby, and taking care to leave not the slightest mark, he climbed up into the crotch and stretching out on one of the broad limbs, after a fashion, rested. Rest brought him new confidence and almost a feeling of security. Even so zealous a hunter as General Zaroff could not trace him there, he told himself; only the devil himself could follow that complicated trail through the jungle after dark. But, perhaps, the general was a devil——

An apprehensive night crawled slowly by like a wounded snake, and sleep did not visit Rainsford, although the silence of a dead world was on the jungle. Toward morning, when a dingy gray was varnishing the sky, the cry of some startled bird focused Rainsford's attention in that direction. Something was coming through the bush, coming slowly, carefully, coming by the same winding way Rainsford had come. He flattened himself down on the limb, and through a screen of leaves almost as thick as tapestry, he watched. The thing that was approaching was a man.

It was General Zaroff. He made his way along with his eyes fixed in utmost concentration on the ground before him. He paused, almost beneath the tree, dropped to his knees and studied the ground. Rainsford's impulse was to hurl himself down like a panther, but he saw the general's right hand held something metallic—a small automatic pistol.

The hunter shook his head several times, as if he were puzzled. Then he straightened up and took from his case one of his black cigarettes; its pungent incenselike smoke floated up to Rainsford's nostrils.

Rainsford held his breath. The general's eyes had left the ground and were traveling inch by inch up the tree. Rainsford froze there, every muscle tensed for a spring. But the sharp eyes of the hunter stopped before they reached the limb where Rainsford lay; a smile spread over his brown face. Very deliberately he blew a smoke ring into the air; then he turned his back on the tree and walked carelessly away, back along the trail he had come. The swish of the underbrush against his hunting boots grew fainter and fainter.

Then pent-up air burst hotly from Rainsford's lungs. His first thought made him feel sick and numb. The general could follow a trail through the woods at night; he could follow an extremely difficult trail; he must have uncanny powers; only by the merest chance had the Cossack failed to see his quarry.

Rainsford's second thought was even more terrible. It sent a shudder of cold horror

---

21. **rowels** (rou'əlz): pointed wheels on the spurs that horseback riders wear on their heels.

through his whole being. Why had the general smiled? Why had he turned back?

Rainsford did not want to believe what his reason told him was true, but the truth was as evident as the sun that had by now pushed through the morning mists. The general was playing with him! The general was saving him for another day's sport! The Cossack was the cat; he was the mouse. Then it was that Rainsford knew the full meaning of terror.

"I will not lose my nerve. I will not."

He slid down from the tree and struck off again into the woods. His face was set and he forced the machinery of his mind to function. Three hundred yards from his hiding place he stopped where a huge dead tree leaned <u>precariously</u> on a smaller living one. Throwing off his sack of food, Rainsford took his knife from its sheath and began to work with all his energy.

The job was finished at last, and he threw himself down behind a fallen log a hundred feet away. He did not have to wait long. The cat was coming again to play with the mouse.

Following the trail with the sureness of a bloodhound came General Zaroff. Nothing escaped those searching black eyes, no crushed blade of grass, no bent twig, no mark, no matter how faint, in the moss. So intent was the Cossack on his stalking that he was upon the thing Rainsford had made before he saw it. His foot touched the protruding bough that was the trigger. Even as he touched it, the general sensed his danger and leaped back with the agility of an ape. But he was not quite quick enough; the dead tree, delicately adjusted to rest on the cut living one, crashed down and struck the general a glancing blow on the shoulder as it fell; but for his alertness, he must have been smashed beneath it. He staggered, but he did not fall; nor did he drop his revolver. He stood there, rubbing his injured shoulder, and Rainsford, with fear again gripping his heart, heard the general's mocking laugh ring through the jungle.

WORDS TO OWN

precariously (prē·ker′ē·əs·lē) *adv.:* unsteadily; in an unstable manner.

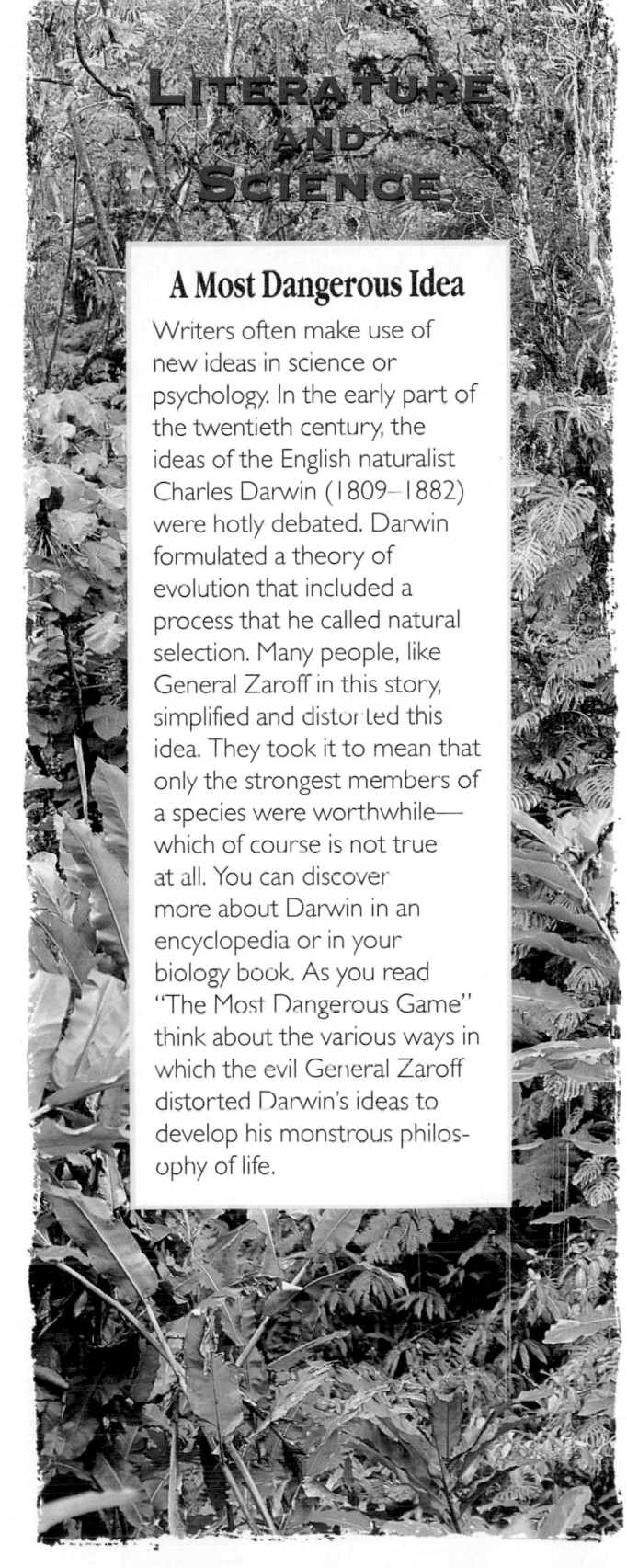

LITERATURE AND SCIENCE

A Most Dangerous Idea

Writers often make use of new ideas in science or psychology. In the early part of the twentieth century, the ideas of the English naturalist Charles Darwin (1809–1882) were hotly debated. Darwin formulated a theory of evolution that included a process that he called natural selection. Many people, like General Zaroff in this story, simplified and distorted this idea. They took it to mean that only the strongest members of a species were worthwhile—which of course is not true at all. You can discover more about Darwin in an encyclopedia or in your biology book. As you read "The Most Dangerous Game" think about the various ways in which the evil General Zaroff distorted Darwin's ideas to develop his monstrous philosophy of life.

"Rainsford," called the general, "if you are within the sound of my voice, as I suppose you are, let me congratulate you. Not many men know how to make a Malay mancatcher. Luckily for me, I too have hunted in Malacca.[22] You are proving interesting, Mr. Rainsford. I am going now to have my wound dressed; it's only a slight one. But I shall be back. I shall be back."

When the general, nursing his bruised shoulder, had gone, Rainsford took up his flight again. It was flight now, a desperate, hopeless flight, that carried him on for some hours. Dusk came, then darkness, and still he pressed on. The ground grew softer under his moccasins; the vegetation grew ranker, denser; insects bit him savagely. Then, as he stepped forward, his foot sank into the ooze. He tried to wrench it back, but the muck sucked viciously at his foot as if it were a giant leech. With a violent effort, he tore loose. He knew where he was now. Death Swamp and its quicksand.

His hands were tight closed as if his nerve were something tangible that someone in the darkness was trying to tear from his grip. The softness of the earth had given him an idea. He stepped back from the quicksand a dozen feet or so, and, like some huge prehistoric beaver, he began to dig.

Rainsford had dug himself in in France,[23] when a second's delay meant death. That had been a placid pastime compared to his digging now. The pit grew deeper; when it was above his shoulders, he climbed out and from some hard saplings cut stakes and sharpened them to a fine point. These stakes he planted in the bottom of the pit with the points sticking up. With flying fingers he wove a rough carpet of weeds and branches and with it he covered the mouth of the pit. Then, wet with sweat and aching with tiredness, he crouched behind the stump of a lightning-charred tree.

He knew his pursuer was coming; he heard the padding sound of feet on the soft earth, and the night breeze brought him the perfume of the general's cigarette. It seemed to Rainsford that the general was coming with unusual swiftness; he was not feeling his way along, foot by foot. Rainsford, crouching there, could not see the general, nor could he see the pit. He lived a year in a minute. Then he felt an impulse to cry aloud with joy, for he heard the sharp crackle of the breaking branches as the cover of the pit gave way; he heard the sharp scream of pain as the pointed stakes found their mark. He leaped up from his place of concealment. Then he cowered back. Three feet from the pit a man was standing, with an electric torch in his hand.

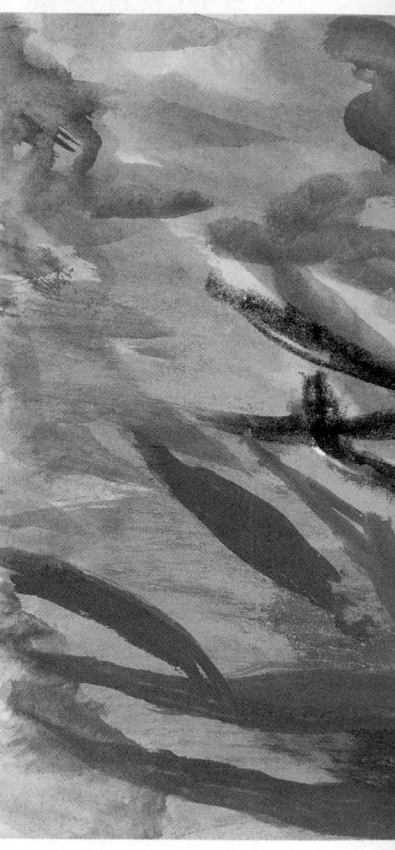

"You've done well, Rainsford," the voice of the general called. "Your Burmese tiger pit has claimed one of my best dogs. Again you score. I think, Mr. Rainsford, I'll see what you can do against my whole pack. I'm going home for a rest now. Thank you for a most amusing evening."

At daybreak Rainsford, lying near the swamp, was awakened by the sound that made him know that he had new things to learn about fear. It was a distant sound, faint and wavering, but he knew it. It was the baying of a pack of hounds.

Rainsford knew he could do one of two things. He could stay where he was and wait. That was suicide. He could flee. That was postponing the inevitable. For a moment he stood there, thinking. An idea that held a wild chance came to him, and, tightening his belt, he headed away from the swamp.

The baying of the hounds drew nearer, then still nearer, nearer, ever nearer. On a ridge

22. **Malacca** (mə·lak′ə): state in what is now the southeastern Asian nation of Malaysia.
23. **dug himself in in France:** dug a hole for shelter from gunfire during World War I (1914-1918).

Rainsford climbed a tree. Down a watercourse, not a quarter of a mile away, he could see the bush moving. Straining his eyes, he saw the lean figure of General Zaroff; just ahead of him Rainsford made out another figure whose wide shoulders surged through the tall jungle weeds. It was the giant Ivan, and he seemed pulled forward by some unseen force. Rainsford knew that Ivan must be holding the pack in leash.

They would be on him any minute now. His

He shinnied excitedly up a tree and looked back. His pursuers had stopped. But the hope that was in Rainsford's brain when he climbed died, for he saw in the shallow valley that General Zaroff was still on his feet. But Ivan was not. The knife, driven by the recoil of the springing tree, had not wholly failed.

"Nerve, nerve, nerve!" he panted, as he dashed along. A blue gap showed between the trees dead ahead. Ever nearer drew the hounds.

mind worked frantically. He thought of a native trick he had learned in Uganda. He slid down the tree. He caught hold of a springy young sapling and to it he fastened his hunting knife, with the blade pointing down the trail; with a bit of wild grapevine he tied back the sapling. Then he ran for his life. The hounds raised their voices as they hit the fresh scent. Rainsford knew now how an animal at bay feels.

He had to stop to get his breath. The baying of the hounds stopped abruptly, and Rainsford's heart stopped too. They must have reached the knife.

Rainsford forced himself on toward that gap. He reached it. It was the shore of the sea. Across a cove he could see the gloomy gray stone of the château. Twenty feet below him the sea rumbled and hissed. Rainsford hesitated. He heard the hounds. Then he leaped far out into the sea. . . .

When the general and his pack reached the place by the sea, the Cossack stopped. For some minutes he stood regarding the blue-green expanse of water. He shrugged his shoulders. Then he sat down, took a drink of brandy from a silver flask, lit a perfumed cigarette, and hummed a bit from *Madama Butterfly*.

General Zaroff had an exceedingly good dinner in his great paneled dining hall that evening. With it he had a bottle of Pol Roger[24] and half a bottle of Chambertin.[25] Two slight annoyances kept him from perfect enjoyment. One was the thought that it would be difficult to replace Ivan; the other was that his quarry had escaped him; of course the American hadn't played the game—so thought the general as he tasted his after-dinner liqueur. In his library he read, to soothe himself, from the works of Marcus Aurelius.[26] At ten he went up to his bedroom. He was deliciously tired, he said to himself as he locked himself in. There was a little moonlight, so before turning on his light, he went to the window and looked down

24. **Pol Roger** (pôl rô·zhā′): brand of champagne.
25. **Chambertin** (shän′ber·tan′): red burgundy wine.
26. **Marcus Aurelius** (mär′kəs ô·rē′lē·əs): emperor of Rome from A.D. 161 to 180, who wrote about the philosophy of Stoicism, which held that people should make themselves indifferent to both pain and pleasure.

at the courtyard. He could see the great hounds, and he called: "Better luck another time," to them. Then he switched on the light.

A man, who had been hiding in the curtains of the bed, was standing there.

"Rainsford!" screamed the general. "How in God's name did you get here?"

"Swam," said Rainsford. "I found it quicker than walking through the jungle."

The general sucked in his breath and smiled. "I congratulate you," he said. "You have won the game."

Rainsford did not smile. "I am still a beast at bay," he said, in a low, hoarse voice. "Get ready, General Zaroff."

The general made one of his deepest bows. "I see," he said. "Splendid! One of us is to furnish a repast for the hounds. The other will sleep in this very excellent bed. On guard, Rainsford. . . ."

He had never slept in a better bed, Rainsford decided.

MEET THE WRITER

Famous for One Story

Richard Connell (1893–1949) started his writing career early. At the age of ten, he began covering baseball games for the newspaper his father edited. He earned ten cents a game. By the age of sixteen he was city editor. As a student at Harvard, Connell edited the humor magazine called the *Lampoon* and the college newspaper. He went on to write novels, hundreds of short stories, and screenplays. Many of his plots, like the one in "The Most

Dangerous Game," trace the exploits of macho adventurers, who bear a strong resemblance to Rainsford. Despite Connell's tremendous output, only one story—"The Most Dangerous Game" (1924)—is still in print. The story keeps showing up in movies. It's been filmed under several titles: *The Most Dangerous Game* (1932); *A Game of Death* (1946); and *Run for the Sun* (1956), a loose adaptation in which a man and a woman crash in the jungle where a Nazi war criminal chases them with guns and hounds. A more recent movie version is titled *Surviving the Game*.

MAKING MEANINGS

First Thoughts

1. What do you think happens to Zaroff? What are some possible endings for the story?

Shaping Interpretations

2. To hook our curiosity, writers drop clues that **foreshadow,** or hint at, what is going to happen later in a story.

   - What clues at the start of the story foreshadow danger ahead for Rainsford?

   - How does Rainsford's discussion about hunting at the start of the story foreshadow later developments?

   - What details in the description of Zaroff's unusual dental features and lips foreshadow the truth about his nature? (How do these details make him seem like a monster?)

3. How are Rainsford and Zaroff alike and how are they different? To help you "see" their **characters** at a glance, fill out a diagram like the one here. List the characteristics of each man in his circle. Then list the characteristics they share in the shaded area.

Rainsford   Zaroff

4. Based on their characters, decide if Rainsford changes his mind about hunting by the end of the story. (Is it possible that he becomes just like Zaroff?)

Connecting with the Text

5. Do the characters in this story make some comments that you felt strongly about? What remarks from the story did you note in your double-entry journal? How did you respond? Be sure to share your responses in class.

Extending the Text

6. Think about Zaroff's civilized tastes and his favorite game. Do "Zaroffs"—people whose appearances mask their true natures—exist in real life? Explain.

Challenging the Text

7. Some stories are so fantastic or contrived that we have to suspend our disbelief. This means that if we do not believe that something in a story is possible, the writer hopes we'll still accept it. Did any details in this story demand that you suspend your disbelief? Share your responses in class.

Reviewing the Text

a. Refer to your Reader's Log: Did you guess the meaning of the story's **title**? What is the most dangerous game?

b. Why is Zaroff glad that it is Rainsford who has come to the island?

c. What happens during the three days of the chase?

d. How is Rainsford's **conflict** with Zaroff finally resolved?

CHOICES: Building Your Portfolio

Writer's Notebook

1. Collecting Ideas for a True Narrative

Finding a conflict. In the Writer's Workshop on page 112, you'll write a true narrative about a conflict. Refer now to the conflicts you listed before you started this collection of stories (see page 11) or make a new list of conflicts you might write about—the conflicts should involve you or someone you know. (Rainsford's physical struggle with the sea might give you new ideas.) Highlight or circle any conflict you'd like to elaborate on and do a cluster diagram to see if you have enough material for a full narrative. Save your notes.

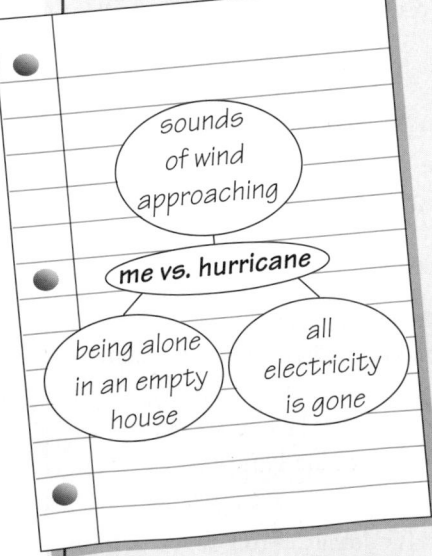

Critical Thinking/ Speaking

2. Looking at Movies

With a partner, prepare for a five-minute TV spot to talk about how this story compares with current movies. To prepare for your conversation, fill out a chart like the one that follows:

	Connell's Tale	A Movie
1. Hero and his/her values		
2. Villain		
3. Setting		
4. What is at stake?		
5. Hero's exploits		
6. Level of violence		

Creative Writing

3. The Sequel

It is morning. Rainsford has just awakened in Zaroff's excellent bed. What happens next? Write the next episode in Rainsford's adventure. (Does he stay on Ship-Trap Island and turn it into a theme park, or does he go home and work on behalf of endangered species? Or does he do something even more surprising?) You might let Rainsford tell his story, using *I*.

Critical Writing

4. Analyzing Characters: Roles for Women?

Suppose you've been asked to cast actors for the roles of Zaroff and Rainsford for yet another movie version of the story. The producer wants a written report on the characteristics of each man and suggestions of actors to play their parts. If you filled out a diagram like the one on page 29, refer to it as you draft your report. Could the roles be played by women?

Drawing

5. Map the Chase

As an illustration for this story, prepare a map of the chase. Before you start, list all the features of the island you want to locate. Include geographical features (jagged crags and dense jungle) and man-made features (the château and all the traps).

LANGUAGE LINK ⬛ MINI-LESSON

Style: Powerful Verbs

Some of Connell's Verbs

• pressed
• strained
• wrestled
• muttered
• dragged
• flung
• tumbled
• floundered
• thrashed
• hurled
• fluttered
• chuckled
• shrugged
• snapped
• plunged
• flattened
• crashed
• staggered

Verbs help give writing its power and color. Richard Connell's verbs propel his story—they help us visualize very specifically what is happening. Compare Connell's vivid verb choices below to the tamer ones above them.

1. He jumped upon the rail and stood there. . . .
   Connell: "He leaped upon the rail and balanced himself there. . . ."

2. . . . his pipe fell from his mouth. He tried to catch it. . . .
   Connell: ". . . his pipe . . . was knocked from his mouth. He lunged for it. . . ."

3. . . . the wash from the speeding yacht hit him in the face and the salt water in his open mouth made him choke.
   Connell: ". . . the wash from the speeding yacht slapped him in the face and the salt water in his open mouth made him gag and strangle."

Find at least five other passages in the story that use good vivid verbs to help you see very specific actions.

Try It Out

➤ Replace the tame, general verbs in these sentences. Change the wording if you wish.

1. Rainsford went to the cellar.

2. Ivan said something under his breath.

3. Zaroff looked around.

4. An animal called in the night.

➤ You might keep a list of strong verbs in your notebook for use when you revise your own writing. Circle the verbs in your own writing that you think could be made more vivid. Then use your list of verbs to find replacements.

VOCABULARY ⬛ HOW TO OWN A WORD

WORD BANK

palpable
indolently
disarming
amenities
imprudent
scruples
solicitously
opiate
deplorable
precariously

Yes or No

Be sure you can justify your yes or no responses.

1. If a lump is palpable, can it be felt?
2. Would someone who worked indolently deserve a raise?
3. Would a disarming leader be able to calm an angry crowd?
4. Are VCRs and fax machines amenities in today's world?
5. Is it imprudent for bicyclists to wear helmets?
6. Is someone without scruples likely to return a lost wallet?
7. If you are treated solicitously, are you treated kindly?
8. Would loud music be an opiate for a tired, crying baby?
9. Would you buy a product described as deplorable?
10. If a pilot flew precariously, would you fly with her?

Elements of Literature

PLOT: "Hooking" Your Reader's Curiosity

When you talk about stories, plot is the element to start with, for plot is story itself. **Plot** is a series of related events, each event connected to the next, like links in a chain. Each event in a plot "hooks" our curiosity and pulls us forward to the next event, to satisfy that curiosity.

> **E**ach event in a plot "hooks" our curiosity and pulls us forward to the next event.

The monster, preparing to paralyze his latest challenger, looked at his victim and saw she was chewing gum.

Right away, we wonder what's going to happen. Why isn't the victim afraid, the way she should be?

The dragon withdrew his venomous talons and asked the young person if she was laughing at him.

Why? the reader wonders. Is the monster especially funny looking? Is he very insecure?

If our curiosity is aroused by these events, we await successive ones with mounting suspense. We want to know: "What happens next?" This buildup of suspense is how a plot works. A series of related events plants the hook of curiosity in us, making us read to find out: "What happens next?"

Conflict: The Fuel of Narrative

Usually, we care about what happens next in a story because we're hooked by a **conflict,** or struggle. This struggle might take place between two characters or it might take place between a character and a whole group of people, or it might take place between a character and something nonhuman—a typhoon or a shark or gas in the mine pit or a computer virus. Conflict can also take place within a character's own mind and heart: The desire to be peaceable might conflict with an urge to knock the stuffing out of a bully. A desire to win someone's friendship might conflict with a fear of rejection. Often, an external conflict results in an internal problem: Facing that typhoon is going to produce fear and perhaps a desire to run away.

When the conflict takes place between a character and another person or between a character and something nonhuman, it is an **external conflict**. When the conflict takes place inside a character's mind, it is an **internal conflict**. Conflict is the fuel of narrative. The greater the conflict, the more we care about the outcome.

> **T**he greater the conflict, the more we care about the outcome.

The "Bare Bones" of a Plot

Stories, like houses and human beings, need a structure or framework to hold them together. Plots are usually built on four major parts, which we might think of as their "bare bones." The first part of a plot can be called the **basic situation**. This is the opening of the story, where the characters and their conflict are usually introduced. (Writers have many names for this part of the story. Some call it **exposition**.)

by John Leggett

Once upon a time there lived a young girl named Cinderella, who was as beautiful as she was good. But she was totally detested by her evil step-mother and two nasty and jealous stepsisters. Cinderella longed to go to the Prince's ball—but it was simply out of the question. After all, Cinderella was just a kitchen servant.

The second part of a plot is the **complication**. Now the main character takes some action to resolve the conflict and meets with more problems or complications: danger, hostility, fear, or even a new threatening situation.

A Fairy Godmother promised to get Cinderella to the ball if she obeyed one rule: "Be home by midnight." Dressed in the most beautiful gown and wearing tiny glass slippers manufactured on the spot by her Fairy Godmother, Cinderella went to the ball. No one knew who this dazzling beauty was. The Prince fell in love with her at first sight, but she had to flee at midnight. One of the dainty glass slippers was left behind as she ran out of the palace.

The third part of a story is the **climax**. This is the key scene of the story—that tense or exciting or terrifying moment when our emotional involvement is greatest. Now we find out what the outcome of the conflict is going to be.

The Prince made a house-to-house search for the foot that fit the tiny shoe. The stepsisters shaved off parts of their big feet to try to squeeze into the slipper, but no luck. The Prince found that small foot on Cinderella.

The final part of the story is the **resolution**. Sometimes this is called the **denouement** (dā'·nōo·män'), a French word for "unraveling the knot." The resolution occurs at the end of the story (perhaps it's only a paragraph). Now all the struggles are over, and we know what is going to happen to the people in the story. The resolution "closes" the story.

Cinderella married the Prince and they lived happily ever after. The stepsisters and the cruel stepmother, however, suffered ghastly punishments for their misdeeds.

These four bare bones support a series of events intended to hook our curiosity. If one of these bare bones is weak, the story falls apart. We are not hooked by the characters and their struggle, and we just might not want to finish the story.

> If one of these bare bones is weak, the story falls apart.

"The plot thickened—and then it congealed."

From The Wall Street Journal. Permission courtesy Cartoon Features Syndicate.

Reading Focus

Facing Fate

Have you ever stood and faced something that you believed would harm you? Have you ever felt that even though you knew a confrontation would be dangerous, you still had to take the risk? Here is a story about a man who spends his life running from his fate. Can he escape the monster in his life? *Should* he?

A Dialogue with the Text

In your Reader's Log, keep track of your responses as you read this story. Record your questions about the plot, your predictions about what will happen next, and your responses to the way the conflict finally is resolved.

Elements of Literature

The Big Moment: Climax

The moment we look forward to in a story is its **climax**—the highly charged moment in the story when our suspense is greatest, when we finally discover how the conflict is going to work out. Be sure to record your emotional responses to the climax in this story. (Did you predict what it would be?)

> T he most emotional moment in a story is its **climax,** when the outcome of the conflict is finally revealed.
>
> *For more on Climax, see page 33.*

THE COLOMBER

Dino Buzzati, *translated by Lawrence Venuti*

That mouth continually opening and closing, those terrible teeth.

When Stefano Roi was twelve years old, he asked his father, a sea captain and the owner of a fine sailing ship, to take him on board as his birthday gift. "When I am grown up," the boy said, "I want to go to sea with you. And I shall command ships even more beautiful and bigger than yours."

"God bless you, my son," the father answered. And since his vessel had to leave that very day, he took the boy with him.

It was a splendid sunny day, and the sea was calm. Stefano, who had never been on a ship, happily wandered around on deck, admiring the complicated maneuvers of the sails. He asked the sailors about this and that, and they gladly explained everything to him.

When the boy had gone astern,[1] he stopped, his curiosity aroused, to observe something that intermittently rose to the surface at a distance of two to three hundred meters, in line with the ship's wake.

Although the ship was indeed moving fast, carried by a great quarter wind, that thing always maintained the same distance. And though the boy did not make out what it was, there was some indefinable air about it, which attracted him intensely.

No longer seeing Stefano on deck, the father came down from the bridge, after having shouted his name in vain, and went to look for him.

"Stefano, what are you doing there, standing so still?" the captain asked his son, finally perceiving him on the stern as he stared at the waves.

"Papa, come here and see."

---

1. **astern:** toward the stern, or back of the ship. The front of the ship is the bow.

The father came, and he too looked in the direction indicated by the boy, but he could not see anything.

"There's a dark thing that rises in the wake every so often," Stefano said, "and it follows behind us."

"Despite my forty years," said the father, "I believe I still have good eyesight. But I see absolutely nothing."

After the boy insisted, the father went to get a telescope, and he scrutinized the surface of the sea, in line with the wake. Stefano saw him turn pale.

"What is it? Why do you make that face?"

"Oh, I wish I had never listened to you," the captain exclaimed. "Now I'm worried about you. What you see rising from the water and following us is not some object. That is a colomber. It's the fish that sailors fear above all others, in every sea in the world. It is a tremendous, mysterious shark, more clever than man. For reasons that perhaps no one will ever know, it chooses its victim, and when it has chosen, it pursues him for years and years, for his entire life, until it has succeeded in devouring him. And the strange thing is this: No one can see the colomber except the victim himself and his blood relations."

"It's not a story?"

"No. I have never seen it. But from descriptions I have heard many times, I immediately recognized it. That bisonlike muzzle, that mouth continually opening and closing, those terrible teeth. Stefano, there's no doubt, the colomber has ominously chosen you, and as long as you go to sea, it will give you no peace. Listen to me: We are going back to land now, immediately; you will go ashore and never leave it again, not for any reason whatsoever. You must promise me you won't. Seafaring is not for you, my son. You must resign yourself. After all, you will be able to make your fortune on land too."

WORDS TO OWN

intermittently (in′tər·mit″nt·lē) *adv.*: from time to time.

scrutinized (skro̅o̅t″n·īzd′) *v.*: looked at carefully.

Having said this, he immediately reversed his course, reentered the port, and on the pretext of a sudden illness, he put his son ashore. Then he left again without him.

Deeply troubled, the boy remained on the shore until the last tip of the masts sank behind the horizon. Beyond the pier that bounded the port, the sea was completely deserted. But looking carefully, Stefano could perceive a small black point which intermittently surfaced on the water: It was "his" colomber, slowly moving back and forth, obstinately waiting for him.

From then on, with every expedient the boy was dissuaded from his desire to go to sea. His father sent him to study at an inland city, hundreds of kilometers away. And for some time, distracted by his new surroundings, Stefano no longer thought about the sea monster. Still, he returned home for summer vacations, and the first thing he did, as soon as he had some free time, was hurry to the end of the pier for a kind of verification, although he fundamentally considered it unnecessary. After so many years, even supposing that all the stories his father told him were true, the colomber had certainly given up its siege.

But Stefano stood there, astonished, his heart pounding. At a distance of two to three hundred meters from the pier, in the open sea, the sinister fish was moving back and forth, slowly, raising its muzzle from the water every now and then and turning toward land, as if it anxiously watched for whether Stefano was coming at last.

So the idea of that hostile creature waiting for him day and night became a secret obsession for Stefano. And even in the distant city it cropped up to wake him with worry in the middle of the night. He was safe, of course; hundreds of kilometers separated him from the colomber. And yet he knew that beyond the mountains, beyond the forests and the plains, the shark was waiting for him. He might have moved even to the most remote continent, and still the colomber would have appeared in the

mirror of the nearest sea, with the inexorable obstinacy of a fatal instrument.

Stefano, who was a serious and eager boy, profitably continued his studies, and as soon as he was a man, he found a dignified and well-paying position at a store in that inland city. Meanwhile, his father died through illness, his magnificent ship was sold by his widow, and his son found himself the heir to a modest fortune. Work, friends, diversions, first love affairs—Stefano's life was now well under way, but the thought of the colomber nonetheless tormented him like a mirage that was fatal and fascinating at the same time; and as the days passed, rather than disappear, it seemed to become more insistent.

Great are the satisfactions of an industrious, well-to-do, and quiet life, but greater still is

WORDS TO OWN

obstinately (äb′stə·nət·lē) *adv.*: stubbornly; persistently.

expedient (ek·spē′dē·ənt) *n.*: means; resource; device used in an emergency.

inexorable (in·eks′ə·rə·bəl) *adj.*: unyielding; immovable; unchangeable.

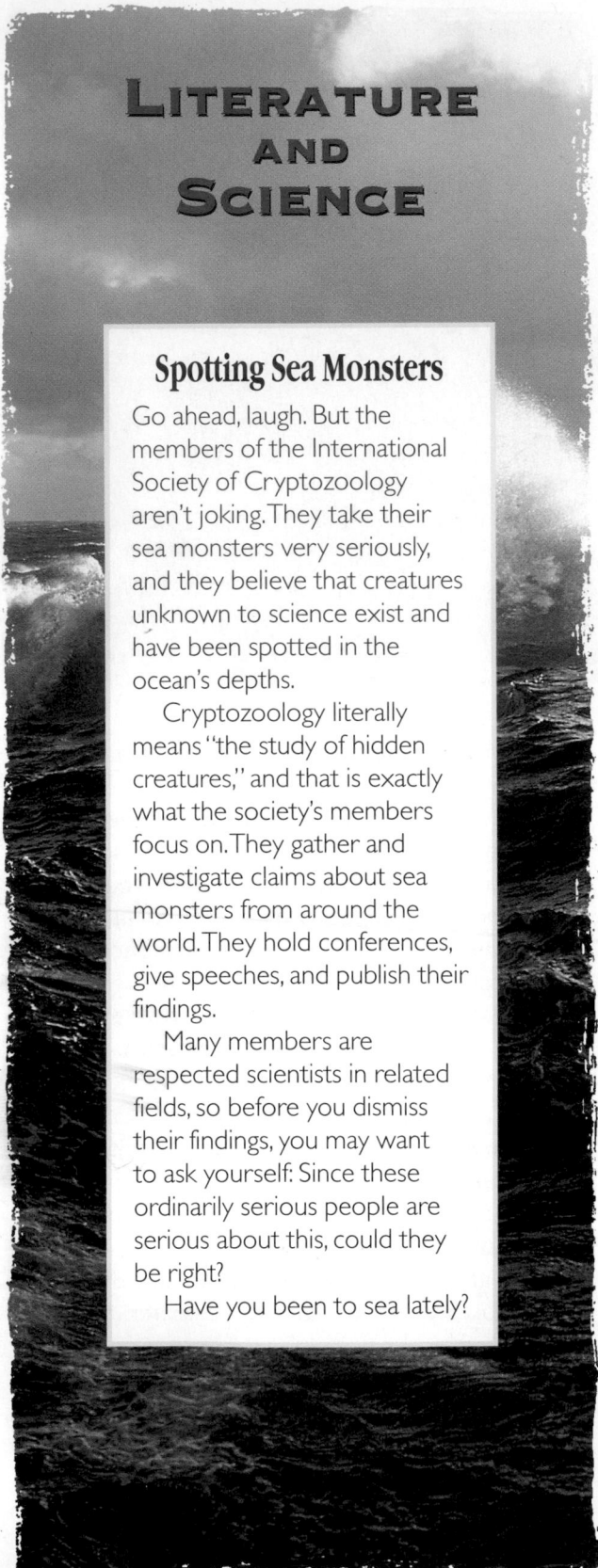

LITERATURE AND SCIENCE

Spotting Sea Monsters

Go ahead, laugh. But the members of the International Society of Cryptozoology aren't joking. They take their sea monsters very seriously, and they believe that creatures unknown to science exist and have been spotted in the ocean's depths.

Cryptozoology literally means "the study of hidden creatures," and that is exactly what the society's members focus on. They gather and investigate claims about sea monsters from around the world. They hold conferences, give speeches, and publish their findings.

Many members are respected scientists in related fields, so before you dismiss their findings, you may want to ask yourself: Since these ordinarily serious people are serious about this, could they be right?

Have you been to sea lately?

the attraction of the abyss. Stefano was hardly twenty-two years old when, having said goodbye to his inland friends and resigned from his job, he returned to his native city and told his mother of his firm intention to follow his father's trade. The woman, to whom Stefano had never mentioned the mysterious shark, joyfully welcomed his decision. To have her son abandon the sea for the city had always seemed to her, in her heart, a betrayal of the family's tradition.

Stefano began to sail, giving proof of his seaworthiness, his resistance to fatigue, and his intrepid spirit. He sailed and sailed, and in the wake of his ship, day and night, in good weather and in storms, the colomber trudged along. He knew that this was his curse and his penalty, and precisely for this reason, perhaps, he did not find the strength to sever himself from it. And no one on board, except him, perceived the monster.

"Don't you see anything over there?" he asked his companions from time to time, pointing at the wake.

"No, we don't see anything at all. Why?"

"I don't know. It seemed to me . . ."

"You didn't see a colomber, by any chance, did you?" the sailors asked, laughing and touching wood.

"Why are you laughing? Why are you touching wood?"

"Because the colomber is an animal that spares no one. And if it has begun to follow this ship, it means that one of us is doomed."

But Stefano did not slacken. The uninterrupted threat that followed on his heels seemed in fact to strengthen his will, his passion for the sea, his courage in times of strife and danger.

When he felt that he was master of his trade, he used his modest inheritance to acquire a small steam freighter with a partner; then he

---

WORDS TO OWN

abyss (ə·bis′) *n.:* bottomless depth; here, something beyond understanding or too deep for measurement.

intrepid (in·trep′id) *adj.:* fearless; brave.

sever (sev′ər) *v.:* separate; break or cut off.

---

became the sole proprietor of it, and thanks to a series of successful shipments, he could subsequently buy a true merchantman,[2] setting out with always more-ambitious aims. But the successes, and the millions, were unable to remove that continual torment from his soul; nor did he ever try, on the other hand, to sell the ship and retire to undertake different enterprises on land.

To sail and sail was his only thought. Just as soon as he set foot on land in some port after a long journey, the impatience to depart again immediately pricked him. He knew that outside the colomber was waiting for him and that the colomber was synonymous with ruin. With nothingness. An indomitable impulse dragged him without rest, from one ocean to another.

Until, one day, Stefano suddenly realized that he had grown old, very old; and no one around him could explain why, rich as he was, he did not finally leave the cursed life of the sea. He was old, and bitterly unhappy, because his entire existence had been spent in that mad flight across the seas, to escape his enemy. But the temptation of the abyss had always been greater for him than the joys of a prosperous and quiet life.

One evening, while his magnificent ship was anchored offshore at the port where he was born, he felt close to death. He then called his second officer, in whom he had great trust, and ordered him not to oppose what he was about to do. The other man promised, on his honor.

Having gotten this assurance, Stefano revealed to the second officer the story of the colomber that had continued to pursue him uselessly for nearly fifty years. The officer listened to him, frightened.

"It has escorted me from one end of the world to the other," Stefano said, "with a faithfulness that not even the noblest friend could have shown. Now I am about to die. The colomber too will be terribly old and weary by now. I cannot betray it."

2. **merchantman:** ship used in trade between cities, states, or countries.

Having said this, he took his leave of the crew, ordered a small boat to be lowered into the sea, and boarded it, after he made them give him a harpoon.

"Now I am going to meet it," he announced. "It isn't right to disappoint it. But I shall struggle, with all my might."

With a few weary strokes of the oars, he drew away from the side of the ship. Officers and sailors saw him disappear down below, on the placid sea, shrouded in the nocturnal shadows. In the sky was a crescent moon.

He did not have to work very hard. Suddenly the colomber's horrible snout emerged at the side of the boat.

"Here I am with you, finally," Stefano said. "Now it's just the two of us." And gathering his remaining strength, he raised the harpoon to strike.

"Uh," the colomber groaned, imploringly, "what a long journey it's taken to find you. I too am wasted with fatigue. How much you made me swim. And you kept on fleeing. You never understood at all."

"What?" asked Stefano, with the point of his harpoon over the colomber's heart.

"I have not pursued you around the world to devour you, as you thought. I was charged by the King of the Sea only to deliver this to you."

And the shark stuck out its tongue, offering the old captain a small phosphorescent[3] sphere.

Stefano picked it up and examined it. It was a pearl of unusual size. And he recognized it as the famous *Perla del Mare*, which brought luck, power, love, and peace of mind to whoever possessed it. But now it was too late.

"Alas!" said the captain, shaking his head sadly. "How wrong it all is. I managed to condemn myself, and I have ruined your life."

"Goodbye, poor man," answered the colomber. And it sank into the black waters forever.

3. **phosphorescent:** glowing.

WORDS TO OWN

indomitable (in·däm′i·tə·bəl) *adj.*: unconquerable; not easily discouraged or defeated.

placid (plas′id) *adj.*: undisturbed; calm; tranquil.

Two months later, pushed by an undertow, a small boat came alongside an abrupt reef. It was sighted by several fishermen, who drew near, curious. In the boat, still seated, was a sun-bleached skeleton; between the little bones of its fingers it grasped a small round stone.

The colomber is a huge fish, frightening to behold and extremely rare. Depending on the sea and the people who live by its shores, the fish is also called the kolombrey, kahloubrha, kalonga, kalu-balu, chalung-gra. Naturalists strangely ignore it. Some even maintain that it does not exist.

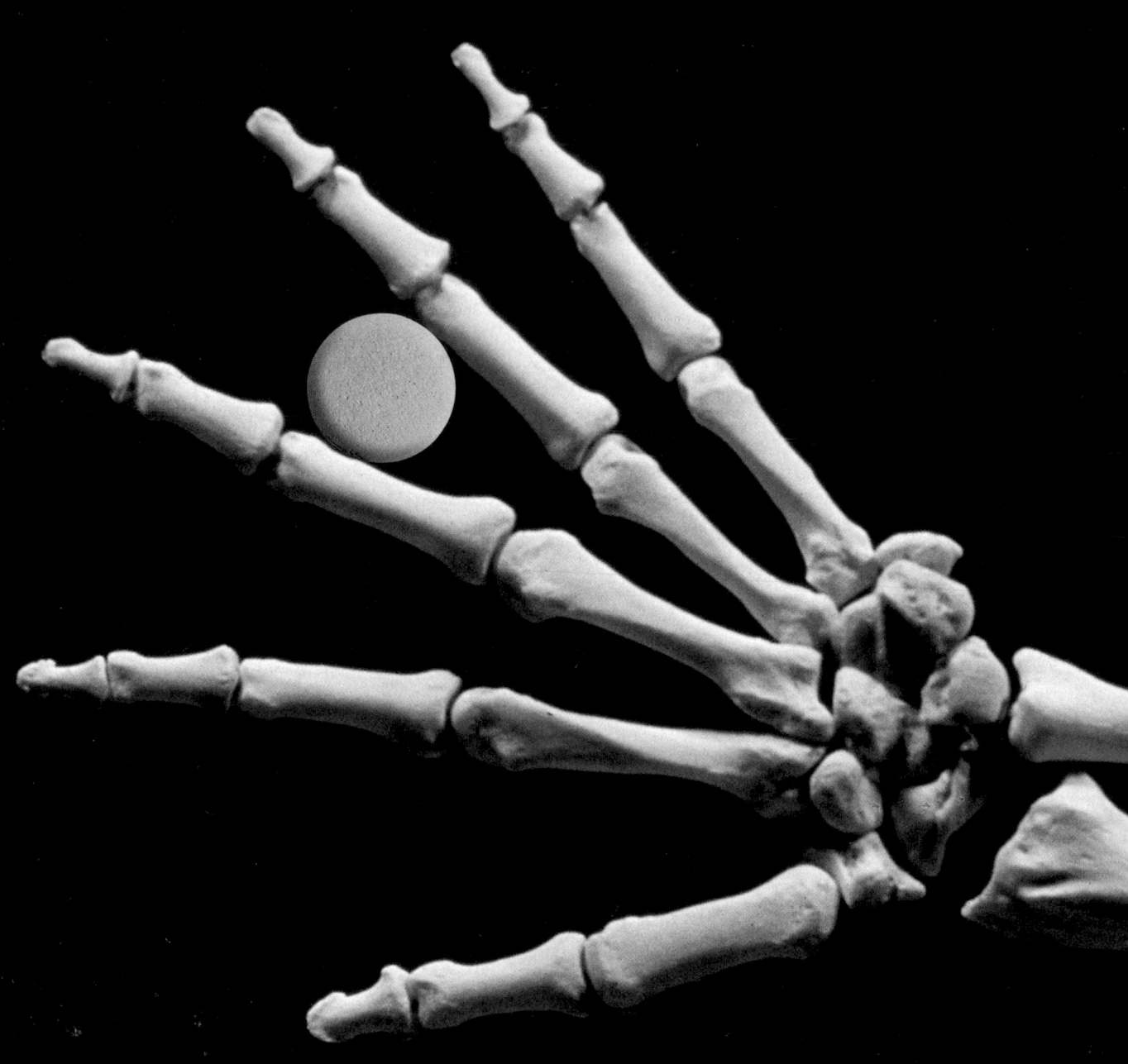

Versatility in Italy

For many years, **Dino Buzzati** (bōō·tsä′tē) (1906–1972) was an editor of a daily newspaper in Milan, Italy. A sort of jack-of-all-trades when it came to his writing career, Buzzati was a successful journalist, novelist, short-story writer, nonfiction writer, and science-fiction writer. In addition, he was a talented painter and illustrator, creating drawings for some of his own work.

Buzzati in English

If you enjoyed "The Colomber" and want to read more of Buzzati's strange stories, look for *The Tartar Steppe* (Avon) and *Restless Nights* (North Point Press), the collection of short stories that includes "The Colomber."

The Orca

I am the Orca
My skin is like a black and white jigsaw
puzzle.
I am the Orca
5   I have fins that cut through the water like
scissors slashing through paper.
I am the Orca
I live in a pod with friends and family.
I am the Orca
10   I was born free to roam the blue waters of the
world.
I am the Orca

—Robynn Waterstrat
Leota Junior High School
Woodinville, Washington

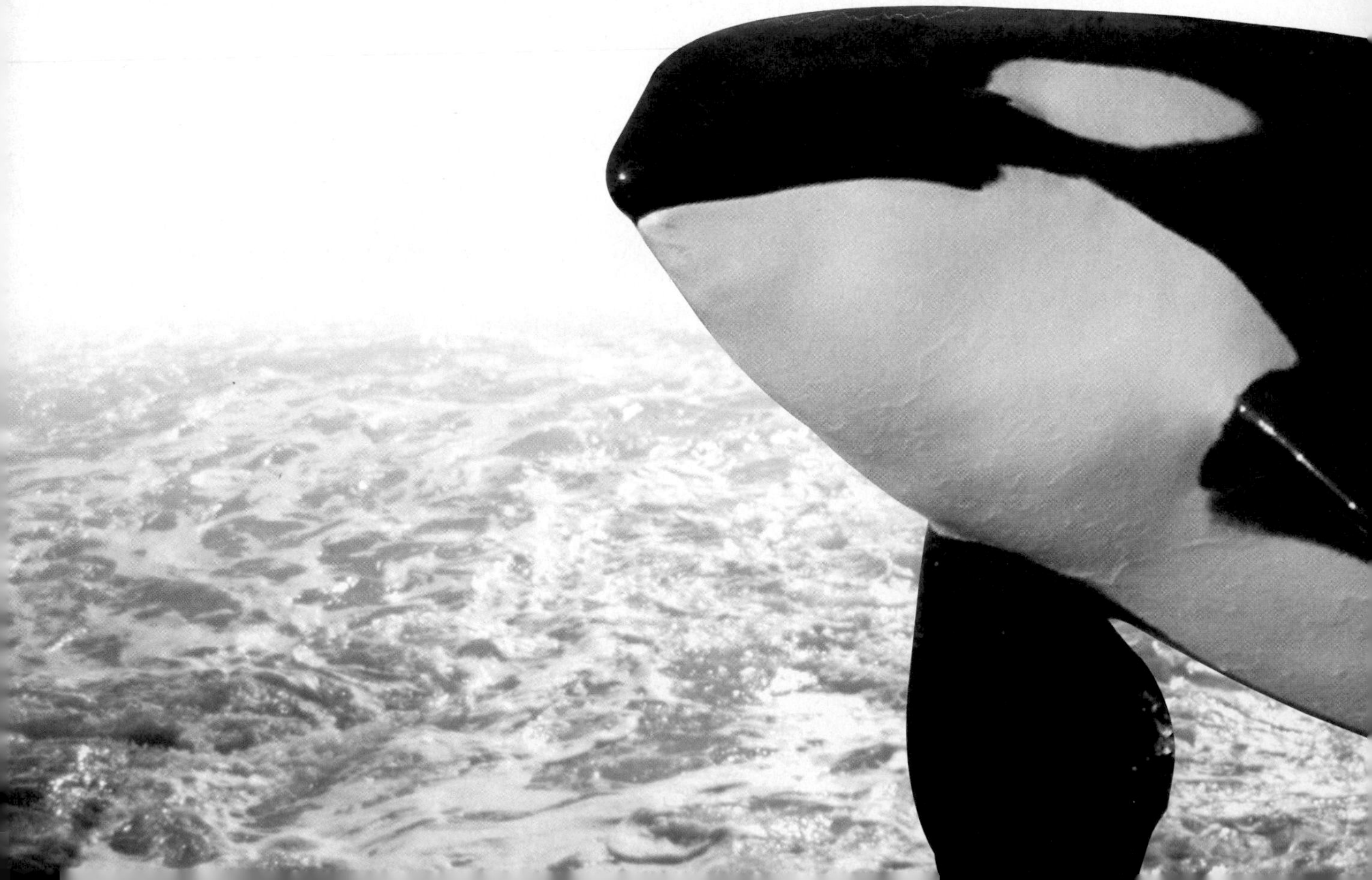

MAKING MEANINGS

First Thoughts

1. Check your Reader's Log. How do the predictions you made as you read compare with Buzzati's surprise ending? What do you think happened at the end?

Shaping Interpretations

2. If you knew that something intended to have you for dinner, you would probably stay as far away from it as you could. How do you explain Stefano's behavior—why would he continue to tempt fate and risk his life at sea?

3. What do you think would have happened if Stefano had faced the colomber earlier in his life?

4. Are you sure that there really was a colomber? Find evidence in the text to prove or disprove its existence. (How about that stone in the skeleton's hand?)

5. If there was no colomber, what *was* Stefano's "monster"?

6. You are already familiar with stories that end with a moral: "He who laughs last laughs best," for instance, or "Slow but steady wins the race." Write two or three morals for Buzzati's story.

Connecting with the Text

7. Is this just an entertaining story, or does it have some message for you? Explain your feelings about the story's possible wider meanings.

Challenging the Text

8. In what other ways could the story have ended? What do you think of stories that have puzzling endings like this one?

Reviewing the Text

Pretend that you're telling your children the story of the colomber as if the events happened to one of your ancestors. Without going back to the text, summarize the story and identify the **climactic** event. Then compare your summaries in class. Refer to the text to settle disagreements. Do you agree on the story's climax?

CHOICES: Building Your Portfolio

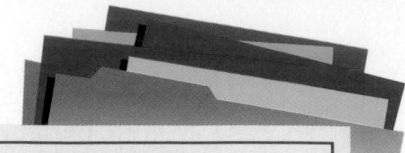

Writer's Notebook

1. Collecting Ideas for a True Narrative

Organizing your main events.

Buzzati begins his story "The Colomber" at the beginning—a young boy on his first ocean voyage—and ends it at the end—a skeleton adrift in a small boat. He chooses to tell his story in **chronological** order, narrating events as they happen. Another writer might include a **flashback,** interrupting the story to bring readers back to earlier times or events.

You should have some notes about a conflict you'll use for the assignment in the Writer's Workshop on page 112. Refer to those notes now and develop a more complete list of the main events of your story. When you've listed the main events, decide if you'll tell your story in chronological order or flash back to tell your readers about something that happened in the past.

News Writing

2. And This Just In

Suppose you are a TV news reporter. Word has just come into the newsroom of the discovery of a skeleton in a small fishing boat. Your assignment is to write the Stefano Roi story. Summarize the important events of the story, giving your report a human-interest slant by including a brief profile of Stefano. In the lead to your news report you must answer the questions Who? What? When? Where? Why? How? The rest of your report should fill in details.

Creative Writing

3. I Am the Colomber . . .

Model a short poem or speech in the style of the student poem "The Orca" on page 42. Write as if you are the colomber. Tell what you look like, where you live, what you like to do—and what happened to Stefano. Add a line telling where you are now.

Research/Science

4. Monster Hunting

Do you think creatures like the colomber really exist—in the sea, in lakes or rivers, or on land? Many people do think so. (See "Spotting Sea Monsters" on page 38.) There are reports of sightings of all kinds of unexplained creatures—such as Bigfoot or the Loch Ness monster. Do some research on the frequency and location of "creature sightings." Try books, newspapers, magazines, television shows, even the Internet for source material. You might compile information on a number of different sightings or concentrate on just one particular creature. Present your findings in written or illustrated form.

MONSTER SIGHTED!

Alien Story: Events

First hear rumors of space landing.

Someone sights a monster in the mountains.

Government reports about an alien are leaked to the press.

Fear and panic start to spread in cities.

Roads become jammed.

Scientists are called in.

Television reports 24 hours a day.

Language Handbook HELP

See Active and Passive Voice, page 1000.

Technology HELP

See Language Workshop CD-ROM. *Key word entry: voice.*

Style: Verbs Play Active and Passive Roles

Like people, verbs may have an active or passive voice.

A verb in the **active** voice expresses an action done *by* its subject: *Tina sent her reply.* A verb in the **passive** voice expresses an action done *to* its subject: *The reply was sent by Tina.*

An active verb takes charge. A passive verb is weaker and doesn't act alone; it needs a helping verb. Here are examples of both voices from "The Colomber":

1. "From then on . . . the boy <u>was dissuaded</u> [passive] from his desire to go to sea."

2. ". . . his magnificent ship <u>was sold</u> [passive] by his widow, and his son <u>found</u> [active] himself the heir to a modest fortune."

3. ". . . a small boat . . . <u>was sighted</u> [passive] by several fishermen. . . ."

Passive voice is useful when the writer or speaker doesn't know who or what performed an action ("My bicycle was taken from the schoolyard") or when the writer or speaker doesn't want other people to know who did the action ("The light was left on all night.").

Try It Out

➤ Make these sentences stronger and more direct by changing the passive voice to active. Notice how the active voice can result in shorter, more vigorous sentences.

1. The pearl was offered by the colomber.
2. The stone was gripped by Stefano's skeleton.
3. The story has been reviewed favorably by most students.
4. My reading of this story will always be remembered.

➤ When you revise your writing, check your verbs. Rewrite those sentences that can be shortened and made more forceful with active verbs.

VOCABULARY   HOW TO OWN A WORD

WORD BANK

intermittently
scrutinized
obstinately
expedient
inexorable
abyss
intrepid
sever
indomitable
placid

Which Word?

Be sure you can justify your answers to "Which Word?"

1. Which adjective describes someone who refuses to give in?
2. Which adjective could be used to describe a quiet pond?
3. Which noun indicates a means to an end?
4. Which noun could be used for the Grand Canyon?
5. Which verb tells how a detective looked at a clue?
6. Which adverb tells how some rain showers fall?
7. Which adjective could describe a brave firefighter?
8. Which verb could you use to say you've broken up with someone?
9. Which adjective describes the march of time?
10. Which adverb tells how a stubborn person acts?

Reading Focus

Nature as a Monster

We human beings have an uneasy relationship with nature. Nature has two faces: We see it as a source of beauty and peace, but we fear its sudden random violence. Extreme weather (hurricanes, droughts, blizzards), volcanoes, earthquakes, even the attacks of tiny creatures (ticks, killer bees, fleas) or viruses can threaten our life on earth. Perhaps this is why, since ancient times, stories have been told about people who find themselves face to face with the dangerous side of nature. In many of these stories, a natural catastrophe threatens to wipe out all evidence of human life on this planet. Such stories reflect our deepest fears, and perhaps for this reason they are, even today, enormously popular.

Quickwrite

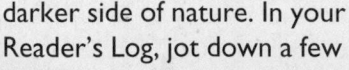

Think about this other, darker side of nature. In your Reader's Log, jot down a few of the ways that nature can threaten human life. If you have ever personally faced nature in its monstrous forms, write briefly about your experience. Save your notes; you'll come back to them later.

Elements of Literature

Danger Signs

Foreshadowing is a technique used by writers to build up suspense, to create anxiety as we read. Foreshadowing hints at what is to come. At the beginning of "The Birds," for example, du Maurier first makes us aware that something might be wrong by saying that the birds are more restless than ever this year. At once we want to know why. Look for other signs of approaching danger as the story continues.

> **F**oreshadowing is the use of clues to hint at events that will occur later.
>
> *For more on Foreshadowing, see the Handbook of Literary Terms.*

THE BIRDS

Daphne du Maurier

On December the third, the wind changed overnight, and it was winter. Until then the autumn had been mellow, soft. The leaves had lingered on the trees, golden-red, and the hedgerows were still green. The earth was rich where the plow had turned it.

Nat Hocken, because of a wartime disability, had a pension and did not work full time at the farm. He worked three days a week, and they gave him the lighter jobs: hedging, thatching, repairs to the farm buildings.

Although he was married, with children, his was a solitary disposition; he liked best to work alone. It pleased him when he was given a bank to build up or a gate to mend at the far end of the peninsula, where the sea surrounded the farmland on either side. Then, at midday, he would pause and eat the pasty[1] that his wife had baked for him and, sitting on the cliff's edge, would watch the birds. Autumn was best for this, better than spring. In spring the birds flew inland, purposeful, intent; they knew where they were bound; the rhythm and ritual of their life brooked no delay. In autumn those that had not migrated overseas but remained to pass the winter were caught up in the same driving urge, but because migration was denied them, followed a pattern of their own. Great flocks of them came to the peninsula, restless, uneasy, spending themselves in motion; now wheeling, circling in the sky, now settling to feed on the rich, new-turned soil; but even when they fed, it was as though they did so without hunger, without desire. Restlessness drove them to the skies again.

Black and white, jackdaw and gull, mingled in strange partnership, seeking some sort of liberation, never satisfied, never still. Flocks of starlings, rustling like silk, flew to fresh pasture, driven by the same necessity of movement, and the smaller birds, the finches and the larks, scattered from tree to hedge as if compelled.

WORDS TO OWN

disposition (dis′pə·zish′ən) *n.*: personality or temperament.

---

1. **pasty** (pas′tē): meat pie.

Nat watched them, and he watched the sea birds too. Down in the bay they waited for the tide. They had more patience. Oystercatchers, redshank, sanderling, and curlew watched by the water's edge; as the slow sea sucked at the shore and then withdrew, leaving the strip of seaweed bare and the shingle[2] churned, the sea birds raced and ran upon the beaches. Then that same impulse to flight seized upon them too. Crying, whistling, calling, they skimmed the placid sea and left the shore. Make haste, make speed, hurry and begone; yet where, and to what purpose? The restless urge of autumn, unsatisfying, sad, had put a spell upon them, and they must flock, and wheel, and cry; they must spill themselves of motion before winter came.

"Perhaps," thought Nat, munching his pasty by the cliff's edge, "a message comes to the birds in autumn, like a warning. Winter is coming. Many of them perish. And like people who, apprehensive of death before their time, drive themselves to work or folly, the birds do likewise."

The birds had been more restless than ever this fall of the year, the agitation more marked because the days were still. As the tractor traced its path up and down the western hills, the figure of the farmer silhouetted on the driving seat, the whole machine and the man upon it, would be lost momentarily in the great cloud of wheeling, crying birds. There were many more than usual; Nat was sure of this. Always, in autumn, they followed the plow, but not in great flocks like these, nor with such clamor.

Nat remarked upon it when hedging was finished for the day. "Yes," said the farmer, "there are more birds about than usual; I've noticed it too. And daring, some of them, taking no notice of the tractor. One or two gulls came so close to my head this afternoon I thought they'd knock my cap off! As it was, I could scarcely see what I was doing when they were overhead and I had the sun in my eyes. I have a notion the

2. **shingle:** beach covered with gravel.

weather will change. It will be a hard winter. That's why the birds are restless."

Nat, tramping home across the fields and down the lane to his cottage, saw the birds still flocking over the western hills, in the last glow of the sun. No wind, and the gray sea calm and full. Campion in bloom yet in the hedges, and the air mild. The farmer was right, though, and it was that night the weather turned. Nat's bedroom faced east. He woke just after two and heard the wind in the chimney. Not the storm and bluster of a sou'westerly gale, bringing the rain, but east wind, cold and dry. It sounded hollow in the chimney, and a loose slate rattled on the roof. Nat listened, and he could hear the sea roaring in the bay. Even the air in the small bedroom had turned chill: A draft came under the skirting of the door, blowing upon the bed. Nat drew the blanket round him, leaned closer to the back of his sleeping wife, and stayed wakeful, watchful, aware of misgiving without cause.

Then he heard the tapping on the window. There was no creeper on the cottage walls to break loose and scratch upon the pane. He listened, and the tapping continued until, irritated by the sound, Nat got out of bed and went to the window. He opened it, and as he did so something brushed his hand, jabbing at his knuckles, grazing the skin. Then he saw the flutter of the wings and it was gone, over the roof, behind the cottage.

WORDS TO OWN

placid (plas′id) *adj.*: calm; untroubled.
apprehensive (ap′rē·hen′siv) *adj.*: fearful.

It was a bird; what kind of bird he could not tell. The wind must have driven it to shelter on the sill.

He shut the window and went back to bed but, feeling his knuckles wet, put his mouth to the scratch. The bird had drawn blood. Frightened, he supposed, and bewildered, the bird, seeking shelter, had stabbed at him in the darkness. Once more he settled himself to sleep.

Presently the tapping came again, this time more forceful, more insistent, and now his wife woke at the sound and, turning in the bed, said to him, "See to the window, Nat, it's rattling."

"I've already seen to it," he told her; "there's some bird there trying to get in. Can't you hear the wind? It's blowing from the east, driving the birds to shelter."

"Send them away," she said, "I can't sleep with that noise."

He went to the window for the second time, and now when he opened it, there was not one bird upon the sill but half a dozen; they flew straight into his face, attacking him.

He shouted, striking out at them with his arms, scattering them; like the first one, they flew over the roof and disappeared. Quickly he let the window fall and latched it.

"Did you hear that?" he said. "They went for me. Tried to peck my eyes." He stood by the window, peering into the darkness, and could see nothing. His wife, heavy with sleep, murmured from the bed.

"I'm not making it up," he said, angry at her suggestion. "I tell you the birds were on the sill, trying to get into the room."

Suddenly a frightened cry came from the room across the passage where the children slept.

"It's Jill," said his wife, roused at the sound, sitting up in bed. "Go to her, see what's the matter."

Nat lit the candle, but when he opened the bedroom door to cross the passage the draft blew out the flame.

There came a second cry of terror, this time from both children, and stumbling into their room, he felt the beating of wings about him in the darkness. The window was wide open. Through it came the birds, hitting first the ceiling and the walls, then swerving in midflight, turning to the children in their beds.

"It's all right, I'm here," shouted Nat, and the children flung themselves, screaming, upon him, while in the darkness the birds rose and dived and came for him again.

"What is it, Nat, what's happened?" his wife called from the further bedroom, and swiftly he pushed the children through the door to the passage and shut it upon them, so that he was alone now in their bedroom with the birds.

He seized a blanket from the nearest bed and, using it as a weapon, flung it to right and left about him in the air. He felt the thud of bodies, heard the fluttering of wings, but they were not yet defeated, for again and again they returned to the assault, jabbing his hands, his head, the little stabbing beaks sharp as pointed forks. The blanket became a weapon of defense; he wound it about his head, and then in greater darkness beat at the birds with his bare hands. He dared not stumble to the door and open it, lest in doing so the birds should follow him.

How long he fought with them in the darkness he could not tell, but at last the beating of the wings about him lessened and then withdrew, and through the density of the blanket he was aware of light. He waited, listened; there was no sound except the fretful crying of one of the children from the bedroom beyond. The fluttering, the whirring of the wings had ceased.

He took the blanket from his head and stared about him. The cold gray morning light exposed the room. Dawn and the open window had called the living birds; the dead lay on the floor. Nat gazed at the little corpses, shocked and horrified. They were all small birds, none of any size; there must have been fifty of them lying there upon the floor. There were robins, finches, sparrows, blue tits, larks, and bramblings, birds that by nature's law kept to their own flock and their own territory, and now, joining one with another in their urge for battle, had destroyed themselves against the bedroom walls or in the strife had been destroyed by him. Some had lost feathers in the fight; others had blood, his blood, upon their beaks.

Sickened, Nat went to the window and stared out across his patch of garden to the fields.

It was bitter cold, and the ground had all the hard, black look of frost. Not white frost, to shine in the morning sun, but the black frost that the east wind brings. The sea, fiercer now with the turning tide, white-capped and steep, broke harshly in the bay. Of the birds there was no sign. Not a sparrow chattered in the hedge beyond the garden gate, no early missel thrush or blackbird pecked on the grass for worms. There was no sound at all but the east wind and the sea.

Nat shut the window and the door of the small bedroom and went back across the passage to his own. His wife sat up in bed, one child asleep beside her, the smaller in her arms, his face bandaged. The curtains were tightly drawn across the window, the candles lit. Her face looked garish in the yellow light. She shook her head for silence.

"He's sleeping now," she whispered, "but only just. Something must have cut him, there was blood at the corner of his eyes. Jill said it was the birds. She said she woke up, and the birds were in the room."

His wife looked up at Nat, searching his face for confirmation. She looked terrified, bewildered, and he did not want her to know that he was also shaken, dazed almost, by the events of the past few hours.

"There are birds in there," he said, "dead birds, nearly fifty of them. Robins, wrens, all the little birds from hereabouts. It's as though a madness seized them, with the east wind." He sat down on the bed beside his wife and held her hand. "It's the weather," he said; "it must be that, it's the hard weather. They aren't the birds, maybe, from here around. They've been driven down from upcountry."

"But, Nat," whispered his wife, "it's only this night that the weather turned. There's been no snow to drive them. And they can't be hungry yet. There's food for them out there in the fields."

"It's the weather," repeated Nat. "I tell you, it's the weather."

His face, too, was drawn and tired, like hers. They stared at one another for a while without speaking.

"I'll go downstairs and make a cup of tea," he said.

The sight of the kitchen reassured him. The cups and saucers, neatly stacked upon the dresser, the table and chairs, his wife's roll of knitting on her basket chair, the children's toys in a corner cupboard.

He knelt down, raked out the old embers, and relit the fire. The glowing sticks brought normality; the steaming kettle and the brown teapot, comfort and security. He drank his tea, carried a cup up to his wife. Then he washed in the scullery[3] and, putting on his boots, opened the back door.

The sky was hard and leaden, and the brown hills that had gleamed in the sun the day before looked dark and bare. The east wind, like a razor, stripped the trees, and the leaves, crackling and dry, shivered and scattered with the wind's blast. Nat stubbed the earth with his boot. It was frozen hard. He had never known a change so swift and sudden. Black winter had descended in a single night.

The children were awake now. Jill was chattering upstairs and young Johnny crying once again. Nat heard his wife's voice, soothing, comforting. Presently they came down. He had breakfast ready for them, and the routine of the day began.

"Did you drive away the birds?" asked Jill, restored to calm because of the kitchen fire, because of day, because of breakfast.

"Yes, they've all gone now," said Nat. "It was the east wind brought them in. They were frightened and lost; they wanted shelter."

"They tried to peck us," said Jill. "They went for Johnny's eyes."

"Fright made them do that," said Nat. "They

3. **scullery:** room next to the kitchen where dishes are washed.

didn't know where they were in the dark bedroom."

"I hope they won't come again," said Jill. "Perhaps if we put bread for them outside the window they will eat that and fly away."

She finished her breakfast and then went for her coat and hood, her schoolbooks, and her satchel. Nat said nothing, but his wife looked at him across the table. A silent message passed between them.

"I'll walk with her to the bus," he said. "I don't go to the farm today."

And while the child was washing in the scullery he said to his wife, "Keep all the windows closed, and the doors too. Just to be on the safe side. I'll go to the farm. Find out if they heard anything in the night." Then he walked with his small daughter up the lane. She seemed to have forgotten her experience of the night before. She danced ahead of him, chasing the leaves, her face whipped with the cold and rosy under the pixie hood.

"Is it going to snow, Dad?" she said. "It's cold enough."

He glanced up at the bleak sky, felt the wind tear at his shoulders.

"No," he said, "it's not going to snow. This is a black winter, not a white one."

All the while he searched the hedgerows for the birds, glanced over the top of them to the fields beyond, looked to the small wood above the farm where the rooks and jackdaws gathered. He saw none.

The other children waited by the bus stop, muffled, hooded like Jill, the faces white and pinched with cold.

Jill ran to them, waving. "My dad says it won't snow," she called, "it's going to be a black winter."

She said nothing of the birds. She began to push and struggle with another little girl. The bus came ambling up the hill. Nat saw her onto it, then turned and walked back toward the farm. It was not his day for work, but he wanted to satisfy himself that all was well. Jim, the cowman, was clattering in the yard.

"Boss around?" asked Nat.

"Gone to market," said Jim. "It's Tuesday, isn't it?"

He clumped off round the corner of a shed. He had no time for Nat. Nat was said to be superior. Read books and the like. Nat had forgotten it was Tuesday. This showed how the events of the preceding night had shaken him. He went to the back door of the farmhouse and heard Mrs. Trigg singing in the kitchen, the wireless[4] making a background to her song.

"Are you there, missus?" called out Nat.

She came to the door, beaming, broad, a good-tempered woman.

"Hullo, Mr. Hocken," she said. "Can you tell me where this cold is coming from? Is it Russia? I've never seen such a change. And it's going on, the wireless says. Something to do with the Arctic Circle."

"We didn't turn on the wireless this morning," said Nat. "Fact is, we had trouble in the night."

"Kiddies poorly?"

"No . . ." He hardly knew how to explain it. Now, in daylight, the battle of the birds would sound absurd.

He tried to tell Mrs. Trigg what had happened, but he could see from her eyes that she thought his story was the result of a nightmare.

"Sure they were real birds," she said, smiling, "with proper feathers and all? Not the funny-shaped kind that the men see after closing hours on a Saturday night?"

"Mrs. Trigg," he said, "there are fifty dead birds, robins, wrens, and such, lying low on the floor of the children's bedroom. They went for me; they tried to go for young Johnny's eyes."

Mrs. Trigg stared at him doubtfully.

"Well there, now," she answered, "I suppose the weather brought them. Once in the bedroom, they wouldn't know where they were to. Foreign birds maybe, from that Arctic Circle."

"No," said Nat, "they were the birds you see about here every day."

"Funny thing," said Mrs. Trigg, "no explaining it, really. You ought to write up and ask the *Guardian.* They'd have some answer for it. Well, I must be getting on."

She nodded, smiled, and went back into the kitchen.

Nat, dissatisfied, turned to the farm gate. Had it not been for those corpses on the bedroom floor, which he must now collect and bury somewhere, he would have considered the tale exaggeration too.

Jim was standing by the gate.

"Had any trouble with the birds?" asked Nat.

"Birds? What birds?"

"We got them up our place last night. Scores of them, came in the children's bedroom. Quite savage they were."

"Oh?" It took time for anything to penetrate Jim's head. "Never heard of birds acting savage," he said at length. "They get tame, like, sometimes. I've seen them come to the windows for crumbs."

"These birds last night weren't tame."

"No? Cold, maybe. Hungry. You put out some crumbs."

Jim was no more interested than Mrs. Trigg had been. It was, Nat thought, like air raids in the war. No one down this end of the country knew what the Plymouth folk had seen and suffered. You had to endure something yourself before it touched you. He walked back along the lane and crossed the stile[5] to his cottage. He found his wife in the kitchen with young Johnny.

"See anyone?" she asked.

"Mrs. Trigg and Jim," he answered. "I don't think they believed me. Anyway, nothing wrong up there."

"You might take the birds away," she said. "I daren't go into the room to make the beds until you do. I'm scared."

5. **stile:** steps over a wall or fence.

4. **wireless:** radio.

"Nothing to scare you now," said Nat. "They're dead, aren't they?"

He went up with a sack and dropped the stiff bodies into it, one by one. Yes, there were fifty of them, all told. Just the ordinary, common birds of the hedgerow, nothing as large even as a thrush. It must have been fright that made them act the way they did. Blue tits, wrens—it was incredible to think of the power of their small beaks jabbing at his face and hands the night before. He took the sack out into the garden and was faced now with a fresh problem. The ground was too hard to dig. It was frozen solid, yet no snow had fallen, nothing had happened in the past hours but the coming of the east wind. It was unnatural, queer. The weather prophets must be right. The change was something connected with the Arctic Circle.

The wind seemed to cut him to the bone as he stood there uncertainly, holding the sack. He could see the white-capped seas breaking down under in the bay. He decided to take the birds to the shore and bury them.

When he reached the beach below the headland he could scarcely stand, the force of the east wind was so strong. It hurt to draw breath, and his bare hands were blue. Never had he known such cold, not in all the bad winters he could remember. It was low tide. He crunched his way over the shingle to the softer sand and then, his back to the wind, ground a pit in the sand with his heel. He meant to drop the birds into it, but as he opened up the sack the force of the wind carried them, lifted them, as though in flight again, and they were blown away from him along the beach, tossed like feathers, spread and scattered, the bodies of the fifty frozen birds. There was something ugly in the sight. He did not like it. The dead birds were swept away from him by the wind.

"The tide will take them when it turns," he said to himself.

He looked out to sea and watched the crested breakers, combing green. They rose stiffly, curled, and broke again, and because it was ebb tide the roar was distant, more remote, lacking the sound and thunder of the flood.

Then he saw them. The gulls. Out there, riding the seas.

What he had thought at first to be the white caps of the waves were gulls. Hundreds, thousands, tens of thousands . . . They rose and fell in the trough of the seas, heads to the wind, like a mighty fleet at anchor, waiting on the tide. To eastward and to the west, the gulls were there. They stretched as far as his eye could reach, in close formation, line upon line. Had the sea been still, they would have covered the bay like a white cloud, head to head, body packed to body. Only the east wind, whipping the sea to breakers, hid them from the shore.

Nat turned and, leaving the beach, climbed the steep path home. Someone should know of this. Someone should be told. Something was happening, because of the east wind and the weather, that he did not understand. He wondered if he should go to the call box by the bus stop and ring up the police. Yet what could they do? What could anyone do? Tens of thousands of gulls riding the sea there in the bay because of storm, because of hunger. The police would think him mad, or drunk, or take the statement from him with great calm. "Thank you. Yes, the matter has already been reported. The hard weather is driving the birds inland in great numbers." Nat looked about him. Still no sign of any other bird. Perhaps the cold had sent them all from upcountry? As he drew near to the cottage his wife came to meet him at the door. She called to him, excited. "Nat," she said, "it's on the wireless. They've just read out a special news bulletin. I've written it down."

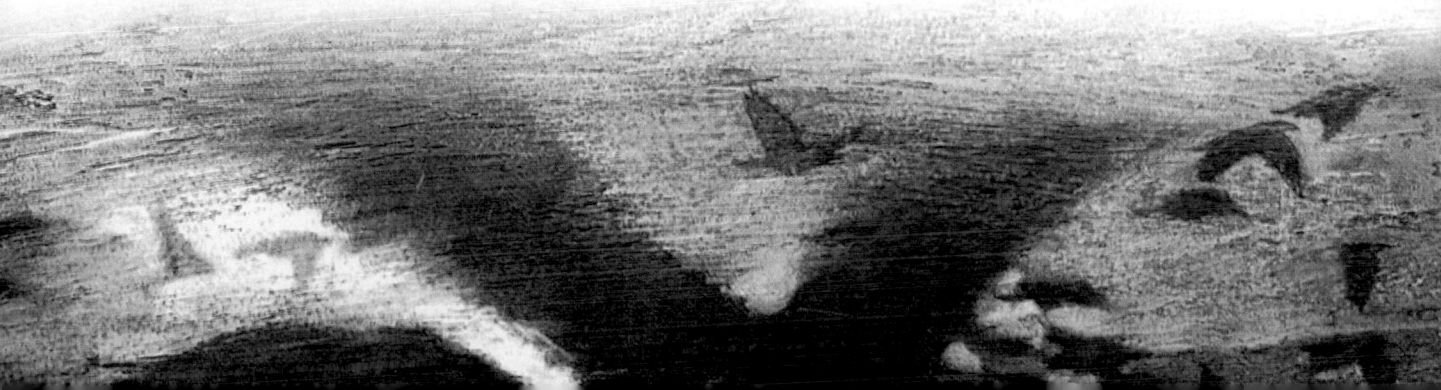

"What's on the wireless?" he said.

"About the birds," she said. "It's not only here; it's everywhere. In London, all over the country. Something has happened to the birds."

Together they went into the kitchen. He read the piece of paper lying on the table.

"Statement from the Home Office at 11 A.M. today. Reports from all over the country are coming in hourly about the vast quantity of birds flocking above towns, villages, and outlying districts, causing obstruction and damage and even attacking individuals. It is thought that the Arctic airstream, at present covering the British Isles, is causing birds to migrate south in immense numbers and that intense hunger may drive these birds to attack human beings. House-holders are warned to see to their windows, doors, and chimneys, and to take reasonable precautions for the safety of their children. A further statement will be issued later."

A kind of excitement seized Nat; he looked at his wife in triumph.

"There you are," he said. "Let's hope they'll hear that at the farm. Mrs. Trigg will know it wasn't any story. It's true. All over the country. I've been telling myself all morning there's something wrong. And just now, down on the beach, I looked out to sea and there are gulls, thousands of them, tens of thousands—you couldn't put a pin between their heads—and they're all out there, riding on the sea, waiting."

"What are they waiting for, Nat?" she asked.

He stared at her, then looked down again at the piece of paper.

"I don't know," he said slowly. "It says here the birds are hungry."

He went over to the drawer where he kept his hammer and tools.

"What are you going to do, Nat?"

"See to the windows and the chimneys too, like they tell you."

"You think they would break in, with the windows shut? Those sparrows and robins and such? Why, how could they?"

He did not answer. He was not thinking of the robins and the sparrows. He was thinking of the gulls. . . .

He went upstairs and worked there the rest of the morning, boarding the windows of the bedrooms, filling up the chimney bases. Good that it was his free day and he was not working at the farm. It reminded him of the old days, at the beginning of the war. He was not married then, and he had made all the blackout boards for his mother's house in Plymouth. Made the shelter too. Not that it had been of any use when the moment came. He wondered if they would take these precautions up at the farm. He doubted it. Too easygoing, Harry Trigg and his missus. Maybe they'd laugh at the whole thing. Go off to a dance or a whist drive.[6]

"Dinner's ready." She called him, from the kitchen.

"All right. Coming down."

He was pleased with his handiwork. The frames fitted nicely over the little panes and at the bases of the chimneys.

When dinner was over and his wife was washing up, Nat switched on the one o'clock news. The same announcement was repeated, the one which she had taken down during the morning, but the news bulletin enlarged upon it. "The flocks of birds have caused dislocation in all areas," read the announcer, "and in London the sky was so dense at ten o'clock this morning that it seemed as if the city was covered by a vast black cloud.

"The birds settled on rooftops, on window ledges, and on chimneys. The species included blackbird, thrush, the common house sparrow, and, as might be expected in the metropolis, a vast quantity of pigeons and starlings and that frequenter of the London river, the black-headed gull. The sight has been so unusual that traffic came to a standstill in many thoroughfares, work was abandoned in shops and offices, and the streets and pavements were crowded with people standing about to watch the birds."

Various incidents were <u>recounted</u>, the suspected reason of cold and <u>hunger</u> stated

6. **whist drive:** card game organized for a large group.

WORDS TO OWN

recounted (ri·kount′id) v.: described in detail; narrated.

again, and warnings to householders repeated. The announcer's voice was smooth and suave. Nat had the impression that this man, in particular, treated the whole business as he would an elaborate joke. There would be others like him, hundreds of them, who did not know what it was to struggle in darkness with a flock of birds. There would be parties tonight in London, like the ones they gave on election nights. People standing about, shouting and laughing, getting drunk. "Come and watch the birds!"

Nat switched off the wireless. He got up and started work on the kitchen windows. His wife watched him, young Johnny at her heels.

"What, boards for down here too?" she said. "Why, I'll have to light up before three o'clock. I see no call for boards down here."

"Better be sure than sorry," answered Nat. "I'm not going to take any chances."

"What they ought to do," she said, "is to call the Army out and shoot the birds. That would soon scare them off."

"Let them try," said Nat. "How'd they set about it?"

"They have the Army to the docks," she answered, "when the dockers strike. The soldiers go down and unload the ships."

"Yes," said Nat, "and the population of London is eight million or more. Think of all the buildings, all the flats and houses. Do you think they've enough soldiers to go around shooting birds from every roof?"

"I don't know. But something should be done. They ought to do something."

Nat thought to himself that "they" were no doubt considering the problem at that very moment, but whatever "they" decided to do in London and the big cities would not help the people here, three hundred miles away. Each householder must look after his own.

"How are we off for food?" he said.

"Now, Nat, whatever next?"

"Never mind. What have you got in the larder?"

"It's shopping day tomorrow, you know that. I don't keep uncooked food hanging about; it goes off. Butcher doesn't call till the day after. But I can bring back something when I go in tomorrow."

Nat did not want to scare her. He thought it possible that she might not go to town tomorrow. He looked in the larder for himself and in the cupboard where she kept her tins. They would do for a couple of days. Bread was low.

"What about the baker?"

"He comes tomorrow too."

He saw she had flour. If the baker did not call she had enough to bake one loaf.

"We'd be better off in the old days," he said, "when the women baked twice a week, and had pilchards[7] salted, and there was food for a family to last a siege, if need be."

"I've tried the children with tinned fish; they don't like it," she said.

Nat went on hammering the boards across the kitchen windows. Candles. They were low in candles too. That must be another thing she meant to buy tomorrow. Well, it could not be helped. They must go early to bed tonight. That was, if . . .

He got up and went out of the back door and stood in the garden, looking down toward the sea. There had been no sun all day, and now, at barely three o'clock, a kind of darkness had already come, the sky <u>sullen</u>, heavy, colorless like salt. He could hear the vicious sea drumming on the rocks. He walked down the path, halfway to the beach. And then he stopped. He could see the tide had turned. The rock that had shown in midmorning was now covered, but it was not the sea that held his eyes. The gulls had risen. They were circling, hundreds of them, thousands of them, lifting their wings against the wind. It was the gulls that made the darkening of the sky. And they were silent. They made not a sound. They just went on soaring and circling, rising, falling, trying their strength against the wind.

Nat turned. He ran up the path, back to the cottage.

"I'm going for Jill," he said. "I'll wait for her at the bus stop."

"What's the matter?" asked his wife. "You've gone quite white."

"Keep Johnny inside," he said. "Keep the door shut. Light up now, and draw the curtains."

"It's only just gone three," she said.

"Never mind. Do what I tell you."

He looked inside the toolshed outside the back door. Nothing there of much use. A spade was too heavy, and a fork no good. He took the hoe. It was the only possible tool, and light enough to carry.

He started walking up the lane to the bus stop and now and again glanced back over his shoulder.

The gulls had risen higher now; their circles were broader, wider; they were spreading out in huge formation across the sky.

He hurried on; although he knew the bus would not come to the top of the hill before four o'clock, he had to hurry. He passed no one on the way. He was glad of this. No time to stop and chatter.

At the top of the hill he waited. He was much too soon. There was half an hour still to go. The east wind came whipping across the fields from the higher ground. He stamped his feet and blew upon his hands. In the distance he could see the clay hills, white and clean, against the heavy pallor of the sky. Something black rose from behind them, like a smudge at first, then widening, becoming deeper, and the smudge became a cloud, and the cloud divided again into five other clouds, spreading north, east, south, and west, and they were not clouds at all; they were birds. He watched them travel across the sky, and as one section passed overhead, within two or three hundred feet of him, he knew, from their speed, they were bound inland, upcountry; they had no business with the people here on the peninsula. They were rooks, crows, jackdaws, magpies, jays, all birds that usually preyed upon the smaller species;

7. **pilchards:** fish similar to sardines.

WORDS TO OWN

sullen (sul′ən) *adj.*: gloomy.

but this afternoon they were bound on some other mission.

"They've been given the towns," thought Nat; "they know what they have to do. We don't matter so much here. The gulls will serve for us. The others go to the towns."

He went to the call box, stepped inside, and lifted the receiver. The exchange would do. They would pass the message on.

"I'm speaking from the highway," he said, "by the bus stop. I want to report large formations of birds traveling upcountry. The gulls are also forming in the bay."

"All right," answered the voice, laconic, weary.

"You'll be sure and pass this message on to the proper quarter?"

"Yes . . . yes . . ." Impatient now, fed up. The buzzing note resumed.

"She's another," thought Nat, "she doesn't care. Maybe she's had to answer calls all day. She hopes to go to the pictures tonight. She'll squeeze some fellow's hand and point up at the sky and say 'Look at all them birds!' She doesn't care."

The bus came lumbering up the hill. Jill climbed out, and three or four other children. The bus went on toward the town.

"What's the hoe for, Dad?"

They crowded around him, laughing, pointing.

"I just brought it along," he said. "Come on now, let's get home. It's cold, no hanging about. Here, you. I'll watch you across the fields, see how fast you can run."

He was speaking to Jill's companions, who came from different families, living in the council houses.[8] A shortcut would take them to the cottages.

"We want to play a bit in the lane," said one of them.

"No, you don't. You go off home or I'll tell your mammy."

They whispered to one another, round-eyed, then scuttled off across the fields. Jill stared at her father, her mouth sullen.

"We always play in the lane," she said.

"Not tonight, you don't," he said. "Come on now, no dawdling."

He could see the gulls now, circling the fields, coming in toward the land. Still silent. Still no sound.

"Look, Dad, look over there, look at all the gulls."

"Yes. Hurry, now."

"Where are they flying to? Where are they going?"

"Upcountry, I dare say. Where it's warmer."

He seized her hand and dragged her after him along the lane.

"Don't go so fast. I can't keep up."

The gulls were copying the rooks and crows. They were spreading out in formation across the sky. They headed, in bands of thousands, to the four compass points.

"Dad, what is it? What are the gulls doing?"

They were not intent upon their flight, as the crows, as the jackdaws had been. They still circled overhead. Nor did they fly so high. It was as though they waited upon some signal. As though some decision had yet to be given. The order was not clear.

8. **council houses:** public housing, built for lower-income families after World War II.

"Do you want me to carry you, Jill? Here, come pick-a-back."

This way he might put on speed; but he was wrong. Jill was heavy. She kept slipping. And she was crying too. His sense of urgency, of fear, had communicated itself to the child.

"I wish the gulls would go away. I don't like them. They're coming closer to the lane."

He put her down again. He started running, swinging Jill after him. As they went past the farm turning, he saw the farmer backing his car out of the garage. Nat called to him.

"Can you give us a lift?" he said.

"What's that?"

Mr. Trigg turned in the driving seat and stared at them. Then a smile came to his cheerful, rubicund[9] face.

"It looks as though we're in for some fun," he said. "Have you seen the gulls? Jim and I are going to take a crack at them. Everyone's gone bird crazy, talking of nothing else. I hear you were troubled in the night. Want a gun?"

Nat shook his head.

The small car was packed. There was just room for Jill, if she crouched on top of petrol tins on the back seat.

"I don't want a gun," said Nat, "but I'd be obliged if you'd run Jill home. She's scared of the birds."

9. **rubicund** (rōō′bə·kund′): reddish, rosy.

He spoke briefly. He did not want to talk in front of Jill.

"OK," said the farmer, "I'll take her home. Why don't you stop behind and join the shooting match? We'll make the feathers fly."

Jill climbed in, and turning the car, the driver sped up the lane. Nat followed after. Trigg must be crazy. What use was a gun against a sky of birds?

Now Nat was not responsible for Jill, he had time to look about him. The birds were circling still above the fields. Mostly herring gull, but the black-backed gull amongst them. Usually they kept apart. Now they were united. Some bond had brought them together. It was the black-backed gull that attacked the smaller birds, and even newborn lambs, so he'd heard. He'd never seen it done. He remembered this now, though, looking above him in the sky. They were coming in toward the farm. They were circling lower in the sky, and the black-backed gulls were to the front, the black-backed gulls were leading. The farm, then, was their target. They were making for the farm.

Nat increased his pace toward his own cottage. He saw the farmer's car turn and come back along the lane. It drew up beside him with a jerk.

"The kid has run inside," said the farmer. "Your wife was watching for her. Well, what do you make of it? They're saying in town the Russians have done it. The Russians have poisoned the birds."

"How could they do that?" asked Nat.

"Don't ask me. You know how stories get around. Will you join my shooting match?"

"No, I'll get along home. The wife will be worried else."

"My missus says if you could eat gull there'd be some sense in it," said Trigg. "We'd have roast gull, baked gull, and pickle 'em into the bargain. You wait until I let off a few barrels into the brutes. That'll scare 'em."

"Have you boarded your windows?" asked Nat.

"No. Lot of nonsense. They like to scare you on the wireless. I've had more to do today than to go round boarding up my windows."

"I'd board them now, if I were you."

"Garn. You're windy. Like to come to our place to sleep?"

"No, thanks all the same."

"All right. See you in the morning. Give you a gull breakfast."

The farmer grinned and turned his car to the farm entrance.

Nat hurried on. Past the little wood, past the old barn, and then across the stile to the remaining field.

As he jumped the stile he heard the whir of wings. A black-backed gull dived down at him from the sky, missed, swerved in flight, and rose to dive again. In a moment it was joined by others, six, seven, a dozen, black-backed and herring mixed. Nat dropped his hoe. The hoe was useless. Covering his head with his arms, he ran toward the cottage. They kept coming at him from the air, silent save for the beating wings. The terrible, fluttering wings. He could feel the blood on his hands, his wrists, his neck. Each stab of a swooping beak tore his flesh. If only he could keep them from his eyes. Nothing else mattered. He must keep them from his eyes. They had not learned yet how to cling to a shoulder, how to rip clothing, how to dive in mass upon the head, upon the body. But with each dive, with each attack, they became bolder. And they had no thought for themselves. When they dived low and missed, they crashed, bruised and broken, on the ground. As Nat ran he stumbled, kicking their spent bodies in front of him.

He found the door; he hammered upon it with his bleeding hands. Because of the boarded windows no light shone. Everything was dark.

"Let me in," he shouted, "it's Nat. Let me in."

He shouted loud to make himself heard above the whir of the gulls' wings.

Then he saw the gannet, poised for the dive, above him in the sky. The gulls circled, retired, soared, one after another, against the wind. Only the gannet remained. One single gannet above him in the sky. The wings folded suddenly to its body. It dropped like a stone. Nat screamed, and the door opened. He stumbled

across the threshold, and his wife threw her weight against the door.

They heard the thud of the gannet as it fell.

His wife dressed his wounds. They were not deep. The backs of his hands had suffered most, and his wrists. Had he not worn a cap they would have reached his head. As to the gannet . . . the gannet could have split his skull.

The children were crying, of course. They had seen the blood on their father's hands.

"It's all right now," he told them. "I'm not hurt. Just a few scratches. You play with Johnny, Jill. Mammy will wash these cuts."

He half shut the door to the scullery so that they could not see. His wife was ashen. She began running water from the sink.

"I saw them overhead," she whispered. "They began collecting just as Jill ran in with Mr. Trigg.

I shut the door fast, and it jammed. That's why I couldn't open it at once when you came."

"Thank God they waited for me," he said. "Jill would have fallen at once. One bird alone would have done it."

Furtively, so as not to alarm the children, they whispered together as she bandaged his hands and the back of his neck.

"They're flying inland," he said, "thousands of them. Rooks, crows, all the bigger birds. I saw them from the bus stop. They're making for the towns."

"But what can they do, Nat?"

"They'll attack. Go for everyone out in the streets. Then they'll try the windows, the chimneys."

"Why don't the authorities do something? Why don't they get the Army, get machine guns, anything?"

"There's been no time. Nobody's prepared. We'll hear what they have to say on the six o'clock news."

Nat went back into the kitchen, followed by his wife. Johnny was playing quietly on the floor. Only Jill looked anxious.

"I can hear the birds," she said. "Listen, Dad."

Nat listened. Muffled sounds came from the windows, from the door. Wings brushing the surface, sliding, scraping, seeking a way of entry. The sound of many bodies, pressed together, shuffling on the sills. Now and again came a thud, a crash, as some bird dived and fell. "Some of them will kill themselves that way," he thought, "but not enough. Never enough."

"All right," he said aloud. "I've got boards over the windows, Jill. The birds can't get in."

He went and examined all the windows. His work had been thorough. Every gap was closed. He would make extra certain, however. He found wedges, pieces of old tin, strips of wood and metal, and fastened them at the sides to reinforce the boards. His hammering helped to deafen the sound of the birds, the shuffling, the

---

WORDS TO OWN

furtively (fur′tiv·lē) *adv.*: stealthily, as if to avoid being seen or heard.

---

tapping, and more ominous—he did not want his wife or the children to hear it—the splinter of cracked glass.

"Turn on the wireless," he said. "Let's have the wireless."

This would drown the sound also. He went upstairs to the bedrooms and reinforced the windows there. Now he could hear the birds on the roof, the scraping of claws, a sliding, jostling sound.

He decided they must sleep in the kitchen, keep up the fire, bring down the mattresses, and lay them out on the floor. He was afraid of the bedroom chimneys. The boards he had placed at the chimney bases might give way. In the kitchen they would be safe because of the fire. He would have to make a joke of it. Pretend to the children they were playing at camp. If the worst happened, and the birds forced an entry down the bedroom chimneys, it would be hours, days perhaps, before they could break down the doors. The birds would be imprisoned in the bedrooms. They could do no harm there. Crowded together, they would stifle and die.

He began to bring the mattresses downstairs. At the sight of them his wife's eyes widened in apprehension. She thought the birds had already broken in upstairs.

"All right," he said cheerfully, "we'll all sleep together in the kitchen tonight. More cozy here by the fire. Then we shan't be worried by those silly old birds tapping at the windows."

He made the children help him rearrange the furniture, and he took the precaution of moving the dresser, with his wife's help, across the window. It fitted well. It was an added safeguard. The mattresses could now be laid, one beside the other, against the wall where the dresser had stood.

"We're safe enough now," he thought. "We're snug and tight, like an air-raid shelter. We can

hold out. It's just the food that worries me. Food, and coal for the fire. We've enough for two or three days, not more. By that time . . ."

No use thinking ahead as far as that. And they'd be giving directions on the wireless. People would be told what to do. And now, in the midst of many problems, he realized that it was dance music only, coming over the air. Not Children's Hour, as it should have been. He glanced at the dial. Yes, they were on the Home Service all right. Dance records. He switched to the Light program. He knew the reason. The usual programs had been abandoned. This only happened at exceptional times. Elections and such. He tried to remember if it had happened in the war, during the heavy raids on London. But of course. The BBC[10] was not stationed in London during the war. The programs were broadcast from other, temporary quarters. "We're better off here," he thought; "we're better off here in the kitchen, with the windows and the doors boarded, than they are up in the towns. Thank God we're not in the towns."

At six o'clock the records ceased. The time signal was given. No matter if it scared the children, he must hear the news. There was a pause after the pips.[11] Then the announcer spoke. His voice was solemn, grave. Quite different from midday.

"This is London," he said. "A national emergency was proclaimed at four o'clock this afternoon. Measures are being taken to safeguard the lives and property of the population, but it must be understood that these are not easy to effect immediately, owing to the unforeseen and unparalleled nature of the present crisis. Every householder must take precautions to his own building, and where several people live together, as in flats and apartments, they must unite to do

10. **BBC:** British Broadcasting Corporation.
11. **pips:** beeping sounds that indicate the exact time.

the utmost they can to prevent entry. It is absolutely <u>imperative</u> that every individual stay indoors tonight and that no one at all remain on the streets or roads or anywhere outdoors. The birds, in vast numbers, are attacking anyone on sight and have already begun an assault upon buildings; but these, with due care, should be impenetrable. The population is asked to remain calm and not to panic. Owing to the exceptional nature of the emergency, there will be no further transmission from any broadcasting station until 7 A.M. tomorrow."

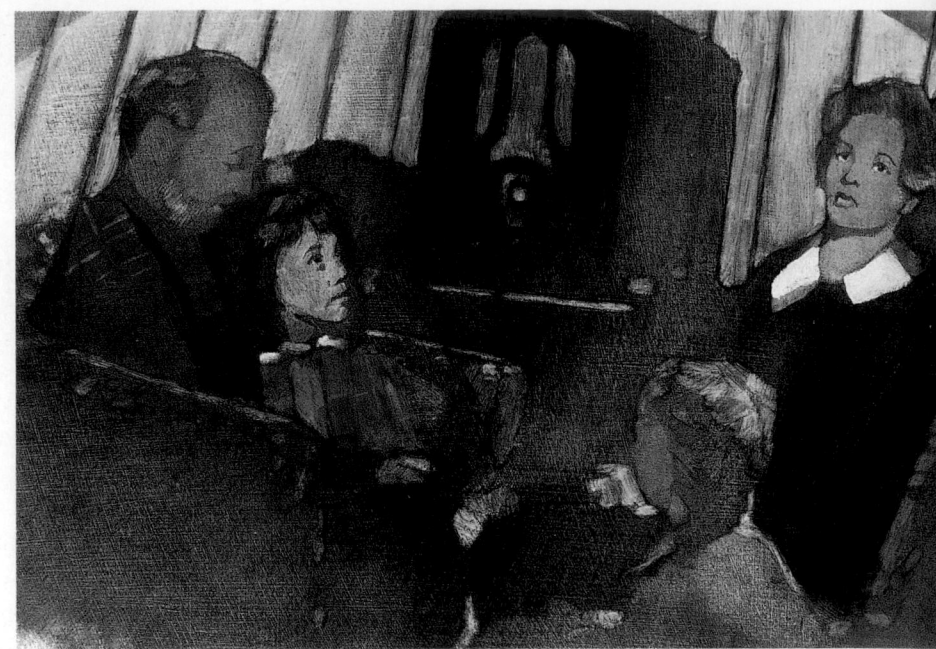

They played the national anthem. Nothing more happened. Nat switched off the set. He looked at his wife. She stared back at him.

"What's it mean?" said Jill. "What did the news say?"

"There won't be any more programs tonight," said Nat. "There's been a breakdown at the BBC."

"Is it the birds?" asked Jill. "Have the birds done it?"

"No," said Nat, "it's just that everyone's very busy, and then of course they have to get rid of the birds, messing everything up, in the towns. Well, we can manage without the wireless for one evening."

"I wish we had a gramophone,"[12] said Jill; "that would be better than nothing."

She had her face turned to the dresser backed against the windows. Try as they did to ignore it, they were all aware of the shuffling, the stabbing, the persistent beating and sweeping of wings.

"We'll have supper early," suggested Nat, "something for a treat. Ask Mammy. Toasted cheese, eh? Something we all like?"

He winked and nodded at his wife. He wanted the look of dread, of apprehension, to go from Jill's face.

12. **gramophone:** phonograph; record player.

He helped with the supper, whistling, singing, making as much clatter as he could, and it seemed to him that the shuffling and the tapping were not so intense as they had been at first. Presently he went up to the bedrooms and listened, and he no longer heard the jostling for place upon the roof.

"They've got reasoning powers," he thought; "they know it's hard to break in here. They'll try elsewhere. They won't waste their time with us."

Supper passed without incident, and then, when they were clearing away, they heard a new sound, droning, familiar, a sound they all knew and understood.

His wife looked up at him, her face alight. "It's planes," she said; "they're sending out planes after the birds. That's what I said they ought to do all along. That will get them. Isn't that gunfire? Can't you hear guns?"

It might be gunfire out at sea. Nat could not

WORDS TO OWN

imperative (im·per′ə·tiv) *adj.*: extremely important; urgent.

tell. Big naval guns might have an effect upon the gulls out at sea, but the gulls were inland now. The guns couldn't shell the shore because of the population.

"It's good, isn't it," said his wife, "to hear the planes?" And Jill, catching her enthusiasm, jumped up and down with Johnny. "The planes will get the birds. The planes will shoot them."

Just then they heard a crash about two miles distant, followed by a second, then a third. The droning became more distant, passed away out to sea.

"What was that?" asked his wife. "Were they dropping bombs on the birds?"

"I don't know," answered Nat. "I don't think so."

He did not want to tell her that the sound they had heard was the crashing of aircraft. It was, he had no doubt, a venture on the part of the authorities to send out reconnaissance forces, but they might have known the venture was suicidal. What could aircraft do against birds that flung themselves to death against propeller and fuselage but hurtle to the ground themselves? This was being tried now, he supposed, over the whole country. And at a cost. Someone high up had lost his head.

"Where have the planes gone, Dad?" asked Jill.

"Back to base," he said. "Come on, now, time to tuck down for bed."

It kept his wife occupied, undressing the children before the fire, seeing to the bedding, one thing and another, while he went round the cottage again, making sure that nothing had worked loose. There was no further drone of aircraft, and the naval guns had ceased. "Waste of life and effort," Nat said to himself. "We can't

destroy enough of them that way. Cost too heavy. There's always gas. Maybe they'll try spraying with gas, mustard gas. We'll be warned first, of course, if they do. There's one thing, the best brains of the country will be onto it tonight."

Somehow the thought reassured him. He had a picture of scientists, naturalists, technicians, and all those chaps they called the back-room boys, summoned to a council; they'd be working on the problem now. This was not a job for the government, for the chiefs of staff—they would merely carry out the orders of the scientists.

"They'll have to be ruthless," he thought. "Where the trouble's worst they'll have to risk more lives if they use gas. All the livestock, too, and the soil—all contaminated. As long as everyone doesn't panic. That's the trouble. People panicking, losing their heads. The BBC was right to warn us of that."

Upstairs in the bedrooms all was quiet. No further scraping and stabbing at the windows. A lull in battle. Forces regrouping. Wasn't that what they called it in the old wartime bulletins? The wind hadn't dropped, though. He could still hear it roaring in the chimneys. And the sea breaking down on the shore. Then he remembered the tide. The tide would be on the turn. Maybe the lull in battle was because of the tide. There was some law the birds obeyed, and it was all to do with the east wind and the tide.

He glanced at his watch. Nearly eight o'clock. It must have gone high water an hour ago. That explained the lull: The birds attacked with the flood tide. It might not work that way inland, upcountry, but it seemed as if it was so this way on the coast. He reckoned the time limit in his head. They had six hours to go without attack. When the tide turned again, around one-twenty in the morning, the birds would come back. . . .

There were two things he could do. The first to rest, with

his wife and the children, and all of them snatch what sleep they could, until the small hours. The second to go out, see how they were faring at the farm, see if the telephone was still working there, so that they might get news from the exchange.

He called softly to his wife, who had just settled the children. She came halfway up the stairs and he whispered to her.

"You're not to go," she said at once, "you're not to go and leave me alone with the children. I can't stand it."

Her voice rose hysterically. He hushed her, calmed her.

"All right," he said, "all right. I'll wait till morning. And we'll get the wireless bulletin then too, at seven. But in the morning, when the tide ebbs again, I'll try for the farm, and they may let us have bread and potatoes, and milk too."

His mind was busy again, planning against emergency. They would not have milked, of course, this evening. The cows would be standing by the gate, waiting in the yard, with the household inside, battened behind boards, as they were here at the cottage. That is, if they had time to take precautions. He thought of the farmer, Trigg, smiling at him from the car. There would have been no shooting party, not tonight.

The children were asleep. His wife, still clothed, was sitting on her mattress. She watched him, her eyes nervous.

"What are you going to do?" she whispered.

He shook his head for silence. Softly, stealthily, he opened the back door and looked outside.

It was pitch dark. The wind was blowing harder than ever, coming in steady gusts, icy, from the sea. He kicked at the step outside the door. It was heaped with birds. There were dead birds everywhere. Under the windows, against the walls. These were the suicides, the divers, the ones with broken necks. Wherever he looked he saw dead birds. No trace of the living. The living had flown seaward with the turn of the tide. The gulls would be riding the seas now, as they had done in the forenoon.

In the far distance, on the hill where the tractor had been two days before, something was burning. One of the aircraft that had crashed; the fire, fanned by the wind, had set light to a stack.

He looked at the bodies of the birds, and he had a notion that if he heaped them, one upon the other, on the windowsills they would make added protection for the next attack. Not much, perhaps, but something. The bodies would have to be clawed at, pecked, and dragged aside before the living birds could gain purchase on the sills and attack the panes. He set to work in the darkness. It was queer; he hated touching them. The bodies were still warm and bloody. The blood matted their feathers. He felt his stomach turn, but he went on with his work. He noticed grimly that every windowpane was shattered. Only the boards had kept the birds from breaking in. He stuffed the cracked panes with the bleeding bodies of the birds.

When he had finished he went back into the cottage. He barricaded the kitchen door, made it doubly secure. He took off his bandages, sticky with the birds' blood, not with his own cuts, and put on fresh plaster.

His wife had made him cocoa and he drank it thirstily. He was very tired.

"All right," he said, smiling, "don't worry. We'll get through."

He lay down on his mattress and closed his eyes. He slept at once. He dreamt uneasily, because through his dreams there ran a thread of something forgotten. Some piece of work, neglected, that he should have done. Some precaution that he had known well but had not taken, and he could not put a name to it in his dreams. It was connected in some way with the burning aircraft and the stack upon the hill. He went on sleeping, though; he did not awake. It was his wife shaking his shoulder that awoke him finally.

"They've begun," she sobbed. "They've started this last hour. I can't listen to it any longer alone. There's something smelling bad too, something burning."

Then he remembered. He had forgotten to make up the fire. It was smoldering, nearly out. He got up swiftly and lit the lamp. The hammering had started at the windows and the doors, but it was not that he minded now. It was the smell of singed feathers. The smell filled the kitchen. He knew at once what it was. The birds were coming down the chimney, squeezing their way down to the kitchen range.

He got sticks and paper and put them on the embers, then reached for the can of paraffin.[13]

"Stand back," he shouted to his wife. "We've got to risk this."

He threw the paraffin onto the fire. The flame roared up the pipe, and down upon the fire fell the scorched, blackened bodies of the birds.

The children woke, crying. "What is it?" said Jill. "What's happened?"

Nat had no time to answer. He was raking the bodies from the chimney, clawing them out onto the floor. The flames still roared, and the danger of the chimney catching fire was one he had to take. The flames would send away the living birds from the chimney top. The lower joint was the difficulty, though. This was choked with the smoldering, helpless bodies of the birds caught by fire. He scarcely heeded the attack on the windows and the door: Let them beat their wings, break their beaks, lose their lives in the attempt to force an entry into his home. They would not break in. He thanked God he had one of the old cottages, with small windows, stout walls. Not like the new council houses. Heaven help them up the lane in the new council houses.

"Stop crying," he called to the children. "There's nothing to be afraid of, stop crying."

He went on raking at the burning, smoldering bodies as they fell into the fire.

"This'll fetch them," he said to himself, "the draft and the flames together. We're all right, as long as the chimney doesn't catch. I ought to be shot for this. It's all my fault. Last thing, I should have made up the fire. I knew there was something."

Amid the scratching and tearing at the window boards came the sudden homely striking of the kitchen clock. Three A.M. A little more than four hours yet to go. He could not be sure of the exact time of high water. He reckoned it would not turn much before half past seven, twenty to eight.

"Light up the Primus,"[14] he said to his wife. "Make us some tea, and the kids some cocoa. No use sitting around doing nothing."

That was the line. Keep her busy, and the children too. Move about, eat, drink; always best to be on the go.

He waited by the range. The flames were dying. But no more blackened bodies fell from the chimney. He thrust his poker up as far as it could go and found nothing. It was clear. The chimney was clear. He wiped the sweat from his forehead.

"Come on now, Jill," he said, "bring me some more sticks. We'll have a good fire going directly." She wouldn't come near him, though. She was staring at the heaped singed bodies of the birds.

14. **Primus:** small portable stove.

13. **paraffin:** British term for "kerosene," a fuel that catches fire easily.

"Never mind them," he said. "We'll put those in the passage when I've got the fire steady."

The danger of the chimney was over. It could not happen again, not if the fire was kept burning day and night.

"I'll have to get more fuel from the farm tomorrow," he thought. "This will never last. I'll manage, though. I can do all that with the ebb tide. It can be worked, fetching what we need, when the tide's turned. We've just got to adapt ourselves, that's all."

They drank tea and cocoa and ate slices of bread and Bovril.[15] Only half a loaf left, Nat noticed. Never mind, though, they'd get by.

"Stop it," said young Johnny, pointing to the windows with his spoon, "stop it, you old birds."

"That's right," said Nat, smiling, "we don't want the old beggars, do we? Had enough of 'em."

They began to cheer when they heard the thud of the suicide birds.

"There's another, Dad," cried Jill. "He's done for."

"He's had it," said Nat. "There he goes, the blighter."

This was the way to face up to it. This was the spirit. If they could keep this up, hang on like this until seven, when the first news bulletin came through, they would not have done too badly.

"Give us a cigarette," he said to his wife. "A bit of a smoke will clear away the smell of the scorched feathers."

"There's only two left in the packet," she said. "I was going to buy you some from the co-op."

"I'll have one," he said, "t'other will keep for a rainy day."

No sense trying to make the children rest. There was no rest to be got while the tapping and the scratching went on at the windows. He sat with one arm round his wife and the other round Jill, with Johnny on his mother's lap and the blankets heaped about them on the mattress.

"You can't help admiring the beggars," he said; "they've got persistence. You'd think they'd tire of the game, but not a bit of it."

15. **Bovril:** thick, beef-flavored liquid that is spread on bread or used to make broth.

Admiration was hard to sustain. The tapping went on and on and a new rasping note struck Nat's ear, as though a sharper beak than any hitherto had come to take over from its fellows. He tried to remember the names of birds; he tried to think which species would go for this particular job. It was not the tap of the woodpecker. That would be light and frequent. This was more serious because if it continued long the wood would splinter, as the glass had done. Then he remembered the hawks. Could the hawks have taken over from the gulls? Were there buzzards now upon the sills, using talons as well as beaks? Hawks, buzzards, kestrels, falcons—he had forgotten the birds of prey. He had forgotten the gripping power of the birds of prey. Three hours to go, and while they waited, the sound of the splintering wood, the talons tearing at the wood.

Nat looked about him, seeing what furniture he could destroy to fortify the door. The windows were safe because of the dresser. He was not certain of the door. He went upstairs, but when he reached the landing he paused and listened. There was a soft patter on the floor of the children's bedroom. The birds had broken through. . . . He put his ear to the door. No mistake. He could hear the rustle of wings and the light patter as they searched the floor. The other bedroom was still clear. He went into it and began bringing out the furniture, to pile at the head of the stairs should the door of the children's bedroom go. It was a preparation. It might never be needed. He could not stack the furniture against the door, because it opened inward. The only possible thing was to have it at the top of the stairs.

"Come down, Nat, what are you doing?" called his wife.

"I won't be long," he shouted. "Just making everything shipshape up here."

He did not want her to come; he did not want her to hear the pattering of the feet in the children's bedroom, the brushing of those wings against the door.

At five-thirty he suggested breakfast, bacon and fried bread, if only to stop the growing look of panic in his wife's eyes and to calm the <u>fretful</u> children. She did not know about the birds upstairs. The bedroom, luckily, was not over the kitchen. Had it been so, she could not have failed to hear the sound of them up there, tapping the boards. And the silly, senseless thud of the suicide birds, the death and glory boys, who flew into the bedroom, smashing their heads against the walls. He knew them of old, the herring gulls. They had no brains. The blackbacks were different; they knew what they were doing. So did the buzzards, the hawks. . . .

He found himself watching the clock, gazing at the hands that went so slowly round the dial. If his theory was not correct, if the attack did not cease with the turn of the tide, he knew they were beaten. They could not continue through the long day without air, without rest, without more fuel, without . . . His mind raced. He knew there were so many things they needed to withstand siege. They were not fully prepared. They were not ready. It might be that it would be safer in the towns, after all. If he could get a message through on the farm telephone to his cousin, only a short journey by train upcountry, they might be able to hire a car. That would be quicker—hire a car between tides . . .

His wife's voice, calling his name, drove away the sudden, desperate desire for sleep.

"What is it? What now?" he said sharply.

"The wireless," said his wife. "I've been watching the clock. It's nearly seven."

"Don't twist the knob," he said, impatient for the first time. "It's on the Home where it is. They'll speak from the Home."

They waited. The kitchen clock struck seven. There was no sound. No chimes, no music. They waited until a quarter past, switching to the Light. The result was the same. No news bulletin came through.

"We've heard wrong," he said. "They won't be broadcasting until eight o'clock."

They left it switched on, and Nat thought of the battery, wondered how much power was left in it. It was generally recharged when his wife went shopping in the town. If the battery failed, they would not hear the instructions.

WORDS TO OWN

fretful (fret′fəl) *adj.*: irritable and discontented.

"It's getting light," whispered his wife. "I can't see it, but I can feel it. And the birds aren't hammering so loud."

She was right. The rasping, tearing sound grew fainter every moment. So did the shuffling, the jostling for place upon the step, upon the sills. The tide was on the turn. By eight there was no sound at all. Only the wind. The children, lulled at last by the stillness, fell asleep. At half past eight Nat switched the wireless off.

"What are you doing? We'll miss the news," said his wife.

"There isn't going to be any news," said Nat. "We've got to depend upon ourselves."

He went to the door and slowly pulled away the barricades. He drew the bolts and, kicking the bodies from the step outside the door, breathed the cold air. He had six working hours before him, and he knew he must reserve his strength for the right things, not waste it in any way. Food and light and fuel; these were the necessary things. If he could get them in suffi-ciency, they could endure another night.

He stepped into the garden, and as he did so he saw the living birds. The gulls had gone to ride the sea, as they had done before; they sought sea food and the buoyancy of the tide, before they returned to the attack. Not so the land birds. They waited and watched. Nat saw them, on the hedgerows, on the soil, crowded in the trees, outside in the field, line upon line of birds, all still, doing nothing.

He went to the end of his small garden. The birds did not move. They went on watching him.

"I've got to get food," said Nat to himself. "I've got to go to the farm to find food."

He went back to the cottage. He saw to the windows and the doors. He went upstairs and opened the children's bedroom. It was empty, except for the dead birds on the floor. The living were out there, in the garden, in the fields. He went downstairs.

"I'm going to the farm," he said.

His wife clung to him. She had seen the living birds from the open door.

"Take us with you," she begged. "We can't stay here alone. I'd rather die than stay here alone."

He considered the matter. He nodded.

"Come on, then," he said. "Bring baskets, and Johnny's pram.[16] We can load up the pram."

They dressed against the biting wind, wore gloves and scarves. His wife put Johnny in the pram. Nat took Jill's hand.

"The birds," she whimpered, "they're all out there in the fields."

"They won't hurt us," he said, "not in the light."

They started walking across the field toward the stile, and the birds did not move. They waited, their heads turned to the wind.

When they reached the turning to the farm, Nat stopped and told his wife to wait in the shelter of the hedge with the two children.

"But I want to see Mrs. Trigg," she protested. "There are lots of things we can borrow if they went to market yesterday; not only bread, and . . ."

"Wait here," Nat interrupted. "I'll be back in a moment."

The cows were lowing, moving restlessly in the yard, and he could see a gap in the fence where the sheep had knocked their way through, to roam unchecked in the front garden before the farmhouse. No smoke came from the chimneys. He was filled with misgiving. He did not want his wife or the children to go down to the farm.

"Don't gib[17] now," said Nat, harshly. "Do what I say."

She withdrew with the pram into the hedge, screening herself and the children from the wind.

He went down alone to the farm. He pushed

16. **pram:** baby carriage.
17. **gib:** balk; hesitate.

his way through the herd of bellowing cows, which turned this way and that, distressed, their udders full. He saw the car standing by the gate, not put away in the garage. The windows of the farmhouse were smashed. There were many dead gulls lying in the yard and around the house. The living birds perched on the group of trees behind the farm and on the roof of the house. They were quite still. They watched him.

Jim's body lay in the yard . . . what was left of it. When the birds had finished, the cows had trampled him. His gun was beside him. The door of the house was shut and bolted, but, as the windows were smashed, it was easy to lift them and climb through. Trigg's body was close to the telephone. He must have been trying to get through to the exchange when the birds came for him. The receiver was hanging loose, the instrument torn from the wall. No sign of Mrs. Trigg. She would be upstairs. Was it any use going up? Sickened, Nat knew what he would find.

"Thank God," he said to himself, "there were no children."

He forced himself to climb the stairs, but halfway he turned and descended again. He could see her legs protruding from the open bedroom door. Beside her were the bodies of the black-backed gulls and an umbrella, broken.

"It's no use," thought Nat, "doing anything. I've only got five hours, less than that. The Triggs would understand. I must load up with what I can find."

He tramped back to his wife and children.

"I'm going to fill up the car with stuff," he said. "I'll put coal in it, and paraffin for the Primus. We'll take it home and return for a fresh load."

"What about the Triggs?" asked his wife.

"They must have gone to friends," he said.

"Shall I come and help you, then?"

"No; there's a mess down there. Cows and sheep all over the place. Wait, I'll get the car. You can sit in it."

Clumsily he backed the car out of the yard and into the lane. His wife and the children could not see Jim's body from there.

"Stay here," he said, "never mind the pram. The pram can be fetched later. I'm going to load the car."

Her eyes watched his all the time. He believed she understood; otherwise she would have suggested helping him to find the bread and groceries.

They made three journeys altogether, backward and forward between their cottage and the farm, before he was satisfied they had everything they needed. It was surprising, once he started thinking, how many things were necessary. Almost the most important of all was planking for the windows. He had to go round searching for timber. He wanted to renew the boards on all the windows at the cottage. Candles, paraffin, nails, tinned stuff; the list was endless. Besides all that, he milked three of the cows. The rest, poor brutes, would have to go on bellowing.

On the final journey he drove the car to the bus stop, got out, and went to the telephone box. He waited a few minutes, jangling the receiver. No good though. The line was dead. He climbed onto a bank and looked over the countryside, but there was no sign of life at all, nothing in the fields but the waiting, watching birds. Some of them slept—he could see the beaks tucked into the feathers.

"You'd think they'd be feeding," he said to himself, "not just standing in that way."

Then he remembered. They were gorged with food. They had eaten their fill during the night. That was why they did not move this morning. . . .

No smoke came from the chimneys of the council houses. He thought of the children who had run across the fields the night before.

"I should have known," he thought; "I ought to have taken them home with me."

He lifted his face to the sky. It was colorless and gray. The bare trees on the landscape looked bent and blackened by the east wind. The cold did not affect the living birds waiting out there in the fields.

"This is the time they ought to get them," said Nat; "they're a sitting target now. They must be doing this all over the country. Why don't our aircraft take off now and spray them with mustard gas? What are all our chaps doing? They must know; they must see for themselves."

He went back to the car and got into the driver's seat.

"Go quickly past that second gate," whispered his wife. "The postman's lying there. I don't want Jill to see."

He accelerated. The little Morris bumped and rattled along the lane. The children shrieked with laughter.

"Up-a-down, up-a-down," shouted young Johnny.

It was a quarter to one by the time they reached the cottage. Only an hour to go.

"Better have cold dinner," said Nat. "Hot up something for yourself and the children, some of that soup. I've no time to eat now. I've got to unload all this stuff."

He got everything inside the cottage. It could be sorted later. Give them all something to do during the long hours ahead. First he must see to the windows and the doors.

He went round the cottage methodically, testing every window, every door. He climbed onto the roof also, and fixed boards across every chimney except the kitchen. The cold was so intense he could hardly bear it, but the job had to be done. Now and again he would look up, searching the sky for aircraft. None came. As he worked he cursed the inefficiency of the authorities.

"It's always the same," he muttered. "They always let us down. Muddle, muddle, from the start. No plan, no real organization. And we don't matter down here. That's what it is. The people upcountry have priority. They're using gas up there, no doubt, and all the aircraft. We've got to wait and take what comes."

He paused, his work on the bedroom

chimney finished, and looked out to sea. Something was moving out there. Something gray and white amongst the breakers.

"Good old Navy," he said, "they never let us down. They're coming down-channel; they're turning in the bay."

He waited, straining his eyes, watering in the wind, toward the sea. He was wrong, though. It was not ships. The Navy was not there. The gulls were rising from the sea. The massed flocks in the fields, with ruffled feathers, rose in formation from the ground and, wing to wing, soared upward to the sky.

The tide had turned again.

Nat climbed down the ladder and went inside the kitchen. The family were at dinner. It was a little after two. He bolted the door, put up the barricade, and lit the lamp.

"It's nighttime," said young Johnny.

His wife had switched on the wireless once again, but no sound came from it.

"I've been all round the dial," she said, "foreign stations, and that lot. I can't get anything."

"Maybe they have the same trouble," he said, "maybe it's the same right through Europe."

She poured out a plateful of the Triggs' soup, cut him a large slice of the Triggs' bread, and spread their dripping upon it.

They ate in silence. A piece of the dripping ran down young Johnny's chin and fell onto the table.

"Manners, Johnny," said Jill, "you should learn to wipe your mouth."

The tapping began at the windows, at the door. The rustling, the jostling, the pushing for position on the sills. The first thud of the suicide gulls upon the step.

"Won't America do something?" said his wife. "They've always been our allies, haven't they? Surely America will do something?"

Nat did not answer. The boards were strong against the windows and on the chimneys too. The cottage was filled with stores, with fuel, with all they needed for the next few days. When he had finished dinner he would put the stuff away, stack it neatly, get everything shipshape, handy like. His wife could help him, and the children too. They'd tire themselves out, between now and a quarter to nine, when the tide would ebb; then he'd tuck them down on their mattresses, see that they slept good and sound until three in the morning.

He had a new scheme for the windows, which was to fix barbed wire in front of the boards. He had brought a great roll of it from the farm. The nuisance was, he'd have to work at this in the dark, when the lull came between nine and three. Pity he had not thought of it before. Still, as long as the wife slept, and the kids, that was the main thing.

The smaller birds were at the window now. He recognized the light tap-tapping of their beaks and the soft brush of their wings. The hawks ignored the windows. They concentrated their attack upon the door. Nat listened to the tearing sound of splintering wood and wondered how many million years of memory were stored in those little brains, behind the stabbing beaks, the piercing eyes, now giving them this instinct to destroy mankind with all the deft precision of machines.

"I'll smoke that last cigarette," he said to his wife. "Stupid of me—it was the one thing I forgot to bring back from the farm."

He reached for it, switched on the silent wireless. He threw the empty packet on the fire and watched it burn.

WORDS TO OWN

deft *adj.*: skillful in a quick, sure and easy way.

MEET THE WRITER

The Urge to Write

Daphne du Maurier (1907–1989) was born in London, the daughter of a famous actor and theater manager and the grand-daughter of George du Maurier, a writer of popular novels. Although she grew up in a stimulating, well-to-do family, she preferred solitude and reading to the busy social lives her sisters enjoyed.

While she was in her early twenties, du Maurier decided to write a novel and secluded herself in an empty house in Cornwall, on the coast of England. The novel turned out to be a romantic family chronicle which grew to 200,000 words in just ten weeks. As she wrote, she discovered something about writing: "Sometimes my book comes so strongly on me that it's like a restless urge within saying 'Get on! Get on!' "

A Shelfful of Books

Du Maurier's first novel revealed an astonishing gift for storytelling, one that readers have since found irresistible. That book, called *The Loving Spirit* (Avon), not only found a publisher at once but also became a best-seller and the forerunner of a shelfful of others, including the three famous romantic novels: *Rebecca* (Avon), *Jamaica Inn* (Buccaneer), and *Frenchman's Creek* (Dell).

Hundreds of Birds Invade Home in California

SANTA PAULA, Calif., May 4 (UPI)—Hundreds of birds swirled "like a tornado" down the chimney of a home twice in one week, creating a fluttering mass invasion reminiscent of the Alfred Hitchcock movie *The Birds,* the home's owners said today.

"They were just swarming around and around," said John Melton, a city councilman in this Ventura County community north of Los Angeles. "Then all of a sudden one went down the chimney. Then they narrowed into a funnel just like a tornado and—shoomp!—right down the chimney."

The birds were identified by ornithologists as Vaux's swifts, now migrating from their winter homes in Mexico and Central America to the Pacific Northwest.

The Meltons returned last Friday from a two-day trip and discovered that the tiny birds had invaded their hillside home by flying down the chimney and through an inch-wide space between the fireplace frame and screen.

"They Were Everywhere"

"They were four deep on our twelve-foot windows," Lucille Melton said. "We walked through the house and they were everywhere. We estimated eight hundred to a thousand birds."

Most of the birds were gone by Saturday afternoon, Mr. Melton said, although the couple continued to find birds "in Kleenex boxes, vases, beneath the kitchen stove, everywhere."

As the family was preparing to go out to dinner Saturday night, a flock of about four hundred swifts returned.

Birds Posed No Danger

The birds finally flew back up the chimney, and the Fire Department installed a heavy steel grate, deterring the flock when they returned a third time Sunday night.

Ornithologists agreed that the Meltons faced no danger from the swifts.

"They couldn't bite you, hurt you, scratch you, if they had to," said Kimball Garrett, bird-collection manager at the Los Angeles County Museum of Natural History.

The birds, flying into foul weather, probably mistook the Meltons' chimney for a tree trunk, their normal roosting place, Mr. Garrett said.

—from *The New York Times*

MAKING MEANINGS

First Thoughts

1. What do you think happens next to Nat and his family?

Shaping Interpretations

2. What resolution to the **conflict** do you think might be suggested in the final scene by the silent radio and the burning cigarette package?

3. Do you think the scene at the Triggs' **foreshadows** what will happen to Nat and his family, or do you think they will survive? In other words, do you read this as a doomsday story (about the end of human life on earth) or as a story in which humans will triumph over nature? Cite details from the text to support your interpretation.

4. Find at least five details that suggest that an evil force might be directing the birds to turn against people. What do you imagine this force could be?

Connecting with the Text

5. In this story du Maurier sometimes seems critical of people and of the way they respond to disaster. Find at least three details that show characters behaving ignorantly or endangering themselves or others. Do you think this is how people really behave?

Extending the Text

6. Look at the notes in your Reader's Log about other threats posed by nature. Why do you think du Maurier chose birds to be the attackers in this story?

Challenging the Text

7. On just a factual level, do you think nature could suddenly turn on us like this? Give the story a credibility rating of 1 to 5:

Possible			Not possible	
1	2	3	4	5

Be ready to support your rating with details from the text and from your own experience. (Be sure to consider the news article on the opposite page.)

Reviewing the Text

a. On December 3, two apparently minor incidents occur—one involving the farmer, the other involving Nat. What are these incidents, and how do they **foreshadow** what the story's conflict will be?

b. In the paragraph beginning "The sky was hard" (page 51), the weather is described. List five details here that strike you as ominous.

c. Nat keeps trying to find a rational explanation for the birds' behavior. What explanations does he think of?

d. How do other people react to the birds—Jim, Mr. Trigg, Jill, Nat's wife?

e. How do the BBC radio announcements create **suspense** as the story progresses?

CHOICES: Building Your Portfolio

Writer's Notebook

1. Collecting Ideas for a True Narrative

Creating a setting. Re-read the paragraph on page 48 beginning "Nat, tramping home." What details help you picture the isolated farmhouse by the sea, hear the wind, feel you are there with Nat in his chilly house? For the narrative you'll write for the Writer's Workshop on page 112, you'll also want to create a vivid setting to help readers feel they are there. Review the notes you've taken for a narrative of your own. Where will your story be set? List as many details about the setting as you can. Try to focus on sights, sounds, smells, even perhaps taste and touch sensations.

WORK IN PROGRESS

> **Setting for a Narrative**
> Peacefulness of the forest
> Smell of pine trees
> Cheerful chirping of birds
> Crunch of pine needles underfoot
> Bright blue sky showing through the umbrella of trees

Creative Writing

2. Who's in Charge?

Du Maurier tells us that the birds are trying to destroy human life, but we never know what is making them do it. Is it really the weather, as some characters in the story think? Is it an evil force, as du Maurier seems to suggest at times? Suppose you are a historian at some future time studying this famous bird attack. Write a feature article summing up the main events of the historical disaster and offering some possible reasons for the birds' sudden frenzy. Be sure to tell why the murderous birds didn't succeed in wiping out the world. (After all, you as the historian are alive on earth. Or are you somewhere else?)

Research/Science

3. Looking at Birds

Find out how the birds in this story act when they are behaving normally. Review the text to locate the types of birds that are attacking. Then use a bird book or an encyclopedia or data bank to chart their characteristics, such as size, physical features, feeding habits, and behavior. Classify the birds according to type: land birds, sea birds, birds of prey, or any other categories you can think of. You might sketch some of the birds to show their appearance or behavior: beaks, talons, wingspans, eating habits, ways of swooping or diving. Imagine that the director of a remake of the movie *The Birds* (see below) wants to use your bird book as a resource.

Speaking and Listening

4. Story vs. Movie

Watch a videotape of Alfred Hitchcock's 1963 movie, *The Birds*. Assume the role of talk-show critic and compare the film with du Maurier's story. You should focus on specific elements such as setting, character, or resolution of the conflict. Conclude your talk by telling which you prefer, and why: the original story or the film. Be ready to take questions on the telephone from your audience.

Scene from the film version of *The Birds*.

LANGUAGE LINK

Language Handbook HELP

See Tense, page 999.

Technology HELP

See Language Workshop CD-ROM. *Key word entry: verb tenses.*

Proofreading: Verb Tenses—What Time Is It?

Every verb in English has six tenses:

Tense	Example
present	I give
past	I gave
future	I will give
present perfect	I have given
past perfect	I had given
future perfect	I will have given

Here are three tenses in sentences from "The Birds."

1. "On December the third, the wind changed overnight, and it was winter." [past tense]
2. " 'It will be a hard winter.' " [future tense]
3. " '. . . a message comes to the birds in autumn. . . .' " [present tense]

Fiction is usually written in the past tense. Notice that du Maurier uses the future and the present only in dialogue. It is rare to find a story told in the present tense, though it has been done.

Try It Out

➤ Choose two narrative paragraphs from the story (try to avoid paragraphs with dialogue) and rewrite them in the present tense. Notice how a change in tense gives the story a "here-and-now" feeling.

➤ When you are writing, the main problem you are likely to have with verb tenses is keeping them consistent. Take out a piece of your own writing and under-line all the verbs. Then label each one according to its tense. Are your tenses consistent?

VOCABULARY HOW TO OWN A WORD

WORD BANK

disposition
placid
apprehensive
garish
recounted
sullen
furtively
imperative
fretful
deft

Own It

1. Write a pet-wanted ad that uses the word *disposition*.
2. Write a description of a park using the word *placid*.
3. Write a journal entry using the word *apprehensive*.
4. Tell what a garish outfit might look like.
5. Write the first sentence of a news report using the word *recounted*.
6. Use the word *sullen* in a sentence from a counselor's report.
7. Describe a burglar's action using the word *furtively*.
8. Write a bulletin-board notice using the word *imperative*.
9. Describe an annoying incident using the word *fretful*.
10. Write two rhyming lines using the words *deft* and *left*.

BEFORE YOU READ
POISON

Reading Focus

Hooking into Our Fears

Three characters confront one another—and danger—in a house in colonial India. As events unfold, we are drawn into their terrible conflicts, and their terror. Suppose you were face to face with grave danger. What might the encounter bring out in you: bravery? fear? or perhaps even something you are ashamed of?

Quickwrite

Write down in your Reader's Log the thoughts you have about the question above. How do you think you would respond to grave danger?

Elements of Literature

The Grip of Suspense

A writer holds us in **suspense** by making us uncertain about—but very interested in—what lies ahead. Suspense is what keeps us turning those pages. The word *suspense* is related to the word *suspended*. When we feel suspense, we feel as if we are hanging in midair, like those characters in a movie who cling by their fingertips to cliffs, their feet kicking out into space.

That's suspense—and that's why stories like this one of Dahl's are called cliffhangers.

> **S**uspense is the uncertainty or anxiety we feel about what is going to happen next in a story.
>
> *For more on Suspense, see pages 32–33 and the Handbook of Literary Terms.*

Background

At one time, the British Empire covered nearly one quarter of the globe. Among the colonies of this powerful empire was the huge subcontinent of India. For the long years that India was under Britain's rule (from 1857 until 1949), many Indians resented the control that the British imposed on all their institutions—their laws, education, army, and government. Religious differences also resulted in conflicts. Most of the Indians were Hindu; a smaller number were Muslim. The English were mostly Christian. Some of the simmering conflicts that eventually resulted in massive bloodshed in India are shown in this story—which is about more than one kind of poison.

"I haven't been bitten," he whispered. "Not yet."

POISON

Roald Dahl

It must have been around midnight when I drove home, and as I approached the gates of the bungalow I switched off the headlamps of the car so the beam wouldn't swing in through the window of the side bedroom and wake Harry Pope. But I needn't have bothered. Coming up the drive, I noticed his light was still on, so he was awake anyway—unless perhaps he'd dropped off while reading.

I parked the car and went up the five steps to the balcony, counting each step carefully in the dark so I wouldn't take an extra one which wasn't there, when I got to the top. I crossed the balcony, pushed through the screen doors into the house itself, and switched on the light in the hall. I went across to the door of Harry's room, opened it quietly, and looked in.

He was lying on the bed and I could see he was awake. But he didn't move. He didn't even turn his head toward me, but I heard him say, "Timber, Timber, come here."

He spoke slowly, whispering each word carefully, separately, and I pushed the door right open and started to go quickly across the room.

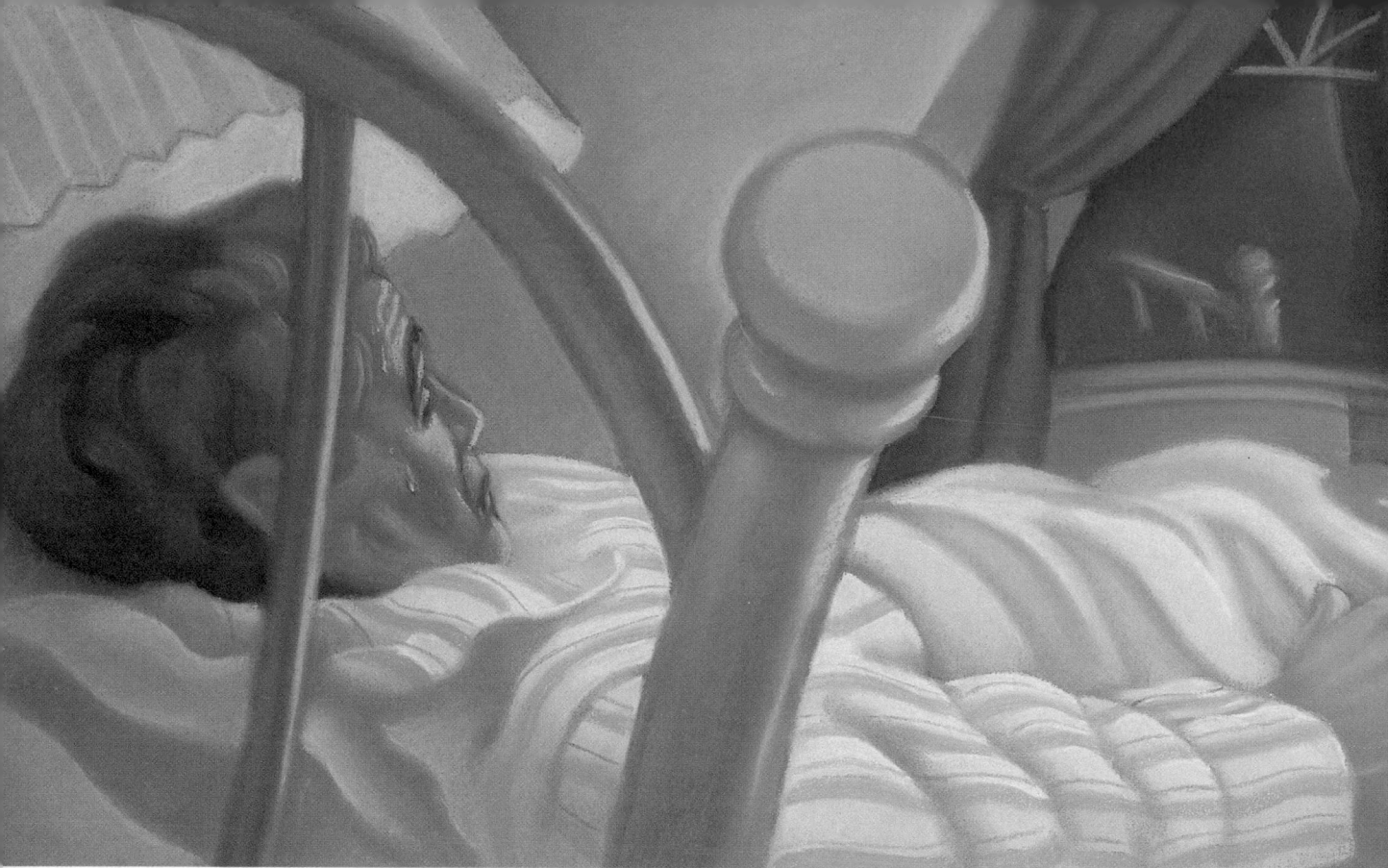

"Stop. Wait a moment, Timber." I could hardly hear what he was saying. He seemed to be straining enormously to get the words out.

"What's the matter, Harry?"

"Sshhh!" he whispered. "Sshhh! For God's sake, don't make a noise. Take your shoes off before you come nearer. *Please* do as I say, Timber."

The way he was speaking reminded me of George Barling after he got shot in the stomach, when he stood leaning against a crate containing a spare airplane engine, holding both hands on his stomach and saying things about the German pilot in just the same hoarse, straining half whisper Harry was using now.

"Quickly, Timber, but take your shoes off first."

I couldn't understand about taking off the shoes but I figured that if he was as ill as he sounded I'd better humor him, so I bent down and removed the shoes and left them in the middle of the floor. Then I went over to his bed.

"Don't touch the bed! For God's sake, don't touch the bed!" He was still speaking like he'd been shot in the stomach, and I could see him lying there on his back with a single sheet covering three quarters of his body. He was wearing a pair of pajamas with blue, brown, and white stripes, and he was sweating terribly. It was a hot night and I was sweating a little myself, but not like Harry. His whole face was wet, and the pillow around his head was sodden with moisture. It looked like a bad go of malaria[1] to me.

"What is it, Harry?"

"A krait,"[2] he said.

"A *krait*! Oh, my God! Where'd it bite you? How long ago?"

"Shut up," he whispered.

"Listen, Harry," I said, and I leaned forward and touched his shoulder. "We've got to be quick. Come on now, quickly, tell me where it bit you." He was lying there very still and tense

1. **malaria** (mə·ler′ē·ə): infectious disease transmitted to humans by the bite of an infected mosquito. Malaria causes frequent sweats and fever.
2. **krait** (krīt): poisonous Asian snake, usually black or dark brown with tan or yellow bands.

as though he were holding on to himself hard because of sharp pain.

"I haven't been bitten," he whispered. "Not yet. It's on my stomach. Lying there asleep."

I took a quick pace backward; I couldn't help it, and I stared at his stomach or rather at the sheet that covered it. The sheet was rumpled in several places and it was impossible to tell if there was anything underneath.

"You don't really mean there's a krait lying on your stomach now?"

"I swear it."

"How did it get there?" I shouldn't have asked the question because it was easy to see he wasn't fooling. I should have told him to keep quiet.

"I was reading," Harry said, and he spoke very slowly, taking each word in turn and speaking it carefully so as not to move the muscles of his stomach. "Lying on my back reading and I felt something on my chest, behind the book. Sort of tickling. Then out of the corner of my eye saw this little krait sliding over my pajamas. Small, about ten inches. Knew I mustn't move.

Couldn't have anyway. Lay there watching it. Thought it would go over top of the sheet." Harry paused and was silent for a few moments. His eyes looked down along his body toward the place where the sheet covered his stomach, and I could see he was watching to make sure his whispering wasn't disturbing the thing that lay there.

"There was a fold in the sheet," he said, speaking more slowly than ever now and so softly I had to lean close to hear him. "See it, it's still there. It went under that. I could feel it through my pajamas, moving on my stomach. Then it stopped moving and now it's lying there in the warmth. Probably asleep. I've been waiting for you." He raised his eyes and looked at me.

"How long ago?"

"Hours," he whispered. "Hours and bloody hours and hours. I can't keep still much longer. I've been wanting to cough."

There was not much doubt about the truth of Harry's story. As a matter of fact it wasn't a surprising thing for a krait to do. They hang around people's houses, and they go for the warm places. The surprising thing was that Harry hadn't been bitten. The bite is quite deadly except sometimes when you catch it at once, and they kill a fair number of people each year in Bengal, mostly in the villages.

"All right, Harry," I said, and now I was whispering too. "Don't move and don't talk anymore unless you have to. You know it won't bite unless it's frightened. We'll fix it in no time."

I went softly out of the room in my stocking feet and fetched a small sharp knife from the kitchen. I put it in my trouser pocket, ready to use instantly in case something went wrong while we were still thinking out a plan. If Harry coughed or moved or did something to frighten the krait and got bitten, I was going to be ready to cut the bitten place and try to suck the venom out. I came back to the bedroom and Harry was still lying there very quiet and sweating all over his face. His eyes followed me as I moved across the room to his bed, and I could see he was wondering what I'd been up to. I stood beside him, trying to think of the best thing to do.

"Harry," I said, and now when I spoke I put my mouth almost on his ear so I wouldn't have to raise my voice above the softest whisper, "I think the best thing to do is for me to draw the sheet back very, very gently. Then we could have a look first. I think I could do that without disturbing it."

"Don't be a fool." There was no expression in his voice. He spoke each word too slowly, too carefully, and too softly for that. The expression was in the eyes and around the corners of the mouth.

"Why not?"

"The light would frighten him. It's dark under there now."

"Then how about whipping the sheet back quick and brushing it off before it has time to strike?"

"Why don't you get a doctor?" Harry said. The way he looked at me told me I should have thought of that myself in the first place.

"A doctor. Of course. That's it. I'll get Ganderbai."

I tiptoed out to the hall, looked up Ganderbai's number in the book, lifted the phone, and told the operator to hurry.

"Doctor Ganderbai," I said. "This is Timber Woods."

"Hello, Mr. Woods. You not in bed yet?"

"Look, could you come round at once? And bring serum—for a krait bite."

"Who's been bitten?" The question came so sharply it was like a small explosion in my ear.

"No one. No one yet. But Harry Pope's in bed, and he's got one lying on his stomach—asleep under the sheet on his stomach."

For about three seconds there was silence on the line. Then speaking slowly, not like an explosion now but slowly, precisely, Ganderbai said, "Tell him to keep quite still. He is not to move or to talk. Do you understand?"

"Of course."

"I'll come at once!" He rang off and I went back to the bedroom. Harry's eyes watched me as I walked across to his bed.

"Ganderbai's coming. He said for you to lie still."

"What does he think I'm doing?"

"Look, Harry, he said no talking. Absolutely no talking. Either of us."

"Why don't you shut up, then?" When he said this, one side of his mouth started twitching with rapid little downward movements that continued for a while after he finished speaking. I took out my handkerchief and very gently I wiped the sweat off his face and neck, and I could feel the slight twitching of the muscle—the one he used for smiling—as my fingers passed over it with the handkerchief.

I slipped out to the kitchen, got some ice from the icebox, rolled it up in a napkin, and began to crush it small. That business of the mouth, I didn't like that. Or the way he talked, either. I carried the ice pack back to the bedroom and laid it across Harry's forehead.

"Keep you cool."

He screwed up his eyes and drew breath sharply through his teeth. "Take it away," he whispered. "Make me cough." His smiling muscle began to twitch again.

The beam of a headlamp shone through the

window as Ganderbai's car swung around to the front of the bungalow. I went out to meet him, holding the ice pack with both hands.

"How is it?" Ganderbai asked, but he didn't stop to talk; he walked on past me across the balcony and through the screen doors into the hall. "Where is he? Which room?"

He put his bag down on a chair in the hall and followed me into Harry's room. He was wearing soft-soled bedroom slippers and he walked across the floor noiselessly, delicately, like a careful cat. Harry watched him out of the sides of his eyes. When Ganderbai reached the bed he looked down at Harry and smiled, confident and reassuring, nodding his head to tell Harry it was a simple matter and he was not to worry but just to leave it to Doctor Ganderbai. Then he turned and went back to the hall and I followed him.

"First thing is to try to get some serum into him," he said, and he opened his bag and started to make preparations. "Intravenously. But I must do it neatly. Don't want to make him flinch."

We went into the kitchen and he sterilized a needle. He had a hypodermic syringe in one hand and a small bottle in the other, and he stuck the needle through the rubber top of the bottle and began drawing a pale yellow liquid up into the syringe by pulling out the plunger. Then he handed the syringe to me.

"Hold that till I ask for it."

He picked up the bag and together we returned to the room. Harry's eyes were bright now and wide open. Ganderbai bent over Harry and very cautiously, like a man handling sixteenth-century lace, he rolled up the pajama sleeve to the elbow without moving the arm. I noticed he stood well away from the bed.

He whispered, "I'm going to give you an injection. Serum. Just a prick but try not to move. Don't tighten your stomach muscles. Let them go limp."

Harry looked at the syringe.

Ganderbai took a piece of red rubber tubing from his bag and slid one end under and up and around Harry's biceps; then he tied the tubing tight with a knot. He sponged a small area of the bare forearm with alcohol, handed the swab to me, and took the syringe from my hand. He held it up to the light, squinting at the calibrations,[3] squirting out some of the yellow fluid. I stood still beside him, watching. Harry was watching too and sweating all over his face so it shone like it was smeared thick with face cream melting on his skin and running down onto the pillow.

I could see the blue vein on the inside of Harry's forearm, swollen now because of the tourniquet, and then I saw the needle above the vein, Ganderbai holding the syringe almost flat against the arm, sliding the needle in sideways through the skin into the blue vein, sliding it slowly but so firmly it went in smooth as into cheese. Harry looked at the ceiling and closed his eyes and opened them again but he didn't move.

When it was finished, Ganderbai leaned forward, putting his mouth close to Harry's ear. "Now you'll be all right even if you *are* bitten. But don't move. Please don't move. I'll be back in a moment."

He picked up his bag and went out to the hall and I followed.

"Is he safe now?" I asked.

"No."

"How safe is he?"

The little Indian doctor stood there in the hall rubbing his lower lip.

"It must give some protection, mustn't it?" I asked.

He turned away and walked to the screen doors that led onto the veranda. I thought he was going through them, but he stopped this side of the doors and stood looking out into the night.

"Isn't the serum very good?" I asked.

---

3. **calibrations** (kal′ə·brā′shənz): markings on a measuring instrument.

- -

WORDS TO OWN

intravenously (in′trə·vē′nəs·lē) *adv.*: directly into a vein.

- -

"Unfortunately not," he answered without turning round. "It might save him. It might not. I am trying to think of something else to do."

"Shall we draw the sheet back quick and brush it off before it has time to strike?"

"Never! We are not entitled to take a risk." He spoke sharply and his voice was pitched a little higher than usual.

"We can't very well leave him lying there," I said. "He's getting nervous."

"Please! Please!" he said, turning round, holding both hands up in the air. "Not so fast, please. This is not a matter to rush into baldheaded."[4] He wiped his forehead with his handkerchief and stood there, frowning, nibbling his lip.

"You see," he said at last, "there is a way to do this. You know what we must do—we must administer an anesthetic to the creature where it lies."

It was a splendid idea.

"It is not safe," he continued, "because a snake is coldblooded, and anesthetic does not work so well or so quick with such animals, but it is better than any other thing to do. We could use ether . . . chloroform.[5] . . ." He was speaking slowly and trying to think the thing out while he talked.

"Which shall we use?"

"Chloroform," he said suddenly. "Ordinary chloroform. That is best. Now quick!" He took my arm and pulled me toward the balcony. "Drive to my house! By the time you get there, I will have waked up my boy on the telephone and he will show you my poisons cupboard. Here is the key of the cupboard. Take a bottle of chloroform. It has an orange label and the name is printed on it. I'll stay here in case anything happens. Be quick now, hurry! No, no, you don't need your shoes!"

I drove fast and in about fifteen minutes I was back with the bottle of chloroform. Ganderbai came out of Harry's room and met me in the hall.

4. **baldheaded:** without being careful or taking precautions.
5. **ether** (ē′thər) . . . **chloroform** (klôr′ə·fôrm′): anesthetics with very strong, suffocating odors. Anesthetics cause loss of feeling or consciousness.

"You got it?" he said. "Good, good. I've just been telling him what we are going to do. But now we must hurry. It is not easy for him in there like that all this time. I am afraid he might move."

He went back to the bedroom and I followed, carrying the bottle carefully with both hands. Harry was lying on the bed in precisely the same position as before, with the sweat pouring down his cheeks. His face was white and wet. He turned his eyes toward me, and I smiled at him and nodded confidently. He continued to look at me. I raised my thumb, giving him the okay signal. He closed his eyes. Ganderbai was squatted down by the bed, and on the floor beside him was the hollow rubber tube that he had previously used as a tourniquet, and he'd got a small paper funnel fitted into one end of the tube.

He began to pull a little piece of the sheet out from under the mattress. He was working directly in line with Harry's stomach, about eighteen inches from it, and I watched his fingers as they tugged gently at the edge of the sheet. He worked so slowly it was almost impossible to discern any movement either in his fingers or in the sheet that was being pulled.

Finally he succeeded in making an opening under the sheet and he took the rubber tube and inserted one end of it in the opening so that it would slide under the sheet along the mattress toward Harry's body. I do not know how long it took him to slide that tube in a few inches. It may have been twenty minutes, it may have been forty. I never once saw the tube move. I knew it was going in because the visible part of it grew gradually shorter, but I doubted that the krait could have felt even the faintest vibration. Ganderbai himself was sweating now, large pearls of sweat standing out all over his forehead and along his upper lip. But his hands were steady, and I noticed that his eyes were watching, not the tube in his hands, but the area of crumpled sheet above Harry's stomach.

WORDS TO OWN

discern (di·zʉrn′) v.: see; detect by looking carefully.

Without looking up, he held out a hand to me for the chloroform. I twisted out the ground-glass stopper and put the bottle right into his hand, not letting go till I was sure he had a good hold on it. Then he jerked his head for me to come closer, and he whispered, "Tell him I'm going to soak the mattress and that it will be very cold under his body. He must be ready for that and he must not move. Tell him now."

I bent over Harry and passed on the message.

"Why doesn't he get on with it?" Harry said.

"He's going to now, Harry. But it'll feel very cold, so be ready for it."

"Oh, get on!" For the first time he raised his voice, and Ganderbai glanced up sharply, watched him for a few seconds, then went back to his business.

Ganderbai poured a few drops of chloroform into the paper funnel and waited while it ran down the tube. Then he poured some more. Then he waited again, and the heavy, sickening smell of chloroform spread out over the room, bringing with it faint unpleasant memories of white-coated nurses and white surgeons standing in a white room around a long white table. Ganderbai was pouring steadily now, and I could see the heavy vapor of the chloroform swirling slowly like smoke above the paper funnel. He paused, held the bottle up to the light, poured one more funnelful, and handed the bottle back to me. Slowly he drew out the rubber tube from under the sheet; then he stood up.

The strain of inserting the tube and pouring the chloroform must have been great, and I recollect that when Ganderbai turned and whispered to me, his voice was small and tired. "We'll give it fifteen minutes. Just to be safe."

I leaned over to tell Harry. "We're going to give it fifteen minutes, just to be safe. But it's probably done for already."

"Then why don't you look and see!" Again he spoke loudly and Ganderbai sprang round, his small brown face suddenly very angry. He had almost pure black eyes and he stared at Harry, and Harry's smiling muscle started to twitch. I took my handkerchief and wiped his wet face, trying to stroke his forehead a little for comfort as I did so.

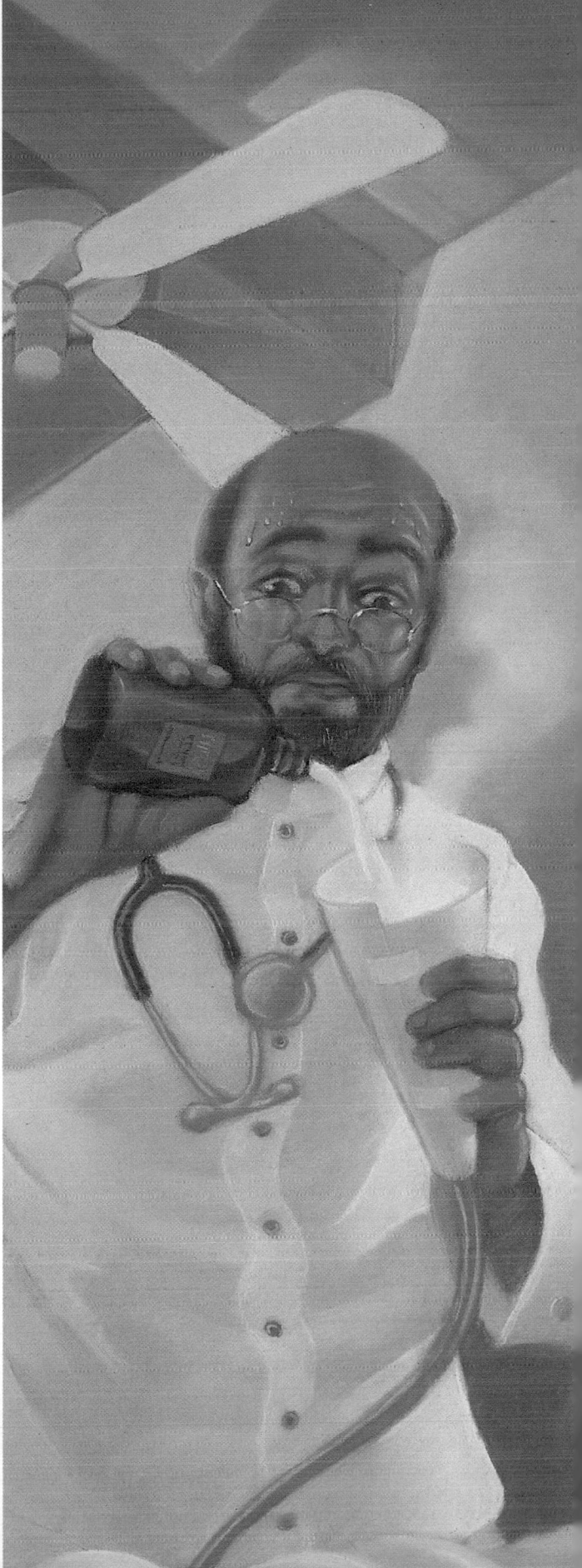

Then we stood and waited beside the bed, Ganderbai watching Harry's face all the time in a curious intense manner. The little Indian was concentrating all his willpower on keeping Harry quiet. He never once took his eyes from the patient and although he made no sound, he seemed somehow to be shouting at him all the time, saying: Now listen, you've got to listen, you're not going to go spoiling this now, d'you hear me; and Harry lay there twitching his mouth, sweating, closing his eyes, opening them, looking at me, at the sheet, at the ceiling, at me again, but never at Ganderbai. Yet somehow Ganderbai was holding him. The smell of chloroform was <u>oppressive</u> and it made me feel sick, but I couldn't leave the room now. I had the feeling someone was blowing up a huge balloon and I could see it was going to burst, but I couldn't look away.

At length Ganderbai turned and nodded and I knew he was ready to proceed. "You go over to the other side of the bed," he said. "We will each take one side of the sheet and draw it back together, but very slowly, please, and very quietly."

"Keep still now, Harry," I said, and I went around to the other side of the bed and took hold of the sheet. Ganderbai stood opposite me, and together we began to draw back the sheet, lifting it up clear of Harry's body, taking it back very slowly, both of us standing well away but at the same time bending forward, trying to peer underneath it. The smell of chloroform was awful. I remember trying to hold my breath, and when I couldn't do that any longer, I tried to breathe shallow so the stuff wouldn't get into my lungs.

The whole of Harry's chest was visible now, or rather the striped pajama top which covered it, and then I saw the white cord of his pajama trousers, neatly tied in a bow. A little farther and I saw a button, a mother-of-pearl button, and that was something I had never had on my pajamas, a fly button, let alone a mother-of-pearl one. This Harry, I thought, he is very refined.

It is odd how one sometimes has <u>frivolous</u> thoughts at exciting moments, and I <u>distinctly</u> remember thinking about Harry being very refined when I saw that button.

Apart from the button there was nothing on his stomach.

We pulled the sheet back faster then, and when we had uncovered his legs and feet we let the sheet drop over the end of the bed onto the floor.

"Don't move," Ganderbai said, "don't move, Mr. Pope"; and he began to peer around along the side of Harry's body and under his legs.

"We must be careful," he said. "It may be anywhere. It could be up the leg of his pajamas."

When Ganderbai said this, Harry quickly raised his head from the pillow and looked down at his legs. It was the first time he had moved. Then suddenly he jumped up, stood on his bed, and shook his legs one after the other violently in the air. At that moment we both thought he had been bitten, and Ganderbai was already reaching down into his bag for a scalpel and a tourniquet when Harry ceased his caperings and stood still and looked at the mattress he was standing on and shouted, "It's not there!"

Ganderbai straightened up and for a moment he too looked at the mattress; then he looked up at Harry. Harry was all right. He hadn't been bitten and now he wasn't going to get bitten and he wasn't going to be killed and everything was fine. But that didn't seem to make anyone feel any better.

"Mr. Pope, you are of course *quite* sure you saw it in the first place?" There was a note of sarcasm in Ganderbai's voice that he would never have employed in ordinary circumstances. "You don't think you might possibly have been dreaming, do you, Mr. Pope?" The way Ganderbai was looking at Harry, I realized that the sarcasm was not seriously intended. He was only easing up a bit after the strain.

Harry stood on his bed in his striped pajamas, glaring at Ganderbai, and the color began to spread out over his cheeks.

"Are you telling me I'm a liar?" he shouted.

WORDS TO OWN

oppressive (ə·pres′iv) *adj.*: heavy; hard to endure.
frivolous (friv′ə·ləs) *adj.*: silly; not as serious as the occasion requires.

Ganderbai remained absolutely still, watching Harry. Harry took a pace forward on the bed and there was a shining look in his eyes.

"Why, you dirty little sewer rat!"

"Shut up, Harry!" I said.

"You dirty black——"

"Harry!" I called. "Shut up, Harry!" It was terrible, the things he was saying.

Ganderbai went out of the room as though neither of us was there, and I followed him and put my arm around his shoulder as he walked across the hall and out onto the balcony.

"Don't you listen to Harry," I said. "This thing's made him so he doesn't know what he's saying."

We went down the steps from the balcony to the drive and across the drive in the darkness to where his old Morris car was parked. He opened the door and got in.

"You did a wonderful job," I said. "Thank you so very much for coming."

"All he needs is a good holiday," he said quietly, without looking at me; then he started the engine and drove off.

MEET THE WRITER

Fighter Pilot

Roald Dahl (1916–1990) was a fighter pilot with Britain's Royal Air Force during World War II. He suffered serious injuries when his Hurricane fighter plane was shot down over North Africa. Eventually he left flying and went to work for the British Embassy in Washington, D.C. There he was interviewed about his flying experiences for a magazine article. Frustrated that the interview was interfering with his lunch, he volunteered to go home and scribble down some notes instead. In fact, what Dahl did was to sit down and write a perfect short story. *The Saturday Evening Post* published it at once. Dahl went on to write several children's books (including *James and the Giant Peach* and *Charlie and the Chocolate Factory*), as well as many other short stories and an autobiography called *Boy*. When the violence in his books for young children was criticized, Dahl said:

66 Children love to be spooked. . . . They like a touch of the macabre as long as it's funny too. . . . And my nastiness is never gratuitous. It's retribution. Beastly people must be punished. **99**

Readers of *Boy* understand some of Dahl's concern about "beastly people." His childhood in an English boarding school was marked by beatings from cruel headmasters.

Like "Poison," Dahl's other short stories almost always place ordinary characters in believable but bizarre situations. Many of his stories have surprise endings—some of them shockers. Several of his stories have been made into TV movies.

Are You Ready for More?

If you'd like to read more by Dahl, take a look at "Dip in the Pool," "Lamb to the Slaughter," and "The Landlady." These three stories are in *The Best of Roald Dahl* (Vintage).

hate

Tato Laviera

watch

out

for

the

venom

of

its

first

bite.

MAKING MEANINGS

First Thoughts

1. How did each of the characters in "Poison" respond to danger? Compare their responses with those you wrote for your Quickwrite.

Shaping Interpretations

2. What is the source of the terrifying **suspense** in this story—that is, what big question does the writer plant in your mind to keep you turning the pages?

3. Is it possible that there really was a krait under the sheet, or do you think Harry imagined it? What evidence can you find in the text to support each interpretation?

4. The major struggle in the story is an **external conflict**. What **internal conflicts** are also at work?

5. By the story's end, what surprising **conflict** between two of the characters is out in the open?

6. We might suspect that the **title** of the story refers to more than the venom of the krait. What other kinds of poison is the story about?

7. How would you explain Harry's response to the generous Indian doctor?

Connecting with the Text

8. Did Harry's response to Ganderbai remind you of any incidents in actual life when cruelty was revealed by people under great pressure?

Extending the Text

9. How does the poem "hate" on the opposite page relate to Timber's experience with Harry and Dr. Ganderbai? What wider conflicts in the world could it also apply to?

Challenging the Text

10. Do you still have some questions unanswered at the end of the story? Talk about whether you found Dahl's ending effective or disappointing or even puzzling.

Reviewing the Text

a. What clues tell us at once that something is wrong with Harry?

b. At what point do we learn precisely what the **external conflict** is in the story?

c. What plan does Dr. Ganderbai finally put into action to resolve the conflict?

d. What is the outcome of the snake search?

e. What cruel things does Harry say to Dr. Ganderbai at the end?

CHOICES: Building Your Portfolio

Writer's Notebook

1. Collecting Ideas for a True Narrative

Using dialogue.  The three characters in "Poison" move the events of the story along with their dialogue. Dahl gives tense, quick sentences to Harry: "'Take it away,' he whispered. 'Make me cough.'" Ganderbai speaks carefully, trying to keep control: "'It might save him. It might not. I am trying to think of something else to do.'" As you take notes for your own narrative, experiment with dialogue. How will your characters speak? Formally? Informally? In slang? What will they say under stress? Remember that not everyone speaks in the same way.

Remember also that speakers often use fragments, especially when they are excited. Be sure to provide "tag lines" to tell who is speaking and *how*.

Creative Writing

2. "What's on His Mind?"

Imagine a final scene that takes place with Dr. Ganderbai in his car as he heads for home. What is he thinking? Will he come to the aid of Harry ever again? Does he understand Harry? What does he think *really* happened—does he believe there was a krait under the sheet? Think of images, words, and symbols that you can put in thought bubbles to show what the doctor is thinking. Then write a brief paragraph to explain your look inside Ganderbai's head.

Role-Playing

3. Hot Seat

Get together with a group of classmates and take turns role-playing the characters Timber, Harry, and Dr. Ganderbai. Begin by choosing your character. Then take turns climbing into the "hot seat" and responding to questions—in character—that the rest of the group members ask. Try to find out why a character acted as he did and how a character felt about the night's events. Keep each person in the hot seat for about two minutes. When you've finished the questioning, discuss what you learned about the characters by stepping into their shoes.

Research/History

4. Investigating India

Dahl's story might have made you curious to know more about colonial India—about the source of Harry's rudeness and the reason for Dr. Ganderbai's response. Plan a small research project in which you compile details about life in India in the 1940s, around the time this story takes place. You might focus on these questions, or others of your own: How did India become independent? What caused the horrible slaughter in Pakistan? What was Gandhi's role in India's independence? Present your report in class. Be sure to tell which questions you decided to focus on.

Dialogue: Narrative About a Meeting

We are waiting for meeting to start. Joan and Jackie are whispering about new girl.

"Here she comes—again," Jackie hissed.

"How I loathe and detest these meetings," answered Joan with a cold look at all of us.

"Hi, how lovely to see you," they both say with bubbly voices when the new girl comes in.

LANGUAGE LINK

MINI-LESSON

Proofreading: An Agreeable Pair—Subject and Verb

Standard American English is the kind of English you most often read in newspapers and hear on the radio and TV. In standard English, verbs agree with their subjects in number—that is, singular subjects take singular verbs, and plural subjects take plural verbs. Here are some sentences with subjects and verbs underlined.

1. The krait's <u>bite</u> <u>is</u> quite deadly. [singular subject, singular verb]

2. <u>They</u> <u>kill</u> a fair number of people each year. [plural subject, plural verb]

3. Harry's <u>face and neck</u> <u>were</u> sweating. [compound subject joined by *and*, plural verb]

4. Ganderbai's <u>bag</u> of medical supplies <u>was</u> needed. [singular subject, singular verb; a prepositional phrase is never the subject]

5. <u>Each</u> of the men <u>was</u> tense. [*Each* is singular.]

6. <u>Few</u> of Harry's friends <u>are</u> so refined. [*Few* is plural.]

Try It Out

Be a test maker. Write six sentences that ask for a choice of singular or plural verbs, using the numbered sentences as models. (You might find some sentences in your writing folder that you can use as test items.) Let a partner take your test. Do you both agree on the correct answers?

Tips for writers: The following pronouns are singular: *each, either, neither, one, everyone, everybody, no one, anyone, someone.*

The following pronouns are plural: *several, few, many.*

Language Handbook HELP

See Agreement of Subject and Verb, page 994.

Technology HELP

See Language Workshop CD-ROM. *Key word entry: subject-verb agreement.*

VOCABULARY

HOW TO OWN A WORD

WORD BANK

intravenously
discern
oppressive
frivolous

Word Maps

Word maps, like the one below, usually include a word's **etymology** (which indicates the origin of each of the word's parts). A word map can also include the word's meaning, related words, and sentences using the word. Work with a partner to produce word maps for the other three words in the Word Bank.

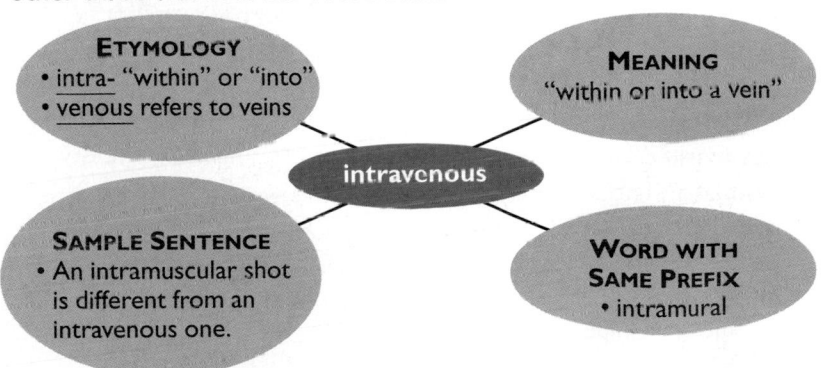

BEFORE YOU READ
MARIGOLDS

Background

In the 1930s a terrible economic depression swept the world. Banks closed their doors. People lost their life savings. The stock market collapsed. Businesses failed all over America, and factories closed their doors. Life was hard for almost every American during those years. As the narrator of this story says, however, the Depression was nothing new to her family—the black workers of rural Maryland were used to hard times.

Reading Focus

The Beginning of Compassion

The Depression forms the backdrop for this story, but it is not just a story about economics and how money— or the lack of it—affects families. The story is also about the passage from childhood to adulthood, a passage that is usually marked with conflicts. In fact, negotiating that passage to adulthood can demand as much courage as a struggle with some outside enemy—or with economic hardships.

Quickwrite

Write down your responses to this question before you read: What fears and conflicts do most young people have to deal with as they move into adult life? Keep your notes for use later when you talk about the story.

Elements of Literature

Internal Conflict

Though there's a violent confrontation in this story, important conflicts also take place inside the mind and heart of fourteen-year-old Lizabeth. Some people would say that Lizabeth is battling her own interior "monsters."

In **internal conflict,** a character struggles to resolve some personal problem, such as fear, shyness, anger, or anxiety.

For more on Conflict, see pages 32–33 and the Handbook of Literary Terms.

Miss Lottie didn't like intruders, especially children.

MARIGOLDS

Eugenia W. Collier

When I think of the hometown of my youth, all that I seem to remember is dust—the brown, crumbly dust of late summer—arid, sterile dust that gets into the eyes and makes them water, gets into the throat and between the toes of bare brown feet. I don't know why I should remember only the dust. Surely there must have been lush green lawns and paved streets under leafy shade trees somewhere in town; but memory is an abstract painting—it does not present things as they are, but rather as they *feel*. And so, when I think of that time and that place, I remember only the dry September of the dirt roads and grassless yards of the shantytown where I lived. And one other thing I remember, another incongruency[1] of memory—a brilliant splash of sunny yellow against the dust—Miss Lottie's marigolds.

Whenever the memory of those marigolds flashes across my mind, a strange nostalgia comes with it and remains long after the picture has faded. I feel again the chaotic emotions of adolescence, illusive as smoke, yet as real as the potted geranium before me now. Joy and rage and wild animal gladness and shame become tangled together in the multicolored skein[2] of fourteen-going-on-fifteen as I recall that devastating moment when I was suddenly more woman than child, years ago in Miss Lottie's yard. I think of those marigolds at the strangest times; I remember them vividly now as I desperately pass away the time. . . .

I suppose that futile waiting was the sorrowful background music of our impoverished little community when I was young. The Depression that gripped the nation was no new thing to us, for the black workers of rural Maryland had always been depressed. I don't know what it was that we were waiting for; certainly not for the prosperity that was "just around the corner," for those were white folks' words, which we never believed. Nor did we wait for hard work and thrift to pay off in shining success, as the American Dream promised, for we knew better than that, too. Perhaps we waited for a miracle, amorphous[3] in concept but necessary if one were to have the grit to rise before dawn each day and labor in the white man's vineyard until after dark, or to wander about in the September

1. **incongruency** (in'kän'grōō·ən·sē): inconsistency; lack of agreement or harmony.

2. **multicolored skein** (skān): The writer is comparing her many feelings to a skein, or long coiled piece of many-colored yarn.
3. **amorphous** (ə·môr'fəs): vague, shapeless.

dust offering one's sweat in return for some meager share of bread. But God was chary[4] with miracles in those days, and so we waited—and waited.

We children, of course, were only vaguely aware of the extent of our poverty. Having no radios, few newspapers, and no magazines, we were somewhat unaware of the world outside our community. Nowadays we would be called culturally deprived and people would write books and hold conferences about us. In those days everybody we knew was just as hungry and ill clad as we were. Poverty was the cage in which we all were trapped, and our hatred of it was still the vague, undirected restlessness of the zoo-bred flamingo who knows that nature created him to fly free.

As I think of those days I feel most poignantly the tag end of summer, the bright, dry times when we began to have a sense of shortening days and the imminence of the cold.

By the time I was fourteen, my brother Joey and I were the only children left at our house, the older ones having left home for early marriage or the lure of the city, and the two babies having been sent to relatives who might care for them better than we. Joey was three years younger than I, and a boy, and therefore vastly inferior. Each morning our mother and father trudged wearily down the dirt road and around the bend, she to her domestic job, he to his daily unsuccessful quest for work. After our few chores around the tumbledown shanty, Joey and I were free to run wild in the sun with other children similarly situated.

For the most part, those days are ill-defined in my memory, running together and combining like a fresh watercolor painting left out in the rain. I remember squatting in the road drawing a picture in the dust, a picture which Joey gleefully erased with one sweep of his dirty foot. I remember fishing for minnows in a muddy creek and watching sadly as they eluded my cupped hands, while Joey laughed uproariously. And I remember, that year, a strange

restlessness of body and of spirit, a feeling that something old and familiar was ending, and something unknown and therefore terrifying was beginning.

One day returns to me with special clarity for some reason, perhaps because it was the beginning of the experience that in some inexplicable[5] way marked the end of innocence. I was loafing under the great oak tree in our yard, deep in some reverie which I have now forgotten, except that it involved some secret, secret thoughts of one of the Harris boys across the yard. Joey and a bunch of kids were bored now with the old tire suspended from an oak limb, which had kept them entertained for a while.

"Hey, Lizabeth," Joey yelled. He never talked when he could yell. "Hey, Lizabeth, let's go somewhere."

I came reluctantly from my private world. "Where you want to go? What you want to do?"

The truth was that we were becoming tired of the formlessness of our summer days. The idleness whose prospect had seemed so beautiful during the busy days of spring now had degenerated to an almost desperate effort to fill up the empty midday hours.

"Let's go see can we find some locusts on the hill," someone suggested.

Joey was scornful. "Ain't no more locusts there. Y'all got 'em all while they was still green."

The argument that followed was brief and not really worth the effort. Hunting locust trees wasn't fun anymore by now.

"Tell you what," said Joey finally, his eyes sparkling. "Let's us go over to Miss Lottie's."

The idea caught on at once, for annoying Miss Lottie was always fun. I was still child enough to scamper along with the group over rickety fences and through bushes that tore our already raggedy clothes, back to where Miss Lottie lived. I think now that we must have made a tragic-comic spectacle, five or six kids of different

5. **inexplicable** (in·eks′pli·kə·bəl): not explainable or understandable.

WORDS TO OWN

clarity (klar′ə·tē) *n.*: clearness.

---

4. **chary** (cher′ē): not generous.

Southern Limited (1976) by Romare Bearden. Collage.

ages, each of us clad in only one garment—the girls in faded dresses that were too long or too short, the boys in patchy pants, their sweaty brown chests gleaming in the hot sun. A little cloud of dust followed our thin legs and bare feet as we tramped over the barren land.

When Miss Lottie's house came into view we stopped, ostensibly[6] to plan our strategy, but actually to reinforce our courage. Miss Lottie's house was the most ramshackle of all our ramshackle homes. The sun and rain had long since faded its rickety frame siding from white to a sullen gray. The boards themselves seemed to remain upright not from being nailed together but rather from leaning together, like a house that a child might have constructed from

cards. A brisk wind might have blown it down, and the fact that it was still standing implied a kind of enchantment that was stronger than the elements. There it stood and as far as I know is standing yet—a gray, rotting thing with no porch, no shutters, no steps, set on a cramped lot with no grass, not even any weeds—a monument to decay.

In front of the house in a squeaky rocking chair sat Miss Lottie's son, John Burke, completing the impression of decay. John Burke was what was known as queer-headed. Black and ageless, he sat rocking day in and day out in a mindless stupor, lulled by the monotonous squeak-squawk of the chair. A battered hat atop his shaggy head shaded him from the sun. Usually John Burke was totally unaware of everything outside his quiet dream world. But if

6. **ostensibly** (ä·sten′sə·blē): seemingly; apparently.

you disturbed him, if you intruded upon his fantasies, he would become enraged, strike out at you, and curse at you in some strange enchanted language which only he could understand. We children made a game of thinking of ways to disturb John Burke and then to elude his violent retribution.

But our real fun and our real fear lay in Miss Lottie herself. Miss Lottie seemed to be at least a hundred years old. Her big frame still held traces of the tall, powerful woman she must have been in youth, although it was now bent and drawn. Her smooth skin was a dark reddish brown, and her face had Indian-like features and the stern stoicism[7] that one associates with Indian faces. Miss Lottie didn't like intruders either, especially children. She never left her yard, and nobody ever visited her. We never knew how she managed those necessities which depend on human interaction—how she ate, for example, or even whether she ate. When we were tiny children, we thought Miss Lottie was a witch and we made up tales that we half believed ourselves about her exploits. We were far too sophisticated now, of course, to believe the witch nonsense. But old fears have a way of clinging like cobwebs, and so when we sighted the tumbledown shack, we had to stop to reinforce our nerves.

"Look, there she is," I whispered, forgetting that Miss Lottie could not possibly have heard me from that distance. "She's fooling with them crazy flowers."

"Yeh, look at 'er."

Miss Lottie's marigolds were perhaps the strangest part of the picture. Certainly they did not fit in with the crumbling decay of the rest of her yard. Beyond the dusty brown yard, in front of the sorry gray house, rose suddenly and shockingly a dazzling strip of bright blossoms, clumped together in enormous mounds, warm and passionate and sun-golden. The old black witch-woman worked on them all summer, every summer, down on her creaky knees, weeding and cultivating and arranging, while the house crumbled and John Burke rocked. For some perverse reason, we children hated those marigolds. They interfered with the perfect ugliness of the place; they were too beautiful; they said too much that we could not understand; they did not make sense. There was something in the vigor with which the old woman destroyed the weeds that intimidated us. It should have been a comical sight—the old woman with the man's hat on her cropped white head, leaning over the bright mounds, her big backside in the air—but it wasn't comical, it was something we could not name. We had to annoy her by whizzing a pebble into her flowers or by yelling a dirty word, then dancing away from her rage, reveling in our youth and mocking her age. Actually, I think it was the flowers we wanted to destroy, but nobody had the nerve to try it, not even Joey, who was usually fool enough to try anything.

"Y'all git some stones," commanded Joey now and was met with instant giggling obedience as everyone except me began to gather pebbles from the dusty ground. "Come on, Lizabeth."

I just stood there peering through the bushes, torn between wanting to join the fun and feeling that it was all a bit silly.

"You scared, Lizabeth?"

I cursed and spat on the ground—my favorite gesture of phony bravado. "Y'all children get the stones, I'll show you how to use 'em."

I said before that we children were not consciously aware of how thick were the bars of our cage. I wonder now, though, whether we were not more aware of it than I thought. Perhaps we had some dim notion of what we were, and how little chance we had of being anything else. Otherwise, why would we have been so preoccupied with destruction? Anyway, the pebbles were collected quickly, and everybody looked at me to begin the fun.

"Come on, y'all."

---

7. **stoicism** (stō′i·siz′əm): calm indifference to pleasure or pain.

WORDS TO OWN
retribution (re′trə·byōō′shən) n.: revenge.
intimidated (in·tim′ə·dāt′id) v.: frightened.

The Magic Garden (1978) by Romare Bearden. Watercolor and collage (10 ⅛″ x 7″).

La Primavera (1967) by Romare Bearden. Collage, oil on board (44″ x 56″).

We crept to the edge of the bushes that bordered the narrow road in front of Miss Lottie's place. She was working placidly, kneeling over the flowers, her dark hand plunged into the golden mound. Suddenly *zing*—an expertly aimed stone cut the head off one of the blossoms.

"Who out there?" Miss Lottie's backside came down and her head came up as her sharp eyes searched the bushes. "You better git!"

We had crouched down out of sight in the bushes, where we stifled the giggles that insisted on coming. Miss Lottie gazed warily across the road for a moment, then cautiously returned to her weeding. *Zing*—Joey sent a pebble into the blooms, and another marigold was beheaded.

Miss Lottie was enraged now. She began struggling to her feet, leaning on a rickety cane and shouting. "Y'all git! Go on home!" Then the rest of the kids let loose with their pebbles, storming the flowers and laughing wildly and senselessly at Miss Lottie's <u>impotent</u> rage. She shook her stick at us and started shakily toward the road crying, "Git 'long! John Burke! John Burke, come help!"

Then I lost my head entirely, mad with the power of inciting such rage, and ran out of the bushes in the storm of pebbles, straight toward Miss Lottie, chanting madly, "Old witch, fell in a

WORDS TO OWN

impotent (im′pə·tənt) *adj.*: powerless; helpless.

ditch, picked up a penny and thought she was rich!" The children screamed with delight, dropped their pebbles, and joined the crazy dance, swarming around Miss Lottie like bees and chanting, "Old lady witch!" while she screamed curses at us. The madness lasted only a moment, for John Burke, startled at last, lurched out of his chair, and we dashed for the bushes just as Miss Lottie's cane went whizzing at my head.

I did not join the merriment when the kids gathered again under the oak in our bare yard. Suddenly I was ashamed, and I did not like being ashamed. The child in me sulked and said it was all in fun, but the woman in me flinched at the thought of the malicious attack that I had led. The mood lasted all afternoon. When we ate the beans and rice that was supper that night, I did not notice my father's silence, for he was always silent these days, nor did I notice my mother's absence, for she always worked until well into evening. Joey and I had a particularly bitter argument after supper; his exuberance got on my nerves. Finally I stretched out upon the pallet[8] in the room we shared and fell into a fitful doze.

When I awoke, somewhere in the middle of the night, my mother had returned, and I vaguely listened to the conversation that was audible through the thin walls that separated our rooms. At first I heard no words, only voices. My mother's voice was like a cool, dark room in summer—peaceful, soothing, quiet. I loved to listen to it; it made things seem all right somehow. But my father's voice cut through hers, shattering the peace.

"Twenty-two years, Maybelle, twenty-two years," he was saying, "and I got nothing for you, nothing, nothing."

"It's all right, honey, you'll get something. Everybody out of work now, you know that."

"It ain't right. Ain't no man ought to eat his woman's food year in and year out, and see his children running wild. Ain't nothing right about that."

"Honey, you took good care of us when you had it. Ain't nobody got nothing nowadays."

"I ain't talking about nobody else, I'm talking about *me*. God knows I try." My mother said something I could not hear, and my father cried out louder, "What must a man do, tell me that?"

"Look, we ain't starving. I git paid every week, and Mrs. Ellis is real nice about giving me things. She gonna let me have Mr. Ellis's old coat for you this winter——"

"Damn Mr. Ellis's coat! And damn his money! You think I want white folks' leavings? Damn, Maybelle"—and suddenly he sobbed, loudly and painfully, and cried helplessly and hopelessly in the dark night. I had never heard a man cry before. I did not know men ever cried. I covered my ears with my hands but could not cut off the sound of my father's harsh, painful, despairing sobs. My father was a strong man who could whisk a child upon his shoulders and go singing through the house. My father whittled toys for us, and laughed so loud that the great oak seemed to laugh with him, and taught us how to fish and hunt rabbits. How could it be that my father was crying? But the sobs went on, un-stifled, finally quieting until I could hear my mother's voice, deep and rich, humming softly as she used to hum to a frightened child.

The world had lost its boundary lines. My mother, who was small and soft, was now the strength of the family; my father, who was the rock on which the family had been built, was sobbing like the tiniest child. Everything was suddenly out of tune, like a broken accordion. Where did I fit into this crazy picture? I do not now remember my thoughts, only a feeling of great bewilderment and fear.

Long after the sobbing and humming had stopped, I lay on the pallet, still as stone with my hands over my ears, wishing that I too could cry and be comforted. The night was silent now except for the sound of the crickets and of Joey's soft breathing. But the room was too crowded with fear to allow me to sleep, and finally, feeling the terrible aloneness of 4 A.M., I decided to awaken Joey.

"Ouch! What's the matter with you? What you want?" he demanded disagreeably when I had pinched and slapped him awake.

"Come on, wake up."

8. **pallet:** small bed or cot.

"What for? Go 'way."

I was lost for a reasonable reply. I could not say, "I'm scared and I don't want to be alone," so I merely said, "I'm going out. If you want to come, come on."

The promise of adventure awoke him. "Going out now? Where to, Lizabeth? What you going to do?"

I was pulling my dress over my head. Until now I had not thought of going out. "Just come on," I replied tersely.

I was out the window and halfway down the road before Joey caught up with me.

"Wait, Lizabeth, where you going?"

I was running as if the Furies[9] were after me, as perhaps they were—running silently and furiously until I came to where I had half known I was headed: to Miss Lottie's yard.

The half-dawn light was more eerie than complete darkness, and in it the old house was like the ruin that my world had become—foul and crumbling, a grotesque caricature. It looked haunted, but I was not afraid, because I was haunted too.

"Lizabeth, you lost your mind?" panted Joey.

I had indeed lost my mind, for all the smoldering emotions of that summer swelled in me and burst—the great need for my mother who was never there, the hopelessness of our poverty and degradation, the bewilderment of being neither child nor woman and yet both at once, the fear unleashed by my father's tears. And these feelings combined in one great impulse toward destruction.

"Lizabeth!"

I leaped furiously into the mounds of marigolds and pulled madly, trampling and pulling and destroying the perfect yellow blooms. The fresh smell of early morning and of dew-soaked marigolds spurred me on as I went tearing and mangling and sobbing while Joey tugged my dress or my waist crying, "Lizabeth, stop, please stop!"

And then I was sitting in the ruined little garden among the uprooted and ruined flowers, crying and crying, and it was too late to undo what I had done. Joey was sitting beside me, silent and frightened, not knowing what to say. Then, "Lizabeth, look."

I opened my swollen eyes and saw in front of me a pair of large, calloused feet; my gaze lifted to the swollen legs, the age-distorted body clad in a tight cotton nightdress, and then the shadowed Indian face surrounded by stubby white hair. And there was no rage in the face now, now that the garden was destroyed and there was nothing any longer to be protected.

"M-miss Lottie!" I scrambled to my feet and just stood there and stared at her, and that was the moment when childhood faded and womanhood began. That violent, crazy act was the last act of childhood. For as I gazed at the immobile face with the sad, weary eyes, I gazed upon a kind of reality which is hidden to childhood. The witch was no longer a witch but only a broken old woman who had dared to create beauty in the midst of ugliness and sterility. She had been born in squalor and lived in it all her life. Now at the end of that life she had nothing except a falling-down hut, a wrecked body, and John Burke, the mindless son of her passion. Whatever verve there was left in her, whatever was of love and beauty and joy that had not been squeezed out by life, had been there in the marigolds she had so tenderly cared for.

Of course I could not express the things that I knew about Miss Lottie as I stood there awkward and ashamed. The years have put words to the things I knew in that moment, and as I look back upon it, I know that that moment marked the end of innocence. Innocence involves an unseeing acceptance of things at face value, an ignorance of the area below the surface. In that humiliating moment I looked beyond myself and into the depths of another person. This was the beginning of compassion, and one cannot have both compassion and innocence.

The years have taken me worlds away from that time and that place, from the dust and squalor of our lives, and from the bright thing that I destroyed in a blind, childish striking out at God knows what. Miss Lottie died long ago

---

9. Furies (fyŏŏr′ēz): in Greek and Roman mythology, spirits who pursue people who have committed crimes, sometimes driving them mad.

and many years have passed since I last saw her hut, completely barren at last, for despite my wild <u>contrition</u> she never planted marigolds again. Yet, there are times when the image of those passionate yellow mounds returns with a painful poignancy. For one does not have to be ignorant and poor to find that his life is as barren as the dusty yards of our town. And I too have planted marigolds.

WORDS TO OWN

contrition (kən·trish′ən) *n.*: deep feelings of guilt and repentance.

MEET THE WRITER

I Must Have Done My Job Well

Eugenia W. Collier
(1928–   ), who has a bachelor's degree, a master's degree, and a Ph.D., has taught English at Howard University, Baltimore Community College, and Morgan State College. Collier wrote this about her story "Marigolds":

❝When I talk with people about 'Marigolds,' someone usually asks me whether the story is autobiographical. I am always pleased with the question, because it means that I must have done my job well —convinced the reader that the incidents in the story are actually happening. However, I always end up admitting that Lizabeth and I are two very different people. I was born and bred in the city of Baltimore, and my family never had the economic problems of Lizabeth's. In some ways we are different in temperament: I was never as daring as Lizabeth, never a leader among my peers. However, I hope that through her I have captured an experience which most young people have— the painful passage from childhood to adulthood, a passage which can be understood only in retrospect. Also, I was tapping into another deeply human experience: hoping desperately for something (planting marigolds) and then having that hope destroyed.

I wrote 'Marigolds' at a time of profound unhappiness. One night I had a tremendous urge to write. I wrote nonstop until the story was finished—about twenty-four hours. Later I sent 'Marigolds' (along with a fee I could hardly afford) to a well-advertised literary agency, which returned the story (not the fee) with a note saying that it had no plot, no conflict, and no hope of publication. Discouraged, I put 'Marigolds' away. Five years later, doing research for a project on black writing of the 1960s, I read stories in *Negro Digest* which were similar in subject matter to 'Marigolds.' I submitted my story, and *Negro Digest* published it. It won the Gwendolyn Brooks Prize for Fiction, it was selected for inclusion in an anthology of black fiction, and since then it has been included in a number of collections. Of all the fiction I have written, 'Marigolds' remains my favorite.❞

Filling Station

Elizabeth Bishop

Oh, but it is dirty!
—this little filling station,
oil-soaked, oil-permeated
to a disturbing, over-all
5   black translucency.
Be careful with that match!
Father wears a dirty,
oil-soaked monkey suit
that cuts him under the arms,
10   and several quick and saucy
and greasy sons assist him
(it's a family filling station),
all quite thoroughly dirty.
Do they live in the station?
15   It has a cement porch
behind the pumps, and on it
a set of crushed and grease-
impregnated wickerwork;
on the wicker sofa
20   a dirty dog, quite comfy.

Some comic books provide
the only note of color—
of certain color. They lie
upon a big dim doily
25   draping a taboret°
(part of the set), beside
a big hirsute° begonia.
Why the extraneous plant?
Why the taboret?
30   Why, oh why, the doily?
(Embroidered in daisy stitch
with marguerites,° I think,
and heavy with gray crochet.)
Somebody embroidered the doily.
35   Somebody waters the plant,
or oils it, maybe. Somebody
arranges the rows of cans
so that they softly say:
ESSO—SO—SO—SO
40   to high-strung automobiles.
Somebody loves us all.

25. taboret (tab'ə·ret'): low footstool.
27. hirsute (hur'sōōt'): shaggy. *Hirsute*
can also mean "hairy."
32. marguerites (mär'gə·rēts'): daisy-
like flowers.

MAKING MEANINGS

First Thoughts

1. Why do you think Lizabeth hated the marigolds? Are her feelings common? Check your Quickwrite.

Shaping Interpretations

2. What are Lizabeth's **internal conflicts**—what personal "monsters" are troubling her?

3. Draw a thought bubble like the one shown opposite. Fill it with words that represent Lizabeth's thoughts as she commits her act of cruel destruction. Be prepared to explain why you chose the words you did.

4. Lizabeth says that destroying the marigolds was her last act of childhood. Why does she think of herself as an adult from that moment on?

Reviewing the Text

a. When and where does this story take place?

b. Who is Miss Lottie and why are the children afraid of her?

c. Describe the children's confrontation with Miss Lottie.

d. What does Lizabeth discover about her parents that night?

e. Years later, what things about Miss Lottie and herself is the narrator able to express?

5. What does Lizabeth mean at the end when she says that she too has planted marigolds? What do you think the marigolds have come to mean in the story? Consider the feelings that the characters have had about the marigolds throughout the story:

   - Miss Lottie loves and cares for them.
   - The children do not understand why they are there.
   - Lizabeth wants to destroy them.

Connecting with the Text

6. Collier makes many general statements about life in this story. Find at least two and talk about your responses to them. Do they trigger any memories or feelings of your own?

7. Compare Miss Lottie's attempts to bring beauty to a drab setting with the efforts of the unknown people in the poem "Filling Station" (opposite). Where do you see such efforts at creating beauty in your own world?

Extending the Text

8. The narrator doesn't tell us much about the effect of the destruction on Miss Lottie. From what she *does* tell us, how do you think Miss Lottie was affected?

9. "The world had lost its boundary lines," Lizabeth writes about her parents' conversation that night. What does she mean? What situations might make a child feel that boundaries have been lost?

CHOICES: Building Your Portfolio

Writer's Notebook

1. Collecting Ideas for a True Narrative

Any inner conflict? You'll be writing a true narrative of your own in the Writer's Workshop on page 112. In your narrative you might want to focus on some inner conflict felt by a character. In "Marigolds," for example, Lizabeth's inner conflict is caused by rage and shame. She's angry because of the poverty and injustice she has suffered throughout her childhood, but she's ashamed of the way she has expressed the anger—by destroying the beautiful marigolds. List some characters who might appear in *your* narrative and make a chart like the one shown here. What are their inner conflicts?

Inner Conflicts	
Myself	Jealousy and admiration of my brother's athletic talent
Mom	Ambition and fear about going back to school
Alex	Lonely and excited after moving across country

Critical Writing

2. A Personal Response

In Meet the Writer on page 99, Collier recalls that the first agency she sent her story to returned it with a note saying the story had no hope of publication. Write a response to that agency in the form of a letter. You might talk about one or all of these:

- how you felt about the story in general
- how you connected with the text
- how you felt about certain passages

Conflict Resolution

3. Resolving Conflicts

An important part of solving problems in actual life is understanding the results, or effects, of certain troublesome actions. Using a chart like the one below, first focus on Lizabeth's actions and their effects on other people and on herself. Then focus on a conflict in your own school or community. Prepare another chart citing specific actions or events and the ways they affect other people.

Actions	Effects
1.	1.
2.	2.
3.	3.

Art

4. Imitating Bearden

The collages on pages 93, 95, and 96 are by Romare Bearden, an African American artist. A **collage**, as you can see from the one below, is a collection of images taken from various sources (magazines, newspapers, photographs, even the artist's own drawings). Collages can also include pieces of cloth, words, or even objects like stones or shells or dried flowers. Create a collage of your own showing Miss Lottie's house and her flowers. For your collage, be sure to add some words from the story.

La Primavera (detail) (1967) by Romare Bearden. Collage, oil on board.

LANGUAGE LINK MINI-LESSON

Handbook of Literary Terms
H E L P

See Figure of Speech.

Style: Figures of Speech—Making It Vivid

Collier's story is remarkable for its vivid figures of speech, which make the place and the characters' feelings come alive. In a figure of speech, one thing is compared to another, very different, thing. There are several kinds of figures of speech. A **simile** states the comparison using words such as *like, as,* or *than:*

> "I feel again the chaotic emotions of adolescence, illusive as smoke. . . ." [Emotions are compared to smoke.]

A **metaphor** compares two unlike things without using the words *like* or *as:*

> ". . . memory is an abstract painting" [Memory is directly compared to a painting.]

At times in a metaphor, only one part of the comparison is directly stated; you have to infer the other part:

> "Joy and rage and wild animal gladness and shame become tangled together in the multicolored skein of fourteen-going-on-fifteen. . . ." [A teenager's mixed emotions are compared to a multicolored skein of wool.]

Try It Out

Complete these sentences with imaginative figures of speech. Remember that a figure of speech compares two *unlike* items.

1. The marigolds were _____.
2. The garden looked like _____.
3. The days were as empty as _____.

Figures of speech are most often visual. Select two or three figures of speech from the story and illustrate them.

A tip for writers: When you create a figure of speech, put it to a test. Ask: "In what specific way are these two unlike things alike?" Ask: "Does this work?"

VOCABULARY   HOW TO OWN A WORD

WORD BANK

clarity
retribution
intimidated
impotent
contrition

How Would You Say It?

Read the following sentences from the story. Then reword them as if you were speaking. Use your everyday language.

1. "One day returns to me with special clarity. . . ."
2. "We children made a game of thinking of ways to disturb John Burke and then to elude his violent retribution."
3. "There was something in the vigor with which the old woman destroyed the weeds that intimidated us."
4. "Then the rest of the kids let loose with their pebbles, storming the flowers and laughing wildly and senselessly at Miss Lottie's impotent rage."
5. "Miss Lottie died long ago and many years have passed since I last saw her hut, completely barren at last, for despite my wild contrition she never planted marigolds again."

Background

This story is from *Black Boy*, an autobiography written by the great African American writer Richard Wright (1908–1960). As this part of his life story opens, Richard and his family are living in a kitchen and bedroom in Memphis, Tennessee, in a run-down tenement. Richard is terrified to go out on the bleak streets alone.

A Dialogue with the Text

As you read remember to pause at least three or four  times to jot down questions and reactions in your Reader's Log. For ideas review the model response, pages 5–10.

> *I began to wake up at night to find hunger standing at my bedside.*

from
Black Boy

Richard Wright

Hunger stole upon me so slowly that at first I was not aware of what hunger really meant. Hunger had always been more or less at my elbow when I played, but now I began to wake up at night to find hunger standing at my bedside, staring at me gauntly. The hunger I had known before this had been no grim, hostile stranger; it had been a normal hunger that had made me beg constantly for bread, and when I ate a crust or two I was satisfied. But this new hunger baffled me, scared me, made me angry and insistent. Whenever I begged for food now, my mother would pour me a cup of tea, which would still the clamor in my stomach for a moment or two; but a little later I would feel hunger nudging my ribs, twisting my empty guts until they ached. I would grow dizzy and my vision would dim. I became less active in my play, and for the first time in my life I had to pause and think of what was happening to me.

"Mama, I'm hungry," I complained one afternoon.

"Jump up and catch a kungry," she said, trying to make me laugh and forget.

"What's a *kungry*?"

"It's what little boys eat when they get hungry," she said.

"What does it taste like?"

"I don't know."

"Then why do you tell me to catch one?"

"Because you said that you were hungry," she said, smiling.

I sensed that she was teasing me and it made me angry.

"But I'm hungry. I want to eat."

"You'll have to wait."

"But I want to eat now."

"But there's nothing to eat," she told me.

"Why?"

"Just because there's none," she explained.

"But I want to eat," I said, beginning to cry.

"You'll just have to wait," she said again.

"But why?"

"For God to send some food."

"When is He going to send it?"

"I don't know."

"But I'm hungry!"

She was ironing and she paused and looked at me with tears in her eyes.

"Where's your father?" she asked me.

I stared in bewilderment. Yes, it was true that my father had not come home to sleep for many days now and I could make as much noise as I wanted. Though I had not known why he was absent, I had been glad that he was not there to shout his restrictions at me. But it had never occurred to me that his absence would mean that there would be no food.

"I don't know," I said.

"Who brings food into the house?" my mother asked me.

"Papa," I said. "He always brought food."

"Well, your father isn't here now," she said.

"Where is he?"

"I don't know," she said.

"But I'm hungry," I whimpered, stomping my feet.

"You'll have to wait until I get a job and buy food," she said.

As the days slid past, the image of my father became associated with my pangs of hunger, and whenever I felt hunger, I thought of him with a deep biological bitterness.

My mother finally went to work as a cook and left me and my brother alone in the flat[1] each day with a loaf of bread and a pot of tea. When she returned at evening, she would be tired and

1. **flat:** apartment.

dispirited and would cry a lot. Sometimes, when she was in despair, she would call us to her and talk to us for hours, telling us that we now had no father, that our lives would be different from those of other children, that we must learn as soon as possible to take care of ourselves, to dress ourselves, to prepare our own food; that we must take upon ourselves the responsibility of the flat while she worked. Half frightened, we would promise solemnly. We did not understand what had happened between our father and our mother, and the most that these long talks did to us was to make us feel a vague dread. Whenever we asked why father had left, she would tell us that we were too young to know.

One evening my mother told me that thereafter I would have to do the shopping for food. She took me to the corner store to show me the way. I was proud; I felt like a grown-up. The next afternoon I looped the basket over my arm and went down the pavement toward the store. When I reached the corner, a gang of boys grabbed me, knocked me down, snatched the basket, took the money, and sent me running home in panic. That evening I told my mother what had happened, but she made no comment; she sat down at once, wrote another note, gave me more money, and sent me out to the grocery again. I crept down the steps and saw the same gang of boys playing down the street. I ran back into the house.

"What's the matter?" my mother asked.

"It's those same boys," I said. "They'll beat me."

"You've got to get over that," she said. "Now, go on."

"I'm scared," I said.

"Go on and don't pay any attention to them," she said.

I went out of the door and walked briskly down the sidewalk, praying that the gang would not molest me. But when I came abreast of them, someone shouted

"There he is!"

They came toward me and I broke into a wild run toward home. They overtook me and flung me to the pavement. I yelled, pleaded, kicked, but they wrenched the money out of my hand. They yanked me to my feet, gave me a few slaps, and sent me home sobbing. My mother met me at the door.

"They b-beat m-me," I gasped. "They t-t-took the m-money."

I started up the steps, seeking the shelter of the house.

"Don't you come in here," my mother warned me.

I froze in my tracks and stared at her.

"But they're coming after me," I said.

"You just stay right where you are," she said in a deadly tone. "I'm going to teach you this night to stand up and fight for yourself."

She went into the house and I waited, terrified, wondering what she was about. Presently she returned with more money and another note; she also had a long, heavy stick.

"Take this money, this note, and this stick," she said. "Go to the store and buy those groceries. If those boys bother you, then fight."

I was baffled. My mother was telling me to fight, a thing that she had never done before.

"But I'm scared," I said.

"Don't you come into this house until you've gotten those groceries," she said.

"They'll beat me; they'll beat me," I said.

"Then stay in the streets; don't come back here!"

I ran up the steps and tried to force my way past her into the house. A stinging slap came on my jaw. I stood on the sidewalk, crying.

"Please, let me wait until tomorrow," I begged.

"No," she said. "Go now! If you come back into this house without those groceries, I'll whip you!"

She slammed the door and I heard the key turn in the lock. I shook with fright. I was alone upon the dark, hostile streets and gangs were after me. I had the choice of being beaten at home or away from home. I clutched the stick, crying, trying to reason. If I were beaten at home, there was absolutely nothing that I could do about it; but if I were beaten in the streets, I had a chance to fight and defend myself. I walked slowly down the sidewalk, coming closer to the gang of boys, holding the stick tightly. I was so full of fear that I could scarcely breathe. I was almost upon them now.

"There he is again!" the cry went up.

They surrounded me quickly and began to grab for my hand.

"I'll kill you!" I threatened.

They closed in. In blind fear I let the stick fly, feeling it crack against a boy's skull. I swung again, lamming[2] another skull, then another. Realizing that they would retaliate if I let up for but a second, I fought to lay them low, to knock them cold, to kill them so that they could not strike back at me. I flayed with tears in my eyes, teeth clenched, stark fear making me throw every ounce of my strength behind each blow. I hit again and again, dropping the money and the grocery list. The boys scattered, yelling, nursing their heads, staring at me in utter disbelief. They had never seen such frenzy. I stood panting, egging them on, taunting them to come on and fight. When they refused, I ran after them and they tore out for their homes, screaming. The parents of the boys rushed into the streets and threatened me, and for the first time in my life I shouted at grown-ups, telling them that I would give them the same if they bothered me. I finally found my grocery list and the money and went to the store. On my way back I kept my stick poised for instant use, but there was not a single boy in sight. That night I won the right to the streets of Memphis.

2. **lamming:** old slang word meaning "beating" or "hitting."

"Only Through Books..."

Richard Wright
(1908–1960) began his life in
poverty. His father, a sharecropper on a Mississippi farm,
abandoned his family when
Wright was five; when the boy
was twelve, his mother could
no longer support her
children. Raised by various relatives, Wright
early learned the bitter lessons of survival on
ghetto streets. He remembered trying alcohol
at the age of six, working in a shabby hotel
while still a child, living with "the sustained
expectation of violence." By borrowing a
library card, he was finally able to gain access

to books. Later, he wrote:

66 . . . it had been only
through books . . . that I had
managed to keep myself
alive. **99**

Black Boy secured Wright's
fame and became a best-seller,
but in the fifteen years following its publication, Wright,
then living abroad, never
wrote another book that
equaled its success. Wright kept trying to
understand the historical and cultural place of
black people in the modern world. He visited
Africa and recorded his observations. But
unfortunately, he felt as alien in Africa as he did
in America. Richard Wright died in Paris, where
he had found as much of a home as he could.

FINDING COMMON GROUND

- Now that you've read the story, meet in a small group and share the
  questions and comments you recorded in your Reader's Logs.

  1. Select a person to speak for your group.

  2. Each of you read aloud your notes (or pass the notes around the
     table so that everyone can read all of the comments).

  3. Identify four or five questions or issues or comments that seem
     most interesting or most widely shared within your group.

  4. Discuss those items, giving a suitable amount of time for each
     (5–10 minutes?).

  5. Reconvene as a full class and share the results of your discussion.

In the Dark

There I was, standing in the dark. No one was there but me and the night. All I could do was stand there and not move. If I moved, I would fall into the black pit. I was scared and cold. I tried to scream, but all you could hear was my echo. I was trying to feel my way without moving, but I couldn't feel anything. I felt something on my shoulder, and it was a hand. I was trying to get away, but it wouldn't let me go. Then the hand pushed me into the black pit. I screamed as loud as I could, but no one heard me. I tried to stop myself from falling, but I kept on falling. Then a hand from under me stopped me from falling; the hand that stopped me was my mother's.

—Leeann Watkins
The Waterways Project
New York, New York

The Lighthouse by Brady Dunklee (U.S.A.). From Yale-New Haven Hospital's collection of international children's art called "Tales of Courage."

READ ON

Just a Little Guy

In J.R.R. Tolkien's fantasy *The Hobbit* (Houghton Mifflin), Bilbo Baggins is just a little guy—a hobbit—who is minding his own business. Then one day, the wizard Gandalf and a gang of thirteen dwarfs arrive at his door and carry him off. So begins Bilbo's great adventure, an adventure with some big challenges for a little guy: bee pastures, giant spiders, icy waterfalls, and the dreaded dragon Smaug.

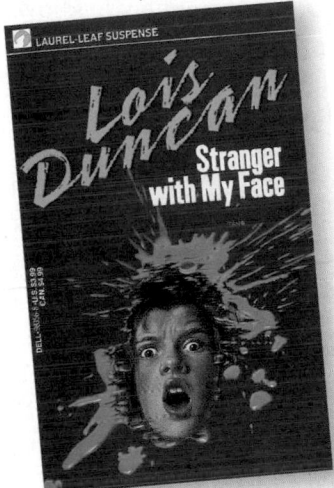

A Suspense Novel

What if you kept feeling that someone was watching you, and your friends blamed you for things you were sure you never did? This happens to a teenage girl in Lois Duncan's *Stranger with My Face* (Dell). The surprise ending of this sinister novel is in the tradition of great writers of suspense like Poe.

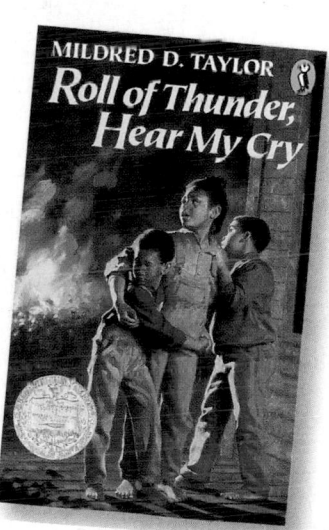

Nobody Said Life Was Fair

You'll get an up-close look at prejudice in Mildred D. Taylor's *Roll of Thunder, Hear My Cry* (Puffin). Too close for comfort—for in this novel, Cassie Logan and her family must fight to hold on to their land and their pride. Emotional and eloquent, Taylor's novel was awarded the Newbery Medal.

NARRATIVE WRITING

TRUE NARRATIVE

In stories, as in real life, first one thing happens, then another, then another. Writing that tells about a series of related events that take place over a period of time is called narrative writing. In this workshop you'll write a narrative about an incident that really happened.

Narration is a very old use of language and is still one of the most popular. You'll use the techniques of narration here to tell a true story about something that happened to you or someone you know. But you can also use narration in directions for fixing or assembling a machine, in scientific reports, in news stories, in historical writing. You can use narration in short stories and novels, in poems, in speeches, and in biographies and autobiographies.

Prewriting

1. A Head Start: Checking Your Notebook

As you were reading the selections in this collection, you should have been gathering material for a narrative. Review your Writer's Notebook entries: You should have a list of possible conflicts, a list of main events, some ideas for dialogue, and some notes on setting. Remember that the story you choose to write about should be an experience you're willing to share with your audience.

2. More Details, Please

Once you've chosen a topic that interests you, see if you have enough to write about.

- Focus on your topic and **brainstorm** for five minutes, listing every detail that whizzes through your brain. Don't stop to think about whether your ideas are dumb or brilliant—just keep on writing.

- Or you can collect more details by **freewriting** on the computer or on paper or by making a **cluster diagram** developing your ideas.

- If friends or relatives shared your experience, **interview** them. Ask what specific details they can recall about events, people, and setting.

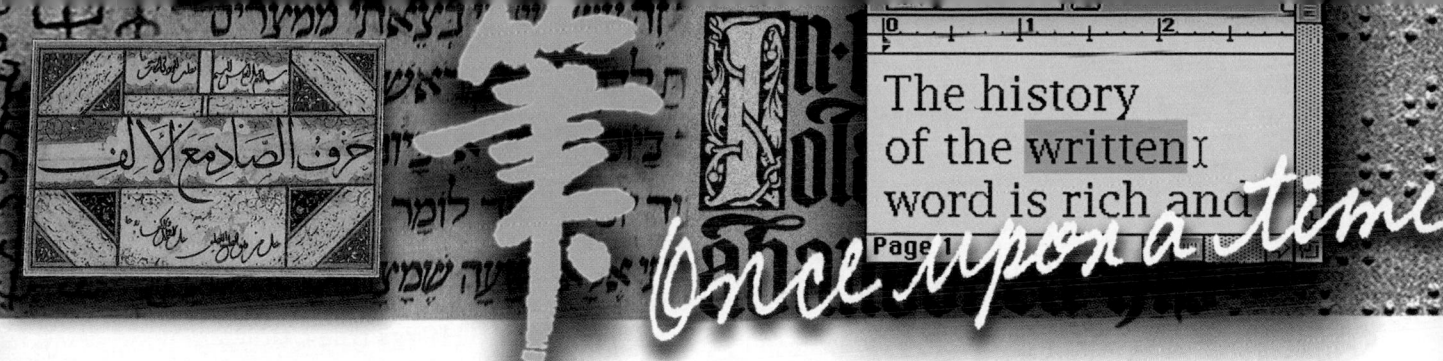
The history
of the written
word is rich and
Page 1

Once upon a time

3. Getting Organized

Richard Wright tells about his experience (page 105) in **chronological order,** the order in which the events occurred. Most narratives follow this first-things-first order. But "Marigolds" (page 91) uses a **flashback.** It begins in the present but then it flashes back to tell about something that happened in an earlier time. The student narrative on the next page opens in the middle of the action and flashes back to explain how the narrator came to be under a car.

A **story map** like the one opposite will help you identify the key events of your narrative. You might circle or highlight events you'll want to elaborate on.

Drafting

1. Show, Don't Tell

The first rule of storytelling is "Show, don't tell." Include many specific details to help readers visualize actions and setting; instead of just naming a feeling, *show* it.

EXAMPLES

I was afraid and ran out of the office. (**Telling**)

"I burst past her through the half-open door, down the hallway and out into the lobby. A scream exploded from my lungs, a scream of terror and panic. Faces, confused and frightened, snapped up from their magazines. I looked down and realized that I was still only wearing my briefs and ran faster—I was nearly flying now." (**Showing**)

—Drake Bennett, "Coward"

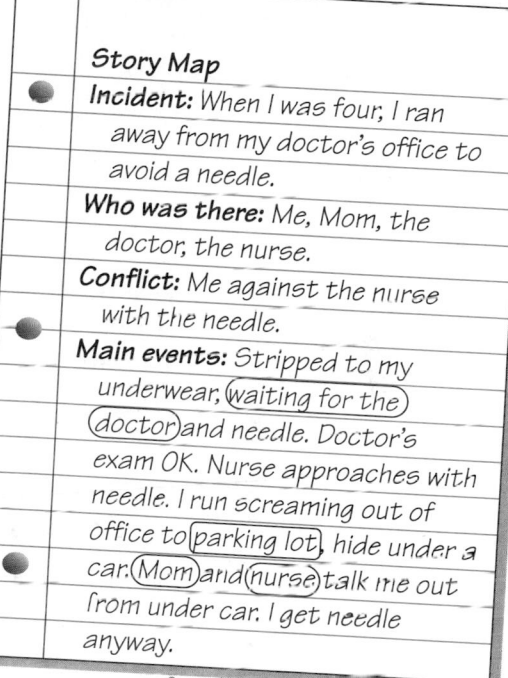

Story Map

Incident: When I was four, I ran away from my doctor's office to avoid a needle.

Who was there: Me, Mom, the doctor, the nurse.

Conflict: Me against the nurse with the needle.

Main events: Stripped to my underwear, waiting for the doctor and needle. Doctor's exam OK. Nurse approaches with needle. I run screaming out of office to parking lot, hide under a car. Mom and nurse talk me out from under car. I get needle anyway.

Language Link
H E L P

Powerful verbs: page 31. Active/passive verbs: page 45. Figures of speech: page 103.

It was a dark and stormy night.

Suddenly, out of the mist a spooky figure appeared.

How spooky was he?

Spooooooooky!

PEANUTS reprinted by permission of UFS, Inc.

2. What People Say

Dialogue lets the reader eavesdrop on actual conversations, which are always more interesting than a summary of what people said. Sometimes dialogue plays an essential part in the story. In "Poison" (page 77), for instance, the muffled, clipped dialogue helps us share Harry's terror. Later, dialogue is used to shock us as it gives us a glimpse into Harry's true character.

3. A Good Beginning Is Half the Battle

If your opening sentences work well, they'll make readers want to know "What's coming next?" Look at the Box of Beginnings on page 115. What do these openings tell you immediately? What can you predict about what might happen next? What questions do these openers put in your mind?

Language Handbook HELP

See Quotation Marks, page 1026.

from COWARD

"Drake, you're making this difficult. You know you're going to have to come out sometime, so you might as well get it over with." Mom's voice had grown impatient. The hard asphalt scraped against my bare body as I turned on my stomach to face her. My nose, pressed against the parking-lot ground, was filled with the dead stench of aging, worn tires and the fumes of burnt gas and dripping oil. I raised my head, hitting it hard on the metal of the muffler above me. A sharp burst of screaming pain shot through my skull. I peered out from under the car at the two sets of feet that imprisoned me. One I recognized immediately: the creased, black leather heels Mom wore to work every day. The white Reebok walking shoes beside them I assumed belonged to the nurse. Mom was wrong. There was no way I was coming out from under that car. It was all that protected me from the pain and terror I had so recently escaped.

The wind picked up, blowing in gusts, skittering freshly fallen leaves across the pavement. A million tiny goose bumps rose all over my body and I shivered. I was cold.

Cold. The bed in the examining room had been cold. The nurse had come into the room and told me to strip down to my underwear and sit on the bed. The

Interesting title.

Opens with dialogue. Makes reader wonder where Drake is.

Shows, doesn't just tell, what his hiding place is like.

Good specific details in this paragraph.

Hooks our interest: Why is he under a car? Why is he in pain and terror?

Makes the setting match his feelings.
Flashes back to an earlier time in the day.

Strategies for Writing a Good Beginning

1. Start with a bit of dialogue, as the Student Model does.

2. Start with an attention-grabber—a statement that will catch your readers' interest, as Richard Wright does on page 105.

3. Start with an especially forceful word.

4. Start with a short, punchy sentence.

A Box of Beginnings

"By seventh grade I knew better than to spit while girls were around."
—Gary Soto, "The Nile"

"One winter morning in the long-ago, four-year-old days of my life I found myself standing before a fireplace, warming my hands over a mound of glowing coals, listening to the wind whistle past the house outside."
—Richard Wright, *Black Boy*

---

bed had been soft but rubbery, and cold, cold like the blubbery, dead flesh of some huge whale. The paper covering stuck to the backs of my naked thighs, and I rumpled and creased it each time I shifted my weight.

I was only four now, but I could remember coming to Dr. Castor's office twice before, and I knew what to expect. In a few minutes Dr. Castor himself would come in and do all the "checkup" sorts of things: the poking and probing and tapping and weighing and feeling sorts of things. After he finished, he would talk to my mom for a while and then leave. I would wait for a few more minutes.

Then came the part I dreaded, the part that made my checkups with Dr. Castor hellish. The nurse would walk into the room carrying a bottle of alcohol and a cotton swab and a little plastic bag. I would bare my trembling arm and she would wet the swab with alcohol. Noticing my clammy palms and tensed face, she would ask if I was scared. I would shake my head quickly; she would smile, a wide, well-rehearsed smile.

"This will only hurt for a second. . . ."

—Drake Bennett
Phillips Exeter Academy
Exeter, New Hampshire

Uses vivid figure of speech that creates a sense of disgust.
Flashback again to explain situation.

Good sensory details.

Here is the conflict. This is what the narrative is going to be about.

First appeared in *Merlyn's Pen: The National Magazines of Student Writing.*

Language Link
H E L P

Powerful verbs: page 31.
Active and passive verbs:
page 45.
Verb tenses: page 75.
Subject-verb agreement:
page 89.

■ *Evaluation Criteria*

A good narrative

1. *has a beginning that captures the reader's interest*

2. *tells a series of related events*

3. *uses description to show the characters and setting*

4. *uses dialogue*

Evaluating and Revising

1. Peer Editing

Get together with three or four classmates to read and comment on one another's drafts. Ask yourself:

• What do I like best about this narrative?

• What would make this narrative more interesting? (Does it have a good beginning and a satisfying ending? Has the writer *shown* me vividly the characters and their setting?)

You might use a colored marker to highlight sentences or passages you think are especially vivid or original. In the margin, write comments and questions that you think will help the writer improve the narrative.

2. Self-Evaluation

You don't have to do everything your readers suggest. The story is yours, after all. Remember to consider your readers' comments carefully as you read through your narrative again. Make changes that you feel will strengthen and improve it.

Proofreading

When you're satisfied your narrative is as good as you can make it, you're still not done. Read it again carefully for mistakes in grammar, usage, spelling, and mechanics. If you're writing on a computer, using the spelling and grammar checkers will help. (But they won't tell you if you've misused a word, such as *threw* instead of *through*.)

Publishing

Find a way to get your narrative to the audience you wrote it for. You might tape-record a reading or help compile a collection of narratives to take home or share with other classes.

Reflecting

If you decide to include this paper in your portfolio, be sure to date it. Then write a brief reflection on your experience, focusing on these questions:

1. What was the most difficult part of writing this narrative?

2. What do I like best about my narrative?

3. What do I want to learn to do better?

4. Why did I include this narrative in my portfolio?

Revision Model

Peer Comments

The asphalt scraped against me as I
hard   *my bare body*

Can you use descriptive words?

turned on my stomach to face her.

My nose, pressed against the

parking-lot ground, was filled with

the dead stench of tires and the
aging, worn

This is great!

fumes of gas and oil. I raised my
burnt   *dripping*

Add more sensory details like these.

head, hitting it hard on the metal of

the muffler above me. Pain shot
A sharp burst of screaming

Another good spot for sensory details.

through my skull. I looked out from
peered

Replace both of these with more vivid verbs.

under the car at the two sets of feet

that held me.
imprisoned

Sentence Workshop
H E L P

Learning from the pros: page 118.

What I've Learned

The toughest part of writing for me is finding words that are just right for what I want to say. The thesaurus on the computer was a big help. I did a lot of planning before I started writing, so the drafting part was pretty easy. I'd never tried a flashback before—I enjoyed the experiment. I think peer revision is great. I've learned a lot about respect for others' writing, and I'm getting better at taking criticism. I've included this narrative because it's about an incident I think is pretty funny—now.

Sentence Workshop

Language Handbook HELP

See Sentence Structure, page 1010.

Technology HELP

See Language Workshop CD-ROM. *Key word entry: sentence structure.*

SENTENCE MODELING: LEARNING FROM THE PROS

To improve your tennis or basketball game, you can watch a tournament or a how-to video made by a pro. You can improve your "writing game" the same way: by analyzing how professional writers put sentences together and by imitating what they do.

In this lesson, you will look at some professionals' sentences and then, for practice, you'll build your own sentences imitating the pros.

In these model sentences, the basic sentence (subject/verb/complement, if there is one) is underlined, and additional "chunks" of meaning (phrases and clauses) are separated by slash marks.

1. "It was a secret place / for us / where nobody else could go / without our permission."

    —Borden Deal, "Antaeus"

2. "Before us / the valley stretched away / into miles / of rocky desolation."

    —James Ramsey Ullman, "Top Man"

3. "In her attic bedroom / Meg regarded Ananda, / who thumped her massive tail / in a friendly manner."

    —Madeleine L'Engle, *A Swiftly Tilting Planet*

Here are some imitations of these professional sentences. The basic sentence in each (subject/verb/complement, if there is one) is underscored.

1. It was a large room, / just for them, / where children could hide / with their books.

2. Before me / the path twisted around / into a maze / of frightening darkness.

3. In the grass, / the snail eyed the cat, / who bared her yellow teeth / in a hungry manner.

Writer's Workshop Follow-up: Revision

Take another look at the narrative you have written for the Writer's Workshop (page 112). Are your sentences interesting? Can you expand any of your basic sentences with phrases and clauses that will add more specific detail to your story?

Try It Out

For each sample below, write your own sentence with the same sentence parts in the same order. Your sentences can be about anything. Exchange your finished sentences with a partner. Underline the basic sentence in your partner's original sentence and add slash marks to separate chunks of meaning. Did you notice any problems?

1. "I remember being startled when I first saw my grandmother rocking away on her porch."

    —Lorraine Hansberry,
    To Be Young, Gifted and Black

2. "When he came back into the room, I was sitting in another machine."

    —Ernest Hemingway,
    "In Another Country"

3. "She listened to the leaves rustling outside the window."

    —Katherine Anne Porter,
    "The Jilting of Granny Weatherall"

Most people are neither villains nor heroes. They aren't vicious enough for the one, and life doesn't give them the opportunity for the other, so their lives aren't as full of excitement as the last good movie you saw. Still, they get through each day. They work; they endure; they perform little acts of kindness and generosity. They help one another and console one another. They may even find themselves surprisingly brave. And they do it without glory or excitement, without applause or notice, until someone stops to pay attention. Their stories, when they are recorded, reveal much that the human spirit is capable of. They also tell us a great deal about who we are and who we may become.

*From what we get,
we can make a living;
what we give,
however, makes a life.*

—Arthur Ashe

Writer's Notebook

You may not realize it, but the people right around you are interesting. In your notebook, jot down quickly the names of some people you know—teachers, relatives, friends, neighbors, a person you see in a store every day. Write as many names as you can think of. Then select a few names to start freewriting about. First, stare at each name for a minute or two, thinking about what that person's spirit is like—how does the person cope with joy and sadness, trouble and success? Then freewrite; try to sketch out one of the people. Save your notes. You might use them later for the assignment in the Writer's Workshop on page 194.

Reading Focus

Way to Go

There's a saying that when the going gets tough, the tough get going. In very tough circumstances, some people do indeed get going. They have a spirit that moves them ahead—that pushes them to do heroic things. What makes these people so tough, so strong in spirit? Why do these people turn out to be good? Why do others go so wrong?

Quickwrite

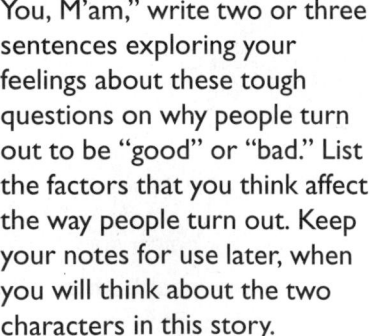

Before you read "Thank You, M'am," write two or three sentences exploring your feelings about these tough questions on why people turn out to be "good" or "bad." List the factors that you think affect the way people turn out. Keep your notes for use later, when you will think about the two characters in this story.

Elements of Literature

Characters Under Stress

People in life and in fiction tend to reveal themselves most dramatically when they are under stress—when they are placed in some situation that presents a problem they must do something about. In this story two characters have a tense encounter. The writer lets their actions and their words (or their silences) tell us about the kind of people they are or could be.

> **C**haracters under stress often reveal themselves and their values by what they say and how they act.
>
> *For more on Character, see pages 130–131 and the Handbook of Literary Terms.*

Thank You, M'am

Langston Hughes

She was a large woman with a large purse that had everything in it but hammer and nails. It had a long strap and she carried it slung across her shoulder. It was about eleven o'clock at night, and she was walking alone, when a boy ran up behind her and tried to snatch her purse. The strap broke with the single tug the boy gave it from behind. But the boy's weight and the

> *"Well, you didn't have to snatch my pocketbook to get some suede shoes."*

Mom Alice (1944) by William H. Johnson.

weight of the purse combined caused him to lose his balance so, instead of taking off full blast as he had hoped, the boy fell on his back on the sidewalk and his legs flew up. The large woman simply turned around and kicked him right square in his blue-jeaned sitter. Then she reached down, picked the boy up by his shirt front, and shook him until his teeth rattled.

After that the woman said, "Pick up my pocketbook, boy, and give it here."

She still held him. But she bent down enough to permit him to stoop and pick up her purse. Then she said, "Now ain't you ashamed of yourself?"

Firmly gripped by his shirt front, the boy said, "Yes'm."

The woman said, "What did you want to do it for?"

The boy said, "I didn't aim to."

She said, "You a lie!"

By that time two or three people passed, stopped, turned to look, and some stood watching.

"If I turn you loose, will you run?" asked the woman.

"Yes'm," said the boy.

"Then I won't turn you loose," said the woman. She did not release him.

"I'm very sorry, lady, I'm sorry," whispered the boy.

"Um-hum! And your face is dirty. I got a great mind to wash your face for you. Ain't you got nobody home to tell you to wash your face?"

"No'm," said the boy.

"Then it will get washed this evening," said the large woman starting up the street, dragging the frightened boy behind her.

He looked as if he were fourteen or fifteen, frail and willow-wild, in tennis shoes and blue jeans.

The woman said, "You ought to be my son. I would teach you right from wrong. Least I can do right now is to wash your face. Are you hungry?"

"No'm," said the being-dragged boy. "I just want you to turn me loose."

"Was I bothering *you* when I turned that corner?" asked the woman.

"No'm."

"But you put yourself in contact with *me*," said the woman. "If you think that that contact is not going to last awhile, you got another thought coming. When I get through with you, sir, you are going to remember Mrs. Luella Bates Washington Jones."

Sweat popped out on the boy's face and he began to struggle. Mrs. Jones stopped, jerked him around in front of her, put a half nelson about his neck, and continued to drag him up the street. When she got to her door, she dragged the boy inside, down a hall, and into a large kitchenette-furnished room at the rear of the house. She switched on the light and left the door open. The boy could hear other roomers laughing and talking in the large house. Some of their doors were open, too, so he knew he and the woman were not alone. The woman still had him by the neck in the middle of her room.

She said, "What is your name?"

"Roger," answered the boy.

"Then, Roger, you go to that sink and wash your face," said the woman, whereupon she turned him loose—at last. Roger looked at the door—looked at the woman—looked at the door—*and went to the sink*.

"Let the water run until it gets warm," she said. "Here's a clean towel."

"You gonna take me to jail?" asked the boy, bending over the sink.

"Not with that face, I would not take you nowhere," said the woman. "Here I am trying to get home to cook me a bite to eat and you snatch my pocketbook! Maybe you ain't been to your supper either, late as it be. Have you?"

"There's nobody home at my house," said the boy.

"Then we'll eat," said the woman. "I believe you're hungry—or been hungry—to try to snatch my pocketbook."

"I wanted a pair of blue suede shoes," said the boy.

"Well, you didn't have to snatch *my* pocketbook to get some suede shoes," said Mrs. Luella Bates Washington Jones. "You could of asked me."

"M'am?"

Digestive System (1989) by James Romberger. Pastel on paper (57″ x 60″).

The water dripping from his face, the boy looked at her. There was a long pause. A very long pause. After he had dried his face and, not knowing what else to do, dried it again, the boy turned around, wondering what next. The door was open. He could make a dash for it down the hall. He could run, run, run, run, *run*!

The woman was sitting on the daybed. After a while she said, "I were young once and I wanted things I could not get."

There was another long pause. The boy's mouth opened. Then he frowned, but not knowing he frowned.

The woman said, "Um-hum! You thought I was going to say *but,* didn't you? You thought I was going to say, *but I didn't snatch people's pocketbooks.* Well, I wasn't going to say that." Pause. Silence. "I have done things, too, which I would not tell you, son—neither tell God, if He didn't already know. So you set down while I fix us something to eat. You might run that comb through your hair so you will look presentable."

In another corner of the room behind a screen was a gas plate and an icebox. Mrs. Jones got up and went behind the screen. The woman did not watch the boy to see if he was going to run now, nor did she watch her purse which she left behind her on the daybed. But the boy took care to sit on the far side of the room where he thought she could easily see him out of the corner of her eye, if she wanted to. He did not trust the woman *not* to trust him. And he did not want to be mistrusted now.

"Do you need somebody to go the store," asked the boy, "maybe to get some milk or something?"

"Don't believe I do," said the woman, "unless you just want sweet milk yourself. I was going to make cocoa out of this canned milk I got here."

"That will be fine," said the boy.

She heated some lima beans and ham she had in the icebox, made the cocoa, and set the table. The woman did not ask the boy anything about where he lived, or his folks, or anything else that would embarrass him. Instead, as they ate, she told him about her job in a hotel beauty shop that stayed open late, what the work was like, and how all kinds of women came in and out, blondes, redheads, and Spanish. Then she cut him a half of her ten-cent cake.

"Eat some more, son," she said.

When they were finished eating she got up and said, "Now, here, take this ten dollars and buy yourself some blue suede shoes. And next time, do not make the mistake of latching onto *my* pocketbook *nor nobody else's*—because shoes come by devilish like that will burn your feet. I got to get my rest now. But I wish you would behave yourself, son, from here on in."

She led him down the hall to the front door and opened it. "Good night! Behave yourself, boy!" she said, looking out into the street.

The boy wanted to say something else other than "Thank you, m'am" to Mrs. Luella Bates Washington Jones, but he couldn't do so as he turned at the barren stoop and looked back at the large woman in the door. He barely managed to say "Thank you," before she shut the door. And he never saw her again.

Mom Sammy (1938) by Henry Bozeman Jones.

The Howard University Gallery of Art, Washington, D.C.

MEET THE WRITER

A Lonely Child

Langston Hughes (1902–1967) was a lonely child who moved often and felt distant from his parents, who eventually divorced. Hughes was born in Joplin, Missouri, graduated from high school in Cleveland, Ohio, and eventually graduated from Lincoln University in Pennsylvania. Early in his adult life Hughes took on a variety of jobs. The man who was later known as one of the great original voices in American literature was at various times a cook, sailor, beachcomber, launderer, doorman, and busboy. Hughes traveled to many parts of the world, but he is chiefly associated with Harlem in New York City. His most creative work was done at his typewriter near a third-floor rear apartment window overlooking a Harlem back yard. We can easily imagine this setting as his inspiration for "Thank You, M'am."

More About Hughes

Hughes has been fortunate in his biographer. Arnold Rampersad, a professor of English at Princeton University, has published the first volume of a very readable biography of Hughes, called *I, Too, Sing America* (Oxford University Press).

A Volunteer Of Love

DENISE CRITTENDON

An old woman is relaxing in a rocking chair, softly humming a lullaby and holding an infant close to her chest. She stares at the baby, gazing into wide eyes, gently stroking wispy strands of hair. She sings to her; whispers to her.

"I see you fighting sleep. Yes I can," the woman says, her sing-songy voice barely above a murmur.

For Fanniedell Peeples, this is a cherished moment. She is one of several Detroit hospital volunteers who take turns caressing the infants who rarely have visitors. Many are crack-cocaine or HIV positive babies. Others are wards of the court, or abandoned children with a host of medical problems. Some have loving family members, some don't. But, says Peeples, "they are human beings and they need human contact."

Peeples won't let them be alone, so sick and so helpless. They won't die alone either. She goes to great lengths to ensure that she is beside her "friends" when they take their final breath. "They feel the love and care and touch you give them because they are sponges of feeling," she explains. "So I stroke and I care and I sing and I rock as they're on their way out. I think that's the least we can do since they have missed so many things. We owe them the dignity to leave as human beings."

—from *The Crisis*

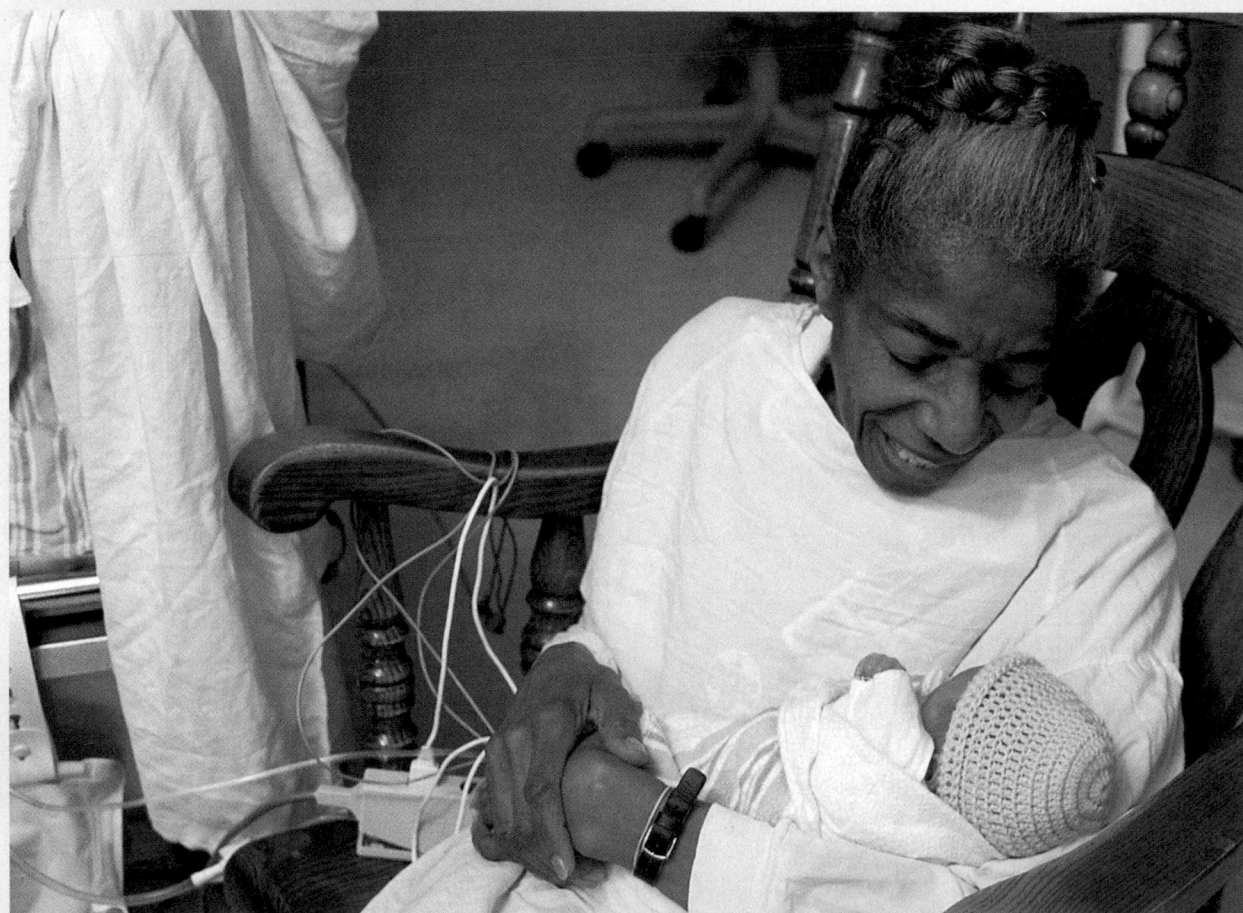

A cherished moment: Fanniedell Peeples with an infant.

MAKING MEANINGS

First Thoughts

1. Which image, or picture, in Hughes's story stands out most clearly in your mind?

Shaping Interpretations

2. The writer never tells us directly what kind of people Roger and Mrs. Jones are. What do the **words** (or dialogue) and **actions** of these two characters reveal about their true natures? Draw and fill in a chart like this one to collect your ideas.

Reviewing the Text

Write down the main events of this story as if you were reporting them for a newspaper. Answer the questions reporters are told to answer in their news articles: What happened? Whom did it happen to? When and where did it happen? Why did it happen?

Then compare your lists of events in class. Did you all remember the same details?

	Dialogue	Actions	What They Reveal
Mrs. Jones			
Roger			

3. Do you think Roger has stolen before? Go back to the story to see if the writer suggests why Roger has gone wrong. Write down the lines that hint at any possible explanations.

4. Why do you think Mrs. Jones tells Roger that she too has done things she is not proud of?

5. What are some of the things the boy might have wanted to say, other than "Thank you, m'am"?

6. How does Mrs. Jones's **setting**—her furnished room, the screen with a gas plate and icebox behind it, the ten-cent cake, the noisy tenement—contribute to your sense of the kind of person she is? What can your imagination add to her surroundings?

Extending the Text

7. Some stories leave us with the feeling that there is more to tell. What past can you create for Mrs. Jones? What do you imagine her future holds?

8. Think back to your Quickwrite and your ideas about what makes some people turn out to be so good while others go wrong. What do you think made the fictional Mrs. Jones and the real-life Fanniedell Peeples (page 126) so good?

Challenging the Text

9. Is the story credible to you—that is, based on your experience, can you believe that these events could happen as Hughes describes them? Why, or why not?

CHOICES: Building Your Portfolio

Writer's Notebook

1. Collecting Ideas for an Observational Essay

Focus on looks and actions.

"She was a large woman with a large purse that had everything in it but hammer and nails." With this description of her appearance, Langston Hughes introduces us to Mrs. Luella Bates Washington Jones—a character who later picks up a boy who's tried to rob her, shakes him till his teeth rattle, and then feeds him cocoa and half of her ten-cent cake. All of these details help us to understand Mrs. Jones—to feel we've met a real person. If you made a list of interesting people before you started this collection of stories (page 119), refer to your notes now. Focus on one person from the list who interests you, or think of a new person. Close your eyes and try to see the person. Then jot down what you see. Describe the person's appearance and behavior—how does she move, what is he wearing, what does her voice sound like, what expression do you see in his eyes? Can you think of something unusual or special the person has done—in other words, why are you interested in this person? Keep your notes. You might be able to use them when you do the assignment in the Writer's Workshop on page 194.

Creative Writing

2. A Letter from Roger

What do you think Roger will be like ten years after his encounter with Mrs. Jones? What might he write in a letter to her? Since Roger is fourteen or fifteen in the story, think of him as a young man of twenty-four or twenty-five. Compose a letter from Roger. Write as *I.* You will have to write Roger's present address inside this letter. Be sure you state the purpose of his communication after all these years.

Role-Playing

3. Interviewing a Character

Imagine you are the host of a TV talk show and can have either Roger or Mrs. Jones on an upcoming show. Choose your guest and prepare a list of questions. You know the story of your guest's late-night adventure, but what else do you want to know? Write specific questions that will encourage your guest to talk freely. Take turns with a classmate role-playing the host and the guests.

Creative Writing

4. Found Poetry

Sometimes poetry is found embedded in prose paragraphs. Sometimes it's found in news articles, even in weather forecasts or recipes. Find the paragraph from "Thank You, M'am" that begins "In another corner of the room" and reformat it so that it looks like a poem. Break the sentences into lines that seem right to you. Use very short lines for dramatic effect. Change any words you wish to. It will be up to you to decide where to end your poem.

Possible Subjects

Greg—dark, short hair, bright eyes, tears around the block on his bike, friendly.

Emily—small, careful voice, shy with the neighbors.

Samantha—marches right up to anyone, short and stocky, firm on the ground, straight hair.

LANGUAGE LINK MINI-LESSON

Style: Modifiers Make Meanings More Definite

Language Handbook HELP

See Using Modifiers, page 1003.

Technology HELP

See Language Workshop CD-ROM. Key word entry: modifiers.

Modifiers make our writing more specific, more exact, or more definite. Notice how adjectives help us clearly visualize those blue suede shoes that Roger wants so much. Adjectives answer the questions *What kind? Which one? How many?* or *How much?* Adverbs answer the questions *Where? When? How often? In what way?* or *To what extent?* The modifiers in Hughes's sentences that follow are single words, compound words, and phrases.

1. "The <u>large</u> woman <u>simply</u> turned <u>around</u> and kicked him <u>right square</u> in his <u>blue-jeaned</u> sitter."

2. "He looked as if he were fourteen or fifteen, <u>frail</u> and <u>willow-wild</u>, <u>in tennis shoes and blue jeans</u>."

3. ". . . she dragged the boy <u>into a large kitchenette-furnished room in the rear of the house</u>."

Try It Out

➤ Rewrite each sentence at the left three times, replacing the underlined modifiers with words and phrases of your own. Each time, give Mrs. Jones or the boy or the setting a totally different appearance. (For example, you might put Roger in combat boots and a leather jacket.)

➤ As you revise your own description of a character, look carefully at your modifiers. Try to find very exact adverbs that will make your character's actions clearer. Search for the best adjectives to describe a detail of your character's appearance or setting. But don't overdo it with modifiers. Sometimes a simple word is best. Notice that Hughes describes Mrs. Jones's stoop—the stairs to her tenement—with one powerful adjective: The stoop was simply "barren."

VOCABULARY HOW TO OWN A WORD

Synonyms

Although a **synonym** is a word that has the same or almost the same meaning as another word, synonyms are not always interchangeable. Often synonyms will have subtle but distinct shades of difference in meaning. Here are three words from the first paragraph of the story: *large, carried,* and *fell.* Find the sentences the words are used in. Then make a map like the one here for each word. Could the synonyms work just as well in each sentence?

barren

DEFINITION empty, devoid of life	**SYNONYMS** bare, sterile
SUBSTITUTIONS He turned at the [bare, sterile] stoop.	**RESPONSE TO SUBSTITUTIONS** *Bare* could work because it can refer to a lack of objects. *Sterile* doesn't work because here it suggests cleanliness, not emptiness. *Barren* is best; it reminds me of something all worn out.

Elements of Literature

CHARACTER: Revealing Human Nature

Creating characters—telling what human beings are like—is the whole point of writing stories. A story is really only interesting to us as readers because of what it tells us about people and how it makes us feel about them.

A magazine editor once said that all you need to tell a story is a character, an adjective, and a series of choices that the character must make. Let's call our character Adam, give him the adjective *cheap,* have him invite Tina out for her birthday, and see what happens.

If we are told that he has fifty dollars yet walks Tina the sixteen blocks to the concert, pretending not to notice the approaching bus, we know our Adam. We are not surprised when Adam chooses cheap seats in the bleachers. Later, at the restaurant, we know he'll be looking anxiously at the right-hand side of the menu (where the prices are listed).

What we are curious about is how Tina will respond to this cheap character. Suppose that at the restaurant, Adam recommends, instead of the four-dollar hamburger, the ten-dollar steak? A surprise, a change in character! Love, that powerful tonic, has done what no amount of reasoning could do—and we recognize with satisfaction a truth, a revelation of how we and our fellow human beings behave.

Of course, people are much more complex than a single adjective can suggest, and that is the joy, and the difficulty, of storytelling. How does a writer build a character out of words, someone who will seem to become flesh and blood and rise off the page, a fully realized Scarlett O'Hara or Ebenezer Scrooge or Huck Finn?

> **A**ll you need to tell a story is a character, an adjective, and a series of choices that the character must make.

Creating Characters

1. The most obvious method of characterization is the character's **speech**. Think of how you can recognize your friends from what they say—not just from their tone of voice, but also from the kinds of words they use (big inflated words or little punchy ones; formal words or slangy ones). Think of how people reveal their values by using words that always allude to what things cost, rather than to how pleasurable or beautiful they are. Reading the characters' dialogue in a story is like listening in on a conversation.

2. Writers also use **appearance** to create character. We can tell so much simply from the way a writer describes how a person looks and sounds. Charles Dickens lets us see Scrooge at once:

   The cold within him froze his old features, nipped his pointed nose, shriveled his cheek, stiffened his gait; made his eyes red, his thin lips blue; and spoke out shrewdly in his grating voice. . . .

   Clearly, Dickens wants us to think of Scrooge as a character whose cold heart is reflected in his whole appearance.

   The kinds of clothes a character wears can give us

by John Leggett

hints too. As readers, we will respond one way to a character wearing a pin-striped suit and carrying a briefcase, and another way to a character wearing faded jeans and carrying a copy of *Of Mice and Men*.

3. In fiction a writer can even take us into the characters' minds to reveal their **private thoughts**. In this sense fiction has an advantage over real life. We might learn that one character detests his brother's drinking or that another one sympathizes with his father for his troubles at his job. We might learn how one character secretly feels when he sees the bully picking on the smallest kid in the schoolyard or how another feels as she watches her grandmother's coffin being lowered into the ground.

4. We can learn about characters by watching **how other characters in the story feel about them**. We might learn, for instance, that a salesman is a good guy in the eyes of his customers and a generous

tipper in the eyes of the local waiter; but he is impatient, cranky, and selfish in the eyes of his family. Dickens tells us how Scrooge affected other people:

Nobody ever stopped him in the street to say, with gladsome looks, "My dear Scrooge, how are you? When will you come to see me?" No beggars implored him to bestow a trifle, no children asked him what it was o'clock, no man or woman ever once in all his life inquired the way to such and such a place, of Scrooge. Even the blind men's dogs appeared to know him; and when they saw him coming on, would tug their owners into doorways. . . .

5. Most of all, we understand characters in fiction from their **actions,** from what we see them doing. How would you react to a girl of sixteen who, when you first meet her in a story, is dyeing her hair green? How would you react to another who, at five-thirty in the morning, is out delivering

newspapers? Scrooge, when we first meet him on Christmas Eve, is working on his accounts—an action that instantly reveals his obsession with money.

6. Some writers use **direct characterization** too. This means that a writer tells us directly what a character is like or what a person's motives are. In a famous listing of adjectives, Dickens tells us directly what kind of person Scrooge is:

Oh, but he was a tightfisted hand at the grindstone, Scrooge! a squeezing, wrenching, grasping, scraping, clutching, covetous old sinner!

Modern writers do not tell us much directly about their characters. They most often use the first five methods listed here, which are called **indirect characterization**. This means that a writer *shows* us a character but allows us to interpret for ourselves the kind of person we are meeting. In fiction, as in life itself, it is much more satisfying to discover for ourselves what characters are truly like.

BEFORE YOU READ
HARRISON BERGERON

Reading Focus

Free to Be . . .

Here are three big "what if's": What if people were so controlled by a powerful government that everyone was just like everyone else? What if all competition were removed from society? What if technology became so advanced that it was used to read thoughts?

Quickwrite

Take a few minutes to write down your thoughts about these "what if" questions. Jot down everything that comes to your mind. Later, you'll see if the story affects any of your responses.

Elements of Literature

Laughing at the Ridiculous

You read and hear satire all the time. **Satire** is the use of language or pictures to mock some weakness in individuals or in society or human nature. Satire is used on late-night talk shows, on TV sitcoms, in the comics, in movies. In fact, satire is so pervasive in modern life that it's hard to find a story or movie or TV show that doesn't use it. The methods of satire are mockery and exaggeration: When something is presented to us as ridiculous, its flaws comically exaggerated, we have to laugh. The satirists hope that this laughter is the first step in bringing about change. It's always important to recognize the exact target of the satire. In this story, the target is almost invisible. But as you'll see, that's part of the point of the satire.

> **S**atire is any kind of writing or speaking or art that ridicules or mocks some weakness in individuals or in society. The main weapon of the satirist is laughter.
>
> *For more on Satire, see the Handbook of Literary Terms.*

Fin de Siecle, II (1989) by Nam June Paik.
201 television sets with four laser discs (480″ x 168″ x 60″).

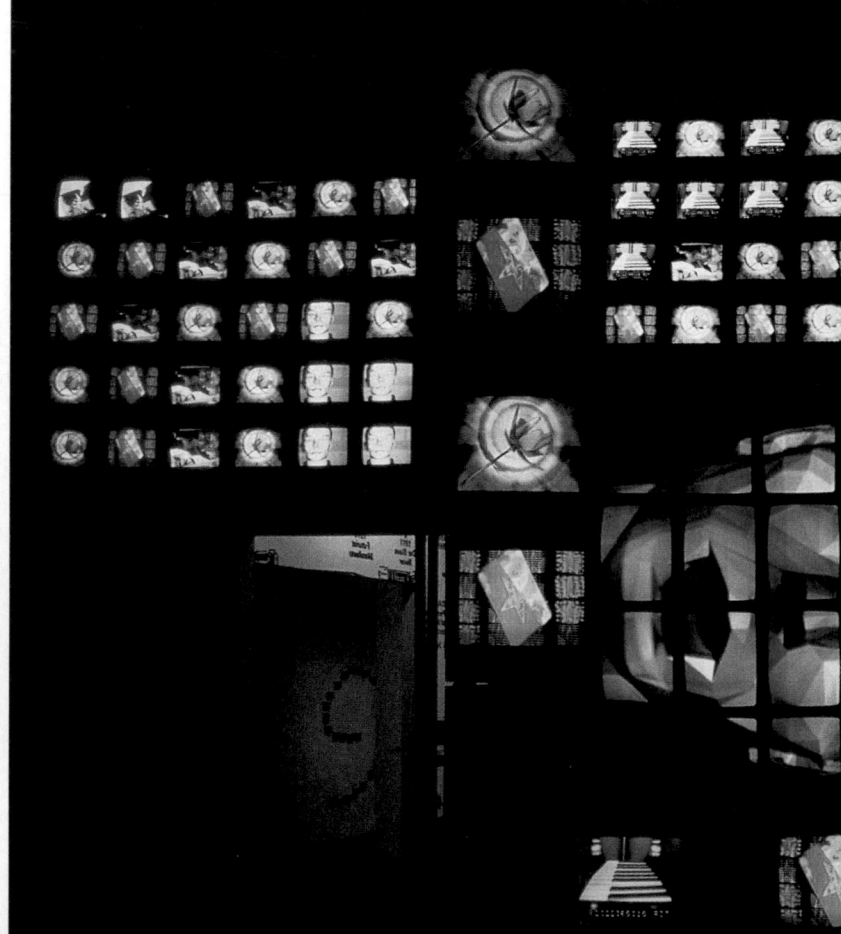

Gift of Laila and Thurston Twigg-Smith. Collection of Whitney Museum of American Art, New York. © 1995 Whitney Museum of American Art. 93.139.

Harrison Bergeron

Kurt Vonnegut

The year was 2081, and everybody was finally equal.

The year was 2081, and everybody was finally equal. They weren't only equal before God and the law. They were equal every which way. Nobody was smarter than anybody else. Nobody was better looking than anybody else. Nobody was stronger or quicker than anybody else. All this equality was due to the 211th, 212th, and 213th Amendments to the Constitution, and to the unceasing vigilance of agents of the United States Handicapper General.

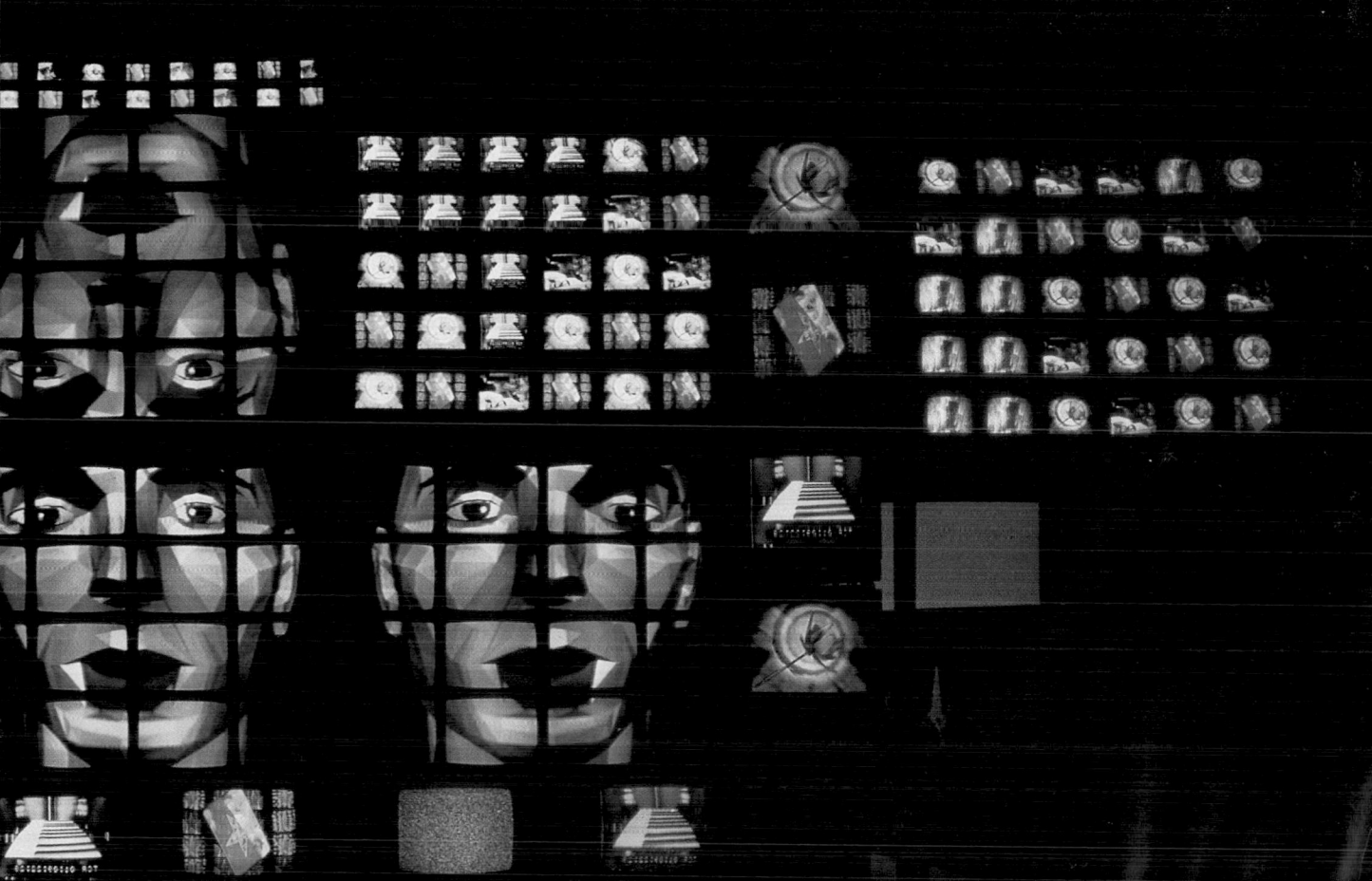

Some things about living still weren't quite right, though. April, for instance, still drove people crazy by not being springtime. And it was in that clammy month that the H-G men took George and Hazel Bergeron's fourteen-year-old son, Harrison, away.

It was tragic, all right, but George and Hazel couldn't think about it very hard. Hazel had a perfectly average intelligence, which meant she couldn't think about anything except in short bursts. And George, while his intelligence was way above normal, had a little mental handicap radio in his ear. He was required by law to wear it at all times. It was tuned to a government transmitter. Every twenty seconds or so, the transmitter would send out some sharp noise to keep people like George from taking unfair advantage of their brains.

George and Hazel were watching television. There were tears on Hazel's cheeks, but she'd forgotten for the moment what they were about.

On the television screen were ballerinas.

A buzzer sounded in George's head. His thoughts fled in panic, like bandits from a burglar alarm.

"That was a real pretty dance, that dance they just did," said Hazel.

"Huh?" said George.

"That dance—it was nice," said Hazel.

"Yup," said George. He tried to think a little about the ballerinas. They weren't really very good—no better than anybody else would have been, anyway. They were burdened with sash weights and bags of birdshot, and their faces were masked, so that no one, seeing a free and graceful gesture or a pretty face, would feel like

something the cat drug in. George was toying with the vague notion that maybe dancers shouldn't be handicapped. But he didn't get very far with it before another noise in his ear radio scattered his thoughts.

George winced. So did two out of the eight ballerinas.

Pachuco (1982) by Ed Paschke.

Hazel saw him wince. Having no mental handicap herself, she had to ask George what the latest sound had been.

"Sounded like somebody hitting a milk bottle with a ball-peen hammer,"[1] said George.

1. **ball-peen hammer:** hammer with a ball-shaped head.

"I'd think it would be real interesting, hearing all the different sounds," said Hazel, a little envious. "All the things they think up."

"Um," said George.

"Only, if I was Handicapper General, you know what I would do?" said Hazel. Hazel, as a matter of fact, bore a strong resemblance to the

Photo: William H. Bengston Courtesy of the Phyllis Kind Gallery, Chicago.

Handicapper General, a woman named Diana Moon Glampers. "If I was Diana Moon Glampers," said Hazel, "I'd have chimes on Sunday—just chimes. Kind of in honor of religion."

"I could think, if it was just chimes," said George.

"Well—maybe make 'em real loud," said Hazel. "I think I'd make a good Handicapper General."

"Good as anybody else," said George.

"Who knows better'n I do what normal is?" said Hazel.

"Right," said George. He began to think glimmeringly about his abnormal son who was now in jail, about Harrison, but a twenty-one-gun salute in his head stopped that.

"Boy!" said Hazel, "that was a doozy, wasn't it?"

It was such a doozy that George was white and trembling, and tears stood on the rims of his red eyes. Two of the eight ballerinas had collapsed to the studio floor and were holding their temples.

"All of a sudden you look so tired," said Hazel. "Why don't you stretch out on the sofa, so's you can rest your handicap bag on the pillows, honeybunch." She was referring to the forty-seven pounds of birdshot in a canvas bag which was padlocked around George's neck. "Go on and rest the bag for a little while," she said. "I don't care if you're not equal to me for a while."

George weighed the bag with his hands. "I don't mind it," he said. "I don't notice it anymore. It's just a part of me."

"You been so tired lately— kind of wore out," said Hazel. "If there was just some way we could make a little hole in the bottom of the bag, and just take out a few of them lead balls. Just a few."

"Two years in prison and two thousand dollars fine for every ball I took out," said George. "I don't call that a bargain."

"If you could just take a few out when you came home from work," said Hazel. "I mean—

you don't compete with anybody around here. You just set around."

"If I tried to get away with it," said George, "then other people'd get away with it—and pretty soon we'd be right back to the Dark Ages again, with everybody competing against everybody else. You wouldn't like that, would you?"

"I'd hate it," said Hazel.

"There you are," said George. "The minute people start cheating on laws, what do you think happens to society?"

If Hazel hadn't been able to come up with an answer to this question, George couldn't have supplied one. A siren was going off in his head.

"Reckon it'd fall all apart," said Hazel.

"What would?" said George blankly.

"Society," said Hazel uncertainly. "Wasn't that what you just said?"

"Who knows?" said George.

The television program was suddenly interrupted for a news bulletin. It wasn't clear at first as to what the bulletin was about, since the announcer, like all announcers, had a serious speech impediment. For about half a minute, and in a state of high excitement, the announcer tried to say, "Ladies and gentlemen——"

He finally gave up, handed the bulletin to a ballerina to read.

"That's all right——" Hazel said of the announcer, "he tried. That's the big thing. He tried to do the best he could with what God gave him. He should get a nice raise for trying so hard."

"Ladies and gentlemen——" said the ballerina, reading the bulletin. She must have been extraordinarily beautiful, because the mask she wore was hideous. And it was easy to see that she was the strongest and most graceful of all the dancers, for her handicap bags were as big as those worn by two-hundred-pound men.

And she had to apologize at once for her voice, which was a very unfair voice for a woman to use. Her voice was a warm, luminous, timeless melody. "Excuse me——" she said, and she began again, making her voice absolutely uncompetitive.

"Harrison Bergeron, age fourteen," she said in a grackle squawk,[2] "has just escaped from jail,

2. **grackle squawk:** loud, harsh cry, like that of a grackle (blackbird).

where he was held on suspicion of plotting to overthrow the government. He is a genius and an athlete, is under-handicapped, and should be regarded as extremely dangerous."

A police photograph of Harrison Bergeron was flashed on the screen—upside down, then sideways, upside down again, then right side up. The picture showed the full length of Harrison against a background calibrated[3] in feet and inches. He was exactly seven feet tall.

The rest of Harrison's appearance was Halloween and hardware. Nobody had ever borne heavier handicaps. He had outgrown hindrances faster than the H-G men could think them up. Instead of a little ear radio for a mental handicap, he wore a tremendous pair of earphones, and spectacles with thick wavy lenses. The spectacles were intended not only to make him half blind, but to give him whanging headaches besides.

Scrap metal was hung all over him. Ordinarily, there was a certain symmetry, a military neatness to the handicaps issued to strong people, but Harrison looked like a walking junkyard. In the race of life, Harrison carried three hundred pounds.

And to offset his good looks, the H-G men required that he wear at all times a red rubber ball for a nose, keep his eyebrows shaved off, and cover his even white teeth with black caps at snaggletooth random.

"If you see this boy," said the ballerina, "do not—I repeat, do not—try to reason with him."

There was the shriek of a door being torn from its hinges.

Screams and barking cries of consternation came from the television set. The photograph of Harrison Bergeron on the screen jumped

3. **calibrated** (kal′ə·brāt′id): marked with measurements.

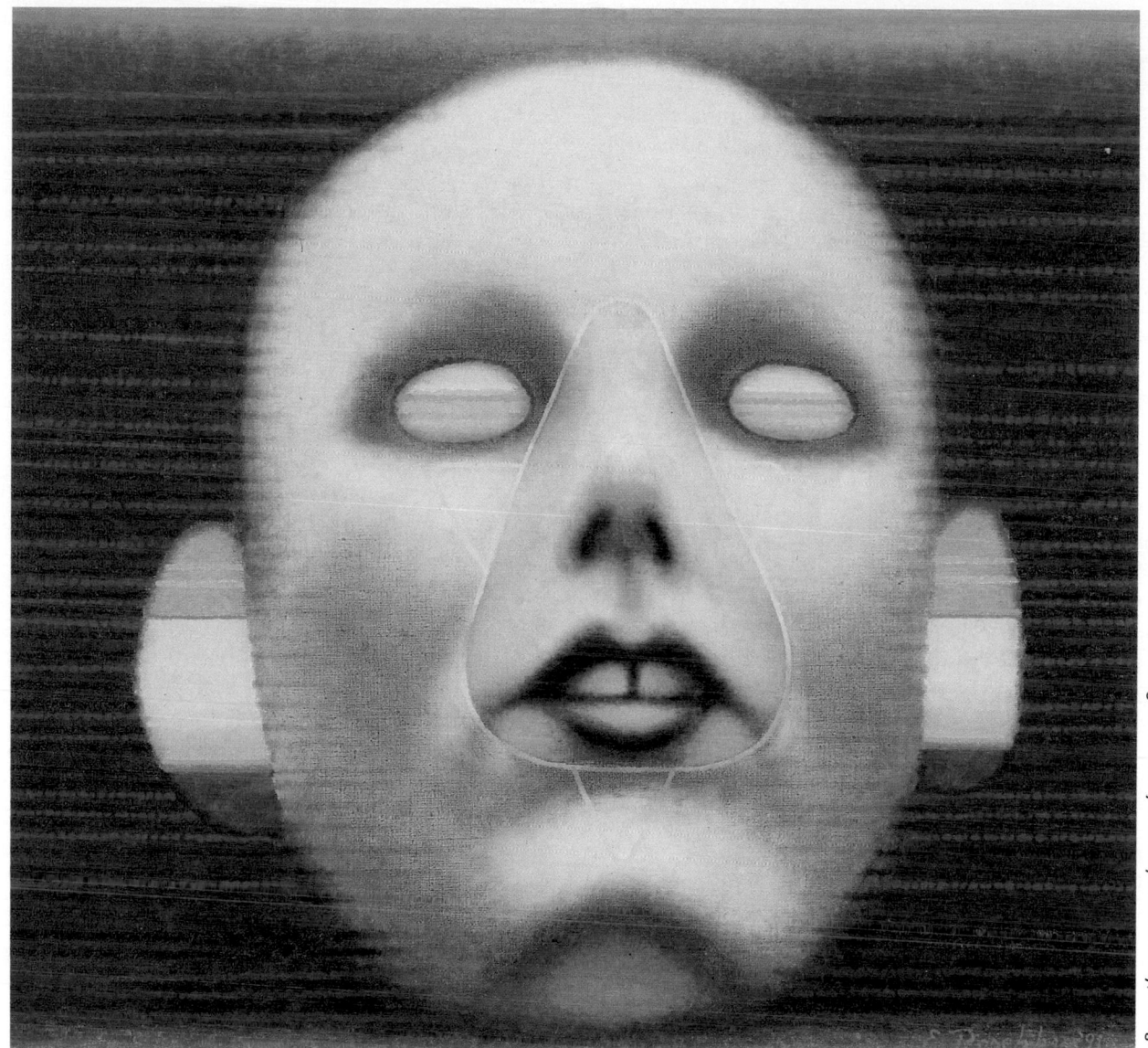

The Triangle (detail) (1991) by Ed Paschke.

again and again, as though dancing to the tune of an earthquake.

George Bergeron correctly identified the earthquake, and well he might have—for many was the time his own home had danced to the same crashing tune. "My God—" said George, "that must be Harrison!"

The realization was blasted from his mind instantly by the sound of an automobile collision in his head.

When George could open his eyes again, the photograph of Harrison was gone. A living, breathing Harrison filled the screen.

Clanking, clownish, and huge, Harrison stood in the center of the studio. The knob of the uprooted studio door was still in his hand. Ballerinas, technicians, musicians, and announcers <u>cowered</u> on their knees before him, expecting to die.

"I am the Emperor!" cried Harrison. "Do you hear? I am the Emperor! Everybody must do

WORDS TO OWN

cowered (kou'ərd) *v.*: drew back or crouched in fear and helplessness.

what I say at once!" He stamped his foot and the studio shook.

"Even as I stand here—" he bellowed, "crippled, hobbled, sickened—I am a greater ruler than any man who ever lived! Now watch me become what I *can* become!"

Harrison tore the straps of his handicap harness like wet tissue paper, tore straps guaranteed to support five thousand pounds.

Harrison's scrap-iron handicaps crashed to the floor.

Harrison thrust his thumbs under the bar of the padlock that secured his head harness. The bar snapped like celery. Harrison smashed his headphones and spectacles against the wall.

He flung away his rubber-ball nose, revealed a man that would have awed Thor, the god of thunder.

"I shall now select my Empress!" he said, looking down on the cowering people. "Let the first woman who dares rise to her feet claim her mate and her throne!"

A moment passed, and then a ballerina arose, swaying like a willow.

Harrison plucked the mental handicap from her ear, snapped off her physical handicaps with marvelous delicacy. Last of all, he removed her mask.

She was blindingly beautiful.

"Now—" said Harrison, taking her hand, "shall we show the people the meaning of the word *dance*? Music!" he commanded.

The musicians scrambled back into their chairs, and Harrison stripped them of their handicaps, too. "Play your best," he told them, "and I'll make you barons and dukes and earls."

The music began. It was normal at first—cheap, silly, false. But Harrison snatched two musicians from their chairs, waved them like batons as he sang the music as he wanted it played. He slammed them back into their chairs.

The music began again and was much improved.

Harrison and his Empress merely listened to

Harrison's scrap-iron handicaps crashed to the floor.

the music for a while—listened gravely, as though synchronizing their heartbeats with it.

They shifted their weights to their toes.

Harrison placed his big hands on the girl's tiny waist, letting her sense the weightlessness that would soon be hers.

And then, in an explosion of joy and grace, into the air they sprang!

Not only were the laws of the land abandoned, but the law of gravity and the laws of motion as well.

They reeled, whirled, swiveled, flounced, capered, gamboled, and spun.

They leaped like deer on the moon.

The studio ceiling was thirty feet high, but each leap brought the dancers nearer to it.

It became their obvious intention to kiss the ceiling.

They kissed it.

And then, neutralizing gravity with love and pure will, they remained suspended in air inches below the ceiling, and they kissed each other for a long, long time.

It was then that Diana Moon Glampers, the Handicapper General, came into the studio with a double-barreled ten-gauge shotgun. She fired twice, and the Emperor and the Empress were dead before they hit the floor.

Diana Moon Glampers loaded the gun again. She aimed it at the musicians and told them they had ten seconds to get their handicaps back on.

It was then that the Bergerons' television tube burned out.

Hazel turned to comment about the blackout to George. But George had gone out into the kitchen for a can of beer.

George came back in with the beer, paused while a handicap signal shook him up. And then he sat down again. "You been crying?" he said to Hazel.

"Yup," she said.

"What about?" he said.

"I forget," she said. "Something real sad on television."

"What was it?" he said.

"It's all kind of mixed up in my mind," said Hazel.

"Forget sad things," said George.

"I always do," said Hazel.

"That's my girl," said George. He winced. There was the sound of a riveting-gun in his head.

"Gee—I could tell that one was a doozy," said Hazel.

"You can say that again," said George.

"Gee—" said Hazel, "I could tell that one was a doozy."

MEET THE WRITER
A Good Citizen

Kurt Vonnegut (1922–) is concerned about the way people treat one another in a world of high technology. So he has written novels, mostly social satires, to express his concerns about morality, about human society, about values. "I consider writing an act of good citizenship," he has said. During World War II, Vonnegut was held prisoner in the underground meat locker of a slaughterhouse in Dresden, Germany. He used that experience in his most famous novel, *Slaughterhouse Five, or the Children's Crusade* (1969), which carries a strong message against all war.

More by Vonnegut

Welcome to the Monkey House (Bantam/Doubleday) is a collection of Vonnegut's stories and essays that includes "EPICAC," about a computer that falls in love, and "Report on the Barnhouse Effect," about a man with astonishing powers.

Don Marquis (1878–1937) was a newspaper columnist who wrote poems that he pretended were written by a cockroach named archy. Archy supposedly lives in the newsroom. At night archy types poems and leaves them on the boss's desk. Since archy is too small to use the shift key on the typewriter at the same time that he uses a letter key, he can't make capital letters. He also, with no excuse, is careless about punctuation.

The Lesson of the Moth

Don Marquis

i was talking to a moth
the other evening
he was trying to break into
an electric light bulb
5   and fry himself on the wires

why do you fellows
pull this stunt i asked him
because it is the conventional
thing for moths or why
10   if that had been an uncovered
candle instead of an electric
light bulb you would
now be a small unsightly cinder
have you no sense
15   plenty of it he answered
but at times we get tired
of using it
we get bored with the routine
and crave beauty
20   and excitement
fire is beautiful
and we know that if we get
too close it will kill us
but what does that matter
25   it is better to be happy
for a moment
and be burned up with beauty

than to live a long time
and be bored all the while
30   so we wad all our life up
into one little roll
and then we shoot the roll
that is what life is for
it is better to be a part of beauty
35   for one instant and then cease to
exist than to exist forever
and never be a part of beauty
our attitude toward life
is come easy go easy
40   we are like human beings
used to be before they became
too civilized to enjoy themselves

and before i could argue him
out of his philosophy
45   he went and immolated himself
on a patent cigar lighter
i do not agree with him
myself i would rather have
half the happiness and twice
50   the longevity

but at the same time i wish
there was something i wanted
as badly as he wanted to fry himself
                        archy

MAKING MEANINGS

First Thoughts

1. At the end of Vonnegut's story, how did you feel about Hazel? George? Harrison?

Shaping Interpretations

2. What details in the story make us infer, or guess, that all does not work very smoothly in this society where everyone is equal "every which way"? Do you think this is a realistic prediction of what would happen if all competition were done away with? Why, or why not?

3. What kinds of societies could be the targets of Vonnegut's **satire** in this story? What attitudes is he mocking?

4. What is the difference between believing that people are equals under the law and believing that everyone is the same?

5. Poor Hazel says of the bumbling announcer, ". . . he tried. That's the big thing." Should people be rewarded for trying or for actually accomplishing something? Talk about your thoughts on this complicated issue. See if talking it over with other readers affects the way you think.

> ### Reviewing the Text
>
> a. What has happened by the year 2081?
> b. What kinds of handicaps have been imposed on people with above-average abilities?
> c. Why has Harrison been put in jail?
> d. What action does Harrison take to resolve his conflict with the government?
> e. At the story's end, who or what has triumphed?

Extending the Text

6. Do you think this story has anything to say to us today? Talk over your responses to Vonnegut's satire.

7. This story is a fantasy. What figures from actual life have tried to save a people from repression the way Harrison does?

8. What connection can you find between the moth in "The Lesson of the Moth" (page 140) and the story of Harrison Bergeron?

Challenging the Text

9. Refer to the Quickwrite you did before reading this story. How do you feel now about these issues? Do you agree with Vonnegut's view of technology, or would you challenge him on some details in the story? Be sure to explain your responses in terms of your own experiences.

Writer's Notebook

1. Collecting Ideas for an Observational Essay

Using dialogue. Notice the way Vonnegut uses dialogue to make his characters sound like real people. Hazel is a bit dazed but sweet: "Why don't you stretch out on the sofa, so's you can rest your handicap bag on the pillows, honeybunch?" George is so distracted by the commotion in his head that he often speaks in near grunts: "Huh?" "Yup." "Um." "Right." Once you've chosen a subject for your own observational essay (see the assignment on page 194), you can begin to gather details about your character's

speech. Write down some of the key words and phrases you might hear your character speak. Maybe you can let your character talk about something important, something that is especially meaningful to him or her. If you can, tape your subject's speech (with permission) so you have a record of his or her special vocabulary and expressions. Try to reproduce distinct pronunciations (like "so's" and "yup").

Critical Writing

2. Why Compete?

Even if it were possible to remove all competition from society, would such an act be a good thing? Consider the effects of such a drastic action on sports, business, and education. Present your ideas in the form of a letter to Vonnegut. Open your letter with a general statement telling what you think of Vonnegut's satire.

Creative Writing

3. Made for TV

Work in a small group to rewrite the story of Harrison Bergeron as a TV movie. Block out scenes for a thirty-minute show with three commercial breaks. As you write, remember the network's policy on violence and language. After your script is written, give it to another group for a "table read." This group will read the script aloud, trying out lines and seeing what works and what doesn't. A sample TV script for "A Christmas Memory" is on page 155.

Drawing

4. The Bergerons: A Cartoon Strip

Plan and draw a cartoon strip of this story. Draw the characters as you imagine them, with all their clunky handicaps, and put their words in speech balloons or captions.

Therese (age 6)
- *asks for "boop" instead of soup, says "heeligoflopter" for helicopter.*
- *always wants to know "what's doin'?"*
- *doesn't like to be left out: "Hey—wait up, you guys!"*
- *wants to be independent: "I can do it by mysauce!"*

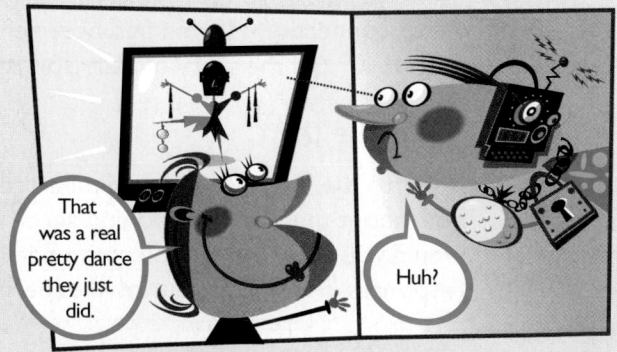

It was 2081, and everyone was finally equal. But some things weren't quite right.

LANGUAGE LINK

Language Handbook HELP

See Placement of Modifiers, page 1005.

Technology HELP

See Language Workshop CD-ROM. *Key word entry: misplaced modifiers.*

Proofreading: Misplaced Modifiers Are Confusing

For clarity, careful writers place modifying phrases and clauses as close as possible to the words they modify.

Misplaced modifiers can be funny. The comedian Groucho Marx used one in the movie *Animal Crackers.* "One morning I shot an elephant in my pajamas," Groucho said. "How he got in my pajamas, I'll never know."

Below are three examples of how descriptions from "Harrison Bergeron" might sound if modifiers were misplaced.

1. Two of the eight ballerinas had collapsed and were holding their temples to the studio floor. [Where should "to the studio floor" be placed?]

2. The photograph of Harrison Bergeron jumped again and again, as though dancing to the tune of an earthquake on the screen. [Where should "on the screen" be placed?]

3. They remained suspended in air, and they kissed each other inches below the ceiling for a long, long time. [Where should "inches below the ceiling" be placed?]

Try It Out

➤ Rewrite each sentence below so that the misplaced modifier that is underlined is placed nearer the word it modifies.

1. George wore a mental handicap and seven pounds of bird shot in his ear.

2. Hazel watched the TV set talking happily about nothing.

3. Harrison stood at the center of the studio with a red rubber ball for a nose.

4. The dancers were gunned down by Diana Moon Glampers kissing the ceiling.

➤ As you proofread your writing, make sure you have placed modifying phrases and clauses near the words they modify. You'll have to read carefully. Misplaced modifiers don't always pop out. You might want to underline modifiers and draw arrows to the words they modify. Can you make the relationship clearer?

VOCABULARY   HOW TO OWN A WORD

WORD BANK

hindrances
symmetry
consternation
cowered
synchronizing

Vocabulary for the Workplace

1. Write a sentence for a political speech using the word *hindrances*.
2. Write a sentence for a car advertisement that uses the word *symmetry*.
3. Use the word *consternation* to say something about people's attitudes toward the media.
4. Use the word *cowered* in a sentence from a veterinarian's report on a sick dog.
5. Write a sentence about an audio system using the word *synchronizing*.

Before You Read
A Christmas Memory

Reading Focus
Those Who Give

One of the mysteries of the human spirit is generosity—especially the generosity of those who don't have very much themselves. Here is a story about an unforgettable character, her young cousin, and their rituals of Christmas generosity. The story also reveals something about the nature of friendship and the endurance of love—even when, to the rest of the world, the friendship seems very odd and the love is not noticed at all.

A Dialogue with the Text

As you read this story, keep a record of your responses in your Reader's Log. Be sure to note the following:

- questions
- predictions
- responses to the characters (Do they remind you of people you know? Do you like them? Dislike them?)
- passages you think are important or well written
- passages or events that puzzle you
- surprises
- feelings about the ending
- connections with your own experiences

Elements of Literature
Characterization— Indirectly

When a writer shows us a character by describing his or her speech, appearance, thoughts, or actions, we say that the characterization is **indirect**. This means that we ourselves have to take all the information we are given about the character and analyze for ourselves the kind of person we are meeting. Direct characterization is something like meeting people in real life. In real life, people do not wear T-shirts with slogans explaining what kind of people they are. In real life, we observe people, we listen to what they say, and we watch how they act. Then we draw our own conclusions about them.

> **I**n **indirect characterization,** a writer reveals what people are like by telling about their speech, their actions, their appearance, their private thoughts, and the ways they affect other characters.
>
> *For more on Character, see pages 130–131 and the Handbook of Literary Terms.*

Christmas Morning 1930 by Charles E. Burchfield.
Watercolor on paper (30″ x 22 ⅛″).

We are each other's
best friend.

A CHRISTMAS MEMORY

TRUMAN CAPOTE

Imagine a morning in late November. A coming of winter morning more than twenty years ago. Consider the kitchen of a spreading old house in a country town. A great black stove is its main feature; but there is also a big round table and a fireplace with two rocking chairs placed in front of it. Just today the fireplace commenced its seasonal roar.

A woman with shorn white hair is standing at the kitchen window. She is wearing tennis shoes and a shapeless gray sweater over a summery calico dress. She is small and sprightly, like a bantam hen; but, due to a long youthful illness, her shoulders are pitifully hunched. Her face is remarkable—not unlike Lincoln's, craggy like that, and tinted by sun and wind; but it is delicate too, finely boned, and her eyes are sherry-colored and timid. "Oh my," she exclaims, her breath smoking the window-pane, "it's fruitcake weather!"

The person to whom she is speaking is myself. I am seven; she is sixty-something. We are cousins, very distant ones, and we have lived together—well, as long as I can remember. Other people inhabit the house, relatives; and though they have power over us, and frequently make us cry, we are not, on the whole, too much aware of them. We are each other's best friend. She calls me Buddy, in memory of a boy who was formerly her best friend. The other Buddy died in the 1880s, when she was still a child. She is still a child.

"I knew it before I got out of bed," she says, turning away from the window with a purposeful excitement in her eyes. "The courthouse bell sounded so cold and clear. And there were no birds singing; they've gone to warmer country, yes indeed. Oh, Buddy, stop stuffing biscuit and fetch our buggy. Help me find my hat. We've thirty cakes to bake."

It's always the same: A morning arrives in November, and my friend, as though officially inaugurating the Christmas time of year that exhilarates her imagination and fuels the blaze of her heart, announces: "It's fruitcake weather! Fetch our buggy. Help me find my hat."

The hat is found, a straw cartwheel corsaged with velvet roses out-of-doors has faded; it once belonged to a more fashionable relative. Together, we guide our buggy, a dilapidated baby carriage, out to the garden and into a grove of pecan trees. The buggy is mine; that is, it was bought for me when I was born. It is made of wicker, rather unraveled, and the wheels wobble like a drunkard's legs. But it is a faithful object; springtimes, we take it to the woods and fill it with flowers, herbs, wild fern for our porch pots; in the summer, we pile it with picnic paraphernalia and sugar-cane fishing poles and roll it down to the edge of the creek; it has its winter uses, too: as a truck for hauling firewood from the yard to the kitchen, as a warm bed for Queenie, our tough little orange and white rat terrier who has survived distemper and two rattlesnake bites. Queenie is trotting beside it now.

Three hours later we are back in the kitchen hulling a heaping buggyload of windfall pecans.[1] Our backs hurt from gathering them: How hard they were to find (the main crop having been shaken off the trees and sold by the orchard's owners, who are not us) among the concealing leaves, the frosted, deceiving grass. Caarackle! A cheery crunch, scraps of miniature thunder sound as the shells collapse and the golden mound of sweet, oily, ivory meat mounts in the milk-glass bowl. Queenie begs to taste, and now and again my friend sneaks her a mite, though insisting we deprive ourselves. "We mustn't, Buddy. If we start, we won't stop. And there's scarcely enough as there is. For thirty cakes." The kitchen is growing dark. Dusk turns the window into a mirror: Our reflections mingle with the rising moon as we work by the fireside in the firelight. At last, when the moon is quite high, we toss the final hull into the fire and, with joined sighs, watch it catch flame. The buggy is empty; the bowl is brimful.

We eat our supper (cold biscuits, bacon, blackberry jam) and discuss tomorrow. Tomorrow the kind of work I like best begins: buying. Cherries and citron, ginger and vanilla and canned Hawaiian pineapple, rinds and raisins and walnuts and whiskey and oh, so much flour, butter, so many eggs, spices, flavorings: Why, we'll need a pony to pull the buggy home.

But before these purchases can be made, there is the question of money. Neither of us has any. Except for skinflint sums persons in the house occasionally provide (a dime is considered very big money); or what we earn ourselves from various activities: holding

1. **windfall pecans:** pecans blown down from the trees by wind.

WORDS TO OWN

inaugurating (in·ô′gyoo·rāt′in) v.: formally beginning.
exhilarates (eg·zil′ə·rāts′) v.: gladdens; excites.
dilapidated (də·lap′ə·dāt′id) adj.: shabby; falling apart.
paraphernalia (par′ə·fər·nāl′yə) n.: equipment; gear.

rummage sales, selling buckets of handpicked blackberries, jars of homemade jam and apple jelly and peach preserves, rounding up flowers for funerals and weddings. Once we won seventy-ninth prize, five dollars, in a national football contest. Not that we know a fool thing about football. It's just that we enter any contest we hear about: At the moment our hopes are centered on the fifty-thousand-dollar Grand Prize being offered to name a new brand of coffee (we suggested "A.M."; and, after some hesitation, for my friend thought it perhaps sacrilegious, the slogan "A.M.! Amen!"). To tell the truth, our only *really* profitable enterprise was the Fun and Freak Museum we conducted in a backyard woodshed two summers ago. The Fun was a stereopticon[2] with slide views of Washington and New York lent us by a relative who had been to those places (she was furious when she discovered why we'd borrowed it); the Freak was a three-legged biddy chicken[3] hatched by one of our own hens. Everybody hereabouts wanted to see that biddy: We charged grown-ups a nickel, kids two cents. And took in a good twenty dollars before the museum shut down due to the decease of the main attraction.

But one way and another we do each year accumulate Christmas savings, a Fruitcake Fund. These moneys we keep hidden in an ancient bead purse under a loose board under the floor

Bouquet and Stove (1929) by Yasuo Kuniyoshi.

The Roland P. Murdock Collection, Wichita Art Museum, Wichita, Kansas.

under a chamber pot[4] under my friend's bed. The purse is seldom removed from this safe location except to make a deposit, or, as happens every Saturday, a withdrawal; for on Saturdays I am allowed ten cents to go to the picture show. My friend has never been to a picture show, nor does she intend to: "I'd rather hear you tell the story, Buddy. That way I can imagine it more. Besides, a person my age shouldn't squander their eyes. When the Lord comes, let me see Him clear." In addition to never having seen a movie, she has never: eaten in a restaurant, traveled more than five miles from home, received or sent a telegram, read anything except funny papers and the Bible, worn cosmetics, cursed, wished someone harm, told a lie on purpose, let a hungry dog go hungry. Here are a few things she has done, does do: killed with a hoe the biggest rattlesnake ever seen in this county (sixteen rattles), dip snuff[5] (secretly), tame hummingbirds (just try it) till they balance on her finger, tell ghost stories (we both believe in ghosts) so tingling they chill you in July, talk to herself, take walks in the rain, grow the prettiest japonicas[6] in town, know the

4. **chamber pot:** Before indoor plumbing and toilets, people used pots, usually kept in their bedrooms, or chambers.
5. **snuff:** powdered tobacco inhaled by sniffing.
6. **japonicas** (jə·pän′i·kəz): flowering shrubs.

2. **stereopticon** (ster′ē·äp′ti·kən): old-fashioned kind of slide projector.
3. **biddy chicken:** young chicken.

WORDS TO OWN

sacrilegious (sak′rə·lij′əs) *adj.*: disrespectful toward religion.

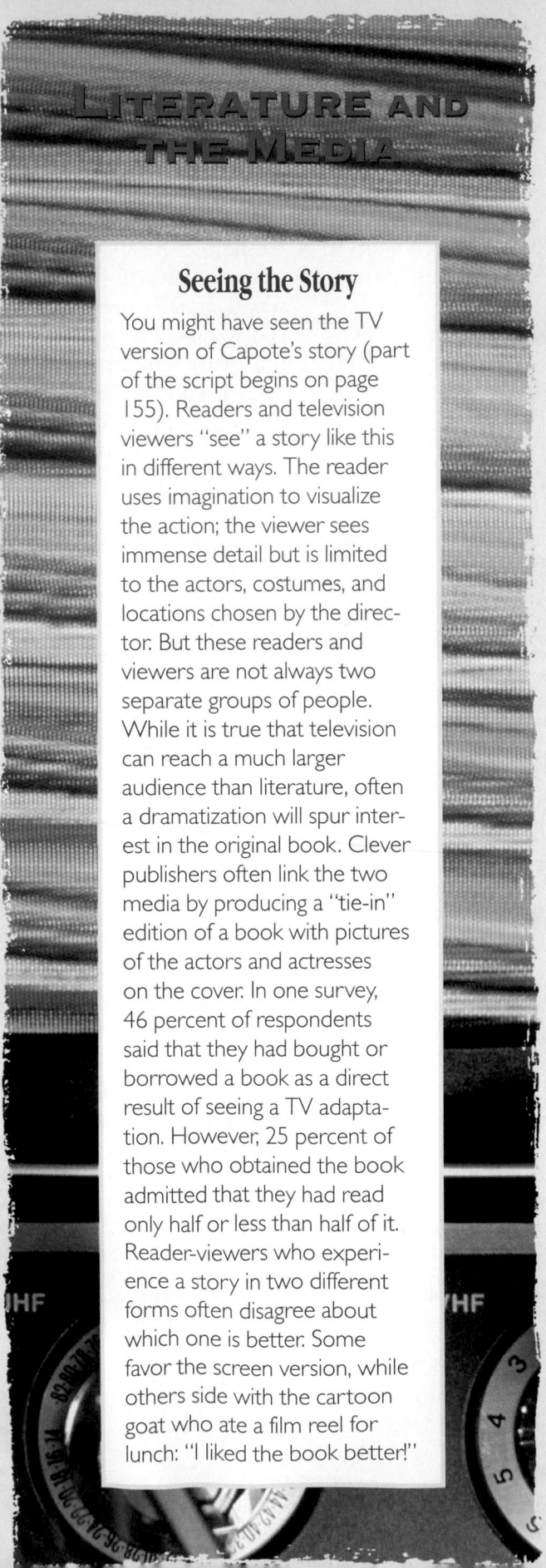

Seeing the Story

You might have seen the TV version of Capote's story (part of the script begins on page 155). Readers and television viewers "see" a story like this in different ways. The reader uses imagination to visualize the action; the viewer sees immense detail but is limited to the actors, costumes, and locations chosen by the director. But these readers and viewers are not always two separate groups of people. While it is true that television can reach a much larger audience than literature, often a dramatization will spur interest in the original book. Clever publishers often link the two media by producing a "tie-in" edition of a book with pictures of the actors and actresses on the cover. In one survey, 46 percent of respondents said that they had bought or borrowed a book as a direct result of seeing a TV adaptation. However, 25 percent of those who obtained the book admitted that they had read only half or less than half of it. Reader-viewers who experience a story in two different forms often disagree about which one is better. Some favor the screen version, while others side with the cartoon goat who ate a film reel for lunch: "I liked the book better!"

recipe for every sort of old-time Indian cure, including a magical wart-remover.

Now, with supper finished, we retire to the room in a faraway part of the house where my friend sleeps in a scrap-quilt-covered iron bed painted rose pink, her favorite color. Silently, wallowing in the pleasures of conspiracy, we take the bead purse from its secret place and spill its contents on the scrap quilt. Dollar bills, tightly rolled and green as May buds. Somber fifty-cent pieces, heavy enough to weight a dead man's eyes. Lovely dimes, the liveliest coin, the one that really jingles. Nickels and quarters, worn smooth as creek pebbles. But mostly a hateful heap of bitter-odored pennies. Last summer others in the house contracted to pay us a penny for every twenty-five flies we killed. Oh, the <u>carnage</u> of August: the flies that flew to heaven! Yet it was not work in which we took pride. And, as we sit counting pennies, it is as though we were back tabulating dead flies. Neither of us has a head for figures; we count slowly, lose track, start again. According to her calculations, we have $12.73. According to mine, exactly $13. "I do hope you're wrong, Buddy. We can't mess around with thirteen. The cakes will fall. Or put somebody in the cemetery. Why, I wouldn't dream of getting out of bed on the thirteenth." This is true: She always spends thirteenths in bed. So, to be on the safe side, we subtract a penny and toss it out the window.

Of the ingredients that go into our fruitcakes, whiskey is the most expensive, as well as the hardest to obtain: State laws forbid its sale. But everybody knows you can buy a bottle from Mr. Haha Jones. And the next day, having completed our more <u>prosaic</u> shopping, we set out for Mr. Haha's business address, a "sinful" (to quote public opinion) fish-fry and dancing cafe down by the river. We've been there before, and on the same errand; but in previous

WORDS TO OWN

carnage (kär′nij) *n.:* slaughter.
prosaic (prō·zā′ik) *adj.:* ordinary.

years our dealings have been with Haha's wife, an iodine-dark Indian woman with brassy peroxided hair and a dead-tired underline disposition. Actually, we've never laid eyes on her husband, though we've heard that he's an Indian too. A giant with razor scars across his cheeks. They call him Haha because he's so gloomy, a man who never laughs. As we approach his cafe (a large log cabin festooned[7] inside and out with chains of garish-gay naked light bulbs and standing by the river's muddy edge under the shade of river trees where moss drifts through the branches like gray mist) our steps slow down. Even Queenie stops prancing and sticks close by. People have been murdered in Haha's cafe. Cut to pieces. Hit on the head. There's a case coming up in court next month. Naturally these goings-on happen at night when the colored lights cast crazy patterns and the Victrola[8] wails. In the daytime Haha's is shabby and deserted. I knock at the door, Queenie barks, my friend calls: "Mrs. Haha, ma'am? Anyone to home?"

Footsteps. The door opens. Our hearts overturn. It's Mr. Haha Jones himself! And he *is* a giant; he *does* have scars; he *doesn't* smile. No, he glowers at us through Satan-tilted eyes and demands to know: "What you want with Haha?"

For a moment we are too paralyzed to tell. Presently my friend half finds her voice, a whispery voice at best: "If you please, Mr. Haha, we'd like a quart of your finest whiskey."

His eyes tilt more. Would you believe it? Haha is smiling! Laughing, too. "Which one of you is a drinkin' man?"

"It's for making fruitcakes, Mr. Haha. Cooking."

This sobers him. He frowns. "That's no way to waste good whiskey." Nevertheless, he retreats into the shadowed cafe and seconds later appears carrying a bottle of daisy-yellow unlabeled liquor. He demonstrates its sparkle in the sunlight and says: "Two dollars."

We pay him with nickels and dimes and pennies. Suddenly, jangling the coins in his hand like a fistful of dice, his face softens. "Tell you what," he proposes, pouring the money back into our bead purse, "just send me one of them fruitcakes instead."

"Well," my friend remarks on our way home, "there's a lovely man. We'll put an extra cup of raisins in *his* cake."

The black stove, stoked with coal and firewood, glows like a lighted pumpkin. Eggbeaters whirl, spoons spin round in bowls of butter and sugar, vanilla sweetens the air, ginger spices it; melting, nose-tingling odors saturate the kitchen, suffuse the house, drift out to the world on puffs of chimney smoke. In four days our work is done. Thirty-one cakes, dampened with whiskey, bask on window sills and shelves.

Who are they for?

Friends. Not necessarily neighbor friends: Indeed, the larger share are intended for persons we've met maybe once, perhaps not at all. People who've struck our fancy. Like President Roosevelt. Like the Reverend and Mrs. J. C. Lucey, Baptist missionaries to Borneo who lectured here last winter. Or the little knife grinder who comes through town twice a year. Or Abner Packer, the driver of the six o'clock bus from Mobile, who exchanges waves with us every day as he passes in a dust-cloud whoosh. Or the young Wistons, a California couple whose car one afternoon broke down outside the house and who spent a pleasant hour chatting with us on the porch (young Mr. Wiston snapped our picture, the only one we've ever had taken). Is it because my friend is shy with everyone *except* strangers that these strangers, and merest acquaintances, seem to us our truest friends? I think yes. Also, the scrapbooks we keep of thank-you's on White House stationery, time-to-time communications from California and Borneo, the knife grinder's penny postcards, make us feel connected to eventful worlds beyond the kitchen with its views of a sky that stops.

WORDS TO OWN

disposition (dis′pə·zish′ən) *n.:* usual frame of mind; temperament.

suffuse (sə·fyo͞oz′) *v.:* spread over or through.

---

7. **festooned** (fes·to͞ond′): decorated.
8. **Victrola** (vik·trō′lə): old term for a record player.

Now a nude December fig branch grates against the window. The kitchen is empty, the cakes are gone; yesterday we carted the last of them to the post office, where the cost of stamps turned our purse inside out. We're broke. That rather depresses me, but my friend insists on celebrating—with two inches of whiskey left in Haha's bottle. Queenie has a spoonful in a bowl of coffee (she likes her coffee chicory-flavored and strong). The rest we divide between a pair of jelly glasses. We're both quite awed at the prospect of drinking straight whiskey; the taste of it brings screwed-up expressions and sour shudders. But by and by we begin to sing, the two of us singing different songs simultaneously. I don't know the words to mine, just: *Come on along, come on along, to the dark-town strutters' ball.* But I can dance: That's what I mean to be, a tap-dancer in the movies. My dancing shadow rollicks on the walls; our voices rock the chinaware; we giggle as if unseen hands were tickling us. Queenie rolls on her back, her paws plow the air, something like a grin stretches her black lips. Inside myself, I feel warm and sparky as those crumbling logs, carefree as the wind in the chimney. My friend waltzes round the stove, the hem of her poor calico skirt pinched between her fingers as though it were a party dress: *Show me the way to go home,* she sings, her tennis shoes squeaking on the floor. *Show me the way to go home.*

Enter: two relatives. Very angry. Potent with eyes that scold, tongues that scald. Listen to what they have to say, the words tumbling together into a wrathful tune: "A child of seven! whiskey on his breath! are you out of your mind? feeding a child of seven! must be loony! road to ruination! remember Cousin Kate? Uncle Charlie? Uncle Charlie's brother-in-law? shame! scandal! humiliation! kneel, pray, beg the Lord!"

Queenie sneaks under the stove. My friend gazes at her shoes, her chin quivers, she lifts her skirt and blows her nose and runs to her room. Long after the town has gone to sleep and the house is silent except for the chimings of clocks and the sputter of fading fires, she is weeping into a pillow already as wet as a widow's handkerchief.

"Don't cry," I say, sitting at the bottom of her bed and shivering despite my flannel nightgown that smells of last winter's cough syrup, "don't cry," I beg, teasing her toes, tickling her

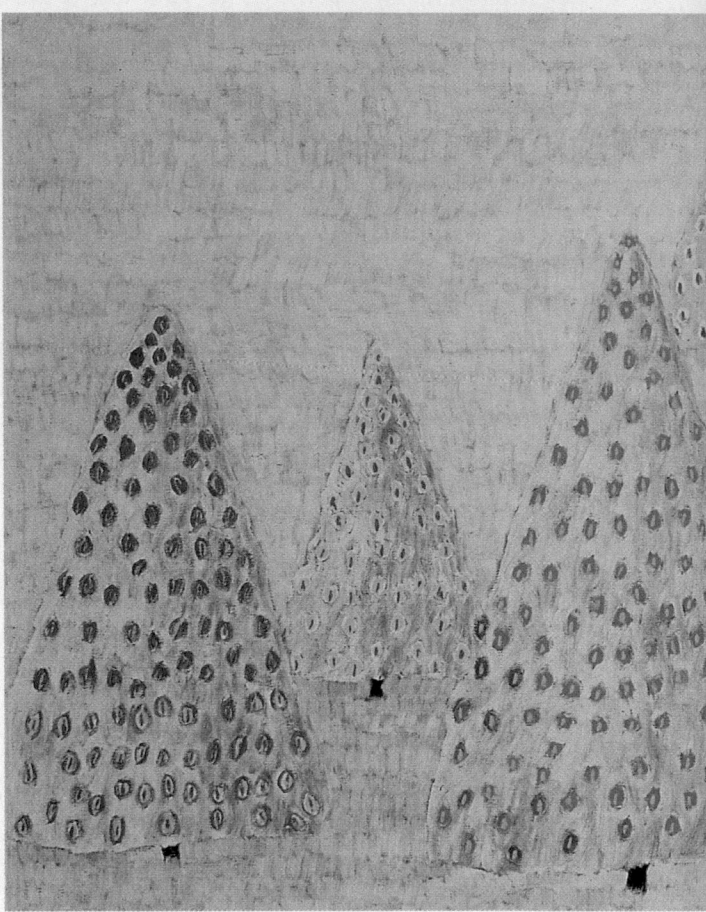

Christmas Trees by Theora Hamblett. Drawing.

feet, "you're too old for that."

"It's because," she hiccups, "I *am* too old. Old and funny."

"Not funny. Fun. More fun than anybody. Listen. If you don't stop crying you'll be so tired tomorrow we can't go cut a tree."

She straightens up. Queenie jumps on the bed (where Queenie is not allowed) to lick her cheeks. "I know where we'll find real pretty trees, Buddy. And holly, too. With berries big as your eyes. It's way off in the woods. Farther than we've ever been. Papa used to bring us

Christmas trees from there: carry them on his shoulder. That's fifty years ago. Well, now: I can't wait for morning."

Morning. Frozen rime[9] lusters the grass; the sun, round as an orange and orange as hot-weather moons, balances on the horizon,

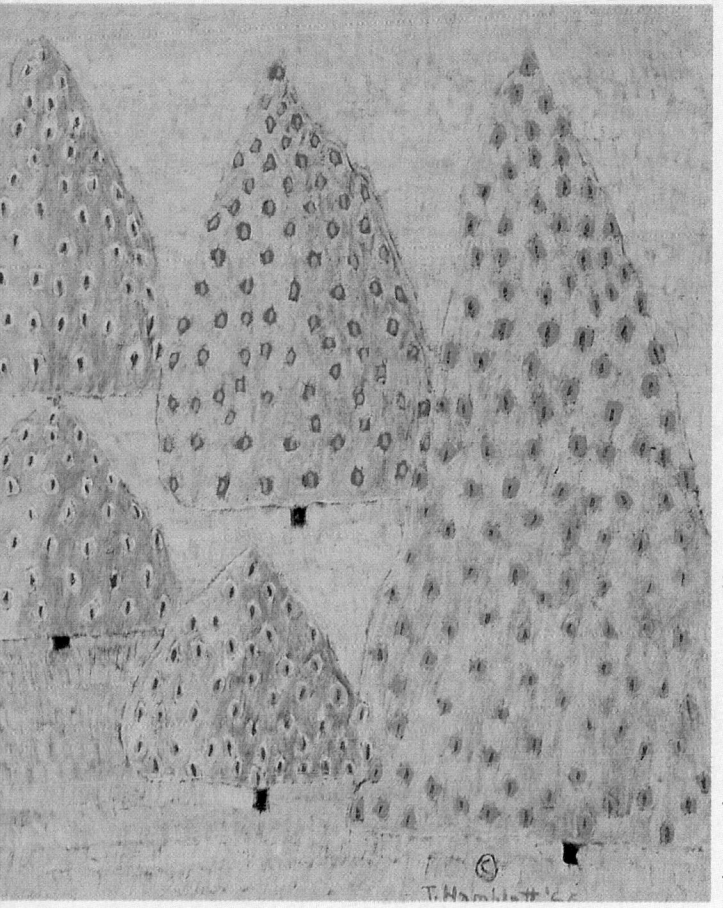

Courtesy of the University Museums, University of Mississippi Cultural Center, University, Mississippi.

burnishes[10] the silvered winter woods. A wild turkey calls. A renegade hog grunts in the undergrowth. Soon, by the edge of knee-deep, rapid-running water, we have to abandon the buggy. Queenie wades the stream first, paddles across, barking complaints at the swiftness of the current, the pneumonia-making coldness of it. We follow, holding our shoes and equipment (a hatchet, a burlap sack) above our heads. A mile more: of chastising thorns, burs and briers that

9. **frozen rime:** frost.
10. **burnishes:** polishes.

catch at our clothes; of rusty pine needles brilliant with gaudy fungus and molted feathers. Here, there, a flash, a flutter, an ecstasy of shrillings remind us that not all the birds have flown south. Always, the path unwinds through lemony sun pools and pitch vine tunnels. Another creek to cross: A disturbed armada[11] of speckled trout froths the water round us, and frogs the size of plates practice belly flops; beaver workmen are building a dam. On the farther shore, Queenie shakes herself and trembles. My friend shivers, too: not with cold but enthusiasm. One of her hat's ragged roses sheds a petal as she lifts her head and inhales the pine-heavy air. "We're almost there; can you smell it, Buddy?" she says, as though we were approaching an ocean.

And, indeed, it is a kind of ocean. Scented acres of holiday trees, prickly-leafed holly. Red berries shiny as Chinese bells: Black crows swoop upon them screaming. Having stuffed our burlap sacks with enough greenery and crimson to garland a dozen windows, we set about choosing a tree. "It should be," muses my friend, "twice as tall as a boy. So a boy can't steal the star." The one we pick is twice as tall as me. A brave, handsome brute that survives thirty hatchet strokes before it keels with a creaking, rending cry. Lugging it like a kill, we commence the long trek out. Every few yards we abandon the struggle, sit down, and pant. But we have the strength of triumphant huntsmen; that and the tree's virile, icy perfume revive us, goad us on. Many compliments accompany our sunset return along the red clay road to town; but my friend is sly and <u>noncommittal</u> when passers-by praise the treasure perched in our buggy: What a fine tree and where did it come from? "Yonderways," she murmurs vaguely. Once a car stops and the rich mill owner's lazy wife leans

11. **armada** (är·mä′də): group, as of warships.

WORDS TO OWN

noncommittal (nän·kə·mit′'l) *adj.*: not admitting or committing to any particular purpose or point of view.

---

out and whines: "Giveya twobits cash for that ol tree." Ordinarily my friend is afraid of saying no; but on this occasion she promptly shakes her head: "We wouldn't take a dollar." The mill owner's wife persists. "A dollar, my foot! Fifty cents. That's my last offer. Goodness, woman, you can get another one." In answer, my friend gently reflects: "I doubt it. There's never two of anything."

Home: Queenie slumps by the fire and sleeps till tomorrow, snoring loud as a human.

A trunk in the attic contains: a shoe box of ermine tails[12] (off the opera cape of a curious lady who once rented a room in the house), coils of frazzled tinsel gone gold with age, one silver star, a brief rope of dilapidated, undoubtedly dangerous candylike light bulbs. Excellent decorations, as far as they go, which isn't far enough: My friend wants our tree to blaze "like a Baptist window," droop with weighty snows of ornament. But we can't afford the made-in-Japan splendors at the five-and-dime. So we do what we've always done: sit for days at the kitchen table with scissors and crayons and stacks of colored paper. I make sketches and my friend cuts them out: lots of cats, fish too (because they're easy to draw), some apples, some watermelons, a few winged angels devised from saved-up sheets of Hershey-bar tinfoil. We use safety pins to attach these creations to the tree; as a final touch, we sprinkle the branches with shredded cotton (picked in August for this purpose). My friend, surveying the effect, clasps her hands together. "Now honest, Buddy. Doesn't it look good enough to eat?" Queenie tries to eat an angel.

After weaving and ribboning holly wreaths for all the front windows, our next project is the fashioning of family gifts. Tie-dye scarves for the ladies, for the men a home-brewed lemon and licorice and aspirin syrup to be taken "at the first Symptoms of a Cold and after Hunting." But

12. **ermine** (ur'min) **tails:** black-tipped white tails of certain kinds of weasels, used to trim clothes.

when it comes time for making each other's gift, my friend and I separate to work secretly. I would like to buy her a pearl-handled knife, a radio, a whole pound of chocolate-covered cherries (we tasted some once and she always swears: "I could live on them, Buddy, Lord yes I could—and that's not taking His name in vain"). Instead, I am building her a kite. She would like to give me a bicycle (she's said so on several million occasions: "If only I could, Buddy. It's bad enough in life to do without something *you* want; but confound it, what gets my goat is not being able to give somebody something you want *them* to have. Only one of these days, I will, Buddy. Locate you a bike. Don't ask how. Steal it, maybe"). Instead, I'm fairly certain that she is building me a kite—the same as last year, and the year before: The year before that we exchanged slingshots. All of which is fine by me. For we are champion kite-fliers who study the wind like sailors; my friend, more accomplished than I, can get a kite aloft when there isn't enough breeze to carry clouds.

Christmas Eve afternoon we scrape together a nickel and go to the butcher's to buy Queenie's traditional gift, a good gnawable beef bone. The bone, wrapped in funny paper, is placed high in the tree near the silver star. Queenie knows it's there. She squats at the foot of the tree, staring up in a trance of greed: When bedtime arrives she refuses to budge. Her excitement is equaled by my own. I kick the covers and turn my pillow as though it were a scorching summer's night. Somewhere a rooster crows: falsely, for the sun is still on the other side of the world.

"Buddy, are you awake?" It is my friend, calling from her room, which is next to mine; and an instant later she is sitting on my bed holding a candle. "Well, I can't sleep a hoot," she declares. "My mind's jumping like a jack rabbit. Buddy, do you think Mrs. Roosevelt will serve our cake at dinner?" We huddle in the bed, and she squeezes my hand I-love-you. "Seems like your hand used to be so much smaller. I guess I hate to see you grow up. When you're grown

up, will we still be friends?" I say always. "But I feel so bad, Buddy. I wanted so bad to give you a bike. I tried to sell my cameo Papa gave me. Buddy—" she hesitates, as though embarrassed. "I made you another kite." Then I confess that I made her one, too; and we laugh. The candle burns too short to hold. Out it goes, exposing the starlight, the stars spinning at the window like a visible caroling that slowly, slowly daybreak silences. Possibly we doze; but the beginnings of dawn splash us like cold water: We're up, wide-eyed and wandering while we wait for others to waken. Quite deliberately my friend drops a kettle on the kitchen floor. I tap-dance in front of closed doors. One by one the household emerges, looking as though they'd like to kill us both; but it's Christmas, so they can't. First, a gorgeous breakfast: just everything you can imagine—from flapjacks and fried squirrel to hominy grits and honey-in-the-comb. Which puts everyone in a good humor except my friend and me. Frankly, we're so impatient to get at the presents we can't eat a mouthful.

Well, I'm disappointed. Who wouldn't be? With socks, a Sunday school shirt, some handkerchiefs, a hand-me-down sweater, and a year's subscription to a religious magazine for children, *The Little Shepherd.* It makes me boil. It really does.

My friend has a better haul. A sack of satsumas,[13] that's her best present. She is proudest, however, of a white wool shawl knitted by her married sister. But she *says* her favorite gift is the kite I built her. And it *is* very beautiful; though not as beautiful as the one she made me, which is blue and scattered with gold and green Good Conduct stars; moreover, my name is painted on it, "Buddy."

"Buddy, the wind is blowing."

The wind is blowing, and nothing will do till we've run to a pasture below the house where Queenie has scooted to bury her bone (and where, a winter hence, Queenie will be buried, too). There, plunging through the healthy,

waist-high grass, we unreel our kites, feel them twitching at the string like sky fish as they swim into the wind. Satisfied, sun-warmed, we sprawl in the grass and peel satsumas and watch our kites cavort. Soon I forget the socks and hand-me-down sweater. I'm as happy as if we'd already won the fifty-thousand-dollar Grand Prize in that coffee-naming contest.

"My, how foolish I am!" my friend cries, suddenly alert, like a woman remembering too late she has biscuits in the oven. "You know what I've always thought?" she asks in a tone of discovery, and smiling not at me but a point beyond. "I've always thought a body would have to be sick and dying before they saw the Lord. And I imagined that when He came it would be like looking at the Baptist window: pretty as colored glass with the sun pouring through, such a shine you don't know it's getting dark. And it's been a comfort: to think of that shine taking away all the spooky feeling. But I'll wager it never happens. I'll wager at the very end a body realizes the Lord has already shown Himself. That things as they are"— her hand circles in a gesture that gathers clouds and kites and grass and Queenie pawing earth over her bone—"just what they've always seen, was seeing Him. As for me, I could leave the world with today in my eyes."

This is our last Christmas together.

Life separates us. Those who Know Best decide that I belong in a military school. And so follows a miserable succession of bugle-blowing prisons, grim reveille-ridden[14] summer camps. I have a new home too. But it doesn't count. Home is where my friend is, and there I never go.

And there she remains, puttering around the kitchen. Alone with Queenie. Then alone. ("Buddy dear," she writes in her wild hard-to-read script, "yesterday Jim Macy's horse kicked Queenie bad. Be thankful she didn't feel much. I wrapped her in a Fine Linen sheet and rode her

13. **satsumas** (sat′sə·mäz′): oranges.

14. **reveille-ridden** (rev′ə·lē rid′′n): ruled by the drum or bugle signal used to rouse sleeping people in a military or summer camp. The writer uses this phrase to suggest a tightly disciplined camp.

in the buggy down to Simpson's pasture where she can be with all her Bones. . . .") For a few Novembers she continues to bake her fruitcakes single-handed; not as many, but some: And, of course, she always sends me "the best of the batch." Also, in every letter she encloses a dime wadded in toilet paper: "See a picture show and write me the story." But gradually in her letters she tends to confuse me with her other friend, the Buddy who died in the 1880s; more and more, thirteenths are not the only days she stays in bed: A morning arrives in November, a leafless birdless coming of winter morning, when she cannot rouse herself to exclaim: "Oh my, it's fruitcake weather!"

And when that happens, I know it. A message saying so merely confirms a piece of news some secret vein had already received, severing from me an irreplaceable part of myself, letting it loose like a kite on a broken string. That is why, walking across a school campus on this particular December morning, I keep searching the sky. As if I expected to see, rather like hearts, a lost pair of kites hurrying toward heaven.

MEET THE WRITER

"A Turtle on Its Back"

Truman Capote (1924–1984) said he was "sort of dragged up" by assorted elderly relatives who lived in "dirt-road Alabama." He was born in New Orleans, but his father deserted the family, and the boy was shunted about while his mother lived in New York. For several years Capote attended military schools, which he hated. When he was seventeen, he abandoned formal schooling for good and moved to New York City to learn to write. He came to national prominence with the publication of his first novel, *Other Voices, Other Rooms* (1948).

Capote's most famous novel is probably *Breakfast at Tiffany's* (1958). It was made into a movie starring Audrey Hepburn as Holly Golightly, the story's unpredictable and "lost" heroine, who goes to New York from the South to make her fortune. His most talked-about book is not fiction at all, but an account of a mass murder that took place in Kansas. Called *In Cold Blood* (1966), the book took Capote seven years of research and writing and involved him in much controversy. Capote called the book a nonfiction novel—a narrative that reads like a novel but with events that are all true.

In a *New York Times Magazine* interview, Capote once said that his frustrations during his early years made him feel "like a turtle on its back."

66 I always felt that nobody was going to understand me, going to understand what I felt about things. I guess that's why I started writing. At least on paper I could put down what I thought. 99

Connections — A Screenplay

from A Christmas Memory

Truman Capote

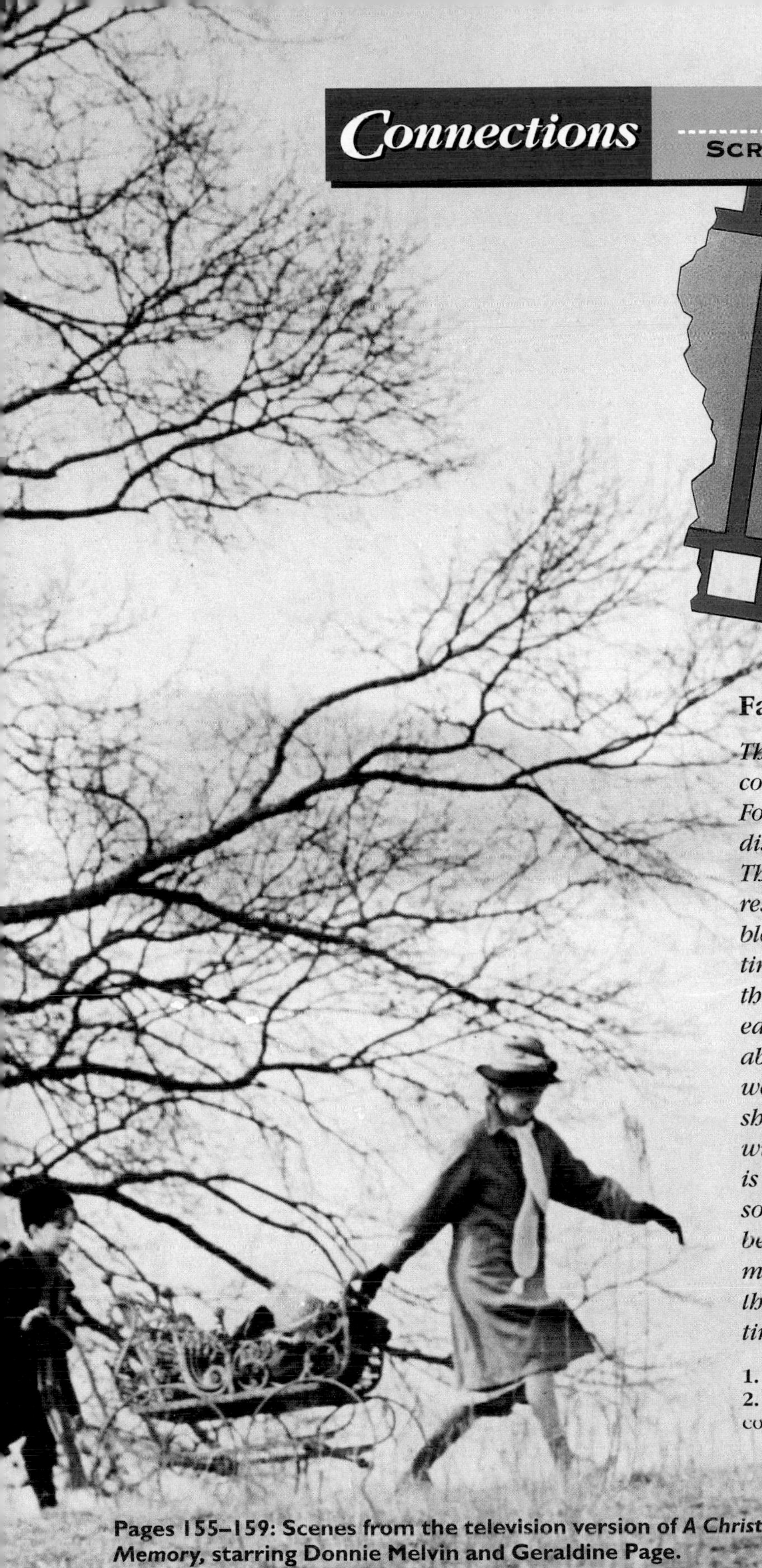

Fade In:

The dark screen slowly begins to assume color: a pale, pastel, washed-out blue. For several beats it is impossible for us to distinguish what it is we are looking at. Then, slowly, the image begins to resolve—a cloudless, predawn sky which blends with a horizon line made indistinguishable because of the limpidity[1] of the light and the softness of a wispy early-morning ground fog. The sun is about to rise, and as the light increases, we begin to distinguish the graceful shapes of the bare trees of a Southern winter landscape. We see that the grass is rimed with morning frost. The first sound now: A distant but clear tolling bell breaks the still, wintry air. The scene must be one of great beauty, reflecting the pastoral and bucolic[2] innocence of a time and place sweetly recalled.

1. **limpidity** (lim·pid′·ə·tē): clearness.
2. **bucolic** (byo͞o·käl′·ik): typical of the countryside.

Pages 155–159: Scenes from the television version of *A Christmas Memory*, starring Donnie Melvin and Geraldine Page.

(Above) American Museum of the Moving Image, New York.

On the horizon comes the first flame of the rising sun, its orange rind in powerful contrast to the blue-gray wash of the landscape. Music gently begins. The sun continues to violate the pellucid[3] unity of ground and sky. Now, slowly, CAMERA PANS, losing the sun, to a large, faded, spreading old house. The architectural grace of the house is emphasized by the softness of light and perhaps even the softness of focus with which we might summon and visualize a precious memory of childhood.

CAMERA begins a slow tracking shot toward the house. We are looking at what must be a kitchen wing. Healthy wood smoke streams from the chimney, while the light from the windows seems warm and inviting. As CAMERA moves closer, music continues and we hear:

and her eyes are sherry-colored and timid. Much of this we shall see in a moment, as the image of her face now is blurred by the scrim[4] of the icy windowpane.

CAMERA draws tighter, concentrating on the reflected rising sun. When its orange nearly fills the screen, we LAP DISSOLVE through to an

EXTREME CLOSE-UP of a roaring fire.

> NARRATOR (voice-over). Just today the fireplace commenced its seasonal roar.

CAMERA pulls back to reveal that we are inside the kitchen. Now we PAN to a CLOSE-UP

> NARRATOR (softly, voice-over). A coming of winter morning more than thirty years ago . . .

Now the CAMERA has drawn in on the kitchen window, concentrating on a particular frosted pane which reflects the half-orb of the still-rising sun. Through the frost and behind the window we see a Woman with almost white hair. Her face is remarkable—not unlike Lincoln's, craggy like that, and tinted by sun and wind; but it is delicate too, finely boned,

of the Woman whose face we half saw from outside. Her eyes sparkle and her breath smokes the windowpane as she exclaims:

> WOMAN. Oh my! It's fruitcake weather!

CAMERA begins a slow pullback from her face, gradually revealing a warm and enormous old-fashioned kitchen. It includes a great

3. **pellucid** (pə·lōō′sid): clear; transparent.

4. **scrim:** curtain used in a theater. It is often semi-transparent.

wood stove and a huge fireplace (both functioning in full fettle this early morning), a large wooden white-scrubbed round table, and an atmosphere of faintly impecunious[5] well-being. As CAMERA continues to pull back it reveals the seated back of a small boy happily involved in eating a large breakfast.

> NARRATOR (voice-over; starts speaking almost immediately after the Woman's line above). The person to whom she is speaking is myself. I am seven; she is sixty-something. We are cousins, very distant ones, and we have lived together—well, as long as I can remember. Other people inhabit the house, relatives; and though they have power over us, and frequently make us cry, we are not, on the whole, too much aware of them. We are each other's best friend. She calls me Buddy, in memory

of a boy who was formerly her best friend. The other Buddy died in the 1880s, when she was still a child. She is still a child.

During the foregoing, the CAMERA completes a thorough investigation of this warm,

5. **impecunious** (im′pi·kyoo′ne·əs): lacking in money.

wonderful room and its two occupants, noting such details as the woman's tennis shoes and her shapeless gray sweater worn over a summery calico dress.

> WOMAN (to the boy, excitedly). It is! It's fruitcake weather! I knew it before I got out of bed. The courthouse bell sounded so cold and clear. And there were no birds singing. They've gone to warmer country, yes indeed!

She sees Buddy is still happily packing his breakfast away. She crosses to him and snatches his plate.

> WOMAN. Oh, Buddy, stop stuffing biscuit and fetch our buggy!

American Museum of the Moving Image, New York.

He runs after her, takes the last biscuit off the plate, and puts it in his mouth. The Woman rushes about clearing the table and piling the dishes in the drainboard. Buddy helps her, but, fast as he moves, it isn't fast enough for her. He has the sugar bowl and is opening the cupboard to put it away.

> WOMAN. Leave it, Buddy. We've got to go. We've thirty cakes to bake!

Buddy drops the sugar bowl on the counter and runs to the coat rack, hurriedly puts on his cap and coat. He takes his long raggedy woolen scarf. The Woman ties it around his neck, the ends hanging down his back.

WOMAN. Raggedy old thing. I've got to knit you a new one.

BUDDY *(anxiously).* Not for my Christmas present?

WOMAN. Would I give you a scarf for *Christmas?* Would I do a thing like that?

He grins and runs out, leaving her still straightening the kitchen.

Buddy comes down the back porch steps and runs to the shed. He opens the door and an instant later comes out wheeling an old rickety wicker baby buggy. Its paint has long ago worn away, and its wheels wobble like a

She rushes back into the house. She is in a hall. She opens a closet stuffed with the outer clothes of other members of the family, umbrellas, boots on the floor, etc., a clutter of hats, caps, gloves, and scarves on a shelf. She rummages around and finally pulls her hat out from under them. It is a straw cartwheel garlanded with faded velvet roses, some of them hanging loosely by a thread. As she claps it on her head, one of the roses falls off. She picks it up and holds it uncertainly. She is torn by her desire to hurry and yet the rose is precious to her. On the narrow hall table there is a vase of flowers

drunkard's legs. The buggy is half filled with firewood. He takes it out and piles it against the shed and then pushes the buggy at a great rate to the back porch. The Woman is just coming down the steps. She is wearing an old hand-me-down ill-fitting coat and carrying her gloves.

BUDDY. Your hat! You forgot your hat!

WOMAN. Oh goodness, my hat!

beneath a dim mirror and perhaps some photographs of relatives. The Woman puts the rose carefully among the flowers in the vase, catches a glimpse of herself in the mirror, straightens the hat from its first crazy angle to another just as odd, and hurries out.

Buddy is down on his hands and knees peering under the house and whistling. Whatever he is whistling at is not answering.

WOMAN. Buddy, Buddy, where are you?

BUDDY. Under here. Queenie won't come out. . . .

WOMAN (*bending down and whistling*). Come on, Queenie, come on, we're going to the pecan grove!

No movement from under the house.

    BUDDY. You shouldn't have told her. She knows it's a long way.

    WOMAN (*to the dog*). Come on, Queenie, I packed a big bone for your lunch!

Reluctantly, a little orange and white rat terrier crawls out from under the house, and the three of them set off. Buddy and the Woman walk as fast as they can, Queenie trails suspiciously behind them.

Here a series of lovely shots of their pilgrimage. The landscape and surrounding country remain a study in early-morning pastel; in our horizon shots of the three we see the cloudless winter sky still the palest shade of blue. Over this montage we:

ROLL MAIN TITLES.

Final shot of montage brings them to a new barbed-wire fence around the pecan grove, prominently featuring a sign "Callahan's Pecan Farm—Private Property—No Trespass-

ing—Trespassers Will Be Prosecuted to the Fullest Extent of the Law."

EXTREME CLOSE-UP of the "No Trespassing" sign.

REVERSE to the faces of the Woman and Buddy.

They are surveying the fence with dismay.

    WOMAN. Buddy, we're going in there!

    BUDDY. How?

The Woman steps forward and picks up the top strand of the fence. Buddy gives her a look.

    WOMAN. Go on!

Buddy looks around. It is clear he is more reluctant about this than she is. Finally he stoops and goes in under the fence. He holds the wire strand for the Woman. She pushes the buggy through and then bends to go under herself. Her sweater catches on a barb. She stops to untangle it.

    WOMAN. I simply do not admire a man who puts up a barbed-wire fence.

    BUDDY. I don't either.

Pushing the buggy, they walk on into the grove.

Photo Album

Can that skinny little boy with
the big ears and the rope belt,
orphaned at seven,
be my grandfather—
5   The grandpa of our loud and boisterous bunch—
Organizer of family reunions that annually weld
nineteen cousins from
Houston,
Chicago,
10   Albany,
Adirondacks,
and me
together—
and keep his five grown sons and their wives
15   unorphaned?

—Gretchen Lund
    Highland Park High School
    Highland Park, New Jersey

MAKING MEANINGS

First Thoughts

1. Refer to your Reader's Log. Share your responses to Capote's characters and to the ways they are treated by others.

Shaping Interpretations

2. Buddy says on page 146 that his friend is "still a child." What do you think this means? Is this a negative trait or a positive one, and why do you think so?

3. How would you describe the **character** of Buddy's friend? Consider

   • what she says

   • the way her face is described

   • the things she does

   • the things she has never done

   • the ways people respond to her

4. Some people feel that this is a story about two people who are in search of love. How do you feel about this interpretation? Explain whether or not you think Buddy and his friend find what they want.

Reviewing the Text

a. What do you know about the person who is telling this story? What is his relationship to the old woman he calls "my friend"?

b. Why do Buddy and his friend make fruitcakes each year?

c. What obstacles must they overcome to make their gifts?

d. What surprises Buddy and his friend about their visit to Mr. Haha Jones?

e. What does Buddy's friend discover while flying her kite on their last Christmas Day together?

Connecting with the Text

5. The ending of "A Christmas Memory" has an emotional impact for most of us—we share in Buddy's sense of loss to a point where we might even feel tears rising. But other readers might find the story too sentimental for their taste. How do you feel about this story and the way it ends?

6. What do you think makes a gift special and meaningful? How important is its cost?

Extending the Text

7. If this is a story about love and generosity, could "Thank You, M'am" (page 120) also be seen as a story with the same message? Talk this over with a partner and share your conclusions in class.

Challenging the Text

8. Some readers feel that Buddy's friend is a realistic character, but others feel she is too good to be believable—that people like this don't exist in real life. Which point of view is closer to yours? Why?

CHOICES: Building Your Portfolio

Writer's Notebook

1. Collecting Ideas for an Observational Essay

Focusing on sensory details.

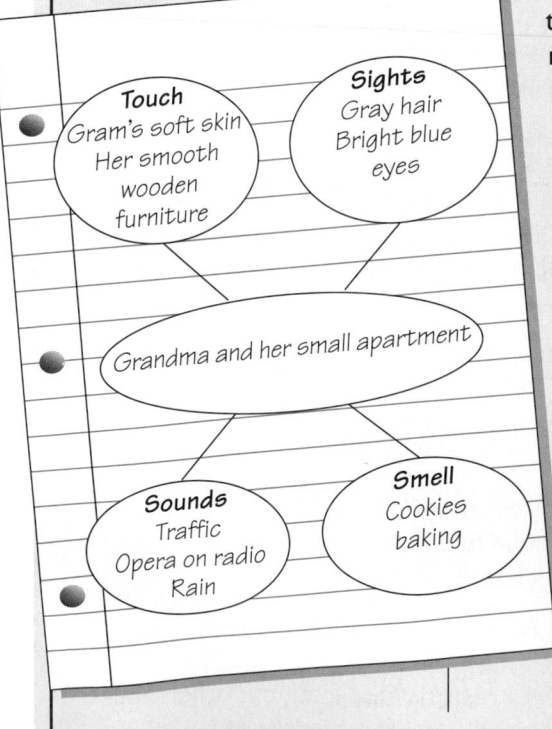

Capote creates a lifelike portrait of Buddy's friend by using **sensory details** to describe her appearance and her setting. Sensory details are details that help us **see** something, **smell** it, **taste** it, **touch** it, **hear** its sounds. When you write your essay about a person you've observed (see the assignment on page 194), you'll want to give your reader sensory information that describes the person and his or her setting. To gather your details, fill out a cluster diagram like the one below. You might also try to think of things your subject reminds you of. Remember that Buddy says that his cousin's eyes are "sherry-colored" and that her face looks like Lincoln's.

Critical Writing/ Character Analysis

2. Made for Television

In 1966, this story was made into a successful TV play that is still shown at Christmastime. (See the excerpt on pages 155–159.) To portray the character of Buddy's friend, the actress had to understand what made her "tick." Prepare a character analysis that would be useful for an actress playing the part. Before you write, brainstorm with a group to come up with Buddy's friend's character traits. Then think of some detail from the story that illustrates each trait. Your answers to question 3 will help.

Creative Writing

3. A Photo of a Friend

In the poem called "Photo Album" on page 160, a writer describes her feelings when she sees a photo of her grandfather as a boy. Write a poem about a photo of a friend of yours (who could be a relative). Tell what you see in the photo and what you wonder about. If you imitate "Photo Album" you will write in free verse and not worry about rhyme and a regular meter.

Art/Oral Presentation

4. A Collage of the Cousin

A **collage** is a collection of images, words, or even objects pasted onto a flat surface. The aim is to create an impression—of a place or a person. The words in a collage can come from stories, poems, newspapers, or just from your own head. Create a collage of Buddy's cousin, showing her in one of the settings described here: the kitchen, the field, Mr. Haha Jones's cafe, the house on Christmas morning, her bedroom. Be prepared to show your collage to the class and explain your choice of objects. See if your audience has picked up the emotional tone you intended.

LANGUAGE LINK

Handbook of Literary Terms
H E L P

See Figure of Speech.

Style: Figures of Speech

Capote's descriptive details help us put our imaginations to work to bring his setting and characters to life. Some of these descriptive details are **figures of speech**—that is, they compare one thing to something else, something very different from it.

In the second paragraph, for example, the narrator compares his friend to a bantam hen. A bantam hen is very different from a human being, but if we use our imaginations, we can picture a person who is small, vigorous, and jumpy, the way a bantam hen is.

As you write your observation of a person, try to use a few carefully chosen figures of speech to tell your readers what your character reminds you of. You might think of an animal, a plant, even a machine. Test your figures of speech to be sure they "work"—how are these two unlike things alike?

Try It Out

For each figure of speech, tell what is compared to what. Does each figure "work"—that is, how are the two different things alike?

1. "... the Christmas time of year ... fuels the blaze of her heart."

2. "Enter: two relatives. Very angry. Potent with eyes that scold, tongues that scald."

3. "... the stars spinning at the window like a visible caroling that slowly, slowly daybreak silences."

4. "... the beginnings of dawn splash us like cold water."

5. "... we unreel our kites, feel them twitching at the string like sky fish as they swim into the wind."

VOCABULARY HOW TO OWN A WORD

WORD BANK

inaugurating
exhilarates
dilapidated
paraphernalia
sacrilegious
carnage
prosaic
disposition
suffuse
noncommittal

Analogies

An analogy is a comparison between two pairs of words. The words in each pair have the same relationship to each other—for example: "*Toe* is to *foot* as *finger* is to *hand*." Copy these analogies on a piece of paper and fill in each blank with a word from the Word Bank.

1. *Amusing* is to *funny* as _____ is to *everyday*.
2. *Biased* is to *neutral* as _____ is to *dedicated*.
3. *Emotion* is to *feeling* as _____ is to *temperament*.
4. *Opening* is to *closing* as _____ is to *ending*.
5. *Inundate* is to *swamp* as _____ is to *soak*.
6. *Soothes* is to *irritates* as _____ is to *disheartens*.
7. *Pollution* is to *contamination* as _____ is to *slaughter*.
8. *Clothing* is to *outfit* as _____ is to *gear*.
9. *Vain* is to *humble* as _____ is to *reverent*.
10. *Disorganized* is to *orderly* as _____ is to *renovated*.

Elements of Literature

SETTING: Putting Us There

A storyteller, like a travel agent, can help gather us up from wherever we are and put us down in another setting on Earth or, for that matter, on a distant planet. That other setting may be a spot we've always wanted to visit, such as a deluxe hotel in Hawaii, or a place where we don't want to be, such as a sinking ship.

Escape—getting away from the same old sights, smells, and obligations—is certainly one of the easy pleasures of reading. But if that is all that happens, our reading experience is just a diversion. In fact, the term *escape reading* suggests that this kind of reading does not have much to do with our lives in the real world.

Setting as a Background

Setting tells us where and when the story takes place. Setting can include the locale of the story, the weather, the time of day, and the time period (past, present, or future). One purpose of setting is to provide background—a place for the characters to live and act in. A good setting helps to make the story real and believable.

Truman Capote opens his story "A Christmas Memory" (page 145) by telling us to imagine a setting: a morning in late November "more than twenty years ago" (he was referring to the early 1930s), a kitchen in a "spreading" old house in a country town, with a black stove, a round table, a fireplace with two rocking chairs—and in the fireplace, the season's first roaring fire. This setting provides the backdrop for the

> **O**ne of the wonders of language is that it can summon up a place for us immediately.

story's characters. Because he describes this setting so vividly, Capote helps us to feel that we are there.

Setting and Character

Places where people live and make their homes can reveal a great deal about their characters. In "A Christmas Memory," for example, we learn that Buddy's friend sleeps in a "scrap-quilt-covered iron bed, painted rose pink" and that she grows the "prettiest japonicas in town." To some readers this setting would suggest her simplicity and her yearning for beauty. (How would you feel about her if she slept in a pile of rags that smelled sour, or if her yard was muddy with no flowers?) Capote has put Mr. Haha Jones in a very different setting. His cafe is "festooned inside and out with chains of garish-gay naked light bulbs." It stands by the river's "muddy edge." The moss on the trees is like "gray mist." His cafe is, in daylight, "shabby and deserted." There is something sinister about Haha's setting, as there is about Haha's character (even though he is also kind).

by John Leggett

Setting and Atmosphere

Setting can also provide **atmosphere** or mood—it can affect the way we feel. Some settings make us feel fear or uneasiness (midnight, a lonely house, the scraping of a branch on the window). Other settings make us feel happy (morning, a garden, the song of a bird). The strange hotel that serves as the setting for Stephen King's novel *The Shining* creates an atmosphere of isolation and terror. We sense that deeds of wickedness can be (and are) committed in the winding, lonely corridors of that huge, old hotel.

How Is Setting Created?

Language is what takes us to King's hotel or to Capote's rural Alabama. One of the wonders of language is that it can summon up a place for us immediately. Language can reach us through our five senses and put us right in the middle of the action, along with the characters themselves.

Like the other elements of storytelling, creating a setting is a skill. To create a believable setting, or one that can make us feel pleasure, mystery, or fear, the writer must select the right details or images. **Images** are words that call forth a response from our senses—sight, smell, touch, hearing, and at times, even taste.

Suppose a writer wants us to imagine a setting as ordinary as the drugstore where Tamara is telling JD she never wants to see him again. We would get tired of a list of all the objects on the shelves. Similarly, we would get tired of a list of all the trees, rocks, and puddles in the mountain pass where the outlaws are waiting for the stagecoach. However, our own imaginations will supply many details if the writer prompts us with the right image. In the drugstore scene, the right image might be a row of bottles, each bearing the label POISON. In the mountain pass the right image might be a circling vulture or the water that seeps into the outlaws' cracked boots.

If we are told that we are landing near a canal on Mars and that the light outside is very harsh, we'll supply not only the glare in the window of the spaceship, but also the intense heat, the dryness of the air, possibly even the sweat trickling down the pilot's back.

When a writer supplies a few right images, we will provide the rest of the scenery. We might draw from our own experience, or we might go beyond our memory into our instincts and into the pool of our subconscious. There we will find all kinds of images—of desert islands, palaces, and planets where, so far as we know, we have never been.

This exercise of our imaginations is what makes fiction a more personal and mind-enhancing experience than, for all their lazy pleasures, the ready-made images of movies and television.

> **A** storyteller, like a travel agent, can help gather us up from wherever we are and put us down in another setting.

BEFORE YOU READ
A MAN CALLED HORSE

Reading Focus

What We Endure

This is a story of the human spirit, of what it can endure and of what it values above all else in life. The story is about a white man who, in 1845, is taken captive by the Crow Indians. Jack Schaefer, author of the novel *Shane,* might have been thinking of this story when he said that no one but Dorothy Johnson could write so perceptively about both the white settlers and the Indians—"those displaced persons who saw their lands being taken and their way of life crumbling before the inevitable white advance. Here is no glamorizing, no romantic gilding, of settlers or of Indians. Here is something finer and more gripping, the honest portrayal of good and bad, of strength and frailty, of the admirable and the contemptible, in both white settlements and Indian villages. . . ."

A Dialogue with the Text

Keep your Reader's Log handy as you read this story. Record your responses to the characters, to the incredible ordeals they face and to the complex beliefs that define their lives. Write down questions you have about the story and its unusual setting. Be sure to note any details that you might want to discuss with others—for example, do you think Johnson is fair to all her characters? Remember that sometimes the most interesting stories are the ones that cause disagreements.

Elements of Literature

Setting Makes It Real

Setting can include the time when the story takes place, its weather, and the customs of the people—how they live, what they do for entertainment, how they dress, what they believe, what they eat. Setting provides background—a place for the characters to live and act in. In some stories—as in this one—setting is so crucial that the story could not take place anywhere else.

> **S**etting tells where and when the story takes place.
>
> *For more on Setting, see pages 164–165 and the Handbook of Literary Terms.*

Background

Before 1845, most of the West was a frontier and not part of the "United States" at all. "A Man Called Horse" begins in 1845 and is set in Indian country. The tribe the story brings to vivid life, the Crows, at this time moved frequently over the northern plains to follow the buffalo herds.

Buffalo hide shield (before 1850), which originally belonged to Arapoosh, head chief of the River Crows.

Courtesy of the National Museum of the American Indian, Smithsonian Institution, New York. 11/7680.

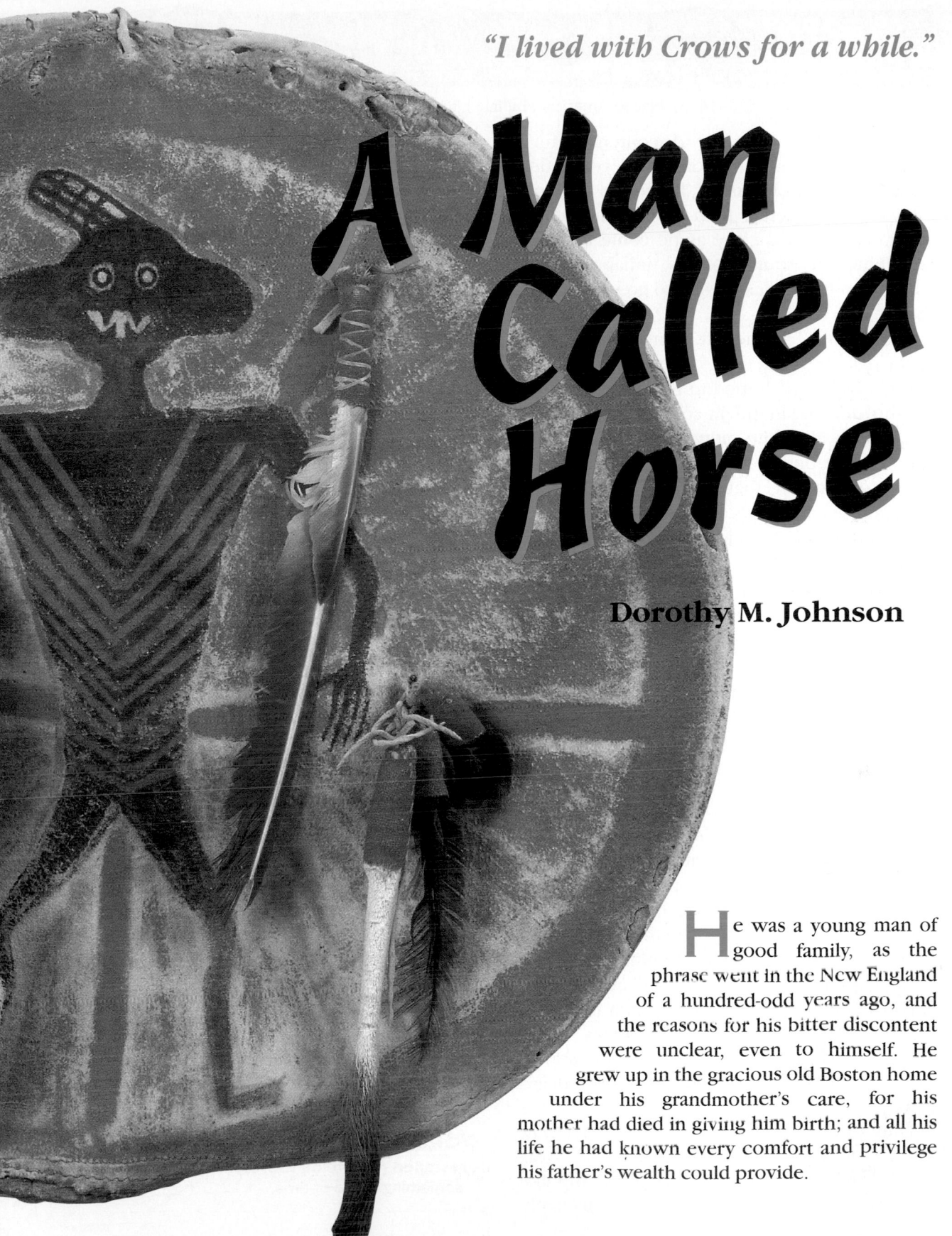

"I lived with Crows for a while."

A Man Called Horse

Dorothy M. Johnson

He was a young man of good family, as the phrase went in the New England of a hundred-odd years ago, and the reasons for his bitter discontent were unclear, even to himself. He grew up in the gracious old Boston home under his grandmother's care, for his mother had died in giving him birth; and all his life he had known every comfort and privilege his father's wealth could provide.

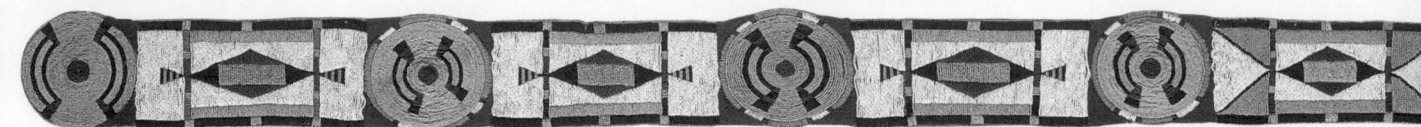

Crow blanket strip (c. 1870–1875). Native American. Buffalo hide, glass beads (63″ x 5.5″). CP-88.

But still there was the discontent, which puzzled him because he could not even define it. He wanted to live among his equals—people who were no better than he and no worse either. That was as close as he could come to describing the source of his unhappiness in Boston and his restless desire to go somewhere else.

In the year 1845, he left home and went out west, far beyond the country's creeping frontier, where he hoped to find his equals. He had the idea that in Indian country, where there was danger, all white men were kings, and he wanted to be one of them. But he found, in the West as in Boston, that the men he respected were still his superiors, even if they could not read, and those he did not respect weren't worth talking to.

He did have money, however, and he could hire the men he respected. He hired four of them, to cook and hunt and guide and be his companions, but he found them not friendly.

They were apart from him and he was still alone. He still brooded about his status in the world, longing for his equals.

On a day in June, he learned what it was to have no status at all. He became a captive of a small raiding party of Crow Indians.

He heard gunfire and the brief shouts of his companions around the bend of the creek just before they died, but he never saw their bodies. He had no chance to fight, because he was naked and unarmed, bathing in the creek, when a Crow warrior seized and held him.

His captor let him go at last, let him run. Then the lot of them rode him down for sport, striking him with their coup sticks. They carried the dripping scalps of his companions, and one had skinned off Baptiste's black beard as well, for a trophy.

They took him along in a matter-of-fact way, as they took the captured horses. He was unshod and naked as the horses were, and like them he had a rawhide thong around his neck.

So long as he didn't fall down, the Crows ignored him.

On the second day they gave him his breeches. His feet were too swollen for his boots, but one of the Indians threw him a pair of moccasins that had belonged to the halfbreed, Henri, who was dead back at the creek. The captive wore the moccasins gratefully. The third day they let him ride one of the

Big Foot's band at Grass Dance on Cheyenne River, August 9, 1890. Photograph.

spare horses so the party could move faster, and on that day they came in sight of their camp.

He thought of trying to escape, hoping he might be killed in flight rather than by slow torture in the camp, but he never had a chance to try. They were more familiar with escape than he was, and knowing what to expect, they forestalled it. The only other time he had tried

WORDS TO OWN

forestalled (fôr·stôld′) v.: prevented by doing something ahead of time.

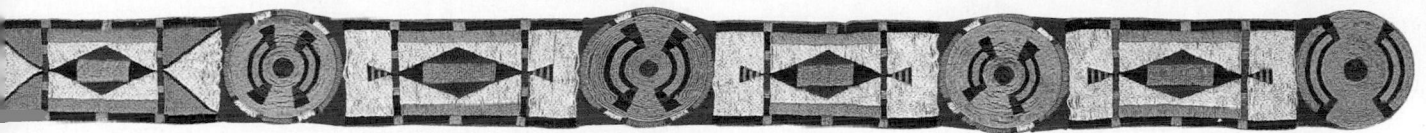

Photograph © 1995 The Detroit Institute of Arts. Richard and Marion Pohrt Collection. © Robert Hensleigh, photographer, DIA.

to escape from anyone, he had succeeded. When he had left his home in Boston, his father had raged and his grandmother had cried, but they could not talk him out of his intention.

The men of the Crow raiding party didn't bother with talk.

Before riding into camp they stopped and dressed in their regalia and in parts of their victims' clothing; they painted their faces black.

Courtesy of the National Museum of the American Indian, Smithsonian Institution, New York.

Then, leading the white man by the rawhide around his neck as though he were a horse, they rode down toward the tepee circle, shouting and singing, brandishing their weapons. He was unconscious when they got there; he fell and was dragged.

He lay dazed and battered near a tepee while the noisy, busy life of the camp swarmed around him and Indians came to stare. Thirst consumed him, and when it rained he lapped rainwater from the ground like a dog. A scrawny, shrieking, eternally busy old woman with ragged graying hair threw a chunk of meat on the grass, and he fought the dogs for it.

When his head cleared, he was angry, although anger was an emotion he knew he could not afford.

It was better when I was a horse, he thought—when they led me by the rawhide around my neck. I won't be a dog, no matter what!

The hag gave him stinking, rancid grease and let him figure out what it was for. He applied it gingerly to his bruised and sun-seared body.

Now, he thought, I smell like the rest of them.

While he was healing, he considered coldly the advantages of being a horse. A man would be humiliated, and sooner or later he would strike back and that would be the end of him. But a horse had only to be <u>docile</u>. Very well, he would learn to do without pride.

He understood that he was the property of the screaming old woman, a fine gift from her son, one that she liked to show off. She did more yelling at him than at anyone else, probably to impress the neighbors so they would not forget what a great and generous man her son was. She was bossy and proud, a dreadful sag of skin and bones, and she was a devilish hard worker.

The white man, who now thought of himself as a horse, forgot sometimes to worry about his danger. He kept making mental notes of things to tell his own people in Boston about this hideous adventure. He would go back a hero, and he would say, "Grandmother, let me fetch your shawl. I've been accustomed to doing little errands for another lady about your age."

Two girls lived in the tepee with the old hag and her warrior son. One of them, the white man concluded, was his captor's wife and the other was his little sister. The daughter-in-law was smug and spoiled. Being beloved, she did not have to be useful. The younger sister had

WORDS TO OWN

docile (däs′əl) *adj.:* easy to manage; submissive.

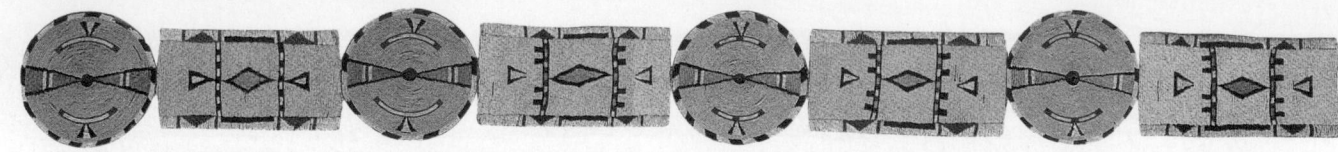

Blackfeet blanket strip (c. 1870–1875). Native American from Montana. Buffalo hide, glass beads (67″x 7″). CP-87.

bright, wandering eyes. Often enough they wandered to the white man who was pretending to be a horse.

The two girls worked when the old woman put them at it, but they were always running off to do something they enjoyed more. There were games and noisy contests, and there was much laughter. But not for the white man. He was finding out what loneliness could be.

That was a rich summer on the plains, with plenty of buffalo for meat and clothing and the making of tepees. The Crows were wealthy in horses, prosperous, and contented. If their men had not been so avid for glory, the white man thought, there would have been a lot more of them. But they went out of their way to court death, and when one of them met it, the whole camp mourned extravagantly and cried to their God for vengeance.

The captive was a horse all summer, a docile bearer of burdens, careful and patient. He kept reminding himself that he had to be better-natured than other horses, because he could not lash out with hoofs or teeth. Helping the old woman load up the horses for travel, he yanked at a pack and said, "Whoa, brother. It goes easier when you don't fight."

The horse gave him a big-eyed stare as if it understood his language—a comforting thought, because nobody else did. But even among the horses he felt unequal. They were able to look out for themselves if they escaped. He would simply starve. He was envious still, even among the horses.

Pair of moccasins.
Courtesy of the National Museum of the American Indian, Smithsonian Institution, New York. 17/8027.

Humbly he fetched and carried. Sometimes he even offered to help, but he had not the skill for the endless work of the women, and he was not trusted to hunt with the men, the providers.

When the camp moved, he carried a pack, trudging with the women. Even the dogs worked then, pulling small burdens on travois[1] of sticks.

The Indian who had captured him lived like a lord, as he had a right to do. He hunted with his peers, attended long ceremonial meetings with much chanting and dancing, and lounged in the shade with his smug bride. He had only two responsibilities: to kill buffalo and to gain glory. The white man was so far beneath him in status that the Indian did not even think of envy.

One day several things happened that made the captive think he might sometime become a man again. That was the day when he began to understand their language. For four months he had heard it, day and night, the joy and the mourning, the ritual chanting and sung prayers, the squabbles and the deliberations. None of it meant anything to him at all.

But on that important day in early fall the two young women set out for the river, and one of them called over her shoulder to the old woman. The white man was startled. She had said she was going to bathe. His understanding was so sudden that he felt as if his ears had come unstopped. Listening to the racket of the camp, he heard fragments of meaning instead of gabble.

1. **travois** (trə·voiz′): sleds. A travois consists of a net or platform dragged along the ground by two poles.

On that same important day the old woman brought a pair of new moccasins out of the tepee and tossed them on the ground before him. He could not believe she would do anything for him because of kindness, but giving him moccasins was one way of looking after her property.

In thanking her, he dared greatly. He picked a little handful of fading fall flowers and took them to her as she squatted in front of her tepee, scraping a buffalo hide with a tool made from a piece of iron tied to a bone. Her hands were hideous—most of the fingers had the first joint missing. He bowed solemnly and offered the flowers.

She glared at him from beneath the short, ragged tangle of her hair. She stared at the flowers, knocked them out of his hand, and went running to the next tepee, squalling the story. He heard her and the other women screaming with laughter.

The white man squared his shoulders and walked boldly over to watch three small boys shooting arrows at a target. He said in English, "Show me how to do that, will you?"

They frowned, but he held out his hand as if there could be no doubt. One of them gave him a bow and one arrow, and they snickered when he missed.

The people were easily amused, except when they were angry. They were amused at him, playing with the little boys. A few days later he asked the hag, with gestures, for a bow that her son had just discarded, a man-sized bow of horn. He scavenged for old arrows. The old woman cackled at his marksmanship and called her neighbors to enjoy the fun.

When he could understand words, he could identify his people by their names. The old woman was Greasy Hand, and her daughter was Pretty Calf. The other young woman's name was not clear to him, for the words were not in his vocabulary. The man who had captured him was Yellow Robe.

Once he could understand, he could begin to talk a little, and then he was less lonely. Nobody had been able to see any reason for talking to him, since he would not understand anyway. He asked the old woman, "What is my name?" Until he knew it, he was incomplete. She shrugged to let him know he had none.

He told her in the Crow language, "My name is Horse." He repeated it, and she nodded. After that they called him Horse when they called him anything. Nobody cared except the white man himself.

They trusted him enough to let him stray out of camp, so that he might have got away and, by unimaginable good luck, might have reached a trading post or a fort, but winter was too close. He did not dare leave without a horse; he needed clothing and a better hunting weapon than he had and more certain skill in using it. He did not dare steal, for then they would surely have pursued him, and just as certainly they would have caught him. Remembering the warmth of the home that was waiting in Boston, he settled down for the winter.

On a cold night he crept into the tepee after the others had gone to bed. Even a horse might try to find shelter from the wind. The old woman grumbled, but without conviction. She did not put him out.

They tolerated him, back in the shadows, so long as he did not get in the way.

He began to understand how the family that owned him differed from the others. Fate had been cruel to them. In a short, sharp argument among the old women, one of them derided Greasy Hand by sneering, "You have no relatives!" and Greasy Hand raved for minutes of the deeds of her father and uncles and brothers. And she had had four sons, she reminded her detractor—who answered with scorn, "Where are they?"

WORDS TO OWN

detractor (dē·trak'tər) *n.*: one who makes something seem less important or valuable.

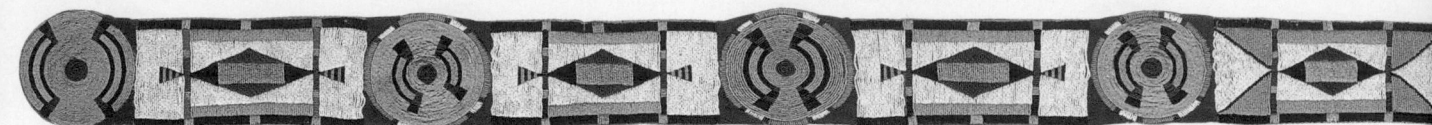

Crow blanket strip (c. 1870–1875). Native American. Buffalo hide, glass beads (63″ x 5.5″). CP-88.

Later the white man found her moaning and whimpering to herself, rocking back and forth on her haunches, staring at her mutilated hands. By that time he understood. A mourner often chopped off a finger joint. Old Greasy Hand had mourned often. For the first time he felt a twinge of pity, but he put it aside as another emotion, like anger, that he could not afford. He thought: What tales I will tell when I get home!

He wrinkled his nose in disdain. The camp stank of animals and meat and rancid grease. He looked down at his naked, shivering legs and was startled, remembering that he was still only a horse.

He could not trust the old woman. She fed him only because a starved slave would die and not be worth boasting about. Just how fitful her temper was he saw on the day when she got tired of stumbling over one of the hundred dogs that infested the camp. This was one of her own dogs, a large, strong one that pulled a baggage travois when the tribe moved camp.

Countless times he had seen her kick at the beast as it lay sleeping in front of the tepee, in her way. The dog always moved, with a yelp, but it always got in the way again. One day she gave the dog its usual kick and then stood scolding at it while the animal rolled its eyes sleepily. The old woman suddenly picked up her ax and cut the dog's head off with one blow. Looking well satisfied with herself, she beckoned her slave to remove the body.

It could have been me, he thought, if I were a dog. But I'm a horse.

His hope of life lay with the girl, Pretty Calf. He set about courting her, realizing how desperately poor he was both in property and honor. He owned no horse, no weapon but the old bow and the battered arrows. He had nothing to give away, and he needed gifts, because he did not dare seduce the girl.

One of the customs of courtship involved sending a gift of horses to a girl's older brother and bestowing much buffalo meat upon her mother. The white man could not wait for some far-off time when he might have either horses or meat to give away. And his courtship had to be secret. It was not for him to stroll past the groups of watchful girls, blowing a flute made of an eagle's wing bone, as the flirtatious young men did.

He could not ride past Pretty Calf's tepee, painted and bedizened;[2] he had no horse, no finery.

Back home, he remembered, I could marry just about any girl I'd want to. But he wasted little time thinking about that. A future was something to be earned.

The most he dared do was wink at Pretty Calf now and then, or state his admiration while she giggled and hid her face. The least he dared do to win his bride was to elope with her, but he had to give her a horse to put the seal of tribal approval on that. And he had no horse until he killed a man to get one. . . .

His opportunity came in early spring. He was casually accepted by that time. He did not belong, but he was amusing to the Crows, like a strange pet, or they would not have fed him through the winter.

His chance came when he was hunting small game with three young boys who were his guards as well as his scornful companions. Rabbits and birds were of no account in a camp well fed on buffalo meat, but they made good targets.

His party walked far that day. All of them at once saw the two horses in a sheltered coulee.[3] The boys and the man crawled forward on their bellies, and then they saw an Indian who lay on the ground, moaning, a lone traveler. From the way the boys inched eagerly forward, Horse knew the man was fair prey—a member of some enemy tribe.

This is the way the captive white man acquired wealth and honor to win a bride and

2. **bedizened:** dressed in a showy way.
3. **coulee** (kōō′lē): ravine.

save his life: He shot an arrow into the sick man, a split second ahead of one of his small companions, and dashed forward to strike the still-groaning man with his bow, to count first coup. Then he seized the hobbled horses.

By the time he had the horses secure, and with them his hope for freedom, the boys had followed, counting coup with gestures and shrieks they had practiced since boyhood, and one of them had the scalp. The white man was grimly amused to see the boy double up with sudden nausea when he had the thing in his hand. . . .

There was a hubbub in the camp when they rode in that evening, two of them on each horse. The captive was noticed. Indians who had ignored him as a slave stared at the brave man who had struck first coup and had stolen horses.

The hubbub lasted all night, as fathers boasted loudly of their young sons' exploits. The white man was called upon to settle an argument between two fierce boys as to which of them had struck second coup and which must be satisfied with third. After much talk that went over his head, he solemnly pointed at the nearest boy. He didn't know which boy it was and didn't care, but the boy did.

The white man had watched warriors in their

Bird's Head Shield (1981) by Kevin Red Star.

Courtesy of the National Museum of the American Indian, Smithsonian Institution, New York. 11/7680.

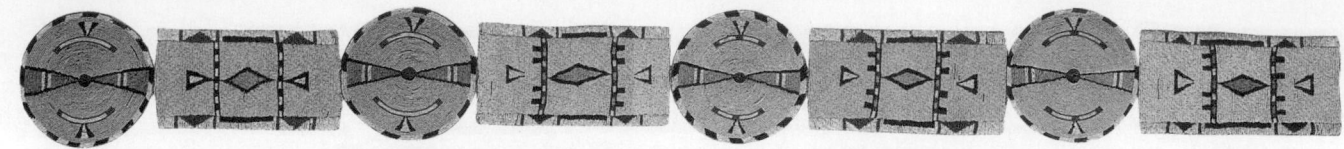

Blackfeet blanket strip (c. 1870–1875). Native American from Montana. Buffalo hide, glass beads (67"x 7"). CP-87.

triumph. He knew what to do. Modesty about achievements had no place among the Crow people. When a man did something big, he told about it.

The white man smeared his face with grease and charcoal. He walked inside the tepee circle, chanting and singing. He used his own language.

"You heathens, you savages," he shouted. "I'm going to get out of here someday! I am going to get away!" The Crow people listened respectfully. In the Crow tongue he shouted, "Horse! I am Horse!" and they nodded.

He had a right to boast, and he had two horses. Before dawn, the white man and his bride were sheltered beyond a far hill, and he was telling her, "I love you, little lady. I love you."

She looked at him with her great dark eyes, and he thought she understood his English words— or as much as she needed to understand.

"You are my treasure," he said, "more precious than jewels, better than fine gold. I am going to call you Freedom."

When they returned to camp two days later, he was bold but worried. His ace, he suspected, might not be high enough in the game he was playing without being sure of the rules. But it served.

Old Greasy Hand raged—but not at him. She complained loudly that her daughter had let herself go too cheap. But the marriage was as good as any Crow marriage. He had paid a horse.

He learned the language faster after that, from Pretty Calf, whom he sometimes called

Crow feather headdress (1890). Native American. Leather, eagle feathers (43.2 cm.). 1988.203.

Photograph © 1995 The Detroit Institute of Arts. Gift of Mr. and Mrs. Richard A. Pohrt. © Robert Hensleigh, photographer, DIA.

Freedom. He learned that his attentive, adoring bride was fourteen years old.

One thing he had not guessed was the difference that being Pretty Calf's husband would make in his relationship to her mother and brother. He had hoped only to make his position a little safer, but he had not expected to be treated with dignity. Greasy Hand no longer spoke to him at all. When the white man spoke to her, his bride murmured in dismay, explaining at great length that he must never do that. There could be no conversation between a man and his mother-in-law. He could not even mention a word that was part of her name.

Having improved his status so magnificently, he felt no need for hurry in getting away. Now that he had a woman, he had as good a chance to be rich as any man. Pretty Calf waited on him; she seldom ran off to play games with other young girls, but took pride in learning from her mother the many women's skills of tanning hides and making clothing and preparing food.

He was no more a horse but a kind of man, a half-Indian, still poor and unskilled but laden with honors, clinging to the buckskin fringes of Crow society.

Escape could wait until he could manage it in comfort, with fit clothing and a good horse, with hunting weapons. Escape could wait until the camp moved near some trading post. He did not plan how he would get home. He dreamed of being there all at once and of telling stories nobody would believe. There was no hurry.

Pretty Calf delighted in educating him. He began to understand tribal arrangements, customs, and why things were as they were. They were that way because they had always been so. His young wife giggled when she told him, in his ignorance, things she had always known. But she did not laugh when her brother's wife was taken by another warrior. She explained that solemnly with words and signs.

Yellow Robe belonged to a society called the Big Dogs. The wife stealer, Cut Neck, belonged to the Foxes. They were fellow tribesmen; they hunted together and fought side by side, but men of one society could take away wives from the other society if they wished, subject to certain limitations.

When Cut Neck rode up to the tepee, laughing and singing, and called to Yellow Robe's wife, "Come out! Come out!" she did as ordered, looking smug as usual, meek and entirely willing. Thereafter she rode beside him in ceremonial processions and carried his coup stick, while his other wife pretended not to care.

"But why?" the white man demanded of his wife, his Freedom. "Why did our brother let his woman go? He sits and smokes and does not speak."

Pretty Calf was shocked at the suggestion. Her brother could not possibly reclaim his woman, she explained. He could not even let her come back if she wanted to—and she probably would want to when Cut Neck tired of her. Yellow Robe could not even admit that his heart was sick. That was the way things were. Deviation meant dishonor.

The woman could have hidden from Cut Neck, she said. She could even have refused to go with him if she had been *ba-wurokee*—a really virtuous woman. But she had been his woman before, for a little while on a berrying expedition, and he had a right to claim her.

There was no sense in it, the white man insisted. He glared at his young wife. "If you go, I will bring you back!" he promised.

She laughed and buried her head against his shoulder. "I will not have to go," she said. "Horse is my first man. There is no hole in my moccasin."

He stroked her hair and said, "*Ba-wurokee.*"

With great daring, she murmured, "*Hayha,*" and when he did not answer, because he did not know what she meant, she drew away, hurt.

"A woman calls her man that if she thinks he will not leave her. Am I wrong?"

The white man held her closer and lied, "Pretty Calf is not wrong. Horse will not leave her. Horse will not take another woman, either." No, he certainly would not. Parting from this one was going to be harder than getting her had been. "*Hayha,*" he murmured. "Freedom."

His conscience irked him, but not very much. Pretty Calf could get another man easily enough when he was gone, and a better provider. His hunting skill was improving, but he was still awkward.

There was no hurry about leaving. He was used to most of the Crow ways and could stand the rest. He was becoming prosperous. He owned five horses. His place in the life of the tribe was secure, such as it was. Three or four young women, including the one who had belonged to Yellow Robe, made advances to him. Pretty Calf took pride in the fact that her man was so attractive.

By the time he had what he needed for a secret journey, the grass grew yellow on the plains and the long cold was close. He was enslaved by the girl he called Freedom and, before the winter ended, by the knowledge that she was carrying his child. . . .

The Big Dog society held a long ceremony in the spring. The white man strolled with his woman along the creek bank, thinking: When I get home I will tell them about the chants and the drumming. Sometime. Sometime.

Pretty Calf would not go to bed when they went back to the tepee.

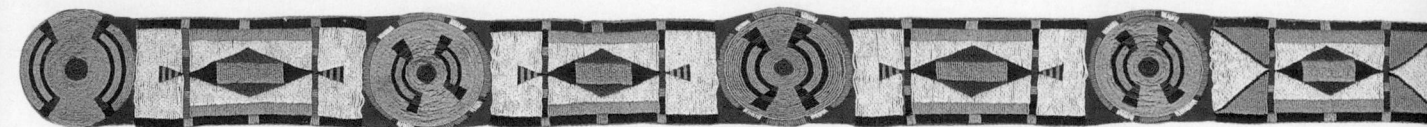

Crow blanket strip (c. 1870–1875). Native American. Buffalo hide, glass beads (63″ x 5.5″). CP-88.

"Wait and find out about my brother," she urged. "Something may happen."

So far as Horse could figure out, the Big Dogs were having some kind of election. He pampered his wife by staying up with her by the fire. Even the old woman, who was a great one for getting sleep when she was not working, prowled around restlessly.

The white man was yawning by the time the noise of the ceremony died down. When Yellow Robe strode in, garish and heathen in his paint and feathers and furs, the women cried out. There was conversation, too fast for Horse to follow, and the old woman wailed once, but her son silenced her with a gruff command.

When the white man went to sleep, he thought his wife was weeping beside him.

The next morning she explained.

"He wears the bearskin belt. Now he can never retreat in battle. He will always be in danger. He will die."

Maybe he wouldn't, the white man tried to convince her. Pretty Calf recalled that some few men had been honored by the bearskin belt, vowed to the highest daring, and had not died. If they lived through the summer, then they were free of it.

"My brother wants to die," she mourned. "His heart is bitter."

Yellow Robe lived through half a dozen clashes with small parties of raiders from hostile tribes. His honors were many. He captured horses in an enemy camp, led two successful raids, counted first coup and snatched a gun from the hand of an enemy tribesman. He wore wolf tails on his moccasins and ermine skins on his shirt, and he fringed his leggings with scalps in token of his glory.

When his mother ventured to suggest, as she did many times, "My son should take a new wife, I need another woman to help me," he ignored her. He spent much time in prayer, alone in the hills or in conference with a medicine man. He fasted and made vows and

kept them. And before he could be free of the heavy honor of the bearskin belt, he went on his last raid.

The warriors were returning from the north just as the white man and two other hunters approached from the south, with buffalo and elk meat dripping from the bloody hides tied on their <u>restive</u> ponies. One of the hunters grunted, and they stopped to watch a rider on the hill north of the tepee circle.

The rider dismounted, held up a blanket and dropped it. He repeated the gesture.

The hunters murmured dismay. "Two! Two men dead!" They rode fast into the camp, where there was already wailing.

A messenger came down from the war party on the hill. The rest of the party delayed to paint their faces for mourning and for victory. One of the two dead men was Yellow Robe. They had put his body in a cave and walled it in with rocks. The other man died later, and his body was in a tree.

There was blood on the ground before the tepee to which Yellow Robe would return no more. His mother, with her hair chopped short, sat in the doorway, rocking back and forth on her haunches, wailing her heartbreak. She cradled one mutilated hand in the other. She had cut off another finger joint.

Pretty Calf had cut off chunks of her long hair and was crying as she gashed her arms with a knife. The white man tried to take the knife away, but she protested so <u>piteously</u> that he let her do as she wished. He was sickened with the lot of them.

Savages! he thought. Now I will go back! I'll go hunting alone, and I'll keep on going.

But he did not go just yet, because he was the

WORDS TO OWN

restive (res′tiv) *adj.*: restless; unsettled.
piteously (pit′ē·əs·lē) *adv.*: in a way that arouses pity or compassion.

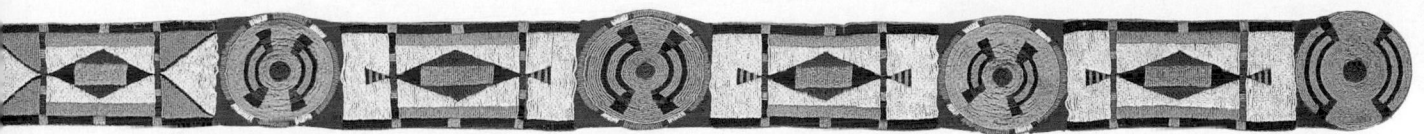

only hunter in the lodge of the two grieving women, one of them old and the other pregnant with his child.

In their mourning, they made him a pauper again. Everything that meant comfort, wealth, and safety they sacrificed to the spirits because of the death of Yellow Robe. The tepee, made of seventeen fine buffalo hides, the furs that should have kept them warm, the white deerskin dress, trimmed with elk teeth, that Pretty Calf loved so well, even their tools and Yellow Robe's weapons—everything but his sacred medicine objects— they left there on the prairie, and the whole camp moved away. Two of his best horses were killed as a sacrifice, and the women gave away the rest.

They had no shelter. They would have no tepee of their own for two months at least of mourning, and then the women would have to tan hides to make it. Meanwhile, they could live in temporary huts made of willows, covered with skins given them in pity by their friends. They could have lived with relatives, but Yellow Robe's women had no relatives.

The white man had not realized until then how terrible a thing it was for a Crow to have no kinfolk. No wonder old Greasy Hand had only stumps for fingers. She had mourned, from one year to the next, for everyone she had ever loved. She had no one left but her daughter, Pretty Calf.

Horse was furious at their foolishness. It had been bad enough for him, a captive, to be naked as a horse and poor as a slave, but that was because his captors had stripped him. These women had voluntarily given up everything they needed.

He was too angry at them to sleep in the willow hut. He lay under a sheltering tree. And on the third night of the mourning he made his plans. He had a knife and a bow. He would go after meat, taking two horses. And he would not come back. There were, he realized, many things he was not going to tell when he got back home.

In the willow hut, Pretty Calf cried out. He heard rustling there, and the old woman's querulous voice.

Some twenty hours later his son was born, two months early, in the tepee of a skilled medicine woman. The child was born without breath, and the mother died before the sun went down.

The white man was too shocked to think whether he should mourn, or how he should mourn. The old woman screamed until she was voiceless. Piteously she approached him, bent and trembling, blind with grief. She held out her knife and he took it.

Crow shield with cover (c. 1865).

Buffalo Bill Historical Center, Cody, Wyoming. Chandler-Pohrt Collection, gift of Mr. and Mrs. Edson W. Spencer. NA.108.105.

She spread out her hands and shook her head. If she cut off any more finger joints, she could do no more work. She could not afford any more lasting signs of grief.

The white man said, "All right! All right!" between his teeth. He hacked his arms with the knife and stood watching the blood run down. It was little enough to do for Pretty Calf, for little Freedom.

Now there is nothing to keep me, he realized. When I get home, I must not let them see the scars.

He looked at Greasy Hand, hideous in her

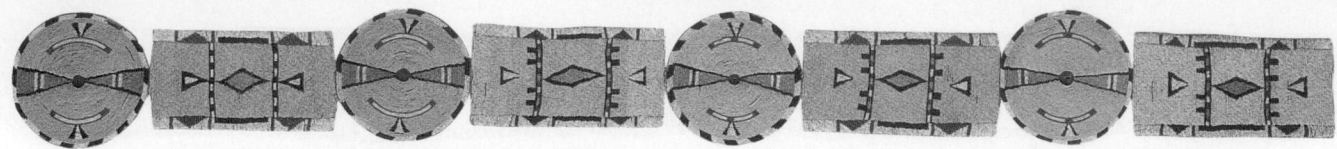

Blackfeet blanket strip (c. 1870–1875). Native American from Montana. Buffalo hide, glass beads (67″ x 7″). CP-87.

Photograph © 1995 The Detroit Institute of Arts. Richard and Marion Pohrt Collection.

grief-burdened age, and thought: I really am free now! When a wife dies, her husband has no more duty toward her family. Pretty Calf had told him so, long ago, when he wondered why a certain man moved out of one tepee and into another.

The old woman, of course, would be a scavenger. There was one other with the tribe, an ancient crone who had no relatives, toward whom no one felt any responsibility. She lived on food thrown away by the more fortunate. She slept in shelters that she built with her own knotted hands. She plodded wearily at the end of the procession when the camp moved. When she stumbled, nobody cared. When she died, nobody would miss her.

Tomorrow morning, the white man decided, I will go.

His mother-in-law's sunken mouth quivered. She said one word, questioningly. She said, "*Eero-oshay?*" She said, "Son?"

Blinking, he remembered. When a wife died, her husband was free. But her mother, who had ignored him with dignity, might if she wished ask him to stay. She invited him by calling him Son, and he accepted by answering Mother.

Greasy Hand stood before him, bowed with years, withered with unceasing labor, loveless and childless, scarred with grief. But with all her burdens, she still loved life enough to beg it from him, the only person she had any right to ask. She was stripping herself of all she had left, her pride.

He looked eastward across the prairie. Two thousand miles away was home. The old woman would not live forever. He could afford to wait, for he was young. He could afford to be magnanimous, for he knew he was a man. He gave her the answer. "*Eegya,*" he said. "Mother."

He went home three years later. He explained no more than to say, "I lived with Crows for a while. It was some time before I could leave. They called me Horse."

He did not find it necessary either to apologize or to boast, because he was the equal of any man on earth.

MEET THE WRITER

Kills-Both-Places

Dorothy M. Johnson (1905–1984) grew up in Montana and then moved east. Though she tried hard to be an Easterner, she finally returned to Montana in the 1950s. At this point, according to Jack Schaefer (see his statement on page 166), she began to write "the stories that only Dorothy Johnson could write."

Johnson was welcomed into the Blackfoot tribe in Montana as an honorary member. Her tribal name reflects her double identity as a white woman and a member of the tribe. The Blackfeet called her Kills-Both-Places.

From Print to Film

Johnson's stories "The Hanging Tree," "The Man Who Shot Liberty Valance," and "A Man Called Horse" were all made into movies.

MAKING MEANINGS

First Thoughts

1. Did you want Horse to get home to Boston, or did you want him to stay with the Crows? Why?

Shaping Interpretations

2. By the end of the story, Horse has changed. In your own words, explain what he discovers about himself—and other people—in his years with the Crows. How do you think becoming a "horse" helped him become a man?

3. Name at least two incidents in the story that remind us that all people share certain feelings.

4. Which character showed you most forcefully what the human spirit is capable of? Explain.

Connecting with the Text

5. How did you respond to the ways the Crows "counted coup" and to how a grieving mother chopped off a joint of one of her fingers for each dead child? How do you think the writer wants you to feel about the Crows?

Reviewing the Text

a. List the few details we are given about the Boston **setting**. Why is the man unhappy there?

b. In contrast to Boston, we are told a great deal about the Crow **setting**. Describe at least five customs of the Crow culture that you learned about in this story.

c. How does the man become a "horse"?

d. Name the two things that happen one day to make Horse think that he might become a man again.

e. Why does Horse marry Pretty Calf? What happens to his status in the Crow community after his marriage?

Extending the Text

6. This could be described as a story about a clash of cultures. What experiences in today's world might result in similar conflicts—where a person must adapt to a new culture? What movies have focused on this theme?

Challenging the Text

7. All that we learn and experience in this story, we learn through the perspective of Horse. At what points in the story do you think you are hearing about Horse's prejudices or perceptions, not necessarily the writer's? How would various episodes of the story differ if we were told how Greasy Hand or Pretty Calf thought or felt?

8. Is the writer fair to all her characters, or did you feel she favors some characters and disapproves of others? Cite passages from the text to support your responses. (Be sure to check the notes in your Reader's Log.)

CHOICES: Building Your Portfolio

Writer's Notebook

1. Collecting Ideas for an Observational Essay

Putting a character in a setting.
In the Writer's Workshop on page 194, you'll write an essay about a person you've observed. You should by now have notes about people you might focus on. Select a person you're especially interested in and think about that person's setting. For a doctor, it might be a hospital; for your grandmother, it might be her room with all the old photographs. To get started, make a diagram like the one shown here. Remember that setting can include clothing, customs, and beliefs, as well as physical surroundings. You may find as you gather notes that you discover something new about the person you've chosen.

Creative Writing

2. Horse's Journal

Imagine that the man called Horse is home in Boston and that he writes an entry in his journal describing his first days back in his "own world." What does he think of his own culture now? Is he critical of any customs? Does he miss anything about the Crows? Write a paragraph that Horse might enter in his journal. Have Horse use the first-person pronoun *I*.

Research/Speaking

3. Exploring Crow Culture

Has spending time in a Crow camp made you curious to know more about the Crows? They were not always a nomadic people. They became buffalo hunters only after moving to the Plains in the eighteenth century. Work with a group of classmates to research the history and culture of the Crows (they call themselves Apsaroke). First outline your areas of interest. For example, you might explore their spiritual beliefs and ceremonies, their distinctive crafts and arts, or the organization of their society. Present your report to the class and invite questions from your audience.

Crow lance case (c. 1890).
Buffalo Bill Historical Center, Cody, Wyoming. NA 108.95.

Speaking and Listening

4. Captivity Stories

Some modern-day true captivity stories have been on the best-seller lists in recent years. Choose a captivity story you have read in the past—or read a new one—and share your findings about it. Prepare a review of the story in which you summarize the reason for the captivity, the main events of the captivity, and how the captive felt about the jailers. How was this captivity different from Horse's? When you are satisfied with your review, you might want to tape it for classmates to listen to. Instead of a book, you may wish to compare Horse's captivity with a movie about the subject. If you wish to read about an American Indian held in a kind of captivity by whites, try *Ishi in Two Worlds* by Theodora Kroeber (University of California).

The diagram (on notebook paper):

Dr. Kimmel

Setting: hospital

smell of medicine
green corridors
shiny floors
green shirt
plastic booties
everyone's respectful

LANGUAGE LINK   MINI-LESSON

Handbook of Literary Terms
H E L P

See Connotation, Imagery.

Technology
H E L P

See Language Workshop CD-ROM. *Key word entry: modifiers.*

Style: Vivid Modifiers—A Definite Choice

Using precise, evocative modifiers is often the most immediate way of creating a clear picture of a character's looks and actions. In the following descriptions from "A Man Called Horse," Johnson's precise adjectives and adverbs are the "brush strokes" that add detail to her word pictures. The modifiers are underscored.

1. "A <u>scrawny, shrieking, eternally busy old</u> woman with <u>ragged graying</u> hair threw a chunk of meat on the grass, and he fought the dogs for it."

2. "He applied it <u>gingerly</u> to his <u>bruised</u> and <u>sun-seared</u> body."

3. "The younger sister had <u>bright, wandering</u> eyes."

Modifiers must be used carefully. Too many modifiers can result in a passage that is "overwritten." (Some critics call such overblown descriptions "purple prose.") For example, Johnson doesn't need a modifier in this sentence to describe how the boys sounded. The verb *snickered* is vivid enough:

"... they <u>snickered</u> when he missed."

In this sentence no adjective is necessary to modify the very precise noun *hag:*

"A few days later he asked the <u>hag</u>, with gestures, for a bow that her son had just discarded. . . ."

Try It Out

➤ Rewrite each of the sentences at the left, replacing Johnson's modifiers with adjectives and adverbs of your own. Try to find modifiers that will give completely different pictures of the characters and their actions. Be sure to compare your descriptions with those of your classmates.

➤ Analyze a piece of your own writing to see how skillfully you have used modifiers. Put a circle around each adjective and adverb, and put a box around each noun or verb that you have left unmodified. Would a modifier help make these nouns and verbs more specific, or do you feel they are vivid enough? Do you have too many circles on your paper—or are you satisfied that those modifiers are just right?

VOCABULARY   HOW TO OWN A WORD

WORD BANK

forestalled
docile
detractor
restive
piteously

What's the Difference?

Write your answers to these questions.

1. What is the difference between *restive* and *restful*?
2. What is the difference between *docile* and *disobedient*?
3. What is the difference between *forestalled* and *forewarned*?
4. What is the difference between *piteously* and *pityingly*?
5. What is the difference between *detractor* and *defender*?

Reading Focus

The Invisible Children

Here, Sandra Cisneros gives us just the quickest glimpse of a boy she names Salvador. There are many "Salvadors" in our world. Sometimes people barely notice these children. The impression they make on most of us is as fleeting as this little story itself.

Quickwrite

In your Reader's Log write a few notes about any children you can think of—in your neighborhood or in the world news—whose difficult lives or small acts of courage go almost unnoticed.

Elements of Literature

A Little Portrait

This picture of Salvador is a vignette (vin·yet′), a very very short literary sketch written in a poetic style. *Vignette* is a French word, referring to a portrait that is made to blur gently into the surrounding color at the edges.

> A **vignette** is a very brief literary sketch, suggestive and poetic in style.

Salvador whose name the teacher cannot remember.

Salvador
Late or Early

Sandra Cisneros

Salvador with eyes the color of caterpillar, Salvador of the crooked hair and crooked teeth, Salvador whose name the teacher cannot remember, is a boy who is no one's friend, runs along somewhere in that vague direction where homes are the color of bad weather, lives behind a raw wood doorway, shakes the sleepy brothers awake, ties their shoes, combs their hair with water, feeds them milk and cornflakes from a tin cup in the dim dark of the morning.

Salvador, late or early, sooner or later arrives with the string of younger brothers ready. Helps his mama, who is busy with the business of the baby. Tugs the arms of Cecilio, Arturito, makes them hurry, because today, like yesterday, Arturito has dropped the cigar box of crayons, has let go the hundred little fingers of red, green, yellow, blue, and nub of black sticks that tumble and spill over and beyond the asphalt puddles until the crossing-guard lady holds back the blur of traffic for Salvador to collect them again.

Salvador inside that wrinkled shirt, inside the throat that must clear itself and apologize each time it speaks, inside that forty-pound body of boy with its geography of scars, its history of hurt, limbs stuffed with feathers and rags, in what part of the eyes, in what part of the heart, in that cage of the chest where something throbs with both fists and knows only what Salvador knows, inside that body too small to contain the hundred balloons of happiness, the single guitar of grief, is a boy like any other disappearing out the door, beside the schoolyard gate, where he has told his brothers they must wait. Collects the hands of Cecilio and Arturito, scuttles off dodging the many schoolyard colors, the elbows and wrists crisscrossing, the several shoes running. Grows small and smaller to the eye, dissolves into the bright horizon, flutters in the air before disappearing like a memory of kites,

MEET THE WRITER

Swan Keeper

Sandra Cisneros (1954–   ) was born in inner-city Chicago to a Mexican father and a Mexican American mother. It is no wonder, given her six boisterous brothers, that Cisneros identified with the lone sister in the fairy tale "Six Swans." (The name *Cisneros* means "swan keeper.") Cisneros graduated from Loyola University in Chicago and the Writers' Workshop at the University of Iowa. Most recently, she has lived in San Antonio, Texas.

Cisneros gives readings of her work all over the country. To see her read is to watch an actress at work. Standing alone at the podium, a tiny figure often wearing

who are you, little i

E. E. Cummings

who are you, little i

(five or six years old)
peering from some high

window; at the gold

of november sunset

(and feeling: that if day
has to become night

this is a beautiful way)

cowboy boots and huge earrings, Cisneros can "fill" the stage with people who speak in her stories.

When asked about her writing, Cisneros recalled a trip to Falfurrias, Texas, where she visited the shrine of a local healer:

66 While I was visiting the shrine, I discovered all of these little notes that people had pinned there—as thanks for something, or as petitions for something. And I was so overwhelmed by the power of the writing. I mean, mine is a community that supposedly can't write, especially the poor, and here was the most beautiful, most moving writing that I have ever read. These were people who weren't trying to pass an English class, or get their GED—they were just writing from their heart. And when your writing is unselfconscious, when it comes from your heart, that's when it's powerful. 99

More by Cisneros

If you would like to meet some of the people that fill the stage at a Cisneros reading, read *The House on Mango Street* (Vintage Books). The vignettes in this book read like a series of journal entries written by a young girl named Esperanza. "In English my name means hope," Esperanza remarks in the first entry. "In Spanish it means too many letters." Cisneros' second book, *Woman Hollering Creek* (Random House), is a collection of her short stories, including some about Latino children whose voices are unmistakably authentic and often touchingly funny.

MAKING MEANINGS

First Thoughts

1. This little sketch about Salvador leaves a great deal unsaid. What questions would you like to ask Sandra Cisneros if you could talk to her?

Shaping Interpretations

2. What exactly do you know from this vignette about the **character** of Salvador and his **setting**?

3. What can you infer, or guess, is the cause of Salvador's "geography of scars" and "history of hurt"?

4. What could it be that "throbs with both fists and knows only what Salvador knows"?

5. How does Cisneros make you feel about Salvador when she describes his eyes as being the color of caterpillars? Think of another comparison that would have made you feel differently about Salvador.

6. Cisneros' short little story and Capote's longer story (page 145) both end with the same **image**. What are the final images in each story? Do they have the same effect on you? Try to explain why, or why not.

> **Reviewing the Text**
>
> Describe the events of Salvador's morning as if he himself were explaining them to another child or an adult. Start with his first action and go on until you have summed up his school day.

Connecting with the Text

7. Try to describe the emotional impact this story had on you. Share your response with your group or with one other reader.

Extending the Text

8. Look back at your Quickwrite. What other "invisible children" could be compared with Salvador?

CHOICES: Building Your Portfolio

Writer's Notebook

1. Collecting Ideas for an Observational Essay

Focus on actions. Salvador seems to be in perpetual motion. If you want to get an idea of how many actions we actually watch Salvador carrying out, list the story's verbs, beginning with "runs" and continuing in the first paragraph with "lives," "shakes," "ties," "combs," "feeds." In fact, Cisneros eventually drops the subject of her sentences (Salvador) and just opens with verbs—with Salvador's actions. You should by now have some notes on a person you might want to write an observational essay about

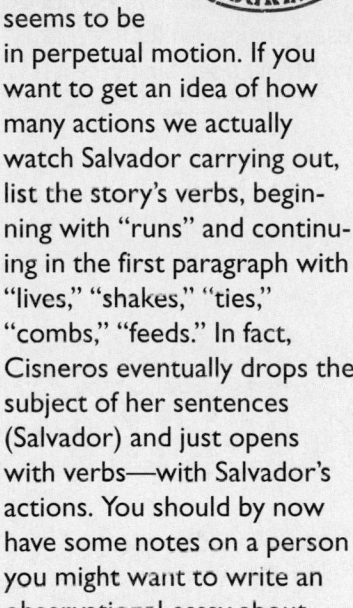

Aunt Kathy
- walks fast
- mumbles to herself
- carries armloads of books and papers
- sometimes skips

Uncle Jack
- careful in his speech
- easily amused
- never stays angry very long

(see the assignment on page 194). Pull out your notes and make a list of specific actions you want to focus on. Concentrate, as Cisneros does, on the things your subject does in a single day or focus on one particular action that reveals your character's nature.

Speaking/ A Group Project

2. A Dramatic Reading

In a group of three (one person for each paragraph), prepare Salvador's story for an oral reading. As a reader, you will have to decide when you will pause, when you will raise or lower your voice, when you will read fast or slow. You will also have to decide how you will present your reading to the class. Some dramatic readings are done in costume. Some readers sit on stools; others stand. After your presentation write a brief reflection on your experience.

Critical Writing

3. A Character Analysis

Suppose you are a counselor in Salvador's school and you must prepare a report on him. All you know about him is what Cisneros has given you. Open your analysis with

a general statement telling what your feelings are for Salvador and what you think his future will be. Be sure to support your analysis of Salvador with details from the text.

Problem Solving/ Community Extension

4. A Panel Discussion

What responsibilities do communities and schools have to children like Salvador? Working with a group, form a panel of "experts"—a student, a parent, a teacher, and a community member. Plan the panel's agenda: What questions or topics will the panel focus on? How long can each panel member talk? How should each "expert" prepare for the discussion? Someone should record the discussion and summarize its conclusions.

Creative Writing

5. Salvador's Poem

Suppose someone asked Salvador: "who are you, little i?" (See E. E. Cummings's poem on page 185.) Write Salvador's answer. You might have Salvador answer in a poem called "i am salvador," using each letter of his name as the first letter of the first word of each line.

Background

The events in this autobiographical essay take place around 1915, in Warsaw, Poland, where most Jews lived in the very old Jewish quarter. At 10 Krochmalna Street, where Isaac Bashevis Singer lived, families shared an outhouse in the courtyard and used kerosene lamps for light. There was no central heating in the dark, old apartments.

A Dialogue with the Text

Be sure to track your responses to this essay in

your Reader's Log. Pay particular attention to passages that seem important or interesting to you. How do details and events in this essay make you feel? What, if anything, does Singer teach you?

The Washwoman

Isaac Bashevis Singer

The old woman did not want to become a burden.

Our home had little contact with Gentiles.[1] The only Gentile in the building was the janitor. Fridays he would come for a tip, his "Friday money." He remained standing at the door, took off his hat, and my mother gave him six groschen.[2]

Besides the janitor there were also the Gentile washwomen who came to the house to fetch our laundry. My story is about one of these.

She was a small woman, old and wrinkled. When she started washing for us, she was already past seventy. Most Jewish women of her age were sickly, weak, broken in body. All the old women in our street had bent backs and leaned on sticks when they walked. But this washwoman, small and thin as she was, possessed a strength that came from generations of peasant forebears. Mother would count out to her a bundle of laundry that had accumulated over several weeks. She would lift the unwieldy pack, load it on her narrow shoulders, and carry it the long way home. She lived on Krochmalna Street too, but at the other end, near the Wola section. It must have been a walk of an hour and a half.

1. **Gentiles** (jen′·tīlz): persons who are not Jewish.
2. **groschen** (grō′·shən): European coin or coins.

Torah binder (1834). Wimpel of Gershon, son of Abraham Seltz (detail 56.341). Germany. Undyed linen, polychrome pigments.

would steal the laundry. The wrung-out wash had to be carried up to the attic and hung on clotheslines. In the winter it would become as brittle as glass and almost break when touched. And there was always a to-do with other housewives and washwomen who wanted the attic clotheslines for their own use. Only God knows all the old woman had to endure each time she did a wash!

She could have begged at the church door or entered a home for the penniless and aged. But there was in her a certain pride and love of labor with which many Gentiles have been blessed. The old woman did not want to become a burden, and so she bore her burden.

My mother spoke a little Polish, and the old woman would talk with her about many things. She was especially fond of me and used to say I looked like Jesus. She repeated this every time she came, and Mother would frown and whisper to herself, her lips barely moving, "May her words be scattered in the wilderness."

The woman had a son who was rich. I no longer remember what sort of business he had. He was ashamed of his mother, the washwoman, and never came to see her. Nor did he ever give her a groschen. The old woman told this without rancor. One day the son was married. It seemed that he had made a good match. The wedding took place in a church. The son had not invited the old mother to his wedding, but she went to the church and waited at the steps to see her son lead the "young lady" to the altar.

The story of the faithless son left a deep impression on my mother. She talked about it for weeks and months. It was an affront not only to the old woman but to the entire institution of motherhood. Mother would argue, "Nu,

She would bring the laundry back about two weeks later. My mother had never been so pleased with any washwoman. Every piece of linen sparkled like polished silver. Every piece was neatly ironed. Yet she charged no more than the others. She was a real find. Mother always had her money ready, because it was too far for the old woman to come a second time.

Laundering was not easy in those days. The old woman had no faucet where she lived but had to bring in the water from a pump. For the linens to come out so clean, they had to be scrubbed thoroughly in a washtub, rinsed with washing soda, soaked, boiled in an enormous pot, starched, then ironed. Every piece was handled ten times or more. And the drying! It could not be done outside because thieves does it pay to make sacrifices for children? The mother uses up her last strength, and he does not even know the meaning of loyalty."

And she would drop dark hints to the effect that she was not certain of her own children: Who knows what they would do some day? This, however, did not prevent her from dedicating her life to us. If there was any delicacy in the house, she would put it aside for the children and invent all sorts of excuses and reasons why she herself did not want to taste it. She knew charms that went back to ancient times, and she used expressions she had inherited from generations of devoted mothers and grandmothers. If one of the children complained of a pain, she would say, "May I be your ransom and may you outlive my bones!" Or she would say, "May I be the atonement for the least of your fingernails!" When we ate, she used to say, "Health and marrow in your bones!" The day before the new moon she gave us a kind of candy that was said to prevent parasitic worms. If one of us had something in his eye, Mother would lick the eye clean with her tongue. She also fed us rock candy against coughs, and from time to time she would take us to be blessed against the evil eye. This did not prevent her from studying *The Duties of the Heart, The Book of the Covenant,* and other serious philosophic works.

But to return to the washwoman. That winter was a harsh one. The streets were in the grip of a bitter cold. No matter how much we heated our stove, the windows were covered with frostwork and decorated with icicles. The newspapers reported that people were dying of the cold. Coal became dear. The winter had become so severe that parents stopped sending children to cheder,[3] and even the Polish schools were closed.

On one such day the washwoman, now nearly eighty years old, came to our house. A good deal of laundry had accumulated during the past weeks. Mother gave her a pot of tea to warm herself, as well as some bread. The old woman sat on a kitchen chair, trembling and shaking, and warmed her hands against the teapot. Her fingers

were gnarled from work, and perhaps from arthritis too. Her fingernails were strangely white. These hands spoke of the stubbornness of mankind, of the will to work not only as one's strength permits but beyond the limits of one's power. Mother counted and wrote down the list: men's undershirts, women's vests, long-legged drawers, bloomers, petticoats, shifts, featherbed covers, pillowcases, sheets, and the men's fringed garments. Yes, the Gentile woman washed these holy garments as well.

The bundle was big, bigger than usual. When the woman placed it on her shoulders, it covered her completely. At first she swayed, as though she were about to fall under the load. But an inner obstinacy seemed to call out: No, you may not fall. A donkey may permit himself to fall under his burden, but not a human being, the crown of creation.

It was fearful to watch the old woman staggering out with the enormous pack, out into the frost, where the snow was dry as salt and the air was filled with dusty white whirlwinds, like goblins dancing in the cold. Would the old woman ever reach Wola?

She disappeared, and Mother sighed and prayed for her.

Usually the woman brought back the wash after two or, at the most, three weeks. But three weeks passed, then four and five, and nothing was heard of the old woman. We remained without linens. The cold had become even more intense. The telephone wires were now as thick as ropes. The branches of the trees looked like glass. So much snow had fallen that the streets had become uneven, and sleds were able to glide down many streets as on the slopes of a hill. Kindhearted people lit fires in the streets for vagrants to warm themselves and roast potatoes in, if they had any to roast.

For us the washwoman's absence was a catastrophe. We needed the laundry. We did not even know the woman's address. It seemed certain that she had collapsed, died. Mother declared she had had a premonition, as the old woman left our house that last time, that we would never see our things again. She found some old torn shirts and washed and mended them. We

3. **cheder** (khā′·dər): Hebrew school for religious instruction.

Destruction of the Ghetto, Kiev (1919) by Abraham Manievich. Oil on canvas (198.1 cm. x 188 cm.).

a priest. Someone had informed the son, and he had contributed money for a coffin and for the funeral. But the Almighty had not yet wanted to take this pain-racked soul to himself. She began to feel better, she became well, and as soon as she was able to stand on her feet once more, she resumed her washing. Not just ours, but the wash of several other families too.

"I could not rest easy in my bed because of the wash," the old woman explained. "The wash would not let me die."

"With the help of God you will live to be a hundred and twenty," said my mother, as a benediction.

"God forbid! What good would such a long life be? The work becomes harder and harder . . . my strength is leaving me . . . I do not want to be a burden on anyone!" The old woman muttered and crossed herself and raised her eyes toward heaven.

Fortunately there was some money in the house, and Mother counted out what she owed. I had a strange feeling: The coins in the old woman's washed-out hands seemed to become as worn and clean and pious as she herself was. She blew on the coins and tied them in a kerchief. Then she left, promising to return in a few weeks for a new load of wash.

But she never came back. The wash she had returned was her last effort on this earth. She had been driven by an indomitable will to return the property to its rightful owners, to fulfill the task she had undertaken.

And now at last her body, which had long been no more than a shard[4] supported only by the force of honesty and duty, had fallen. Her soul passed into those spheres where all holy souls meet, regardless of the roles they played on this earth, in whatever tongue, of whatever creed. I cannot imagine paradise without this Gentile washwoman. I cannot even conceive of a world where there is no recompense for such effort.

mourned, both for the laundry and for the old, toilworn woman who had grown close to us through the years she had served us so faithfully.

More than two months passed. The frost had subsided, and then a new frost had come, a new wave of cold. One evening, while Mother was sitting near the kerosene lamp mending a shirt, the door opened and a small puff of steam, followed by a gigantic bundle, entered. Under the bundle tottered the old woman, her face as white as a linen sheet. A few wisps of white hair straggled out from beneath her shawl. Mother uttered a half-choked cry. It was as though a corpse had entered the room. I ran toward the old woman and helped her unload her pack. She was even thinner now, more bent. Her face had become more gaunt, and her head shook from side to side as though she were saying no. She could not utter a clear word, but mumbled something with her sunken mouth and pale lips.

After the old woman had recovered somewhat, she told us that she had been ill, very ill. Just what her illness was, I cannot remember. She had been so sick that someone had called a doctor, and the doctor had sent for

4. **shard** (shärd): fragment, as of a clay pot.

MEET THE WRITER

The Storyteller

Grandson of two rabbis and son of another, **Isaac Bashevis Singer** (1904–1991) was born in Radzymin, near Warsaw, Poland. Because his family wanted him to continue the tradition, Singer studied to be a rabbi, but he soon discovered that his real love was writing.

He began writing in Hebrew. Later he switched to Yiddish, the language spoken by many Eastern European Jews, and wrote for the Yiddish press in Poland. In 1935, Singer became alarmed at the rise of antisemitism in Europe, and he sailed to America. There he eventually married, became a U.S. citizen, and settled in New York City.

Success as a novelist and short-story writer came late in his life—when he was forty-five. Eventually, in 1978, Singer was awarded the Nobel Prize for literature. Despite his great success as a writer, Singer continued his

practice of rewriting. He once told an interviewer that as a writer he considered the wastebasket one of his friends.

Singer saw himself as a storyteller (see also his comments about storytelling on page 2):

66 The idea that literature consists only of a man revealing his inner self and complaining about his complexes is a modern kind of idea, and the truth is that people are not interested. If I sit down and write a book about how unhappy I am that I did not marry my first love, only my second love, and there is no plot, the reader will say 'Who cares?' There has to be a story. 99

No Complaining Here

If you enjoy Singer's storytelling, read the book from which "The Washwoman" is taken, *A Day of Pleasure* (Farrar, Straus & Giroux). Or try *The Family Moskat* (Farrar, Straus & Giroux), a novel about several generations of a Jewish family living in the Warsaw Ghetto.

FINDING COMMON GROUND

1. For you, what was "The Washwoman" about? Take a quick look at this list and make an impulsive decision. Don't reflect; just decide—what was the major topic in this story?

work	dignity
acceptance of people who are different	generosity
	faith
pride	God's love for everyone

2. Now take a few minutes to think about the topic you chose. Why did you identify that as the central topic of the essay? Find a passage or two in the story that might have caused you to focus on this idea. Write brief discussion notes elaborating on your thoughts about the passage you identified. Before you write your notes, be sure to check the responses you recorded in your Reader's Log.

3. Finally, meet with a few other readers and compare your responses. As you talk, be alert for differences of opinion. As the discussion draws to a close, note the questions you've raised and the points you'd like to discuss further with the entire class.

READ ON

Crisis in a Small Town

Scout Finch is only a child—eight years old. She's vulnerable and funny. But it is her intelligence and sensitivity that will touch you in Harper Lee's *To Kill a Mockingbird* (Warner). There's a trial in this Pulitzer Prize–winning novel that you're not likely to forget. Set in a small Southern town, Lee's novel is a riveting story of race relations.

Man's Best Friend

Can you imagine enduring a temperature of −50°F—or lower—on a dog sled that covers a thousand-mile course? Gary Paulsen brings an experience like this to life in his book *Woodsong* (Puffin). In this account of his experiences on the Iditarod, a dog-sled race through Alaska, Paulsen whisks us along on his long and lonely journey. His only friends are a team of dogs, and they turn out to be the best friends he has ever had.

Taking Her Place

Charlayne Hunter-Gault was the first African American woman to attend the University of Georgia. As you'll see in her autobiography, *In My Place* (Farrar, Straus & Giroux), it wasn't easy. After the triumph of gaining admittance came the pain of prejudice. Even though she was enrolled, there were classmates and professors who didn't want her there. Was it worth the struggle? Hunter-Gault explains why her answer is a definite yes.

Facing the World

Growing up, most of us think about our looks: our clothes, our hair, our growing bodies, our faces. But Lucy Grealy had a rare type of cancer that made her think about her face even more than most young people do. Her *Autobiography of a Face* (Houghton Mifflin) is the story of a girl who found herself suddenly different at the age of nine. It's the story of a girl struggling to learn to accept and love herself. Lucy Grealy has something to teach the world—about what it values and what it ridicules.

Writer's Workshop

Technology HELP

See Writer's Workshop 2 CD-ROM. *Assignment: Observational Writing.*

ASSIGNMENT

Write a description of a person you can observe, so that your reader has the experience of "seeing" the subject too.

AIM

To give information, to express your feelings.

AUDIENCE

Your classmates or readers of a magazine of student writing. (You choose.)

DESCRIPTIVE WRITING

OBSERVATIONAL ESSAY

Observational writing is used in many ways. It can be used in a character profile, a journal entry, a news report, or a firsthand account in a history book. In this workshop you'll focus on writing a close observation of a person.

In your observation you'll use **description** (the kind of writing that includes sensory details to help the reader see, hear, smell, taste, or touch someone or something) and perhaps **narration** (the kind of writing that tells about a series of related events).

Prewriting

1. Review Your Writer's Notebook

You've already made some Writer's Notebook entries about various subjects, their appearance, their setting, their actions, their dialogue. Look over these notes now. You can make changes or add to them; or you may want to choose a new subject for this paper.

2. Brainstorm or Cluster or Freewrite

If your notebook entries haven't helped you identify a subject, choose a partner and brainstorm ideas for possible subjects. Or prepare clusters of possible subjects and see which ones offer the best possibilities. Think of people you know at home, at school, at work, on the bus, in the store, on the street. List all the subjects you can think of. Then look over your subject possibilities, and choose the one you think you'll most enjoy developing.

3. You're the Camera

Take notes as you observe your subject closely. Choose someone you know well who won't mind your observation and note taking (a neighbor taking out the garbage, friends in the lunchroom, family members having breakfast). Focus on all kinds of **sensory details,** not just visual details. As an observer, you see things from a definite viewpoint, or position. Where are you in relation to your subject? When you zoom in for a closer look, what do you see?

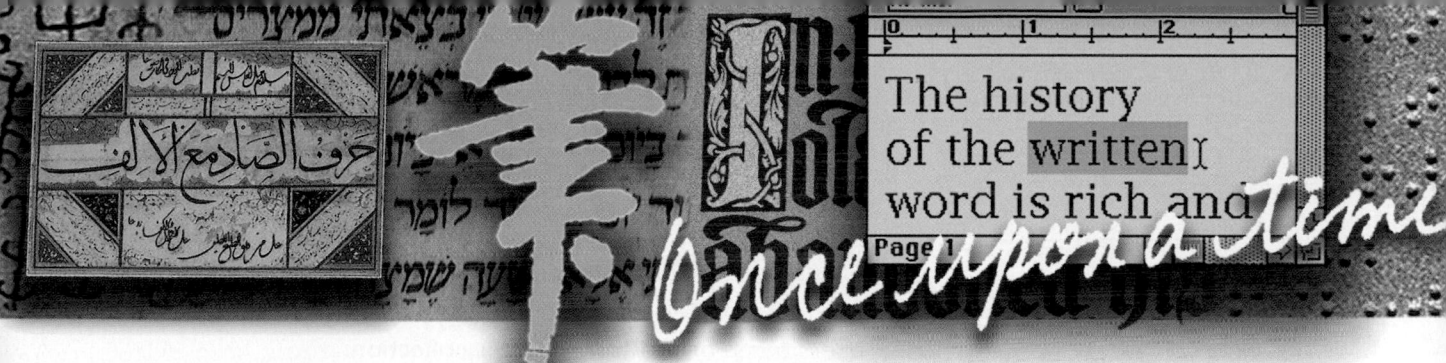

The history
of the written
word is rich and

Page 1

Once upon a time

4. Draw What You See

Newspaper writers often draw a quick sketch as another way of taking notes. A sketch will help you focus on details of the subject's appearance and setting.

5. Describe the Context or Location

Artists and photographers know that people aren't seen as cutouts; they're part of a whole scene. So establish a location, or **setting,** for your subject at the moment you're describing him or her. On page 145, for example, Truman Capote tells you right off to imagine a morning in late November and to consider the kitchen of a spreading old house in a country town.

Drafting
1. Show, Don't Tell

General descriptions won't help your reader see your subject. Give concrete, sensory details that *show* how your subject looks, what he or she sounds like, maybe even how he or she smells or feels (the silky dress your grandma wears). Express those details with precise, vivid nouns, verbs, and modifiers, as in this passage:

> "Sweat popped out on the boy's face and he began to struggle. Mrs. Jones stopped, jerked him around in front of her, put a half nelson about his neck, and continued to drag him up the street."

—Langston Hughes, "Thank You, M'am" (page 122)

2. Avoid Clichés

If you find yourself about to write a familiar-sounding expression (such as "eyes like stars" or "pretty as a picture"), STOP! It's probably a wilted, gasping cliché. Clichés are expressions that were once fresh and original but use has worn them out. Search for new comparisons and figures of speech like the ones underlined in these sentences:

> "She is small and sprightly, like a bantam hen; but, due to a long youthful illness, her shoulders are pitifully hunched. Her face is remarkable—not unlike Lincoln's, craggy like that, and

---

A Box of Descriptive Words

Sight: *towering, rusty, jagged, shadowy, silver, fluorescent*

Sound: *jingling, hoarse, echoing, musical, loud, murmuring*

Smell: *musty, cut-grass, putrid, garlicky, earthy, lemony*

Touch: *frozen, satiny, splintered, mushy, slimy*

Taste: *curried, tart, syrupy, pickled, fiery, salty*

Language Link
H E L P

Modifiers: pages 129 and 181. Figures of speech: page 163.

---

tinted by sun and wind; but it is delicate too, finely boned, and her eyes are sherry-colored and timid.

—Truman Capote, "A Christmas Memory" (page 145)

3. Catch Their Interest

Try to find an interesting way to open your essay. Here are three openers based on the stories in this collection:

"She was . . ."

"The year was . . ."

"Imagine . . ."

However you begin, be sure that the subject of your essay is introduced right away.

4. Let Your People Speak

If you can, let us hear how your subject talks. You might want to have the person speak directly and tell his or her philosophy of life, as Buddy's friend does in "A Christmas Memory."

Try It Out

Expand these "empty," generalized descriptions by adding concrete images and sensory details. Use precise and vivid words to *show* the characters, their actions and settings.

EXAMPLE

General: She walked up the street.

Specific: Her tiny leather shoes patted over the cobblestone sidewalk and her long, straight navy skirt brushed the many parked scooters.

1. The boy jumped into water cold as ice.
2. A woman and child got on the bus and sat down.
3. A man answered the door.

Student Model

PARA MI EMILIO, SEÑOR

The wrinkled old woman hurried across the narrow street without looking up. A white and red Madrid city taxi screeched to a stop, and the driver honked his horn impatiently. He yelled at her, but the old lady was already scurrying past the metro station, jewelry stores, hotels, and tapas bars. Her tiny leather shoes patted over the cobblestone sidewalk and her long, straight navy skirt brushed the many parked scooters. She slowly pushed through a crowd of young businesspeople and stopped in front of the Iglesia de Santa Cruz.

Identifies and locates subject in a specific setting.

Observes from a distance.

Image of sound.

Details of subject's appearance.

The gray-haired woman straightened her shawl, pulled on her gloves, and mounted the steps to the church. Just inside the massive carved oak doors, she paused a moment and pulled on her

Follows subject's movements.

Or you might let your subject say some things that are very typical: Perhaps your grandmother, for example, always says goodbye with "God bless you." Adding that detail would tell something about her character.

5. A Strong Ending

Both Capote and Cisneros end their stories in this collection with images of kites soaring to heaven. Try to find a strong ending for your essay. You'll know your ending is right when it sounds right to you—when it feels like a definite closure. You might find your ending by asking yourself: What image of this person do I want my readers to go away with?

6. How Do You Feel?

You might want to add a reflection at the end of your essay to let your readers know how you feel about this person. Why did you choose this person? What does he or she mean to you?

handkerchief. She looked at the gray rainy sky, crossed herself, and fearfully marched into the church.

Narrates subject's actions in chronological order.

The old woman slipped into the back row and knelt. She crossed herself and said a "Hail Mary." She rose, glanced both ways, and scuffled into the side altar. The señora bowed her head before the gaudy painted statue of Jesus and then, with great determination, stepped toward the tablelike wooden box in the corner. Five out of the thirty red electric candles on top were lit. The woman carefully placed 250 pesetas into the slot and watched the candles begin to glow.

Writer is close enough to hear what the woman is saying.

Details of setting.

"Para mi Emilio, Señor," she said glancing at the statue of Christ, and she left the Iglesia de Santa Cruz with a tear in her eye.

Image of sight. A mystery here—who is Emilio? What's happened to him?

—Kate Wilkinson
Sheridan High School
Sheridan, Montana

■ *Evaluation Criteria*

A good essay of observation

1. *clearly identifies the subject*
2. *shows the subject in a specific context or setting*
3. *establishes the writer as an observer*
4. *uses descriptive and narrative details*
5. *includes dialogue*
6. *reveals the writer's feelings about the subject*

Language Link
HELP

Misplaced modifiers:
page 143.

Sentence Workshop
HELP

Revising sentence
fragments: page 200.

Writing is hard work. A clear
sentence is no accident. Very
few sentences come out right
the first time, or even the third
time. Remember this in
moments of despair. If you find
that writing is hard, it's because
it is hard. It's one of the hardest
things people do.

—William Zinsser

Evaluating and Revising

1. Peer Review

Work with a small group to read and comment on one another's drafts. As you read, ask yourself the following questions:

- Does the writer clearly identify the subject? Who is it?
- Does the writer locate the subject in a specific setting (place and time)? What is that setting?

Revision Model

	Peer Comments
The ~~old~~ [gray-haired] woman straightened her	Draw a clearer picture.
shawl[, pulled on her gloves, and mounted] ~~and went up~~ the steps to the	Give more details if you can.
church. Just inside the doors, she [massive carved oak]	Help me <u>see</u> this church.
paused a moment and pulled on her	
handkerchief. She looked at the [gray rainy] sky,	Help me see the sky.
crossed herself, and ~~went~~ [fearfully marched] into the	Can you use a more exact verb?
church.	
The old woman ~~went~~ [slipped] into the	Ditto.
back row and knelt. She crossed	
herself and said a "Hail Mary." She	Nice details.
rose~~, She~~ glanced both ways[, and scuffled] ~~She~~	Sounds choppy—combine? You've used "went" four times. Replace?
~~went to~~ [into] the side altar.	

- Does the writer tell us where he or she is—what is the writer's point of view as the subject is being observed?

- What details in the description hold my interest? Are there enough specific details? Does the writer *show* the character in action? Would dialogue help?

Peer reviewers should be sure also to comment on details, sentences, and wording they think are especially good.

2. Self-Evaluation

Consider your writing group's comments as you go back over your first draft. Sometimes "less is more"; cutting wordy sentences sharpens your focus.

Proofreading

Double-check your final draft to make sure it has no mistakes in grammar, usage, spelling, or mechanics. You might read your paper aloud to a partner or writing group to see if it sounds right. If you're keeping a proofreading log of the mistakes you often make, check your error list.

Publishing

Here are some suggestions for sharing your paper with an audience:

- Create a classroom Gallery of Characters. Combine each essay with an illustration (a drawing, cartoon, photograph, or collage).

- Give your essay to the person you've written about or give it to the person's family.

- Share your essay with your writing group. You might want to talk about which of the characters in your group's essays might provide material for a short story.

Reflecting

Will you add this piece of observational writing to your portfolio? If you do, date your work and write a brief reflection on your writing experience.

1. What was the most difficult part of writing this description?

2. What do I like best about the description?

3. What do I want to learn to do better?

What I've Learned

It's really hard to describe a character without being boring. My writing group helped a lot by pointing out where I was too general. They kept pushing me to get more specific, and I learned that I could. Whenever I was stuck for a good descriptive word, I used a thesaurus. I never knew there were so many choices. Some readers thought I should use more dialogue, but I think one really strong quote is good. I've included this description because I'm proud of the way it turned out.

Sentence Workshop

Basic Ingredients of a Sentence

1. a subject
2. a verb
3. a complete thought

Language Handbook HELP

See Sentence Structure, page 1010.

Technology HELP

See Language Workshop CD-ROM. *Key word entry: sentence fragments.*

Try It Out

Edit the following paragraph so that all fragments are corrected. Do you want to keep any fragments for dramatic effect? Be sure to compare your edited versions.

The girl stood on the edge of the high diving board. Her thin arms stretched in front of her. She was nine. Small for her age. She hesitated. Wobbled. Swayed a little. Stared straight ahead of her. Not looking down at the water. Her lips moved. As if she were talking to herself. Angry voices yelled from below. "C'mon, Angie." "Whadya waiting for?" "Jump!" Nothing. After what seemed like hours. She took a deep breath, stepped forward. And plunged into the pool feet first.

REVISING SENTENCES: FRAGMENTS

The pros do it. In the second sentence of "A Christmas Memory," the narrator says, "A coming of winter morning more than twenty years ago." That's a **sentence fragment,** not a sentence.

Truman Capote uses fragments to help create the narrator's "voice," his special way of talking and thinking.

But beware! Fragments probably aren't welcome in the writing you do for school, especially critical writing. You can correct fragments in two ways:

1. Attach the fragment to the sentence that is before or after it.

FRAGMENT "And there she remains, puttering around the kitchen. Alone with Queenie. Then alone."

SENTENCE And there she remains, puttering around the kitchen, alone with Queenie, then alone.

2. Add words to make the fragment a complete sentence.

FRAGMENT "A coming of winter morning more than twenty years ago."

SENTENCE Imagine a morning in late November, a coming of winter morning more than twenty years ago.

Writer's Workshop Follow-up: Proofreading

Look again at the observational essay you wrote for the Writer's Workshop. Check your sentences to be sure each one has a subject and a verb and expresses a complete thought. One way to test your sentences is to draw an arrow from each subject to its verb. If you want to use a fragment for dramatic effect, the way Capote does, think of your audience and be sure your teacher approves.

EXPECT THE UNEXPECTED

*It ain't over
till it's over.*

—Yogi Berra,
speaking of a
ball game

Things don't always turn out the way we plan them. Sometimes, just when we think that we have taken charge of our lives, we are thrown yet another curveball. Some of us love these surprises; others of us try to plan our lives and predict what's going to happen next.

In some ways fiction is just like real life. Fiction is also full of surprises—twists and turns that catch characters unawares and turn their expectations upside down.

The writers of the stories in this collection are not afraid of surprising you with characters whose behavior is unusual, whose motives are sometimes not the best, and whose problems are resolved in ways you least expect.

Writer's Notebook

WORK IN PROGRESS

Think back to a day that was different— when something happened that you never could have predicted. You might remember a time when you were fooled by someone's unpredictable behavior, or perhaps a time when *you* surprised someone else. Write freely, recording as much of the event as you can remember. Save your notes. You might find a story idea there to use in the Writer's Workshop assignment on page 250.

Reading Focus

The Perfect Gift

Fiction, like life, brings surprises. O. Henry liked to put a surprise twist or "snapper" in his plots. In "The Gift of the Magi" each character plans to give the other a gift, and because they love each other very much, each one searches for the perfect gift. What happens is not at all what they expected.

Quickwrite

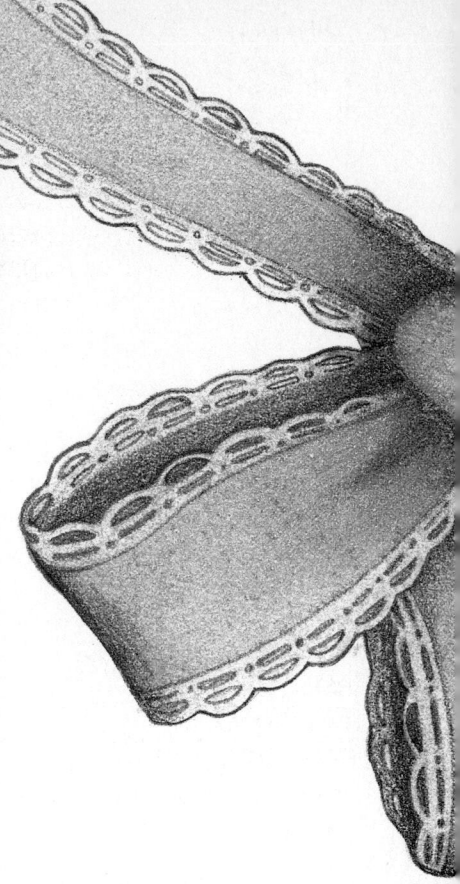

If you could save one item from a disaster—a fire, a flood, an earthquake—what would it be? In your Reader's Log, describe your most cherished possession. Tell why you treasure it. Was it a gift?

Elements of Literature

Ironic Situations

Often when we read a story, we think one thing will happen, only to be taken by surprise when something entirely different takes place. This is an **ironic situation,** and it reminds us that even though we think we can control our lives, chance or the unexpected often has the last word.

> **A**n **ironic situation** is one that turns out to be the opposite of what we expected.
>
> *For more on Irony, see pages 212–213 and the Handbook of Literary Terms.*

Background

The Magi that O. Henry refers to in the title of this story were the three "wise men" from the East who brought gifts of gold, frankincense, and myrrh to the Christ child. Traditionally, these have been regarded as the first Christmas gifts.

The Magi, as you know, were wise men.

The Gift of the Magi

O. Henry

A Woman's Work (1912) by John Sloan (American, 1871–1951).
Oil on canvas, 31 ⅝″ x 25 ¾″ (80.3 cm. x 65.4 cm.).

O ne dollar and eighty-seven cents. That was all. And sixty cents of it was in pennies. Pennies saved one and two at a time by bulldozing the grocer and the vegetable man and the butcher until one's cheeks burned with the silent imputation of parsimony[1] that such close dealing implied. Three times Della counted it. One dollar and eighty-seven cents. And the next day would be Christmas.

1. **imputation** (im′pyoo·tā′shən) **of parsimony** (pär′sə·mō′nē): suggestion of stinginess.

There was clearly nothing to do but flop down on the shabby little couch and howl. So Della did it. Which instigates the moral reflection that life is made up of sobs, sniffles, and smiles, with sniffles predominating.

While the mistress of the home is gradually subsiding from the first stage to the second, take a look at the home. A furnished flat[2] at $8 per week. It did not exactly beggar description, but it certainly had that word on the lookout for the mendicancy squad.[3]

In the vestibule[4] below was a letter box into which no letter would go, and an electric button from which no mortal finger could coax a ring. Also appertaining[5] thereunto was a card bearing the name "Mr. James Dillingham Young."

The "Dillingham" had been flung to the breeze during a former period of prosperity when its possessor was being paid $30 per week. Now, when the income was shrunk to $20, the letters of "Dillingham" looked blurred, as though they were thinking seriously of contracting to a modest and unassuming *D*. But whenever Mr. James Dillingham Young came home and reached his flat above, he was called Jim and greatly hugged by Mrs. James Dillingham Young, already introduced to you as Della. Which is all very good.

Della finished her cry and attended to her cheeks with the powder rag. She stood by the window and looked out dully at a gray cat walking a gray fence in a gray back yard. Tomorrow would be Christmas Day and she had only $1.87 with which to buy Jim a present. She had been saving every penny she could for months, with this result. Twenty dollars a week doesn't go far. Expenses had been greater than she had calculated. They always are. Only $1.87 to buy a present for Jim. Her Jim. Many a happy hour she had spent planning for something nice for him. Something fine and rare and sterling— something just a little bit near to being worthy of the honor of being owned by Jim.

There was a pier glass[6] between the windows of the room. Perhaps you have seen a pier glass in an $8 flat. A very thin and very agile person may, by observing his reflection in a rapid sequence of longitudinal strips, obtain a fairly accurate conception of his looks. Della, being slender, had mastered the art.

Suddenly she whirled from the window and stood before the glass. Her eyes were shining brilliantly, but her face had lost its color within twenty seconds. Rapidly she pulled down her hair and let it fall to its full length.

Now, there were two possessions of the James Dillingham Youngs in which they both took a mighty pride. One was Jim's gold watch that had been his father's and his grandfather's. The other was Della's hair. Had the Queen of Sheba lived in the flat across the air shaft,[7] Della would have let her hair hang out the window some day to dry just to depreciate Her Majesty's jewels and gifts. Had King Solomon been the janitor, with all his treasures piled up in the basement, Jim would have pulled out his watch every time he passed, just to see him pluck at his beard from envy.

So now Della's beautiful hair fell about her rippling and shining like a cascade of brown waters. It reached below her knee and made itself almost a garment for her. And then she did it up again nervously and quickly. Once she faltered for a minute and stood still while a tear or two splashed on the worn red carpet.

On went her old brown jacket; on went her old brown hat. With a whirl of skirts and with the brilliant sparkle still in her eyes, she fluttered out the door and down the stairs to the street.

Where she stopped, the sign read: "Mme. Sofronie. Hair Goods of All Kinds." One flight

---

6. **pier glass:** tall mirror hung between two windows.
7. **air shaft:** narrow gap between two buildings.

- -

WORDS TO OWN

instigates (in′stə·gāts′) *v.*: gives rise to. *Instigates* is generally used to mean "provokes or urges on to some action."

depreciate (dē·prē′shē·āt′) *v.*: belittle; lower the value of.

- -

2. **flat:** apartment.
3. **mendicancy** (men′di·kən·sē) **squad:** police who arrested beggars and homeless people.
4. **vestibule:** small entrance hall.
5. **appertaining** (ap′ər·tān′iŋ): belonging.

Snow in New York (1902) by Robert Henri.

inside out. It was a platinum fob chain,[8] simple and chaste in design, properly proclaiming its value by substance alone and not by meretricious[9] ornamentation—as all good things should do. It was even worthy of The Watch. As soon as she saw it she knew that it must be Jim's. It was like him. Quietness and value—the description applied to both. Twenty-one dollars they took from her for it, and she hurried home with the 87 cents. With that chain on his watch Jim might be properly anxious about the time in any company. Grand as the watch was, he sometimes looked at it on the sly on account of the old leather strap that he used in place of a chain.

When Della reached home, her intoxication gave way a little to prudence and reason. She got out her curling irons and lighted the gas and went to work repairing the ravages made by generosity added to love. Which is always a tremendous task, dear friends—a mammoth task.

Within forty minutes her head was covered with tiny, close-lying curls that made her look wonderfully like a truant schoolboy. She looked at her reflection in the mirror long, carefully, and critically.

"If Jim doesn't kill me," she said to herself, "before he takes a second look at me, he'll say I look like a Coney Island chorus girl. But what could I do—oh! what could I do with a dollar and eighty-seven cents?"

At 7 o'clock the coffee was made and the frying pan was on the back of the stove hot and ready to cook the chops.

up Della ran, and collected herself, panting. Madame, large, too white, chilly, hardly looked the "Sofronie."

"Will you buy my hair?" asked Della.

"I buy hair," said Madame. "Take yer hat off and let's have a sight at the looks of it."

Down rippled the brown cascade.

"Twenty dollars," said Madame, lifting the mass with a practiced hand.

"Give it to me quick," said Della.

Oh, and the next two hours tripped by on rosy wings. Forget the hashed metaphor. She was ransacking the stores for Jim's present.

She found it at last. It surely had been made for Jim and no one else. There was no other like it in any of the stores, and she had turned all of them

8. fob chain: short chain meant to be attached to a pocket watch.
9. meretricious (mer'ə·trish'əs): attractive in a cheap, flashy way.

Jim was never late. Della doubled the fob chain in her hand and sat on the corner of the table near the door that he always entered. Then she heard his step on the stair away down on the first flight, and she turned white for just a moment. She had a habit of saying little silent prayers about the simplest everyday things, and now she whispered: "Please God, make him think I am still pretty."

The door opened and Jim stepped in and closed it. He looked thin and very serious. Poor fellow, he was only twenty-two—and to be burdened with a family! He needed a new overcoat and he was without gloves.

Jim stepped inside the door, as immovable as a setter at the scent of quail. His eyes were fixed upon Della, and there was an expression in them that she could not read, and it terrified her. It was not anger, nor surprise, nor disapproval, nor horror, nor any of the sentiments that she had been prepared for. He simply stared at her fixedly with that peculiar expression on his face.

Della wriggled off the table and went for him.

"Jim, darling," she cried, "don't look at me that way. I had my hair cut off and sold it because I couldn't have lived through Christmas without giving you a present. It'll grow out again—you won't mind, will you? I just had to do it. My hair grows awfully fast. Say 'Merry Christmas!' Jim, and let's be happy. You don't know what a nice—what a beautiful, nice gift I've got for you."

"You've cut off your hair?" asked Jim, laboriously, as if he had not arrived at that patent[10] fact yet even after the hardest mental labor.

"Cut it off and sold it," said Della. "Don't you like me just as well, anyhow? I'm me without my hair, ain't I?"

Jim looked about the room curiously.

"You say your hair is gone?" he said, with an air almost of idiocy.

"You needn't look for it," said Della. "It's sold, I tell you—sold and gone, too. It's Christmas Eve, boy. Be good to me, for it went for you. Maybe the hairs on my head were numbered," she went on with a sudden serious sweetness, "but nobody could ever count my love for you.

Shall I put the chops on, Jim?"

Out of his trance Jim seemed quickly to wake. He enfolded his Della. For ten seconds let us regard with discreet scrutiny some inconsequential object in the other direction. Eight dollars a week or a million a year—what is the difference? A mathematician or a wit would give you the wrong answer. The Magi brought valuable gifts, but that was not among them. This dark assertion will be illuminated later on.

Jim drew a package from his overcoat pocket and threw it upon the table.

"Don't make any mistake, Dell," he said, "about me. I don't think there's anything in the way of a haircut or a shave or a shampoo that could make me like my girl any less. But if you'll unwrap that package, you may see why you had me going awhile at first."

White fingers and nimble tore at the string and paper. And then an ecstatic scream of joy; and then, alas! a quick feminine change to hysterical tears and wails, necessitating the immediate employment of all the comforting powers of the lord of the flat.

For there lay The Combs—the set of combs, side and back, that Della had worshiped for long in a Broadway window. Beautiful combs, pure tortoise shell, with jeweled rims—just the shade to wear in the beautiful vanished hair. They were expensive combs, she knew, and her heart had simply craved and yearned over them without the least hope of possession. And now, they were hers, but the tresses that should have adorned the coveted adornments were gone.

But she hugged them to her bosom, and at length she was able to look up with dim eyes and a smile and say: "My hair grows so fast, Jim!"

And then Della leaped up like a little singed cat and cried, "Oh, oh!"

Jim had not yet seen his beautiful present. She held it out to him eagerly upon her open palm. The dull

---

10. **patent** (pāt''nt): obvious.

WORDS TO OWN

scrutiny (skr‾oot''n·ē) n.: close inspection.
coveted (kuv'it·id) v. used as adj.: longed-for.

precious metal seemed to flash with a reflection of her bright and ardent spirit.

"Isn't it a dandy, Jim? I hunted all over town to find it. You'll have to look at the time a hundred times a day now. Give me your watch. I want to see how it looks on it."

Instead of obeying, Jim tumbled down on the couch and put his hands under the back of his head and smiled.

"Dell," said he, "let's put our Christmas presents away and keep 'em a while. They're too nice to use just at present. I sold the watch to get the money to buy your combs. And now suppose you put the chops on."

The Magi, as you know, were wise men—wonderfully wise men—who brought gifts to the Babe in the manger. They invented the art of giving Christmas presents. Being wise, their gifts were no doubt wise ones, possibly bearing the privilege of exchange in case of duplication. And here I have lamely related to you the uneventful chronicle of two foolish children in a flat who most unwisely sacrificed for each other the greatest treasures of their house. But in a last word to the wise of these days, let it be said that of all who give gifts, these two were the wisest. Of all who give and receive gifts, such as they are wisest. Everywhere they are wisest. They are the Magi.

MEET THE WRITER

He ♥ New York

O. Henry (1862–1910), whose real name was William Sydney Porter, was brought up in Greensboro, North Carolina. At the age of twenty, he went to Texas, where he became a rancher, worked as a bank teller, and founded a humorous weekly called *The Rolling Stone*.

When he was accused of stealing a thousand dollars from the First National Bank of Austin, where he was a teller, Porter panicked and fled to Central America. In Honduras he traveled with the outlawed Jennings brothers and helped them spend the loot from a recent robbery. But news of his wife's illness brought him back to Austin. There he was arrested, tried, and sentenced to five years in prison. Ironically, if he had not run away, Porter might have been acquitted. The bank was poorly run, and the loss of money might have been a case of mismanagement, not a crime.

Porter served only three years of his sentence. In prison he wrote more than a dozen stories and absorbed the underworld lore that he would use in stories such as "A Retrieved Reformation." He also may have found his pen name there: One of the prison guards was named Orrin Henry.

Porter left prison in 1901 and went to New York. He loved the city at once, and he wrote about it and its inhabitants for the few years remaining in his life. He once remarked:

❝ There are stories in everything. I've got some of my best yarns from park benches, lampposts, and newspaper stands. ❞

O. Henry wrote more than six hundred stories altogether—sixty-five in 1904 alone. But he also drank heavily, and tuberculosis killed him when he was only forty-seven. His last words were, "Pull up the shades so I can see New York. I don't want to go home in the dark."

More Snappers by O. Henry

"A Retrieved Reformation"
"The Furnished Room"
"The Ransom of Red Chief"

But It Was

Wing Tek Lum

We were in the old house in the kitchen.
I was sitting at the dining table
and they were cooking by the stoves.

And somehow it was me, the cupid,
5   who reminded them
that it was their anniversary.

And he uttered a surprise
and embraced her
with a smooch right on her lips.

10   And she pushed him away
flustered and complaining about his stubble
and how this was no big deal.

But it was.
It was the only time
15   I ever did see them kiss.

MAKING MEANINGS

First Thoughts

1. What do you think of O. Henry's comments in the last paragraph of this story?

Shaping Interpretations

2. An **ironic situation** is one that turns out to be just the opposite of what we—or the characters in the story—expect. Describe the situational irony in this story. What lesson about life and love do you think it teaches Della and Jim?

3. What is the real "gift" referred to in the **title**? (Notice that O. Henry says "gift," not "gifts.")

Reviewing the Text

Suppose you are telling the story of Della and Jim to a group of your friends. Identify the two **characters,** tell what each one **wants** to do, and summarize the **main events**— and the **outcome**—of their story.

Connecting with the Text

4. Under what circumstances would you give up the cherished possession you wrote about in your Reader's Log—as Jim and Della did?

Extending the Text

5. What do you think this little story, written almost a century ago, has to say about our consumer society today? Do you think that we often equate love with money? Consider:

   - advertising
   - the amount of money we spend on gifts
   - the value placed on having many possessions

6. O. Henry's poverty-stricken couple are so sustained by love that it is hard to imagine a cross word between them. Suppose a writer with a view of the world different from O. Henry's—someone who viewed human nature as selfish—were to write this same story. How might it change?

Challenging the Text

7. Describe your response to O. Henry's ending—the "snapper." Do you enjoy this kind of **irony** in stories or movies, or does it seem contrived—a trick on the reader?

CHOICES: Building Your Portfolio

Writer's Notebook

1. Collecting Ideas for a Short Short Story

A menu of story ideas.
O. Henry said he got ideas for his stories from "anything." In the Writer's Workshop on page 250, you'll get the opportunity to write a short short story of your own. See if you, like O. Henry, can make up a story from "anything." Here's a technique for generating story ideas that you can try yourself or with a group. Make three columns on a piece of paper or on the chalkboard. Label the columns **character, conflict,** and **setting**. Then fill in the columns with all the ideas you can think of. Your columns don't have to match or make sense across each row. When your list is as long as you can make it, choose one item from each column and see if you can use these items to create a story. You can vary your story ideas any way you want, but at least you'll have a start.

Character	Conflict	Setting
mother	hurricane	year 2010
alien	grizzly	mall
teenager	mob	year 400
virus	bully	sewer

Creative Writing

2. Life Goes On

The glimpse O. Henry gives us of Della and Jim is of just one brief time in their lives—early in their marriage. But life goes on and people change and grow—sometimes in different directions from each other. Suppose you want to provide readers with a glimpse of Della and Jim ten years later. In what ways has each character changed or stayed the same? What is each one doing? Where do they live? Write a paragraph about Della and Jim called "Life Goes On."

(Do you think they'll be like the older couple in the poem on page 208?)

Creative Writing/ Economics

3. Updating the Story

How would the details of O. Henry's love story be different if it were set in Dallas or Los Angeles or some other place (even New York City) today? Consider wages, prices, rents, and living quarters. Would Della have a job? Work with a partner to write a brief update of the story. Begin with the famous first sentence, but alter the amount of money that Della would have saved and still have found insufficient.

Research/Social Studies

4. Turn of the Century

What was America like in the early 1900s? Suppose you find a time capsule—a collection of objects sealed up at a certain time in history—from that era. What objects are in it? Research the time period and use what you learn to make a list of the capsule's contents. See what you can find out about the government, economics, communications, and transportation. Will your capsule contain anything that shows what forms of entertainment were popular? You might want to put in your capsule some details about what was happening in Europe, Asia, and South America as Della and Jim were scrimping in New York.

Handbook of Literary Terms
H E L P

See Diction.

Style: Diction—Ornate or Plain?

Diction, or word choice, can make a great difference in a piece of writing. A realistic writer might use slang. A science reporter might have to be precise and technical. A romantic might want to be poetic.

O. Henry loved flowery language and ornate diction. In the first paragraph he writes:

> ". . . one's cheeks burned with the silent imputation of parsimony that such close dealing implied."

By using such formal language, O. Henry is showing off his literary skills in a way that was once considered funny. A writer who preferred the plain style might have said:

> . . . you'd blush to think that this haggling over money suggested you were stingy.

Try It Out

➤ Find three ornate sentences in the story and rewrite each of them using plain, straightforward diction, as if you were modernizing the story for today's readers. Compare your edited versions in class.

➤ William Strunk and E. B. White, the authors of a famous writing handbook called *The Elements of Style,* tell writers never to use a twenty-dollar word when a ten-cent word will do just as well. As you work on your writing, think about your diction. Consider the diction that is most appropriate for your characters, for your setting, and for your tone. Can a strong, simple word work just as well as that fancy one?

VOCABULARY   HOW TO OWN A WORD

WORD BANK	**In Your Own Words**
instigates	**1.** Describe a time when you <u>instigated</u> something.
depreciate	**2.** What would <u>depreciate</u> a car?
scrutiny	**3.** What might an airport guard's <u>scrutiny</u> reveal?
coveted	**4.** Describe something you once <u>coveted</u>.

PEANUTS reprinted by permission of UFS, Inc.

Elements of Literature

IRONY: Twists and Surprises

Surprise is often an important ingredient in a good story, just as it is in life itself. In our own lives we are forever expecting events to develop in a certain way, only to see them turn out otherwise. The election is won by an underdog. The firehouse goes up in flames. The shortest kid is the best basketball center. This kind of surprise—the difference between what we expect and what actually happens—is **irony**.

Verbal Irony: Meaning Something Else

The simplest kind of irony is **verbal irony**. You use it yourself every day when you say one thing but mean something else. "Nice clean water you've got here," you might say, standing at the edge of a polluted river. Remember General Zaroff, who hunts and kills other humans in "The Most Dangerous Game" (page 13)? He uses verbal irony when he says: "Oh, yes . . . I have electricity. We try to be civilized here." Zaroff, of course, is anything but civilized.

Situational Irony: Reversing Expectations

Situational irony occurs when a situation turns out to be just the opposite of what we expect. We feel this kind of irony, for example, when the police chief's son turns out to be a thief or when the quietest student in the class turns up on a TV talk show.

A famous example of situational irony is found in O. Henry's story "The Gift of the Magi" (page 202). This situational irony is so important to the story's plot that if we described it we'd be giving away the story. You see this kind of irony in movies. You might remember how, in *The Wizard of Oz*, everyone trembles at the thought of the mighty, terrible ruler of Oz. But when we meet "the wizard," he turns out to be a little con man.

Situational irony cuts deeply into our feelings. When irony is put to work in fiction, it is often what touches us most. Irony can move us toward tears or laughter because we sense we are close to the truth of life. A good example of this kind of irony is Somerset Maugham's retelling of the old tale "Appointment in Samarra." Here it is:

Death speaks: There was a merchant in Baghdad who sent his servant to market to buy provisions, and in a little while the servant came back, white and trembling, and said, "Master, just now when I was in the marketplace I was jostled by a woman in the crowd, and when I turned I saw it was Death that jostled me. She looked at me and made a threatening gesture; now, lend me your horse, and I will ride away from this city and avoid my fate. I will go to Samarra, and there Death will not find me." The merchant lent him his horse, and the

---

"How ironic!"

The election is won by an underdog.

The firehouse goes up in flames.

The shortest kid is the best basketball center.

by John Leggett

servant mounted it, and he dug his spurs in its flanks, and as fast as the horse could gallop he went. Then the merchant went down to the marketplace and he saw me standing in the crowd and he came to me and said, "Why did you make a threatening gesture to my servant when you saw him this morning?" "That was not a threatening gesture," I said. "It was only a start of surprise. I was astonished to see him in Baghdad, for I had an appointment with him tonight in Samarra."

There is a childish, or perhaps cowardly, logic in the belief that we can avoid the consequences of bad news simply by running away from it. This is what the servant believes when he tries to outwit fate by being out of town when Death calls. But a surprise awaits the servant when he reaches Samarra: He thinks that when he gets there he will have escaped Death. Ironically, just the opposite happens. By running to Samarra, he has actually run to meet Death.

Dramatic Irony: Withholding Knowledge

Irony comes from the Greek word *eirōneia,* which means "a withholding of knowledge." This is the kind of irony that we see most often in plays, films, and TV programs; we call it **dramatic irony**. We sense this kind of irony when we in the audience know something that characters on stage or screen do *not* know. In a stage comedy, for example, *we* know (but the leading man doesn't know) that the young woman he's flirting with is really his male roommate in disguise. In an action movie, *we* know (but the heroine doesn't know) that one of the cables of the elevator she's about to enter has been cut.

Dramatic irony is used in novels and short stories, too. What about Little Red Riding Hood knocking innocently on Grandma's front door? We know about the wolf under the bedclothes wearing Grandma's bonnet, but Little Red is unaware of the toothy surprise that awaits her.

"... the good news is that we now have a phone in the car."

Reprinted from *The Saturday Evening Post* © 1988.

Reading Focus

An Unexpected Experience

It might be the sight of a winter sky filled with snow. It might be the feel of the tropical sun in December. Whatever the setting, a new climate can bring surprises. "Snow" is narrated by a girl who has just moved to New York City from the tropical climate of the Dominican Republic, a small country southeast of Florida. There will be other surprises for Yolanda as she tries to understand a new city, a new culture, and a new climate.

Quickwrite

In your Reader's Log write about some features of your area that might surprise someone from another country who is new to your school. Think about your climate, customs, food, and clothing. If you are from another country yourself, write about some of the things that surprised you in your new setting.

Elements of Literature

A Character as Narrator

A writer may choose to let one of the characters in a story narrate the events. This **narrator** talks to us directly and uses the first-person pronoun *I*. When the narrator of the story is one of its characters, we can share the person's innermost thoughts and feelings. But there are limits to what we know. The only information we get about the events in the story is what this narrator tells us. In many stories the choice of a first-person narrator can lead to surprises, since we make discoveries at the same time the character is making them.

> The **narrator** is the person telling the story. A **first-person narrator** is a character in the story.
>
> *For more on Point of View, see pages 218–219 and the Handbook of Literary Terms.*

Background

The Cuban missile crisis took place in October 1962, when the United States discovered that Soviet missiles had been installed in Cuba, only ninety miles from the U.S. mainland. John F. Kennedy was then president of the United States, and Fidel Castro was prime minister of Cuba. Both Cuba and the Soviet Union had Communist governments, and the missiles were considered a threat to the United States. At times during the crisis, it seemed as if war might break out. Many Americans fully expected the missiles to be launched against their cities.

*"Why,
Yolanda dear,
that's snow!"*

S❄N❄O❄W

Julia Alvarez

Our first year in New York we rented a small apartment with a Catholic school nearby, taught by the Sisters of Charity, hefty women in long black gowns and bonnets that made them look peculiar, like dolls in mourning. I liked them a lot, especially my grandmotherly fourth-grade teacher, Sister Zoe. I had a lovely name, she said, and she had me teach the whole class how to pronounce it. *Yo-lan-da.* As the only immigrant in my class, I was put in a special seat in the first row by the window, apart from the other children, so that Sister Zoe could tutor me without disturbing them. Slowly, she enunciated the new words I was to repeat: *laundromat, cornflakes, subway, snow.*

Soon I picked up enough English to understand holocaust[1] was in the air. Sister Zoe explained to a wide-eyed classroom what was happening in Cuba. Russian missiles were being assembled, trained supposedly on New York City. President Kennedy, looking worried too, was on the television at home, explaining we might have to go to war against the Commu-

1. **holocaust** (häl′ə·kôst′): great or total destruction of life.

nists. At school, we had air-raid drills: An ominous bell would go off and we'd file into the hall, fall to the floor, cover our heads with our coats, and imagine our hair falling out, the bones in our arms going soft. At home, Mami and my sisters and I said a rosary[2] for world peace. I heard new vocabulary: *nuclear bomb, radioactive fallout, bomb shelter.* Sister Zoe explained how it would happen. She drew a picture of a mushroom on the blackboard and dotted a flurry of chalk marks for the dusty fallout that would kill us all.

The months grew cold, November, December. It was dark when I got up in the morning, frosty when I followed my breath to school.

2. **rosary** (rō′zər·ē): in the Roman Catholic religion, series of prayers counted off on a special set of beads.

One morning, as I sat at my desk daydreaming out the window, I saw dots in the air like the ones Sister Zoe had drawn—random at first, then lots and lots. I shrieked, "Bomb! Bomb!" Sister Zoe jerked around, her full black skirt ballooning as she hurried to my side. A few girls began to cry.

But then Sister Zoe's shocked look faded. "Why, Yolanda dear, that's snow!" She laughed. "Snow."

"Snow," I repeated. I looked out the window warily. All my life I had heard about the white crystals that fell out of American skies in the winter. From my desk I watched the fine powder dust the sidewalk and parked cars below. Each flake was different, Sister Zoe had said, like a person, irreplaceable and beautiful.

MEET THE WRITER

"Listening Closely to Words"

At the age of ten, **Julia Alvarez** (1950–   ) left her home in the Dominican Republic and moved with her family to New York City. The Alvarez children went to Catholic schools and learned English, sometimes with difficulty. "Snow" is from Alvarez's book of fiction called *How the García Girls Lost Their Accents*. The other García girls—besides Yolanda—are Carla, Sandra, and Sofia. Alvarez, who teaches at her alma mater, Middlebury College, in Vermont, has this to say about one of her own teachers:

❝ In sixth grade, I had one of the first of a lucky line of great English teachers who began to nurture a love of the language, a love that had been there since a childhood of listening closely to words. Sister Bernadette did not make our class interminably diagram sentences from a workbook or learn a catechism of grammar rules. Instead, she asked us to write little stories imagining we were snowflakes, birds, pianos, a stone in the pavement, a star in the sky. What would it feel like to be a flower with the roots in the ground? If the clouds could talk, what would they say? She had an expressive, dreamy look that was accentuated by her face being framed in a wimple. Supposing, just supposing. My mind would take off, soaring into possibilities, a flower with roots, a star in the sky, a cloud full of sad sad tears, a piano crying out each time its back was tapped, music only to our ears. ❞

MAKING MEANINGS

First Thoughts

1. What **images** did you see as you read this story? Describe the image you saw most clearly.

Shaping Interpretations

2. Suppose that Sister Zoe was the **narrator** of the story instead of Yolanda. What might she be able to tell you that Yolanda can't?

3. Yolanda tells us about two new sets of English words that she learns from Sister Zoe. How do the "war words" differ from the "peacetime words"? How would the "war words" make a child feel?

4. As much as anything, this story reveals the **character** of Sister Zoe. What does the last sentence of the story tell you about the way she treats her students?

Extending the Text

5. How do you think people today would respond to a crisis like the one in the story? How do you think such situations affect young children?

Reviewing the Text

How would you summarize the main events in this story to an artist who is going to illustrate it? Be sure the artist understands Yolanda's mix-up and what caused it.

CHOICES: Building Your Portfolio

Writer's Notebook

1. Collecting Ideas for a Short Short Story

Creating characters. When Julia Alvarez uses the adjective *grandmotherly* to describe Sister Zoe, we get an immediate impression of someone who's warm and loving. Look over any story ideas you've recorded in your notebook. Make word diagrams containing adjectives that describe people who might be main characters in one of those stories. Save your notes. You might want to use these characters for the assignment in the Writer's Workshop on page 250.

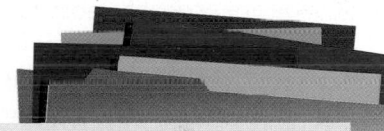

Interviewing

2. Cultural Diversity

There may be some students at your school who have come from other countries or other parts of the United States. Interview one of these students for your school paper. Plan the questions you want to ask. (Use your Quickwrite notes for ideas, if you like.) If you want to write up your interview in question and answer format, you should tape the conversation or take careful notes. (If *you* are the student from another country, you might interview yourself.)

Elements of Literature

POINT OF VIEW: Who's Talking?

Every story has a voice—a **narrator** whose view is the one we share. A writer must decide early on who is going to tell the story. The choice is an important one.

There are three basic points of view available to a writer: **omniscient** (äm·nish'ənt); **first-person;** and **third-person limited**.

The Omniscient Point of View: "All-Knowing"

You are probably most familiar with the omniscient point of view. *Omniscient* means "all-knowing." The all-knowing narrator is not a character in the story and never refers to himself or herself with the first-person pronoun *I*. This omniscient narrator is able to tell us everything about every character (including how each one thinks and feels). Let's look at a story told from the omniscient point of view:

One sunny day, a young woman looked down from her apartment window and saw a young man playing a saxophone. "Cool," she thought as she swayed in time with his tune. Shortly, a large brown dog sauntered up, sat in front of the musician, and howled along with the music.

Then a man in his pajamas yelled from another window. He said that the noise woke him up and he was going to call the police. This man worked the night shift and had to sleep all day and liked cats better than dogs anyway. The young saxophonist left. Soon the young woman appeared in the street and hurried off in the direction taken by the departing horn player. In a year's time, the young woman married the talented saxophonist, he had a hit CD, and they adopted a large brown dog.

The First-Person Point of View: "I" Tells the Story

In the first-person point of view, one of the characters in a story talks to us, using *I*, the first-person pronoun. When a character in the story is the narrator, we can know only what this person sees and hears about events and about other characters. We learn only what "I" chooses—or is able—to tell us. Suppose the saxophonist is

Drawing by Ziegler: © 1991 The New Yorker Magazine, Inc.

"We can't imagine what a spider thinks, Louisa, because it's a whole different life style."

the first-person narrator of the story.

I took the subway to Clancy Street, found a spot in front of Park View Apartments, and started to play my sax. I was hoping to attract an audience and, if I was lucky, earn some money. The morning started out great. This girl opened her window and applauded madly. Later, I had a duet with this big howling dog—what a riot! I had to move on, however, when a guy slammed his window shut and called the police—not a music lover. He said I was disturbing the peace. Give me a break.

by John Leggett

Third-Person Limited: Focus on One Character

The third-person limited point of view means that the story-teller zooms in on just one character. With this point of view, we witness the events of a story just as this one charac-ter witnesses them. We share intensely this character's reactions to everything that happens in the story, but what we know about the other characters is limited. Suppose we hear the saxophone story from this point of view, focus-ing on the man in pajamas.

The man couldn't take any more. It was noon, but he had just fallen asleep, because he had worked the night shift. He had trouble getting to sleep because he was worried—he had just lost his job at the warehouse. And why was he fired? Because he fell asleep on the job. And why had he been so sleepy? Because a barking dog had kept him awake the day before. And here it was again, a barking, howling dog right outside his window! And some beggar playing a horn besides. The man picked up his phone and dialed 911.

Why Is Point of View Important?

The more you think about it, the more you realize what a huge difference point of view makes to a story. When you are reading, ask yourself how the story would differ if someone else were telling it. Whose opinions are being shared? Whose emotions are being expressed? Where do the storyteller's sympathies lie?

While readers are rarely even aware of the techniques of point of view, writers and student writers talk about it constantly, and the best of them are always experimenting with it. In telling the saxophon-ist's story, they would probably be tempted to let the large brown dog tell it, just to see the difference.

I remember well my sensation as we first entered the house. I knew instantly that something was very wrong. I realized that my father's chair had been sat in, as well as my mother's and my own. The porridge we had left on the table to cool had been partially eaten. None of this, however, pre-pared me for what we were about to discover up-stairs. . . .

BEFORE YOU READ
THE NECKLACE

Reading Focus

The Grass Is Greener

All of us, at one time or another, have felt that the grass is greener on the other side of the fence—in other words, that someone else's life is better than our own. For some of us it is wealth and the possessions of others that we envy. We believe that having what they have will make us happy—until we experience the unexpected results of envy.

Quickwrite

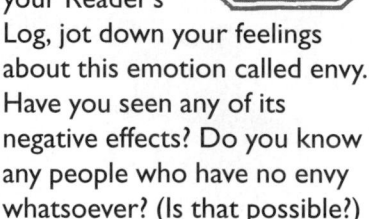

In a few lines in your Reader's Log, jot down your feelings about this emotion called envy. Have you seen any of its negative effects? Do you know any people who have no envy whatsoever? (Is that possible?)

Elements of Literature

A Limited Point of View

De Maupassant was interested in the psychology of his characters, so it's not surprising that he tells this famous story from the limited point of view of Mathilde Loisel. This narrator zooms in at once on Mathilde. We learn in the first seven paragraphs about her past, her dreams, what makes her unhappy, what she envies in other people, what she thinks will make her happy. We follow Mathilde so closely through a crisis in her life that the irony revealed at the story's end hits us almost as powerfully as it strikes the unsuspecting Mathilde.

> A **third-person limited** point of view focuses on the thoughts and feelings of a single character in the story.
>
> *For more on Point of View, see pages 218–219 and the Handbook of Literary Terms.*

Background

"The Necklace" takes place in Paris in the late 1880s. At that time and in that place, social classes were all-important; people were born into a certain class, and that was usually where they remained. For more information on the kind of world the characters in this story lived in, read "Separate Spheres" on page 223 before you start the story.

THE NECKLACE

Guy de Maupassant

She was one of those pretty and charming girls, born, as if by an accident of fate, into a family of clerks. With no dowry,[1] no prospects, no way of any kind of being met, understood, loved, and married by a man both prosperous and famous, she was finally married to a minor clerk in the Ministry of Education.

She dressed plainly because she could not afford fine clothes, but she was as unhappy as a woman who has come down in the world; for women have no family rank or social class. With them, beauty, grace, and charm take the place of birth and breeding. Their natural poise, their instinctive good taste, and their mental cleverness are the sole guiding principles which make daughters of the common people the equals of ladies in high society.

She grieved <u>incessantly</u>, feeling that she had been born for all the little niceties and luxuries of living. She grieved over the shabbiness of her apartment, the dinginess of the walls, the worn-out appearance of the chairs, the ugliness of the draperies. All these things, which another woman of her class would not even have

She so much longed to please, be envied, be fascinating.

noticed, gnawed at her and made her furious. The sight of the little Breton girl[2] who did her humble housework roused in her <u>disconsolate</u> regrets and wild daydreams. She would dream of silent chambers, draped with Oriental tapestries[3] and lighted by tall bronze floor lamps, and of two handsome butlers in knee breeches, who, drowsy from the heavy warmth cast by the central stove, dozed in large overstuffed armchairs.

She would dream of great reception halls hung with old silks, of fine furniture filled with priceless curios,[4] and of small, stylish, scented sitting rooms just right for the four o'clock chat with intimate friends, with distinguished and sought-after men whose attention every woman envies and longs to attract.

---

2. **Breton** (bret''n) **girl:** girl from Brittany, a region in northwestern France.
3. **tapestries** (tap'əs·trēz): heavy cloths woven with decorative designs and pictures, used as wall hangings or furniture coverings.
4. **curios** (kyoor'ē·ōz'): unusual items.

WORDS TO OWN

incessantly (in·ses'ənt·lē) *adv.:* constantly; continually.
disconsolate (dis·kän'sə·lit) *adj.:* very unhappy.

---

1. **dowry** (dou'rē): property that a woman brings to her husband at marriage.

When dining at the round table, covered for the third day with the same cloth, opposite her husband, who would raise the cover of the soup tureen, declaring delightedly, "Ah! a good stew! There's nothing I like better . . . ," she would dream of fashionable dinner parties, of gleaming silverware, of tapestries making the walls alive with characters out of history and strange birds in a fairyland forest; she would dream of delicious dishes served on wonderful china, of gallant compliments whispered and listened to with a sphinxlike[5] smile as one eats the rosy flesh of a trout or nibbles at the wings of a grouse.

She had no evening clothes, no jewels, nothing. But those were the things she wanted; she felt that was the kind of life for her. She so much longed to please, be envied, be fascinating and sought after.

She had a well-to-do friend, a classmate of convent-school days whom she would no longer go to see, simply because she would feel so distressed on returning home. And she would weep for days on end from vexation, regret, despair, and anguish.

Then one evening, her husband came home proudly holding out a large envelope.

"Look," he said, "I've got something for you."

She excitedly tore open the envelope and pulled out a printed card bearing these words:

"The Minister of Education and Mme. Georges Ramponneau beg M. and Mme. Loisel[6] to do them the honor of attending an evening reception at the Ministerial Mansion on Friday, January 18."

Instead of being delighted, as her husband had hoped, she scornfully tossed the invitation on the table, murmuring, "What good is that to me?"

"But, my dear, I thought you'd be thrilled to death. You never get a chance to go out, and this is a real affair, a wonderful one! I had an awful time getting a card. Everybody wants one;

it's much sought after, and not many clerks have a chance at one. You'll see all the most important people there."

She gave him an irritated glance and burst out impatiently, "What do you think I have to go in?"

He hadn't given that a thought. He stammered, "Why, the dress you wear when we go to the theater. That looks quite nice, I think."

He stopped talking, dazed and distracted to see his wife burst out weeping. Two large tears slowly rolled from the corners of her eyes to the corners of her mouth; he gasped, "Why, what's the matter? What's the trouble?"

By sheer willpower she overcame her outburst and answered in a calm voice while wiping the tears from her wet cheeks, "Oh, nothing. Only I don't have an evening dress and therefore I can't go to that affair. Give the card to some friend at the office whose wife can dress better than I can."

He was stunned. He resumed, "Let's see, Mathilde. How much would a suitable outfit cost—one you could wear for other affairs too—something very simple?"

She thought it over for several seconds, going over her allowance and thinking also of the amount she could ask for without bringing an immediate refusal and an exclamation of dismay from the thrifty clerk.

Finally, she answered hesitatingly, "I'm not sure exactly, but I think with four hundred francs I could manage it."

He turned a bit pale, for he had set aside just that amount to buy a rifle so that the following summer, he could join some friends who were getting up a group to shoot larks on the plain near Nanterre.[7]

However, he said, "All right. I'll give you four hundred francs. But try to get a nice dress."

As the day of the party approached, Mme. Loisel seemed sad, moody, ill at ease. Her outfit was ready, however. Her husband said to her one evening, "What's the matter? You've been all out of sorts for three days."

5. **sphinxlike:** mysterious. The sphinx was a creature in Greek mythology who asked riddles.
6. **Mme. Georges Ramponneau** (mȧ·dȧm′ zhôrzh rȧm′pə·nō̄) . . . **M.** (mə·syr̂′) . . . **Mme. Loisel** (mȧ·dȧm′ lwä·zel′): M. and *Mme.* are abbreviations for "Monsieur" and "Madame" and are the French equivalents of *Mr.* and *Mrs.*

7. **Nanterre** (nän·ter′): town near Paris.

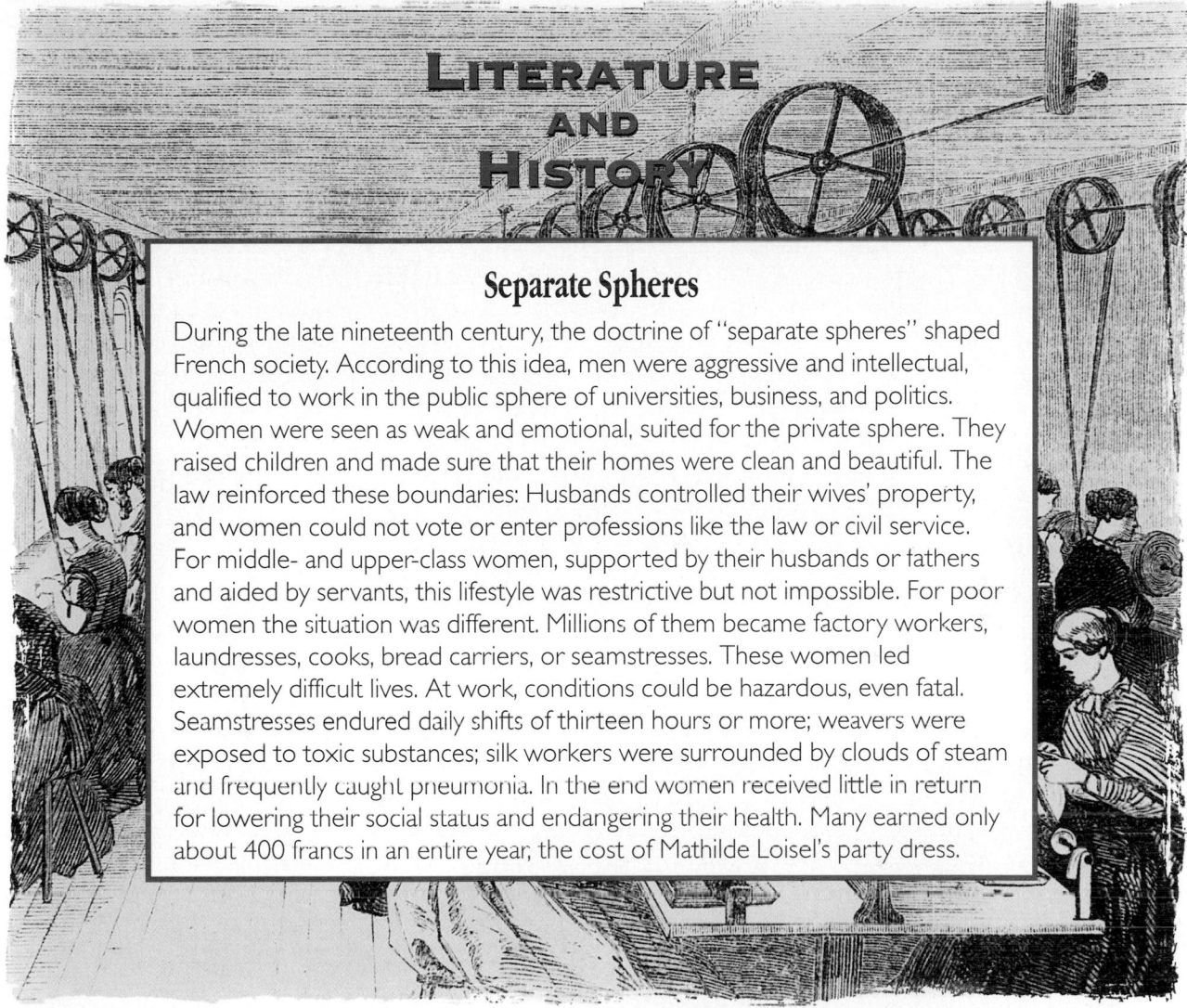

Separate Spheres

During the late nineteenth century, the doctrine of "separate spheres" shaped French society. According to this idea, men were aggressive and intellectual, qualified to work in the public sphere of universities, business, and politics. Women were seen as weak and emotional, suited for the private sphere. They raised children and made sure that their homes were clean and beautiful. The law reinforced these boundaries: Husbands controlled their wives' property, and women could not vote or enter professions like the law or civil service. For middle- and upper-class women, supported by their husbands or fathers and aided by servants, this lifestyle was restrictive but not impossible. For poor women the situation was different. Millions of them became factory workers, laundresses, cooks, bread carriers, or seamstresses. These women led extremely difficult lives. At work, conditions could be hazardous, even fatal. Seamstresses endured daily shifts of thirteen hours or more; weavers were exposed to toxic substances; silk workers were surrounded by clouds of steam and frequently caught pneumonia. In the end women received little in return for lowering their social status and endangering their health. Many earned only about 400 francs in an entire year, the cost of Mathilde Loisel's party dress.

And she answered, "It's embarrassing not to have a jewel or a gem—nothing to wear on my dress. I'll look like a pauper. I'd almost rather not go to the party."

He answered, "Why not wear some flowers? They're very fashionable this season. For ten francs you can get two or three gorgeous roses."

She wasn't at all convinced. "No. . . . There's nothing more humiliating than to look poor among a lot of rich women."

But her husband exclaimed, "My, but you're silly! Go see your friend Mme. Forestier,[8] and ask her to lend you some jewelry. You and she know each other well enough for you to do that."

8. **Forestier** (fô·rəs·tyā′).

She gave a cry of joy. "Why, that's so! I hadn't thought of it."

The next day she paid her friend a visit and told her of her predicament.

Mme. Forestier went toward a large closet with mirrored doors, took out a large jewel box, brought it over, opened it, and said to Mme. Loisel, "Pick something out, my dear."

At first her eyes noted some bracelets, then a pearl necklace, then a Venetian cross, gold and gems, of marvelous workmanship. She tried on these adornments in front of the mirror, but

WORDS TO OWN
pauper (pô′pər) *n.:* very poor person.

Interrupted Reading (c. 1870) by Jean-Baptiste Camille Corot. French, 1796–1875.
Oil on canvas mounted on board (92.2 cm. x 65.1 cm.).

hesitated, unable to decide which to part with and put back. She kept on asking, "Haven't you something else?"

"Oh, yes, keep on looking. I don't know just what you'd like."

All at once she found, in a black satin box, a superb diamond necklace; and her pulse beat faster with longing. Her hands trembled as she took it up. Clasping it around her throat, outside her high-necked dress, she stood in ecstasy looking at her reflection.

Then she asked, hesitatingly, pleading, "Could I borrow that, just that and nothing else?"

"Why, of course."

She threw her arms around her friend, kissed her warmly, and fled with her treasure.

The day of the party arrived. Mme. Loisel was a sensation. She was the prettiest one there, fashionable, gracious, smiling, and wild with joy. All the men turned to look at her, asked who she was, begged to be introduced. All the Cabinet officials wanted to waltz with her. The minister took notice of her.

She danced madly, wildly, drunk with pleasure, giving no thought to anything in the triumph of her beauty, the pride of her success, in a kind of happy cloud composed of all the adulation, of all the admiring glances, of all the awakened longings, of a sense of complete victory that is so sweet to a woman's heart.

She left around four o'clock in the morning. Her husband, since midnight, had been dozing in a small, empty sitting room with three other gentlemen whose wives were having too good a time.

He threw over her shoulders the wraps he had brought for going home, modest garments of everyday life whose shabbiness clashed with the stylishness of her evening clothes. She felt this and longed to escape unseen by the other women, who were draped in expensive furs.

Loisel held her back.

"Hold on! You'll catch cold outside. I'll call a cab."

But she wouldn't listen to him and went rapidly down the stairs. When they were on the street, they didn't find a carriage; and they set out to hunt for one, hailing drivers whom they saw going by at a distance.

They walked toward the Seine,[9] disconsolate and shivering. Finally, on the docks, they found one of those carriages that one sees in Paris only after nightfall, as if they were ashamed to show their drabness during daylight hours.

It dropped them at their door in the Ruc des Martyrs,[10] and they climbed wearily up to their apartment. For her, it was all over. For him, there was the thought that he would have to be at the Ministry at ten o'clock.

Before the mirror, she let the wraps fall from her shoulders to see herself once again in all her glory. Suddenly she gave a cry. The necklace was gone.

Her husband, already half undressed, said, "What's the trouble?"

She turned toward him despairingly, "I . . . I . . . I don't have Mme. Forestier's necklace."

"What! You can't mean it! It's impossible!"

They hunted everywhere, through the folds of the dress, through the folds of the coat, in the pockets. They found nothing.

He asked, "Are you sure you had it when leaving the dance?"

"Yes, I felt it when I was in the hall of the Ministry."

"But if you had lost it on the street, we'd have heard it drop. It must be in the cab."

"Yes, quite likely. Did you get its number?"

"No. Didn't you notice it either?"

"No."

They looked at each other aghast. Finally Loisel got dressed again.

"I'll retrace our steps on foot," he said, "to see if I can find it."

And he went out. She remained in her evening clothes, without the strength to go to bed, slumped in a chair in the unheated room, her mind a blank.

Her husband came in around seven o'clock. He had had no luck.

He went to the police station, to the newspapers to post a reward, to the cab companies,

9. **Seine** (sen): river that runs through Paris.
10. **Ruc des Martyrs** (rü dā mär·tēr'): street in Paris. The name means "Street of the Martyrs."

everywhere the slightest hope drove him.

That evening Loisel returned, pale, his face lined; still he had learned nothing.

"We'll have to write your friend," he said, "to tell her you have broken the catch and are having it repaired. That will give us a little time to turn around."

She wrote to his dictation.

At the end of a week, they had given up all hope.

And Loisel, looking five years older, declared, "We must take steps to replace that piece of jewelry."

The next day they took the case to the jeweler whose name they found inside. He consulted his records. "I didn't sell that necklace, madame," he said. "I only supplied the case."

Then they went from one jeweler to another hunting for a similar necklace, going over their recollections, both sick with despair and anxiety.

They found, in a shop in Palais Royal,[11] a string of diamonds which seemed exactly like the one they were seeking. It was priced at forty thousand francs. They could get it for thirty-six.

They asked the jeweler to hold it for them for three days. And they reached an agreement that he would take it back for thirty-four thousand if the lost one was found before the end of February.

Loisel had eighteen thousand francs he had inherited from his father. He would borrow the rest.

He went about raising the money, asking a thousand francs from one, four hundred from another, a hundred here, sixty there. He signed notes, made ruinous deals, did business with loan sharks, ran the whole gamut of money-lenders. He compromised the rest of his life, risked his signature without knowing if he'd be able to honor it, and then, terrified by the outlook of the future, by the blackness of despair about to close around him, by the prospect of all the <u>privations</u> of the body and tortures of the spirit, he went to claim the new necklace with

The Boulevard Montmartre at Night (c. 1897) by Camille Pissarro.

the thirty-six thousand francs, which he placed on the counter of the shopkeeper.

When Mme. Loisel took the necklace back, Mme. Forestier said to her frostily, "You should have brought it back sooner; I might have needed it."

WORDS TO OWN

privations (prī·vā′shənz) *n.:* hardships; lack of the things needed for a happy, healthy life.

---

11. Palais Royal (pȧ·lā′ rwä·yȧl′): fashionable shopping district in Paris.

perform the hateful duties of cooking. She washed dishes, wearing down her shell-pink nails scouring the grease from pots and pans; she scrubbed dirty linen, shirts, and cleaning rags, which she hung on a line to dry; she took the garbage down to the street each morning and brought up water, stopping on each landing to get her breath. And, clad like a peasant woman, basket on arm, guarding sou[13] by sou her scanty allowance, she bargained with the fruit dealers, the grocer, the butcher, and was insulted by them.

Each month notes had to be paid, and others renewed to give more time.

Her husband labored evenings to balance a tradesman's accounts, and at night, often, he copied documents at five sous a page.

And this went on for ten years.

Finally, all was paid back, everything including the <u>exorbitant</u> rates of the loan sharks and accumulated compound interest.

Mme. Loisel appeared an old woman now. She became heavy, rough, harsh, like one of the poor. Her hair untended, her skirts askew, her hands red, her voice shrill, she even slopped water on her floors and scrubbed them herself. But, sometimes, while her husband was at work, she would sit near the window and think of that long-ago evening when, at the dance, she had been so beautiful and admired.

What would have happened if she had not lost that necklace? Who knows? Who can say? How strange and unpredictable life is! How little there is between happiness and misery!

Then, one Sunday, when she had gone for a walk on the Champs Élysées[14] to relax a bit from the week's labors, she suddenly noticed a woman strolling with a child. It was Mme. Forestier, still young looking, still beautiful, still charming.

She didn't open the case, an action her friend was afraid of. If she had noticed the substitution, what would she have thought? What would she have said? Would she have thought her a thief?

Mme. Loisel experienced the horrible life the needy live. She played her part, however, with sudden heroism. That frightful debt had to be paid. She would pay it. She dismissed her maid; they rented a garret under the eaves.[12]

She learned to do the heavy housework, to

12. **garret under the eaves:** attic under the overhanging lower edges of a roof.

13. **sou** (so͞o): old French coin of little value.
14. **Champs Élysées** (shän zā·lē·zā′): famous avenue in Paris.

- -

WORDS TO OWN

exorbitant (eg·zôr′bi·tənt) *adj.*: much too high in price or amount.

- -

Mme. Loisel felt a rush of emotion. Should she speak to her? Of course. And now that everything was paid off, she would tell her the whole story. Why not?

She went toward her. "Hello, Jeanne."

The other, not recognizing her, showed astonishment at being spoken to so familiarly by this common person. She stammered, "But . . . madame . . . I don't recognize . . . You must be mistaken."

"No, I'm Mathilde Loisel."

Her friend gave a cry, "Oh, my poor Mathilde, how you've changed!"

"Yes, I've had a hard time since last seeing you. And plenty of misfortunes—and all on account of you!"

"Of me . . . How do you mean?"

"Do you remember that diamond necklace you loaned me to wear to the dance at the Ministry?"

"Yes, but what about it?"

"Well, I lost it."

"You lost it! But you returned it."

"I brought you another just like it. And we've been paying for it for ten years now. You can imagine that wasn't easy for us who had nothing. Well, it's over now, and I am glad of it."

Mme. Forestier stopped short. "You mean to say you bought a diamond necklace to replace mine?"

"Yes. You never noticed, then? They were quite alike."

And she smiled with proud and simple joy.

Mme. Forestier, quite overcome, clasped her by the hands. "Oh, my poor Mathilde. But mine was fake. Why, at most it was worth only five hundred francs!"

MEET THE WRITER

Hectic Pace

One of the world's greatest short-story writers, **Guy de Maupassant** (1850–1893) was born in Normandy, the French province that is the setting for much of his fiction. After his parents separated, de Maupassant was raised by his mother, who was a close friend of the great novelist Gustave Flaubert.

Flaubert set out to instruct the young de Maupassant in the art of fiction. He explained that good writing depends upon seeing things anew, rather than recording what people before us have thought. Flaubert also gave his student this advice:

66 Whatever you want to say, there is only one word to express it, only one verb to give it movement, only one adjective to qualify it. 99

For years de Maupassant sent Flaubert his writing exercises every week, and then they met to discuss his work over lunch. With the success of his story "Ball of Fat," de Maupassant, now aged thirty, quit his job as a clerk with the Naval Ministry and began to put great energy into writing. He quickly achieved enormous popularity. For eleven years he wrote at a hectic pace and produced nearly three hundred stories and six novels. Advising writers, de Maupassant said, "Get black on white."

His novel *The Horla* has been called one of the most terrifying stories of madness ever written. It foretold de Maupassant's own tragic fate of illness, insanity, and early death. He died in a Paris asylum when he was only forty-two years old.

MAKING MEANINGS

First Thoughts

1. Describe how you felt about Mathilde at the beginning of the story, and how you felt about her by the time the story ended.

Shaping Interpretations

2. When Mme. Forestier reveals that the necklace was a fake, the reader feels the force of the **irony**. Explain why her revelation is ironic. How did you respond to this surprise twist in the story?

3. How do you feel about Mathilde's husband? Consider the things you know about him:

   - his loyalty to Mathilde
   - the way he indulges her
   - his years of sacrifice and hard work
   - his plans to buy things for himself

4. Do you think this story is critical of Mathilde only, or do you think the writer is criticizing the values of a whole society? Tell why you think as you do.

5. Think about the characters and circumstances of two women—Mathilde in "The Necklace" and Della in "The Gift of the Magi" (page 202). Use a diagram like the one at the right to see how the women are alike and how they're different.

Mathilde — Both — Della

Reviewing the Text

a. What important facts did you learn about the **character** of Mathilde in the first two paragraphs?

b. What kind of life does Mathilde want?

c. How do Mathilde's dreams contrast with the life she really leads?

d. What **actions** do the Loisels take to resolve their problem?

e. As a result of losing the necklace, what kind of life do the Loisels begin to lead?

Connecting with the Text

6. Look back at your Quickwrite about envy. Does this story remind you of any experience in your life or in the lives of your friends? Explain.

Extending the Text

7. Could a young woman today be unhappy with her "class," as Mathilde was? What choices do women have today that can help them change their lives?

Challenging the Text

8. Did you find de Maupassant's **plot** believable and the motives of his **characters** convincing? Use specific incidents from the story to support your evaluations.

CHOICES: Building Your Portfolio

Writer's Notebook

1. Collecting Ideas for a Short Short Story

Choosing a point of view. When you plan the story you'll write for the Writer's Workshop on page 250, you'll have to think seriously about your point of view. Who will tell your story? Will it be a character (or even an animal) in the story, speaking as *I*? Will you choose an omniscient narrator who tells everything about all characters? Or you might want to zoom in on just one character, and really get into that person's psychology. Review the story ideas you've collected in your notebook and experiment with point of view (writers call it POV). Jot down notes about how different points of view would affect the story. You'll be surprised at how a change in POV can change the focus of the story.

Creative Writing

2. Extending the Story

Write a paragraph telling what might happen after Mme. Forestier reveals that the necklace was a fake. Does she return the difference in value between the original necklace and the one she received as a replacement? Do the Loisels now begin to lead a different kind of life? Is it too late for Mathilde to recapture the past—her beauty and social triumph? Has she learned something during those ten years that makes her unwilling to try?

Creative Writing

3. Another Point of View

Experiment with this story's **point of view,** as if you were de Maupassant trying to decide how to tell your story. Write a paragraph telling how the story would change if it were told in the first person by

a. Mathilde's husband

b. Mathilde herself

Critical Thinking/ Debating

4. What's the Difference?

Do you think Mme. Forestier should return the difference in value between the original necklace and the one she received as a replacement? Take one side of this question and write a position statement for or against a payment to the Loisels. Form a debate team and work together to prepare your arguments. Focus on the reasons for your position and try to anticipate what the other team will say. Be ready for them.

Music

5. Mood Music

Suppose you were to make a short film of "The Necklace" and wanted to add songs to the soundtrack as a way of expressing Mathilde's feelings. Select the songs you would use at these three moments: Mathilde at home before learning of the invitation; Mathilde at the party; Mathilde on the Champs Élysées ten years later. Play recordings of the songs you choose or read the lyrics to the class.

One of the two students tells the story years later. He quit in midterm and became a poet.

The principal tells the story. She really likes the kids but feels she has to act tough.

A student in the hallway was an unwilling witness. He remembers different details.

LANGUAGE LINK ▌MINI-LESSON▐

Technology HELP

See Language Workshop CD-ROM. *Key word entry: homonyms.*

Words Often Confused

- its, it's
- their, they're
- whose, who's
- your, you're

Proofreading: Pronoun Problems

Some pronouns in English sound exactly like other words: *its* and *it's*; *their* and *they're*; *whose* and *who's*; *your* and *you're*. Words that sound alike are no problem when you are speaking, but they can be troublesome when you are writing. To avoid trouble, you must be aware of the difference between a possessive pronoun and a pronoun contraction.

- A possessive pronoun (such as *its, their, whose, your*) shows ownership or relationship.

- A pronoun contraction (such as *it's, they're, who's,* and *you're*) is a shortened form of a pronoun and another word (*it is, they are, who is,* and *you are*). A pronoun contraction always has an apostrophe.

Try It Out

➤ Choose the correct word from the pair in parentheses.

1. "But her husband exclaimed, 'My, but (your, you're) silly!' "

2. " 'Everybody wants one; (its, it's) much sought after, and not many clerks have a chance at one.' "

3. "It dropped them at (their, they're) door in the Rue des Martyrs, and they climbed wearily up to (their, they're) apartment."

4. "The next day they took the case to the jeweler (whose, who's) name they found inside."

➤ Check the pronouns in your writing. Any problems? Highlight any pronoun contractions and then substitute the words they stand for. Do the substitutions make sense? Have you used a possessive where a contraction should be used?

VOCABULARY ▌HOW TO OWN A WORD▐

WORD BANK

incessantly
disconsolate
pauper
privations
exorbitant

Scaling Words

You can reinforce your ownership of a word by comparing it to other words with similar meanings. One way to compare words is to arrange them on a scale from high to low intensity.

Work with a partner to make an intensity scale for each word listed in the Word Bank. Add at least two words that mean more or less the same thing but that show a decrease in intensity. Be sure to compare and defend your "intensity scales" in class.

High Intensity	Medium Intensity	Low Intensity
incessantly	constantly	always

BEFORE YOU READ
THE CASK OF AMONTILLADO

Reading Focus

Revenge—Its Grisly Effects

During his brief and tormented life, Edgar Allan Poe searched in vain for love and acceptance. Perhaps to get even with a world that he thought rejected him, Poe became a master at writing stories of revenge. Think about the idea of revenge. What experiences could lead someone to seek revenge? How could an obsession with vengeance lead to tragedy?

Quickwrite

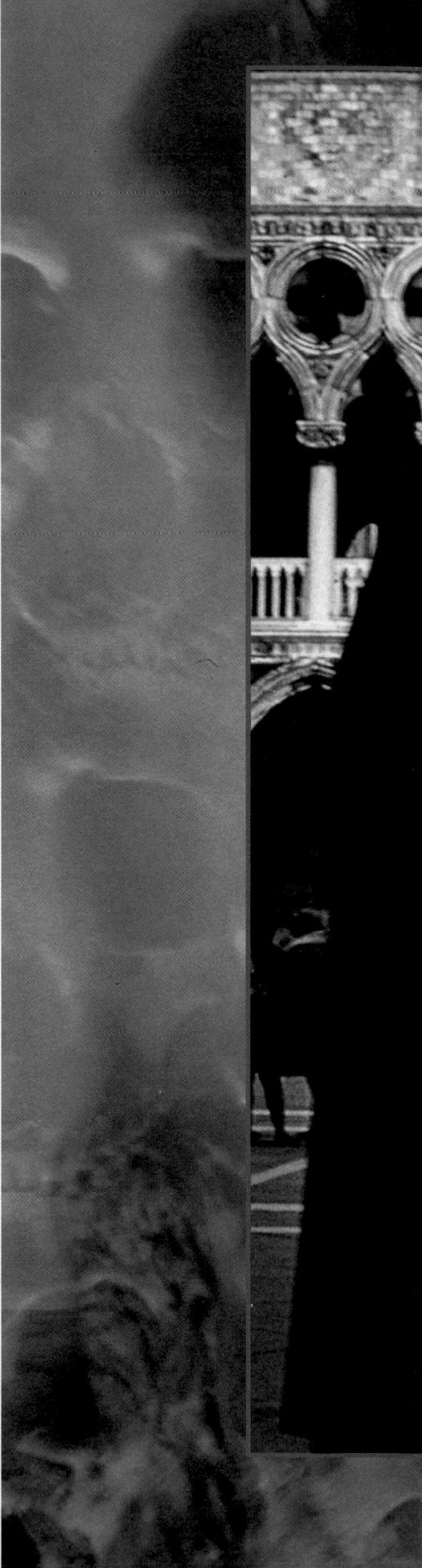

Brainstorm to share your ideas about these questions on revenge. Jot your responses down in your Reader's Log. Include any movies, TV programs, and stories that are built around this idea of the avenger.

Elements of Literature

Is the Narrator Reliable?

One of the first questions we ask on reading a story is "Who's telling me this story?" or "Who's speaking?" Poe's story is told by a man who reveals who he is and what he is up to as he and a friend wind down twisted stairways to an underground tunnel. Over the years since Poe wrote this now-famous story, people have asked: Is the narrator reliable? Is he telling the truth? Are we being deceived by a liar—or a madman?

> **A**n **unreliable narrator** is someone who is not always perceptive about what's going on in a story, or someone who is deliberately not telling the whole truth.
>
> *For more on Point of View, see pages 218–219 and the Handbook of Literary Terms.*

Background

Centuries ago, in Italy, the early Christians buried their dead in catacombs, which are long, winding underground tunnels. Later, wealthy families built private catacombs beneath their homes. Dark and cool, these chambers were suitable not only for burial but also for the storage of fine wine such as, in this story, amontillado (ə·män′tə·lä′dō). Poe's story happens during carnival, a celebration that still takes place in many countries, including parts of the United States. Carnival is celebrated in February or March, before Ash Wednesday and the start of Lent, the season of penitence. During carnival people wear masks and costumes. They dance and drink on the streets before giving up meat and other pleasures to do penance for their sins.

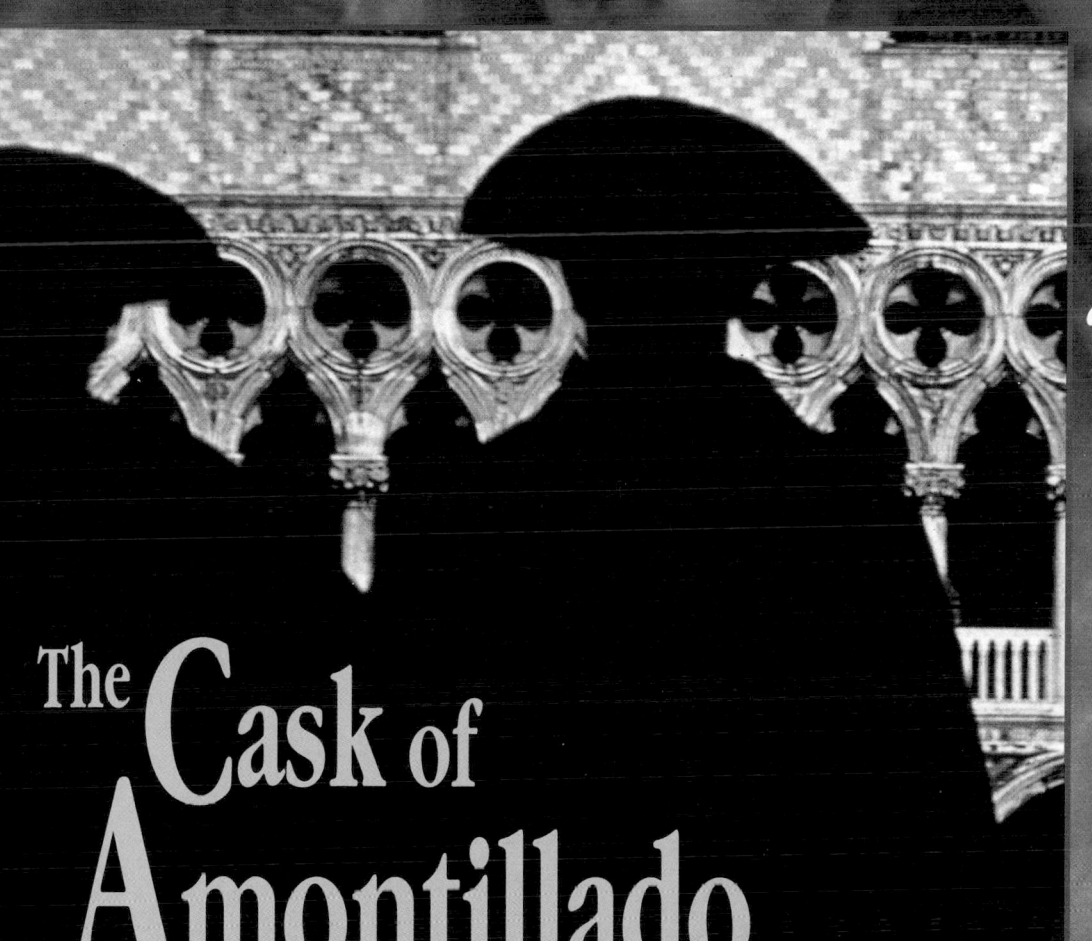

The Cask of Amontillado

Edgar Allan Poe

It was about dusk, one evening during the supreme madness of the carnival season.

The thousand injuries of Fortunato I had borne as best I could; but when he ventured upon insult, I vowed revenge. You, who so well know the nature of my soul, will not suppose, however, that I gave utterance to a threat. At length I would be avenged; this was a point definitively settled—but the very definitiveness with which it was resolved <u>precluded</u> the idea of risk. I must not only punish, but punish with <u>impunity</u>. A wrong is unredressed when <u>retribution</u> overtakes its redresser. It is equally unredressed when the avenger fails to make himself felt as such to him who has done the wrong.

WORDS TO OWN
precluded (prē·klōōd'id) *v.*: made impossible in advance; prevented.
impunity (im·pyōō'ni·tē) *n.*: freedom from punishment.
retribution (re'trə·byōō'shən) *n.*: punishment.

It must be understood that neither by word nor deed had I given Fortunato cause to doubt my goodwill. I continued, as was my wont, to smile in his face, and he did not perceive that my smile *now* was at the thought of his immolation.

He had a weak point—this Fortunato—although in other regards he was a man to be respected and even feared. He prided himself on his connoisseurship in wine. Few Italians have the true virtuoso spirit. For the most part their enthusiasm is adopted to suit the time and opportunity—to practice imposture upon the British and Austrian millionaires. In painting and gemmary, Fortunato, like his countrymen, was a quack—but in the matter of old wines he was sincere. In this respect I did not differ from him materially: I was skillful in the Italian vintages myself and bought largely whenever I could.

It was about dusk, one evening during the supreme madness of the carnival season, that I encountered my friend. He accosted me with excessive warmth, for he had been drinking much. The man wore motley.[1] He had on a tight-fitting parti-striped dress, and his head was surmounted by the conical cap and bells. I was so pleased to see him that I thought I should never have done wringing his hand.

I said to him, "My dear Fortunato, you are luckily met. How remarkably well you are looking today! But I have received a pipe[2] of what passes for amontillado, and I have my doubts."

"How?" said he. "Amontillado? A pipe? Impossiblc! And in the middle of the carnival!"

"I have my doubts," I replied; "and I was silly enough to pay the full amontillado price without consulting you in the matter. You were not to be found, and I was fearful of losing a bargain."

"Amontillado!"

"I have my doubts."

"Amontillado!"

"And I must satisfy them."

"Amontillado!"

"As you are engaged, I am on my way to Luchesi. If anyone has a critical turn, it is he. He will tell me——"

"Luchesi cannot tell amontillado from sherry."

"And yet some fools will have it that his taste is a match for your own."

"Come, let us go."

"Whither?"

"To your vaults."[3]

---

1. **motley** (mät′lē): multicolored costume worn by a clown or jester.
2. **pipe:** barrel.
3. **vaults** (vôlts): storage cellars.

WORDS TO OWN

immolation (im′ə·lā′shən) *n.*: destruction.
connoisseurship (kän′ə·sʉr′ship) *n.*: expert knowledge.

"My friend, no; I will not impose upon your good nature. I perceive you have an engagement. Luchesi——"

"I have no engagement; come."

"My friend, no. It is not the engagement, but the severe cold with which I perceive you are afflicted. The vaults are insufferably damp. They are encrusted with niter."[4]

"Let us go, nevertheless. The cold is merely nothing. Amontillado! You have been imposed upon. And as for Luchesi, he cannot distinguish sherry from amontillado."

Thus speaking, Fortunato possessed himself of my arm. Putting on a mask of black silk and drawing a roquelaure[5] closely about my person, I suffered him to hurry me to my *palazzo*.[6]

There were no attendants at home; they had absconded to make merry in honor of the time. I had told them that I should not return until the morning and had given them explicit orders not to stir from the house. These orders were sufficient, I well knew, to ensure their immediate disappearance, one and all, as soon as my back was turned.

I took from their sconces two flambeaux[7] and, giving one to Fortunato, bowed him through several suites of rooms to the archway that led into the vaults. I passed down a long and winding staircase, requesting him to be cautious as he followed. We came at length to the foot of the descent and stood together on the damp ground of the catacombs of the Montresors.

The gait of my friend was unsteady, and the bells upon his cap jingled as he strode.

"The pipe," said he.

"It is farther on," said I; "but observe the white web-work which gleams from these cavern walls."

4. **niter** (nīt′ər): salt deposits.
5. **roquelaure** (räk′ə·lôr′): heavy knee-length cloak.
6. *palazzo* (pä·lät′sô): Italian for "palace."
7. **sconces** (skän′siz): wall fixtures that hold **flambeaux** (flam′bōz′), candlesticks or flaming pieces of wood.

He turned toward me, and looked into my eyes with two filmy orbs that distilled the rheum[8] of intoxication.

"Niter?" he asked, at length.

"Niter," I replied. "How long have you had that cough?"

"Ugh! ugh! ugh!—ugh! ugh! ugh!—ugh! ugh! ugh!—ugh! ugh! ugh!—ugh! ugh! ugh!"

My poor friend found it impossible to reply for many minutes.

"It is nothing," he said, at last.

"Come," I said, with decision, "we will go back; your health is precious. You are rich, respected, admired, beloved; you are happy, as once I was. You are a man to be missed. For me it is no matter. We will go back; you will be ill, and I cannot be responsible. Besides, there is Luchesi——"

"Enough," he said; "the cough is a mere nothing; it will not kill me. I shall not die of a cough."

"True—true," I replied; "and, indeed, I had no intention of alarming you unnecessarily—but you should use all proper caution. A draft of this Médoc[9] will defend us from the damps."

Here I knocked off the neck of a bottle which I drew from a long row of its fellows that lay upon the mold.

"Drink," I said, presenting him the wine.

He raised it to his lips with a leer. He paused and nodded to me familiarly, while his bells jingled.

"I drink," he said, "to the buried that repose around us."

"And I to your long life."

He again took my arm, and we proceeded.

"These vaults," he said, "are extensive."

"The Montresors," I replied, "were a great and numerous family."

8. **rheum** (rōōm): watery discharge.
9. **Médoc** (mā·dôk′): type of red wine.

WORDS TO OWN

impose (im·pōz′) **upon** v.: take advantage of.

The Other Man in the Wall

On July 12, 1845, a letter appeared in a New York newspaper. The letter writer was describing his recent travels in Italy. He said that he had an amazing experience in the little town of San Giovanni when he visited the church of San Lorenzo. In the wall of the church he was shown a niche covered with a sort of trapdoor. Inside the niche was an upright human skeleton. The writer examined the skeleton and concluded that the victim had been walled up alive and suffocated. The writer also supposed that the motive had been revenge. He guessed that the man had been tied securely and then walled up, brick by brick. The writer also guessed that the men involved (like Fortunato and Montresor) were nobles—no one else, he figured, could have gotten control of a church to perform the gruesome deed.

The year after this letter was published, Poe wrote his famous revenge story, "The Cask of Amontillado."

"I forget your arms."[10]

"A huge human foot d'or, in a field azure; the foot crushes a serpent rampant whose fangs are embedded in the heel."[11]

"And the motto?"

Nemo me impune lacessit.[12]

"Good!" he said.

The wine sparkled in his eyes and the bells jingled. My own fancy grew warm with the Médoc. We had passed through walls of piled bones, with casks and puncheons[13] intermingling, into the inmost recesses of the catacombs. I paused again, and this time I made bold to seize Fortunato by an arm above the elbow.

"The niter!" I said. "See, it increases. It hangs like moss upon the vaults. We are below the river's bed. The drops of moisture trickle among the bones. Come, we will go back ere it is too late. Your cough——"

"It is nothing," he said; "let us go on. But first, another draft of the Médoc."

I broke and reached him a flagon of de Grâve.[14] He emptied it at a breath. His eyes

10. **arms:** coat of arms, a group of symbols used to represent a family.
11. **foot d'or . . . heel:** The Montresor coat of arms shows a huge golden foot against a blue background, with the foot crushing a snake that is rearing up and biting the heel.
12. **Nemo me impune lacessit** (nā′mō mā im·poo′nā lä·ke′sit): Latin for "Nobody attacks me without punishment."
13. **puncheons** (pun′chənz): large wine casks.
14. **flagon of de Grâve:** narrow-necked bottle with a handle and sometimes a lid, containing a wine from the Graves region of France.

flashed with a fierce light. He laughed and threw the bottle upward with a gesticulation I did not understand.

I looked at him in surprise. He repeated the movement—a grotesque one.

"You do not comprehend?" he said.

"Not I," I replied.

"Then you are not of the brotherhood."

"How?"

"You are not of the Masons."[15]

"Yes, yes," I said, "yes, yes."

"You? Impossible! A Mason?"

"A mason," I replied.

"A sign," he said.

"It is this," I answered, producing a trowel from beneath the folds of my roquelaure.

"You jest," he exclaimed, recoiling a few paces. "But let us proceed to the amontillado."

"Be it so," I said, replacing the tool beneath the cloak and again offering him my arm. He leaned upon it heavily. We continued our route in search of the amontillado. We passed through a range of low arches, descended, passed on, and, descending again, arrived at a deep crypt in which the foulness of the air caused our flambeaux rather to glow than flame.

---

15. **Masons** (māʹsənz): Freemasons, a secret society of people who believe in brotherhood, giving to the poor, and helping one another. Members use secret signs and gestures to recognize one another.

WORDS TO OWN

recoiling (ri·koilʹiŋ) v. used as adj.: moving backward, as if in horror.

At the most remote end of the crypt there appeared another less spacious. Its walls had been lined with human remains, piled to the vault overhead, in the fashion of the great catacombs of Paris. Three sides of this interior crypt were still ornamented in this manner. From the fourth the bones had been thrown down and lay promiscuously[16] upon the earth, forming at one point a mound of some size. Within the wall thus exposed by the displacing of the bones, we perceived a still interior recess, in depth about four feet, in width three, in height six or seven. It seemed to have been constructed for no especial use within itself, but formed merely the interval between two of the colossal supports of the roof of the catacombs and was backed by one of their circumscribing walls of solid granite.

It was in vain that Fortunato, uplifting his dull torch, endeavored to pry into the depth of the recess. Its termination the feeble light did not enable us to see.

"Proceed," I said; "herein is the amontillado. As for Luchesi——"

"He is an ignoramus," interrupted my friend, as he stepped unsteadily forward, while I followed immediately at his heels. In an instant he had reached the extremity of the niche, and finding his progress arrested by the rock, stood stupidly bewildered. A moment more and I had fettered[17] him to the granite. In its surface were two iron staples, distant from each other about two feet horizontally. From one of these depended a short chain, from the other a padlock. Throwing the links about his waist, it was but the work of a few seconds to secure it. He was too much astounded to resist. Withdrawing the key, I stepped back from the recess.

"Pass your hand," I said, "over the wall; you cannot help feeling the niter. Indeed it is *very* damp. Once more let me *implore* you to return. No? Then I must positively leave you. But I must first render you all the little attentions in my power."

16. **promiscuously** (prō·mis′kyoo̅·əs·lē): randomly; in a disorganized way.
17. **fettered** (fet′ərd): chained.

"The amontillado!" ejaculated my friend, not yet recovered from his astonishment.

"True," I replied; "the amontillado."

As I said these words, I busied myself among the pile of bones of which I have before spoken. Throwing them aside, I soon uncovered a quantity of building stone and mortar. With these materials and with the aid of my trowel, I began vigorously to wall up the entrance of the niche.

I had scarcely laid the first tier of the masonry when I discovered that the intoxication of Fortunato had in a great measure worn off. The earliest indication I had of this was a low moaning cry from the depth of the recess. It was *not* the cry of a drunken man. There was then a long and obstinate silence. I laid the second tier, and the third, and the fourth; and then I heard the furious vibrations of the chain. The noise lasted for several minutes, during which, that I might hearken to it with the more satisfaction, I ceased my labors and sat down upon the bones. When at last the clanking subsided, I resumed the trowel and finished without interruption the fifth, the sixth, and the seventh tier. The wall was now nearly upon a level with my breast. I again paused and, holding the flambeaux over the mason-work, threw a few feeble rays upon the figure within.

A succession of loud and shrill screams, bursting suddenly from the throat of the chained form, seemed to thrust me violently back. For a brief moment I hesitated—I trembled. Unsheathing my rapier,[18] I began to grope with it about the recess; but the thought of an instant reassured me. I placed my hand upon the solid fabric of the catacombs and felt satisfied. I reapproached the wall; I replied to the yells of him who clamored. I reechoed—I

18. **rapier** (rā′pē·ər): slender two-edged sword.

- -

WORDS TO OWN
endeavored (en·dev′ərd) *v.*: tried.
obstinate (äb′stə·nət) *adj.*: stubborn.
succession (sək·sesh′ən) *n.*: series.

- -

aided—I surpassed them in volume and in strength. I did this, and the clamorer grew still.

It was now midnight, and my task was drawing to a close. I had completed the eighth, the ninth, and the tenth tier. I had finished a portion of the last and the eleventh; there remained but a single stone to be fitted and plastered in. I struggled with its weight; I placed it partially in its destined position. But now there came from out the niche a low laugh that erected the hairs upon my head. It was succeeded by a sad voice, which I had difficulty in recognizing as that of the noble Fortunato. The voice said—

"Ha! ha! ha!—he! he! he!—a very good joke indeed—an excellent jest. We will have many a rich laugh about it at the *palazzo*—he! he! he!—over our wine—he! he! he!"

"The amontillado!" I said.

"He! he! he!—he! he! he!—yes, the amontillado. But is it not getting late? Will not they be awaiting us at the *palazzo*—the Lady Fortunato and the rest? Let us be gone."

"Yes," I said, "let us be gone."

"For the love of God, Montresor!"

"Yes," I said, "for the love of God!"

But to these words I hearkened in vain for a reply. I grew impatient. I called aloud—

"Fortunato!"

No answer. I called again—

"Fortunato!"

No answer still. I thrust a torch through the remaining aperture and let it fall within. There came forth in return only a jingling of the bells. My heart grew sick—on account of the dampness of the catacombs. I hastened to make an end of my labor. I forced the last stone into its position; I plastered it up. Against the new masonry I reerected the old rampart[19] of bones. For the half of a century no mortal has disturbed them. *In pace requiescat.*[20]

19. **rampart** (ram'pärt'): wall resembling one built for protection or defense.
20. *In pace requiescat* (in pä'chā rä'kwē·es'kät): Latin for "May he rest in peace."

MEET THE WRITER

A Haunted Life

Edgar Allan Poe (1809–1849) was the son of traveling actors. His father deserted the family, and his beautiful young mother died in a theatrical rooming house in Richmond, Virginia, before Edgar was three years old. The little boy was taken in as a foster child by the wealthy and childless Allan family of Richmond.

At first, Edgar's foster parents were pleased with his brilliant scholarship and athletic ability. But later they became angry at his moodiness and irresponsibility with money. Poe went to the University of Virginia but dropped out with heavy gambling debts. (John Allan apparently refused to support him any longer.) Eventually, Poe and his foster father split up completely, and Poe was left penniless. After several failed courtships, Poe married his thirteen-year-old cousin, Virginia Clemm, and moved to New York City. There, in 1837, they set up house, together with Virginia's mother, whom Poe fondly called Muddy.

Poe drank excessively, and he was always in need of money. But he wrote regularly and had increasing success, although his unusual poems and stories were mocked by conservative critics. "The Cask of Amontillado" was published in 1846 during a time when Poe was enduring vicious insults from critics. The story might have been Poe's way of getting even not only with hostile critics but also with his foster father. The Montresors' motto is the motto of Scotland; John Allan was Scottish and, like the hated Fortunato, a businessman and a Mason.

Poe's one refuge in life was threatened when Virginia became ill with tuberculosis. (Almost 25 percent of Americans in the nineteenth century died from tuberculosis.) When she died, Poe broke down completely. Two years later, he was found delirious in a tavern in Baltimore on a rainy election day. The great master of horror died a few days later.

A Second Helping of Poe

If you like Poe, you might also read "The Tell-Tale Heart," "The Masque of the Red Death," and "The Gold Bug."

MAKING MEANINGS

First Thoughts

1. Draw a head with thought bubbles like the one shown opposite, and fill in the bubbles with words and pictures that show what you think Montresor is thinking as he says, *"In pace requiescat."* Be prepared to explain your interpretation.

Shaping Interpretations

2. To whom could Montresor be talking, fifty years after the murder, and for what reasons?

3. Part of the story's horrifying effect comes from Poe's use of **irony**. What do *we* know that Fortunato does *not* know about why he has been invited into the vaults? When did *you* figure out what Montresor was up to?

4. Which of Montresor's comments to the unsuspecting Fortunato are **ironic**— that is, which ones mean something different from what they seem to mean?

5. The story is full of other examples of **irony**. Think about these uses of irony and how they made you feel:

   - Fortunato's name

   - his costume

   - the fact that a carnival takes place in the streets above the murder

6. Think about whether or not Montresor is a **reliable narrator**. Do any details suggest that he might have imagined "the thousand injuries" and the insult—or even the whole story? Can you find evidence in the story to support Montresor's claim that Fortunato *did* in fact injure and insult him? Talk about your interpretations with a group of classmates.

Extending the Text

7. Is this Just a gripping horror story told only for entertainment, or do you think it reveals some truth about life and the way people sometimes behave? Give reasons for your opinions. (Refer to the notes you made in your Reader's Log.)

Challenging the Text

8. What do you think of the way the story ends? Consider this question: Do writers have an obligation to punish murderers for their fictional crimes?

9. Some people feel that violence in fiction and on TV (like the violence in Poe's story) results in real-life violence. How do you feel about this?

> **Reviewing the Text**
>
> a. According to Montresor, what makes a perfect crime?
>
> b. How does Montresor lure Fortunato into the catacombs?
>
> c. What does Montresor admit is his motive for this crime?
>
> d. According to Montresor, what kind of person is Fortunato?
>
> e. What evidence suggests that Montresor committed the perfect crime?

CHOICES: Building Your Portfolio

Writer's Notebook

1. Collecting Ideas for a Short Short Story

Writing dialogue. A large part of Poe's story is told in dialogue. Poe uses dialogue to reveal important facts about his characters and to advance his plot. In Poe's dialogue *something happens.* Refer to the story ideas you've jotted down in your notebook. Can you *show* any of your characters in action by letting us hear their conversation? You might sketch comic-strip panels (stick figures are fine) and write the characters' words in bubbles. Remember that dialogue is easier to write if you place your characters in stressful circumstances, such as an argument or a dangerous situation. Decide if you want to add tag lines telling how your characters are talking (Emma whispered hoarsely, John shrieked). Save your notes for the Writer's Workshop on page 250.

Creative Writing

2. From Fortunato's Point of View

Suppose this story was being told by the gullible Fortunato instead of by Montresor. Write a new beginning. Start when the two men meet at dusk, and end when they begin their journey underground. Let Fortunato tell what *he* thinks of Montresor. Is he guilty of the thousand injuries and the insult?

Critical Writing

3. Finding a Motive

Suppose a detective assigned to the case at the time it happened wrote a report with this theory about the disappearance of Fortunato:

"Montresor is the last member of an old aristocratic Catholic family that lost its money. Fortunato was a businessman who recently became wealthy and wasn't above cheating to make money. Fortunato also was a member of the Masons, a secret Protestant organization that Catholics are forbidden to join. These facts explain Montresor's hatred of Fortunato. They also supply him with a motive for murder."

Now you are another detective assigned to the still unsolved case a few years later. In a report to your supervisor, explain exactly what you think of this theory. If you agree or disagree, tell why and find reasons in the story to support your interpretation of the case.

Critical Thinking/ Role-Playing

4. Crime and Punishment

Suppose the person to whom Montresor is telling his story has turned him over to the police. Montresor's lawyer might argue that his client is insane. The prosecution will argue that Montresor knew exactly what he was doing, even planned it in advance. Write a speech for either lawyer. Then role-play the courtroom scene.

Drawing

5. Designing a Stage Set

Suppose Poe's story is to be dramatized for TV and you are in charge of set design. Before you present your design to your director, decide on an exact time period for the story.

LANGUAGE LINK MINI-LESSON

Language Handbook HELP

See Quotation Marks, page 1026.

Technology HELP

See Language Workshop CD-ROM. *Key word entry: quotation marks.*

Style: Dialogue—Who's Talking?

One way writers make things happen in a story is by using dialogue. Dialogue can advance the plot, reveal the thoughts and words of a character, or even be the tool a writer uses to present important facts to a reader. In American usage, dialogue is enclosed in double quotation marks (" "). Usually, a new paragraph lets us know when a different person begins to speak, as in this example from "The Cask of Amontillado":

> "You do not comprehend?" he said.
> "Not I," I replied.
> "Then you are not of the brother-hood."

Most writers use tag lines ("he said," "I replied") to identify the speakers in a dialogue. But some writers don't. Poe, for example, has written long passages of conversation between Montresor and Fortunato in which neither speaker is directly identified.

Try It Out

Look back at page 234, at the dialogue beginning "Amontillado!" and at page 237 at the dialogue beginning "You do not comprehend?"

1. Get together with a partner and read the dialogue aloud. Use your voices to distinguish one speaker from another.

2. Now add tag lines to Poe's dialogue. Compare your edited versions of Poe's dialogue in class.

3. Finally, look at what Poe's dialogue accomplished. What did you learn about the characters or plot from this exchange?

VOCABULARY HOW TO OWN A WORD

WORD BANK

precluded
impunity
retribution
immolation
connoisseurship
impose upon
recoiling
endeavored
obstinate
succession

Yes or No

Be sure you can justify your responses to these questions.

1. If Robin loses her passport, is her trip to Japan precluded?
2. Should bank robbers be free to do their work with impunity?
3. Do you expect retribution if you never do your homework?
4. Could an earthquake cause the immolation of an entire city?
5. Would connoisseurship of horses help someone recognize a thoroughbred?
6. If a guest were to impose upon you, would you invite him back?
7. If a cobra was attacking, would you be recoiling?
8. If you endeavored to do something, did you give up immediately?
9. Would an obstinate person make a good negotiator?
10. Would a hitter's succession of strikeouts make him popular with fans?

Quickwrite

Write a few
sentences
summing up a fairy tale or fable
you remember from your childhood. What moral lesson does
the story teach?

The Princess and the Tin Box

James Thurber

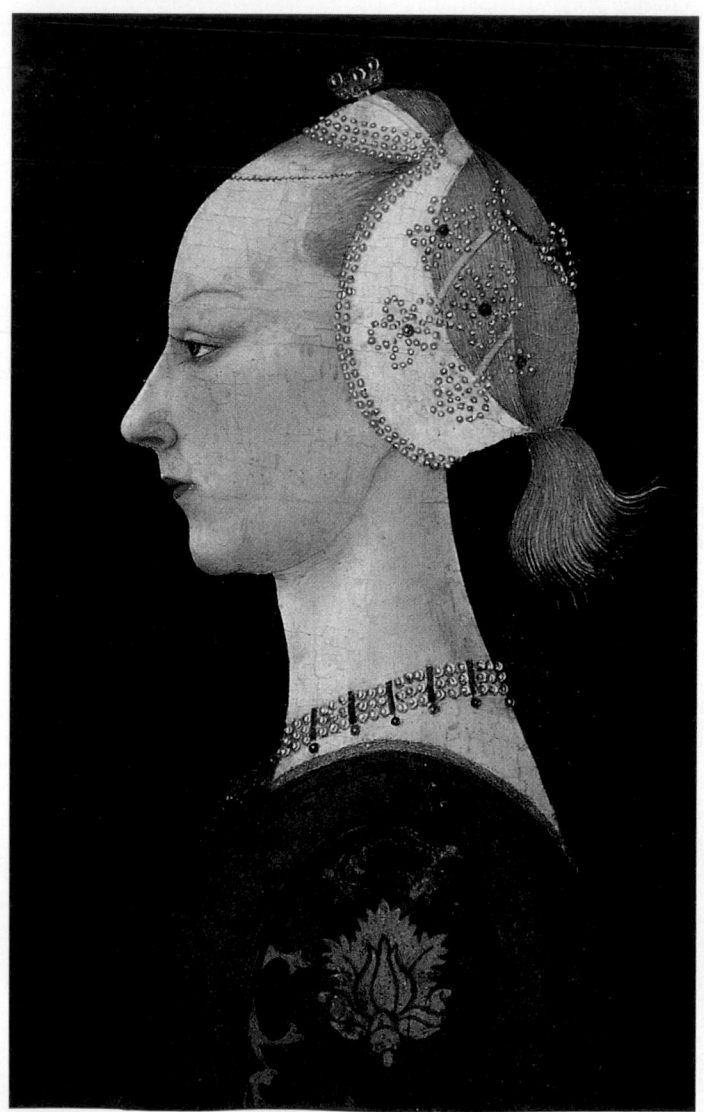

O nce upon a time, in a far
country, there lived a King
whose daughter was the prettiest
princess in the world. Her eyes were
like the cornflower, her hair was
sweeter than the hyacinth, and her
throat made the swan look dusty.

From the time she was a year old,
the Princess had been showered with
presents. Her nursery looked like
Cartier's[1] window. Her toys were all
made of gold or platinum or diamonds
or emeralds. She was not permitted to
have wooden blocks or china dolls or
rubber dogs or linen books, because
such materials were considered cheap
for the daughter of a king.

When she was seven, she was
allowed to attend the wedding of her
brother and throw real pearls at the
bride instead of rice. Only the nightingale, with his lyre of gold, was permitted to sing for the Princess. The
common blackbird, with his boxwood
flute, was kept out of the palace
grounds. She walked in silver-and-
samite[2] slippers to a sapphire-and-

1. **Cartier's** (kär′tē·āz): store selling
expensive jewelry in New York City.
2. **samite** (sam′īt): heavy silk fabric.

Young Lady of Fashion (15th century) by Paolo Uccello.

The Bettmann Archive.

topaz bathroom and slept in an ivory bed inlaid with rubies.

On the day the Princess was eighteen, the King sent a royal ambassador to the courts of five neighboring kingdoms to announce that he would give his daughter's hand in marriage to the prince who brought her the gift she liked the most.

The first prince to arrive at the palace rode a swift white stallion and laid at the feet of the Princess an enormous apple made of solid gold which he had taken from a dragon who had guarded it for a thousand years. It was placed on a long ebony table set up to hold the gifts of the Princess' suitors. The second prince, who came on a gray charger, brought her a nightingale made of a thousand diamonds, and it was placed beside the golden apple. The third prince, riding on a black horse, carried a great jewel box made of platinum and sapphires, and it was placed next to the diamond nightingale. The fourth prince, astride a fiery yellow horse, gave the Princess a gigantic heart made of rubies and pierced by an emerald arrow. It was placed next to the platinum-and-sapphire jewel box.

Now the fifth prince was the strongest and handsomest of all the five suitors, but he was the son of a poor king whose realm had been overrun by mice and locusts and wizards and mining engineers so that there was nothing much of value left in it. He came plodding up to the palace of the Princess on a plow horse, and he brought her a small tin box filled with mica and feldspar and hornblende[3] which he had picked up on the way.

The other princes roared with disdainful laughter when they

3. **mica . . . feldspar . . . hornblende:** types of ordinary rocks.

© Guy Marche/FPG International.

saw the tawdry gift the fifth prince had brought to the Princess. But she examined it with great interest and squealed with delight, for all her life she had been glutted with precious stones and priceless metals, but she had never seen tin before or mica or feldspar or hornblende. The tin box was placed next to the ruby heart pierced with an emerald arrow.

"Now," the King said to his daughter, "you must select the gift you like best and marry the prince that brought it."

The Princess smiled and walked up to the table and picked up the present she liked the most. It was the platinum-and-sapphire jewel box, the gift of the third prince.

"The way I figure it," she said, "is this. It is a very large and expensive box, and when I am married, I will meet many admirers who will give me precious gems with which to fill it to the top. Therefore, it is the most valuable of all the gifts my suitors have brought me, and I like it the best."

The Princess married the third prince that very day in the midst of great merriment and high revelry. More than a hundred thousand pearls were thrown at her and she loved it.

Moral: All those who thought that the Princess was going to select the tin box filled with worthless stones instead of one of the other gifts will kindly stay after class and write one hundred times on the blackboard, "I would rather have a hunk of aluminum silicate than a diamond necklace."

Drawing for "The Princess and the Tin Box" (1948) by James Thurber.

MEET THE WRITER

He Walked into Himself

When he was asked by an editor to write his own biography, **James Thurber** (1894–1961) came up with these details:

❝ James Thurber was born on a night of wild portent and high wind in the year 1894, at 147 Parsons Avenue, Columbus, Ohio. The house, which is still standing, bears no tablet or plaque of any description and is never pointed out to visitors. Once Thurber's mother, walking past the place with an old lady from Fostoria, Ohio, said to her, 'My son James was born in that house,' to which the old lady, who was extremely deaf, replied, 'Why, on the Tuesday morning train, unless my sister is worse.' Mrs. Thurber let it go at that.

The infant Thurber was brought into the world by an old practical nurse named Margery Albright, who had delivered the babies of neighbor women before the Civil War. He was, of course, much too young at the time to have been affected by the quaint and homely circumstances of his birth. . . . Not a great deal is known about his earliest years, beyond the fact that he could walk when he was only two years old and was able to speak whole sentences by the time he was four.

Thurber's boyhood (1900–1913) was pretty well devoid of significance. I see no reason why it should take up much of our time. There is no clearly traceable figure or pattern in this phase of his life. If he knew where he was going, it is not apparent from this distance. He fell down a great deal during this period, because of a trick he had of walking into himself. His gold-rimmed glasses forever needed straightening, which gave him the appearance of a person who hears somebody calling but can't make out where the sound is coming from. Because of his badly focused lenses, he saw, not two of everything, but one and a half. Thus, a four-wheeled wagon would not have eight wheels for him, but six. How he succeeded in preventing these two extra wheels from getting into his work, I have no way of knowing.

Thurber's life baffles and irritates the biographer because of its lack of design. One has the disturbing feeling that the man contrived to be some place without actually having gone there. His drawings, for example, sometimes seem to have reached completion by some other route than the common one of intent.

The writing is, I think, different. In his prose pieces he appears always to have started from the beginning and to have reached the end by way of the middle. It is impossible to read any of the stories from the last line to the first without experiencing a definite sensation of going backward. This seems to me to prove that the stories were written and did not, like the drawings, just suddenly materialize.

Thurber's very first bit of writing was a so-called poem entitled 'My Aunt Mrs. John T. Savage's Garden at 185 South Fifth Street, Columbus, Ohio.' It is of no value or importance except insofar as it demonstrates the man's appalling memory for names and numbers. He can tell you to this day the names of all the children who were in the fourth grade when he was. He remembers the phone numbers of several of his high school chums. He knows the birthdays of all his friends and can tell you the date on which any child of theirs was christened. He can rattle off the names of all the persons who attended the lawn fete of the First M.E. Church of Columbus in 1907. This ragbag of precise but worthless information may have helped him in his work, but I don't see how. . . . ❞

- Work in groups to create your own updated versions of old fairy tales like "Little Red Ridinghood" or "Cinderella." Your Reader's Log entries might give you ideas.

  1. Choose a familiar fairy tale. What is its moral lesson?

  2. Retell the story with a new, modern setting (like Los Angeles or Puerto Rico) and real-life characters. Remember to follow Thurber's example and give the fairy tale a modern twist at the end. How does this twist change the moral lesson of the fairy tale?

  3. If you have an artist in your group, ask him or her to illustrate your twenty-first-century fairy tale. You might prefer to tell your modern fairy tale in the form of cartoon panels.

  4. Choose someone from your group to share the results with the class.

a chance meeting

i was walking through the forest and came
upon a cockroach
allen, he said
i walked on
i don't talk to cockroaches.

—Halley Wheeless
Worland High School
Worland, Wyoming

Drawing by John O'Brien; © 1994 The New Yorker Magazine, Inc.

New Light on an Old Monster

Was Dr. Frankenstein's creation a monster, a miracle, or just a misunderstood outsider? You might know a monster from the movie version of Mary Shelley's *Frankenstein* (Signet)—a huge creature lurking at the window, wandering the dark lanes. But do you know who the real monster is in this story? You may be in for a surprise when you read the book *Frankenstein*.

Other Worlds

H. G. Wells specializes in fantasy worlds. Once upon a time Wells invented the Time Traveler, put him in a Time Machine, and propelled him from Victorian England thousands of years into the future. If that isn't fantastic enough, another of Wells's stories—about an invasion from Mars—is so convincing that it created a panic when Orson Welles read it on the radio more than forty years after it was first published. Escape to other worlds with Wells's *The Time Machine* and *The War of the Worlds* (Fawcett Premier).

Twilight Zones

A whistling night train and a shrieking dragon just miss crossing each other's path, garbage trucks clean up the aftermath of nuclear annihilation, rainy days on Venus never end. Expect thirty-one excursions into twilight zones when you read Ray Bradbury's *Classic Stories 1* (Bantam Spectra), where everyday life is hauntingly transformed into strange and fantastic tales. You may find your way back from these twilight zones, but the world you knew will never seem the same.

Writer's Workshop

ASSIGNMENT

Write a short short story. Your story can be a realistic one about everyday life; a science fiction, horror, or mystery story; a fantasy; a satire; or a story with a surprise ending.

AIM

To create an original story.

AUDIENCE

Your friends; class-mates; young children; or readers of a magazine of student writing. (You choose.)

NARRATIVE WRITING

SHORT SHORT STORY

In this collection you've read stories with various plots, set in various places, and filled with various characters. Now you'll do some creative thinking to write a short short story of your own.

Prewriting

1. Find Your Ideas

You might have already started on a story of your own or you may have lots of ideas collected in your Writer's Notebook. Flip through your notes to see if there's an idea waiting to be turned into a story. If you're not satisfied with your notes, try these strategies:

• Check the newspaper for some interesting situations that could be turned into stories. (Remember, Poe's idea might have come from a newspaper.)

• Check current magazines. You might find some ideas in the photographs or even in the advertisements.

• Try brainstorming with other people. Some notes about story ideas are in the notebook on the opposite page.

2. Make Some Decisions

Once you have an idea, it's time to settle these basic questions:

• **Audience.** Are you writing for children, teenagers, or adults? Design your vocabulary, sentence length, and details to suit your audience. If you're writing for your classmates, you're already an expert on the language, interests, and humor of your readers. If you're writing for children, browse through some children's books to get a sense of vocabulary level and sentence length.

• **Characters.** Who are your main characters and what is each one's problem or conflict? What are they like—what kind of people are they?

• **Point of view.** Who will tell your story? Will you have an

The history
of the written
word is rich and *Once upon a time*

Page 1

omniscient narrator tell it, someone not in the story? Or will you let one of the characters speak as *I* and tell the story?

- **Order of events.** Will you start at the beginning and move your readers in chronological, or time, order right to the end of the story? Or will you tell the whole story as a flashback to an earlier time?

- **Suspense.** Will you withhold information? Try not telling your readers some important piece of information until the story's end.

3. Now Map the Story

Focus on your characters and their conflict, and start planning the story's events. Ask yourself, "What happens to my characters first? What happens next? What happens then?" Make a story map like the one shown here, and try out your plot ideas on your writing group or partner. Even if you aren't writing a story with a surprise ending, you still have to keep your readers guessing about what will happen next.

Drafting
1. Jump-Start the Action

In a short short story you won't have the space to develop your characters slowly or in depth. Instead, focus on plot and start your action moving right away with a bit of interesting dialogue or a startling event. Try to hook your reader's attention at once.

2. Add Dialogue

Let your readers eavesdrop on what the characters actually say to each other. In the short short story that follows, notice how dialogue moves the action along and at the same time keeps you guessing about the setting and the situation.

3. Elaborate

Will more sensory details help readers experience the story's **sights, sounds, smells, touches,** and **tastes**?

> **Story Ideas**
> Sleeping Beauty is brought up to date.
> Dogs can talk, but people can't.
> The whole earth turns to sand.
> An alien lands in the Grand Canyon.

> **Story Map**
> **Characters:** 2 college admission people; student.
> **Setting:** Far in the future, very hi-tech (keep setting a surprise).
> **Conflict:** Admission to college totally automated, people vs. computers.
> **Main Events:** 2 characters discuss applicants. Dispose of rejected CDs. Talk a lot, very regimented. Finally accept student.
> **Point of View:** Omniscient.

WAITING FOR THE BEEP

The two individuals, one male, one female, sat opposite each other in the small office. Between them lay a large pile of papers reeking of bureaucracy, each with a small compact disc attached.

"Next," Mr. Thanatogenos said.

"Number 123,456," Mrs. Hedon said.

Mr. Thanatogenos glanced at the paper for a few seconds. "No, no, no," he said immediately, a sharp edge to his voice. "How did this get in here? This one's only a Good Person! You know we take only Superior Persons!"

"I'm sorry, Mr. Thanatogenos," Mrs. Hedon said, dumping the paper and the CD down the disposal chute conveniently located next to her. "I'll see that it never happens again."

"You'd better. Next."

"Number 123,457," Mrs. Hedon said. "This one's a Superior Person."

Mr. Thanatogenos ran his eyes rapidly over the sheet. "Hmm," he said.

"Ha!" he said. "Hm. Ha. Uh-huh. Well."

"Look promising?" Mrs. Hedon asked.

"Member of the National Conglomeration of Incredible People," he said, mulling it over. "Member of the forty-three other prestigious-sounding organizations, all listed in the Great Handbook of Prestigious Organizations."

"Impressive," Mrs. Hedon agreed, nodding her head.

"Uh-oh," Mr. Thanatogenos said at once. "This one's only a 1590. The cutoff is 1591."

Mrs. Hedon clicked her tongue several times consecutively, producing a sound not unlike that of an M-60 heavy machine gun. "Too bad. It looked so good, too."

The disposal chute whirred as it greedily consumed yet another package.

"Next," Mr. Thanatogenos said.

"Number 123,458," Mrs. Hedon said, handing him the package.

Mr. Thanatogenos scanned it with bored eyes. Glancing at his chrono, he saw that it was 4:57:08 P.M. Just a few more minutes . . . and seconds . . .

"Hm. Ah. 1595. Once personally met with an individual who had a rating of Interesting. Was given an award for Extreme Service to Frogs."

Story situation given in two sentences.

The phrase "reeking of bureaucracy" catches interest.

The details begin to get humorously absurd.

Numbers are mysterious. They raise questions.

The dialogue moves the plot forward and reveals character. It's very realistic.

Humorous description of a character.

Notice the characters' obsession with time, measured to the second. More humor.

"Your decision?" Mrs. Hedon prompted, her own eyes on her own chrono.

"Wait. What's this?" Mr. Thanatogenos pointed to a blank space on the sheet. "There's no reference number for the rank index."

Dialogue is used to advance the action.

"It must have gone to one of those places where they don't have reference numbers for the rank index."

"Hm. Unbelievable, the laxity of some units, excuse me, people, these days. Well, I can't make a decision without a reference number for the rank index."

The disposal chute whirred again. 4:58:32 P.M.

"Next."

"Number 123,459," Mrs. Hedon announced.

Mr. Thanatogenos's eyes ate up the paper before him. "1599. Extra-Special Superior rating. And—" He grinned at this, almost forgetting his chrono for a moment. "—has actually flattered three Official Representatives."

Dialogue is used to provide information and to reveal a character's values.

Even Mrs. Hedon smiled at this.

"So we accept?" she asked.

"Yes."

Mrs. Hedon turned and opened the slot on the materializer. Sliding the CD inside, she shut it and pressed PLAY. The human passenger which had been encoded upon its groove by the transportation division was being returned to life at the touch of a button.

On the acceptance platform before the two of them, a young man of eighteen appeared, accompanied by a loud popping sound. An anxious expression dominated his face, which was attempting to avoid drowning in nervous perspiration.

A good descriptive sentence.

"Number 123,459," Mrs. Hedon said, feigning a smile of pleasure, "as of 4:59:42 P.M. on Tuesday, August 28, 2021, you are hereby granted the place of B-2 Grade Underclassman at Princeton University. Classes will commence at precisely 8:00:00 A.M. on Monday, September 3, 2021."

The climax: Now we know what this was all about.

The relieved student on the platform wanted to thank them, but their chronos beeped simultaneously as they hit 5:00:00 P.M., and both were out the door before he could say a word.

The ending is clever—the future setting is a complete surprise.

—John Morgan
Half Hollow Hills High School
Dix Hills, New York

Language Link
H E L P

Diction: page 211.
Pronouns and pronoun
contractions: page 231.
Dialogue: page 243.

Jim's Journal
by Jim

After my classes today I started a story for my creative-writing class.

The story isn't due till next Wednesday, but I had an idea for it today.

It's a science-fiction story in which everything in the universe disappears.

But I can't think of where to take it from there.

Reprinted from *I Went to College and It Was Okay* by permission of the author. Publisher: Andrews and McMeel.

Evaluating and Revising

1. Reading the Story Aloud

Try reading your draft aloud to yourself. Your sentences, especially the dialogue, should flow smoothly, as if someone were talking comfortably. Then try to "tighten" the story, eliminating padding. All of the details and dialogue should move your story along to its climax.

2. Peer Editing

Get together with three or four classmates to read and comment on one another's drafts. Focus on the following questions:

- Is the beginning interesting? Does it make you want to know more? How can it be improved?
- Is the sequence of events clear?
- Is the point of view effective? Is it consistent?
- Does the story move quickly or drag? If it drags, identify where you got bogged down.
- Does the dialogue sound realistic?
- Does the story have impact—or does it fall flat?

Proofreading

If you're writing on a computer, use the spelling and grammar checkers. Or exchange papers with your writing group and hunt for overlooked mistakes. Check the Language Handbook (pages 993–1039) and/or a dictionary when in doubt, and make sure you understand the grammar or usage rules behind any corrections you make. It's never too late to make changes, so if you get a brilliant idea, try it out.

Publishing

- You might make class anthologies of each type of short short story—science fiction, mystery, fairy tale, and so on. Donate your anthologies to the school library.
- If you've written a children's story, you might volunteer to read it aloud to children at a day-care center, elementary school, or shelter. With others in your class, present a storytelling or reading hour.
- Send your story to one of the magazines of student writing. "Waiting for the Beep" (pages 252–253) was published in a school literary magazine.

The two individuals, one male, one

<u>opposite each other</u>〉 <u>Between</u>〉
(in the small (them lay
female, sat ~~in an~~ office. ~~There was~~
∧ ∧

<u>reeking of bureaucracy</u>
a large pile of papers, each with a
∧

small compact disc attached.

"Next," Mr. Thanatogenos said.
"Number 123,456," Mrs. Hedon said.

Mr. Thanatogenos glanced at
∧
the paper for a few seconds. "No, no, no," he〉
(said immediately, a sharp edge to his voice.
~~one of the papers and said,~~
∧

here
"How did this get in ~~hear~~? This
∧

one's only a Good Person! You

know we take only Superior

Persons!"

Peer Comments

Can you tell us more?

You could add some dialogue.

Misspelling.

I like the mystery. We need to know more, though.

■ *Evaluation Criteria*

A short short story should

1. **introduce the main characters and their conflicts quickly**

2. **capture the reader's interest by starting the action right away**

3. **relate a series of events that peak in a climax**

4. **have a satisfying ending, perhaps a surprise**

5. **maintain a consistent point of view**

Sentence Workshop
H E L P

Varying sentence beginnings: page 256.

Reflecting

If you are putting this story in your portfolio, add a brief reflection on your writing and include it in your portfolio. Your reflection could answer these questions:

1. How did I get my idea for this story?
2. What was the hardest part of writing this short short story?
3. Which part was the most fun?
4. Next time I write a story, what will I do differently?
5. What skills do I need to work on?

I got the idea for the story from some fantasy stories I'd been reading. I like fantasy and especially stories that use a lot of technology. The hardest part of writing is finding enough to write about. At times I thought my ideas had dried up, but going back to the story a few days later helped. The most fun is dialogue. I think I have a knack for it. Also the satire. I like that. I need to work on writing a story set in the real world.

Sentence Workshop

Language Handbook HELP

See Writing Effective Sentences, page 1015.

REVISING SENTENCES: BEGINNINGS

The normal word order for English sentences is subject + verb + complement (if there is one), as in this sentence from "The Cask of Amontillado" (page 237).

     S   V   C

"He repeated the movement—a grotesque one."

Subject-verb-complement sentences are fine, but a whole series of them, bumper to bumper, dulls a paragraph. A good paragraph has variety, and one way to achieve variety is to vary your sentence beginnings.

  Possible variations. Each of these sentences from "The Gift of the Magi" begins in a different way. To see how the opening word or group of words receives extra emphasis, try rewriting each sentence so that it begins with the subject.

ADVERB	"<u>Suddenly</u> she whirled from the window and stood before the glass." (page 204)
PREPOSITIONAL PHRASE	"<u>With that chain on his watch</u> Jim might be properly anxious about the time in any company." (page 205)
ADVERB CLAUSE	"<u>When Della reached home</u>, her intoxication gave way a little to prudence and reason." (page 205)

Writer's Workshop Follow-up: Proofreading

Are your sentences stuck in a rut of the same beginnings? When you revise the story you've written for the Writer's Workshop (page 250), go over each sentence. Highlight words and phrases that you think could be placed at the beginnings of your sentences to make them more forceful. Then recast your story and read it aloud to a partner. Do the sentences sound as if they fit together smoothly?

Try It Out

Rewrite the following sentences so that each one begins with the part specified in parentheses. Is there a change in emphasis?

1. "An arm seems to reach out from behind her and snatch her backward." (prepositional phrase)
—Alice Walker, "Roselily"

2. "The sight I saw when I entered that large hall was new and strange to me." (adverb clause)
—Mark Twain, "Life on the Mississippi"

3. "The priest approached the grave slowly, wondering how they had managed to dig into the frozen ground." (adverb)
—Leslie Marmon Silko, "The Man to Send Rain Clouds"

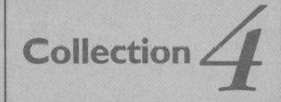
Collection 4

Every once in a while close friends or parents or teachers do something that surprises us. We've been around them a lot and think we know them well. Then a kind and gentle friend reveals a selfish streak, a hard teacher gives us a break, or someone we never trusted comes through for us suddenly. At such moments we discover something about people and life, and the discoveries can be wonderful or painful. More startling still can be the moments when we discover something about ourselves. It may happen when we're suddenly angry at something that never bothered us before, or when we suddenly understand why we're nervous at parties. We might realize that we admire someone we've never noticed before, or want something we never thought we would want. Every story is in some way or other also about a discovery. If the story works, we realize by its end that we, along with the characters, have discovered (or rediscovered) something important about life.

A lie hides the truth.
A story tries to find it.

—Paula Fox

Writer's Notebook

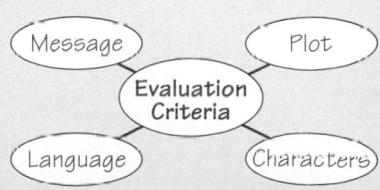

Every time we read a story (or see a movie) we evaluate it: It was good. It was slow. It was hard to understand. In the Writer's Workshop on page 332, you'll be using these judgment skills to write an evaluation of a short story. Get started early by thinking back to the stories you have read. What did you like about some stories? What did you dislike about others? Review the stories you remember. Gather your criteria about what makes a good or poor story (in your opinion) in a cluster like the one below. Keep your notes and add to them as you read the stories that follow.

```
  Message           Plot
        \         /
        Evaluation
         Criteria
        /         \
  Language        Characters
```

BEFORE YOU READ
THE GIFT

Reading Focus

What Endures

We may not celebrate holidays today in quite the same way our ancestors did. We shop for different gifts, cook with new recipes, and travel in airplanes instead of covered wagons. Still, traditions have a way of enduring—the old meanings are still there. We still choose gifts for people we love and rearrange our schedules to share holidays with them. In Ray Bradbury's "The Gift" the holidays have changed on the outside, but the true meaning of Christmas endures.

Quickwrite

Think for a few minutes about the next holiday in your life. What are your plans? Will you do anything that simply couldn't have been done two hundred years ago—like taking pictures or listening to CDs? Write for a few minutes in your Reader's Log about holidays past, present, and future. If things are different today from what they once were, what might they become in, say, another two hundred years?

Elements of Literature

Climax

The **climax** of a story is its key scene—that tense, terrifying, or just plain exciting moment when our emotional involvement is greatest because we are about to discover the outcome of the story's conflict. It's the moment when Cinderella's foot fits into the slipper or when Dorothy clicks her heels together and finds herself back home in Kansas. Very often, at the climax, we readers discover something right along with the characters.

> The **climax** is that moment when we realize what the outcome of the story will be.
>
> *For more on Plot, see pages 32–33 and the Handbook of Literary Terms.*

It was the boy's first flight into space.

THE GIFT

Ray Bradbury

Tomorrow would be Christmas, and even while the three of them rode to the rocket port the mother and father were worried. It was the boy's first flight into space, his very first time in a rocket, and they wanted everything to be perfect. So when, at the customs table, they were forced to leave behind his gift, which exceeded the weight limit by no more than a few ounces, and the little tree with the lovely white candles, they felt themselves deprived of the season and their love.

The boy was waiting for them in the Terminal room. Walking toward him, after their unsuccessful clash with the Inter-planetary officials, the mother and father whispered to each other.

"What shall we do?"

"Nothing, nothing. What *can* we do?"

"Silly rules!"

"And he so wanted the tree!"

The siren gave a great howl and people pressed forward into the Mars Rocket. The mother and father walked at the very last, their small pale son between them, silent.

"I'll think of something," said the father.

"What . . .?" asked the boy.

And the rocket took off and they were flung headlong into dark space.

The rocket moved and left fire behind

Life in Outer Space?

On October 12, 1992, the 500th anniversary of Columbus's landing in the Americas, the National Aeronautics and Space Administration began a project called SETI, the Search for Extraterrestrial Intelligence. SETI scientists do not hunt for spaceships or little green men; they listen to the static in outer space, hoping to detect a radio signal from an unknown civilization somewhere in the universe. The main tool in this search is the radio telescope, which looks like a huge bowl made of perforated aluminum surrounded by movable antennae. A super computer processes every radio wave that hits the bowl. The computer does billions of tests a second, discarding the random waves given off by stars and carefully scanning any regular patterns. Some scientists dream of discovering an "encyclopedia galactica," a collection of advanced scientific knowledge sent by sophisticated aliens. This dream may be intriguing, but there's no guarantee that humans would be able to recognize or interpret such information if it actually arrived. To date, there is no proof that anyone is out there, and in 1993, Congress ended all federal funding for the project. Still, scientists at three privately supported SETI programs continue to point their telescopes at the stars and to listen.

and left Earth behind on which the date was December 24, 2052, heading out into a place where there was no time at all, no month, no year, no hour. They slept away the rest of the first "day." Near midnight, by their Earth-time New York watches, the boy awoke and said, "I want to go look out the porthole."

There was only one port, a "window" of immensely thick glass of some size, up on the next deck.

"Not quite yet," said the father. "I'll take you up later."

"I want to see where we are and where we're going."

"I want you to wait for a reason," said the father.

He had been lying awake, turning this way and that, thinking of the abandoned gift, the problem of the season, the lost tree and the white candles. And at last, sitting up, no more than five minutes ago, he believed he had found a plan. He need only carry it out and this journey would be fine and joyous indeed.

"Son," he said, "in exactly one half-hour it will be Christmas."

"Oh," said the mother, dismayed that he had mentioned it. Somehow she had rather hoped that the boy would forget.

The boy's face grew feverish and his lips trembled. "I know, I know. Will I get a present, will I? Will I have a tree? Will I have a tree? You promised——"

"Yes, yes, all that, and more," said the father.

The mother started. "But——"

"I mean it," said the father. "I really mean it. All and more, much more. Excuse me, now. I'll be back."

He left them for about twenty minutes. When he came back, he was smiling. "Almost time."

"Can I hold your watch?" asked the boy, and

the watch was handed over and he held it ticking in his fingers as the rest of the hour drifted by in fire and silence and unfelt motion.

"It's Christmas *now*! Christmas! Where's my present?"

"Here we go," said the father and took his boy by the shoulder and led him from the room, down the hall, up a rampway, his wife following.

"I don't understand," she kept saying.

"You will. Here we are," said the father.

They had stopped at the closed door of a large cabin. The father tapped three times and then twice in a code. The door opened and the light in the cabin went out and there was a whisper of voices.

"Go on in, son," said the father.

"It's dark."

"I'll hold your hand. Come on, Mama."

They stepped into the room and the door shut, and the room was very dark indeed. And before them loomed a great glass eye, the porthole, a window four feet high and six feet wide, from which they could look out into space.

The boy gasped.

Behind him, the father and the mother gasped with him, and then in the dark room some people began to sing.

"Merry Christmas, son," said the father.

And the voices in the room sang the old, the familiar carols, and the boy moved slowly until his face was pressed against the cool glass of the port. And he stood there for a long, long time, just looking and looking out into space and the deep night at the burning and the burning of ten billion billion white and lovely candles. . . .

MEET THE WRITER

Teller of Tales

Ray Bradbury (1920–   ) calls himself a teller of tales and a magic realist. He also claims to remember everything—every book he's read, every movie he's seen, all the events of his life back to and including his birth in Waukegan, Illinois, on August 22, 1920. All those memories and a big imagination are the materials for the "magic realist" fiction and poetry he's been writing for more than fifty years. Bradbury gives credit for all his writing to his boyhood self:

66 I don't know if I believe in previous lives; I'm not sure I can live forever. But that young boy believed in both, and I have let him have his head. He has written my stories and books for me. **99**

Bradbury's work is full of childhood imaginings, fantasies, and nightmares—portraits of Venus and Mars, time traveling, ageless children, never-ending rains—but Bradbury the grown-up is a concerned citizen.

His fantasy stories are often warnings against blind faith in science, but they're optimistic. By giving strange twists to everyday objects and events, Bradbury challenges his readers to look at them as if for the first time. As a writer, he entertains, leading readers to see science through the excited eyes of children, but he also informs, suggesting ways adults might use technology more responsibly.

More Magic Realism

Other books by Bradbury include *Something Wicked This Way Comes* (Simon & Schuster), *I Sing the Body Electric* (Buccaneer), and *R Is for Rocket* (Buccaneer).

While We're Young

GREGG EASTERBROOK

ARLINGTON, Va.—Lights in the distance—candles on a window-sill, a twinkling decorated tree, the street lights of a small town seen from a snowy hill above—have long evoked a feeling of hope that is the best universal feature of the Christmas season. Yet our rational impulse tells us that this notion comes from sentiment, not reasoning—that a distant light can't reveal anything about the human prospect. Or can it?

Researchers working with the Hubble Space Telescope this fall fixed their gaze on the light emitted by a class of stars called cepheids, located in a galaxy that sky charts designate M100, and made a discovery that, if confirmed, could have tremendous implications for the way we think about the future of our species and our planet.

Galaxy M100 appears to the eye as a dot in the constellation Virgo. The cepheids are pulsating stars; they twinkle more emphatically than any object known to mankind, and scientists can use them to gauge distance. Applying their studies of the cepheids to theories of cosmology, the researchers estimated that the universe is only eight billion years old.

As tools of astronomy have improved—especially with the launching of the Hubble telescope, which orbits above the Earth's distorting atmosphere—discoveries have tended to lower the postulated cosmic age. But the findings connected with the M100 cepheids are astounding: No previously accepted data had put the age of the firmament at less than fourteen billion years.

A universe eight billion years old may seem fantastically ancient to our sensibilities. (It seems old, too, by most religious notions, especially those typified by the seventeenth-century dictum of James Ussher, an Irish archbishop, who calculated that the heavens and the Earth were forged in precisely 4004 B.C.) Yet in cosmological terms, a universe of eight billion years glistens with the dew of creation.

According to the pessimistic main current of contemporary thought, mankind has encountered the natural world late in a long, exhausting journey of decline. The environment is running down, we are told, and the heavens already exhibit entropic decay. Renewal is impossible; the Sun can only set.

But the findings from galaxy M100 raise the prospect that we are greeting creation in its morning hours. "If there will ever be any re-collapse that ends the universe, that event is a long way off, perhaps thousands of billions of years," said Alan Dressler, an astronomer at the Carnegie Observatory in Pasadena, California. "People have come to the cosmos very close to the beginning of time."

Our species may have arrived on the planet mere moments after dawn: Perhaps less than 1 percent of the time available on the cosmic clock has expired. If the universe is much newer than once supposed, it is also possible that life on Earth may have arisen relatively rapidly in cosmic terms.

If so, almost everything important that's going to happen to mankind—and many other creatures—lies ahead. And if treated with proper respect, the Earth will sustain its people, plants, and animals much longer than is now assumed.

What will happen over very long spans of time may not seem directly relevant to how we live and think today. Yet people have always been influenced by whether there is a positive or negative conception of the human prospect. Prominent thinkers who have bemoaned humanity's inevitable decline have often cited what they took to be the decaying natural order. With findings like those in galaxy M100, this metaphor increasingly seems dead wrong.

At this time of year, nearly everyone pauses to wonder on the future of humanity and the message of common hope some of our ancestors believed they received long ago. This year, pause on a starry night. Look overhead at the twinkling enormity of the firmament and consider the data from galaxy M100 and that from another recent finding: Improved instruments have given evidence of new stars coalescing practically everywhere astronomers look, even in our own galaxy, the Milky Way.

The universe is young, stars are still forming—some right in our neighborhood. When we raise our eyes to the night sky, what we behold is the light of sunrise.

—from *The New York Times*, December 23, 1994

MAKING MEANINGS

First Thoughts

1. What do you think the family discovers at the **climax** of "The Gift"?

Shaping Interpretations

2. What does the story suggest is most important about the observation of Christmas?

3. What is the gift referred to in the story's **title**?

Extending the Text

4. What traditions would you miss—the way this boy misses his tree and candles and gifts—if you were in outer space on your favorite holiday? Why are those traditions important? What do they do for you? Be sure to check your Quick-write.

CHOICES: Building Your Portfolio

Writer's Notebook

1. Collecting Ideas for an Evaluation

Where are we? In the Writer's Workshop on page 332, you'll write an evaluation of a short story. If you compiled a list of criteria for story evaluation before beginning this collection, you might find **setting** on the list. Some readers like to lose themselves in strange and fantastic settings. Others prefer to read about places close to home. What appeals to *you* in a story setting? What makes a setting weak? What do you think about stories that don't have any special setting at all? Jot down your criteria for enjoyable or boring settings and save your notes.

Storyboard

2. A TV Special

Your job is to write a proposal for a half-hour television special based on "The Gift." Retell the main events of the story so that it will sound unique and compelling to a TV producer. Describe a few of the special effects that will convey its unusual setting. Which actors do you see in the main roles? Remember, TV producers can be very picky, so give the specific information they'll be looking for:

- What feeling will you be conveying in the special?
- Who will the audience be?
- What time slot would you aim for?

- Who are the characters and what do they want?
- What complications keep them from getting what they want?
- How are their problems resolved?

Critical Writing

3. A Letter to the Editor

Suppose you read "While We're Young" (page 262) in your newspaper. Write a letter to the editor telling how you feel about the writer's main idea, or about any details in the editorial. Do you have any questions you'd like to ask the writer? Do you think the newspaper should publish more editorials like this?

Elements of Literature

THEME: What Does It Mean?

A story can excel in any number of ways—in the strength of its plot, in the reality of its characters, in the gracefulness of its language. But what often makes us remember a story long after we've read it is the idea on which it's built.

This central idea of a story is called its **theme**. The theme of a story is not the same as its subject. The **subject** is simply the topic of the story. A topic can be stated in one or two words: love, war, growing up. The theme makes some revelation about the subject. A theme is always a statement; it must always be something that can be expressed in at least one sentence.

Revealing a Truth About Human Behavior

Usually, the theme reveals a truth about human behavior. That truth is often one that the writer has discovered from experience or perhaps in the act of writing—for example, that in certain circumstances it is a mistake to marry only for love; or that as one grows old, death becomes less terrifying. To communicate—perhaps to discover—this idea, the writer tells a story.

The theme is usually not stated directly in the story at all. An essayist often states a theme directly as a way of getting the main idea across clearly, but the fiction writer has a different purpose. The fiction writer can let the story's characters act the idea out for us. The fiction writer hopes that we will feel the characters' experiences so strongly that the truth revealed to them will be revealed to us as well.

When the theme of a story seems fresh and true, we say, "Yes, I see what the writer means, but I hadn't quite thought of it that way before," or "I hadn't felt quite so strongly about it before." Then we have penetrated the surface of human behavior and seen what the writer wants us to recognize about our lives. Although a theme is usually invisible and unstated, it can be the story's most forceful element. A powerful theme can be the reason that a story gets to our hearts and lingers in our minds.

> A powerful theme can be the reason that a story gets to our hearts and lingers in our minds.

A Conflict Between What Ought to Be and What Is

In previous eras fiction was widely regarded as a way to teach morality—the right and wrong ways to behave. One could usually be sure in those days that a wicked character in a story would be punished and a virtuous one would be rewarded. Today, fiction is not usually regarded as a way to teach morality. Yet that conflict between what we know *would be* in a perfect world and what *is* in a disorderly, imperfect world is still the central business of literature. The theme in a story can be seen as a reflection of this basic conflict in human experience.

by John Leggett

Thinking Critically About Theme

Sometimes it is wise to question the writer's presentation of a theme. We need to discover whether the writer is presenting a truth about life or trying to force us to accept a view of life that we think is false.

The wise reader makes a judgment about a writer's view of the world and doesn't accept a story's theme as valid just because it's in print. The wise reader asks: Is this story's view of life too romantic? Is it too cynical? Is it too simple? Is it narrow-minded? Is this writer an overzealous salesperson who is trying to get me to buy an idea that is false or shoddy? Is this writer using violent incidents just to sell the story and make money?

Much of the fiction in popular magazines is weak in this way. It is often referred to as "slick" fiction, not only because it is usually found in magazines printed on slick paper, but because such stories have a smooth, shiny surface but little depth.

"Formula fiction" is another way of putting it—many of these stories are written to a plan that satisfies the general preference for happy or upbeat stories over true-to-life ones. Think of the typical romance novel in which a happy outcome is assured, and you'll have one commercially successful formula.

> **I**s this writer an overzealous salesperson who is trying to get me to buy an idea that is false or shoddy?

As wise readers we learn to make our own critical judgments about the fiction we read—just as we do with the television we watch and the movies we see.

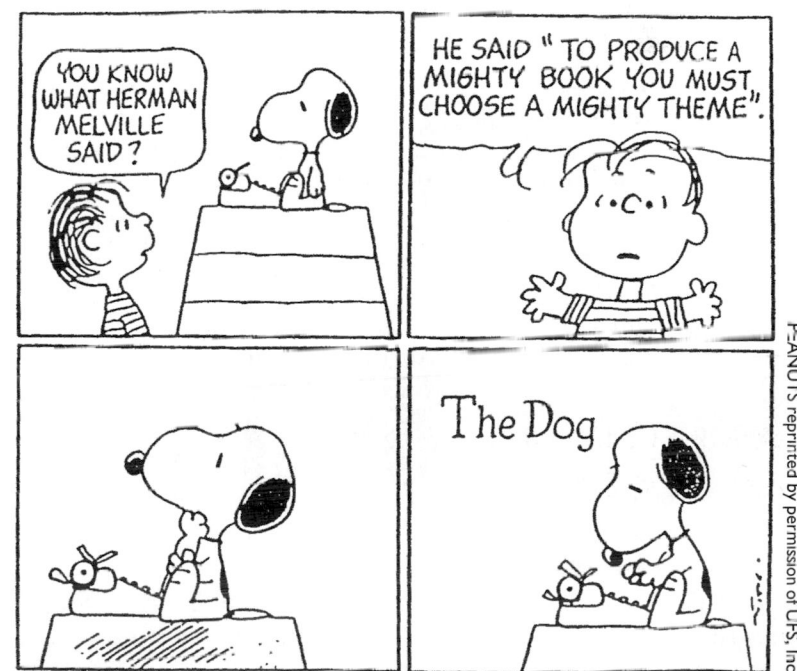

Reading Focus

Singing the Blues

The title of this story comes from an old Mississippi blues song sung by African Americans as a response to trouble. The song tells us that the blues are not self-pitying, nor are they songs about death (as the song of the mockingbird is said to be). The blues are really fighting songs. The blues help people get through.

Quickwrite

The grown-ups in this story have plenty of reasons to sing the blues. One of their problems comes from a camera-man who wants to take pictures of them. Jot down quickly your feelings on the ways the media sometimes interferes with people's private lives and private sufferings. On the other hand, do you think people like to watch other people's troubles on the TV news?

Elements of Literature

Title and Theme

The title of a story or novel is part of the text—in fact, it is the first part of the text that we read, though often it is the last thing a writer thinks up. In the past, titles of novels were often the names of people, which made the novels sound like biographies (*David Copperfield*, for example). Then writers began using titles that suggested mystery or a setting (*The Secret Garden*). Some titles, like the one for this story, are quotations. Today many writers like unusual titles. Some titles almost seem like riddles (*The Catcher in the Rye, Tuck Everlasting*). Whatever title the writer chooses, it should bring into sharper focus what the story is about. Sometimes choosing a title isn't easy. Charles Dickens once listed fourteen possible titles for the novel he eventually called *Hard Times*.

> The **title** often gives a clue to a story's theme.
>
> *For more on Theme, see pages 264–265 and the Handbook of Literary Terms.*

Blues Ain't No Mockin Bird

Toni Cade Bambara

"Just people here is what I tend to consider."

The puddle had frozen over, and me and Cathy went stompin in it. The twins from next door, Tyrone and Terry, were swingin so high out of sight we forgot we were waitin our turn on the tire. Cathy jumped up and came down hard on her heels and started tap-dancin. And the frozen patch splinterin every which way underneath kinda spooky. "Looks like a plastic spider web," she said. "A sort of weird spider, I guess, with many mental problems."

Li'l Sis (1944) by William H. Johnson.
Oil on board. (26″ x 21 ¼″).
National Museum of American Art, Washington, D.C.

But really it looked like the crystal paperweight Granny kept in the parlor. She was on the back porch, Granny was, making the cakes drunk. The old ladle dripping rum into the Christmas tins, like it used to drip maple syrup into the pails when we lived in the Judsons' woods, like it poured cider into the vats when we were on the Cooper place, like it used to scoop buttermilk and soft cheese when we lived at the dairy.

"Go tell that man we ain't a bunch of trees."

"Ma'am?"

"I said to tell that man to get away from here with that camera." Me and Cathy look over toward the meadow where the men with the station wagon'd been roamin around all mornin. The tall man with a huge camera lassoed to his shoulder was buzzin our way.

"They're makin movie pictures," yelled Tyrone, stiffenin his legs and twistin so the tire'd come down slow so they could see.

"They're makin movie pictures," sang out Terry.

"That boy don't never have anything original to say," say Cathy grown-up.

By the time the man with the camera had cut across our neighbor's yard, the twins were out of the trees swingin low and Granny was onto the steps, the screen door bammin soft and scratchy against her palms. "We thought we'd get a shot or two of the house and everything and then——"

"Good mornin," Granny cut him off. And smiled that smile.

"Good mornin," he said, head all down the way Bingo does when you yell at him about the bones on the kitchen floor. "Nice place you got here, aunty. We thought we'd take a——"

"Did you?" said Granny with her eyebrows. Cathy pulled up her socks and giggled.

"Nice things here," said the man, buzzin his camera over the yard. The pecan barrels, the sled, me and Cathy, the flowers, the printed stones along the driveway, the trees, the twins, the toolshed.

"I don't know about the thing, the it, and the stuff," said Granny, still talkin with her eyebrows. "Just people here is what I tend to consider."

Camera man stopped buzzin. Cathy giggled into her collar.

"Mornin, ladies," a new man said. He had come up behind us when we weren't lookin. "And gents," discoverin the twins givin him a nasty look. "We're filmin for the county," he said with a smile. "Mind if we shoot a bit around here?"

"I do indeed," said Granny with no smile. Smilin man was smiling up a storm. So was Cathy. But he didn't seem to have another word to say, so he and the camera man backed on out the yard, but you could hear the camera buzzin still. "Suppose you just shut that machine off," said Granny real low through her teeth and took a step down off the porch and then another.

"Now, aunty," Camera said, pointin the thing straight at her.

"Your mama and I are not related."

Smilin man got his notebook out and a chewed-up pencil. "Listen," he said movin back into our yard, "we'd like to have a statement from you . . . for the film. We're filmin for the county, see. Part of the food stamp campaign. You know about the food stamps?"

Granny said nuthin.

"Maybe there's somethin you want to say for the film. I see you grow your own vegetables," he smiled real nice. "If more folks did that, see, there'd be no need——"

Granny wasn't sayin nuthin. So they backed on out, buzzin at our clothesline and the twins' bicycles, then back on down to the meadow. The twins were danglin in the tire, lookin at Granny. Me and Cathy were waitin, too, cause Granny always got somethin to say. She teaches steady with no let-up. "I was on this bridge one time," she started off. "Was a crowd cause this man was goin to jump, you understand. And a minister was there and the police and some other folks. His woman was there, too."

"What was they doin?" asked Tyrone.

"Tryin to talk him out of it was what they was doin. The minister talkin about how it was a mortal sin, suicide. His woman takin bites out of her own hand and not even knowin it, so nervous and cryin and talkin fast."

The Blues—Music of Survival

You know that the "blues ain't no mockin bird," but then what are they? The blues are many things: music, protest, survival, triumph—all these and more.

The first blues songs were sung in the rural South by African Americans—the ancestors of Granny Cain and her family. It wasn't long, though, before the blues had traveled to cities and small towns across the United States and Europe. Today there are different styles of blues, but all blues songs are about hard times and how they make people feel. Blues are not just mournful. They can be hopeful too, even funny. Blues lyrics like the ones below may sound hopeless at first:

Woke up this morning, feeling sad and blue,
Woke up this morning, feeling sad and blue,
Didn't have nobody to tell my troubles to.

I've got the blues but I'm too darn mean to cry,
I've got the blues but I'm too darn mean to cry,
Before I'd cry I'd rather lay down and die.

What sounds hopeless may actually make audiences laugh and rejoice. Blues singers create characters when they sing. The characters may sound as if they've given up, but the singer hasn't—and neither has the audience. By singing and listening to the blues, people keep hope alive. No matter how hard things get—no matter how poor or lonely or heartbroken people are   tomorrow is a new day. Many people believe the first blues songs were the mournful and spiritual songs of slaves working in the fields—hoping for a better day, singing to survive.

The blues and the struggle of African Americans have influenced many American writers, including Toni Cade Bambara. Like the blues singers, her characters in this story are survivors—they defend their way of life against the intrusive eye of the camera.

"So what happened?" asked Tyrone.

"So here comes . . . this person . . . with a camera, takin pictures of the man and the minister and the woman. Takin pictures of the man in his misery about to jump, cause life so bad and people been messin with him so bad. This person takin up the whole roll of film practically. But savin a few, of course."

"Of course," said Cathy, hatin the person. Me standin there wonderin how Cathy knew it was "of course" when I didn't and it was *my* grandmother.

After a while Tyrone say, "Did he jump?"

"Yeh, did he jump?" say Terry all eager.

And Granny just stared at the twins till their faces swallow up the eager and they don't even care any more about the man jumpin. Then she goes back onto the porch and lets the screen door go for itself. I'm lookin to Cathy to finish the story cause she knows Granny's whole story before me even. Like she knew how come we move so much and Cathy ain't but a third cousin we picked up on the way last Thanksgivin visitin. But she knew it was on account of people drivin Granny crazy till she'd get up in the night and start packin. Mumblin and packin and wakin everybody up sayin, "Let's get on away from here before I kill me somebody." Like people wouldn't pay her for things like they said they would. Or Mr. Judson bringin us boxes of old clothes and raggedy magazines. Or Mrs. Cooper comin in our kitchen and touchin everything and sayin how clean it all was. Granny goin crazy, and Granddaddy Cain pullin her off the people, sayin, "Now, now, Cora." But next day loadin up the truck, with rocks all in his jaw, madder than Granny in the first place.

"I read a story once," said Cathy soundin like Granny teacher. "About this lady Goldilocks who barged into a house that wasn't even hers. And not invited, you understand. Messed over the people's groceries and broke up the people's furniture. Had the nerve to sleep in the folks' bed."

"Then what happened?" asked Tyrone. "What they do, the folks, when they come in to all this mess?"

"Did they make her pay for it?" asked Terry, makin a fist. "I'd've made her pay me."

I didn't even ask. I could see Cathy actress was very likely to just walk away and leave us in mystery about this story, which I heard was about some bears.

"Did they throw her out?" asked Tyrone, like his father sounds when he's bein extra nasty-plus to the washin-machine man.

"Woulda," said Terry. "I woulda gone upside her head with my fist and——"

"You woulda done whatcha always do—go cry to Mama, you big baby," said Tyrone. So naturally Terry starts hittin on Tyrone, and next thing you know they tumblin out the tire and rollin on the ground. But Granny didn't say a thing or send the twins home or step out on the steps to tell us about how we can't afford to be fightin amongst ourselves. She didn't say nuthin. So I get into the tire to take my turn.

And I could see her leanin up against the pantry table, starin at the cakes she was puttin up for the Christmas sale, mumblin real low and grumpy and holdin her forehead like it wanted to fall off and mess up the rum cakes.

Behind me I hear before I can see Grand-daddy Cain comin through the woods in his field boots. Then I twist around to see the shiny black oilskin[1] cuttin through what little left there was of yellows, reds, and oranges. His great white head not quite round cause of this bloody thing high on his shoulder, like he was wearin a cap on sideways. He takes the shortcut through the pecan grove, and the sound of twigs snapping overhead and underfoot travels clear and cold all the way up to us. And here comes Smilin and Camera up behind him like they was goin to do somethin. Folks like to go for him sometimes. Cathy say it's because he's so tall and quiet and like a king. And people just can't stand it. But Smilin and Camera don't hit him in the head or nuthin. They just buzz on him as he stalks by with the chicken hawk slung over his shoulder, squawkin, drippin red down the back of the oilskin. He passes the porch and stops a second for Granny to see he's caught the hawk at last, but she's just starin and mumblin, and not at the hawk. So he nails the bird to the toolshed door, the hammerin crackin through the eardrums. And the bird flappin himself to death and droolin down the door to paint the gravel in the driveway red, then brown, then black. And the two men movin up on tiptoe like they was invisible or we were blind, one.

"Get them persons out of my flower bed, Mister Cain," say Granny, moanin real low like at a funeral.

"How come your grandmother calls her husband Mister Cain all the time?" Tyrone whispers all loud and noisy and from the city and don't know no better. Like his mama, Miss Myrtle, tell us never mind the formality as if we had no better breeding than to call her Myrtle, plain. And then this awful thing—a giant hawk—come wailin up over the meadow, flyin

1. **oilskin:** waterproof coat.

Family (1955) by Charles H. Alston. Oil on canvas (48 ¼″ x 35 ¾″).

low and tilted and screamin, zigzaggin through the pecan grove, breakin branches and hollerin, snappin past the clothesline, flyin every which way, flyin into things reckless with crazy.

"He's come to claim his mate," say Cathy fast, and ducks down. We all fall quick and flat into the gravel driveway, stones scrapin my face. I squinch my eyes open again at the hawk on the door, tryin to fly up out of her death like it was just a sack flown into by mistake. Her body

holdin her there on that nail, though. The mate beatin the air overhead and clutchin for hair, for heads, for landin space.

The camera man duckin and bendin and runnin and fallin, jigglin the camera and scared. And Smilin jumpin up and down swipin at the huge bird, tryin to bring the hawk down with just his raggedy ole cap. Granddaddy Cain straight up and silent, watchin the circles of the hawk, then aimin the hammer off his wrist. The

Gee's Bend (1947) by Jacob Lawrence. Tempera on gesso on wood (20″ x 24″).

giant bird fallin, silent and slow. Then here comes Camera and Smilin all big and bad now that the awful screechin thing is on its back and broken, here they come. And Granddaddy Cain looks up at them like it was the first time noticin, but not payin them too much mind cause he's listenin, we all listenin, to that low groanin music comin from the porch. And we figure any minute, somethin in my back tells me any minute now, Granny gonna bust through that screen with somethin in her hand and murder on her mind. So Granddaddy say above the buzzin, but quiet, "Good day, gentlemen." Just like that. Like he'd invited them in to play cards and they'd stayed too long and all the sandwiches were gone and Reverend Webb was droppin by and it was time to go.

They didn't know what to do. But like Cathy say, folks can't stand Granddaddy tall and silent and like a king. They can't neither. The smile the men smilin is pullin the mouth back and showin the teeth. Lookin like the wolf man, both of them. Then Granddaddy holds his hand out—this huge hand I used to sit in when I was a baby and he'd carry me through the house to my mother like I was a gift on a tray. Like he used to on the trains. They called the other men just waiters. But they spoke of Granddaddy separate and said, The Waiter. And said he had engines in his feet and motors in his hands and couldn't no train throw him off and couldn't nobody turn him round. They were big enough for motors, his hands were. He held that one hand out all still and it gettin to be not at all a hand but a person in itself.

"He wants you to hand him the camera," Smilin whispers to Camera, tiltin his head to talk secret like they was in the jungle or somethin and come upon a native that don't speak the language. The men start untyin the straps, and they put the camera into that great hand speckled with the hawk's blood, all black and crackly now. And the hand don't even drop with the weight, just the fingers move, curl up around the machine. But Granddaddy lookin straight at the men. They lookin at each other and everywhere but at Granddaddy's face.

"We filmin for the county, see," say Smilin. "We puttin together a movie for the food stamp program . . . filmin all around these parts. Uhh, filmin for the county."

"Can I have my camera back?" say the tall man with no machine on his shoulder, but still keepin it high like the camera was still there or needed to be. "Please, sir."

Then Granddaddy's other hand flies up like a sudden and gentle bird, slaps down fast on top of the camera and lifts off half like it was a calabash[2] cut for sharing.

"Hey," Camera jumps forward. He gathers up the parts into his chest and everything unrollin and fallin all over. "Whatcha tryin to do? You'll ruin the film." He looks down into his chest of metal reels and things like he's protectin a kitten from the cold.

"You standin in the missus' flower bed," say Granddaddy. "This is our own place."

The two men look at him, then at each other, then back at the mess in the camera man's chest, and they just back off. One sayin over and over all the way down to the meadow, "Watch it, Bruno. Keep ya fingers off the film." Then Granddaddy picks up the hammer and jams it into the oilskin pocket, scrapes his boots, and goes into the house. And you can hear the squish of his boots headin through the house. And you can see the funny shadow he throws from the parlor window onto the ground by the string-bean patch. The hammer draggin the pocket of the oilskin out so Granddaddy looked even wider. Granny was hummin now—high, not low and grumbly. And she was doin the cakes again, you could smell the molasses from the rum.

"There's this story I'm goin to write one day," say Cathy dreamer. "About the proper use of the hammer."

"Can I be in it?" Tyrone say with his hand up like it was a matter of first come, first served.

"Perhaps," say Cathy, climbin onto the tire to pump us up. "If you there and ready."

---

2. **calabash:** large tropical fruit.

MEET THE WRITER

Writing on the Upbeat

Toni Cade Bambara
(1939–1995) said she wrote upbeat fiction because she was raised on stories of champions: Harriet Tubman, Ida B. Wells, Paul Robeson, and her grandmother Annie. She grew up in Harlem, Brooklyn, and Jersey City, attended schools in New York City and the South, and graduated from Queens College in New York.

In the sixties, Bambara studied theater in Italy and mime in France. When she returned to New York, she became interested in dance but also did social work in local hospitals and community centers. Eventually she turned to teaching, and over the years she taught at various colleges and universities, including Rutgers University in New Brunswick, New Jersey, and Spelman College in Atlanta, Georgia.

"Blues Ain't No Mockin Bird" comes from Bambara's first collection of stories: *Gorilla, My Love* (1972). Many of these stories are told in the voice of a sassy young girl who is tough, compassionate, and brave.

Bambara had her own very definite ideas about writing:

66 Folks come up to me 'lowing as how since I am a writer I would certainly want to hear blah, blah, blah, blah. They . . . tell me about every ugly overheard and lived-through nightmare imaginable. They've got the wrong writer. The kid can't use it. I straightaway refer them to the neighborhood healer, certain that anyone so intoxicated would surely welcome a cleansing. But they persist— 'Hey, this is for real, square business. The truth.' I don't doubt that the horror tales are factual. I don't even doubt that ugly is a truth for somebody . . . somehow. But I'm not convinced that ugly is *the* truth that can save us, redeem us. The old folks teach that. Be triflin' and ugly and they say, 'Deep down, gal, you know that ain't right,' appealing to a truth about our deep-down nature. Good enough for me. Besides, I can't get happy writing ugly weird. If I'm not laughing while I work, I conclude that I am not communicating nourishment, since laughter is the most sure-fire healant I know. I don't know all my readers, but I know well for whom I write. And I want for them—no less than I want for myself—wholesomeness.

It all sounds so la-di-da and tra-la-la. I can afford to be sunny. I'm but one voice in the chorus. The literature(s) of our time are a collective effort, dependent on so many views, on so many people's productions. There's a lot of work to do, a lot of records to get straight, a lot of living to share, a lot to plumb. This reader wants it all—the oddball, the satiric, the grim, the ludicrous, what have you. As for my own writing, I prefer the upbeat. It pleases me to blow three or four choruses of just sheer energetic fun and optimism. . . . 99

MAKING MEANINGS

First Thoughts

1. Which detail of the story was the most memorable for you? Was it an image, a statement, a character, or something else? Pair up with another student and share your major memory from the story.

Shaping Interpretations

2. When Smilin and Camera return to the county office, what do you think they tell their supervisor? How do you think they portray the characters of Granny and Granddaddy Cain?

3. Have you ever said one thing while thinking something else? What do you imagine Granddaddy Cain is thinking when he says, "Good day, gentlemen"? What about when he says, "You standin in the missus' flower bed. This is our own place"?

4. Writers create powerful impressions with concrete dramatic images. What do the suffering hawks in the story suggest to you? (Are they like any characters in the story?)

5. How would you state the **theme** of the story as you see it—that is, what does the story reveal to you about our need for respect and sympathy and privacy? Consider these elements of the story:

   • the **title**

   • the story Granny tells about the man on the bridge

   • Cathy's story about Goldilocks

6. What did you learn about the **first-person narrator** in this story? What else would you know if Granny or her husband were narrating the story?

Reviewing the Text

a. Which characters play a part in this story's conflict? Which are onlookers?

b. What details in the story explain why Granny has moved so often?

c. Why do the two men want to film the family?

d. Why does Granny resent the film crew?

e. What action does Granddaddy Cain finally take to resolve Granny's conflict with the camera crew?

Connecting with the Text

7. A family's privacy is invaded in this story. Invasion of privacy has become commonplace in today's media. When have you felt that someone's privacy was invaded by TV cameras or reporters? What would you do if you were in Granny's situation? (Be sure to refer to your Quickwrite notes.)

Challenging the Text

8. Toni Cade Bambara says she prefers upbeat fiction and likes energetic fun and optimism. Do you think this story is upbeat and optimistic? Why or why not?

CHOICES: Building Your Portfolio

Writer's Notebook

1. Establishing Criteria for an Evaluation

What's in a title? In the Writer's Workshop on page 332, you'll be using certain criteria to evaluate a short story. If **title** is not on your list of criteria, you should add it. A good title can make us want to read a story, and a dull one can make us pass it by. What do you think makes a good title? Skim the table of contents in the front of this book. Make a list of three titles that you especially like and three that would not make you want to read the story. Jot down reasons for your reactions.

Like
- *"Salvador Late or Early"*
  Unusual, makes me wonder.
- *"The Most Dangerous Game"*
  Sounds exciting—good!
- *"Blues Ain't No Mockin Bird"*
  Not sure—it might be different and interesting. (Why is the "g" missing?)

Not appealing
- *"The Necklace"*
  Too common, uninteresting.
- *"The Scarlet Ibis"*
  What's an ibis?

Critical Writing

2. Character Analysis

By now you may have speculated on what Smilin and Camera reported to their supervisor about Granny. Suppose you, as an observer, decide the supervisor needs to hear another point of view. Write an analysis of Granny's character as you interpret it. Look in the story for examples of Granny's **words,** her **actions,** and her **effect on others**.

Creative Writing/Speaking

3. "I Am" Poem

Writing as either Granny or Granddaddy Cain, complete the following lines of an "I Am" poem:

I am _____
I wonder _____
I hear _____
I try _____
I wish _____
I dream _____
I see _____
I hope _____

Research/Social Studies

4. Compiling a Report

The two men who came out to Granny's place said they were filming for the county as part of the food stamp program. Food stamps are certificates that are issued by the federal government and traded for food at grocery stores. However, most poor people in the United States do not receive any form of government assistance. Do some research of your own. Find out the regulations that govern food stamps and write a summary of your findings. Be sure to include a list of your sources.

Critical Writing

5. "I'm Not a Wall"

In a paragraph, compare the speaker of the following poem with Granny. The chart below should help you outline their similarities. Fill this out before you write.

Silent, but . . .
I may be silent, but
I'm thinking.
I may not talk, but
Don't mistake me for a wall.
—Tsuboi Shigeji

	Bambara	Shigeji
Line from beginning of story that sounds like line from poem.		
How Granny and speaker of poem do **not** want to be treated.		
How they **do** want to be treated.		

LANGUAGE LINK MINI-LESSON

Handbook of Literary Terms
H E L P

See Dialect.

If it doesn't sound right to the ear, if it doesn't come out the way a ranch hand might say it with a pipe in one hand and a cup of coffee in the other, then I change it.
—Louis
  L'Amour

Style: Dialect Reveals Character

While language is being spoken, it changes. All of us, in fact, alter language slightly. We take the sounds we first learn from our parents, brothers, and sisters, and then we add what we hear at school, at work, on the radio, on TV, and in the movies.

Thus, our own particular speech soon becomes as distinctive as the features on our faces. We sometimes can even recognize a person simply by overhearing a single spoken word. When we meet new people for the first time, their speech can tell us about the region they come from and about their social, economic, and educational backgrounds. For this reason, a writer tries to breathe life into a fictional character by letting us hear *how* the person speaks, as well as *what* the person says.

Suppose a writer is setting a story in a particular region—for instance, the deep South or a barrio in Los Angeles or the Flatbush section of Brooklyn. The way people in the story speak must persuade us (even if we've never been to these places) that they are using the region's special grammar and expressions and pronunciations—in other words, that they are speaking its **dialect**.

Having an "ear" for dialect—being able to hear the peculiarities of speech, its rhythm and flow, the words that are emphasized, the contractions, the slang, the pronunciations—is vital for a writer. The writer with a sensitive ear will record Bostonians' broad *a*'s and the way they pronounce *r*'s for *h*'s and *h*'s for *r*'s so that "idea" becomes "idear" and "dear" becomes "deah." In a story set in a rural black neighborhood in Arkansas, the writer will hear "ask" become "aks" and "my" become "mah," and will notice how final consonants are dropped so that "don't" becomes "don."

Even in her comment on page 274 about writing, Bambara reproduces a dialect with its peculiar pronunciations, its special vocabulary, its special syntax, and its rhythms.

Try It Out

1. Look through the story and find at least five good examples of dialect. Arrange your examples under two headings.

Nonstandard Grammar	Nonstandard Pronunciation

2. Try this experiment: Take one of Granny's speeches or conversations in "Blues Ain't No Mockin Bird" and rewrite it in standard, formal English without Granny's usual pronunciations and grammar. How much of Granny's character is lost when her dialect is taken away from her?

A tip for writers: If you are interested in creating realistic speech, always keep your notebook handy. When professional writers hear talk that they might want to use someday, they write it down.

BEFORE YOU READ
INDEPENDENCE

Reading Focus

Yearn and Learn

The chance to be independent—that's what the teenaged characters in this story yearn for. All of us, at some time or another, have had the same longing. We want independence even if we can't really define what we mean by it, even if we don't know exactly what we want to do once we get it.

Quickwrite

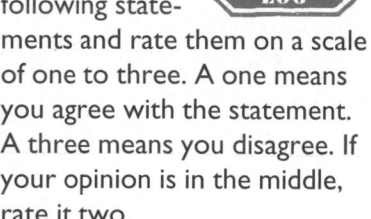

Read the following statements and rate them on a scale of one to three. A one means you agree with the statement. A three means you disagree. If your opinion is in the middle, rate it two.

agree	in the middle	disagree
1	2	3

- Once people have made a decision, they should stick it out and face the consequences.

- Older siblings have a responsibility to protect younger ones.

- Independence = freedom.

Elements of Literature

Learning with Characters

Discoveries in fiction usually come at the end of the action. In describing a character's discovery, a writer wants to make us, the readers, discover something too—in fact, at these moments of discovery we may grasp the whole meaning of the story itself. A discovery often happens when a character *sees* or *experiences* or *does* something that brings about a sudden, intense feeling—a realization about life that often changes the character in some way.

> **Theme** in fiction is often revealed by what a character has learned or discovered as a result of the action.
>
> *For more on Theme, see pages 264–265 and the Handbook of Literary Terms.*

Independence

Ruth Sasaki

In the summer of '64, I was eleven. I had just finished my first semester of junior high. My eldest sister, Linda, was spending her last summer at home before going away to college, to the big, wide world of Berkeley[1] that lay just across the bay. She was working at the Franchise Tax Board[2] and saving money. My other two sisters, Cathy and Sharon, were in the tenth and ninth grades and yearned for adventure and romance, preferably on the beach.

I was a lowly preteen and was perfectly content to loaf the summer away reading, hanging out with friends, and swimming at the Y. Cathy and Sharon, in their advanced years, wanted to go away.

1. **Berkeley:** city near San Francisco; site of one of the campuses of the University of California.
2. **Franchise Tax Board:** government office.

Cathy and Sharon never did talk much about their summer at Lake Tahoe.

Of course there were certain obstacles. The most apparent of these to my sisters was that Mom and Daddy would never let them just take off. Then there was the question of money. My sisters had none to speak of.

"Besides," Cathy complained, "how would we get there?"

"Get where?" I asked.

"Wherever," she said. "I'll go absolutely anywhere. But we don't have any wheels."

The obstacles were so numerous that it looked as though their adventure would have to be postponed a few more years, at least until one of them was old enough to get her driver's license. But the more impossible the situation seemed, the more obsessed my sisters became, until they felt they would die if they didn't get away that summer.

One Saturday in early June, Cathy came triumphantly into the sun room, where Sharon and I were sprawled reading Nancy Drew mysteries.

"This is it," she announced dramatically, waving a copy of the *Nichibei Times.*

"This is what?" I asked.

"This is our summer vacation. Listen to this: 'Young man, for housework at Lake Tahoe cabin. July–August.'" She was ecstatic.

"I don't get it," I said. "What does that have to do with you?"

"It's perfect," she said. "Sharon and I can do housework. And a cabin! At Lake Tahoe! I mean, how much housework can there be? We can go to the beach every day!"

I hated to spoil her fun, but I was immediately struck by several glaring inconsistencies. First of all, I had serious reservations about my sisters' qualifications to do housework, but I thought I would pass over that as Cathy was sometimes prone to fits of violent temper. I proceeded to the next objection on my list.

"It says 'young man.' Did you notice that?"

"Man, woman, what's the difference? We're young, all right." Cathy was an optimist.

"Yeah, but there's two of you. It says 'man.' Singular."

"You take things too literally, Jo. Just think, they can get two of us for the price of one.

They'll jump at the chance."

They began by approaching my mother, who could usually be won over and whose aid could then be enlisted in approaching my father. Looking back on it, I'm amazed my father even listened to the proposition. It must have been my sisters' determination. Never once did they consider that the job might fall into other hands; if my dad said yes, it was theirs. He could not disappoint them, but neither would he allow them to go off into the unknown. He would find out the details first.

The details served to fire my sisters to greater heights of anticipation. The cabin was the property of Dr. Cluett, of San Francisco, but only his wife would be occupying it during the summer. The cabin was on the north shore of Lake Tahoe, about two miles from the town of Homewood. The two girls would do light house-keeping chores and cooking (I was aghast) in return for their own room, board, and after-noons free. Cathy would receive sixty dollars for the six-week period; Sharon, as the younger, would receive fifty. My dad arranged for an inter-view. He wanted to check the lady out.

The Cluetts lived in Pacific Heights, and we drove by their house, days before the interview, to check it out. It was a very respectable-looking mansion.

When my sisters came home with my dad after the interview, they were ecstatic. Daddy had felt Mrs. Cluett to be trustworthy. Cathy and Sharon were to appear at the Cluett cabin on the first Saturday in July, in the early afternoon.

I felt betrayed, now that my sisters' departure was a reality. Here I had looked forward to a long summer of their companionship while engaging in traditional summer rituals: sprawl-ing on the stairway with a stack of mysteries, snacking on Cap'n Crunch cereal (we had just discovered it and were addicted), listening to Giants games in the sun room, and knitting. And now my sisters were going off to have a great adventure. It was no fun listening to Giants games by yourself.

My parents made Linda promise to move into the bedroom that I usually shared with Sharon so that I would not feel too deserted, and so

I cheered up somewhat at the prospect of a summer-long slumber party.

The night before the great adventure was to begin, my mother stayed up preparing our traditional family vacation picnic lunch of teriyaki Spam,[3] rice balls, and potato salad. Early the next morning, we got up and left for Lake Tahoe. Cathy and Sharon had spent the week packing. After all the fuss and bother, I was amazed by how small their suitcases looked in the trunk of my dad's car. My dad also loaded the ice chest, the lunch, and the folding picnic table, which we were convinced was jinxed, because every time we took it out, it would rain. And we were off.

We had our lunch by the lake, and sure enough, as soon as we had unpacked the picnic table, large raindrops began to fall. We finished eating in the car and set out for the north shore.

We went several miles past Homewood before we decided we must have missed the turnoff. We turned around. Cathy and Sharon were silent.

It took several passes, back and forth, before my sharp-eyed mother spotted the Cluetts' name on a large tree, in an area that was so dense with trees that we had not thought people would live there. My dad turned in, and several trees deep we found ourselves in front of the Cluett cabin.

A young Japanese man came out to greet us.

"Terasaki-san?"[4] he inquired. He introduced himself as Noguchi, Mrs. Cluett's houseboy.

I had never seen a real houseboy before—only on TV—so I studied him carefully. He was a lot younger than the ones on TV—probably in his early twenties. He didn't look like the houseboys on television. He wasn't subservient, sinister, or stupid. In short, I was rather disappointed. He just looked like a regular Japanese person. In fact, I thought he was rather cute. I looked at Linda to see if she thought so,

too. I could usually tell when she thought a guy was cute. She would start to act weird. But Linda didn't even seem to notice Noguchi.

---

3. **teriyaki** (ter'ē·yä'kē) **Spam:** Teriyaki Spam is Spam (a kind of canned ham loaf) soaked Japanese style in spiced soy sauce before cooking.
4. **Terasaki-san** (ter·ə·sa'kē·sän'): The houseboy is greeting the father, Mr. Terasaki. Using the suffix *-san* is a respectful way of addressing a person.

WORDS TO OWN

subservient (səb·sur'vē·ənt) *adj.*: submissive; showing too great a willingness to serve or obey.

Then Mrs. Cluett came out. She was a large middle-aged woman. She did not smile. "Would you like to see your room?" she said.

I noticed Cathy craning her neck around as we entered the cabin. I thought she must be looking for the lake, which was nowhere in sight.

The trees were particularly dense around the cabin, and that, on top of the rainy weather, gave the cabin a dark, gloomy atmosphere. There was a cold, damp smell when we entered.

I watched Cathy and Sharon carefully. They were <u>ominously</u> silent.

One by one, we followed Mrs. Cluett up the stairs.

"Nice wood," I said.

"This will be your room," Mrs. Cluett said, opening a door onto a narrow chamber with bunk beds against one wall.

"Bunk beds! How neat!" I cried. We had always wanted bunk beds. "Look, Cathy—bunk beds!"

"Oh boy," she said, but she didn't sound too enthusiastic.

In fact, Cathy and Sharon didn't say anything until we were leaving. Mrs. Cluett asked us to give Noguchi a ride back to the city. He was leaving her employment and had some friends in San Francisco. Noguchi got into the front seat with my dad. My mother got into the back with Linda and me.

Linda and I were dismayed. There was nothing like the presence of a total stranger to ruin the fun of a family car trip, especially this stranger, who seemed straight from Japan, very stiff and formal. He didn't even speak much English.

As my dad started the engine, Cathy and Sharon managed to say goodbye.

"See you in six weeks," Cathy said, as if she were already counting them.

It must have been hard for my dad to drive away and leave them there, but he did.

Noguchi and my dad conversed for a while in Japanese, but even that was hard going, and after a few of his pleasant inquiries were met with <u>monosyllabic</u> replies, my dad lapsed into silence. Linda and I were glad Noguchi was sitting in the front seat; we could make faces at

---

WORDS TO OWN

ominously (ăm′ə·nəs·lē) *adv.:* suspiciously; in a way that suggests future problems.
monosyllabic (măn′ō·si·lab′ik) *adj.:* one-syllable.

each other behind his back. It was going to be a long trip.

We stopped halfway for A&W root beers. Noguchi loosened up some, and my dad explained to us that he was from Yokohama[5] and had been in the States for three months. He wanted to improve his English and go into business here, but he missed Japan. He had heard that being a houseboy was a good way to learn English, but he just couldn't get used to taking orders from a woman. He would have to find another job. I felt more kindly toward him when I heard he was homesick, and vowed to stop making faces whenever he did something weird. Linda looked as if she felt bad about it, too, but when he took one sip of his root beer and said it tasted more like medicine than beer, we forgot about kindness and exchanged looks of utter disgust.

When we got to the city, we dropped Noguchi off in front of a house on Sacramento Street. A friend lived there, he said.

My dad told him we would wait to make sure his friend was home, but Noguchi insisted that it wasn't necessary. He thanked us for the ride. My dad gave him our telephone number, and told him to come over on Thanksgiving.

"Gambatte, ne," my dad said. "Don't give up."

Noguchi stood on the sidewalk, bowing after us as we drove away.

"His friend must be rich," I said, looking back at the large Victorian in front of which Noguchi, growing smaller, remained standing.

"I wonder if he really has a friend living there," my dad said.

"What do you mean?" Linda asked.

My dad didn't answer.

"Why did you invite him to Thanksgiving?" I asked. "We don't even know him."

My dad seemed surprised by the question and searched for an answer.

"It's hard to be away from home," he said finally.

"Do you think he'll really come?" I asked. I didn't think I would go to a strange family's house for Thanksgiving.

"He might," my dad said, "if he's doing well. Otherwise, he'll probably enryo.[6] That's the way Japanese people are."

---

5. Yokohama (yō′kə·hä′mə): seaport on Tokyo Bay, Japan.

6. enryo (en′rē·yō): decline or "bow out" politely. Noguchi probably feels that Mr. Terasaki is just being polite in asking him, since they are so different in income and status. In Japan, society is very rigid and movement between classes is difficult.

The summer resumed for me with swimming, reading, and writing an occasional letter to Cathy and Sharon. We got letters from them, telling of afternoons on the beach, which wasn't far from the cabin, and of walks into Homewood to pick up their mail. They would stop at the general store for a milkshake. They spent most nights in their room, talking and reading movie magazines. That sounded wonderful. Our mother had a low opinion of movie magazines, and to be able to read all the movie magazines you wanted to sounded like paradise.

Cathy's letters became humorous. They had begun calling Mrs. Cluett "Plicket," an abbreviation for "picky Cluett." She wanted everything done just so. Her patio furniture had to be moved every time it looked like rain and moved back again when the sky cleared. Her rugs had to be continually beaten out. She went after blue jays with a BB gun, much to my sisters' amusement at first, then disgust as the novelty wore off.

The letters became increasingly contemptuous, dark. Plicket washed her hair every day and pin-curled it, and it was like steel wool. Their "beach" was rocky and frequented by packs of slobbering dogs.

At the end of three weeks, there was a phone call. I answered it and was surprised to hear Sharon's voice.

"Hey, what's happening?" I said.

Her voice broke and I realized that she was crying. I listened, shocked, as there were scuffling noises and Cathy came on the line.

"Hey, Jo—how's it going? Listen—let me talk to Daddy."

I knew it was serious. I got my dad. My mom and Linda gathered around the phone. My dad made several one-word replies, then concluded, "All right. We'll come get you this Saturday. You wanna talk to Mommy?"

I was incredulous. There must be forces at work in the world that I could not imagine, much less comprehend, forces that could overcome even big sisters. It was an occasion for solemnity.

The following Saturday we packed our picnic table and my mom's lunch and set out again for the Cluett cabin. When we got there, Cathy and Sharon came out immediately with their suitcases. Mrs. Cluett came out to see them off.

"Thank you, Mrs. Cluett," Cathy said politely. She got into the car after Sharon. "Let's get out of here."

We drove into Homewood so that Cathy and Sharon could stop to check their mail one last time.

"There's the post office," Sharon said.

"And that's the general store where we used to get milkshakes," Cathy added. Though anxious to leave, they also wanted us to know the town as they did.

I looked around at the post office and the general store, the sidewalks of raised wooden slats like in an old cowboy movie. So this had been the scene of their independence.

They went into the general store for the last time. When they came out, Sharon handed me a brown paper bag.

WORDS TO OWN

contemptuous (kən·temp′chōō·əs) *adj.*: scornful.
incredulous (in·krej′oo·ləs) *adj.*: unwilling to believe or unable to believe.

"Look what we found," she said.

There was a box of Cap'n Crunch cookies inside.

"Try 'em," she said. "They're real good."

"Later," Cathy said. "Let's get out of here."

We stopped to have lunch along the Truckee River. My dad got out his fishing pole as Cathy got the old picnic table out of the trunk and set it up under a tree. When the rain started coming down, we just kept right on eating and fishing. When you're eating and fishing, what's a little rain?

Cathy and Sharon never did talk much about their summer at Lake Tahoe. I never found out what it was that had made their summer with Plicket so unbearable. They both knew, or perhaps they didn't know either, at least in so many words; so the experience remained locked within the silence of their deepest understanding. All they had chosen to share with me were the good things: the Cap'n Crunch cookies, the movie magazines, and memories of chocolate milkshakes. And my dad was right about Noguchi—when Thanksgiving came around that year, he didn't call. We wondered if he had stuck it out and had his own business somewhere or if he had gone back to Japan.

At the end of that summer Linda went away to Berkeley, and within the next six years, we all followed in her footsteps. In her junior year at Cal, Cathy, still pursuing a yen for adventure, fell to her death while rock climbing. Years later, when I saw a vending machine selling Cap'n Crunch cookies in the empty corridor of an impersonal university building, I bought them immediately. And for a magical moment I was eleven years old again, feeling my sisters' love.

MEET THE WRITER

Restoring a History

Ruth Sasaki (1952–   ) was born in San Francisco and grew up without a sense of her Japanese heritage. Her grand-parents' and parents' generations did not speak of Japanese culture and history—out of fear and shame. Sasaki would later learn about World War II—she would hear about the Japanese attack on Pearl Harbor and about the Japanese on the West Coast who were held in internment camps in the United States until the war was over. She would also learn about the Japanese who were bombed in Hiroshima and Nagasaki. Sasaki says:

66 I wandered ghostlike amidst the mainstream of America, treading unaware on a culture that lay buried like a lost civilization beneath my feet, unaware of the cultural amnesia inflicted on my parents' generation by the internment and the atomic bomb. 99

She hopes that her stories will help "restore a history that was almost lost."

More by Sasaki

"Independence" is included in *The Loom and Other Stories* (Graywolf). In 1983, "The Loom" won an American Japanese National Literary Award.

Childhood

When I was a child, I knew

    how to call Mama and Papa,
    how to look like an upper-class lady
    by wearing Mama's dress
5   and Mama's jewels.
    I knew how to be a working man
    by wearing Papa's suit and
    carrying Papa's briefcase.

When I was no longer a child, I knew

10   how to be myself
    how to laugh at the right time

and cry in a hiding place.
I knew about sadness and love
when Mama and Grandma died.
15 Love came when someone in the street
asked me how I felt,
when a friend offered a piece of candy,
when a neighbor bought me a dress
for New Year.
20 But I don't want anything now.
I only want the good old times
when a mama, a papa
and a little girl lived together.

—Mai Trang
Thomas Jefferson High School
Portand, Oregon

The Family (detail) by Gustav Vigeland.

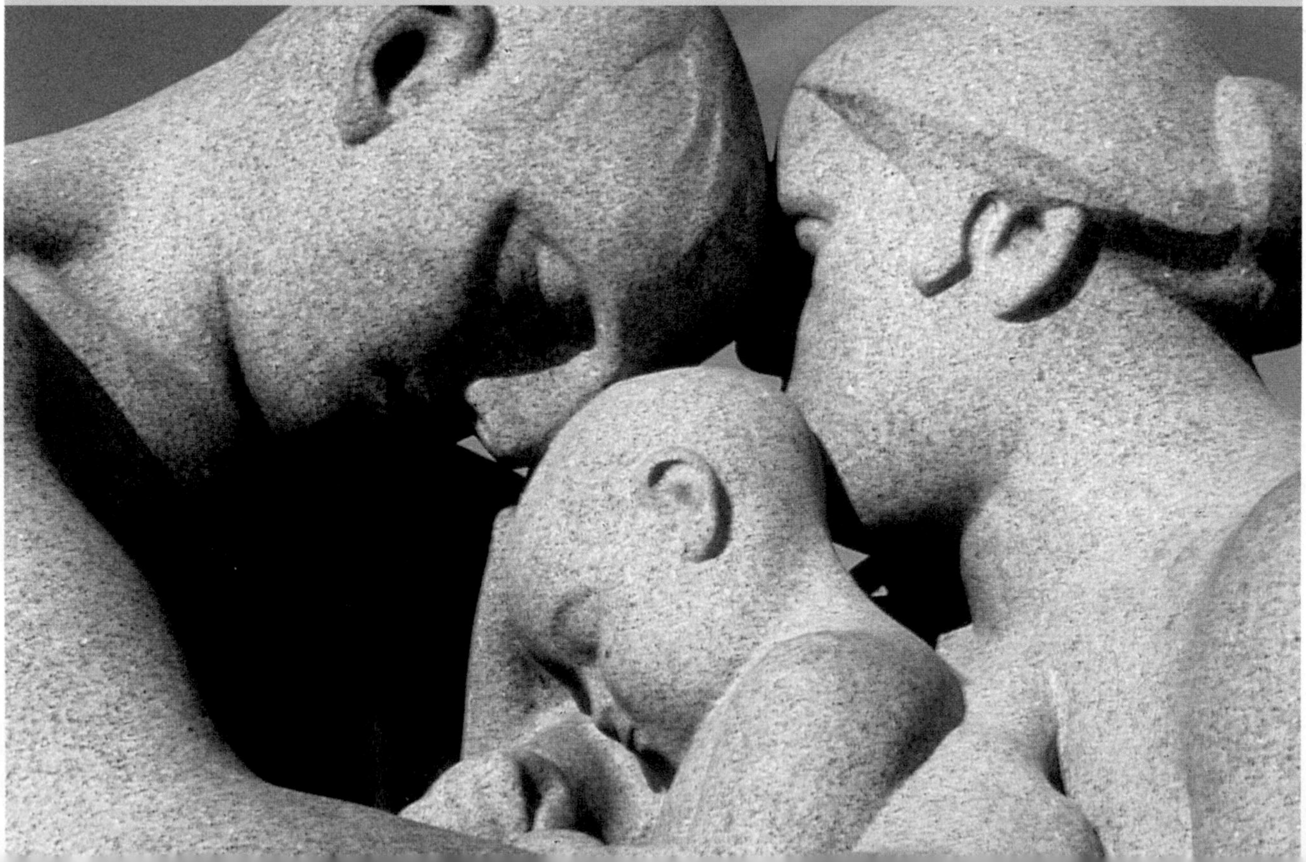

Making Meanings

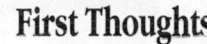

• **First Thoughts**

1. Draw thought bubbles containing words and images that show what Cathy and Sharon *hoped for* in their summer of independence, and what they *actually experienced.*

Shaping Interpretations

2. What kind of person do you think the girls' father is? Draw a character web for the father like the one here. List at least four **character traits** and note a specific incident from the text where Daddy reveals each trait.

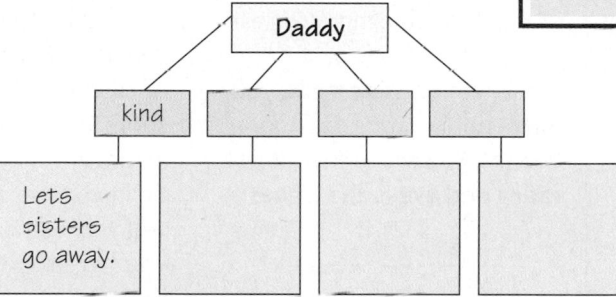

Reviewing the Text

The bare bones of a story usually are something like this:

Characters (1) want something badly enough to (2) take action to get it; they then (3) meet with complications and finally (4) either get what they want or lose it.

Work with a partner to outline the bare bones of "Independence." Compare your outline with those of your classmates. Do you all agree?

3. Cathy and Sharon do not talk about their summer with Plicket. Jo says, ". . . the experience remained locked within the silence of their deepest understanding." What explanations can you imagine for their experience being so "unbearable"?

4. What do you think Cathy and Sharon learn during this summer of independence? What about Jo—what does she discover at the story's end?

5. Write down what you learned about human behavior from this story—in other words, what is the story's central idea or **theme**? Compare your statements of theme in class. Can you reach any general agreement on what the story reveals about our lives?

Connecting with the Text

6. Go back to the opinions you marked in your Reader's Log. Did your opinions change after you read the story? Or did the story reinforce what you felt?

Challenging the Text

7. Cathy's death is mentioned almost casually at the story's end. How did you feel about the way the writer announces this? When you realize what happens later to Cathy, do your feelings about the whole story change in any way? (How would you have felt about the story if you'd been told this at the start?)

CHOICES: Building Your Portfolio

Writer's Notebook

1. Establishing Criteria for an Evaluation

Judging themes. If you prepared a list of criteria at the beginning of this story collection, did you include **theme**—a story's main idea? Here's your chance to think more about using theme in the short-story evaluation you'll write for the Writer's Workshop on page 332. Jot down notes evaluating the theme of "Independence." Base them on the notes below about "Blues Ain't No Mockin Bird." If you don't think all the questions listed in the notes are appropriate, add some of your own.

WORK IN PROGRESS

Critical Writing

2. You the Reviewer

Suppose you are a member of a team of readers deciding if you want to use Sasaki's story in a schoolbook. Write a brief statement about the story in which you (a) say if you think the story will appeal to high school students, (b) give at least one reason for your opinion, (c) tell how the story compares in appeal with other stories you have read. As part of your opinion statement, you might add a rating scale for this story. Zero is the lowest rating and five is the highest.

0 1 2 3 4 5

Writing/Drawing

3. Making a Storyboard

Filmmakers use storyboards to plan their camera shots. Imagine you are the director of a thirty-minute feature film of "Independence," with a classmate as your cinematographer. Together, create a storyboard showing each scene you will shoot. First sketch the major story events on cards, one camera shot per card. Then arrange the cards in sequence on a sheet of cardboard and discuss the shots. How do you want to arrange the events? Will they be in chronological order? Or will you add flashbacks? Will you have to add or cut a scene?

Creative Writing

4. A Missing Scene

For every story there are scenes that could have been shown but weren't. Think of a scene in "Independence"—either in San Francisco or in Tahoe—that Sasaki omitted. Be sure to specify the time and place of your new scene. The missing scene might take place before the main action begins, during the main action, or afterward. Compare your additional scene with those of your classmates. Did any two writers choose the same scene?

Theme of "Blues Ain't No Mockin Bird"
Outsiders often fail to understand the struggles and feelings of other people.
Do I accept the theme?
I think it's very tough to see life as others live it.
Is it clearly revealed in the story?
Not sure. Parts of the story still puzzle me—like the hawks. Why are they there?

Proofreading: Transitions—Bridge Work Ahead

Transitions are words or phrases that connect one idea to another. Transitions are like road signs, guiding readers over bridges and helping them cross from one sentence or paragraph to another.

What Transitions Can Do:
Compare/contrast ideas also, and, too, although, but, however, instead, on the other hand
Show cause and effect as a result, because, since, therefore
Show time after, before, finally, last, first, next
Show place above, below, across, nearby, next to
Show importance mainly, first, last, more important

In the following passage from "Independence," the transitions are underscored.

"I hated to spoil her fun, but I was immediately struck by several glaring inconsistencies. First of all, I had serious reservations about my sisters' qualifications to do housework. . . ."

Try It Out

➤ Following is a series of statements about the story. Make them into a coherent paragraph by adding transitions to show the connections from one idea to another. Be sure to compare your revised paragraphs.

Cathy and Sharon want to be independent. They take a job working for a Mrs. Cluett. Mrs. Cluett is picky. She wants the rugs beaten. She washes her hair every day. The girls quit the job. Their motives are not entirely clear.

➤ Pull out a piece of your own writing and circle all the transitional words you've used. Are there spots where a better transitional word would smooth choppy sentences? Are there passages that would be clearer if transitions were added?

VOCABULARY ▪ HOW TO OWN A WORD

WORD BANK
subservient
ominously
monosyllabic
contemptuous
incredulous

Explain Why

Be sure you can defend your response to each query.

1. How would you feel if someone described you as subservient?
2. How would you feel if you reported an ominous sound outside and the police were incredulous?
3. How would you feel if someone was contemptuous of you?
4. How would you feel if someone thought you could understand only monosyllabic words?

Reading Focus

Missed Chances

It seems simple enough. You'd like to be friends with somebody who seems interesting from a distance—nice, smart, talented—but very different from you. Say that person is much older or younger, or is from another country, or speaks a different language. It might not be so easy to start a friendship.

Quickwrite

READER'S LOG

As you read "American History," jot down your thoughts, questions, and predictions. Be sure especially to record your responses to some of the statements made by adults in the story. Perhaps some of them strike you as biased or unfair, or perhaps you feel they are all true. You might note these passages and your reactions in a double-entry journal:

Passage	My Response

Elements of Literature

Theme and Key Passages

A writer can reveal theme in many ways. Sometimes theme is directly stated in the text. But in most fiction you have to think about all the story events and then infer, or guess at, the meaning of the whole story for yourself. Very often a key passage in the story helps you discover the theme.

Not everyone sees the same theme in the same story. Some writers say that they themselves don't know the meaning of a story until their characters beg them to reveal it.

> **A** story may contain several passages that reveal the essence of the **theme**.
>
> *For more on Theme, see pages 264–265 and the Handbook of Literary Terms.*

Background

President John F. Kennedy was assassinated on November 22, 1963, while riding in a motorcade in Dallas, Texas. No one expected the explosion of bullets that killed the young president as he greeted enthusiastic citizens on the sunny streets. That unforgettable day has become an important piece of American mythology—that is, it has become a part of what we think of ourselves as a nation. Even today, people from all walks of life share stories about where they were and what they were doing when Kennedy was killed. Elena, in this story, has a very personal reason to remember later the day Kennedy died.

"Listen," he repeated, "something awful has happened."

Teach Our Children (1990) by Juan Sanchez. Oil and mixed media on canvas.

Collection of the Museum of Tourism, San Juan, Puerto Rico.

American History

Judith Ortiz Cofer

I once read in a "Ripley's Believe It or Not" column that Paterson, New Jersey, is the place where the Straight and Narrow (streets) intersect. The Puerto Rican tenement known as El Building was one block up on Straight. It was, in fact, the corner of Straight and Market; not "at" the corner, but *the* corner. At almost any hour of the day, El Building was like a monstrous jukebox, blasting out salsas from open windows as the residents, mostly new immigrants just up from the island, tried to drown out whatever they were currently enduring with loud music. But the day President Kennedy was shot, there was a profound silence in El Building; even the abusive tongues of viragoes,[1] the cursing of the

1. **viragoes** (vi·rā′gōz): quarrelsome women.

unemployed, and the screeching of small children had been somehow muted. President Kennedy was a saint to these people. In fact, soon his photograph would be hung alongside the Sacred Heart and over the spiritist altars that many women kept in their apartments. He would become part of the hierarchy of martyrs[2] they prayed to for favors that only one who had died for a cause would understand.

On the day that President Kennedy was shot, my ninth-grade class had been out in the fenced playground of Public School Number 13. We had been given "free" exercise time and had been ordered by our PE teacher, Mr. DePalma, to "keep moving." That meant that the girls should jump rope and the boys toss basketballs through a hoop at the far end of the yard. He in the meantime would "keep an eye" on us from just inside the building.

It was a cold gray day in Paterson. The kind that warns of early snow. I was miserable, since I had forgotten my gloves and my knuckles were turning red and raw from the jump rope. I was also taking a lot of abuse from the black girls for not turning the rope hard and fast enough for them.

"Hey, Skinny Bones, pump it, girl. Ain't you got no energy today?" Gail, the biggest of the black girls, had the other end of the rope, yelled, "Didn't you eat your rice and beans and pork chops for breakfast today?"

The other girls picked up the "pork chop" and made it into a refrain: "Pork chop, pork chop, did you eat your pork chop?" They entered the double ropes in pairs and exited without tripping or missing a beat. I felt a burning on my cheeks and then my glasses fogged up so that I could not manage to coordinate the jump rope with Gail. The chill was doing to me what it always did: entering my bones, making me cry, humiliating me. I hated the city, especially in winter. I hated Public School Number 13. I hated my skinny, flat-chested body, and I envied the

black girls, who could jump rope so fast that their legs became a blur. They always seemed to be warm, while I froze.

There was only one source of beauty and light for me that school year—the only thing I had anticipated at the start of the semester. That was seeing Eugene. In August, Eugene and his family had moved into the only house on the block that had a yard and trees. I could see his place from my window in El Building. In fact, if I sat on the fire escape I was <u>literally</u> suspended above Eugene's back yard. It was my favorite spot to read my library books in the summer. Until that August the house had been occupied by an old Jewish couple. Over the years I had become part of their family, without their knowing it, of course. I had a view of their kitchen and their back yard, and though I could not hear what they said, I knew when they were arguing, when one of them was sick, and many other things. I knew all this by watching them at mealtimes. I could see their kitchen table, the sink, and the stove. During good times, he sat at the table and read his newspapers while she fixed the meals. If they argued, he would leave and the old woman would sit and stare at nothing for a long time. When one of them was sick, the other would come and get things from the kitchen and carry them out on a tray. The old man had died in June. The last week of school I had not seen him at the table at all. Then one day I saw that there was a crowd in the kitchen. The old woman had finally emerged from the house on the arm of a stocky middle-aged woman, whom I had seen there a few times before, maybe her daughter. Then a man had carried out suitcases. The house had stood empty for weeks. I had had to resist the temptation to climb down into the yard and water the flowers the old lady had taken such good care of.

By the time Eugene's family moved in, the yard was a tangled mass of weeds. The father had spent several days mowing, and when he

---

2. **hierarchy** (hī′ər·är′kē) **of martyrs** (märt′ərz): Martyrs are people who have suffered or died rather than give up their faith or principles; here, the author refers to martyrs who are honored and worshiped by Roman Catholics. *Hierarchy* means "ranking in order of importance."

WORDS TO OWN
literally (lit′ər·əl·ē) *adv.*: actually; in fact.

finished, from where I sat I didn't see the red, yellow, and purple clusters that meant flowers to me. I didn't see this family sit down at the kitchen table together. It was just the mother, a redheaded, tall woman who wore a white uniform—a nurse's, I guessed it was; the father was gone before I got up in the morning and was never there at dinner time. I only saw him on weekends, when they sometimes sat on lawn chairs under the oak tree, each hidden behind a section of the newspaper; and there was Eugene. He was tall and blond, and he wore glasses. I liked him right away because he sat at the kitchen table and read books for hours. That summer, before we had even spoken one word to each other, I kept him company on my fire escape.

Once school started, I looked for him in all my classes, but PS 13 was a huge, over-populated place and it took me days and many discreet questions to discover that Eugene was in honors classes for all his subjects, classes that were not open to me because English was not my first language, though I was a straight-A student. After much maneuvering I managed to "run into him" in the hallway where his locker was—on the other side of the building from mine—and in study hall at the library, where he first seemed to notice me but did not speak, and finally, on the way home after school one day when I decided to approach him directly, though my stomach was doing somersaults.

I was ready for rejection, snobbery, the worst. But when I came up to him, practically panting in my nervousness, and blurted out: "You're Eugene. Right?" he smiled, pushed his

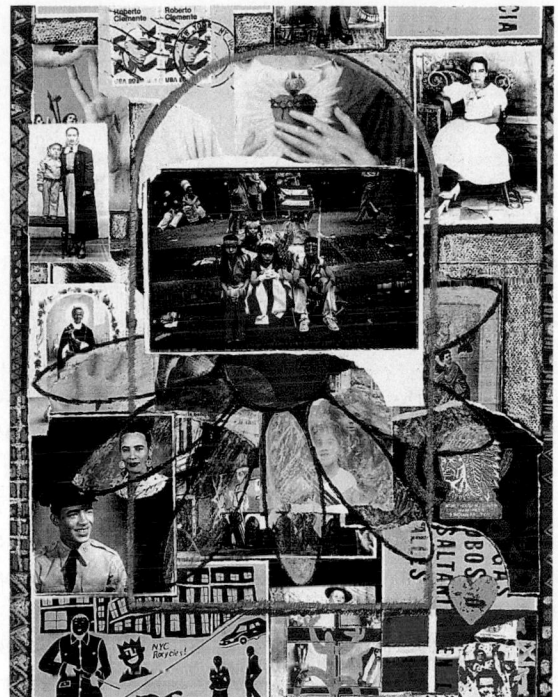

Untitled (1992) by Juan Sanchez.
Mixed media on paper.

Originally commissioned for the Testimonio Exhibit, New Museum of Contemporary Art, New York.

glasses up on his nose, and nodded. I saw then that he was blushing deeply. Eugene liked me, but he was shy. I did most of the talking that day. He nodded and smiled a lot. In the weeks that followed, we walked home together. He would linger at the corner of El Building for a few minutes, then walk down to his two-story house. It was not until Eugene moved into that house that I noticed that El Building blocked most of the sun and that the only spot that got a little sunlight during the day was the tiny square of earth the old woman had planted with flowers.

I did not tell Eugene that I could see inside his kitchen from my bedroom. I felt dishonest, but I liked my secret sharing of his evenings, especially now that I knew what he was reading since we chose our books together at the school library.

One day my mother came into my room as I was sitting on the windowsill staring out. In her abrupt way she said: "Elena, you are acting 'moony.'" "Enamorada" was what she really said, that is—like a girl stupidly <u>infatuated</u>. Since I had turned fourteen . . . , my mother had been more <u>vigilant</u> than ever. She acted as if I was going to go crazy or explode or something if she didn't watch me and nag me all the time about being a señorita now. She kept talking about virtue, morality, and other subjects that did not

WORDS TO OWN

infatuated (in·fach′ōō·āt′id) *adj.*: carried away by shallow or foolish love.
vigilant (vij′ə·lənt) *adj.*: watchful.

interest me in the least. My mother was unhappy in Paterson, but my father had a good job at the bluejeans factory in Passaic and soon, he kept assuring us, we would be moving to our own house there. Every Sunday we drove out to the suburbs of Paterson, Clifton, and Passaic, out to where people mowed grass on Sundays in the summer and where children made snowmen in the winter from pure white snow, not like the gray slush of Paterson, which seemed to fall from the sky in that hue. I had learned to listen to my parents' dreams, which were spoken in Spanish, as fairy tales, like the stories about life in the island paradise of Puerto Rico before I was born. I had been to the island once as a little girl, to Grandmother's funeral, and all I remembered was wailing women in black, my mother becoming hysterical and being given a pill that made her sleep two days, and me feeling lost in a crowd of strangers all claiming to be my aunts, uncles, and cousins. I had actually been glad to return to the city. We had not been back there since then, though my parents talked constantly about buying a house on the beach someday, retiring on the island— that was a common topic among the residents of El Building. As for me, I was going to go to college and become a teacher.

But after meeting Eugene I began to think of the present more than of the future. What I wanted now was to enter that house I had watched for so many years. I wanted to see the other rooms where the old people had lived and where the boy spent his time. Most of all I wanted to sit at the kitchen table with Eugene like two adults, like the old man and his wife had done, maybe drink some coffee and talk about books. I had started reading *Gone With the Wind*. I was <u>enthralled</u> by it, with the daring and the passion of the beautiful girl living in a mansion, and with her devoted parents and the slaves who did everything for them. I didn't believe such a world had ever really existed, and I wanted to ask Eugene some questions since he and his parents, he had told me, had come up from Georgia, the same place where the novel was set. His father worked for a company that had transferred him to Paterson.

His mother was very unhappy, Eugene said, in his beautiful voice that rose and fell over words in a strange, lilting way. The kids at school called him "the Hick" and made fun of the way he talked. I knew I was his only friend so far, and I liked that, though I felt sad for him sometimes. "Skinny Bones and the Hick" was what they called us at school when we were seen together.

The day Mr. DePalma came out into the cold and asked us to line up in front of him was the day that President Kennedy was shot. Mr. DePalma, a short, muscular man with slicked-down black hair, was the science teacher, PE coach, and disciplinarian at PS 13. He was the teacher to whose homeroom you got assigned if you were a troublemaker, and the man called out to break up playground fights and to escort violently angry teenagers to the office. And Mr. DePalma was the man who called your parents in for "a conference."

That day, he stood in front of two rows of mostly black and Puerto Rican kids, brittle from their efforts to "keep moving" on a November day that was turning bitter cold. Mr. DePalma, to our complete shock, was crying. Not just silent adult tears, but really sobbing. There were a few titters from the back of the line where I stood shivering.

"Listen," Mr. DePalma raised his arms over his head as if he were about to conduct an orchestra. His voice broke, and he covered his face with his hands. His barrel chest was heaving. Someone giggled behind me.

"Listen," he repeated, "something awful has happened." A strange gurgling came from his throat, and he turned around and spat on the cement behind him.

"Gross," someone said, and there was a lot of laughter.

"The president is dead, you idiots. I should have known that wouldn't mean anything to a bunch of losers like you kids. Go home." He was shrieking now. No one moved for a minute or

WORDS TO OWN
enthralled (en·thrôld′) v.: fascinated.

two, but then a big girl let out a "Yeah!" and ran to get her books piled up with the others against the brick wall of the school building. The others followed in a mad scramble to get to their things before somebody caught on. It was still an hour to the dismissal bell.

A little scared, I headed for El Building. There was an eerie feeling on the streets. I looked into Mario's drugstore, a favorite hangout for the high school crowd, but there were only a couple of old Jewish men at the soda bar talking with the short-order cook in tones that sounded almost angry, but they were keeping their voices low. Even the traffic on one of the busiest intersections in Paterson—Straight Street and Park Avenue—seemed to be moving slower. There were no horns blasting that day. At El Building, the usual little group of unemployed men were not hanging out on the front stoop making it difficult for women to enter the front door. No music spilled out from open doors in the hallway. When I walked into our apartment, I found my mother sitting in front of the grainy picture of the television set.

She looked up at me with a tear-streaked face and just said: "Dios mío," turning back to the set as if it were pulling at her eyes. I went into my room.

Though I wanted to feel the right thing about President Kennedy's death, I could not fight the feeling of elation that stirred in my chest. Today was the day I was to visit Eugene in his house. He

Retroactive I (1964) by Robert Rauschenberg. Oil on canvas (84″ x 60″).

had asked me to come over after school to study for an American history test with him. We had also planned to walk to the public library together. I looked down into his yard. The oak tree was bare of leaves and the ground looked gray with ice. The light through the large kitchen window of his house told me that El Building blocked the sun to such an extent that they had to turn lights on in the middle of the day. I felt ashamed about it. But the white kitchen table with the lamp hanging just above it looked cozy and inviting. I would soon sit there, across from Eugene, and I would tell him about my perch just above his house. Maybe I should

In the next thirty minutes I changed clothes, put on a little pink lipstick, and got my books together. Then I went in to tell my mother that I was going to a friend's house to study. I did not expect her reaction.

"You are going out *today*?" The way she said "today" sounded as if a storm warning had been issued. It was said in utter disbelief. Before I could answer, she came toward me and held my elbows as I clutched my books.

"Hija,[3] the president has been killed. We must show respect. He was a great man. Come to church with me tonight."

She tried to embrace me, but my books were in the way. My first impulse was to comfort her, she seemed so distraught, but I had to meet Eugene in fifteen minutes.

3. **hija** (ē′hä): Spanish for "daughter."

"I have a test to study for, Mama. I will be home by eight."

"You are forgetting who you are, Niña.[4] I have seen you staring down at that boy's house. You are heading for humiliation and pain." My mother said this in Spanish and in a resigned tone that surprised me, as if she had no intention of stopping me from "heading for humiliation and pain." I started for the door. She sat in front of the TV holding a white handkerchief to her face.

I walked out to the street and around the chain-link fence that separated El Building from Eugene's house. The yard was neatly edged around the little walk that led to the door. It always amazed me how Paterson, the inner core of the city, had no apparent logic to its architecture. Small, neat single residences like this one could be found right next to huge, dilapidated apartment buildings like El Building. My guess was that the little houses had been there first, then the immigrants had come in droves, and the monstrosities had been raised for them—the Italians, the Irish, the Jews, and now us, the Puerto Ricans and the blacks. The door was painted a deep green: verde, the color of hope. I had heard my mother say it: verde-esperanza.

I knocked softly. A few suspenseful moments later the door opened just a crack. The red, swollen face of a woman appeared. She had a halo of red hair floating over a delicate ivory

Originally commissioned for the Center for Puerto Rican Studies at Hunter College, New York.

Untitled (1993) by Juan Sanchez.
Mixed media on paper.

face—the face of a doll—with freckles on the nose. Her smudged eye makeup made her look unreal to me, like a mannequin[5] seen through a warped store window.

"What do you want?" Her voice was tiny and sweet sounding, like a little girl's, but her tone was not friendly.

"I'm Eugene's friend. He asked me over. To study." I thrust out my books, a silly gesture that embarrassed me almost immediately.

"You live there?" She pointed up to El Building, which looked particularly ugly, like a gray prison, with its many dirty windows and rusty fire escapes. The woman had stepped halfway out and I could see that she wore a white nurse's uniform with "St. Joseph's Hospital" on the name tag.

"Yes. I do."

She looked intently at me for a couple of heartbeats, then said as if to herself, "I don't know how you people do it." Then directly to me: "Listen. Honey. Eugene doesn't want to study with you. He is a smart boy. Doesn't need help. You understand me. I am truly sorry if he told you you could come over. He cannot study with you. It's nothing personal. You understand? We won't be in this place much longer, no need for him to get close to people—it'll just make it harder for him later. Run back home now."

I couldn't move. I just stood there in shock at hearing these things said to me in such a honey-drenched voice. I had never heard an accent like hers, except for Eugene's softer version. It was as if she were singing me a little song.

4. **niña** (nē′nyä): Spanish for "girl."

5. **mannequin** (man′i·kin): life-size model of a person.

"What's wrong? Didn't you hear what I said?" She seemed very angry, and I finally snapped out of my trance. I turned away from the green door and heard her close it gently.

Our apartment was empty when I got home. My mother was in someone else's kitchen, seeking the solace she needed. Father would come in from his late shift at midnight. I would hear them talking softly in the kitchen for hours that night. They would not discuss their dreams for the future, or life in Puerto Rico, as they often did; that night they would talk sadly about the young widow and her two children, as if they were family. For the next few days, we would observe luto in our apartment; that is, we would practice restraint and silence—no loud music or laughter. Some of the women of El Building would wear black for weeks.

That night, I lay in my bed trying to feel the right thing for our dead president. But the tears that came up from a deep source inside me were strictly for me. When my mother came to the door, I pretended to be sleeping. Sometime during the night, I saw from my bed the street-light come on. It had a pink halo around it. I went to my window and pressed my face to the cool glass. Looking up at the light, I could see the white snow falling like a lace veil over its face. I did not look down to see it turning gray as it touched the ground below.

WORDS TO OWN

solace (säl′is) *n.:* comfort; easing of grief.

MEET THE WRITER

Mastering English

Judith Ortiz Cofer (1952–   ) was born in Puerto Rico but her family moved to the mainland United States when she was a child. For her, this meant learning English. As Cofer explains it:

66 The 'infinite variety' and power of language interest me. I never cease to experiment with it. As a native Puerto Rican, my first language was Spanish. It was a challenge not only to learn English, but to master it enough to teach it and—the ultimate goal—to write poetry in it. 99

Cofer achieved her goal. She earned a master's degree, and she attended Oxford University in England, where she received recognition as a Scholar of the English Speaking Union. She has taught English at various colleges in Florida and Georgia and has published several books of poetry. In 1989, she published her first novel, *The Line of the Sun,* and in 1990, she published *Silent Dancing,* a remembrance of her early years in Puerto Rico. "American History" paints a picture of mainland United States seen through the eyes of a little girl from Puerto Rico.

this morning
(For the girls of Eastern High School)

Lucille Clifton

this morning
this morning
               i met myself
coming in

5   a bright
jungle girl
shining
quick as a snake
a tall
10 tree girl a
me girl
               i met myself
this morning
coming in

15 and all day
i have been
a black bell
ringing
i survive
20   survive
survive

MAKING MEANINGS

First Thoughts

1. What do you think happens to Elena and Eugene after the story is over?

Shaping Interpretations

2. Eugene, nicknamed "the Hick," and Elena, nicknamed "Skinny Bones," come from entirely different worlds, yet they have something important in common. What is it?

3. Review your Reader's Log: Which statements in the story seem important or controversial to you? Share the passages and your responses to them in class. Does sharing your reactions to the text change your feelings about it?

> **Reviewing the Text**
>
> Imagine that it is fifty years later. Elena now has grand-children who are studying the 1960s in history class. Their assignment is to interview someone who was alive at that time. Stage the interview with a partner. One of you will play Elena's grandchild and will ask the other (grandmother Elena) questions about the sixties. Elena will answer by telling about her experience on the day Kennedy was killed.

4. If someone who hadn't read the story asked you what the **title** means, what would you say?

5. Why do you think Elena is turned away from Eugene's house?

6. Look at the last statement in the story. Why do you think Elena doesn't want to see the snow turning gray? Could this statement reveal something important about Elena—about how she faces a loss in her life? Think about the whole story and try to state in your own words your interpretation of the story's **theme**.

Connecting with the Text

7. What would you say to Elena about her experience with Eugene's mother? What would you advise her to do?

Extending the Text

8. Do you think that Elena's rejection is something that others have experienced? Explain.

9. Imagine it is the week after Elena's heartbreak and she has to go to school. How do you think she will manage? What does the narrator of the poem "this morning" (page 298) have to say to Elena?

10. Eugene disappears from the story after page 295. What do you suppose he thinks that evening, when Elena doesn't show up? Do you think he knows what his mother did?

CHOICES: Building Your Portfolio

Writer's Notebook

1. Collecting Ideas for an Evaluation

Focusing on character. When people evaluate fiction, they often focus on characters. In fact, you might have listed "believable characters" as one of the criteria you'd use in evaluating a story (see page 257). With a partner or group, brainstorm all the things that you think make a character in a story seem alive. Try to think of examples (perhaps from stories in this book) of believable characters and of characters who are not convincing at all. As you brainstorm, you might focus on "American History." Save your notes for use in the Writer's Workshop on page 332.

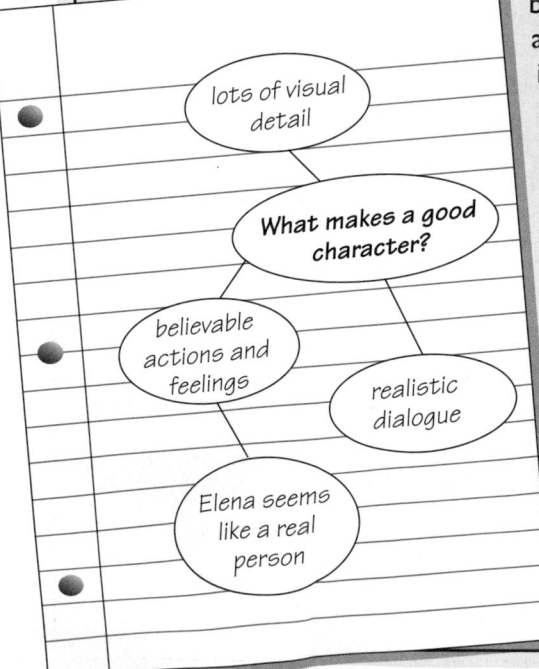

lots of visual detail

What makes a good character?

believable actions and feelings

realistic dialogue

Elena seems like a real person

Writing/Social Studies

2. Oral History: "Where Were You When . . . ?"

At the beginning of the story the author states, "President Kennedy was a saint to these people." She also describes the "profound silence" in El Building the day President Kennedy was shot. Interview at least three people who remember that day. Ask them: "Where were you and what were you doing when you heard that President Kennedy had been assassinated?" Write your report in a question-and-answer format that might be published as a magazine article. Include a short introduction to each person you interview. Begin the article with a paragraph or two about that period in American history.

Creative Writing

3. Just the One I'm Looking For

Elena is attracted to Eugene for several reasons. Think about the qualities in a person that are attractive to you. Use this chart to come up with ideas. (If some of these details are not important, say so.) Then write a character sketch of your ideal friend—either a boy or a girl.

Appearance	
Thoughts or attitudes	
Way of talking	
Way of treating others	
Actions	
Other people's feelings about the person	

Drawing/Social Studies

4. La puerta de la esperanza (Door of Hope)

Elena knocked on Eugene's door, which was green, "the color of hope." Draw two green doors that are beginning to open. Under one door write "Door of Hope for the United States." Under the other door write "Door of Hope for Me." Fill in the opening with images and words that describe your hopes for this nation and for yourself. You might also draw a third green door, "Door of Hope for the World."

LANGUAGE LINK MINI-LESSON

Language Handbook HELP

See Clauses, page 1009.

Technology HELP

See Language Workshop CD-ROM. *Key word entry: adverb clauses.*

Style: All for a Good Clause

To avoid writing a series of short, choppy sentences, and to show relationships between ideas, writers use adverb clauses.

An adverb clause is a dependent clause that tells *where, when, how, why, to what extent,* or *under what conditions.* Cofer uses adverb clauses (underlined below) and a variety of subordinating conjunctions (such as *if, because,* and *when*) to make the relationships between her ideas clear. The first sentence in each pair shows how a passage from Cofer's story would look if she did not put one of her ideas in a subordinate clause.

1. I sat on the fire escape. In fact, I was literally suspended above Eugene's back yard.

   Cofer: "In fact, if I sat on the fire escape, I was literally suspended above Eugene's back yard."

2. He sat at the kitchen table and read books for hours. I liked him right away.

   Cofer: "I liked him right away because he sat at the kitchen table and read books for hours."

3. I got home. Our apartment was empty.

   Cofer: "Our apartment was empty when I got home."

Try It Out

➤ Jot down four observations about Elena and Eugene's friendship. Then make those four statements more precise by reshaping them into sentences using any of the subordinating conjunctions from the list below.

- after
- although
- because
- since
- than
- until
- when
- while

➤ When you revise your own writing, experiment with subordinating conjunctions. Find exactly the right conjunction to express your ideas. Notice that in some of the example sentences, other conjunctions could have been used. (Cofer could have written "*When* I sat on the fire escape . . .")

VOCABULARY HOW TO OWN A WORD

WORD BANK

literally
infatuated
vigilant
enthralled
solace

Which Word?

Follow the instructions below by writing a sentence for each item that uses one word from the Word Bank.

1. Describe the guard at a prison camp.
2. Describe your reaction to a mystery novel you're recommending to a friend.
3. Explain why some people like to talk about a loved one who has died.
4. Write the first line of a letter telling about a friend who's in love.
5. Tell what you would say to let a police officer know that your description of a crime scene is exact.

BEFORE YOU READ
TRAIN TIME

Background

In the late nineteenth century, the United States government established boarding schools for American Indians. Children were taken from their parents and sent to live in schools hundreds of miles away from their homes. Officials of the Bureau of Indian Affairs believed the children would more quickly learn and adopt white values if they were separated from their own culture. Most American Indian parents did not want their children to be taken away.

Here is an account of one child's experience of the day the children were sent away from their Arizona village:

"We were now loaded into wagons hired from and driven by our enemies. . . . We were taken to the schoolhouse in New Oraibi, with military escort. We slept on the floor of the dining room that night. . . .

"It was after dark when we reached the Keams Canyon boarding school and were unloaded and taken into the big dormitory, lighted with electricity. I had never seen so much light at night. I was all mixed up and thought it was daytime. . . . There were not enough beds so they put mattresses on the floor. . . .

"Evenings we would gather in a corner and cry softly so the matron would not hear and scold or spank us. I would try to be a comforter, but in a little while I would be crying too. I can still hear the plaintive little voices saying, 'I want to go home. I want my mother.' We didn't understand a word of English and didn't know what to say or do. . . ."

Reading Focus

Good Intentions

Most American Indian boarding schools were probably established with good intentions. But can we cause pain to other people even if we have all the good intentions in the world?

Quickwrite

Preview this story by looking at the illustrations. Write down one word, then one phrase, then one sentence to describe how you feel about the boarding schools right now.

Elements of Literature

Point of View: Whose Is It?

Whenever we read a story, we should ask "Whose **point of view** am I getting?" This story is told from the limited point of view of a man we know only as the Major. We know he is a white man who works for the Bureau of Indian Affairs on a reservation in the West. The Major doesn't tell the story himself: A narrator relates the events but limits what we see and know to what the Major sees and knows (and remembers). What we soon realize is that what the Major knows and speaks about is not the whole picture.

In the **third-person limited** point of view, the writer focuses on the thoughts and perceptions of just one character in the story. With this point of view, we share intensely what the character experiences, but we may not know what other people in the story are thinking.

For more on Point of View, see pages 218–219 and the Handbook of Literary Terms.

Train Time

D'Arcy McNickle

On the depot platform everybody stood waiting, listening. The train has just whistled, somebody said. They stood listening and gazing eastward, where railroad tracks and creek emerged together from a tree-choked canyon.

Twenty-five boys, five girls, Major Miles—all stood waiting and gazing eastward. Was it true that the train had whistled?

The Chemawa Indian Training School, north of Salem, Oregon.

The boy was no taller than an ax handle.

"That was no train!" a boy's voice explained. "It was a steer bellowing."

"It was the train!"

Girls crowded backward against the station building, heads hanging, tears starting; boys pushed forward to the edge of the platform. An older boy with a voice already turning heavy stepped off the weather-shredded boardwalk and stood wide-legged in the middle of the track. He was the doubter. He had heard no train.

Major Miles boomed, "You! What's your name? Get back here! Want to get killed? All of you, stand back!"

The Major strode about, soldierlike, and waved commands. He was exasperated. He was tired. A man driving cattle through timber had it easy, he was thinking. An animal trainer had no idea of trouble. Let anyone try corralling twenty, thirty Indian kids, dragging them out of hiding places, getting them away from relatives and together in one place, then holding them, without tying them, until train time! Even now, at the last moment, when his worries were almost over, they were trying to get themselves killed!

Major Miles was a man of conscience. Whatever he did he did earnestly. On this hot end-of-summer day he perspired and frowned and wore his soldier bearing. He removed his hat from his wet brow and thoughtfully passed his hand from the hairline backward. Words tumbled about in his mind. Somehow, he realized, he had to vivify° the moment. These children were about to go out from the reservation and get a new start. Life would change. They ought to realize it, somehow——

"Boys—and girls——" There were five girls, he remembered. He had got them all lined up against the building, safely away from the edge of the platform. The air was <u>stifling</u> with end-of-summer heat. It was time to say something, never mind the heat. Yes, he would have to make

°**vivify** (viv′ə·fī′): give life to.

the moment real. He stood soldierlike and thought that.

"Boys and girls——" The train whistled, dully but unmistakably. Then it repeated more clearly. The rails came to life; something was running through them and making them sing.

Just then the Major's eye fell upon little Eneas and his sure voice faltered. He knew about little Eneas. Most of the boys and girls were mere names; he had seen them around the agency with their parents or had caught sight of them scurrying behind tepees and barns when he visited their homes. But little Eneas he knew. With him before his eyes, he paused.

He remembered so clearly the winter day, six months ago, when he first saw Eneas. It was the boy's grandfather, Michel Lamartine, he had gone to see. Michel had contracted to cut wood for the agency but had not started work. The Major had gone to discover why not.

It was the coldest day of the winter, late in February, and the cabin, sheltered as it was among the pine and cottonwood of a creek bottom, was shot through by frosty drafts. There was wood all about them. Lamartine was a woodcutter besides, yet there was no wood in the house. The fire in the flat-topped cast-iron stove burned weakly. The reason was apparent. The Major had but to look at the bed where Lamartine lay twisted and shrunken by rheumatism. Only his black eyes burned with life. He tried to wave a hand as the Major entered.

"You see how I am!" the gesture indicated. Then a nerve-strung voice faltered. "We have it bad here. My old woman, she's not much good."

Clearly she wasn't, not for wood chopping. She sat close by the fire, trying with a good-natured grin to lift her <u>ponderous</u> body from a low-seated rocking chair. The Major had to motion

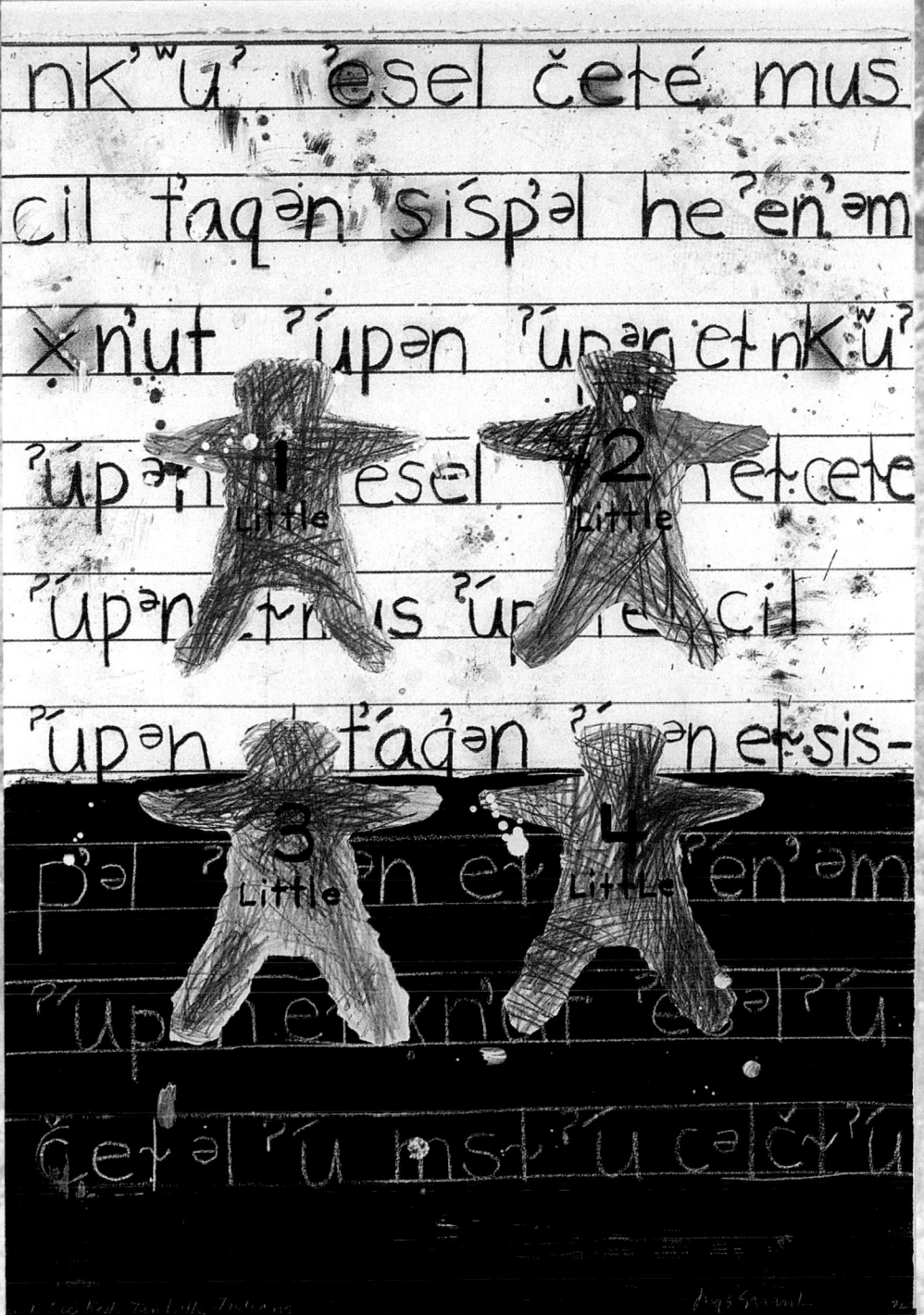

I See Red: Ten Little Indians (1992) by Jaune Quick-to-See Smith.
Mixed media, collage on paper (41 ½″ x 29 ½″).

her back to her ease. She breathed with an asthmatic roar. Wood chopping was not within her range. With only a squaw hatchet to work with, she could scarcely have come within striking distance of a stick of wood. Two blows, if she had struck them, might have put a stop to her laboring heart.

"You see how it is," Lamartine's eyes flashed.

The Major saw clearly. Sitting there in the frosty cabin, he pondered their plight and at the same time wondered if he would get away without coming down with pneumonia. A stream of wind seemed to be hitting him in the back of the neck. Of course, there was nothing to do. One saw too many such situations. If one undertook to provide <u>sustenance</u> out of one's own pocket, there would be no end to the demands. Government salaries were small; resources were limited. He could do no more than shake his head sadly, offer some vague hope, some small sympathy. He would have to get away at once.

Then a hand fumbled at the door; it opened. After a moment's struggle, little Eneas appeared, staggering under a full armload of pine limbs hacked into short lengths. The boy was no taller than an ax handle, his nose was running, and he had a croupy cough. He dropped the wood into the empty box near the old woman's chair, then straightened himself.

A soft chuckling came from the bed. Lamartine was full of pride. "A good boy, that. He keeps the old folks warm."

Something about the boy made the Major forget his determination to depart. Perhaps it was his wordlessness, his uncomplaining wordlessness. Or possibly it was his loyalty to the old people. Something drew his eyes to the boy and set him to thinking. Eneas was handing

---

WORDS TO OWN

sustenance (sus'tə·nəns) *n.:* support.

sticks of wood to the old woman and she was feeding them into the stove. When the firebox was full, a good part of the boy's armload was gone. He would have to cut more, and more, to keep the old people warm.

The Major heard himself saying suddenly: "Sonny, show me your woodpile. Let's cut a lot of wood for the old folks."

It happened just like that, inexplicably. He went even further. Not only did he cut enough wood to last through several days, but when he had finished, he put the boy in the agency car and drove him to town, five miles there and back. Against his own principles, he bought a week's store of groceries and excused himself by telling the boy, as they drove homeward, "Your grandfather won't be able to get to town for a few days yet. Tell him to come see me when he gets well."

That was the beginning of the Major's interest in Eneas. He had decided that day that he would help the boy in any way possible, because he was a boy of quality. You would be shirking your duty if you failed to recognize and to help a boy of his sort. The only question was, how to help?

When he saw the boy again, some weeks later, his mind saw the problem clearly. "Eneas," he said, "I'm going to help you. I'll see that the old folks are taken care of, so you won't have to think about them. Maybe the old man won't have rheumatism next year, anyhow. If he does, I'll find a family where he and the old lady can move in and be looked after. Don't worry about them. Just think about yourself and what I'm going to do for you. Eneas, when it comes school time, I'm going to send you away. How do you like that?" The Major smiled at his own happy idea.

There was silence. No shy smiling, no look of gratitude, only silence. Probably he had not understood.

"You understand, Eneas? Your grandparents will be taken care of. You'll go away and learn things. You'll go on a train."

The boy looked here and there and scratched at the ground with his foot. "Why do I have to go away?"

"You don't have to, Eneas. Nobody will make you. I thought you'd like to. I thought——" The Major paused, confused.

"You won't make me go away, will you?" There was fear in the voice, tears threatened.

"Why, no, Eneas. If you don't want to go. I thought——"

The Major dropped the subject. He didn't see the boy again through spring and summer, but he thought of him. In fact, he couldn't forget the picture he had of him that first day. He couldn't forget either that he wanted to help him. Whether the boy understood what was good for him or not, he meant to see to it that the right thing was done. And that was why, when he made up a quota of children to be sent to the school in Oregon, the name of Eneas Lamartine was included. The Major did not discuss it with him again but he set the wheels in motion. The boy would go with the others. In time to come, he would understand. Possibly he would be grateful.

Thirty children were included in the quota, and of them all Eneas was the only one the Major had actual knowledge of, the only one in whom he was personally interested. With each of them, it was true, he had had difficulties. None had wanted to go. They said they "liked it at home," or they were "afraid" to go away, or they would "get sick" in a strange country; and the parents were no help. They too were frightened

WORDS TO OWN

inexplicably (in·eks′pli·kə·blē) *adv.*: unexplainably; without apparent reason.

and uneasy. It was a tiresome, hard kind of duty, but the Major knew what was required of him and never hesitated. The difference was that in the cases of all these others, the problem was routine. He met it and passed over it. But in the case of Eneas, he was bothered. He wanted to make clear what this moment of going away meant. It was a breaking away from fear and doubt and ignorance. Here began the new. Mark it; remember it.

His eyes lingered on Eneas. There he stood, drooping, his nose running as on that first day, his stockings coming down, his jacket in need of buttons. But under that shabbiness, the Major knew, was real quality. There was a boy who, with the right help, would blossom and grow strong. It was important that he should not go away hurt and resentful.

The Major called back his straying thoughts and cleared his throat. The moment was important.

"Boys and girls——"

The train was pounding near. Already it had emerged from the canyon and from moment to moment the headlong-flying locomotive loomed blacker and larger. A white plume flew upward—*whoo-oo, whoo-oo.*

The Major realized in sudden sharp remorse that he had waited too long. The vital moment had come, and he had paused, looked for words, and lost it. The roar of rolling steel was upon them.

Lifting his voice in desperate haste, his eyes fastened on Eneas, he bellowed: "Boys and girls—be good——"

That was all anyone heard.

MEET THE WRITER

Man from Montana

D'Arcy McNickle (1904–1977) was one-quarter American Indian— he had Salish and Kutenai ancestors—and he devoted most of his life to American Indian affairs.

Born on the Flathead Indian Reservation in St. Ignatius, Montana, McNickle knew what he was talking (and writing) about. He gained a wider perspective on his own upbringing when he studied at the University of Montana and later in England, France, and New York City. He spent several years in Washington, D.C., and Boulder, Colorado, working with the Bureau of Indian Affairs. Later he became program director of the Center for the History of the American Indian at the Newberry Library in Chicago. McNickle became an influential professor in the growing field of anthropology— the study of human beings, especially their culture, customs, and social relationships. In many ways all his writing about American Indian life—nonfiction, short stories, and novels—is just that, a study of human beings.

More About American Indians

If you'd like to learn more about American Indian history, read McNickle's novel *Wind from an Enemy Sky* (University of New Mexico Press). His books for young people include *Runner in the Sun* (University of New Mexico Press) and *The Hawk Is Hungry* (University of Arizona Press).

The School Days of an Indian Girl

Zitkala-Sa (Gertrude Bonnin)

Born in 1876 and brought up as a Yankton Sioux in South Dakota, Zitkala-Sa left the reservation to attend a Quaker school when she was eight years old. The transition from her childhood home to the painful early days in school is the subject of an autobiography that is excerpted here.

The old Indian School at Elbowoods, on the Mandan Indian Reservation in North Dakota.

There were eight in our party of bronzed children who were going east with the missionaries. Among us were three young braves, two tall girls, and we three little ones, Judéwin, Thowin, and I.

We had been very impatient to start on our journey to the Red Apple Country, which, we were told, lay a little beyond the great circular horizon of the Western prairie. Under a sky of rosy apples we dreamed of roaming as freely and happily as we had chased the cloud shadows on the Dakota plains. We had anticipated much pleasure from a ride on the iron horse,° but the throngs of staring palefaces disturbed and troubled us.

On the train, fair women, with tottering babies on each arm, stopped their haste and

°**iron horse:** train.

scrutinized the children of absent mothers. Large men, with heavy bundles in their hands, halted nearby and riveted their glassy blue eyes upon us.

I sank deep into the corner of my seat, for I resented being watched. Directly in front of me, children who were no larger than I hung themselves upon the backs of their seats, with their bold white faces toward me. Sometimes they took their forefingers out of their mouths and pointed at my moccasined feet. Their mothers, instead of reproving such rude curiosity, looked closely at me and attracted their children's further notice to my blanket. This embarrassed me and kept me constantly on the verge of tears.

I sat perfectly still, with my eyes downcast, daring only now and then to shoot long glances around me. Chancing to turn to the window at my side, I was quite breathless upon seeing one familiar object. It was the telegraph pole which strode by at short paces. Very near my mother's dwelling, along the edge of a road thickly bordered with wild sunflowers, some poles like these had been planted by white men. Often I had stopped, on my way down the road, to hold my ear against the pole, and hearing its low moaning, I used to wonder what the paleface had done to hurt it. Now I sat watching for each pole that glided by to be the last one.

In this way I had forgotten my uncomfortable surroundings, when I heard one of my comrades call out my name. I saw the missionary standing very near, tossing candies and gums into our midst. This amused us all, and we tried to see who could catch the most of the sweetmeats.

Though we rode several days inside of the iron horse, I do not recall a single thing about our luncheons.

It was night when we reached the school grounds. The lights from the windows of the large buildings fell upon some of the icicled trees that stood beneath them. We were led toward an open door, where the brightness of the lights within flooded out over the heads of the excited palefaces who blocked our way. My body trembled more from fear than from the snow I trod upon.

Entering the house, I stood close against the wall. The strong, glaring light in the large white-washed room dazzled my eyes. The noisy hurrying of hard shoes upon a bare wooden floor increased the whirring in my ears. My only safety seemed to be in keeping next to the wall. As I was wondering in which direction to escape from all this confusion, two warm hands grasped me firmly, and in the same moment I was tossed high in midair. A rosy-cheeked paleface woman caught me in her arms. I was both frightened and insulted by such trifling. I stared into her eyes, wishing her to let me stand on my own feet, but she jumped me up and down with increasing enthusiasm. My mother had never made a plaything of her wee daughter. Remembering this, I began to cry aloud.

They misunderstood the cause of my tears and placed me at a white table loaded with food. There our party was united again. As I did not hush my crying, one of the older ones whispered to me, "Wait until you are alone in the night."

It was very little I could swallow besides my sobs, that evening.

"Oh, I want my mother and my brother Dawée! I want to go to my aunt!" I pleaded; but the ears of the palefaces could not hear me.

From the table we were taken along an upward incline of wooden boxes, which I learned afterward to call a stairway. At the top was a quiet hall, dimly lighted. Many narrow beds were in one straight line down the entire length of the wall. In them lay sleeping brown faces, which peeped just out of the coverings. I was tucked into bed with one of the tall girls, because she talked to me in my mother tongue and seemed to soothe me.

I had arrived in the wonderful land of rosy skies, but I was not happy, as I had thought I should be. My long travel and the bewildering sights had exhausted me. I fell asleep, heaving deep, tired sobs. My tears were left to dry themselves in streaks, because neither my aunt nor my mother was near to wipe them away.

Center: Sioux doll (c. 1890) from South Dakota. Tanned cowhide, beads (20″ x 14″). Native American. CP-122. Richard and Marion Pohrt Collection.

MAKING MEANINGS

First Thoughts

1. What do you think of Major Miles's decision to send Eneas away?

Shaping Interpretations

2. "Train Time" is told from the **limited point of view** of the Major. Find places where you are taken right into the Major's mind and told what he is thinking and feeling.

3. List all the **character** traits you see revealed in Major Miles. Make a pie graph (an example is shown here) indicating how important each trait is in making him the kind of person he is. Be sure to compare your "Major Miles Pies" in class.

Reviewing the Text

a. Who is Major Miles employed by and what duty is he carrying out in this story?

b. Describe living conditions on the reservation as Major Miles sees them.

c. Why does Major Miles believe Eneas is a "boy of quality"?

d. How do the children feel about leaving the reservation?

4. What does Major Miles want the children to realize before the train arrives to take them away?

5. How do you think Eneas might describe what happens to him? How do you imagine he thinks and feels about Major Miles?

6. McNickle doesn't tell us directly what *he* thinks of Major Miles—if he had done so, what might he have said?

Connecting with the Text

7. Look back at the responses to the illustrations in this story that you recorded in your Quickwrite notes. How did reading the story affect your responses? Now write a word, a phrase, and a sentence to describe your final responses to "Train Time."

Extending the Text

8. In "The School Days of an Indian Girl" (page 309), a young American Indian describes her journey away from home to a boarding school. According to this account, what is in store for Eneas?

CHOICES: Building Your Portfolio

Writer's Notebook

1. Collecting Ideas for an Evaluation

Storytellers. In the short-story evaluation you'll be writing in the Writer's Workshop on page 332, you'll probably want to think about **point of view** and how it affects the way you feel about the characters and what happens to them. Make a chart like the one here, listing three stories in this collection and the point of view they are written from. For each one, describe how the point of view affected your reading of the story.

Creative Writing

2. Journal of a Journey

Pretend you are a screenwriter who has been working on a script for "Train Time." You've been asked to add a final scene in which Eneas is on the train heading for Oregon. As a way to express his thoughts, you have Eneas writing a journal. In the movie, his thoughts will be presented by a narrator's voice-over. Write entries for the boy's journal including

- his feelings about leaving home
- his thoughts about Oregon and a new school
- events that occur during the trip
  - observations of other children on the train

Critical Writing/ Social Studies

3. Research—Indian Boarding Schools

Use the following questions, or write questions of your own, to gather information on American Indian boarding schools. Present your findings in the form of a research paper or an oral report.

- What became of the American Indian boarding schools?
- Where were they located?
- What were conditions like at the schools? What was a day like at the schools?
- Who taught at the schools?
- How did most American Indians feel about the schools?
- What other attempts were made to assimilate American Indians in the late 1800s and early 1900s?

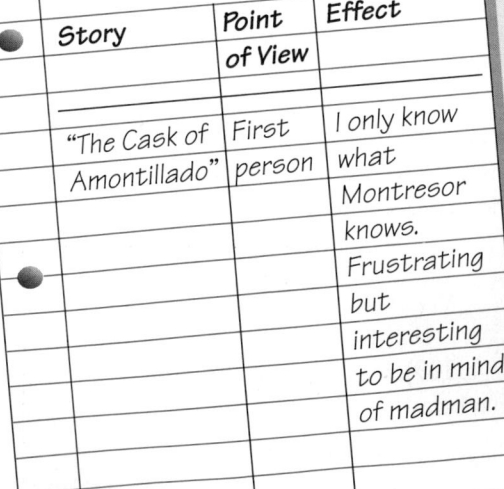

Story	Point of View	Effect
"The Cask of Amontillado"	First person	I only know what Montresor knows. Frustrating but interesting to be in mind of madman.

Old St. Labre Indian School in Ashland, Montana.

LANGUAGE LINK `MINI-LESSON`

Language Handbook HELP

See Sentence Combining, page 1015.

Technology HELP

See Language Workshop CD-ROM. *Key word entry:* coordinating conjunctions.

Style: Coordinating Conjunctions—Getting It Together

You probably didn't notice the coordinating conjunctions as you read "Train Time," but they were there doing their job. Writers use coordinating conjunctions to join words, phrases, or clauses of equal importance. Suppose the writer of this story had these ideas about the Major in his notes.

> Major on the platform
> - hot day
> - end of summer
> - he perspired
> - he frowned
> - soldier bearing

Here is how he put these ideas together in a sentence using coordinating conjunctions to join a series of verbs:

> "On this hot end-of-summer day he perspired <u>and</u> frowned <u>and</u> wore his soldier bearing."

Here are two other sentences from the story that use coordinating conjunctions to join ideas of equal importance. Break these sentences into smaller ones to see how many details the writer combined.

1. "Most of the boys <u>and</u> girls were mere names; he had seen them around the agency with their parents <u>or</u> had caught sight of them scurrying behind tepees <u>and</u> barns when he visited their homes."

2. "Michel had contracted to cut wood for the agency <u>but</u> had not started work."

Try It Out

Using each of the seven coordinating conjunctions listed below, summarize the events in "Train Time."

- and
- but
- for
- nor
- or
- so
- yet

VOCABULARY `HOW TO OWN A WORD`

WORD BANK

stifling
ponderous
sustenance
inexplicably

Descriptive Responses

Write detailed answers to the following questions.

1. How do people behave if they have to sit for a long time in a <u>stifling</u> room?
2. Describe the difference between a <u>ponderous</u> person and someone who's carefree.
3. Name some things that provide <u>sustenance</u> and some that don't.
4. If your best friend <u>inexplicably</u> started ignoring you, what would you do?

BEFORE YOU READ
THE SCARLET IBIS

Reading Focus

Southern Exposure

Some people say "The Scarlet Ibis" is a story they will never forget. The story is set in the American South. Its climax takes place in 1918, the year World War I ended in Europe. You'll find references in the story to battles being fought in parts of the world far from this peaceful Southern setting, but the story is not about the wider war. It is about a small but still tragic struggle that takes place between two young brothers.

A Dialogue with the Text

Read to the end of the paragraph that starts "It was bad enough" (page 317). Then

stop and write down at least three questions that the story-teller has made you wonder about. When you finish the story, see if your questions have been answered.

Elements of Literature

Symbols

We communicate by means of symbols. We use groups of sounds or letters to stand for things in the outer physical world and for ideas in our own inner worlds. The sounds or letters themselves are not the things or ideas; they only symbolize, or stand for, these things or ideas.

In literature a symbol is somewhat different. It's a specific object, person, or event that stands for something more than itself. In the story "Marigolds" on page 91, those sturdy, pungent flowers could stand for hope and endurance. But, as is the way with

all symbols, you might have other ideas about what the marigolds stand for. In fact, symbols in literature may have different shades of meaning for each of us.

> A **symbol** is an object, a person, or an event that functions as itself but also stands for something more than itself.
>
> *For more on Symbol, see the Handbook of Literary Terms.*

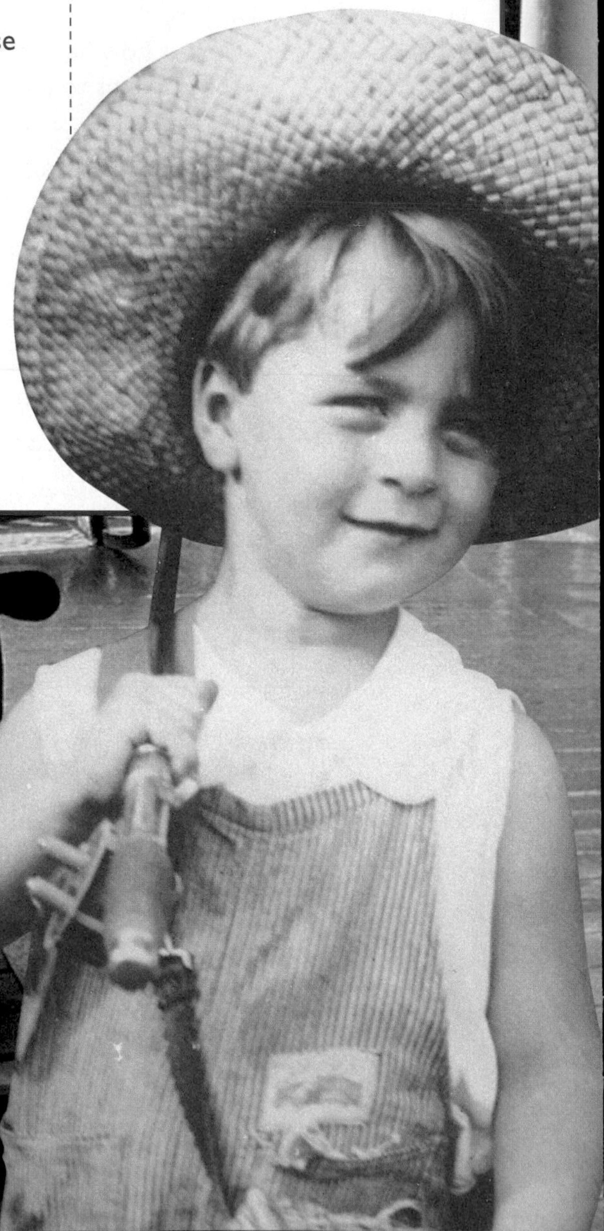

THE Scarlet Ibis

James Hurst

Doodle was just about the craziest brother a boy ever had.

It was in the clove of seasons, summer was dead but autumn had not yet been born, that the ibis lit in the bleeding tree. The flower garden was stained with rotting brown magnolia petals, and ironweeds grew rank[1] amid the purple phlox. The five o'clocks by the chimney still marked time, but the oriole nest in the elm was untenanted and rocked back and forth like an empty cradle. The last graveyard flowers were blooming, and their smell drifted across the cotton field and through every room of our house, speaking softly the names of our dead.

1. **rank:** thick and wild. *Rank* also means "smelly" or "overripe."

Uptown Street (1890) by Lulu Saxon. Oil on canvas (90″ x 68″).

with all its changes is ground away—and I remember Doodle.

Doodle was just about the craziest brother a boy ever had. Of course, he wasn't a crazy crazy like old Miss Leedie, who was in love with President Wilson and wrote him a letter every day, but was a nice crazy, like someone you meet in your dreams. He was born when I was six and was, from the outset, a disappointment. He seemed all head, with a tiny body which was red and shriveled like an old man's. Everybody thought he was going to die—everybody except Aunt Nicey, who had delivered him. She said he would live because he was born in a caul[2] and cauls were made from Jesus' nightgown. Daddy had Mr. Heath, the carpenter, build a little mahogany coffin for him. But he didn't die, and when he was three months old, Mama and Daddy decided they might as well name him. They named him William Armstrong, which was like tying a big tail on a small kite. Such a name sounds good only on a tombstone.

I thought myself pretty smart at many things, like holding my breath, running, jumping, or climbing the vines in Old Woman Swamp, and I wanted more than anything else someone to

It's strange that all this is still so clear to me, now that that summer has long since fled and time has had its way. A grindstone stands where the bleeding tree stood, just outside the kitchen door, and now if an oriole sings in the elm, its song seems to die up in the leaves, a silvery dust. The flower garden is prim, the house a gleaming white, and the pale fence across the yard stands straight and spruce. But sometimes (like right now), as I sit in the cool, green-draped parlor, the grindstone begins to turn, and time

2. **caul:** membrane (thin, skinlike material) that sometimes covers a baby's head at birth.

race to Horsehead Landing, someone to box with, and someone to perch with in the top fork of the great pine behind the barn, where across the fields and swamps you could see the sea. I wanted a brother. But Mama, crying, told me that even if William Armstrong lived, he would never do these things with me. He might not, she sobbed, even be "all there." He might, as long as he lived, lie on the rubber sheet in the center of the bed in the front bedroom where the white marquisette[3] curtains billowed out in the afternoon sea breeze, rustling like palmetto fronds.[4]

It was bad enough having an invalid brother, but having one who possibly was not all there was unbearable, so I began to make plans to kill him by smothering him with a pillow. However, one afternoon as I watched him, my head poked between the iron posts of the foot of the bed, he looked straight at me and grinned. I skipped through the rooms, down the echoing halls, shouting, "Mama, he smiled. He's all there! He's all there!" and he was.

When he was two, if you laid him on his stomach, he began to try to move himself, straining terribly. The doctor said that with his weak heart this strain would probably kill him, but it didn't. Trembling, he'd push himself up, turning first red, then a soft purple, and finally collapse back onto the bed like an old worn-out doll. I can still see Mama watching him, her hand pressed tight across her mouth, her eyes wide and unblinking. But he learned to crawl (it was his third winter), and we brought him out of the front bedroom, putting him on the rug before the fireplace. For the first time he became one of us.

As long as he lay all the time in bed, we called him William Armstrong, even though it was formal and sounded as if we were referring to one of our ancestors, but with his creeping around on the deerskin rug and beginning to talk, something had to be done about his name. It was I who renamed him.

When he crawled, he crawled backward, as if he were in reverse and couldn't change gears. If you called him, he'd turn around as if he were going in the other direction, then he'd back right up to you to be picked up. Crawling backward made him look like a doodlebug[5] so I began to call him Doodle, and in time even Mama and Daddy thought it was a better name than William Armstrong. Only Aunt Nicey disagreed. She said caul babies should be treated with special respect since they might turn out to be saints. Renaming my brother was perhaps the kindest thing I ever did for him, because nobody expects much from someone called Doodle.

Although Doodle learned to crawl, he showed no signs of walking, but he wasn't idle. He talked so much that we all quit listening to what he said. It was about this time that Daddy built him a go-cart, and I had to pull him around. At first I just paraded him up and down the piazza,[6] but then he started crying to be taken out into the yard and it ended up by my having to lug him wherever I went. If I so much as picked up my cap, he'd start crying to go with me, and Mama would call from wherever she was, "Take Doodle with you."

He was a burden in many ways. The doctor had said that he mustn't get too excited, too hot, too cold, or too tired and that he must always be treated gently. A long list of don'ts went with him, all of which I ignored once we got out of the house. To discourage his coming with me, I'd run with him across the ends of the cotton rows and careen him around corners on two wheels. Sometimes I accidentally turned him over, but he never told Mama. His skin was very sensitive, and he had to wear a big straw hat whenever he went out. When the going got rough and he had to cling to the sides of the go-cart, the hat slipped all the way down over his ears. He was a sight. Finally, I could see I was licked. Doodle was my brother, and he was going to cling to me forever, no matter what I

3. **marquisette** (mär'ki·zet'): thin, netlike fabric.
4. **palmetto fronds:** fanlike leaves of a palm tree.

5. **doodlebug:** larva of a type of insect; also, a shuttle train that goes back and forth between stations.
6. **piazza:** large covered porch.

did, so I dragged him across the burning cotton field to share with him the only beauty I knew, Old Woman Swamp. I pulled the go-cart through the sawtooth fern, down into the green dimness where the palmetto fronds whispered by the stream. I lifted him out and set him down in the soft rubber grass beside a tall pine. His eyes were round with wonder as he gazed about him, and his little hands began to stroke the rubber grass. Then he began to cry.

"For heaven's sake, what's the matter?" I asked, annoyed.

"It's so pretty," he said. "So pretty, pretty, pretty."

After that day Doodle and I often went down into Old Woman Swamp. I would gather wild-flowers, wild violets, honeysuckle, yellow jasmine, snakeflowers, and waterlilies, and with wire grass we'd weave them into necklaces and crowns. We'd bedeck ourselves with our handi-work and loll about thus beautified, beyond the touch of the everyday world. Then when the slanted rays of the sun burned orange in the tops of the pines, we'd drop our jewels into the stream and watch them float away toward the sea.

There is within me (and with sadness I have watched it in others) a knot of cruelty borne by the stream of love, much as our blood sometimes bears the seed of our destruction, and at times I was mean to Doodle. One day I took him up to the barn loft and showed him his casket, telling him how we all had believed he would die. It was covered with a film of Paris green[7] sprinkled to kill the rats, and screech owls had built a nest inside it.

Doodle studied the mahogany box for a long time, then said, "It's not mine."

"It is," I said. "And before I'll help you down from the loft, you're going to have to touch it."

"I won't touch it," he said sullenly.

"Then I'll leave you here by yourself," I threatened, and made as if I were going down.

Doodle was frightened of being left. "Don't go leave me, Brother," he cried, and he leaned toward the coffin. His hand, trembling, reached

7. **Paris green:** poisonous green powder used to kill insects.

out, and when he touched the casket, he screamed. A screech owl flapped out of the box into our faces, scaring us and covering us with Paris green. Doodle was paralyzed, so I put him on my shoulder and carried him down the ladder, and even when we were outside in the bright sunshine, he clung to me, crying, "Don't leave me. Don't leave me."

When Doodle was five years old, I was embarrassed at having a brother of that age who couldn't walk, so I set out to teach him. We were down in Old Woman Swamp and it was spring and the sick-sweet smell of bay flowers hung everywhere like a mournful song. "I'm going to teach you to walk, Doodle," I said.

He was sitting comfortably on the soft grass, leaning back against the pine. "Why?" he asked.

I hadn't expected such an answer. "So I won't have to haul you around all the time."

"I can't walk, Brother," he said.

"Who says so?" I demanded.

"Mama, the doctor—everybody."

"Oh, you can walk," I said, and I took him by the arms and stood him up. He collapsed onto the grass like a half-empty flour sack. It was as if he had no bones in his little legs.

"Don't hurt me, Brother," he warned.

"Shut up. I'm not going to hurt you. I'm going to teach you to walk." I heaved him up again, and again he collapsed.

This time he did not lift his face up out of the rubber grass. "I just can't do it. Let's make honeysuckle wreaths."

"Oh yes you can, Doodle," I said. "All you got to do is try. Now come on," and I hauled him up once more.

It seemed so hopeless from the beginning that it's a miracle I didn't give up. But all of us must have something or someone to be proud of, and Doodle had become mine. I did not know then that pride is a wonderful, terrible thing, a seed that bears two vines, life and death. Every day that summer we went to the pine beside the stream of Old Woman Swamp, and I put him on his feet at least a hundred times each afternoon. Occasionally I too became discouraged because it didn't seem as if he was trying, and I would say, "Doodle, don't you *want* to learn to walk?"

He'd nod his head, and I'd say, "Well, if you don't keep trying, you'll never learn." Then I'd paint for him a picture of us as old men, white-haired, him with a long white beard and me still pulling him around in the go-cart. This never failed to make him try again.

Finally, one day, after many weeks of practicing, he stood alone for a few seconds. When he fell, I grabbed him in my arms and hugged him, our laughter pealing through the swamp like a ringing bell. Now we knew it could be done. Hope no longer hid in the dark palmetto thicket but perched like a cardinal in the lacy tooth-brush tree, brilliantly visible. "Yes, yes," I cried, and he cried it too, and the grass beneath us was soft and the smell of the swamp was sweet.

With success so <u>imminent</u>, we decided not to tell anyone until he could actually walk. Each day, barring rain, we sneaked into Old Woman Swamp, and by cotton-picking time Doodle was ready to show what he could do. He still wasn't able to walk far, but we could wait no longer. Keeping a nice secret is very hard to do, like holding your breath. We chose to reveal all on October eighth, Doodle's sixth birthday, and for weeks ahead we mooned around the house, promising everybody a most spectacular surprise. Aunt Nicey said that, after so much talk, if we produced anything less tremendous than the Resurrection, she was going to be disappointed.

At breakfast on our chosen day, when Mama, Daddy, and Aunt Nicey were in the dining room, I brought Doodle to the door in the go-cart just as usual and had them turn their backs, making them cross their hearts and hope to die if they peeked. I helped Doodle up, and when he was standing alone I let them look. There wasn't a sound as Doodle walked slowly across the room and sat down at his place at the table. Then Mama began to cry and ran over to him, hugging him and kissing him. Daddy hugged him too, so I went to Aunt Nicey, who was thanks-praying in the doorway, and began to waltz her around. We danced together quite well until she came down on my big toe with

her brogans,[8] hurting me so badly I thought I was crippled for life.

Doodle told them it was I who had taught him to walk, so everyone wanted to hug me, and I began to cry.

"What are you crying for?" asked Daddy, but I couldn't answer. They did not know that I did it for myself; that pride, whose slave I was, spoke to me louder than all their voices; and that Doodle walked only because I was ashamed of having a crippled brother.

Within a few months Doodle had learned to walk well and his go-cart was put up in the barn loft (it's still there) beside his little mahogany coffin. Now, when we roamed off together, resting often, we never turned back until our destination had been reached, and to help pass the time, we took up lying. From the beginning Doodle was a terrible liar, and he got me in the habit. Had anyone stopped to listen to us, we would have been sent off to Dix Hill.

My lies were scary, involved, and usually pointless, but Doodle's were twice as crazy. People in his stories all had wings and flew wherever they wanted to go. His favorite lie was about a boy named Peter who had a pet peacock with a ten-foot tail. Peter wore a golden robe that glittered so brightly that when he walked through the sunflowers they turned away from the sun to face him. When Peter was ready to go to sleep, the peacock spread his magnificent tail, enfolding the boy gently like a closing go-to-sleep flower, burying him in the gloriously iridescent,[9] rustling vortex.[10] Yes, I must admit it. Doodle could beat me lying.

Doodle and I spent lots of time thinking about our future. We decided that when we were grown, we'd live in Old Woman Swamp and pick dog's-tongue[11] for a living. Beside the

8. **brogans** (brō'gənz): heavy ankle-high shoes.
9. **iridescent** (ir'i·des'ənt): rainbowlike; displaying a shifting range of colors.
10. **vortex:** something resembling a whirlpool.
11. **dog's-tongue:** wild vanilla.

WORDS TO OWN

imminent (im'ə·nənt) *adj.*: near; about to happen.

stream, he planned, we'd build us a house of whispering leaves and the swamp birds would be our chickens. All day long (when we weren't gathering dog's-tongue) we'd swing through the cypresses on the rope vines, and if it rained we'd huddle beneath an umbrella tree and play stickfrog. Mama and Daddy could come and live with us if they wanted to. He even came up with the idea that he could marry Mama and I could marry Daddy. Of course, I was old enough to know this wouldn't work out, but the picture he painted was so beautiful and serene that all I could do was whisper yes, yes.

Once I had succeeded in teaching Doodle to walk, I began to believe in my own infallibility and I prepared a terrific development program for him, unknown to Mama and Daddy, of course. I would teach him to run, to swim, to climb trees, and to fight. He, too, now believed in my infallibility, so we set the deadline for these accomplishments less than a year away, when, it had been decided, Doodle could start to school.

That winter we didn't make much progress, for I was in school and Doodle suffered from one bad cold after another. But when spring came, rich and warm, we raised our sights again. Success lay at the end of summer like a pot of gold, and our campaign got off to a good start. On hot days, Doodle and I went down to Horsehead Landing, and I gave him swimming lessons or showed him how to row a boat. Sometimes we descended into the cool greenness of Old Woman Swamp and climbed the rope vines or boxed scientifically beneath the pine where he had learned to walk. Promise hung about us like leaves, and wherever we looked, ferns unfurled and birds broke into song.

That summer, the summer of 1918, was blighted.[12] In May and June there was no rain and the crops withered, curled up, then died under the thirsty sun. One morning in July a hurricane came out of the east, tipping over the oaks in the yard and splitting the limbs of the elm trees. That afternoon it roared back out of the west, blew the fallen oaks around, snapping their roots and tearing them out of the earth like a hawk at the entrails[13] of a chicken. Cotton bolls were wrenched from the stalks and lay like green walnuts in the valleys between the rows, while the cornfield leaned over uniformly so that the tassels touched the ground. Doodle and I followed Daddy out into the cotton field, where he stood, shoulders sagging, surveying the ruin. When his chin sank down onto his chest, we were frightened, and Doodle slipped his hand into mine. Suddenly Daddy straightened his shoulders, raised a giant knuckly fist, and with a voice that seemed to rumble out of the earth itself began cursing heaven, hell, the weather, and the Republican party.[14] Doodle and I, prodding each other and giggling, went back to the house, knowing that everything would be all right.

And during that summer, strange names were heard through the house: Château-Thierry, Amiens, Soissons, and in her blessing at the supper table, Mama once said, "And bless the Pearsons, whose boy Joe was lost in Belleau Wood."[15]

So we came to that clove of seasons. School was only a few weeks away, and Doodle was far behind schedule. He could barely clear the ground when climbing up the rope vines, and his swimming was certainly not passable. We decided to double our efforts, to make that last drive and reach our pot of gold. I made him swim until he turned blue and row until he couldn't lift an oar. Wherever we went, I purposely walked fast, and although he kept up, his face turned red and his eyes became glazed.

12. **blighted** (blīt′id): suffering from conditions that destroy or prevent growth.

13. **entrails** (en′trālz): inner organs; guts.
14. **Republican party:** At this time most Southern farmers were loyal Democrats.
15. **Château-Thierry** (sha′tō tē·er′ē), **Amiens** (á·myan′), **Soissons** (swä·sôn′), **Belleau** (be·lô′) **Wood:** World War I battle sites in France.

WORDS TO OWN

infallibility (in·fal′ə·bil′ə·tē) *n.*: inability to make a mistake.

Once, he could go no further, so he collapsed on the ground and began to cry.

"Aw, come on, Doodle," I urged. "You can do it. Do you want to be different from everybody else when you start school?"

"Does it make any difference?"

"It certainly does," I said. "Now, come on," and I helped him up.

As we slipped through the dog days, Doodle began to look feverish, and Mama felt his forehead, asking him if he felt ill. At night he didn't sleep well, and sometimes he had nightmares, crying out until I touched him and said, "Wake up, Doodle. Wake up."

It was Saturday noon, just a few days before school was to start. I should have already admitted defeat, but my pride wouldn't let me. The excitement of our program had now been gone for weeks, but still we kept on with a tired doggedness. It was too late to turn back, for we had both wandered too far into a net of expectations and had left no crumbs behind.

Daddy, Mama, Doodle, and I were seated at the dining-room table having lunch. It was a hot day, with all the windows and doors open in case a breeze should come. In the kitchen Aunt Nicey was humming softly. After a long silence, Daddy spoke. "It's so calm, I wouldn't be surprised if we had a storm this afternoon."

"I haven't heard a rain frog," said Mama, who believed in signs, as she served the bread around the table.

"I did," declared Doodle. "Down in the swamp."

"He didn't," I said contrarily.

"You did, eh?" said Daddy, ignoring my denial.

"I certainly did," Doodle reiterated, scowling at me over the top of his iced-tea glass, and we were quiet again.

Suddenly, from out in the yard came a strange croaking noise. Doodle stopped eating, with a piece of bread poised ready for his mouth, his eyes popped round like two blue buttons. "What's that?" he whispered.

I jumped up, knocking over my chair, and had reached the door when Mama called, "Pick up the chair, sit down again, and say excuse me."

By the time I had done this, Doodle had excused himself and had slipped out into the yard. He was looking up into the bleeding tree. "It's a great big red bird!" he called.

The bird croaked loudly again, and Mama and Daddy came out into the yard. We shaded our eyes with our hands against the hazy glare of the sun and peered up through the still leaves. On the topmost branch a bird the size of a chicken, with scarlet feathers and long legs, was perched precariously. Its wings hung down loosely, and as we watched, a feather dropped away and floated slowly down through the green leaves.

"It's not even frightened of us," Mama said.

"It looks tired," Daddy added. "Or maybe sick."

Doodle's hands were clasped at his throat, and I had never seen him stand still so long. "What is it?" he asked.

Daddy shook his head. "I don't know, maybe it's——"

At that moment the bird began to flutter, but the wings were uncoordinated, and amid much flapping and a spray of flying feathers, it tumbled down, bumping through the limbs of the bleeding tree and landing at our feet with a thud. Its long, graceful neck jerked twice into an S, then straightened out, and the bird was still. A white veil came over the eyes, and the long white beak unhinged. Its legs were crossed and its clawlike feet were delicately curved at rest. Even death did not mar its grace, for it lay on the earth like a broken vase of red flowers, and we stood around it, awed by its exotic beauty.

"It's dead," Mama said.

"What is it?" Doodle repeated.

"Go bring me the bird book," said Daddy.

I ran into the house and brought back the bird book. As we watched, Daddy thumbed through its pages. "It's a scarlet ibis," he said, pointing to a picture. "It lives in the tropics—South America to Florida. A storm must have brought it here."

Sadly, we all looked back at the bird. A scarlet ibis! How many miles it had traveled to die like this, in *our* yard, beneath the bleeding tree.

"Let's finish lunch," Mama said, nudging us back toward the dining room.

"I'm not hungry," said Doodle, and he knelt down beside the ibis.

"We've got peach cobbler for dessert," Mama tempted from the doorway.

Doodle remained kneeling. "I'm going to bury him."

"Don't you dare touch him," Mama warned. "There's no telling what disease he might have had."

"All right," said Doodle. "I won't."

Daddy, Mama, and I went back to the dining-room table, but we watched Doodle through the open door. He took out a piece of string from his pocket and, without touching the ibis, looped one end around its neck. Slowly, while singing softly "Shall We Gather at the River," he carried the bird around to the front yard and dug a hole in the flower garden, next to the petunia bed. Now we were watching him through the front window, but he didn't know it. His awkwardness at digging the hole with a shovel whose handle was twice as long as he was made us laugh, and we covered our mouths with our hands so he wouldn't hear.

When Doodle came into the dining room, he found us seriously eating our cobbler. He was pale and lingered just inside the screen door. "Did you get the scarlet ibis buried?" asked Daddy.

Doodle didn't speak but nodded his head.

"Go wash your hands, and then you can have some peach cobbler," said Mama.

"I'm not hungry," he said.

"Dead birds is bad luck," said Aunt Nicey, poking her head from the kitchen door. "Specially *red* dead birds!"

As soon as I had finished eating, Doodle and I hurried off to Horsehead Landing. Time was short, and Doodle still had a long way to go if he

was going to keep up with the other boys when he started school. The sun, gilded with the yellow cast of autumn, still burned fiercely, but the dark green woods through which we passed were shady and cool. When we reached the landing, Doodle said he was too tired to swim, so we got into a skiff and floated down the creek with the tide. Far off in the marsh a rail was scolding, and over on the beach locusts were singing in the myrtle trees. Doodle did not speak and kept his head turned away, letting one hand trail limply in the water.

After we had drifted a long way, I put the oars in place and made Doodle row back against the tide. Black clouds began to gather in the southwest, and he kept watching them, trying to pull the oars a little faster. When we reached Horsehead Landing, lightning was playing across half the sky and thunder roared out, hiding even the sound of the sea. The sun disappeared and darkness descended, almost like night. Flocks of marsh crows flew by, heading inland to their roosting trees, and two egrets, squawking, arose from the oyster-rock shallows and careened away.

Doodle was both tired and frightened, and when he stepped from the skiff he collapsed onto the mud, sending an armada[16] of fiddler crabs rustling off into the marsh grass. I helped him up, and as he wiped the mud off his trousers, he smiled at me ashamedly. He had failed and we both knew it, so we started back home, racing the storm. We never spoke (what are the words that can solder[17] cracked pride?), but I knew he was watching me, watching for a sign of mercy. The lightning was near now, and from fear he walked so close behind me he kept stepping on my heels. The faster I walked, the faster he walked, so I began to run. The rain was coming, roaring through the pines, and then, like a bursting Roman candle, a gum tree ahead of us was shattered by a bolt of lightning. When the deafening peal of thunder had died, and in the moment before the rain arrived, I heard Doodle,

---

16. **armada** (är·mä′də): group. *Armada* is generally used to mean "fleet, or group, of warships."
17. **solder** (säd′ər): patch or repair. Solder is a mixture of metals melted and used to repair metal parts.

who had fallen behind, cry out, "Brother, Brother, don't leave me! Don't leave me!"

The knowledge that Doodle's and my plans had come to naught was bitter, and that streak of cruelty within me awakened. I ran as fast as I could, leaving him far behind with a wall of rain dividing us. The drops stung my face like nettles, and the wind flared the wet, glistening leaves of the bordering trees. Soon I could hear his voice no more.

I hadn't run too far before I became tired, and the flood of childish spite evanesced[18] as well. I stopped and waited for Doodle. The sound of rain was everywhere, but the wind had died and it fell straight down in parallel paths like ropes hanging from the sky. As I waited, I peered through the downpour, but no one came. Finally I went back and found him huddled beneath a red nightshade bush beside the road. He was sitting on the ground, his face buried in his arms, which were resting on his drawn-up knees. "Let's go, Doodle," I said.

18. **evanesced** (ev′ə·nest′): faded away; disappeared.

He didn't answer, so I placed my hand on his forehead and lifted his head. Limply, he fell backward onto the earth. He had been bleeding from the mouth, and his neck and the front of his shirt were stained a brilliant red.

"Doodle! Doodle!" I cried, shaking him, but there was no answer but the ropy rain. He lay very awkwardly, with his head thrown far back, making his vermilion[19] neck appear unusually long and slim. His little legs, bent sharply at the knees, had never before seemed so fragile, so thin.

I began to weep, and the tear-blurred vision in red before me looked very familiar. "Doodle!" I screamed above the pounding storm, and threw my body to the earth above his. For a long, long time, it seemed forever, I lay there crying, sheltering my fallen scarlet ibis from the heresy[20] of rain.

19. **vermilion** (vər·mil′yən): bright red.
20. **heresy** (her′i·se): here, mockery. *Heresy* generally means "denial of what is commonly believed to be true" or "rejection of a church's teaching."

Connections   A POEM

If There Be Sorrow

Mari Evans

If there be sorrow
let it be
for things undone . . .
undreamed
   unrealized
    unattained
to these add one;
Love withheld . . .
. . . restrained

The Kiss (1922–1940)
by Constantin Brancusi.

MAKING MEANINGS

First Thoughts

1. How were the questions you noted in your journal answered in "The Scarlet Ibis"? Were you left with unanswered questions when you finished the story?

Shaping Interpretations

2. How do you feel about the narrator's behavior at the end of the story? Is he responsible for Doodle's death? Could he be partially responsible? Is his emotion at the very end sorrow, guilt, or something else?

3. By the end of the story, whom do you pity more—the narrator or Doodle? Why?

4. Do you think the narrator makes any kind of discovery at the story's end, as he cradles his brother's little body?

5. In Meet the Writer (page 324), there is an indication of what Hurst thinks his famous story means. How would you state the **theme** of his story—what truth about our lives do the story's events reveal to you? Find passages from the story to support your response.

6. In the last sentence, the narrator calls his brother his "fallen scarlet ibis." In what ways could the ibis be a **symbol** for Doodle?

   Consider:

   • how Doodle and the ibis resemble each other

   • how Doodle's and the ibis's deaths are similar

   • how Doodle himself identifies with the bird

   • how both Doodle and the ibis are put in worlds where they can't survive

Connecting with the Text

7. Why do you think this story is so popular and is remembered for a long time by many readers? What feelings do you think it taps into?

Extending the Text

8. Re-read what the storyteller says on page 318 about human pride. What incidents from life could illustrate the good and bad effects of human pride? Does pride lead to the kinds of sorrow that Mari Evans writes about in her poem "If There Be Sorrow" (page 324)?

Reviewing the Text

a. What do we know about the narrator of the story?

b. What details at the start of the story tell us that the events he is about to relate took place many years ago?

c. Why does the narrator teach Doodle to walk, and why does he cry when his family congratulates him for his effort?

d. After Doodle has learned to walk, what does his brother try to teach him, to prepare him for school?

e. How does Doodle respond to the scarlet ibis and to its death?

CHOICES: Building Your Portfolio

Writer's Notebook

1. Collecting Ideas for an Evaluation

How did it make you feel? As

you've read the stories in this collection, you may have been making notes on criteria to use when you write an evaluation for the Writer's Workshop on page 332. Now focus on those criteria—the aspects of the story that struck you most strongly. Working with a partner, set up scales like the one shown here that evaluates a story's emotional content. You may choose to rank the sympathy you feel for a partic-ular character, the effective-ness of the symbols in the story, or your feelings about the selfish or generous actions in the story. Remember that when you use scales like this one, you won't agree with all

your classmates. When you write an evaluation, you'll have to justify your rating. Be sure to compare your ratings with those of your classmates.

Critical Writing

2. A Character's Inner Life

Doodle's inner life is revealed in the "lies" he tells. Write a paragraph analyzing these stories. Before you write, be sure to review the passage on page 319 where the stories are described. Consider these questions in your analysis:

- What do Doodle's characters want?
- What kind of world do they live in?
- Why does Doodle tell this kind of story?
- What do his stories reveal about his own wants?

Creative Writing

3. Doodle's Point of View

"The Scarlet Ibis" would be a different story if it were told from Doodle's point of view. Pick a key scene from the story and tell it from the third-person limited point of view, through Doodle's senses and feelings. Write a paragraph or two.

Research/Drawing

4. Flora of the American South

There is a distinct feeling of nature in "The Scarlet Ibis"—the seasons, the drought, the varied vegetation, the details of Old Woman Swamp. Make a list of all the plants mentioned in the story: trees, flowers, and grasses. In an encyclopedia or botanical reference book, find out what these plants look like and then use them in a series of illustrations that will capture the story's lush setting.

Creative Writing/ Interviewing

5. Meeting the Challenge

You might want to interview a person who, like Doodle, is physically challenged in some way. Before the interview, be sure you have your questions ready. Tape the interview if you can. Try to publish it in your local or school paper.

Emotional Scale

no emotional appeal	some emotional appeal		too emotional	
0	1	2	3	4	5

Reasons:

LANGUAGE LINK MINI-LESSON

**Handbook of
Literary
Terms
H E L P**

*See Figure of
Speech.*

Style: Figurative Language—Picture This

". . . like a bursting Roman candle, a gum tree ahead of us was shattered by a bolt of lightning." How is a Roman candle like a tree struck by lightning? That's not a joke. James Hurst is using a **simile**—the simplest form of figurative language—to help us see what a tree struck by lightning looks like. In a simile, two dissimilar things are compared by words such as *like, as,* or *resembles*. Similes, like other forms of figurative language, help us see things in fresh, vivid ways.

Here are five more sentences containing similes from "The Scarlet Ibis":

1. ". . . the oriole nest in the elm was untenanted and rocked back and forth like an empty cradle."

2. "They named him William Armstrong, which was like tying a big tail on a small kite."

3. ". . . the white marquisette curtains billowed out in the afternoon sea breeze, rustling like palmetto fronds."

4. ". . . [the ibis] lay on the earth like a broken vase of red flowers. . . ."

5. ". . . the sick-sweet smell of bay flowers hung everywhere like a mournful song."

Try It Out

1. In each passage at the left, locate the simile and tell what is being compared to what. What exactly do the two things have in common?

2. Reword each passage using new similes. Can you change the whole emotional tone of the passage with a different comparison?

➤ Select a piece of descriptive writing from your Writer's Notebook and highlight at least two places where you could make your writing more vivid and interesting by using a simile. Rewrite each passage with a fresh comparison.

A tip for writers: When you use figurative language, be sure to avoid trite, or overused, expressions such as "proud as a peacock" or "like two peas in a pod." Try to find new comparisons that say what *you* want to say.

VOCABULARY HOW TO OWN A WORD

WORD BANK

*imminent
infallibility
doggedness
reiterated
precariously*

Own It

1. Write a headline for a newspaper using the word *imminent.*
2. Use the word *infallibility* in a description of a person.
3. Write a sentence supporting a political candidate, using the word *doggedness.*
4. Write an instruction your teacher might give using the word *reiterate.*
5. Write a sentence about Doodle using the word *precariously.*

EXTENDING *the theme*

A MEMORY

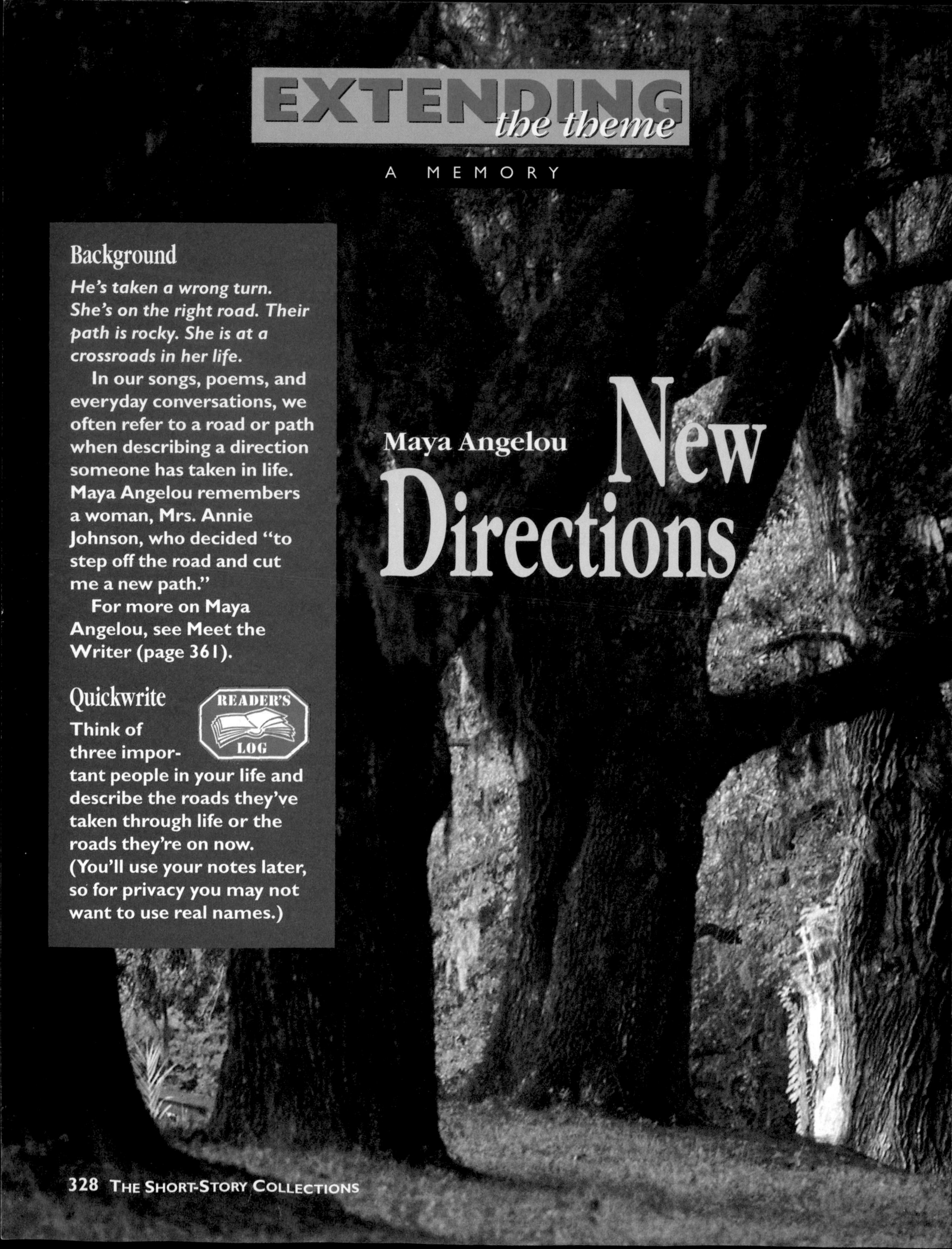

Background

He's taken a wrong turn. She's on the right road. Their path is rocky. She is at a crossroads in her life.

In our songs, poems, and everyday conversations, we often refer to a road or path when describing a direction someone has taken in life. Maya Angelou remembers a woman, Mrs. Annie Johnson, who decided "to step off the road and cut me a new path."

For more on Maya Angelou, see Meet the Writer (page 361).

Quickwrite

READER'S LOG

Think of three important people in your life and describe the roads they've taken through life or the roads they're on now. (You'll use your notes later, so for privacy you may not want to use real names.)

Maya Angelou

New Directions

"I decided to step off the road."

In 1903 the late Mrs. Annie Johnson of Arkansas found herself with two toddling sons, very little money, a slight ability to read and add simple numbers. To this picture add a disastrous marriage and the burdensome fact that Mrs. Johnson was a Negro.

When she told her husband, Mr. William Johnson, of her dissatisfaction with their marriage, he conceded that he too found it to be less than he expected, and had been secretly hoping to leave and study religion. He added that he thought God was calling him not only to preach but to do so in Enid, Oklahoma. He did not tell her that he knew a minister in Enid with whom he could study and who had a friendly, unmarried daughter. They parted amicably, Annie keeping the one-room house and William taking most of the cash to carry himself to Oklahoma.

Annie, over six feet tall, big-boned, decided that she would not go to work as a domestic and leave her "precious babes" to anyone else's care. There was no possibility of being hired at the town's cotton gin or lumber mill, but maybe there was a way to make the two factories work for her. In her words, "I looked up the road I was going and back the way I come, and since I wasn't satisfied, I decided to step off the road and cut me a new path." She told herself that she wasn't a fancy cook but that she could "mix groceries well enough to scare hungry away and keep from starving a man."

She made her plans meticulously[1] and in secret. One early evening to see if she was ready, she placed stones in two five-gallon pails and carried them three miles to the cotton gin. She rested a little, and then, discarding some rocks, she walked in the darkness to the sawmill five miles farther along the dirt road. On her way back to her little house and her babies, she dumped the remaining rocks along the path.

That same night she worked into the early hours boiling chicken and frying ham. She made dough and filled the rolled-out pastry with meat. At last she went to sleep.

The next morning she left her house carrying the meat pies, lard, an iron brazier,[2] and coals for a fire. Just before lunch she appeared in an empty lot behind the cotton gin. As the dinner noon bell rang, she dropped the savors into boiling fat and the aroma rose and floated over to the workers who spilled out of the gin, covered with white lint, looking like specters.

1. **meticulously** (mə·tik′·yo̅o·ləs·lē): extremely carefully; with great attention to detail.
2. **brazier** (brā′·zhər): metal container that holds burning coals or charcoal to warm a room or grill food.

Most workers had brought their lunches of pinto beans and biscuits or crackers, onions and cans of sardines, but they were tempted by the hot meat pies which Annie ladled out of the fat. She wrapped them in newspapers, which soaked up the grease, and offered them for sale at a nickel each. Although business was slow, those first days Annie was determined. She balanced her appearances between the two hours of activity.

So, on Monday if she offered hot fresh pies at the cotton gin and sold the remaining cooled-down pies at the lumber mill for three cents, then on Tuesday she went first to the lumber mill presenting fresh, just-cooked pies as the lumbermen covered in sawdust emerged from the mill.

For the next few years, on balmy spring days, blistering summer noons, and cold, wet, and wintry middays, Annie never disappointed her customers, who could count on seeing the tall, brown-skin woman bent over her brazier, carefully turning the meat pies. When she felt certain that the workers had become dependent on her, she built a stall between the two hives of industry and let the men run to her for their lunchtime provisions.

She had indeed stepped from the road which seemed to have been chosen for her and cut herself a brand-new path. In years that stall became a store where customers could buy cheese, meal, syrup, cookies, candy, writing tablets, pickles, canned goods, fresh fruit, soft drinks, coal, oil, and leather soles for worn-out shoes.

Each of us has the right and the responsibility to assess the roads which lie ahead, and those over which we have traveled, and if the future road looms ominous or unpromising, and the roads back uninviting, then we need to gather our resolve and, carrying only the necessary baggage, step off that road into another direction. If the new choice is also unpalatable,[3] without embarrassment, we must be ready to change that as well.

Center: *Field Trilogy* (1985) by Viola Burley Leak.
Appliqué, tapestry, and soft sculpture (38″ x 25″).
Courtesy of the artist.

3. **unpalatable** (un·pal′·ə·tə·bəl): unpleasant. *Unpalatable* often means "tasting bad."

FINDING COMMON GROUND

1. Re-read your Quickwrite and add new details to your notes, if you wish. In a small group take turns and read your notes about the roads people have chosen.

2. Are there any people you wrote about who might benefit from reading about Mrs. Annie Johnson's new direction? Discuss your responses in your group.

3. With your group, write a song or a poem about traveling the road of life. Tell about the forks in the road that people come to. What choices are available? What might wait at the end of each person's road? What rough places might lie along the way? Share your songs and poems with the class.

READ ON

A Sapling Stands Tall

In Betty Smith's novel, a tree grows in Brooklyn—and so does young Francie Nolan. Living in a poor neighborhood with her parents and brother, Francie finds joys and an assortment of troubles as she comes of age. Her experiences are sometimes painful, but they become the building blocks of wisdom. *A Tree Grows in Brooklyn* (HarperCollins) takes place between 1902 and 1919, but don't be surprised if Francie and the Nolan family remind you of people you know today.

America Has Many Streets

Reading the stories in *America Street* (Persea) is like taking a walk in fourteen neighborhoods. On one street Toni Cade Bambara will introduce you to Squeaky, who's determined to win the neighborhood race if it kills her. On another street you'll meet Gary Soto's Fausto who's busy scraping pennies together to buy a guitar. Duane Big Eagle will take you to Raoul's neighborhood where he is boarding a train in search of his mysterious medicine-woman aunt. Why not go for a walk and meet your neighbors?

Be Yourself

When you read the stories, poems, and plays in *American Dragons* (HarperCollins), you'll hear the voices of twenty-five Asian American teenagers expressing their feelings. They are trying to figure out how to fit in and how to be themselves at the same time. Their struggle is expressed in a range of feelings—from rage to sorrow, from worry to wonder.

Not Enough Time

The absence of her father was always painful to Bebe Moore Campbell while she was growing up. She saw him during the summers, but she desperately wished they could have more time together. In *Sweet Summer: Growing Up with and Without My Dad* (Ballantine), the story of her youth, Campbell tells how she learned to deal with the pain of missing him. Read it and find out how her father came to be a constant presence in her life in spite of their separation.

Writer's Workshop

Technology HELP

See Writer's Workshop 2 CD-ROM. *Assignment: Evaluation.*

ASSIGNMENT

Imagine that you've been asked to evaluate a story for possible use in a school textbook. Write an essay in which you evaluate one story in this book. Use specific reasons to convince your audience to include the story or to reject it.

AIM

To evaluate a story and support your opinion.

AUDIENCE

A committee made up of teachers or a review board that decides on textbook materials.

PERSUASIVE WRITING

EVALUATION

"I love it." "I hate it." "It's too hard." "It's too silly." Whenever you make a critical assessment, judging whether something is good or bad, successful or unsuccessful (a movie, TV show, pizza, car), you're making an evaluation. In this workshop you'll apply evaluation skills and strategies to a short story.

Throughout your life you'll face occasions when you must evaluate something: You might have to evaluate job offers, career choices, a new product, perhaps even a proposed piece of legislation, a new management system, or, if you're an English teacher, the writing of your students.

Prewriting

1. Choose a Story

Writing your evaluation will be interesting if you choose a story you feel strongly about. Select one that you either love or hate, one that you'll always remember, or one that you could barely finish.

Don't worry if your choice of best or worst story is different from the choices of your classmates. In your essay you'll have a chance to present evidence to show how you arrived at your judgment.

2. Establish Your Criteria

"I really like this story a lot" is a subjective evaluation—a statement based on personal preference. An objective evaluation, on the other hand, is a judgment based on **objective criteria,** or particular standards of excellence. Your evaluation will have elements of both. Review the criteria already listed in your Writer's Notebook. If you feel your criteria aren't well enough developed, get together with your writing group to brainstorm ideas.

When you work on your criteria, ask yourself: What are the qualities that make a short story excellent? Then turn each quality into a statement. What can you say, for example, about the plot of an excellent story? If you say the plot is believable, one

The history
of the written
word is rich and

Page 1

Once upon a time

of your criteria would be: *A good short story must have a believable plot.* Compare your group's criteria with those of other groups, and see if you want to revise your list.

3. Apply the Criteria

Once you've established your criteria, apply them to the story you want to focus on. How does the story measure up? Or doesn't it? Dig into your story, using your criteria as a guide for what to take notes on. Complete a chart like the one shown here for "The Scarlet Ibis" (page 315). On the left side, list all of your criteria. On the right, list the story's weaknesses and strengths and find details from the text that support your evaluation.

The Scarlet Ibis		
Criterion	Meets Criterion	Fails to Meet Criterion
Character development: Must be believable and original; motivation must be clear.	Narrator is believable; how he grows and changes is believable. Reasons for pushing brother are clear.	
Plot: Must not be contrived; must have surprises and be suspenseful.		
Setting: Must be realistic and create atmosphere.		

If you wish, give your story a rating: On a scale of one to ten, ten would be the highest rating.

The Scarlet Ibis = 9.5

Failure as a story

Perfect story

0 ——————————————— 10

My Rating

4. So, What Do You Think?

After you have listed the ways your story meets the criteria, or fails to, and after you have given your story a rating (if you wish to), draft a judgment statement that expresses your overall evaluation. This statement about your topic will be the most

■ *Kinds of Evidence*

- *your personal reasons*
- *brief plot summary*
- *analysis of characters*
- *analysis of theme*
- *quotations from the text*
- *reference to specific scenes and dialogue*
- *comparison with other stories*
- *references to experts' opinions*

Yes, it's the talking pig, "Babe." He's pink, he oinks, and he has his own movie.

The movie starts at a pig farm. The star, Babe (voiced by Christine Cavanaugh), is sitting in his pen with his mother and siblings. Suddenly his mom is swiftly taken to pig paradise.

The little pig is taken to a carnival where Mr. Hoggins wins him and takes him to the Hogginses' farm.

While he's on the farm, many different adventures happen to the little pig and his farm friends. Some of his friends include sheep, sheep dogs, ducks, and singing mice.

You may think pigs are considered stinky, muddy, ugly, and stupid. "Babe" is none of these. He is actually very smart, but because he is young, he doesn't know a lot of things.

As you know, animals don't talk like we do, except in this movie. The animals talk to each other. Apparently the animals were given vocal cords and were taught a very advanced English.

Since this wasn't a cartoon you might not expect it to be a "G" movie. Well, today is your lucky day. "Babe" is a G-rated movie, so everyone can go, even adults.

I give this movie a thumbs up because it was funny, made me feel happy, and wasn't what I expected from a "G" movie.

—Bob Tester
North Middle School
Great Falls, Montana

---

important part of your introductory paragraph. Note that it should cite the story you'll focus on, its author, and your general assessment of the story's effectiveness. The statement can consist of more than one sentence.

Make your judgment statement specific. Here are three statements that are so general they're almost meaningless.

- "The Most Dangerous Game" has an interesting plot.
- The narrator in "The Scarlet Ibis" has a problem.
- "The Necklace" is a good story.

This judgment, on the other hand, is specific and interesting:

- I think that this popular story, "The Most Dangerous Game" by Richard Connell, is a fine example of an escape story. It's fun to read; it helps us pass an hour or two. But does it reveal much about human life and the complex world we live in? My answer to that is a strong NO. I rate this story ten for fun and three for significance.

5. Select the Criteria You Want to Focus On

You might want to avoid any discussion of setting, for example, because in the story you are recommending, you don't feel it's important. You should have at least three strong criteria to apply to your story.

Student Model

Following are the opening and closing paragraphs of an evaluation of "The Scarlet Ibis."

James Hurst's short story "The Scarlet Ibis" is the poignant tale of a boy torn between the love and hate he feels for his younger brother. The protagonist, motivated by embarrassment and pride, forcefully, sometimes cruelly, pushes his handicapped younger brother to learn to walk and run. Despite his evident affection and concern for his brother, the protagonist feels that Doodle is somehow a disgrace and a burden. Moments of tenderness between the siblings are marred by the protagonist's shame for his brother's disabilities as well as for his own lack of compassion. The	*Identifies title and author and indicates (briefly) how the story affected her. Begins a plot summary.* *This creates interest.* *Touches on character and motivation.*

6. Support Your Evaluation

The rest of your essay will support your judgment statement with as many details as you can assemble. An essay of evaluation, like a persuasive essay, should provide sufficient evidence to convince your readers that your opinion is justified. Cite passages from the story or refer to pages that provide examples of what you are focusing on.

Drafting
1. Watch Your Tone

Remember that you want your readers to accept your evaluation as a fair one. You'll sound more confident if you avoid "hedge words" like *probably, maybe, perhaps, seems,* and *might.* State your ideas clearly, directly, and positively. Here are some useful judgment words—some positive, some negative—that you could use in evaluating a story.

Positive Words

poignant	*unforgettable*
exciting	*moving*
intense	*well-crafted*

Negative Words

tedious	*pointless*
irritating	*confusing*
contrived	*dull*

Communications Handbook H E L P

Taking notes and documenting sources: pages 983–984.

---

traumatic end to the story, in which the protagonist leaves his frail brother behind him during a storm, results in two tragedies: Doodle's death and the protagonist's flood of guilt. . . .

"Traumatic" suggests how ending affected her.

[*conclusion*]

"The Scarlet Ibis" is a moving, well-written story. The writer has created a flawed, believable character with whom readers can identify and sympathize. Hurst's use of metaphor and irony contributes to the intensity of the text and to the potency of the prose. Well-crafted and poignant, "The Scarlet Ibis" is an excellent character study and story.

Summarizes her general judgment of story. Includes effect on reader. "Intensity of the text" and "potency of the prose" are effective judgment statements.

—Erin-Elizabeth Tadie
The Potomac School
McLean, Virginia

2. Follow a Plan

Organize your essay so that your readers will be able to follow your thoughts easily. Here is one possible way to organize it.

- A forceful introduction that identifies the title and author and contains your judgment statement and your rating (if you've used one).
- A brief plot summary (no more than three or four sentences).
- A discussion of how the story measures up against three or four criteria (a paragraph for each). Provide evidence from the text to support your points.
- A conclusion that restates your evaluation.

Evaluating and Revising
1. Peer Editing

Ask classmates to read and comment on your draft. Have them write suggestions in the margin for improving the paper (see the Evaluation Criteria) and note questions they think you should

Language Link
H E L P

Transitions: page 289.
Adverb clauses: page 301.
Conjunctions: page 313.

Sentence Workshop
H E L P

Revising run-on
sentences: page 338.

Revision Model

Peer Comments

"The Scarlet Ibis" is very much a

character study. The story spans *of the protagonist, the narrator*

Tell who the main character is.

eight years covering the narrator's

life between ages six and

fourteen—delicate and confusing

years, which for the narrator were

made / more difficult. The protagonist comes *by his brother's problems*

Why were they difficult?

because he grows and changes / over the course of the story

across as very believable.

Tell why you find him believable.

answer. Peer reviewers should give positive feedback, too. As a peer reviewer, you could highlight sections of your classmates' papers that you think are especially well done.

2. Self-Evaluation

Read your essay aloud to yourself several times. Does the paper sound like you (your own voice) or someone else? Check your transitions—words like *also, besides, in addition to, so*—to be sure your ideas are clearly connected.

Proofreading

Re-read your essay slowly to check for mistakes in grammar, usage, spelling, and mechanics. Ask a friend to double-check for errors. If you're writing on a computer, consult the "magic" tools: the grammar and spelling checkers.

Tip to computer users: The spelling checker on your computer will not tell you if you've used the wrong word. It won't catch *it's* for *its* or *they're* for *there* or *threw* for *through*. Even though you use a spelling checker, you have to proofread.

Publishing

Add your paper to a class book of evaluative essays. Which stories were nominated for use in a school textbook? Which ones were rejected? Was there much agreement? Share your evaluations with other English classes. You might even find that the publisher of your textbook will be interested in receiving copies of your evaluations.

Reflecting

If you decide to include your evaluation in your writing portfolio, date it and attach a brief reflection:

1. How workable were my criteria? Do they need revising?

2. What writing skills do I still need to work on?

3. What did I learn about storytelling itself from this writing experience?

4. What did I learn about my own thinking process?

THE QUIGMANS   by Buddy Hickerson

I'M SORRY, BOB. YOUR WORK OF FICTION LACKS DIRECTION, HAS A GLARING ABSENCE OF CHARACTER DEVELOPMENT, AND NO DISCERNIBLE PLOT.

GREENBACK PUBLISHING COMPANY

IT'S...MY...AUTOBIOGRAPHY.

© 1995 Los Angeles Times Syndicate. Reprinted with permission.

I think I found enough evidence from the text to be convincing. But I realize that I need to dig a little more. Thinking up the criteria was fun—and easy because we discussed the elements in class. My criteria worked OK, and I'm keeping them to apply to new stories. Digging into a story made me appreciate how hard it is to write a good one. The hardest part of this assignment was writing my first draft. My writing group nagged a lot. What do I need to improve? Sometimes my writing isn't clear, though it always seems clear to me.

Sentence Workshop

Language Handbook HELP

See Run-on Sentences, page 1014.

Technology HELP

See Language Workshop CD-ROM. Key word entry: run-on sentences.

REVISING SENTENCES: STOPPING IN ALL THE RIGHT PLACES

Sentences that run together with no end punctuation between them are **run-on sentences**. When the sentences have no punctuation between them, they are **fused**. When the sentences are separated only by a comma, the run-on is called a **comma splice**.

EXAMPLES   His brother crawls backward like a doodlebug the narrator calls him Doodle. [fused]

His brother crawls backward like a doodlebug, the narrator calls him Doodle. [comma splice]

Strategies for revising run-ons:

1. Separate the sentences with a period.

   EXAMPLE
   His brother crawls backward like a doodlebug. The narrator calls him Doodle.

2. Connect the sentences with a semicolon or with a coordinating conjunction (*and, but, or, so, for, yet*).

   EXAMPLES
   His brother crawls backward like a doodlebug; the narrator calls him Doodle.

   His brother crawls backward like a doodlebug, so the narrator calls him Doodle.

3. Change one of the sentences into a subordinate clause.

   EXAMPLE
   Because his brother crawls backward like a doodlebug, the narrator calls him Doodle.

Writer's Workshop Follow-up: Revision

An effective way of spotting run-ons is to read your work aloud. Usually, you will naturally pause at the end of a full sentence. Stop and be sure it's punctuated correctly.
Warning: Watch the relationships between your run-on sentences. You do not want to link ideas that are not related. In those situations, separate the run-ons with a period.

Try It Out

Act as an editor and correct the run-ons in this report. Be sure to compare your edited versions.

The first American Indian boarding school was the Carlisle Indian Industrial School it was established in 1879, in the 1880s and 1890s American Indian children were sent to faraway federal boarding schools, many American Indian families hid their children, at school the children were made to wear military uniforms they were punished for speaking their native languages, John Collier was the Commissioner of Indian Affairs from 1933 to 1945, he began reforms, these included bilingual education and day schools instead of boarding schools.

LEARNING FOR LIFE

Oral History

Problem

All the short stories in these collections were published, so they are available to a wide audience and will be preserved for years in libraries. But many people have stories in them that are never recorded and so are lost as time passes. What are some ways you can preserve the stories of older people in your community (or even in your own family)?

Project

Interview at least three older people from your community or family and preserve some of their stories (even their brief anecdotes—don't look for full-fledged short stories like the ones in this unit!).

Preparation

1. Think carefully about the people you would like to interview. Ask for suggestions from your teacher or family or friends. When you have chosen your subjects, tell them about your project and arrange a meeting with each one.

2. Prepare a list of questions to encourage each person to recall some stories. You may want to help the person by asking questions like these:

• How did you come to live in this community?

• What was this community or neighborhood like years ago?

• What was your most memorable experience?

• Who is the most unforgettable character you ever met?

• What is your favorite place in the world?

Procedure

1. Use the questions you prepared as a general guide. But be ready to forget your questions and pursue any interesting memories that your subject mentions.

2. Your interview should be taped. You can take notes immediately after the interview to record anything of interest you noticed about your storyteller (setting, appearance, etc.).

3. Depending on the presentation you choose to make, you might want to take photographs of your storyteller.

Presentation

Present your oral history in one of the following formats (or another that your teacher approves):

1. Newspaper Article

Write a feature article for your community or school newspaper about your storytellers and the tales and life experiences they shared with you. Begin with an introduction that supplies interesting background information on your storytellers and on the place where you talked to each of them. Send photographs, with captions, along with your copy, which should be neatly typed, double-spaced, and carefully proofread.

2. Tape Recording

Edit your stories and present them on tape to your local museum or historical society. You might want to introduce each speaker using your own voice. Design a cover for the tape cassette. On the cover identify your speakers and the places where the stories were recorded.

3. A Display

Plan a storytellers' wall to be set up in some community building—a church, school, town hall, library. Mount photographs of the storytellers and paste their stories under the photos.

Processing

What did you learn about your community by doing this project? Write a reflection in your portfolio.

The Nonfiction Collections

If you believe in the power of words, you can bring about physical changes in the universe.

—N. Scott Momaday

Indian petroglyphs, or rock carvings, on Newspaper Rock, State Historic Monument, Utah.

A Writer on Nonfiction
A CONVERSATION WITH SANDRA CISNEROS

When you begin to read the selections in this collection, you will be entering the world of nonfiction. Before you begin, read what Sandra Cisneros, a writer who writes from her personal experience, has to say about the line between fiction and nonfiction. (You will find selections by Cisneros on pages 183 and 475.)

Q: What would you say nonfiction is?

Cisneros: When I was little and spent a lot of time in the Chicago Public Library, I always had a hard time remembering the difference between the books marked "Fiction" and the books marked "Nonfiction." I think somebody told me the difference once, but I kept forgetting.

The way I made myself remember was like this: *Fiction* means "fake" and *nonfiction* means "nonfake." This definition seemed to satisfy me then.

Q: What about your own writing—is it fiction or nonfiction?

Cisneros: Of course, the question students ask the most is "Is this story real?" In other words, how much of this story is "true" (nonfiction)? Well, all of it is true—kind of. All my fiction stories are based on nonfiction, but I add and cut and paste and change the details to make them "more real"—to make the story more interesting. Does this make sense?

Whenever I read my stories from *The House on Mango Street,* my six brothers and my mother say, "It wasn't like that." Or, "We weren't that poor!" They think I'm writing autobiography (nonfiction) about the real house we once lived in at 1525 N. Campbell Street in Chicago. But I'm doing what every good fiction writer does. I'm taking "real" people and "real" events and rearranging them so as to *create* a better story, because "real" life doesn't have

shape. But real stories do. No wonder they call writers liars.

On the other hand, while writing an article for a magazine the other day, I had to rewrite my essay (nonfiction) and add characters that hadn't really been a part of the true event. It was an essay about my father, but the editor kept asking me, "What about your mother? Where is she? Is she still alive?" Yes, she's very much alive, but she played no part in the story I was telling. However, for the sake of the public that might wonder, "What about your mother?" I had to change the facts a bit and add my mother to the story.

See what I mean? Fiction. Nonfiction. Fake? Nonfake? Such rubbery meanings! What is the difference? Now, *you* tell *me.*

BECOMING A STRATEGIC READER

• ## Critical Reading

When we read nonfiction, we are engaged in an active process. We interact with the text just as we do when we read fiction or poetry, but with nonfiction we read more critically. We bring our experiences, knowledge, and memories to nonfiction, but we also bring questions, expectations, and even biases. Here are some of the strategies we use when we read nonfiction.

1. **We ask about the writer.** We don't believe everything we read. We ask if the writer is qualified, if the writer has a bias or a special purpose. Is the writer informing or trying to persuade?

2. **We try to determine if what we are reading is fact or opinion.** Statements of fact can be verified, but opinions cannot.

3. **We interpret.** It's important that we trust our own knowledge and judgment when we read. We try to figure out the writer's main idea, and we decide if we agree with it.

4. **We extend the text.** We put the new information to work. We might want to search for more information or look for another point of view.

5. **We challenge the text.** We reflect on the vision of the world the text offers us, questioning it, perhaps disagreeing with it, but always binding ourselves to the rules of evidence and reason.

HOW TO OWN A WORD

How can you get to own a word—really own it? You might figure out its meaning from context. Or read a footnote that defines it and then look for more details in a dictionary. But the most important thing is to start using the word and listening to the way other people use it. After a while you'll be surprised to find you feel you own the word.

You May Know More Than You Think

Elizabeth Wong, in her memoir about going to Chinese school (page 344), says that Chinatown sounds chaotic. Below are four questions you might ask about the word *chaotic,* and some answers.

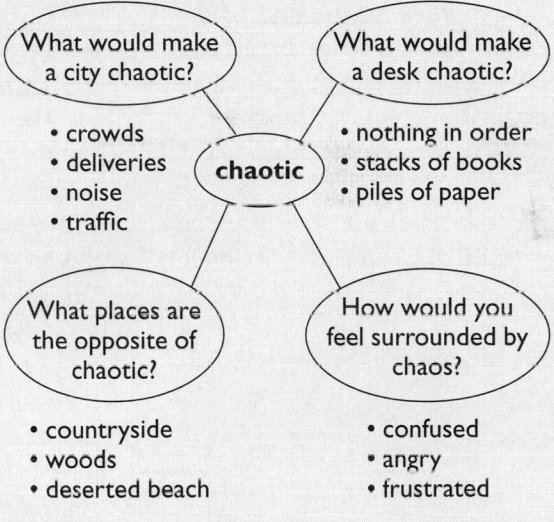

What would make a city chaotic?
- crowds
- deliveries
- noise
- traffic

chaotic

What would make a desk chaotic?
- nothing in order
- stacks of books
- piles of paper

What places are the opposite of chaotic?
- countryside
- woods
- deserted beach

How would you feel surrounded by chaos?
- confused
- angry
- frustrated

Extending Your Store of Words

From what you know about *chaotic,* what would you guess about the primeval time that the Greeks called Chaos—the time before the universe was formed? How is chaos worse than mere confusion?

THE *Struggle* TO BE AN *All-American Girl*

READER'S LOG

The notes that follow show the thoughts of one reader as she reads this memoir for the first time. When you read the selection yourself for the first time, cover her responses. Track your own responses in your Reader's Log and then compare your responses with Janelle's.

Why did they have to go to school instead of playing with the other children?

Oh, it was to learn Chinese.

She probably saw him in this manner because she was frightened.

I preferred tacos to egg rolls.

Elizabeth Wong

It's still there, the Chinese school on Yale Street where my brother and I used to go. Despite the new coat of paint and the high wire fence, the school I knew ten years ago remains remarkably, stoically[1] the same.

Every day at 5 P.M., instead of playing with our fourth- and fifth-grade friends or sneaking out to the empty lot to hunt ghosts and animal bones, my brother and I had to go to Chinese school. No amount of kicking, screaming, or pleading could dissuade my mother, who was solidly determined to have us learn the language of our heritage.

Forcibly, she walked us the seven long, hilly blocks from our home to school, depositing our defiant, tearful faces before the stern principal. My only memory of him is that he swayed on his heels like a palm tree, and he always clasped his impatient, twitching hands behind his back. I recognized him as a repressed maniacal child killer and knew that if we ever saw his hands we'd be in big trouble.

We all sat in little chairs in an empty auditorium. The room

1. **stoically** (stō′ik·lē): indifferently; calmly.

smelled like Chinese medicine, an imported faraway mustiness. Like ancient mothballs or dirty closets. I hated that smell. I favored crisp new scents. Like the soft French perfume that my American teacher wore in public school.

There was a stage far to the right, flanked by an American flag and the flag of the Nationalist Republic of China,[2] which was also red, white, and blue but not as pretty.

Although the emphasis at the school was mainly language—speaking, reading, writing—the lessons always began with an exercise in politeness. With the entrance of the teacher, the best student would tap a bell and everyone would get up, kowtow,[3] and chant, "Sing san ho," the phonetic for "How are you, teacher?"

Being ten years old, I had better things to learn than ideographs[4] copied painstakingly in lines that ran right to left from the tip of a *moc but,* a real ink pen that had to be held in an awkward way if blotches were to be avoided. After all, I could do the multiplication tables, name the satellites of Mars, and write reports on *Little Women* and *Black Beauty.* Nancy Drew, my favorite book heroine, never spoke Chinese.

The language was a source of embarrassment. More times than not, I had tried to disassociate myself from the nagging loud voice that followed me wherever I wandered in the nearby American supermarket outside Chinatown. The voice belonged to my grandmother, a fragile woman in her seventies who could outshout the best of the street vendors. Her humor was raunchy, her Chinese rhythmless, patternless. It was quick, it was loud, it was unbeautiful. It was not like the quiet, lilting romance of French or the gentle refinement of the American South. Chinese sounded pedestrian. Public.

2. **Nationalist Republic of China:** Republic of China, consisting mainly of Taiwan.
3. **kowtow** (kou′tou′): show respect by kneeling and touching the ground with the forehead.
4. **ideographs** (id′ē·ō·grafs′): written symbols representing objects or ideas. The Chinese write in ideographs.

It sounds like she would rather try to fit in and be an "All-American" girl rather than a Chinese American girl.

In this culture the elders and parents are treated with great respect and politeness.

She compares everything Chinese with American. American seems to be outweighing Chinese so far.

Her grandmother appears to be overprotective, following her around.

She really wants to fit in in America, but everything is holding her back.

She has a lot of potential in the real world, but she is locked up in her own Chinatown world.

This is the complete opposite of what usually happens. Mothers usually correct their children in their English.

Everyone tries to find a scape-goat when they make a mistake.

She fits in now, mostly, but she is still Chinese. She should be proud of the fact that she has a unique heritage.

—Janelle Jones
Southeast High School
Bradenton, Florida

In Chinatown, the comings and goings of hundreds of Chinese on their daily tasks sounded chaotic[5] and frenzied. I did not want to be thought of as mad, as talking gibberish. When I spoke English, people nodded at me, smiled sweetly, said encouraging words. Even the people in my culture would cluck and say that I'd do well in life. "My, doesn't she move her lips fast," they would say, meaning that I'd be able to keep up with the world outside Chinatown.

My brother was even more fanatical than I about speaking English. He was especially hard on my mother, criticizing her, often cruelly, for her pidgin speech—smatterings of Chinese scattered like chop suey in her conversation. "It's not 'what it is,' Mom," he'd say in exasperation. "It's 'What *is* it, what *is* it, what *is* it!'" Sometimes Mom might leave out an occasional "the" or "a," or perhaps a verb of being. He would stop her in midsentence: "Say it again, Mom. Say it right." When he tripped over his own tongue, he'd blame it on her: "See, Mom, it's all your fault. You set a bad example."

What infuriated my mother most was when my brother cornered her on her consonants, especially "r." My father had played a cruel joke on Mom by assigning her an American name that her tongue wouldn't allow her to say. No matter how hard she tried, "Ruth" always ended up "Luth" or "Roof."

After two years of writing with a *moc but* and reciting words with multiples of meanings, I finally was granted a cultural divorce. I was permitted to stop Chinese school.

I thought of myself as multicultural. I preferred tacos to egg rolls; I enjoyed Cinco de Mayo[6] more than Chinese New Year.

At last, I was one of you; I wasn't one of them.
Sadly, I still am.

5. **chaotic** (kā·ät′ik): completely confused; in total disorder.
6. **Cinco de Mayo** (siŋ′kô de mä′yô): holiday celebrated by Mexicans and Mexican Americans in honor of a Mexican military victory in 1862. *Cinco de Mayo* is Spanish for "May 5."

Most of us are only half aware of the days we're living through. We barely notice their flavor and their rhythms. We don't realize that gradually these days will transform themselves into memories and will fade into vague shadows in our minds. There we will catch a glimpse of them only occasionally, perhaps when a song brings back, for just a second, the person who sang it long ago, or a scene calls to mind a place we visited long ago. Almost all writers start with memories. A French writer, Marcel Proust, wrote his greatest work after a taste of cake released a flood of childhood memories.

Writer's Notebook

"Life," the saying goes, "is what happens while you're making other plans." What does that mean? Perhaps it means that we don't pay enough attention to the present. Perhaps it means that we lose today because we're thinking about tomorrow—or about what we want instead of what we have. If you're busy making other plans, lay them aside for a few minutes and think about where you are right now. Write down what you want to remember about the present moment. Keep your notes for possible use in the Writer's Workshop on page 386, where you'll be writing an autobiographical incident.

*Some memories are realities
and are better than anything
that can ever happen to one again.*

BEFORE YOU READ
NOT MUCH OF ME
WITH A TASK BEFORE ME

Reading Focus

In His Own Words

You probably know a lot about Abraham Lincoln from what biographers and historians have written, from what teachers have said, and from what you've seen on TV. All of this information comes from people other than Lincoln. What do you think you might learn about Lincoln from Lincoln himself—from his own words?

Quickwrite

Think about all the things you have heard or read about Abraham Lincoln. You probably know that he was president during the Civil War. What else? Do you know anything about his appearance? His family? Using a chart like the one in the next column, record some of the things you know about him. Then, when you have finished reading these autobiographical notes, record the new information Lincoln has given you about himself.

What I Know	New Information

Elements of Literature

Tone

In speech, tone is expressed through voice, body language, and word choice. In writing, tone is expressed primarily through the writer's choice of words. When you write about yourself, your tone is especially revealing. You can be modest about your accomplishments or boastful; you can be satirical about other people or sweet; you can be comical about your life or serious. When you read any piece of writing, you must be sensitive to the writer's tone. If you misinterpret tone, you've missed the whole point.

Tone is the attitude a writer takes toward an audience, a subject, or a character.

For more on Tone, see pages 586–587 and the Handbook of Literary Terms.

Not Much of Me
Abraham Lincoln

Background

Just five months before his nomination to the presidency in 1860, Lincoln wrote this sketch as background for newspaper writers in the eastern United States. "There is not much of it," Lincoln apologized, "for the reason, I suppose, that there is not much of me." It is one of the few things that he ever wrote about himself. It is reproduced here just as Lincoln wrote it—you will find some unusual spellings and punctuation.

I was born Feb. 12, 1809, in Hardin County, Kentucky. My parents were both born in Virginia, of undistinguished families—second families, perhaps I should say. My mother, who died in my tenth year, was of a family of the name of Hanks, some of whom now reside in Adams and others in Macon counties, Illinois. My paternal grandfather, Abraham Lincoln, emigrated from Rockingham County, Virginia, to Kentucky, about 1781 or 2, where, a year or two later, he was killed by indians, not in battle, but by stealth, when he was laboring to open a farm in the forest. His ancestors, who were quakers, went to Virginia from Berks County, Pennsylvania. An effort to identify them with the New-England family of the same name ended in nothing more definite than a similarity of Christian names in both families, such as Enoch, Levi, Mordecai, Solomon, Abraham, and the like.

My father, at the death of his father, was but six years of age; and he grew up, litterally without education. He removed from Kentucky to what is now Spencer county, Indiana, in my eighth year. We reached our new home about the time the State came in the Union. It was a wild region, with many bears and other wild animals still in the woods. There I grew up. There were some schools, so called; but no qualification was ever required of a teacher, beyond "*readin, writin,* and *cipherin,*" to the Rule of Three. If a straggler supposed to understand latin, happened to sojourn in the neighborhood, he was looked upon as a wizzard. There was absolutely nothing to excite ambition for education. Of course when I came of age I did not know much. Still somehow, I could read, write, and cipher to the Rule of Three; but that was all. I have not been to school since. The little advance I now have upon this store of education, I have picked up from time to time under the pressure of necessity.

I was raised to farm work, which I continued till I was twenty-two. At twenty-one I came to Illinois, and passed the first year in Illinois—Macon county. Then I got to New-Salem, (at that time in Sangamon, now in Menard county), where I remained a year as a sort of Clerk in a store. Then came the Black-Hawk war;[1] and I was elected a Captain of Volunteers—a success which gave me more pleasure than any I have had since. I went the campaign, was elated, ran for the Legislature the same year (1832) and was beaten—the only time I have been beaten by the people. The next, and three succeeding biennial[2] elections, I was elected to the Legislature. I was not a candidate afterwards. During this Legislative period I had studied law, and removed to Springfield to practice it. In 1846 I was once elected to the lower House of Congress. Was not a candidate for re-election. From 1849 to 1854, both inclusive, practiced law more assiduously than ever before. Always a whig[3] in politics, and generally on the whig electoral tickets, making active canvasses.[4] I was losing interest in politics, when the repeal of the Missouri Compromise[5] aroused me again. What I have done since then is pretty well known.

If any personal description of me is thought desirable, it may be said, I am, in height, six feet, four inches, nearly; lean in flesh, weighing, on an average, one hundred and eighty pounds; dark complexion, with coarse black hair, and grey eyes—no other marks or brands recollected. Yours very truly,

A. Lincoln

1. **Black-Hawk war:** war between the United States and the Sauk and Fox tribes in 1832. Black Hawk (1767–1838) was chief of the Sauk people and a leader in the war.
2. **biennial** (bī·en'ē·əl): happening every two years.
3. **whig:** Whigs favored a less powerful presidency than Democrats, but both parties split over the question of slavery.
4. **canvasses:** requests for votes.
5. **Missouri Compromise:** agreement reached in 1820 admitting Maine to the Union as a free state (one where slavery was illegal) and Missouri as a slave state, but limiting the creation of other slave states to the area south of Missouri.

WORDS TO OWN

elated (ē·lāt'id) *adj.:* very happy.
assiduously (ə·sij'oo·əs·lē) *adv.:* industriously; in a careful and hard-working manner.

With a Task Before Me

Abraham Lincoln

Background

Elected president in 1860, Lincoln had the sad task of bidding farewell to his home—Springfield, Illinois. He delivered the emotional address "With a Task Before Me" from the back of the train he boarded for the long trip to his new life in Washington. As you read, imagine Lincoln delivering these simple, eloquent words over the noisy chaos of a train depot. There is a particular sadness to this speech. In Washington four years later, Lincoln was assassinated. He was buried in Springfield.

My friends—No one, not in my situation, can appreciate my feeling of sadness at this parting. To this place, and the kindness of these people, I owe every thing. Here I have lived a quarter of a century, and have passed from a young to an old man. Here my children have been born, and one is buried. I now leave, not knowing when, or whether ever, I may return, with a task before me greater than that which rested upon Washington. Without the assistance of that Divine Being, who ever attended him, I cannot succeed. With that assistance I cannot fail. Trusting in Him, who can go with me, and remain with you and be every where for good, let us confidently hope that all will yet be well. To His care commending you, as I hope in your prayers you will commend me, I bid you an affectionate farewell.

MEET THE WRITER

A Way with Words

Abraham Lincoln (1809–1865) had a way with words and loved to tell stories. People listened to him and people liked him.

When Lincoln ran for the U.S. Senate against Stephen A. Douglas in 1858, he lost the election but won recognition for his brilliant speeches during their now-famous debates. Lincoln's way with words continued after he was elected president in 1860.

His Gettysburg Address (1863), for example, is less than three hundred words in length but is considered one of the greatest speeches by an American political leader. The speech is notable especially for its vision of American democracy: ". . . that this nation, under God, shall have a new birth of freedom—and that government of the people, by the people, for the people, shall not perish from the earth."

Lincoln had four children, all boys; three of his boys died young. The following words are said to have been written on the day one of his sons started school:

66 World, take my son by the hand—he starts to school today. . . .

Try to give my son the strength not to follow the crowd when everyone else is getting on the bandwagon. Teach him to listen to all men, but to filter all he hears on a screen of truth and to take only the good that comes through.

Teach him gently, World, but don't coddle him, because only the test of fire makes fine steel.

This is a big order, World, but see what you can do.

He's such a nice little fellow. . . . 99

N Y
Westfield Chatauque Co
Oct 15. 1860

Hon A B Lincoln
Dear Sir

My father has just [come] home from the fair and brought home your picture and Mr. [Hannibal] Hamlin's [Lincoln's running mate]. I am a little girl only eleven years old, but want you should be President of the United States very much so I hope you wont think me very bold to write to such a great man as you are. Have you any little girls about as large as I am if so give them my love and tell her to write to me if you cannot answer this letter. I have got 4 brother's and part of them will vote for you any way and if you will let your whiskers grow I will try and get the rest of them to vote for you you would look a great deal better for your face is so thin. All the ladies like whiskers and they would tease their husband's to vote for you and then you would be President. My father is a going to vote for you and if I was a man I would vote for you to but I will try and get every one to vote for you that I can I think that rail fence around your picture makes it look very pretty. I have got a little baby sister she is nine weeks old and is just as cunning as can be. When you direct your letter dir[e]ct to Grace Bedell Westfield Chatauque County New York

I must not write any more answer this letter right off Good bye

Grace Bedell

Presidential candidate Lincoln answered this letter—probably the most famous piece of advice he ever received—with an equally well-known reply.

PRIVATE

Springfield, Ills.
Oct. 19. 1860

Miss. Grace Bedell
My dear little Miss.

Your very agreeable letter of the 15th. is received.

I regret the necessity of saying I have no daughters. I have three sons—one seventeen, one nine, and one seven, years of age. They, with their mother, constitute my whole family.

As to the whiskers, never having worn any, do you not think people would call it a piece of silly affect[at]ion if I were to begin it now? Your very sincere well-wisher

A. Lincoln.

- ### First Thoughts

    1. Did these two pieces tell you anything new about Abraham Lincoln? Did they affect the way you feel about him? Be sure to complete the chart you filled in for your Quick-write.

Shaping Interpretations

2. People reveal a great deal about themselves when they look back on their lives. Which of the following words would you use to describe Lincoln's **tone** as he writes about himself in "Not Much of Me"? Find details in the selection to support your answers.

bitter	critical	serious
playful	humorous	awed
regretful	affectionate	sad
nostalgic	humble	sarcastic

3. How does Lincoln describe his education? What do you think enabled him to achieve so much?

4. Someone once said that Lincoln omitted from this thumbnail autobiography all that gave his life direction. What do you think this means—what would you like to ask Lincoln about his life that he failed to tell you about?

Extending the Texts

5. If someone asked any of the recent presidents to sum up their lives, what might they focus on? What **tone** do you think these modern presidents might take?

6. In 1860, when Lincoln ran for president, television was not available. Most of his speeches were delivered to local crowds and then published, sometimes days later, in newspapers or on posters. Suppose Abraham Lincoln were alive today and planned to run for president of the United States. What do you think his chances would be? What kind of platform do you think he would run on? How would the media treat him? How would he do in television campaigning?

From *Harper's Weekly,* November 26, 1864.

Long Abraham Lincoln a Little Longer by Frank Bellew.

CHOICES: Building Your Portfolio

Writer's Notebook

1. Collecting Ideas for an Autobiographical Incident

It happened to you. When you write your autobiographical incident for the Writer's Workshop on page 386, you'll be writing about an event that happened to *you*—you'll be your own main character. Before you started reading this collection, you did some thinking about what you would like to remember about the present moment. Now think about all the important **events** that have happened to you since you were born. Think also of the **places** you've known and perhaps even of your family's **history** before your arrival in their midst. Take notes to see if there is something in your past you'd like to use in your autobiographical incident.

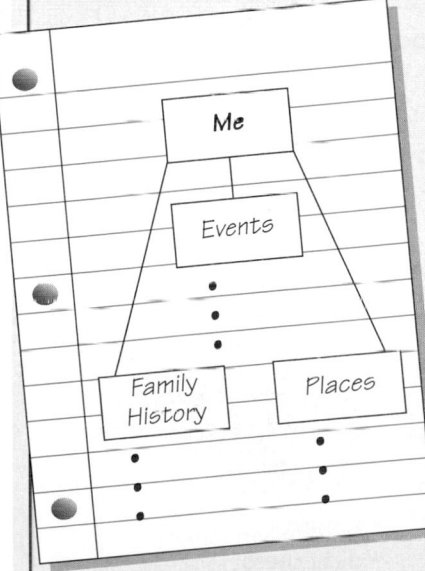

Creative Writing

2. Dear Mr. President

Grace Bedell (see page 351) wrote a letter of advice to Lincoln just before he was elected president. If you were to write a letter to Lincoln from the twentieth century, what would you tell him about equal opportunity in the Union he struggled to preserve? What advice would you ask him for?

Research/History

3. A Life on the Line

Several dates are mentioned in these selections. Use the dates to create a time line showing significant events in Lincoln's life, beginning with his birth in 1809 and continuing to his election to Congress in 1846. Then research the rest of Lincoln's life in Illinois and Washington and add important dates to the time line. Illustrate the time line, if you wish.

Creative Writing

4. The Campaign Trail

You're Abraham Lincoln's campaign manager. Your job is to convince the public to elect him sixteenth president of the United States. Write an appeal to voters—to be printed in newspapers around the country—urging them to vote for him. "Sell" Lincoln to the public by emphasizing his qualifications: his character, background, achievements, and plans for the country's future.

Research/Speaking

5. A Lincoln Celebration

With a group of classmates, prepare a Lincoln celebration. For your presentations, you should include speeches by Lincoln and a poem or two about Lincoln. Give a brief introduction to each speech and poem to set the scene (time, place, occasion). For some of the selections, you might consider a choral reading. You could include music in your celebration, focusing perhaps on Civil War songs. Here are some ideas:

- The "House Divided" Speech (Abraham Lincoln, 1858)
- The Gettysburg Address (Abraham Lincoln, 1863)
- The Second Inaugural (Abraham Lincoln, 1865)
- "Abraham Lincoln Walks at Midnight" (poem by Vachel Lindsay)
- "O Captain, My Captain" (poem by Walt Whitman)

LANGUAGE LINK   MINI-LESSON

**Language
Handbook
H E L P**

*See Capital-
ization,
pages
1018–1022;
Punctua-
tion, pages
1022–1031;
Spelling,
pages
1031–1034.*

**Technology
H E L P**

See Language
Workshop
CD-ROM.
*Key word
entry: punc-
tuation.*

Proofreading: Punctuation, Capitalization, Spelling

Our language is always changing. We add new words (such as *camcorder*) and we use old words in new ways (such as *voice mail*). We also adjust the mechanics for writing our language—experts are continually publishing new rules for capitalization, punctuation, and spelling. You can get an idea of how the mechanics of our language have evolved over the years if you compare the following sentence from Lincoln's "Not Much of Me" with the way we would write the sentence today.

> *Lincoln:* "If a straggler supposed to understand <u>latin</u>, happened to sojourn in the neighborhood, he was looked upon as a <u>wizzard</u>."

> *Modern version:* If a straggler supposed to understand <u>Latin</u> [no comma] happened to sojourn in the neighborhood, he was looked upon as a <u>wizard</u>.

Try It Out

Suppose you are an editor and you want to update Lincoln's capitalization, punctuation, and spelling. Write part of the text on a piece of paper, leaving extra space between the lines for your corrections. Then edit the text to make it conform to modern style. Pages 1018–1034 of the Language Handbook and a good dictionary will help you check up-to-date rules on capitalization, punctuation, and spelling. Exchange your edited copy with a classmate. As editors, do you agree on the rules?

VOCABULARY   HOW TO OWN A WORD

WORD BANK

*elated
assiduously*

What Do You Know About a Word?

This cluster diagram organizes some ideas about the word *sincere*. Try it with the words *elated* and *assiduously*.

How would a sincere person behave?

• would tell the truth
• be reliable

How would an insincere person behave?

• might tell lies
• two-faced

sincere

When would it be important to know if someone is sincere?

• if you need advice
• if person is a friend

What other characteristics would a sincere person probably have?

• honesty
• directness

Elements of Literature

BIOGRAPHY AND AUTOBIOGRAPHY *by* Janet Burroway

In Greek the word *bios* means "life" and *graphia* means "writing." A **biography** is therefore a "written life," or the story of a life. *Auto* in the same language means "self," so an **autobiography** is the written story of the writer's own life.

Biography: Someone Else's Life

A biographer who sets out to write the story of someone else's life must do a great deal of study and research. We'd expect someone who is going to write a biography of Anne Frank, for example, to read all about the rise of Nazism in Germany in the 1930s. We'd expect the biographer to find out what kinds of schools Anne went to and what kinds of books and newspapers she read. We'd expect the writer to interview people who knew Anne, people who helped her family hide, and people who were with her in the camp where she died. We'd expect that the biographer would visit the places where Anne lived and the prison where she died. And then we would expect that all this knowledge would be recorded accurately in a way that would make all the places, people, atmospheres, and events of Anne's life come alive.

Autobiography: Getting Personal

When Anne Frank sat down to write her own diary, she needed no such research. Her "research" was the daily living of her very own life. She already knew which people, places, and events were at the center of her life. Her purpose as a writer was to record the personal reactions and emotions of her experience, day by day.

A diary like Anne's is one sort of autobiography. The life is recorded as it is lived, a day or a week at a time. A person may also write an autobiography that is a record from memory of his or her entire life up to the time of writing. In either case, what we expect from autobiography is the kind of personal, internal knowledge that cannot be researched, because no one can get into another person's mind.

> **N**o one can get into another person's mind.

Objectivity or Subjectivity?

What we usually look for in biography is factual accuracy and **objectivity**. This means that we want an unbiased account of the person the biography deals with—we do not want the account distorted by the writer's own prejudices.

But in autobiography, we look for **subjectivity**—that is, we want this writer to "get personal." We want to know what the writer thinks about her grandmother or how the writer feels about his hometown or why the writer has always been afraid of cats.

The advantage of other kinds of biography is their perspective: An outsider can tell us things about the background, history, influences, and effectiveness of another person—things that this person may not have realized or cared to write about. The advantage of autobiography, on the other hand, is that it reveals the motives, emotions, fears, hopes, doubts, and joys that only the writer can know.

Reading Focus

Memories Stay with Us

We all remember people we've admired—people who were wise, funny, or especially kind. We also remember people who were less than perfect—people who were uneasy, demanding, even unkind. All of these memories—good and bad—stay with us and become part of who we are. Here, Maya Angelou reflects on an incident from her childhood, when she witnessed her beloved grandmother's encounter with some mean-spirited children. Why has this experience stayed with her?

Quickwrite

What are some effective re-actions to insults or bullying? Could you respond without causing trouble—and still keep your dignity? Suppose you were advising a younger person about how to deal with bullying. In your log, write down the advice you would give. Consider these options:

- run away
- be rude back
- fight
- ignore the person
- try to reason with the person
- report the incident to an adult

Background

"When I Lay My Burden Down" is an excerpt from Maya Angelou's autobiography *I Know Why the Caged Bird Sings*. When Angelou was three years old, her parents divorced and she was sent on a train from Long Beach, California, to live with her grandmother and uncle in the small town of Stamps, Arkansas. Life in this segregated Southern town took some getting used to, but it wasn't long before Maya and her older brother were calling their grandmother Momma and pulling their weight by working in her general store. In this selection, Maya is ten years old.

Elements of Literature

Imagery: Words Make It Real

Angelou uses images to make the people and the places that are so real to her seem just as immediate and real to her readers. Descriptions of "cold, molasses-slow minutes," of an apron so stiff with starch that it could have stood alone, and of children with "greasy, uncolored hair" help us see and experience what Angelou herself saw and experienced as a little girl so many years ago.

> **I**magery is language that appeals to one or more of our senses—to our sight, hearing, smell, taste, or touch.
>
> *For more on Imagery, see pages 492–493 and the Handbook of Literary Terms.*

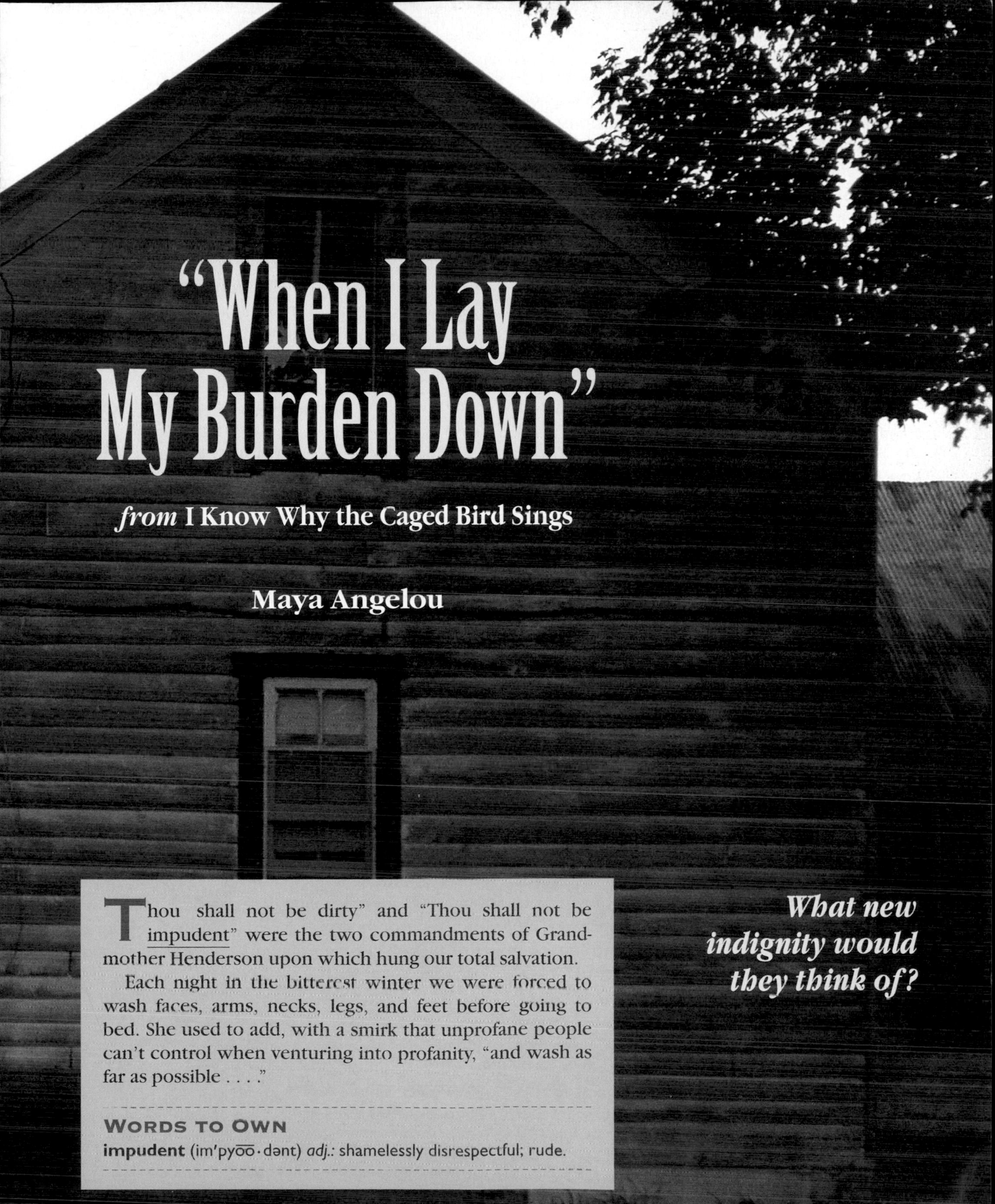

"When I Lay My Burden Down"

from I Know Why the Caged Bird Sings

Maya Angelou

What new indignity would they think of?

Thou shall not be dirty" and "Thou shall not be impudent" were the two commandments of Grandmother Henderson upon which hung our total salvation.

Each night in the bitterest winter we were forced to wash faces, arms, necks, legs, and feet before going to bed. She used to add, with a smirk that unprofane people can't control when venturing into profanity, "and wash as far as possible . . . ."

WORDS TO OWN

impudent (im′pyo͞o·dənt) *adj.:* shamelessly disrespectful; rude.

We would go to the well and wash in the ice-cold, clear water, grease our legs with the equally cold, stiff Vaseline, then tiptoe into the house. We wiped the dust from our toes and settled down for schoolwork, corn bread, clabbered milk,[1] prayers, and bed, always in that order. Momma was famous for pulling the quilts off after we had fallen asleep to examine our feet. If they weren't clean enough for her, she took the switch (she kept one behind the bedroom door for emergencies) and woke up the offender with a few aptly placed burning reminders.

The area around the well at night was dark and slick, and boys told about how snakes love water, so that anyone who had to draw water at night and then stand there alone and wash knew that moccasins and rattlers, puff adders and boa constrictors were winding their way to the well and would arrive just as the person washing got soap in her eyes. But Momma convinced us that not only was cleanliness next to godliness, dirtiness was the inventor of misery.

The impudent child was detested by God and a shame to its parents and could bring destruction to its house and line. All adults had to be addressed as Mister, Missus, Miss, Auntie, Cousin, Unk, Uncle, Buhbah, Sister, Brother, and a thousand other appellations indicating familial relationship and the lowliness of the addressor.

Everyone I knew respected these customary laws, except for the powhitetrash children.

Some families of powhitetrash lived on Momma's farmland behind the school. Sometimes a gaggle of them came to the Store, filling the whole room, chasing out the air, and even changing the well-known scents. The children crawled over the shelves and into the potato and onion bins, twanging all the time in their sharp voices like cigar-box guitars. They took liberties in my Store that I would never dare. Since Momma told us that the less you say to whitefolks (or even powhitetrash) the better, Bailey and I would stand, solemn, quiet, in the displaced air. But if one of the playful apparitions got close to us, I pinched it. Partly out of

1. **clabbered milk:** thickly clotted sour milk.

angry frustration and partly because I didn't believe in its flesh reality.

They called my uncle by his first name and ordered him around the Store. He, to my crying shame, obeyed them in his limping dip-straight-dip fashion.

My grandmother, too, followed their orders, except that she didn't seem to be servile because she anticipated their needs.

"Here's sugar, Miz Potter, and here's baking powder. You didn't buy soda last month, you'll probably be needing some."

Momma always directed her statements to the adults, but sometimes, Oh painful sometimes, the grimy, snotty-nosed girls would answer her.

"Naw, Annie . . ."—to Momma? Who owned the land they lived on? Who forgot more than they would ever learn? If there was any justice in the world, God should strike them dumb at once!—"Just give us some extry sody crackers, and some more mackerel."

At least they never looked in her face, or I never caught them doing so. Nobody with a smidgen of training, not even the worst roustabout,[2] would look right in a grown person's face. It meant the person was trying to take the words out before they were formed. The dirty little children didn't do that, but they threw their orders around the Store like lashes from a cat-o'-nine-tails.[3]

When I was around ten years old, those scruffy children caused me the most painful and confusing experience I had ever had with my grandmother.

One summer morning, after I had swept the dirt yard of leaves, spearmint-gum wrappers, and Vienna-sausage labels, I raked the yellow-

2. **roustabout** (roust′ə·bout′): unskilled or temporary laborer.
3. **cat-o'-nine-tails:** whip made of nine knotted cords attached to a handle.

WORDS TO OWN
appellations (ap′ə·lā′shənz) *n.:* names; titles.
apparitions (ap′ə·rish′ənz) *n.:* strange, ghostlike figures.
servile (sʉr′vəl) *adj.:* humbly submissive; like a slave.

The Hoe Cake (c. 1946) by Horace Pippin. Oil on canvas (14″ x 18″).

red dirt and made half-moons carefully, so that the design stood out clearly and masklike. I put the rake behind the Store and came through the back of the house to find Grandmother on the front porch in her big, wide white apron. The apron was so stiff by virtue of the starch that it could have stood alone. Momma was admiring the yard, so I joined her. It truly looked like a flat redhead that had been raked with a big-toothed comb. Momma didn't say anything but I knew she liked it. She looked over toward the school principal's house and to the right at Mr. McElroy's. She was hoping one of those community pillars would see the design before the day's business wiped it out. Then she looked upward to the school. My head had swung with hers, so at just about the same time we saw a troop of the powhitetrash kids marching over the hill and down by the side of the school.

I looked to Momma for direction. She did an excellent job of sagging from her waist down, but from the waist up she seemed to be pulling for the top of the oak tree across the road. Then she began to moan a hymn. Maybe not to moan, but the tune was so slow and the meter so strange that she could have been moaning. She didn't look at me again. When the children reached halfway down the hill, halfway to the Store, she said without turning, "Sister, go on inside."

I wanted to beg her, "Momma, don't wait for them. Come on inside with me. If they come in the Store, you go to the bedroom and let me wait on them. They only frighten me if you're around. Alone I know how to handle them." But of course I couldn't say anything, so I went in and stood behind the screen door.

Before the girls got to the porch, I heard their laughter crackling and popping like pine logs in a cooking stove. I suppose my lifelong paranoia[4] was born in those cold, molasses-slow minutes. They came finally to stand on the ground in front of Momma. At first they pretended seriousness. Then one of them wrapped her right arm in the crook of her left, pushed out her mouth, and started to hum. I realized that she was aping my grandmother. Another said, "Naw, Helen, you ain't standing like her. This here's it." Then she lifted her chest, folded her arms and mocked that strange carriage that was Annie Henderson. Another laughed, "Naw, you can't do it. Your mouth ain't pooched out enough. It's like this."

I thought about the rifle behind the door, but I knew I'd never be able to hold it straight, and the .410, our sawed-off shotgun, which stayed loaded and was fired every New Year's night, was locked in the trunk and Uncle Willie had the key on his chain. Through the fly-specked screen door, I could see that the arms of Momma's apron jiggled from the vibrations of her humming. But her knees seemed to have locked as if they would never bend again.

She sang on. No louder than before, but no softer either. No slower or faster.

The dirt of the girls' cotton dresses continued on their legs, feet, arms, and faces to make them all of a piece. Their greasy uncolored hair hung down, uncombed, with a grim finality. I knelt to see them better, to remember them for all time. The tears that had slipped down my dress left unsurprising dark spots and made the front yard blurry and even more unreal. The world had taken a deep breath and was having doubts about continuing to revolve.

The girls had tired of mocking Momma and turned to other means of agitation. One crossed her eyes, stuck her thumbs in both sides of her mouth, and said, "Look here, Annie." Grandmother hummed on and the apron strings trembled. I wanted to throw a handful of black pepper in their faces, to throw lye on them, to scream that they were dirty, scummy pecker-

woods,[5] but I knew I was as clearly imprisoned behind the scene as the actors outside were confined to their roles.

One of the smaller girls did a kind of puppet dance while her fellow clowns laughed at her. But the tall one, who was almost a woman, said something very quietly, which I couldn't hear. They all moved backward from the porch, still watching Momma. For an awful second I thought they were going to throw a rock at Momma, who seemed (except for the apron strings) to have turned into stone herself. But the big girl turned her back, bent down, and put her hands flat on the ground—she didn't pick up anything. She simply shifted her weight and did a handstand.

Her dirty bare feet and long legs went straight for the sky. Her dress fell down around her shoulders, and she had on no drawers. . . . She hung in the vacuum of that lifeless morning for only a few seconds, then wavered and tumbled. The other girls clapped her on the back and slapped their hands.

Momma changed her song to "Bread of Heaven, bread of Heaven, feed me till I want no more."

I found that I was praying too. How long could Momma hold out? What new indignity would they think of to subject her to? Would I be able to stay out of it? What would Momma really like me to do?

Then they were moving out of the yard, on their way to town. They bobbed their heads and shook their slack behinds and turned, one at a time:

"'Bye, Annie."

"'Bye, Annie."

"'Bye, Annie."

Momma never turned her head or unfolded her arms, but she stopped singing and said, "'Bye, Miz Helen, 'bye, Miz Ruth, 'bye, Miz Eloise."

I burst. A firecracker July-the-Fourth burst.

5. **peckerwoods:** hostile term for "poor white people."

4. **paranoia** (par'ə·noi'ə): mental disorder that often causes people to believe they are being persecuted. The author is using the term in an informal sense, to mean "suspiciousness" or "distrustfulness."

WORDS TO OWN

agitation (aj'ə·tā'shən) *n.*: stirring up disturbance or excitement.

How could Momma call them Miz? The mean, nasty things. Why couldn't she have come inside the sweet, cool store when we saw them breasting the hill? What did she prove? And then if they were dirty, mean, and impudent, why did Momma have to call them Miz?

She stood another whole song through and then opened the screen door to look down on me crying in rage. She looked until I looked up. Her face was a brown moon that shone on me. She was beautiful. Something had happened out there which I couldn't completely understand, but I could see that she was happy. Then she bent down and touched me as mothers of the church "lay hands on the sick and afflicted" and I quieted.

"Go wash your face, Sister." And she went behind the candy counter and hummed, "Glory, glory, hallelujah, when I lay my burden down."

I threw the well water on my face and used the weekday handkerchief to blow my nose. Whatever the contest had been out front, I knew Momma had won.

I took the rake back to the front yard. The smudged footprints were easy to erase. I worked for a long time on my new design and laid the rake behind the wash pot. When I came back in the Store, I took Momma's hand and we both walked outside to look at the pattern.

It was a large heart with lots of hearts growing smaller inside, and piercing from the outside rim to the smallest heart was an arrow. Momma said, "Sister, that's right pretty." Then she turned back to the Store and resumed, "Glory, glory, hallelujah, when I lay my burden down."

MEET THE WRITER

Born Winner

66 One would say of my life, 'born loser, had to be'—but it's not the truth. In the black community, however bad it looks, there's a lot of love and so much humor. 99

Maya Angelou (1928–   ) is anything but a loser. After she left Stamps, Arkansas, she won a scholarship to the California Labor School, where she took evening classes in dance and drama. In 1954 and 1955, she toured Europe and Africa in a State Department–sponsored production of the opera *Porgy and Bess*. She later wrote and produced a ten-part television series on Africanisms in American life, wrote songs that were recorded by B. B. King, and published short stories, magazine articles, and poems. In 1992, she was asked to write a poem for the inauguration of President Clinton. On Inauguration Day of 1993, Maya Angelou presented her eloquent poem "On the Pulse of Morning." Here are the final lines:

66 Here on the pulse of this new day
You may have the grace to look up and out
And into your sister's eyes,
And into your brother's face,
Your country,
And say simply
Very simply
With hope—
Good morning. 99

Angelou is an imposing woman, six feet tall, with a gracious, formal manner. She speaks six languages fluently. Although she declares a continuing interest in exploring the character of the black woman, Angelou's focus is not narrow:

66 I speak to the black experience, but I am always talking about the human condition—about what we can endure, dream, fail at, and still survive. 99

Sympathy
Paul Laurence Dunbar

I know what the caged bird feels, alas!
   When the sun is bright on the upland slopes;
When the wind stirs soft through the springing grass,
And the river flows like a stream of glass;
5   When the first bird sings and the first bud opes,°
And the faint perfume from its chalice° steals—
I know what the caged bird feels!

I know why the caged bird beats his wing
   Till its blood is red on the cruel bars;
10 For he must fly back to his perch and cling
When he fain° would be on the bough a-swing;
   And a pain still throbs in the old, old scars
And they pulse again with a keener sting—
I know why he beats his wing!

15 I know why the caged bird sings, ah me,
   When his wing is bruised and his bosom sore,—
When he beats his bars and he would be free;
It is not a carol of joy or glee,
   But a prayer that he sends from his heart's deep core,
20 But a plea, that upward to Heaven he flings—
I know why the caged bird sings!

  5. opes: opens.
  6. chalice (chal′is): cup-shaped flower.
11. fain (fān): gladly.

MAKING MEANINGS

First Thoughts

1. What does Angelou mean when she says "Whatever the contest had been out front, I knew Momma had won"? Do you agree? Why, or why not?

Shaping Interpretations

2. Look back at the advice you wrote in your Quickwrite. Do you think Momma would agree with you? Explain.

3. During the incident, Momma doesn't say a word until the girls are leaving. What do you imagine she is thinking? Draw a thought bubble like the one shown opposite, and fill it with words and pictures that might represent Momma's thoughts. Be ready to explain your choices.

4. Why do you think the girls mock Momma? Talk about why people would be so cruel to another person. Why are children occasionally cruel to an innocent adult? (You might think of the story "Marigolds" on page 91.)

5. On page 359 Angelou says that when Momma sees the girls approaching, she sags from the waist down but from the top seems to be pulling for the top of an oak tree. Exactly what does this **image** make you see? What do you think Momma is feeling?

6. Angelou takes some time to tell us about what is considered good behavior and courtesy in her family. Why do you think she does this? How do you feel about her family's rules?

Connecting with the Text

7. At one point Angelou says that she is afraid of the kids only when Momma is around, and that she knows how to handle them when she's alone. What do you suppose she means? Would you feel the same way?

Extending the Text

8. The speaker of Paul Laurence Dunbar's poem "Sympathy" (page 362) says he knows why the caged bird sings at springtime, when nature is blooming and other birds fly freely. Why do you think Angelou chose Dunbar's image as the **title** of her life story? What might a caged bird be praying for? How is the narrator like a caged bird in this incident?

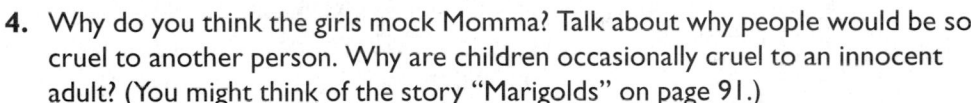

> **Reviewing the Text**
>
> a. List all the things you know about the setting of this incident.
>
> b. How do the "powhitetrash" children behave in the Store?
>
> c. What is the narrator's reaction as the rude girls insult her grandmother?
>
> d. What is Momma's response to the insult?

CHOICES: Building Your Portfolio

Writer's Notebook

1. Collecting Ideas for an Autobiographical Incident

People and places. When you write an auto-biographical incident for the Writer's Workshop on page 386, you'll want to help your readers visualize people and places, just as Angelou does. Look over your notes: Do you have an incident you would like to elaborate on? Gather notes on the people involved in the incident and on the place where it occurred. Try to find images that will help your readers see the scene, hear it, smell it, maybe even taste it and feel it.

WORK IN PROGRESS

Creative Writing

2. Look Who's Talking

Retell the events of "When I Lay My Burden Down" from Momma's point of view. What is Momma thinking and feeling as the girls taunt her? Be sure to consider why Momma sings when her ordeal is over. Write as *I*.

Speaking and Listening

3. A Found Poem

Find a poem in the text of "When I Lay My Burden Down." Meet with two or more classmates and look through the selection for "illuminating" words or phrases—words that you think are especially moving or that create particularly vivid pictures. Take five minutes and create a list of about eight words or phrases. Then narrow your choices to the four you like most. Get together with other groups and read your words aloud. If your group's choices are the same as the others', that's OK; it means the words are important. Read one word or phrase at a time, moving without interruption from group to group. There you have it—a found poem.

Drawing

4. TV Set

Design a set for a TV show based on "When I Lay My Burden Down." Draw a few renderings—color sketches—to show how you visualize the store, inside and outside, including the yard. Label the details in your drawings—furniture, family possessions, the yard. That way the location scouts, carpenters, decorators, and "prop masters" will know exactly what you need to set your scene.

Incident/I Am 6
The parking lot was crowded and hot. Waves of heat rose off the pavement. People looked irritable as they wrestled with their grocery carts. I got locked in trunk.

Photograph by Walker Evans (1936).

LANGUAGE LINK MINI-LESSON

Handbook of Literary Terms
H E L P

See Metaphor, Simile, and Personification.

Style: Comparisons—Seeing Unusual Connections

Writers use imaginative comparisons to create striking images. These comparisons are "special-effects" language that is not meant to be taken literally. When Maya Angelou says, for example, that the world "had taken a deep breath and was having doubts about continuing to revolve," she doesn't *really* mean that the planet Earth was about to stop spinning on its axis. Angelou uses **personification** here, a type of comparison that gives human characteristics to nonhuman things.

Other types of comparisons are similes and metaphors. A **simile** compares two unlike things, using a word like *like* or *as*. A **metaphor,** on the other hand, says that one thing *is* something else, something very different. A metaphor does not use *like* or *as*. Here are some similes and metaphors from Angelou's story:

1. ". . . sharp voices like cigar-box guitars."

2. ". . . threw their orders around the Store like lashes from a cat-o'-nine-tails."

3. ". . . laughter crackling and popping like pine logs in a cooking stove."

4. ". . . I knew I was as clearly imprisoned behind the scene as the actors outside were confined to their roles."

5. "Her face was a brown moon that shone on me."

Try It Out

➤ What two different things is Angelou comparing in each passage opposite? What does each comparison make you see or hear?

➤ Write your own comparisons to describe voices; laughter; an observer who feels trapped; a face.

VOCABULARY   HOW TO OWN A WORD

WORD BANK
impudent
appellations
apparitions
servile
agitation

Semantic Mapping

Semantic mapping is a simple strategy that can help you own new words. A semantic map includes (1) the word's definition, (2) its synonyms, if any, (3) use of the word in a sentence, (4) a response to the use of the synonyms in the sentence. A sample is shown here. Make a semantic map for the other words in the Word Bank.

> **impudent**

> **DEFINITION**
> "shamelessly disrespectful"

> **SYNONYMS**
> rude, bold, impolite, fresh

> **SENTENCE**
> A child who makes nasty faces at an adult is impudent.

> **RESPONSE TO SYNONYMS**
> *Rude* could be used but other words are too mild for this situation.

BEFORE YOU READ
CHOICE: A TRIBUTE TO DR. MARTIN LUTHER KING, JR.

Reading Focus

Tribute

With eloquence and style Martin Luther King, Jr., brought the message of civil rights to a world television audience. His voice sounded a call for the elimination of racism in the United States through non-violent resistance. To a generation of African Americans, he became a symbol of the struggle to fulfill at last the century-old promise of emancipation.

As you read, be aware of the setting and the audience for Walker's tribute to King, who was killed by an assassin on April 4, 1968, as he stood on a motel balcony in Memphis, Tennessee.

A Dialogue with the Text

Form groups and brainstorm for a few minutes to make a list of the positive changes you think have happened as a result of Martin Luther King's work and life. Record your list in your Reader's Log. As you read this speech, add to your list the things Walker says King gave her.

Elements of Literature

Main Idea

Speeches, essays, and editorials all are focused on a **main idea**—a message, an opinion, or an idea that the writer wants to communicate to the reader. Some writers, especially editorial writers, state their main ideas directly. But in most cases the main idea is implied or suggested. We readers discover it on our own by making inferences about what all the separate details in the piece of writing add up to. When you read a speech like this one, look for key statements that give you clues to the speaker's broader meaning. One of the key elements in this speech is a story—why does Walker tell us this story?

> The **main idea** is the message, opinion, or idea that a writer wants to communicate.

This address was given in 1972 at a Jackson, Mississippi, restaurant that had refused to serve African Americans until forced to do so by the civil rights movement a few years earlier.

Choice: A Tribute to Dr. Martin Luther King, Jr.

Alice Walker

Alice Walker's "three greats"–grandmother Mary Poole, who was born some time before 1800 and died in 1921.

He gave us home.

My great-great-great-grandmother walked as a slave from Virginia to Eatonton, Georgia—which passes for the Walker ancestral home—with two babies on her hips. She lived to be a hundred and twenty-five years old and my own father knew her as a boy. (It is in memory of this walk that I choose to keep and to embrace my "maiden" name, Walker.)

There is a cemetery near our family church where she is buried; but because her marker was made of wood and rotted years ago, it is impossible to tell exactly where her body lies. In the same cemetery are most of my mother's people, who have lived in Georgia for so long nobody even remembers when they came. And all of my great-aunts and -uncles are there, and my grandfather and grandmother, and very recently, my own father.

If it is true that land does not belong to anyone until they have buried a body in it, then the land of my birthplace belongs to me, dozens of times over. Yet the history of my family, like that of all black Southerners, is a history of dispossession. We loved the land and worked the land, but we never owned it; and even if we bought land, as my great-grandfather did after the Civil War, it was always in danger of being taken away, as his was, during the period following Reconstruction.°

My father inherited nothing of material value from his father, and when I came of age in the early sixties I awoke to the bitter knowledge that in order just to continue to love the land of my birth, I was expected to leave it. For black people—including my parents—had learned a long time ago that to stay willingly in a beloved but brutal place is to risk losing the love and being forced to acknowledge only the brutality.

It is a part of the black Southern sensibility that we treasure memories; for such a long time, that is all of our homeland those of us who at one time or another were forced away from it have been allowed to have.

I watched my brothers, one by one, leave our home and leave the South. I watched my sisters do the same. This was not unusual; abandonment, except for memories, was the common thing, except for those who "could not do any better" or those whose strength or stubbornness was so colossal they took the risk that others could not bear.

In 1960, my mother bought a television set, and each day after school I watched Hamilton Holmes and Charlayne Hunter as they struggled to integrate—fair-skinned as they were—the University of Georgia. And then, one day, there appeared the face of Dr. Martin Luther King, Jr. What a funny name, I thought. At the moment I first saw him, he was being handcuffed and shoved into a police truck. He had dared to claim his rights as a native son and had been arrested. He displayed no fear, but seemed calm and serene, unaware of his own extraordinary courage. His whole body, like his conscience, was at peace.

°**Reconstruction:** the period after the Civil War, lasting from 1867 to 1877, during which the Southern states were brought back into the Union and the former slaves were granted citizenship and certain other civil and political rights. African Americans were deprived of many of these rights after Reconstruction.

At the moment I saw his resistance I knew I would never be able to live in this country without resisting everything that sought to disinherit me, and I would never be forced away from the land of my birth without a fight.

He was The One, The Hero, The One Fearless Person for whom we had waited. I hadn't even realized before that we *had* been waiting for Martin Luther King, Jr., but we had. And I knew it for sure when my mother added his name to the list of people she prayed for every night.

I sometimes think that it was literally the prayers of people like my mother and father, who had bowed down in the struggle for such a long time, that kept Dr. King alive until five years ago. For years we went to bed praying for his life and awoke with the question "Is the 'Lord' still here?"

The public acts of Dr. King you know. They are visible all around you. His voice you would recognize sooner than any other voice you have heard in this century—this in spite of the fact that certain municipal libraries, like the one in downtown Jackson, do not carry recordings of his speeches, and the librarians chuckle cruelly when asked why they do not.

You know, if you have read his books, that his is a complex and revolutionary philosophy that few people are capable of understanding fully or have the patience to embody in themselves. Which is our weakness, which is our loss.

And if you know anything about good Baptist preaching, you can imagine what you missed if you never had a chance to hear Martin Luther King, Jr., preach at Ebenezer Baptist Church.

You know of the prizes and awards that he tended to think very little of. And you know of his concern for the disinherited—the American Indian, the Mexican American, and the poor American white—for whom he cared much.

WORDS TO OWN

dispossession (dis′pə·zesh′ən) *n.*: taking away of one's possessions.

sensibility (sen′sə·bil′ə·tē) *n.*: consciousness; awareness. *Sensibility* also means "emotional responsiveness."

embody (em·bäd′ē) *v.*: make real, give form to, or include.

The Civil Rights Memorial in Montgomery, Alabama.

You know that this very room, in this very restaurant, was closed to people of color not more than five years ago. And that we eat here together tonight largely through his efforts and his blood. We accept the common pleasures of life, assuredly, in his name.

But add to all of these things the one thing that seems to me second to none in importance: He gave us back our heritage. He gave us back our homeland; the bones and dust of our ancestors, who may now sleep within our caring *and* our hearing. He gave us the blueness of the Georgia sky, in autumn as in summer; the colors of the Southern winter as well as glimpses of the green of vacation-time spring. Those of our relatives we used to invite for a visit we now can ask to stay. . . . He gave us full-time use of our own woods and restored our memories to those of us who were forced to run away, as realities we might each day enjoy and leave for our children.

He gave us continuity of place, without which community is <u>ephemeral</u>. He gave us home.

WORDS TO OWN

ephemeral (e·fem′ər·əl) *adj.*: short-lived; passing quickly.

MEET THE WRITER
Pulitzer Prize Winner

Alice Walker (1944–   ) is a novelist, short-story writer, poet, and essayist. She is best known for her novel *The Color Purple,* which won a Pulitzer Prize in 1983 and was made into a popular movie starring Whoopi Goldberg and Oprah Winfrey. Alice Walker was born in Eatonton, a small town in Georgia. Her father was a sharecropper, and her mother was a maid. Walker was the youngest of eight children.

In a letter Walker wrote this about other heroes:

   ❝ I stood looking at a picture of Frederick Douglass I have on my wall. And I asked myself: Where is your picture of Harriet Tubman, the General? Where is your drawing of Sojourner Truth? And I thought that if black women would only start asking questions like that, they'd soon—all of them—have to begin reclaiming their mothers and grandmothers—and what an enrichment that would be! **❞**

For more on Alice Walker, see page 557.

No One Ever Told Me Not to Dream

from In My Place

Charlayne Hunter-Gault

Charlayne Hunter-Gault grew up in a big family in the Deep South. As one of two black students who bravely integrated the all-white University of Georgia, she was a leading civil rights figure. Eventually, she became a national correspondent for PBS.

On January 9, 1961, I walked onto the campus at the University of Georgia to begin registering for classes. Ordinarily, there would not have been anything unusual about such a routine exercise, except, in this instance, the officials at the university had been fighting for two and a half years to keep me out. I was not socially, intellectually, or morally undesirable. I was black. And no black student had ever been admitted to the University of Georgia in its 176 year history. Until the landmark *Brown* v. *Board of Education* decision that in 1954 declared separate but equal schools unconstitutional, the university was protected by law in its exclusion of people like me. In applying to the university, Hamilton Holmes and I were making one of the first major tests of the court's ruling in Georgia, and no one was sure just how hard it would be to challenge nearly two hundred years of exclusive white privilege. It would take us two and a half years of fighting our way through the system and the courts, but finally, with the help of the NAACP Legal Defense and Educational Fund, Inc., and with the support of our family and friends, we won the right that should have been ours all along. With the ink barely dry on the court

order of three days before, Hamilton Holmes and I walked onto the campus and into history.

We would be greeted by mobs of white students, who within forty-eight hours would hurl epithets, burn crosses and black effigies, and finally stage a riot outside my dormitory while, nearby, state patrolmen ignored the call from university officials to come and intervene. Tear gas would disperse the crowd, but not before I got word in my dorm room, now strewn with glass from a rock through my window, that Hamilton and I were being suspended for our own safety. It might have been the end of the story but for the fact that the University of Georgia was now the lead case in a series of events that would become Georgia's entry into the Civil Rights Revolution. And we—like the legions of young black students to follow in other arenas—were now imbued with an unshakable determination to take control of our destiny and force the South to abandon the wretched Jim Crow laws it had perpetuated for generations to keep us in our place.

The newfound sense of mission that now motivated us evolved for me out of a natural desire to fulfill a dream I had nurtured from an early age. With a passion bordering on obsession, I wanted to be a journalist, a dream that would have been, if not unthinkable, at least undoable in the South of my early years. But no one ever told me not to dream, and when the time came to act on that dream, I would not let anything stand in the way of fulfilling it.

MAKING MEANINGS

First Thoughts

1. What picture of Martin Luther King, Jr., did Walker's tribute give you?

Shaping Interpretations

2. Did Walker's speech tell you anything new about Martin Luther King, Jr., and his effect on American life? Check your Reader's Log and compare your final list of King's contributions with the lists made by other readers.

3. What choice do you think Walker is referring to in the **title** of her speech?

4. In the first eight paragraphs, Alice Walker talks about her own family. What is her point in telling you about these memories?

> ### Reviewing the Text
>
> **a.** When and where did Alice Walker give this speech? What is the significance of the location?
>
> **b.** According to Walker, why did African Americans once have to leave the South?
>
> **c.** How did Walker first learn about Martin Luther King, Jr.? How did this affect her life?
>
> **d.** According to Walker, what gifts did Martin Luther King, Jr., leave behind? List the things he gave us.

5. Alice Walker says that King was concerned for the "disinherited" of all ethnic backgrounds. What do you think she means by *disinherited*?

6. What is Walker's **main idea**? How does the story she tells support that main idea?

7. What larger meaning do you read into the word *home* in the last sentence?

Connecting with the Text

8. Did anything Walker says here about her family and their dreams remind you of your own family and friends and their hopes for the future?

Extending the Text

9. Although heroism is never easy to define, few Americans would deny that King is an authentic hero. In literature, heroes are often portrayed as deliverers of their people. How does King qualify as a deliverer? What other people in history do you think of as deliverers?

10. Alice Walker tells us what it meant to her to watch Charlayne Hunter and Hamilton Holmes struggle to integrate the University of Georgia in 1961. In the prologue to *In My Place* (page 371), Charlayne Hunter-Gault describes her walk onto the campus of the university—to be greeted by rocks, mobs, and riots. What other people can you think of—people like Hunter-Gault and Holmes—who are heroes even though they did not lead armies or nations?

 CHOICES: Building Your Portfolio

Writer's Notebook

1. Collecting Ideas for an Autobiographical Incident

Cast of characters.  When you write your own autobiographical incident in the Writer's Workshop at the end of this collection (page 386), you may find that the other people involved in the incident are as important as the incident itself. Think back to an event that you will always remember. You probably had a major role, but who else was there? What did each person do or say? What feelings did the person have about the incident? About you? Perhaps it was the actions, words, or feelings of another person that changed you or made the event memorable. Make a list like the one shown here, identifying an autobiographical Incident and the other people involved in it.

Speaking and Listening

2. Telling It Aloud

Read Alice Walker's speech to your class. As you rehearse, decide which words you will emphasize, what tone you will adopt, what gestures you will use. When you are part of the audience for a classmate's presentation, take notes so that you can make helpful suggestions. When the presentations are over, discuss how hearing the speech and delivering it affected the way you feel about it.

Creative Writing

3. A Place Called Home

Walker obviously loves the South, the place she and her family call home. She evokes the blueness of the Georgia sky in autumn and summer, the colors of the southern winter, the green of spring. Write a brief reflection on a place you love: Tell your readers how you came to know this place, what it looks like and sounds like and feels like. Is it a place connected in your mind with people?

Critical Writing

4. Reporting on the Speech

Suppose you were a reporter who went to the restaurant to hear Alice Walker deliver this speech in memory of Martin Luther King. Write a feature story about the occasion. Summarize the main idea of Walker's speech, tell how she supported her idea, and quote any particularly interesting details from the speech. It's possible you might have questions about some of the things Walker says. If so, be sure to include your questions in the report. As a feature writer, you will want to present not only objective facts about the occasion, but your own subjective feelings as well.

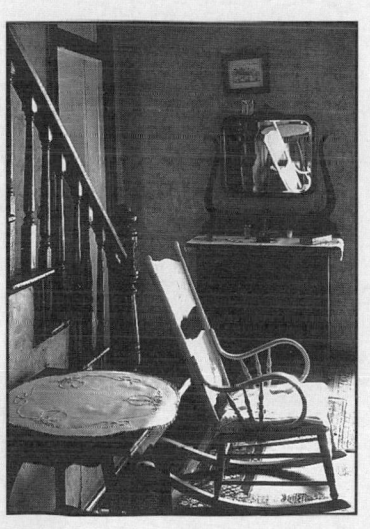

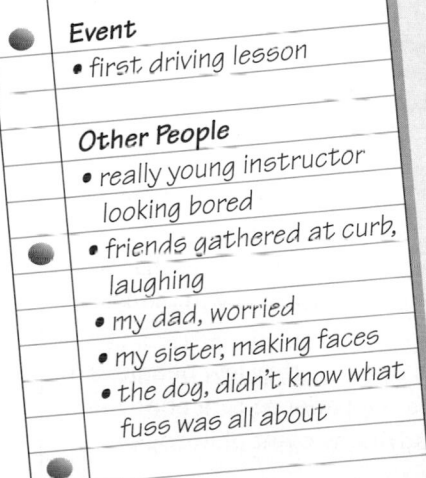

Event
- first driving lesson

Other People
- really young instructor looking bored
- friends gathered at curb, laughing
- my dad, worried
- my sister, making faces
- the dog, didn't know what fuss was all about

CHOICE: A TRIBUTE TO DR. MARTIN LUTHER KING, JR. **373**

LANGUAGE LINK

Handbook of Literary Terms
H E L P

See Connotation.

Style: Emotional Context

Many words affect us in powerful ways. The associations and emotional responses that some words call up are their **connotations**. Those same words also have strict dictionary meanings, which are their **denotations**. Consider the name *New York,* which has a dictionary meaning (a city on the Hudson River) but also a whole range of connotations, from negative (overcrowding and crime) to positive (glamour and excitement).

The following passages from Walker's speech carry strong emotional connotations.

1. "My great-great-great-grandmother walked as a slave from Virginia to Eatonton, Georgia—which passes for the Walker ancestral home—with two babies on her hips."

2. "He was The One, The Hero, The One Fearless Person for whom we had waited."

3. "He gave us back our homeland; the bones and dust of our ancestors, who may now sleep within our caring and our hearing."

4. "He gave us the blueness of the Georgia sky, in autumn as in summer; the colors of the Southern winter as well as glimpses of the green of vacation-time spring."

Try It Out

➤ Look at the sentences opposite. Discuss the feeling or impression that each sentence evokes for you. Find the sentence's key words. Think: Why did Walker choose this precise word or phrase? Try asking other people how these sentences make them feel.

➤ Pull out any of the notes you've taken for an autobiographical incident (for the Work in Progress assignments). Now list at least four strong words or phrases you could use to describe a person, a place, or an episode in any of those incidents.

VOCABULARY   HOW TO OWN A WORD

WORD BANK

dispossession
sensibility
embody
ephemeral

Back to the Text

1. Walker states that the history of her family ". . . is a history of dispossession." How would a victim of dispossession feel?

2. Walker says, "It is a part of the black Southern sensibility that we treasure memories. . . ." What sort of memories do you think are part of this sensibility?

3. Walker explains King's philosophy as one ". . . that few people are capable of understanding fully or have the patience to embody in themselves." If people were to embody nonviolent philosophy, how might their behavior change?

4. Walker says that King ". . . gave us continuity of place, without which community is ephemeral." Do you agree?

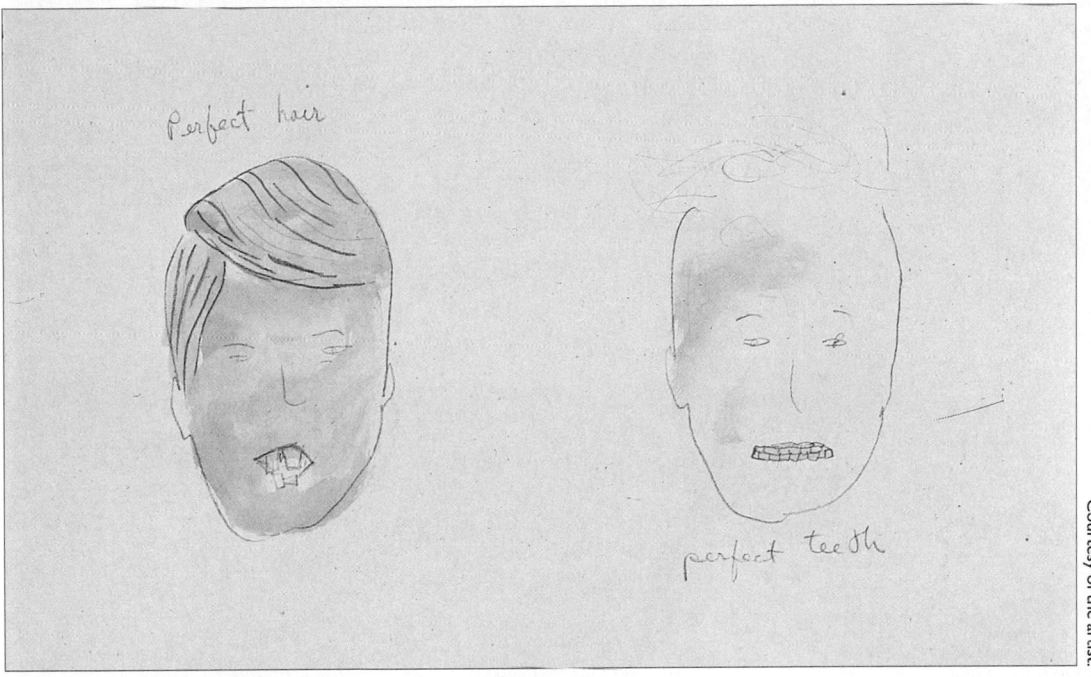

Perfect Hair, Perfect Teeth (1975) by William Wegman. Drawing.

Courtesy of the artist.

Reading Focus

Do People Like Nice Faces?

In the autobiography you are about to read, a twelve-year-old boy who is disgusted with his own looks says, "People like people with nice faces." Is he right? How much emphasis does our society place on appearances?

Quickwrite

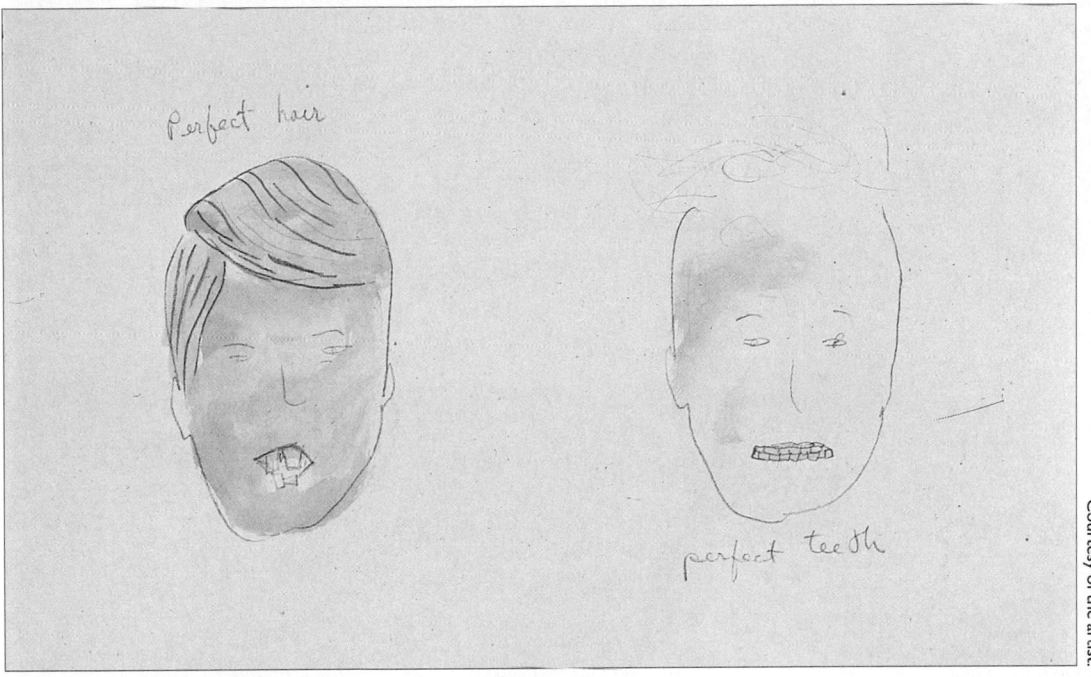

READER'S LOG

Write down some of your own thoughts in your Reader's Log about this boy's statement. Think about how important appearance is

- in the media
- in your own school
- in the workplace
- in your own reactions to people

Elements of Literature

Exaggeration Is a Big Deal

In literature, **exaggeration** is overstating something in order to create some effect: to express a strong emotion, to be funny, to emphasize a point. Exaggeration can bring humor to almost anything. In "The Talk," Soto exaggerates when he describes his eyes as pencil dots and his arms as nearly touching his kneecaps. We know these statements are not true, but they let us know in a forceful way how Soto felt about his looks.

Writers have been amusing (and sometimes irritating) readers by making the most of exaggeration for thousands—make that billions—of years.

> **E**xaggeration means overstating something in a big way—make that "in a *colossal* way."

Washing a Dish (1986) by Candida Alvarez. Acrylic/gel on paper (44 ¼″ x 30 ¾″).

THE TALK

Gary Soto

My best friend and I knew that we were going to grow up to be ugly. On a backyard lawn—the summer light failing west of the mulberry tree where the house of the most beautiful girl on our street stood—we talked about what we could do: shake the second-base dirt from our hair, wash our hands of frog smells and canal water, and learn to smile without showing our crooked teeth. We had to stop spitting when girls were looking and learn not to pile food onto a fork and into a fat cheek already churning hot grub.

We were twelve, with lean bodies that were beginning to grow in weird ways. First, our heads got large, but our necks wavered, frail as crisp tulips. The eyes stayed small as well, receding into pencil dots on each side of an unshapely nose that cast remarkable shadows when we turned sideways. It seemed that Scott's legs sprouted muscle and renegade veins, but his arms, blue with ink markings, stayed short and hung just below his waist. My gangly arms nearly touched my kneecaps. In this way, I was built for picking up grounders and doing cartwheels, my arms swaying just inches from the summery grass.

We sat on the lawn, with the porch light off, waiting for the beautiful girl to turn on her bedroom light and read on her stomach with one leg stirring the air. This stirred us, and our dream was a clean dream of holding hands and airing out our loneliness by walking up and down the block.

When Scott asked whom I was going to marry, I said a brown girl from the valley. He said that he was going to marry a strawberry blonde who would enjoy Millerton Lake, dirty as it was. I said mine would like cats and the sea and would think nothing of getting up at night from a warm, restless bed and sitting in the yard under the icy stars. Scott said his wife would work for the first year or so, because he would go to trade school in refrigeration. Since our town was made with what was left over after God made hell, there was money in air conditioning, he reasoned.

I said that while my wife would clean the house and stir pots of nice grub, I would drive a truck to my job as a carpenter, which would allow me to use my long arms. I would need only a stepladder to hand a fellow worker on the roof a pinch of nails. I could hammer, saw, lift beams into place, and see the work I got done at the end of the day. Of course, she might like to work, and that would be okay, because then we could buy two cars and wave at each other if we should see the other drive by. In the evenings, we would drink Kool-Aid and throw a slipper at our feisty dog at least a hundred times before we went inside for a Pop-Tart and hot chocolate.

Scott said he would work hard too, but now and then he would find money on the street and the two of them could buy extra things like a second TV for the bedroom and a Doughboy swimming pool for his three kids. He planned on having three kids and a ranch house on the river, where he could dip a hand in the water, drink, and say, "Ahh, tastes good."

But that would be years later. Now we had to do something about our looks. We plucked at the grass and flung it into each other's faces.

"Rotten luck," Scott said. "My arms are too short. Look at 'em."

"Maybe we can lift weights. This would make up for our looks," I said.

"I don't think so," Scott said, depressed. "People like people with nice faces."

He was probably right. I turned onto my stomach, a stalk of grass in my mouth. "Even if I'm ugly, my wife's going to be good-looking," I said. "She'll have a lot of dresses and I'll have more shirts than I have now. Do you know how much carpenters make?"

Then I saw the bedroom light come on and the beautiful girl walk into the room drying her hair with a towel. I nudged Scott's short arm and he saw what I saw. We flicked the stalks of grass, stood up, and walked over to the fence to look at her scrub her hair dry. She plopped onto the bed and began to comb it, slowly at first because it was tangled. With a rubber band, she tied it back, and picked up a book that was thick as a good-sized sandwich.

Scott and I watched her read a book, now both legs in the air and twined together, her painted toenails like red petals. She turned the pages slowly, very carefully, and now and then lowered her face into the pillow. She looked sad but beautiful, and we didn't know what to do except nudge each other in the heart and creep away to the front yard.

"I can't stand it anymore. We have to talk about this," Scott said.

"If I try, I think I can make myself better looking," I said. "I read an article about a girl whitening her teeth with water and flour."

So we walked up the street, depressed. For every step I took, Scott took two, his short arms pumping to keep up. For every time Scott said, "I think we're ugly," I said two times, "Yeah, yeah, we're in big trouble."

MEET THE WRITER

A California Boy

Gary Soto (1952–) grew up in a Mexican American family in Fresno, a city in California's San Joaquin Valley. He went to college planning to major in geography. Then a poem—"Unwanted" by Edward Field—changed his life. The poem helped him discover the power of language. He began to see how he could reach other people by writing about his own experience, and that's exactly what he did— and is still doing today. Soto even called his first book, *The Elements of San Joaquin* (1977), after his birthplace. Much of his award-winning fiction and poetry draws on childhood memories, the everyday details of Mexican American life. As Soto puts it:

❝ I tried to remain faithful to the common things of my childhood—dogs, alleys, my baseball mitt, curbs, and the fruit of the valley. . . . I wanted to give these things life. ❞

More Everyday Stories

If you enjoyed "The Talk," take a look at the book it came from: *A Summer Life* (Dell). You might also enjoy Soto's stories in *Baseball in April* (Harcourt Brace) and his collection of poems for young adults, *A Fire in My Hands* (Scholastic).

So Much Better Back Then

I remember Christmas cookies.
Grandma's elf on Christmas Eve,
Innocent hands creating self-proclaimed
Cookie-cutter masterpieces of clumsy dough.
5 Standing guard at the oven's gate,
Slowly succumbing to fugitive smells
Of angels singing, stars glistening, reindeer prancing.
Amazed by Grandma's successful magic,
Producing plates stacked with smiles.
10 I remember Christmas cookies.
They tasted so much better back then.

—Whit Hughes
Jackson Preparatory School
Jackson, Mississippi

The Christmas Tree (late 19th or early 20th century) by Albert Chevallier Tayler.

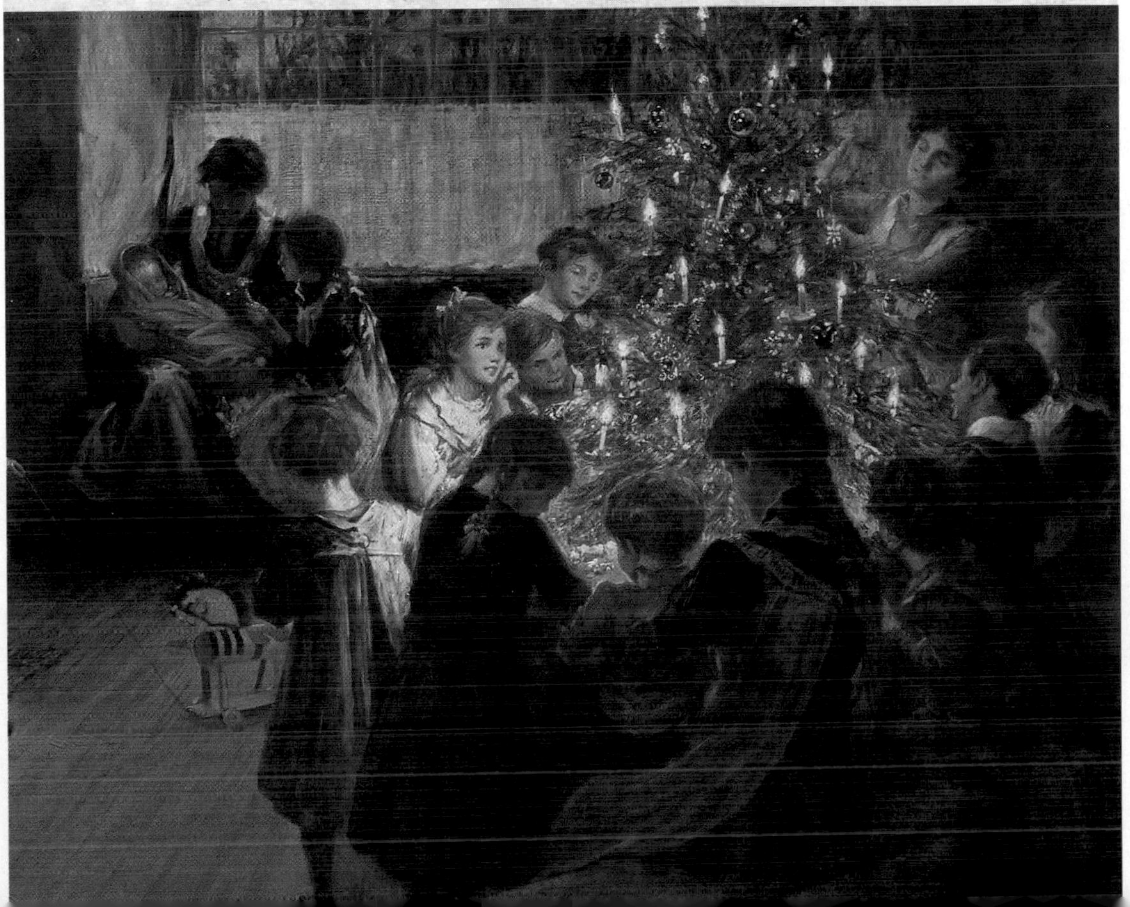

Private Collection.

MAKING MEANINGS

First Thoughts

1. Do any of Soto's characters remind you of yourself—or someone you know? Explain.

Shaping Interpretations

2. Soto uses **exaggeration** to describe himself and his friend Scott. Find two exaggerated statements in the text. What do they tell you about how the boys feel about themselves?

Reviewing the Text

Imagine that in ten years Scott and Gary happen to meet in a restaurant. They reminisce about their talk. With a partner, take the parts of Scott and Gary. Retell what they recall about their talk.

Extending the Text

3. Look over the notes you made in your Reader's Log about the importance of looks in our society. How important *are* good looks? What about other factors—such as good character, honesty, hard work, money? Rate some factors on a scale, with 5 being very important and 0 being not important at all. Be sure to discuss your ratings in class.

| 0 | 1 | 2 | 3 | 4 | 5 |

CHOICES: Building Your Portfolio

Writer's Notebook

1. Collecting Ideas for an Autobiographical Incident

At the tone. You're going to be writing an autobiographical incident like Soto's in the Writer's Workshop on page 386. Do you want to write humorously like Soto or will you try for some other **tone**? You may want to be serious, sad, sarcastic, or something else altogether. List one or more incidents you might write about (you should have some ideas in your notebook already). Tell why they were important to you, and describe the tone you'd aim for if you wrote about them.

Creative Writing

2. Free Advice

With a partner, imagine that the boys from Soto's true story are writing to a newspaper for advice. One of you will write the letter. The other partner will be the columnist and will write a reply.

Drawing

3. Caricatures

Draw caricatures of what you think Gary and Scott look like. Because a caricature exaggerates certain features, you might want to re-read the selection to get ideas. You'll probably find that a cartoon style gives the amusing touch you want. Use a brief passage from the essay as a caption for your caricature.

Analogies

You can reach a better understanding of many words by completing an analogy. An analogy shows the relationship between two pairs of words, stating the relationship in a sentence or expressing the relationship using symbols (: and ::). There are many ways that two things can be related, but the most common types of analogies are shown opposite.

Which word is the logical choice? To complete an analogy, you analyze the relationship between the first pair of words and then choose a word to make a second pair with a similar relationship. Here is how you can decide which word fits in the following analogy:

KIND OF RELATIONSHIP	EXAMPLE
Degree	Pink is to red as lavender is to purple. (pink : red :: lavender : purple)
Size	Puddle is to lake as anthill is to mountain.
Parts and wholes	Branch is to tree as petal is to flower.
Cause and effect	Cold is to shiver as danger is to tremble.
Synonyms	Brave is to courageous as friendly is to amicable.
Antonyms	Brave is to cowardly as friendly is to hostile.

Whacked is to tapped as shoved is to _____.

flicked   nudged   plucked   plopped

1. The relationship between the first pair of words is one of degree. *Whacked* indicates a strong hit, while *tapped* indicates a light one.
2. In the second pair, *shoved* indicates a rough push. Of the word choices, the one that indicates a gentle push is *nudged*.

Sharpening your reasoning skills. When you use analogies as a vocabulary strategy, you are putting your reasoning and logic abilities to work. Give yourself and your classmates a mental workout by creating analogies. Try coming up with analogies for the following words from "The Talk": *renegade, gangly, feisty, grub.*

"One of the main forms of social and recreational activities in which the migrants indulged occurred in the church." Panel 54 from *The Migration Series* by Jacob Lawrence (1940–1941; text and title revised by the artist, 1993). Tempera on gesso on composition board (12″ x 18″, 30.5 cm. x 45.7 cm.).

Background

On Sunday morning, September 15, 1963, in the midst of the struggle for civil rights for African Americans, a bomb exploded in the Sixteenth Street Baptist Church in Birmingham, Alabama. Four little girls were killed.

A Dialogue with the Text

Keep a record of your responses to this ballad and to the historical account of the bombing that appears on page 384. Respond to details in each account and record any questions you'd like to ask about the explosion.

Ballad of Birmingham

(On the bombing of a church in Birmingham, Alabama, 1963)

Dudley Randall

"Mother dear, may I go downtown
Instead of out to play,
And march the streets of Birmingham
In a Freedom March today?"

5   "No, baby, no, you may not go,
For the dogs are fierce and wild,
And clubs and hoses, guns and jails
Aren't good for a little child."

"But, mother, I won't be alone.
10   Other children will go with me,
And march the streets of Birmingham
To make our country free."

"No, baby, no, you may not go,
For I fear those guns will fire.
15   But you may go to church instead
And sing in the children's choir."

She has combed and brushed her
     night-dark hair,
And bathed rose-petal sweet,
And drawn white gloves on her small
     brown hands,
20   And white shoes on her feet.

The mother smiled to know her child
Was in the sacred place,
But that smile was the last smile
To come upon her face

25   For when she heard the explosion,
Her eyes grew wet and wild.
She raced through the streets of Birmingham
Calling for her child.

She clawed through bits of glass and brick,
30   Then lifted out a shoe.
"O, here's the shoe my baby wore,
But, baby, where are you?"

THE STORY BEHIND THE BALLAD

In Parting the Waters, *a book that won the Pulitzer Prize for history in 1989, Taylor Branch writes about the tragedy of the Birmingham bombing:*

That Sunday was the annual Youth Day at the Sixteenth Street Baptist Church. Mamie H. Grier, superintendent of the Sunday school, stopped in at the basement ladies' room to find four young girls who had left Bible classes early and were talking excitedly about the beginning of the school year. All four were dressed in white from head to toe, as this was their day to run the main service for the adults at eleven o'clock. Grier urged them to hurry along and then went upstairs to sit in on her own women's Sunday-school class. They were engaged in a lively debate on the lesson topic, "The Love That Forgives," when a loud earthquake shook the entire church and showered the classroom with plaster and debris. Grier's first thought was that it was like a ticker-tape parade. Maxine McNair, a schoolteacher sitting next to her, reflexively went stiff and was the only one to speak. "Oh, my goodness!" she said. She escaped with Grier, but the stairs down to the basement were blocked and the large stone staircase on the outside literally had vanished. They stumbled through the church to the front door and then made their way around outside through the gathering noise of moans and sirens. A hysterical church member shouted to Grier that her husband had already gone to the hospital in the first ambulance. McNair searched desperately for her only child until finally she came upon a sobbing old man and screamed, "Daddy, I can't find Denise!" The man helplessly replied, "She's dead, baby. I've got one of her shoes." He held a girl's white dress shoe, and the look on his daughter's face made him scream out, "I'd like to blow the whole town up!"

MEET THE WRITER

Poet and Publisher

Dudley Randall (1914–   ) was born in Washington, D.C., and educated at Wayne State University and the University of Michigan. He has lived for many years in Detroit. As publisher of Broadside Press, Randall has been influential in presenting many important works by African American writers, including poets Gwendolyn Brooks and Nikki Giovanni.

FINDING COMMON GROUND

1. Check your Reader's Log and decide on two or three questions you'd like to discuss about the historical extract from *Parting the Waters* and about the ballad.

2. Place your questions on a large sheet of paper and around each question write some possible answers. Even if you don't know the answer exactly, write down what you *think* the answer might be.

3. Share your questions in class. Can you reach a consensus on the key question to be asked about these two selections? Prepare a class map with the key question in the middle and possible answers spinning off from it.

READ ON

A Lost World

Life for young Isaac Bashevis Singer was sometimes treacherous, but as he reveals in *A Day of Pleasure: Stories of a Boy Growing Up in Warsaw* (Farrar, Straus and Giroux), it was also filled with delight. Singer recalls days crowded with fascinating characters—scholars, rabbis, soldiers, panhandlers. Follow him in these autobiographical stories through breezy forests and across filthy gutters, in a world later wiped out forever by the Holocaust.

In Her Mother's Words

Karen was a quiet, well-behaved baby, weighing just under two pounds at birth. She was the delight of family and friends, and when they discovered that she had cerebral palsy, her struggle became their struggle. Karen's mother, Marie Killilea, tells her daughter's story in *Karen* (Dell), sharing special moments in the life of a special child: Karen taking her first shaky steps, Karen writing her first words. This award-winning book has become a classic, touching and inspiring millions of readers.

New York Stories

Mami stands in the kitchen of a New York City tenement, singing about the faraway, sunny island of Puerto Rico. Her singing drifts out the open window onto the streets of the South Bronx, or "El Bronx." In Nicholasa Mohr's *El Bronx Remembered* (Harper-Collins), you'll meet Jasmine the Gypsy girl, Uncle Luis with his roach-killer shoes, and teenage Hannibal and his rambunctious friends.

This Boy's Life

You might already know Roald Dahl's fantasy stories: *James and the Giant Peach,* for starters, or *Charlie and the Chocolate Factory*. Did you ever wonder about the childhood of the writer who created—from scratch—such fantastic worlds? You can read about it in *Boy* (Penguin). Follow Dahl around England, Wales, and Norway, through "sweetshops," magic islands, and public-school days, as he tells of his adventures with all the humor, enchantment, and sometimes even horror, of his fiction.

Writer's Workshop

Technology HELP

See Writer's Workshop 2
CD-ROM. *Assignment:
Autobiographical
Incident.*

ASSIGNMENT

**Write about an
incident from your life
that is vivid to you—
perhaps something
that taught you an
important lesson or
that made you feel
something deeply.**

AIM

**To express yourself; to
inform.**

AUDIENCE

**Your classmates or
younger readers or
readers of a magazine
for teenagers. (You
choose.)**

NARRATIVE WRITING

AUTOBIOGRAPHICAL INCIDENT

If you wrote down everything that ever happened to you, how many books would your autobiography fill? Of course, some events are more memorable than others. "My mother woke me at 6 A.M. and I got ready to go to school" isn't nearly so interesting as "The earthquake hit at 4:36 A.M. and I heard screams as I found myself falling through the air."

Writing that tells about an incident in your life is a special kind of narrative writing called an autobiographical incident.

Prewriting

1. Find a Topic

Narrow your focus to a single incident that happened in a short time—maybe just a few minutes or several hours or a day. Look through your Writer's Notebook for ideas. Or, brainstorm some lists—"Six Memories of Food," "Three Horrible Vacations," "Four School Experiences," "Three Things I Wish I Could Do Again." Write a sentence or two about several incidents and present them to your writing group. Ask for feedback: Which one would they like to read about? Ask yourself which incident gives you most to write about.

2. Jog Your Memory

Once you find a topic, replay the incident in your memory and take notes.

• **Context:** Who was there? How old was I? Where did the incident happen?

• **Sensory details:** What sights, smells, sounds, tastes can I recall?

• **Dialogue/monologue:** Who said what?

• **Events:** Exactly what happened? (List the events in the order they occurred.) What was the most exciting or tense moment?

The history
of the written
word is rich and

Page 1

Once upon a time

- **Significance:** What did I think or feel about the incident at the time? What do I think or feel about it now?

Here is how one writer in this collection uses specific **images** to help us see the people and places in her writing:

> "One summer morning, after I had swept the dirt yard of leaves, spearmint-gum wrappers, and Vienna-sausage labels, I raked the yellow-red dirt and made half-moons carefully, so that the design stood out clearly and masklike. I put the rake behind the Store and came through the back of the house to find Grandmother on the front porch in her big, wide white apron. The apron was so stiff by virtue of the starch that it could have stood alone."

—Maya Angelou, "When I Lay My Burden Down" (page 358)

A quickwrite like the one in the margin at the right, below, can help you discover how you feel about an incident and what the incident means to you.

3. Map Your Story

Like other narratives, an autobiographical incident has **characters,** a series of **related events** usually told in chronological order, and a **setting**.

To plan your story, try using a story map (see page 113).

Drafting

There comes a time when you just have to sit down and start writing. The novelist Louise Erdrich remembers that she wrote only poems at first because she couldn't sit still long enough to write prose. Here is her description of how she wrote her first draft:

> "One raw and rainy Baltimore evening, in an apartment that smelled of wet wool, I hit upon the solution to my problem and tied myself to my chair. A long scarf, knotted at the waist, allowed me to finish the first piece of prose I'd ever done."

—Louise Erdrich, "What My Mother Taught Me: Nests"

Four Incidents I'd Rather Forget

1. the time I almost drowned
2. the worst haircut ever
3. when Pete got hit by a car
4. the fire in our kitchen

Quickwrite

Visiting the homeless shelter with my mother. Sorry for the sad-looking women—especially the children. But I'm glad to get away, leave, go home. Very very very grateful—for my home and family, for the ordinary, everyday calmness of my life. Security, safety. My cozy, warm room—the good smells of the house.

Language Link
H E L P

Comparisons: page 365.
Connotations: page 374.

Use your story map and the details you've collected to finish your first draft at one sitting. Here are the steps in that difficult drafting process:

1. **Set the stage.** Choose a few details—just enough to give the incident a **context**. Let readers know where and when the incident took place and who was there.

2. **Entice the reader.** Try for an opening that catches your reader's interest: perhaps a line of dialogue or a quotation or an interesting detail, or even one dramatic word.

Student Model

DRIVER'S ED?

The accident was reminiscent of a clip straight out of one of Mr. Brooks's supposedly enlightening driver's ed movies— maybe the one I had watched only an hour before.

It was a beautiful day, dry and sunny, not a cloud in the sky. My half-hour driving lesson with my mother thus far matched the weather: It was near perfect. I drove at the speed limit, stopped at all the stop signs, and even landed in the proper lane after a turn. As I pulled onto my driveway, I was really proud of myself. But what started out as the perfect driving lesson ended in a terrible tragedy when I inadvertently pressed down on the accelerator instead of the brake.

The long driveway lay ahead of me. Unfortunately for my sake, it was not as long as it originally seemed to be. That didn't matter because with the help of my mother's 1982 Oldsmobile station wagon, I elongated it, thus decreasing the length of the garage. But that didn't matter; the car had shortened also. In those seemingly endless seconds, the garage door and the corner of my house disappeared.

It was a thunderous crash that brought everyone out as quick as lightning. My little brother, who had witnessed the entire catastrophe from two feet away, just stood in awe. My other brother came running out faster than he does on the soccer field to see what had happened. My sister, as always, took pride in pointing out another one of my major mistakes by screaming about how stupid I was. And unfortunately, my good friend and next-door neighbor had the foresight to be playing ball on his driveway at four that afternoon, such an unlikely occurrence for this nonathletic person. He watched without commenting. My mother just sat in the car, speechless. As for me, I was out of the car in a dash, cradling my head in my hands, uttering the same phrase over and over— "Why me? Why me?"

After what seemed like an eternity, during which time the

Beginning generates interest.

Here is where the incident begins. The stage is set.

There is lots of humor here.

Tells how other people react to the incident.

Focuses on each person, then goes on to the next.

Writer tells his own reaction last.

3. **Tell what happened.** Narrate the events in chronological order, the order in which they happened. If necessary, add a **flashback** to an earlier time to explain something.

4. **Reflect on meaning and feelings.** In your conclusion, tell what the incident means to you, how you feel about it now, and how you felt about it then. Say this as directly and simply as you can.

initial shock had worn off, I swore I would never drive again and then began to get nervous all over, thinking about my father's anticipated arrival within the next half-hour. The only saving grace was that my family was to immediately leave for a holiday dinner at my grandmother's. My father wouldn't have the nerve to start a scene in front of all those people: He would just give me the eye all night. I made sure to sit at an angle, not conducive to good eye contact. Actually, my father surprised me by saying the accident wasn't completely my fault. It was those cloddy sneakers that he's always despised.

I realized later that this tragedy was a blessing in disguise. The thought of my little brother standing between the car and the garage door rather than a few feet off to the side as he was, kept playing over and over in my mind like a scratched record. Until this day, the thought still terrifies me. Driving is not as easy and carefree as the average sixteen-year-old thinks. I am extra cautious now, realizing that there is no margin for error. A car can truly be a lethal weapon.

My road-training class recently scheduled a field trip past my now infamous garage doors with me as their tour guide: "To the right is the Balsam estate, which is undergoing extensive renovation to the front of the house. . . ."

I have since learned that mine was the most common accident of sixteen-year-olds learning to drive. Because of inexperience, they tend to panic in emergency situations, thus pressing the accelerator. I have learned, however, that I must be responsible for my actions. I cannot rationalize my driving mistakes. Fortunately, my accident was a valuable lesson. Cars are not toys and driving is not a game. Furthermore, accidents don't just happen to the other guy. They can hit home.

—Howie Balsam
Half Hollow Hills High School East
Dix Hills, New York

Suspense—how will the father react?

What the incident means to the writer—serious tone here.

A humorous note again.

The conclusion is serious: The writer draws a generalization from the incident.

Evaluating and Revising

Look at your draft carefully. Have you used enough details? Have you used images to describe the setting and people so readers can visualize them? Do your sentences flow smoothly? Read your draft to your writing group and ask for specific suggestions. Or ask two peer editors to read your paper and to write their comments in the margin.

Language Link
H E L P

Punctuation, capitalization, spelling: page 354.

Sentence Workshop
H E L P

Expanding sentences with prepositional phrases: page 392.

Revision Model

	Peer Comments
The accident) reminiscent of) straight out of) ~~It~~ was ~~like~~ a clip ~~from~~ one of Mr. Brooks'ˢ supposedly ~~educational~~ enlightening driver's ed movies—maybe the one I had watched only an hour before. It ¶ beautiful , dry and sunny, not a cloud in the sky. was a ~~nice~~ day. My half-hour driving lesson with my mother ~~was~~ thus far matched ~~as good as~~ the weather: It was near perfect. I drove at the speed limit ~~that was required~~, stopped at all the stop signs, and even landed in the proper ~~right~~ lane after a turn.	*What is "it"? Can you be more specific?* *Say more about the day. Use descriptive words.* *Nice comparison. I like the way you link the lesson and the weather. It's a little wordy. Can you simplify?*

PEANUTS reprinted by permission of UFS, Inc.

Proofreading

Here is a technique used by professional proofreaders. Read through your paper at least twice. Focus first on sentence structure. Look for run-ons and fragments. Next focus on spelling and capitalization. If you used a word processor, remember that the spelling checker can't tell you if you've misused a word (it can't correct *its* when you mean *it's*).

Publishing

Consider writing your memoirs—several autobiographical incidents—and binding them in a folder. Think of them as a time capsule and bury them in a drawer—to be re-read many years from now. Share them first with your family. Do others remember the incidents the same way you do?

Reflecting

If you add your autobiographical incident to your portfolio, date it and reflect on your experience:

1. I had the most trouble _____.

2. The easiest part of writing this was _____.

3. I'm adding this to my portfolio because _____.

4. The next time I write an autobiographical incident, I'll _____.

> Definitely the hardest thing for me was thinking of an incident. Next time I'll try to add dialogue. I'm adding this paper to my portfolio because I don't ever want to forget this incident and how it made me feel.

Sentence Workshop

Language Handbook HELP

See Prepositional Phrases, page 1006.

Technology HELP

See Language Workshop CD-ROM. *Key word entry: prepositional phrases.*

EXPANDING SENTENCES: PREPOSITIONAL PHRASES

A **prepositional phrase** begins with a preposition (a word such as *above, across, behind, between, during, from, in, into, like, of, on, over, to, under, with*) and ends with the object of that preposition. It may also contain words that modify the object of the preposition. Prepositional phrases are usually used the same way as adjectives or adverbs.

An **adjective phrase** is a prepositional phrase that modifies a noun or a pronoun. An adjective phrase tells *what kind* or *which one*.

EXAMPLES   1. "At 7:30 the couple <u>in the next room</u> began to quarrel. . . ." [which one?]

—O. Henry, "Springtime à la Carte"

2. "The morning <u>of June 27th</u> was clear and sunny. . . ." [which one?]

—Shirley Jackson, "The Lottery"

An **adverb phrase** is a prepositional phrase that modifies a verb, an adjective, or an adverb. An adverb phrase tells *how, when, where, why,* or *to what extent* (*how long* or *how far*).

EXAMPLES   1. "Her face was gnarled <u>around a beautiful sharp nose</u>." [where?]

—Louise Erdrich, "Snares"

2. "She had filled the room <u>with magnolia blossoms</u> . . ." [how?]

—Zora Neale Hurston, "Spunk"

Writer's Workshop Follow-up: Revision

Usually you elaborate on your sentences during the revision process. Look at the autobiographical incident you wrote for the Writer's Workshop on page 386. Find at least three sentences that you can expand with further details supplied by prepositional phrases.

Try It Out

Expand these empty sentences by adding prepositional phrases that answer the questions in brackets. Underline the prepositional phrases in your sentences. Be sure to compare your expanded versions in class.

1. The woman waited. [Tell *when* and *where*.]

2. One is missing. [Tell *which one* and *from where*.]

3. Some cheered. [Tell *who* and *how*.]

4. The driver stopped. [Tell *who, how, where,* and *when*.]

5. The couple began to move. [Tell *which one, where,* and *how*.]

Home is where one starts from.

—*T. S. Eliot*

M uch of life seems to be a search for some small place in the world where we fit and feel safe, where we can be comfortably ourselves. When we are young, we need a private place where we can nurse our wounds and dream about the future; and when we are older and the future has come, we want a home of our own, a place that we can shape to fit ourselves. That home we search for is more than just a place to live. It's also a place among people who provide us with friendship and love, and a place in the working world that lets us accomplish something satisfying.

Writer's Notebook

In your Writer's Notebook, freewrite your responses to the quotation from T. S. Eliot above. What do you hope to find in a place called home? How would you express your own idea of what home is? Save your notes for possible use in the Writer's Workshop on page 438.

Reading Focus

Somewhere Else

The essay you are about to read begins, "I think my idea of heaven when I was a kid was Christy Sanders's home." A quick prediction might lead you to realize that this essay was written by someone who, at least at that time in her life, longed to live somewhere else.

Quickwrite

Write down and complete this statement. Add reasons for your choice. (Your answer might be "where I live right now.")

If I could live anywhere in the world it would be . . .

Elements of Literature

Objective and Subjective Writing

A nonfiction writer can write objectively or subjectively. In **subjective writing,** writers reveal their feelings, judgments, and even biases. We look for subjective writing in personal essays and autobiographies and in the editorial pages of a newspaper, where writers express opinions about news events. In **objective writing,** writers report just the facts; they reveal no personal emotions, opinions, or judgments. We expect objectivity when we read news reports, encyclopedia articles, and history.

> **S**ubjective writing reveals the writer's feelings, opinions, or biases. **Objective writing** focuses on facts and contains no expression of personal feelings or opinions.

The Best Gift of My Life

from **But I'll Be Back Again**

Cynthia Rylant

I think my idea of heaven when I was a kid was Christy Sanders's home. She lived in a new brick house with carpeting in it and a bar in the kitchen you could eat on and a picture window in the living room. Her dad wore suits and her mother was queen of the PTA. Christy's house always smelled like those chocolate-covered marshmallow cookies you can get at the grocery. Everything in it was new and it matched and it worked.

In the apartment my mother and I shared, there were old gas heaters you had to light with a match and which threatened to blow you up every time you did. We didn't have carpet. We had old green-and-brown linoleum with cigarette burns in it. Every morning, there would be at least one spider in the bathtub, and it would take every ounce of nerve I had to look in and check. Once, a really big spider crawled out from under our old couch and I was too scared to step on him; instead I dropped a Sears catalog on his head and left it there

I was ashamed of where I lived.

for a week, just to make sure he was dead.

If you looked out our front window, you would have seen Todd's warehouse and junkyard. It was a long metal building enclosed by a high chain-link fence, and on the outside were rusting barrels and parts of bulldozers and all manner of rotten equipment. There was some talk that the ghost of Mr. Todd's old father walked around that warehouse at night, but I was too worried about spiders in my bathtub to give it much thought.

Wanting Christy Sanders's brick house was just a symptom of the overall desire I had for better things. I read a lot of magazines, and I wanted to live in houses with yellow drapes and backyard pools. I was ashamed of where I lived and felt the world would judge me unworthy because of it. I wouldn't even go to the library in the nearby city because I felt so unequal to city kids. Consequently, I lived on comic books for most of my childhood, until I moved into drugstore paperback romances as a teenager.

As long as I stayed in Beaver, I felt I was somebody important. I felt smart and pretty and fun. But as soon as I left town to go anywhere else, my sense of being somebody special evaporated into nothing, and I became dull and ugly and poor. This feeling would stick with me for years, and when I went away to college and met students who had grown up in big Northern cities and could breeze through the world talking like they owned it, I realized that no matter how much I studied or how many college degrees I got, there was one thing I might never fully learn: I might never fully learn that it would be all right for me to have a house that smelled like chocolate-covered marshmallow cookies.

One year, the New Orleans Symphony Orchestra came to play in our junior high school gymnasium. What that orchestra was doing in my little town I cannot imagine, for surely they were all fresh out of London and New York and Los Angeles and didn't need any extra publicity in Beaver, West Virginia.

But the visit of that orchestra was something I have never forgotten. I was not familiar with any real sort of culture. No one I knew played classical records. I had never been to a museum of any kind. In fact, it would not be until I went to college in Charleston, West Virginia, that I set foot in a library or art museum.

The New Orleans Symphony was for me like a visit from God himself, so full of awe and humility was I. We sat on the hard bleachers our bottoms usually warmed for junior varsity games, and we watched these elegant people who seemed long and fluid, like birds, play their marvelous instruments. Their music bounced off the blue-and-gold picture of our school tiger on the wall and the time clock and the heavy velvet curtains we used for school plays, and the gym was transformed into a place of wonder for me.

The conductor was a slender, serious man with a large nose and a lot of dark hair swept back from his forehead. I watched him and I wanted to live in his pink house in New Orleans, surrounded by maids carrying iced tea and peanuts, sleeping each night in a white canopy bed, greeting at the door of our home such notable musicians as Elvis Presley, Paul McCartney, and The Monkees.

Watching the conductor and his beautiful orchestra, I felt something in me that wanted more than I had. Wanted to walk among musicians and artists and writers. Wanted a life beyond Saturdays at G. C. Murphy's department store and Sundays with the Baptist Youth Fellowship.

I wanted to be someone else, and that turned out to be the worst curse and the best gift of my life. I would finish out my childhood forgetting who I really was and what I really thought, and I would listen to other people and repeat their ideas instead of finding my own. That was the curse. The gift was that I would be willing to try to write books when I grew up.

MEET THE WRITER

"Nothing to Write About"

66 I didn't know I was a writer. I always felt inferior to friends who wrote poetry and short stories. Always felt my life had been too limited. Nothing to write about. 99

In her early twenties, **Cynthia Rylant** (1954–   ) started writing about all the things she once thought were nothing to write about. She wrote about growing up in Beaver, West Virginia, and called her memoirs *When I Was Young in the Mountains* (1982). She has this to say about her hometown:

66 In Beaver I lived in a three-room apartment with my mother, who was a nurse. The boy next door and I became quick friends. We knocked on the walls with certain codes, we played Beatles records in our shared basement, and I had popcorn and drank Kool-Aid with his family on Friday nights while we watched their black-and-white TV. Beaver was full of kids and I knew them all. . . . Beaver was without a doubt a small, sparkling universe that gave me a lifetime's worth of material for my writing. 99

More by Rylant

Rylant talks about her characters as if they're real. "I think Ellie in *A Blue-Eyed Daisy* is wonderful. I enjoy her a lot, admire her. She doesn't know, though, that she is admirable." And of Pete, the fourteen-year-old narrator in *A Fine White Dust*, Rylant says, "I worry about him. I see a lot of beauty in him and I hope he doesn't change too much."

My Room

I would be willing to sacrifice every other room in the house, if necessary, to salvage my bedroom. My room is a reflection of me. As I grow, my room does too. As I expand, so does my room. When I was little, it was a place of secret kingdoms, faraway lands, and toys. As I grew older, my room became a safe haven where I could escape. I used to sit on my bed with the comforting voice of a friend on the phone. In my room, I ruled. I had a place in this world that was wholly mine. It felt good to know that I would always have a place to which I could escape.

As I got older, so did my room. The toys were put up in the attic, and I got adult furniture. Some of my childhood memories left with the old furniture, but I was glad to have new furniture with which to make new memories.

Now my room has shed its teenage appearance. There are no longer posters on the wall or mismatched furniture. There are no "I love so-and-so's" scrawled on the bedpost or stickers on the side of the dresser. There is matching furniture and a large, simple bed.

Looking into my room, one sees a reflection of me. On the surface it is simple; but on the floor, the bed, the dresser, the entertainment center, and the rocking chair are bits and pieces of my life. They are beautiful things strewn about hopelessly. But that is exactly what I am. A simple person on the outside with beautiful things scattered about within myself, just waiting to be discovered.

—Brooke Olson
Alief-Hastings High School
Houston, Texas

MAKING MEANINGS

First Thoughts

1. Jot down some phrases that describe your impression of the narrator of "The Best Gift of My Life."

Shaping Interpretations

2. In this very **subjective** excerpt from her autobiography, Rylant is not afraid to let her feelings show. Find some passages that reveal personal details no one else could know.

3. Rylant tells a story to show us how she came to be a writer. Why was the concert a peak experience for her?

4. Describe Rylant's feelings about herself when she was a teenager. What did those feelings prevent her from doing?

5. Express Rylant's **main idea** (or ideas, if you think she makes more than one main point) in your own words. How close did you come to predicting what Rylant's best gift was?

Connecting with the Text

6. What advice would you give to a young person who is not happy with where he or she lives, or who wishes to be someone else?

Reviewing the Text

Suppose you have to summarize this excerpt for a classmate who's been home sick for a week. In three or four sentences, explain what Rylant's problem was and what the best gift was.

CHOICES: Building Your Portfolio

Writer's Notebook

1. Collecting Ideas for a Reflective Essay

What to write about. In the Writer's Workshop on page 438, you'll write a **reflective essay** about your thoughts (reflections) on a specific subject. The subject can be just about anything—a personal experience you'd like to share, a place you love to visit, a news story, a passage from a book. Brainstorm a list of subjects and circle the ones you'd most like to explore. (Rylant's story and your Quickwrite jottings might give you ideas.) Save your notes.

Creative Writing

2. Describing a Place

Rylant tells about the people, the buildings, the objects, and even the bugs and smells she remembers. Describe a place that you love, real or imagined. It might be your room, your home, the town or city you live in, or a secret hiding spot. Help your readers see, smell, hear, maybe even taste and touch the place you're describing. Find a visual means to show your special place. Before you write, decide if you will be mostly subjective, mostly objective, or a combination of both. The essay "My Room" on page 397 might give you some ideas.

Elements of Literature

ESSAYS: Thoughts About a Subject *by* Janet Burroway

Over four hundred years ago, a French lawyer named Michel de Montaigne got tired of his practice, sold it, and retired to his country estate. To amuse himself there, he began to write short prose pieces about various topics that came into his mind—cannibals, smells, names, sleeping, friendship, prayers. Probably he had no intention of publishing these pieces at first, but eventually he published three volumes of what he called his *Essais*. Today, only historians are interested in the fact that Montaigne was at the court of King Charles IX and was mayor of Bordeaux, but his *Essais* are translated, read, and studied in every language of the Western world.

Essais means "tries" or "attempts" in French, and the name too has lasted. *Essays* or *tries* is a good way to describe these short pieces of nonfiction prose, since no essay will ever say everything there is to say about any subject.

> He began to write about various topics that came into his mind—cannibals, smells, names, sleeping, friendship, prayers.

There are as many ways of looking at and writing about cannibals, smells, names, and so forth, as there are people to write about them. Montaigne himself understood that a personal essay presents not only its subject but also its writer's personality. He said about his essays, "I have here only made a small bouquet of flowers and have brought nothing of my own but the thread that ties them together."

The essays in this collection were written many centuries after Montaigne wrote his *Essais,* but each one still reflects a writer's "attempt" or "try" to talk about a subject with the reader. In "Riding Is an Exercise of the Mind," N. Scott Momaday talks about the best home of his childhood. In "The Round Walls of Home," Diane Ackerman writes about the planet we all share. Like Montaigne's essays, these are conversational in style and personal in tone and feeling. In all of them, we hear the voice of one particular writer responding in a personal way to some experience that is part of the real world we live in.

Drawing by W. Miller; © 1937 The New Yorker Magazine, Inc.

BEFORE YOU READ
RIDING IS AN EXERCISE OF THE MIND

Reading Focus

Surrounded by the Landscape

What's the landscape like where you live? Are there hills or mountains, or is the land basically flat? Do you see buildings and roads or a lot of wide-open space? What kinds of trees and flowers grow? For N. Scott Momaday, remembering "the last, best home" of his childhood is an occasion to reflect on how powerfully its landscape colored his daydreams.

Quickwrite

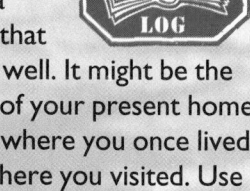

Describe a landscape that you know well. It might be the landscape of your present home or a place where you once lived or somewhere you visited. Use details to describe what you see, smell, and hear when you imagine that place.

Elements of Literature

Sensory Images

Sensory images add color and life to description, helping readers see, hear, smell, taste, and touch what the writer is describing. Momaday's descriptions show us the caravan of Navajo riders and let us hear their songs; we smell pine and cedar smoke and see the "angles of geese" above Jemez (hā′mās) Pueblo. As you read this essay, let the descriptive paragraphs dense with imagery work on your imagination.

> **S**ensory details are images that appeal to our senses of sight, taste, smell, hearing, and touch.
>
> *For more on Description, see the Handbook of Literary Terms.*

Background

When N. (Novarro) Scott Momaday was born in the Kiowa and Comanche Indian Hospital in Lawton, Oklahoma, his birth certificate described him as "7/8th degree Indian blood." Momaday grew up on Kiowa and Navajo reservations in the Southwest, equally fluent in the English, Kiowa, and Navajo languages. In September 1946, Momaday's parents began teaching at the two-room Navajo school at Jemez Pueblo, in the canyon country in the foothills of the Jemez Mountains, fifty miles from Albuquerque, New Mexico.

RIDING
Is an Exercise of the Mind

I had found
the best home
of my childhood.

N. Scott Momaday

One autumn morning in 1946 I woke up at Jemez Pueblo.[1] I had arrived there in the middle of the night and gone to sleep. I had no idea of the landscape, no sense of where in the world I was. Now, in the bright New Mexican morning, I began to look around and settle in. I had found the last, best home of my childhood.

1. In the Southwestern United States, pueblos are American Indian communities of flat-roofed, terraced houses made from stone or sun-dried brick.

When my parents and I moved to Jemez, I was twelve years old. The world was a different place then, and Jemez was the most exotic corner within it. The village and the valley, the canyons and the mountains, had been there from the beginning of time, waiting for me. So it seemed. Marco Polo in the court of Kublai Khan[2] had nothing on me. I was embarked upon the greatest adventure of all; I had come to the place of my growing up.

The landscape was full of mystery and of life. The autumn was in full bloom. The sun cast a golden light upon the adobe walls and the cornfields; it set fire to the leaves of willows and cottonwoods along the river; and a fresh, cold wind ran down from the canyons and carried the good scents of pine and cedar smoke, of bread baking in the beehive ovens, and of rain in the mountains. There were horses in the plain and angles of geese in the sky.

One November, on the feast of San Diego, Jemez took on all the color of a Renaissance fair. I lived on the southwest corner of the village, on the wagon road to San Ysidro.[3] I looked southward into the plain; there a caravan of covered wagons reached as far as the eye could see. These were the Navajos, coming in from Torreon. I had never seen such a pageant; it was as if that whole proud people, the Diné,[4] had been concentrated into one endless migration. There was a great dignity to them, even in revelry. They sat tall in the wagons and on horseback, going easily with laughter and singing their riding songs. And when they set up camp in the streets, they were perfectly at home, their dogs about them. They made coffee and fried bread and roasted mutton on their open fires.

Gradually and without effort I entered into the motion of life there. In the winter dusk I heard coyotes barking away by the river, the sound of the drums in the kiva,[5] and the voice of the village crier, ringing at the rooftops.

And on summer nights of the full moon I saw old men in their ceremonial garb, running after witches—and sometimes I saw the witches themselves in the forms of bats and cats and owls on fence posts.

I came to know the land by going out upon it in all seasons, getting into it until it became the very element in which I lived my daily life.

I had a horse named Pecos, a fleet-footed roan gelding, which was my great glory for a time. Pecos could outrun all the other horses in the village, and he wanted always to prove it. We two came to a good understanding of each other, I believe. I did a lot of riding in those days, and I got to be very good at it. My Kiowa ancestors, who were centaurs,[6] should have been proud of me.

Riding is an exercise of the mind. I dreamed a good deal on the back of my horse, going out into the hills alone. Desperadoes were everywhere in the brush. More than once I came upon roving bands of hostile Indians and had, on the spur of the moment, to put down an uprising. Now and then I found a wagon train in trouble, and always among the settlers there was a lovely young girl from Charleston or Philadelphia who needed simply and more than anything else in the world to be saved. I saved her.

After a time Billy the Kid was with me on most of those adventures. He rode on my right

---

2. **Marco Polo in the court of Kublai Khan** (ko͞o′blī kän): Marco Polo (1254–1324) was one of the first Europeans to visit China, where he served as a government official during the rule of the emperor Kublai Khan.
3. **San Ysidro** (san ē·sēd′rō).
4. **Diné** (də·nā′): the Navajos' name for themselves, meaning "the people."

5. **kiva** (kē′və): underground room in a pueblo, used for ceremonies and other purposes.
6. **centaurs** (sen′tôrz′): creatures from Greek mythology that are half man and half horse. The Kiowa were great horsemen.

WORDS TO OWN

exotic (eg·zät′ik) *adj.*: fascinating; strangely beautiful. *Exotic* also means "foreign."
revelry (rev′əl·rē) *n.*: noisy, lively celebration.

---

side and a couple of steps behind. I watched him out of the corner of my eye, for he bore watching. We got on well together in the main, and he was a good man to have along in a fight. We had to be careful of glory-seeking punks. Incredibly, there were those in the world who were foolish enough to oppose us, merely for the sake of gaining a certain reputation.

When it came time for me to leave home and venture out into the wider world, I sold my horse to an old gentleman at Vallecitos. I like to think that Pecos went on with our games long afterward, that in his old age he listened for the sound of bugles and of gunfire—and for the pitiful weeping of young ladies in distress—and that he heard them as surely as I do now.

MEET THE WRITER

Rock-Tree Boy

When **N. Scott Momaday** (1934–   ) was six months old, his parents took him to a sacred place—Devils Tower in Wyoming, which the Kiowa people call Tsoai (Rock Tree). There an old storyteller gave Momaday the name Tsoai-talee, which means "Rock-Tree Boy." (If you saw the movie *Close Encounters of the Third Kind,* you know what Devils Tower looks like: a steep-sided volcanic rock tower 865 feet high.)

Momaday says that schooling was a problem at Jemez because there were no high schools nearby. He recalls his mother's influence:

66 My mother has been the inspiration of many people . . . certainly she was mine at Jemez, when inspiration was the nourishment I needed most. I was at that age in which a boy flounders. I had not much sense of where I must go or of what I must do and be in my life, and there were for me moments of great, growing urgency, in which I felt that I was imprisoned in the narrow quarters of my time and place. I wanted, needed, to conceive of what my destiny might be, and my mother allowed me to believe that it might be worthwhile. 99

Momaday received his B.A. from New Mexico State University and his Ph.D. in creative writing from Stanford University. While teaching at several universities, he has created novels, memoirs, poems, and paintings that draw upon his American Indian heritage. *House Made of Dawn* (1968), his first novel, won the Pulitzer Prize for fiction. His memoir *The Way to Rainy Mountain* (1969) combines Kiowa legend, history, personal memories, and poetry.

MAKING MEANINGS

First Thoughts

1. How would you feel about growing up in a place like Jemez Pueblo?

Shaping Interpretations

2. What **sensory details** help you see, smell, and feel the landscape Momaday loves?

3. Find where the **title** is mentioned in the essay. What do you think the title means? What other titles would you suggest for this essay?

4. Skim the essay again. What word or passage do you think is the most important? Why do you think so?

Challenging the Text

5. Someone complains: "Momaday writes about imaginary events and real ones mixed up together." How would you respond?

Reviewing the Text

a. In the first three paragraphs, what facts do we learn about Jemez Pueblo?

b. Who was Pecos and why was he important?

c. Why would Momaday's ancestors have been proud of him?

d. Which paragraphs describe imagined events?

CHOICES: Building Your Portfolio

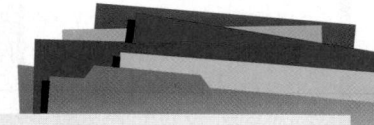

Writer's Notebook

1. Collecting Ideas for a Reflective Essay

Concrete description.  In the reflective essay you'll write for the Writer's Workshop on page 438, you might describe something that happened to you or something you've observed in nature. If you do, you'll want to use sensory details to create images in your reader's mind. Notice how Momaday shows us the Navajos sitting tall in their wagons and helps us smell coffee and fried bread and hear the sounds of laughter and singing. What incident or observation would give you a starting-off place for your reflective essay? Collect your sensory details in a chart. Your Quickwrite notes might give you a start.

Creative Writing

2. Your Name

What does *your* first name mean, and why was it chosen for you? If you don't already know, find out. Write a brief essay about your name and how you feel about it. (See the details about Momaday's name in Meet the Writer on page 403.)

Research/Oral History

3. Who We Are

Interview relatives or family friends or neighbors, starting with the oldest ones. Take notes or tape-record their answers to questions about who your ancestors are or where people in your community came from or how your town was first settled. You could donate your oral histories to your school library, so future students can share your celebrations.

LANGUAGE LINK

Language Handbook HELP

See Tense, page 999.

Technology HELP

See Language Workshop CD-ROM. Key word entry: verb tenses.

Style: Showing Time

Momaday's essay is a journey back in time as well as a journey back to a special place. He uses these devices to capture time in words:

1. **Verb tenses.** The tense of verbs can show past, present, future, and various shades of continuing action. Most of the verbs in this essay are in the past ("I woke up") and past perfect ("I had arrived there") tenses.

2. **Time words and phrases.** When a writer wants to be specific, time can be indicated with words and phrases: "One autumn morning in 1946 . . . ," "Now and then . . . ," "And on summer nights of the full moon. . . ."

3. **Chronological order.** Most writers who use the narrative mode write in chronological order, the order in which events happened, from start to finish. (When such writers want to tell us about something that happened in the past, they use a **flashback**.)

Try It Out

1. Most narratives are told in the past tense, but writers often like to experiment with the present tense. Rewrite one paragraph of Momaday's narrative in the present tense. What parts of the narrative will you have to keep in the past? Does a change of tense change your feeling of participating in the story?

2. Illustrate the events Momaday links with the seasons, by describing them in a seasonal "wheel": Note that Momaday misses a season. What events can you supply from your imagination?

3. Do you wish that Momaday had flashed back to an earlier time to explain anything? What would you like to know?

VOCABULARY   HOW TO OWN A WORD

WORD BANK

exotic
revelry

Word Play

There are only two words in this Word Bank, so take a break and think of some entertaining ways to learn them. Here are two suggestions for starters:

1. You could create two cartoons that use the words *exotic* and *revelry* in captions or in thought bubbles.
2. You might write verses that have words rhyming with *exotic* (*hypnotic? periodic?*) and *revelry* (*celery? bravery?*).

Riddles, raps, puns, puzzles—anything goes. Think of some ways to use these two words just for fun and share your ideas with your classmates.

BEFORE YOU READ
"HAVEN'T I MADE A DIFFERENCE!"

Reading Focus

Who Cares?

Throughout history and in almost all cultures, pets have made people feel happy. Probably more than fifty thousand years ago cave dwellers had dogs as household—"cavehold"—pets. Ancient Egyptians tamed baboons and worshiped cats. Before the first Europeans arrived in Mexico, the Aztecs kept pet parrots. Why do people make animals part of their homes? Is it because pets seem to care about us, or is it because they give us something to care about?

A Dialogue with the Text

Keep a double-entry journal as you read this true story. In one column, write passages or sentences that you find particularly interesting or moving. In the second column, jot down your comments and responses.

Elements of Literature

Nonfiction Narratives

Usually we think of narratives as fiction, but nonfiction writers often tell true stories and anecdotes to make a point. **Nonfiction narratives** are used in news reports, biographies, and histories. The narrative you're about to read tells a lively story that's as entertaining as if it were fiction. The narrator is a veterinarian who uses the pen name James Herriot, and Darrowby is a town in Yorkshire, in northeast England.

> **A** nonfiction narrative tells about a series of related events that actually happened.
>
> *For more on Narration, see the Handbook of Literary Terms.*

I saw in his eyes only a calm trust.

"HAVEN'T I MADE A DIFFERENCE!"

from **All Things Bright and Beautiful**

James Herriot

Old Mrs. Donovan was a woman who really got around. No matter what was going on in Darrowby—weddings, funerals, house sales—you'd find the dumpy little figure and walnut face among the spectators, the darting, black-button eyes taking everything in. And always, on the end of its lead, her terrier dog.

When I say "old," I'm only guessing, because she appeared ageless; she seemed to have been around a long time but she could have been anything between fifty-five and seventy-five. She certainly had the vitality of a young woman because she must have walked vast distances in her dedicated quest to keep abreast of events. Many people took an uncharitable view of her acute curiosity, but whatever the motivation, her activities took her into almost every channel of life in the town. One of these channels was our veterinary practice.

Because Mrs. Donovan, among her other widely ranging interests, was an animal doctor. In fact I think it would be safe to say that this facet of her life transcended all the others.

She could talk at length on the ailments of small animals, and she had a whole armory of medicines and remedies at her command, her two specialties being her miracle-working condition powders and a dog shampoo of unprecedented value for improving the coat. She had an <u>uncanny</u> ability to sniff out a sick animal, and it was not uncommon when I was on my rounds to find Mrs. Donovan's dark Gypsy face poised intently over what I had thought was my patient while she administered calf's-foot jelly or one of her own patent nostrums.[1]

I suffered more than Siegfried[2] because I took a more active part in the small-animal side of our practice. I was anxious to develop this aspect and to improve my image in this field and Mrs. Donovan didn't help at all. "Young Mr. Herriot," she would confide to my clients, "is all right with cattle and suchlike, but he don't know nothing about dogs and cats."

And of course they believed her and had <u>implicit</u> faith in her. She had the irresistible mystic appeal of the amateur and on top of that there was her habit, particularly endearing in Darrowby, of never charging for her advice, her medicines, her long periods of <u>diligent</u> nursing.

Older folk in the town told how her husband, an Irish farm worker, had died many years ago and how he must have had a "bit put away" because Mrs. Donovan had apparently been able to indulge all her interests over the years without financial strain. Since she inhabited the streets of Darrowby all day and every day, I often encountered her and she always smiled up at me sweetly and told me how she had been sitting up all night with Mrs. So-and-so's dog that I'd been treating. She felt sure she'd be able to pull it through.

There was no smile on her face, however, on the day when she rushed into the surgery[3] while Siegfried and I were having tea.

"Mr. Herriot!" she gasped. "Can you come? My little dog's been run over!"

I jumped up and ran out to the car with her. She sat in the passenger seat with her head bowed, her hands clasped tightly on her knees.

"He slipped his collar and ran in front of a car," she murmured. "He's lying in front of the school halfway up Cliffend Road. Please hurry."

I was there within three minutes but as I bent over the dusty little body stretched on the pavement, I knew there was nothing I could do. The fast-glazing eyes, the faint, gasping respirations, the ghastly pallor of the mucous membranes[4] all told the same story.

"I'll take him back to the surgery and get some saline[5] into him, Mrs. Donovan," I said. "But I'm afraid he's had a massive internal hemorrhage.[6] Did you see what happened exactly?"

She gulped. "Yes, the wheel went right over him."

Ruptured liver, for sure. I passed my hands under the little animal and began to lift him gently, but as I did so the breathing stopped and the eyes stared fixedly ahead.

Mrs. Donovan sank to her knees and for a few moments she gently stroked the rough hair of the head and chest. "He's dead, isn't he?" she whispered at last.

"I'm afraid he is," I said.

She got slowly to her feet and stood bewilderedly among the little group of bystanders on the pavement. Her lips moved but she seemed unable to say any more.

---

3. **surgery:** British term for "doctor's office."
4. **pallor of the mucous membranes:** unnatural paleness of the tissue lining body cavities that connect with outside air, such as those in the nose.
5. **saline** (sā′līn): salt solution used in medical treatment.
6. **hemorrhage** (hem′ər·ij′): heavy bleeding.

- -

WORDS TO OWN

uncanny (un·kan′ē) *adj.:* eerily remarkable.
implicit (im·plis′it) *adj.:* absolute; unquestioning.
   Implicit is also used to describe something that is
   implied or suggested but not expressed in words.
diligent (dil′ə·jənt) *adj.:* careful and hard-working.

- -

---

1. **patent nostrums** (pat′′nt näs′trəmz): trademarked medicines of doubtful effectiveness that can be bought without a doctor's prescription.
2. Siegfried and Herriot are partners in the veterinary practice.

I took her arm, led her over to the car, and opened the door. "Get in and sit down," I said. "I'll run you home. Leave everything to me."

I wrapped the dog in my calving overall and laid him in the boot[7] before driving away. It wasn't until we drew up outside Mrs. Donovan's house that she began to weep silently. I sat there without speaking till she had finished. Then she wiped her eyes and turned to me.

"Do you think he suffered at all?"

"I'm certain he didn't. It was all so quick—he wouldn't know a thing about it."

She tried to smile. "Poor little Rex. I don't know what I'm going to do without him. We've traveled a few miles together, you know."

"Yes, you have. He had a wonderful life, Mrs. Donovan. And let me give you a bit of advice—you must get another dog. You'd be lost without one."

She shook her head. "No, I couldn't. That little dog meant too much to me. I couldn't let another take his place."

"Well, I know that's how you feel just now, but I wish you'd think about it. I don't want to seem callous—I tell everybody this when they lose an animal and I know it's good advice."

"Mr. Herriot, I'll never have another one." She shook her head again, very decisively. "Rex was my faithful friend for many years and I just want to remember him. He's the last dog I'll ever have."

I often saw Mrs. Donovan around the town after this, and I was glad to see she was still as active

as ever, though she looked strangely incomplete without the little dog on its lead. But it must have been over a month before I had the chance to speak to her.

It was on the afternoon that Inspector Halliday of the RSPCA[8] rang me.

"Mr. Herriot," he said, "I'd like you to come and see an animal with me. A cruelty case."

"Right, what is it?"

"A dog, and it's pretty grim. A dreadful case of neglect." He gave me the name of a row of old brick cottages down by the river and said he'd meet me there.

Halliday was waiting for me, smart and businesslike in his dark uniform, as I pulled up in the back lane behind the houses. He was a big blond man with cheerful blue eyes, but he didn't smile as he came over to the car.

"He's in here," he said, and led the way toward one of the doors in the long, crumbling wall. A few curious people were hanging around and with a feeling of inevitability I recognized a gnomelike brown face. Trust Mrs. Donovan, I thought, to be among those present at a time like this.

We went through the door into the long garden. I had found that even the lowliest dwellings in Darrowby had long strips of land at

8. **RSPCA:** Royal Society for the Prevention of Cruelty to Animals.

7. **boot:** British term for "trunk of a car."

WORDS TO OWN

callous (kal′əs) *adj.:* unfeeling; insensitive.

the back, as though the builders had taken it for granted that the country people who were going to live in them would want to occupy themselves with the pursuits of the soil; with vegetable and fruit growing, even stock keeping[9] in a small way. You usually found a pig there, a few hens, often pretty beds of flowers.

But this garden was a wilderness. A chilling air of desolation hung over the few gnarled apple and plum trees standing among a tangle of rank grass, as though the place had been forsaken by all living creatures.

Halliday went over to a ramshackle wooden shed with peeling paint and a rusted corrugated-iron roof. He produced a key, unlocked the padlock, and dragged the door partly open.

9. **stock keeping:** raising farm animals.

There was no window and it wasn't easy to identify the jumble inside: broken gardening tools, an ancient mangle, rows of flowerpots, and partly used paint tins. And right at the back, a dog sitting quietly.

I didn't notice him immediately because of the gloom and because the smell in the shed started me coughing, but as I drew closer I saw that he was a big animal, sitting very upright, his collar secured by a chain to a ring in the wall. I had seen some thin dogs but this advanced emaciation[10] reminded me of my textbooks on anatomy; nowhere else did the bones of pelvis,

10. **emaciation** (ē·mā′shē·ā′shən): extreme, abnormal thinness.

Words to Own
desolation (des′ə·lā′shən) *n.*: loneliness; ruin.

face, and rib cage stand out with such horrifying clarity. A deep, smoothed-out hollow in the earth floor showed where he had lain, moved about, in fact lived for a very long time.

The sight of the animal had a <u>stupefying</u> effect on me; I only half took in the rest of the scene—the filthy shreds of sacking scattered nearby, the bowl of scummy water.

"Look at his back end," Halliday muttered.

I carefully raised the dog from his sitting position and realized that the stench in the place was not entirely due to the piles of excrement. The hindquarters were a welter of pressure sores which had turned gangrenous[11] and strips of sloughing tissue[12] hung down from them.

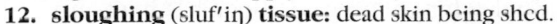

11. **gangrenous** (gaŋ′grə·nəs): decayed because of blockage of the blood supply caused by disease or injury.
12. **sloughing** (sluf′iŋ) **tissue:** dead skin being shed.

There were similar sores along the sternum[13] and ribs. The coat, which seemed to be a dull yellow, was matted and caked with dirt.

The inspector spoke again. "I don't think he's ever been out of here. He's only a young dog—about a year old—but I understand he's been in this shed since he was an eight-week-old pup. Somebody out in the lane heard a whimper or he'd never have been found."

I felt a tightening of the throat and a sudden nausea which wasn't due to the smell. It was the thought of this patient animal sitting starved and forgotten in the darkness and filth for a year. I looked again at the dog and saw in his eyes only a calm trust. Some dogs would have barked their heads off and soon been discovered, some would have become terrified and vicious, but this was one of the totally undemanding kind, the kind which had complete faith in people and accepted all their actions without complaint. Just an occasional whimper perhaps as he sat <u>interminably</u> in the empty blackness which had been his world and at times wondered what it was all about.

"Well, Inspector, I hope you're going to throw the book at whoever's responsible," I said.

Halliday grunted. "Oh, there won't be much done. It's a case of diminished responsibility. The owner's definitely simple. Lives with an aged mother who hardly knows what's going on either. I've seen the fellow and it seems he threw in a bit of food when he felt like it and that's about all he did. They'll fine him and stop him keeping an animal in the future but nothing more than that."

"I see." I reached out and stroked the dog's head and he immediately responded by resting a paw on my wrist. There was a pathetic dignity about the way he held himself erect, the calm eyes regarding me, friendly and unafraid. "Well, you'll let me know if you want me in court."

13. **sternum** (stʉr′nəm): breastbone.

WORDS TO OWN

stupefying (stoo′pə·fi′iŋ) v. used as *adj*.: paralyzing; numbing.
interminably (in·tʉr′mi·nə·blē) *adv*.: endlessly.

"Of course, and thank you for coming along." Halliday hesitated for a moment. "And now I expect you'll want to put this poor thing out of his misery right away."

I continued to run my hand over the head and ears while I thought for a moment. "Yes . . . yes, I suppose so. We'd never find a home for him in this state. It's the kindest thing to do. Anyway, push the door wide open, will you, so that I can get a proper look at him."

In the improved light I examined him more thoroughly. Perfect teeth, well-proportioned limbs with a fringe of yellow hair. I put my stethoscope on his chest and as I listened to the slow, strong thudding of the heart, the dog again put his paw on my hand.

I turned to Halliday. "You know, Inspector, inside this bag of bones there's a lovely, healthy golden retriever. I wish there was some way of letting him out."

As I spoke, I noticed there was more than one figure in the door opening. A pair of black pebble eyes were peering intently at the dog from behind the inspector's broad back. The other spectators had remained in the lane, but Mrs. Donovan's curiosity had been too much for her. I continued conversationally as though I hadn't seen her.

"You know, what this dog needs first of all is a good shampoo to clean up his matted coat."

"Huh?" said Halliday.

"Yes. And then he wants a long course of some really strong condition powders."

"What's that?" The inspector looked startled.

"There's no doubt about it," I said. "It's the only hope for him, but where are you going to find such things? Really powerful enough, I mean." I sighed and straightened up. "Ah well, I suppose there's nothing else for it. I'd better put him to sleep right away. I'll get the things from my car."

When I got back to the shed, Mrs. Donovan was already inside examining the dog despite the feeble remonstrances of the big man.

"Look!" she said excitedly, pointing to a name roughly scratched on the collar. "His name's Roy." She smiled up at me. "It's a bit like Rex, isn't it, that name."

"You know, Mrs. Donovan, now you mention it, it is. It's very like Rex, the way it comes off your tongue." I nodded seriously.

She stood silent for a few moments, obviously in the grip of a deep emotion, then she burst out.

"Can I have 'im? I can make him better, I know I can. Please, please let me have 'im!"

"Well I don't know," I said. "It's really up to the inspector. You'll have to get his permission."

Halliday looked at her in bewilderment; then he said, "Excuse me, madam," and drew me to one side. We walked a few yards through the long grass and stopped under a tree.

"Mr. Herriot," he whispered, "I don't know what's going on here, but I can't just pass over an animal in this condition to anybody who has a casual whim. The poor beggar's had one bad break already—I think it's enough. This woman doesn't look a suitable person. . . ."

I held up a hand. "Believe me, Inspector, you've nothing to worry about. She's a funny old stick but she's been sent from heaven today. If anybody in Darrowby can give this dog a new life, it's her."

Halliday still looked very doubtful. "But I still don't get it. What was all that stuff about him needing shampoos and condition powders?"

"Oh, never mind about that. I'll tell you some other time. What he needs is lots of good grub, care, and affection and that's just what he'll get. You can take my word for it."

"All right, you seem very sure." Halliday looked at me for a second or two, then turned and walked over to the eager little figure by the shed.

I had never before been deliberately on the lookout for Mrs. Donovan; she had just cropped up wherever I happened to be, but now I scanned the streets of Darrowby anxiously day by day without sighting her. I didn't like it when Gobber Newhouse got drunk and drove his bicycle determinedly through a barrier into a

WORDS TO OWN
remonstrances (ri·män'strən·siz) *n.*: protests.

ten-foot hole where they were laying the new sewer and Mrs. Donovan was not in evidence among the happy crowd who watched the council workmen and two policemen trying to get him out; and when she was nowhere to be seen when they had to fetch the fire engine to the fish-and-chip shop the night the fat burst into flames, I became seriously worried.

Maybe I should have called round to see how she was getting on with that dog. Certainly I had trimmed off the necrotic[14] tissue and dressed the sores before she took him away, but perhaps he needed something more than that. And yet at the time I had felt a strong conviction that the main thing was to get him out of there and clean him and feed him

and nature would do the rest. And I had a lot of faith in Mrs. Donovan—far more than she had in me—when it came to animal doctoring; it was hard to believe I'd been completely wrong.

It must have been nearly three weeks and I was on the point of calling at her home when I noticed her stumping briskly along the far side of the marketplace, peering closely into every shop window exactly as before. The only difference was that she had a big yellow dog on the end of the lead.

I turned the wheel and sent my car bumping over the cobbles till I was abreast of her. When she saw me getting out, she stopped and smiled impishly but she didn't speak as I bent over Roy and examined him. He was still a skinny dog but

he looked bright and happy, his wounds were healthy and granulating,[15] and there was not a speck of dirt in his coat or on his skin. I knew then what Mrs. Donovan had been doing all this time; she had been washing and combing and teasing at that filthy tangle till she had finally conquered it.

As I straightened up, she seized my wrist in a grip of surprising strength and looked up into my eyes.

"Now Mr. Herriot," she said. "Haven't I made a difference to this dog!"

"You've done wonders, Mrs. Donovan," I said. "And you've been at him with that marvelous shampoo of yours, haven't you?"

She giggled and walked away, and from that day I saw the two of them frequently but at a distance, and something like two months went by before I had a chance to talk to her again. She was passing by the surgery as I was coming down the steps and again she grabbed my wrist.

"Mr. Herriot," she said, just as she had done before. "Haven't I made a difference to this dog!"

I looked down at Roy with something akin to awe. He had grown and filled out and his coat, no longer yellow but a rich gold, lay in luxuriant, shining swaths over the well-fleshed ribs and

14. **necrotic** (ne·krät′ik): dead; decayed.

15. **granulating** (gran′yoo·lāt′iŋ): forming new capillaries, or tiny blood vessels, in the process of healing.

- -

WORDS TO OWN

luxuriant (lug·zhoor′ē·ənt) *adj.*: thick; growing in great abundance.

- -

back. A new brightly studded collar glittered on his neck, and his tail, beautifully fringed, fanned the air gently. He was now a golden retriever in full magnificence. As I stared at him, he reared up, plunked his forepaws on my chest, and looked into my face, and in his eyes I read plainly the same calm affection and trust I had seen back in that black, noisome[16] shed.

"Mrs. Donovan," I said softly, "he's the most beautiful dog in Yorkshire." Then, because I knew she was waiting for it, "It's those wonderful condition powders. Whatever do you put in them?"

"Ah, wouldn't you like to know!" She bridled and smiled up at me coquettishly and indeed she was nearer being kissed at that moment than for many years.

I suppose you could say that that was the start of Roy's second life. And as the years passed, I often pondered on the beneficent providence[17] which had decreed that an animal which had spent his first twelve months abandoned and unwanted, staring uncomprehendingly into that unchanging, stinking darkness, should be whisked in a moment into an existence of light and movement and love. Because I don't think any dog had it quite so good as Roy from then on.

His diet changed dramatically, from odd bread crusts to best stewing steak and biscuit, meaty bones, and a bowl of warm milk every evening. And he never missed a thing. Garden fetes,[18] school sports, evictions, gymkhanas[19]—he'd be there. I was pleased to note that as time went on, Mrs. Donovan seemed to be clocking up an even greater daily mileage. Her expenditure on shoe leather must have been phenomenal, but of course it was absolute pie for Roy—a busy round in the morning, home for a meal, then straight out again; it was all go.

Mrs. Donovan didn't confine her activities to the town center; there was a big stretch of common land down by the river where there were seats, and people used to take their dogs for a gallop and she liked to get down there fairly regularly to check on the latest developments on the domestic scene. I often saw Roy loping majestically over the grass among a pack of assorted canines, and when he wasn't doing that he was submitting to being stroked or patted or generally fussed over. He was handsome and he just liked people; it made him irresistible.

It was common knowledge that his mistress had bought a whole selection of brushes and combs of various sizes with which she labored over his coat. Some people said she had a little brush for his teeth, too, and it might have been true, but he certainly wouldn't need his nails clipped—his life on the roads would keep them down.

Mrs. Donovan, too, had her reward; she had a faithful companion by her side every hour of the day and night. But there was more to it than that; she had always had the compulsion to help and heal animals and the salvation of Roy was the high point of her life—a blazing triumph which never dimmed.

I know the memory of it was always fresh because many years later I was sitting on the sidelines at a cricket match and I saw the two of them; the old lady glancing keenly around her, Roy gazing placidly out at the field of play, apparently enjoying every ball. At the end of the match I watched them move away with the dispersing crowd; Roy would be about twelve then and heaven only knows how old Mrs. Donovan must have been, but the big golden animal was trotting along effortlessly and his mistress, a little more bent, perhaps, and her head rather nearer the ground, was going very well.

When she saw me, she came over and I felt the familiar tight grip on my wrist.

"Mr. Herriot," she said, and in the dark probing eyes the pride was still as warm, the triumph still as bursting new, as if it had all happened yesterday.

"Mr. Herriot, haven't I made a difference to this dog!"

---

16. **noisome** (noi′səm): foul-smelling.
17. **beneficent** (bə·nef′ə·sənt) **providence:** kindly care and protection provided by God or nature; favorable fate.
18. **fetes** (fāts): outdoor parties or festivals.
19. **gymkhanas** (jim·kä′nəz): athletic events.

WORDS TO OWN

dispersing (di·spʉrs′iŋ) v. used as adj.: breaking up; scattering.

MEET THE WRITER

Tales of a Veterinarian

When he was thirteen, **James Herriot** (1916–1995) read a magazine article about veterinarians and made up his mind to become one, even though he had what he described as a "poor science record." He trained as a vet in Glasgow, Scotland, and took his first job in Yorkshire in northern England. For twenty-five years he talked about writing a book on his work but never wrote a word until his wife challenged him one day: "Who are you kidding? Vets of fifty don't write first books." He bought some paper, chose a pen name (his real name was James Alfred Wight), and began to write.

❝ I suppose I started out with the intention of just writing a funny book, because veterinary life was funny in those days, but as I progressed I found that there were so many other things I wanted to say. I wanted to tell about the sad things, too, because they are inseparable from a vet's experiences; about the splendid old characters among the animal owners of that time and about the magnificent Yorkshire countryside . . . [whose] wildness and peace captivated me instantly. ❞

Eager readers made Herriot's entertaining tales best-sellers, and soon there were a TV series and a movie. Four of Herriot's most popular books (all published by St. Martin's Press) take their titles from this nineteenth-century hymn:

All things bright and beautiful,
    All creatures great and small,
All things wise and wonderful,
    The Lord God made them all.

The World Is Not a Pleasant Place to Be

Nikki Giovanni

the world is not a pleasant place
to be without
someone to hold and be held by

5   a river would stop
its flow if only
a stream were there
to receive it

an ocean would never laugh
10   if clouds weren't there
to kiss her tears

the world is not
a pleasant place to be without
someone

MAKING MEANINGS

First Thoughts

1. List several words that you think describe Mrs. Donovan in Herriot's story. Did you like her? Why or why not?

Shaping Interpretations

2. If Herriot has a **main idea** (or ideas) in mind, he doesn't tell us directly. Brainstorm with a group of students to come up with some statements of what the main idea might be.

3. Which passages did you list in your Reader's Log as especially moving or beautiful or terrible? Read these passages aloud in class and share your comments.

4. To hook our interest and keep it, Herriot uses many of the elements of fiction you studied in the short-story collections. Find examples of each of the following. What other fictional elements does Herriot use in this **nonfiction narrative**?

Elements of Fiction	Examples
Characterization	
Dialogue	
Suspense	

Reviewing the Text

Make a cause-and-effect chart to map the important events in this story. Begin like this:

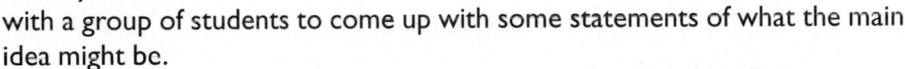

Connecting with the Text

5. Are you a "dog person," a "cat person," or neither? Tell about an experience that has shaped your attitude toward pets and other animals.

Extending the Text

6. Do you agree or disagree with this statement? "According to this story, one person can make a big difference in the life of a dog. But people's problems are usually so complicated that one person can't make a difference in their lives." Support your opinion with examples, facts, and/or anecdotes.

7. What do you think James Herriot's response would be to the message of "The World Is Not a Pleasant Place to Be" (page 416)? Would you count a pet as "someone" (see line 13) who helps make a place home? Explain.

CHOICES: Building Your Portfolio

Writer's Notebook

1. Collecting Ideas for a Reflective Essay

Thought connections. Once you've decided on an occasion for your reflective essay (an incident, an observation, a quotation, an abstract idea), focus on it. What does it make you think of or remind you of? What's your opinion about it? Capture your thought connections in a cluster diagram like the one below. Don't stop to decide whether your ideas are useful or not; just get them down on paper. Save your notes for possible use in the Writer's Workshop on page 438.

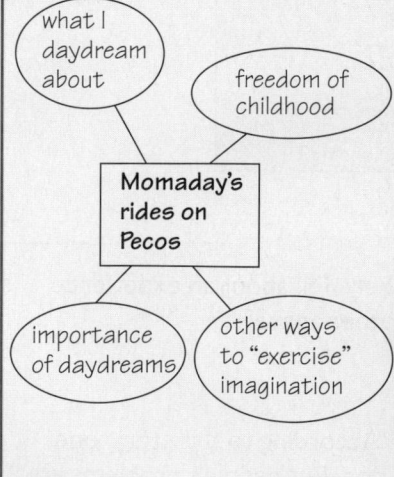

Creative Writing

2. A Pet Story

Tell a pet story of your own, using an animal—your own pet or someone else's—as the main character. Try to describe your pet in a way that brings him or her to life. In your narrative, tell what happened to the pet, when and where it happened, and how you felt about it.

Critical Writing

3. Do Animals Have Rights?

What do you think should be done to people who treat animals badly? How do you feel about the use of animals for medical research? for psychological research? for testing cosmetics? Choose one of these animal rights issues, and write at least one paragraph stating your opinion. Try to support your opinion with facts and examples. Read your paragraph in class and ask for questions (and challenges) from your audience.

Drawing

4. Cartoon Chronicle

The comics are full of famous animals, from Pogo (the possum) to Snoopy (the dog) to Hobbes (the tiger). You might work with a partner or small group to create a cartoon strip called "Roy." Choose scenes that you think summarize Roy's story, and draw the characters as you imagine them, sketching in background details. Write a caption for each frame or write dialogue in speech balloons, keeping in mind the humor and the drama of Roy's story. Post your cartoon strips on a bulletin board.

LANGUAGE LINK   MINI-LESSON

Handbook of Literary Terms
H E L P

See Description.

Style: Description Makes It Live

Descriptive writing uses sensory details, vivid verbs, and precise nouns and modifiers to help readers form a sharp mental image of a subject. Herriot introduces his animal and human characters with descriptions that appeal to our senses of sight, smell, taste, hearing, and touch. We seem to step along at the doctor's side, seeing what he sees, observing small details. Which specific words in these sentences help you picture Mrs. Donovan and Roy? (What details of your own do you supply?)

1. "... you'd find the dumpy little figure and walnut face among the spectators, the darting, black-button eyes taking everything in."

2. "He had grown and filled out and his coat, no longer yellow but a rich gold, lay in luxuriant, shining swaths over the well-fleshed ribs and back."

3. "I often saw Roy loping majestically over the grass among a pack of assorted canines, and when he wasn't doing that he was submitting to being stroked or patted or generally fussed over."

> **Try It Out**
>
> You're a newspaper reporter. Write two or three sentences describing each of the following characters, who play an important part in the true story you're writing. Use sensory details, vivid verbs, and precise nouns and modifiers.
>
> 1. a bus driver
> 2. a teenage musician
> 3. an animal
> 4. someone who lives in your neighborhood

VOCABULARY   HOW TO OWN A WORD

WORD BANK

uncanny
implicit
diligent
callous
desolation
stupefying
interminably
remonstrances
luxuriant
dispersing

Vocabulary for the Workplace

1. List some sights a veterinarian would find stupefying.
2. What remonstrances might a vet have for someone planning to adopt a lion cub?
3. What would diligent pet owners do about their pets' fleas?
4. What advice might a vet give to someone with a cat that howls interminably?
5. In what ways would a flood cause desolation?
6. What did Mrs. Donovan do to transform Roy's dull coat into a luxuriant one?
7. How might a callous person react to a litter of kittens?
8. If a pack of wild dogs was dispersing, what would they be doing?
9. What's implicit in this message: "Save the whales"?
10. What special jobs can dogs do because of their uncanny sense of smell?

Reading Focus

A View from Space

With our feet planted firmly here on Earth, it's hard to hold onto the thought that our complicated lives take place on a planet spinning in space. But it's all a matter of perspective. Picture yourself cruising in outer space. What might you think and feel as you looked back at your home on Earth?

A Dialogue with the Text

As you read, jot down your responses to passages that you find striking or puzzling or controversial.

READER'S
LOG

Passage	My Response
"Home is the Guatemalan jungle, at times deadly as an arsenal."	I don't understand this reference. Is it to politics?

Elements of Literature

Exposition: Informative Writing

Exposition, writing that explains or gives information, is a main ingredient in most kinds of nonfiction. Essayists often combine exposition with description and narration.

Exposition is the kind of factual writing that explains a subject, gives information, or clarifies an idea.

For more on Exposition, see the Handbook of Literary Terms.

THE ROUND WALLS OF HOME

from A Natural History of the Senses

Diane Ackerman

Picture this: everyone you've ever known, everyone you've ever loved, your whole experience of life, floating in one place, on a single planet underneath you. On that dazzling oasis, swirling with blues and whites, the weather systems form and travel. You watch the clouds tingle and swell above the Amazon and know the weather that develops there will affect the crop yield half a planet away in Russia and China. Volcanic eruptions make tiny spangles below. The rain forests are disappearing in Australia, Hawaii, and South America. You see dust bowls developing in Africa and the Near East. Remote sensing devices, judging the humidity in the desert, have already warned you there will be plagues of locusts[1] this year. To your amazement, you identify the lights of Denver and

1. **plagues of locusts:** swarms of large grasshoppers that eat all plants in their path.

WORDS TO OWN
oasis (ō·ā′sis) *n.:* fertile place. *Ousis* may also mean "place or thing offering welcome relief."

Home is springtime.

hoarse threats at the neighbor's dog. Home is the exquisite torment of love and all the lesser mayhems of the heart. But what you long for is to stand back and see it whole. You want to live out that age-old yearning, portrayed in myths and legends of every culture, to step above the Earth and see the whole world fidgeting and blooming below you.

I remember my first flying lesson, in the doldrums of summer in upstate New York. Pushing the throttle forward, I zoomed down the runway until the undercarriage began to dance; then the ground fell away below and I was airborne, climbing up an invisible flight of stairs. To my amazement, the horizon came with me (how could it not, on a round planet?). For the first time in my life I understood what a valley was, as I floated above one at 7,000 feet. I could see plainly the devastation of the gypsy moth, whose hunger had leeched[3] the forests to a mottled gray. Later on, when I flew over Ohio, I was saddened to discover the stagnant ocher[4] of the air, and to see that the long expanse of the Ohio River, dark and chunky, was the wrong texture for water, even flammable at times, thanks to the fumings of plastics factories, which I could also see, standing like pustules[5] along the river. I began to understand how people settle a landscape, in waves and at crossroads, how they survey a land and irrigate it. Most of all, I discovered that there are things one can learn about the world only from certain perspectives. How can you understand the ocean without becoming part of its intricate fathoms? How can you understand the planet without walking upon it, sampling its marvels

Cairo. And though you were taught about them one by one, as separate parts of a jigsaw puzzle, now you can see that the oceans, the atmosphere, and the land are not separate at all, but part of an <u>intricate</u> recombining web of nature. Like Dorothy in *The Wizard of Oz,* you want to click your magic shoes together and say three times: "There's no place like home."

You know what home is. For many years, you've tried to be a modest and eager watcher of the skies and of the Earth, whose green <u>anthem</u> you love. Home is a pigeon strutting like a <u>petitioner</u> in the courtyard in front of your house. Home is the law-abiding hickories out back. Home is the sign on a gas station just outside Pittsburgh that reads "If we can't fix it, it ain't broke." Home is springtime on campuses all across America, where students sprawl on the grass like the war-wounded at Gettysburg.[2] Home is the Guatemalan jungle, at times deadly as an arsenal. Home is the pheasant barking

2. **Gettysburg:** town in Pennsylvania where a bloody Civil War battle was fought in 1863. Some 48,000 men were killed or wounded in the battle.

3. **leeched:** drained. Leeches are worms that suck blood.
4. **stagnant ocher** (stag′nənt ō′kər): foul, motionless dark yellow.
5. **pustules** (pus′tyo͞olz′): pimples or blisters.

WORDS TO OWN
intricate (in′tri·kit) *adj.:* complicated; elaborately detailed.
anthem (an′thəm) *n.:* song of praise. Here, the writer is imagining the vivid greenness of Earth itself as a song of praise.
petitioner (pə·tish′ən·ər) *n.:* person seeking favors.

one by one, and then floating high above it, to see it all in a single eye-gulp?

Most of all, the twentieth century will be remembered as the time when we first began to understand what our address was. The "big, beautiful blue, wet ball" of recent years is one way to say it. But a more profound way will speak of the orders of magnitude of that bigness, the shades of that blueness, the arbitrary delicacy of beauty itself, the ways in which water has made life possible, and the fragile euphoria of the complex ecosystem[6] that is Earth, an Earth on which, from space, there are no visible fences, or military zones, or national borders. We need to send into space a flurry of artists and naturalists, photographers and painters, who will turn the mirror upon ourselves and show us Earth as a single planet, a single organism that's buoyant, fragile, blooming, buzzing, full of spectacles, full of fascinating human beings, something to cherish. Learning our full address may not end all wars, but it will enrich our sense of wonder and pride. It will remind us that the human context is not tight as a noose, but large as the universe we have the privilege to inhabit. It will change our sense of what a neighborhood is. It will persuade us that we are citizens of something larger and more profound than mere countries, that we are citizens of Earth, her joy riders and her caretakers, who would do well to work on her problems together. The view from space is offering us the first chance we evolutionary toddlers have had to cross the cosmic street and stand facing our own home, amazed to see it clearly for the first time.

6. **ecosystem** (ek′ō·sis′təm): community of animals and plants and their physical and chemical environment.

WORDS TO OWN

euphoria (yōō·fôr′ē·ə) *n.*: feeling of vigor or well-being.

MEET THE WRITER

"A Great Fan of the Universe"

To gather material for her writing, **Diane Ackerman** (1948–　　) has stood in the midst of millions of bats, straddled alligators, and swum right up to a whale's mouth. Sometimes, she admits, she's been truly frightened.

❝ I try to give myself passionately, totally, to whatever I'm observing, with as much affectionate curiosity as I can muster, as a means of understanding a little better what being human is, and what it was like to have once been alive on the planet. . . . I appear to have a lot of science in my work, I suppose, but I think of myself as a Nature poet, if what we mean by nature is . . . the full sum of creation. ❞

Ackerman grew up in a small Chicago suburb and walked to school through its deep, dark woods instead of staying on the sidewalks, as she was supposed to do. She remembers creating her first metaphor in those forests: Bats hanging from the trees, she told her horrified friends, were "living plums."

Ackerman, an award-winning poet, published four books of poetry before she began writing nonfiction. She has taught at Cornell, Columbia, and New York universities and is now a staff writer for *The New Yorker*. "The Round Walls of Home," from *A Natural History of the Senses* (1990), reveals her concerns about nature:

❝ I'm a great fan of the Universe, which I take literally: as one. All of it interests me, and it interests me in detail. ❞

Prologue

Edward Field

Look, friend, at this universe
With its spiral clusters of stars
Flying out all over space
Like bedsprings suddenly busting free;
5 And in this galaxy, the sun
Fissioning° itself away,
Surrounded by planets, prominent in their dignity,
And bits and pieces running wild;
And this middling planet
10 With a lone moon circling round it.

Look, friend, through the fog of gases at this world
With its skin of earth and rock, water and ice,
With various creatures and rooted things;
And up from the bulging waistline
15 To this land of concrete towers,
Its roads swarming like a hive cut open,
Offshore to this island, long and fish shaped,
Its mouth to a metropolis,
And in its belly, this village,
20 A gathering of families at a crossways,
And in this house, upstairs and through the wide-open door
Of the front bedroom with a window on the world,
Look, friend, at me.

6. fissioning: splitting apart.

MAKING MEANINGS

First Thoughts

1. Which statement did you find most interesting—or most controversial—in Ackerman's essay? Why? (Check your Reader's Log.)

Shaping Interpretations

2. What **metaphors** does Ackerman use to say what home is?

3. Find some sentences that convey facts and some that express opinions. Would you say that Ackerman's purpose here is mainly **expository** (explaining and informing) or do you think she has a different aim? Explain.

4. Try to state Ackerman's **main idea** in one or two sentences.

Extending the Text

5. How do Ackerman's ideas compare with those in the poem on page 423?

Reviewing the Text

a. Explain Ackerman's **title**.

b. When Ackerman takes her first flying lesson, what does she discover?

c. List the global problems that Ackerman alludes to or mentions directly in paragraphs three and four.

d. What new "address" does she want us to accept?

CHOICES: Building Your Portfolio

Writer's Notebook

1. Collecting Ideas for a Reflective Essay

Start with a quotation. A passage from a literary work can be the starting point of a reflective essay like the one you'll write for the Writer's Workshop on page 438. Look through Ackerman's excerpt for one statement or idea that you have some feelings about. Freewrite your thoughts and responses. Do you strongly agree or disagree? What does the passage make you think of? Save your notes.

Scientific Writing

2. Changing Perspective

As precisely as you can, describe an object or natural phenomenon that you see every day. Look at the object from a different perspective—up very close (try a magnifying glass) and from different angles. Describe what you observe. You might want to add your thoughts about the object.

Speaking and Listening

3. Debate the Issues

As a class, brainstorm some debatable topics that Ackerman's essay suggests (environmental issues, space travel, life on other planets). Then write an affirmative statement about each topic, such as "The United Nations should enforce worldwide rules to limit air pollution." Form opposing teams that will either support or challenge one of the statements. For help in running the debate, see the Communications Handbook.

LANGUAGE LINK ▸ MINI-LESSON

Language Handbook HELP

See Commas, page 1023.

Technology HELP

See Language Workshop CD-ROM. *Key word entry: commas.*

Proofreading: Series—Three or More in a Row

Ackerman uses many items in a series. Here are the comma rules she followed.

1. Use commas to separate items in a series:

   "The rain forests are disappearing in Australia, Hawaii, and South America." [commas separate a series of nouns]

   "How can you understand the planet without walking upon it, sampling its marvels one by one, and then floating high above it . . . ?" [commas separate a series of phrases]

2. When *and* or *or* joins all the items in a series, no comma is necessary:

   "For many years you've tried to be a modest <u>and</u> eager watcher of the skies. . . ." [no comma between <u>modest</u> and <u>and eager</u>]

3. No comma is used between an adjective and the noun it modifies:

   "You see <u>dust bowls</u> developing in Africa. . . ." [no comma between <u>dust</u> and <u>bowls</u>]

Try It Out

Practice using commas to separate items in a series. Be sure to have your partner proofread your work.

1. Ackerman says that "big, beautiful blue, wet ball" is one way to describe Earth. Write a sentence containing another series of adjectives describing Earth or one of its features.

2. In her last paragraph, Ackerman calls human beings joy riders, caretakers, and evolutionary toddlers. Write a sentence containing a series of verbs that describe what human beings have done to Earth.

3. Write a sentence in which you include a series of nouns naming at least four places you'd like to visit someday.

4. Describe yourself to a pen pal, using a series of phrases.

VOCABULARY ▸ HOW TO OWN A WORD

WORD BANK

oasis
intricate
anthem
petitioner
euphoria

In Your Own Words

How would you answer these questions about this essay?

1. In what way is Earth a dazzling <u>oasis</u>?
2. When Ackerman says the oceans, atmosphere, and land are part of an <u>intricate</u> web, what does she mean?
3. What <u>anthems</u> do you know?
4. How is a pigeon like a <u>petitioner</u>?
5. If the ecosystem is experiencing a "fragile <u>euphoria</u>," how does it feel? (What kind of figure of speech is this?)

Reading Focus

Trapped

Imagine a place so small you can't stand up, with little air and no light. You don't see the rats, mice, and bugs crawling on you, but you can feel them. Then imagine that this is a place you've chosen to be in. What could bring you to such a place—and keep you there?

A Dialogue with the Text

Divide a page of your Reader's Log into three columns for a KWL entry on slavery in America. KWL stands for "what I already *know* about slavery," "what I *want* to find out," and "what I've *learned* from reading this selection." Fill in the K and W columns now; save the L column until after you read "The Loophole of Retreat."

K	W	L

Elements of Literature

Setting: Where and When?

Setting can be crucial in nonfiction. Sometimes, the setting actually *causes* what happens. In the true narrative you're about to read, the narrator's "home" setting is key, and you should try to picture

exactly what it looks like. Another, wider setting is also important: To understand this story, you must also know about the time in history when these events took place.

> **S**etting is the time and place in which specific events occur.
>
> *For more on Setting, see pages 164–165 and the Handbook of Literary Terms.*

Background

In August 1835, in Edenton, North Carolina, a twenty-two-year-old woman held in slavery hid in a swamp and then crept into the crawl space above her grandmother's storeroom. She went into hiding to escape the abuse of her owner (called Dr. Flint in her narrative).

The title of this chapter from Jacobs's autobiography comes from these lines by the English poet William Cowper:

> 'Tis pleasant, through the
>   loopholes of retreat,
> To peep at such a world; to see
>   the stir
> Of the great Babel, and not feel
>   the crowd.

The rats and mice ran over my bed.

from Incidents in the Life of a Slave Girl

The LOOPHOLE of RETREAT

Harriet A. Jacobs

A small shed had been added to my grandmother's house years ago. Some boards were laid across the joists[1] at the top, and between these boards and the roof was a very small garret,[2] never occupied by anything but rats and mice. It was a pent roof,[3] covered with nothing but shingles, according to the Southern custom for such buildings. The garret was only nine feet long and seven wide. The highest part was three feet high and sloped down abruptly to the loose board floor. There was no admission for either light or air. My uncle Phillip, who was a carpenter, had very skillfully made a concealed trapdoor, which communicated with the storeroom. He had been doing this while I was waiting in the swamp. The storeroom opened upon a piazza.[4]

To this hole I was conveyed as soon as I entered the house. The air was stifling; the darkness, total. A bed had been spread on the floor. I could sleep quite comfortably on one side, but the slope was so sudden that I could not turn on the other without hitting the roof. The rats and mice ran over my bed; but I was weary, and I slept such sleep as the wretched may when a tempest[5] has passed over them. Morning came. I knew it only by the noises I heard; for in my small den, day and night were all the same. I suffered for air even more than for light. But I was not comfortless. I heard the voices of my children. There was joy and there was sadness in the sound. It made my tears flow. How I longed to speak to them! I was eager to look on their faces; but there was no hole, no crack, through which I could peep. This continued darkness was oppressive. It seemed horrible to sit or lie in a cramped

1. **joists:** parallel beams.
2. **garret** (gar′it): attic.
3. **pent roof:** roof sloping on only one side.
4. **piazza** (pē·az′ə): large covered porch.
5. **tempest** (tem′pist): violent storm.

Database: Slavery in America

First Africans arrive: Dutch ship brings 20 African indentured servants to Jamestown, Virginia, 1619.

First legalization of slavery: In 1641, Massachusetts is the first state to legalize slavery.

Places that Africans were taken from: present African nations of Senegal, Gambia, Guinea, Sierra Leone, Liberia, Burkina Faso, Ivory Coast, Ghana, Togo, Benin, Nigeria, Cameroon, Gabon, Congo

Total number of Africans brought to America as slaves: 10 million to 12 million (estimate)

Percentage of Africans who died during the Middle Passage (from Africa to West Indies): 10–20 percent

Percentage of Africans who died "in training" in West Indies: 30 percent

Landmark laws and court decisions:

- Fugitive Slave Act of 1793 (runaway slaves, even in a free state, can be forcibly returned to their owners)
- Compromise of 1850 (some new states to be free, some to be slave states)
- Dred Scott decision, 1857 (slavery is legal in the territories)
- Emancipation Proclamation, January 1, 1863 (frees slaves in seceded states)
- Fourteenth Amendment, 1868 (African Americans born in the United States are citizens)
- Fifteenth Amendment, 1870 (African American men have the right to vote)

position day after day, without one gleam of light. Yet I would have chosen this rather than my lot as a slave, though white people considered it an easy one; and it was so compared with the fate of others. I was never cruelly overworked; I was never <u>lacerated</u> with the whip from head to foot; I was never so beaten and bruised that I could not turn from one side to the other; I never had my heel strings[6] cut to prevent my running away; I was never chained to a log and forced to drag it about, while I toiled in the fields from morning till night; I was never branded with hot iron or torn by bloodhounds. On the contrary, I had always been kindly treated and tenderly cared for, until I came into the hands of Dr. Flint. I had never wished for freedom till then. But though my life in slavery was comparatively <u>devoid</u> of hardships, God pity the woman who is compelled to lead such a life!

My food was passed up to me through the trapdoor my uncle had contrived;[7] and my grandmother, my uncle Phillip, and my aunt Nancy would seize such opportunities as they could to mount up there and chat with me at the opening. But of course this was not safe in the daytime. It must all be done in darkness. It was impossible for me to move in an erect position, but I crawled about my den for exercise. One day I hit my head against something and found it was a gimlet.[8] My uncle had left it sticking there when he made the trapdoor. I was as rejoiced as Robinson Crusoe[9] could have been at finding such a treasure. It put a lucky thought into my head. I said to

---

6. heel strings: The writer is referring to her Achilles' tendons, the tough, stiff cords of tissue connecting the backs of the heels to the muscles of the calves.
7. contrived (kən·trīvd′): constructed skillfully.
8. gimlet (gim′lit): hand tool used to bore holes.
9. Robinson Crusoe: character in a novel of the same name by Daniel Defoe (1660–1731); Crusoe is shipwrecked on a small tropical island, where he survives for many years.

WORDS TO OWN

lacerated (las′ər·āt′id) v.: torn.
devoid (di·void′) adj.: empty.

myself, "Now I will have some light. Now I will see my children." I did not dare to begin my work during the daytime, for fear of attracting attention. But I groped round; and having found the side next the street, where I could frequently see my children, I stuck the gimlet in and waited for evening. I bored three rows of holes, one above another; then I bored out the interstices[10] between. I thus succeeded in making one hole about an inch long and an inch broad. I sat by it till late into the night, to enjoy the little whiff of air that floated in. In the morning I watched for my children. The first person I saw in the street was Dr. Flint. I had a shuddering, superstitious feeling that it was a bad omen. Several familiar faces passed by. At last I heard the merry laugh of children, and presently two sweet little faces were looking up at me, as though they knew I was there and were conscious of the joy they imparted. How I longed to *tell* them I was there!

My condition was now a little improved. But for weeks I was tormented by hundreds of little red insects, fine as a needle's point, that pierced through my skin and produced an intolerable burning. The good grandmother gave me herb teas and cooling medicines, and finally I got rid of them. The heat of my den was intense, for nothing but thin shingles protected me from the scorching summer's sun. But I had my consolations. Through my peeping hole I could watch the children, and when they were near enough, I could hear their talk. Aunt Nancy brought me all the news she could hear at Dr. Flint's. From her I learned that the doctor had written to New York to a colored woman who had been born and raised in our neighborhood and had breathed his contaminating atmosphere. He offered her a reward if she could find out anything about me. I know not what was the nature of her reply; but he soon after started for New York in haste, saying to his family that he had business of importance to transact. I peeped at him as he passed on his way to the steamboat. It was a satisfaction to have miles of land and water between us, even

10. **interstices** (in·tur′stə·siz′): small spaces.

for a little while; and it was a still greater satisfaction to know that he believed me to be in the Free States. My little den seemed less dreary than it had done. He returned, as he did from his former journey to New York, without obtaining any satisfactory information. When he passed our house next morning, Benny was standing at the gate. He had heard them say that he had gone to find me, and he called out, "Dr. Flint, did you bring my mother home? I want to see her." The doctor stamped his foot at him in a rage and exclaimed, "Get out of the way, you little damned rascal! If you don't, I'll cut off your head."

Benny ran terrified into the house, saying, "You can't put me in jail again. I don't belong to you now."[11] It was well that the wind carried the words away from the doctor's ear. I told my grandmother of it, when we had our next conference at the trapdoor, and begged of her not to allow the children to be impertinent to the irascible old man.

Autumn came, with a pleasant abatement of heat. My eyes had become accustomed to the dim light, and by holding my book or work in a certain position near the aperture, I contrived to read and sew. That was a great relief to the tedious monotony of my life. But when winter came, the cold penetrated through the thin shingle roof, and I was dreadfully chilled. The winters there are not so long or so severe as in northern latitudes; but the houses are not built

11. The freedom of Jacobs's two children, Benny and Louisa Matilda, had been bought by their father, a lawyer. The children were living with Harriet Jacobs's grandmother.

WORDS TO OWN

omen (ō′mən) *n.*: sign; thing or happening believed to foretell an event.
intolerable (in·täl′ər·ə·bəl) *adj.*: unbearable; too painful or severe to be endured.
consolations (kän′sə·lā′shənz) *n.*: things that comfort.
contaminating (kən·tam′ə·nāt′in) *v.* used as *adj.*: polluting; poisoning.
impertinent (im·purt′'n·ənt) *adj.*: shamelessly disrespectful; rude.
irascible (i·ras′ə·bəl) *adj.*: irritable; easily angered.
abatement (ə·bāt′mənt) *n.*: lessening; reduction.
aperture (ap′ər·chər) *n.*: opening; gap.

---

to shelter from cold, and my little den was peculiarly comfortless. The kind grandmother brought me bedclothes and warm drinks. Often I was obliged to lie in bed all day to keep comfortable; but with all my precautions, my shoulders and feet were frostbitten. Oh, those long, gloomy days, with no object for my eye to rest upon and no thoughts to occupy my mind except the dreary past and the uncertain future! I was thankful when there came a day sufficiently mild for me to wrap myself up and sit at the loophole to watch the passers-by. Southerners have the habit of stopping and talking in the streets, and I heard many conversations not intended to meet my ears. I heard slave hunters planning how to catch some poor fugitive. Several times I heard allusions to Dr. Flint, myself, and the history of my children, who, perhaps, were playing near the gate. One would say, "I wouldn't move my little finger to catch her, as old Flint's property." Another would say, ". . . A man ought to have what belongs to him, even if he *is* a damned brute." The opinion was often expressed that I was in the Free States. Very rarely did anyone suggest that I might be in the vicinity. Had the least suspicion rested on my grandmother's house, it would have been burned to the ground. But it was the last place they thought of. Yet there was no place, where slavery existed, that could have afforded me so good a place of concealment.

Reproduced by permission of Harvard University Press.

MEET THE WRITER

A Horrible Word

Harriet A. Jacobs (1813–1897), born into slavery in Edenton, North Carolina, was taught to read, spell, and sew by her first mistress. (Reading and writing were forbidden to slaves.) When she was a teenager, Jacobs's second owner harassed her repeatedly. Furious at her refusals, he sent her away to hard labor as a plantation slave and threatened to do the same with her two young children.

She ran away from the plantation and hid for seven years in the crawl space she describes in her autobiography. All she ever sought, she said, was freedom and a home for her children and herself. In 1842, Jacobs escaped to New York City, where she found work as a nursemaid.

She began writing the story of her life in 1853 and published it herself in 1861, using the pen name Linda Brent. This quotation, attributed to "A Woman of North Carolina," appears on the title page:

66 Northerners know nothing at all about Slavery. They think it is perpetual bondage only. They have no conception of the depth of *degradation* involved in that word, *slavery*; if they had, they would never cease their efforts until so horrible a system was overthrown. 99

MAKING MEANINGS

First Thoughts

1. Jot down some words and phrases that describe your feelings as you read this selection from Jacobs's autobiography.

Shaping Interpretations

2. In a short story a writer sometimes chooses details of **setting** to create a mood or atmosphere. How would you describe the mood of this selection? Which details of the setting contribute to that mood?

3. Think of some words and phrases you'd use to describe the narrator's **character**. Find details in the text that show us the sort of person she is.

4. Compare Jacobs's "loophole of retreat" with William Cowper's "loopholes" (see his three lines of poetry in the Background, page 426). What do you think of Jacobs's **title**? What other titles would you suggest?

5. What **main idea** do you think this selection reveals? Is the main idea directly stated, or is it implied?

Extending the Text

6. Jacobs faces great hardship but doesn't give up. What do you think keeps some people going in the face of great hardship? Why do others give up?

Reviewing the Text

a. Draw a picture of Jacobs's hiding place as you see it. Show its dimensions. Where is it?

b. Why is she hiding there?

c. Why is the gimlet a lucky find?

d. Who is Dr. Flint, and what news of him does Aunt Nancy bring?

e. Where do people imagine that Jacobs has gone?

Slave Auction, Virginia (19th century) by Lefevre James Cranstone.

Virginia Historical Society, Richmond.

CHOICES: Building Your Portfolio

Writer's Notebook

1. Collecting Ideas for a Reflective Essay

Making a general-ization. At the end of a reflective essay (see the Writer's Workshop on page 438), you must add a general-ization or insight about life and people. A **generalization** is a statement that applies not just to a specific situation, but to all individuals in a similar situa-tion. (See page 439 for more about generalizations.) Think of some generalizations about life and people you would make, based on "The Loophole of Retreat."

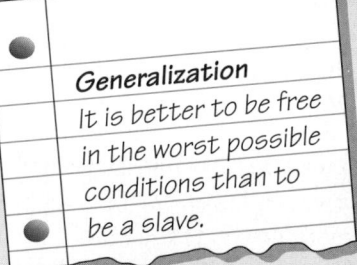

Generalization

It is better to be free in the worst possible conditions than to be a slave.

Creative Writing

2. Dear Ms. Jacobs

Write a letter to Harriet A. Jacobs, telling what you think and feel after reading this episode from her true narra-tive. In your letter include any questions you would like to ask her. Be sure to read Jacobs's biography (page 430).

Research/History/Speaking and Listening

3. Finding More Facts

Go back to the KWL chart in your Reader's Log and fill in the L column. What new facts about slavery did you learn from Jacobs's essay? What questions (from your W column) remain unanswered? (Be sure to check the database on page 428.) With a partner or small group, research the questions you still have. Use reference books, histories, books about slavery, the Internet, even television shows and movies. Present the answers to your own questions in a brief oral report to the class.

Research/Music

4. Spiritual Sing-Along

No one knows who first sang the African American spiri-tuals, or "sorrow songs," as W.E.B. Du Bois called them. Many spirituals, like the one below, are based on Biblical stories. Many express faith that one day freedom will come. Others are "signal songs," used to carry messages (about meetings and escapes) that overseers would not understand. Many spirituals, like the one below, are still sung as gospel hymns. If you enjoy singing, get together with other students and sing several spirituals for the class. Introduce each song with a note on its origins and meanings.

Swing Low, Sweet Chariot

Swing low, sweet chariot,
Coming for to carry me
   home,
Swing low, sweet chariot,
Coming for to carry me
   home.

I looked over Jordan and
   what did I see
Coming for to carry me
   home,
A band of angels, coming
   after me,
Coming for to carry me
   home.

If you get there before I do,
Coming for to carry me
   home,
Tell all my friends I'm
   coming too,
Coming for to carry me
   home.

Swing low, sweet chariot,
Coming for to carry me
   home,
Swing low, sweet chariot,
Coming for to carry me
   home.

LANGUAGE LINK MINI-LESSON

**Language
Handbook
HELP**

*See Clauses,
page 1009.*

**Technology
HELP**

See Language
Workshop
CD-ROM.
*Key word
entry: adjec-
tive clauses.*

Proofreading: Adjective Clauses—Essential and Not

Adjective clauses, which modify nouns and pronouns, are either essential or nonessential. If an adjective clause is necessary, or **essential,** to the meaning of the sentence, it is not set off with commas. Read these sentences without the underlined essential clauses. Do they make sense?

1. "But though my life in slavery was compara-tively devoid of hardships, God pity the woman who is compelled to lead such a life!"

2. For seven years Harriet Jacobs lived in condi-tions that seem impossible to us.

If an adjective clause gives only extra informa-tion and is **nonessential** to the meaning of the sentence, it is set off by commas. If the sentence's sense is not affected when the clause is omitted, then you have a nonessential clause, one that should be set off by commas.

3. "My uncle Phillip, who was a carpenter, had very skillfully made a concealed trapdoor. . . ."

Try It Out

Add an adjective clause to each sentence and punctuate it correctly. Begin the clause with the word in parentheses.

1. Harriet Jacobs hid in a crawl space. (which)

2. She was hiding from Dr. Flint. (who)

3. She was eager to see her children. (who)

4. Harriet Jacobs's grand-mother, aunt, and uncle were the only people. (who)

VOCABULARY HOW TO OWN A WORD

WORD BANK

lacerated
devoid
omen
intolerable
consolations
contaminating
impertinent
irascible
abatement
aperture

Word Meanings

Work with a group to find out what you know about the meanings of the Word Bank words. To do this, make up three questions about each word (similar to the questions below) and organize your answers in a chart. After you have completed charts for all the words, invite another group to answer some of your questions.

LACERATED	
Questions	**Answers**
What would you do for some-one who has been lacerated?	• comfort the person • get medical help for wounds
How might wild animals lacerate something?	• tear with claws • rip with teeth
If your feelings were lacerated, how would you feel?	• hurt (emotionally) • distressed • depressed

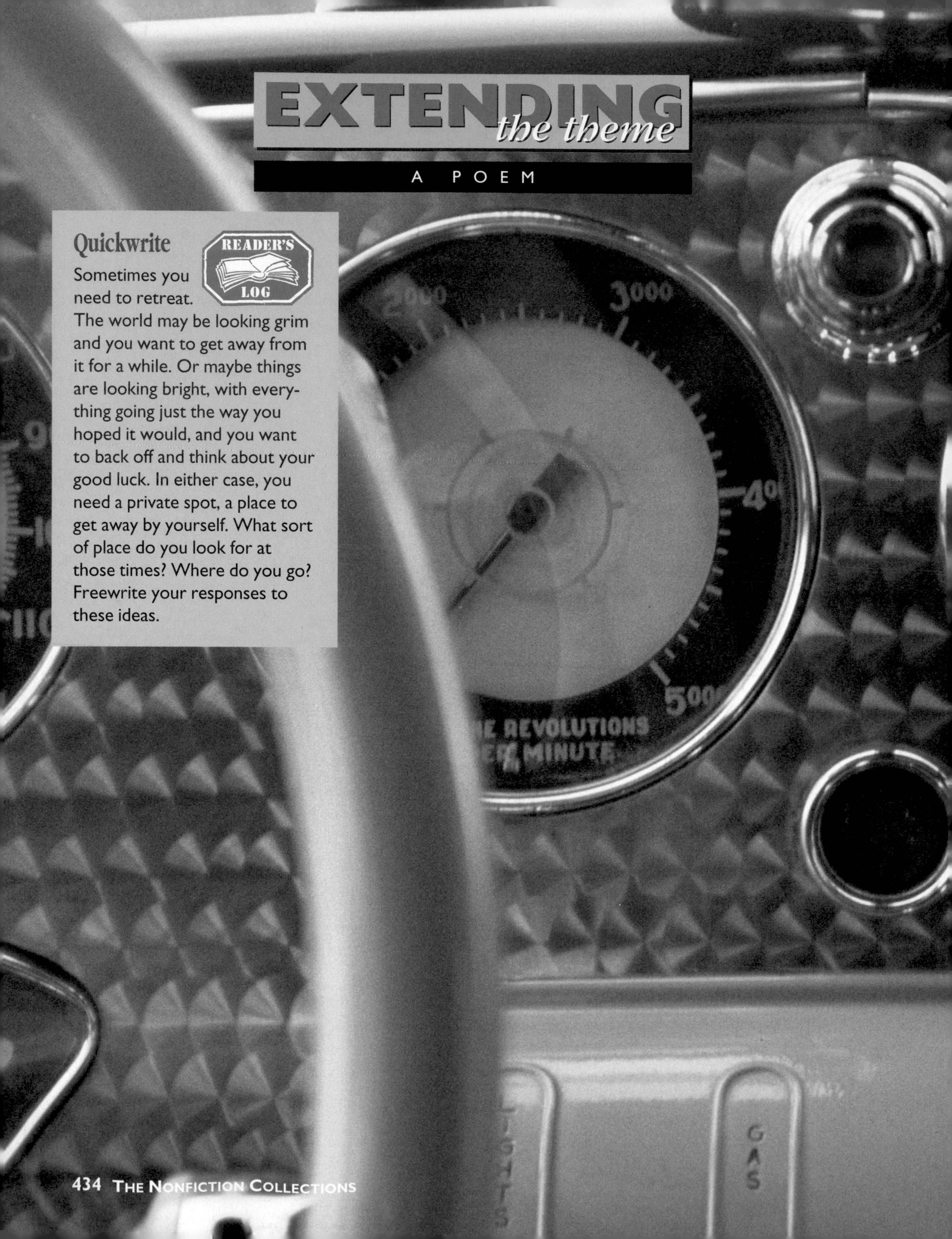

Quickwrite

READER'S LOG

Sometimes you need to retreat. The world may be looking grim and you want to get away from it for a while. Or maybe things are looking bright, with everything going just the way you hoped it would, and you want to back off and think about your good luck. In either case, you need a private spot, a place to get away by yourself. What sort of place do you look for at those times? Where do you go? Freewrite your responses to these ideas.

THE SACRED

Stephen Dunn

After the teacher asked if anyone had
  a sacred place
and the students fidgeted and shrank

in their chairs, the most serious of them all
5   said it was his car,
being in it alone, his tape deck playing

things he'd chosen, and others knew the truth
  had been spoken
and began speaking about their rooms,

10 their hiding places, but the car kept coming up,
  the car in motion,
music filling it, and sometimes one other person

who understood the bright altar of the dashboard
  and how far away
15 a car could take him from the need

to speak, or to answer, the key
  in having a key
and putting it in, and going

Poet of Everyday Life

When **Stephen Dunn** (1939–   ) graduated from college with a degree in history, his first job was playing professional basketball for the Williamsport (Pennsylvania) Billies for a year. Then he wrote advertising copy for a few years. When he was twenty-five, he went to Spain "to try to change my life and see if I could write poetry." He could and did, becoming an award-winning poet whose many books of poetry celebrate the stuff of everyday life.

66 . . . For the most part, because I'm lucky or unlucky enough to live where and how I do, I'm mostly dealing with local things, like getting through a day, or trying to deal with the demands and failures of relationships, the normal difficulties and pleasures of ordinary living. . . . To get that kind of experience right—to somehow deliver it and also say what it might mean—seems to me a large thing. **99**

Dunn teaches at Stockton State College in New Jersey.

FINDING COMMON GROUND

Look back at the notes you made for the Quickwrite. Do this boy's feelings and needs correspond in any way with yours? Then read the poem "Fifteen" on page 571.

Freewrite for a few more minutes about the need to find a place where you can be yourself. Here are some questions to respond to.

1. Dunn's student may be both escaping and seeking, both running away *from* something and running *toward* something else. When he pulls out of his driveway, what is he leaving behind—or trying to leave behind—and what is he trying to find?

2. If it were *you* in the poem, what would the "bright altar of the dashboard" represent, and what would be your equivalent of the "need to speak, or to answer"?

After you've written briefly about these issues, discuss them with other readers. How varied are your responses to the questions and to this poem? Are there any points on which you all agree?

READ ON

Searching for Home

Meet Dicey, James, Sammy, and Maybeth—two sisters and two brothers. In Cynthia Voigt's *Homecoming* (Fawcett Juniper), you'll follow their struggle to stay together and look out for one another. They grow up fast because they have to, and their moving story will surprise you.

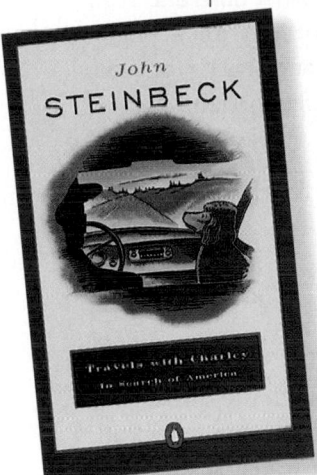

On the Road in Search of America

Some people say that you don't know what home means until you leave it. Travel along in a camper with the Nobel Prize–winning writer John Steinbeck and Charley, his "gallant" poodle, as they set off to rediscover America. In *Travels with Charley in Search of America* (Bantam), Steinbeck records his adventures as he journeys across America from coast to coast and back home again.

A Lost Home

In *The Land I Lost* (HarperCollins), Huynh Quang Nhuong paints a detailed picture of his boyhood in a small village in Vietnam. In these brief stories—some humorous, some serious—villagers outwit the wild hogs, crocodiles, tigers, and horse snakes that threaten them as they farm and hunt.

To Save a Home

In the movie *Places in the Heart* (1984), a young widow (Sally Field) struggles to keep her Texas farm during the Great Depression with the help of a field hand (Danny Glover) and a blind boarder (John Malkovich). Writer/director Robert Benton won an Oscar for his moving screenplay; Field won one for best actress.

Writer's Workshop

ASSIGNMENT

Write an essay that begins with an occasion (a personal experience, an observation, or a quotation). In the rest of the essay, explore your thoughts about the occasion.

AIM

To inform.

AUDIENCE

Your classmates, family members, or readers of a magazine of student writing. (You choose.)

EXPOSITORY WRITING

REFLECTIVE ESSAY

In this Writer's Workshop you'll write a **reflective essay**, an essay that expresses your thoughts. (One of the meanings of *to reflect* is "to think," so your *reflections* are your thoughts—somewhat different from the kind of *reflections* you see in mirrors or quiet waters.) Reflecting involves thinking about a subject from many angles and staying focused on that subject until you reach a conclusion. You reflect whenever you wonder about the meaning of something or when you explore different solutions to a problem or even when you daydream.

Prewriting

1. Start Here

A reflective essay starts with something specific, which is called an **occasion**. If you're not happy with the occasion (or occasions) you've been working with throughout this collection, check your Writer's Notebook and Reader's Log for other ideas:

- something you've experienced—an ordinary or extraordinary event
- something (good or bad) you've observed—an incident in someone else's life, a world event
- an occurrence or feature in nature
- an abstract idea—a quality (such as dignity) or concept (such as justice)
- something you've read (in this book or even in a newspaper) or have seen on TV or in the movies
- a quotation or reference to a specific literary work

2. Now Explore Your Thoughts

As you think about the occasion, what **thought connections** can you make? (On the next page you'll see a sample of the thought connections that the writer of the essay on page 440 might have made.) Make your own connections as you consider these questions:

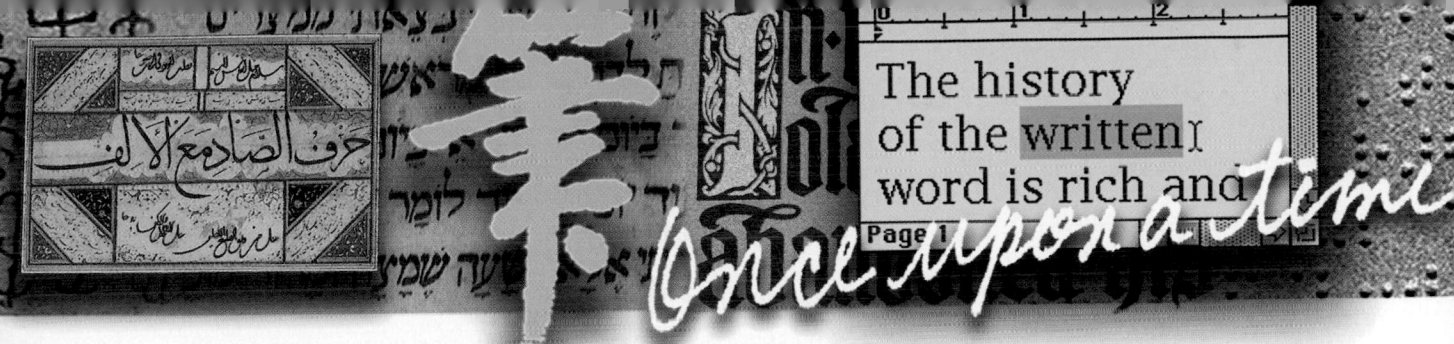

The history
of the written
word is rich and
Page 1

- What does the occasion (experience, observation, concept, or quotation) mean to me? What are my thoughts and feelings about it? What do I associate with it?

- What can I compare the occasion to?

- What does it teach me?

Try It Out

If each of the following were the occasion (the starting point) for a reflective essay, what might you say about it? Make a cluster diagram like the one to the left to capture your thoughts. To get started, ask yourself the questions at the top of this page.

1. waiting in line (at a movie theater, bank, bus stop)

2. "There is no calamity greater than lavish desires."—Laotzu

3. the idea of responsibility

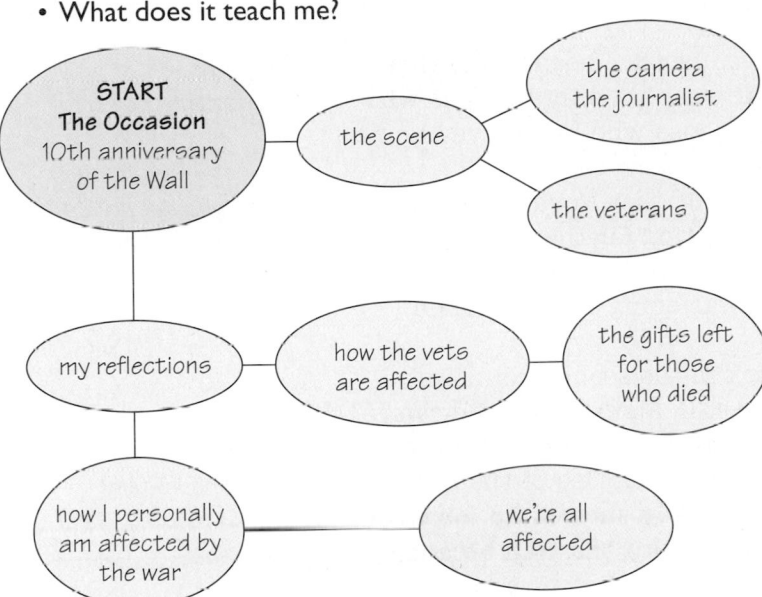

3. Take a Giant Leap

The end of every reflective essay is an insight or understanding about life or people in general. If you ask yourself "What can I learn from this occasion?" you'll be on your way to making the leap from something very specific to a **generalization** (see page 432). Here's a generalization at the end of the essay by Diane Ackerman that begins on page 420:

> "Learning our full address may not end all wars, but it will enrich our sense of wonder and pride. It will remind us that the human context is not tight as a noose, but large as the universe we have the privilege to inhabit. It will change our sense of what a neighborhood is. It will persuade us that we are citizens of something larger and more profound than mere countries, that we are citizens of Earth, her joy riders and her caretakers, who would do well to work on her problems together."

Language Link
H E L P

Showing time: page 405.
Description: page 419.

Drafting

1. Find Your Own Voice

Try to write the way you talk—with a confident, informal tone, using contractions and everyday words.

2. Explore Your Thoughts

Don't let the occasion take over your whole essay; it's just the starting place. Most of your essay should be an exploration of your thoughts and where they lead you. You might also include quotations or examples to develop your ideas, as Diane

Student Model

A VIETNAM REMEMBRANCE

Looking back on yesterday, November 8, I began to realize how important the Vietnam War was, not only to those who had gone and fought, but also to those who had stayed home and prayed for their loved ones to return safely.

It was an extremely cold morning, that November day. My stepfather, Michael, and I were waiting for the cameraman and Anne Taylor Fleming to arrive. Michael works for the MacNeil/Lehrer NewsHour and was doing a piece on the tenth anniversary of the Wall.

Cold and uncomfortable, I took in the scene around me. I saw veterans standing perfectly still, almost as if they were frozen in time. I had no idea whether they were thinking or not. All I know is that they had the memories of the war.

The cameraman and Anne eventually showed up. However, we weren't able to go straight to shooting the Wall because there was a ceremony going on. Jesse Jackson was leading a prayer service for all the Vietnam vets who had died. He sent a message to them saying that although they were gone, they would not be forgotten. After his prayer, people came up on stage and read off some names of the people who had died during the war. Some people had a list of twenty names and while they recited the names, they would say every once in a while, "I knew that man." Some people would only have one name on their list. There was a lady who had been married the day before who read off her father's name. It seemed as if she wanted her father to be part of her wedding. This calling of names would continue for twenty-four hours a day until the 11th of November. In rain or shine, whether people showed up or not, the litany of names would echo across the Mall.

About half of the people I saw were Vietnam vets. Surprisingly, they were all wearing their uniforms. One vet found a name of a friend or a brother or someone with whom he was

The writer begins with a powerful event and states its significance. She describes a particular occasion and gives background.

The scene is specifically described. We know how she felt.

The writer includes specific details to help us visualize the scene. The writer narrates the series of events that she's reflecting on.

Ackerman does when she gives many examples of what *home* means (page 421). Remember that thoughts have a way of zigging and zagging all over the place, so stay focused on your occasion.

Evaluating and Revising
1. Self-Evaluation

Once your draft is on paper, let it sit for a while so you can evaluate it with fresh eyes. Tighten your paragraphs. Get rid of unnecessary words and ideas that stray from the subject.

close during the war. He simply stood there and cried for a long time. A father saw his son's name imprinted on the wall. I remembered seeing him feel the inscription of his son's name while he rested his head on his arm. I also saw a woman who commented to everyone who passed by, saying repeatedly, "This is my husband."

> *The writer looks at the ceremony from several perspectives. She is very specific in describing what she sees.*

Out of this whole wall, one name stood out the most to me. That name was Billy Frank Dodd, an old friend of my mom's. When I saw his name, I fell to my knees. I wasn't crying, however, until a vet came up to me, put his hand on my shoulder, and said, "May he rest in peace." I stayed at this section of the Wall thinking, "My mom knew you. She came here once, but had to leave before she made it to the Wall because she was crying so hard. She misses you." After I was done crying, I gave Billy a kiss goodbye. I can still remember the feel of the smooth marble surface on my lips.

> *A personal anecdote illustrates the writer's personal connection to the event.*

> *Another sensory detail.*

After I left the Wall, I went to look around and it surprised me that people had left gifts—roses, Tabasco sauce, a teddy bear, even a bottle of whiskey. However, the one gift that touched me the most was a letter written by a man to his brother. In this letter he assured his brother of his love and wished that he could see him just one last time.

> *A list of specific sights.*

Visiting this Wall made me realize many things. I understand what an important event this was in a vet's life. It also made me realize that a war can bring people closer together and yet pull them apart. However, what the Wall made me appreciate the most was that the war still haunts people. Looking back on yesterday, November 8, I began to realize how important the Vietnam War is.

> *The conclusion summarizes the writer's reflections.*

> *A strong conclusion that echoes the beginning.*

—Alicia Guevara
Marymount School
New York, New York

Sentence Workshop
H E L P

Combining sentences by using participial phrases: page 444.

■ *Evaluation Criteria*

A good reflective essay

1. *begins with an observation, event, quotation, or abstract idea*

2. *explores the occasion and its meaning from different perspectives*

3. *includes the writer's thoughts and feelings about the subject*

4. *concludes with some insight or new awareness about people or life in general*

5. *has a natural, confident tone*

Although your essay shouldn't read like a newspaper headline, it shouldn't go on and on—and on and on and on—either. Pare your draft down to its best parts, as if you were adjusting a pair of binoculars to bring a blurry picture into sharp focus.

You might ask someone to read your paper aloud as you listen for awkward-sounding sentences (too many short ones in a row, sentences that are too long and complicated) and words that don't sound like your own voice.

2. Peer Editing

Before the members of your writing group read (or listen to you read) your draft, ask them to focus on parts of the paper you're not sure about. For example:

- Does the language sound natural?
- Can you follow my train of thought easily?
- Is the beginning strong enough?
- Do you think I spend enough (or too much) time developing the occasion/incident?
- Does the conclusion bring the essay to a satisfying end?

Revision Model

	Peer Comments
After I left the Wall, I went to look	*Can you combine your first two sentences so they're not so choppy?*
around/ ^and^ It surprised me that	
roses, Tabasco sauce, a teddy bear, even a bottle of whiskey. people had left gifts/ However, the	*It would be nice to know what the gifts were. Frags.*
one gift touched me the most/ ^that^ A ^was^	
letter written by a man to his	*Tell us why the gift touched you so much.*
In this letter he assured his brother of his love and wished that he could see him just one last time. brother. ^	

Proofreading

Run the spelling and grammar checkers if you're writing on a computer, but force yourself to read every word and punctuation mark *very slowly* anyway, since computers won't catch some kinds of mistakes—like using *their* instead of *they're*. Exchange papers with a partner to double-check for mistakes. Watch out for overuse or underuse of commas in a series and in adjective clauses.

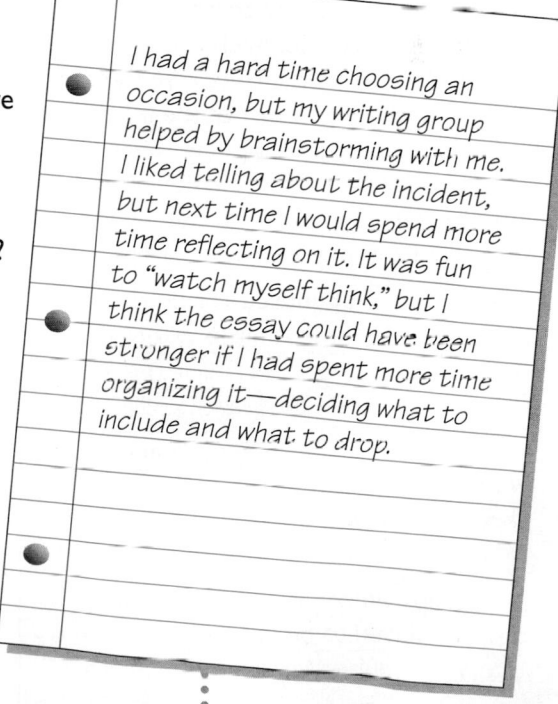

Language Link
H E L P

Punctuating a series: page 425. Adjective clauses: page 433.

Publishing

Share your essay with the audience you had in mind when you wrote it, or try one of these publishing ideas:

- **Make a class anthology.** Student artists might submit designs for a logo and a cover. Then have the winning design chosen by the pub (short for *publications*) board, which is made up of everyone in class. Place everyone's reflective essay in a binder and donate your anthology to the school library.

- **Send it away.** Mail your essay to a contest or one of the national magazines that publish student writing. Ask your teacher or school librarian for addresses and advice.

- **Record your essay.** Have everyone read his or her essay on an audiotape or videotape. Share the tape with your family but leave it with your teacher to inspire future reflective essay writers.

Reflecting

Think about what it was like to write your reflective essay. If you include it in your portfolio, date it, and attach a brief reflection.

1. Did I learn anything about the way I think? Did I enjoy searching for meanings in my experiences?

2. What do I like best about my reflective essay? What still needs work?

3. What was the most difficult part of writing this essay? What will I do differently next time?

I had a hard time choosing an occasion, but my writing group helped by brainstorming with me. I liked telling about the incident, but next time I would spend more time reflecting on it. It was fun to "watch myself think," but I think the essay could have been stronger if I had spent more time organizing it—deciding what to include and what to drop.

Sentence Workshop

Language Handbook HELP

See Participles and Participial Phrases, page 1007.

Technology HELP

See Language Workshop CD-ROM. *Key word entry:* participial phrases.

COMBINING SENTENCES: PARTICIPIAL PHRASES

N. Scott Momaday might have written these short sentences:

> These were the Navajos. They were coming in from Torreon. They sat tall in the wagons and on horseback. They went easily with laughter. They sang their riding songs.

Instead, he uses participial phrases to combine ideas and create a smoother-sounding paragraph:

> "These were the Navajos, <u>coming in from Torreon</u>. . . . They sat tall in the wagons and on horseback, <u>going easily with laughter</u> and <u>singing their riding songs</u>."

A **participle** is a verb form that is used as an adjective. Participles come in two varieties: **present participles** (<u>baking</u> bread, <u>running</u> men) and **past participles** (<u>covered</u> wagons, <u>imagined</u> adventures).

A **participial phrase** is made up of a participle followed by its modifiers and objects. Participial phrases, which are always used as adjectives, should be placed close to the noun or pronoun they modify. An introductory participial phrase is always followed by a comma.

> <u>Finding a gimlet</u>, Harriet Jacobs bored a small hole through which she could watch her children.

> <u>Tormented by hundreds of tiny biting insects</u>, Harriet Jacobs suffered for weeks until she got rid of them.

Writer's Workshop Follow-up: Revision

Take another look at the reflective essay you wrote for the Writer's Workshop. See if there are short sentences you can combine by using participial phrases. Read both versions aloud (with and without the participial phrase). Which version sounds better?

Try It Out

First, to see how ideas are combined by professional writers, take each sentence that follows and make it into two sentences; one sentence should consist of the information now in the participial phrase. Then, write an original sentence modeled after each professional sentence. Underline the participial phrases in your own sentences.

1. "We watched a hundred-ton shaft <u>plunging down to that place where the water was</u>."
   —Joan Didion, "At the Dam"

2. "We are at our human finest, <u>dancing with our minds</u>, when there are more choices than two."
   —Lewis Thomas, "To Err Is Human"

3. "He sleeps almost as soon as he lies down, <u>relieved to be at last alone</u>."
   —V. S. Naipaul, *A Way in the World*

Collection 7

WHAT I THINK

Writing Focus: Persuasive Essay

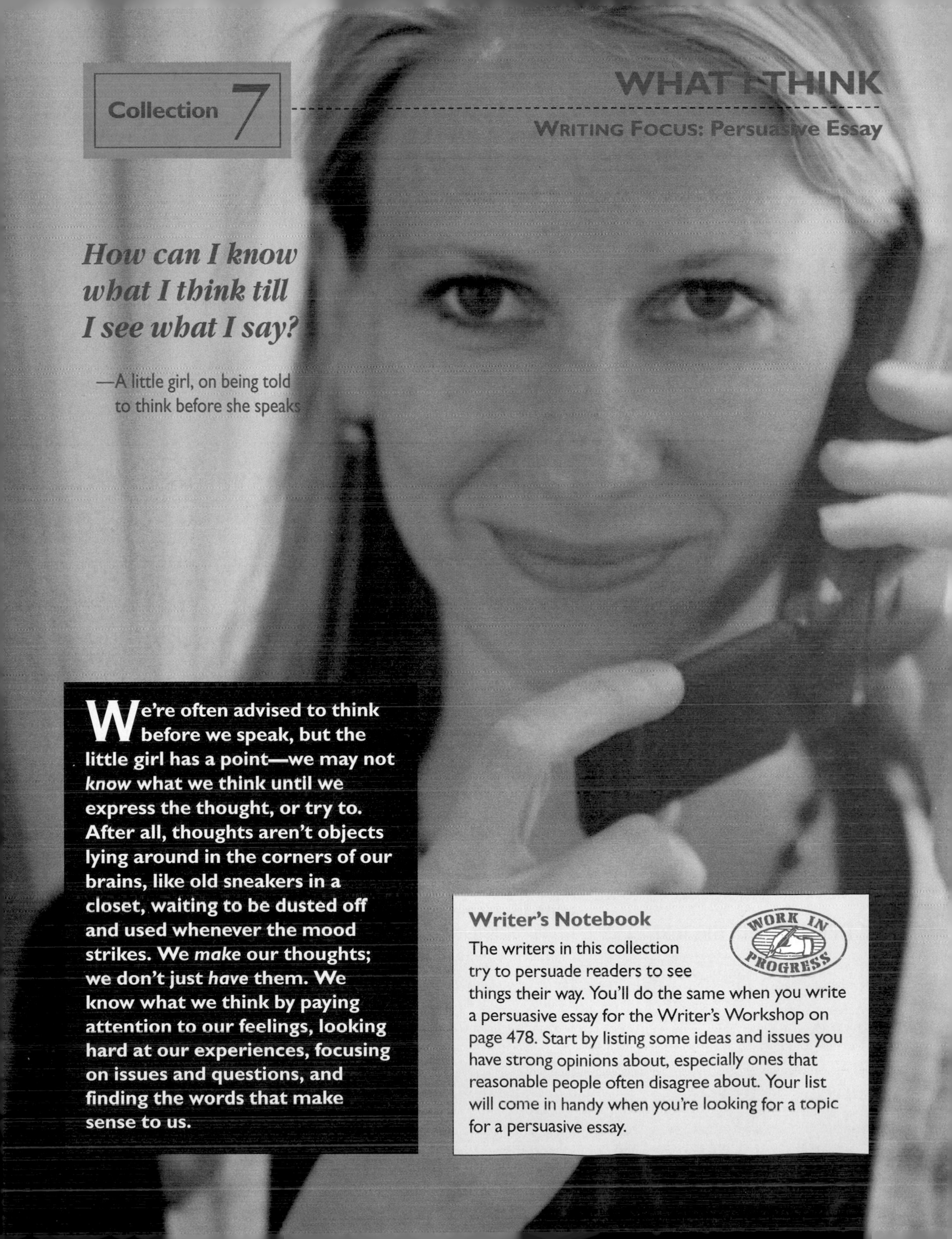

How can I know what I think till I see what I say?

—A little girl, on being told to think before she speaks

We're often advised to think before we speak, but the little girl has a point—we may not *know* what we think until we express the thought, or try to. After all, thoughts aren't objects lying around in the corners of our brains, like old sneakers in a closet, waiting to be dusted off and used whenever the mood strikes. We *make* our thoughts; we don't just *have* them. We know what we think by paying attention to our feelings, looking hard at our experiences, focusing on issues and questions, and finding the words that make sense to us.

Writer's Notebook

WORK IN PROGRESS

The writers in this collection try to persuade readers to see things their way. You'll do the same when you write a persuasive essay for the Writer's Workshop on page 478. Start by listing some ideas and issues you have strong opinions about, especially ones that reasonable people often disagree about. Your list will come in handy when you're looking for a topic for a persuasive essay.

Reading Focus

Broken Promises

When the first Europeans arrived, about ten million American Indians lived in what is the United States today. The history of the government's relationship with the people who lived here first is long and tragic. In the speech you are about to read, a Nez Percé (nez' pʉrs') leader pleads with the government for better treatment for his people.

Background

In 1877, when three young braves killed four white settlers, Chief Joseph fled the Wallowa Valley in Oregon with some 250 warriors and their families. For more than three months and 1,400 miles, they outmaneuvered federal troops, finally surrendering 40 miles from the Canadian border.

Exiled to a reservation in Oklahoma, Chief Joseph spent the rest of his life trying to persuade the government to let his people return to their home.

A Dialogue with the Text

In your Reader's Log, make a KWL chart like the one shown. In the K column, write what you already *know* about "Indian affairs." In the W column, fill in what you *want* to know—some questions you'd like answered. Complete the L column (what you *learned*) after you read Chief Joseph's speech.

K	W	L

Elements of Literature

Appealing to the Head and Heart

When you're trying to persuade, you can use **logical appeals** (reasons, facts, statistics, and examples) or **emotional appeals** (words, phrases, and anecdotes that appeal strongly to your audience's feelings—their fears, hopes, even prejudices) or a combination of both techniques.

Persuasive writers use **logical** and **emotional appeals** to convince the reader or listener to think or act in a certain way.

For more on Logical and Emotional Appeals, see page 453.

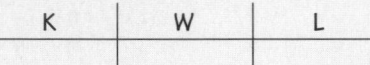

Words do not pay for my dead people.

National Portrait Gallery, Smithsonian Institution, Washington, D.C.

Portrait of In-mut-too-yah-lat-lat (Chief Joseph), Indian Chief, by Cyrenius Hall.

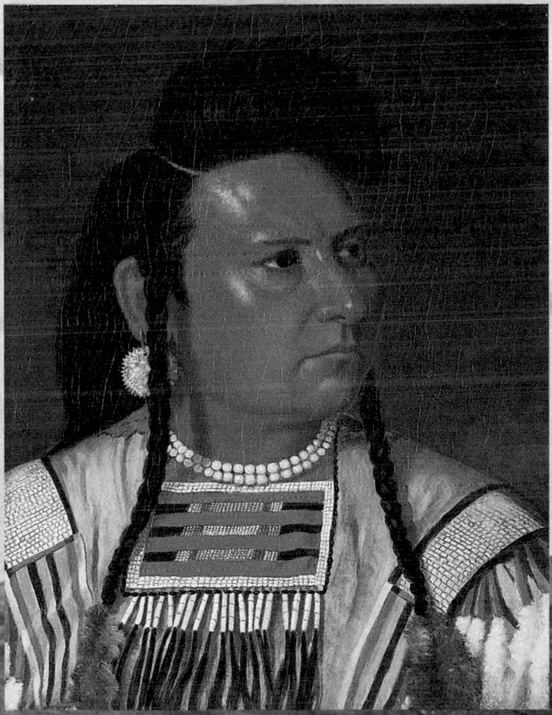

from

An Indian's Views of Indian Affairs

Chief Joseph

. . . I have heard talk and talk, but nothing is done. Good words do not last long unless they amount to something. Words do not pay for my dead people. They do not pay for my country, now overrun by white men. They do not protect my father's grave. They do not pay for all my horses and cattle. Good words will not give me back my children. Good words will not make good the promise of your war chief General Miles.° Good words will not give my people good health and stop them from dying. Good words will not get my people a home where they can live in peace and take care of themselves.

I am tired of talk that comes to nothing. It makes my heart sick when I remember all the good words and all the broken promises. There has been too much talking by men who had no right to talk. Too many misrepresentations have been made, too many misunderstandings have come up between the white men about the Indians.

If the white man wants to live in peace with the Indian, he can live in peace. There need be no trouble. Treat all men alike. Give them the same law. Give them an even chance to live and grow. All men were made by the same Great Spirit Chief. They are all brothers. The earth is the mother of all people, and all people should have equal rights upon it.

You might as well expect the rivers to run backward as that any man who was born a free man should be contented when penned up and denied liberty to go where he pleases. If you tie

°**General Miles:** Nelson Appleton Miles (1839–1925), an army officer who led many military campaigns against American Indians. In 1877, he led a campaign against the Nez Percé warriors and captured Chief Joseph.

a horse to a stake, do you expect he will grow fat? If you pen an Indian up on a small spot of earth and compel him to stay there, he will not be contented, nor will he grow and prosper. I have asked some of the great white chiefs where they get their authority to say to the Indian that he shall stay in one place while he sees white men going where they please. They cannot tell me.

I only ask of the government to be treated as all other men are treated. If I cannot go to my own home, let me have a home in some country where my people will not die so fast. . . .

When I think of our condition, my heart is heavy. I see men of my race treated as outlaws and driven from country to country or shot down like animals.

I know that my race must change. We cannot hold our own with white men as we are. We ask only an even chance to live as other men live. We ask to be recognized as men. We ask that the same law shall work alike on all men. If the Indian breaks the law, punish him by the law. If the white man breaks the law, punish him also.

Let me be a free man—free to travel, free to stop, free to work, free to trade where I choose, free to choose my own teachers, free to follow the religion of my fathers, free to think and talk and act for myself—and I will obey every law or submit to the penalty.

Whenever white men treat Indians as they treat each other, then we will have no more wars. We shall all be alike—brothers of one father and one mother, with one mother, with one sky above us and one country around us, and one government for all. Then the Great Spirit Chief who rules above will smile upon this land and send rain to wash out the bloody spots made by brothers' hands from the face of the earth.

For this time the Indian race is waiting and praying. I hope that no more groans of wounded men and women will ever go to the ear of the Great Spirit Chief above and that all people may be one people.

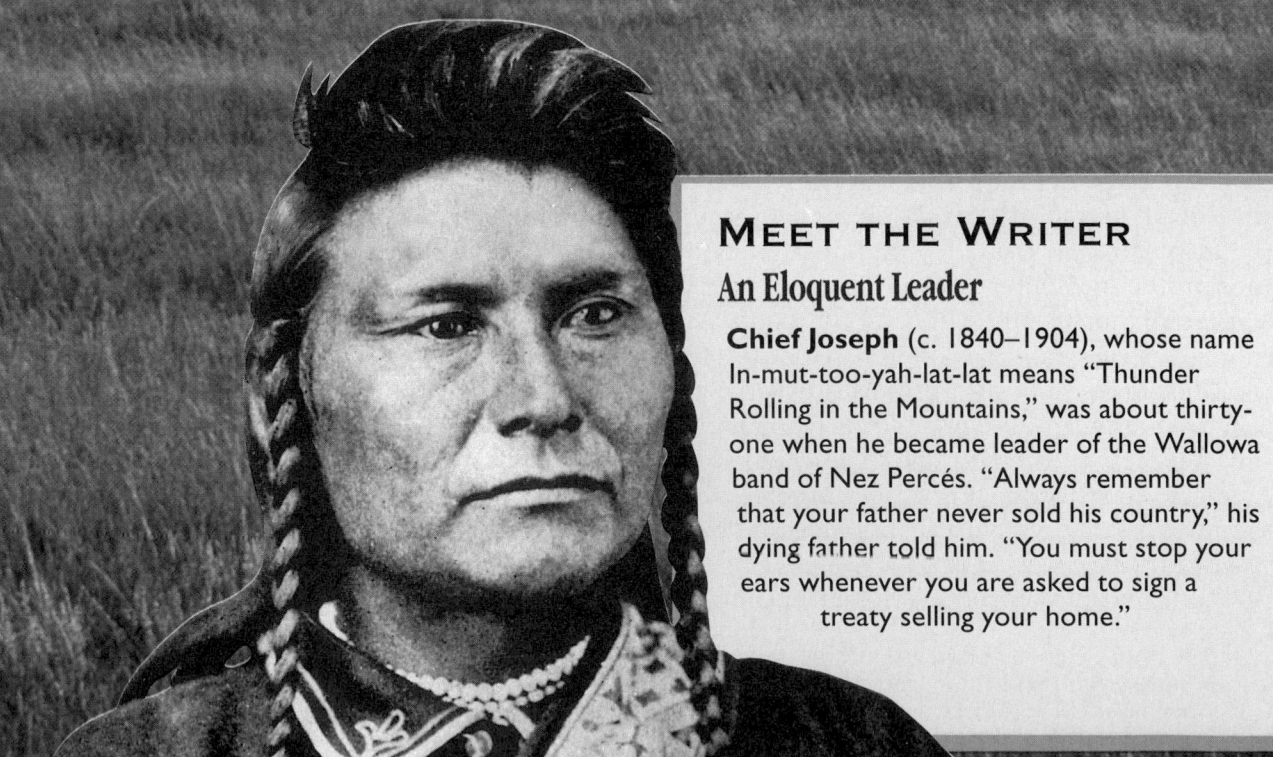

MEET THE WRITER
An Eloquent Leader

Chief Joseph (c. 1840–1904), whose name In-mut-too-yah-lat-lat means "Thunder Rolling in the Mountains," was about thirty-one when he became leader of the Wallowa band of Nez Percés. "Always remember that your father never sold his country," his dying father told him. "You must stop your ears whenever you are asked to sign a treaty selling your home."

The Man from Washington

James Welch

The end came easy for most of us.
Packed away in our crude beginnings
in some far corner of a flat world,
we didn't expect much more
5   than firewood and buffalo robes
to keep us warm. The man came down,
a slouching dwarf with rainwater eyes,
and spoke to us. He promised
that life would go on as usual,
10   that treaties would be signed, and everyone—
man, woman, and child—would be inoculated
against a world in which we had no part,
a world of money, promise, and disease.°

13. Epidemics of smallpox and chickenpox, caused by contact with white settlers, wiped out whole American Indian villages.

In October 1877, Chief Joseph surrendered his band of Nez Percés, who had refused to sign the latest government treaty, with these now-famous words:

❝ I am tired of fighting. Our chiefs are killed. . . . The old men are all dead. . . . It is cold, and we have no blankets. The little children are freezing to death. My people, some of them, have run away to the hills, and have no blankets, no food. No one knows where they are—perhaps freezing to death. I want to have time to look for my children and see how many of them I can find. Maybe I shall find them among the dead. Hear me, my chiefs! I am tired. My heart is sick and sad. From where the sun now stands I will fight no more forever. **❞**

Chief Joseph continued to fight—not with weapons but with words—traveling twice to the nation's capital to plead for his people's return to their ancestral lands. After eight years 150 surviving Nez Percés (all of Joseph's children had died by then) were allowed to return to the Northwest but not to their beloved Wallowa Valley. When Chief Joseph died on the Colville Reservation in Washington, the doctor said he had died of a broken heart.

MAKING MEANINGS

First Thoughts

1. Were you persuaded? Tell how you responded to Chief Joseph's speech.

Shaping Interpretations

2. Does Chief Joseph use **logical** or **emotional appeals** or both? Find some examples.

Connecting with the Text

3. Are actions always more important than "good words"? Support your opinion with examples from history or from your own experience.

4. Who *is* "The Man from Washington" (page 449) and who is the speaker? Using what you know of American Indians' history, tell how this poem affects you.

5. Fill in the L column in your KWL chart (see page 446). If you have any unanswered questions, do some research and share your findings with the class.

Reviewing the Text

In a chart like the one below, state each main idea in the speech and list its supporting details.

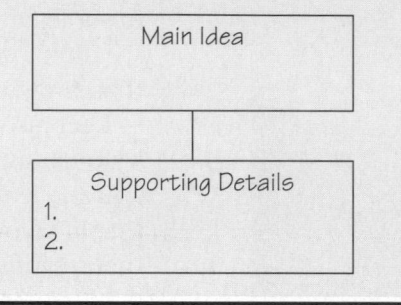

Main Idea

Supporting Details
1.
2.

CHOICES: Building Your Portfolio

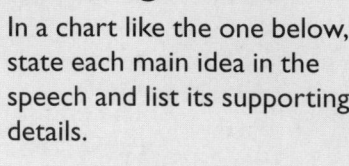

Writer's Notebook

1. Collecting Ideas for a Persuasive Essay

Pinning down what you think.

In the persuasive essay you'll write for the Writer's Workshop on page 478, you'll choose a debatable topic, decide what you think about it, and try to convince your audience you're right. With a small group, brainstorm debatable topics (topics that people have opposing opinions about). (A topic might be suggested by Chief Joseph's speech.) Choose two topics that interest you and decide what you think about each one. For each topic write a **thesis statement,** a sentence that clearly states your opinion. Save your notes.

Critical Writing/ Speaking

2. Dear Chief Joseph

You are one of the members of Congress who listened to Chief Joseph plead his case. Write a letter or deliver a brief speech responding to his statements.

Art

3. Good Words

Choose one sentence from the speech that you found especially powerful and create a poster based on it. Experiment with different design elements (lettering, color, symbols, images, decorative patterns) to express Chief Joseph's ideas.

LANGUAGE LINK MINI-LESSON

Handbook of Literary Terms
H E L P

See Connotation.

Style: Connotations and Loaded Words

Many English words have **connotations** (feelings and associations) in addition to their **denotations** (dictionary meanings). Connotations stir people's feelings in a positive or negative way. When such words are used in persuasive writing or speaking, they're called **loaded words**. For example:

Senator Blank is <u>rigid</u>.
Senator Blank is <u>firm</u>.

Both of these sentences really say the same thing (Senator Blank does not change her mind easily). Which sentence uses a loaded word designed to make you approve of her, and which one is meant to make you disapprove?

You should be aware of loaded words in advertisements and political speeches. Someone may be trying to sway your feelings so that you'll buy a product or support a candidate.

Try It Out

1. If you can think of a word to fill each empty space in this chart, you'll have a list of words that mean more or less the same but are loaded either positively or negatively.

Positive	Negative
slender	
	cheap
	stubborn
	timid

2. Look for loaded words in Chief Joseph's speech and in line 7 in Welch's poem. Are the words positive or negative? Can you substitute other words that would change the tone of each text?

VOCABULARY HOW TO OWN A WORD

Synonyms

Synonyms are words that have the same, or nearly the same, meaning (*protect/shield, equal/alike*). The English language has few exact synonyms, but many words that mean almost the same. Choose five words from the speech and make a diagram like the one here for each. Write the word, one synonym, and a sentence for each. Can the synonyms be used interchangeably, or are there important differences in meaning?

Prosper wouldn't be right in second sentence, unless Nedra wants to get rich.

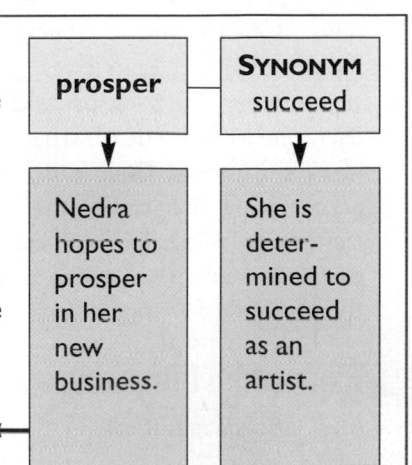

Elements of Literature

THE WRITER'S PURPOSE

by Janet Burroway

Every good writer of nonfiction has a purpose when he or she sits down to write. The purpose may be to explain or inform; to create a mood or stir an emotion; to tell about a series of events; to persuade the reader to believe something or do something. A writer may want to do several of these things in a single essay or report, but he or she will know what the primary purpose of the piece of writing is and will select and arrange words and details that best accomplish that purpose.

Suppose, for instance, that Jim Greene breaks Terry Lewis's arm in the gym on Friday afternoon during a judo workout. Jim says it was an accident; Terry says Jim did it on purpose. Mrs. Jeffords, the judo instructor, wasn't looking. Another student, Stan Jones, was looking. The principal asks each one to write down what he or she knows. Their four accounts are all based on the same facts. What differs in each case is the writer's purpose and the method of writing.

Exposition: Informing

Mrs. Jeffords is not taking sides. She simply wants to explain how such an accident could have happened. Most of her report is **exposition,** the method of writing that explains or informs.

Judo throws require both precise timing and exact balance. At this level (yellow belt) there is always a slight possibility that the participants have insufficient agility or coordination.

Description: Sensing It

Stan Jones, the only witness, writes a more detailed and dramatic piece. He adds a great deal of **description,** the kind of writing that uses images to help us experience something with our senses.

The air conditioner in the gym was broken, and the place was like a giant oven. Jim was sweating heavily after the last throw. Terry lunged for Jim, but his fingers slipped on Jim's glistening skin.

Narration: What Happens

Jim Greene, who feels innocent and wants to appear as reasonable as possible, sticks to a straight **narration**.

This method of writing tells about a series of events, usually in chronological order.

I had just come out of the last throw and had turned toward Terry, who was getting up to come at me from the left. I made a quarter-turn and moved my left leg forward when he reached for my neck and his hand slipped.

Persuasion: Influencing People

Terry's arm hurts and he's angry that he'll miss the spring tournament. His purpose is **persuasion,** so he'll select all the evidence he can to persuade the principal that Jim broke his arm on purpose.

Jim's jealous of me and always has been. I got my yellow belt three meets ahead of him, and I'm the only one who's ever thrown him three-out-of-four.

In general, **exposition** answers "What is it, and how does it work?" **Description** answers "What does it look, sound, smell, feel, taste like?" **Narration** answers "What happened?" **Persuasion** answers "What should I feel or do about it?"

PERSUASIVE TECHNIQUES: Watch for the Tricks

When your purpose is **persuasion,** you'll develop a **logical argument,** a series of statements made up of your opinion supported by reasons and evidence. You'll find step-by-step techniques for developing such an argument in the Writer's Workshop (page 478).

Fallacies: How Not to Argue

Beware of **fallacies,** which are errors in logical thinking. They'll weaken your argument and make your audience doubt *everything* you say. Suppose, for instance, the school board has announced plans to cut all after-school sports. Here are four fallacies to avoid.

1. Attacking the Person

Mr. McAloo, who proposed these cuts, hates sports and is a pennypinching meanie.

Don't attack an opponent's character or judgment. Stay focused on the issue.

2. Circular Reasoning

After-school sports are essential because they're a necessary part of school activities.

This may look like a reason but it's not. The part of the sentence that follows *because* just restates the writer's opinion.

3. False Cause and Effect

When after-school sports were dropped at Adams High School, the dropout rate increased immediately.

Just because Event 2 happens *after* Event 1, you can't conclude that Event 1 *caused* Event 2. The two events may be (and usually are) unrelated.

4. Hasty Generalization

Everyone in school agrees that dropping after-school sports is a dumb idea. I know because I asked my friend Chad, and he agrees with me.

You can't generalize about "everyone" or "everything" based on only one or two cases. You need a great many observations before you can make a valid generalization.

Emotional Appeals

In a persuasive essay or speech, **emotional appeals** add an extra persuasive push, but they're not a substitute for a logical argument. In this collection, you'll learn about two useful types of emotional appeals: loaded words (page 451) and anecdotes (page 454). Here are others that you'll recognize from advertisements and campaign speeches.

1. Bandwagon

Everyone's throwing a Spiro-cylinder, the best thing since a boomerang. Get yours today before they're all gone.

The bandwagon appeal suggests that unless you "jump on the bandwagon" and act right now, you'll be left out, the only one who's different.

2. Testimonial

Carrie, the Most Valuable Player in the soccer league, starts every morning with Brand X Cereal.

Entertainers and athletes are paid to endorse products they often know little about. Advertisers hope they'll persuade their fans to "Be like me; do what I do."

3. "Plain Folks"

I'm just an average guy who values his family, and I know we're all safe on Giant-Tread Tires.

People tend to believe people who look and sound like themselves, so advertisers hire ordinary-looking actors and actresses.

Check It Out

Find and display examples of these fallacies and emotional appeals. Look for them in television and radio commercials, magazine and newspaper advertisements, political messages and campaign speeches.

Reading Focus

Seeing What He Means

In this essay the narrator tells some humorous stories about how people have reacted to his blindness. Although he claims to have a "saintlike disposition," some reactions clearly annoy him, while others please him. As you read this essay, you'll discover how Krents wants to be treated.

Quickwrite

What do you think is the right way to treat a person who has impaired sight or hearing or who uses a wheelchair? Quickwrite for a few minutes in your Reader's Log.

Elements of Literature

Stories with a Point

Anecdotes are very brief stories that have some of the elements of a short story: characters, plot, and dialogue. In a persuasive essay, anecdotes usually help the writer make some kind of point. Look for anecdotes in "Darkness at Noon."

An **anecdote** is a very brief story that is used to make a point or provide an example.

DARKNESS at NOON

Harold Krents

> *Others know that I can hear, but believe that I can't talk.*

Blind from birth, I have never had the opportunity to see myself and have been completely dependent on the image I create in the eye of the observer. To date it has not been narcissistic.[1]

There are those who assume that since I can't see, I obviously also cannot hear. Very often people will converse with me at the top of their lungs, enunciating each word very carefully. Conversely, people will also often whisper, assuming that since my eyes don't work, my ears don't either.

For example, when I go to the airport and ask the ticket agent for assistance to the plane, he or she will <u>invariably</u> pick up the phone, call a ground hostess, and whisper: "Hi, Jane, we've got a 76 here." I have concluded that the word blind is not used, for one of two reasons: Either they fear that if the dread word is spoken, the ticket agent's retina will immediately detach,[2] or they are reluctant to inform me of my condition, of which I may not have been previously aware.

---

1. narcissistic (när′sə·sis′tik): here, flattering. Narcissism is self-love or an excessive interest in one's own appearance.

2. retina (ret′'n·ə) **will immediately detach:** The retina is the innermost lining of the eyeball. A detached retina can cause blindness.

WORDS TO OWN
invariably (in·ver′ē·ə·blē) *adv.:* always; without exception.

LITERATURE AND THE LAW

A Time Line on Rights for the Disabled

1962: Ed Roberts, a quadriplegic, appeals his rejection by the University of California at Berkeley. Roberts enters Berkeley, and the disability rights movement is born.

1970: Twenty-two-year-old Judy Heumann, a quadriplegic, founds Disabled in Action, a rights group for the disabled.

1971: An episode of Julia Child's *The French Chef* is the first TV show captioned for hearing-impaired viewers.

1973: Rehabilitation Act forbids federal agencies and federally funded institutions to make hiring decisions "solely by reason of . . . handicap"; final regulations delayed.

1975: Education of All Handicapped Children Act guarantees free appropriate public education; final regulations delayed.

1977: Activists occupy San Francisco offices of the Department of Health, Education and Welfare for twenty-five days. Final regulations are issued, and the 1973 and 1975 acts are more strictly enforced.

1988: Students at Gallaudet University for the hearing-impaired demand a deaf president; their protests shut down the campus. I. King Jordan, a deaf man, is appointed president.

1990: President Bush signs the Americans with Disabilities Act, banning discrimination in jobs, transportation, and government services.

On the other hand, others know that of course I can hear, but believe that I can't talk. Often, therefore, when my wife and I go out to dinner, a waiter or waitress will ask Kit if "he would like a drink" to which I respond that "indeed he would."

This point was graphically driven home to me while we were in England. I had been given a year's leave of absence from my Washington law firm to study for a diploma in law at Oxford University. During the year I became ill and was hospitalized. Immediately after admission I was wheeled down to the X-ray room. Just at the door sat an elderly woman—elderly I would judge from the sound of her voice. "What is his name?" the woman asked the orderly who had been wheeling me.

"What's your name?" the orderly repeated to me.

"Harold Krents," I replied.

"Harold Krents," he repeated.

"When was he born?"

"When were you born?"

"November 5, 1944," I responded.

"November 5, 1944," the orderly <u>intoned</u>.

This procedure continued for approximately five minutes, at which point even my saintlike disposition deserted me. Looking I finally blurted out, "this is absolutely ridiculous. Okay, granted I can't see, but it's got to have become pretty clear to both of you that I don't need an interpreter."

"He says he doesn't need an interpreter," the orderly reported to the woman.

The toughest misconception of all is the view that because I can't see, I can't work. I was turned down by over forty law firms because of my blindness, even though my qualifications included a cum laude[3]

3. ***cum laude*** (koom lou′dā): Latin phrase meaning "with praise," used in college or university diplomas to indicate above-average grades.

WORDS TO OWN

intoned (in·tōnd′) *v.*: said or recited in a dull, unchanging tone.

degree from Harvard College and a good ranking in my Harvard Law School class.

The attempt to find employment, the continuous frustration of being told that it was impossible for a blind person to practice law, the rejection letters, based not on my lack of ability but rather on my disability, will always remain one of the most disillusioning experiences of my life.

Fortunately, this view of limitation and exclusion is beginning to change. On April 16, [1978,] the Department of Labor issued regulations that mandate equal-employment opportunities for the handicapped. By and large, the business community's response to offering employment to the disabled has been enthusiastic.

I therefore look forward to the day, with the expectation that it is certain to come, when employers will view their handicapped workers as a little child did me years ago when my family still lived in Scarsdale.

I was playing basketball with my father in our back yard according to procedures we had developed. My father would stand beneath the hoop, shout, and I would shoot over his head at the basket attached to our garage. Our next-door neighbor, aged five, wandered over into our yard with a playmate. "He's blind," our neighbor whispered to her friend in a voice that could be heard distinctly by Dad and me. Dad shot and missed; I did the same. Dad hit the rim; I missed entirely; Dad shot and missed the garage entirely. "Which one is blind?" whispered back the little friend.

I would hope that in the near future when a plant manager is touring the factory with the foreman and comes upon a handicapped and a nonhandicapped person working together, his comment after watching them work will be, "Which one is disabled?"

WORDS TO OWN

disillusioning (dis'i·loo'zhən·iŋ) v. used as *adj.*: disappointing; making one feel bitter.
mandate (man'dāt') v.: require; formally order.

MEET THE WRITER

Independent and Proud of It

Harold Krents (1944–1987) titled his autobiography *To Race the Wind* (1972) because when he was three, he used to try to run faster than the wind, racing ahead of his mother. Because he was almost totally blind and was running on city sidewalks, he sometimes crashed into lampposts and parking meters. His family raised him to be independent. When Krents was nine, for example, his older brother threw passes at him until Krents could catch the football he couldn't see:

66 It was this confidence, which I received from every member of my family, that gave me the strength to attempt, to fail, and to try again until the goal, whatever it happened to be, was achieved. 99

Playwright Leonard Gershe, who heard Krents being interviewed on the radio, was "bowled over by this boy's humor and healthy attitude about his situation." This inspired Gershe to write *Butterflies Are Free* (1969), a successful play about a visually impaired young man living alone in a city.

Krents practiced law in Washington, D.C., and was a lifelong advocate for the rights of all people with disabilities. He advised presidents and helped establish Mainstream, Inc., an organization that works for legal rights for the disabled.

MAKING MEANINGS

First Thoughts

1. Jot down some words or phrases that describe Harold Krents's character and personality as you see them.

Shaping Interpretations

2. Krents deals with a serious personal issue in a way that's designed to appeal to readers. Describe his essay's **tone**. What details create that tone?

3. Tell what point you think Krents is making with each of the **anecdotes** about events at the airport, in the hospital, in a backyard basketball game.

4. How would you state the essay's **main idea** (you may find more than one)? What do you think the unusual **title** means?

Connecting with the Text

5. Look back at your Reader's Log entry. How does a disabled person really want to be treated? Would you want to add anything to Krents's main point?

Reviewing the Text

a. Summarize one anecdote that shows how Krents doesn't want to be treated.

b. Which anecdote shows how he *wants* to be treated?

c. Describe his job-hunting experience after law school.

d. What rules did the Department of Labor issue about jobs for people with disabilities?

CHOICES: Building Your Portfolio

Writer's Notebook

1. Collecting Ideas for a Persuasive Essay

Anecdotes to persuade. Professional writers often advise: "Write what you know." Review your notebook and find a controversial topic you have firsthand knowledge about. Think of some anecdotes—your own experiences or observations, true

stories you've read or heard—that will help convince your readers that your opinion on this issue is correct. List these anecdotes in your notebook. Save your notes for possible use in the Writer's Workshop on page 478.

Critical Writing

2. Expressing Your Views

Look around you—at your school and at your community's sidewalks, streets, transportation system, and public buildings. How easily can a person with a disability get around? Write a letter to the editor of your local newspaper expressing your views about what changes need to be made. Be sure you don't use the fallacies mentioned on page 453.

Style: Euphemisms—Language That Covers Up

On page 454 Harold Krents suggests two humorous reasons that airline employees might use a code term instead of the straightforward word *blind.* When a less direct word or phrase is used as a substitute for a term some people find offensive or distasteful, it is called a **euphemism** (yōō′fə‧miz′əm). *Passed away,* for example, is a euphemism for *died;* a *pre-need arrangement* with a funeral home is really a prepaid funeral. Euphemisms aren't used only to spare feelings; sometimes they're used to mislead people or hide the facts. A *pre-owned car,* for instance, is a used car with a classier name.

Use each of the following euphemisms in a sentence, and then substitute the more direct word each one replaces. Do you notice the difference?

Euphemism	Direct Term
house of correction	prison
disinformation	lies
downsizing	firings, layoffs
depressed socio-economic area	slum

Try It Out

➤ For three TV programs in a row, listen carefully to every commercial. Then read your newspaper or news magazine very carefully. Pay attention to political speeches and quotes from public officials. List any euphemisms you discover. What, in each case, is the speaker or writer *really* saying? Be sure to share your findings with the class.

➤ Look for euphemisms in your own writing. In the revision stage, or when you review a peer's work, bracket any words or phrases you think are not direct enough. Then go back over your paper and see if you can find clearer, more forceful ways of saying what you mean.

VOCABULARY `HOW TO OWN A WORD`

WORD BANK

invariably
intoned
disillusioning
mandate

Vocabulary for the Workplace

You're a speech writer who's been asked to write several paragraphs for the president's State of the Union speech.

1. What topics would you guess are <u>invariably</u> discussed in this speech?
2. Demonstrate to a partner how the president would sound if he <u>intoned</u> his speech.
3. List some current situations the president will focus on that some people find <u>disillusioning</u>.
4. Write a sentence for the president's speech, using the word *mandate.*

Reading Focus

"The Worst Thing"

In this essay Anna Quindlen takes a new approach to a problem she calls the worst thing. Instead of our talking about the problem, gathering statistics, complaining, and hoping it will go away, what does Quindlen want us to do?

A Dialogue with the Text

As you read, jot down some of the statements you agree or disagree with (you'll probably find some of each) and any statements you find puzzling.

Statements	My Comments
"You are where you live."	That doesn't sound right to me—people can be better than terrible places they live in.

Elements of Literature

More Than Just the Facts

A **fact** is something that can be proved true, so what more do you need to persuade someone? Anna Quindlen does *not* stick just to the facts. In this essay, she states her opinions, tells stories, and shares her feelings. As you read, notice what Quindlen is trying to persuade you to believe or do and how she goes about it.

> **A fact** is something that can be proved true. An **opinion** is a personal belief that can't be proved, only supported.

HOMELESS

Home is where the heart is.

Anna Quindlen

Her name was Ann, and we met in the Port Authority Bus Terminal several Januaries ago. I was doing a story on homeless people. She said I was wasting my time talking to her; she was just passing through, although she'd been passing through for more than two weeks. To prove to me that this was true, she rummaged through a tote bag and a manila envelope and finally unfolded a sheet of typing paper and brought out her photographs.

They were not pictures of family, or friends, or even a dog or cat, its eyes brown-red in the flashbulb's light. They were pictures of a house. It was like a thousand houses in a hundred towns, not suburb, not city, but somewhere in between, with aluminum siding and a chain-link fence, a narrow driveway running up to a one-car garage and a patch of back yard. The house was yellow. I looked on the back for a date or a name, but neither was there. There was no

Quilt for a crib (c. 1885).

need for discussion. I knew what she was trying to tell me, for it was something I had often felt. She was not adrift, alone, anonymous, although her bags and her raincoat with the grime shadowing its creases had made me believe she was. She had a house, or at least once upon a time had had one. Inside were curtains, a couch, a stove, potholders. You are where you live. She was somebody.

I've never been very good at looking at the big picture, taking the global view, and I've always been a person with an overactive sense of place, the legacy of an Irish grandfather. So it

WORDS TO OWN

legacy (leg′ə·sē) *n.*: inheritance; something handed down from an ancestor or from the past.

is natural that the thing that seems most wrong with the world to me right now is that there are so many people with no homes. I'm not simply talking about shelter from the elements or three square meals a day or a mailing address to which the welfare people can send the check—although I know that all these are important for survival. I'm talking about a home, about precisely those kinds of feelings that have wound up in cross-stitch and French knots on samplers[1] over the years.

Home is where the heart is. There's no place like it. I love my home with a <u>ferocity</u> totally out of proportion to its appearance or location. I love dumb things about it: the hot-water heater, the plastic rack you drain dishes in, the roof over my head, which occasionally leaks. And yet it is precisely those dumb things that make it what it is—a place of certainty, stability, predictability, privacy, for me and for my family. It is where I live. What more can you say about a place than that? That is everything.

Yet it is something that we have been edging away from gradually during my lifetime and the lifetimes of my parents and grandparents. There was a time when where you lived often was where you worked and where you grew the food you ate and even where you were buried. When that era passed, where you lived at least was where your parents had lived and where you would live with your children when you became <u>enfeebled</u>. Then, suddenly, where you lived was where you lived for three years, until you could move on to something else and something else again.

And so we have come to something else again, to children who do not understand what it means to go to their rooms because they have never had a room, to men and women whose

1. **cross-stitch and French knots on samplers:** embroidery designs sewn on cloth with sayings like "Home Sweet Home."

WORDS TO OWN

ferocity (fə·räs′ə·tē) *n.:* fierceness.
enfeebled (en·fē′bəld) *adj.:* weakened, usually by old age or illness.

Collection of Jean-Christophe Castelli, New York. © 1997 Jasper Johns/Licensed by VAGA, New York.

Fool's House (1962) by Jasper Johns. Oil on canvas with objects (72″ x 36″).

fantasy is a wall they can paint a color of their own choosing, to old people reduced to sitting on molded-plastic chairs, their skin blue-white in the lights of a bus station, who pull pictures of houses out of their bags. Homes have stopped being homes. Now they are real estate.

People find it curious that those without homes would rather sleep sitting up on benches or huddled in doorways than go to shelters. Certainly some prefer to do so because they are emotionally ill, because they have been locked in before and they are damned if they will be locked in again. Others are afraid of the violence and trouble they may find there. But some seem to want something that is not available in shelters, and they will not <u>compromise</u>, not for a cot, or oatmeal, or a shower with special soap that kills the bugs. "One room," a woman with a baby who was sleeping on her sister's floor once told me, "painted blue." That was the crux[2] of it: not size or location, but pride of ownership. Painted blue.

This is a difficult problem, and some wise and compassionate people are working hard at

2. **crux** (kruks): basic or deciding point.

it. But in the main I think we work around it, just as we walk around it when it is lying on the sidewalk or sitting in the bus terminal—the problem, that is. It has been <u>customary</u> to take people's pain and lessen our own participation in it by turning it into an issue, not a collection of human beings. We turn an adjective into a noun: the poor, not poor people; the homeless, not Ann or the man who lives in the box or the woman who sleeps on the subway grate.

Sometimes I think we would be better off if we forgot about the broad strokes and concentrated on the details. Here is a woman without a bureau. There is a man with no mirror, no wall to hang it on. They are not the homeless. They are people who have no homes. No drawer that holds the spoons. No window to look out upon the world. My God. That is everything.

WORDS TO OWN

compromise (käm′prə·mīz′) v.: give up something to receive something desired; settle for less than what one wants.

customary (kus′tə·mer′ē) adj.: usual; established by custom.

MEET THE WRITER

"The Unknown and the Everyday"

Even before she graduated from Barnard College, **Anna Quindlen** (1953–) sold a story to *Seventeen* magazine and landed a job as a staff reporter at the *New York Post*. In 1977, she moved to *The New York Times,* starting as a reporter and later becoming a columnist. Her columns, "Life in the 30s" and "Public and Private," addressed personal and political issues that affect us all. Quindlen is an avid reader and the mother of three children.

Books and children appear frequently in her writing:

66 Reading has always been life unwrapped to me, a way of understanding the world and understanding myself through both the unknown and the everyday. If being a parent consists often of passing along chunks of ourselves to unwitting—often unwilling—recipients, then books are, for me, one of the simplest and most sure-fire ways of doing that. 99

Quindlen's pursuit of "the unknown and the everyday" won her the Pulitzer Prize for commentary in 1991. These days Quindlen is a full-time novelist living in New Jersey.

A House Is Not a Home

Several months ago, when the weather was still warm and many people were trying to get the most out of the remaining days of summer, my mother and I volunteered to be part of a group bringing food for a picnic to The Haven. The Haven is the only home in Oakland County for battered women and their children. I didn't know what to expect, and I must confess that I was a little reluctant to go.

The Haven is actually a big old house on a heavily shaded street. From the outside it could be any old house. The mighty trees manage to keep the house cool. I suspect these tall, full trees have tales of despair and fear to tell, but they, like the residents who stay there, are silent. The yard has been turned into a playground. It is not the colorful state-of-the-art kind you find in the suburbs. Instead it is a grassless area with a few rickety swings and a basketball hoop without a net.

We brought chicken, potato chips, and chocolate chip cookies. We set the food on a picnic table, and the mothers and their children joined us. It was a bit awkward at first, not so much for the children, who didn't seem to care, but for the women, who seemed quiet and self-conscious. They were average-looking women with not-so-average experiences. I wondered about the very young children. I wondered what they must think about the kind of world this is. . . .

—Layne Sakwa
Andover High School
Bloomfield Hills, Michigan

College student volunteers help to clean up a neighborhood.

MAKING MEANINGS

First Thoughts

1. Which statement or passage in Quindlen's essay did you find most important or significant or disturbing? Look back at your Reader's Log entries and share them with the class.

Shaping Interpretations

2. How does Quindlen try to persuade you to think the way she does about the homeless? Where does she use **facts** and where does she state **opinions**? Do you think her editorial would have been more forceful if she'd presented her ideas some other way? Talk about the details she's chosen for her editorial.

3. What do you think Quindlen wants the reader to do or to believe when she says, "It has been customary to take people's pain and lessen our own participation in it by turning it into an issue, not a collection of human beings"?

4. Suppose you are reorganizing the selections in this book. Look at the titles of the collections. Could Quindlen's editorial and the student essay (opposite) fit somewhere else? Why or why not?

Challenging the Text

5. What do you think of Quindlen's choice of homelessness as "the thing that seems most wrong with the world to me right now"? What seems most wrong in the world to you?

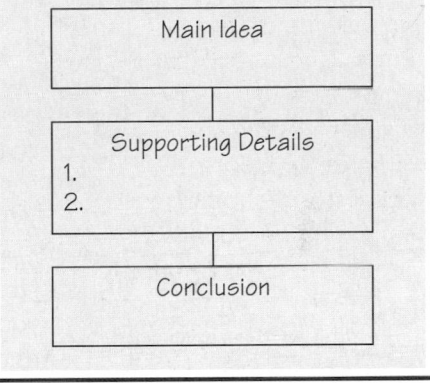

Reviewing the Text

Using a chart like the one that follows, summarize the main idea, the supporting details, and the conclusion of Quindlen's editorial. Use your own words and as many boxes as you need.

Main Idea

Supporting Details
1.
2.

Conclusion

House and Tree II (c. 1900). Quilt. Maker unknown. Virginia.

Writer's Notebook

1. Collecting Ideas for a Persuasive Essay

Supporting your opinion.

WORK IN PROGRESS

Remember that you can't *prove* an opinion. The closest you can come is to support your opinion with incredibly convincing evidence. Examples, anecdotes, statistics, and quotations from experts are kinds of evidence that you can use to persuade your readers. You should have a list of possible

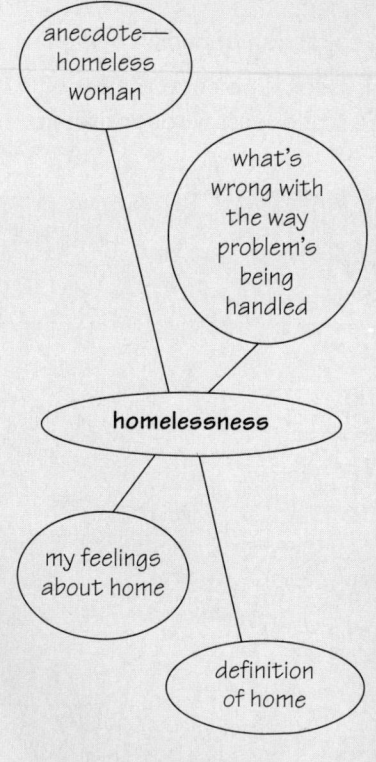

anecdote—homeless woman

what's wrong with the way problem's being handled

homelessness

my feelings about home

definition of home

topics for a persuasive essay for the Writer's Workshop on page 478. Select a topic you have especially strong feelings about and collect some evidence to support your opinion.

Critical Writing

2. This Is Just to Say

How did Anna Quindlen's essay affect you? Did it change your thinking or feelings about homelessness? Will it affect your actions? Let the author know. Write a letter to Quindlen, sharing your thoughts about her essay and the problem of homelessness.

Social History/ Speaking and Listening

3. Speaking Up

What problems do you see in this country, in your

community, or in your school that you feel people are "working around"? Take a stand on one issue and make notes on what you think should be done. Then present your ideas in a brief, informal report to the class. Be sure to state your opinion clearly and back it up.

Social History/ Speaking and Listening

4. What to Do?

Homelessness hasn't gone away; in many cities, it's increased. With a group, brainstorm three possible reasons for homelessness and then discuss possible solutions. See if you can reach a consensus (agreement from everybody). Share your ideas with the class.

White House Dreamer (1983) by Michael Lucero.

LANGUAGE LINK   MINI-LESSON

Style: Parallel Structure—Keeping Things Balanced

Equal or related items in the same sentence must be expressed in a similar way. Single words should be matched with other single words, phrases with phrases, and clauses with clauses. This kind of balanced writing is called **parallel structure**. Careful writers make sure they use parallel structure when equal or related ideas are doing the same work in a sentence.

FAULTY   She was not adrift, alone, and not someone without a name.

PARALLEL   "She was not <u>adrift, alone, anonymous. . . .</u>" [three single-word predicate adjectives]

FAULTY   Quindlen writes about her feelings, her impressions, and thinking.

PARALLEL   Quindlen writes <u>about her feelings, her impressions, and her thoughts.</u> [three phrases]

Try It Out

Edit the following sentences for parallel structure. There's more than one way to create parallel structure in each sentence. Be sure to compare your revisions in class.

1. Let's solve this problem quickly and to be efficient.

2. Everyone complains that homelessness is serious, urgent, and a problem that's difficult.

3. People can't seem to agree about what should be done first or solutions to eliminate the problem.

VOCABULARY   HOW TO OWN A WORD

WORD BANK

legacy
ferocity
enfeebled
compromise
customary

Mapping an Unfamiliar Word

One trick to owning a word is figuring out what you already know about it. Take *customary*, for example. A word map like the one here, which organizes some ideas about *customary*, will help you get to know a new word better. Fill out this map for *customary* and then make word maps of your own for the other words in the Word Bank.

meaning
things that are customary for me
customary
things that aren't customary for me
sample sentence

Reading Focus

Signs of the Times

You've probably heard many times that it's important to spell words correctly, but it isn't always easy. See what Charles Kuralt has discovered about spelling "on the road" in the United States.

Quickwrite

Suppose we suddenly toss out all spelling rules, dictionaries, and spelling checkers. You are free to spell words any way you want. Quickwrite for a few minutes about what the results might be.

Elements of Literature

Humor

Persuasive writers sometimes use **humor**—to make us laugh, of course, but also to make a point. If we find something funny, we'll keep on reading and maybe think twice about the writer's ideas. How can the topic of correct spelling possibly be funny? See what you think of the signs Kuralt mentions and his wry comments on them.

"How can it be misspelled? I just made it up!"

© 1992; Reprinted courtesy of Bunny Hoest and *Parade* Magazine.

Misspelling

Charles Kuralt

They say this is an age of conformity, but wherever we go, we keep finding refreshing evidence of individualism, even on the roadside signs. You know that no stuffy conformist painted this sign: PARK HEAR. It is spelled wrong, but it does tell you where to park: "hear"! MACHANIC ON DUTY. FRONT END REPAIRES. This mechanic may not be good at spelling, but he's probably fine at making "repaires." Anything which can be sold, we have found, can also be misspelled . . . ANTIQES . . . anything from "antiques" to "souvenirs" . . . SOUVINERS . . . especially "souvenirs" . . . SOUVENIERS. How *do* you spell "souvenirs"? SOUVENIRES. This is the American answer: just exactly as you please!

We have found our country's spelling to be horrible, and entirely excusable. ACERAGE FOR SAIL—we may excuse this man

because he's a farmer, not a schoolteacher. RASBERIES—so is this man. SPEGHETTI AND PIZZA—and this man because he's probably from across the sea. BEER AVAILALBE HERE—and this man because, like as not, he was sampling his own product while he painted the sign. BAR DRINKS 55¢ ANEYTIME—that can blur anybody's memory of how to spell.

Some misspellings are quiet and private, like this one in the back room of an Oklahoma diner: BE CURTEOUS AND SMILE. Others are spectacular, like this one in Oregon—(*huge lighted sign*) BAR AND RESTRUANT—and proclaim their error proudly for half a mile in every direction. HUNGARY? MARION'S SNACK SHACK 6 MILES. If you are hungary enough, of course, it doesn't matter much.

NO TRESSPASSING. We like the snappy, rude signs. NO TRASPASSING. You get the idea. NO TRUSTPASSING. Keep out. NO BOATS ALOUD—silent boats OK, but no boats aloud.

The point about American spelling is that, however awful, it serves the cause of individualism and serves the purpose. We read this one at a gas station in Tennessee: NO CONGRETATING ON THE DRIVEWAY. VIALTORS WILL BE PROSCUATED. Well, naturally we didn't congretate. Fearing proscuation, we paid for our gas and pulled right out of there and headed on down the road.

MEET THE WRITER

A Roving Reporter

When **Charles Kuralt** (1934–1997) was a boy on his grandparents' North Carolina farm, he "traveled" the world by reading *National Geographic* magazines. As an adult, he spent his life on the road—first as a radio and TV reporter in Europe and Latin America covering political strife, war, and terrorism. In 1967, Kuralt decided to change direction:

❝ I got the idea . . . one night in an airplane as I looked down at the lights in the country-side and wondered . . . what was going on down there. There are a lot of Americans who don't live in cities and don't make headlines. I was interested in finding out about them. ❞

He started reporting offbeat, human-interest stories for radio and TV and stayed on the road for the next thirty years. He traveled in a secondhand camper from one end of the country to the other, searching for what he jokingly called unimportant, irrelevant, and even "resolutely insignificant" stories for his program *On the Road*. His wit and unusual perspective on everything from lumberjacks to unicyclists made his audience see an America they never knew existed.

Hints on Pronunciation
for Foreigners

T.S.W.

I take it you already know
Of tough and bough and cough and dough?
Others may stumble but not you,
On hiccough, thorough, lough, and through?
5 Well done! And now you wish, perhaps,
To learn of less familiar traps?

Beware of heard, a dreadful word
That looks like beard and sounds like bird,
And dead: it's said like bed, not bead—
10 For goodness sake don't call it "deed"!
Watch out for meat and great and threat.
(They rhyme with suite and straight and debt.)
A moth is not a moth in mother
Nor both in bother, broth in brother,
15 And here is not a match for there
Nor dear and fear for bear and pear,
And then there's dose and rose and lose—
Just look them up—and goose and choose,
And cork and work and card and ward,
20 And font and front and word and sword,
And do and go and thwart and cart—
Come, come, I've hardly made a start!
A dreadful language? Man alive!
I'd mastered it when I was five!

Drawing by Modell; © 1970
The New Yorker Magazine, Inc.

MAKING MEANINGS

First Thoughts

1. Do you think Kuralt's essay belongs in a collection called "What I Think"?

Shaping Interpretations

2. How do you think Kuralt feels about misspellings? Does he describe his attitude directly or let the reader infer it?

3. How do you feel about the need to spell English words correctly? Look back at your Reader's Log entries.

4. Do you agree that we live in an "age of conformity"? Why, or why not? Besides the misspellings on roadside signs, how do you think Americans show "refreshing evidence of individualism"?

Extending the Text

5. How is the problem described in "Hints on Pronunciation . . ." (page 471) related to English spelling? (Don't miss the chance to read this poem aloud.) What other pronunciation problems can you add to this list?

> **Reviewing the Text**
>
> Summarize the **main idea** of this essay. If you find it humorous, give examples of details you smiled at.

CHOICES: Building Your Portfolio

Writer's Notebook

1. Collecting Ideas for a Persuasive Essay

Be prepared for opposing views. You have your opinion; others may hold opposing views. Check your notebook for topics you've been considering for the Writer's Workshop on page 478. Select a topic and formulate your opinion on it. Now imagine what people who disagree with your

opinion might say. How would they attack your reasons and evidence? Take notes for the **counter-arguments** you could use to refute your opponents (attacks on what they say and further defense of your position).

Creative Writing

2. Going Places

Using "Misspelling" as a model, choose a place (your hometown or a place you've visited) and write a short feature about it. What is

unique or unusual about the place and its residents?

Research/Speaking

3. Spelling's History

Who decides what's correct and not correct? What's a lexicographer? Who wrote the first dictionaries, and how are they written now? With a small group, research some aspect of the history of English spelling and share your findings with the class. You might want to report on the work of Samuel Johnson and Noah Webster.

LANGUAGE LINK

**Technology
HELP**

See Language
Workshop
CD-ROM.
*Key word
entry:
homonyms.*

Proofreading: Homonyms—Words That Sound Alike

Some of the spelling mistakes Kuralt discovers are pesky **homonyms** (häm′ə·nimz′), words that are pronounced alike but spelled differently. How would you correct these signs?

NO BOATS ALOUD   PARK HEAR

A spelling checker won't catch these mistakes; the words are spelled correctly but they're the wrong words.

As if that's not bad enough, the same sound can be spelled in many ways. The poem on page 471 illustrates these "eye rhymes," words that look as if they're pronounced alike but aren't.

So whenever you write, proofread your work carefully to make sure you've got the right word in the right place and that you've spelled it correctly. Use a dictionary whenever you're in doubt.

Try It Out

1. Correct all the misspelled signs Kuralt mentions.

2. Make up a dozen signs, some containing misspellings, and exchange your signs with a partner. Correct each other's misspellings.

➤ Which homonyms cause you trouble? Keep a list of trouble-makers in your proofreading log, and refer to it whenever you use these sound-alike words in your writing.

VOCABULARY   HOW TO OWN A WORD

Powerful Prefixes, Stupendous Suffixes

Prefixes and suffixes can't usually stand alone, but they can totally change the words they're attached to. A **prefix** is a word part that is added before a word; a **suffix** is a word part that's added to the end of a word.

1. *Mis-* turns a word into its opposite. Describe a <u>misfortune</u>. Name three things you wouldn't do with someone you <u>mistrusted</u>.

2. *Dis-, non-,* and *un-* also mean "no" or "not." Which ones give each of these words a negative meaning: <u>likely</u>, <u>appear</u>, <u>important</u>, <u>sense</u>?

3. Don't confuse the look-alike prefixes *ante-* (before) and *anti-* (against). Which prefix would you use to describe someone who is against smoking? What does <u>antedate</u> mean?

4. The suffix *-ist* means "someone who (does a particular action)." Give an example of how two people—a <u>conformist</u> and a <u>nonconformist</u>—might behave at a wedding.

5. The suffixes *-ism* and *-ion* turn words into nouns. They mean "the act or condition of (doing or being something)." How would you turn the verb <u>correct</u> into a noun? What does <u>tourism</u> mean?

EXTENDING *the theme*

A REFLECTION

Quickwrite

READER'S LOG

Them and us. We some- times divide the world that way. What makes people suspicious or even afraid of other people? Is it the way they look, the place they live in, the way they talk, or something else? Write your ideas in your Reader's Log.

Those Who Don't

Sandra Cisneros

Those who don't know any better come into our neighborhood scared. They think we're dangerous. They think we will attack them with shiny knives. They are stupid people who are lost and got here by mistake.

But we aren't afraid. We know the guy with the crooked eye is Davey the Baby's brother, and the tall one next to him in the straw brim, that's Rosa's Eddie V., and the big one that looks like a dumb grown man, he's Fat Boy, though he's not fat anymore nor a boy.

All brown all around, we are safe. But watch us drive into a neighborhood of another color and our knees go shakity-shake and our car windows get rolled up tight and our eyes look straight. Yeah. That is how it goes and goes.

They think we're dangerous.

MEET THE WRITER

Sandra Cisneros (1954–   ), poet, essayist, and short-story writer, began writing at the age of ten. "Those Who Don't" is a vignette from her first book, *The House on Mango Street* (Vintage). For a biography of Cisneros, see page 184.

FINDING COMMON GROUND

1. Compare the notes from your Quickwrite with Cisneros' little reflection.

2. In a group, discuss and compare your responses.

3. With your group, talk about ways mutual suspicion and fear can be dealt with. Bring in examples from your own experience and from what you've learned from history and from stories—perhaps from some selections in this book.

4. Write down and present to the class at least one way your group feels people can learn to live together with more tolerance and respect.

READ ON

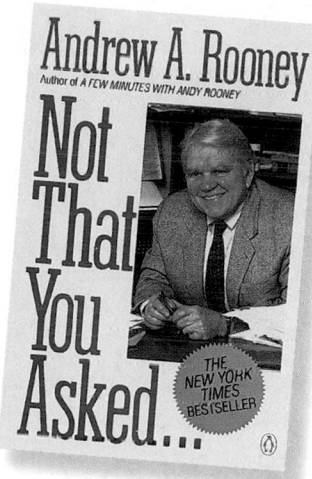

Ask Andy

If you've ever watched CBS's *60 Minutes* on Sunday night, you've heard Andy Rooney's wry, offbeat observations of the world around him. In his best-selling collection of essays, *Not That You Asked . . .* (Penguin), Rooney tries to persuade you to see things his way. His topics range from textbooks to leftovers, from baseball to holiday cards.

A Seat at the Front of the Bus

When Rosa Parks boarded a bus in Montgomery, Alabama, on December 1, 1955, she was about to play an important role in the civil rights movement. She sat in an empty seat and quietly refused to give it up to a white passenger. *Quiet Strength* (Zondervan) is Parks's own story of the civil rights movement, a story of pride, commitment, and courage.

Everyday Laughs

In *Dave Barry's Greatest Hits* (Fawcett/Columbine), Dave Barry makes fun of TV commercials, mutant fleas, newspaper columnists (like himself), and just about anything else you might encounter.

One Woman's Views

In *In Search of Our Mothers' Gardens* (Harcourt Brace), you'll meet Alice Walker up close and personal. In this collection of essays, she writes about her life, her family, her writing, and her political views.

Writer's Workshop

Technology HELP

See Writer's Workshop 2
CD-ROM. *Assignment:
Controversial Issue.*

ASSIGNMENT

Write a persuasive
essay about a debatable
issue you feel strongly
about.

AIM

To persuade.

AUDIENCE

Your classmates,
members of a club,
readers of a local news-
paper. (You choose.)

PERSUASIVE WRITING

PERSUASIVE ESSAY

Have you ever been sure you were right but you couldn't convince
the person you were talking to? You'll sharpen your skills of **persuasion** as you write this essay, and you'll be able to use the same skills
with your friends and family (when you're trying to persuade your
brother to lend you his car), in school (when you're trying to
convince your teacher to give an essay test as a final), and at work
(when you're trying to persuade your boss that you deserve a raise).

Prewriting

1. Choose a Topic

Check your Writer's Notebook for topic ideas.
If you're still undecided, brainstorm with a small
group for more ideas. The topic that you choose should meet
these criteria:

- **You care about the issue.** To be convincing, you need to feel
  strongly about your topic.

- **Reasonable people disagree on the issue.** "War is bad"
  and "Eating is important" aren't topics that most people have
  serious disagreements on.

- **You can research the issue.** Choose a current topic so you
  can easily find evidence to support your views (facts, examples,
  quotations).

2. What Do You Think?

Before you take a stand on an issue, you may need to do some
research. Once you figure out what you think, write a **thesis
statement** that clearly states your view.

3. Who's Your Audience?

Tailor your argument to fit your specific audience. What are their
main concerns? What are their biases? What do they know about
the issue? What reasons will they find most convincing?

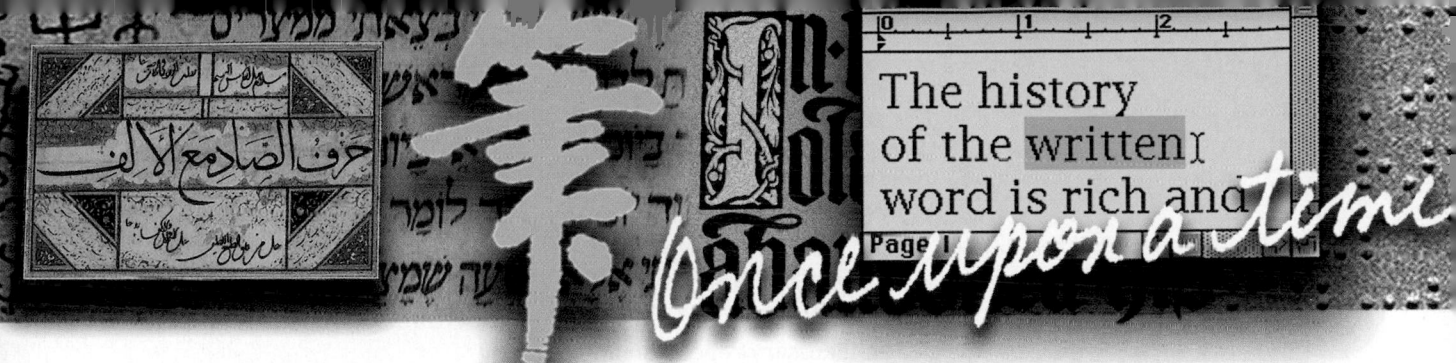
4. Use Logical Appeals

Find two or three good **reasons** to back up your thesis statement and enough **supporting evidence** to be convincing. As you plan your argument, avoid all **fallacies** (see page 453), which are errors in logical thinking.

5. Use Emotional Appeals

It helps to appeal to your audience's feelings as well as to their minds. In both "Homeless" (page 460) and "Darkness at Noon" (page 454), personal **anecdotes** make the writers' points more powerfully than facts or statistics could. **Loaded words** can also influence your audience's emotional response.

6. Plan What You'll Say

- The **introduction** should grab the reader's attention and contain your thesis statement.

- The **body** states your argument clearly, point by point, and gives reasons in the **order of importance,** often ending with the most important reason. As in debate, you'll attack the arguments of those who hold opposing views; your responses to their arguments are called **counterarguments**. A Pro/Con chart like the one below will help you plan your essay.

Con: Against Curfew	Pro: For Curfew	Counterarguments
Innocent teens will be punished.	It will decrease crime and violence.	Are there statistics to prove this?
Teens who work late at necessary jobs will be stopped by police.	Smaller number of teenagers on street means less crime.	Crime occurs at home, other places.

- The **conclusion** may include a **call to action** that asks your audience to do something specific, like writing a letter.

Try It Out

The daily news is a good source of topics for a persuasive essay. Write a thesis statement expressing your opinion on each of these recent laws.

- In an Oregon city parents are held responsible for crimes committed by their children under eighteen. Parents may be fined $1,000 and required to attend classes on effective parenting and/or alcohol and drug abuse.

- In an Indiana city it's illegal to wear gang colors or emblems in school and to carry a cellular phone or pager to communicate with a gang member.

Find two more news stories and write a thesis statement for each one.

Language Link
H E L P

Connotations and loaded words: page 451.

Drafting

1. Say It Simply and Clearly

Wordiness weakens your argument by making it hard for your audience to follow your reasoning, so be as clear and direct as Chief Joseph (page 447). The repetition of a catchy phrase may be effective, because it stays in the reader's mind, but you should cut unnecessary repetition and padding.

2. Watch Your Tone

No one will believe you if you sound unsure of yourself, so eliminate "hedge words" (like *probably, possibly, maybe,* and *perhaps*) and phrases like "I think," "I feel," "I believe," "in my opinion," and "it seems to me."

Student Model

TICK TOCK

Headlines: The *Atlanta Constitution* newspaper reports that an eleven o'clock curfew will be imposed upon persons sixteen years of age and younger who live in the city of Atlanta. Young people who do not comply with this order may be detained by the police. Further, fines may be imposed upon the parent(s). Throughout the ages, youth have had to watch the clock. They have lived under the "Cinderella" beliefs of guardians who seem to think that when the clock strikes twelve, the adolescents' "Air Jordans" will turn into brogans or combat boots, leading them to trouble and shame.

Surely a curfew serves some beneficial purposes. For example, requiring that a youth be in a designated place as expected by his or her parents helps to teach discipline and responsibility. Clearly, there are times when circumstances may necessitate that groups of people obey laws imposed on them for the safety of society. However, this usually occurs when a state of emergency exists, and other means of control have failed. In the case of Atlanta, one may question whether there is a state of emergency, or whether the rights of adolescents are being violated by the city-imposed curfew. One thing is certain, many teens and parents are watching the clock—tick tock. The question is whether the assumption that "early to bed" (or home) results in fewer crimes is fair and therefore should be enforced on adolescents.

Despite the seemingly good intentions of a curfew for Atlanta's urban teens, there are many disadvantages that accompany this approach. For example, as is true with all mass punishments, some innocent teens will be forced to bear the embarrassment and constraints of having to abide

Attention-grabbing introduction.

Fairy tale allusion is clever idea.

Here are two opposing arguments supporting the curfew. Counter-arguments.

Clock sounds repeated throughout the essay, a kind of refrain.

Reason 1 and evidence.

WEAK	There are four reasons that I can think of that state why I think that the curfew probably isn't a good idea.
STRONGER	The curfew is a bad idea for four reasons.
WEAK	In my opinion, students in this school should probably wear uniforms.
STRONGER	Students in this school should wear uniforms.

Evaluating and Revising

1. Peer Review

Read your draft aloud to your writing group or give it to them to read. Ask them for feedback on parts of your essay that concern

by a curfew for which they have no need. The teens who followed the rules given by their guardians and enjoyed a later curfew than is now allowed by the city of Atlanta are being unduly punished. Indeed, such a state of affairs may result in the "good" teen rebelling. Tick tock—parents and teens are watching the clock.

Many adolescents are gainfully employed, helping pay for such things as their clothes, cars, and entertainment. Some youths are even helping to sustain the family household or pay for their education. Even if these youths are able to verify why they are out past curfew, this does not spare them the humiliation of being stopped and questioned by the police. Nonetheless, tick tock—these youths must watch the clock.

Reason 2.

Many crimes do not occur on the street. Often, crimes are as prevalent in the household, at neighboring residences, or establishments where people congregate. Bringing the adolescent "home" does not necessarily yield the desired "safe and sound" outcome that people concerned about public safety in Atlanta are searching for. In spite of this, tick tock—teens must be off the street at the stroke of the clock.

Reason 3.

While the leaders of Atlanta may be applauded for good intentions in terms of public safety, the imposition of a curfew on a select group of people based solely on their age, as a means to prevent crime, is questionable. Until it is proven that teens are more likely than any other age group to commit offenses after eleven o'clock, they should not have to be watchful of the ticking of the clock.

Conclusion.

—Ashaki M. Brown
Brookwood High School
Snellville, Georgia

Sentence Workshop
H E L P

Combining sentences using clauses: page 484.

■ *Evaluation Criteria*

A good persuasive essay

1. *has an attention-grabbing introduction and a clear thesis statement*

2. *provides at least two strong reasons that are supported by evidence*

3. *may also contain emotional appeals*

4. *states the opposition's arguments and refutes them*

5. *presents an effective conclusion that may include a call to action*

you. For example: Do you think the anecdote works better at the beginning or at the end of the essay? Is my third reason strong enough? Is there enough supporting evidence?

2. Self-Evaluation

As you read your essay to yourself, focus first on content. Are your reasons clearly identified? (You might state them as topic sentences or add transitions, such as *first, second, most important,*

Revision Model

	Peer Comments
Many crimes do not occur on the	*Clear topic sentence.*
are as prevalent in the household, at ^	
street. Often, crimes ~~occur in other~~	
neighboring residences, or establishments ⌐ ⌐*where people congregate.*⌐	
~~places~~. Bringing the adolescent ^	*What places? Be specific.*
"home" does not necessarily yield	
"safe and sound" ⌐ ⌐*concerned about public safety in Atlanta*⌐	*What outcome? What people?*
the desired ⌐outcome that people⌐ are ^ ^	
In spite of this,	
searching for. ~~Tick tock—teens~~ ^	*A transition here would help.*
must be off the street at the stroke	
of the clock.	

CALVIN AND HOBBES © 1993 Waterson. Distributed by UNIVERSAL PRESS SYNDICATE. Reprinted with permission. All rights reserved.

finally.) Read your draft a second time for style, paying attention to the way the sentences sound together. Are the ideas smoothly connected? Maybe you can combine some sentences by using participial phrases or adjective or adverb clauses.

Proofreading

Before you write your final version, look over your paper for mistakes in spelling, usage, capitalization, and punctuation. If something looks strange to you, use your spelling checker, a dictionary, or the Language Handbook. Be sure to go through your proofreading log and watch for mistakes you've made before.

Publishing

- **Turn your essay into a speech.** Read it (better yet, practice delivering it without reading it word for word) to a school club or another English class.

- **Conduct a panel discussion or debate.** Get together with classmates who've written on the same issue and discuss it in front of your class. For help in running a debate, see the Communications Handbook.

- **Write a letter.** Shorten your paper to three paragraphs and deliver it to the editor of your local or school newspaper. Or write to your mayor, school board, or anyone else who has the power to act on your suggestions.

Reflecting

If you add this essay to your portfolio, date it and attach a brief reflection on your writing experience:

1. What was difficult for me? What will I do differently next time?

2. What is the strongest part of my argument? What is the weakest?

3. Why am I including this essay in my portfolio?

Language Link
H E L P

Homonyms: page 473.
Parallel structure: page 467.

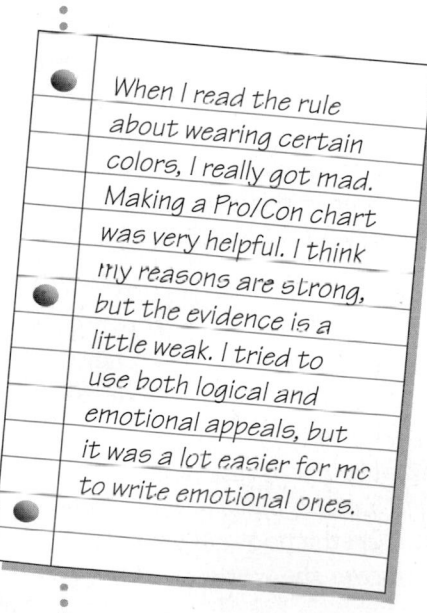

When I read the rule about wearing certain colors, I really got mad. Making a Pro/Con chart was very helpful. I think my reasons are strong, but the evidence is a little weak. I tried to use both logical and emotional appeals, but it was a lot easier for me to write emotional ones.

Sentence Workshop

Language Handbook
H E L P

See Clauses, page 1009.

Technology
H E L P

See Language Workshop CD-ROM. *Key word entry: clauses.*

COMBINING SENTENCES: CLAUSES

When you want to combine two short sentences and make their relationship clearer, you can often make one of them into a clause.

You can make a sentence into an **adjective clause** by inserting *who, which,* or *that* in place of the subject and moving the clause so that it clearly modifies a noun or pronoun.

They are people. They have no homes.

"They are people <u>who have no homes</u>." (page 463)

An **adverb clause** may modify a verb, an adjective, or another adverb. You can make a sentence into an adverb clause by using a subordinating conjunction like *if, because, until, unless, when,* and *although.*

This point was graphically driven home to me. We were in England.

"This point was graphically driven home to me <u>while we were in England</u>." (page 456)

When you combine sentences using subordination, you usually have many choices. Notice in the sentences above that the subordinate clause could be some other group of words or it could be placed at another spot in the sentence.

1. When the point was graphically driven home to me, we were in England.

2. We were in England when the point was graphically driven home to me.

Writer's Workshop Follow-up: Proofreading

To see how useful clauses are in combining sentences, go back to a piece of writing you are currently working on. Find at least three sets of sentences you could combine by making one sentence into a clause. Then exchange papers. See if your peer reviewer can suggest variations.

Try It Out

Act as an editor and combine the following sentences by using adjective or adverb clauses. Be sure to compare your rewritten sentences in class to see if any variations are possible.

1. The Nobel Committee awarded Elie Wiesel the peace prize in 1986. They called him "a messenger to mankind."

2. Mother Teresa began her work in India. Her work to aid the poor has spread all over the world.

LEARNING FOR LIFE

You and the Law

Problem

Consumers and laborers are protected by local, state, and federal laws. What about teenagers who work part-time? How about teenagers as consumers? What does the law have to say about your rights and responsibilities in the workplace and the marketplace?

Project

Find out how local, state, and federal laws affect what you can and cannot do as a teenage consumer and producer.

Preparation

1. Working with a small group, brainstorm to explore what you already know about such laws.

2. Develop a list of questions to guide your search for facts. Questions like these will get you started:

   In the workplace. How many hours a week can I work? What should I do if my boss insists that I work longer hours? What kinds of machines can I operate? What happens if I get hurt on the job? Is there a minimum wage law?

   In the marketplace. Is joining a mail-order CD club the same as signing a contract? Can teenagers use layaway plans and get credit cards? If I want to start a business, what laws do I need to know about?

3. Decide which questions your group will tackle and how you'll divide them among the group members.

Procedure

1. Research and take notes on the questions you've chosen. Possible sources:

   • magazine and newspaper articles

   • law guides and handbooks written for the average person

   • interviews with lawyers

2. As you look for answers, keep an eye out for anecdotes as well as facts and figures. They're a good way to clarify and enliven legal jargon.

Presentation

Present your findings in one of the following formats (or another that your teacher approves):

1. On-Line Q & A

Work with your group to prepare a question-and-answer "page" for your school's database system. Be sure to cite the sources you used, so that other students will know where to go for more information. Ask the editor of the school paper to print a notice about the new page and the way to access it.

2. Fact Forum

Present a panel discussion explaining your findings. Meet with your group to choose a question for discussion, prepare an outline, and elect a leader. Hold the discussion in front of the rest of the class, a school-wide assembly, or a class of eighth-graders at a nearby middle school.

3. Letter

Write a letter to an elected official who can influence laws that affect teenagers. Express your view of one such law and try to persuade the official to agree with you. Suggest steps the official can take to change the law so that it conforms to your point of view.

Processing

What did you learn about your own rights and responsibilities by doing this project? What about the rights and responsibilities of others? Write a brief reflection for your portfolio.

Dialogue of Two Poets Disguised as Birds (1988) by Alfredo Castañeda.
Oil on canvas (15 ¾″ x 19 ¾″).

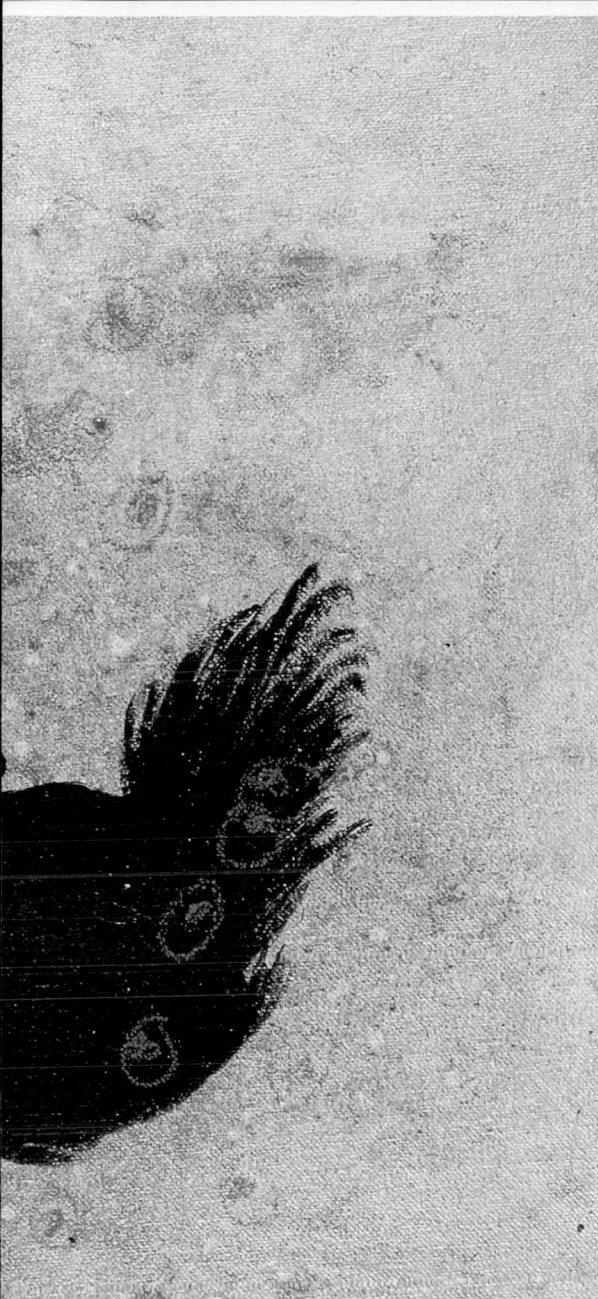

THE
POETRY
COLLECTIONS

A word is dead
When it is said,
Some say.
I say it just
Begins to live
That day.

—Emily Dickinson

A Writer on Poetry
A CONVERSATION WITH GLADYS CARDIFF

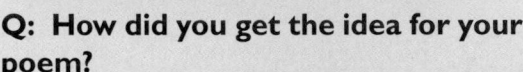

As you read the poems in these collections, you may wonder what inspired the poets, how they set to work on the poems, or how they got their ideas so clearly and brightly down on paper.

Gladys Cardiff has this to say about her poem "Combing" (page 567).

Q: How did you get the idea for your poem?

Cardiff: As a young mother, I often helped my small daughter comb out the tangles in her bright orange, curly hair after it was washed. My mother used to reminisce about combing *her* grandmother's hair. . . .

Q: How did you set to work on this poem?

Cardiff: When I write, I write alone and where it is quiet. At the time of this poem, that was usually at night when everyone was settled into bed and I was settled at the dining-room table with lots of clean paper and a pen. Several weeks had gone by during which I had sort of rolled the feelings and ideas around in my head. The idea of myself doing something so ordinary, something all of the women on the maternal side of my family had done for each other for generations, was part of what interested me. But it was trying to pinpoint the feelings I had when I stood behind my seated daughter and her clean, lively hair that fascinated me. I realized I felt lucky, and thankful. Lucky to have her, to be able to care for her, and thankful to have learned this kind of love from my own mother. At the dining-room table

that feeling of thanksgiving was called up again. I felt it as I leaned over the page. "Bending, I bow my head. . . ."

Q: Did you revise your poem?

Cardiff: It is very rare for a poem to set itself upon the page as a finished work. This poem did. It is the only poem I have ever written that did not require additional labor and revision. When I look at it now as a writer—and see how the lines all fell into three beats to the line, its three stanzas, and ending triad, how the color orange was true to the facts and also a refrain that, like the experience itself, reverberated down through the poem—I take no conscious credit for its craft.

Q: How does someone become a writer?

Cardiff: People often say writing is a gift. And it is a gift, but not one that you own. I have never successfully forced a poem into being. My experience is that writing is often like playing, sometimes pretty rough playing, as if the poem has a mind of its own. In that sense, poems are gifts, ones which I work hard to prepare myself for so they can be received, and then passed on. Like the braided rug in "Combing," what starts them is often a tangle of rags, dull and colorful, ordinary or special, that want to be put together in some form that is right for them. You try to stay alert for that time when your attention is grabbed— and you've been practicing how to catch what comes your way.

BECOMING A STRATEGIC READER

Making a Poem Your Own

When you read a poem, you respond to it just the way you respond to fiction and nonfiction. You connect it with your own memories and feelings and experiences; you interpret; you shape your own meanings.

But reading poetry also demands certain strategies.

1. **Look for punctuation in the poem telling you where sentences begin and end.** Most poems are written in full sentences.

2. **Do not make a full stop at the end of a line if there is no period, comma, colon, semicolon, or dash there.** If a line of poetry has no punctuation at its end, most poets intend us to read right on to the next line to complete the sense of the sentence.

3. **If a passage of a poem is difficult to understand, look for the subject, verb, and complement of each sentence.** Try to decide what words the clauses and phrases modify.

4. **Be alert for comparisons—for figures of speech.** Try to see what the poet is describing for you.

5. **Read the poem aloud.** Poets are not likely to work in silence. The sound of a poem is very important.

6. **After you have read the poem, talk about it and read it again.** This time, the poem's meaning will change, slightly or dramatically. You'll see things in the poem you didn't see before.

7. **Read the poem a third time.** This time, the poem should become "yours."

HOW TO OWN A WORD

Playing with Words

Motto for a Dog House

I love this little house because

   It offers, after dark,

A pause for rest, a rest for paws,

   A place to moor my bark.

   —Arthur Guiterman

One of the things you must remember about poetry is that it is a form of playing. Poets play with rhymes, rhythms, and *words*.

The simplest kind of play with meanings is **punning**. One kind of punning uses a word that can have two different meanings at once. You'll see one of the puns in Guiterman's little poem if you know two meanings for the word *bark*. Another kind of punning uses words that sound the same but are spelled differently. If you spotted two words that sound alike, you caught the other pun in this poem.

A Narrow Fellow in the Grass

Emily Dickinson

A narrow fellow in the grass
Occasionally rides;
You may have met him—did you not?
His notice sudden is.

5   The grass divides as with a comb,
A spotted shaft is seen;
And then it closes at your feet
And opens further on.

He likes a boggy acre,
10   A floor too cool for corn.
Yet when a boy, and barefoot,
I more than once, at noon,

Have passed, I thought, a whip-lash
Unbraiding in the sun—
15   When, stooping to secure it,
It wrinkled, and was gone.

Several of nature's people
I know, and they know me;
I feel for them a transport
20   Of cordiality;

But never met this fellow,
Attended or alone,
Without a tighter breathing,
And zero at the bone.

These notes show the thoughts of one reader as she read this poem for the first time. Her next step would be to talk about the poem with her classmates and then read it again. On this second reading, her responses would probably change.

Snake, evil, representing an evil person.

He's quiet, sneaky.

What opens and closes? How can it close at your feet and open further on at the same time?

What does a floor too cool for corn represent?
Isn't Emily Dickinson female? Is she supposed to be writing this from a boy's point of view?
What's a whip-lash unbraiding in the sun?

She loves nature and almost all of its creatures.

She's petrified.
What does zero at the bone mean?

Erika Cole

—Erika Cole
Southeast High School
Bradenton, Florida

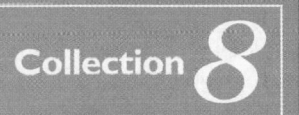
SEE THE MIRACLES

To me every hour of the light and dark is a miracle,
Every cubic inch of space is a miracle.

— *Walt Whitman*

Every molecule and moment of life is a miracle. Children are good at seeing miracles—but as people grow older, they often stop noticing them. Not so the poet. Noticing miracles is the poet's specialty. Describing them in the right words is the poet's job. How can you do it? First, keep your ears and eyes and heart as open as a child's. Second, work on developing special skills with words and images. A few people seem to be born with these skills—just as some people are "born athletes." But most writers have to learn and practice, just as most ballplayers have to learn to hit grounders and catch fly balls before they can play the game.

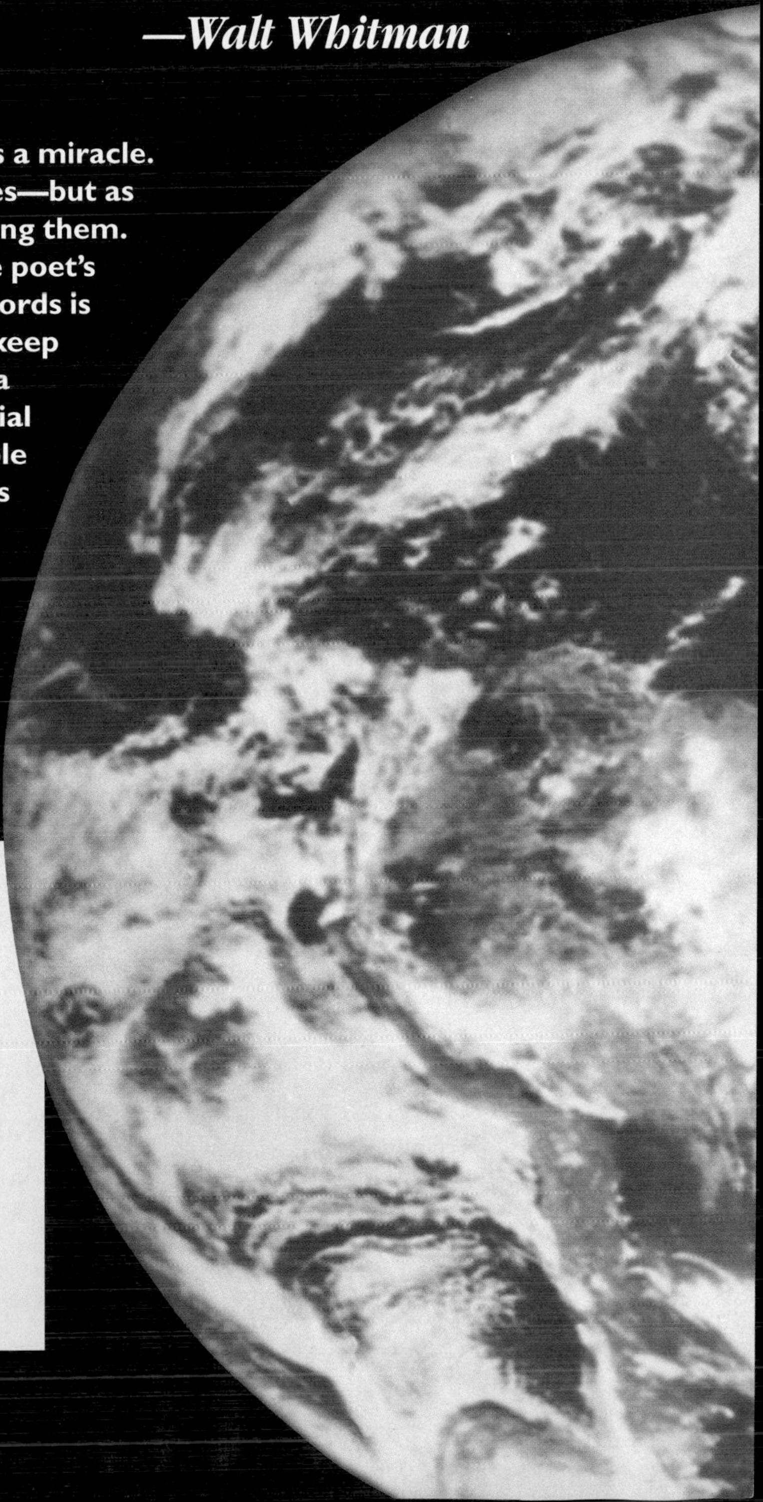

Writer's Notebook

If Whitman is right, and every cubic inch is a miracle, then looking closely at even the most familiar sight should reveal something new. Take a notebook and pencil, find a comfortable spot, focus on some place or person or creature, and watch closely for five or ten minutes. Try to capture in words every detail you can. Look hard for something you would normally miss. Record what you see and hear, and possibly even smell, taste, and touch.

Elements of Literature

IMAGERY: Seeing Things Freshly

Imagery is one of the elements that give poetry its forcefulness. Images are basically copies of things you can see. But images in poetry can do even more than help us see things. An **image** is a single word or a phrase that appeals to one of our senses. An image can help us see color or motion. Sometimes it can also help us hear a sound, smell an odor, feel texture or temperature, or even taste a sweet, sour, or salty flavor.

Suppose you were an artist and wanted to paint a picture of a house. You would emphasize certain aspects of the house. You might emphasize the age of the house by making its shingles look as worn and wrinkled and cracked as an old shoe. Or you might emphasize the emptiness of the house by painting curtainless windows that reflect the clouds, and doors opening onto empty hallways. In each case, as an artist, you would give the actual image (the house) a certain twist, a particular shading.

Poets do the same thing. Edwin Arlington Robinson in "The House on the Hill" saw an empty house and emphasized its loneliness:

House by the Railroad (1925) by Edward Hopper. Oil on canvas 24″ x 29″ (61 cm. x 73.7 cm.).

The Museum of Modern Art, New York. Given anonymously. Photograph © 1995 The Museum of Modern Art, New York.

by John Malcolm Brinnin

Through broken walls and gray
The winds blow bleak and shrill;
They are all gone away.

Robert Frost in "The Black Cottage" saw an empty house and emphasized the new life that had moved in:

"There are bees in this wall."
  He struck the clapboards,
Fierce heads looked out; small
  bodies pivoted.
We rose to go. Sunset blazed
  on the windows.

Imagery is part of a poet's style. It is the product of the poet's own way of seeing the world. Just as we learn to recognize certain painters at once by noticing the colors and shapes that mark their works, so we learn to identify poets by paying attention to their imagery. Of course, the time and place in which poets live influence the kind of imagery they use. Poets who live in cities will usually draw upon the street scenes and industrial landscapes they know so well. Poets who live far from cities will usually draw their images from what they see of country life.

Imagery and Feelings

An image can be so fresh, so powerful, that it can speak to our deepest feelings. An image can be so phrased that it makes us feel joy or grief, wonder or horror, love or disgust.

Here is a poem that uses images to help us see a scene on the Great Lakes and hear the sounds made by a boat lost in the mist. But what readers remember most about this little poem is the way the images make them feel:

> **A**n image can be so fresh, so powerful, that it can speak to our deepest feelings.

Lost

Desolate and lone
All night long on the lake
Where fog trails and mist creeps,
The whistle of a boat
Calls and cries unendingly,
Like some lost child
In tears and trouble
Hunting the harbor's breast
And the harbor's eyes.
              —Carl Sandburg

The poet . . . should stop and examine what others have missed, whether it be veins on a leaf or the surge of a mob; he should hear what others miss— not just skylarks but the breath of an old man or sleet against the window; he should respond to the feel of a rusted iron railing, a cut, or a gull's feather; he should identify the variety of city smells and country odors and consider what it is that makes an unoccupied house different from one lived in; and he should taste not only food but pine gum and smog.

              —Stephen Minot

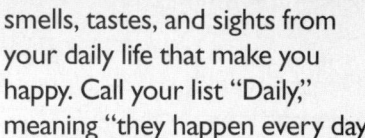

The Grinder (1924) by Diego Rivera (Mexican, 1886–1957). Encaustic on canvas (90 cm. x 117 cm.).

Courtesy Museo de Arte Moderno (INBA), Mexico City. © Dirk Bakker, Photographer. P-34.

Photograph © The Detroit Institute of Arts, 1995.

BEFORE YOU READ
DAILY

Reading Focus

Days Are Nouns

Since your life is different from everyone else's, your special miracles are unique. At any moment, nobody is standing exactly where you're standing, and nobody is thinking what you're thinking, feeling what you're feeling, or seeing, smelling, hearing, touching exactly the way you do. No one but Naomi Nye would have made this exact list of daily miracles.

Quickwrite

READER'S LOG

Make a list of the sounds, smells, tastes, and sights from your daily life that make you happy. Call your list "Daily," meaning "they happen every day."

Keep your notes. For questions and activities on this poem, see page 498.

Elements of Literature

Catalogs

One of America's greatest poets, Walt Whitman, wrote in catalogs—long rolling lists of things that he saw and wondered at and wanted to share. One of the interesting things about catalogs is that they can bring together very different items in one list.

A **catalog** poem is built on a list of images. The repetition of items in the list creates a rolling rhythm when the poem is read aloud.

Daily

Naomi Shihab Nye

These shriveled seeds we plant,
corn kernel, dried bean,
poke into loosened soil,
cover over with measured fingertips
5 These T-shirts we fold
into perfect white
squares
These tortillas we slice and fry to crisp strips
This rich egg scrambled in a gray clay bowl
10 This bed whose covers I straighten
smoothing edges till blue quilt fits brown blanket
and nothing hangs out
This envelope I address
so the name balances like a cloud
15 in the center of the sky
This page I type and retype
This table I dust till the scarred wood shines
This bundle of clothes I wash and hang and wash again
like flags we share, a country so close
20 no one needs to name it
The days are nouns: touch them
The hands are churches that worship the world

MEET THE WRITER

Noticing the World

Naomi Shihab Nye (1952–   ), born and raised in St. Louis, Missouri, has written several collections of poems, including *Red Suitcase* (1994) and *Words Under the Words: Selected Poems* (1995). Also a song-writer, she has two albums to her credit—*Rutabaga-Roo* and *Lullaby Raft*. Many of Nye's poems are inspired by childhood memories and by her travels, including visits to her Palestinian grandmother in Jerusalem. Nye lives in San Antonio, Texas, with her husband and her son, Madison Cloudfeather. She regularly reads her poetry in schools, where she also runs workshops to help students find the poetry hiding in their own imaginations. She says:

66 Being alive is a common road. It's what we notice makes us different. 99

Reading Focus

The Real Thing

If you have ever wanted to be outdoors enjoying a fine spring day instead of wrestling with tenses and equations in school, you will know how the speaker in this poem felt as he sat in a lecture hall and listened to the cold facts of astronomy, while outside was the real thing—the beautiful starry night.

To place the poem in its time, remember that astronomy was of great interest to many nineteenth-century Americans, who followed scientific lectures and debates as eagerly as their great-grandchildren would follow television serials.

Quickwrite

Find at least one image from the world of nature that fills you with wonder. Your image could be as big as the starry sky or as small as an ant.

Keep your notes. For questions and activities on this poem, see page 498.

Elements of Literature

Setting the Scene

Images are used to set the scene of a poem. A scene can be an external physical setting— a hillside, a city, a pond. A scene can also be internal—it can take you inside the speaker's mind. In this poem, how many scenes do you see and share?

> Every poem has a **scene,** or location. The scene can be internal, external, or both.

When I Heard the Learn'd Astronomer

Walt Whitman

When I heard the learn'd astronomer,
When the proofs, the figures, were ranged in
      columns before me,
When I was shown the charts and diagrams, to add,
      divide, and measure them,
When I sitting heard the astronomer where he
      lectured with much applause in the lecture room,
How soon unaccountable I became tired and sick,
Till rising and gliding out I wandered off by myself,
In the mystical moist night air, and from time to time,
Looked up in perfect silence at the stars.

MEET THE WRITER

An American Treasure

Walt Whitman (1819–1892), born on Long Island, New York, was one of the first world-class poets America ever produced. He transformed the language of literature, especially poetry, forever—by writing it in free verse and using common speech and slang. Nobody would publish his radical book *Leaves of Grass,* so he published it himself in 1855. He even wrote glowing reviews of it himself. In one review he said:

66 Very devilish to some, and very divine to some, will appear the poet of these new poems. . . . 99

Whitman left school at the age of eleven and went to work. But on weekends he read Sir Walter Scott, the Bible, Shakespeare, Homer, Dante, and "the ancient Hindoo poems." In his thirties, he described himself as "a Fine Brute." He dressed differently from most people and is said, on one occasion, to have driven a horse-drawn carriage up and down Broadway reciting passages of Shakespeare at the top of his lungs. For years Whitman kept notebooks of his thoughts and experiences. He drew heavily on these notebooks when he created *Leaves of Grass.*

The great naturalist John Burroughs, who often saw Whitman on the street, wrote: "The first and last impression which his personal presence always made upon one was of a nature wonderfully gentle, tender, and benignant. . . . I was impressed by the fine grain and clean, fresh quality of the man. . . . He always had the look of a man who had just taken a bath."

Certainly, Walt Whitman gave old-fashioned poetry a good hard scrubbing, but at first not many people thanked him for it. As a poor old man, he was reduced to selling his book out of a basket on the streets of Philadelphia. But he never stopped working on his *Leaves of Grass,* revising and adding to it until his death. Today, Whitman's *Leaves* is one of the treasures of American literature.

MAKING MEANINGS

DAILY
WHEN I HEARD THE LEARN'D ASTRONOMER

First Thoughts

1. When you think of **images** in the world that give you joy or that fill you with wonder, do you look at ordinary things, as Nye does, or at cosmic things, as Whitman does? Or do you find wonder in abstractions like math (or astronomy)? Talk over your responses to each poet's source of wonder and joy.

Shaping Interpretations

2. What do Nye's particular **images** tell you about her life and where she lives?

3. What **scenes** do you share in Whitman's poem?

4. What do you think *sick* means in Whitman's poem—what was bothering the speaker as he listened to the astronomer? At the end of the poem, what part of the speaker has been restored by the "mystical" starry night?

Challenging the Texts

5. Suppose you, the learn'd astronomer, came upon Whitman's poem a week after your lecture. How would you respond to the poet?

CHOICES: Building Your Portfolio

Writer's Notebook
1. Keeping a Journal

Getting started.  Whitman kept a "memoranda book" he called *Specimen Days*. As an introduction to your own journal, describe yourself and where you live. You might want to name your journal.

Creative Writing
2. Looking Up (or Down)

Refer to notes you made in the Quickwrite for Whitman's poem (page 496).

Expand your notes into a poem or paragraph that imitates the structure of Whitman's poem: A speaker tells where he or she is and how he or she feels and what he or she does to capture a sense of mystery. Try to set two scenes: one actual place (where is your speaker?) and one place inside the speaker's mind.

Creative Writing
3. Daily

Refer to notes you made in your Quickwrite for Nye's poem (page 494). Expand your notes into a **catalog** poem or paragraph that lists images of things in your daily life that are miracles or that make you happy to be alive.

Science/Drawing
4. Drawing the Stars

A lot of constellations are named after people or animals. Choose a famous constellation—Ursa Major, Cassiopeia, Orion, Cancer—and find out where its name came from. Then locate your constellation on a star map, draw your own simple diagram of its principal stars, and on top of that draw the person or animal it is named after.

BEFORE YOU READ
HAIKU

Reading Focus

Snapshot Album

Haiku, the most famous form of Japanese poetry, capture moments of life with all the speed and precision of a snapshot. But haiku are better than snapshots. Cameras don't lie about the outside of people, but they can't tell you what's going on inside them. Haiku are different. To unlock a haiku, read one word or phrase at a time, pausing long enough to let yourself see, hear, smell, taste, or touch that single element of the original moment. In the end you will find yourself standing inside a special moment in someone else's life—whether that experience was captured three minutes ago or three hundred years ago.

Quickwrite

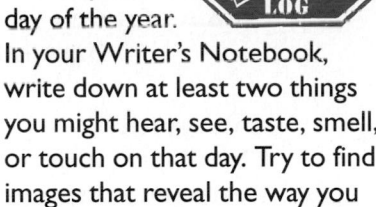

Pick a special day of the year. In your Writer's Notebook, write down at least two things you might hear, see, taste, smell, or touch on that day. Try to find images that reveal the way you feel at this moment, on this day.

Keep your notes. For questions and activities on these poems, see pages 507–508.

Elements of Literature

Haiku

Haiku work by suggestion. The scene in the haiku—that special moment of someone else's life—is supposed to serve as a starting-off place for your own thoughts and associations.

Haiku are written as if they were telegrams and each word cost money. The Japanese language has no articles (*a, an, the*), uses practically no pronouns, and in general does not indicate whether a noun is singular or plural.

A Japanese **haiku**

1. has seventeen syllables, five in lines one and three and seven in line two

2. presents images from everyday life

3. usually contains a seasonal word or symbol (*kigo*)

4. presents a moment of discovery or enlightenment (*satori*)

The Original Language

Here, in the original Japanese, with the English translation, is Bashō's haiku from the next page. You might want to try your own version. (*Ya* is a word frequently used in haiku to mean something like "Lo!" Some translators indicate it with a colon, since it suggests a kind of equation.)

古池や蛙飛び込む水の音

Furu	ike	ya
old	pond	:
Kawazu	tobikomu	
frog	jump in	
Mizu	no	oto
water	sound	

Haiku

Get out of my road
and allow me to plant these
bamboos, Mr. Toad.
   —Miura Chora

A morning glory
Twined round the bucket:
I will ask my neighbor
 for water.
    —Chiyo

The old pond;
A frog jumps in:
Sound of water.
    —Matsuo Bashō

A dragonfly!
The distant hills
Reflected in his eyes.
    —Kobayashi Issa

Morning Glories (19th century) by Suzuki Kiitsu. Japanese screen, six-fold, one of a pair. Color and gold leaf on paper.

MEET THE WRITERS

Captured Moments

Miura Chora (1729–1780), like most writers of haiku, drew his images from the ordinary objects and activities of daily life—in this case, the work of planting bamboo shoots. In Japanese, every haiku has exactly seventeen syllables, but English translators can't always keep to that. Check the number of syllables here and see if this translator has performed a miracle of translation.

Chiyo (1703–1775) is the most celebrated of the women writers of haiku. Some critics say her poems are too explicit and unmysterious to be true haiku. They want their haiku to be more subtle, indirect, and suggestive—like the classical Bashō poem here. But Chiyo's admirers remind us that some people mistake "haziness" in haiku for profound thought.

Matsuo Bashō (1644–1694) is considered the developer of the haiku form as well as its greatest master. Bashō was a deeply spiritual man who became a Zen monk in his later years. His haiku show a zest for every mote and speck of life—a sense that nothing in this world is unimportant.

群鷺

A Magician Turning Paper into Cranes (1819) from the *Manga* (a book of humorous sketches), vol. 10, by Katsushika Hokusai.

Kobayashi Issa (1763–1827) had a very sad life. Despite his poverty and the fact that he saw all his beloved children die, Issa's extraordinarily simple poems are full of human tenderness and wry humor.

BEFORE YOU READ
FOG

Reading Focus

Images People Treasure

One day, a CBS morning weather report began with the words "It's little cat feet out there for large swatches of the country." People listening knew exactly what that meant. Fog. Creeping fog. And they knew because they knew this poem.

Quickwrite

READER'S LOG

Choose a weather condition—a hurricane, tornado, blizzard, thunderstorm, drought. In your Writer's Notebook, write the name of a creature that might serve as an image for that kind of weather. Describe how that weather-animal looks, smells, sounds, and behaves, especially when hungry or angry or moving.

Keep your notes. For questions and activities on this poem, see pages 507–508.

Elements of Literature

Extended Images

Sandburg never comes right out and says, "The fog is a cat." But after the first line, every line in the poem describes some aspect of a cat's anatomy or behavior. Of course, Sandburg has said all he wants to in these six short lines—but can you think of at least one other thing a cat does that might fit into the extended image of "Fog"?

An **extended image** is an image developed over several lines of a poem or even throughout an entire poem.

For more on Imagery, see pages 492–493 and the Handbook of Literary Terms.

Fog

Carl Sandburg

The fog comes
on little cat feet.

It sits looking
over harbor and city
on silent haunches
and then moves on.

MEET THE WRITER

An American Singer

Carl Sandburg (1878–1967) wrote a poem called "Ten Definitions of Poetry." Here are four of the definitions:

> Poetry is a search for syllables to shoot at the barriers of the unknown and the unknowable. . . .
> Poetry is the silence and speech between a wet struggling root of a flower and a sunlit blossom of that flower. . . .
> Poetry is the synthesis of hyacinths and biscuits. . . .
> Poetry is the opening and closing of a door, leaving those who look through to guess about what is seen during a moment. **99**

Sandburg, the son of Swedish immigrants, was born in Galesburg, Illinois. Between the ages of thirteen and nineteen, he worked on a milk wagon, in a barbershop, theater, and brickyard, and as a hotel dishwasher and a harvest hand. He became known as the poet of Chicago in the days when that city was the expanding center of steel mills, stockyards, and railroads. Sandburg helped change American poetry by insisting that the rhythms of American speech could best be caught in free verse (see page 555). Though he was unknown to the poetry world until he was thirty-six, by the time he died, Sandburg's name was a household word. His sometimes tough, often tender poems about nature and the American people, especially working-class people, were known and loved by millions. Still a landmark in American musical history is Sandburg's book called *The American Songbag*—in which, for the very first time, are printed more than a hundred songs gathered from people who sing "because they must." Sandburg often gave public recitals of his poems and these songs, accompanying himself on the guitar. Sandburg loved Lincoln, another son of Illinois, and won a Pulitzer Prize for part of his massive lifework: a six-volume biography of the Great Emancipator.

BEFORE YOU READ

IN JUST-

Reading Focus

The Mysterious Stranger

Poets don't like to repeat the same old images that others have used. So sometimes they do make-overs—especially on irresistible but common subjects like spring. At first glance, "in Just-" looks and sounds like an old-fashioned spring poem. But Cummings has given spring a new look.

Sure, there's plenty of mud and water. And the kids are outdoors playing, and the balloon man is back in town. But just who is this mysterious stranger?

He's lame and goat-footed. If you know your Greek mythology, you should be hearing little bells right now. Hephaestus, god of fire, was lame. And here he is thousands of years later— to throw a little heat on this year's spring. And Pan, the remarkably homely god of nature who loved to dance with all the nymphs, was goat-footed. Here he is, calling the kids to dance.

By the way, Pan invented the flute. Can you hear its echoes in this poem?

Quickwrite

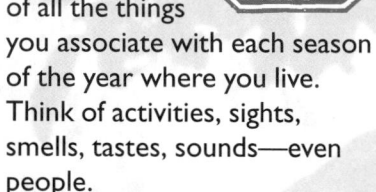

Make a catalog of all the things you associate with each season of the year where you live. Think of activities, sights, smells, tastes, sounds—even people.

Keep your notes. For questions and activities on this poem, see pages 507–508.

Elements of Literature

Refreshed Images

Part of any good poet's job is to find fresh new images, to avoid those old, worn-out phrases called **clichés**. Notice how Cummings combines words to make brand-new images of springtime. "Mud-luscious" and "puddle-wonderful" are refreshed images. They make us remember how much fun it was to play in the mud and splash in puddles when we were kids.

> A **cliché** is an overused, worn-out expression or phrase. Poets want to find **fresh images** that help us see the world in an unusual or original way.
>
> *For more on Imagery, see pages 492–493 and the Handbook of Literary Terms.*

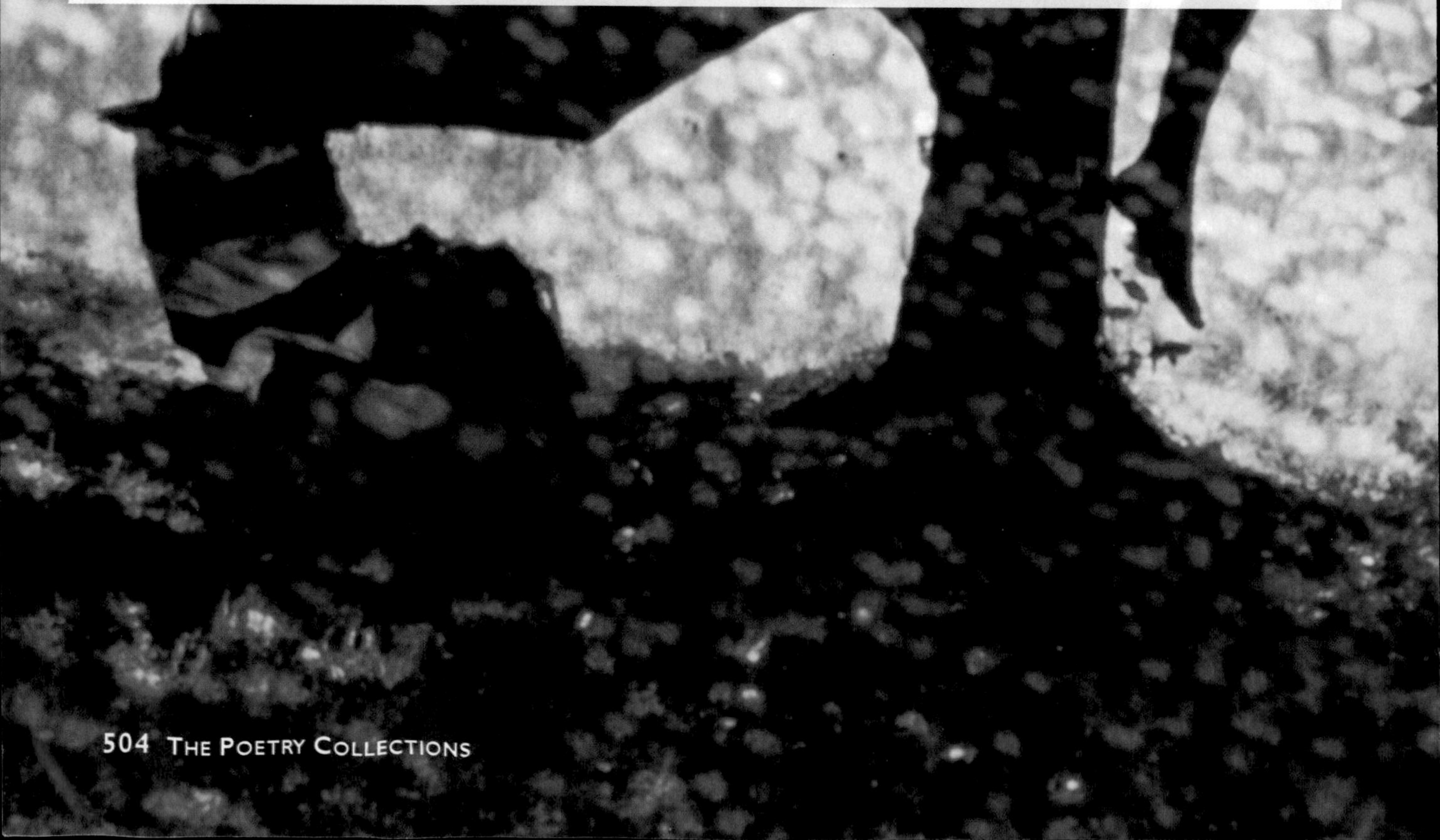

in Just-

E. E. Cummings

in Just-
spring   when the world is mud-
luscious the little
lame balloonman

5   whistles   far   and wee

and eddieandbill come
running from marbles and
piracies and it's
spring

10   when the world is puddle-wonderful

the queer
old balloonman whistles
far   and   wee
and bettyandisbel come dancing

15   from hop-scotch and jump-rope and

it's
spring
and
    the

20   goat-footed

balloonMan   whistles
far
and
wee

MEET THE WRITER

Nobody-but-Himself

E. E. Cummings (1894–1962) began writing a poem a day when he was eight years old— and kept at it until he was twenty-two. Multiply 365 poems a year by fourteen and see what you get! Many of these poems were very short, and a lot of them weren't very good. But if practice makes perfect, then Cummings must have been perfect—on some days, anyhow.

Cummings once got a letter from a high school editor asking him what advice he had for young people who wanted to become poets. The poet's reply tells us something of what poetry meant to him:

66 A poet is somebody who feels, and who expresses his feelings through words. This may sound easy. It isn't . . . [because] the moment you feel, you're nobody-but-yourself. To be nobody-but-yourself—in a world which is doing its best, night and day, to make you everybody else—means to fight the hardest battle which any human being can fight; and never stop fighting. . . . If, at the end of your first ten or fifteen years of fighting and working and feeling, you find you've written one line of one poem, you'll be very lucky indeed. . . . Does this sound dismal? It isn't. It's the most wonderful life on earth. 99

My Grandmother's House

The car rumbles across the bridge along with the other hundred cars. As usual everyone remarks how beautiful the bay is. Mac says hello to the seagulls that seem to greet us by standing on all the posts of the bridge.

We glance and see what's playing at the movies, and pass through the section which always has the putrid smell of bay mud. There's a quick look at the flume and the amusement park. Then we make the turn, and there is my grandmother's house.

Almost at the same time, my family gives a sigh of relief. The brown-shingled house always makes everyone feel at ease. It looks small from the front, except for the addition which sticks out but still seems to blend in.

We all step out on the freshly mowed grass. The grass is green and lush and has a nice squishy feeling to it. There is an exchange of hugs and kisses and an "Oh my, haven't you grown!"

We kids dash up the stairs that would give you a bad scrape if you stepped on one of the many nails that stick up dangerously. We run down the hall and jump into the Charlie Brown bedroom. It is a small room, so all three of us have a bit of trouble standing side by side, yet it is the most popular room. The Charlie Brown bedspread is on, and the old broken radio is still under the bedside table. The number one plus is that there is a great view of the family-room window. You can have a great time spying on everyone.

As the boys rush down to grab a Coke and I slide out of the room on the hard wooden floor, I glance into my grandmother's room. The two single beds are neatly made, the cats are quietly sleeping on the chaise longue, the weeping willow ruffles its leaves against the window, and the chest of old clothes is still there.

Last of the rooms upstairs is my Aunt Kappy's room. This is my favorite room. For at night you can hear the flip-flops crunching against the sandy sidewalks and the talk of the local bomb playing at the movies. In the morning you can smell the bacon cooking downstairs, and maybe hear the chimes of the church bell and the crashing of the waves.

The kitchen always smells delicious. There is always something being prepared. There are always dishes in the drying rack and the red floor shines brightly.

The house would not be complete if a single detail were taken away. To me, my grandmother's house is perfect.

—Kate Daniel
Radnor Middle School
Wayne, Pennsylvania

MAKING MEANINGS

HAIKU
FOG
IN JUST-

First Thoughts

1. All of these poems contain **images** of moments and miracles in nature. What image in the haiku, in "Fog," and in "in Just-" did you find most striking, original, or powerful? Compare your choices with those of your classmates.

Shaping Interpretations

2. One of the characteristics of a **haiku** is that it presents a moment of discovery or revelation. In your own words, describe the moment frozen in each of the haiku on page 500.

3. In Chiyo's haiku, the plant is a "morning glory." How could these words also describe what the poet experienced at her morning encounter?

4. Why do you think Sandburg thought the fog was like a cat? What other cat actions could fit into "Fog"?

5. E. E. Cummings is famous for his unusual punctuation and arrangements of words. What are the children doing in "in Just-" that matches the leaps and jumps of the words? Why do you think Cummings made single words out of the names "eddieandbill" and "bettyandisbel"?

Connecting with the Texts

6. Inside each of the haiku there is a person. Put yourself in each person's shoes, one by one. Consider:

   - In the first haiku, do you wait for the toad to move, or do you poke it?

   - In the second haiku, do you ever use that bucket again?

   - In the third haiku, what do you think you were doing the minute before the frog jumped in?

   - In the fourth haiku, how long are you able to see the hills?

7. Read Sandburg's "Fog" again. Pretend you are actually standing at the edge of a harbor and watching the fog come in across the water. How do you feel about everything around you disappearing? How does the fog feel against your skin?

8. Both Pan and Hephaestus, like most of the Greek gods, were pretty tricky customers. Do you think Cummings depicts the balloon man as completely harmless and kind? Which of the poem's words and images support your response?

Turquoise frog-shaped snuff bottle, Qing dynasty (18th–19th century), Chinese.

CHOICES: Building Your Portfolio

Writer's Notebook

1. Keeping a Journal

Look around. Take notes describing a particular part of your world on a particular day in your life. Be as specific as you can. The student who wrote the essay on page 506 found something to write about on a trip to her grandmother's.

Creative Writing

2. A Special-Day Haiku

Look at the notes you made about your sensations on a special day of the year for the Quickwrite on page 499.

Now write a haiku about your special day. Keep in mind that a haiku brings two images together for comparison, contains a seasonal or weather word, and presents a moment of discovery.

Creative Writing

3. A Weather Change!

Using the notes you made for the "Fog" Quickwrite on page 502, compose a television weather report that describes how tomorrow's weather will look, sound, smell, and behave—in terms of the animal you chose. Sample: "The storm will exhibit early morning rattles followed by one swift bite by noon, followed by increasing pain tonight."

Creative Writing

4. A Seasonal Salute

Imitate the style of Cummings's poem on page 505 and write a poem presenting images and people that you associate with a particular season. Your notes for the Quickwrite on page 504 should give you a start. You might open the way Cummings did: "in Just- . . . when the world is . . ." Play with words and punctuation and typography just as Cummings did.

VOCABULARY   HOW TO OWN A WORD

The Class Word Bank

Set up a class word bank in which you enter any unusual and unfamiliar words you come across. To get started, tear up an old magazine or newspaper, with you and your classmates each taking one page. Each person defines and enters in the class word bank any unusual or interesting word from that page. Set your words up in a computer or in a scrapbook. Map each word as shown here. Be sure to write down the sentence you found the word in.

"The <u>implacable</u> opposition of property owners put a stop to the developer's plans to drain the marsh."

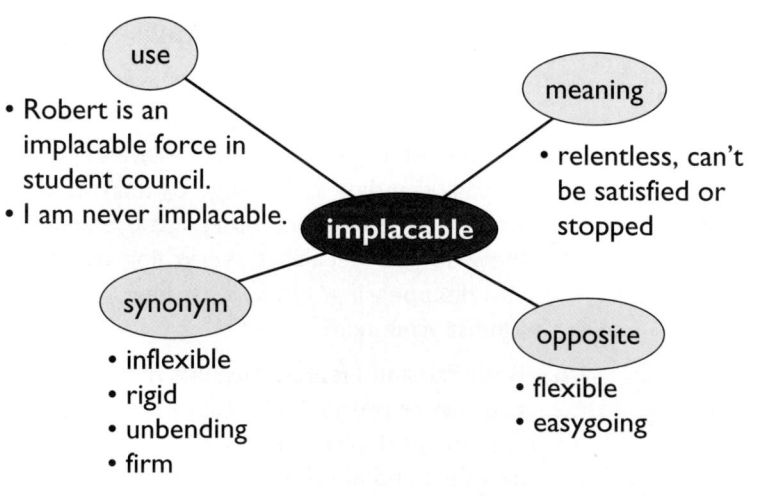

Reading Focus

Two People/One Miracle

This poem captures with enormous precision a special moment that occurred almost two hundred years ago—on April 15, 1802, to be precise. And we *can* be precise because there was another witness to that miracle—the poet's sister Dorothy, also a wonderful writer—who captured the very same miracle in her journal.

Quickwrite

Remember when you saw some scene that made a big impression on you: the earth from a plane window, the ocean, the desert, a city blackout, a mountain peak, snow blanketing city streets? Close your eyes and be there again. What time of year is it? What time of day is it? Is anybody with you? Do they say anything? Can you smell anything? Hear anything? Why do you remember the scene?

Keep your notes. For questions and activities on this poem, see page 513.

Elements of Literature

Figures of Speech

This poem uses two kinds of figures of speech. In a **simile,** the writer compares two unlike things using a word such as *like, as,* or *resembles.* The first line of this poem has become a famous simile. In **personification,** the writer speaks of something nonhuman as if it has human qualities. This poet uses personification when he imagines the daffodils dancing, as if they're in a chorus line.

"'I wandered lonely as a cloud.' Hey, wild!"

Drawing by Donald Reilly; ©1970.
The New Yorker Magazine, Inc.

> **F**igures of speech are words or phrases that describe one thing in terms of another, very different thing. Figures of speech are not meant to be taken literally.
>
> *For more on Figures of Speech, see pages 520–521 and the Handbook of Literary Terms.*

I Wandered Lonely as a Cloud

William Wordsworth

I wandered lonely as a cloud
That floats on high o'er vales and hills,
When all at once I saw a crowd,
A host, of golden daffodils,
5   Beside the lake, beneath the trees,
Fluttering and dancing in the breeze.

Continuous as the stars that shine
And twinkle on the Milky Way,
They stretched in never-ending line
10   Along the margin of a bay;
Ten thousand saw I at a glance,
Tossing their heads in sprightly dance.

The waves beside them danced, but they
Outdid the sparkling waves in glee;
15   A poet could not but be gay,
In such a jocund° company;
I gazed—and gazed—but little thought
What wealth the show to me had brought:

For oft, when on my couch I lie
20   In vacant or in pensive mood,
They flash upon that inward eye
Which is the bliss of solitude;
And then my heart with pleasure fills,
And dances with the daffodils.

16. jocund: merry.

Study of Cumulus Clouds (1822) by John Constable.

MEET THE WRITER

Nature: The Best Teacher

66 One impulse from a vernal wood
May teach you more of man,
Of moral evil and of good,
Than all the sages can. 99

The English Romantic poet **William Wordsworth** (1770–1850) believed that nature was the best teacher. And he believed that common, uneducated people who lived close to nature had at least as much to teach us as people with college degrees.

Wordsworth's mother died when he was seven. Six years later his father was also dead. William had started writing poems by the time he was fifteen. When he was twenty-eight, he and his close friend Samuel Taylor Coleridge published a collection of poems called *Lyrical Ballads*. This slim

William Wordsworth (1842) by B. R. Haydon.

book contained only twenty-four poems, but it was very different from the fancy, aristocratic poetry that most poets then wrote. Wordsworth and Coleridge used simple people and ordinary experiences as their subjects. They used common speech. They said that the human mind was intimately related to the workings of the natural world. They said that God is revealed in the laws and forces of nature.

According to Wordsworth, poetry begins when we get in touch with a memory and relive the experience:

66 . . . poetry is the spontaneous overflow of powerful feelings: It takes its origin from emotion recollected in tranquillity. 99

"In tranquillity," Wordsworth says, meaning that it's better to write about something later than when you're right in the middle of it. Of course, you can still take notes, as Wordsworth and his sister Dorothy regularly did. Then you can take your time to relive what you experienced and put it down on paper exactly the way you want to.

Connections A JOURNAL

I Never Saw Daffodils So Beautiful

Dorothy Wordsworth

April 15, 1802: . . . The wind seized our breath. The lake was rough. There was a boat by itself floating in the middle of the bay below Water Millock. We rested again in the Water Millock Lane. The hawthorns are black and green, the birches here and there greenish, but there is yet more of purple to be seen on the twigs. We got over into a field to avoid some cows—people working. A few primroses by the roadside—wood sorrel flower, the anemone, scentless violets, strawberries, and that starry, yellow flower which Mrs. C. calls pile wort. When we were in the woods beyond Gowbarrow Park, we saw a few daffodils close to the waterside. We fancied that the lake had floated the seeds ashore, and that the little colony had so sprung up. But as we went along there were more and yet more; and at last, under the boughs of the trees, we saw that there was a long belt of them along the shore, about the breadth of a country turnpike road. I never saw daffodils so beautiful. They grew along the mossy stones about and about them; some rested their heads upon these stones as on a pillow for weariness; and the rest tossed and reeled and danced, and seemed as if they verily laughed with the wind that blew upon them over the lake, they looked so gay, ever glancing, ever changing. This wind blew directly over the lake to them. There was here and there a little knot, and a few stragglers a few yards higher up; but they were so few as not to disturb the simplicity, unity, and life of that one busy highway. We rested again and again. The bays were stormy, and we heard the waves at different distances, and in the middle of the water. Rain came on—we were wet when we reached Luff's. . . .

A Worcestershire Cottage (late 19th to early 20th century) by Arthur Claude Strachan.

First Thoughts

1. Listen to Wordsworth's poem read aloud, and draw a picture of what you see.

Shaping Interpretations

2. What **simile** does the poem's speaker use to help you imagine the number of daffodils he saw?

3. Which words in the poem **personify** the daffodils—make them seem like people, even friends and companions, for the lonely speaker?

4. In your own words, how would you explain the "inward eye" in line 21?

5. The word *wealth* can mean several things. What kind of wealth is the speaker referring to in line 18? How do people accumulate this kind of wealth?

Connecting with the Text

6. When could people use an "inward eye" to get through difficult times?

CHOICES: Building Your Portfolio

Writer's Notebook

1. Keeping a Journal

A remembered scene. Refer to the notes in your Quickwrite and compose a journal entry using the details of your remembered scene. See if you can add a comparison to make your scene vivid to a person who might read your journal two hundred years from now.

Creative Writing

2. A Change of Mood

Imitate the first verse of this poem and write four lines or a paragraph that opens with a simile describing how you once felt and what you saw that changed your mood. Open with the words "I wandered [lonely as? happy as? silly as?]. . . ."

Critical Writing

3. Journal and Poem

Write at least one paragraph comparing Dorothy Wordsworth's journal entry with her brother's poem. Before you write, use the following chart to identify the similarities and differences between the two accounts.

	Journal Entry
Details not in poem	
Details that contradict poem	
Figurative language similar to that in poem	
Figurative language that is different	
Lesson drawn from experience (if any)	

I Saw a Wonderful Thing

Annie Dillard

Quickwrite

Some people see things that others would not even notice— little things or things so common they hardly seem worth looking at. Annie Dillard's reflection is about butterflies, the ordinary kind called monarchs, which are only four inches wide when their wings are spread. Butterflies, as you know, seem as fragile as a piece of tissue paper. Notice the comparisons this observer uses to help you see her butterflies.

Before you read, jot down some lessons or insights that you think nature could give you—any form of nature: tides, seasons, earthworms, city pigeons, weeds, ants, a blade of grass.

Monarchs were everywhere. They skittered and bobbed, rested in the air, lolled on the dust—but with none of their usual insouciance.[1] They had but one unwearying thought: South. I watched from my study window: three, four . . . eighteen, nineteen, one every few seconds, and some in tandem.[2] They came fanning straight toward my window from the northwest, and from the northeast, materializing from behind the tips of high hemlocks, where Polaris[3] hangs by night. They appeared as Indian horsemen appear in movies: first dotted, then massed, silent, at the rim of a hill.

Each monarch butterfly had a brittle black body and deep orange wings limned[4] and looped in black bands. A monarch at rest looks like a fleck of tiger, stilled and wide-eyed. A monarch in flight looks like an autumn leaf with a will, vitalized and cast upon the air from which it seems to suck some thin sugar of energy, some leaf-life or sap. As each one climbed up the air outside my window, I could see the more delicate, ventral[5] surfaces of its wings, and I had a sense of bunched legs and straining thorax,[6] but I could never focus well into the flapping and jerking before it vaulted up past the window and out of sight over my head.

1. **insouciance** (in·sōō′sē·əns): carefree attitude.
2. **in tandem** (in tan′dəm): one behind the other.
3. **Polaris** (pō·lar′is): bright star, also called the North Star.
4. **limned** (limd): painted.
5. **ventral** (ven′trəl): front.
6. **thorax** (thôr′aks′): center of an insect's body, between the head and the abdomen.

I walked out and saw a monarch do a wonderful thing: It climbed a hill without twitching a muscle. I was standing at the bridge over Tinker Creek, at the southern foot of a very steep hill. The monarch beat its way beside me over the bridge at eye level, and then, flailing[7] its wings exhaustedly, ascended straight up in the air. It rose vertically to the enormous height of a bankside sycamore's crown. Then, fixing its wings at a precise angle, it glided *up* the steep road, losing altitude extremely slowly, climbing by checking its fall, until it came to rest at a puddle in front of the house at the top of the hill.

I followed. It panted, skirmished briefly westward, and then, returning to the puddle, began its assault on the house. It struggled almost straight up the air next to the two-story brick wall, and then scaled the roof. Wasting no effort, it followed the roof's own slope, from a distance of two inches. Puff, and it was out of sight. I wondered how many more hills and houses it would have to climb before it could rest. From the force of its will it would seem it could flutter through walls.

7. **flailing** (flāl'iŋ): waving wildly.

MEET THE WRITER

A Sounding Bell

Annie Dillard
(1945–   ) had written a few articles for magazines and had produced a small book of poetry when she wrote a series of essays called *Pilgrim at Tinker Creek*. At that time she was living by Tinker Creek in a valley of Virginia's Blue Ridge Mountains. In 1975, much to her surprise, her book of essays won the Pulitzer Prize for general nonfiction. Dillard says:

66 I walk out. I see something, some event that would otherwise have been utterly missed and lost; or something sees me, some enormous power brushes me with its clean wing, and I resound like a beaten bell. I am an explorer. . . . 99

FINDING COMMON GROUND

Annie Dillard made her discoveries after close observation of butterflies.

1. Spend some time outside just looking at something, the way Dillard did. Take a notebook with you and write down all you see, even if you think it's boring. Just keep writing. (You may want to check your Quickwrite notes before deciding what you want to look at.)

2. Write a brief reflection on what you saw and what it taught you. Use your observation notes, just as Dillard did.

3. Be sure to share your reflections in class. Did any of you observe the same natural event or creature? Were your reflections mostly similar, or do you notice great differences in what you saw and what you thought?

Writer's Workshop

ASSIGNMENT
Keep a journal.

AIM
To express yourself.

AUDIENCE
Yourself.

JOURNAL WRITING

Walt Whitman kept a journal during the Civil War in America, and when he published it, he called it *Specimen Days*. Anne Frank, who kept a journal in Amsterdam during another war, in the 1940s, called her red-and-white-checkered diary Kitty. Latoya Hunter, who kept a diary in the 1990s in New York City, called her journal Janice. Probably every writer in this book has kept a journal—whether it had a name or not. Here are some questions and answers about journals.

Q: What exactly is a journal?

A: *Journal* is a very loose term for a collection of your thoughts, memories, experiences, and responses to things you read or see. A journal is usually added to every day.

Q: What's in a journal?

A: A journal can contain

- a day-to-day record of your life
- a record of your feelings, concerns, joys, hopes, fears, disappointments, triumphs
- ideas that strike you during the day (or night)
- descriptions of things you notice in the world that please you
- illustrations
- news headlines, photographs, snatches of dialogue, interesting words—anything that catches your attention and that you want to keep

Q: Are there different kinds of journals?

A: There are many kinds of journals, including these:

- **Diaries** are mostly records of events that have happened to you. Strictly speaking, diaries tend to be more specific and thorough than journals. Journals are freer, more creative, sometimes more personal. But many people use the terms interchangeably.

The history
of the written
word is rich and *Once upon a time*

Page 1

- **Travel journals** preserve your memories of a trip (so you can remember where all those pictures were taken). You may also list your expenses, the names and addresses of people you'd like to see again, and details of places you'd like to revisit.

- **Learning logs** record what you're learning or having trouble with or having a lot of good ideas about. In learning logs you record discussions, respond to what you read, evaluate your progress, and reflect on your learning process.

But the most popular kind of journal is the one that serves as a confidant to the writer, or a place where the writer can reflect on, describe, evaluate, or challenge something. A journal can be a storehouse for the writer's hopes and dreams. It can also be a rich resource. Most professional writers use their journals for inspiration or for details when they write for publication.

Q: What do I need to write a journal?

A: A blank book or notebook is the best place to keep your writings. Many writers keep journals on computers. Some people even keep journals on scraps of paper. You also need a pen or pencil, and you need to set aside time to write—about five minutes a day will do. Most journal keepers write at night, before going to sleep.

Q: Do I have to watch my grammar and all that?

A: No. You'll find more ideas to write about if you freewrite nonstop, without bothering to correct yourself. Your journal is a resource; it is not for publication (even though the journals of many people have been published).

Q: How do I start?

A: Put the date and time of day at the top of the page. The weather, if you like. One word will do. Now write down the very first thing you saw when you opened your eyes this morning. You also had a first thought. Write it down. Now write down the first thing you ate. Then write the name of the first person you saw at school this morning, one thing he or she was wearing, what was said, and how you felt about meeting that person. Now write down where you'd want to be if you weren't right here.

Saturday, 20 June, 1942

I haven't written for a few days, because I wanted first of all to think about my diary. It's an odd idea for someone like me to keep a diary; not only because I have never done so before, but because it seems to me that neither I—nor for that matter anyone else—will be interested in the unbosomings of a thirteen-year-old schoolgirl. Still, what does that matter? I want to write, but more than that, I want to bring out all kinds of things that lie buried deep in my heart.

—Anne Frank

There. You're writing a journal.

Write in your journal every night. If you're really tired and sleepy, just write down the single most important thing that happened to you. That's what most writers do. Sometimes their journals become more famous than their poems!

By permission of Doug Marlette and Creators Syndicate.

Student Model

Latoya Hunter was a teenager living in New York City when she wrote her diary. Latoya focuses on herself and her feelings, though from time to time she describes a part of her world (she thinks the street she lives on is ugly, she thinks winter is the most depressing time of year, and she loves summer "with no trembling teeth"). She calls her journal Janice.

September 20, 1990

Dear Diary,

I spent the day helping out my friend Anika. She's moving out of her apartment. I'll still get to see her though, she's still going to go to my school.

We met an old lady on the street. We walked with her to the bus stop. I think in that short time we spent walking, she actually told us her life story. She told us she's going back to high school and she seemed to be proud of herself. She told us about God and that He had been her best friend ever since she was our age. It was really interesting to listen to someone who has lived and experienced so much. At first, I was just trying not to be rude so I listened, but soon I found myself wanting to hear what she had to say. I realize now that everyone has a life to them. I see so many faces every day, it was nice to go beyond the face for once.

—Latoya Hunter

Think with your body
And dance with your mind.

—Victor Hernandez Cruz

Can dogs imagine?
Can whales
imagine? Can cats imagine?
Maybe. Maybe not. But you can
imagine that they can, even if they
can't—and that's what's important.
Your imagination is a time-and-space
ship more powerful than *Star Trek*'s *Voyager*.
Your ship can take you anywhere, any time—
backward, forward, upside down and inside
out—and you are the captain. Want to visit
Mars? China? Win a million dollars? Go on a
date? See Timbuktu? You can. For everything
we imagine is real—at least as real as our
dreams and hopes and fears.

Writer's Notebook

Exercise your imagination. Pick a hungry insect, bird, or animal and put yourself in its
shoes (or feet). Close your eyes and picture
what time of year it is, what time of day it is,
and what the weather is like. Write these down in your
Writer's Notebook. Now close your eyes again, look around
carefully, make notes on exactly where you—the hungry insect,
bird, or animal—are located, and tell what you want, right this
minute. Save your notes.

WORK IN PROGRESS

FIGURES OF SPEECH: Seeing Connections

One of the ways that poets play with words is by using figurative language—expressions that put aside literal meanings in favor of imaginative connections. A **figure of speech** is always based on a comparison, and it is not literally true. If someone says to you, "Listen, I'm going to give you a piece of my mind," you don't say, "OK, I'll bring a plate to put it on." You understand that the speaker is using a figure of speech, that he's going to tell you what he's *really* thinking, and that it's not going to be nice.

Figurative language can be a kind of shorthand. It can take a lot of words to express an idea in literal terms. But the same idea can be communicated instantly by a figure of speech. Think of all the words you'd have to use to explain literally what these common expressions say: "Judy's uptight." "The check bounced." "Gilford's laid back." "Cool it."

Figures of Speech in Everyday Language

Many figures of speech that were once fresh and original have been completely absorbed into our everyday language. We use them without realizing that they aren't literally true. When we think about our language, in fact, we realize that figures of speech are the foundation of thousands of expressions.

When we refer to the "roof of the mouth" or the "arm of the chair" or the "foot of the bed," we are using figurative language. In each case, we are imaginatively relating a part of the body to something that has nothing to do with the body.

Even the languages of science and business are based on figures of speech. Dentists talk about "building bridges." Biologists talk about "the bloodstream." Stockbrokers talk about "the market crash." Even our newest technology, computer science, already has its own figures of speech in terms such as *menu, virus, window,* and *mouse.*

Similes: "X Is Like Y"

A simile is the simplest form of figurative language. In a **simile,** two dissimilar things are compared using a word such as *like, as, than,* or *resembles.* "The moon shines *like* a fifty-cent piece." "Eva's eyes are *as* glassy *as* marbles." "Lucy feels lighter *than* a grasshopper."

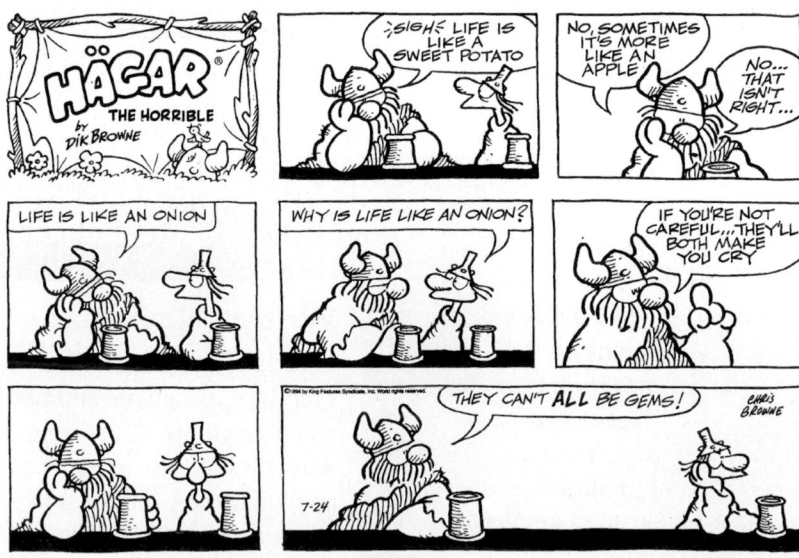

Reprinted with special permission of King Features Syndicate.

by John Malcolm Brinnin

Here is a poet who looked at an ordinary fork and thought of a simile.

Fork

This strange thing must have
  crept
Right out of hell.
It resembles a bird's foot
Worn around the cannibal's
  neck.
As you hold it in your hand,
As you stab with it into a piece
  of meat,
It is possible to imagine the
  rest of the bird:
Its head which like your fist
Is large, bald, beakless, and
  blind.

—Charles Simic

Metaphors: "X Is Y"

Similes are easily recognized because of their connectives (*like, as, than, resembles*): "You eat like a pig!" When the connective is omitted, we have a metaphor: "You're a pig!" A **metaphor,** then, is a comparison between two unlike things, in which one thing becomes another thing without the use of the word *like, as, than,* or *resembles.* The difference between a metaphor and a simile is a matter of emphasis.

In a simile, the two things remain separate, but in a metaphor they are united.

A metaphor can be direct or implied. A **direct metaphor** directly compares the two things by the use of a verb such as *is.* An **implied metaphor** implies or suggests the comparison between the two things without stating it directly. If we say, "The city is a sleeping woman," we are using a direct metaphor. If we say, "The city sleeps peacefully," we use an implied metaphor. Both metaphors identify a city that has its lights out with a person who has quietly fallen into the darkness of sleep.

Metaphor is the most flexible and suggestive element of figurative language. It is a means by which all experience can be imaginatively connected.

According to an old Hebrew saying, "The world is a wedding"—and in that, we have a single metaphor that defines all metaphors.

Personification: Making the World Human

Personification is a special kind of metaphor in which human qualities are given to something that is not human—an animal, an object, or even an idea. What personifications can you find in these headlines?

- Every Computer "Whispers" Its Secrets

- China Now a Struggling Giant

- White House Digs In Its Heels on Budget Issue

> According to an old Hebrew saying, "The world is a wedding"—and in that, we have a single metaphor that defines all metaphors.

Sometimes personification simply involves giving life and feelings to things that are inanimate, or lifeless. When we say that a tooth is angry or a cough is stubborn or a computer is friendly or love is blind, we are using a kind of personification. Personification is yet another example of how we use our imaginations to give meaning to the whole nonhuman world.

Reading Focus

Imagining Things Unseen

Every day each of us travels in imagination. (Yes, that includes thinking about running the marathon or dreaming of being a hoop star.) Being a poet means tuning in and paying attention to these journeys—and writing down what they look and feel like as they flash by.

Quickwrite

Name two things that you've never seen first-hand but that you can imagine clearly. Describe what you see, hear, smell, taste, touch.

Keep your notes. For questions and activities on this poem, see pages 528–529.

Elements of Literature

Diction: Words Count

After Emily Dickinson's death, her friends set to work copying her poems (Dickinson's handwriting was often hard to make out) and trying to get them published. In this process, they made changes. In "I Never Saw a Moor" the word *Billow* was changed to *Wave*. The word *Checks* was changed to *Chart*. The changes in diction made a difference.

> **D**iction is a writer's or speaker's choice of words.
>
> *For more on Diction, see the Handbook of Literary Terms.*

I Never Saw a Moor

Emily Dickinson

I never saw a Moor—
I never saw the Sea—
Yet know I how the Heather looks
And what a Billow be.

I never spoke with God
Nor visited in Heaven—
Yet certain am I of the spot
As if the Checks° were given—

8. Checks: slips of paper that railway conductors gave to passengers after collecting their tickets.

MEET THE WRITER

She Knows Poetry

Unlike most people today, **Emily Dickinson** (1830–1886) was born, lived most of her life, and died in the same house. After she was twenty-six, she rarely went out of that house in Amherst, Massachusetts. But for the next thirty years she traveled to the ends of the earth and the universe in her imagination. She jotted down poems in the margins of newspapers, on brown paper bags, and even on the insides of envelopes.

Dickinson also wrote many letters. In one of them, she defined poetry:

66 If I read a book and it makes my whole body so cold no fire can ever warm me, I know it is poetry. If I feel physically as if the top of my head were taken off, I know that it is poetry. These are the only ways I know it. **99**

A famous editor, T. W. Higginson, once asked Emily Dickinson for a photograph of herself. In her reply the poet created a photograph in words.

66 Could you believe me—without? I had no portrait, now, but am small, like the Wren, and my Hair is bold, like the Chestnut Bur— and my eyes like the Sherry in the Glass, that the Guest leaves. **99**

While she was alive, only seven of her poems were published—all anonymously. Dickinson died not knowing that she would become recognized as one of the greatest poets who ever wrote in English.

BEFORE YOU READ
KIDNAP POEM

Reading Focus

Taken for a Ride

Poets and children like to play games with words—listen to any four-year-old. In "Kidnap Poem" a poet pretends to abduct you into her world, and she turns nouns into verbs to help her do it. Actually, there's as much kidding around as kidnapping in this poem.

Quickwrite

Imagine a job you'd like to have—jet pilot, teacher, writer, plumber, diver, actor, home-maker, DJ. Anything you want. Then, list all the words you can think of that are associated with that job. If you choose musician, you might start with *symphony, notes, strings, keys, chorus.*

Keep your notes. For questions and activities on this poem, see pages 528–529.

Elements of Literature

Puns for Fun

As you saw on page 491, poets play with words—this poet plays with nouns and makes them verbs, she plays with words that sound the same but are spelled differently, and she plays with words that have several meanings. Read carefully—this poem is like one of those word games that contain hidden tricks.

A pun is a play on the multiple meanings of a word (*flies, club, kid*) or on two words that sound alike but have different meanings (*pause/paws*).

For more on Pun, see the Hand-book of Literary Terms.

Serenade (1969) by Romare Bearden. Collage and paint on panel (45 ⅓″ × 32 ½″).

Kidnap Poem

Nikki Giovanni

ever been kidnapped
by a poet
if i wcre a poet
i'd kidnap you

5   put you in my phrases
and meter you to jones beach
or maybe coney island
or maybe just to my house

lyric you in lilacs
10   dash you in the rain
alliterate the beach
to complement my see

play the lyre for you
ode you with my love song
15   anything to win you
wrap you in the red Black green
show you off to mama

yeah if i were
a poet i'd kid
20   nap you

MEET THE WRITER

"The Princess of Black Poetry"

Nikki Giovanni (1943–   ) was born in Knoxville, Tennessee, and grew up in Cincinnati, Ohio. She is affectionately called the Princess of Black Poetry because of the large, enthusiastic crowds she attracts whenever she gives public readings of her work. Behind all of Giovanni's poetry, according to one critic, are "the creation of raclal pride and the communication of individual love." Giovanni herself says:

66 I write out of my own experiences—which also happen to be the experiences of my people. 99

Not flattered when students who take her classes try to write poems that sound like hers, she says:

66 I already sound like me. I want my students to hear their own voices. 99

BEFORE YOU READ
SOUTHBOUND ON THE FREEWAY

Reading Focus

Imagination on Location

This poem opens with a long traveling shot, zooms in, hovers, and takes a series of close-ups. If that sounds like making a movie, it is. Just like a movie, the imagination can do long shots, jump-cuts, splices, wide-angle shots, and close-ups. Here's a creature feature about... well, you have to discover that for yourself.

Quickwrite

You are an extremely intelligent alien from outer space, but you have never seen a human before. For the very first time, you watch a human get out of bed, brush his or her teeth, sing in a chorus, or play softball. Choose a few of these activities (or some others you think of) and jot down how the alien might describe what is going on.

Keep your notes. For questions and activities on this poem, see pages 528–529.

Elements of Literature

Speaker: Who's Talking?

In Emily Dickinson's poem on page 490, we hear a voice who calls himself "I." We know this speaker is a boy because he tells us so in line 11—but the writer of the poem is a female. Poets can imagine anyone or anything as the speaker of their poems. In Don Marquis's poem on page 140, the speaker is a cockroach. When you start to read a poem, ask yourself: Who is speaking to me?

> The **speaker** is the voice talking to us in a poem.

Highway Patrol (1986) by James Doolin.
Courtesy of Koplin Gallery, Santa Monica, California.

Southbound on the Freeway

May Swenson

A tourist came in from Orbitville,
parked in the air, and said:

The creatures of this star
are made of metal and glass.

5   Through the transparent parts
you can see their guts.

Their feet are round and roll
on diagrams—or long

measuring tapes—dark
10 with white lines.

They have four eyes.
The two in the back are red.

Sometimes you can see a 5-eyed
one, with a red eye turning

15 on the top of his head.
He must be special—

the others respect him,
and go slow,

when he passes, winding
20 among them from behind.

They all hiss as they glide,
like inches, down the marked

tapes. Those soft shapes,
shadowy inside

25 the hard bodies—are they
their guts or their brains?

MAKING MEANINGS

I NEVER SAW A MOOR
KIDNAP POEM
SOUTHBOUND ON THE FREEWAY

First Thoughts

1. What are the poets imagining in "I Never Saw a Moor," "Kidnap Poem," and "Southbound on the Freeway"?

Shaping Interpretations

2. What sound effect would be lost in "I Never Saw a Moor" if "Billow be" was changed to "Wave must be"?

3. Dickinson's editors changed the word *Checks* in "I Never Saw a Moor" to *Chart,* meaning "map." How does this change in **diction** change the sense of lines 5–8?

4. "Kidnap Poem" uses terms associated with writing, especially with poetry. See if you can find five nouns connected with writing and poetry that are used here as verbs.

5. "Kidnap Poem" is full of word tricks. Can you spot the **puns** in lines 11, 12, 13, and 19–20?

6. Red, black, and green are the colors of Kenya's and Malawi's flags. How could knowing this fact add to your reading of line 16 in "Kidnap Poem"?

7. Who is the **speaker** in the poem "Southbound on the Freeway"?

8. Each detail in "Southbound on the Freeway" is a clue to the riddle. What *is* the "tourist" looking at? See if you can identify all the clues by filling out these equations:

   guts =   tapes =   5-eyed one =   feet =   eyes =

Extending the Texts

9. Suppose you are driving one of the cars southbound on the freeway. You look up and see this tourist parked in the air. Think of some **figures of speech** you'd use to describe this vision to your skeptical friends.

10. Look at what May Swenson said about cars and people on page 527. How do you feel about her opinion?

CHOICES: Building Your Portfolio

Writer's Notebook

1. Collecting Ideas for a Poem

Finding a subject.
Poetry is first of all about feelings. Make a list of all the feelings you can think of: hate, love, anger, honesty, grief, joy, and so on. Choose five feelings from this list that could be starting points for a poem. Try making up five similes that compare the feelings to an object, animal, or person. If you want, try to extend your comparison—in other words, show several ways in which your two things are alike.

> Hate is like ice.
> It freezes feelings.
> Makes the eyes
>   like stones.
> Hardens the heart.

Creative Writing

2. "I Never Saw . . ."

Imitate the structure of Dickinson's poem and write at least four lines describing things you can imagine even though you have never seen them, and things you have faith in even though you've never seen or touched them. Your Quickwrite notes should give you a start.

Creative Writing

3. Your Alien Riddle

Using the notes you made in the Quickwrite for "Southbound on the Freeway," write a paragraph that describes some everyday human activities from your alien's point of view. Open with the line "I came in from _____, parked in the air, and saw _____." Before you write, take notes on all the specific features of the human activities your speaker will observe. Try not to give away what the speaker is looking at. See if a classmate can guess.

Creative Writing

4. Your "Kidnap Poem"

Refer to the notes you took before reading "Kidnap Poem" and, using the words and phrases associated with your job, write a "kidnap poem" to someone you like.

Use some of your nouns as verbs, if you're inspired:

Ever been kidnapped by a
  singer?
I'd music you to meet my
  mom
put you in my chorus . . .

Research/Collaboration

5. Class Notebook for Figures of Speech

With your classmates, start a group notebook in which you gather striking and original figures of speech—metaphors, similes, and personifications. Start by looking in one issue of a daily newspaper. (The sports and entertainment sections are usually riddled with figures of speech.) Schedule a few minutes each week to read new entries aloud and try to identify the terms of the figures of speech—that is, tell what is compared to what. Just as starters, here are some metaphoric news headlines. If these were taken literally, what would be happening?

"Taxpayers Are Drained"
"Senate Committee Grills
  President"
"President Puts Lid on
  News Leaks"

BEFORE YOU READ
BEWARE: DO NOT READ THIS POEM

Reading Focus

Swallowed Alive

Mirrors can do many things—in real life or in people's imaginations. This poem is like one of those houses of mirrors in an amusement park, where you don't know where in the world *you* are.

Quickwrite

Write down quickly your first response to this poem's title.

Keep your notes. For questions and activities on this poem, see page 535.

Elements of Literature

Narration in Poetry

This unusual poem tells *two* stories. The external story is strange enough: It is about a woman and some other people who disappear into a mirror. But this only sets the stage for the internal story—the tale of what happens to *you*, the reader, as you disappear into the poem. Like all stories, this one is meant to be told aloud.

Narration is any kind of writing or speaking that tells a story—a series of related events.

For more on Narration, see the Handbook of Literary Terms.

Beware: Do Not Read This Poem

Ishmael Reed

tonite, *thriller* was
abt an ol woman, so vain she
surrounded her self w/
    many mirrors

5   It got so bad that finally she
locked herself indoors & her
whole life became the
    mirrors

one day the villagers broke
10   into her house, but she was too
swift for them. she disappeared
    into a mirror
each tenant who bought the house
after that lost a loved one to
15   the ol woman in the mirror:
    first a little girl
    then a young woman
    then the young woman/s husband
the hunger of this poem is legendary
20   it has taken in many victims
back off from this poem
it has drawn in yr feet
back off from this poem
it has drawn in yr legs
25   back off from this poem

it is a greedy mirror
you are into this poem. from
    the waist down
nobody can hear you can they?
30   this poem has had you up to here
    belch
this poem aint got no manners
you cant call out frm this poem
relax now & go w/ this poem
35   move & roll on to this poem

    do not resist this poem
    this poem has yr eyes
    this poem has his head
    this poem has his arms
40   this poem has his fingers
    this poem has his fingertips
this poem is the reader & the
    reader this poem

statistic: the us bureau of missing persons reports
45   that in 1968 over 100,000 people disappeared
    leaving no solid clues
      nor trace   only
  a space   in the lives of their friends

MEET THE WRITER

"Writin' Is Fightin' "

Ishmael Reed (1938–   ),
as a fellow poet noted, "alters
our notion of what is possible."
Known for his bold, brash, and
blunt style, Reed has written
several satiric novels that blend
African American vernacular with standard
English and hip jargon. As the title of one of his
books indicates, Reed believes
"writin' is fightin'" and ought to
stir up controversy. A native of
Tennessee (his daughter is named
for her father's home state), Reed
lives in Oakland, California. You
probably won't be surprised that
Reed says:

66 My novels and poems are
meant to be read aloud. That's
why jazz musicians have been able to adapt
my stuff. 99

Eyeglasses for the Mind

from **Feast of Fear: Conversations with Stephen King**

Stephen King

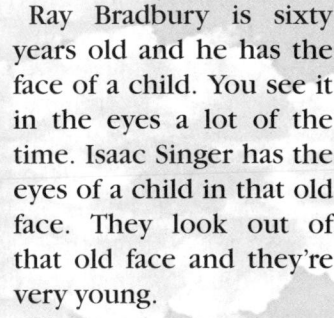

I did the Mike Wallace radio show in New York at the CBS building. We went in and the electric eye had a case of the hiccups. The door was one of these doors where you'd step on the pad and the door would slide open. And this door was almost pitching a fit. It was jerking back and forth, not closing or opening all the way.

And my feeling about that is that somebody else would look at that and say: "Oh, that door has the hiccups." Whereas a little kid would walk up to that door and might very well shrink away from even going near it. And say: "It wants to eat me, it's alive!" Children see things from a different perspective.

And in that sense I'm childlike. I looked at the door and I thought: "Gee, that would make a good story if that thing came alive and somebody walked up to it and CHUNG!" Which is a very childish sort of fantasy.

People respond to this perspective. It doesn't really die. It atrophies[1] and lies dormant.[2] And I get paid to show people that different perspec-

tive. It's like exercising a muscle, rather than letting it go slack. But I'll tell you a funny thing. There are writers who look like children. They've used this facility so much for so long that they literally look like children.

Ray Bradbury is sixty years old and he has the face of a child. You see it in the eyes a lot of the time. Isaac Singer has the eyes of a child in that old face. They look out of that old face and they're very young.

That's why people pay writers and artists. That's the only reason we're around. We're excess baggage. I can't even fix a pipe in my house when it freezes. I am a dickey bird on the back of civilization.

I have no skill that improves the quality of life in a physical sense at all. The only thing I can do is say: "Look here, this is the way you didn't look at it before. It's just a cloud to you, but look at it, doesn't it look like an elephant?" Somebody says: "Boy! it does look like an elephant!" And for that, people pay because they've lost all of it themselves.

You know, I'm like a person who makes eyeglasses for the mind.

---

1. **atrophies** (a'trə·fēz): wastes away.
2. **dormant** (dôr'mənt): inactive.

BEFORE YOU READ
THE SECRET

Reading Focus

The Secret Never Told

If you knew the secret of life, you'd be superhuman. And you're not. But certain poems can put you in touch with matters bigger than yourself. Remember, poems capture bits of life the way plants capture sunlight in their leaves. Once written, those poems wait quietly for some reader to open them so they can release that stored-up light. Of course, poems reveal different things to different people. There is, after all, no one big secret to life, but thousands of little ones.

Quickwrite

Quickly write down what *you* think are some of the secrets of life. Try to say what you feel.

Keep your notes. For questions and activities on this poem, see page 535.

Elements of Literature

Implied Ideas: Speaking Indirectly

Poetry uses the language of suggestion, not the language of direct statement. This means that a good poem never comes right out and says: "This is my main idea." Instead, a good poem lets us, the readers, enter the poem and discover its meanings for ourselves.

Landscape with Two Who Are Lost (1938) by Paul Klee.

Oeffentliche Kunstsammlung, Basel. Kupferstichkabinett.

The Secret

Denise Levertov

Two girls discover
the secret of life
in a sudden line of
poetry.

5   I who don't know the
secret wrote
the line. They
told me

(through a third person)
10 they had found it
but not what it was
not even

what line it was. No doubt
by now, more than a week
15 later, they have forgotten
the secret,

the line, the name of
the poem. I love them for
finding what
20 I can't find,
and for loving me
for the line I wrote,
and for forgetting it
so that

25 a thousand times, till death
finds them, they may
discover it again, in other
lines

in other
30 happenings. And for
wanting to know it,
for

assuming there is
such a secret, yes,
35 for that
most of all.

MEET THE WRITER

"Members of One Another"

66 I believe poets are instruments on which the power of poetry plays . . . it is given to the seer to see, but it is then his responsibility to communicate what he sees, that they who cannot see may see, since we are members of one another. 99

For most of her education, **Denise Levertov** (1923–   ) relied on her mother's reading aloud to the family such writers as Tolstoy, Conrad, Dickens, and Cather. Levertov, who was born in England, was a nurse during the bombing of London in World War II. For years, she has been active in antiwar and antinuclear protest movements. Of the relation of poets and poetry to life, she once said:

66 The spring sunshine, the new leaves: [Poets] still see them, still love them; but in what poignant contrast is their beauty and simple goodness to the evil we are conscious of day and night. . . . 99

Levertov met an American writer in a Swiss youth hostel, married him, and moved to the United States in 1948. She became an American citizen in 1956.

MAKING MEANINGS
BEWARE: DO NOT READ THIS POEM
THE SECRET

First Thoughts

1. Suppose you could ask Reed and Levertov one question each about their poems. What would you ask? Your Quickwrites might give you ideas.

Shaping Interpretations

2. According to the last stanza of "Beware: Do Not Read This Poem," what has become of all those missing persons?

3. How is "Beware: Do Not Read This Poem" like a greedy mirror? What words do you think **personify** the poem as some kind of greedy monster?

4. Can poetry be dangerous? Talk about Reed's ideas.

5. Who is the **speaker** in "The Secret"? What can you **infer** about how the speaker feels about the two girls?

6. In your own words tell what "The Secret" reveals to *you* about poetry.

CHOICES: Building Your Portfolio

Writer's Notebook

1. Collecting Ideas for a Poem

Finding a subject.
These poets probably found their subjects in something that happened in ordinary life. Perhaps Ishmael Reed read a news article about missing persons. Perhaps Denise Levertov was told by a friend about two girls who liked her poetry. Look through the newspaper, or think about what people have said to you today. Take notes on something that might be interesting to express in a poem. Try to take notes on at least three things.

Creative Writing

2. A Shoe

To prove that poems can be made out of anything, look at your shoes. If they're new, write a birth-announcement poem for your "twins." Give their names, sex, length, and weight. Don't forget to describe details such as soles, tongues, heels, and laces. Use as many figures of speech as you like. Or, if your shoes are old, write an epitaph poem, announcing the end of your shoes and giving highlights of their lives. Or, write a poem in which your shoes take over your life and go wherever they please.

Creative Writing

3. More of the Story

What happens next? Use narration to write another stanza for "Beware: Do Not Read This Poem" describing what happens next. Write as "I," the reader who has become the poem. If you wish, imitate Reed's typography and spelling.

Critical Writing

4. Dear Stephen King . . .

Write King a letter telling him how you feel about the ideas he expresses in the interview on page 532. What do *you* think writers and artists do for us?

Reading Focus

Life in Seven Acts

Seven acts. Yes, that's how long this poet imagines the play of your life is going to be. According to this speaker, you're already in the middle of the second act. See what Jaques (pronounced jā′kwēz) predicts about the rest of your life in this speech from Shakespeare's comedy *As You Like It*.

Quickwrite

Second-guess Shakespeare.

Write down what *you* think are the seven stages of a man's or woman's life.

Keep your notes. For questions and activities on this poem, see pages 538–539.

Elements of Literature

Extended Metaphor

Jaques opens with one of the most famous metaphors ever written—"All the world's a stage." Then he extends that metaphor to compare the stages of our lives to seven actors who say their parts and then exit from the stage.

> **A**n **extended metaphor** is a comparison developed over several lines of a poem.
>
> *For more on Metaphors, see pages 520–521 and the Handbook of Literary Terms.*

The Seven Ages of Man

William Shakespeare

　　　　　　　All the world's a stage,
And all the men and women merely players;
They have their exits and their entrances,
And one man in his time plays many parts,
5　　His acts being seven ages. At first the infant,
Mewling and puking in the nurse's arms;
And then the whining schoolboy, with his satchel
And shining morning face, creeping like snail
Unwillingly to school. And then the lover,
10　Sighing like furnace, with a woeful ballad
Made to his mistress' eyebrow. Then a soldier,
Full of strange oaths, and bearded like the pard,° 　　　　**12. pard:** leopard.
Jealous in honor, sudden and quick in quarrel,
Seeking the bubble reputation
15　Even in the cannon's mouth. And then the justice,° 　　**15. justice:** judge.
In fair round belly with good capon° lined, 　　　　　　**16. capon:** fat chicken.
With eyes severe and beard of formal cut,
Full of wise saws° and modern instances; 　　　　　　**18. saws:** sayings.
And so he plays his part. The sixth age shifts

First Steps (19th century), after Millet by Vincent van Gogh. Dutch. Oil on canvas.

The Metropolitan Museum of Art, New York. Gift of George N. and Helen M. Richard, 1964 (64.165.2). Photograph by Malcolm Varon.

20   Into the lean and slippered pantaloon,°
       With spectacles on nose and pouch on side;
       His youthful hose,° well saved, a world too wide
       For his shrunk shank; and his big manly voice,
       Turning again toward childish treble, pipes
25   And whistles in his sound. Last scene of all,
       That ends this strange eventful history,
       Is second childishness and mere oblivion,
       Sans° teeth, sans eyes, sans taste, sans everything.

20. pantaloon: silly old man.

22. hose: stockings.

28. sans: without.

MAKING MEANINGS
THE SEVEN AGES OF MAN

First Thoughts

1. Jaques is a gloomy character, so it's not surprising that he views people (especially men—he pretty much ignores women) as ridiculous. What characteristics of our lives has Jaques left out of his speech?

Shaping Interpretations

2. In the first two acts, what **images** help you picture childhood as Jaques sees it? What **simile** describes the schoolboy's attitude toward school? How do you feel about these pictures of childhood?

3. In Shakespeare's day, it was fashionable to compose serious love poems celebrating the perfection of a woman's eyes, lips, or complexion. Find the lines where Jaques makes fun of this type of poetry. What **simile** describes the sighs of the person who writes it?

4. In lines 13 and 14, what does Jaques compare "reputation" to? What point about the permanence of a reputation is he making by using this **metaphor**? What people seek reputation "even in the cannon's mouth"?

5. If the justice's belly is lined "with good capon," what do we know about him? What details make the justice seem like a ridiculous character?

6. According to Jaques, what physical and mental changes take place as a man reaches the sixth and seventh ages?

Extending the Text

7. These famous lines were written nearly four hundred years ago. Of all the seven ages of man that Shakespeare characterizes, which do you think have remained true to life in the twentieth century? Have any changed?

Challenging the Text

8. Do you find Jaques' descriptions of old age horrifying? What alternate, equally valid descriptions of old age can you think of?

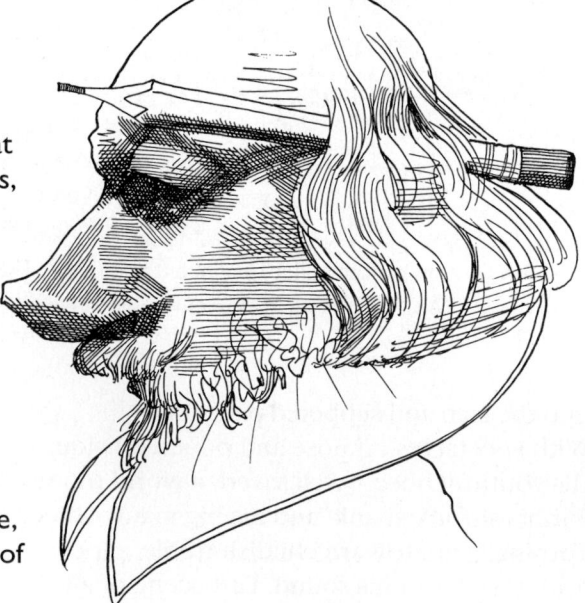

William Shakespeare.

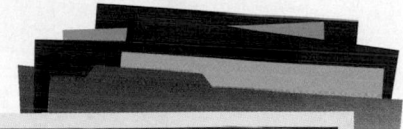

Writer's Notebook

1. Collecting Ideas for a Poem

An imitation.
Some poems are perfect for imitation, even parody, which is humorous mockery. Take notes on how you could adapt this poem to focus on women, not men. Stick with seven ages. Extend your metaphor, comparing life to a stage as far as you can logically take it.

Speaking/Creative Writing

2. Talking Stages

Suppose each stage of life is assigned to a different actor and each of the seven actors has a chance to deliver one speech as he (or she) occupies the spotlight for a second on the stage of life. Write seven one-line comments and, with a group of classmates, act each player entering and leaving the stages of life. You might want to add costumes and props (for example, each character could hold something symbolic).

Critical Thinking

3. Paraphrasing a Poem

To **paraphrase** a passage means to restate it in your own words. Because a paraphrase restates complex ideas in plainer words, it is often longer than the original passage (and never as interesting). Write a paraphrase of Jaques' speech. Explain in your own words each figure of speech. Pretend you are writing the paraphrase for a reader who has had trouble understanding Jaques' language.

VOCABULARY   HOW TO OWN A WORD

WORD BANK

strange
fair
saws
hose

Multiple Meanings

Those very ordinary words in the Word Bank at left have several meanings. Each word is used at least once by Jaques. Find where he uses each word and then explore the meaning of the words by drawing a map for each word like the one opposite. You will have to do two maps for *strange*.

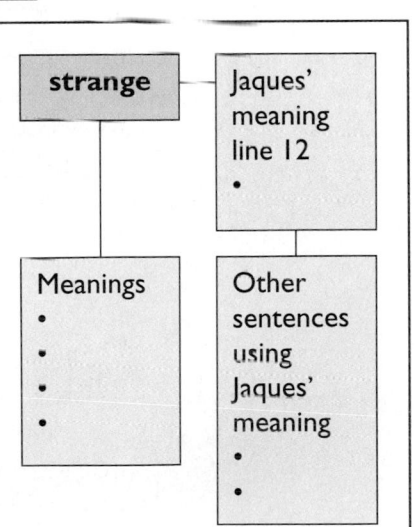

BEFORE YOU READ
FIRE AND ICE

Reading Focus

Whose Fault Is It?

From the beginning of time, people have imagined—and often predicted—the end of the world. Today, scientists tell us that the sun will burn itself out in about six billion years. That may be a bit far off to worry about—but what about terrorists? And the hole in the ozone layer? And global warming?

Quickwrite

Fill out a diagram like the one in the next column. In the larger part of the circles, list the characteristics of fire and ice. Where the circles overlap, list the characteristics they share.

Keep your notes. For questions and activities on this poem, see pages 544–545.

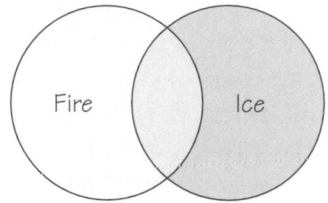

Fire   Ice

Elements of Literature

Implied Metaphor

"Fire and Ice" is built around two metaphors, but the comparisons are never directly stated. Use your powers of inference to figure this out: What emotions do fire and ice stand for?

> **A**n **implied metaphor** does not tell us directly that one thing *is* something else. Instead, it uses words that suggest the nature of the comparison.
>
> *For more on Metaphors, see pages 520–521 and the Handbook of Literary Terms.*

MEET THE WRITER
A "Stay Against Confusion"

Robert Frost (1874–1963) lived and wrote in New England most of his life. New England still bears the scars of the Ice Age glacier that stripped the land bare and buried everything in its path. Enormous boulders still litter the landscape where the glacier dropped them millions of years ago.

Indeed, Frost had only to look out his farmhouse window to see the destructive effects of

Fire and Ice

Robert Frost

Some say the world will end in fire,
Some say in ice.
From what I've tasted of desire
I hold with those who favor fire.
But if it had to perish twice,
I think I know enough of hate
To say that for destruction ice
Is also great
And would suffice.

ice—and had only to take a short walk to find the charred clearing and the blackened cellar holes left by lightning fires. And then, like all human beings, he had only to look inside himself to discover the destructive forces of desire and hate.

In his essay "The Figure a Poem Makes," Frost talks about poetry:

> 66 [A poem] . . . begins in delight and ends in wisdom . . . a clarification of life—not necessarily a great clarification, such as sects and cults are founded on, but in a momentary stay against confusion. 99

Frost certainly doesn't give us any definite answers in "Fire and Ice." However, like other puzzling poems by Frost, "Fire and Ice" does make us think about how little we really know about the forces that shape the world.

Despite the dark side of his poetry, Robert Frost was the last American poet to achieve the status of a national figure on the order of certain sports or movie stars. As an old man, he recited one of his poems on the cold windy day of John F. Kennedy's inauguration as president in 1961.

BEFORE YOU READ
ALL WATCHED OVER
BY MACHINES OF LOVING GRACE

Reading Focus

Imagination to the Rescue

Machines free us and improve our incomes and our minds. Machines enslave us, invade our privacy, and are destroying the environment at a rapid rate. Both statements are true. In this poem Richard Brautigan imagines a world like the Biblical vision of a peaceable kingdom (see the art on page 544), where the lion lies down with the lamb. But Brautigan's vision includes technology.

Quickwrite

READER'S LOG

Name three machines you feel you couldn't live without. Pretend these machines disappear from the face of the earth. Write down quickly what you would miss.

Keep your notes. For questions and activities on this poem, see pages 544–545.

Elements of Literature

Tone: An Attitude

You've read poems in these collections that reveal many tones, from cynical to sincere to playful. It is important to be sensitive to tone: If you are talking to a friend and you mistake a tone of sarcasm for a tone of sincerity, you've made a serious mistake. In speech, tone is revealed by voice and body language. In writing, tone can be revealed only by words.

> **T**one is a writer's or speaker's attitude toward a subject, a character, or an audience.
>
> *For more on Tone, see pages 586–587 and the Handbook of Literary Terms.*

All Watched Over by Machines of Loving Grace

Richard Brautigan

I like to think (and
the sooner the better!)
of a cybernetic° meadow
where mammals and computers
5   live together in mutually
programming harmony
like pure water
touching clear sky.

I like to think
10 (right now, please!)
of a cybernetic forest
filled with pines and electronics
where deer stroll peacefully
past computers
15 as if they were flowers
with spinning blossoms.

I like to think
(it has to be!)
of a cybernetic ecology
20 where we are free of our labors
and joined back to nature,
returned to our mammal
brothers and sisters,
and all watched over
25 by machines of loving grace.

3. cybernetic: having to do with
computers.

MEET THE WRITER

"Please Plant This Book"

Richard Brautigan (1935–1984) published his
first books of poetry himself and sold them on
the street corners of Berkeley and San Francisco.
He said he "wrote poetry for seven
years to learn how to write a
sentence" and he called his eleven
volumes of poetry his diary. He
loved to invent unusual figures of
speech, such as "Your alligator
looks like a handbag filled with
harmonicas." He also used
metaphors in titles such as *Please
Plant This Book, Loading Mercury
with a Pitchfork,* and *All Watched
Over by Machines of Loving Grace.*
Born in Tacoma, Washington,
Brautigan spent most of his
adult life in California and on
his ranch in Montana.

MAKING MEANINGS
FIRE AND ICE
ALL WATCHED OVER BY MACHINES OF LOVING GRACE

First Thoughts

1. Both Frost and Brautigan think about what is going to happen to us and to the planet. Which view comes closer to yours?

Shaping Interpretations

2. Frost uses two **implied metaphors** to make his point. What emotion does he compare to fire? What emotion does he compare to ice?

3. How would you define desire as Frost uses the word in his poem? How is desire like fire?

4. Explain why Frost's speaker might feel that hate and ice have something in common.

5. In the Quickwrite you wrote before you read "Fire and Ice," you thought of how fire and ice share some characteristics. How could each of them cause the world to end? How could desire and hate also do the job?

6. Brautigan also has a vision of the future. How are machines usually thought of in relation to nature? As enemies? As guardians? How does Brautigan think of them?

Extending the Texts

7. Brautigan's poem is a vision of the future, but in what sense do we already live under the guardianship of machines? Do you think of them as "loving" machines? Explain why or why not.

8. Do you think any part of Brautigan's vision of the future can come true? Would you want it to come true— or do you find it unappealing? Explain.

9. Would you call Brautigan's poem optimistic in **tone,** or pessimistic, or neither? Why? How about Frost's?

The Peaceable Kingdom (c. 1848) by Edward Hicks. Oil on canvas (23 ⅞" x 31 ⅞").

CHOICES: Building Your Portfolio

Writer's Notebook

1. Collecting Ideas for a Poem

A first line. Sometimes it's just a matter of getting started. Use Brautigan's opening line and list some things you like to imagine could happen to make the world a better place. You might want to add "(and the sooner the better!)."

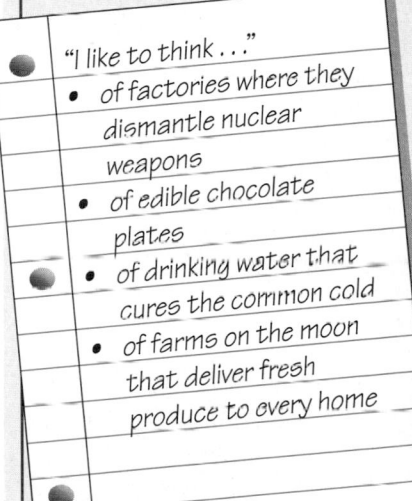

"I like to think . . ."
- of factories where they dismantle nuclear weapons
- of edible chocolate plates
- of drinking water that cures the common cold
- of farms on the moon that deliver fresh produce to every home

Creative Writing

2. A Machine Fantasy

Using your notes from the Quickwrite for "All Watched Over by Machines of Loving Grace," write a paragraph about how your life would be different without your favorite machines. Think hair dryer, washing machine, toaster, car, computer, popcorn popper, chain saw, lawn mower, snow blower, water heater, oil furnace, electric lights.

Creative Writing

3. Creating Your Own Metaphors

Add to Frost's list of destructive human acts and qualities. Don't forget jealousy and greed. For each item, choose an element of nature that might express or stand for that human act or quality. Set the items up as equations:

$$\text{anger} = \text{volcano}$$
$$\text{sadness} = \text{rain}$$

Then make a parallel list of equations for positive and constructive human acts and qualities.

$$\text{loyalty} = \text{rock}$$
$$\text{kiss} = \text{rain}$$

(Don't be surprised if some of the things on your lists, like rain in the examples, can be both destructive and beneficial. Metaphors are famous for being hard to pin down. That's what makes them interesting.)

Critical Writing

4. Your Choice

0   1   2   3   4   5

We all write best when we feel passionately about a subject. Look back at the poems you've read so far. Select one poem that you would rank high on this scale, or low. Write an evaluation of the poem, explaining your rating. You might want to focus on the poem's message, attitude toward life, language, images, metaphors, or sounds. You can't just say "I love it" or "I hate it." You have to find at least one reason for your response. (For help in writing an evaluation, see pages 332–337.)

A Dialogue with the Text

In this reflection, a poet named Diane Glancy writes directly to someone, anyone, who also wants to be a poet. She might be writing directly to you. While you read, keep your Reader's Log handy. As Glancy makes her suggestions, and even gives orders, write down your responses. Include questions you'd like to ask her. Pretend that Glancy is talking directly to you. What do you want to say back? You should read the essay twice, at least.

Claiming Breath

Diane Glancy

How do you begin writing poetry? I would say after all these years I'm not sure. First of all, you read. You have to be aware of what's being written. Poetry is a conversation. Often while I'm reading, I start a poem. An image will set off another image, or I think of something I want to say. It also helps to know the tradition of poetry, though often there's something about it that gets in the way. You strain for a rhyme without thought for the fire, the energy of the poem, the originality of voice. Yet I've heard others say that structure forces them to work in ways they would have missed on their own.

Begin by getting words down. What have you got to say? Even if you want to remain obscure there has to be coherence on some level. I remember hearing Gerald Stern say, if you get your words in order on the first row, you make room for a craziness later on, deeper in the poem, in a more important place.

Work with what you've experienced. I think sometimes, who cares about my ordinary life? But often, that's exactly what matters.

What idea, impression, image, do you want to convey? Why should I listen to you? Again, (1) read, (2) write what you have to say, & (3) read it to someone. Listen to their reaction, their criticism, & write again. So much of writing is rewriting.

Contemporary poetry says what you have to say in whatever way you want to say. Make sure you have a style, a voice, a certain way of expressing yourself. Where's your uniqueness, your individuality? You have a thumbprint different from other thumbprints. You have a way of seeing & a way of expressing what you see that is also different. Develop that difference. Take chances with unusual words & combinations. Writing is a long process. Reveal what it's like to be you.

Do you have something bothering you? Get into it. That will save the trouble of writing boring poems.

Remember imagery, the mental pictures your writing makes, usually thru metaphor & simile. Make sure they haven't been said before. They have to be new. Tell me something in a way I haven't heard before. Let an image connect with a thought, sometimes a memory. Get rid of weak verbs. Watch tenses; make them consistent. Use DETAIL! A cotton dress printed with crocuses is usually better than "a dress." Look for the right word. The inevitable one. Ask what your poem means. What conclusion is drawn from it? Even if not a logical thought, but an impression. Good poems are sometimes simple, on at least onc level.

What is life like for you? That's what you should begin writing about.

Remember also the richness of language. Make sure there's a lot in your writing. Read your words to yourself. Listen to them on a tape recorder.

The form a poem takes on the page is also integral. Experiment with line breaks, stanzas, the square or prose poem, the words wiggling over the page.

Then workshop a poem. Critiques are usually common sense. Does the poem work? Do you like it? Does it begin at the first stanza or do you really get into the poem several lines later? Do all the parts form a whole? What central thought holds the poem together? What emotion or impression is shared? What stays in your mind after you've heard it? Is it in the form it should be in? Is the poem clear? Have you said the same thing too many times? Is the reader rewarded for reading it?

Be interested in a lot of things. Be an interesting person; live a responsible life. Start keeping notes.

I think it's also important to know why you write. When I go into a bookstore & see shelves full of books, I think why do I do this? Hasn't it been done better than I can do it? That's when I have to be able to look in myself & decide, I have something to say too—these other books can move over & make room for mine.

A manuscript page showing Sara Teasdale's revisions of her poem "Spring."

Manuscripts Department, Lilly Library, Indiana University, Bloomington.

"A Pencil Is a Buffalo Migration"

Like the poets of long ago, **Diane Glancy** (1941–   ) has spent much of her life traveling. For years she earned her living by driving through Oklahoma and Arkansas to teach poetry in schools. The prose reflections in *Claiming Breath* (1992) are a diary of one of those years. Now Diane Glancy teaches creative writing and American Indian literature at Macalaster College in St. Paul, Minnesota. Here she talks about being an American Indian woman and a poet:

66 I often write about being in the middle ground between two cultures, not fully a part of either. I write with a split voice, often experimenting with language until the parts equal some sort of a whole. I would say a pencil is a buffalo migration under the sky with its stars turning like a jar-lid poked with holes. Writing affects my life, my Real life, while the rest spins through the lone pines. I write from everyday circumstances, old ordinary life, and the stampede of the past. **99**

FINDING COMMON GROUND

1. Referring to the notes in your Reader's Log, quickly write a brief answer to Glancy. Speak directly to her, as if you were talking face to face. Ask her questions. Tell her about the problems you have with creative writing. Tell her what you don't understand about her suggestions, and what you especially like. Maybe she says some things you disagree with: Tell her why you disagree.

2. When you finish writing your personal reflections, share your responses in class. Do you all agree on what's important and interesting about Glancy's reflection? Or do people have very different responses? How do you account for the differences in responses?

3. One thing you must do: Talk about her title.

Writer's Workshop

ASSIGNMENT

Write a poem or group of poems.

AIM

To express yourself; to be creative.

AUDIENCE

Yourself, classmates, family, readers of a magazine of student writing. (You choose.)

I don't look at anything as being insignificant. I think that's another overlooked gift of poetry. Many times people imagine that poets wait for some splendid experience to overtake them, but I think the tiniest moments are the most splendid. This is the wisdom that all these small things have to teach.

—Naomi Shihab Nye

POETRY

Where poems come from is a mystery. All we know is that a poem is a kind of wedding between something in the outside world that can be observed and pointed to, and some feeling inside the poet that lives like an untold secret in the mind and heart. In a sense, all poems are revelations—they help poets and their readers discover connections between inside feelings and the outside world.

Getting Started

1. Check Your Reader's Log and Journal

You've been collecting ideas for poems and doing exercises on imagery and figurative language as you worked with the poems in these two collections. See if any of that work interests you enough to develop it further.

If you still need help, the exercises that follow might give you some ideas. Begin with the confidence that you have feelings that can be expressed in a poem. You just have to find a subject that will urge them into expression.

2. Find an Occasion

Start by listing moments or days in your life that you associate with some feeling. Any one of these moments may provide that spark, that connection between outside events and inside feelings that may lead you to a poem.

a. You learn that your family is moving to another city and you know you'll have to give up friends and neighborhood and everything familiar.

b. Your grandmother has died and you realize you'll never see her face again or open the birthday and Christmas presents she never failed to send.

c. You smile at someone you like a lot, and you see that person looking back and smiling at you.

d. You go back to your old playground and find that all the kids there look so young.

e. You have a wonderful dream.

The history
of the written
word is rich and
Page 1
Once upon a time

3. Look Around

If those occasions won't work for you, there are other ways of finding topics for poems:

a. Look through a newspaper for items that catch your imagination.

b. Pretend you are Cinderella, a rock star, the last dinosaur (or any other figure from a story or a movie or real life).

c. Begin with a question:

- "What kind of house would I have lived in in 1600?"

- "How would I be remembered if I disappeared this very moment?"

- "Twenty years from now, who will I be?"

d. Choose an object or a creature and speak to it as though it were capable of understanding what you say. You might call your poem "A Conversation with a House" or "To a Pizza Pie" or "Words for an Old Dog."

e. Write a poem consisting of a series of images. Its title might be "A Catalog of Sounds" or "A List of Memories." Or its first line might be "I see —" (or "I smell," "I taste," "I touch," "I hear").

f. Write a poem consisting of a series of contrasting metaphors.

- "A cat seems to be _____, but it really is _____."

- "Fog seems to be _____, but it really is _____."

- "An onion seems to be _____, but it really is _____."

Finding a Form

Once you have an idea for a poem, you have to find a form to write it in.

1. Free Verse: Imitate Natural Speech

The simplest form for a beginning poet to use is **free verse**—poetry written in lines that imitate the natural rhythms of speech (see page 555). If you use free verse, take special care in deciding

Poetry can do a hundred and one things, delight, sadden, disturb, amuse, instruct—it may express every possible shade of emotion, and describe every conceivable kind of event, but there is only one thing that all poetry must do: It must praise all it can for being and for happening.

—W. H. Auden

How Poetry Comes to Me

*It comes blundering over the
Boulders at night, it stays
Frightened outside the
Range of my campfire
I go to meet it at the
Edge of the light*

—Gary Snyder

where to break your lines, and be sure that no one line is so long that it almost runs off the page. Begin with a statement to catch the reader's attention. Then keep your reader's interest, not only by what you say, but also by using question marks (?), by using dots (. . .) to continue a thought, by using dashes (—) to add a thought, even by using exclamation marks (!).

2. Try Rhyme

Almost as simple are poems in **rhymed couplets** (two rhyming lines) or **quatrains** (four rhyming lines). If you use couplets, the last words in each line should rhyme:

> I wish I could unlOCK
> The secrets of a clOCK.

If you use quatrains, you can rhyme just two of the four lines, or you can rhyme the last words in every line. Here is a quatrain in which only two lines are rhymed:

This morning, late for class, I skipped	a
My cornflakes and, gung-ho, departed.	b
Nice timing! I made history	c
Before the Civil War got started.	b

For more on rhyme, see pages 559–560.

3. Meter: A Challenge

Perhaps you'll want a challenge and will try to write a poem in **meter**—that is, to give each line a regular pattern of stressed and unstressed syllables. For beginners, one of these two meters is best:

a. Each line has six syllables, alternating an unstressed syllable with a stressed syllable: da/DAH, da/DAH, da/DAH ("The dead began to speak").

b. Each line has eight syllables, also alternating an unstressed syllable with a stressed syllable: da/DAH, da/DAH, da/DAH, da/DAH ("I wandered lonely as a cloud").

If you write in meter, maintain your beat, but at times add a little variation so your verse doesn't become singsong. For instance, you can reverse the beat of the first two syllables in any line without doing serious harm to your pattern (from da/DAH to DAH/da).

For more on meter, see pages 554–555.

Opposite is a poem by a famous American poet who found a feeling, a moment that he associated with that feeling, and a form to write his thoughts in.

Running
1933
(North Caldwell, New Jersey)

What were we playing? Was it
*   prisoner's base?*
I ran with whacking keds
Down the cart-road past
*   Rickard's place,*
And where it dropped beside the
*   tractor-sheds*

Leapt out into the air above a
*   blurred*
Terrain, through jolted light,
Took two hard lopes, and at the
*   third*
Spanked off a hummock-side
*   exactly right,*

And made the turn, and with
*   delighted strain*
Sprinted across the flat
By the bull-pen, and up the
*   lane.*
Thinking of happiness, I think
*   of that.*

—Richard Wilbur

THE WAYS WE ARE

The people who speak in poems will tell you that they sometimes are afraid, envious, confused, sad. And, oh yes, sometimes suffused with joy and kindness and compassion and gratitude and love. You may feel you don't have much in common with some of the people who speak in poems. Or, you may not like it when one of them hits a nerve or comes too close to home. But whatever happens, when you read a poem, you win. For you get to know people of all kinds, without moving anything (except your brain). All of this may give you a better handle on your own relationships—starting with how you feel about yourself.

Reader's Theater

You already know a lot of poetry. Most of us can recite a nursery rhyme, a prayer, a jump-rope chant, or a football cheer, and we can sing a few songs or hymns. Start preparing for a poetry performance now by finding one poem you like the sound of, and memorizing it.

Each of us inevitable;
Each of us limitless—each of us
* with his or her right upon the earth . . .*
Each of us here as divinely as any is here.
                    —*Walt Whitman*

Elements of Literature

THE SOUNDS OF POETRY: You've Got Rhythm

Poetry is not irregular lines in a book, but something very close to dance and song, something to walk down the street keeping time to.

—Northrop Frye

As long as your heart is beating, you've got rhythm. Musicians and poets, perhaps in imitation of that heartbeat, also create rhythm. Rhythm is based on repetition. In poetry, rhythmic patterns can be organized either as meter or as free verse.

> As long as your heart is beating, you've got rhythm.

Meter: A Pattern of Stressed Syllables

One way to think of meter in poetry is to compare it with a metronome. A metronome is an instrument that often sits on top of a piano. It has an upside-down pendulum that moves back and forth, ticking and tocking like a clock, at whatever speed the musician has chosen.

The metronome gives the musician a basic beat that must be kept—but not exactly. Music that followed the beat of the metronome exactly would be dull and monotonous. Musicians must learn to keep the beat but also to make variations on it. Every musician knows you must be *offbeat*—without ever forgetting that you can't be "off" until you have a sense of what's "on."

The same is true for poets. When a poet chooses to write in a meter, that meter, like the metronome's beat, is "given." The meter sets the basic mechanical beat, around which, and over which, and even against which, the poet's own voice must play.

Poetry that is written in **meter** has a regular pattern of stressed and unstressed syllables in each line.

The following poem is written in meter. The stressed syllables are marked ´; the unstressed syllables are marked ˘. Read Frost's poem aloud, to feel its steady beat.

> If you listen to spoken English, you will find that very often we speak in iambs.

Dust of Snow
Thĕ wáy ă crów
Shóok dówn ŏn mé
Thĕ dúst ŏf snów
Frŏm ă hémlŏck treé

Has given my heart
A change of mood
And saved some part
Of a day I had rued.

—Robert Frost

Frost wrote his poem mostly in iambs. An **iamb** (ī′amb′) is an unstressed syllable followed by a stressed syllable (da DAH). (You may think meter is artificial, but if you listen to spoken English, you will find that very often we speak in iambs.)

An iamb is an example of a poetic foot—a **foot** being the basic building block of meter. A foot usually consists of one stressed syllable and one or more unstressed syllables.

English poetry has other kinds of feet. A **trochee** (trō′kē) is a stressed syllable followed by an unstressed syllable (DAH da); it is the

by John Malcolm Brinnin

opposite of an iamb. Here is a line from Edgar Allan Poe's famous poem "The Raven" that uses trochees:

Once upŏn ă mídnĭght dréaŏy

An **anapest** is two unstressed syllables followed by a stressed syllable (da da DAH). Here is a line from Byron's poem "The Destruction of Sennacherib" that uses anapests:

Thĕ Ăssýrĭan cǎme dówn lĭke thĕ wolf ŏn thĕ fóld

A **dactyl** is one stressed syllable followed by two unstressed syllables (DAH da da). Here is the beginning of a nursery rhyme that uses dactyls:

Híckŏry, díckŏry, dóck

A **spondee** is two stressed syllables (DAH DAH). Here are some lines from "We Real Cool" by Gwendolyn Brooks that use spondees:

Wé reál coól. Wé
léft schoól. Wé
Lúrk láte. . . .

When you analyze a poem to show its meter, you are **scanning** the poem. Scanning a poem is like analyzing the construction of a song. You are trying to take the poem apart to see how the poet has created the music.

Free Verse Isn't Free

Until the last century, all poetry in English was written with a strict concern for meter. But eventually, some poets began to rebel against the old poetic "rules." They insisted that new rhythms were necessary to create new moods. Many poets abandoned meter and began writing what is called free verse.

Free verse is poetry that is free of regular meter—that is, free of a strict pattern of stressed syllables and unstressed syllables. This new kind of poetry sounds very close to prose and to everyday spoken language. But free verse is free only in the sense that it is liberated from the formal rules governing meter. Poets writing in free verse pay close attention to the rhythmic rise and fall of the voice, to pauses, and to the balance between long and short phrases.

Walt Whitman's poem on page 496 is written in free verse. When you read it aloud, you'll notice how close to ordinary spoken language it sounds at first. But then you'll notice how it soars into the kind of language used by preachers and orators. That's free verse at its most eloquent.

"The Bagel" by David Ignatow.

POETRY IN MOTION

The Bagel

I stopped to pick up the bagel
rolling away in the wind,
annoyed with myself
for having dropped it
as it were a portent.
Faster and faster it rolled,
with me running after it

David Ignatow

bent low, gritting my teeth,
and I found myself doubled over
and rolling down the street
head over heels, one complete somersault
after another like a bagel
and strangely happy with myself.

MTA New York City Transit

Reading Focus

What We Are Given

Very few of us are born into this world with lots of money. Yet every one of us inherits incalculable treasure, for we are the living beneficiaries of every person who has ever lived. What they did with their lives affects ours. If we inherit a polluted planet, they are partially responsible. If they spent their lives struggling to make the world a better place, that's part of their legacy too.

Quickwrite

READER'S LOG

Take notes about people who helped you become the person you are today. You'll probably think of relatives, teachers, and church people—but think also about others, even people from the past.

Keep your notes. For questions and activities on this poem, see page 558.

Elements of Literature

Metaphor: Battering Doors

Walker's famous poem is built around a metaphor that is first suggested in line 12 and then extended through line 18. The metaphor is based on a comparison that is never openly stated. After you read the poem, talk about what Walker is comparing her women and their struggle to.

An **implied metaphor** does not directly state that one thing *is* something else. Instead it uses words to suggest the comparison.

For more on Metaphor, see pages 520–521 and the Handbook of Literary Terms.

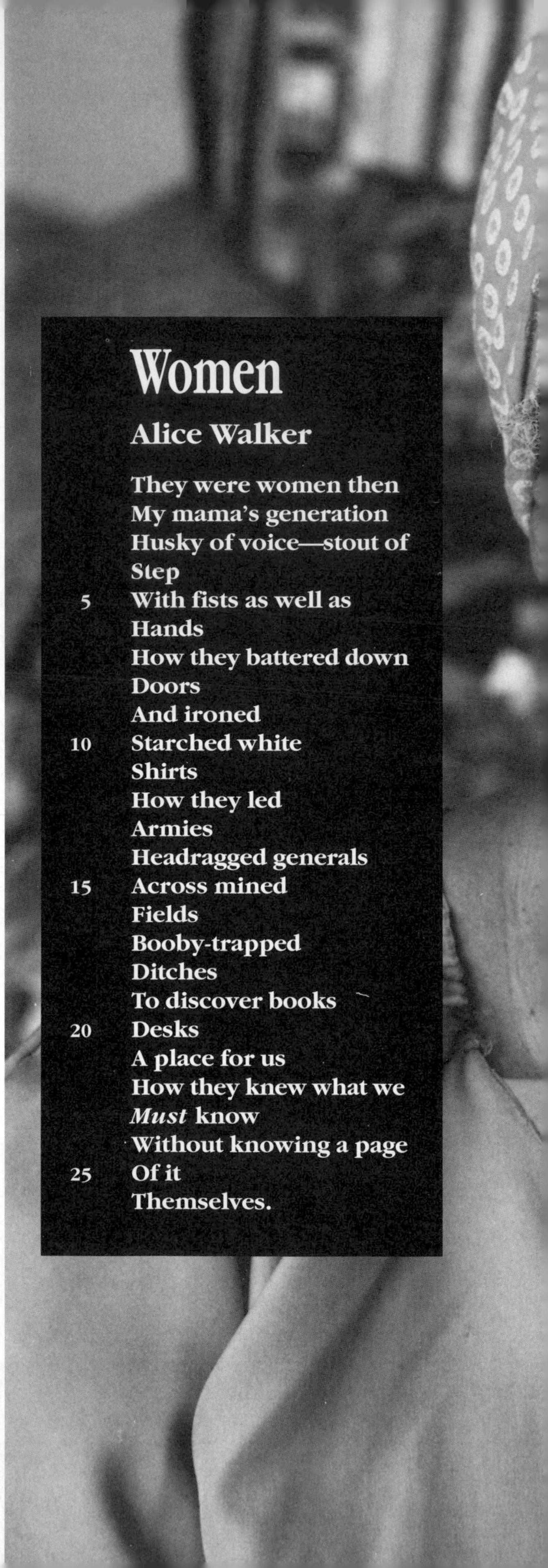

Women
Alice Walker

They were women then
My mama's generation
Husky of voice—stout of
Step
5 With fists as well as
Hands
How they battered down
Doors
And ironed
10 Starched white
Shirts
How they led
Armies
Headragged generals
15 Across mined
Fields
Booby-trapped
Ditches
To discover books
20 Desks
A place for us
How they knew what we
Must know
Without knowing a page
25 Of it
Themselves.

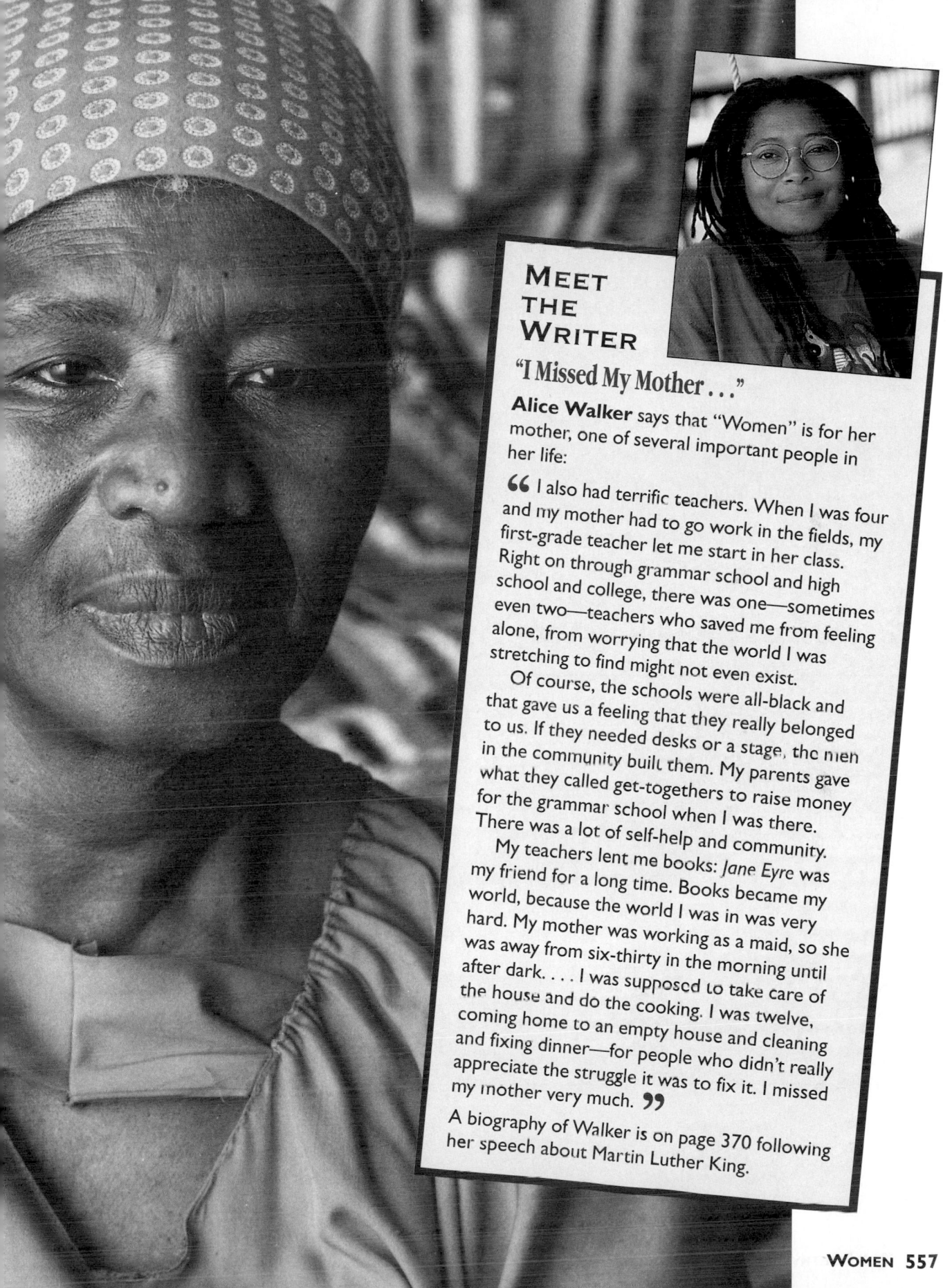

MEET THE WRITER

"I Missed My Mother..."

Alice Walker says that "Women" is for her mother, one of several important people in her life:

66 I also had terrific teachers. When I was four and my mother had to go work in the fields, my first-grade teacher let me start in her class. Right on through grammar school and high school and college, there was one—sometimes even two—teachers who saved me from feeling alone, from worrying that the world I was stretching to find might not even exist.

Of course, the schools were all-black and that gave us a feeling that they really belonged to us. If they needed desks or a stage, the men in the community built them. My parents gave what they called get-togethers to raise money for the grammar school when I was there. There was a lot of self-help and community.

My teachers lent me books: *Jane Eyre* was my friend for a long time. Books became my world, because the world I was in was very hard. My mother was working as a maid, so she was away from six-thirty in the morning until after dark. . . . I was supposed to take care of the house and do the cooking. I was twelve, coming home to an empty house and cleaning and fixing dinner—for people who didn't really appreciate the struggle it was to fix it. I missed my mother very much. 99

A biography of Walker is on page 370 following her speech about Martin Luther King.

First Thoughts

1. What do you *see* happening in this poem? Compare your images in class. Are your mental pictures very different?

Shaping Interpretations

2. Alice Walker uses a **metaphor** to compare two kinds of actions or struggles. What does she compare the women's struggle to?

3. What doors did these women really batter down?

4. What do you think the mined fields and booby-trapped ditches stand for?

5. What do you think these women knew their children had to know?

Extending the Text

6. What other people in the world could be described as generals leading armies? What do these people fight against?

CHOICES: Building Your Portfolio

Reader's Theater

1. Preparing for a Performance

Feeling the rhythm.
Repetition is what gives poetry its rhythm. Walker creates rhythm in her poem by repeating certain words and by alternating long and short lines.

Write Walker's poem on a separate piece of paper. This is your script for oral reading. On your script, mark the ends of lines where you will pause briefly. Do not put a mark if you will keep right on reading on to the next line without a pause. Underscore the words or phrases in the poem that you will emphasize in your reading.

Practice reading the poem aloud until you feel you are expressing its natural rhythms.

Save your script. You might choose to present this poem in the Reader's Theater discussed on page 582.

Creative Writing

2. Celebrate Other Heroes

How would you describe the heroic women and men of today? What do they struggle for? What do they want for their children? Write a poem or paragraph describing these men and women. What would you compare your heroes to? Use your Quickwrite notes for ideas about who is important to you.

Elements of Literature

THE SOUNDS OF POETRY: Rhyme and Other Sound Effects

Everyone loves rhyme—babies respond to rhyme, and your first books (like Dr. Seuss's *Hop on Pop*) were probably written in rhyme. Rhyme is easy to recognize. **Rhyme** is the repetition of the sound of a stressed vowel and any sounds that follow it within a word: *nails* and *whales; material* and *cereal; icicle* and *bicycle*.

Until very recently, poets thought rhyme was essential, and readers expected it. Today, rhyme is a matter of choice—except for those versifiers who grind out the little singsong messages found on some greeting cards.

Modern poets who use rhyme feel that it not only helps to make a poem sing, but that it also defines the shape of a poem and holds it together. Rhyme enhances the music of a poem with chiming sounds. It sets up in the reader a sense of expectation. We expect that the pattern of sounds introduced in the opening lines of a poem will be skillfully sustained until the poem is concluded. Readers also know that poems with a regular pattern of rhyme, or a **rhyme scheme,** are especially easy to memorize.

> **M**any poets have turned away from rhyme because they feel that just about all of the words in the English language that can be rhymed have long ago been used up.

Many poets have turned away from rhyme because they feel that just about all of the words in the English language that can be rhymed have long ago been used up. The contemporary poet who would like to continue the practice of using rhyme is faced with having to repeat rhymes that have echoed down the centuries. Or the poet faces the challenge of making new rhymes that might sound strained.

Approximate Rhyme: Not Quite Exact

Some poets have solved this problem by using **approximate rhyme**—that is, words that repeat some sounds but are not exact echoes. These approximate rhymes are also called half rhymes, off rhymes, or slant rhymes. Readers who dislike them call them imperfect rhymes. In any case, all of them are substitutes for familiar "head-on" rhymes like *June* and *moon* or *hollow* and *follow*. Instead of being an exact echo, approximate rhyme is a partial echo: *moon* and *morn* or *hollow* and *mellow*.

Internal Rhyme: Chimes Inside Lines

Rhymes usually occur at the ends of lines. They are seldom spaced more than four lines apart—an interval longer than that is too long for the chiming sound to be clearly heard. But rhyme can also occur inside the lines. This is called **internal rhyme**. Here are some lines from "The Raven" by Edgar Allan Poe in which two internal rhymes (*remember* and *ember*) chime with *December:*

Ah, distinctly I remember it
   was in the bleak December;
And each separate dying
   ember wrought its ghost
upon the floor.

[Continued on next page]

Elements of Literature

[Continued from previous page]

by John Malcolm Brinnin

Onomatopoeia: Imitating Sounds

Beyond rhythm and the forms it may take, the most important aspect of sound in poetry is the one with the very unusual name: onomatopoeia (än′ō·mat′ō·pē′ə). **Onomatopoeia** is the use of words that sound like what they mean.

Literally, *onomatopoeia* means "the making of words." Long ago, it came into the English language from the Greek. It eventually came to mean not merely word-making, but word-making by the imitation of sounds. We use onomatopoeia when we say a gun "bangs" or a cannon "booms." We use onomatopoeia when we say that bacon "sizzles."

In its simplest form onomatopoeia is a single word that echoes a natural sound (*hiss, slap, rumble, snarl, moan, drip*) or a mechanical sound (*zing, whack, clickety-clack, putt-putt, toot*).

Alliteration: Repeating Sounds

Alliteration is the repetition of the same consonant sound in several words: *money mad,* *hot and heavy, dog days, drip dry, wash and wear, ready and raring to go.* Alliteration can also be the repetition of similar, but not identical, sounds: a series of *p*'s and *b*'s, or *s*'s and *z*'s, or *d*'s and *t*'s, or *m*'s and *n*'s. Alliteration can also be used to echo sounds. Here is another example from "The Raven":

The silken sad uncertain
    rustling of each purple
    curtain

Alliteration (the repetition of rustling *s* sounds in *silken sad uncertain*) and onomatopoeia (the word *rustling*) together imitate the sound wind makes when it blows past heavy silk draperies.

Onomatopoeia comes naturally to us. Suppose we want to describe the movement of a snake through the grass. We wouldn't say it goes "bumping along like a bicycle," because that's not what a snake in the grass sounds like. We are more likely to say the snake "slithers swiftly across the grass." Then we would be imitating in words the sound we might actually hear.

"Griping, greedy, grasping, grotesque, gruesome, grisly—
do you know any other good 'grr' words?"

Drawing by Ed Fisher; © 1984 The New Yorker Magazine, Inc.

BEFORE YOU READ
FORGIVE MY GUILT

Reading Focus

Something Thoughtless

We've all made mistakes. We've all done something we wish we could undo—something reckless, or careless, or thoughtless. We've all found that some of our actions had lasting consequences for ourselves or for others. Perhaps worst of all, sometimes we've found that our actions have shown us to be something we don't want to be.

Quickwrite

READER'S LOG

Recall a mistake from your own history, or from the life of someone you know, and make notes on the experience. What happened and how did you or the other person feel? If the experience taught you anything, what was it?

Keep your notes. For questions and activities on this poem, see page 563.

Elements of Literature

Rhyme: Chiming Sounds

Of course, nothing in poetry works in isolation. The rhythm, the subject matter, the speaker's attitude, even the length of the poem—all these elements combine to produce effects on us. **Rhyme,** however, is often what we notice first. Rhyme can have widely varying effects. In some poems, it may create humor. In some poems it may sound solemn and serious; in others it may sound haunting or songlike. In bad poems rhyme can seem singsong and mechanical. Listen for Coffin's rhymes. Do they have one syllable or many? Are they placed in some pattern?

Rhyme is the repetition of accented vowel sounds and all sounds following them, in words that are close together in a poem. **Rhyme scheme** is the pattern of rhymes in a poem.

For more on Rhyme, see pages 559–560 and the Handbook of Literary Terms.

Forgive My Guilt

Robert P. Tristram Coffin

Not always sure what things called sins may be,
I am sure of one sin I have done.
It was years ago, and I was a boy,
I lay in the frostflowers with a gun,
5   The air ran blue as the flowers, I held my breath,
Two birds on golden legs slim as dream things
Ran like quicksilver on the golden sand,
My gun went off, they ran with broken wings
Into the sea, I ran to fetch them in,
10   But they swam with their heads high out to sea,
They cried like two sorrowful high flutes,
With jagged ivory bones where wings should be.

For days I heard them when I walked that headland
Crying out to their kind in the blue,
15   The other plovers were going over south
On silver wings leaving these broken two.
The cries went out one day; but I still hear them
Over all the sounds of sorrow in war or peace
I ever have heard, time cannot drown them,
20   Those slender flutes of sorrow never cease.
Two airy things forever denied the air!
I never knew how their lives at last were spilt,
But I have hoped for years all that is wild,
Airy, and beautiful will forgive my guilt.

MEET THE WRITER

The Simple Subjects of Every Day

Robert P. Tristram Coffin (1892–1955) was a New Englander through and through. From a Puritan background, Coffin was a poet and scholar who combined the best of the classics with the poetry of everyday speech, sights, and people. He said:

66 When I began to write poetry, I had the mistaken idea that a poet must always be on the mountaintop. Only in maturity did I learn to come down upon the plain and choose for my poems the simple subjects of every day. 99

MAKING MEANINGS
FORGIVE MY GUILT

First Thoughts

1. In the Quickwrite you recalled an experience that you or someone else regrets. Did that memory influence the way you reacted to the poem? Explain.

Shaping Interpretations

2. What sin is the speaker certain he has committed?

3. Considering all the crimes and sins people commit, the one reported in this poem might seem rather minor. Do you suppose the poem is about more than a boy's cruelty to two birds? Talk over your interpretations.

4. How did the **rhymes** affect your response to the poem? Try this experiment:

   • Read line 4 substituting *rifle* for *gun*.

   • Read line 6 substituting *shapes* for *things*.

   • Read line 10 substituting *through the water* for *out to sea*.

   Read the first stanza again with those substitutions. The ideas are roughly the same; but is there a difference in the effect? Make similar substitutions in the second stanza and see how they affect the poem's music.

CHOICES: Building Your Portfolio

Reader's Theater

1. Preparing for a Performance

Make a script. Prepare this poem for performance, just as a professional actor would. Your first step is to prepare your script. Then, think about who the speaker in the poem is, what he is trying to say, and what tone of voice you want to use. Will you change your tone at different points in the poem? Decide where the *slowest*, the *fastest*, the *softest*, and the *loudest* points of your performance will be. Mark these parts of your script. Save your script for possible use in a Reader's Theater (see page 582).

Creative Writing

2. A Remembered Moment

Intense moments—those when we are very happy or extremely sad, when we are triumphant or defeated—are probably captured in poetry more effectively than in any other form of writing. Take your Quickwrite, or some other remembered moment that seems right, and turn it into a poem. You might open with "I remember."

Creative Writing

3. Asking Forgiveness

Many people, past and present, have asked forgiveness of the animals they've had to kill in order to survive. Write a poem asking the forgiveness of a pesky plant or animal—for instance, an allergy-causing weed that you are about to pull up by the roots, or a biting mosquito you are about to slap.

BEFORE YOU READ
THE GIFT

Reading Focus

Tenderness and Discipline

It seems to be the very intense moments, when things are going wonderfully well or terribly wrong, that give us the sharpest images of the people we know. A lot of what we remember of people comes from those specific moments that are vivid in our minds because of what we discover about those people's pain or kindness or fear or courage.

In moments like these, people show us who they are and who we may become.

Quickwrite

Try to recall one incident in which the actions of a parent, teacher, or friend were a model for something you would like to become yourself.

Keep your notes. For questions and activities on this poem, see pages 568–569.

Elements of Literature

Breath Groupings

Free-verse poems create rhythm by organizing words in breath groups. Breath groups are usually defined by punctuation. Watch for punctuation marks in this poem. Pause briefly for breath at commas. Make full stops at periods. Let your voice rise and fall in a natural way, just like the voice of an oral storyteller. Do you feel the rhythm?

I**n free verse,** rhythm can be created by breath groupings, which are signaled by marks of punctuation.

For more on Free Verse, see pages 554–555 and the Handbook of Literary Terms.

The Gift

Li-Young Lee

To pull the metal splinter from my palm
my father recited a story in a low voice.
I watched his lovely face and not the blade.
Before the story ended he'd removed
5 the iron sliver I thought I'd die from.

I can't remember the tale
but hear his voice still, a well
of dark water, a prayer.
And I recall his hands,
10 two measures of tenderness
he laid against my face,
the flames of discipline
he raised above my head.

Had you entered that afternoon
15 you would have thought you saw a man
planting something in a boy's palm,
a silver tear, a tiny flame.

20 Had you followed that boy
you would have arrived here,
where I bend over my wife's right hand.

Look how I shave her thumbnail down
so carefully she feels no pain.
Watch as I lift the splinter out.
I was seven when my father
25 took my hand like this,
and I did not hold that shard
between my fingers and think,
Metal that will bury me,
christen it Little Assassin,
30 Ore Going Deep for My Heart.
And I did not lift up my wound and cry,
Death visited here!
I did what a child does
when he's given something to keep.
35 I kissed my father.

MEET THE WRITER

"The Winged Seed"

The great-grandfather of **Li-Young Lee** (1957–   ) was the first president of the Republic of China. His father, on whom the character in "The Gift" is based, was personal physician to the revolutionary leader Mao Tse-tung. In the 1950s, the family had to flee the political turmoil of China when the Communist People's Republic was established. They went first to Indonesia; Li-Young Lee was born in Jakarta. But there his father was thrown into jail by the corrupt dictator Sukarno. The father spent nineteen months in prison, seventeen of them in a leper colony. When the family fled again, they went to Hong Kong. When Li-Young Lee was six, they arrived in the United States where his father became a Presbyterian minister.

Li-Young Lee has recorded his family's history in *The Winged Seed: A Remembrance* (1995). His first book of poems, *Rose,* won

the 1986 Delmore Schwartz Memorial Poetry Award, and a second book, *The City in Which I Love You,* was the 1990 Lamont Poetry Selection of the Academy of American Poets.

Lee now lives in Chicago with his family.

“ I know I am not a poet. How do I know this? Because I know a poet when I read one. There are living poets in the world today. I am not one of them. But I want to be one, and I know only of one path: serious and passionate apprenticeship, which involves a strange combination of awe and argument, with the Masters.

Other than this, I don't know anything about poetry, though if space permitted, I could go on earnestly, and to the boredom and horror of everyone, about all those things I don't know. ”

Reading Focus

A Portrait in Words

Many families keep an album of photos of family members collected through the years. Maybe your family does this. In "Combing" we are given word portraits of several generations of a family, all connected by the same action that is learned and repeated and passed on. Can you imagine how pleased this poet's grandchildren will be to have this poem-portrait of those who came before them? Perhaps you'll be inspired to plait (braid, or weave) a poem to pass on to the people who come after you.

Quickwrite

Make notes on one or more legacies you have received from the past, including where the legacy came from and why you are glad to have it. Hint: a photograph, jewelry, clothing, a song or poem, a prayer, a recipe, a special way of observing a holiday.

Keep your notes. For questions and activities on this poem, see pages 568–569.

Elements of Literature

Repetition

Repetition is basic to the sound of all poetry. When you repeat vowel sounds, you get **assonance**. When you repeat consonants, you get **alliteration**. You can also repeat words and phrases. After you read "Combing," go back and read it aloud and count the number of sounds you hear repeated—start with *b*.

> **R**epetition in poetry includes assonance, alliteration, and the repetition of words, phrases, and even entire lines.
>
> *For more on Assonance, Alliteration, and Repetition, see pages 559–560 and the Handbook of Literary Terms.*

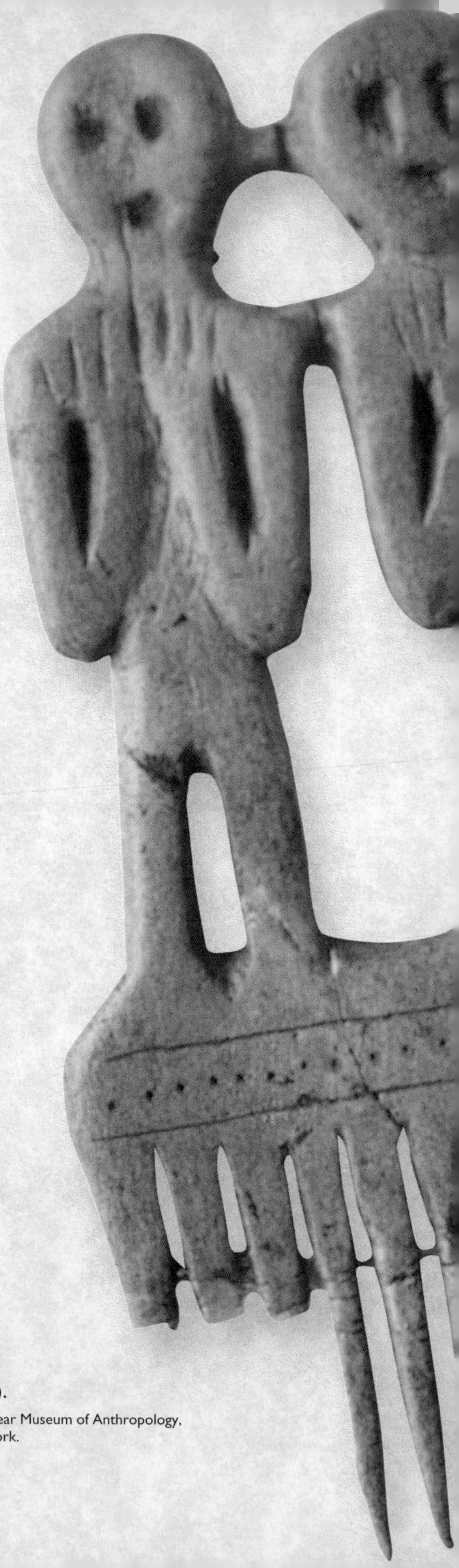

Iroquois bone comb (1556).

Herbert Bigford Sr. Collection, Longyear Museum of Anthropology, Colgate University, Hamilton, New York.

Combing

Gladys Cardiff

Bending, I bow my head
And lay my hand upon
Her hair, combing, and think
How women do this for
5 Each other. My daughter's hair
Curls against the comb,
Wet and fragrant—orange
Parings. Her face, downcast,
Is quiet for one so young.

10 I take her place. Beneath
My mother's hands I feel
The braids drawn up tight
As a piano wire and singing,

Vinegar-rinsed. Sitting
15 Before the oven I hear
The orange coils tick
The early hour before school.

She combed her grandmother
Mathilda's hair using
20 A comb made out of bone.
Mathilda rocked her oak-wood
Chair, her face downcast,
Intent on tearing rags
In strips to braid a cotton
25 Rug from bits of orange
And brown. A simple act,

Preparing hair. Something
Women do for each other,
Plaiting the generations.

MEET THE WRITER

"Paths from Every Direction"

On page 488 you'll find a conversation with **Gladys Cardiff** (1942–   ), in which she tells how she came to write "Combing." Gladys Cardiff had a Cherokee father and an Irish/Welsh mother. She was born in Montana, where her parents taught on the Blackfoot Reservation, and she grew up in Seattle, Washington. Cardiff earned a bachelor's degree and a master's degree in creative writing from the University of Washington. She says that writing for her is an art of celebration, and she especially connects her poetry with an old Cherokee blessing and prayer: "Let the paths from every direction recognize each other."

An Open Mind

She sits by the window, rocking back and forth in the early morning light. I look at her hands. They are old, rough and wrinkled, not like my hands, which are young and smooth, yet hers are stronger. There's a story behind the left index finger, the one with half a nail. That's where a parrot bit her, on the outskirts of a small Central American village.

I look at her arms, round and firm. They are strong from those nights she would swim with her sisters, proud and graceful as dolphins, in the lake by their country house.

I look now at her face, so much like my own, like my mother's. I'm not fooled by the crow's-feet and deep creases on her forehead, because her eyes are young, alive with a shining vitality.

Who is she? I call her Abuela. She is my grandmother. She knows many things, like how to catch fish with her bare hands, pan for gold, cook a soufflé. She can dance a waltz and climb a cliff.

Born of wealthy Spanish-Arabic parents in Honduras, she traveled far and wide in her childhood, picking up several languages. As an adult, she lived in different countries like India, Norway, France, and even Australia. In each of these places she did not bring preconceived notions of what her particular culture considered "normal." In fact, she never did, and still doesn't, judge people based on their appearance or cultural background, but waits until she knows their personality.

I hope one day I'm as strong and wise as my grandmother.

—Nicole A. Plumail
Stuyvesant High School
New York, New York

MAKING MEANINGS
THE GIFT
COMBING

- ### First Thoughts

    1. What gifts are given in "The Gift" and "Combing"?

Shaping Interpretations

    2. Whom do you think the speaker in "The Gift" is talking to, when he says "you"? What scene is taking place in the present?

    3. What does the speaker of "The Gift" say he *didn't* do with that shard, or piece of metal, in his hand? Why, instead, does he kiss his father?

    4. What do you think the poet means in "Combing" when she refers in the last line to women "plaiting the generations"?

Extending the Texts

    5. What other things do family members do that tie or braid generations? What other gifts do parents give children? Be sure to check your Quickwrites.

CHOICES: Building Your Portfolio

Reader's Theater

1. Preparing for a Performance

Practice your diction. All professional  actors and singers pay attention to their diction—because they wish to be understood by their audiences. The secret is to *extra*-pronounce every one of your consonants—eX-aGG-eR-aTe! It will feel funny at first, but it will sound just right to the audience. Next time you see singers or actors on TV, listen to them land on their consonants. To practice your diction, chant some tongue twisters. Start slowly, then build up speed. If you begin losing consonants, slow down. Ask for feedback from your listeners. Taping your tongue-twister chant will help you evaluate your own diction.

Critical Thinking

2. Verbal Music

Many poets use **free verse** because it gives them room to create their own individual voices—and make their own rules. Both "The Gift" and "Combing" are written in free verse. Notice that the poets have used all kinds of strategies to create verbal music.

Working with a group, make a chart for each poem. Map all the examples of **repetition** you can find—**alliteration, internal rhymes,** and **onomatopoeia**. If a poet uses a strategy repetitively, you can bet it's for a reason. For example, you should be able to find four words in "Combing" that sound like *hair*. Those words evoke an image in the reader's mind and sound musical to the ear. Once your chart is finished, read the poems aloud, emphasizing the verbal strategies you've found in them.

Creative Writing

3. Rhyme Crime

Write a poem about a mystery—a crime that needs solving. Make your poem at least four lines long and use exact rhymes, either from this list or from a list you make up:

begun, done, fun, gun, Hun, none, one, outdone, outrun, pun, run, shun, son, spun, stun, sun, ton, undone, won

If there's a rhyming dictionary within reach, don't hesitate to use it.

Creative Writing

4. How Does It Sound?

Write a sentence describing the sounds made by each of the following things. Try to use onomatopoeia and alliteration to echo the sounds you hear.

- a rainy, windy night
- a cat eating dry pet food
- a drummer practicing
- a city street
- a person eating soup

Research

5. Poetry in Pop Culture

Advertisers know how powerful poetry is: They use the strategies of poetry to fix in our memories the names of their products. Make a class collection of brand names that use rhyme, alliteration, or onomatopoeia. Next, think of a song that's popular now, or any song that you particularly like or know well. How does it use rhyme, alliteration, and onomatopoeia? Add the song to the class "Poetry in Pop Culture" collection.

BEFORE YOU READ
FIFTEEN

Reading Focus
Coming Close

We sometimes come close to things that we want but can't have. We may not be old enough, strong enough, or brave enough to possess the things yet. Or we may not yet have earned the right to them. Still, coming close to what we long to possess can leave us with strange conflicting feelings.

Quickwrite

When you're young, a great many things seem out of reach. Think of some moment when you were close to something you wanted badly but you couldn't quite achieve or acquire it. What was it? What feelings did you have after the moment passed? Did the incident present you with any choices?

Keep your notes. For questions and activities on this poem, see pages 574–575.

Elements of Literature
Conflict

Conflict comes in two flavors—external and internal.
External: You are taking your neighbor to court for planting poison ivy between your houses. You and a large bear have just found a terrific raspberry patch.
Internal: The ship is sinking, and a mother with an infant begs you to give up your place in the lifeboat. If you tell your buddies what you really think of how they behave, they'll drop you.

> **I**n an **external conflict,** a character struggles against some outside force. An **internal conflict** is a struggle between opposing needs or desires or emotions within a single person.
>
> *For more on Conflict, see pages 32–33 and the Handbook of Literary Terms.*

Fifteen

William Stafford

South of the Bridge on Seventeenth
I found back of the willows one summer
day a motorcycle with engine running
as it lay on its side, ticking over
5   slowly in the high grass. I was fifteen.

I admired all that pulsing gleam, the
shiny flanks, the demure headlights
fringed where it lay; I led it gently
to the road and stood with that
10   companion, ready and friendly. I was fifteen.

We could find the end of a road, meet
the sky out on Seventeenth. I thought about
hills and, patting the handle, got back a
confident opinion. On the bridge we indulged
15   a forward feeling, a tremble. I was fifteen.

Thinking, back farther in the grass I found
the owner, just coming to, where he had flipped
over the rail. He had blood on his hand, was pale—
I helped him walk to his machine. He ran his hand
20   over it, called me a good man, roared away.

I stood there, fifteen.

MEET THE WRITER

"One of the Great Free Human Activities"

William Stafford (1914–1993), born in Hutchinson, Kansas, of Native American heritage, grew up in several small Kansas towns. The people, animals, and landscapes of his childhood became lifelong subjects for his poetry. Early in his adult life, Stafford worked as a laborer in sugar-beet fields, on construction jobs, and in an oil refinery. He also spent four years in prison during World War II because of his conscientious objection to war. Stafford's poetry is marked by his concern about choices and tough decisions, especially those involving our aggression toward nature and other human beings. He believes that "writing is one of the great free human activities."

Starting in 1948, Stafford taught at Lewis and Clark College in Portland, Oregon. For more than forty years, he instructed and influenced several generations of students. Many of these students went on to make their own reputations as poets. They never forgot William Stafford.

BEFORE YOU READ

AMERICAN HERO

Reading Focus

Seeing Stars

We all have expectations of our heroes. We expect firefighters to race at the first sound, police officers to answer every plea for help, sport stars to win every game, movie and television stars to be perfect and beautiful all the time. After all, that is what we see and we can't look inside their heads to know what they are thinking. But what *are* they thinking? How do they see themselves? What thoughts do firefighters have as they rush into a burning building? Or rock stars as the applause rises around them? Or basketball players when they make a three-point shot? Our heroes may be seeing things from a different angle.

Quickwrite

READER'S LOG

Before you read this poem, take a few minutes to write down what a hero in action might be feeling. For example, what do you think the player opposite is thinking at the moment he is photographed?

Keep your notes. For questions and activities on this poem, see pages 574–575.

Elements of Literature

Onomatopoeia

It quacks like a duck. It must be a duck. The sounds of certain words tell you unmistakably what is being described. *Racketa-racketa-racketa. Chug-chug. Toot-toot.* It's got to be a train. *Choke, slap, slam, holler.* Those are four of the ono-matopoetic words Hemphill uses to give us the sound of a basketball game. *Double dribble* would sound great, too. Can you think of others?

> **O**nomatopoeia is the use of a word whose sound imitates or suggests its meaning: *bang, bow-wow, buzz, chug, clack, clang, crash, crunch, glug, honk, moo, murmur, neigh, rat-a-tat, slurp, splat, squeak, thud.*
>
> *For more on Onomatopoeia, see pages 559–560 and the Hand-book of Literary Terms.*

American Hero

Essex Hemphill

I have nothing to lose tonight.
All my men surround me, panting,
as I spin the ball above our heads
on my middle finger.
5   It's a shimmering club light
and I'm dancing, slick in my sweat.
Squinting, I aim at the hole
fifty feet away. I let the tension go.
Shoot for the net. Choke it.
10   I never hear the ball
slap the backboard. I slam it
through the net. The crowd goes wild
for our win. I scored
thirty-two points this game
15   and they love me for it.
Everyone hollering
is a friend tonight.
But there are towns,
certain neighborhoods
20   where I'd be hard pressed
to hear them cheer
if I move on the block.

MEET THE WRITER

Writer, Poet, Activist

Essex Hemphill (1957–1995),
born in Chicago and later a
Philadelphian, was a writer, poet, and cultural
activist. Hemphill was the author of two books
of poetry and a collection of prose and poetry.
He received a Fellowship in Literature from the
National Endowment for the Arts in 1986.

MAKING MEANINGS
FIFTEEN
AMERICAN HERO

• First Thoughts

1. How do you think the writers of "Fifteen" and "American Hero" felt about the **conflicts** that they made into poems?

Shaping Interpretations

2. How does the boy in "Fifteen" feel about the motorcycle? What lines convey that feeling? What have *you* experienced that allows you to understand his emotion?

3. What do you think the boy in "Fifteen" means in lines 11–12 when he says that he and the motorcycle could "meet the sky out on Seventeenth"? What else could "meet the sky" mean?

4. The writer uses "Fifteen" as the title of the poem, and the phrase "I was fifteen" as a **refrain,** or chorus. What is the significance of that number? Could it as well have been sixteen? How about twelve or eighteen?

5. The American hero in Hemphill's poem says he has "nothing to lose *tonight,*" and "Everyone hollering / is a friend *tonight.*" What does this repetition of the word *tonight* suggest about tomorrow?

6. Look at the last five lines of "American Hero." How has the speaker's mood changed? What **conflict** is the speaker feeling now? What is he saying about his fans?

7. Read "American Hero" aloud. See if you can feel how the pattern of short and long lines creates a kind of tension.

Connecting with the Texts

8. Suppose you are the person who finds the motorcycle in "Fifteen." The man who owns the motorcycle calls you a good man or a good woman. Given what you were just thinking about doing, how does that make you feel?

9. If you had a chance to speak to the "American Hero," what would you say? Did you predict his thoughts in your Quickwrite?

Basketball Collage (1992) by Josh Falley, Topeka West High School, Topeka, Kansas. Oil pastels.

Courtesy of the artist.

CHOICES: Building Your Portfolio

Reader's Theater

1. Preparing for a Performance

A group reading.  Find a poem from this book that you think would be effective read by more than one voice. (You might try Alice Walker's "Women" on page 556.) To prepare for a group reading, you must first prepare your script. You'll have to make these decisions: How many readers will you need? Will you have the whole poem read by several voices? Or will you have some lines read by individual voices? Will you need males and females? Mark up your script, draft a few friends into reading it with you, and rehearse it for presentation to the class.

Critical Writing

2. Moral Dilemmas

If you think one or both of these poems say something important that students in your school should think about, write your ideas in the form of a letter to your school newspaper. Open your letter with a statement telling why you are writing. Be sure to sum up briefly what happens in each poem you write about, before you get into details about why you think the poem is important. Check what you wrote for the Quickwrites before you read these poems.

Creative Writing

3. Poetry in Sports

Hemphill's poem is about more than sports, but you may find the game part as exciting to read as the sports page of your newspaper. Try reporting a game you've watched closely (or better, played in) using free verse and all the musical strategies available to the poet. When you're describing action, use short, fast sentences. Try to find words that sound like the sounds of your game. (Maybe you started a list before you read the poem. See page 572.)

Creative Writing

4. Personify That Machine

Stafford's motorcycle is described as if it's a horse or even a person. Describe a machine you like a lot in terms that make the machine seem human. Before you write, list the parts of the machine and think of how they could seem human. The engine of a car, for example, could be its lungs. The bottom of a boat could be its fat belly. The vacuum cleaner's suction could be its breath. Write three sentences or more.

Creative Writing

5. The Class Onomatopoeia Collection

Establish a class **onomatopoeia** collection on a bulletin board or computer. Collect words you hear or read, but also try to invent new onomatopoetic words or phrases for things such as the sounds of skates, skateboards, computers and computer games, VCRs, copying machines, home appliances, smoke alarms or car alarms, sports sounds, classroom sounds—or any other special or unusual sounds you want to imitate. Inventors should sign their contributions.

BEFORE YOU READ
THE GIRL WHO LOVED THE SKY

Reading Focus

Seeing the World Clearly

The two second-graders in this poem deal in different ways with the lives they've been given. Before you read, you might want to see what the poet says about her story on page 577.

Quickwrite

Do you know anyone who has felt like an outsider? Maybe you have had that feeling from time to time—most people have. Write down your thoughts about being inside and outside.

Keep your notes. For questions and activities on this poem, see page 578.

Elements of Literature

Images: Sharing Sensations

As you read, let the poet's words create pictures in your mind—pictures that also help you smell, hear, touch, and even taste the vivid world this lonely little girl shared with her best friend.

> **I**mages are words that create sensory impressions.
>
> *For more on Imagery, see pages 492–493 and the Handbook of Literary Terms.*

The Girl Who Loved the Sky

Anita Endrezze

Outside the second-grade room,
the jacaranda tree blossomed
into purple lanterns, the papery petals
drifted, darkening the windows.
5   Inside, the room smelled like glue.
The desks were made of yellowed wood,
the tops littered with eraser rubbings,
rulers, and big fat pencils.
Colored chalk meant special days.
10   The walls were covered with precise
bright tulips and charts with shiny stars
by certain names. There, I learned
how to make butter by shaking a jar
until the pale cream clotted
15   into one sweet mass. There, I learned
that numbers were fractious° beasts
with dens like dim zeros. And there,
I met a blind girl who thought the sky
tasted like cold metal when it rained
20   and whose eyes were always covered
with the bruised petals of her lids.
She loved the formless sky, defined
only by sounds, or the cool umbrellas
of clouds. On hot, still days
25   we listened to the sky falling
like chalk dust. We heard the noon
whistle of the pig-mash factory,
smelled the sourness of homebound men.
I had no father; she had no eyes;
30   we were best friends. The other girls
drew shaky hopscotch squares
on the dusty asphalt, talked about
pajama parties, weekend cookouts,
and parents who bought sleek-finned cars.
35   Alone, we sat in the canvas swings,
our shoes digging into the sand, then pushing,
until we flew high over their heads,
our hands streaked with red rust
from the chains that kept us safe.

16. fractious: hard to manage; rebellious.

40   I was born blind, she said, an act of nature.
      Sure, I thought, like birds born
      without wings, trees without roots.
      I didn't understand. The day she moved
      I saw the world clearly; the sky
45   backed away from me like a departing father.
      I sat under the jacaranda, catching
      the petals in my palm, enclosing them
      until my fist was another lantern
      hiding a small and bitter flame.

MEET THE WRITER

Different from the Rest

Anita Endrezze (1952–   ) bridges the two worlds of visual arts and literary arts. "The Girl Who Loved the Sky" is from her book *At the Helm of Twilight* (1992). Her paintings have been widely shown and have appeared on book covers in the United States and in Europe.

In the early 1980s, Endrezze and her husband lived in a home they built out of logs in the middle of a pine forest. They now live with their two children, Aaron Joseph Sunhawk and Maja Sierra Rose, in Spokane, Washington.

66 'The Girl Who Loved the Sky' was written about my early life. My parents divorced when I was very young, in a time when divorce was unusual. Not one other kid in my class came from a divorced family. My situation was also different because my parents were from two different races. My father was Yaqui Indian and my mother is white (European-mixed background). I didn't find it easy to make friends.

We also moved a lot. Finally, I did make friends with a blind girl who was also lonely and not accepted by the other kids. In her case, I don't think they knew how to relate to her. I don't remember them being actively cruel; they just didn't know how to play with someone who could not see. We became friends because we were the only two girls who were left outside the 'circle.' After I got to know her, though, I began to understand her and what her life was like. I tried to imagine myself in her position. Maybe we would have gone on to be great friends, but my family moved again and I no longer saw her.

To write this poem, I needed to remember the smells, sights, feelings, and sounds of my childhood and of elementary school. I tried to use my five senses to evoke images others could identify with. I wanted to express the loneliness of a child who is different from the rest. 99

MAKING MEANINGS
THE GIRL WHO LOVED THE SKY

First Thoughts

1. If you had a chance, what would you say to the little girl who speaks in this poem? (Check your Quickwrite notes.)

Shaping Interpretations

2. What has each girl in this poem lost?

3. Do you think the girl who was blind taught her friend anything? Is the poem clear on this point? Explain your response.

4. What **images** does Endrezze create for you in her poem? What can you *see*? *hear*? almost *taste*?

5. How could chains keep the girls safe—safe from what?

Connecting with the Text

6. What do you think the little girl means in lines 43–44 when she says that the day her friend moved she "saw the world clearly"? Do you agree with her vision of what the world is like? Why, or why not?

CHOICES: Building Your Portfolio

Reader's Theater

1. Preparing for a Performance

Pauses.
Prepare a script for a reading of "The Girl Who Loved the Sky," either for a group performance or for a single voice (see page 582). Your main challenge will be to decide on places in the text where you must make pauses: full pauses or brief pauses. Punctuation marks will guide you. On your script, write *p* in the places where you'll make a full pause and *b* in the spots where you'll stop briefly for a breath.

Art

2. Views of the Jacaranda

The tree with the odd name opens and closes the poem, shedding both light and darkness on the two little girls. Suppose you are asked to illustrate this poem. Paint or draw the tree as the speaker sees it, but first be sure you know exactly what it looks like yourself. Include in your painting one important line from the poem.

Creative Writing

3. Mixing Senses

The blind girl knew how the sky tasted and how the clouds felt. Write a series of images in which you describe some ordinary object as it would appear to a sense you wouldn't associate with it— just as you probably wouldn't associate the sky with the sense of taste. Here are some ideas:

How does math smell?
How does the sun taste?
How does a pizza sound?

Americans All

Michael Dorris

Quickwrite

READER'S LOG

Here's another way of looking at "The Ways We Are." Before you read what Michael Dorris says about Americans, write down quickly your own ideas of "what we are"—what are Americans? When you think of the word *American,* what do you see and perhaps hear? Save your notes.

I recognize them instantly abroad: on the street, in crowded rooms, on airplanes, at restaurants—but how? It's emphatically not skin color, not clothing, not little red-white-and-blues stitched to their breast pockets. They don't have to say anything, to show a passport, or to sing the "Star-Spangled Banner," but nevertheless they're unmistakable in any foreign setting.

Americans. We come in all varieties of size, age, and style. We travel singly and in groups. We're alternately loud and disapproving or humble and apologetic. We seek each other out or self-consciously avoid each other's company. We pack our gear in Gucci bags or stuff it into Patagonia backpacks, travel first-class or on Eurailpasses,

stay in youth hostels or in luxury hotels, but none of that matters. It's as though we're individually implanted with some invisible beeper, some national homing device, that's activated by the proximity of similar equipment.

This common denominator is manifest in shared knowledge (we all know who Mary Tyler Moore is), topics of mutual interest or dispute (guns, the environment, choice), and popular culture (do we or do we not deserve a thousand-calorie break today?). In other words, we take the same things seriously or not seriously, are capable of speaking, when we choose to, not merely a common language but a common idiom, and know the melodies, if not all the words, to many of the same songs.

Why, then, doesn't any of this count when we're *not* overseas? Why, at home, do we seem so different from each other, so mutually incompatible, so strange and forbidding? Do we have to recognize each other in Tokyo or Cairo

in order to see through the distinctions and into the commonalities? How does that "we," so obvious anywhere else in the world, get split into "us" and "them" when we're stuck within our own borders?

The answer is clear: To be Americans means to be not the clone of the people next door. I fly back from any homogeneous country, from a place where every person I see is blond, or black, or belongs to only one religion, and then disembark at JFK. I revel in the cadence of many accents, catch a ride to the city with a Nigerian American or Russian American cabdriver. Eat Thai food at a Greek restaurant next to a table of Chinese American conventioneers from Alabama. Get directions from an Iranian American cop and drink a cup of Turkish coffee served by a Navajo student at Fordham who's majoring in Japanese literature. Argue with everybody about everything. I'm home.

— from *Newsday*, October 1992

From Within

Michael Dorris
(1945–1997), novelist
and nonfiction writer,
was the husband and collaborator of poet
and novelist Louise Erdrich. A member of the
Modocs, a Native American people originally
from Lost River Valley on the California-
Oregon border, Dorris was a professor of
cultural anthropology and Native American
studies at Dartmouth College before taking a
leave to devote full time to his writing.

One of Dorris's nonfiction books, *The
Broken Cord* (1989), is about his adopted son
Adam, who was born with fetal alcohol syn-
drome (FAS). Dorris said: "As with all hard
challenges, motivation must come from
within." That's a motto Dorris lived by—
in his personal and professional lives. It's
also a motto he passed on to his
children, his students, and his
readers.

Dorris adopted Adam and two
other children before he was
married to Erdrich. The house-
keeping and parenting duties didn't
faze him:

66 I have this very rich background of grandmothers and aunts and a mother, a wonderful
extended family who made nothing seem impossible or out of reach. We were poor when
I was growing up, but I never felt it. They
could kill me for telling this, but sometimes
on Sunday afternoons they'd lock the door to
the house, everyone would dress up and we'd
sit at the dining-room table and have lunch. If
it were later at night, they'd call it the Stork
Club. Everything they did was wonderful.
When you don't have a lot of things, every
event becomes special, like The Adventure of
Getting the Deep Fryer. 99

FINDING COMMON GROUND

1. Review the notes you made in your Quickwrite and then meet with a group of
   other readers to discuss Dorris's article. Talk over what you agree with and
   what you would question in Dorris's article.

2. Using your Quickwrite notes and any new ideas you got from Dorris and from
   your discussion, write your own article about "Americans and the Ways We
   Are." You can write it as a response to Dorris, or as an independent essay of
   your own. You can include some reference to poems in this collection, if you
   think they are relevant.

3. Put aside some class time to read aloud your essays—and Dorris's. Dorris
   says "We come in all varieties." Do your essays come in all varieties too?

Speaking and Listening Workshop

Perform at least one of the poems in this collection before an audience.

. . . poetry readings have moved out of smoky cafes and into libraries, bookstores, and cafes (nonsmoking, of course) around the country. With help from MTV's poetry videos and poetry slams at places like Nuyorican Poets Cafe on East Third Street in the East Village [of New York City], where audiences rate performances like Olympic judges, poetry readings—as opposed to reading poetry—are becoming a staple of the country's cultural scene.

—Diana Jean Schemo,
   from *The New York Times*

READER'S THEATER
POETRY READING

Reprinted by permission: Tribune Media Services.

"So what I get from acting is using it for others, using it for people. I find that when I work well, people enjoy it and . . . things happen to them."

—Sidney Poitier

How is "reader's" theater different from "regular" theater? The main difference is the text that the performer shares with the audience. In regular theater, the actor performs a play, which is written in dramatic form with dialogue and stage directions. In reader's theater, one or more actors perform works of nondramatic literature as they were originally written—poems, stories, even whole novels that are read aloud over several performances.

Preparation

Your first job in preparing for a reader's theater performance is to build your private, personal understanding of the poem.

1. Making Your Choice

As you worked through this collection, you might already have chosen a poem you feel a connection with. If you still haven't selected a text, read a few poems from this collection out loud to see which one you'd most enjoy reading in public.

2. Shaping Interpretations

• Make a copy of the poem and use it as a working script. Underline the parts you find most dramatic—words, phrases, images,

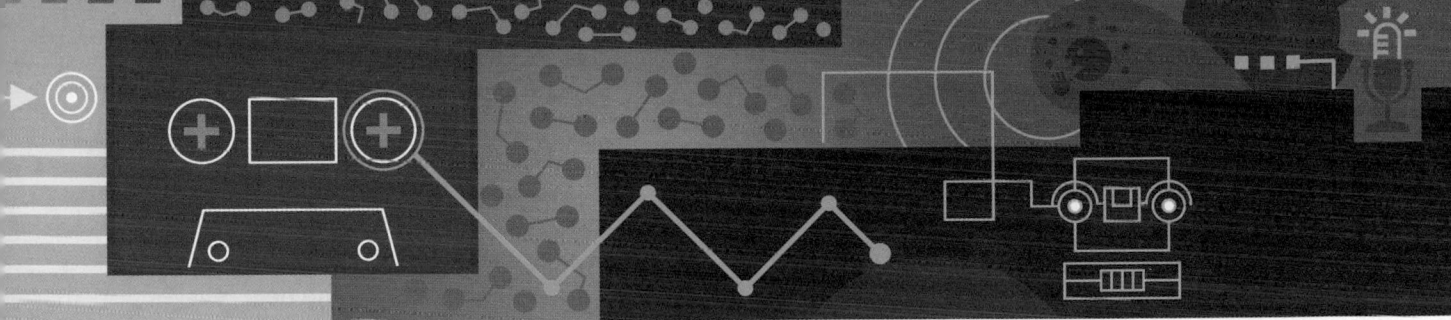

sounds, rhythms. Note places where you want to go slowly or speed up or pause. Be sure to note which lines do *not* end with a punctuation mark. This means that you don't come to a full pause but read on to the next line to complete the thought.

- Make notes describing the speaker in the poem. Is the speaker a particular age? How does the speaker feel in the poem, and do his or her feelings change as the poem goes on?

- What will your own tone or attitude be? Thoughtful? Serious? Sad? Sarcastic? How will you use your voice to convey your tone?

- Complete this statement: If my audience gets just one single impression from my reading, I want them to . . .

Planning and Rehearsing

Now it's time to develop ways to communicate your private, personal, unique experience of the poem to your audience.

1. Memorizing (or Not)

You may or may not decide to memorize the poem. Even if you plan to hold a copy of the poem throughout your reading, you should be extremely familiar with it. And if you choose to memorize your poem, an actors' secret will help you: Thoroughly understanding a text makes it much easier to memorize.

2. Planning Your Movements

You may feel most comfortable standing still and speaking to your audience. Or you may want to move around, to act out parts of the poem. You may want to sit. Make eye contact with your audience: Don't keep your head buried in your script.

Naomi Shihab Nye stood under the bright lights at Waterloo Village [New Jersey] on Thursday night, a television camera hovering around her like a mobile X-ray, to read her work into a microphone. The poet could not hear herself; the wind whipping the tent's plastic walls, the rain's ping-ping drumbeat on the roof and the expanse of empty seats seemed to swallow the sound of her.

I want to be famous in the
    way a pulley is famous,

or a buttonhole, not
    because it did anything
    spectacular,

but because it never forgot
    what it could do.

It was only the anticipation on the faces in the audience and the final applause that made Ms. Nye realize she had struck the right mix of words, gestures, and pauses in performing her poetry, a talent that has become crucial to a poet's success.

    —Diana Jean Schemo,
      from *The New York Times*

FRANK & ERNEST reprinted by permission of Newspaper Enterprise Association, Inc.

3. Using Props, Scenery, Costumes

Props—objects that are significant in the poem—can help establish the speaker's identity or setting. For example, if you are reading "American Hero" (page 573), you may want to handle a basketball and then toss it away near the poem's end. During a performance, props can provide a focus for you and help relieve your nervousness. If you use props, however, you should definitely memorize the poem.

You may want to use costumes and even special makeup to bring a speaker to life. Scenery pieces (a bench, a rug, a table) will help define your performing area and give you ideas for movement. If you use music or sound effects (a purring motorcycle for "Fifteen"), keep them subtle and don't let them distract your audience.

4. Rehearsing Your Reading

Make a clean copy of the poem. Across the top write your finished version of the sentence that begins "If the audience gets just one single impression." Add any important interpretive and performance notes. This is your script.

Reflecting: How Did It Go?

If you decide to include a tape of your reading in your portfolio, date the tape and attach a brief reflection:

1. Was my poem a good choice?

2. Do I still need to work on some performance skills?

3. What did I learn about performing for an audience?

4. What did I learn about myself as a public speaker?

Even though I didn't win the slam, I found out that I enjoy performing. Of course, I was nervous, just before I went on. I'm glad I picked this poem. I really got into it during the "understanding" stage. That helped me not be too self-conscious when I began to think about actually performing it. If I could do it one more time, I'd try to use my props more—it relaxed me a lot to have something to hold on to.

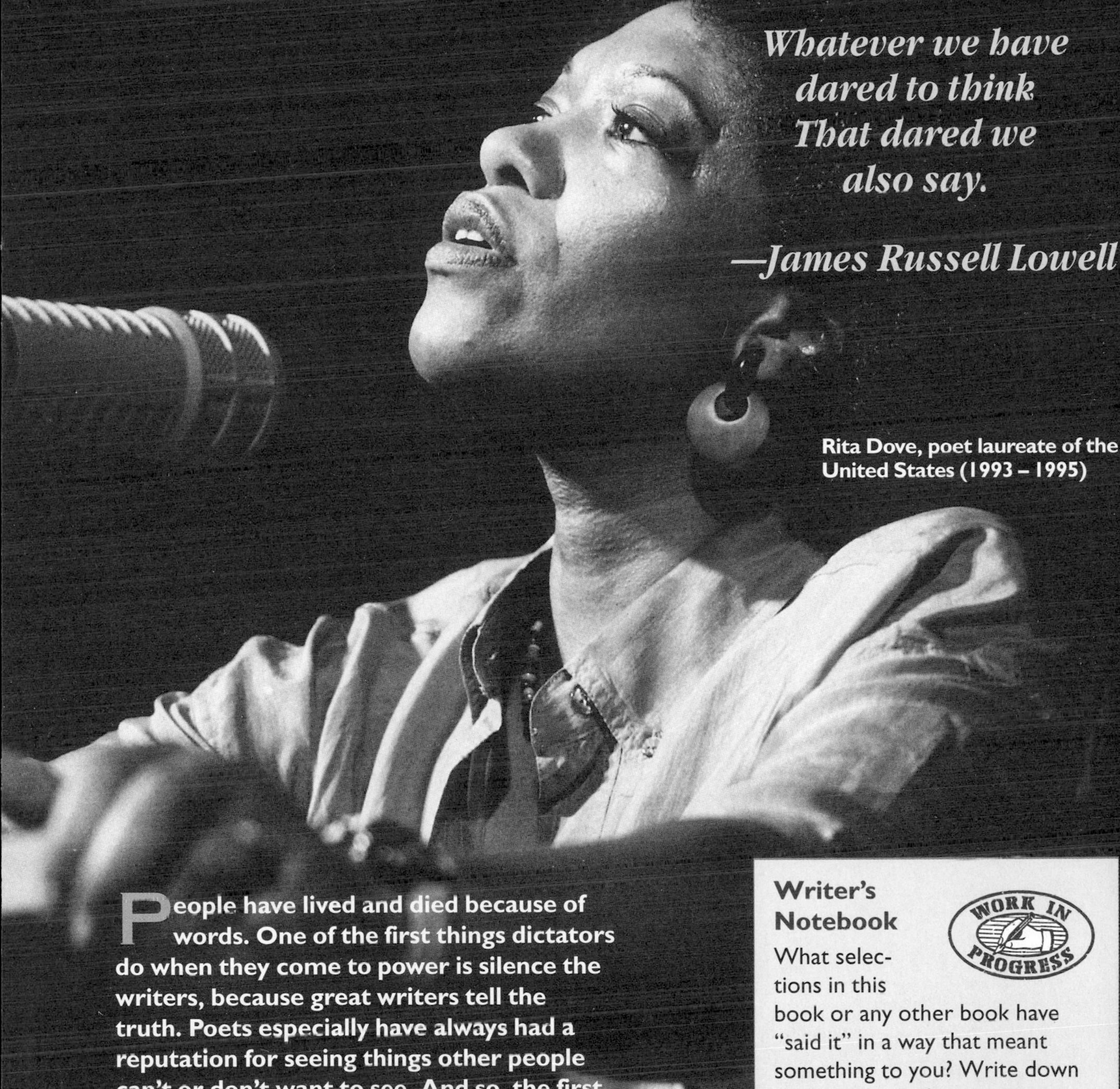

Whatever we have dared to think That dared we also say.

—James Russell Lowell

Rita Dove, poet laureate of the United States (1993 – 1995)

People have lived and died because of words. One of the first things dictators do when they come to power is silence the writers, because great writers tell the truth. Poets especially have always had a reputation for seeing things other people can't or don't want to see. And so, the first rule of writing, or of any art, is: Say it! Say it with your own words. Remember that you are the only person who can see things from your angle. Share your vision!

Writer's Notebook

What selections in this book or any other book have "said it" in a way that meant something to you? Write down the titles and a few notes on what they said and how they were alike, or different. Save your notes.

Elements of Literature

TONE: It's an Attitude

Tone is not easy to define, because it's a quality of language that is suggested, not stated. Tone is a speaker's attitude—toward a subject or toward an audience. Tone can be sarcastic, teasing, critical, serious, playful, angry, admiring, ironic, and so on. (Painters can also reveal tones. The artist whose work is shown below takes a mocking tone toward the poor poet, who counts out his syllables in a leaky attic.)

When we speak out loud, we reveal tone by the way we use our voices and bodies. We use our voices to create emphasis—that is, we give importance to particular words by pausing and by varying our pitch and volume.

Take a simple sentence such as "School starts next week." By emphasizing different words and by varying your pitch, volume, and pauses, you can change your tone. Try it.

- School starts next week. (sincere)
- School starts next week? (disbelieving)
- School starts next week! (excited)
- School starts next week. (disgusted)

When a poem is printed on a page, we can't hear its tone in the way we can hear a tone of voice. But a poem does convey a tone, and until you've heard its tone, you haven't grasped the poet's complete message.

Look at the Words

One way tone is revealed is through word choice, or **diction**. If a poet sees a red face and describes it as beefy, the tone is unsympathetic, maybe even sarcastic—no one

The Poor Poet (1839) by Carl Spitzweg. Oil.
Nationalgalerie, Staatliche Museen, Preussischer Kulturbesitz, Berlin.

by John Malcolm Brinnin

wants to look like a piece of steak. But if the poet describes the face as rosy or robust, the tone is positive and approving.

If a poet compares the world to a rose, the tone is approving—the world seems beautiful. But if a poet compares the world to a prickly cactus, the world does not seem so beautiful, and we sense a cynical tone.

If the poet describes a gaping wound as a minor scratch, we sense an ironic tone—we know the poet is saying one thing but really means something else.

William Wordsworth's tone was solemn when he said, "A slumber did my spirit seal." If you said, "I blanked out," you'd be saying more or less the same thing, but your tone would be completely different.

William Shakespeare was adoring when he asked his lover, "Shall I compare thee to a summer's day?" But when he stated in another poem, "My mistress' eyes are nothing like the sun," he was mocking

poets who use such exaggerated comparisons.

Listen to the Sounds

Until you have heard a poem's tone, you haven't grasped the poet's complete message.

Rhythms and rhymes can also convey tone. If we hear a lively, bouncy rhythm and jingly rhymes, we know the poet is probably not feeling solemn about the subject. If a poem is slow-moving and stately, we figure the poet is not looking at the subject in a light, humorous way.

When Ogden Nash writes: "Any hound a porcupine nudges/Can't be blamed for harboring grudges," we laugh. The bouncy rhythm and jingly rhyme reveal to us at once that Nash is being silly and funny.

When you read a poem, try to hear the poet's tone of voice and what he or she is emphasizing. Look at the words the poet has chosen and listen to the way the poem sounds. Once you catch the poet's tone of voice, you become aware of a particular attitude, and the meaning of the poem will become clearer for you.

" 'Born in conservation,' if you don't mind. 'Captivity' has negative connotations."

Drawing by Handelsman; ©1993 The New Yorker Magazine, Inc.

Reading Focus

Lesson from a Puppy

The most serious subjects are sometimes presented in a light way. Here the Russian writer Aleksandr Solzhenitsyn (sōl′zhə·nēt′sin) offers a simple description of a puppy who is permitted to play in the snow. Solzhenitsyn spent eight years in a labor camp for criticizing dictator Joseph Stalin, and his writings were banned in Russia for much of his lifetime. Knowing this makes us realize how much more serious than a romping puppy his real subject is.

Quickwrite

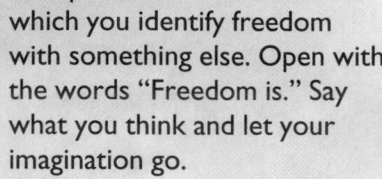

Write three metaphors in which you identify freedom with something else. Open with the words "Freedom is." Say what you think and let your imagination go.

Keep your notes. For questions and activities on this poem, see pages 596–597.

Elements of Literature

A Prose Poem

Solzhenitsyn has written his light and delicate description in the form of a **prose poem**—a compact composition that creates the rhythms of free verse. Here, the writer uses the sight of a small puppy, unchained for a few moments on a snowy day, to convey a message. See if the words he uses to describe the puppy could apply just as well to a bear, the traditional symbol of Russia.

> A **prose poem** is a compact and rhythmic composition written in the form of a prose paragraph. Like any poem, a prose poem often presents its message by means of a vivid figure of speech.

MEET THE WRITER

He Wrote in a Prison Hut

Aleksandr Solzhenitsyn (1918–   ) was sentenced to prison for eight years when he was twenty-six years old because he wrote a letter to a friend criticizing the Russian dictator Joseph Stalin.

Denied writing materials, he managed to compose in his head and commit to memory a verse novel of 10,000 lines and a play of some 2,500 lines in iambic rhymed couplets. The first thing he did when released from prison was to write these compositions down on paper. Here is what he said later about his writing:

66 I myself had learned long ago in the camp to compose and to write as I marched in a column under escort; out on the frozen

The Puppy

Aleksandr Solzhenitsyn

translated by Michael Glenny

In our back yard a boy keeps his little dog Sharik chained up, a ball of fluff shackled since he was a puppy.

One day I took him some chicken bones that were still warm and smelled delicious. The boy had just let the poor dog off his lead to have a run round the yard. The snow there was deep and feathery; Sharik was bounding about like a hare, first on his hind legs, then on his front ones, from one corner of the yard to the other, back and forth, burying his muzzle in the snow.

He ran toward me, his coat all shaggy, jumped up at me, sniffed the bones—then off he went again, belly-deep in the snow.

I don't need your bones, he said. Just give me my freedom. . . .

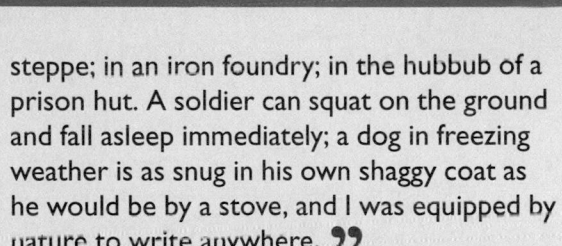

steppe; in an iron foundry; in the hubbub of a prison hut. A soldier can squat on the ground and fall asleep immediately; a dog in freezing weather is as snug in his own shaggy coat as he would be by a stove, and I was equipped by nature to write anywhere. **"**

Solzhenitsyn's novel *One Day in the Life of Ivan Denisovich* (1962)—set in a forced-labor camp very much like the one he endured—made him famous. After the fall of Nikita Khrushchev in 1964, however, Solzhenitsyn's writings were banned from publication in the Soviet Union. Awarded the Nobel Prize for literature in 1970, he did not even dare to go to Sweden to accept it, for fear that he would not be allowed back into Russia.

In 1974, Solzhenitsyn was stripped of his Soviet citizenship and exiled. He moved to a small village in Vermont and continued to write and lecture. In 1990, his citizenship was restored, and Solzhenitsyn has returned to the land of his birth.

BEFORE YOU READ
HARLEM

Reading Focus

"A Dream Deferred"

We all have dreams for the future. We all need to believe that these dreams can come true. But what happens when we have to give up these dreams? Langston Hughes has written a poem that answers the question "What happens to a dream deferred?"

Quickwrite

What happens when you have to give up or postpone a dream? Freewrite your answers to the question posed in the opening line of the poem. Use the sharpest words and images that you can think of.

Keep your notes. For questions and activities on this poem, see pages 596–597.

Elements of Literature

Figures of Speech

When the playwright Lorraine Hansberry wrote about the hopes and courage and defeats of an African American family, she found her title, *A Raisin in the Sun,* in one of the lines from this poem. By using a figure of speech, Hansberry chose to put aside literal meaning in favor of an imaginative connection.

Figures of speech are always based on comparisons and they are not literally true. A **simile** creates a comparison by using a connective word such as *like, as, than,* or *resembles.* A **metaphor** compares two unlike things without the use of these specific connective words. See if you can find the five similes that Hughes uses to describe a dream deferred. What powerful metaphor tells what the dream might become?

> **A figure of speech** is a word or phrase that describes one thing in terms of something very different from it.
>
> *For more on Figurative Language, see pages 520–521 and the Handbook of Literary Terms.*

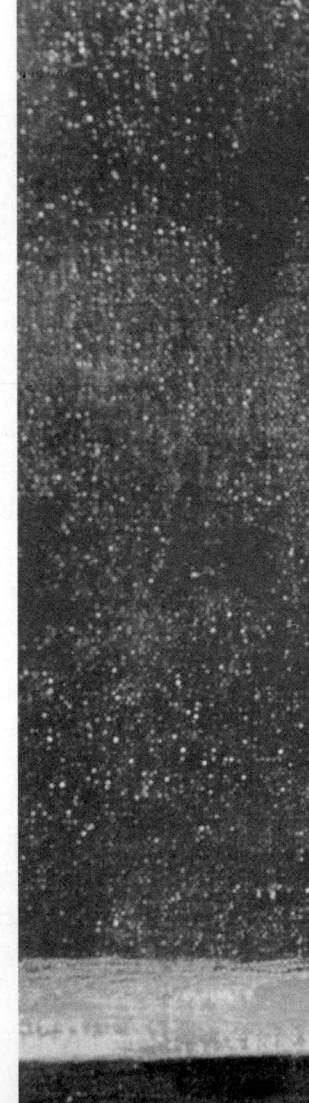

Slum Song (1944) by Hughie Lee-Smith.
Courtesy of the Golden State Mutual Life Insurance Company, Los Angeles. African-American Collection.

Harlem

**Langston
Hughes**

What happens to a dream deferred?

Does it dry up
like a raisin in the sun?
Or fester like a sore—
5   And then run?
Does it stink like rotten meat?
Or crust and sugar over—
like a syrupy sweet?

Maybe it just sags
10 like a heavy load.

Or does it explode?

MEET THE WRITER

Speaking to People's Hearts

Langston Hughes (1902–1967) was voted class poet before he had ever written a single poem. But the position inspired him to write some poems—and he went on to become one of the most important American writers of the twentieth century. Hughes broke barriers in writing and in race relations—bringing the blues, jazz rhythms, and street slang into American literature and gaining an audience of millions of people of every race. In an early collection of his poems, he wrote:

> 66 . . . I have felt that there has been a distinct lack of rhymed poems dramatizing current racial interests in simple, understandable verse, pleasing to the ear, and suitable for reading aloud. . . . I have felt that much of our poetry has been aimed at the heads of the highbrows, rather than at the hearts of the people. 99

Hughes, in his boldly different poems, lets ordinary people speak for themselves. His poems are often written in slang—his speakers say what is on their minds and they say it in the language they use every day. As might be expected, Hughes had to put up with a lot of scorn: "Langston Hughes's Book of Poems Trash," said a Pittsburgh *Courier* headline long ago.

Just before he died Hughes asked:

> 66 What is poetry? 99

And then he answered his own question:

> 66 It is the human soul entire squeezed like a lemon into atomic words. 99

A story by Hughes appears on page 120.

Langston Hughes on the IRT

A Poem Arouses Many Feelings.

JOE SEXTON

The New York City Transit Authority's program is called "Poetry in Motion," and on this particular morning eight lines of Langston Hughes rumble along the length of the IRT No. 3 line.

> *Sometimes a crumb falls*
> *From the tables of joy*
> *Sometimes a bone*
> *Is flung*
> *To some people*
> *Love is given*
> *To others*
> *Only heaven.*

The poem, titled "Luck," is in the last days of its singular urban life on Car No. 2000, which sits awash in filtered morning sunlight in the outdoor New Lots Avenue station in Brooklyn. It is scheduled to be taken down, replaced by poems No. 26 and 27 in the series that began sixteen months ago in the subways.

Wendy Richards is the first person to glance at the poem poster this morning. She reads it quietly and then both smiles and cries. Ms. Richards is two hours late for work. She had spent the morning attending to the details of the death of a neighbor who used to ride the subway with her. Lois Russell, who had talked with Ms. Richards recently about the Hughes poem, had died in her sleep only hours before. She was forty-five years old.

"She was with me yesterday," Ms. Richards said of her neighbor. "We both loved the poem. It seems full of knowledge, and it's nice to be offered a bit of it."

The No. 3 train courses through the cold. There are stops at Van Siclen Avenue and then Pennsylvania Avenue. The poem is posted above the exit doors in the center of the car, helping to frame a frozen East New York. The car at nearly 11:00 A.M. is crowded, rush hour evidently as free-form as the verse.

Lakiesha McNeil, twenty-two years old, sits across from the poem, along with her husband. She does not read poetry beyond what interrupts her stares on the subway. She re-reads "Luck" and waits a long time before talking.

"I can't express it, but I get it," Ms. McNeil says of the poem. "Everybody has luck, although sometimes you can't be happy. Everything is not good in this world."

The world of the moment for Car No. 2000 changes with each stop. Daylight vanishes as the train descends again under-ground. Above, the neighborhoods are shifting, and the population of the car undergoes the constant, arbitrary, oddball integration that happens throughout the city.

Hughes, who died in 1967, lived in New York for significant parts of his life, and "mightily did he use the streets," another poet, Gwendolyn Brooks, once said of him. "He found its multiple heart, its tastes, smells, alarms, formulas, flowers, garbage, and convulsions," she said.

Now on this day, on this train, a construction worker stands under "Luck" and never happens to look up. A man with a briefcase rummages through computer printouts in his lap. A mother and child peer curiously into a blackened window, each peacefully deciphering the darkness.

—from *The New York Times*
March 2, 1994

BEFORE YOU READ
"HOPE" IS THE THING WITH FEATHERS

Reading Focus

On Wings of Hope

Emily Dickinson says that hope doesn't use words. But *she* certainly does—special words, carefully chosen to bring hope alive—perched, feathered, singing—before our very eyes.

"In Extremity," she says in this poem. Her poems are full of extremities—sorrow, grief, loss, death, joy, exaltation, despair, frustration, loneliness, unrequited love, longing—extremities she might not have been able to bear, much less put down on paper, had hope not perched in her soul, as it does in each of ours.

A Dialogue with the Text

As you read this poem, track your responses in your Reader's Log. Ask questions, note details that match your own experiences, and respond to Dickinson's words as they speak to you.

Keep your notes. For questions and activities on this poem, see pages 596–597.

Elements of Literature

Denotation and Connotation

This poem about hope has a calm tone, at least when it's talking about hope. But wherever hope is, there's got to be trouble to begin with. And there's plenty of trouble here. The words *gale* and *storm* literally mean "a strong wind" and "a disturbance of the atmosphere." These are the dictionary definitions—the **denotations** of the words. But what do you also get with your usual gale and storm? **Connotations,** that's what.

Thunder. Lightning. Rain, snow, hail, sleet. Howling wind. Downed trees. Snapped power lines. Sunken ships. Flattened buildings. Flooded fields. Destruction. Death.

Whenever we use a word we use all its connotations—the associations and feelings that are attached to it. Poets, who know words well, choose them carefully.

> **D**enotation is the literal, dictionary definition of a word. **Connotation** is all the meanings, associations, or emotions suggested by a word.
>
> *For more on Connotation, see the Handbook of Literary Terms.*

For a biography of Emily Dickinson, see page 523.

Bird Singing in the Moonlight (1938–1939) by Morris Graves.
Tempera and watercolor on mulberry paper (26 ¾″ x 30 ⅛″, 68 cm. x 76.5 cm.).

"Hope"
Is the Thing
with Feathers

Emily Dickinson

"Hope" is the thing with feathers—
That perches in the soul—
And sings the tune without the words—
And never stops—at all—

5   And sweetest—in the Gale—is heard—
And sore must be the storm—
That could abash the little Bird
That kept so many warm—

I've heard it in the chillest land—
10   And on the strangest Sea—
Yet, never, in Extremity,
It asked a crumb—of Me.

MAKING MEANINGS

THE PUPPY

HARLEM

"HOPE" IS THE THING WITH FEATHERS

First Thoughts

1. Which of the three poems comes closest to describing feelings you've had?

Shaping Interpretations

2. Look back at the details in Solzhenitsyn's prose poem. Do you think this is only about a puppy or do you think it refers to a broader subject? Find details to justify your response.

3. The word *deferred* in line 1 of "Harlem" means "delayed," "postponed." What is the dream that is being postponed here?

4. The first line of "Harlem" is calm and moderate in **tone**. What adjective would you choose to describe the tone of lines 2 through 10? What words in the poem support your choice?

5. What final **metaphor** is implied when Hughes uses the word *explode*—what are we to understand that the dream might become? Why might a "dream deferred" one day explode?

6. What **metaphor** does Dickinson use to speak of hope throughout her poem? What do you think of her metaphor?

7. Think about why Dickinson chose the word *strangest* to describe the sea and *chillest* to describe the land. What **connotations** do these words have for you? What feelings and associations do they evoke? Check your Reader's Log for your first reactions. What other words could Dickinson have chosen—words that would have different connotations for you?

Extending the Texts

8. Solzhenitsyn's puppy prefers freedom to food. What people in history might agree with him?

9. "Harlem" was published in 1951. What conditions still exist that make this poem relevant to people's lives today?

10. Think back on Dickinson's poem: What extremities can you think of in which hope keeps people warm?

11. Read the article on page 593, about the Langston Hughes poem in the subway for busy commuters to enjoy. Where else could you imagine poems being displayed? Which poems that you've read would you recommend for a public display?

CHOICES: Building Your Portfolio

Writer's Notebook

1. Collecting Ideas for a Comparison/Contrast Essay

Finding a topic. The first thing to do when you are preparing to compare two texts (see the Writer's Workshop on page 614) is to look at their elements. Look, for example, at the metaphor in Hughes's poem "Harlem" and the one in Dickinson's poem on hope. Take notes now on these metaphors: Tell what the poets are basing their comparisons on and how each metaphor makes you feel. Save your notes. (The model below is based on other poems.)

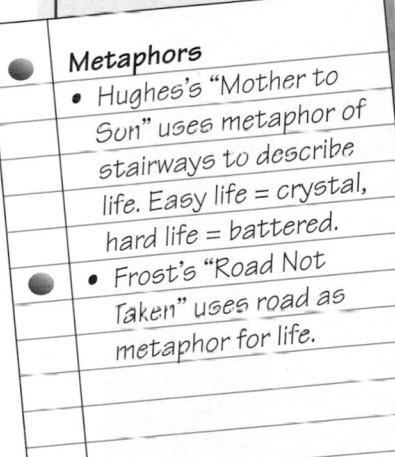

Metaphors
- Hughes's "Mother to Son" uses metaphor of stairways to describe life. Easy life = crystal, hard life = battered.
- Frost's "Road Not Taken" uses road as metaphor for life.

Creative Writing

2. Your Own Dream, Your Own Hope

Write two poems. One should be about your own dream or dreams and should open with the words "I dream." The other should be about what happens when those dreams are taken away or "deferred." (Be sure to check the notes you made in the Quickwrite on page 590 before you started to read Hughes's poem.) Before you write your poems, think carefully about your tone. Here are some shades of feeling you might want to convey: *angry, glad, cheerful, joyous, sorrowful, confident, thankful, awed.*

Creative Writing

3. Your Own Prose Poem

Solzhenitsyn probably got the idea for his prose poem on page 589 when he saw the puppy frolicking in the snow. Write a prose poem of your own about freedom. Base it on something you've observed in everyday life. Be sure to check the notes you made for the Quickwrite on page 588 for ideas.

Speaking/Research

4. A "Speak-in"

Contribute quotations, poems, and news stories to a class freedom-of-speech collection. Share that collection in a "speak-in," in which you read aloud your selections and then exchange views on the freedom of speech guaranteed to Americans under the First Amendment.

Art

5. "I Dream" Collage

Using lines or ideas from the notes you took for the Quickwrite on page 590, plus drawings or found images as illustrations, create your personal "Dream" collage. Then, with your classmates, contribute to a "We Have Dreams" class poster.

Reading Focus

Between Worlds

Each of us belongs to several different worlds—of gender, ethnicity, economic status. The combinations are infinite. The speaker in "Legal Alien" is a Mexican American who lives in two worlds at once—the world of her Mexican ancestry and heritage and the Anglo world all around her. A legal alien is a person who enters the United States via legal channels.

Quickwrite

Think of all the worlds you belong to: worlds of home, family, school, church, sports, friends. Make lists in which you cite at least three ways you feel or behave in two of your worlds. A sample is started below.

My Worlds	
School	Sports
Sometimes feel slow.	Feel special, successful, free.

Keep your notes. For questions and activities on this poem, see page 600.

Elements of Literature

Tone: Look at Word Choice

Bilingual, bicultural. These seem like innocent, OK things to be. But what follows in this poem is anything but calm. Look at the choice of words: *exotic, inferior, definitely different, alien.* These are disturbing words—deliberately chosen by Pat Mora to let you know how passionate she feels.

When you read, you can't see the writer's face or gestures. You can't hear the writer's voice. So writers have to make words do the job of showing you how they feel—of getting across their **tone**. Tone may be simple or complicated—and very changeable.

Tone is the attitude a writer takes toward the audience, the subject, or a character. Tone can be conveyed through the writer's choice of words.

For more on Tone, see pages 586–587 and the Handbook of Literary Terms.

Legal Alien

Pat Mora

Bi-lingual, Bi-cultural,
able to slip from "How's life?"
to *"Me'stan volviendo loca,"*
able to sit in a paneled office
5   drafting memos in smooth English,
able to order in fluent Spanish
at a Mexican restaurant,
American but hyphenated,
viewed by Anglos as perhaps exotic,
10 perhaps inferior, definitely different,
viewed by Mexicans as alien
(their eyes say, "You may speak
Spanish but you're not like me"),
an American to Mexicans
15 a Mexican to Americans
a handy token
sliding back and forth
between the fringes of both worlds
by smiling
20 by masking the discomfort
of being pre-judged
Bi-laterally.

Extranjera legal

Pat Mora

Bi-lingüe, bi-cultural,
capaz de deslizarse de *"How's life?"*
a "Me'stan volviendo loca",
capaz de ocupar un despacho bien apuntado,
5   redactando memorandums en inglés liso,
capaz de ordenar la cena en español fluido
en restaurante mexicano,
americana pero con guión,
vista por los anglos como exótica,
10 quizás inferior, obviamente distinta,
vista por mexicanos como extranjera
(sus ojos dicen "Hablas español
pero no eres como yo"),
americana para mexicanos
15 mexicana para americanos
una ficha servible
pasando de un lado al otro
de los márgenes de dos mundos
sonriéndome
20 disfrazando la incomodidad
del pre-juicio
bi-lateralmente.

MEET THE WRITER

Beyond Borders

Pat Mora (1942–   ) maintains that people's identities grow out of all the worlds they inhabit— the ones they inherit from the past as well as the ones they encounter as they go through life. Born and raised in the border town of El Paso, Texas, Mora has spent her life observing the interactions between Mexican and Anglo cultures. While never denying the painful side of bicultural existence, Mora stresses the harmonies between the cultures—harmonies that are the result of centuries of shared living.

Often inspired by the high-desert landscape of the Southwest as a source of renewal and connection, Mora finds differences between people less important than the things all cultures share— living, loving, marrying, raising children, working, growing old, and dying.

The poem "Legal Alien" is from *Chants* (1984), Mora's first book of poems. Her other books include *Communion* (1991), a book of poems; *Tomas and the Library Lady* (1989) and *A Birthday Basket for Tía* (1992), both children's books.

MAKING MEANINGS
LEGAL ALIEN/EXTRANJERA LEGAL

First Thoughts

1. How would you respond to these questions: How am I like or unlike the person in "Legal Alien"? What could we learn from each other?

Shaping Interpretations

2. How do Anglos view the speaker? How do Mexicans view her?

3. According to lines 20–22, what is the speaker "masking," or hiding?

4. In line 16, what two meanings of the word *token* is Mora suggesting?

5. Of the following adjectives, which two best describe the speaker's **tone** in this poem: *sad, impatient, understanding, critical, angry, amused, accepting*? Which particular words and phrases tip you off to the speaker's tone?

6. English and Spanish may have more in common than you think. Take a look at the Spanish version of "Legal Alien"—"Extranjera legal." List the words you recognize as similar to English words.

Connecting with the Text

7. The speaker says "American but hyphenated." What does she mean? What hyphenated words, if any, might describe your own identity?

8. Do you ever feel you are being prejudged? In what ways do people prejudge other people?

CHOICES: Building Your Portfolio

Writer's Notebook

1. Collecting Ideas for a Comparison/Contrast Essay

Looking at tones. One way to compare two texts is to look at how each uses a common element. Make a list of adjectives to describe the tones you hear in Hughes's poem on page 591 and in Mora's poem. Jot down details from each poem that contribute to that tone. Save your notes.

Creative Writing

2. Use Mora as a Model

Look at the notes you made for the Quickwrite on page 598. Use your notes and any additions as the basis of a poem of your own, about *your* worlds. Here is a framework you might want to use for your poem.

In the world of _____
I am _____.
In the world of _____
I am _____.
Some people think _____
But I am really _____.

Find specific things to say in your poem, as Mora does. Think also of your word choice: What tone do you want to give your poem? Create a suitable title for your poem.

BEFORE YOU READ
THE ROAD NOT TAKEN

Reading Focus

"If Only..."

"If only I'd been born a genius. Or staggeringly beautiful. Or fabulously talented or rich. Or made this decision instead of that one. Or had gone to a different school. Then my life would be different."

Quickwrite

Think of a turning point in your life (or in someone else's life)—moving to a new place, meeting a special person, learning a sport, changing your mind about something, having someone help you at the right time. Go back to that moment and pretend it never happened. Make notes on how you imagine your life might have been different if that turning point had never happened.

Keep your notes. For questions and activities on this poem, see pages 604–605.

Elements of Literature

Verbal Irony

Verbal irony is a contrast between what a writer or a speaker says and what is really meant. Verbal irony can range from gentle to sarcastic. Robert Frost is a master of the subtle uses of irony. Perhaps that's why he called "The Road Not Taken" a tricky poem. Read it several times and try to figure out exactly what Frost's attitude is about life and the choices we make.

Irony is the contrast between expectation and reality. In **verbal irony,** the writer or the speaker says one thing but really means something different.

For more on Irony, see pages 212–213 and the Handbook of Literary Terms.

For a biography of Robert Frost, see page 540.

The Road Not Taken

Robert Frost

Two roads diverged in a yellow wood,
And sorry I could not travel both
And be one traveler, long I stood
And looked down one as far as I could
5   To where it bent in the undergrowth;

Then took the other, as just as fair,
And having perhaps the better claim,
Because it was grassy and wanted wear;
Though as for that the passing there
10   Had worn them really about the same,

And both that morning equally lay
In leaves no step had trodden black.
Oh, I kept the first for another day!
Yet knowing how way leads on to way,
15   I doubted if I should ever come back.

I shall be telling this with a sigh
Somewhere ages and ages hence:
Two roads diverged in a wood, and I—
I took the one less traveled by,
20   And that has made all the difference.

Crossing Paths

Robert Frost

Robert Frost wrote this letter to the literary editor Susan Hayes Ward.

Plymouth, New Hampshire
10 February 1912

Dear Miss Ward:

. . . Two lonely crossroads that themselves cross each other I have walked several times this winter without meeting or overtaking so much as a single person on foot or on runners. The practically unbroken condition of both for several days after a snow or a blow proves that neither is much traveled. Judge then how surprised I was the other evening as I came down one to see a man, who to my own unfamiliar eyes and in the dusk looked for all the world like myself, coming down the other, his approach to the point where our paths must intersect being so timed that unless one of us pulled up we must inevitably collide. I felt as if I was going to meet my own image in a slanting mirror. Or say I felt as we slowly converged on the same point with the same noiseless yet laborious strides as if we were two images about to float together

with the uncrossing of someone's eyes. I verily expected to take up or absorb this other self and feel the stronger by the addition for the three-mile journey home. But I didn't go forward to the touch. I stood still in wonderment and let him pass by; and that, too, with the fatal omission of not trying to find out by a comparison of lives and immediate and remote interests what could have brought us by crossing paths to the same point in the wilderness at the same moment of nightfall. Some purpose I doubt not, if we could but have made it out. I like a coincidence almost as well as an incongruity. . . .

Nonsensically yours,

Robert Frost

MAKING MEANINGS
THE ROAD NOT TAKEN

First Thoughts

1. Are this speaker's feelings about the choices he's made in life familiar to you? Compare the speaker's thoughts with your Quickwrite notes.

Shaping Interpretations

2. Instead of roads through a garden or a wide open plain, why do you think the poet writes about roads that go through a wood? (Think about what the word *wood* suggests, as in the statement "We're not out of the woods yet.")

3. What do you think the speaker means when he says that he "kept" the first road for another day? How do we know that he realizes his choice of paths is utterly final?

4. Why do you think the speaker's choice "has made all the difference"?

5. How does Frost's speaker contradict himself in lines 8 through 10? In what other ways does this speaker **ironically** contradict himself?

6. Some adjectives that describe **tone** are listed below. Which adjectives would you choose to describe the tone of this poem? What words, phrases, or lines in the poem make you feel this tone? *Angry, awed, bitter, cynical, fearful, hopeful, ironic, playful, positive, puzzled, regretful, sad.*

Connecting with the Text

7. What might happen if someone chooses a "less traveled" road? Do you know people who have made choices like this—and people who have chosen well-traveled roads? What kinds of lives did they have?

8. Do you think people ever have a chance to go back and try another road? Talk about your responses. What decisions could you have made since you got up this morning that might have changed the course of your life? Are any life decisions harder to alter or reverse than others?

Challenging the Text

9. Talk over your responses to Frost's letter on page 603. What questions would you ask him if you were able to?

CHOICES: Building Your Portfolio

Writer's Notebook

1. Collecting Ideas for a Comparison/Contrast Essay

Looking for details.

When you compare and contrast poems (see the Writer's Workshop on page 614), you might want to talk about the form of each poem. Is one rhymed and written in meter? Is one written in free verse? How do the forms affect the way you respond to the poems? Take notes on the form of Frost's poem and of one other poem in these collections. Be specific in the details you gather.

> Form of "Hope Is the Thing . . ."
> 1. Written in meter.
> 2. Iambic (˘ ´).
> 3. Alternates 3 & 4 stresses a line.
> 4. Some lines rhyme at end.
> 5. Some half rhymes.
> 6. Can sing this poem to "The Yellow Rose of Texas."

Creative Writing

2. Your Own Road Poem

Think of another setting, another traveler (maybe a younger person, maybe a female), and another attitude toward life and all the roads life offers its travelers. Put all these details into your own road poem (maybe it's a Road Taken). Open with "Two roads diverged. . . ."

VOCABULARY   HOW TO OWN A WORD

Word Map

Diverge is a key word in Frost's poem. It looks like certain other words but has a different meaning. Here is a word map exploring *diverge*—what it means, examples of its use, and examples of its opposites. Use this vocabulary strategy to create similar word maps for these words: *diverge, divert, diverse, divulge,* and *divest.*

You might add to your word map an illustration for each word.

diverge

meanings
- move in different directions
- become different
- depart from some viewpoint

opposites
- run parallel
- meet

what things diverge?
- roads
- opinions
- careers
- lives
- lifestyles

BEFORE YOU READ
LUCINDA MATLOCK

Reading Focus

"It Takes Life"

Here is a message from beyond the grave from a very outspoken old woman. How do you feel about Lucinda's advice to the younger generation?

Quickwrite

Write a short speech for a person who is complaining about "kids today." Think manners, slang, music, grooming, eating habits, cars, video games, attitudes toward money and work.

Keep your notes. For questions and activities on this poem, see pages 608–609.

Elements of Literature

Dramatic Monologue

"Lucinda Matlock" is one of more than two hundred portraits created by Edgar Lee Masters in *Spoon River Anthology,* a book of **dramatic monologues** spoken by the dead in a small-town cemetery. These housewives, bankers, poets, druggists, losers, ministers, and laborers are "saying it" to anybody who will listen. And since the book's publication in 1915, hundreds of thousands of readers have listened intently.

A dramatic **monologue** is a poem in which a character speaks to one or more listeners. The reactions of the listener must be inferred by the reader.

All Had a Good Time (c. 1910). Wool on burlap hooked rug (17 ½″ × 45 ½″).

Shelburne Museum, Shelburne, Vermont. Photograph by Ken Burris.

Lucinda Matlock

Edgar Lee Masters

I went to the dances at Chandlerville,
And played snap-out at Winchester.
One time we changed partners,
Driving home in the moonlight of middle June,
5   And then I found Davis.
We were married and lived together for seventy years,
Enjoying, working, raising the twelve children,
Eight of whom we lost
Ere I had reached the age of sixty.
10   I spun, I wove, I kept the house, I nursed the sick,
I made the garden, and for holiday
Rambled over the fields where sang the larks,
And by Spoon River gathering many a shell
And many a flower and medicinal weed—
15   Shouting to the wooded hills, singing to the green valleys.
At ninety-six I had lived enough, that is all,
And passed to a sweet repose.
What is this I hear of sorrow and weariness,
Anger, discontent, and drooping hopes?
20   Degenerate sons and daughters,
Life is too strong for you—
It takes life to love Life.

MEET THE WRITER

Speaker from a Small Town

Edgar Lee Masters (1869–1950) wasn't afraid to look under the surface of small-town American life. His *Spoon River Anthology* was an enormous success but it angered many people. Although Masters lets many good people speak, he also lets us hear from people who are intolerant, small-minded, mean, and hypocritical. But the book outlived its attackers and is now considered a classic of American literature.

Born in Garnett, Kansas, and raised in Petersburg and Lewistown, Illinois, Edgar Lee Masters became a lawyer with a flourishing practice. The idea for *Spoon River Anthology* came to him after a visit from his mother reminded him of the people he grew up with.

By the time Masters died, *Spoon River Anthology* had been translated into at least eight languages, including Arabic, Korean, Czech, and Chinese. It has even been made into an opera.

Masters is now buried next to his grandparents, Squire Davis Masters and Lucinda Masters. "Lucinda Matlock" is based on his grandmother, who represented his ideal of the undaunted pioneer woman. The real Lucinda also gave birth to twelve children and lived a very long life.

MAKING MEANINGS
LUCINDA MATLOCK

First Thoughts

1. What do you think of this old woman's final words?

Shaping Interpretations

2. What adjectives would you choose to describe Matlock's **tone** in lines 1–17? What different adjectives best describe her tone in lines 18–22?

3. As Langston Hughes would put it, life for Lucinda Matlock "ain't been no crystal stair." Identify the details in the text that describe the blows and hardships Matlock has endured. Then pick out the details that depict her joys and pleasures.

4. What two meanings does the word *life* have in "It takes life to love Life"—the last line of the poem? Why do you suppose the second *Life* is capitalized?

5. How do you think Masters feels about his outspoken Lucinda?

Connecting with the Text

6. How many people do you know who go around "shouting to the wooded hills"? How does this startling image affect your feelings about this woman?

Challenging the Text

7. How fair is it for Lucinda Matlock to insist that other people deal with sorrow, weariness, anger, and depression the way she has dealt with them in her own life?

8. What kinds of Lucindas do you know in life today? Be sure to refer to your Quickwrite responses. What do you admire about these people? Do you have other feelings about them too?

Woman with Plants (1929) by Grant Wood. Oil on upsom board.

CHOICES: Building Your Portfolio

Writer's Notebook

1. Collecting Ideas for a Comparison/Contrast Essay

Looking at speakers. Take notes on the speakers you hear in various poems in these collections. Who are they? What do you think of them? What attitudes do you find in the words they speak? (Notice the strong contrast between Frost's speaker and the bold Lucinda.)

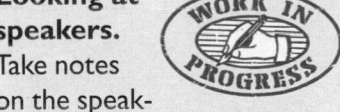

Speakers in "The Gift" and "Combing": Son/Mother. Loving, tender, caring. Both talk of passing on love from generation to generation.
Supporting details:
• a childhood memory; speaker remembers his father gently removing a splinter from his hand
• combing her daughter's hair, remembering her mother combing her hair

Creative Writing

2. A Dramatic Monologue in Response

What do you think of Lucinda's speech? In a paragraph (or a poem, if you like), respond to this voice from the old Spoon River cemetery. Open your own dramatic monologue with *I*. Be sure you make clear who your speaker is and where your speaker lives.

Creative Writing

3. Send a Letter Back

Lucinda Matlock probably died more than a hundred years ago—before there were movies, telephones, television, computers, cars, or even electric light. Write Lucinda a letter comparing and contrasting the details of her rural life and those of most people's lives today. Hint: Take each part of Matlock's story and think of how it would be different if it were happening today. For instance, it was probably a wagon drawn by horses that was being driven home in line 4. What would it be today? Have many people alive today been married for seventy years? Do many have twelve children? Why would it be unlikely today that eight of Matlock's children would die (as they did) before they were forty or so years old? Talk to Lucinda from your perch in time a hundred years later.

Interviewing

4. Class Oral History Project

With a group, form a class oral history collection. You could contribute a written, taped, or videotaped interview of an older person, possibly a relative or friend. Prepare your questions carefully; in fact, the person might appreciate seeing a copy of your questions in advance. Each interviewer should be sure to ask the subject how life was different in his or her youth from what life is like today. You may want to invite some of your subjects to present their histories directly to the class. Preserve your collection for future classes. You might even donate it to your local library or museum.

Research/Community Connections

5. How It Was

Museums around the country have exhibits showing American life as it was many years, even centuries, ago. Probably the most famous is the immigration museum on Ellis Island in New York City. Find out if there is a museum in your area. What does it focus on? How is it funded? Does it need volunteers? If you can, visit the museum and report on what you learn there.

Quickwrite

Before you read this speech, take some time to write down what you know about the history of women's rights in this country. Do you know that women had to struggle for some of the rights that everyone enjoys now? Write down any questions you have about that struggle.

Background

In 1852, a women's rights convention was held in Akron, Ohio. Various speakers, many of them members of the clergy, used the Bible to argue that men had superior rights and, moreover, that men held superior principles to those held by women. Sojourner Truth, who had not been invited, stood up and walked to the platform to attack those arguments. This is the speech she made. It is probably the only speech at that event that is still remembered today. Sojourner Truth knew what she wanted to say—and she said it!

Unfortunately, there is no exact copy of the speech in existence today. It has been adapted here in the form of a poem.

Sharecropper (1970) by Elizabeth Catlett. Woodcut.
Courtesy of the Evans-Tibbs Collection, Washington, D.C.

Ain't I a Woman?

Sojourner Truth

That man over there say
    a woman needs to be helped into carriages
and lifted over ditches
    and to have the best place everywhere.
5   Nobody ever helped me into carriages
    or over mud puddles
        or gives me a best place. . . .

And ain't I a woman?
    Look at me
10   Look at my arm!
    I have plowed and planted
and gathered into barns
    and no man could head me. . . .
And ain't I a woman?
15   I could work as much
and eat as much as a man—
    when I could get to it—
and bear the lash as well
    and ain't I a woman?
20   I have borne 13 children
    and seen most all sold into slavery
and when I cried out a mother's grief
    none but Jesus heard me . . .
and ain't I a woman?
25   that little man in black there say
a woman can't have as much rights as a man
    cause Christ wasn't a woman
Where did your Christ come from?
    From God and a woman!
30   Man had nothing to do with him!
    If the first woman God ever made
was strong enough to turn the world
    upside down, all alone
together women ought to be able to turn it
35   rightside up again.

MEET THE WRITER

Up and Down the Land

Sojourner Truth (c. 1797–1883) was born in slavery in Ulster County, New York, and was named Isabella. Just before New York State abolished slavery in 1827, she was sold to a man named Isaac van Wagener, who gave her her freedom.

Isabella and her two youngest children moved in 1829 to New York City where she worked as a servant until 1843. Then she had a vision that changed her life. According to her own testimony, God instructed her to take the name Sojourner Truth and "travel up and down the land," spreading a message against slavery and in favor of women's rights.

That's exactly what she did, and her speeches drew huge crowds, whether she was an invited speaker or, as was often the case, a zealous impromptu preacher.

Sophiia Smith Collection, Smith College, Northampton, Massachusetts.

In the 1850s, Sojourner Truth settled in Battle Creek, Michigan. When the Civil War broke out, she gathered supplies for African American volunteer regiments. In 1864, Abraham Lincoln received her at the White House. A painting that records that meeting is below.

FINDING COMMON GROUND

How might Sojourner Truth update her speech "Ain't I a Woman?" for today? Meet in groups to discuss these questions and report on your answers.

1. Who might her audience be? What issues might she choose to address?

2. How do you think she would feel about the lives of women today? Look at your own community and school. What progress would she notice? What would she like to see changed?

3. Rewrite the speech in prose or verse. Use your own words but remember that you are writing as Sojourner Truth, from her point of view.

The Schomberg Center for Research in Black Culture/New York Public Library.

READ ON

Distant Times and Remote Places

Ever read any African chants, European lullabies, or American Indian myths set to verse? If you'd like to, *Talking to the Sun* (The Metropolitan Museum of Art/Henry Holt) is the place to start. The collection is full of art from New York's Metropolitan Museum of Art and poetry from all over the world.

Almost There

Discover some of the best of Robert Frost's poetry in *You Come Too: Favorite Poems for Young Readers—Robert Frost* (Henry Holt). In poems like "Christmas Tree" and "Hyla Brook," Frost brings to life the trees, mountains, cliffs, dirt roads, old fences, grassy fields, and abandoned houses of his part of New England. Reading his work, you'll almost believe you're there—in the woods or at the edge of the brook.

All Twisted Up

Drumbeats, dreamers, and skyscrapers—those are the stuff of Carl Sandburg's poetry. In *Harvest Poems: 1910–1960* (Harcourt Brace) you'll find everyday subjects described in everyday language—but it all sounds brand new. Sandburg's poems appeal to everyday people but are in no way ordinary.

The Spoken Word

Julie Harris won a Tony Award for her portrayal of Emily Dickinson in the Broadway play *The Belle of Amherst*. You can listen to her interpretation of Dickinson's letters and poems on audiotape. *The Poems and Letters of Emily Dickinson* (HarperCollins/Caedmon) contains forty-eight minutes of Harris as Dickinson—reciting her most famous poems and most personal correspondence.

Writer's Workshop

EXPOSITORY WRITING

COMPARISON-CONTRAST ESSAY

How is football like soccer? How are you different from your best friend, and what do you have in common? You answer questions like these all the time. Without being aware of it, you're comparing and contrasting. Your ability to recognize similarities (compare) and differences (contrast) is what lets you recognize your dog in a roomful of dogs, or define a word, or explain how the Civil War was different from all other American wars. In this workshop you'll compare two poems and write an essay discussing their similarities and their differences. A comparison-contrast essay is one kind of expository writing—writing that explains or gives information. Remember:

- *Comparing* means "seeing similarities."

- *Contrasting* means "seeing differences."

- *Comparing* is often used to mean both comparing and contrasting.

Prewriting

1. Choose Two Poems

You should already have some notes on comparing and contrasting various poems. Pull your notes out now to see if you'd like to develop any of your notes into an essay. The poems you compare might have similar subjects or themes. They might have similar figures of speech. They might even be written by the same person. The important thing is to find two poems with something in common. The next important thing is to find poems you want to write about.

If you don't feel satisfied with the notes you've been taking, try these strategies:

- Review the poems in these collections. Briefly list the subjects of all the poems you've read. Which poems are about similar subjects?

- Look at the titles of the collections of poems. Under each title you should be able to find poems with similar themes or concerns.

ASSIGNMENT

Write an essay comparing and contrasting two poems. Choose any two poems that are alike in at least one important way.

AIM

To give information.

AUDIENCE

Your classmates and teacher, other English classes, readers of a magazine of student writing. (You choose.)

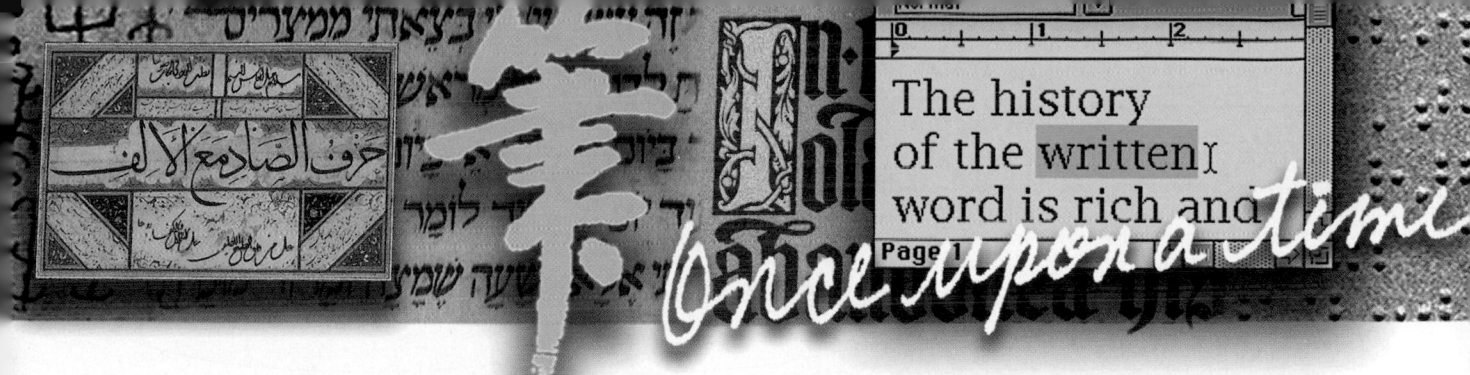

ARLO AND JANIS reprinted by permission of Newspaper Enterprise Association, Inc.

- Look at the sections called Elements of Literature. Clustered around these sections you should find poems that make prominent use of the same element.

2. Find the Features

Once you have your poems, look closely at the features you'll compare. A **feature** is a part that you can examine and talk about separately from the whole. If you were a dog breeder, for instance, you might compare dogs by these features: type of breed, size, color of coat, body shape, and special abilities. In this workshop you'll use the elements of poetry (such as **subject, speaker, figures of speech, imagery, sound effects, tone**) as your main features. Your essay will focus on how each poem you choose uses one or more features.

EXAMPLES

- Shakespeare's "The Seven Ages of Man" and Dickinson's "'Hope' Is the Thing with Feathers" both begin with a metaphor that extends throughout the poem.

- "Daily" and "When I Heard the Learn'd Astronomer" both express tones of awe and wonder and joy.

- "Lucinda Matlock" and "Women" are both about courageous women.

3. Analyze Both Poems and Take Notes

Analysis is the thinking skill that breaks a whole into its parts and examines each part separately. One reading isn't enough to analyze a poem. Re-read each poem you're comparing until you feel you understand it and can discuss each of its major elements.

One way to collect details to support your main idea is to use a Venn diagram like the one below. This will help you focus on all the ways the poems are different and on the important features they share.

4. Organize Your Information

Think of the details you've collected as building blocks of information. You can build the essay's body in either of two ways. Use the one that feels more comfortable to you.

- **Block method.** First, you say *everything* you have to say about poem 1. Then you say *everything* you have to say about poem 2. Discuss the features in the same order for both poems. (The student model on the next page, which compares and contrasts two stories, uses the block method.)

- **Point-by-point method.** You discuss the *features* one at a time. First, you might talk about sound effects in poem 1; then you talk about sound effects in poem 2. Next, you might discuss imagery in poem 1 and go on to discuss imagery in poem 2. You follow this same neat and tidy organization in discussing each feature.

5. Write a Thesis Statement

Are the two texts more alike than different? In what ways? Write a **thesis statement,** a summary of what you've discovered.

EXAMPLE

Naomi Nye's poem "Daily" and Walt Whitman's poem "When I Heard the Learn'd Astronomer" both communicate tones of awe and wonder and joy, but Nye's poem is very domestic while Whitman goes cosmic.

Drafting

1. A Formula for a Comparison/Contrast Essay

Like all essays, a comparison/contrast essay has three basic parts:

- The **introduction** captures the reader's attention, identifies the two works by title and author, and provides background information if the works are new to the reader. The thesis statement usually appears in the introductory paragraph.

- The **body** discusses at least two features, using either the block method or the point-by-point method of organization. Specific details, facts, examples, and quotations support your statements.

Characters in "Snow" and "Thank You, M'am"

When I first read "Snow" and "Thank You, M'am," I didn't really see any similarities in any of the characters. But after re-reading both stories, I realize that there are actually more similarities than differences in the characters.

Mrs. Luella Bates Washington Jones, a character in "Thank You, M'am," is a very caring and sincere person. When Roger tries to steal her pocketbook, she could have him arrested, but instead she takes him home with her, makes him dinner, and talks to him, which I think is very kind of her. She doesn't ask any embarrassing questions, so he won't feel uncomfortable. She tells him that she can understand how he wanted to steal money to buy shoes. She says that she too wanted things. Because of his talk with Mrs. Jones, I don't think Roger will ever steal again. Mrs. Jones isn't just a person to talk to. She is more than that. She makes Roger feel accepted by inviting him into her home. I know Roger feels comfortable with Mrs. Jones because he has every opportunity to run away but he doesn't.

The experience Yolanda has with her teacher Sister Zoe in the story "Snow" is similar to Roger's experience with Mrs. Jones. Sister Zoe is very motherly. She tries to make Yolanda feel accepted when she is the only immigrant in her class. She takes the time to tutor Yolanda when she doesn't have to. She also teaches Yolanda new words. Both women have the same basic effect on the children.

Sister Zoe and Mrs. Jones are also different. Though they both make significant differences in the lives of two young people, they go about it in two different ways. In the few hours Mrs. Jones is with Roger, I feel she may have given him a new outlook on life, whereas the change in Yolanda is gradual, over a long period of time. The changes are made in different ways by different people.

Though Sister Zoe and Mrs. Jones are different, they have many similar traits, and I feel they both changed the lives of two young people. I wonder how different Yolanda's and Roger's lives would have been without Sister Zoe and Mrs. Jones.

—Jessica Preston
Hamden High School
Hamden, Connecticut

Identifies the works and makes a general statement about the characters.

Introduces first character. Block method.

Supplies supporting details.

Second character is introduced. Supplies supporting details.

Sums up how characters are alike. Shows differences as well as similarities between the characters.

Conclusion adds a personal note.

• The **conclusion,** usually a single paragraph, summarizes the essay's main ideas or adds a final thought to close the essay.

2. Say It Clearly; Back It Up

A comparison/contrast essay has a formal, objective tone, but that doesn't mean you need to use long words and complicated sentences. As you draft your essay, concentrate on expressing your ideas clearly (see the Sentence Workshop on page 620). Eliminate padding, unnecessary repetition, and vague words.

Evaluating and Revising

Share your paper with your writing group or with a partner. Ask your reader(s) to focus especially on these points:

1. What organization did I use? Is it clear?

2. What are the features I used for comparison? Are they clear?

3. Can you follow everything I've said? Do you have questions?

Proofreading

Before you proofread, check your proofreading log to make sure you don't miss the same old spelling and grammar mistakes. If you're using a computer, run the spelling and grammar checkers. Be careful to use the correct forms of comparison and avoid making double comparisons.

Publishing

• If you're pleased with your essay, submit it to a magazine that publishes student writing.

• Meet with others who've compared the same two poems you did, and discuss your findings. See if you can reach a consensus about similarities and differences to present to the rest of the class.

• If you've written about poems the class hasn't read, read the poems aloud and then read your paper aloud.

• Put all the class essays in a Comparison/Contrast folder to share with other English classes or with parents at a Back-to-School Night.

Reflecting

If you include this essay in your portfolio, date it and write a brief reflection on your writing experience:

1. What do I like best about my essay? What part or parts am I less satisfied with? Why?

2. Did writing the essay increase my understanding of the text?

3. Which part of the writing assignment was easiest for me? Which part was most difficult? Why?

Sentence Workshop
H E L P

Revising sentences for structure and length: page 620.

Communications Handbook
H E L P

Taking notes and documenting sources: pages 983-984.

Revision Model

Peer Comments

Sister Zoe and Mrs. Jones
~~The two characters are also differ-~~
                        ∧

make significant differences in the lives of two
ent. Though they both ~~affect~~ young
                        ∧

people, they go about it in two

different ways. In the few hours

I feel
Mrs. Jones is with Roger, she helps
                        ∧

may have given him a new outlook on life,
~~him a lot~~, whereas the change in
                        ∧

Yolanda is gradual, over a long

made in
period of time. The changes are
                        ∧

ways by different people.
different ~~in each case.~~
        ∧

        Though Sister Zoe and Mrs.

many
Jones are different, they have
                        ∧

similar traits, and I feel they both

changed the lives of two young

*I wonder how different Yolanda's
and Roger's lives would have been
without Sister Zoe and Mrs. Jones.*
people.
    ∧

Be more specific. Use names.

How exactly did she help him?

What makes the cases different?

Can you come up with a more powerful ending?

I think I found my own unique way of looking at the two texts, and I made interesting connections between them. However, looking back, I realize that my essay would have benefited from quotations from both texts. Quotations would have helped me support my ideas.

Sentence Workshop

Language Handbook HELP

See Sentence Structure, page 1010.

Technology HELP

See Language Workshop CD-ROM. *Key word entry: sentence.*

REVISING SENTENCES: STRUCTURE AND LENGTH

Professional writers vary their sentences to create a pleasing rhythm and to keep readers interested. They write short sentences and long ones. They open their sentences with subjects or with modifying phrases and clauses. The possibilities are almost endless. (Writer Jay McInerney says that every sentence is potentially revisable in thirty directions!) Think of sentences as falling into four basic types:

1. **Simple** (one independent clause)
2. **Compound** (two or more independent clauses combined)
3. **Complex** (one independent clause combined with one dependent clause)
4. **Compound-complex** (two or more independent clauses combined with one or more dependent clauses)

Below are examples of sentences from the work of professional writers. (The slash marks divide the clauses.)

1. "Drifting down the river of grass, Billie Wind could see the sun and the water and soils at work." [simple sentence, opens with a participial phrase]

    —Jean Craighead George, *The Talking Earth*

2. "They had won, / but they were weary and bleeding." [compound sentence]

    —George Orwell, *Animal Farm*

3. "When they were arranging him for his last rest, / they found upon his bosom a small, plain miniature-case, opening with a spring." [complex sentence, opens with a dependent clause]

    —Harriet Beecher Stowe, *Uncle Tom's Cabin*

Writer's Workshop Follow-up: Revision

Read aloud your comparison/contrast essay. Do the sentences have a pleasing rhythm? Do they vary or are many of them put together the same way? Try combining some simple sentences into compound ones. Would a short dramatic sentence add emphasis?

Try It Out

1. Model the professional sentences at the right: That is, write a sentence of your own that imitates the structure of each professional example. When you have completed your own sentences, go back to them and rewrite each one so that it opens in a different way—or becomes two short punchy sentences. Compare your sentences in class.

2. Rewrite the following paragraph to give it variety.

    I got lost on the way to Corky's shop. She sells magnets at her shop. I wanted to buy a magnet for Grandma Trumble. She has a collection of magnets on her refrigerator. I thought this would be a short trip. It took two hours. I bought a dolphin magnet. Grandma Trumble loves dolphins.

LEARNING FOR LIFE

Music and Change

Problem

Poetry is in the air—and on the airwaves. Popular music is big business in the United States. What do the lyrics of this century's popular songs reveal about American society?

Project

With the approval of your teacher, investigate the century's most popular songs and determine what they reveal about our country's tastes in music and its changing concerns and values.

Preparation

1. Working with a partner or a small group, decide how you'll divide up these tasks:

   • determining the most popular song of each decade—1901–1910, 1911–1920, and so on

   • finding recordings of the songs

2. Identify possible resources for your project such as

   • anthologies of popular music

   • songbooks

   • newspaper and magazine articles

Procedure

1. Find out which song was most popular in each decade. For the early decades of the century, look at sales of sheet music. For later decades, look at sales of records, tapes, and CDs.

2. Find the lyrics and the music of the most popular song of each decade, and make notes. Pay special attention to the songs' use of

   • imagery

   • figures of speech

   • sound effects

   • tone

3. Decide what each song says and why it was so popular at the time. To do this, think about what you know of the decade from other sources, such as

   • books and movies set in the same time

   • history and social studies classes

   • stories you've heard from friends and family

Presentation

Do one of the following activities (or another that your teacher approves).

1. Found Poem

Present your findings in a poem of your own. You could combine snatches of lyrics from each of the songs in chronological order. Give your poem an original title and read it to the rest of the class or submit it to the school paper.

2. Musical Medley

Create a musical medley by combining soundtracks of the songs. Write a brief introduction and conclusion to your soundtrack. Give the tape to a senior citizens' center or a retirement residence.

3. Time-Line Wall Display

With a group of classmates, create a wall display of the hit songs and major events of the century. (Be sure to plan your design before you begin.) Put your display in your school's lobby or a hallway, along with cards on which viewers can write their responses.

Processing

What did you learn about twentieth-century American society by doing this project? Write a brief reflection for your portfolio.

Modern Drama

*What does theater give us that nothing else can—
not so intensely anyway, or so pleasurably?
It gives us human beings in three dimensions:
bodies that live in front of us, that move, speak,
change shape, create tension, or bestow peace.*

—Margo Jefferson

Ann Mabrey as Helen Keller and Sarah Prud-Homme
as Annie Sullivan, in a performance of *The Miracle Worker*
at the Virginia Museum Theatre in Richmond in 1967.

A Writer on Writing Plays

WILLIAM GIBSON
TALKS ABOUT
THE MIRACLE WORKER

*The following comments about
The Miracle Worker were made by
playwright William Gibson the night that
a film version of his famous play was
scheduled for a rerun on TV.*

Gibson:

Tonight at eight on NBC, *The Miracle Worker* will be broadcast in
its second television incarnation. Set in 1887, the play recounts
the critical events in the first months of Annie Sullivan's struggle
to teach the young deaf, mute, and blind Helen Keller how to
communicate with the rest of humanity. Its first telecast was live.
I wrote that version twenty-three summers ago when *all* television was live, rehearsal time was scant, unwritten pages were
improvised, actors went blank over missing props, cameras
photographed each other, and everything was sprightlier. So, for
example, our first chance to hear the score was in dress rehearsal,
violins sobbing away in another studio piped in to us in the control
booth; our director, Arthur Penn, groaned, "This music is killing
us!" and an hour later on the air was—unbeknownst to the
musicians giving their all—dialing most of it out ad lib. . . .

No such misadventures will occur in tonight's filmed production. This cast rehearsed in Los Angeles for three weeks, played
on stage in Palm Beach for two, and went back to the Coast for
another month of filming. But one surprise, for audiences who

two decades ago saw Patty Duke as young Helen Keller, may be that she grew up to portray her teacher Annie; her pupil now is played by Melissa Gilbert, at age fifteen, a most familiar figure to viewers of *Little House on the Prairie*.

I never thought much of the play, till last year. My opinion is hardly objective; after opening night, I can't stand any of my plays and do my best to avoid seeing them. With *The Miracle Worker* I got trapped in venality.[1] I wrote it a second time as a stage play, and a third time as a movie; the present teleplay is my fourth trek through it. My favorite editions now are in those exotic languages I can't tell front from back of. Last year I saw it in Afrikaans, couldn't comprehend a word, and for the first time thought it looked like a real play—by somebody else. . . .

What makes for a hit is always an enigma,[2] but one element certainly is common ground between the writer and his audience. The author of *The Miracle Worker* believed in children, was young, energetic, incorrigibly[3] optimistic, no stranger to the "uplift-ing" in life; these are not objection-able qualities, and they flowed naturally into the script.

And it was obviously a love letter. To whom, I would learn later. I like to fall a little in love with my heroines, and the title—from Mark Twain, who said, "Helen is a miracle, and Miss Sullivan is the miracle worker"—was meant to show where my affections lay. This stubborn girl of twenty, who six years earlier could not write her name, and in one month salvaged Helen's soul, and lived thereafter in its shadow, seemed to me to deserve a star bow.

Patty Duke and Melissa Gilbert in *The Miracle Worker* on NBC in 1979.

1. **venality** (vi·nal′ə·tē): willingness to waste one's talents for financial gain.
2. **enigma** (i·nig′mə): something puzzling.
3. **incorrigibly** (in·kôr′ə·jə·blē): in a way that cannot be corrected.

Elements of Drama

by Robert Anderson

Eugene O'Neill, America's first great playwright, said that a play should reveal the most intense basic human interrelationships. Perhaps this is why, over the years, so many playwrights have written about families. Probably nowhere else do we find such intense feelings as those we find within the family.

Even the happiest families have conflicts, great and small. Parents have dreams for their children. Children have dreams of their own. Children need to belong to the family and to feel its support; they also need to be independent. Families feel the strains from living closely together. Families face the problems of aging. The conflicts in a family range from mild, funny blowups to battles royal which break families apart.

Conflict: The Basis of Drama

Let's imagine a typical family situation:

The Nortons have just finished dinner. Then Sara starts the trouble: She tells her brother that she's going to ask for the family car tonight. Her brother, knowing that Sara disobeyed her parents and kept the car out too late the night before, feels a sense of dread and warns Sara not to ask for it. But Sara is going ahead. It is important to her. She fears she'll lose her friends if she can't drive them—she *promised*.

Here we have all the elements for the beginning of a drama. One character, Sara, expresses a want. ("I want the car.") She is our protagonist. A **protagonist** is generally the person who drives the action, who has the want, who takes the step to get what she (or he) wants. Sara has something at stake (her friends), and there is an obstacle in her way—her parents (the **antagonists**) and their probable refusal to let her have the car.

In dramatic terms, then, we have the **exposition**—the presentation of the characters and their basic situation; we have the foreshadowing, or suggestions, of a **conflict** (Sara's brother has asked her not to ask for the car); and we have a basic **dramatic question:** "Will Sara get what she wants?"

Sara goes to her ally, her mother, and tells her that she wants the car. Her mother says no: The roads are slick with ice. Then, in irritation, the mother adds something else: She doesn't care for Sara's friends.

The protagonist has now taken her first step and has met an obstacle and an unexpected **complication:** She's discovered that her mother doesn't like her friends.

Sara ignores what her brother and mother say (as the protagonist, she has to, if we're to have a story) and she asks her father.

Now we are moving toward the drama's **climax**—that moment when our tension and emotions are at a peak, when we watch the characters engage in the final struggle that is going to determine the **resolution** of the problem. (In cowboy movies this is the moment of the big shootout on Main Street.)

Sara makes her request. The battle begins. Her father not only says no because the roads are bad, but he goes on to reveal other feelings; he says that Sara is showing poor judgment and has become irresponsible. Under the pressure of the situation, Mr. Norton, like Mrs. Norton, reveals what he never would have said under other circumstances.

Now an argument may follow. The mother at first sides with the father; then she starts to defend her daughter. The brother may run away from the argument, or join in on Sara's side. "You don't understand her. You don't understand either of us." Blowup. Tears. The pressure-cooker situation has exposed all the characters to themselves and to one another. Sara storms out of the house. The question asked at the beginning of the story is answered: Sara does *not* get the car. In most homes the daughter would return and some compromise would be worked out. In a serious drama Sara might be gone forever.

During the working out of the conflict in this family story, something else has taken place. Relationships have changed. Relationships and what happens to them are one of the main elements of a play. Sara, who always thought her parents trusted her, finds out what they really think.

Characters We Care About

Writing about the family can help the playwright with a basic task—to organize the emotions of the audience, to arouse our interest or sympathy for one or more of the characters. (In the old melodramas, where there were real, detestable villains, writers organized the emotions of the audience very simply: Early in the play they would turn the audience against the villain by having him kick a dog.)

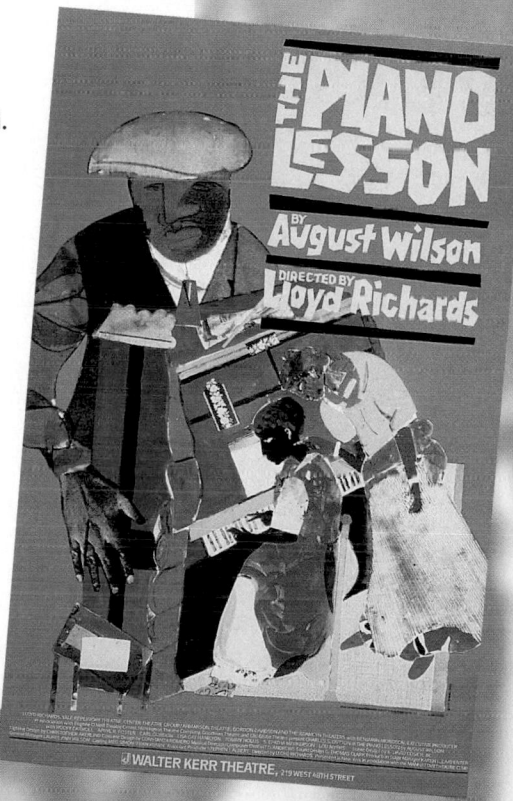

Poster courtesy of Triton Gallery/Courtesy Estate of Romare Bearden, ACA Galleries/New York and Munich.

Scene from *I Never Sang for My Father.*

We are all more or less familiar with the "cast of characters" in families. Though these characters are as unique as thumbprints, they are all as similar as thumbs. When my play *I Never Sang for My Father* was produced, I received letters from people asking questions like "How did you know my father?" Of course, I didn't know *their* fathers, but I knew my own. Thus playwrights may write out of feelings for their own particular family, and if they write truly, they sometimes achieve a universality. They may make the audience understand something about all families.

This, of course, is one of the aims of art—to reveal the universal through the particular. The characters in plays may seem larger than life, but they are not bizarre, theatrical creatures. The great plays are able to revitalize the familiar. They help us to see our own lives in perspective—our own parents, our own wives or husbands, our own friends. Playwrights strike notes from their own feelings and experiences, and they hope for a responsive chord from the audience.

The "Shock of Recognition"

A play, then, actually exists halfway between the stage and the audience. By choosing the familiar ground of the family, the playwright sometimes finds it easier to reach an audience. Spectators in the theater are often doing two things at once: They are watching a play on the stage, and at the same time they are relating to their own experiences. They are feeling what is known as the shock of recognition. *"How did you know my father?"*

The two plays in this book dramatize conflicts within the general framework of the family. They examine easily recognized situations about which hundreds of plays, films, and television dramas have been written. In *The Miracle Worker* there is a family with a severely handicapped child and an outsider who comes to help. In *Romeo and Juliet* there are the two young lovers who will marry despite all obstacles. In the case of *Romeo and Juliet,* the protagonists' obstacle is an old feud between their families. In more modern plays based on this situation, the obstacles might be race, religion, or class, as in the musical version of Shakespeare's play—the Bernstein-Sondheim-Laurents *West Side Story.*

PLAYBILL®

THE BOOTH THEATRE

Having Our Say

"Is It True?"

While playwrights write out of what they know, out of what concerns them, probably very little of their work is strictly autobiographical. The Nobel Prize–winning novelist William Faulkner said that a writer needs experience, observation, and imagination. Writers rarely limit themselves to re-creating an actual person as a character in a play. Playwrights may base a character on a person they know, but then they invent and expand to suit the needs of the story. Painters may use models for poses or outlines, but after a while they become more interested in what is on the canvas. Artists develop their paintings so that they may end up scarcely resembling the original model.

An example of a dramatist who expanded and invented to suit the particular aims of each play was Eugene O'Neill. He used his family as the basis for two plays: the comic and sentimental play called *Ah, Wilderness!* and the tragic play called *Long Day's Journey into Night.* The same family—very different plays!

Drama Is a Verb

The dynamic, or drive, of each play in this book is the same: People we care about struggle through crucial situations because they have something important at stake. Note the word *struggle. Drama* is, in a sense, a verb. Drama should involve action, and that action can be verbal or physical. In our Norton family story, the action was verbal, as each person in the family tried to achieve his or her ends with words. (The gunfight in the dusty Western town at high noon would be physical action.)

A Playwright's Concerns: Feeling, Story, and Form

When playwrights sit down to write plays, they have many things to consider. First, they must decide if their feeling about the material is strong enough. Will it hold their interest for the time it takes to write the play—which might be as long as three years? Will they be able to convey their excitement or humor or emotion to an audience? Mildness is a curse in the theater, and playwrights have to decide if the feelings they are communicating will have a strong impact.

Next, playwrights must ask whether the story they want to tell is dramatic. Does it involve interesting people in a conflict which moves to a crisis and a climax?

Finally, playwrights must consider the form in which they'll write. Probably most of us are more aware of form in painting than in

writing. We know that a picture may be painted in the more or less realistic style of a Rembrandt or in the impressionistic style of a Monet or in the cubist style of a Picasso.

In somewhat the same way, the story of a play can be told in various forms. It can be told in a conventional straightforward way (often called linear style), with a beginning, a middle, and an end, presented in chronological order. Or the story can move back and forth in time, with such devices as flashbacks or dream sequences. One contemporary play, *Betrayal* by Harold Pinter, actually begins at the end of the story and ends at the beginning.

The two plays in this book—*The Miracle Worker* and *Romeo and Juliet*—are more or less conventional in their form. They tell their stories from beginning to end. *The Miracle Worker* uses some memory flashbacks in which we hear the voices that Annie remembers from her childhood. Otherwise, the play moves ahead in a straightforward chronological manner.

Although these two plays are different in style and tone, the shock of recognition awaits you in each. See how these particular characters and their conflicts reveal truths that are still important today. See if you ask: "How did that writer know *my* family?"

Manuscript of *Our Town* by Thornton Wilder, showing author's revisions.

The Yale Collection of American Literature, Beinecke Rare Book and Manuscript Library, Yale University, New Haven.

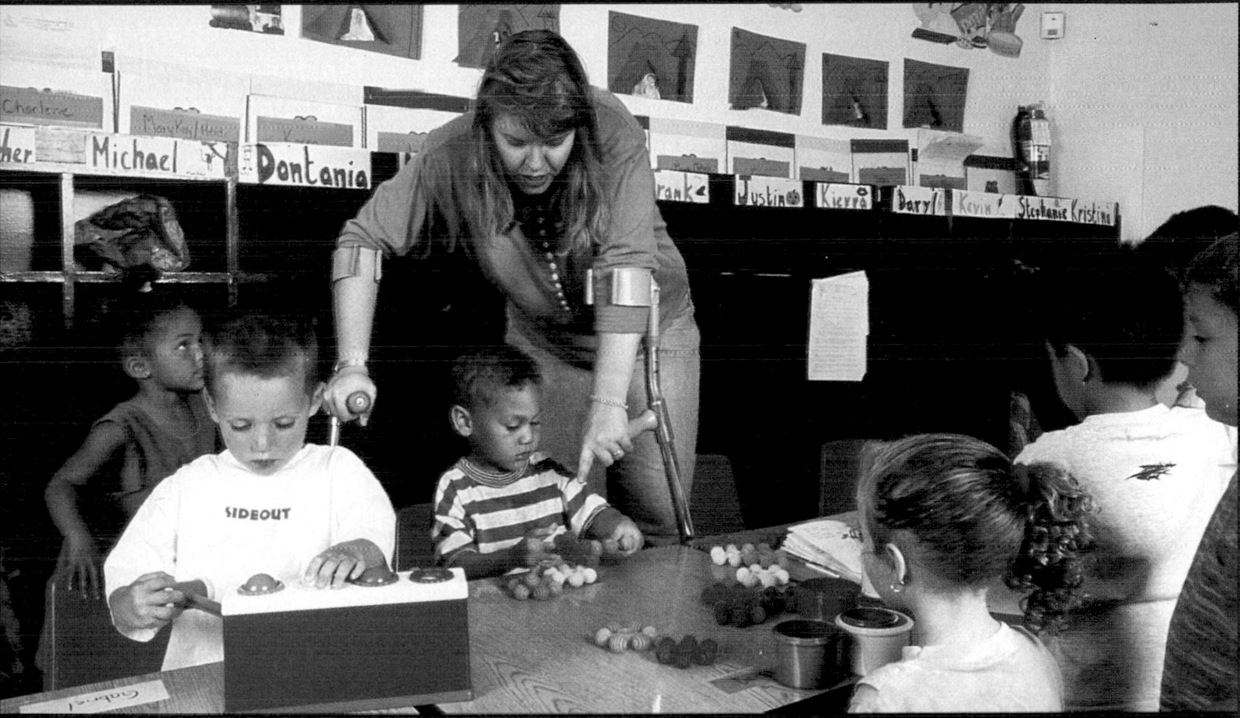

We come across many doors in a lifetime—doors into relationships, responsibilities, opportunities. If life is easy, the doors all open smoothly. If life is more difficult, we find that some doors require a lot of effort to open—some stay locked and bolted no matter how we pound at them. Often, even with those doors we struggle to open, we aren't really sure what we'll find on the other side.

But sometimes opening a door can change our lives. In this play, which is based on a true story, a young teacher tries to open a door that will give a little girl a fully human life. Behind the door, the little girl is locked out of the world of words. Behind that door, Helen is totally alone.

A journey of a thousand miles must begin with a single step.

—Laotzu

Writer's Notebook

In the Writer's Workshop on page 716 you'll write an interpretation of *The Miracle Worker*. Before you start reading the play, think about its title and the theme of this collection: Opening Doors. In a few words, give your first impressions of what the title might mean and how it might relate to "opening doors." Save your notes.

THE MIRACLE WORKER: BACKGROUND

Young Helen Keller.

William Gibson's *The Miracle Worker*, a true story, is based on the early life of the blind and deaf Helen Keller and of her teacher, Annie Sullivan. The play was first presented in 1957 on a **CBS** television program called *Playhouse 90*, which fostered excellent work by many of the emerging young playwrights of the period.

William Gibson later expanded his teleplay into the full-length stage play we have here, which opened on Broadway on October 10, 1959. The play retains the fluid quality of its original television form: Short, highly dramatic scenes flow into one another, each scene developing conflicts and crises and decisions that move the story into the next scene.

Note particularly the arresting opening scene—evidence of the play's original television form. With no preparation, we are immediately hooked by the family crisis. The play plunges us at once into a desperate situation with "She can't see! . . . She can't hear . . . !" One of the principles of television writing is that you have to capture the attention of the viewers immediately, or they will turn to another channel.

Annie Sullivan arriving at the Kellers' house, in a 1967 stage production in Richmond, Virginia.

A playwright tells a story by letting us hear what characters say and by letting us watch what they do. This play is an outstanding example of the use of theatrical activity and action. **Activity** is simply any movement on stage: picking up a cup, closing a door. **Action** is dramatically meaningful activity, which helps to move the story forward or which deepens our understanding of characters or of their relationships. A man may close the door just to

Annie spelling into Helen's hand, in the movie.

close the door, or he may close the door to keep someone from leaving the room. The first is activity; the second is action.

Because this play deals with a main character who cannot speak or hear, much of the action must be worked out in physical activity, which is indicated in the long stage directions. Anyone reading what Annie and Helen are expected to do on stage should not be surprised to hear that the actresses who played their roles found the physical exertion exhausting. During the Broadway production, Helen and Annie had to wear padding under their clothing to protect themselves from each other's blows.

Throughout the play, Annie hears voices from her past. In the stage production, these voices that haunt Annie were taped and amplified. Speakers placed on the side walls of the theater projected the voices with an echo effect that sounded ghostly and otherworldly. The result was that the people in the theater seemed to hear the voices and their disturbing echo effect in the same way that Annie heard them.

The Miracle Worker was made into an Academy Award–winning movie and later was turned back into a television play. This time, on television, Patty Duke, who originally played the child Helen on stage, played the part of Annie. Anne Bancroft originated the part of Annie Sullivan on Broadway.

Helen and Annie at the pump, in the NBC television movie.

"She is like a little safe,
locked, that no one can open.
Perhaps there is a treasure inside."

THE *Miracle* WORKER

WILLIAM GIBSON

Most of the photographs that illustrate the play are from the film version starring Patty Duke as Helen and Anne Bancroft as Annie.

The photographs on pages 645, 683, and 703 are from the Broadway production of the play.

The playing space is divided into two areas by a more or less diagonal line, which runs from downstage right to upstage left.

The area behind this diagonal is on platforms and represents the Keller house; inside we see, down right, a family room, and up center, elevated, a bedroom. On stage level near center, outside a porch, there is a water pump.

The other area, in front of the diagonal, is neutral ground; it accommodates various places as designated at various times—the yard before the Keller home, the Perkins Institution for the Blind, the garden house, and so forth.

The less set there is, the better. The stage should be free, airy, unencumbered by walls. Apart from certain practical items—such as the pump, a window to climb out of, doors to be locked—locales should be only skeletal suggestions, and the movement from one to another should be accomplishable by little more than lights.

Characters

A Doctor
Kate, *Helen's mother*
Keller, *Helen's father*
Helen
Martha
Percy } *children of servants*
Aunt Ev
James, *Captain Keller's son by his first marriage*
Anagnos, *Director of the Perkins Institution for the Blind, in Boston*
Annie Sullivan
Viney, *a servant*
Blind Girls
A Servant
Offstage Voices

Time: *The 1880s.*
Place: *In and around the Keller homestead in Tuscumbia, Alabama; also, briefly, the Perkins Institution for the Blind, in Boston.*

Act ONE

SCENE 1

It is night over the Keller homestead.

Inside, three adults in the bedroom are grouped around a crib, in lamplight. They have been through a long vigil, and it shows in their tired bearing and disarranged clothing. One is a young gentlewoman with a sweet girlish face, KATE KELLER; *the second is an elderly* DOCTOR, *stethoscope at neck, thermometer in fingers; the third is a hearty gentleman in his forties with chin whiskers,* CAPTAIN ARTHUR KELLER.

Doctor. She'll live.
Kate. Thank God.

[The DOCTOR *leaves them together over the crib, packs his bag.]*

Doctor. You're a pair of lucky parents. I can tell you now, I thought she wouldn't.
Keller. Nonsense, the child's a Keller, she has the constitution[1] of a goat. She'll outlive us all.
Doctor (*amiably*). Yes, especially if some of you Kellers don't get a night's sleep. I mean you, Mrs. Keller.
Keller. You hear, Katie?
Kate. I hear.

1. **constitution** (kän′stə·tōō′shən): here, physical makeup.

"She can't see. Look at her eyes. She can't see!"

Keller (*indulgent*). I've brought up two of them, but this is my wife's first, she isn't battle-scarred yet.

Kate. Doctor, don't be merely considerate, will my girl be all right?

Doctor. Oh, by morning she'll be knocking down Captain Keller's fences again.

Kate. And isn't there anything we should do?

Keller (*jovial*). Put up stronger fencing, ha?

Doctor. Just let her get well, she knows how to do it better than we do. (*He is packed, ready to leave.*) Main thing is the fever's gone, these things come and go in infants, never know why. Call it acute congestion[2] of the stomach and brain.

Keller. I'll see you to your buggy, Doctor.

Doctor. I've never seen a baby with more vitality, that's the truth.

[*He beams a good night at the baby and* KATE, *and* KELLER *leads him downstairs with a lamp. They go down the porch steps and across the yard, where the* DOCTOR *goes off left;* KELLER *stands with the lamp aloft.* KATE *meanwhile is bent lovingly over the crib, which emits a bleat; her finger is playful with the baby's face.*]

Kate. Hush. Don't you cry now, you've been trouble enough. Call it acute congestion, indeed, I don't see what's so cute about a congestion, just because it's yours. We'll have your father run an editorial in his paper, the wonders of modern medicine, they don't know what they're curing even when they cure it. Men, men and their battle scars, we women will have to—— (*But she breaks off, puzzled, moves her finger before the baby's eyes.*) Will have to—Helen? (*Now she moves her hand, quickly.*) Helen. (*She snaps her fingers at the baby's eyes twice, and her hand falters; after a moment she calls out, loudly.*) Captain. Captain, will you come—— (*But she stares at the baby, and her next call is directly at her ears.*) Captain!

[*And now, still staring,* KATE *screams.* KELLER *in the yard hears it and runs with the lamp*

2. **acute congestion** (ə·kyōōt′ kən·jes′chən): severe blockage (an old-fashioned medical diagnosis).

back to the house. KATE *screams again, her look intent on the baby and terrible.* KELLER *hurries in and up.*]

Keller. Katie? What's wrong?

Kate. Look. (*She makes a pass with her hand in the crib, at the baby's eyes.*)

Keller. What, Katie? She's well, she needs only time to——

Kate. She can't see. Look at her eyes. (*She takes the lamp from him, moves it before the child's face.*) She can't *see!*

Keller (*hoarsely*). Helen.

Kate. Or hear. When I screamed she didn't blink. Not an eyelash——

Keller. Helen. Helen!

Kate. She can't *hear* you!

Keller. *Helen!*

[*His face has something like fury in it, crying the child's name;* KATE, *almost fainting, presses her knuckles to her mouth, to stop her own cry. The room dims out quickly.*]

SCENE 2

Time, in the form of a slow tune of distant belfry chimes which approaches in a crescendo and then fades, passes; the light comes up again on a day five years later, on three kneeling children and an old dog outside around the pump.

The dog is a setter named BELLE, *and she is sleeping. Two of the children are Negroes,* MARTHA *and* PERCY. *The third child is* HELEN, *six and a half years old, quite unkempt, in body a* vivacious *little person with a fine head, attractive, but noticeably blind, one eye larger and protruding; her gestures are abrupt, insistent, lacking in human restraint, and her face never smiles. She is flanked by the other two, in a litter of paper-doll cutouts, and while they speak* HELEN'S *hands thrust at their faces in turn, feeling baffledly at the movements of their lips.*

Martha (*snipping*). First I'm gonna cut off this doctor's legs, one, two, now then——

Percy. Why you cuttin' off that doctor's legs?

Martha. I'm gonna give him a operation. Now I'm gonna cut off his arms, one, two. Now I'm gonna fix up—— (*She pushes* HELEN'S *hand away from her mouth.*) You stop that.

Percy. Cut off his stomach, that's a good operation.

Martha. No, I'm gonna cut off his head first, he got a bad cold.

Percy. Ain't gonna be much of that doctor left to fix up, time you finish all them opera——

[*But* HELEN *is poking her fingers inside his mouth, to feel his tongue; he bites at them, annoyed, and she jerks them away.* HELEN *now fingers her own lips, moving them in imitation, but soundlessly.*]

Martha. What you do, bite her hand?

Percy. That's how I do, she keep pokin' her fingers in my mouth, I just bite 'em off.

Martha. What she tryin' do now?

Percy. She tryin' *talk.* She gonna get mad. Looka her tryin' talk.

[HELEN *is scowling, the lips under her fingertips moving in ghostly silence, growing more and more frantic, until in a bizarre rage she bites at her own fingers. This sends* PERCY *off into laughter, but alarms* MARTHA.]

Martha. Hey, you stop now. (*She pulls* HELEN'S *hand down.*) You just sit quiet and——

[*But at once* HELEN *topples* MARTHA *on her back, knees pinning her shoulders down, and grabs the scissors.* MARTHA *screams.* PERCY *darts to the bell string on the porch, yanks it, and the bell rings.*]

WORDS TO OWN
vivacious (vī·vā′shəs) *adj.:* very lively.

Six and a half years old, quite unkempt...

SCENE 3

Inside, the lights have been gradually coming up on the main room, where we see the family informally gathered, talking, but in pantomime: KATE *sits darning socks near a cradle, occasionally rocking it;* CAPTAIN KELLER, *in spectacles, is working over newspaper pages at a table; a* <u>benign</u> *visitor in a hat,* AUNT EV, *is sharing the sewing basket, putting the finishing touches on a big shapeless doll made out of towels; an* <u>indolent</u> *young man,* JAMES KELLER, *is at the* <u>window</u> *watching the children.*

With the ring of the bell, KATE *is instantly on her feet and out the door onto the porch, to take in the scene; now we see what these five years have done to her: The girlish playfulness is gone, she is a woman steeled in grief.*

Kate (*for the thousandth time*). Helen. (*She is down the steps at once to them, seizing* HELEN'S *wrists and lifting her off* MARTHA; MARTHA *runs off in tears and screams for momma, with* PERCY *after her.*) Let me have those scissors.

[*Meanwhile the family inside is alerted,* AUNT EV *joining* JAMES *at the window;* CAPTAIN KELLER *resumes work.*]

James (*blandly*). She only dug Martha's eyes out. Almost dug. It's always almost, no point worrying till it happens, is there?

[*They gaze out, while* KATE *reaches for the scissors in* HELEN'S *hand. But* HELEN *pulls the scissors back, they struggle for them a moment, then* KATE *gives up, lets* HELEN *keep them. She tries to draw* HELEN *into the house.* HELEN *jerks away.* KATE *next goes down on her knees, takes* HELEN'S *hands gently, and using the scissors like a doll, makes* HELEN *caress and cradle them; she points* HELEN'S *finger houseward.* HELEN'S *whole body now becomes eager; she surrenders the scissors.* KATE *turns her toward the door and gives her a little push.* HELEN *scrambles up and toward the house, and* KATE, *rising, follows her.*]

Aunt Ev. How does she stand it? Why haven't you seen this Baltimore man? It's not a thing you can let go on and on, like the weather.

James. The weather here doesn't ask permission of me, Aunt Ev. Speak to my father.

Aunt Ev. Arthur. Something ought to be done for that child.

Keller. A refreshing suggestion. What?

[KATE, *entering, turns* HELEN *to* AUNT EV, *who gives her the towel doll.*]

Aunt Ev. Why, this very famous oculist[3] in Baltimore I wrote you about, what was his name?

Kate. Dr. Chisholm.

Aunt Ev. Yes, I heard lots of cases of blindness people thought couldn't be cured he's cured, he just does wonders. Why don't you write to him?

Keller. I've stopped believing in wonders.

Kate (*rocks the cradle*). I think the Captain will write to him soon. Won't you, Captain?

Keller. No.

James (*lightly*). Good money after bad, or bad after good. Or bad after bad——

Aunt Ev. Well, if it's just a question of money, Arthur, now you're marshal you have this Yankee money. Might as well——

Keller. Not money. The child's been to specialists all over Alabama and Tennessee. If I thought it would do good I'd have her to every fool doctor in the country.

Kate. I think the Captain will write to him soon.

Keller. Katie. How many times can you let them break your heart?

Kate. Any number of times.

[HELEN *meanwhile sits on the floor to explore the doll with her fingers, and her hand pauses over the face: This is no face, a blank area of towel, and it troubles her. Her hand searches for features and taps questioningly for eyes, but no one notices. She then yanks*

---

3. **oculist** (äk′yoo·list): formerly, eye doctor.

WORDS TO OWN

benign (bi·nīn′) *adj.:* good-natured; harmless.
indolent (in′də·lənt) *adj.:* lazy, idle.

at her AUNT'S *dress and taps again vigorously for eyes.*]

Aunt Ev. What, child?

[*Obviously not hearing,* HELEN *commences to go around, from person to person, tapping for eyes, but no one attends or understands.*]

Kate (*no break*). As long as there's the least chance. For her to see. Or hear, or——
Keller. There isn't. Now I must finish here.
Kate. I think, with your permission, Captain, I'd like to write.
Keller. I said no, Katie.
Aunt Ev. Why, writing does no harm, Arthur, only a little bitty letter. To see if he can help her.
Keller. He can't.
Kate. We won't know that to be a fact, Captain, until after you write.
Keller (*rising, emphatic*). Katie, he can't. (*He collects his papers.*)
James (*facetiously*). Father stands up, that makes it a fact.
Keller. You be quiet! I'm badgered enough here by females without your <u>impudence</u>. (JAMES *shuts up, makes himself scarce.* HELEN *now is groping among things on* KELLER'S *desk and paws his papers to the floor.* KELLER *is exasperated.*) Katie. (KATE *quickly turns* HELEN *away and retrieves the papers.*) I might as well try to work in a henyard as in this house——
James (*placating*). You really ought to put her away, Father.
Kate (*staring up*). What?
James. Some asylum. It's the kindest thing.
Aunt Ev. Why, she's your sister, James, not a nobody——
James. Half sister, and half—mentally defective, she can't even keep herself clean. It's not pleasant to see her about all the time.
Kate. Do you dare? Complain of what you *can* see?
Keller (*very annoyed*). This discussion is at an end! I'll thank you not to broach it again, Ev. (*Silence descends at once.* HELEN *gropes her way with the doll, and* KELLER *turns back for a final word, explosive.*) I've done as much as I can bear, I can't give my whole life to it! The house is at sixes and sevens[4] from morning till night over the child. It's time some attention was paid to Mildred[5] here instead!
Kate (*gently dry*). You'll wake her up, Captain.
Keller. I want some peace in the house. I don't care how, but one way we won't have it is by rushing up and down the country every time someone hears of a new quack. I'm as sensible to this affliction as anyone else. It hurts me to look at the girl.
Kate. It was not our affliction I meant you to write about, Captain.

[HELEN *is back at* AUNT EV, *fingering her dress, and yanks two buttons from it.*]

Aunt Ev. Helen! My buttons.

[HELEN *pushes the buttons into the doll's face.* KATE *now sees, comes swiftly to kneel, lifts* HELEN'S *hand to her own eyes in question.*]

Kate. Eyes? (HELEN *nods energetically.*) She wants the doll to have eyes.

[*Another kind of silence now, while* KATE *takes pins and buttons from the sewing basket and attaches them to the doll as eyes.* KELLER *stands, caught, and watches morosely.* AUNT EV *blinks, and conceals her emotion by inspecting her dress.*]

Aunt Ev. My goodness me, I'm not decent.
Kate. She doesn't know better, Aunt Ev. I'll sew them on again.
James. Never learn with everyone letting her do anything she takes it into her mind to——
Keller. You be quiet!
James. What did I say now?
Keller. You talk too much.
James. I was agreeing with you!
Keller. Whatever it was. Deprived child, the least she can have are the little things she wants.

---

4. **at sixes and sevens:** in disorder and confusion.
5. **Mildred:** the Kellers' second child.

- -

WORDS TO OWN

impudence (im′pyoo·dəns) *n.:* disrespect; rudeness.

- -

[JAMES, *very wounded, stalks out of the room onto the porch; he remains here, sulking.*]

Aunt Ev (*indulgently*). It's worth a couple of buttons, Kate, look. (HELEN *now has the doll with eyes and cannot contain herself for joy; she rocks the doll, pats it vigorously, kisses it.*) This child has more sense than all these men Kellers, if there's ever any way to reach that mind of hers.

[*But* HELEN *suddenly has come upon the cradle and unhesitatingly overturns it; the swaddled baby tumbles out, and* CAPTAIN KELLER *barely manages to dive and catch it in time.*]

Keller. Helen!

[*All are in commotion, the baby screams, but* HELEN, *unperturbed, is laying her doll in its place.* KATE *on her knees pulls her hands off the cradle, wringing them;* HELEN *is bewildered.*]

Kate. Helen, Helen, you're not to do such things, how can I make you understand——
Keller (*hoarsely*). Katie.
Kate. How can I get it into your head, my darling, my poor——
Keller. Katie, some way of teaching her an iota of discipline has to be——
Kate (*flaring*). How can you discipline an afflicted child? Is it her fault?

[HELEN'S *fingers have fluttered to her* MOTHER'S *lips, vainly trying to comprehend their movements.*]

Keller. I didn't say it was her fault.
Kate. Then whose? I don't know what to do! How can I teach her, beat her—until she's black and blue?
Keller. It's not safe to let her run around loose. Now there must be a way of confining her, somehow, so she can't——
Kate. Where, in a cage? She's a growing child, she has to use her limbs!

Keller. Answer me one thing, is it fair to Mildred here?
Kate (*inexorably*). Are you willing to put her away?

[*Now* HELEN'S *face darkens in the same rage as at herself earlier, and her hand strikes at* KATE'S *lips.* KATE *catches her hand again, and* HELEN *begins to kick, struggle, twist.*]

Keller. Now what?
Kate. She wants to talk, like—*be* like you and me. (*She holds* HELEN *struggling until we hear from the child her first sound so far, an inarticulate weird noise in her throat such as an animal in a trap might make; and* KATE *releases her. The second she is free* HELEN *blunders away, collides violently with a chair, falls, and sits weeping.* KATE *comes to her, embraces, caresses, soothes her, and buries her own face in her hair, until she can control her voice.*) Every day she slips further away. And I don't know how to call her back.
Aunt Ev. Oh, I've a mind to take her up to Baltimore myself. If that doctor can't help her, maybe he'll know who can.
Keller (*presently, heavily*). I'll write the man, Katie. (*He stands with the baby in his clasp, staring at* HELEN'S *head hanging down on* KATE'S *arm.*)

[*The lights dim out, except the one on* KATE *and* HELEN. *In the twilight,* JAMES, AUNT EV, *and* KELLER *move off slowly, formally, in separate directions;* KATE *with* HELEN *in her arms remains, motionless, in an image which overlaps into the next scene and fades only when it is well under way.*]

- -
WORDS TO OWN
inarticulate (in'är·tik'yo͞o·lit) *adj.:* not expressed clearly enough to be understood.
- -

SCENE 4

Without pause, from the dark down left we hear a man's voice with a Greek accent speaking:

Anagnos. ——who could do nothing for the girl, of course. It was Dr. Bell[6] who thought she might somehow be taught. I have written the family only that a suitable governess, Miss Annie Sullivan, has been found here in Boston——

[*The lights begin to come up, down left, on a long table and chair. The table contains equipment for teaching the blind by touch—a small replica of the human skeleton, stuffed animals, models of flowers and plants, piles of books. The chair contains a girl of twenty,* ANNIE SULLIVAN, *with a face which in repose is grave and rather obstinate, and when active is impudent, combative, twinkling with all the life that is lacking in* HELEN'S, *and handsome; there is a crude vitality to her. Her suitcase is at her knee.* ANAGNOS, *a stocky bearded man, comes into the light only toward the end of his speech.*]

Anagnos. ——and will come. It will no doubt be difficult for you there, Annie. But it has been difficult for you at our school too, hm? Gratifying, yes, when you came to us and could not spell your name, to accomplish so much here in a few years, but always an Irish battle. For independence. (*He studies* ANNIE, *humorously; she does not open her eyes.*) This is my last time to counsel you, Annie, and you do lack some—by some I mean *all*—what, tact or talent to bend. To others. And what has saved you on more than one occasion here at Perkins is that there was nowhere to expel you to. Your eyes hurt?

Annie. My ears, Mr. Anagnos. (*And now she has opened her eyes; they are inflamed, vague, slightly crossed, clouded by the granular growth of trachoma,[7] and she often keeps them closed to shut out the pain of light.*)

Anagnos (*severely*). Nowhere but back to Tewksbury, where children learn to be saucy. Annie, I know how dreadful it was there, but that battle is dead and done with, why not let it stay buried?

Annie (*cheerily*). I think God must owe me a resurrection.

Anagnos (*a bit shocked*). What?

Annie (*taps her brow*). Well, he keeps digging up that battle!

Anagnos. That is not a proper thing to say, Annie. It is what I mean.

Annie (*meekly*). Yes. But I know what I'm like. What's this child like?

Anagnos. Like?

Annie. Well—bright or dull, to start off.

Anagnos. No one knows. And if she is dull, you have no patience with this?

Annie. Oh, in grown-ups you have to, Mr. Anagnos. I mean in children it just seems a little—precocious, can I use that word?

Anagnos. Only if you can spell it.

Annie. Premature. So I hope at least she's a bright one.

Anagnos. Deaf, blind, mute—who knows? She is like a little safe, locked, that no one can open. Perhaps there is a treasure inside.

Annie. Maybe it's empty, too?

Anagnos. Possibly. I should warn you, she is much given to tantrums.

Annie. Means something is inside. Well, so am I, if I believe all I hear. Maybe you should warn *them*.

Anagnos (*frowns*). Annie. I wrote them no word of your history. You will find yourself among strangers now, who know nothing of it.

Annie. Well, we'll keep them in a state of blessed ignorance.

Anagnos. Perhaps *you* should tell it?

Annie (*bristling*). Why? I have enough trouble with people who don't know.

6. **Dr. Bell:** Alexander Graham Bell, inventor of the telephone, who also developed methods for teaching the deaf.

7. **trachoma** (trə·kō′mə): eye disease that results in "grainy" scar tissue.

WORDS TO OWN

resurrection (rez′ə·rek′shən) *n.*: rebirth.

Anagnos. So they will understand. When you have trouble.

Annie. The only time I have trouble is when I'm right. (*But she is amused at herself, as is* ANAGNOS.) Is it my fault it's so often? I won't give them trouble, Mr. Anagnos, I'll be so ladylike they won't notice I've come.

Anagnos. Annie, be—humble. It is not as if you have so many offers to pick and choose. You will need their affection, working with this child.

Annie (*humorously*). I hope I won't need their pity.

Anagnos. Oh, we can all use some pity. (*Crisply*) So. You are no longer our pupil, we throw you into the world, a teacher. *If* the child can be taught. No one expects you to work miracles, even for twenty-five dollars a month. Now, in this envelope a loan, for the railroad, which you will repay me when you have a bank account. But in this box, a gift. With our love. (ANNIE *opens the small box he extends and sees a garnet ring. She looks up, blinking, and down.*) I think other friends are ready to say goodbye. (*He moves as though to open doors.*)

Annie. Mr. Anagnos. (*Her voice is trembling.*) Dear Mr. Anagnos, I—— (*But she swallows over getting the ring on her finger, and cannot continue until she finds a woebegone joke.*) Well, what should I say, I'm an ignorant, opinionated girl, and everything I am I owe to you?

Anagnos (*smiles*). That is only half true, Annie.

Annie. Which half? I crawled in here like a drowned rat, I thought I died when Jimmie died, that I'd never again—come alive. Well, you say with love so easy, and I haven't *loved* a soul since and I never will, I suppose, but this place gave me more than my eyes back. Or taught me how to spell, which I'll never learn anyway, but with all the fights and the trouble I've been here it taught me what help is, and how to live again, and I don't want to say goodbye. Don't open the door, I'm crying.

Anagnos (*gently*). They will not see.

[*He moves again as though opening doors, and in comes a group of girls, eight-year-olds to seventeen-year-olds; as they walk we see they are blind.* ANAGNOS *shepherds them in with a hand.*]

A Child. Annie?

Annie (*her voice cheerful*). Here, Beatrice.

[*As soon as they locate her voice they throng joyfully to her, speaking all at once;* ANNIE *is down on her knees to the smallest, and the following are the more intelligible fragments in the general hubbub.*]

Children. There's a present. We brought you a going-away present, Annie!

Annie. Oh, now you shouldn't have——

Children. We did, we did, where's the present?

Smallest Child (*mournfully*). Don't go, Annie, away.

Children. Alice has it. Alice! Where's Alice? Here I am! Where? Here!

[*An arm is aloft out of the group, waving a present;* ANNIE *reaches for it.*]

Annie. I have it. I have it, everybody. Should I open it?

Children. Open it! Everyone be quiet! Do, Annie! She's opening it. Ssh! (*A settling of silence while* ANNIE *unwraps it. The present is a pair of smoked glasses, and she stands still.*) Is it open, Annie?

Annie. It's open.

Children. It's for your eyes, Annie. Put them on, Annie! 'Cause Mrs. Hopkins said your eyes hurt since the operation. And she said you're going where the sun is *fierce*.

Annie. I'm putting them on now.

Smallest Child (*mournfully*). Don't go, Annie, where the sun is fierce.

Children. Do they fit all right?

Annie. Oh, they fit just fine.

Children. Did you put them on? Are they pretty, Annie?

Annie. Oh, my eyes feel hundreds of percent better already, and pretty, why, do you know how I look in them? Splendiloquent. Like a racehorse!

Children (*delighted*). There's another present! Beatrice! We have a present for Helen, too! Give it to her, Beatrice. Here, Annie! (*This present is*

"*It's for Helen. And we took up a collection to buy it.*"

an elegant doll, with movable eyelids and a momma sound.) It's for Helen. And we took up a collection to buy it. And Laura dressed it.

Annie. It's beautiful.

Children. So don't forget, you be sure to give it to Helen from us, Annie!

Annie. I promise it will be the first thing I give her. If I don't keep it for myself, that is, you know I can't be trusted with dolls!

Smallest Child (*mournfully*). Don't go, Annie, to her.

Annie (*her arm around her*). Sarah, dear. I don't *want* to go.

Smallest Child. Then why are you going?

Annie (*gently*). Because I'm a big girl now, and big girls have to earn a living. It's the only way I can. But if you don't smile for me first, what I'll just have to do is—— (*She pauses, inviting it.*)

Smallest Child. What?

Annie. Put *you* in my suitcase, instead of this doll. And take *you* to Helen in Alabama!

[*This strikes the children as very funny, and they begin to laugh and tease the smallest child, who after a moment does smile for* ANNIE.]

Anagnos (*then*). Come, children. We must get the trunk into the carriage and Annie into her train, or no one will go to Alabama. Come, come.

[*He shepherds them out, and* ANNIE *is left alone on her knees with the doll in her lap. She reaches for her suitcase, and by a subtle change in the color of the light, we go with her thoughts into another time. We hear a boy's voice whispering; perhaps we see shadowy intimations[8] of these speakers in the background.*]

Boy's Voice. Where we goin', Annie?

Annie (*in dread*). Jimmie.

Boy's Voice. Where we goin'?

Annie. I said—I'm takin' care of you——

Boy's Voice. Forever and ever?

Man's Voice (*impersonal*). Annie Sullivan,

aged nine, virtually blind. James Sullivan, aged seven—— What's the matter with your leg, Sonny?

Annie. Forever and ever.

Man's Voice. Can't he walk without that crutch? (ANNIE *shakes her head and does not stop shaking it.*) Girl goes to the women's ward. Boy to the men's.

Boy's Voice (*in terror*). Annie! Annie, don't let them take me—Annie!

Anagnos (*offstage*). Annie! Annie?

[*But this voice is real, in the present, and* ANNIE *comes up out of her horror, clearing her head with a final shake; the lights begin to pick out* KATE *in the* KELLER *house, as* ANNIE *in a bright tone calls back.*]

Annie. Coming!

[*This word catches* KATE, *who stands half turned and attentive to it, almost as though hearing it. Meanwhile* ANNIE *turns and hurries out, lugging the suitcase.*]

---

8. **intimations** (in′tə·mā′shənz): suggestions or hints.

SCENE 5

The room dims out; the sound of railroad wheels begins from off left and maintains itself in a constant rhythm underneath the following scene; the remaining lights have come up on the KELLER *homestead.* JAMES *is lounging on the porch, waiting. In the upper bedroom, which is to be* ANNIE'S, HELEN *is alone, puzzledly exploring, fingering and smelling things, the curtains, empty drawers in the bureau, water in the pitcher by the washbasin, fresh towels on the bedstead. Downstairs in the family room* KATE *turning to a mirror hastily adjusts her bonnet, watched by a servant in an apron,* VINEY.

Viney. Let Mr. Jimmie go by hisself, you been pokin' that garden all day, you ought to rest your feet.

Kate. I can't wait to see her, Viney.

Viney. Maybe she ain't gone be on this train neither.

Kate. Maybe she is.

Viney. And maybe she ain't.

Kate. And maybe she is. Where's Helen?

Viney. She upstairs, smellin' around. She know somethin' funny's goin' on.

Kate. Let her have her supper as soon as Mildred's in bed, and tell Captain Keller when he comes that we'll be delayed tonight.

Viney. Again.

Kate. I don't think we need say *again*. Simply delayed will do.

[She runs upstairs to ANNIE'S *room,* VINEY *speaking after her.]*

Viney. I mean that's what he gone say. "What, again?"

*[*VINEY *works at setting the table. Upstairs* KATE *stands in the doorway, watching* HELEN'S *groping explorations.]*

Kate. Yes, we're expecting someone. Someone for my Helen. (HELEN *happens upon her skirt, clutches her leg;* KATE *in a tired dismay kneels to tidy her hair and soiled pinafore.)*[9] Oh, dear,

9. **pinafore** (pin′ə·fôr′): sleeveless, apronlike garment worn by little girls over a dress.

this was clean not an hour ago. (HELEN *feels her bonnet, shakes her head darkly, and tugs to get it off.* KATE *retains it with one hand, diverts* HELEN *by opening her other hand under her nose.)* Here. For while I'm gone. (HELEN *sniffs, reaches, and pops something into her mouth, while* KATE *speaks a bit guiltily.)* I don't think one peppermint drop will spoil your supper.

[She gives HELEN *a quick kiss, evades her hands, and hurries downstairs again. Meanwhile* CAPTAIN KELLER *has entered the yard from around the rear of the house, newspaper under arm, cleaning off and munching on some radishes; he sees* JAMES *lounging at the porch post.]*

Keller. Jimmie?

James (*unmoving*). Sir?

Keller (*eyes him*). You don't look dressed for anything useful, boy.

James. I'm not. It's for Miss Sullivan.

Keller. Needn't keep holding up that porch; we have wooden posts for that. I asked you to see that those strawberry plants were moved this evening.

James. I'm moving your—Mrs. Keller, instead. To the station.

Keller (*heavily*). Mrs. Keller. Must you always speak of her as though you haven't met the lady?

*[*KATE *comes out on the porch, and* JAMES *inclines his head.]*

James (*ironic*). Mother. (*He starts off the porch, but sidesteps* KELLER'S *glare like a blow.*) I said mother!

Kate. Captain.

Keller. Evening, my dear.

Kate. We're off to meet the train, Captain. Supper will be a trifle delayed tonight.

Keller. What, again?

Kate (*backing out*). With your permission, Captain?

[And they are gone. KELLER *watches them offstage, morosely. Upstairs* HELEN *meanwhile has groped for her mother, touched her cheek*

in a meaningful gesture, waited, touched her cheek, waited, then found the open door and made her way down. Now she comes into the family room, touches her cheek again; VINEY *regards her.*]

Viney. What you want, honey, your momma? (HELEN *touches her cheek again.* VINEY *goes to the sideboard, gets a tea cake, gives it into* HELEN'S *hand;* HELEN *pops it into her mouth.*) Guess one little tea cake ain't gone ruin your appetite.

[*She turns* HELEN *toward the door.* HELEN *wanders out onto the porch, as* KELLER *comes up the steps. Her hands encounter him, and she touches her cheek again, waits.*]

Keller. She's gone. (*He is awkward with her; when he puts his hand on her head, she pulls away.* KELLER *stands regarding her, heavily.*) She's gone, my son and I don't get along, you don't know I'm your father, no one likes me,

and supper's delayed. (HELEN *touches her cheek, waits.* KELLER *fishes in his pocket.*) Here. I brought you some stick candy, one nibble of sweets can't do any harm.

[*He gives her a large stick of candy;* HELEN *falls to it.* VINEY *peers out the window.*]

Viney (*reproachfully*). Cap'n Keller, now how'm I gone get her to eat her supper you fill her up with that trash?

Keller (*roars*). Tend to your work!

[VINEY *beats a rapid retreat.* KELLER *thinks better of it and tries to get the candy away from* HELEN, *but* HELEN *hangs on to it; and when* KELLER *pulls, she gives his leg a kick.* KELLER *hops about,* HELEN *takes refuge with the candy down behind the pump, and* KELLER *then irately flings his newspaper on the porch floor, stamps into the house past* VINEY, *and disappears.*]

Courtesy George Jenkins.

Courtesy George Jenkins.

Set designs by George Jenkins for the movie (above) and Broadway (right) productions of *The Miracle Worker*. In the play, the dining room was placed close to the audience because several important scenes are set there. An unexpected result was that the food hurled about during Act Two often hit the first-row viewers.

SCENE 6

The lights half dim on the homestead, where VINEY *and* HELEN *going about their business soon find their way off. Meanwhile, the railroad sounds off left have mounted in a crescendo to a climax typical of a depot at arrival time, the lights come up on stage left, and we see a suggestion of a station. Here* ANNIE *in her smoked glasses and disarrayed by travel is waiting with her suitcase, while* JAMES *walks to meet her; she has a battered paperbound book, which is a Perkins report,[10] under her arm.*

James (*coolly*). Miss Sullivan?
Annie (*cheerily*). Here! At last. I've been on trains so many days I thought they must be backing up every time I dozed off——
James. I'm James Keller.
Annie. James? (*The name stops her.*) I had a brother Jimmie. Are you Helen's?
James. I'm only half a brother. You're to be her governess?
Annie (*lightly*). Well. Try!
James (*eying her*). You look like half a governess. (KATE *enters.* ANNIE *stands moveless, while* JAMES *takes her suitcase.* KATE'S *gaze on her is doubtful, troubled.*) Mrs. Keller, Miss Sullivan.

[KATE *takes her hand.*]

Kate (*simply*). We've met every train for two days.

[ANNIE *looks at* KATE'S *face, and her good humor comes back.*]

Annie. I changed trains every time they stopped. The man who sold me that ticket ought to be tied to the tracks——
James. You have a trunk, Miss Sullivan?
Annie. Yes. (*She passes* JAMES *a claim check, and he bears the suitcase out behind them.* ANNIE *holds the battered book.* KATE *is studying her face, and* ANNIE *returns the gaze; this is a* mutual *appraisal*, *Southern gentlewoman and working-class Irish girl, and* ANNIE *is not quite comfortable under it.*) You didn't bring Helen, I was hoping you would.
Kate. No, she's home.

[*A pause.* ANNIE *tries to make ladylike small talk, though her energy now and then erupts; she catches herself up whenever she hears it.*]

Annie. You—live far from town, Mrs. Keller?
Kate. Only a mile.
Annie. Well. I suppose I can wait one more mile. But don't be surprised if I get out to push the horse!
Kate. Helen's waiting for you, too. There's been such a bustle in the house, she expects something, heaven knows what. (*Now she voices part of her doubt, not as such, but* ANNIE *understands it.*) I expected—a desiccated[11] spinster. You're very young.
Annie (*resolutely*). Oh, you should have seen me when I left Boston. I got much older on this trip.
Kate. I mean, to teach anyone as difficult as Helen.
Annie. *I* mean to try. They can't put you in jail for trying!
Kate. Is it possible, even? To teach a deaf-blind child *half* of what an ordinary child learns—has that ever been done?
Annie. Half?
Kate. A tenth.
Annie (*reluctantly*). No. (KATE'S *face loses its remaining hope; still appraising her youth.*) Dr. Howe did wonders, but—an ordinary child? No, never. But then I thought when I was going over his reports—(*She indicates the one in her hand.*)—he never treated them like ordinary children. More like—eggs everyone was afraid would break.
Kate (*a pause*). May I ask how old you are?

11. desiccated (des′i·kāt′id): dried up.

---

10. **Perkins report:** report on methods of teaching the blind, prepared by the director of the Perkins Institution for the Blind in Boston.

Annie. Well, I'm not in my teens, you know! I'm twenty.

Kate. All of twenty.

[ANNIE *takes the bull by the horns, valiantly.*]

Annie. Mrs. Keller, don't lose heart just because I'm not on my last legs. I have three big advantages over Dr. Howe that money couldn't buy for you. One is his work behind me. I've read every word he wrote about it and he wasn't exactly what you'd call a man of few words. Another is to *be* young, why, I've got energy to do anything. The third is, I've been blind. (*But it costs her something to say this.*)

Kate (*quietly*). Advantages.

Annie (*wry*). Well, some have the luck of the Irish, some do not.

[KATE *smiles; she likes her.*]

Kate. What will you try to teach her first?

Annie. First, last, and—in between—language.

Kate. Language.

Annie. Language is to the mind more than light is to the eye. Dr. Howe said that.

Kate. Language. (*She shakes her head.*) We can't get through to teach her to sit still. You *are* young, despite your years, to have such—confidence. Do you, inside?

[ANNIE *studies her face; she likes her, too.*]

Annie. No, to tell you the truth I'm as shaky inside as a baby's rattle!

[*They smile at each other, and* KATE *pats her hand.*]

Kate. Don't be. (JAMES *returns to usher them off.*) We'll do all we can to help, and to make you feel at home. Don't think of us as strangers, Miss Annie.

Annie (*cheerily*). Oh, strangers aren't so strange to me. I've known them all my life!

[KATE *smiles again,* ANNIE *smiles back, and they precede* JAMES *offstage.*]

SCENE 7

The lights dim on them, having simultaneously risen full on the house; VINEY *has already entered the family room, taken a water pitcher, and come out and down to the pump. She pumps real water. As she looks offstage, we hear the clop of hoofs, a carriage stopping, and voices.*

Viney. Cap'n Keller! Cap'n Keller, they comin'! (*She goes back into the house, as* KELLER *comes out on the porch to gaze.*) She sure 'nuff came, Cap'n.

[KELLER *descends and crosses toward the carriage; this conversation begins offstage and moves on.*]

Keller (*very courtly*). Welcome to Ivy Green, Miss Sullivan. I take it you are Miss Sullivan——

Kate. My husband, Miss Annie, Captain Keller.

Annie (*her best behavior*). Captain, how do you do.

Keller. A pleasure to see you, at last. I trust you had an agreeable journey?

Annie. Oh, I had several! When did this country get so big?

James. Where would you like the trunk, Father?

Keller. Where Miss Sullivan can get at it, I imagine.

Annie. Yes, please. Where's Helen?

Keller. In the hall, Jimmie——

Kate. We've put you in the upstairs corner room, Miss Annie, if there's any breeze at all this summer, you'll feel it——

[*In the house the setter* BELLE *flees into the family room, pursued by* HELEN *with groping hands; the dog doubles back out of the same door, and* HELEN, *still groping for her, makes her way out to the porch; she is messy, her hair tumbled, her pinafore now ripped, her shoelaces untied.* KELLER *acquires the suitcase, and* ANNIE *gets her hands on it too, though still endeavoring to live up to the general air of propertied[12] manners.*]

Keller. *And* the suitcase——
Annie (*pleasantly*). I'll take the suitcase, thanks.

12. **propertied** (präp'ər·tēd): like rich people who own a lot of property.

Keller. Not at all, I have it, Miss Sullivan.
Annie. I'd like it.
Keller (*gallantly*). I couldn't think of it, Miss Sullivan. You'll find in the South we——
Annie. Let me.
Keller. ——view women as the flowers of civiliza——
Annie (*impatiently*). I've got something in it for Helen! (*She tugs it free;* KELLER *stares.*) Thank you. When do I see her?
Kate. There. There is Helen.

[ANNIE *turns and sees* HELEN *on the porch. A moment of silence. Then* ANNIE *begins across the yard to her, lugging her suitcase.*]

Keller (*sotto voce*).[13] Katie——

13. **sotto voce** (sät'ō vō'chē): in a low voice.

Annie turns and sees Helen on the porch.

[KATE *silences him with a hand on his arm. When* ANNIE *finally reaches the porch steps she stops, contemplating* HELEN *for a last moment before entering her world. Then she drops the suitcase on the porch with intentional heaviness;* HELEN *starts with the jar and comes to grope over it.* ANNIE *puts forth her hand and touches* HELEN'S. HELEN *at once grasps it and commences to explore it, like reading a face. She moves her hand on to* ANNIE'S *forearm, and dress; and* ANNIE *brings her face within reach of* HELEN'S *fingers, which travel over it, quite without timidity, until they encounter and push aside the smoked glasses.* ANNIE'S *gaze is grave, unpitying, very attentive. She puts her hands on* HELEN'S *arms, but* HELEN *at once pulls away, and they confront each other with a distance between. Then* HELEN *returns to the suitcase, tries to open it, cannot.* ANNIE *points* HELEN'S *hand overhead.* HELEN *pulls away, tries to open the suitcase again;* ANNIE *points her hand overhead again.* HELEN *points overhead, a question, and* ANNIE, *drawing* HELEN'S *hand to her own face, nods.* HELEN *now begins tugging the suitcase toward the door; when* ANNIE *tries to take it from her, she fights her off and backs through the doorway with it.* ANNIE *stands a moment, then follows her in, and together they get the suitcase up the steps into* ANNIE'S *room.*]

Kate. Well?

Keller. She's very rough, Katie.

Kate. I like her, Captain.

Keller. Certainly rear a peculiar kind of young woman in the North. How old is she?

Kate (*vaguely*). Ohh—Well, she's not in her teens, you know.

Keller. She's only a child. What's her family like, shipping her off alone this far?

Kate. I couldn't learn. She's very closemouthed about some things.

Annie brings her face within reach of Helen's fingers. . . .

Keller. Why does she wear those glasses? I like to see a person's eyes when I talk to——

Kate. For the sun. She was blind.

Keller. Blind.

Kate. She's had nine operations on her eyes. One just before she left.

Keller. Blind, good heavens, do they expect one blind child to teach another? Has she experience at least? How long did she teach there?

Kate. She was a pupil.

Keller (*heavily*). Katie, Katie. This is her first position?

Kate (*bright voice*). She was valedictorian——

Keller. Here's a houseful of grown-ups can't cope with the child. How can an inexperienced half-blind Yankee schoolgirl manage her?

[JAMES *moves in with the trunk on his shoulder.*]

James (*easily*). Great improvement. Now we have two of them to look after.

Keller. You look after those strawberry plants!

[JAMES *stops with the trunk.* KELLER *turns from him without another word and marches off.*]

James. Nothing I say is right.

Kate. Why say anything? (*She calls.*) Don't be long, Captain, we'll have supper right away——

[*She goes into the house and through the rear door of the family room.* JAMES *trudges in with the trunk, takes it up the steps to* ANNIE'S *room, and sets it down outside the door. The lights elsewhere dim somewhat.*]

SCENE 8

Meanwhile, inside, ANNIE *has given* HELEN *a key; while* ANNIE *removes her bonnet,* HELEN *unlocks and opens the suitcase. The first thing she pulls out is a* voluminous *shawl. She fingers it until she perceives what it is; then she wraps it around her, and acquiring* ANNIE'S *bonnet and smoked glasses as well, dons the lot: The shawl swamps her, and the bonnet settles down upon the glasses, but she stands before a mirror cocking her head to one side, then to the other, in a mockery of adult action.* ANNIE *is amused, and talks to her as one might to a kitten, with no trace of company manners.*

Annie. All the trouble I went to and that's how I look? (HELEN *then comes back to the suitcase, gropes for more, lifts out a pair of female drawers.*) Oh, no. Not the drawers! (*But* HELEN, *discarding them, comes to the elegant doll. Her fingers explore its features, and when she raises it and finds that its eyes open and close,* she is at first startled, then delighted. She picks it up, taps its head vigorously, taps her own chest, and nods questioningly.* ANNIE *takes her finger, points it to the doll, points it to* HELEN, *and touching it to her own face, also nods.* HELEN *sits back on her heels, clasps the doll to herself, and rocks it.* ANNIE *studies her, still in bonnet and smoked glasses, like a* caricature *of herself, and addresses her humorously.*) All right, Miss O'Sullivan. Let's begin with doll. (*She takes* HELEN'S *hand; in her palm* ANNIE'S *forefinger points, thumb holding her other fingers clenched.*) D. (*Her thumb next holds all her fingers clenched, touching* HELEN'S *palm.*) O. (*Her thumb and forefinger extend.*) L. (*Same contact repeated.*) L. (*She puts* HELEN'S *hand to the doll.*) Doll.

- -

WORDS TO OWN

voluminous (və·lōōm′ə·nəs) *adj.*: large and bulky.

caricature (kar′i·kə·chər) *n.*: exaggerated portrait.

- -

James. You spell pretty well. (ANNIE *in one hurried move gets the drawers swiftly back into the suitcase, the lid banged shut, and her head turned, to see* JAMES *leaning in the doorway.*) Finding out if she's ticklish? She is.

[ANNIE *regards him stonily, but* HELEN *after a scowling moment tugs at her hand again, imperious.*[14] ANNIE *repeats the letters, and* HELEN *interrupts her fingers in the middle, feeling each of them, puzzled.* ANNIE *touches* HELEN'S *hand to the doll, and begins spelling into it again.*]

James. What is it, a game?
Annie (*curtly*). An alphabet.
James. Alphabet?
Annie. For the deaf. (HELEN *now repeats the finger movements in air, exactly, her head cocked to her own hand, and* ANNIE'S *eyes suddenly gleam.*) Ho. How *bright* she is!
James. You think she knows what she's doing? (*He takes* HELEN'S *hand, to throw a meaningless gesture into it; she repeats this one too.*) She imitates everything, she's a monkey.
Annie (*very pleased*). Yes, she's a bright little monkey, all right.

[*She takes the doll from* HELEN *and reaches for her hand;* HELEN *instantly grabs the doll back.* ANNIE *takes it again, and* HELEN'S *hand next, but* HELEN *is incensed now; when* ANNIE *draws her hand to her face to shake her head no, then tries to spell to her,* HELEN *slaps at* ANNIE'S *face.* ANNIE *grasps* HELEN *by both arms and swings her into a chair, holding her pinned there, kicking, while glasses, doll, bonnet fly in various directions.* JAMES *laughs.*]

James. She wants her doll back.
Annie. When she spells it.
James. Spell, she doesn't know the thing has a name, even.
Annie. Of course not, who expects her to, now? All I want is her fingers to learn the letters.
James. Won't mean anything to her. (ANNIE *gives him a look. She then tries to form* HELEN'S *fingers*

into the letters, but* HELEN *swings a haymaker*[15] *instead, which* ANNIE *barely ducks, at once pinning her down again.*) Doesn't like that alphabet, Miss Sullivan. You invent it yourself?

[HELEN *is now in a rage, fighting tooth and nail to get out of the chair, and* ANNIE *answers while struggling and dodging her kicks.*]

Annie. Spanish monks under a—vow of silence. Which I wish *you'd* take! (*And suddenly releasing* HELEN'S *hands, she comes and shuts the door in* JAMES'S *face.* HELEN *drops to the floor, groping around for the doll.* ANNIE *looks around desperately, sees her purse on the bed, rummages in it, and comes up with a battered piece of cake wrapped in newspaper; with her foot she moves the doll deftly out of the way of* HELEN'S *groping, and going on her knee she lets* HELEN *smell the cake. When* HELEN *grabs for it,* ANNIE *removes the cake and spells quickly into the reaching hand.*) Cake. From Washington up north, it's the best I can do. (HELEN'S *hand waits, baffled.* ANNIE *repeats it.*) C, a, k, e. Do what my fingers do, never mind what it means. (*She touches the cake briefly to* HELEN'S *nose, pats her hand, presents her own hand.* HELEN *spells the letters rapidly back.* ANNIE *pats her hand enthusiastically and gives her the cake;* HELEN *crams it into her mouth with both hands.* ANNIE *watches her, with humor.*) Get it down fast, maybe I'll steal that back too. Now. (*She takes the doll, touches it to* HELEN'S *nose, and spells again into her hand.*) D, o, l, l. Think it over. (HELEN *thinks it over, while* ANNIE *presents her own hand. Then* HELEN *spells three letters.* ANNIE *waits a second, then completes the word for* HELEN *in her palm.*) L. (*She hands over the doll, and* HELEN *gets a good grip on its leg.*) Imitate now, understand later. End of the first les—— (*She never finishes, because* HELEN *swings the doll with a furious energy. It hits* ANNIE *squarely in the face, and she falls back with a cry of pain, her knuckles up to her mouth.* HELEN *waits, tensed for further combat. When* ANNIE *lowers her knuckles she looks at blood on them; she works her lips, gets to her feet, finds the mirror, and bares her teeth*

---

14. imperious (im·pir′ē·əs): demanding.

15. haymaker: powerful punch, as if to knock someone out.

at herself. Now she is furious herself.) You little wretch, no one's taught you *any* manners? I'll—— (*But rounding from the mirror she sees the door slam,* HELEN *and the doll are on the outside, and* HELEN *is turning the key in the lock.* ANNIE *darts over, to pull the knob; the door is locked fast. She yanks it again.*) Helen! Helen, let me out of——

[*She bats her brow at the folly of speaking, but* JAMES, *now downstairs, hears her and turns to see* HELEN *with the key and doll groping her way down the steps;* JAMES *takes in the whole situation, makes a move to intercept* HELEN, *but then changes his mind, lets her pass, and amusedly follows her out onto the porch. Upstairs* ANNIE *meanwhile rattles the knob, kneels, peers through the keyhole, gets up. She goes to the window, looks down, frowns.* JAMES *from the yard sings gaily up to her:*]

James. Buffalo girl, gonna come out tonight,
Come out tonight,
Come out——

[*He drifts back into the house.* ANNIE *takes a handkerchief, nurses her mouth, stands in the middle of the room, staring at door and window in turn, and so catches sight of herself in the mirror, her cheek scratched, her hair disheveled, her handkerchief bloody, her face disgusted with herself. She addresses the mirror, with some irony.*]

Annie. Don't worry. They'll find you, you're not lost. Only out of place. (*But she coughs, spits something into her palm, and stares at it, outraged.*) And toothless. (*She winces.*) Oo! It hurts.

[*She pours some water into the basin, dips the handkerchief, and presses it to her mouth. Standing there, bent over the basin in pain— with the rest of the set dim and unreal, and the lights upon her taking on the subtle color of the past—she hears again, as do we, the faraway voices, and slowly she lifts her head to them; the boy's voice is the same, the others are cracked old crones in a nightmare, and perhaps we see their shadows.*]

Boy's Voice. It hurts. Annie, it hurts.
First Crone's Voice. Keep that brat shut up, can't you, girlie, how's a body to get any sleep in this damn ward?
Boy's Voice. It hurts. It hurts.
Second Crone's Voice. Shut up, you!
Boy's Voice. Annie, when are we goin' home? You promised!
Annie. Jimmie——
Boy's Voice. Forever and ever, you said forever—— (ANNIE *drops the handkerchief, adverts to the window, and is arrested there by the next cry.*) Annie? Annie, you there? Annie! It *hurts*!
Third Crone's Voice. Grab him, he's fallin'!
Boy's Voice. *Annie!*
Doctor's Voice (*a pause, slowly*). Little girl. Little girl, I must tell you your brother will be going on a——

[*But* ANNIE *claps her hands to her ears, to shut this out; there is instant silence. As the lights bring the other areas in again,* JAMES *goes to the steps to listen for any sound from upstairs.* KELLER *reentering from left crosses toward the house; he passes* HELEN *en route to her retreat under the pump.* KATE *reenters the rear door of the family room, with flowers for the table.*]

Kate. Supper is ready, Jimmie, will you call your father?
James. Certainly. (*But he calls up the stairs, for* ANNIE'S *benefit.*) Father! Supper!
Keller (*at the door*). No need to shout, I've been cooling my heels for an hour. Sit down.
James. Certainly.
Keller. Viney!

[VINEY *backs in with a roast, while they get settled around the table.*]

Viney. Yes, Cap'n, right here.
Kate. Mildred went directly to sleep, Viney?
Viney. Oh yes, that babe's a angel.
Kate. And Helen had a good supper?
Viney (*vaguely*). I dunno, Miss Kate, somehow she didn't have much of a appetite tonight——
Kate (*a bit guilty*). Oh. Dear.
Keller (*hastily*). Well, now. Couldn't say the same for my part, I'm famished. Kate, your plate.

Kate (*looking*). But where is Miss Annie?

[*A silence.*]

James (*pleasantly*). In her room.

Keller. In her room? Doesn't she know hot food must be eaten hot? Go bring her down at once, Jimmie.

James (*rises*). Certainly. I'll get a ladder.

Keller (*stares*). What?

James. I'll need a ladder. Shouldn't take me long.

Kate (*stares*). What shouldn't take you——

Keller. Jimmie, do as I say! Go upstairs at once and tell Miss Sullivan supper is getting cold——

James. She's locked in her room.

Keller. Locked in her——

Kate. What on earth are you——

James. Helen locked her in and made off with the key.

Kate (*rising*). And you sit here and say nothing.

James. Well, everyone's been telling me not to say anything.

[*He goes serenely out and across the yard, whistling.* KELLER *thrusting up from his chair makes for the stairs.*]

Kate. Viney, look out in back for Helen. See if she has that key.

Viney. Yes, Miss Kate. (VINEY *goes out the rear door.*)

Keller (*calling down*). She's out by the pump. (KATE *goes out on the porch after* HELEN, *while* KELLER *knocks on* ANNIE'S *door, then rattles the knob, imperiously.*) Miss Sullivan! Are you in there?

Annie. Oh, I'm in here, all right.

Keller. Is there no key on your side?

Annie (*with some asperity*). Well, if there was a key in here, *I* wouldn't be in here. Helen took it. The only thing on my side is me.

Keller. Miss Sullivan. I—— (*He tries, but cannot hold it back.*) Not in the house ten minutes, I don't see *how* you managed it!

"*She's out by the pump.*"

[*He stomps downstairs again, while* ANNIE *mutters to herself.*]

Annie. And even I'm not on my side.

Keller (*roaring*). Viney!

Viney (*reappearing*). Yes, Cap'n?

Keller. Put that meat back in the oven!

[VINEY *bears the roast off again, while* KELLER *strides out onto the porch.* KATE *is with* HELEN *at the pump, opening her hands.*]

Kate. She has no key.

Keller. Nonsense, she must have the key. Have you searched in her pockets?

Kate. Yes. She doesn't have it.

Keller. Katie, she must have the key.

Kate. Would you prefer to search her yourself, Captain?

Keller. No, I would not prefer to search her! She almost took my kneecap off this evening, when I tried merely to—— (JAMES *reappears carrying a long ladder, with* PERCY *running after him to be in on things.*) Take that ladder back!

James. Certainly.

[*He turns around with it.* MARTHA *comes skipping around the upstage corner of the house to be in on things, accompanied by the setter* BELLE.]

Kate. She could have hidden the key.

Keller. Where?

Kate. Anywhere. Under a stone. In the flower beds. In the grass——

Keller. Well, I can't plow up the entire grounds to find a missing key! Jimmie!

James. Sir?

Keller. Bring me a ladder!

James. Certainly.

[VINEY *comes around the downstage side of the house to be in on things; she has* MILDRED *over her shoulder, bleating.* KELLER *places the ladder against* ANNIE'S *window and mounts.* ANNIE *meanwhile is running about making herself presentable, washing the blood off her mouth,*

WORDS TO OWN

asperity (ə·sper′ə·tē) *n.:* sharpness of temper.

straightening her clothes, tidying her hair. Another servant enters to gaze in wonder, increasing the gathering ring of spectators.]

Kate (*sharply*). What is Mildred doing up?
Viney. Cap'n woke her, ma'am, all that hollerin'.
Keller. Miss Sullivan!

[ANNIE *comes to the window, with as much air of gracious normality as she can manage;* KELLER *is at the window.*]

Annie (*brightly*). Yes, Captain Keller?
Keller. Come out!
Annie. I don't see how I can. There isn't room.
Keller. I intend to carry you. Climb onto my shoulder and hold tight.
Annie. Oh, no. It's—very chivalrous of you, but I'd really prefer to——
Keller. Miss Sullivan, follow instructions! I will not have you also tumbling out of our windows. (ANNIE *obeys, with some misgivings.*) I hope this is not a sample of what we may expect from you. In the way of simplifying the work of looking after Helen.
Annie. Captain Keller, I'm perfectly able to go down a ladder under my own——
Keller. I doubt it, Miss Sullivan. Simply hold onto my neck. (*He begins down with her, while the spectators stand in a wide and somewhat awestricken circle, watching.* KELLER *half misses a rung, and* ANNIE *grabs at his whiskers.*) My neck, Miss Sullivan!
Annie. I'm sorry to inconvenience you this way——
Keller. No inconvenience, other than having that door taken down and the lock replaced, if we fail to find that key.
Annie. Oh, I'll look everywhere for it.
Keller. Thank you. Do not look in any rooms that can be locked. There.

[*He stands her on the ground.* JAMES *applauds.*]

Annie. Thank you very much.

[*She smooths her skirt, looking as composed and ladylike as possible.* KELLER *stares around at the spectators.*]

Keller. Go, go, back to your work. What are you looking at here? There's nothing here to look at. (*They break up, move off.*) Now would it be possible for us to have supper, like other people? (*He marches into the house.*)
Kate. Viney, serve supper. I'll put Mildred to sleep.

[*They all go in.* JAMES *is the last to leave, murmuring to* ANNIE *with a gesture.*]

James. Might as well leave the l, a, d, d, e, r, hm?

[ANNIE *ignores him, looking at* HELEN; JAMES *goes in too. Imperceptibly the lights commence to narrow down.* ANNIE *and* HELEN *are now alone in the yard,* HELEN *seated at the pump, where she has been oblivious to it all, a battered little savage, playing with the doll in a picture of innocent contentment.* ANNIE *comes near, leans against the house, and taking off her smoked glasses, studies her, not without awe. Presently* HELEN *rises, gropes around to see if anyone is present;* ANNIE *evades her hand, and when* HELEN *is satisfied she is alone, the key suddenly protrudes out of her mouth. She takes it in her fingers, stands thinking, gropes to the pump, lifts a loose board, drops the key into the well, and hugs herself gleefully.* ANNIE *stares. But after a moment she shakes her head to herself; she cannot keep the smile from her lips.*]

Annie. You *devil.* (*Her tone is one of great respect, humor, and acceptance of challenge.*) You think I'm so easily gotten rid of? You have a thing or two to learn, first. I have nothing else to do. (*She goes up the steps to the porch, but turns for a final word, almost of warning.*) And nowhere to go.

[*And presently she moves into the house to the others, as the lights dim down and out, except for the small circle upon* HELEN *solitary at the pump, which ends the act.*]

> *"Miss Sullivan, follow instructions! I will not have you also tumbling out of our windows."*

MAKING MEANINGS   ACT ONE

First Thoughts

1. It has been said that in a play we must have someone to root for. So far, whom are you rooting for in this play? Is there anyone you dislike? Explain.

Shaping Interpretations

2. If Annie is the play's **protagonist,** who or what would you say are her **antagonists** or obstacles—the forces that block her from getting what she wants?

3. Helen's action of putting her fingers to others' mouths is **symbolic**—it stands for Helen's desire for communication. What would you say is symbolic in the fact that the first thing Annie gives Helen is a key?

4. In Scene 5 three people give sweets to Helen. What does this tell you about the way Helen has been treated by her family? What might Annie do for Helen that others cannot?

5. By the end of Act One, what questions do you have about what will happen next?

Reviewing the Text

a. This play begins with a crisis. What do we learn in the first scene?

b. What do Helen's **actions** in Scene 2 indicate about her wants?

c. By the end of Scene 3, what decision has been reached about Helen? What **action** has been taken?

d. New pressures are introduced in Scenes 6 and 7 when the Kellers meet Annie. How does each family member respond to this addition to their already troubled household?

e. You can see **conflicts** developing between Annie and Helen and between Annie and the Kellers. What hints of another conflict do you notice between James and his father?

6. What "doors" are closed to Annie and Helen in this act? Have any "doors" opened? Did you predict in your Writer's Notebook what the title "Opening Doors" would mean?

Connecting with the Text

7. If you were Annie or Mrs. Keller, how would you be feeling at this point in the story?

The Playhouse

PLAYBILL
a weekly magazine for theatregoers

THE MIRACLE WORKER

CHOICES: Building Your Portfolio

Writer's Notebook

1. Collecting Ideas for an Interpretive Essay

Finding a topic. When you interpret a work (see the Writer's Workshop on page 716), you need to focus on key passages that illuminate the theme or that reveal something important about the characters. A double-entry journal will help you note these key passages and record your responses to them. Making a double-entry journal is simple. Draw a line down the center of a page of your notebook. On the left side, quote directly or summarize the passage you're interested in. On the right, jot down your reactions—what you make of it. Later, when it's time to interpret the play, your double-entry journal will help you locate key passages.

Speaking

2. Act It Out

Form a group interested in acting and prepare a scene from the first act of the play for presentation to the rest of the class. Assign parts and choose a director. Work as a group to rehearse ways you can bring the scene and the characters to life. If the scene calls for special effects (such as the voices from Annie's past), be sure to assign someone to provide them. You will also have to assign someone to find props and to design costumes. If you wish, you can perform your scene as a dramatic reading rather than as an enactment.

Creative Writing

3. Just One Person

Begin a diary for one of the characters in this play (Helen's mother, father, aunt, or half brother or one of the servants) and record the events that are taking place from that person's point of view. Start on the day Annie arrives. Your diary can reveal things about the character that are only hinted at in the play. Be sure to date your diary entries.

VOCABULARY   HOW TO OWN A WORD

WORD BANK

vivacious
benign
indolent
impudence
inarticulate
resurrection
appraisal
voluminous
caricature
asperity

Semantic Mapping

Work with a partner to create a semantic map for each word in the Word Bank. You will have to make up your own questions about each word and provide your own answers. A sample map is done for *vivacious*. There are two rules: You have to relate each word to *The Miracle Worker,* and you have to come up with an antonym for each.

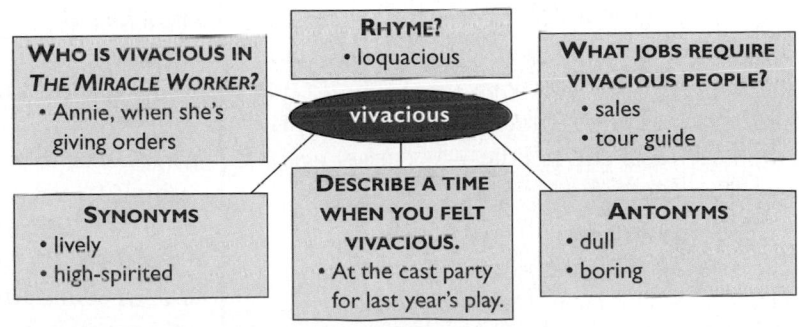

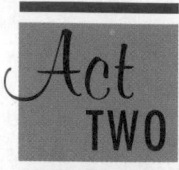

Act TWO

SCENE 1

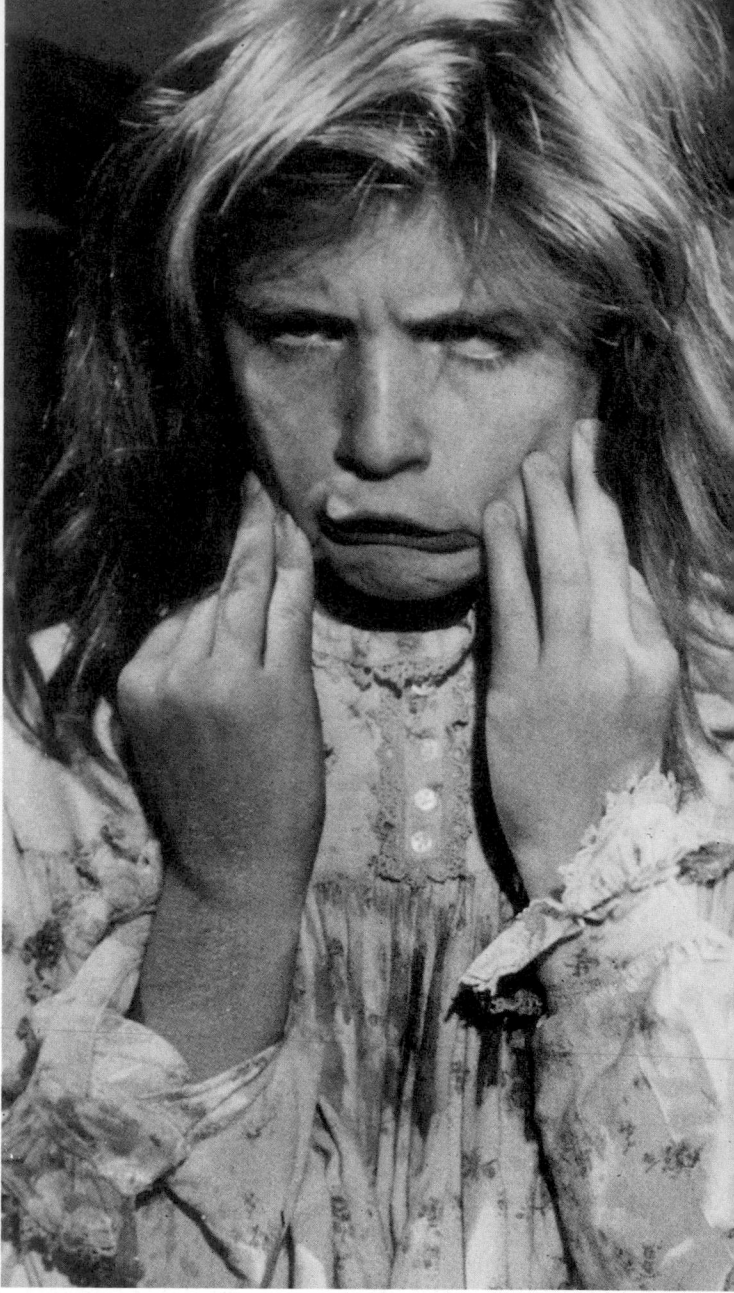

It is evening.

The only room visible in the KELLER *house is* ANNIE'S, *where by lamplight* ANNIE *in a shawl is at a desk writing a letter; at her bureau* HELEN *in her customary unkempt state is tucking her doll in the bottom drawer as a cradle, the contents of which she has dumped out, creating as usual a fine disorder.*

ANNIE *mutters each word as she writes her letter, slowly, her eyes close to and almost touching the page, to follow with difficulty her penwork.*

Annie. ". . . and, nobody, here, has, attempted, to, control, her. The, greatest, problem, I, have, is, how, to, discipline, her, without, breaking, her, spirit." (*Resolute voice*) "But, I, shall, insist, on, reasonable, obedience, from, the, start——" (*At which point* HELEN, *groping about on the desk, knocks over the inkwell.* ANNIE *jumps up, rescues her letter, rights the inkwell, grabs a towel to stem the spillage, and then wipes at* HELEN'S *hands;* HELEN *as always pulls free, but not until* ANNIE *first gets three letters into her palm.*) Ink. (HELEN *is enough interested in and puzzled by this spelling that she proffers her hand again, so* ANNIE *spells and* impassively *dunks it back in the spillage.*) Ink. It has a name. (*She wipes the hand clean and leads* HELEN *to her bureau, where she looks for something to engage her. She finds a sewing card, with needle and thread, and going to her knees, shows* HELEN'S *hand how to connect one row of holes.*) Down. Under. Up. And be careful of the needle—— (HELEN *gets it,* and ANNIE *rises.*) Fine. You keep out of the ink and perhaps I can keep out of—the soup. (*She returns to the desk, tidies it, and resumes writing her letter, bent close to the page.*) "These, blots, are, her, handiwork. I——" (*She is interrupted by a gasp:* HELEN *has stuck her finger and sits sucking at it, darkly. Then with vengeful resolve she seizes her doll and is about to dash its brains out on the floor when* ANNIE, *diving, catches it in one hand, which she at once shakes with hopping pain but otherwise ignores, patiently.*) All right, let's try

WORDS TO OWN

impassively (im·pas′iv·lē) *adv.*: without emotion; calmly.

She lets Helen feel the grieved expression on her face. Helen imitates it.

temperance. (*Taking the doll, she kneels, goes through the motion of knocking its head on the floor, spells into* HELEN'S *hand.*) Bad, girl. (*She lets* HELEN *feel the grieved expression on her face.* HELEN *imitates it. Next she makes*

WORDS TO OWN

temperance (tĕm′pər·əns) *n.*: self-restraint.

HELEN *caress the doll and kiss the hurt spot and hold it gently in her arms, then spells into her hand.*) Good, girl. (*She lets* HELEN *feel the smile on her face.* HELEN *sits with a scowl, which suddenly clears; she pats the doll, kisses it, wreathes her face in a large artificial smile, and bears the doll to the washstand, where she carefully sits it.* ANNIE *watches, pleased.*) Very good girl——

[*Whereupon* HELEN *elevates the pitcher and dashes it on the floor instead.* ANNIE *leaps to her feet and stands inarticulate;* HELEN *calmly gropes back to the sewing card and needle.*

ANNIE *manages to achieve self-control. She picks up a fragment or two of the pitcher, sees* HELEN *is puzzling over the card, and resolutely kneels to demonstrate it again. She spells into* HELEN'S *hand.*

KATE *meanwhile coming around the corner with folded sheets on her arm, halts at the doorway and watches them for a moment in silence; she is moved, but level.*]

Kate (*presently*). What are you saying to her?

[ANNIE *glancing up is a bit embarrassed and rises from the spelling, to find her company manners.*]

Annie. Oh, I was just making conversation. Saying it was a sewing card.
Kate. But does that—(*She imitates with her fingers.*)—mean that to her?
Annie. No. No, she won't know what spelling is till she knows what a word is.
Kate. Yet you keep spelling to her. Why?
Annie (*cheerily*). I like to hear myself talk!
Kate. The Captain says it's like spelling to the fence post.
Annie (*a pause*). Does he, now.
Kate. Is it?
Annie. No, it's how I watch you talk to Mildred.
Kate. Mildred.
Annie. Any baby. Gibberish, grown-up gibberish, baby-talk gibberish, do they understand one word of it to start? Somehow they begin to. If they hear it. I'm letting Helen hear it.
Kate. Other children are not—impaired.
Annie. Ho, there's nothing impaired in that head. It works like a mousetrap!
Kate (*smiles*). But after a child hears how many words, Miss Annie, a million?
Annie. I guess no mother's ever minded enough to count.

[*She drops her eyes to spell into* HELEN'S *hand, again indicating the card;* HELEN *spells back, and* ANNIE *is amused.*]

Kate (*too quickly*). What did she spell?
Annie. I spelled card. She spelled cake! (*She takes in* KATE'S *quickness and shakes her head, gently.*) No, it's only a finger game to her, Mrs. Keller. What she has to learn first is that things have names.
Kate. And when will she learn?
Annie. Maybe after a million and one words.

[*They hold each other's gaze;* KATE *then speaks quietly.*]

Kate. I should like to learn those letters, Miss Annie.
Annie (*pleased*). I'll teach you tomorrow morning. That makes only half a million each!
Kate (*then*). It's her bedtime. (ANNIE *reaches for the sewing card,* HELEN *objects,* ANNIE *insists, and* HELEN *gets rid of* ANNIE'S *hand by jabbing it with the needle.* ANNIE *gasps and moves to grip* HELEN'S *wrist; but* KATE *intervenes with a proffered sweet, and* HELEN *drops the card, crams the sweet into her mouth, and scrambles up to search her mother's hands for more.* ANNIE *nurses her wound, staring after the sweet.*) I'm sorry, Miss Annie.
Annie (*indignantly*). Why does she get a reward? For stabbing me?
Kate. Well—— (*Then, tiredly*) We catch our flies with honey, I'm afraid. We haven't the heart for much else, and so many times she simply cannot be compelled.
Annie (*ominous*). Yes. I'm the same way myself. (KATE *smiles and leads* HELEN *off around the corner.* ANNIE *alone in her room picks up things and in the act of removing* HELEN'S *doll gives way to unmannerly temptation: She throttles it. She drops it on her bed and stands pondering. Then she turns back, sits decisively, and writes again, as the lights dim on her. Grimly:*) "The, more, I, think, the, more, certain, I, am, that, obedience, is, the, gateway, through, which, knowledge, enters, the, mind, of, the, child——"

WORDS TO OWN

ominous (äm′ə·nəs) *adj.*: threatening.

SCENE 2

On the word obedience *a shaft of sunlight hits the water pump outside, while* ANNIE'S *voice ends in the dark, followed by a distant cockcrow; daylight comes up over another corner of the sky, with* VINEY'S *voice heard at once.*

Viney. Breakfast ready!

[VINEY *comes down into the sunlight beam and pumps a pitcherful of water. While the pitcher is brimming we hear conversation from the dark; the light grows to the family room of the house where all are either entering or already seated at breakfast, with* KELLER *and* JAMES *arguing the war.*[1] HELEN *is wandering around the table to explore the contents of the other plates. When* ANNIE *is in her chair, she watches* HELEN. VINEY *reenters, sets the pitcher on the table;* KATE *lifts the almost empty biscuit plate with an inquiring look,* VINEY *nods and bears it off back, neither of them interrupting the men.* ANNIE *meanwhile sits with fork quiet, watching* HELEN, *who at her mother's plate pokes her hand among some scrambled eggs.* KATE *catches* ANNIE'S *eyes on her, smiles with a wry gesture.* HELEN *moves on to* JAMES'S *plate, the male talk continuing,* JAMES *deferential and* KELLER *overriding.*]

James. —no, but shouldn't we give the devil his due, Father? The fact is we lost the South two years earlier when he outthought us behind Vicksburg.[2]

Keller. *Outthought* is a peculiar word for a butcher.

James. Harness maker, wasn't he?

Keller. I said butcher, his only virtue as a soldier was numbers and he led them to slaughter with no more regard than for so many sheep.

James. But even if in that sense he was a butcher, the fact is he——

Keller. And a drunken one, half the war.

---

1. **the war:** the Civil War.
2. **Vicksburg:** On July 4, 1863, at Vicksburg, Mississippi, General Ulysses S. Grant's Northern army won a decisive victory in the Civil War.

James. Agreed, Father. If his own people said he was I can't argue he——

Keller. Well, what is it you find to admire in such a man, Jimmie, the butchery or the drunkenness?

James. Neither, Father, only the fact that he beat us.

Keller. He didn't.

James. Is it your contention we won the war, sir?

Keller. He didn't beat us at Vicksburg. We lost Vicksburg because Pemberton gave Bragg five thousand of his cavalry, and Loring, whom I knew personally for a nincompoop before you were born, marched away from Champion's Hill with enough men to have held them. We lost Vicksburg by stupidity verging on treason.

James. I would have said we lost Vicksburg because Grant was one thing no Yankee general was before him——

Keller. Drunk? I doubt it.

James. Obstinate.

Keller. Obstinate. Could any of them compare even in that with old Stonewall?[3] If he'd been there we would still have Vicksburg.

James. Well, the butcher simply wouldn't give up; he tried four ways of getting around Vicksburg and on the fifth try he got around. Anyone else would have pulled north and——

Keller. He wouldn't have got around if we'd had a Southerner in command, instead of a half-breed Yankee traitor like Pemberton—— (*While this background talk is in progress,* HELEN *is working around the table, ultimately toward* ANNIE'S *plate. She messes with her hands in* JAMES'S *plate, then in* KELLER'S, *both men taking it so for granted they hardly notice. Then* HELEN *comes groping with soiled hands past her own plate, to* ANNIE'S; *her hand goes to it, and* ANNIE, *who has*

---

3. **Stonewall:** General Thomas J. Jackson, nicknamed "Stonewall" by his Southern troops because of his stubborn refusal to give up.

- -

WORDS TO OWN

deferential (def′ər·en′shəl) *adj.:* showing polite respect.

- -

been waiting, deliberately lifts and removes her hand. HELEN *gropes again,* ANNIE *firmly pins her by the wrist and removes her hand from the table.* HELEN *thrusts her hands again,* ANNIE *catches them, and* HELEN *begins to flail and make noises; the interruption brings* KELLER'S *gaze upon them.*) What's the matter there?

Kate. Miss Annie. You see, she's accustomed to helping herself from our plates to anything she——

Annie (*evenly*). Yes, but *I'm* not accustomed to it.

Keller. No, of course not. Viney!

Kate. Give her something, Jimmie, to quiet her.

James (*blandly*). But her table manners are the best she has. Well.

Annie firmly pins her by the wrist and removes her hand from the table.

[*He pokes across with a chunk of bacon at* HELEN'S *hand, which* ANNIE *releases; but* HELEN *knocks the bacon away and stubbornly thrusts at* ANNIE'S *plate.* ANNIE *grips her wrists again. The struggle mounts.*]

Keller. Let her this time, Miss Sullivan, it's the only way we get any adult conversation. If my son's half merits that description. (*He rises.*) I'll get you another plate.

Annie (*gripping* HELEN). I have a plate, thank you.

Kate (*calling*). Viney! I'm afraid what Captain Keller says is only too true. She'll persist in this until she gets her own way.

Keller (*at the door*). Viney, bring Miss Sullivan another plate——

Annie (*stonily*). I have a plate, nothing's wrong with the *plate*, I intend to keep it.

[*Silence for a moment, except for* HELEN'S *noises as she struggles to get loose; the* KELLERS *are a bit nonplused,[4] and* ANNIE *is too darkly intent on* HELEN'S *manners to have any thoughts now of her own.*]

James. Ha. You see why they took Vicksburg?

Keller (*uncertainly*). Miss Sullivan. One plate or another is hardly a matter to struggle with a deprived child about.

Annie. Oh, I'd sooner have a more—(HELEN *begins to kick,* ANNIE *moves her ankles to the opposite side of the chair*)—heroic issue myself, I——

Keller. No, I really must insist you—— (HELEN *bangs her toe on the chair and sinks to the floor, crying with rage and feigned injury;* ANNIE *keeps hold of her wrists, gazing down, while* KATE *rises.*) Now she's hurt herself.

Annie (*grimly*). No, she hasn't.

Keller. Will you please let her hands go?

Kate. Miss Annie, you don't know the child well enough yet, she'll keep——

Annie. I know an ordinary tantrum well enough, when I see one, and a badly spoiled child——

James. Hear, hear.

Keller (*very annoyed*). Miss Sullivan! You would have more understanding of your pupil if you had some pity in you. Now kindly do as I——

Annie. Pity? (*She releases* HELEN *to turn equally annoyed on* KELLER *across the table; instantly* HELEN *scrambles up and dives at* ANNIE'S *plate. This time* ANNIE *intercepts her by pouncing on her wrists like a hawk, and her*

4. **nonplused** (nän'plust'): puzzled; uncertain what to do next.

WORDS TO OWN

feigned (fānd) *adj.:* pretended or faked.

temper boils.) For this *tyrant*? The whole house turns on her whims. Is there anything she wants she doesn't get? I'll tell you what I pity, that the sun won't rise and set for her all her life, and every day you're telling her it will. What good will your pity do her when you're under the strawberries, Captain Keller?

Keller (*outraged*). Kate, for the love of heaven will you——

Kate. Miss Annie, please, I don't think it serves to lose our——

Annie. It does you good, that's all. It's less trouble to feel sorry for her than to teach her anything better, isn't it?

Keller. I fail to see where you have taught her anything yet, Miss Sullivan!

Annie. I'll begin this minute, if you'll leave the room, Captain Keller!

Keller (*astonished*). Leave the——

Annie. Everyone, please.

[*She struggles with* HELEN, *while* KELLER *endeavors to control his voice.*]

Keller. Miss Sullivan, you are here only as a paid teacher. Nothing more, and not to lecture——

Annie. I can't *un*teach her six years of pity if you can't stand up to one tantrum! Old Stonewall, indeed. Mrs. Keller, you promised me help.

Kate. Indeed I did, we truly want to——

Annie. Then leave me alone with her. Now!

Keller (*in a wrath*). Katie, will you come outside with me? At once, please.

[*He marches to the front door.* KATE *and* JAMES *follow him. Simultaneously* ANNIE *releases* HELEN'S *wrists, and the child again sinks to the floor, kicking and crying her weird noises.* ANNIE *steps over her to meet* VINEY *coming in the rear doorway with biscuits and a clean plate, surprised at the general commotion.*]

Viney. Heaven sakes——

Annie. Out, please.

[*She backs* VINEY *out with one hand, closes the door on her astonished mouth, locks it, and removes the key.* KELLER *meanwhile snatches his hat from a rack, and* KATE *follows him down the porch steps.* JAMES *lingers in the doorway to address* ANNIE *across the room with a bow.*]

James. If it takes all summer, general.

[ANNIE *comes over to his door in turn, removing her glasses grimly; as* KELLER *outside begins speaking,* ANNIE *closes the door on* JAMES, *locks it, removes the key, and turns with her back against the door to stare ominously at* HELEN, *kicking on the floor.* JAMES *takes his hat from the rack, and going down the porch steps joins* KATE *and* KELLER *talking in the yard,* KELLER *in a sputter of ire.*]

Keller. This girl, this—cub of a girl—*presumes*! I tell you, I'm of half a mind to ship her back to Boston before the week is out. You can inform her so from me!

Kate (*eyebrows up*). I, Captain?

Keller. She's a *hireling.*[5] Now I want it clear. Unless there's an apology and complete change of manner, she goes back on the next train! Will you make that quite clear?

Kate. Where will you be, Captain, while I am making it quite——

Keller. At the office!

[*He begins off left, finds his napkin still in his irate hand, is uncertain with it, dabs his lips with dignity, gets rid of it in a toss to* JAMES, *and marches off.* JAMES *turns to eye* KATE.]

James. Will you? (KATE'S *mouth is set, and* JAMES *studies it lightly.*) I thought what she said was exceptionally intelligent. I've been saying it for years.

Kate (*not without scorn*). To his face? (*She comes to relieve him of the white napkin, but reverts again with it.*) Or will you take it, Jimmie? As a flag?

5. **hireling** (hīr′liŋ): paid servant. Here, the word shows a lack of respect.

JAMES *stalks out, much offended, and* KATE *turning stares across the yard at the house; the lights narrowing down to the following pantomime in the family room leave her motionless in the dark.*

ANNIE *meanwhile has begun by slapping both keys down on a shelf out of* HELEN'S *reach; she returns to the table, upstage.* HELEN'S *kicking has subsided, and when from the floor her hand finds* ANNIE'S *chair empty she pauses.* ANNIE *clears the table of* KATE'S, JAMES'S, *and* KELLER'S *plates; she gets back to her own across the table just in time to slide it deftly away from* HELEN'S *hand. She lifts the hand and moves it to* HELEN'S *plate, and after an instant's exploration,* HELEN *sits again on the floor and drums her heels.* ANNIE *comes around the table and resumes her chair. When* HELEN *feels her skirt again, she ceases kicking, waits for whatever is to come, renews some kicking, waits again.* ANNIE, *retrieving her plate, takes up a forkful of food, stops it halfway to her mouth, gazes at it devoid of appetite, and half lowers it; but after a look at* HELEN *she sighs, dips the forkful toward* HELEN *in a for-your-sake toast, and puts it in her own mouth to chew, not without an effort.*

HELEN *now gets hold of the chair leg, and half succeeds in pulling the chair out from under her.* ANNIE *bangs it down with her rear, heavily, and sits with all her weight.* HELEN'S *next attempt to topple it is unavailing, so her fingers dive in a pinch at* ANNIE'S *flank.* ANNIE *in the middle of her mouthful almost loses it with startle, and she slaps down her fork to round on* HELEN. *The child comes up with curiosity to feel what* ANNIE *is doing, so* ANNIE *resumes eating, letting* HELEN'S *hand follow the movement of her fork to her mouth; whereupon* HELEN *at once reaches into* ANNIE'S *plate.* ANNIE *firmly removes her hand to her own plate.* HELEN *in reply pinches* ANNIE'S *thigh, a good mean pinchful that makes* ANNIE *jump.* ANNIE *sets the fork down and sits with her mouth tight.* HELEN *digs another pinch into her thigh, and this time* ANNIE *slaps her hand*

smartly away; HELEN *retaliates with a roundhouse fist that catches* ANNIE *on the ear, and* ANNIE'S *hand leaps at once in a forceful slap across* HELEN'S *cheek;* HELEN *is the startled one now.* ANNIE'S *hand in compunction falters to her own face, but when* HELEN *hits at her again,* ANNIE *deliberately slaps her again.* HELEN *lifts her fist irresolute for another roundhouse,* ANNIE *lifts her hand resolute for another slap, and they freeze in this posture while* HELEN *mulls it over. She thinks better of it, drops her fist, and giving* ANNIE *a wide berth gropes around to her mother's chair, to find it empty; she blunders her way along the table upstage, and encountering the empty chairs and missing plates, she looks bewildered; she gropes back to her mother's chair, again touches her cheek and indicates the chair, and waits for the world to answer.*

ANNIE *now reaches over to spell into her hand but* HELEN *yanks it away; she gropes to the front door, tries the knob, and finds the door locked, with no key. She gropes to the rear door and finds it locked, with no key. She commences to bang on it.* ANNIE *rises, crosses, takes her wrists, draws her resisting back to the table, seats her, and releases her hands upon her plate; as* ANNIE *herself begins to sit,* HELEN *writhes out of her chair, runs to the front door, and tugs and kicks at it.* ANNIE *rises again, crosses, draws her by one wrist back to the table, seats her, and sits;* HELEN *escapes back to the door, knocking over her mother's chair en route.* ANNIE *rises again in pursuit, and this time lifts* HELEN *bodily from behind and bears her kicking to her chair. She deposits her, and once more turns to sit.* HELEN *scrambles out, but as she passes,* ANNIE *catches her up again from behind and deposits her in the chair;* HELEN *scrambles out on the other side, for the*

WORDS TO OWN

retaliates (ri·tal′ē·āts′) v.: returns an injury or wrong.
compunction (kəm·puŋk′shən) n.: feeling of guilt and regret.

---

rear door, but ANNIE *at her heels catches her up and deposits her again in the chair. She stands behind it.* HELEN *scrambles out to her right, and the instant her feet hit the floor* ANNIE *lifts and deposits her back; she scrambles out to her left and is at once lifted and deposited back. She tries right again and is deposited back, and tries left again and is deposited back, and now feints* ANNIE *to the right but is off to her left, and is promptly deposited back. She sits a moment and then starts straight over the tabletop, dishware notwithstanding;* ANNIE *hauls her in and deposits her back, with her plate spilling in her lap, and she melts to the floor and crawls under the table, laborious among its legs and chairs; but* ANNIE *is swift around the table and waiting on the other side when she surfaces, immediately bearing her aloft;* HELEN *clutches at* JAMES'S *chair for anchorage, but it comes with her, and halfway back she abandons it to the floor.* ANNIE *deposits her in her chair, and waits.* HELEN *sits tensed, motionless. Then she tentatively puts out her left foot and hand,* ANNIE *interposes her own hand, and at the contact* HELEN *jerks hers in. She tries her right foot,* ANNIE *blocks it with her own, and* HELEN *jerks hers in. Finally, leaning back, she slumps down in her chair, in a sullen biding.*

ANNIE *backs off a step and watches:* HELEN *offers no move.* ANNIE *takes a deep breath. Both of them and the room are in considerable disorder, two chairs down and the table a mess; but* ANNIE *makes no effort to tidy it; she only sits on her own chair and lets her energy refill. Then she takes up knife and fork and resolutely addresses her food.* HELEN'S *hand comes out to explore, and seeing it,* ANNIE *sits without moving; the child's hand goes over her hand and fork, pauses—*ANNIE *still does not move—and withdraws. Presently it moves for her own plate, slaps about for it, and stops, thwarted. At this,* ANNIE *again rises, recovers* HELEN'S *plate from the floor and a handful of scattered food from the deranged tablecloth, drops it on the plate, and pushes the plate into contact with* HELEN'S *fist. Neither of them now moves for a pregnant moment—until* HELEN *suddenly takes a grab of food and wolfs it down.* ANNIE *permits herself the humor of a minor bow and warming of her hands together; she wanders off a step or two, watching.* HELEN *cleans up the plate.*

After a glower of indecision, she holds the empty plate out for more. ANNIE *accepts it, and crossing to the removed plates, spoons food from them onto it; she stands debating the spoon, tapping it a few times on* HELEN'S *plate; and when she returns with the plate she brings the spoon, too. She puts the spoon first into* HELEN'S *hand, then sets the plate down.* HELEN *discarding the spoon reaches with her hand, and* ANNIE *stops it by the wrist; she replaces the spoon in it.* HELEN *impatiently discards it, and again* ANNIE *stops her hand, to replace the spoon in it. This time* HELEN *throws the spoon on the floor.* ANNIE, *after considering it, lifts* HELEN *bodily out of the chair, and in a wrestling match on the floor closes her fingers upon the spoon and returns her with it to the chair.* HELEN *again throws the spoon on the floor.* ANNIE *lifts her out of the chair again; but in the struggle over the spoon* HELEN, *with* ANNIE *on her back, sends her sliding over her head;* HELEN *flees back to her chair and scrambles into it. When* ANNIE *comes after her she clutches it for dear life;* ANNIE *pries one hand loose, then the other, then the first again, then the other again, and then lifts* HELEN *by the waist, chair and all, and shakes the chair loose.* HELEN *wrestles to get free, but* ANNIE *pins her to the floor, closes her fingers upon the spoon, and lifts her kicking under one arm; with her other hand she gets the chair in place again and plunks* HELEN *back on it. When she releases her hand,* HELEN *throws the spoon at her.*

ANNIE *now removes the plate of food.* HELEN *grabbing finds it missing and commences to bang with her fists on the table.* ANNIE *collects a fistful of spoons and descends with them and the plate on* HELEN; *she lets her smell the plate, at which* HELEN *ceases banging, and* ANNIE *puts the plate down and a spoon in* HELEN'S *hand.* HELEN *throws it on the floor.* ANNIE *puts another spoon in her hand.* HELEN *throws it on the floor.*

She puts the spoon first into Helen's hand. . . .

*The pain brings Annie to her knees, and Helen pummels her;
they roll under the table....*

ANNIE *puts another spoon in her hand.* HELEN *throws it on the floor. When* ANNIE *comes to her last spoon, she sits next to* HELEN *and, gripping the spoon in* HELEN'S *hand, compels her to take food in it up to her mouth.* HELEN *sits with lips shut.* ANNIE *waits a stolid moment, then lowers* HELEN'S *hand. She tries again;* HELEN'S *lips remain shut.* ANNIE *waits, lowers* HELEN'S *hand. She tries again; this time* HELEN *suddenly opens her mouth and accepts the food.* ANNIE *lowers the spoon with a sigh of relief, and* HELEN *spews the mouthful out at her face.* ANNIE *sits a moment with eyes closed, then takes the pitcher and dashes its water into* HELEN'S *face,* *who gasps astonished.* ANNIE *with* HELEN'S *hand takes up another spoonful and shoves it into her open mouth.* HELEN *swallows involuntarily, and while she is catching her breath* ANNIE *forces her palm open, throws four swift letters into it, then another four, and bows toward her with devastating pleasantness.*

Annie. Good girl.

[ANNIE *lifts* HELEN'S *hand to feel her face nodding;* HELEN *grabs a fistful of her hair, and yanks. The pain brings* ANNIE *to her knees, and* HELEN *pummels her; they roll under the table, and the lights commence to dim out on them.*]

SCENE 4

Simultaneously the light at left has been rising, slowly, so slowly that it seems at first we only imagine what is intimated in the yard: a few ghostlike figures, in silence, motionless, waiting. Now the distant belfry chimes commence to toll the hour, also very slowly, almost—it is twelve— interminably; the sense is that of a long time passing. We can identify the figures before the twelfth stroke, all facing the house in a kind of watch; KATE *is standing exactly as before, but now with the baby* MILDRED *sleeping in her arms, and placed here and there, unmoving, are* AUNT EV *in her hat with a hankie to her nose, and the two children,* PERCY *and* MARTHA, *with necks outstretched eagerly, and* VINEY *with a knotted kerchief on her head and a feather duster in her hand.*

The chimes cease, and there is silence. For a long moment none of the group moves.

Viney (*presently*). What am I gone do, Miss Kate? It's noontime, dinner's comin', I didn't get them breakfast dishes out of there yet.

[KATE *says nothing, stares at the house.* MARTHA *shifts* HELEN'S *doll in her clutch, and it plaintively says "Momma."*]

Kate (*presently*). You run along, Martha.

[AUNT EV *blows her nose.*]

Aunt Ev (*wretchedly*). I can't wait out here a minute longer, Kate, why, this could go on all afternoon, too.
Kate. I'll tell the captain you called.
Viney (*to the children*). You hear what Miss Kate say? Never you mind what's going on here. (*Still no one moves.*) You run along tend your own bizness. (*Finally* VINEY *turns on the children with the feather duster.*) Shoo!

[*The two children divide before her. She chases them off.* AUNT EV *comes to* KATE, *on her dignity.*]

Aunt Ev. Say what you like, Kate, but that child is a *Keller*. (*She opens her parasol, preparatory to leaving.*) I needn't remind you that all the Kellers are cousins to General Robert E. Lee. I

don't know *who* that girl is. (*She waits; but* KATE, *staring at the house, is without response.*) The only Sullivan I've heard of—from Boston too, and I'd think twice before locking her up with that kind—is that man John L.[6]

[*And* AUNT EV *departs, with head high. Presently* VINEY *comes to* KATE, *her arms out for the baby.*]

Viney. You give me her, Miss Kate, I'll sneak her in back, to her crib.

[*But* KATE *is moveless, until* VINEY *starts to take the baby;* KATE *looks down at her before relinquishing her.*]

Kate (*slowly*). This child never gives me a minute's worry.
Viney. Oh yes, this one's the angel of the family, no question 'bout *that*.

[*She begins off rear with the baby, heading around the house; and* KATE *now turns her back on it, her hand to her eyes. At this moment there is the slamming of a door, and when* KATE *wheels,* HELEN *is blundering down the porch steps into the light, like a ruined bat out of hell.* VINEY *halts, and* KATE *runs in;* HELEN *collides with her mother's knees and reels off and back to clutch them as her savior.* ANNIE *with smoked glasses in hand stands on the porch, also much undone, looking as though she had indeed just taken Vicksburg.* KATE, *taking in* HELEN'S *ravaged state, becomes steely in her gaze up at* ANNIE.]

Kate. What happened?

[ANNIE *meets* KATE'S *gaze and gives a factual report, too exhausted for anything but a flat voice.*]

Annie. She ate from her own plate. (*She thinks a moment.*) She ate with a spoon. Herself. (KATE

6. **John L. Sullivan:** heavyweight boxing champion of the 1880s.

WORDS TO OWN
interminably (in·tɜr′mi·nə·blē) *adv.:* endlessly.

frowns, uncertain with thought, and glances down at HELEN.) And she folded her napkin.

[KATE'S *gaze now wavers, from* HELEN *to* ANNIE, *and back.*]

Kate (*softly*). Folded—her napkin?
Annie. The room's a wreck, but her napkin is folded. (*She pauses, then*) I'll be in my room, Mrs. Keller. (*She moves to reenter the house; but she stops at* VINEY'S *voice.*)
Viney (*cheery*). Don't be long, Miss Annie. Dinner be ready right away!

[VINEY *carries* MILDRED *around the back of the house.* ANNIE *stands unmoving, takes a deep breath, stares over her shoulder at* KATE *and* HELEN, *then inclines her head graciously and goes with a slight stagger into the house. The lights in her room above steal up in readiness for her.*

KATE *remains alone with* HELEN *in the yard, standing protectively over her, in a kind of wonder.*]

Kate (*slowly*). Folded her napkin. (*She contemplates the wild head in her thighs and moves her fingertips over it, with such a tenderness, and something like a fear of its strangeness, that her own eyes close; she whispers, bending to it.*) My Helen—folded her napkin——

[*And still erect, with only her head in surrender,* KATE *for the first time that we see loses her protracted war with grief; but she will not let a sound escape her, only the grimace of tears comes, and sobs that shake her in a grip of silence. But* HELEN *feels them, and her hand comes up in its own wondering, to interrogate her mother's face, until* KATE *buries her lips in the child's palm.*]

SCENE 5

Upstairs, ANNIE *enters her room, closes the door, and stands back against it; the lights, growing on her with their special color, commence to fade on* KATE *and* HELEN. *Then* ANNIE *goes wearily to her suitcase and lifts it to take it toward the bed. But it knocks an object to the floor, and she turns back to regard it. A new voice comes in a cultured murmur, hesitant as with the effort of remembering a text:*[7]

7. **text:** The text is from the writings of Dr. Samuel Gridley Howe, former director of the Perkins Institution, who had died before Annie arrived there. The words that follow refer to a blind, deaf, and mute woman whom Howe visited in an institution in England.

Man's Voice. This—soul—(ANNIE *puts the suitcase down and kneels to the object: It is the battered Perkins report, and she stands with it in her hand, letting memory try to speak.*) This—blind, deaf, mute—woman—(ANNIE *sits on her bed, opens the book, and finding the passage, brings it up an inch from her eyes to read, her face and lips following the overheard words, the voice quite factual now.*) Can nothing be done to disinter[8] this

8. **disinter** (dis′in·tûr′): dig up from the grave. Here, the speaker uses the word figuratively to mean "find the soul hidden within a person."

human soul? The whole neighborhood would rush to save this woman if she were buried alive by the caving in of a pit, and labor with zeal until she were dug out. Now if there were one who had as much patience as zeal, he might awaken her to a consciousness of her immortal—— (*When the boy's voice comes,* ANNIE *closes her eyes, in pain.*)

Boy's Voice. Annie? Annie, you there?
Annie. Hush.
Boy's Voice. Annie, what's that noise? (ANNIE *tries not to answer; her own voice is drawn out of her, unwilling.*)
Annie. Just a cot, Jimmie.
Boy's Voice. Where they pushin' it?
Annie. To the deadhouse.
Boy's Voice. Annie. Does it hurt, to be dead?

[ANNIE *escapes by opening her eyes, her hand works restlessly over her cheek; she retreats into the book again, but the cracked old crones interrupt, whispering.* ANNIE *slowly lowers the book.*]

First Crone's Voice. There is schools.
Second Crone's Voice. There is schools outside——
Third Crone's Voice. ——schools where they teach blind ones, worse'n you——
First Crone's Voice. To read——
Second Crone's Voice. To read and write——
Third Crone's Voice. There is schools outside where they——
First Crone's Voice. There is schools——

[*Silence.* ANNIE *sits with her eyes shining, her hand almost in a caress over the book. Then:*]

Boy's Voice. You ain't goin' to school, are you, Annie?
Annie (*whispering*). When I grow up.
Boy's Voice. You ain't either, Annie. You're goin' to stay here take care of me.
Annie. I'm goin' to school when I grow up.
Boy's Voice. You said we'll be together, forever and ever and ever——
Annie (*fierce*). I'm goin' to school when I grow up!
Doctor's Voice (*slowly*). Little girl. Little girl, I must tell you. Your brother will be going on a journey, soon.

[ANNIE *sits rigid, in silence. Then the boy's voice pierces it, a shriek of terror.*]

Boy's Voice. *Annie!*

[*It goes into* ANNIE *like a sword, she doubles onto it; the book falls to the floor. It takes her a racked moment to find herself and what she was engaged in here; when she sees the suitcase she remembers and lifts it once again toward the bed. But the voices are with her, as she halts with suitcase in hand.*]

First Crone's Voice. Goodbye, Annie.
Doctor's Voice. Write me when you learn how.
Second Crone's Voice. Don't tell anyone you came from here. Don't tell anyone——
Third Crone's Voice. Yeah, don't tell anyone you came from——
First Crone's Voice. Yeah, don't tell anyone——
Second Crone's Voice. Don't tell any——

[*The echoing voices fade. After a moment* ANNIE *lays the suitcase on the bed; and the last voice comes faintly, from far away.*]

Boy's Voice. Annie. It hurts, to be dead. Forever.

[ANNIE *falls to her knees by the bed, stifling her mouth in it. When at last she rolls blindly away from it, her palm comes down on the open report; she opens her eyes, regards it dully, and then, still on her knees, takes in the print.*]

Man's Voice (*factual*). ——might awaken her to a consciousness of her immortal nature. The chance is small indeed; but with a smaller chance they would have dug desperately for her in the pit; and is the life of the soul of less import than that of the body?

[ANNIE *gets to her feet. She drops the book on the bed and pauses over her suitcase; after a moment she unclasps and opens it. Standing before it, she comes to her decision; she at once turns to the bureau, and taking her things out of its drawers, commences to throw them into the open suitcase.*]

SCENE 6

In the darkness down left a hand strikes a match and lights a hanging oil lamp. It is KELLER'S *hand, and his voice accompanies it, very angry; the lights rising here before they fade on* ANNIE *show* KELLER *and* KATE *inside a suggestion of a garden house, with a bay window seat toward center and a door at back.*

Keller. Katie, I will not *have* it! Now you did not see when that girl after supper tonight went to look for Helen in her room——

Kate. No.

Keller. The child practically climbed out of her window to escape from her! What kind of teacher *is* she? I thought I had seen her at her worst this morning, shouting at me, but I come home to find the entire house disorganized by her—Helen won't stay one second in the same room, won't come to the table with her, won't let herself be bathed or undressed or put to bed by her, or even by Viney now, and the end result is that *you* have to do more for the child than before we hired this girl's services! From the moment she stepped off the train she's been nothing but a burden, incompetent, impertinent, ineffectual, immodest——

Kate. She folded her napkin, Captain.

Keller. What?

Kate. Not ineffectual. Helen did fold her napkin.

Keller. What in heaven's name is so extraordinary about folding a napkin?

Kate (*with some humor*). Well. It's more than you did, Captain.

Keller. Katie. I did not bring you all the way out here to the garden house to be frivolous. Now, how does Miss Sullivan propose to teach a deaf-blind pupil who won't let her even touch her?

Kate (*a pause*). I don't know.

Keller. The fact is, today she scuttled any chance she ever had of getting along with the child. If you can see any point or purpose to her staying on here longer, it's more than——

Kate. What do you wish me to do?

Keller. I want you to give her notice.

Kate. I can't.

Keller. Then if you won't, I must. I simply will not—— (*He is interrupted by a knock at the back door.* KELLER *after a glance at* KATE *moves to open the door;* ANNIE *in her smoked glasses is standing outside.* KELLER *contemplates her, heavily.*) Miss Sullivan.

Annie. Captain Keller. (*She is nervous, keyed up to seizing the bull by the horns again, and she assumes a cheeriness which is not unshaky.*) Viney said I'd find you both over here in the garden house. I thought we should—have a talk?

Keller (*reluctantly*). Yes. I—— Well, come in. (ANNIE *enters and is interested in this room; she rounds on her heel, anxiously, studying it.* KELLER *turns the matter over to* KATE, *sotto voce.*) Katie.

Kate (*turning it back, courteously*). Captain.

[KELLER *clears his throat, makes ready.*]

Keller. I, ah—wanted first to make my position clear to Mrs. Keller, in private. I have decided I—am not satisfied—in fact, am deeply dissatisfied—with the manner in which——

Annie (*intent*). Excuse me, is this little house ever in use?

Keller (*with patience*). In the hunting season. If you will give me your attention, Miss Sullivan. (ANNIE *turns her smoked glasses upon him; they hold his unwilling stare.*) I have tried to make allowances for you because you come from a part of the country where people are—women, I should say—come from who— well, for whom—(*It begins to elude him.*)— allowances must—be made. I have decided, nevertheless, to—that is, decided I—(*vexedly*) Miss Sullivan, I find it difficult to talk through those glasses.

Annie (*eagerly, removing them*). Oh, of course.

Keller (*dourly*). Why do you wear them? The sun has been down for an hour.

Annie (*pleasantly, at the lamp*). Any kind of light hurts my eyes.

[*A silence;* KELLER *ponders her, heavily.*]

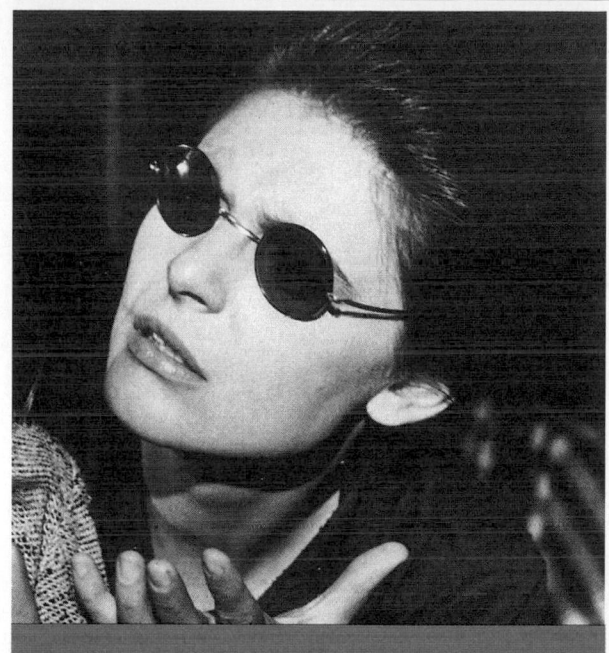

"Mrs. Keller, I don't think Helen's worst handicap is deafness or blindness. I think it's your love. And pity."

Keller. Put them on. Miss Sullivan, I have decided to—give you another chance.
Annie (*cheerfully*). To do what?
Keller. To—remain in our employ. (ANNIE'S *eyes widen.*) But on two conditions. I am not accustomed to rudeness in servants or women, and that is the first. If you are to stay, there must be a radical change of manner.
Annie (*a pause*). Whose?
Keller (*exploding*). Yours, young lady, isn't it obvious? And the second is that you persuade me there's the slightest hope of your teaching a child who flees from you now like the plague, to anyone else she can find in this house.
Annie (*a pause*). There isn't.

[KATE *stops sewing and fixes her eyes upon* ANNIE.]

Kate. What, Miss Annie?
Annie. It's hopeless here. I can't teach a child who runs away.
Keller (*nonplused*). Then—do I understand you—propose——

Annie. Well, if we all agree it's hopeless, the next question is what——
Kate. Miss Annie. (*She is leaning toward* ANNIE, *in deadly earnest; it commands both* ANNIE *and* KELLER.) I am not agreed. I think perhaps you—underestimate Helen.
Annie. I think everybody else here does.
Kate. She did fold her napkin. She learns, she learns, do you know she began talking when she was six months old? She could say "water." Not really—"wahwah." "Wahwah," but she meant water, she knew what it meant, and only six months old, I never saw a child so—bright, or outgoing—— (*Her voice is unsteady, but she gets it level.*) It's still in her, somewhere, isn't it? You should have seen her before her illness, such a good-tempered child——
Annie (*agreeably*). She's changed.

[*A pause,* KATE *not letting her eyes go; her appeal at last is unconditional, and very quiet.*]

Kate. Miss Annie, put up with it. And with us.
Keller. Us!
Kate. Please? Like the lost lamb in the parable, I love her all the more.
Annie. Mrs. Keller, I don't think Helen's worst handicap is deafness or blindness. I think it's your love. And pity.
Keller. Now what does that mean?
Annie. All of you here are so sorry for her you've kept her—like a pet, why, even a dog you housebreak. No wonder she won't let me come near her. It's useless for me to try to teach her language or anything else here. I might as well——
Kate (*cuts in*). Miss Annie, before you came we spoke of putting her in an asylum.

[ANNIE *turns back to regard her. A pause.*]

Annie. What kind of asylum?
Keller. For mental defectives.
Kate. I visited there. I can't tell you what I saw, people like—animals, with—*rats,* in the halls, and—— (*She shakes her head on her vision.*) What else are we to do, if you give up?
Annie. Give up?
Kate. You said it was hopeless.

Annie. Here. Give up, why, I only today saw what has to be done, to begin! (*She glances from* KATE *to* KELLER, *who stare, waiting; and she makes it as plain and simple as her nervousness permits.*) I—want complete charge of her.

Keller. You already have that. It has resulted in——

Annie. No, I mean day and night. She has to be dependent on me.

Kate. For what?

Annie. Everything. The food she eats, the clothes she wears, fresh—(*She is amused at herself, though very serious.*)—air, yes, the air she breathes, whatever her body needs is a—primer,[9] to teach her out of. It's the only way, the one who lets her have it should be her teacher. (*She considers them in turn; they digest it,* KELLER *frowning,* KATE *perplexed.*) Not anyone who *loves* her, you have so many feelings they fall over each other like feet, you won't use your chances and you won't let me.

Kate. But if she runs from you—*to us*——

Annie. Yes, that's the point. I'll have to live with her somewhere else.

Keller. What!

Annie. Till she learns to depend on and listen to me.

Kate (*not without alarm*). For how long?

Annie. As long as it takes. (*A pause. She takes a breath.*) I packed half my things already.

Keller. Miss—Sullivan!

[*But when* ANNIE *attends him he is speechless, and she is merely earnest.*]

Annie. Captain Keller, it meets both your conditions. It's the one way I can get back in touch with Helen, and I don't see how I can be rude to you again if you're not around to interfere with me.

Keller (*red-faced*). And what is your intention if I say no? Pack the other half, for home, and abandon your charge to—to——

Annie. The asylum? (*She waits, appraises* KELLER'S *glare and* KATE'S *uncertainty, and decides to use her weapons.*) I grew up in

such an asylum. The state almshouse. (KATE'S *head comes up on this, and* KELLER *stares hard;* ANNIE'S *tone is cheerful enough, albeit level as gunfire.*) Rats—why, my brother Jimmie and I used to play with the rats because we didn't have toys. Maybe you'd like to know what Helen will find there, not on visiting days? One ward was full of the—old women, crippled, blind, most of them dying, but even if what they had was catching there was nowhere else to move them, and that's where they put us. There were younger ones across the hall, prostitutes mostly, with T.B.,[10] and epileptic fits, and a couple of the kind who—keep after other girls, especially young ones, and some insane. Some just had the D.T.'s.[11] The youngest were in another ward to have babies they didn't want, they started at thirteen, fourteen. They'd leave afterward, but the babies stayed and we played with them, too, though a lot of them had—sores all over from diseases you're not supposed to talk about, but not many of them lived. The first year we had eighty, seventy died. The room Jimmie and I played in was the deadhouse, where they kept the bodies till they could dig——

Kate (*closes her eyes*). Oh, my dear——

Annie. ——the graves. (*She is immune to* KATE'S *compassion.*) No, it made me strong. But I don't think you need send Helen there. She's strong enough. (*She waits again; but when neither offers her a word, she simply concludes.*) No, I have no conditions, Captain Keller.

Kate (*not looking up*). Miss Annie.

Annie. Yes.

Kate (*a pause*). Where would you—take Helen?

Annie. Ohh—(*brightly*) Italy?

Keller (*wheeling*). What?

Annie. Can't have everything, how would this garden house do? Furnish it, bring Helen here after a long ride so she won't recognize

---

9. **primer** (prim′ər): simple book that gives basic information on a subject. Here, Annie is comparing Helen's surroundings to a book she can learn from.

10. **T.B.:** abbreviation for "tuberculosis," an infectious disease that most often affects the lungs.
11. **D.T.'s:** abbreviation for "delirium tremens," hallucinations and trembling caused by alcoholism.

it, and you can see her every day. If she doesn't know. Well?

Kate (*a sigh of relief*). Is that all?

Annie. That's all.

Kate. Captain. (KELLER *turns his head; and* KATE's *request is quiet but firm.*) With your permission?

Keller (*teeth in cigar*). Why must she depend on you for the food she eats?

Annie (*a pause*). I want control of it.

Keller. Why?

Annie. It's a way to reach her.

Keller (*stares*). You intend to *starve* her into letting you touch her?

Annie. She won't starve, she'll learn. All's fair in love and war, Captain Keller. You never cut supplies?

Keller. This is hardly a war!

Annie. Well, it's not love. A siege is a siege.

Keller (*heavily*). Miss Sullivan. Do you *like* the child?

Annie (*straight in his eyes*). Do you?

[*A long pause.*]

Kate. You could have a servant here——

Annie (*amused*). I'll have enough work without looking after a servant! But that boy Percy could sleep here, run errands——

Kate (*also amused*). We can let Percy sleep here, I think, Captain?

Annie (*eagerly*). And some old furniture, all our own——

Kate (*also eager*). Captain? Do you think that walnut bedstead in the barn would be too——

Keller. I have not yet consented to Percy! Or to the house, or to the proposal! Or to Miss Sullivan's—staying on when I—(*But he erupts in an irate surrender.*) Very well, I consent to everything! (*He shakes the cigar at* ANNIE.) For two weeks. I'll give you two weeks in this place, and it will be a miracle if you get the child to tolerate you.

Kate. Two weeks? Miss Annie, can you accomplish anything in two weeks?

Keller. Anything or not, two weeks, then the child comes back to us. Make up your mind, Miss Sullivan, yes or no?

Annie. Two weeks. For only one miracle? (*She nods at him, nervously.*) I'll get her to tolerate me.

[KELLER *marches out, and slams the door.* KATE *on her feet regards* ANNIE, *who is facing the door.*]

Kate (*then*). You can't think as little of love as you said. (ANNIE *glances questioning.*) Or you wouldn't stay.

Annie (*a pause*). I didn't come here for love. I came for money!

[KATE *shakes her head to this, with a smile; after a moment she extends her open hand.* ANNIE *looks at it, but when she puts hers out it is not to shake hands, it is to set her fist in* KATE's *palm.*]

Kate (*puzzled*). Hm?

Annie. A. It's the first of many. Twenty-six!

[KATE *squeezes her fist, squeezes it hard, and hastens out after* KELLER. ANNIE *stands as the door closes behind her, her manner so apprehensive that finally she slaps her brow, holds it, sighs, and, with her eyes closed, crosses herself[12] for luck.*]

12. **crosses herself:** makes the sign of the cross, touching her forehead, chest, and both shoulders.

- - - - - - - - - - - - - - - - - - - -

WORDS TO OWN

siege (sēj) n.: stubborn, continued effort to win or control something.

- - - - - - - - - - - - - - - - - - - -

SCENE 7

The lights dim into a cool silhouette scene around her, the lamp paling out, and now, in formal entrances, persons appear around ANNIE *with furniture for the room:* PERCY *crosses the stage with a rocking chair and waits;* MARTHA *from another direction bears in a stool,* VINEY *bears in a small table, and the other servant rolls in a bed partway from left; and* ANNIE, *opening her eyes to put her glasses back on, sees them. She turns around in the room once and goes into action, pointing out locations for each article; the servants place them and leave, and* ANNIE *then darts around, interchanging them. In the midst of this— while* PERCY *and* MARTHA *reappear with a tray of food and a chair, respectively—* JAMES *comes down from the house with* ANNIE'S *suitcase and stands viewing the room and her quizzically;* ANNIE *halts abruptly under his eyes, embarrassed, then seizes the suitcase from his hand, explaining herself brightly.*

Annie. I always wanted to live in a doll's house!

[*She sets the suitcase out of the way and continues;* VINEY *at left appears to position a rod with drapes for a doorway, and the other servant at center pushes in a wheelbarrow loaded with a couple of boxes of* HELEN'S *toys and clothes.* ANNIE *helps lift them into the room, and the servant pushes the wheelbarrow off. In none of this is any heed taken of the imaginary walls of the garden house; the furniture is moved in from every side and itself defines the walls.*

ANNIE *now drags the box of toys into center, props up the doll conspicuously on top; with the people melted away, except for* JAMES, *all is again still. The lights turn again without pause, rising warmer.*]

James. You don't let go of things easily, do you? How will you—win her hand now, in this place?
Annie (*curtly*). Do I know? I lost my temper, and here we are!
James (*lightly*). No touching, no teaching. Of course, you *are* bigger——

Annie. I'm not counting on force, I'm counting on her. That little imp is dying to know.
James. Know what?
Annie. Anything. Any and every crumb in God's creation. I'll have to use that appetite too. (*She gives the room a final survey, straightens the bed, arranges the curtains.*)
James (*a pause*). Maybe she'll teach you.
Annie. Of course.
James. That she isn't. That there's such a thing as—dullness of heart. Acceptance. And letting go. Sooner or later we all give up, don't we?
Annie. Maybe you all do. It's my idea of the original sin.
James. What is?
Annie (*witheringly*). Giving up.
James (*nettled*).[13] You won't open her. Why can't you let her be? Have some—pity on her, for being what she is——
Annie. If I'd ever once thought like that, I'd be dead!
James (*pleasantly*). You will be. Why trouble? (ANNIE *turns to glare at him; he is mocking.*) Or will you teach me?

[*And with a bow, he drifts off.*

Now in the distance there comes the clopping of hoofs, drawing near, and nearer, up to the door; and they halt. ANNIE *wheels to face the door. When it opens this time, the* KELLERS—KATE *in traveling bonnet,* KELLER *also hatted—are standing there with* HELEN *between them; she is in a cloak.* KATE *gently cues her into the room.* HELEN *comes in groping, baffled, but interested in the new surroundings;* ANNIE *evades her exploring hand, her gaze not leaving the child.*]

Annie. Does she know where she is?
Kate (*shakes her head*). We rode her out in the country for two hours.
Keller. For all she knows, she could be in another town——

[HELEN *stumbles over the box on the floor and in it discovers her doll and other battered toys, is*

---

13. nettled: irritated. A nettle is a prickly plant that irritates the skin.

pleased, sits to them, then becomes puzzled and suddenly very wary. She scrambles up and back to her mother's thighs, but ANNIE *steps in, and it is hers that* HELEN *embraces.* HELEN *recoils, gropes, and touches her cheek instantly.*]

Kate. That's her sign for me.

Annie. I know. (HELEN *waits, then recommences her groping, more urgently.* KATE *stands indecisive and takes an abrupt step toward her, but* ANNIE'S *hand is a barrier.*) In two weeks.

Kate. Miss Annie, I—— Please be good to her. These two weeks, try to be very good to her——

Annie. I will. (KATE, *turning then, hurries out. The* KELLERS *cross back of the main house.* ANNIE *closes the door.* HELEN *starts at the door jar and rushes it.* ANNIE *holds her off.* HELEN *kicks her, breaks free, and careens around the room like an imprisoned bird, colliding with furniture, groping wildly, repeatedly touching her cheek in a growing panic. When she has covered the room, she commences her weird screaming.* ANNIE *moves to comfort her, but her touch sends* HELEN *into a paroxysm of rage: She tears away, falls over her box of toys, flings its contents in handfuls in* ANNIE'S *direction, flings the box too, reels to her feet, rips curtains from the window, bangs and kicks at the door, sweeps objects off the mantelpiece and shelf, a little tornado incarnate,*[14] *all destruction, until she comes upon her doll and, in the act of hurling it, freezes. Then she clutches it to herself, and in exhaustion sinks sobbing to the floor.* ANNIE *stands contemplating her, in some awe.*) Two weeks. (*She shakes her head, not without a touch of disgusted bewilderment.*) What did I get into now?

[*The lights have been dimming throughout, and the garden house is lit only by moonlight now, with* ANNIE *lost in the patches of dark.*]

14. **tornado incarnate** (in·kär′nit): tornado in human form.

- -

WORDS TO OWN

paroxysm (par′əks·iz′əm) *n.*: sudden outburst; spasm.

"I'm not counting on force, I'm counting on her. That little imp is dying to know."

SCENE 8

KATE, *now hatless and coatless, enters the family room by the rear door, carrying a lamp.* KELLER, *also hatless, wanders simultaneously around the back of the main house to where* JAMES *has been waiting, in the rising moonlight, on the porch.*

Keller. I can't understand it. I had every intention of dismissing that girl, not setting her up like an empress.

James. Yes, what's her secret, sir?

Keller. Secret?

James (*pleasantly*). That enables her to get anything she wants out of you? When I can't.

[JAMES *turns to go into the house, but* KELLER *grasps his wrist, twisting him half to his knees.* KATE *comes from the porch.*]

Keller (*angrily*). She does *not* get anything she——

James (*in pain*). Don't—don't——

Kate. Captain.

Keller. He's afraid. (*He throws* JAMES *away from him, with contempt.*) What *does* he want out of me?

James (*an outcry*). My God, don't you know? (*He gazes from* KELLER *to* KATE.) Everything you forgot, when you forgot my mother.

Keller. What! (JAMES *wheels into the house.* KELLER *takes a stride to the porch, to roar after him.*) One thing that girl's secret is not, she doesn't fire one shot and disappear! (KATE *stands rigid, and* KELLER *comes back to her.*) Katie. Don't mind what he——

Kate. Captain, *I* am proud of you.

Keller. For what?

Kate. For letting this girl have what she needs.

Keller. Why can't my son be? He can't bear me, you'd think I treat him as hard as this girl does Helen—— (*He breaks off, as it dawns in him.*)

Kate (*gently*). Perhaps you do.

Keller. But he has to learn some respect!

Kate (*a pause, wryly*). Do you like the child? (*She turns again to the porch, but pauses, reluctant.*) How empty the house is, tonight.

[*After a moment she continues on in,* KELLER *stands moveless, as the moonlight dies on him.*]

SCENE 9

The distant belfry chimes toll, two o'clock, and with them, a moment later, comes the boy's voice on the wind, in a whisper:

Boy's Voice. Annie. Annie.

[*In her patch of dark* ANNIE, *now in her nightgown, hurls a cup into a corner as though it were her grief, getting rid of its taste through her teeth.*]

Annie. No! No pity, I won't have it. (*She comes to* HELEN, *prone on the floor.*) On either of us. (*She goes to her knees, but when she touches* HELEN'S *hand the child starts up awake, recoils, and scrambles away from her under the bed.* ANNIE *stares after her. She strikes her palm on the floor, with passion.*) I *will* touch you! (*She gets to her feet, and paces in a kind of anger around the bed, her hand in her hair, and confronting* HELEN *at each turn.*) How, how? How do I—— (ANNIE *stops. Then she calls out urgently, loudly.*) Percy! Percy! (*She moves swiftly to the drapes, at left.*) Percy, wake up! (PERCY'S *voice comes in a thick sleepy mumble, unintelligible.*) Get out of bed and come in here, I need you. (ANNIE *darts away, finds and strikes a match, and touches it to the hanging lamp; the lights come up dimly in the room,* and PERCY *stands bare to the waist in torn overalls between the drapes, with eyes closed, swaying.* ANNIE *goes to him, pats his cheeks vigorously.*) Percy. You awake?

Percy. No'm.

Annie. How would you like to play a nice game?

Percy. Whah?

Annie. With Helen. She's under the bed. Touch her hand.

[*She kneels* PERCY *down at the bed, thrusting his hand under it to contact* HELEN'S; HELEN *emits an animal sound and crawls to the opposite side, but commences sniffing.* ANNIE *rounds the bed with* PERCY *and thrusts his hand again at* HELEN; *this time* HELEN *clutches it, sniffs in recognition, and comes scrambling out after* PERCY, *to hug him with delight.* PERCY, *alarmed, struggles, and* HELEN'S *fingers go to his mouth.*]

Percy. Lemme go. Lemme go—— (HELEN *fingers her own lips, as before, moving them in dumb imitation.*) She tryin' talk. She gonna hit me——

Annie (*grimly*). She *can* talk. If she only knew, I'll show you how. She makes letters. (*She opens* PERCY'S *other hand, and spells into it.*) This one is C, C. (*She hits his palm with it a couple of times, her eyes upon* HELEN *across him;* HELEN *gropes to feel what* PERCY'S *hand is doing, and when she encounters* ANNIE'S *she falls back from them.*) She's mad at me now, though, she won't play. But she knows lots of letters. Here's another, A. C, a. C, a. (*But she is*

Annie rounds the bed with Percy and thrusts his hand again at Helen.

Language in Three Dimensions

Sign language is used more often than you might realize. Take a close look at football games on TV: Players and coaches often communicate by sign language.

Annie Sullivan taught Helen Keller to communicate by spelling words onto the hand, since Helen was not able to see the hand movements of traditional sign language.

American Sign Language (ASL) is the main way that people with impaired hearing communicate with one another in the United States. Many people think sign language is the same in all countries, but it is not. Users of ASL, for example, cannot easily understand users of Chinese Sign Language. When foreign signers learn ASL, they tend to use it with an "accent." ASL is more closely related to French Sign Language than to British Sign Language, so for hearing-impaired people, communication is easier between Americans and French people than between Americans and British people.

Apart from such differences, is ASL a language in the same way that spoken English is? Or is it a pale reflection of language, a type of "broken English on the hands"? By studying the way the brain deals with language, scientists have found that ASL *is* a distinct language, not simply a collection of hand pictures. Research suggests that *all* languages, both spoken and signed, are based in the left side of the brain—contrary to the widely accepted theory that visual and spatial relationships are perceived by the brain's *right* side.

Like other languages, ASL has its own distinctive rules, or grammar. Instead of being based on the order and forms of words, however, ASL grammar is based on the shapes and movements of hands and their positions in space. ASL is language in three dimensions.

For example, take the two statements "The girl looks at the boy" and "The girl is looking at the boy." To express the first statement, a signer places the sign for *girl* at one position in space and the sign for *boy* at another, and then moves the *look* sign (two splayed fingers bent horizontally) from the first point to the second. To express the continuous action *is looking,* the signer modifies the *look* sign, moving it like a Ferris wheel from the first position to the second and then back again.

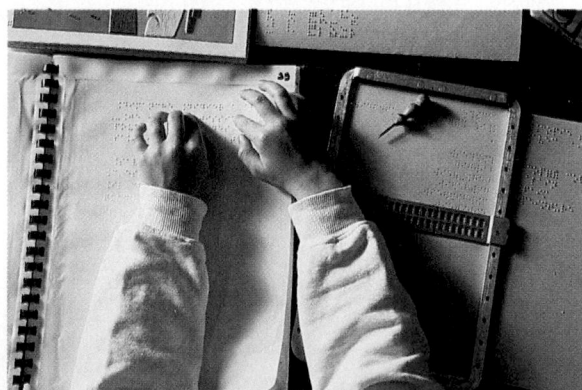

Braille is another way to use language. Here a child reads with his hands.

watching HELEN, *who comes groping, consumed with curiosity;* ANNIE *makes the letters in* PERCY'S *hand, and* HELEN *pokes to question what they are up to. Then* HELEN *snatches* PERCY'S *other hand, and quickly spells four letters into it.* ANNIE *follows them aloud.*) C, a, k, e! She spells cake, she gets cake. (*She is swiftly over to the tray of food, to fetch cake and a jug of milk.*) She doesn't know yet it means this. Isn't it funny she knows how to spell it and doesn't *know* she knows? (*She breaks the cake in two pieces, and extends one to each;* HELEN *rolls away from her offer.*) Well, if she won't play it with me, I'll play it with you. Would you like to learn one she doesn't know?
Percy. No'm.

[*But* ANNIE *seizes his wrist and spells to him.*]

Annie. M, i, l, k. M is this. I, that's an easy one, just the little finger. L is this—— (*And* HELEN *comes back with her hand, to feel the new word.* ANNIE *brushes her away and continues spelling aloud to* PERCY. HELEN'S *hand comes back again and tries to get in;* ANNIE *brushes it away again.* HELEN'S *hand insists, and* ANNIE *puts it away rudely.*) No, why should I talk to you? I'm teaching Percy a new word. L. K is this—— (HELEN *now yanks their hands apart; she butts* PERCY *away and thrusts her palm out insistently.* ANNIE'S *eyes are bright, with glee.*) Ho, you're *jealous,* are you! (HELEN'S *hand waits, intractably*[15] *waits.*) All right. (ANNIE *spells into it, milk; and* HELEN *after a moment spells it back to* ANNIE. ANNIE *takes her hand, with her whole face shining. She gives a great sigh.*) Good! So I'm finally back to where I can touch you, hm? Touch and go! No love lost, but here we go. (*She puts the jug of milk into* HELEN'S *hand and squeezes* PERCY'S *shoulder.*) You can go to bed now, you've earned your sleep. Thank you. (PERCY, *stumbling up, weaves his way out through the drapes.* HELEN *finishes drinking and holds the jug out for* ANNIE; *when* ANNIE *takes it,* HELEN *crawls onto the bed and makes for sleep.* ANNIE *stands, looks down at her.*) Now all I have to teach you

is—one word. Everything. (*She sets the jug down. On the floor now* ANNIE *spies the doll, stoops to pick it up, and with it dangling in her hand, turns off the lamp. A shaft of moonlight is left on* HELEN *in the bed, and a second shaft on the rocking chair; and* ANNIE, *after putting off her smoked glasses, sits in the rocker with the doll. She is rather happy and dangles the doll on her knee, and it makes its momma sound.* ANNIE *whispers to it in mock solicitude.*) Hush, little baby. Don't—say a word—— (*She lays it against her shoulder and begins rocking with it, patting its diminutive behind; she talks the lullaby to it humorously at first.*)

Momma's gonna buy you—a mockingbird:
If that—mockingbird don't sing——

[*The rhythm of the rocking takes her into the tune, softly, and more tenderly.*]

Momma's gonna buy you a diamond ring:
If that diamond ring turns to brass——

[*A third shaft of moonlight outside now rises to pick out* JAMES *at the main house, with one foot on the porch step; he turns his body, as if hearing the song.*]

Momma's gonna buy you a looking glass:
If that looking glass gets broke——

[*In the family room a fourth shaft picks out* KELLER *seated at the table, in thought; and he, too, lifts his head, as if hearing.*]

Momma's gonna buy you a billy goat:
If that billy goat don't pull——

[*The fifth shaft is upstairs in* ANNIE'S *room and picks out* KATE, *pacing there; and she halts, turning her head, too, as if hearing.*]

Momma's gonna buy you a cart and bull:
If that cart and bull turns over,
Momma's gonna buy you a dog named
    Rover:
If that dog named Rover won't bark——

[*With the shafts of moonlight on* HELEN, *and* JAMES, *and* KELLER, *and* KATE, *all moveless, and* ANNIE *rocking the doll, the curtain ends the act.*]

---

15. intractably (in·trak'tə·blē): stubbornly.

MAKING MEANINGS ACT TWO

First Thoughts

1. How do you feel about the characters Annie, Helen, and Kate at this point in the play?

Shaping Interpretations

2. Why does Annie feel that if she teaches Helen only one word, she has taught her everything?

3. Annie's voices reveal her **internal conflict**. Why does she feel guilty about her dead brother, Jimmie?

4. Why do you think Annie is so determined to teach Helen, no matter what? What does Annie have at stake? Look for clues in the voices of Annie's past that speak in her **flashbacks**.

5. After a while the conflicts in a play wouldn't hold our interest unless the characters involved were also developing and changing. What **changes,** if any, do you see in the main members of the Keller family by the end of Act Two?

6. Someone once said that the art of play writing is to get your character up a tree in Act One, throw stones at him (or her) in Act Two, and get the character down in Act Three. What new "stones," or serious problems, are hurled at Annie in this act?

Reviewing the Text

a. According to Annie's letter and her conversation with Kate Keller in Scene 1, what must be done to help Helen?

b. In contrast, what actions at the breakfast table in Scene 2 reveal the way the Kellers treat Helen?

c. What is Annie's goal in the struggle with Helen in Scene 3?

d. **Reversals** are an important part of drama. We think something is going well, and then suddenly it is going badly. Or something is going badly, and then suddenly it goes well. When Annie packs her suitcase in Scene 5, what does it look as if she intends to do? What does she really intend?

e. What bargain has been struck by Annie and the Kellers by the end of Act Two?

Extending the Text

7. When might taking children like Helen out of their familiar environment be a good way to help them? Why is this a difficult thing to do, and what are the risks?

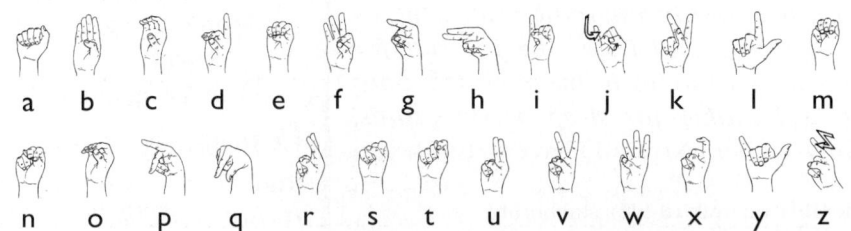

a b c d e f g h i j k l m

n o p q r s t u v w x y z

CHOICES: Building Your Portfolio

Writer's Notebook

1. Collecting Ideas for an Interpretive Essay

Finding a topic. A **symbol** is an object or event that stands for itself and for something broader than itself as well. How do you know what the symbols in a work are and what they stand for? One way is to keep track of any object or event that seems to come up in meaningful and interesting ways. Taking notes now on

possible symbols in the play will help you draw conclusions later about why they are important. In the Writer's Workshop on page 716, you might use your notes and your tracking of the symbols in an interpretive essay.

Creative Writing

2. What's Happening

If you have started a diary for one of the characters in the play, add to your entries now. Is your character changing in any way? Think about your character's opinions and feelings. What episodes in this act would your character comment on? What else is going on in his or her life?

Speaking/Listening

3. The Sound of Voices

Make a tape recording of the ghostly voices Annie hears from time to time in the play. Will you use additional sound effects? What mood will you aim for? Will you use real children's voices or your own and your classmates'? Be sure to play your tape for an audience and get feedback.

VOCABULARY   HOW TO OWN A WORD

WORD BANK

impassively
temperance
ominous
deferential
feigned
retaliates
compunction
interminably
siege
paroxysm

Synonyms: Nearly the Same

Synonyms are words that mean more or less the same thing. But there are often subtle differences between synonyms, and the words are not always interchangeable. Find the place in Act Two where each word in the Word Bank at left is used. Then find a synonym for each word. Use a chart like the following to indicate if the synonym could be used in place of the word in the play.

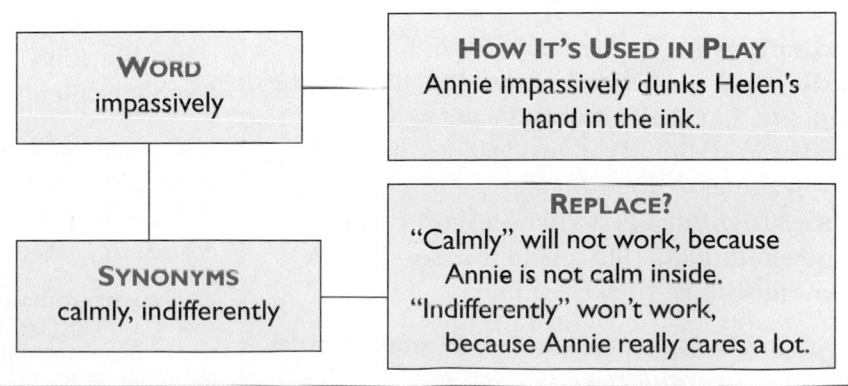

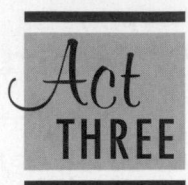

Act THREE

SCENE 1

The stage is totally dark, until we see ANNIE *and* HELEN *silhouetted on the bed in the garden house.* ANNIE'S *voice is audible, very patient, and worn; it has been saying this for a long time.*

Annie. Water, Helen. This is water. W, a, t, e, r. It has a *name.* (*A silence. Then:*) Egg, e, g, g. It has a *name,* the name stands for the thing. Oh, it's so simple, simple as birth, to explain. (*The lights have commenced to rise, not on the garden house but on the homestead. Then:*) Helen, Helen, the chick *has* to come out of its shell, sometime. You come out, too. (*In the bedroom upstairs, we see* VINEY *unhurriedly washing the window, dusting, turning the mattress, readying the room for use again; then in the family room a diminished group at one end of the table—*KATE, KELLER, JAMES—*finishing up a quiet breakfast; then outside, down right, the other servant on his knees, assisted by* MARTHA, *working with a trowel around a new trellis and wheelbarrow. The scene is one of everyday calm, and all are oblivious to* ANNIE'S *voice.*) There's only one way out, for you, and it's language. To learn that your fingers can talk. And say anything, anything you can name. This is mug. Mug, m, u, g. Helen, it has a *name.* It—has—a—*name.*

[KATE *rises from the table.*]

Keller (*gently*). You haven't eaten, Katie.
Kate (*smiles, shakes her head*). I haven't the appetite. I'm too—restless, I can't sit to it.
Keller. You should eat, my dear. It will be a long day, waiting.
James (*lightly*). But it's been a short two weeks. I never thought life could be so—noiseless, went much too quickly for me.

[KATE *and* KELLER *gaze at him, in silence.* JAMES *becomes uncomfortable.*]

Annie. C, a, r, d. Card. C, a——
James. Well, the house has been practically normal, hasn't it?
Keller (*harshly*). Jimmie.
James. Is it wrong to enjoy a quiet breakfast, after five years? And you two even seem to enjoy each other——
Keller. It could be even more noiseless, Jimmie, without your tongue running every minute. Haven't you enough feeling to imagine what Katie has been undergoing, ever since——

[KATE *stops him, with her hand on his arm.*]

Kate. Captain. (*To* JAMES) It's true. The two weeks have been normal, quiet, all you say. But not short. Interminable. (*She rises and wanders out; she pauses on the porch steps, gazing toward the garden house.*)
Annie (*fading*). W, a, t, e, r. But it means *this.* W, a, t, e, r. *This.* W, a, t——
James. I only meant that Miss Sullivan is a boon. Of contention,[1] though, it seems.
Keller (*heavily*). If and when you're a parent, Jimmie, you will understand what separation means. A mother loses a—protector.
James (*baffled*). Hm?
Keller. You'll learn, we don't just keep our children safe. They keep us safe. (*He rises, with his empty coffee cup and saucer.*) There are of course all kinds of separation. Katie has lived with one kind for five years. And another is disappointment. In a child.

[*He goes with the cup out the rear door.* JAMES *sits for a long moment of stillness. In the garden house the lights commence to come up;* ANNIE, *haggard at the table, is*

1. **boon of contention:** James is making a joke. A "boon" is a blessing. A "bone of contention" is a subject that causes an argument or disagreement, like a bone dogs might fight over.

"Helen, it has a name. It—has—a—name."

writing a letter, her face again almost in contact with the stationery; HELEN, apart on the stool, and for the first time as clean and neat as a button, is quietly crocheting an endless chain of wool, which snakes all around the room.]

Annie. "I, feel, every, day, more, and, more, in—" (*She pauses, and turns the pages of a dictionary open before her; her finger descends the words to a full stop. She elevates her eyebrows, then copies the word.*) "—adequate."

[*In the main house* JAMES *pushes up and goes to the front doorway, after* KATE.]

James. Kate? (KATE *turns her glance.* JAMES *is rather wary.*) I'm sorry. Open my mouth, like that fairy tale, frogs jump out.

Kate. No. It has been better. For everyone. (*She starts away, up center.*)

Annie (*writing*). "If, only, there, were, someone, to, help, me, I, need, a, teacher, as, much, as, Helen——"

James. Kate. (KATE *halts, waits.*) What does he want from me?

Kate. That's not the question. Stand up to the world, Jimmie, that comes first.

James (*a pause, wryly*). But the world is him.
Kate. Yes. And no one can do it for you.
James. Kate. (*His voice is humble.*) At least we—— Could you—be my friend?
Kate. I am.

[KATE *turns to wander, up back of the garden house.* ANNIE'S *murmur comes at once; the lights begin to die on the main house.*]

Annie. "—My, mind, is, undisciplined, full, of, skips, and, jumps, and——" (*She halts, re-reads, frowns.*) Hm. (ANNIE *puts her nose again in the dictionary, flips back to an earlier page, and fingers down the words;* KATE *presently comes down toward the bay window with a trayful of food.*) Disinter—disinterested—disjoin—dis—— (*She backtracks, indignant.*) Disinterested, disjoin—Where's disipline? (*She goes a page or two back, searching with her finger, muttering.*) What a dictionary, have to know how to spell it before you can look up how to spell it, disciple, *discipline*! Diskipline. (*She corrects the word in her letter.*) Undisciplined.

[*But her eyes are bothering her. She closes them in exhaustion and gently fingers the eyelids.* KATE *watches her through the window.*]

Kate. What are you doing to your eyes?

[ANNIE *glances around; she puts her smoked glasses on and gets up to come over, assuming a cheerful energy.*]

Annie. It's worse on my vanity! I'm learning to spell. It's like a surprise party, the most unexpected characters turn up.
Kate. You're not to overwork your eyes, Miss Annie.
Annie. Well. (*She takes the tray, sets it on her chair, and carries chair and tray to* HELEN.) Whatever I spell to Helen I'd better spell right.
Kate (*almost wistful*). How—serene she is.
Annie. She learned this stitch yesterday. Now I can't get her to stop! (*She disentangles one foot from the wool chain and sets the chair before* HELEN. HELEN, *at its contact with her knee, feels the plate, promptly sets her crocheting down, and tucks the napkin in at her neck, but* ANNIE *withholds the spoon. When* HELEN *finds it missing, she folds her hands in her lap and quietly waits.* ANNIE *twinkles at* KATE *with mock devoutness.*) Such a little lady, she'd sooner starve than eat with her fingers.

[*She gives* HELEN *the spoon, and* HELEN *begins to eat, neatly.*]

Kate. You've taught her so much, these two weeks. I would never have——
Annie. Not enough. (*She is suddenly gloomy, shakes her head.*) Obedience isn't enough. Well, she learned two nouns this morning, key and water, brings her up to eighteen nouns and three verbs.
Kate (*hesitant*). But—not——
Annie. No. Not that they mean things. It's still a finger game, no meaning. (*She turns to* KATE, *abruptly.*) Mrs. Keller—— (*But she defers it; she comes back, to sit in the bay, and lifts her hand.*) Shall we play our finger game?
Kate. How will she learn it?
Annie. It will come.

[*She spells a word;* KATE *does not respond.*]

Kate. How?
Annie (*a pause*). How does a bird learn to fly? (*She spells again.*) We're born to use words, like wings, it has to come.
Kate. How?
Annie (*another pause, wearily*). All right. I don't know how. (*She pushes up her glasses, to rub her eyes.*) I've done everything I could think of. Whatever she's learned here—keeping herself clean, knitting, stringing beads, meals, setting-up exercises each morning, we climb trees, hunt eggs, yesterday a chick was born in her hands—all of it I spell, everything we do, we never stop spelling. I go to bed with—writer's cramp from talking so much!
Kate. I worry about you, Miss Annie. You must rest.
Annie. Now? She spells back in her *sleep,* her fingers make letters when she doesn't know! In her bones those five fingers know, that hand aches to—speak out, and something in her mind is asleep, how do I—nudge that awake? That's the one question.

Katc. With no answer.

Annie (*long pause*). Except keep at it. Like this.

[*She again begins spelling—I, need—and* KATE'S *brows gather, following the words.*]

Kate. More—time? (*She glances at* ANNIE, *who looks her in the eyes, silent.*) Here?

Annie. Spell it.

[KATE *spells a word—no—shaking her head;* ANNIE *spells two words—why, not—back, with an impatient question in her eyes; and* KATE *moves her head in pain to answer it.*]

Kate. Because I can't——

Annie. Spell it! If she ever lcarns, you'll have a lot to tell each other, start now.

[KATE *painstakingly spells in air. In the midst of this the rear door opens, and* KELLER *enters with the setter* BELLE *in tow.*]

Keller. Miss Sullivan? On my way to the office, I brought Helen a playmate——

Annie. Outside please, Captain Keller.

Keller. My dear child, the two weeks are up today, surely you don't object to——

Annie (*rising*). They're not up till six o'clock.

Keller (*indulgent*). Oh, now. What difference can a fraction of one day——

Annie. An agreement is an agreement. Now you've been very good, I'm sure you can keep it up for a few more hours.

[*She escorts* KELLER *by the arm over the threshold; he obeys, leaving* BELLE.]

Keller. Miss Sullivan, you are a tyrant.

Annie. Likewise, I'm sure. You can stand there, and close the door if she comes.

Kate. I don't think you know how eager we are to have her back in our arms——

Annie. I do know, it's my main worry.

Keller. It's like expecting a new child in the house. Well, she *is,* so—composed, so—(*gently*) attractive. You've done wonders for her, Miss Sullivan.

Annie (*not a question*). Have I.

Keller. If there's anything you want from us in repayment tell us, it will be a privilege to——

Annie. I just told Mrs. Keller. I want more time.

Kate. Miss Annie——

Annie. Another week.

[HELEN *lifts her head, and begins to sniff.*]

Keller. We miss the child. *I* miss her, I'm glad to say, that's a different debt I owe you——

Annie. Pay it to Helen. Give *her* another week.

Kate (*gently*). Doesn't she miss us?

Keller. Of course she does. What a wrench this unexplainable—exile must be to her, can you say it's not?

Annie. No. But I——

[HELEN *is off the stool, to grope about the room; when she encounters* BELLE, *she throws her arms around the dog's neck in delight.*]

Kate. Doesn't she need affection too, Miss Annie?

Annie (*wavering*). She—never shows me she needs it, she won't have any—caressing or——

Kate. But you're not her mother.

Keller. And what would another week accomplish? We are more than satisfied, you've done more than we ever thought possible, taught her constructive——

Annie. I can't promise anything. All I can——

Keller (*no break*). ——things to do, to behave like—even look like—a human child, so manageable, contented, cleaner, more——

Annie (*withering*). Cleaner.

Keller. Well. We say cleanliness is next to godliness, Miss——

Annie. Cleanliness is next to nothing. She has to learn that everything has its name! That words can be her *eyes,* to everything in the world outside her, and inside too. What is she without words? With them she can think, have ideas, be reached. There's not a thought or fact in the world that can't be hers. You publish a newspaper, Captain Keller, do I have to tell you what words are? And she has them already——

Keller. Miss Sullivan.

Annie. ——eighteen nouns and three verbs, they're in her fingers now, I need only time to push *one* of them into her mind! One, and everything under the sun will follow. Don't you see what she's learned here is only clearing the way for that? I can't risk her unlearning it, give me more time alone with her, another week to——

Keller. Look. (*He points, and* ANNIE *turns.* HELEN *is playing with* BELLE'S *claws; she makes letters with her fingers, shows them to* BELLE, *waits with her palm, then manipulates the dog's claws.*) What is she spelling?

[*A silence.*]

Kate. Water?

[ANNIE *nods.*]

Keller. Teaching a dog to spell. (*A pause*) The dog doesn't know what she means, any more than she knows what you mean, Miss Sullivan. I think you ask too much, of her and yourself. God may not have meant Helen to have the— eyes you speak of.

Annie (*toneless*). I mean her to.

Keller (*curiously*). What is it to you? (ANNIE'S *head comes slowly up.*) You make us see how we indulge her for our sake. Is the opposite true, for you?

Annie (*then*). Half a week?

Keller. An agreement *is* an agreement.

Annie. Mrs. Keller?

Kate (*simply*). I want her back.

[*A wait;* ANNIE *then lets her hands drop in surrender, and nods.*]

Keller. I'll send Viney over to help you pack.

Annie. Not until six o'clock. I have her till six o'clock.

Keller (*consenting*). Six o'clock. Come, Katie.

[KATE, *leaving the window, joins him around back, while* KELLER *closes the door; they are shut out. Only the garden house is daylit now, and the light on it is narrowing down.* ANNIE *stands watching* HELEN *work* BELLE'S *claws. Then she settles beside them on her knees and stops* HELEN'S *hand.*]

Annie (*gently*). No. (*She shakes her head, with* HELEN'S *hand to her face, then spells.*) Dog. D, o, g, dog. (*She touches* HELEN'S *hand to* BELLE. HELEN *dutifully pats the dog's head and resumes spelling to its paw.*) Not water. (ANNIE

rolls to her feet, brings a tumbler of water back from the tray, and kneels with it, to seize HELEN'S hand and spell.) Here. Water. Water. (*She thrusts* HELEN'S *hand into the tumbler.* HELEN *lifts her hand out dripping, wipes it daintily on* BELLE'S *hide, and taking the tumbler from* ANNIE, *endeavors to thrust* BELLE'S *paw into it.* ANNIE *sits watching, wearily.*) I don't know how to tell you. Not a soul in the world knows how to tell you. Helen, Helen. (*She bends in compassion to touch her lips to* HELEN'S *temple, and instantly* HELEN *pauses, her hands off the dog, her head slightly averted. The lights are still narrowing, and* BELLE *slinks off. After a moment* ANNIE *sits back.*) Yes, what's it to me? They're satisfied. Give them back their child and dog, both housebroken, everyone's satisfied. But me, and you. (HELEN'S *hand comes out into the light, groping.*) Reach. *Reach!* (ANNIE *extending her own hand grips* HELEN'S; *the two hands are clasped, tense in the light, the rest of the room changing in shadow.*) I wanted to teach you—oh, everything the earth is full of, Helen, everything on it that's ours for a wink and it's gone, and what we are on it, the—light we bring to it and leave behind in—words, why, you can see five thousand years back in a light of words, everything we feel, think, know—and share, in words, so not a soul is in darkness, or done with, even in the grave. And I know, I *know*, one word and I can—put the world in your hand—and whatever it is to me, I won't take less! How, how, how do I tell you that *this*—— (*She spells*) ——means a *word*, and the word means this *thing*, wool? (*She thrusts the wool at* HELEN'S *hand;* HELEN *sits, puzzled.* ANNIE *puts the crocheting aside.*) Or this—s, t, o, o, l— means this *thing*, stool? (*She claps* HELEN'S *palm to the stool.* HELEN *waits, uncomprehending.* ANNIE *snatches up her napkin, spells:*) Napkin! (*She forces it on* HELEN'S *hand, waits, discards it, lifts a fold of the child's dress, spells:*) Dress! (*She lets it drop, spells:*) F, a, c, e, face! (*She draws* HELEN'S *hand to her cheek, and pressing it there, staring into the child's responseless eyes, hears the distant belfry begin to toll, slowly: one, two, three, four, five, six.*)

She makes letters with her fingers, shows them to Belle, waits with her palm. . . .

SCENE 2

On the third stroke the lights stealing in around the garden house show us figures waiting: VINEY, *the other servant,* MARTHA, PERCY *at the drapes, and* JAMES *on the dim porch.* ANNIE *and* HELEN *remain, frozen. The chimes die away. Silently* PERCY *moves the drape rod back out of sight;* VINEY *steps into the room—not using the door—and unmakes the bed; the other servant brings the wheelbarrow over, leaves it handy, rolls the bed off;* VINEY *puts the bed linens on top of a waiting boxful of* HELEN'S *toys and loads the box on the wheelbarrow;* MARTHA *and* PERCY *take out the chairs, with the trayful, then the table; and* JAMES, *coming down and into the room, lifts* ANNIE'S *suitcase from its corner.* VINEY *and the other servant load the remaining odds and ends on the wheelbarrow, and the servant wheels it off.* VINEY *and the children, departing, leave only* JAMES *in the room with* ANNIE *and* HELEN. JAMES *studies the two of them, without mockery, and then, quietly going to the door and opening it, bears the suitcase out, and houseward. He leaves the door open.*

KATE *steps into the doorway, and stands.* ANNIE, *lifting her gaze from* HELEN, *sees her; she takes* HELEN'S *hand from her cheek and returns it to the child's own, stroking it there twice, in her mother sign, before spelling slowly into it.*

Annie. M, o, t, h, e, r. Mother. (HELEN, *with her hand free, strokes her cheek, suddenly forlorn.* ANNIE *takes her hand again.*) M, o, t, h—— (*But* KATE *is trembling with such impatience that her voice breaks from her, harsh.*) Let her *come!*

[ANNIE *lifts* HELEN *to her feet, with a turn, and gives her a little push. Now* HELEN *begins groping, sensing something, trembling herself; and* KATE, *falling one step in onto her knees, clasps her, kissing her.* HELEN *clutches her, tight as she can.* KATE *is inarticulate, choked, repeating* HELEN'S *name again and again. She wheels with her in her arms, to stumble away out the doorway;* ANNIE *stands unmoving, while* KATE *in a blind walk carries* HELEN *like a baby behind the main house, out of view.*

ANNIE *is now alone on the stage. She turns, gazing around at the stripped room, bidding it silently farewell, impassively, like a defeated general on the deserted battlefield. All that remains is a stand with a basin of water; and here* ANNIE *takes up an eyecup, bathes each of her eyes, empties the eyecup, drops it in her purse, and tiredly locates her smoked glasses on the floor. The lights alter subtly; in the act of putting on her glasses* ANNIE *hears something that stops her, with head lifted. We hear it too, the voices out of the past, including her own now, in a whisper:*]

Boy's Voice. You said we'd be together, forever—You promised, forever and—*Annie!*
Anagnos's Voice. But that battle is dead and done with, why not let it stay buried?
Annie's Voice (*whispering*). I think God must owe me a resurrection.
Anagnos's Voice. What?

[*A pause, and* ANNIE *answers it herself, heavily.*]

Annie. And I owe God one.
Boy's Voice. Forever and ever—— (ANNIE *shakes her head.*) ——forever, and ever, and—— (ANNIE *covers her ears.*) —— forever, and ever, and ever——

[*It pursues* ANNIE; *she flees to snatch up her purse, wheels to the doorway, and* KELLER *is standing in it. The lights have lost their special color.*]

Keller. Miss—Annie. (*He has an envelope in his fingers.*) I've been waiting to give you this.
Annie (*after a breath*). What?
Keller. Your first month's salary. (*He puts it in her hand.*) With many more to come, I trust. It doesn't express what we feel, it doesn't pay our debt. For what you've done.
Annie. What have I done?
Keller. Taken a wild thing, and given us back a child.

Kate, falling one step in onto her knees, clasps her, kissing her.

Annie (*presently*). I taught her one thing, no. Don't do this, don't do that——

Keller. It's more than all of us could, in all the years we——

Annie. I wanted to teach her what language is. I wanted to teach her yes.

Keller. You will have time.

Annie. I don't know how. I know without it to do nothing but obey is—no gift, obedience without understanding is a—blindness, too. Is that all I've wished on her?

Keller (*gently*). No, no——

Annie. Maybe. I don't know what else to do. Simply go on, keep doing what I've done, and have—faith that inside she's—— That inside it's waiting. Like water, underground. All I can do is keep on.

Keller. It's enough. For us.

Annie. You can help, Captain Keller.

Keller. How?

Annie. Even learning no has been at a cost. Of much trouble and pain. Don't undo it.

Keller. Why should we wish to——

Annie (*abruptly*). The world isn't an easy place

for anyone. I don't want her just to obey, but to let her have her way in everything is a lie, to *her,* I can't——(*Her eyes fill, it takes her by surprise, and she laughs through it.*) And I don't even love her, she's not my child! Well. You've got to stand between that lie and her.

Keller. We'll try.

Annie. Because *I* will. As long as you let me stay, that's one promise I'll keep.

Keller. Agreed. We've learned something too, I hope. (*A pause*) Won't you come now, to supper?

Annie. Yes. (*She wags the envelope, ruefully.*) Why doesn't God pay his debts each month?

Keller. I beg your pardon?

Annie. Nothing. I used to wonder how I could—— (*The lights are fading on them, simultaneously rising on the family room of the main house, where* VINEY *is polishing glassware at the table set for dinner.*) ——earn a living.

Keller. Oh, you do.

Annie. I really do. Now the question is, can I survive it!

[KELLER *smiles, offers his arm.*]

Keller. May I?

[ANNIE *takes it, and the lights lose them as he escorts her out.*]

WORDS TO OWN

simultaneously (sī′məl·tā′nē·əs·lē) *adv.:* at the same time.

SCENE 3

Now in the family room the rear door opens, and HELEN *steps in. She stands a moment, then sniffs in one deep grateful breath, and her hands go out vigorously to familiar things, over the door panels, and to the chairs around the table, and over the silverware on the table, until she meets* VINEY; *she pats her flank approvingly.*

Viney. Oh, we glad to have you back too, prob'ly.

[HELEN *hurries, groping, to the front door, opens and closes it, removes its key, opens and closes it again to be sure it is unlocked, gropes back to the rear door and repeats the procedure, removing its key and hugging herself gleefully.*

AUNT EV *is next in by the rear door, with a relish tray; she bends to kiss* HELEN'S *cheek.* HELEN *finds* KATE *behind her, and thrusts the keys at her.*]

Kate. What? Oh. (*To* EV) Keys. (*She pockets them, lets* HELEN *feel them.*) Yes, *I'll* keep the keys. I think we've had enough of locked doors, too.

[JAMES, *having earlier put* ANNIE'S *suitcase inside her door upstairs and taken himself out of view around the corner, now reappears and comes down the stairs as* ANNIE *and* KELLER *mount the porch steps. Following them into the family room, he pats* ANNIE'S *hair in passing, rather to her surprise.*]

James. Evening, general.

[*He takes his own chair opposite.*

VINEY *bears the empty water pitcher out to the porch. The remaining suggestion of garden house is gone now, and the water pump is unobstructed;* VINEY *pumps water into the pitcher.*

KATE, *surveying the table, breaks the silence.*]

Kate. Will you say grace, Jimmie?

[*They bow their heads, except for* HELEN, *who palms her empty plate and then reaches to be sure her mother is there.* JAMES *considers a moment, glances across at* ANNIE, *lowers his head again, and obliges.*]

James (*lightly*). And Jacob was left alone, and wrestled with an angel until the breaking of the day; and the hollow of Jacob's thigh was out of joint, as he wrestled with him; and the angel said, Let me go, for the day breaketh. And Jacob said, I will not let thee go, except thou bless me. Amen. (ANNIE *has lifted her eyes suspiciously at* JAMES, *who winks expressionlessly and inclines his head to* HELEN.) Oh, you angel.

[*The others lift their faces;* VINEY *returns with the pitcher; setting it down near* KATE, *then goes out the rear door; and* ANNIE *puts a napkin around* HELEN.]

Aunt Ev. That's a very strange grace, James.
Keller. Will you start the muffins, Ev?
James. It's from the Good Book, isn't it?
Aunt Ev (*passing a plate*). Well, of course it is. Didn't you know?
James. Yes, I knew.
Keller (*serving*). Ham, Miss Annie?
Annie. Please.
Aunt Ev. Then why ask?
James. I meant it *is* from the Good Book, and therefore a fitting grace.
Aunt Ev. Well. I don't know about *that*.
Kate (*with the pitcher*). Miss Annie?
Annie. Thank you.
Aunt Ev. There's an awful *lot* of things in the Good Book that I wouldn't care to hear just before eating.

[*When* ANNIE *reaches for the pitcher,* HELEN *removes her napkin and drops it to the floor.*

ANNIE *is filling* HELEN'S *glass when she notices it; she considers* HELEN'S *bland expression a moment, then bends, retrieves it, and tucks it around* HELEN'S *neck again.*]

James. Well, fitting in the sense that Jacob's thigh was out of joint, and so is this piggie's.
Aunt Ev. I declare, James——
Kate. Pickles, Aunt Ev?
Aunt Ev. Oh, I should say so, you know my opinion of your pickles——
Kate. This is the end of them, I'm afraid. I didn't put up nearly enough last summer, this year I intend to——

[*She interrupts herself, seeing* HELEN *deliberately lift off her napkin and drop it again to the floor. She bends to retrieve it, but* ANNIE *stops her arm.*]

Keller (*not noticing*). Reverend looked in at the office today to complain his hens have stopped laying. Poor fellow, *he* was out of joint, all he could——

[*He stops too, to frown down the table at* KATE, HELEN, *and* ANNIE *in turn, all suspended in mid-motion.*]

James (*not noticing*). I've always suspected those hens.
Aunt Ev. Of what?
James. I think they're Papist.[2] Has he tried——

[*He stops, too, following* KELLER'S *eyes.* ANNIE *now stoops to pick the napkin up.*]

Aunt Ev. James, now you're pulling my—lower extremity,[3] the first thing you know we'll be——

[*She stops, too, hearing herself in the silence.* ANNIE, *with everyone now watching, for the third time puts the napkin on* HELEN. HELEN *yanks it off and throws it down.* ANNIE *rises, lifts* HELEN'S *plate, and bears it away.* HELEN, *feeling it gone, slides down and commences to kick up under the table; the dishes jump.* ANNIE *contemplates this for a moment, then coming*

---

2. **Papist** (pā′pist): term for "Roman Catholic" that suggests dislike. James jokingly suspects the Papist hens of making trouble for the Protestant reverend.
3. **lower extremity** (ek·strem′ə·tē): leg.

"And ask outsiders not to interfere."

back, takes HELEN'S *wrists firmly and swings her off the chair.* HELEN, *struggling, gets one hand free and catches at her mother's skirt; when* KATE *takes her by the shoulders,* HELEN *hangs quiet.*]

Kate. Miss Annie.
Annie. No.
Kate (*a pause*). It's a very special day.
Annie (*grimly*). It will be, when I give in to that.

[*She tries to disengage* HELEN'S *hand;* KATE *lays hers on* ANNIE'S.]

Kate. Please. I've hardly had a chance to welcome her home——
Annie. Captain Keller.
Keller (*embarrassed*). Oh. Katie, we—had a little talk, Miss Annie feels that if we indulge Helen in these——
Aunt Ev. But what's the child done?
Annie. She's learned not to throw things on the floor and kick. It took us the best part of two weeks and——
Aunt Ev. But only a napkin, it's not as if it were breakable!
Annie. And everything she's learned *is*? Mrs. Keller, I don't think we should—play tug-of-war for her, either give her to me or you keep her from kicking.
Kate. What do you wish to do?
Annie. Let me take her from the table.
Aunt Ev. Oh, let her stay, my goodness, she's only a child, she doesn't have to wear a napkin if she doesn't want to her first evening——
Annie (*level*). And ask outsiders not to interfere.
Aunt Ev (*astonished*). Out—outsi—I'm the child's *aunt*!
Kate (*distressed*). Will once hurt so much, Miss Annie? I've—made all Helen's favorite foods, tonight.

[*A pause.*]

Keller (*gently*). It's a homecoming party, Miss Annie.

[ANNIE *after a moment releases* HELEN. *But she cannot accept it; at her own chair she shakes*

her head and turns back, intent on KATE.]

Annie. She's testing you. You realize?
James (*to* ANNIE). She's testing you.
Keller. Jimmie, be quiet. (JAMES *sits, tense.*) Now she's home, naturally she——
Annie. And wants to see what will happen. At your hands. I said it was my main worry. Is this what you promised me not half an hour ago?
Keller (*reasonably*). But she's *not* kicking, now——
Annie. And not learning not to. Mrs. Keller, teaching her is bound to be painful, to everyone. I know it hurts to watch, but she'll live up to just what you demand of her, and no more.
James (*palely*). She's testing *you*.
Keller (*testily*). Jimmie.
James. I have an opinion, I think I should——
Keller. No one's interested in hearing your opinion.
Annie. *I'm* interested. Of course she's testing me. Let me keep her to what she's learned and she'll go on learning from me. Take her out of my hands and it all comes apart. (KATE *closes her eyes, digesting it;* ANNIE *sits again, with a brief comment for her.*) *Be* bountiful, it's at her expense. (*She turns to* JAMES, *flatly.*) Please pass me more of—her favorite foods.

[*Then* KATE *lifts* HELEN'S *hand, and turning her toward* ANNIE, *surrenders her;* HELEN *makes for her own chair.*]

Kate (*low*). Take her, Miss Annie.
Annie (*then*). Thank you.

[*But the moment* ANNIE, *rising, reaches for her hand,* HELEN *begins to fight and kick, clutching to the tablecloth and uttering laments.* ANNIE *again tries to loosen her hand, and* KELLER *rises.*]

Keller (*tolerant*). I'm afraid you're the difficulty, Miss Annie. Now I'll keep her to what she's learned, you're quite right there—— (*He takes* HELEN'S *hands from* ANNIE, *pats them;* HELEN *quiets down.*) ——but I don't see that we need send her from the table. After all, she's the guest of honor. Bring her plate back.
Annie. If she was a seeing child, none of you would tolerate one——

Keller. Well, she's not, I think some compromise is called for. Bring her plate, please. (ANNIE'S *jaw sets, but she restores the plate, while* KELLER *fastens the napkin around* HELEN'S *neck; she permits it.*) There. It's not unnatural, most of us take some aversion to our teachers, and occasionally another hand can smooth things out. (*He puts a fork in* HELEN'S *hand;* HELEN *takes it. Genially.*) Now. Shall we start all over?

[*He goes back around the table and sits.* ANNIE *stands watching.* HELEN *is motionless, thinking things through, until with a wicked glee she deliberately flings the fork on the floor. After another moment she plunges her hand into her food and crams a fistful into her mouth.*]

James (*wearily*). I think we've started all over——

[KELLER *shoots a glare at him, as* HELEN *plunges her other hand into* ANNIE'S *plate.* ANNIE *at once moves in to grasp her wrist, and* HELEN, *flinging out a hand, encounters the pitcher; she swings with it at* ANNIE; ANNIE, *falling back, blocks it with an elbow, but the water flies over her dress.* ANNIE *gets her breath, then snatches the pitcher away in one hand, hoists* HELEN *up bodily under the other arm, and starts to carry her out, kicking.* KELLER *stands.*]

Annie (*savagely polite*). Don't get up!
Keller. Where are you going?
Annie. Don't smooth anything else out for me, don't interfere in any way! I treat her like a seeing child because I *ask* her to see, I *expect* her to see, don't undo what I do!
Keller. Where are you taking her?
Annie. To make her fill this pitcher again!

[*She thrusts out with* HELEN *under her arm, but* HELEN *escapes up the stairs and* ANNIE *runs after her.* KELLER *stands rigid.* AUNT EV *is astounded.*]

> *Annie has pulled Helen downstairs again by one hand, the pitcher in her other hand, down the porch steps. . . .*

Aunt Ev. You let her speak to you like that, Arthur? A creature who *works* for you?
Keller (*angrily*). No, I don't.

[*He is starting after* ANNIE *when* JAMES, *on his feet with shaky resolve, interposes his chair between them in* KELLER'S *path.*]

James. Let her go.
Keller. What!
James (*a swallow*). I said—let her go. She's right. (KELLER *glares at the chair and him.* JAMES *takes a deep breath, then headlong.*) She's right, Kate's right, I'm right, and you're wrong. If you drive her away from here it will be over my dead—chair, has it never occurred to you that on one occasion you might be <u>consummately</u> wrong?

[KELLER'S *stare is unbelieving, even a little fascinated.* KATE *rises in* <u>trepidation</u> *to* <u>mediate</u>.]

Kate. Captain.

[KELLER *stops her with his raised hand; his eyes stay on* JAMES'S *pale face, for a long hold. When he finally finds his voice, it is gruff.*]

Keller. Sit down, everyone. (*He sits.* KATE *sits.* JAMES *holds onto his chair.* KELLER *speaks mildly.*) Please sit down, Jimmie.

[JAMES *sits, and a moveless silence prevails;* KELLER'S *eyes do not leave him.* ANNIE *has pulled* HELEN *downstairs again by one hand, the pitcher in her other hand, down the porch steps, and across the yard to the pump. She puts* HELEN'S *hand on the pump handle, grimly.*]

Annie. All right. Pump. (HELEN *touches her cheek, waits uncertainly.*) No, she's not here. Pump! (*She forces* HELEN'S *hand to work the handle, then lets go. And* HELEN *obeys. She pumps till the water comes, then* ANNIE *puts the pitcher in her other hand and guides it under the spout, and the water, tumbling half into*

WORDS TO OWN

consummately (kən·sum′it·lē) *adv.*: completely.
trepidation (trep′ə·dā′shən) *n.*: fearful uncertainty.
mediate (mē′dē·āt′) *v.*: settle a dispute or argument by bringing the two sides together.

and half around the pitcher, douses HELEN's hand. ANNIE takes over the handle to keep water coming, and does automatically what she has done so many times before, spells into HELEN's free palm.) Water. W, a, t, e, r. Water. It has a—name——

[And now the miracle happens. HELEN drops the pitcher on the slab under the spout; it shatters. She stands transfixed. ANNIE freezes on the pump handle: There is a change in the sundown light, and with it a change in HELEN's face, some light coming into it we have never seen there, some struggle in the depths behind it; and her lips tremble, trying to remember something the muscles around them once knew, till at last it finds its way out, painfully, a baby sound buried under the debris of years of dumbness.]

Helen. Wah. Wah. (And again, with great effort) Wah. Wah.

[HELEN plunges her hand into the dwindling water, spells into her own palm. Then she gropes frantically; ANNIE reaches for her hand, and HELEN spells into ANNIE's hand.]

Annie (whispering). Yes. (HELEN spells into it again.) Yes! (HELEN grabs at the handle, pumps for more water; plunges her hand into its spurt, and grabs ANNIE's to spell it again.) Yes! Oh, my dear—— (She falls to her knees to clasp HELEN's hand, but HELEN pulls it free, stands almost bewildered, then drops to the ground, pats it swiftly, holds up her palm, imperious. ANNIE spells into it.) Ground. (HELEN spells it back.) Yes! (HELEN whirls to the pump, pats it, holds up her palm, and ANNIE spells into it.) Pump. (HELEN spells it back.) Yes! Yes! (Now HELEN is in such an excitement she is possessed, wild, trembling, cannot be still, turns, runs, falls on the porch step, claps it, reaches out her palm, and ANNIE is at it instantly to spell.) Step. (HELEN has no time to spell back now, she whirls groping, to touch anything, encounters the trellis, shakes it, thrusts out her palm, and ANNIE, while spelling to her, cries wildly at the house.) Trellis. Mrs. Keller! Mrs. Keller! (Inside, KATE starts to her feet. HELEN scrambles back

onto the porch, groping, and finds the bell string, tugs it; the bell rings, the distant chimes begin tolling the hour, all the bells in town seem to break into speech while HELEN reaches out and ANNIE spells feverishly into her hand. KATE hurries out, with KELLER after her; AUNT EV is on her feet, to peer out the window; only JAMES remains at the table, and with a napkin wipes his damp brow. From up right and left the servants—VINEY, the two children, the other servant—run in and stand watching from a distance as HELEN, ringing the bell, with her other hand encounters her mother's skirt; when she throws a hand out, ANNIE spells into it.) Mother. (KELLER now seizes HELEN's hand, she touches him, gestures a hand, and ANNIE again spells.) Papa—— She knows! (KATE and KELLER go to their knees, stammering, clutching HELEN to them, and ANNIE steps unsteadily back to watch the threesome, HELEN spelling wildly into KATE's hand, then into KELLER's, KATE spelling back into HELEN's; they cannot keep their hands off her, and rock her in their clasp. Then HELEN gropes, feels nothing, turns all around, pulls free, and comes with both hands groping, to find ANNIE. She encounters ANNIE's thighs, ANNIE kneels to her, HELEN's hand pats ANNIE's cheek impatiently, points a finger, and waits; and ANNIE spells into it.) Teacher. (HELEN spells it back, slowly; ANNIE nods.) Teacher.

[She holds HELEN's hand to her cheek. Presently HELEN withdraws it, not jerkily, only with reserve, and retreats a step. She stands thinking it over, then turns again and stumbles back to her parents. They try to embrace her, but she has something else in mind. It is to get the keys, and she hits KATE's pocket until KATE digs them out for her.

ANNIE, with her own load of emotion, has retreated, her back turned, toward the pump, to sit; KATE moves to HELEN, touches her hand questioningly, and HELEN spells a word to her.

And now the miracle happens.

KATE *comprehends it, their first act of verbal communication, and she can hardly utter the word aloud, in wonder, gratitude, and deprivation; it is a moment in which she simultaneously finds and loses a child.*]

Kate. Teacher?

[ANNIE *turns; and* KATE, *facing* HELEN *in her direction by the shoulders, holds her back, holds her back, and then* relinquishes *her.* HELEN *feels her way across the yard, rather shyly, and when her moving hands touch* ANNIE'S *skirt she stops. Then she holds out the keys and places them in* ANNIE'S *hand. For a moment neither of them moves. Then* HELEN *slides into* ANNIE'S *arms, and lifting away her smoked glasses, kisses her on the cheek.* ANNIE *gathers her in.*

KATE, *torn both ways, turns from this, gestures the servants off, and makes her way into the house on* KELLER'S *arm. The servants go, in separate directions.*

The lights are half down now, except over the pump. ANNIE *and* HELEN *are here, alone in the yard.* ANNIE *has found* HELEN'S *hand, almost without knowing it, and she spells slowly into it, her voice unsteady, whispering:*]

Annie. I, love, Helen. (*She clutches the child to her, tight this time, not spelling, whispering into her hair.*) Forever, and—— (*She stops. The lights over the pump are taking on the color of the past and it brings* ANNIE'S *head up, her eyes opening in fear; and as slowly as though drawn she rises to listen, with her hand on* HELEN'S *shoulder. She waits, waits, listening with ears and eyes both, slowly here, slowly there, and hears only silence. There are no voices. The color passes on, and when her eyes come back to* HELEN *she can breathe the end of her phrase without fear.*) ——ever.

[*In the family room* KATE *has stood over the table, staring at* HELEN'S *plate, with* KELLER *at her shoulder; now* JAMES *takes a step to move her chair in, and* KATE *sits, with head erect, and* KELLER *inclines his head to* JAMES; *so it is* AUNT EV, *hesitant and rather humble, who moves to the door.*

Outside HELEN *tugs at* ANNIE'S *hand, and* ANNIE *comes with it.* HELEN *pulls her toward the house, and hand in hand, they cross the yard and ascend the porch steps, in the rising lights, to where* AUNT EV *is holding the door open for them. The curtain ends the play.*]

MEET THE WRITER

In Love with His Heroines

William Gibson (1914–   ) has also written a light, touching comedy called *Two for the Seesaw* (1958), which starred Henry Fonda and Anne Bancroft. He is also the author of *A Cry of Players* (1968), a play about the young Shakespeare; *Golda* (1977), a play about Golda Meir, who became prime minister of Israel; and *A Mass for the Dead* (1968), a book about his family. In 1982, *Monday After the Miracle,* a sequel to *The Miracle Worker,* had a brief run on Broadway. Gibson's reflections on *The Miracle Worker* appear on page 624.

Everything Had a Name

from The Story of My Life

Helen Keller

Helen Keller went on to graduate cum laude from Radcliffe College. Annie Sullivan was with her—she "spelled" every lecture for Helen. In 1954 Helen published her autobiography, The Story of My Life. *This excerpt is her version of the miracle, the moment when the mystery of language was revealed to her.*

One day, while I was playing with my new doll, Miss Sullivan put my big rag doll into my lap also, spelled "d-o-l-l" and tried to make me understand that "d-o-l-l" applied to both. Earlier in the day we had had a tussle over the words "m-u-g" and "w-a-t-e-r." Miss Sullivan had tried to impress it upon me that "m-u g" is *mug* and that "w-a-t-e-r" is *water*, but I persisted in confounding the two. In despair she had dropped the subject for the time, only to renew it at the first opportunity.

I became impatient at her repeated attempts and, seizing the new doll, I dashed it upon the floor. I was keenly delighted when I felt the fragments of the broken doll at my feet. Neither sorrow nor regret followed my passionate outburst. I had not loved the doll. In the still, dark world in which I lived there was no strong sentiment or tenderness. I felt my teacher sweep the fragments to one side of the hearth, and I had a sense of satisfaction that the cause of my discomfort was removed. She brought me my hat, and I knew I was going out into the warm sunshine. This thought, if a wordless sensation may be called a thought, made me hop and skip with pleasure.

We walked down the path to the well-house, attracted by the fragrance of the honeysuckle with which it was covered. Someone was drawing water and my teacher placed my hand under the spout. As the cool stream gushed over one hand she spelled into the other the word *water,* first slowly, then rapidly. I stood still, my whole attention fixed upon the motions of her fingers. Suddenly I felt a misty consciousness as of something forgotten—a thrill of returning thought; and somehow the mystery of language was revealed to me. I knew then that "w-a-t-e-r" meant the wonderful cool something that was flowing over my hand. That living word awakened my soul, gave it light, hope, joy, set it free! There were barriers still, it is true, but barriers that could in time be swept away.

I left the well-house eager to learn. Everything had a name, and each name gave birth to a new thought. As we returned to the house every object which I touched seemed to quiver with life. That was because I saw everything with the strange, new sight that had come to me. On entering the door I remembered the doll I had broken. I felt my way to the hearth and picked up the pieces. I tried vainly to put them together. Then my eyes filled with tears; for I realized what I had done, and for the first time I felt repentance and sorrow.

I learned a great many new words that day. I do not remember what they all were; but I do know that *mother, father, sister, teacher* were among them—words that were to make the world blossom for me, "like Aaron's rod, with flowers." It would have been difficult to find a happier child than I was as I lay in my crib at the close of that eventful day and lived over the joys it had brought me, and for the first time longed for a new day to come.

> In the still, dark world in which I lived there was no tenderness.

MAKING MEANINGS   ACT THREE

First Thoughts

1. If you had to select one scene to present as the most important in the play, which would it be?

Shaping Interpretations

2. What is significant about the fact that Annie no longer hears the voices at the end of the play?

3. Whenever a character announces early in a play that she (or he) will never love again, we sense that she will change her mind before the end, and we wait to see what will cause the change. Earlier in this play, Annie says she'll never love again. Why does she say this? What happens to change her mind?

4. How is the play's **climax** the resurrection that Annie feels she owes God and God owes her?

5. How has Helen been reborn by the end of the play?

6. The relationship of James to his father has constituted a **subplot**, a smaller story within the major plot. How is James's **conflict** resolved?

7. What do the stage directions mean when they say that Kate has simultaneously found and lost a child?

Connecting with the Text

8. What do you think of the methods Annie uses to teach Helen? If someone said Annie is cruel, how would you answer?

9. By the end of the play, how do you feel about all the characters?

Extending the Text

10. Is there a **message** in *The Miracle Worker* that is still important today? What do you think this play reveals about love, disabilities, and courage?

11. How many "doors" are opened for people in this play? What people in real life suffer because doors are closed to them?

Reviewing the Text

a. The two weeks are now up. (A time limit is always a good way of increasing pressure.) What startling **change** do we see when Helen appears in Scene 1?

b. In Scene 3, at the dining-room table, what surprising **reversal** do we see in Helen's behavior?

c. How does James now reveal a major **change** in his character?

d. The **climax** of the play takes place at the pump—in one of the most moving scenes in the history of the theater. We have been lured into feeling that Helen has gone as far as she can go—that this is good, but still a defeat for Annie *and* Helen. Explain what Helen learns at the pump.

e. Where in Act Two did the playwright establish the word *wahwah*, so that its simple utterance can score in this final scene?

CHOICES: Building Your Portfolio

Writer's Notebook

1. Collecting Ideas for an Interpretive Essay

Finding a topic. When you interpret a play, story, or novel (see the Writer's Workshop on page 716), you'll want to look closely at the characters and at how they've changed in the grip of events. What have they learned? Is the change for better or for worse? Take notes now on one of the characters in this play whom you're particularly interested in. Track the character's experiences in a time line.

Captain Keller

Act 1: Scene 7

Thinks Annie too young and inexperienced—"half-blind Yankee schoolgirl"

Act 2: Scene 2

Furious. Sees Annie as stubborn, rude.

Scene 6

Wants to fire Annie.

Act 3: Scene 1

Appreciates her work; thinks she expects too much.

Scene 3

Falls to knees over Annie's miracle.

Creative Writing

2. What Happens Next?

Write a scene that could be a sequel for *The Miracle Worker*. Begin by thinking of a new conflict that will give dramatic tension to the scene. Do Annie and the Kellers disagree about Helen's education? Will Annie hear more voices? What about James? In stage directions, state the time and setting of the sequel. Gibson called his own sequel *Monday After the Miracle*. What will you call yours?

Critical Writing

3. All You Need Is Love

Love is an important theme in *The Miracle Worker*. Use one of the following statements as the topic sentence of a short essay about the play. Support the statement with details from the play.

- When Annie was young, she loved Jimmie so much that when he died, she thought she would never love again. Jimmie's death haunts Annie until love for Helen helps her face her past.

- Captain Keller learns that obedience, respect, and proper behavior are not proof of love.

- Kate Keller learns that real love can mean letting go of the one you love so much.

Critical Writing

4. Heralding the Heroine

In his comment on page 625, the playwright says that *The Miracle Worker* is a love letter. In an essay, tell which character the love letter is directed to and explain how *you* responded to her.

Critical Writing

5. Comparing the Miracles

Gibson used the letters of Annie Sullivan and Helen Keller's autobiography as sources for the play. Annie wrote the following letter on the climactic day that Helen learned that everything had a name. In one paragraph, cite at least four details that the playwright altered in writing the scene at the pump. In a second paragraph, tell how Annie's firsthand version of the miracle compares with Helen's (page 705). In a final paragraph, tell which you preferred reading, and why: the scene in the play, Annie's letter, or Helen's autobiography.

April 5. 1887

I must write you a line this morning because something very important has happened. Helen has taken the second great step in her education. She has learned that everything has a name, and that the manual alphabet is the key to everything she wants to know.

In a previous letter I think I wrote you that "mug" and "milk" had given Helen more trouble than all the rest. She confused the nouns with the verb "drink." She didn't know the word for "drink," but went through the pantomime of drinking whenever she spelled "mug" or "milk." This morning, while she was washing, she wanted to know the name for "water." When she wants to know the name of anything, she points to it and pats my hand. I spelled "w-a-t-e-r" and thought no more about it until after breakfast. Then it occurred to me that with the help of this new word I might succeed in straightening out the "mug-milk" difficulty. We went out to the pump house, and I made Helen hold her mug under the spout while I pumped. As the cold water gushed forth, filling the mug, I spelled "w-a-t-e-r" in Helen's free hand. The word coming so close to the sensation of cold water rushing over her hand seemed to startle her. She dropped the mug and stood as one transfixed. A new light came into her face. She spelled "water" several times. Then she dropped on the ground and asked for its name and pointed to the pump and the trellis, and suddenly turning around she asked for my name. I spelled "Teacher."

Annie Sullivan

VOCABULARY — HOW TO OWN A WORD

WORD BANK

simultaneously
consummately
trepidation
mediate
relinquishes

Roots and Affixes: Taking Words Apart

Roots are core words with fairly constant meanings. Many word roots have come into English from other languages—often from Greek and Latin. When you know some roots, you can figure out the meanings of many words. Fill out a chart like the one below for each word in the Word Bank at the left. In your chart, show the word's root and any affixes. Affixes may be prefixes (word parts added to the front of a word, such as *mis-* or *anti-*) or suffixes (word parts added to the end of a word, such as *-ation* or *-ment*). In one part of your chart, see if you can list some words that have the same root.

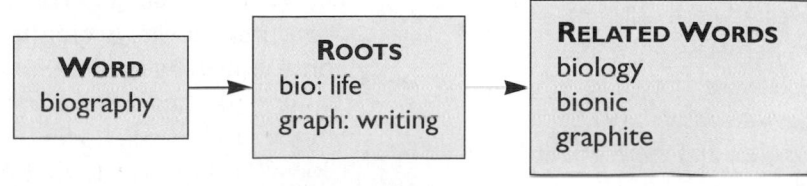

WORD	**ROOTS**	**RELATED WORDS**
biography	bio: life graph: writing	biology bionic graphite

EXTENDING *the theme*

A BIOGRAPHY

ANNIE

from Helen and Teacher

Joseph P. Lash

Annie was born in April 1866 in Feeding Hills, a village outside Springfield, Massachusetts, in circumstances of poverty that were not uncommon among Irish immigrants. But the destitution of the Sullivans was starker and more desolate than even that of their compatriots. Annie's father, red-haired Thomas Sullivan, was not only illiterate and unskilled but a drinker and a brawler, and shiftless. Her gentle mother, born Alice Cloesy (spelled Cloahassy on Annie's baptismal certificate), was tubercular and, after a fall when Annie was three or four, was unable to walk again except on crutches. She bore five children. Annie, christened Johanna, was the oldest. The fifth, John, died before he was three months old. A sister, Nellie, had died before that. Her little brother Jimmie was born with a tubercular hip. Only Mary, next to the youngest, did not ail. Annie, although physically robust, contracted trachoma when she was about five. Untreated, this was gradually destroying her vision. One of her earliest memories was a neighbor saying, "She would be so pretty if it were not for her eyes." A woman urged her mother to wash them in geranium water, and Annie remembers thin hands dabbing her "bad" eyes.

Half-blind, hot-tempered like her father, Annie responded to the miseries within and about her by lashing out childishly, throwing things, going into tantrums. "What a terrible child," the neighbors said. "You little devil," her father often shouted and tried to control her by beatings so severe that, to save her, Annie's mother would try to hide her little daughter. Horror followed horror. Her mother, "gentle Alice Cloesy," as her neighbors from Limerick called her, died.

Helen Keller, aged thirteen, and Annie Sullivan.

There was no money for the funeral, and the town helped to defray the expenses. She was buried in Potter's Field,[1] a kinswoman told Annie years later. She remembered her father saying after the funeral, "God put a curse on me for leaving Ireland and the old folks." Then he would rage wildly against "the landlords" and weep.

On February 22, 1876, Annie and Jimmie, who was on a crutch because of his diseased hip, were delivered in a Black Maria[2] to the state poorhouse in Tewksbury. It was an isolated, forbidding huddle of grimy structures. The attendant who received them proposed to separate them, sending Annie to the women's ward and Jimmie to the men's; but Annie, whose whole childhood had been one abandonment after another, protested with such passionate sobs that the attendant relented and sent them both to a women's ward. No matter that it was unpainted, overcrowded, peopled with misshapen, diseased, often manic women; they were together.

> Annie's whole childhood had been one abandonment after another.

Somehow it all seemed "very homelike" to Annie. The children's cots were next to each other. They had the "dead house," where corpses were prepared for burial, to play in, and old issues of *Godey's Lady's Book* and the *Police Gazette* to cut up. It seemed homelike to Annie, too, because most of the women were Irish, the Catholic priest was always about—and she was no stranger to filth and disease.

Death was a common occurrence, and all her life Annie remembered the clatter of the cots being wheeled over the wooden floor in the dead house. Then the dead house claimed Jimmie. She awoke suddenly in the middle of the night and, sensing the empty space next to her, knew immediately what had happened. She began to tremble. She crept to the dead room and, feeling his cold body under the sheets, began to scream, wakening everyone. As the women dragged her away, she clung to the lifeless body and kicked and screamed. Only when it was light was she permitted to go into the dead room again and sit on a chair beside the bed. Then the sheet was lifted for her, and again she flung herself on the little body "and kissed and kissed and kissed his face—the dearest thing in the world—the only thing I had ever loved." Later the matron allowed her to go outside to pick an armful of flowers. These she placed on the little body. She begged to be allowed to follow the coffin to the burial ground. No priest was there as it was lowered

---

1. **Potter's Field:** public land set aside for burial of very poor or unknown persons.
2. **Black Maria:** police van.

into the bare, sandy spot. "When I got back, I saw that they had put Jimmie's bed back in its place. I sat down between my bed and his empty bed, and I hoped desperately to die. I believe very few children have ever been so completely left alone as I was."

Maggie Hogan, the quiet little woman in charge of her ward, took a special interest in her. She introduced Annie to Tewksbury's small library and persuaded a mildly deranged girl, Tilly, to read to Annie books that she selected, mostly by Irish authors.

Annie's overriding ambition was to get out of the almshouse and go to school. Her chance to escape from Tewksbury came when she heard that an investigating commission headed by Frank B. Sanborn, chairman of the State Board of Charities, had arrived to inspect the institution. Gruesome stories about Tewksbury were rife in the state, even rumors of skins being sold from dead bodies to make shoes. She followed the group from ward to ward, trying to screw up her courage to approach it directly. Finally, as the men stood at the gate, she acted. Without knowing which figure was the exalted Mr. Sanborn, she flung herself into the group, crying, "Mr. Sanborn, Mr. Sanborn, I want to go to school!" "What's the matter with you?" a voice asked. "I can't see very well." "How long have you been here?" She was unable to tell him. The men left, but soon afterward a woman came and told her she was to leave Tewksbury and go to school.

Two calico dresses were found for her. The red one she wore; the blue one, along with a coarse-grained chemise and two pairs of black cotton stockings, was tied up in a newspaper bundle. The women in the ward crowded around her shouting advice as she walked to the Black Maria. "Don't tell anyone you came from the poorhouse." "Keep your head up, you're as good as any of them." "Be a good girl and mind your teachers." When Tim, the driver, handed her over to a state charity official, he added his own bit of advice: "Don't ever come back to this place. Do you hear? Forget this and you will be all right."

In Boston, the charity worker handed her over to another official. When he told her Annie came from Tewksbury, she patted the girl on the head. "Poor child," she said pityingly. Annie's face burned. She had thought the calico dress pretty, but the woman's pity suddenly aroused in her a sense of how poorly dressed she must be. "The essence of poverty," she told Nella Braddy, "is shame. Shame to have been overwhelmed by ugliness, shame to be a hole in the perfect pattern of the universe."

That day—October 7, 1880—she entered the Perkins Institution for the Blind.

> "The essence of poverty," she told Nella Braddy, "is shame."

Joseph P. Lash

(1909–1987) was at work
on one of his biographies of
Franklin Delano Roosevelt
when the president of
Radcliffe College asked if he
would write a biography of
Radcliffe's famous graduate Helen Keller. Lash
at first refused, but his wife pointed out to
him that it was an unusual honor for a man
to be asked by a women's college to write a
book about a woman. He read and was
enchanted by Helen Keller's autobiography,
The Story of My Life. He
decided that it would be
good for him "to get away
for a time from those power-
oriented men, Roosevelt,
Churchill, and Stalin."

Lash's research took him
from Massachusetts to New
York, Washington, Iowa,
Illinois, California, and
Tuscumbia, Alabama. He
read newspapers and letters,
studied journals, and interviewed friends and
relatives of Helen Keller. He found that it was
impossible to write a book about Helen
Keller that was not also a book about her
teacher. Therefore, his book *Helen and
Teacher* starts with Annie.

FINDING COMMON GROUND

1. Get together with a partner or a group and talk about your responses to this
   true story. Be sure to refer to your journals.

2. Then, on your own, write about your responses to Annie's experiences. Your
   response might take the form of an essay, or an article that you can publish in
   your school newspaper. You might even want to write a poem or a short
   story. Before you write, be sure to check your journal for passages that caught
   your attention.

3. You might also set up a read-in, in which each final written response to Annie's
   story is read aloud in class.

READ ON

A Different Mountain to Conquer

In 1955, Jill Kinmont, beautiful and already famous, was a promising candidate for the U.S. Olympic ski team. Then, in the last qualifying race before tryouts, she crashed. Jill, only eighteen years old, was paralyzed from the shoulders down. She would never stand up again. Here is her story, with photographs: *The Other Side of the Mountain* told by E. G. Valens (HarperCollins).

Doors to Freedom

The underground railroad was really a collection of "safe houses" placed along the perilous route north that was taken by Africans escaping slavery in the South. Born a slave herself, Harriet Tubman made it her personal mission to open the doors of freedom for more than three hundred others. Ann Petry's *Harriet Tubman: Conductor on the Underground Railroad* (Pocket/Simon and Schuster) tells Tubman's story. All her passengers successfully escaped—and Tubman was never caught, though she had a price on her head.

Mission Impossible

Twenty-eight men defied all the odds. Shipwrecked in the Antarctic, the surviving passengers of the H.M.S. *Endurance* made homes out of flimsy tents and battered lifeboats for fourteen months. For company they had circling killer whales, riptides, frostbite—and of course, hunger and thirst. Ernest Shackleton and five others were sent in a small boat through freezing waters to scout for help. What they didn't know was that their rescue mission would make history—and become a classic: F. A. Worsley's *Shackleton's Boat Journey* (Norton).

A Struggle to Communicate

In *My Left Foot* (Heinemann), Christy Brown, born with severe cerebral palsy, tells the courageous—and funny—story of his life. Brown grew up with a large and lively family in the slums of Dublin. With fierce discipline, he learned to read and to write, paint, and finally type with the toes of his left foot. His story was made into a motion picture in 1989 starring Daniel Day-Lewis.

Writer's Workshop

Technology HELP

See Writer's Workshop 2 CD-ROM. *Assignment: Interpretation.*

ASSIGNMENT

Write an essay in which you interpret the meaning of some aspect of *The Miracle Worker*. You can focus on the play as a whole or on a single character or symbol.

AIM

To inform.

AUDIENCE

Your classmates and teacher; the Drama Club; readers of a magazine of student writing. (You choose.)

EXPOSITORY WRITING

INTERPRETIVE ESSAY

What is an interpretation? It is a meaning; it's what we make of something. Scientists interpret data. Politicians interpret polls. Historians interpret events. Audiences interpret movies. And certainly, readers interpret literature.

When you write an essay of interpretation, you try to show other people a meaning that you see in a work of literature. To do so, you have to think carefully about the text. You have to find passages to support your sense of what the text means. In the end, if you are persuasive, others will see your meaning too.

Prewriting

1. Review Your Writer's Notebook and Reader's Log

The first thing you'll decide is your focus—what *you* make of an aspect of the play. For insights, browse through your Writer's Notebook and your Reader's Log. Jot notes about the issues you raised or explored while reading this play.

2. Discuss the Play with a Partner

Talk about the play with a partner and see where you disagree or go off in different directions. Zero in on the parts you disagree most strongly about. They may point you toward your own interpretation of the play.

3. Shape an Interpretive Claim

Now develop a statement or claim about the play based on your discussion and notes (or write several claims and choose the best one). Think of an interesting interpretation that goes beyond the literal facts. Good interpretive statements might deal with the following:

- **Motive.** Why do certain characters behave as they do?

- **Changes.** Who changes in the course of the play?

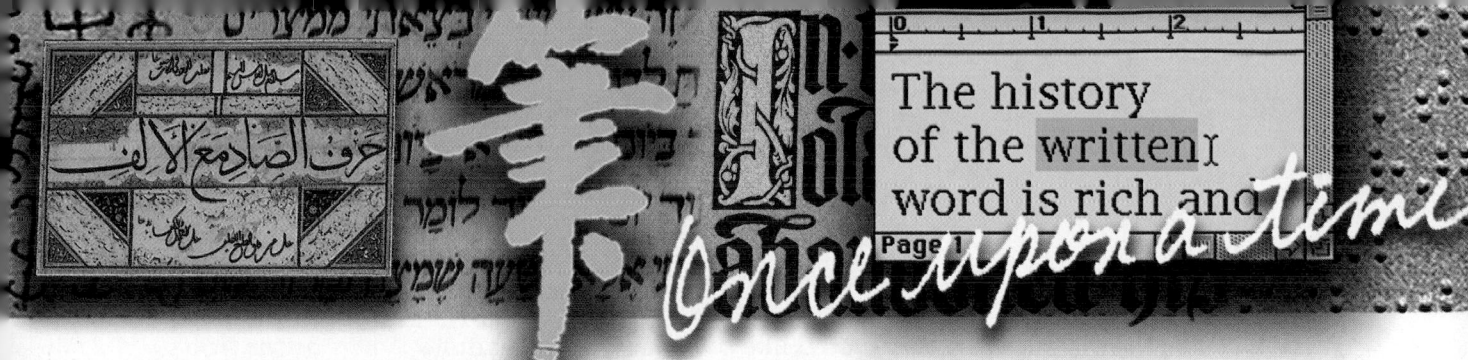

The history of the written word is rich and
Once upon a time
Page 1

- **Theme.** What statement about life is the play making?
- **Relevance.** How does this play relate to our own lives?
- **Symbols.** What things keep recurring in the play that seem to stand for broad subjects such as life, death, growth, communication?
- **Judgment.** Is the play believable?

Drafting

1. Establish Your Subject and Focus

Start by giving your readers a context. Tell them what literary work you are going to discuss and who wrote it. Tell if you are going to explain the whole play or just one part. Which part? Try to hook your reader's interest in your opening paragraph.

2. Make Your Claim

Basically, an interpretive essay issues a challenge. It tells the reader: "Here's something that may not be obvious, but it's true and I can prove it." This claim is your **thesis,** the core of your interpretation. Get it on the table early. In fact, you might include a **thesis statement,** which is a sentence that directly states your point. Here, for example, are thesis statements from three essays about Harper Lee's novel *To Kill a Mockingbird.*

- Scout, Jem, and Dill learn valuable lessons from adults in *To Kill a Mockingbird.*
- Though Dill may seem like a minor character in the book, he has great impact on the lives of Jem and Scout.
- Tom Robinson is just one of many victims of the prejudice that runs throughout *To Kill a Mockingbird.*

3. Make Your Case

Now back up your claim. Think of yourself as a guide, giving your readers a tour of the play *your* way—a tour in which you point out the details that support your thesis. For every statement you make *about* the play, present supporting evidence *from* the play. Direct quotations work well if they go right to your point. Paraphrase long passages.

Try It Out

Support each of the following statements with evidence from *The Miracle Worker.* Provide the type of evidence called for in parentheses.

1. As a young child, Helen Keller was a troublemaker. (Report an action.)

2. Annie was torn with doubt. (Provide a direct quotation.)

3. James felt ignored and unloved. (Paraphrase some dialogue.)

HARPER LEE'S TO KILL A MOCKINGBIRD

As children grow older, the beliefs and values of the adults around them help them decide what kind of people they would like to become. These adults serve as examples, so that younger generations can learn from their various experiences. This way children are offered many different perspectives of the world around them.

Nice intro-duction. Elaborates on the thesis of the essay.

Throughout Harper Lee's novel To Kill a Mockingbird, Jem and Scout Finch are exposed to the insight and wisdom of loved ones. Yet they are also faced with the ignorance of those who are racially and morally biased. One of the positive influences in their lives is their father, Atticus, a lawyer who has accepted the case of a black man despite the racially explosive times. By standing by Tom, no matter what his color, Atticus shows Jem and Scout what it means to remain stead-fast to what they believe in their hearts is right.

Main idea, or thesis, is established. Detail backs up main idea.

During Tom Robinson's trial, however, brother and sister find it isn't always easy to stand up for what you believe. When the Finches' neigh-bor, Miss Maudie, is publicly berated for working in her garden, Jem and Scout are shown how cruel people can truly be to one another just because they believe different things. But Miss Maudie tries to help them see that even though different races, sexes, and religious denominations can sometimes be unfair to each other, they are all human and therefore are allowed to make mistakes—and be forgiven. Jem and Scout begin to realize that many people make uninformed decisions about others based on prejudices.

Another detail supports main idea.

Main idea is supported with more details.

Throughout the story, the siblings also face negative influences. They live in an era when racial acceptance isn't common. The two are scared, chased, and hated because of their family's position in the Robinson trial. One night, Scout, Jem, and their friend Dill witness firsthand the danger of hatred when the local "posse" goes to the jail to bring Tom what they consider justice. The group of men threatens Atticus, despite the fact that he is a man once well respected by the entire town. They ignore his reputation and his desire for understanding. As the children discover, people can turn on each other at a moment's notice.

Probably the biggest influence for Jem and Scout turns out to be Boo Radley, the town recluse. Although they feared and misunderstood Boo because he is "different," he comes through for the children when they need somebody most. From Boo they learn not to be afraid of what they do not know, and not to close their hearts to people in need.

These people, both good and bad, serve as guides for the children and the choices they will have to make in life. The influences they provide help teach Jem and Scout the basics of right and wrong, good and bad. These are the influences they will draw upon when they need to make decisions or need support in the future.

—Meg Tracy
Cape Coral High School
Cape Coral, Florida

Deals with possible objections to the main idea.

Sums up a point.

Begins to develop major supporting detail.

Main Idea restated and extended to show its significance in the children's lives.

Sentence Workshop
H E L P

Revising sentences using parallel structure: page 722.

Communications Handbook
H E L P

Taking notes and documenting sources: pages 983-984.

Evaluating and Revising

1. Peer Review

Your classmates who have read and written about the play make good sounding boards. Trade drafts in groups of three, and write detailed comments and suggestions for one another, keeping in mind the checklist of Evaluation Criteria. (Consider writing your comments on tracing paper laid over your partner's draft, or ask permission to write in the margin with pencil.)

2. Self-Evaluation

Sometimes you can hear problems that don't pop out when you see them. So try reading your essay aloud to yourself and listening for problems (or tape yourself reading and then make notes as you listen to the tape).

Proofreading

Comb your draft for errors in usage, mechanics, and spelling. Professional proofreaders, in one stage of their work, do not think about the content of a text. Try doing the same: Just look at each sentence and word by itself. You might cut a hole in a blank piece of paper and proofread your essay through that window. If you're using a word-processing program on a computer, be sure to run the spelling checker and grammar checker, no matter how long it may take.

Publishing

You might conduct a symposium or gathering of experts on *The Miracle Worker*. Read your essay to your classmates and listen to their essays. Or present your paper to the Drama Club if your school has one. Also, consider sending your essay to a magazine that publishes student writing.

Reflecting

Will you add your essay to your portfolio? If you do, date it and attach a brief reflection on your writing experience, focusing on questions like these:

1. How did I come up with my thesis for this essay?

2. What did I realize about the text that had not occurred to me before?

3. What was the most difficult part of writing this paper?

4. What do I like best about the final version of my essay?

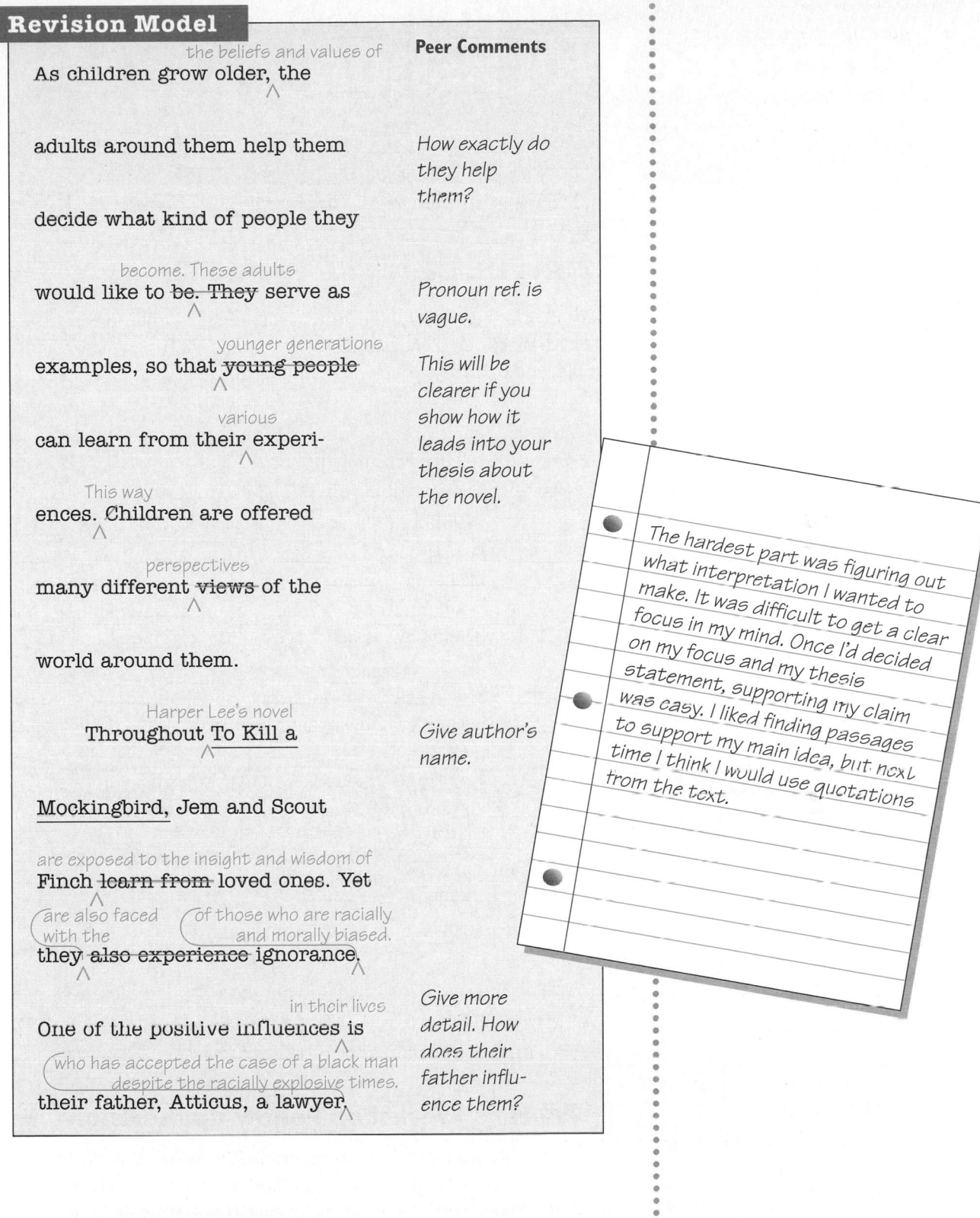

the beliefs and values of
As children grow older, the

adults around them help them

decide what kind of people they

become. These adults
would like to ~~be. They~~ serve as

younger generations
examples, so that ~~young people~~

various
can learn from their experi-

This way
ences. Children are offered

perspectives
many different ~~views~~ of the

world around them.

Harper Lee's novel
Throughout To Kill a

Mockingbird, Jem and Scout

are exposed to the insight and wisdom of
Finch ~~learn from~~ loved ones. Yet

are also faced   _of those who are racially_
with the   _and morally biased._
they ~~also experience~~ ignorance.

in their lives
One of the positive influences is

who has accepted the case of a black man
despite the racially explosive times.
their father, Atticus, a lawyer.

Peer Comments

How exactly do they help them?

Pronoun ref. is vague.

This will be clearer if you show how it leads into your thesis about the novel.

Give author's name.

Give more detail. How does their father influence them?

The hardest part was figuring out what interpretation I wanted to make. It was difficult to get a clear focus in my mind. Once I'd decided on my focus and my thesis statement, supporting my claim was easy. I liked finding passages to support my main idea, but next time I think I would use quotations from the text.

Sentence Workshop

**Technology
HELP**

See Language Workshop
CD-ROM. *Key word entry:
parallel structure.*

REVISING SENTENCES: PARALLEL STRUCTURE

When you combine several ideas in one sentence, it is important to make sure that your combinations are grammatically balanced. For example, you balance a noun with a noun, a phrase with a phrase, and a clause with a clause. This balance is called **parallel structure**.

FAULTY	I enjoy reading but I don't like mysteries, or to read science fiction. [a noun and a phrase]
PARALLEL	I enjoy reading but I don't like mysteries or science fiction. [two nouns]
FAULTY	Jason does not have enough time to eat dinner, do his homework, and piano. [two phrases and a noun]
PARALLEL	Jason does not have enough time to eat dinner, do his homework, and practice the piano. [three phrases]
FAULTY	He promised that he would spend more time studying and to help around the house. [clause and phrase]
PARALLEL	He promised that he would spend more time studying and that he would help around the house. [two clauses]

Some examples of parallel structure are underlined in the following sentences.

1. "I love to <u>sail forbidden seas</u>, and <u>land on barbarous coasts</u>."
—Herman Melville, *Moby-Dick*

2. "They <u>hugged her</u>, and <u>kissed her</u>, and <u>clapped their hands</u>, and <u>shouted</u>."
—Harriet Jacobs, *Incidents in the Life of a Slave Girl*

Writer's Workshop Follow-up: Revision

Review your essay of interpretation, looking carefully for faulty parallel structure. If you find problems, decide how to correct them. You must make sure that the items that should be parallel are in the same grammatical form.

Try It Out

Write two sentences of your own, modeled on the two numbered sentences at the right. For example, a sentence modeled on number 1 might read: "I try to dunk the basketball and land on my feet." Compare your modeled sentences in class to see the variety possible.

Next, pretend you're an editor and use parallel structure to correct the following sentences.

1. Gabriel likes playing soccer in summer and to ski in winter.

2. The boss promised Anita more vacation time and that she would work fewer hours.

3. The guests enjoyed the wedding reception more than to sit through the long ceremony.

4. The food was cold and too much salt in it.

5. I like to see it lap the miles and licking up the valleys.

LEARNING FOR LIFE

Teaching Others

Problem

Helen Keller suffered from severe disabilities: She could neither hear nor see. Fortunately, Helen's family had the money to hire a special teacher for their child. Today, people with visual and hearing handicaps have other options. What are some of the ways society today assists those with disabilities?

Project

Find out what is being done to help people with disabilities lead full, rewarding lives.

Preparation

Using *who, what, where, when,* and *why* questions, brainstorm to find a specific topic that interests you. These ideas will get you started.

People: *Who* provides services to people with disabilities? *Who* is eligible? *What* about children?

Places: *Where* in your community have buildings been modified to comply with the Americans with Disabilities Act (ADA)? *What* services do schools supply?

Things: *What* devices for people with limited sight, hearing, speech, or mobility are available or under development?

Procedure

On your own or with a group of classmates, do one of the following activities or think up an information-gathering activity of your own.

1. Find someone in your community or school who can answer your questions. Arrange a time and place to meet with this expert, and take notes.

2. Take photographs of two public buildings, one that has been modified to make it more accessible to people using wheelchairs or crutches and one that hasn't.

3. Listen for public service announcements (PSAs) on your favorite radio station. Think about the kind of programming the station features and the characteristics of its audience (age, sex, income, etc.).

Presentation

Use one of the following formats (or another that your teacher approves).

1. Photo Essay

Create a photo essay showing the differences between a building that has been modified to meet the requirements of the ADA and one that hasn't. Write captions explaining what problems the unmodified building presents and how the modifications solve those problems in the other building. Send your photo essay to your community or school newspaper.

2. Public Service Announcement

Prepare and tape a thirty-second PSA to raise public awareness about treating people with disabilities as individuals. Target the PSA to the audience of your favorite radio station and ask the station manager to schedule air time for it.

3. Demonstration

Build or make detailed drawings of a model of a device used by people with a particular disability. With other students who have chosen this option, demonstrate or explain the workings of the device to your classmates.

Processing

Reflect on your work. What conclusions can you draw about what society is doing for citizens with disabling conditions?

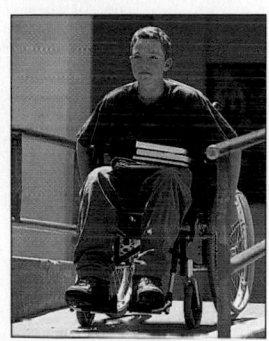

WILLIAM SHAKESPEARE

All the world's a stage . . .
—As You Like It
(Act II, Scene 7)

WILLIAM SHAKESPEARE'S LIFE:
A GENIUS FROM STRATFORD

BY ROBERT ANDERSON

William Shakespeare (1783). Sketch by Ozias Humphrey.
From the Art Collection of the Folger Shakespeare Library, Washington, D.C.

He is the most famous writer in the world, but he left us no journals or letters—he left us only his poems and his plays. What we know about William Shakespeare's personal life comes mostly from church and legal documents—a baptismal registration, a marriage license, and records of real-estate transactions. We also have a few remarks that others wrote about him during his lifetime.

We know that William was born the third of eight children, around April 23, 1564, in Stratford, a market town about one hundred miles northwest of London. His father, John, was a shopkeeper and a man of some importance in Stratford, serving at various times as justice of the peace and high bailiff (mayor).

William attended grammar school, where he studied Latin grammar, Latin literature, and rhetoric (the uses of language). As far as we know, he had no further formal education.

At the age of eighteen, he married Anne Hathaway, who was eight years older than he was. Some time after the birth of their second and third children (twins), Shakespeare moved to London, apparently leaving his family in Stratford.

We know that several years later, by 1592, Shakespeare had already become an actor and a playwright. By 1594, he was a charter member of the theatrical company called the Lord Chamberlain's Men, which was later to become the King's Men. (As the names of these acting companies indicate, theatrical groups depended on the support of a wealthy patron—the King's Men were supported by King James himself.) Shakespeare worked with this company for the rest of his writing life. Year after year, he provided it with plays, almost on demand. Shakespeare was the ultimate professional writer. He had a theater that needed plays, actors who needed parts, and a family that needed to be fed.

Romeo and Juliet was probably among the early plays that Shakespeare wrote, between 1594 and 1596. By 1612, when he returned to Stratford to live the life of a prosperous retired gentleman, Shakespeare had written thirty-seven plays, including such masterpieces as *Julius Caesar, Hamlet, Othello, King Lear,* and *Macbeth.*

Shakespeare's plays are still produced all over the world. During a Broadway season in the 1980s, one critic estimated that if Shakespeare were alive, he would be receiving $25,000 a week in royalties for a production of *Othello* alone. The play was attracting larger audiences than any other nonmusical production in town.

Shakespeare died on April 23, 1616, at the age of fifty-two. He is buried under the old stone floor in the chancel of Holy Trinity church in Stratford. Carved over his grave is the following verse (the spelling is modernized):

Good friend, for Jesus' sake forbear
To dig the dust enclosed here.
Blessed be the man that spares these stones
And cursed be he that moves my bones.

These are hardly the best of Shakespeare's lines (if indeed they are his at all), but like his other lines, they seem to have worked. His bones lie undisturbed to this day.

Shakespeare and His Theater: A Perfect Match

by Robert Anderson

Sometimes playwrights influence the shape and form of a theater, but more often, existing theaters seem to influence the shape and form of plays. It is important that we understand Shakespeare's theater because it influenced how he wrote his plays. Shakespeare took the theater of his time, and he used it brilliantly.

The Globe Theater (18th century), based on C. J. Visscher's engraved panoramic view of London (published 1616).

British Museum, London. The Granger Collection, New York.

THE "WOODEN O"

In 1576, outside the city walls of London, an actor-manager named James Burbage built the first permanent theater in England. He called it The Theater. Up to that time, touring acting companies had played wherever they could rent space. Usually this would be in the courtyards of inns. There the actors would erect a temporary platform stage at one end of the yard and play to an audience which stood around the stage or sat in the tiers of balconies that surrounded the courtyard. (Normally, these balconies were used as passageways to the various rooms of the inn.) It was natural, then, that the first theater built by Burbage should derive its shape and form from the inns.

In 1599, Burbage's theater was torn down and its timbers were used by Shakespeare and his company to build the Globe Theater. This was the theater for which Shakespeare wrote most of his plays.

In his play *Henry V*, Shakespeare called his theater a "wooden O." It was a large, round (or polygonal) building, three stories high, with a large platform stage that projected from one end into a yard open to the sky. In the back wall of this stage was a curtained-off inner stage. Flanking the inner stage were two doors for entrances and exits. Above this inner stage was a small balcony or upper stage, which could be used to suggest Juliet's balcony or the high walls of a castle or the bridge of a ship. Trapdoors were placed in the floor of the main stage for the entrances and exits of ghosts and for descents into hell.

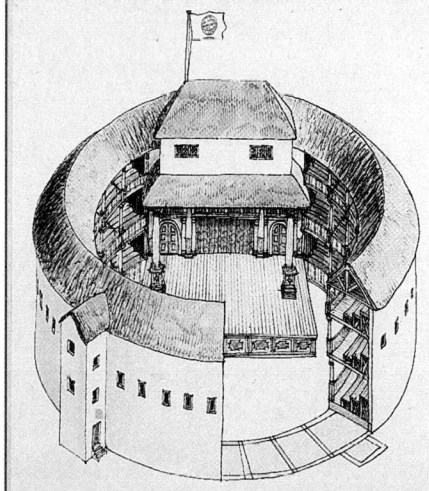

"The Wooden O," the Globe Theater. Drawing by David Gentleman.

The plays were performed in the afternoon. Since the stage was open to the sky, there was no need for stage illumination. There were very few sets (scenery, furniture, etc.). The stage was "set" by the language. A whole forest scene is created in one play when a character announces: "Well, this is the Forest of Arden." But costumes were often elaborate, and the stage might be hung with colorful banners and trappings. (The groundlings, those eight hundred or more people who stood shoulder to shoulder around the stage for the price of a penny, loved a good show. Most people still do.)

We can see that this stage, with its few sets and many acting areas—forestage, inner stage, and upper stage—made for a theater of great fluidity. That is, scene could follow scene with almost cinematic ease.

In one interesting aspect, the theater in Shakespeare's day was very different from the theater we know today. Acting wasn't considered entirely respectable by the English Puritans, so all women's parts were played by boys. Not for many years did women appear on stage in the professional English theater. In Shakespeare's day, Juliet would have been played by a trained boy actor.

THE MODERN STAGE: BACK TO SHAKESPEARE'S THEATER

It has been said that all you need for a theater is "two planks and a passion." Since Shakespeare's time "the planks" (the stage) have undergone various changes. First, the part of the stage which projected into the yard grew narrower, and the

(Background) Panoramic view of London in 1616 (detail) by C. J. Visscher. Globe Theater shown in lower center, page 729.

A cutaway of the Globe, showing the three stage levels and the dressing and prop rooms. Drawing by David Gentleman.

small curtained inner stage grew larger, until there developed what is called the **proscenium stage**. Here, there is no outer stage; there is only the inner stage, and a large curtain separates it from the audience. The effect is like looking inside a window or inside a picture frame. This is the stage most of us know today. It has been standard for well over a hundred years.

But recently, we have seen a reversal of this design. Now, more and more theaters (especially university and regional theaters) are building "thrust" stages, or arena stages. In this kind of theater, the audience once again sits on three or even four sides of the stage.

THE MOVIES AND THE THEATER: WORDS VS. ACTION

Like Shakespeare's stage, this kind of "thrust" stage, with its minimal scenery, allows playwrights (if they want) to move their stories rapidly from place to place. They can establish each new scene with a line like "Well, this is the Forest of Arden." As a result, playwrights have been tempted to write plays that imitate the style of movies. But this imitation rarely works. Theater and movies are two different media. A theater audience does not necessarily want to be whisked from place to place. People who go to plays often prefer to spend a long, long time watching the subtle development of conflicts among a small group of people, all in one setting. For example, all of the action in Lorraine Hansberry's play *A Raisin in the Sun* takes place inside one small apartment on Chicago's South Side.

Movies are basically a *visual* medium and so must chiefly engage and delight the eye, rather than the ear. (One movie director once referred to a dialogue in a movie as "foreground *noise*"!) The theater is much more a medium of *words*. When we go to see a play, it is the movement of the *words* rather than the movement of the scenery that delights us.

This difference between the appeal of a movie and the appeal of a play may account for the failure of some successful plays when they are translated to the screen. The movie producer will say: "Open up the story." In "opening up the story," the producer sometimes loses the concentration, the intensity, which was the prime virtue of the play.

THE DESTRUCTION OF INNOCENCE

SPEAKING AND LISTENING FOCUS: Staging the Play
WRITING FOCUS: Informative Report

What can anyone tell you about love? There's nothing anyone can say that will let you know how wonderful—and horrible—it is. When you fall in love, and you know that it's reciprocated, the world's a bright and glorious place. But if love falls apart, if you begin to feel abandoned or excluded, or if someone else interferes, the agony can be intense. You feel betrayal and loss, and they hurt worse than you ever imagined they would.

Love does strange things to people. The lovers in this play stumble into it, full of hope and innocence. But they learn a hard lesson: that hopes can be ruined and innocence can be destroyed, in part by the very people they trust the most.

Whoever loved that loved not at first sight?

—Christopher Marlowe

Pages 731 and 734–849: Olivia Hussey as Juliet and Leonard Whiting as Romeo in Franco Zeffirelli's film *Romeo and Juliet* (1968).

Writer's Notebook

In the Writer's Workshop on page 870, you'll write an informative report. Your topic will probably come from something that interested you about Shakespeare or about *Romeo and Juliet*. Just from what you've thought about so far, and from what you notice in the illustrations as you flip through the play, jot down some ideas you'd be interested in pursuing. Think about what you know, and what you'd like to know more about.

WORK IN PROGRESS

BEFORE YOU READ
THE TRAGEDY OF ROMEO AND JULIET

Reading Focus

"Kids These Days . . ."

"Kids these days! They think that love conquers all, that nothing matters except how they feel about each other. They have no sense of responsibility to their families, no respect for tradition, no regard for those who are older and wiser. They don't know the problems they're going to have that all the love in the world won't solve for them."

Quickwrite

READER'S LOG

What do you think of this complaint? Have you heard older people say these things about kids today? How would one of the "kids" respond to this speaker? Write a quick response from the kids' point of view.

Background

Most of Shakespeare's plays are based on stories that were already well known to his audiences. (He never wrote a play about a contemporary subject.) *Romeo and Juliet* is based on a long narrative poem by Arthur Brooke, which was published in 1562 as *The Tragicall Historye of Romeus and Juliet.* Brooke's popular poem itself was based on older Italian stories.

The balcony scene and the party scene, from *West Side Story,* an American musical based on *Romeo and Juliet,* set in New York City.

Romeo and Juliet, a very young man and a nearly fourteen-year-old girl, fall in love at first sight. They are caught up in an idealized, almost unreal, passionate love. They are in love with love. In his Prologue, Brooke preaches a moral, which people of his time expected. He says that Romeo and Juliet had to die because they broke the laws and married unwisely, against their parents' wishes. But Shakespeare does away with this moralizing. He presents the couple as "star-crossed lovers," doomed to disaster by fate.

To understand what *star-crossed* means, you have to realize that most people of Shakespeare's time believed in astrology. They believed that the course of their lives was partly determined by the hour, day, month, and year of their birth—hence, "the star" under which they were born. But Shakespeare may not have shared this belief. In a later play, *Julius Caesar*, Shakespeare has a character question this old idea about astrology and the influence of the stars:

The fault, dear Brutus, is not in our stars,
But in ourselves that we are underlings.

Although Shakespeare says in the Prologue that Romeo and Juliet are star-crossed, he does not make them mere victims of fate. Romeo and Juliet make decisions that lead to their disaster. More important, other characters have a hand in the play's tragic ending. How important do *you* think fate is in affecting what happens to us? To what degree do you think we control our own destinies?

A Word List

Shakespeare wrote this play about four hundred years ago. It's not surprising, then, that many words are by now **archaic,** which means that they (or their particular meanings) have disappeared from common use. The side notes in the play will help you with these archaic words and with other words and expressions that might be unfamiliar to you. Here are some of the archaic words that are repeatedly used in the play.

'a: he.
a': on.
an' or **and:** if.
Anon!: Soon! Right away! Coming!
but: if, or only.
Good-den or **go-den** or **God-den:** Good evening. (This was said in the late afternoon.)

hap or **happy:** luck, or lucky.
humor: mood, or moisture.
Jack: common fellow, ordinary guy.
maid: unmarried girl.
mark: listen to.
Marry!: mild oath, shortened from "By the Virgin Mary!"
nice: trivial, foolish.
owes: owns.

shrift: confession or forgiveness for sins that have been confessed to a priest. After confession a person was said to be **shriven.**
Soft!: Quiet! Hush! Slow up!
Stay!: Wait!
withal: with that, with.
wot: know.

CHARACTERS

" A pair of star-crossed lovers "

The Montagues

Lord Montague
Lady Montague
Romeo, son of Montague
Benvolio, nephew of Montague and friend of Romeo
Balthasar, servant of Romeo
Abram, servant of Montague

The Capulets

Lord Capulet
Lady Capulet
Juliet, daughter of Capulet
Tybalt, nephew of Lady Capulet
Nurse to Juliet
Peter, servant to the Nurse
Sampson
Gregory } servants of Capulet
An Old Man of the Capulet family

The Others

Prince Escalus, ruler of Verona
Mercutio, a relative of the Prince and friend of Romeo
Friar Laurence, a Franciscan priest
Friar John, another Franciscan priest
Count Paris, a young nobleman, a relative of the Prince
An Apothecary (a druggist)
Page to Paris
Chief Watchman
Three Musicians
An Officer

Citizens of Verona, Relatives of both families, **Maskers, Guards, Watchmen,** and **Attendants**

Scene: Verona and Mantua, cities in northern Italy

THE TRAGEDY OF ROMEO AND JULIET

William Shakespeare

THE PROLOGUE

Enter CHORUS.

Chorus.

Two households, both alike in dignity,°
   In fair Verona, where we lay our scene,
From ancient grudge break to new mutiny,
   Where civil blood makes civil hands unclean.°
5 From forth the fatal loins of these two foes
   A pair of star-crossed lovers take their life;
Whose misadventured piteous overthrows
   Do with their death bury their parents' strife.
The fearful passage of their death-marked love,
10   And the continuance of their parents' rage,
Which, but° their children's end, naught could remove,
   Is now the two hours' traffic° of our stage;
The which if you with patient ears attend,
What here shall miss, our toil shall strive to mend.

                                                              [Exit.]

1. dignity: status.

4. That is, where civilians' passions ("civil blood") make their hands unclean (because they have been used for killing).

11. but: unless.

12. traffic: business.

? 14. *This Prologue is spoken by a single actor called "the chorus." The Prologue welcomes the audience and gives them a taste of the story. What will the "two hours' traffic" of this stage be about? What will happen to the two lovers?*

ACT I

Scene 1. *Verona. A public place.*

Enter SAMPSON *and* GREGORY, *of the house of Capulet, with swords and bucklers (shields).*

Sampson. Gregory, on my word, we'll not carry coals.°
Gregory. No, for then we should be colliers.°
Sampson. I mean, and° we be in choler,° we'll draw.°
Gregory. Ay, while you live, draw your neck out of
5   collar.°
Sampson. I strike quickly, being moved.
Gregory. But thou art not quickly moved to strike.
Sampson. A dog of the house of Montague moves me.
Gregory. To move is to stir, and to be valiant is to stand.
10   Therefore, if thou art moved, thou run'st away.
Sampson. A dog of that house shall move me to stand. I
    will take the wall° of any man or maid of Montague's.
Gregory. That shows thee a weak slave; for the weakest
    goes to the wall.°
15 **Sampson.** 'Tis true; and therefore women, being the
    weaker vessels, are ever thrust to the wall. Therefore I
    will push Montague's men from the wall and thrust his
    maids to the wall.
Gregory. The quarrel is between our masters and us
20   their men.
Sampson. 'Tis all one. I will show myself a tyrant. When
    I have fought with the men, I will be civil with the
    maids—I will cut off their heads.
Gregory. The heads of the maids?
25 **Sampson.** Ay, the heads of the maids or their maiden-
    heads. Take it in what sense thou wilt.
Gregory. They must take it in sense that feel it.
Sampson. Me they shall feel while I am able to stand; and
    'tis known I am a pretty piece of flesh.
30 **Gregory.** 'Tis well thou art not fish; if thou hadst, thou
    hadst been Poor John.° Draw thy tool!° Here comes
    two of the house of Montagues.

[Enter two other servingmen, ABRAM *and* BALTHASAR.]

Sampson. My naked weapon is out. Quarrel! I will back
    thee.
35 **Gregory.** How? Turn thy back and run?
Sampson. Fear me not.°
Gregory. No, marry. I fear thee!

? *Stage direction: The two servants enter, bragging and teasing each other. What actions do you imagine they are engaged in as they cross the city square?*

1. carry coals: do dirty work (put up with insults). People often made jokes about men who carted coal.
2. colliers: coal dealers (men with dirty jobs). Notice how the servants start making jokes based on words that sound similar (*colliers, choler,* and *collar*).
3. and: if. **choler:** anger. **draw:** pull out swords.
5. collar: the hangman's noose.

12. take the wall: take the best place on the path (which is closest to the wall).
14. goes to the wall: is defeated.

31. Poor John: kind of salted fish, a poor person's food. **tool:** sword.

? *Stage direction: Sampson's and Gregory's swaggering stops when they spy their enemies. How do their next speeches show that they are really cowards? What's Sampson doing when he says "Quarrel! I will back thee"?*

36. Fear me not: Do not distrust me.

Sampson. Let us take the law of our sides;° let them begin.

40 **Gregory.** I will frown as I pass by, and let them take it as they list.

Sampson. Nay, as they dare. I will bite my thumb° at them, which is disgrace to them if they bear it.

Abram. Do you bite your thumb at us, sir?

45 **Sampson.** I do bite my thumb, sir.

Abram. Do you bite your thumb at us, sir?

Sampson (*aside to* GREGORY). Is the law of our side if I say ay?

Gregory (*aside to* SAMPSON). No.

50 **Sampson.** No, sir, I do not bite my thumb at you, sir; but I bite my thumb, sir.

Gregory. Do you quarrel, sir?

Abram. Quarrel, sir? No, sir.

Sampson. But if you do, sir, I am for you. I serve as good

55 a man as you.

Abram. No better.

Sampson. Well, sir.

[*Enter* BENVOLIO.]

Gregory. Say "better." Here comes one of my master's kinsmen.

60 **Sampson.** Yes, better, sir.

Abram. You lie.

Sampson. Draw, if you be men. Gregory, remember thy swashing° blow.

[*They fight.*]

Benvolio.
　Part, fools!
65　Put up your swords. You know not what you do.

[*Enter* TYBALT.]

Tybalt.
　What, art thou drawn among these heartless hinds?°
　Turn thee, Benvolio; look upon thy death.
Benvolio.
　I do but keep the peace. Put up thy sword,
　Or manage it to part these men with me.
Tybalt.
70　What, drawn, and talk of peace? I hate the word
　As I hate hell, all Montagues, and thee.
　Have at thee, coward!

[*They fight.*]

38. That is, stay on the right side of the law.

42. bite my thumb: an insulting gesture.

? 44. *It takes the Montague servants some time to speak. How do their actions show that these four servants are very wary of one another?*

? 58. *How does Gregory change when he spots Tybalt in the distance?*

63. swashing: slashing.

? 65. *What action is Benvolio involved in here?*

66. heartless hinds: cowardly hicks.

? 67. *Sometimes Tybalt's second line is spoken after a dramatic silence. Why should this line demand our attention?*

? 70. *This is a key speech. What is Tybalt's mood? How is he shown to be opposite in nature to Benvolio?*

[*Enter an* OFFICER, *and three or four* CITIZENS *with clubs, bills, and partisans, or spears.*]

Officer. Clubs, bills, and partisans! Strike! Beat them down! Down with the Capulets! Down with the Mon-
75 tagues!

[*Enter old* CAPULET *in his gown, and his wife,* LADY CAPULET.]

Capulet.
What noise is this? Give me my long sword, ho!
Lady Capulet.
A crutch, a crutch! Why call you for a sword?
Capulet.
My sword, I say! Old Montague is come
And flourishes his blade in spite of° me.

[*Enter old* MONTAGUE *and his wife,* LADY MONTAGUE.]

Montague.
80 Thou villain Capulet!—Hold me not; let me go.
Lady Montague.
Thou shalt not stir one foot to seek a foe.

[*Enter* PRINCE ESCALUS, *with his* TRAIN.]

Prince.
Rebellious subjects, enemies to peace,
Profaners of this neighbor-stainèd steel—
Will they not hear? What, ho! You men, you beasts,
85 That quench the fire of your pernicious rage
With purple fountains issuing from your veins!
On pain of torture, from those bloody hands
Throw your mistempered° weapons to the ground
And hear the sentence of your movèd prince.
90 Three civil brawls, bred of an airy° word
By thee, old Capulet, and Montague,
Have thrice disturbed the quiet of our streets
And made Verona's ancient citizens
Cast by their grave beseeming° ornaments
95 To wield old partisans, in hands as old,
Cankered with peace, to part your cankered° hate.
If ever you disturb our streets again,
Your lives shall pay the forfeit of the peace.
For this time all the rest depart away.
100 You, Capulet, shall go along with me;
And, Montague, come you this afternoon,
To know our farther pleasure in this case,
To old Freetown, our common judgment place.
Once more, on pain of death, all men depart.

77. *In the midst of the tension over Tybalt, we have a comic touch. Why is Lady Capulet talking about crutches?*
79. in spite of: in defiance of.

80. *Who is holding Montague back?*

Stage direction: *If you were directing this play, how would you stage the entrance of the prince? His dignified procession must contrast with the bloody rioting. How do you know from the next speech that the prince is at first ignored by the brawlers?*

88. mistempered: used with bad temper.
89. *There is a dramatic pause before the next line is spoken. What are the brawlers doing now?*
90. airy: light or harmless.

94. grave beseeming: dignified, as they should be.

96. cankered: The first "cankered" means "rusted" (from lack of use in peaceful times); the second means "diseased," like a canker, a running sore.

104. *What has been happening in Verona? What is the prince's warning?*

" Throw your mistempered weapons to the ground.... "

[Exeunt all but MONTAGUE, LADY MONTAGUE, *and* BENVOLIO.]

Montague.

105 Who set this ancient quarrel new abroach?°
  Speak, nephew, were you by when it began?

Benvolio.

  Here were the servants of your adversary
  And yours, close fighting ere I did approach.
  I drew to part them. In the instant came
110 The fiery Tybalt, with his sword prepared,
  Which, as he breathed defiance to my ears,
  He swung about his head and cut the winds,
  Who, nothing hurt withal, hissed him in scorn.
  While we were interchanging thrusts and blows,
115 Came more and more, and fought on part and part,°
  Till the prince came, who parted either part.

Lady Montague.

  O, where is Romeo? Saw you him today?
  Right glad I am he was not at this fray.

Benvolio.

  Madam, an hour before the worshiped sun
120 Peered forth the golden window of the East,
  A troubled mind drave me to walk abroad;
  Where, underneath the grove of sycamore
  That westward rooteth from this city side,
  So early walking did I see your son.
125 Towards him I made, but he was ware° of me
  And stole into the covert of the wood.
  I, measuring his affections by my own,
  Which then most sought where most might not be
   found,°
  Being one too many by my weary self,
130 Pursued my humor not pursuing his,
  And gladly shunned who gladly fled from me.

Montague.

  Many a morning hath he there been seen,
  With tears augmenting the fresh morning's dew,
  Adding to clouds more clouds with his deep sighs;
135 But all so soon as the all-cheering sun

---

105. new abroach: newly opened.

115. on part and part: some on one side, some on the other.

? **118.** *For the first time, Romeo is mentioned, and by his mother, whose parental concern is accented by a rhyme. Lady Montague does not say anything else in this scene. What do you imagine she is doing while her husband and Benvolio discuss her son?*

125. ware: aware.

128. He sought a place where no one could be found. (He wanted to be alone.)

How to Read Shakespeare

THE POETRY

Whatever Shakespeare learned of rhetoric, or language, in grammar school, he parades with relish in *Romeo and Juliet.* He is obviously having a fine time here with puns and wordplay and all the other variations he can ring on the English language.

Romeo and Juliet is written in both prose and poetry. Prose is for the most part spoken by the common people and occasionally by Mercutio when he is joking. Most of the other characters speak in poetry.

Blank verse. The poetry is largely written in unrhymed iambic pentameter. In **iambic meter** each unstressed syllable is followed by a stressed syllable, as in the word *prefér.* In **iambic pentameter** there are five of these iambic units in each line. Unrhymed iambic pentameter is called **blank verse.** The word *blank* just means that there is no rhyme at the end of lines.

Read aloud this perfect example of iambic pentameter, spoken by Romeo. The syllables marked (') should be stressed.

But soft! What light through yonder window breaks?

Couplets. When Shakespeare uses rhymes, he generally uses **couplets,** two consecutive lines of poetry that rhyme. The couplets often punctuate a character's exit or signal the end of a scene. Read aloud Juliet's exit line from the balcony.

Good night, good night! Parting is such sweet sorrow
That I shall say good night till it be morrow.

Reading the lines. We have all heard people ruin a good poem by mechanically pausing at the end of each line, whether or not the meaning of the line called for such a pause. (Maxwell Anderson, who wrote verse plays, had his plays typed as though they were prose, so that actors would not be tempted to pause at the end of

---

Should in the farthest East begin to draw
The shady curtains from Aurora's° bed,
Away from light steals home my heavy° son
And private in his chamber pens himself,
140 Shuts up his windows, locks fair daylight out,
And makes himself an artificial night.
Black and portentous must this humor prove
Unless good counsel may the cause remove.
Benvolio.
My noble uncle, do you know the cause?
Montague.
145 I neither know it nor can learn of him.
Benvolio.
Have you importuned° him by any means?
Montague.
Both by myself and many other friends;
But he, his own affections' counselor,
Is to himself—I will not say how true—
150 But to himself so secret and so close,

137. Aurora is goddess of the dawn.
138. heavy: heavy-hearted.

? **143.** *Romeo has been described by his father and his friend. What do we know of him so far?*

146. importuned: questioned.

each line. Directors of Shakespeare's plays today often advise actors to do the same.)

Lines of poetry are either end-stopped lines or run-on lines. An **end-stopped line** has some punctuation at its end. A **run-on line** has no punctuation at its end. In a run-on line, the meaning is completed in the line or lines that follow.

Try reading aloud this passage from Act II, Scene 2, where Juliet speaks in end-stopped lines—lines ending with punctuation that requires her to pause:

> O, Romeo, Romeo! Wherefore art thou Romeo?
> Deny thy father and refuse thy name;
> Or, if thou wilt not, be but sworn my love,
> And I'll no longer be a Capulet.

But Romeo's speech in the same scene has many run-on lines. Read these lines aloud; where does Romeo pause?

> The brightness of her cheek would shame those stars
> As daylight doth a lamp; her eyes in heaven
> Would through the airy region stream so bright
> That birds would sing and think it were not night.

The glory of *Romeo and Juliet* is its poetry and its theatricality. The play is fast-moving, and the poetry suits the story of young people dealing with a matter very important to them— passionate, once-in-a-lifetime love.

". . . be but sworn my love . . ."

So far from sounding° and discovery,
As is the bud bit with an envious° worm
Ere he can spread his sweet leaves to the air
Or dedicate his beauty to the sun.
155 Could we but learn from whence his sorrows grow,
We would as willingly give cure as know.

[*Enter* ROMEO.]

Benvolio.
See, where he comes. So please you step aside;
I'll know his grievance, or be much denied.
Montague.
I would thou wert so happy° by the stay
160 To hear true shrift.° Come, madam, let's away.

[*Exeunt* MONTAGUE *and* LADY MONTAGUE.]

Benvolio.
Good morrow, cousin.
Romeo.   Is the day so young?

151. So far from sounding: so far from being sounded out for his mood (as a river is sounded for its depth).
152. envious: evil.

? **Stage direction:** *Romeo at first doesn't see his parents or Benvolio. How do you think he would be acting as he enters?*

159. happy: lucky.
160. shrift: confession.

? **161.** *Benvolio is trying to be casual. What attitude should Romeo convey by his answer to Benvolio's cheery greeting?*

Benvolio.

But new struck nine.

Romeo.   Ay me! Sad hours seem long.

Was that my father that went hence so fast?

Benvolio.

It was. What sadness lengthens Romeo's hours?

Romeo.

165   Not having that which having makes them short.

Benvolio. In love?

Romeo. Out——

Benvolio. Of love?

Romeo.

Out of her favor where I am in love.

Benvolio.

170   Alas that love, so gentle in his view,°

Should be so tyrannous and rough in proof!°

Romeo.

Alas that love, whose view is muffled still,°

Should without eyes see pathways to his will!

Where shall we dine? O me! What fray was here?

175   Yet tell me not, for I have heard it all.

Here's much to do with hate, but more with love.°

Why then, O brawling love, O loving hate,

O anything, of nothing first created!

O heavy lightness, serious vanity,

180   Misshapen chaos of well-seeming forms,

Feather of lead, bright smoke, cold fire, sick health,

Still-waking sleep, that is not what it is!

This love feel I, that feel no love in this.

Dost thou not laugh?

169. *Romeo blurts out the truth. What is the cause of his strange behavior?*

170. view: appearance.

171. in proof: in reality.

172. muffled still: always blindfolded. Romeo is talking about Cupid, who was depicted as blindfolded.

174. *Romeo wants to change the subject. Then he notices the signs of the street fighting. What does he say about the rivalry between the two families?*

176. more with love: They enjoyed fighting.

180–182. *All of these are contradictions, things that are really the opposite of the way they are described. How does Romeo bitterly relate these to the love he feels?*

" *Here's much to do with hate, but more with love.* "

Benvolio.   No, coz,° I rather weep.

Romeo.

Good heart, at what?

185   **Benvolio.**   At thy good heart's oppression.

Romeo.

Why, such is love's transgression.

Griefs of mine own lie heavy in my breast,

Which thou wilt propagate,° to have it prest°

With more of thine. This love that thou hast shown

190   Doth add more grief to too much of mine own.

184. coz: cousin (or other relative).

188. propagate: increase. **prest:** pressed; burdened.

Love is a smoke made with the fume of sighs;
Being purged, a fire sparkling in lovers' eyes;
Being vexed, a sea nourished with loving tears.
What is it else? A madness most discreet,°
195 A choking gall, and a preserving sweet.
Farewell, my coz.

Benvolio.   Soft!° I will go along.
And if you leave me so, you do me wrong.

Romeo.
Tut! I have lost myself; I am not here;
This is not Romeo, he's some other where.

Benvolio.
200 Tell me in sadness,° who is that you love?

Romeo.
What, shall I groan and tell thee?

Benvolio.   Groan? Why, no;
But sadly tell me who.

Romeo.
Bid a sick man in sadness make his will.
Ah, word ill urged to one that is so ill!
205 In sadness, cousin, I do love a woman.

Benvolio.
I aimed so near when I supposed you loved.

Romeo.
A right good markman. And she's fair I love.

Benvolio.
A right fair mark, fair coz, is soonest hit.

Romeo.
Well, in that hit you miss. She'll not be hit
210 With Cupid's arrow. She hath Dian's wit,°
And, in strong proof° of chastity well armed,
From Love's weak childish bow she lives uncharmed.
She will not stay° the siege of loving terms,
Nor bide th' encounter of assailing eyes,
215 Nor ope her lap to saint-seducing gold.°
O, she is rich in beauty; only poor
That, when she dies, with beauty dies her store.°

Benvolio.
Then she hath sworn that she will still live chaste?

Romeo.
She hath, and in that sparing makes huge waste;
220 For beauty, starved with her severity,
Cuts beauty off from all posterity.
She is too fair, too wise, wisely too fair,
To merit bliss° by making me despair.
She hath forsworn to love, and in that vow

194. **discreet:** discriminating.

? 195. *Romeo refuses to reveal more about his troubles and suggests to Benvolio that he is driven mad by love. What things does he compare love to, before he tries to get away from Benvolio?*
196. **Soft!:** Wait!

200. **sadness:** seriousness.

210. **Dian's wit:** the cunning of Diana, the goddess of chastity, who was not interested in men.
211. **proof:** armor.
213. **stay:** submit to.

215. **Nor ope . . . gold:** In myth, the god Zeus visited Danae in the form of a shower of gold, and Danae bore Zeus a son.
217. **when she dies . . . her store:** Her store of beauty dies with her, since she'll have no children.

223. **bliss:** heaven.

225   Do I live dead that live to tell it now.

Benvolio.

     Be ruled by me; forget to think of her.

   Romeo.

     O, teach me how I should forget to think!

Benvolio.

     By giving liberty unto thine eyes.

     Examine other beauties.

   Romeo.   'Tis the way

230   To call hers, exquisite, in question° more.

     These happy masks° that kiss fair ladies' brows,

     Being black, put us in mind they hide the fair.

     He that is strucken blind cannot forget

     The precious treasure of his eyesight lost.

235   Show me a mistress that is passing fair:

     What doth her beauty serve but as a note

     Where I may read who passed that passing fair?

     Farewell. Thou canst not teach me to forget.

Benvolio.

     I'll pay that doctrine, or else die in debt.°

                               [*Exeunt.*]

225. *What vow has the young woman made?*

230. call . . . in question: bring her beauty to mind.
231. masks: Women often wore masks to protect their faces from the sun.

237. *Why won't looking at other women help Romeo?*

239. or else die in debt: or die trying.
239. *Benvolio can exit here as if he is running after Romeo. The pair will reenter later, Romeo still being pursued. How would the audience feel about Benvolio?*

Scene 2. *A street.*

Enter CAPULET, COUNT PARIS, *and the clown, his* SERVANT.

Capulet.

     But Montague is bound° as well as I,

     In penalty alike; and 'tis not hard, I think,

     For men so old as we to keep the peace.

Paris.

     Of honorable reckoning° are you both,

5   And pity 'tis you lived at odds so long.

     But now, my lord, what say you to my suit?

Capulet.

     But saying o'er what I have said before:

     My child is yet a stranger in the world,

     She hath not seen the change of fourteen years;

10   Let two more summers wither in their pride

     Ere we may think her ripe to be a bride.

1. is bound: is pledged to keep the peace.

4. reckoning: reputation.

Paris.
　　Younger than she are happy mothers made.
Capulet.
　　And too soon marred are those so early made.
　　Earth hath swallowed all my hopes but she;
15　　She is the hopeful lady of my earth.
　　But woo her, gentle Paris, get her heart;
　　My will to her consent is but a part.
　　And she agreed, within her scope of choice°
　　Lies my consent and fair according° voice.
20　　This night I hold an old accustomed° feast,
　　Whereto I have invited many a guest,
　　Such as I love; and you among the store,
　　One more, most welcome, makes my number more.
　　At my poor house look to behold this night
25　　Earth-treading stars° that make dark heaven light.
　　Such comfort as do lusty young men feel
　　When well-appareled April on the heel
　　Of limping winter treads, even such delight
　　Among fresh fennel° buds shall you this night
30　　Inherit° at my house. Hear all, all see,
　　And like her most whose merit most shall be;
　　Which, on more view of many, mine, being one,
　　May stand in number,° though in reck'ning none.°
　　Come, go with me.

> ❝ *Earth hath swallowed all my hopes but she;*
> *She is the hopeful lady of my earth.* ❞

[*To* SERVANT, *giving him a paper.*]

　　　　　　　Go, sirrah, trudge about
35　Through fair Verona; find those persons out
　　Whose names are written there, and to them say
　　My house and welcome on their pleasure stay.°

　　　　　　　　[*Exit with* PARIS.]

Servant. Find them out whose names are written here?
　　It is written that the shoemaker should meddle with
40　his yard and the tailor with his last, the fisher
　　with his pencil and the painter with his nets;° but I
　　am sent to find those persons whose names are here
　　writ, and can never find° what names the writing

12. *Paris is very much at ease with old Capulet and more composed than the lovesick Romeo we just saw. What does Paris want?*

15. *Why doesn't Capulet want his daughter to marry right away? How is Capulet now different from the man who drew his sword in Scene 1?*

18. within her scope of choice: among all she can choose from.
19. according: agreeing.
20. accustomed: traditional.

25. Earth-treading stars: that is, young girls.

29. fennel: an herb. Capulet compares the young girls to fennel flowers.
30. Inherit: have.

33. stand in number: be one of the crowd (of girls). **though in reck'ning none:** though none will be worth more than Juliet is.

34. *Capulet can be played many ways by actors. Some play him here as a loving, considerate father. Other actors interpret him as a man who chiefly wants a socially advantageous marriage for his daughter. How would you play this scene?*

37. stay: wait.

38. *Like the other servants, this one plays for comedy. He can't read or write. How should he show his bewilderment?*

39–41. shoemaker . . . nets: The servant is quoting mixed-up proverbs. He's trying to say that people should attend to what they do best.

43. find: understand.

45 person hath here writ. I must to the learned. In good time!°

[*Enter* BENVOLIO *and* ROMEO.]

Benvolio.
Tut, man, one fire burns out another's burning;
  One pain is less'ned by another's anguish;
Turn giddy, and be holp by backward turning;°
  One desperate grief cures with another's languish.
50 Take thou some new infection to thy eye,
And the rank poison of the old will die.

Romeo.
Your plantain leaf is excellent for that.

Benvolio.
For what, I pray thee?

Romeo.   For your broken° shin.

Benvolio.
Why, Romeo, art thou mad?

Romeo.
55 Not mad, but bound more than a madman is;
Shut up in prison, kept without my food,
Whipped and tormented and—God-den,° good fellow.

Servant. God gi' go-den. I pray, sir, can you read?

Romeo.
Ay, mine own fortune in my misery.

60 **Servant.** Perhaps you have learned it without book. But, I pray, can you read anything you see?

Romeo.
Ay, if I know the letters and the language.

Servant. Ye say honestly. Rest you merry.

Romeo. Stay, fellow; I can read.

[*He reads the letter.*]

65 "Signior Martino and his wife and daughters;
County Anselm and his beauteous sisters;
The lady widow of Vitruvio;
Signior Placentio and his lovely nieces;
Mercutio and his brother Valentine;
70 Mine uncle Capulet, his wife and daughters;
My fair niece Rosaline; Livia;
Signior Valentio and his cousin Tybalt;
Lucio and the lively Helena."
A fair assembly. Whither should they come?

75 **Servant.** Up.

Romeo. Whither? To supper?

Servant. To our house.

Romeo. Whose house?

Servant. My master's.

44–45. In good time!: Just in time!

45. *The servant looks up from the note to see the young gentlemen enter. He now tries to get them to read the note, while one chases the other across the stage. How do Romeo's comments in the next conversation show that he is trying to change the subject?*

48. be holp by backward turning: be helped by turning in the opposite direction.

53. broken: scratched.

57. God-den: good evening.

57. *Romeo turns to get away and runs into the servant, who has been listening to them in stupefied silence. How should the two gentlemen treat the servant in this little encounter?*

71. *Rosaline, Capulet's niece, is the woman Romeo is in love with. Some actors read this line to betray to the audience Romeo's secret. How would you have Romeo read this letter? How would he ask his question?*

Romeo.
80   Indeed I should have asked you that before.
Servant. Now I'll tell you without asking. My master is
      the great rich Capulet; and if you be not of the house of
      Montagues, I pray come and crush a cup of wine. Rest
      you merry.

                                                    [*Exit.*]

Benvolio.
85   At this same ancient° feast of Capulet's
      Sups the fair Rosaline whom thou so loves;
      With all the admirèd beauties of Verona.
      Go thither, and with unattainted° eye
      Compare her face with some that I shall show,
90   And I will make thee think thy swan a crow.
Romeo.
      When the devout religion of mine eye
          Maintains such falsehood, then turn tears to fires;
      And these, who, often drowned, could never die,
          Transparent heretics,° be burnt for liars!
95   One fairer than my love? The all-seeing sun
      Ne'er saw her match since first the world begun.
Benvolio.
      Tut! you saw her fair, none else being by,
      Herself poised° with herself in either eye;
      But in that crystal scales° let there be weighed
100   Your lady's love against some other maid
      That I will show you shining at this feast,
      And she shall scant° show well that now seems best.
Romeo.
      I'll go along, no such sight to be shown,
      But to rejoice in splendor of mine own.

                                                [*Exeunt.*]

« One fairer than my love? The
all-seeing sun
Ne'er saw her match since
first the world begun. »

---

85. ancient: old; established by an old custom.

88. unattainted: untainted (by prejudice).

? 90. *What does Benvolio say to lure Romeo to the party?*

94. transparent heretics: His eyes would be easily "seen through"—they would betray the truth.

98. poised: balanced (for comparison).
99. crystal scales: Romeo's eyes.

102. scant: scarcely.

? 104. *If we know from the letter that Rosaline is to be at the party and that she is the one Romeo loves, we know why Romeo decides to go to Capulet's. Actors usually say these lines to indicate that the decision to go is crucial and fateful. What mood is Romeo in?*

Scene 3. *A room in Capulet's house.*

Enter Capulet's wife, LADY CAPULET, *and* NURSE.

Lady Capulet.
Nurse, where's my daughter? Call her forth to me.
Nurse.
Now, by my maidenhead at twelve year old,
I bade her come. What,° lamb! What, ladybird!
God forbid, where's this girl? What, Juliet!

[*Enter* JULIET.]

Juliet.
How now? Who calls?
Nurse.   Your mother.
5   **Juliet.**   Madam, I am here.
What is your will?
Lady Capulet.
This is the matter.—Nurse, give leave awhile;
We must talk in secret. Nurse, come back again.
I have rememb'red me; thou's° hear our counsel.
10   Thou knowest my daughter's of a pretty age.
Nurse.
Faith, I can tell her age unto an hour.
Lady Capulet.
She's not fourteen.
Nurse.   I'll lay fourteen of my teeth—
And yet, to my teen° be it spoken, I have but four—
She's not fourteen. How long is it now
To Lammastide?°
15   **Lady Capulet.**   A fortnight and odd days.
Nurse.
Even or odd, of all days in the year,
Come Lammas Eve at night shall she be fourteen.
Susan and she (God rest all Christian souls!)
Were of an age.° Well, Susan is with God;
20   She was too good for me. But, as I said,
On Lammas Eve at night shall she be fourteen;
That shall she, marry; I remember it well.
'Tis since the earthquake now eleven years;
And she was weaned (I never shall forget it),
25   Of all the days of the year, upon that day;
For I had then laid wormwood to my dug,°
Sitting in the sun under the dovehouse wall.
My lord and you were then at Mantua.
Nay, I do bear a brain. But, as I said,

3. What: impatient call, like
"Hey!" or "Where are you?"

9. thou's: thou shalt.

[?] 10. *The nurse and Lady Capulet are opposites in nature.
Lady Capulet sends the nurse off
and then calls her back. Some
actresses use this impulsive move
to indicate Lady Capulet's reluc-
tance to speak to her daughter
about marriage. In contrast, how
does the nurse react in this next
scene?*
13. teen: sorrow.
15. Lammastide: church feast, on
August 1.

19. Were of an age: were the
same age.

26. laid wormwood to my dug:
applied a bitter substance (wormwood) to her breast to wean the
baby.

« Tell me, daughter Juliet,
How stands your disposition to be married? »

30 When it did taste the wormwood on the nipple
    Of my dug and felt it bitter, pretty fool,
    To see it tetchy° and fall out with the dug!
    Shake, quoth the dovehouse!° 'Twas no need, I trow,
    To bid me trudge.
35 And since that time it is eleven years,
    For then she could stand high-lone;° nay, by th'
        rood,°
    She could have run and waddled all about;
    For even the day before, she broke her brow;
    And then my husband (God be with his soul!
40 'A was a merry man) took up the child.
    "Yea," quoth he, "dost thou fall upon thy face?
    Thou wilt fall backward when thou hast more wit;°

32. tetchy: angry.

33. Shake, quoth the dovehouse:
The dovehouse shook (from the
earthquake).

36. high-lone: alone. **by th' rood:**
by the cross (a mild oath).

42. wit: understanding.

Wilt thou not, Jule?" and, by my holidam,°
The pretty wretch left crying and said, "Ay."

45 To see now how a jest shall come about!
I warrant, and I should live a thousand years,
I never should forget it. "Wilt thou not, Jule?" quoth
    he,
And, pretty fool, it stinted° and said, "Ay."

Lady Capulet.
Enough of this. I pray thee hold thy peace.

Nurse.
50 Yes, madam. Yet I cannot choose but laugh
To think it should leave crying and say, "Ay."
And yet, I warrant, it had upon its brow
A bump as big as a young cock'rel's stone;
A perilous knock; and it cried bitterly.

55 "Yea," quoth my husband, "fall'st upon thy face?
Thou wilt fall backward when thou comest to age,
Wilt thou not, Jule?" It stinted and said, "Ay."

Juliet.
And stint thou too, I pray thee, nurse, say I.

Nurse.
Peace, I have done. God mark thee to his grace!
60 Thou wast the prettiest babe that e'er I nursed.
And I might live to see thee married once,
I have my wish.

Lady Capulet.
Marry, that "marry" is the very theme
I came to talk of. Tell me, daughter Juliet,
65 How stands your disposition to be married?

Juliet.
It is an honor that I dream not of.

Nurse.
An honor? Were not I thine only nurse,
I would say thou hadst sucked wisdom from thy teat.

Lady Capulet.
Well, think of marriage now. Younger than you,
70 Here in Verona, ladies of esteem,
Are made already mothers. By my count,
I was your mother much upon these years
That you are now a maid. Thus then in brief:
The valiant Paris seeks you for his love.

Nurse.
75 A man, young lady! Lady, such a man
As all the world.—Why, he's a man of wax.°

Lady Capulet.
Verona's summer hath not such a flower.

Nurse.
Nay, he's a flower, in faith—a very flower.

43. by my holidam: by my holy
relic (object associated with a
saint).

48. stinted: stopped.
? **48.** *The nurse must make a
strong impression with this
speech, which leaves her helpless
with laughter. The nurse directs
her chatter to Lady Capulet, but
Juliet is listening too. How would
Juliet react to her fond nurse's
memories, which cannot be stifled?*

? **62.** *This short line suggests
another dramatic pause.
Often, a director will have Juliet
rush to the nurse and kiss her. Her
fondness for and gaiety with the
nurse must contrast with her
reserve toward her mother. How
should Juliet react when she
speaks in line 66?*

76. man of wax: man like a wax
statue, with a perfect figure.

Lady Capulet.

80

What say you? Can you love the gentleman?
This night you shall behold him at our feast.
Read o'er the volume of young Paris' face,
And find delight writ there with beauty's pen;
Examine every married lineament,°
And see how one another lends content;°

85

And what obscured in this fair volume lies
Find written in the margent of his eyes.
This precious book of love, this unbound lover,
To beautify him only lacks a cover.
The fish lives in the sea, and 'tis much pride

90

For fair without the fair within to hide.°
That book in many's eyes doth share the glory,
That in gold clasps locks in the golden story;
So shall you share all that he doth possess,
By having him, making yourself no less.

Nurse.

95

No less? Nay, bigger! Women grow by men.

Lady Capulet.

Speak briefly, can you like of Paris' love?

Juliet.

I'll look to like, if looking liking move;
But no more deep will I endart mine eye
Than your consent gives strength to make it fly.

[Enter SERVINGMAN *]*

100

Servingman. Madam, the guests are come, supper served up, you called, my young lady asked for, the nurse cursed in the pantry, and everything in extremity. I must hence to wait. I beseech you follow straight.

[Exit.]

Lady Capulet.

105

We follow thee. Juliet, the county stays.°

Nurse.

Go, girl, seek happy nights to happy days.

[Exeunt.]

———

❝ Go, girl, seek happy nights to happy days. ❞

———

---

79. *Notice that Juliet isn't answering. How do you suppose she is feeling during the conversation between the nurse and her mother about this man they want her to marry?*

83. married lineament: harmonious feature.

84. how one another lends content: how one feature makes another look good.

90. For fair without the fair within to hide: for those who are handsome outwardly to also be handsome inwardly.

94. *Lady Capulet has made an elegant appeal to Juliet, to persuade her to consider marrying Paris. Which images in this speech compare Paris to a fine book?*

99. *Juliet says she'll look at Paris to see if she likes him (if liking is brought about by looking). How does she show that she is a dutiful daughter?*

100. *Another comical servant enters, speaking breathlessly, but our attention still must be on Juliet. In some productions, we now hear the sounds of music coming offstage, and Juliet exits excitedly, with little dancing motions. Do we really know much about Juliet yet?*

105. the county stays: the count waits.

106. *We meet Juliet for the first time in this scene. What is your first impression of her?*

Scene 4. *A street.*

Enter ROMEO, MERCUTIO, BENVOLIO, *with five or six other*
 MASKERS; TORCHBEARERS.

Romeo.
    What, shall this speech be spoke for our excuse?°
    Or shall we on without apology?

Benvolio.
    The date is out of such prolixity.°
    We'll have no Cupid hoodwinked° with a scarf,
5   Bearing a Tartar's painted bow of lath,
    Scaring the ladies like a crowkeeper;°
    Nor no without-book prologue,° faintly spoke
    After the prompter, for our entrance;
    But, let them measure° us by what they will,
10   We'll measure them a measure° and be gone.

Romeo.
    Give me a torch. I am not for this ambling.
    Being but heavy, I will bear the light.

Mercutio.
    Nay, gentle Romeo, we must have you dance.

Romeo.
    Not I, believe me. You have dancing shoes
15   With nimble soles; I have a soul of lead
    So stakes me to the ground I cannot move.

Mercutio.
    You are a lover. Borrow Cupid's wings
    And soar with them above a common bound.

Romeo.
    I am too sore enpiercèd with his shaft
20   To soar with his light feathers; and so bound
    I cannot bound a pitch° above dull woe.
    Under love's heavy burden do I sink.

Mercutio.
    And, to sink in it, should you burden love—
    Too great oppression for a tender thing.

Romeo.
25   Is love a tender thing? It is too rough,
    Too rude, too boist'rous, and it pricks like thorn.

Mercutio.
    If love be rough with you, be rough with love;
    Prick love for pricking, and you beat love down.
    Give me a case to put my visage in.
30   A visor° for a visor! What care I

? *Stage direction: It's night.
The stage is lit with torches
and filled with grotesquely masked
young men. The mood is one of
excitement—but we are watching
Romeo. What does he say in the
next speeches to indicate that he is
still heavy-hearted?*
  **1. shall this speech be spoke
for our excuse?:** Shall we introduce ourselves with the usual
speeches? (Uninvited maskers were
usually announced by a messenger.)
  **3. The date is out of such
prolixity:** Such long-winded
speeches are out of fashion now.
  4. hoodwinked: blindfolded.
  6. crowkeeper: scarecrow.
  7. without-book prologue:
memorized speech.
  9. measure: examine.
10. measure them a measure:
dance one dance.

? *13. Mercutio is a key character. Here he comes out of the
crowd and speaks to Romeo. They
engage in a verbal duel about love.
In the following dialogue, how do
Mercutio and Romeo differ in their
attitudes toward love?*

21. bound a pitch: fly as high as a
falcon.

? *23. In what ways does
Mercutio show that he is a
good friend to Romeo? Would you
want to be Mercutio's friend?*

? *29. Mercutio pauses and
asks for a mask. What activity would he be engaged in here?*
30. visor: mask.

What curious eye doth quote deformities?°
Here are the beetle brows shall blush° for me.
Benvolio.
Come, knock and enter; and no sooner in
But every man betake him to his legs.°
Romeo.
35   A torch for me! Let wantons light of heart
Tickle the senseless rushes° with their heels;
For I am proverbed with a grandsire phrase,°
I'll be a candleholder and look on;
The game was ne'er so fair, and I am done.°

31.   quote deformities: see imper-
fections (in the way he looks).
**32.   Here are the beetle brows
shall blush:** The mask's heavy
eyebrows will blush for him.
34.   betake him to his legs: begin
dancing.

36.   rushes: The dance floor is
covered with rushes.
37.   grandsire phrase: old man's
saying.
39.   The game . . . I am done: The
game (dancing) was never very
good, and I'm exhausted.

? **39.** *Despite Mercutio's teasing and Benvolio's urging,
what is Romeo determined to do
at the dance?*

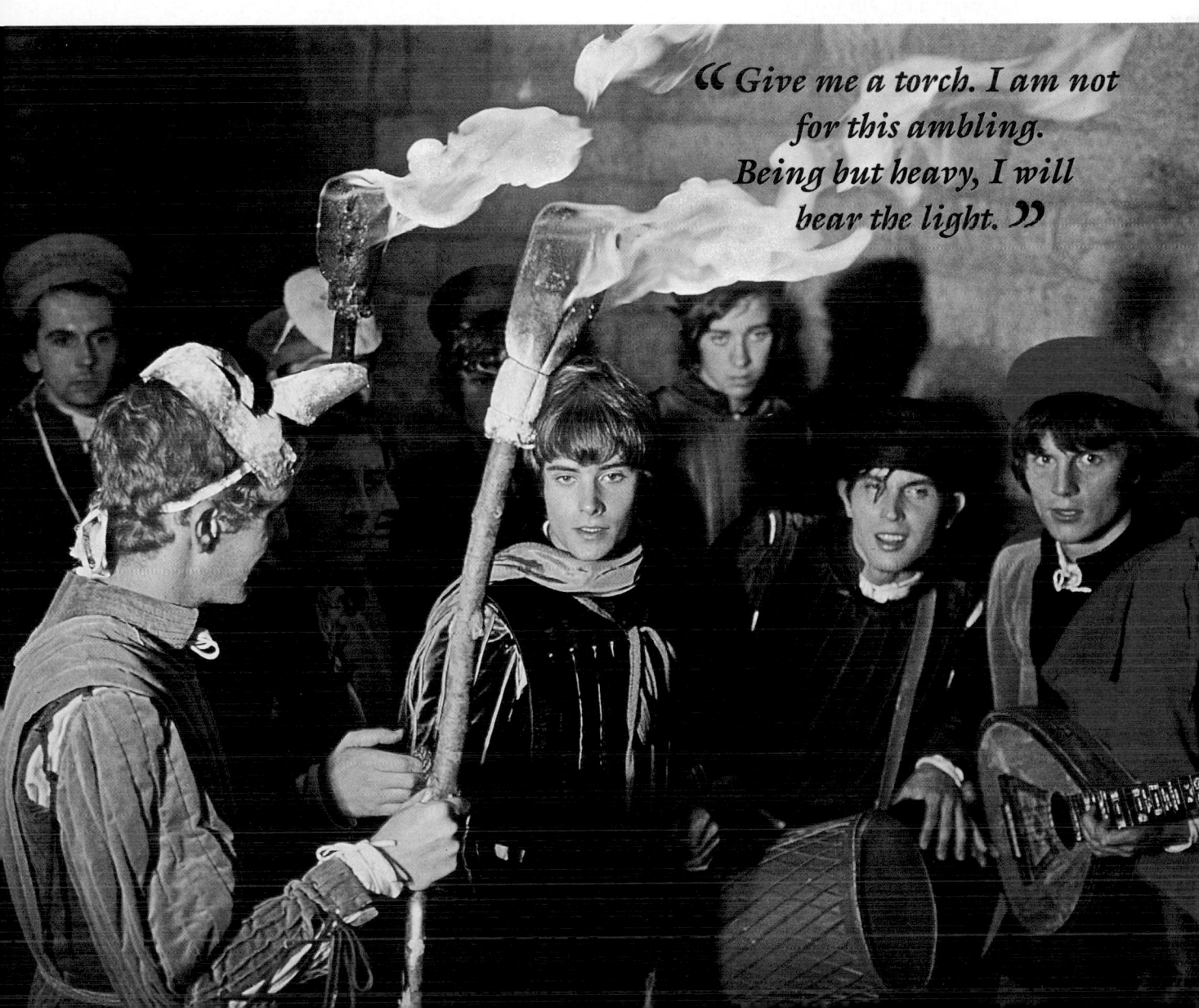

*« Give me a torch. I am not
for this ambling.
Being but heavy, I will
bear the light. »*

Mercutio.

40   Tut! Dun's the mouse, the constable's own word!
      If thou art Dun,° we'll draw thee from the mire
      Of this sir-reverence love,° wherein thou stickest
      Upon to the ears. Come, we burn daylight, ho!

Romeo.

      Nay, that's not so.

Mercutio.   I mean, sir, in delay

45   We waste our lights° in vain, like lights by day.
      Take our good meaning, for our judgment sits
      Five times in that° ere once in our five wits.

Romeo.

      And we mean well in going to this masque,
      But 'tis no wit° to go.

Mercutio.   Why, may one ask?

Romeo.

      I dreamt a dream tonight.

50 **Mercutio.**   And so did I.

Romeo.

      Well, what was yours?

Mercutio.   That dreamers often lie.

Romeo.

      In bed asleep, while they do dream things true.

Mercutio.

      O, then I see Queen Mab hath been with you.
      She is the fairies' midwife, and she comes
55   In shape no bigger than an agate stone
      On the forefinger of an alderman,
      Drawn with a team of little atomies°
      Over men's noses as they lie asleep;
      Her wagon spokes made of long spinners'° legs,
60   The cover, of the wings of grasshoppers;
      Her traces,° of the smallest spider web;
      Her collars, of the moonshine's wat'ry beams;
      Her whip, of cricket's bone; the lash, of film;°
      Her wagoner, a small gray-coated gnat,
65   Not half so big as a round little worm
      Pricked from the lazy finger of a maid;°
      Her chariot is an empty hazelnut,
      Made by the joiner squirrel or old grub,
      Time out o' mind the fairies' coachmakers.
70   And in this state she gallops night by night
      Through lovers' brains, and then they dream of love;
      On courtiers' knees, that dream on curtsies straight;
      O'er lawyers' fingers, who straight dream on fees;
      O'er ladies' lips, who straight on kisses dream,
75   Which oft the angry Mab with blisters plagues,
      Because their breaths with sweetmeats tainted are.

41. Dun: pun on Romeo's "done"; Dun was the common name used for a horse in an old game called "Dun is in the mire."

42. sir-reverence love: "Save your reverence" is an apologetic expression. Mercutio means, "We'll save you from—pardon me for saying so—love."

45. lights: torches.

47. in that: in our good meaning.

49. no wit: not a good idea.

? 50. *Romeo's mood seems to have changed abruptly, and he has a sense of approaching doom. How would he speak this line about a dream? Would Mercutio's reply be kindly or sharp?*

? 53. *Mercutio is a ringleader and a born entertainer. As he tells this story about Queen Mab, everyone stops and listens in fascinated silence. For the moment, Romeo is in the background. How is Mercutio, in this famous speech, trying to get Romeo's mind off serious thoughts about dreams and their significance? What gestures will he use to embellish his speech? According to Mercutio, what does Queen Mab have to do with Romeo? Be sure to read the speech aloud. (You might want to draw pictures of Mab.)*

57. atomies: tiny creatures.

59. spinners': spiders'.

61. traces: reins and harnesses for a wagon.

63. film: filament, or thread.

66. lazy finger of a maid: Lazy maids were said to have worms breeding in their fingers.

Sometime she gallops o'er a courtier's nose,
And then dreams he of smelling out a suit;°
And sometime comes she with a tithe pig's° tail
80 Tickling a parson's nose as 'a lies asleep,
Then dreams he of another benefice.°
Sometime she driveth o'er a soldier's neck,
And then dreams he of cutting foreign throats,
Of breaches, ambuscadoes, Spanish blades,
85 Of healths° five fathom deep; and then anon
Drums in his ear, at which he starts and wakes,
And being thus frighted, swears a prayer or two
And sleeps again. This is that very Mab
That plaits the manes of horses in the night
90 And bakes the elflocks° in foul sluttish hairs,
Which once untangled much misfortune bodes.
This is the hag,° when maids lie on their backs,
That presses them and learns them first to bear,
Making them women of good carriage.°
This is she——
95 **Romeo.**   Peace, peace, Mercutio, peace!
Thou talk'st of nothing.
Mercutio.   True, I talk of dreams;
Which are the children of an idle brain,
Begot of nothing but vain fantasy;
Which is as thin of substance as the air,
100 And more inconstant than the wind, who woos
Even now the frozen bosom of the North
And, being angered, puffs away from thence,
Turning his side to the dewdropping South.
Benvolio.
This wind you talk of blows us from ourselves.
105 Supper is done, and we shall come too late.
Romeo.
I fear, too early; for my mind misgives
Some consequence yet hanging in the stars
Shall bitterly begin his fearful date
With this night's revels and expire the term
110 Of a despisèd life, closed in my breast,
By some vile forfeit of untimely death.
But he that hath the steerage of my course
Direct my sail! On, lusty gentlemen!
Benvolio. Strike, drum.

[*They march about the stage, and retire to one side.*]

78. suit: person who might want to buy his influence at court.
79. tithe pig's: A tithe is a tenth of one's income given to the church. Farmers often gave the parson one pig as a tithe.
81. benefice: church office that enabled a minister to make a living.

85. healths: toasts to his health.

90. elflocks: locks of hair that were tangled by mischievous elves.

92. hag: nightmare. Nightmares were thought to be spirits who molested women at night.
94. women of good carriage: women who can bear children well.

? **94.** *Mercutio's tone changes here. How are these last details getting into subjects that are more shocking and cynical? Romeo doesn't like this turn of events and cuts Mercutio off.*

? **103.** *Mercutio could be comparing Romeo to the frozen North. If he is, what warning does he give his friend about remaining cold too long?*

? **106.** *Romeo again expresses feelings that something terrible will happen. Does he give any reasons for his fears? Which words in this speech suggest that he is going to the party because he is in the hands of fate?*

Scene 5. *A hall in Capulet's house.*

SERVINGMEN *come forth with napkins.*

First Servingman. Where's Potpan, that he helps not
to take away? He shift a trencher!° He scrape a
trencher!

Second Servingman. When good manners shall lie all in
5   one or two men's hands, and they unwashed too, 'tis a
foul thing.

First Servingman. Away with the join-stools,° remove
the court cupboard, look to the plate. Good thou, save
me a piece of marchpane,° and as thou loves me, let
10   the porter let in Susan Grindstone and Nell, Anthony,
and Potpan!

Second Servingman. Ay, boy, ready.

First Servingman. You are looked for and called for,
asked for and sought for, in the great chamber.

15 **Third Servingman.** We cannot be here and there
too. Cheerly, boys! Be brisk awhile, and the longer liver
take all.

                            [*Exeunt.*]

[*Enter* CAPULET, LADY CAPULET, JULIET, TYBALT, NURSE, *and all
the* GUESTS *and* GENTLEWOMEN, *meeting the* MASKERS.]

Capulet.
    Welcome, gentlemen! Ladies that have their toes
    Unplagued with corns will walk a bout° with you.
20   Ah, my mistresses, which of you all
    Will now deny to dance? She that makes dainty,°
    She I'll swear hath corns. Am I come near ye now?
    Welcome, gentlemen! I have seen the day
    That I have worn a visor and could tell
25   A whispering tale in a fair lady's ear,
    Such as would please. 'Tis gone, 'tis gone, 'tis gone.
    You are welcome, gentlemen! Come, musicians, play.

[*Music plays, and they dance.*]

    A hall,° a hall! Give room! And foot it, girls.
    More light, you knaves, and turn the tables up,
30   And quench the fire; the room is grown too hot.
    Ah, sirrah, this unlooked-for sport° comes well.
    Nay, sit; nay, sit, good cousin Capulet;
    For you and I are past our dancing days.
    How long is't now since last yourself and I
    Were in a mask?

? Stage direction: *As you read
these servants' speeches, note
that one speaks in short emphatic
sentences and bosses everyone else
around. Which one is this? What
mood do you think is suggested in
this short scene?*
2. trencher: wooden plate.

7. join-stools: wooden stools
made by a carpenter (a joiner).
9. marchpane: marzipan.

19. bout: dance.

21. makes dainty: pretends to
be shy.

? Stage direction: *The dance,
slow and stately, takes place
at center stage. Old Capulet and
his relative reminisce at one side,
but our attention is focused on
Romeo (in a mask) and Juliet,
who is dancing with someone else.
How does the following conversation contrast the two old men
with Romeo and Juliet?*
28. A hall: clear the floor (for
dancing).
31. unlooked-for sport: He
hadn't expected to find some of
the dancers masked.

Second Capulet. By'r Lady, thirty years.
Capulet.
    What, man? 'Tis not so much, 'tis not so much;
    'Tis since the nuptial of Lucentio,
    Come Pentecost as quickly as it will,
    Some five-and-twenty years, and then we masked.
Second Capulet.
    'Tis more, 'tis more. His son is elder, sir;
    His son is thirty.
Capulet.   Will you tell me that?
    His son was but a ward° two years ago.
Romeo (*to a* SERVINGMAN).
    What lady's that which doth enrich the hand
    Of yonder knight?
Servingman. I know not, sir.
Romeo.
    O, she doth teach the torches to burn bright!
    It seems she hangs upon the cheek of night
    As a rich jewel in an Ethiop's ear—
    Beauty too rich for use, for earth too dear!
    So shows a snowy dove trooping with crows
    As yonder lady o'er her fellows shows.
    The measure° done, I'll watch her place of stand
    And, touching hers, make blessèd my rude° hand.
    Did my heart love till now? Forswear it, sight!
    For I ne'er saw true beauty till this night.
Tybalt.
    This, by his voice, should be a Montague.
    Fetch me my rapier, boy. What! Dares the slave
    Come hither, covered with an antic face,°
    To fleer° and scorn at our solemnity?
    Now, by the stock and honor of my kin,
    To strike him dead I hold it not a sin.
Capulet.
    Why, how now, kinsman? Wherefore storm you so?
Tybalt.
    Uncle, this is a Montague, our foe,
    A villain, that is hither come in spite
    To scorn at our solemnity this night.
Capulet.
    Young Romeo is it?
Tybalt.   'Tis he, that villain Romeo.
Capulet.
    Content thee, gentle coz, let him alone.
    'A bears him like a portly° gentleman,
    And, to say truth, Verona brags of him
    To be a virtuous and well-governed youth.
    I would not for the wealth of all this town

35
40
45
50
55
60
65
70

42. ward: minor.

? 43. *In some productions, Romeo puts his torch down here, to draw our attention to his urgent question. Where would Juliet be on stage at this point?*

52. measure: dance.
53. rude: rough or simple.

? 55. *What has happened to Romeo?*

? 56. *Why would we feel a sense of fear when we see Tybalt stepping onto center stage again?*
58. antic face: grotesque mask.
59. fleer: jeer.

68. portly: well-mannered.

Here in my house do him disparagement.
Therefore be patient; take no note of him.
It is my will, the which if thou respect,
75   Show a fair presence and put off these frowns,
An ill-beseeming semblance for a feast.

Tybalt.
It fits when such a villain is a guest.
I'll not endure him.

Capulet.   He shall be endured.
What, goodman boy!° I say he shall. Go to!°
80   Am I the master here, or you? Go to!
You'll not endure him, God shall mend my soul!
You'll make a mutiny among my guests!
You will set cock-a-hoop.° You'll be the man!

Tybalt.
Why, uncle, 'tis a shame.

Capulet.   Go to, go to!
85   You are a saucy boy. Is't so, indeed?
This trick may chance to scathe° you. I know what.
You must contrary me! Marry, 'tis time—
Well said, my hearts!—You are a princox°—go!
Be quiet, or—More light, more light!—For shame!
90   I'll make you quiet. What!—Cheerly, my hearts!

Tybalt.
Patience perforce° with willful choler meeting
Makes my flesh tremble in their different greeting.
I will withdraw; but this intrusion shall,
Now seeming sweet, convert to bitt'rest gall.

                                                        [*Exit.*]

Romeo.
95   If I profane with my unworthiest hand
        This holy shrine, the gentle sin is this:°
My lips, two blushing pilgrims, ready stand
        To smooth that rough touch with a tender kiss.

Juliet.
Good pilgrim, you do wrong your hand too much,
100   Which mannerly devotion shows in this;
For saints have hands that pilgrims' hands do touch,
        And palm to palm is holy palmers'° kiss.

Romeo.
Have not saints lips, and holy palmers too?

Juliet.
Ay, pilgrim, lips that they must use in prayer.

Romeo.
105   O, then, dear saint, let lips do what hands do!
They pray; grant thou, lest faith turn to despair.

Juliet.
Saints do not move,° though grant for prayers' sake.

78. *What is Capulet's sensible reply to Tybalt's hostility? What feelings is Capulet revealing in his next speeches? Have Capulet's feelings about the Montagues changed since Scene 1?*

79. goodman boy: a scornful phrase. *Goodman* is below the rank of gentleman; *boy* is insulting. **Go to!:** similar to "Go on!" or "Cut it out!"

83. set cock-a-hoop: start trouble.

86. scathe: hurt.

88. princox: rude youngster.

91. patience perforce: enforced patience.

94. *Paraphrase lines 56–94, putting the exchange between Capulet and Tybalt in modern-day language.*

95. *In contrast to the raging Tybalt is Romeo, now on center stage with Juliet. Romeo takes Juliet's hand, and in their next 14 lines, the two young speakers' words form a sonnet. Romeo pretends to be a pilgrim going to a saint's shrine. Exactly where do the two young lovers use religious images to talk of their feelings for each other?*

96. the gentle sin is this: this is the sin of a gentleman.

98. *Romeo and Juliet bring the palms of their hands together here. What in their words suggests that this is what they are doing?*

102. palmers': pilgrims going to a holy place. They often carried palm leaves to show they had been to the Holy Land.

107. do not move: do not make the first move.

> *For saints have hands*
> *that pilgrims' hands do touch,*
> *And palm to palm is holy*
> *palmers' kiss.*

Romeo.
  Then move not while my prayer's effect I take.
  Thus from my lips, by thine my sin is purged.

[*Kisses her.*]

Juliet.
110 Then have my lips the sin that they have took.
Romeo.
  Sin from my lips? O trespass sweetly urged!
  Give me my sin again. [*Kisses her.*]
Juliet.   You kiss by th' book.°
Nurse.
  Madam, your mother craves a word with you.
Romeo.
  What is her mother?
Nurse.   Marry, bachelor,
115 Her mother is the lady of the house,
  And a good lady, and a wise and virtuous.
  I nursed her daughter that you talked withal.°
  I tell you, he that can lay hold of her
  Shall have the chinks.°

? 109. *In the midst of the swirling dancers, Romeo and Juliet kiss. All of the audience's attention must be on this kiss. What do you fear as you watch, remembering that Tybalt is nearby?*

112. You kiss by th' book: You take my words literally (to get more kisses).

? 113. *As the nurse interrupts, the dance ends. Juliet runs off, and Romeo is left alone with the nurse. What do we know about the Capulets' plans for Juliet that Romeo does not know?*

117. withal: with.

119. chinks: money.

« *Thus from my lips, by thine my sin is purged.* »

Romeo. Is she a Capulet?

120   O dear account! My life is my foe's debt.°

Benvolio.

Away, be gone; the sport is at the best.

Romeo.

Ay, so I fear; the more is my unrest.

Capulet.

Nay, gentlemen, prepare not to be gone;
We have a trifling foolish banquet towards.°

125   Is it e'en so? Why then, I thank you all.
I thank you, honest gentlemen. Good night.
More torches here! Come on then; let's to bed.
Ah, sirrah, by my fay,° it waxes late;
I'll to my rest.

                    [*Exeunt all but* JULIET *and* NURSE.]

Juliet.

130   Come hither, nurse. What is yond gentleman?

Nurse.

The son and heir of old Tiberio.

Juliet.

What's he that now is going out of door?

Nurse.

Marry, that, I think, be young Petruchio.

Juliet.

What's he that follows there, that would not dance?

Nurse.

135   I know not.

Juliet.

Go ask his name.—If he be married,
My grave is like to be my wedding bed.

Nurse.

His name is Romeo, and a Montague,
The only son of your great enemy.

Juliet.

140   My only love, sprung from my only hate!
Too early seen unknown, and known too late!
Prodigious° birth of love it is to me
That I must love a loathèd enemy.

Nurse.

What's this? What's this?

Juliet.   A rhyme I learnt even now
Of one I danced withal.

[*One calls within,* "Juliet."]

145   **Nurse.**   Anon, anon!°
Come, let's away; the strangers all are gone.

                                        [*Exeunt.*]

---

120. My life is my foe's debt:
My foe now owns my life.

122. *Romeo stands alone here, horrified. What activity goes on around him?*

124. towards: in preparation.

128. fay: faith.

130. *Juliet has moved to the side of the stage. What feelings must she convey in this question? (She is not pointing to Romeo.)*

142. prodigious: huge and monstrous.

145. *What tone of voice would Juliet use here? What has she just realized?*

145. anon: at once.

MAKING MEANINGS   ACT I

First Thoughts

1. Did you find the "love at first sight" scene convincing? Why, or why not?

Shaping Interpretations

2. Scene 1 is a brilliant example of how information can be conveyed through theatrical activity. Look at these three segments of the scene: Gregory-Sampson and the Montague servants; Benvolio-Tybalt; and the prince's warning. To examine the scene, use a chart like the one following. List each episode on the left. On the right, explain how the episode clarifies the forces at work in the play (some of them deadly).

Episode	What It Shows

3. Before Romeo and Juliet meet in Scene 4, Shakespeare must set up obstacles to their love, so that when they do meet, we will groan at the problems they are going to face. What problem or **complication** is presented in Scenes 2 and 3?

4. Scene 4 does not seem to advance the story, but it does introduce us to Mercutio, who will play an important part in the play later. How would you **characterize** Mercutio, based on what he has said and done so far? Is he a believable character? Have you known people like him?

5. Mercutio is used as a **foil** to Romeo. The word *foil* in drama means "a character or scene that is set up as a contrast to another so that each will stand out vividly." In what specific ways is Mercutio a foil to Romeo?

6. Scene 4 sets up a sense of **foreboding**—a feeling that something bad is about to happen. Identify Romeo's specific expressions of foreboding, as he sets off for the party.

7. By the end of Act I, a lot of **suspense** has been generated. If you were watching this play, what questions would you be asking at this point?

Extending the Text

8. The action of this play takes place in Italy in the fourteenth century. Which episodes in Act I could you imagine taking place today? What details would have to change, if any?

CHOICES: Building Your Portfolio

Writer's Notebook

1. Collecting Ideas for an Informative Report

Finding a topic. You'll be writing an informative report in the Writer's Workshop on page 870. The play itself can give you some possible topics.

Shakespeare set his play in Verona, Italy, in the fourteenth century, but the play really reflects the attitudes and customs of Elizabethan England, at the time when Shakespeare lived. The early productions of the play (like the modern production illustrated on these pages) used costumes worn in England in Shakespeare's time. From looking at the photographs here, you can get an idea of how the Elizabethans dressed. From reading about Capulet's party, you can get an idea of Renaissance parties. Study all the photos and make a list of questions you have about the period costumes. Or, if you prefer, re-read Scene 4 and make a list of things you would like to know about the music, dancing, and party masks of the time. Keep your notes and add to them as you continue the play.

Creative Writing

2. Society Column

Imagine that you are a columnist for the local Verona newspaper. Write a column in which you cover the party at the Capulets' house, noting the guests and their outfits. Include any "hot" gossip from the party that you think would interest your readers.

Critical Thinking/ Creative Writing

3. Keeping a Journal

Choose a character and begin a diary for him or her that you will keep throughout the action of the play. Make journal entries for the key moments of the play, plus any others that you wish to include. Since it is a private diary, your character will be able to speak honestly and openly, even if he or she does not speak that way in public.

VOCABULARY   MINI-LESSON

Shakespeare's Words and Their Relatives

As you see by the word list on page 733, many words in Shakespeare's plays have different meanings today. The word *humor,* for example, comes from a Latin word for "moisture" or "fluid." In Shakespeare's time, people believed there were four fluids, or humors, in the body. These regulated a person's temperament. The four fluids were blood, phlegm (flem), yellow bile, and black bile. The word *humorous* eventually came to refer to the kind of temperament that is able to see comedy in situations.

Choose five words from the list on page 733 and make a diagram showing what each word meant in Shakespeare's day and what it generally means today. *Humor* is done as a sample. Use a dictionary if you need help.

| humor | → | **SHAKESPEARE'S MEANING** "fluid, moisture" |

↓

TODAY'S MEANING "ability to see the funny side of things"

ACT II

Enter CHORUS.

Chorus.
    Now old desire doth in his deathbed lie,
        And young affection gapes to be his heir;
    That fair° for which love groaned for and would die,
        With tender Juliet matched, is now not fair.
5   Now Romeo is beloved and loves again,
        Alike° bewitchèd by the charm of looks;
    But to his foe supposed he must complain,°
        And she steal love's sweet bait from fearful hooks.
    Being held a foe, he may not have access
10   To breathe such vows as lovers use to swear,°
    And she as much in love, her means much less
        To meet her new belovèd anywhere;
    But passion lends them power, time means, to meet,
    Temp'ring extremities° with extreme sweet.° [*Exit.*]

3. That fair: Rosaline.

6. Alike: both (both Romeo and Juliet).
7. complain: ask Juliet's father, his foe, for her hand in marriage.

10. use to swear: are used to promising.

14. extremities: difficulties. **extreme sweet:** very sweet delights.
? **14.** *According to the chorus, what has happened to Romeo's old love? What is his new problem? What line suggests what the love of these young people is based on?*

Scene 1. *Near Capulet's orchard.*

Enter ROMEO *alone.*

Romeo.
    Can I go forward when my heart is here?
    Turn back, dull earth, and find thy center° out.

[*Enter* BENVOLIO *with* MERCUTIO. ROMEO *retires.*]

Benvolio.
    Romeo! My cousin Romeo! Romeo!
Mercutio.   He is wise
    And, on my life, hath stol'n him home to bed.
Benvolio.
5   He ran this way and leapt this orchard wall.
    Call, good Mercutio.
Mercutio.   Nay, I'll conjure too.
    Romeo! Humors! Madman! Passion! Lover!

2. center: Juliet. The "dull earth" is Romeo, and Juliet is his soul.
? *Stage direction: Though the stage direction says that Romeo "retires," Shakespeare did not mean for him to retire quietly, for a few lines later Benvolio says he was running. Romeo has often been played by actors in middle age, and leaping over the wall has been a problem for them. Many older Romeos have in fact chosen to "retire" behind the wall. How might this wall be arranged on stage so that we continue to see Romeo hiding in Capulet's orchard and Benvolio and Mercutio in the lane?*

Appear thou in the likeness of a sigh;
Speak but one rhyme, and I am satisfied!
Cry but "Ay me!" pronounce but "love" and
10   "dove";
Speak to my gossip° Venus one fair word,
One nickname for her purblind° son and heir,
Young Abraham Cupid,° he that shot so true
When King Cophetua loved the beggar maid!°
15 He heareth not, he stirreth not, he moveth not;
The ape is dead,° and I must conjure him.
I conjure thee by Rosaline's bright eyes,
By her high forehead and her scarlet lip,
By her fine foot, straight leg, and quivering thigh,
20 And the demesnes° that there adjacent lie,
That in thy likeness thou appear to us!

Benvolio.
And if he hear thee, thou wilt anger him.

Mercutio.
This cannot anger him. 'Twould anger him
To raise a spirit in his mistress' circle°
25 Of some strange nature, letting it there stand
Till she had laid it and conjured it down.
That were some spite;° my invocation
Is fair and honest: in his mistress' name,
I conjure only but to raise up him.

Benvolio.
30 Come, he hath hid himself among these trees
To be consorted° with the humorous° night.
Blind is his love and best befits the dark.

Mercutio.
If love be blind, love cannot hit the mark.
And wish his mistress were that kind of fruit
35 As maids call medlars when they laugh alone.
O, Romeo, that she were, O that she were
An open et cetera, thou a pop'rin pear!
Romeo, good night. I'll to my truckle bed;
This field bed is too cold for me to sleep.
Come, shall we go?

40 **Benvolio.**   Go then, for 'tis in vain
To seek him here that means not to be found.

[*Exit with others.*]

---

11. gossip: good friend. Venus is the goddess of love.
12. purblind: blind.
13. Young Abraham Cupid: To Mercutio, Romeo seems the very figure of love—old like Abraham in the Bible and young like Cupid.
14. When . . . maid: from a popular ballad.
16. The ape is dead: Romeo is "playing" dead.

20. demesnes: domains; regions.

? **22.** *What is Benvolio's tone here? Why would Romeo be angry at Mercutio's remarks?*

24. circle: magical place.

27. spite: cause to be angry.

31. consorted: familiar. **humorous:** damp.

**❝ *Blind is his love and*
best befits the dark. ❞**

Scene 2. *Capulet's orchard.*

Romeo (*coming forward*).
He jests at scars that never felt a wound.

[*Enter* JULIET *at a window.*]

But soft! What light through yonder window breaks?
It is the East, and Juliet is the sun!
Arise, fair sun, and kill the envious moon,
5   Who is already sick and pale with grief
That thou her maid° art far more fair than she.
Be not her maid, since she is envious.
Her vestal livery° is but sick and green,°
And none but fools do wear it. Cast it off.
10 It is my lady! O, it is my love!
O, that she knew she were!
She speaks, yet she says nothing. What of that?
Her eye discourses;° I will answer it.
I am too bold; 'tis not to me she speaks.
15 Two of the fairest stars in all the heaven,
Having some business, do entreat her eyes
To twinkle in their spheres till they return.
What if her eyes were there, they in her head?
The brightness of her cheek would shame those stars
20 As daylight doth a lamp; her eyes in heaven
Would through the airy region stream so bright
That birds would sing and think it were not night.
See how she leans her cheek upon her hand!
O, that I were a glove upon that hand,
That I might touch that cheek!
Juliet.   Ay me!
25 **Romeo.**   She speaks.
O, speak again, bright angel, for thou art
As glorious to this night, being o'er my head,
As is a wingèd messenger of heaven
Unto the white-upturnèd wond'ring eyes
30 Of mortals that fall back to gaze on him
When he bestrides the lazy puffing clouds
And sails upon the bosom of the air.
Juliet.
O Romeo, Romeo! Wherefore art thou Romeo?°
Deny thy father and refuse thy name;
35 Or, if thou wilt not, be but sworn my love,
And I'll no longer be a Capulet.

? 1. *This begins the balcony scene, one of the most famous scenes in all dramatic literature. In 190 magical lines, the two lovers woo and win each other. (In the wide-open Elizabethan theater, the balcony scene presented no staging problems. In modern theaters, however, it is often difficult to have a balcony high enough and yet still visible to people sitting in the back of the theater.) Romeo has heard all the joking. Whom is he referring to here, and what kind of "wound" is he talking about?*

6. thou her maid: Juliet, whom Romeo sees as the servant of the virgin goddess of the moon, Diana.

8. vestal livery: maidenly clothing. **sick and green:** Unmarried girls supposedly had "greensickness," or anemia.

13. discourses: speaks.

? 25. *Romeo and Juliet rarely talk of each other in straightforward prose. What are some of the metaphors and images that Romeo uses to express his love here?*

33. In other words, "Why is your name Romeo?" (It is the name of her enemy.)

« O Romeo, Romeo! Wherefore art thou Romeo? »

Romeo (*aside*).
　　Shall I hear more, or shall I speak at this?
Juliet.
　　'Tis but thy name that is my enemy.
　　Thou art thyself, though not° a Montague.
40　What's Montague? It is nor hand, nor foot,
　　Nor arm, nor face. O, be some other name
　　Belonging to a man.
　　What's in a name? That which we call a rose
　　By any other word would smell as sweet.
45　So Romeo would, were he not Romeo called,
　　Retain that dear perfection which he owes°
　　Without that title. Romeo, doff thy name;
　　And for thy name, which is no part of thee,
　　Take all myself.

> **❝ What's in a name? That which we**
> **call a rose**
> **By any other word would smell**
> **as sweet. ❞**

Romeo.　　　　I take thee at thy word.
50　Call me but love, and I'll be new baptized;
　　Henceforth I never will be Romeo.
Juliet.
　　What man art thou, that, thus bescreened in night,
　　So stumblest on my counsel?°
Romeo.　　　　　　By a name
　　I know not how to tell thee who I am.
55　My name, dear saint, is hateful to myself
　　Because it is an enemy to thee.
　　Had I it written, I would tear the word.
Juliet.
　　My ears have yet not drunk a hundred words
　　Of thy tongue's uttering, yet I know the sound.
60　Art thou not Romeo, and a Montague?
Romeo.
　　Neither, fair maid, if either thee dislike.
Juliet.
　　How camest thou hither, tell me, and wherefore?
　　The orchard walls are high and hard to climb,
　　And the place death, considering who thou art,
65　If any of my kinsmen find thee here.

37. *Juliet does not know Romeo is standing beneath her balcony. What has Romeo now learned about her feelings for him?*
39. though not: even if you were not.

42. *Short lines like this one usually indicate an interruption or pause. Here, Juliet pauses to think about a question. What does she say in answer to this question about the true significance of a "name"?*
46. owes: owns.

53. counsel: private thoughts.
53. *How do you know Romeo has finally spoken aloud to Juliet? What are her feelings in this speech?*

Romeo.
> With love's light wings did I o'erperch° these walls;
> For stony limits cannot hold love out,
> And what love can do, that dares love attempt.
> Therefore thy kinsmen are no stop to me.

Juliet.
70
> If they do see thee, they will murder thee.

Romeo.
> Alack, there lies more peril in thine eye
> Than twenty of their swords! Look thou but sweet,
> And I am proof° against their enmity.

Juliet.
> I would not for the world they saw thee here.

Romeo.
75
> I have night's cloak to hide me from their eyes;
> And but° thou love me, let them find me here.
> My life were better ended by their hate
> Than death prorogued,° wanting of thy love.

Juliet.
> By whose direction found'st thou out this place?

Romeo.
80
> By Love, that first did prompt me to inquire.
> He lent me counsel, and I lent him eyes.
> I am no pilot; yet, wert thou as far
> As that vast shore washed with the farthest sea,
> I should adventure for such merchandise.

Juliet.
85
> Thou knowest the mask of night is on my face;
> Else would a maiden blush bepaint my cheek
> For that which thou hast heard me speak tonight.
> Fain would I dwell on form—fain, fain deny
> What I have spoke; but farewell compliment.°
90
> Dost thou love me? I know thou wilt say "Ay";
> And I will take thy word. Yet, if thou swear'st,
> Thou mayst prove false. At lovers' perjuries,
> They say Jove laughs. O gentle Romeo,
> If thou dost love, pronounce it faithfully.
95
> Or if thou think'st I am too quickly won,
> I'll frown and be perverse and say thee nay,
> So thou wilt woo; but else, not for the world.
> In truth, fair Montague, I am too fond,°
> And therefore thou mayst think my havior° light;
100
> But trust me, gentleman, I'll prove more true
> Than those that have more cunning to be strange.°
> I should have been more strange, I must confess,
> But that thou overheard'st, ere I was ware,
> My truelove passion. Therefore pardon me,
105
> And not impute this yielding to light love,

66. o'erperch: fly over.

73. proof: armored.

[?] **74.** *Juliet is practical. She fears Romeo will be murdered. What is Romeo's tone— is he also fearful and cautious, or is he reckless and elated?*
76. but: if only.

78. prorogued: postponed.
[?] **78.** *The two lovers will repeatedly remind us that they prefer death to separation. What does this speech tell us of Romeo's intentions? Do you think he is seriously thinking of death here, or is he being impulsive and exaggerating—as many people are when they've fallen head over heels in love?*

[?] **85.** *Juliet's thoughts race now, and she probably speaks rapidly here. Read this speech aloud. Where does she shift from embarrassment to frankness, to pleading, to anxiety, to doubt? Why is she worried that Romeo will think poorly of her?*
89. compliment: good manners.

98. fond: affectionate, tender.
99. havior: behavior.

101. strange: aloof or cold.

« *O, swear not by the moon, the inconstant moon,*
That monthly changes in her circle orb,
Lest that thy love prove likewise variable. **»**

Which the dark night hath so discoverèd.° 106. **discoverèd:** revealed.

Romeo.
    Lady, by yonder blessèd moon I vow,
    That tips with silver all these fruit-tree tops——

Juliet.
    O, swear not by the moon, the inconstant moon,
110   That monthly changes in her circle orb,
    Lest that thy love prove likewise variable.

? 109. *Why is Juliet afraid of having Romeo swear by the moon? If you were speaking these lines, would you make them comic, or would you make Juliet sound genuinely frightened?*

Romeo.
    What shall I swear by?

Juliet.   Do not swear at all;
    Or if thou wilt, swear by thy gracious self,
    Which is the god of my idolatry,
    And I'll believe thee.

115 **Romeo.**   If my heart's dear love——

Juliet.
    Well, do not swear. Although I joy in thee,
    I have no joy of this contract tonight.
    It is too rash, too unadvised, too sudden;
    Too like the lightning, which doth cease to be
120   Ere one can say it lightens. Sweet, good night!
    This bud of love, by summer's ripening breath,
    May prove a beauteous flower when next we meet.
    Good night, good night! As sweet repose and rest
    Come to thy heart as that within my breast!

? 120. *Romeo is quick with vows and promises. Why has Juliet become fearful and cautious?*

Romeo.
125   O, wilt thou leave me so unsatisfied?

Juliet.
    What satisfaction canst thou have tonight?

Romeo.
    The exchange of thy love's faithful vow for mine.

Juliet.
    I gave thee mine before thou didst request it;
    And yet I would it were to give again.

Romeo.
130   Wouldst thou withdraw it? For what purpose, love?

Juliet.
    But to be frank° and give it thee again.
    And yet I wish but for the thing I have.
    My bounty° is as boundless as the sea,
    My love as deep; the more I give to thee,
135   The more I have, for both are infinite.
    I hear some noise within. Dear love, adieu!

131. **frank:** generous.

133. **bounty:** capacity for giving.

[NURSE *calls within.*]

    Anon, good nurse! Sweet Montague, be true.
    Stay but a little, I will come again.   [*Exit.*]

Romeo.
    O blessèd, blessèd night! I am afeard,
140   Being in night, all this is but a dream,
    Too flattering-sweet to be substantial.

[*Enter* JULIET *again.*]

Juliet.
    Three words, dear Romeo, and good night indeed.
    If that thy bent° of love be honorable,
    Thy purpose marriage, send me word tomorrow,
145   By one that I'll procure to come to thee,
    Where and what time thou wilt perform the rite;
    And all my fortunes at thy foot I'll lay
    And follow thee my lord throughout the world.
Nurse (*within*). Madam!
Juliet.
150   I come anon.—But if thou meanest not well,
    I do beseech thee——
Nurse (*within*). Madam!
Juliet.   By and by I come.—
    To cease thy strife° and leave me to my grief.
    Tomorrow will I send.
Romeo.   So thrive my soul——
Juliet.
155   A thousand times good night!   [*Exit.*]
Romeo.
    A thousand times the worse, to want thy light!
    Love goes toward love as schoolboys from their books;
    But love from love, toward school with heavy looks.

[*Enter* JULIET *again.*]

Juliet.
    Hist! Romeo, hist! O for a falc'ner's voice
160   To lure this tassel gentle° back again!
    Bondage is hoarse° and may not speak aloud,
    Else would I tear the cave where Echo° lies
    And make her airy tongue more hoarse than mine
    With repetition of "My Romeo!"
Romeo.
165   It is my soul that calls upon my name.
    How silver-sweet sound lovers' tongues by night,
    Like softest music to attending ears!
Juliet.
    Romeo!
Romeo.
        My sweet?

143. bent: intention.

148. *What is Juliet making clear to Romeo here? Where does she show that she still fears he may be false with her?*

153. strife: efforts to win her.

154. *With this fervent vow, Romeo swears by his immortal soul. What lines that follow indicate that Romeo turns around and heads away from her balcony?*

160. tassel gentle: male falcon.
161. Bondage is hoarse: Juliet is in "bondage" to her parents and must whisper.
162. Echo: mythical girl who could only repeat others' final words.

Juliet.   What o'clock tomorrow
Shall I send to thee?

Romeo.   By the hour of nine.

Juliet.
170   I will not fail. 'Tis twenty years till then.
       I have forgot why I did call thee back.

Romeo.
       Let me stand here till thou remember it.

Juliet.
       I shall forget, to have thee still stand there,
       Rememb'ring how I love thy company.

Romeo.
175   And I'll still stay, to have thee still forget,
       Forgetting any other home but this.

Juliet.
       'Tis almost morning. I would have thee gone—
       And yet no farther than a wanton's° bird,
       That lets it hop a little from his hand,
180   Like a poor prisoner in his twisted gyves,°
       And with a silken thread plucks it back again,
       So loving-jealous of his liberty.

Romeo.
       I would I were thy bird.

Juliet.   Sweet, so would I.
       Yet I should kill thee with much cherishing.
185   Good night, good night! Parting is such sweet sorrow
       That I shall say good night till it be morrow.   [*Exit.*]

Romeo.
       Sleep dwell upon thine eyes, peace in thy breast!
       Would I were sleep and peace, so sweet to rest!
       Hence will I to my ghostly friar's° close cell,
190   His help to crave and my dear hap° to tell.   [*Exit.*]

---

178. wanton's: careless child's.

180. gyves: chains, like the threads that hold the bird captive.

? **184.** *What terrible future event does this line foreshadow?*

? **185.** *Why is parting "sweet" to Juliet? (Is she enjoying this prolonged farewell?)*

189. ghostly friar's: spiritual father's.
190. hap: luck.

**❝ Parting is such sweet sorrow
That I shall say good night till it be morrow. ❞**

Scene 3. *Friar Laurence's cell.*

Enter FRIAR LAURENCE *alone, with a basket.*

Friar.

    The gray-eyed morn smiles on the frowning night,
    Check'ring the eastern clouds with streaks of light;
    And fleckèd darkness like a drunkard reels
    From forth day's path and Titan's burning wheels.°
5   Now, ere the sun advance his burning eye
    The day to cheer and night's dank dew to dry,
    I must upfill this osier cage° of ours
    With baleful° weeds and precious-juicèd flowers.
    The earth that's Nature's mother is her tomb.
10 What is her burying grave, that is her womb;
    And from her womb children of divers kind
    We sucking on her natural bosom find,
    Many for many virtues excellent,
    None but for some, and yet all different.
15 O, mickle° is the powerful grace that lies
    In plants, herbs, stones, and their true qualities;
    For naught so vile that on the earth doth live
    But to the earth some special good doth give;
    Nor aught so good but, strained° from that fair use,
20 Revolts from true birth,° stumbling on abuse.
    Virtue itself turns vice, being misapplied,
    And vice sometime by action dignified.

    [*Enter* ROMEO.]

    Within the infant rind° of this weak flower
    Poison hath residence and medicine° power;
25 For this, being smelt, with that part cheers each part;°
    Being tasted, stays all senses with the heart.
    Two such opposèd kings encamp them still°
    In man as well as herbs—grace and rude will;
    And where the worser is predominant,
30 Full soon the canker° death eats up that plant.

Romeo.

    Good morrow, father.

Friar.   Benedicite!°

    What early tongue so sweet saluteth me?
    Young son, it argues a distemperèd head°
    So soon to bid good morrow to thy bed.
35 Care keeps his watch in every old man's eye,
    And where care lodges, sleep will never lie;
    But where unbruisèd° youth with unstuffed° brain
    Doth couch his limbs, there golden sleep doth reign.

1. *In the absence of lighting, Shakespeare had his characters "set the stage" in their speeches. What "scene" does the friar set? How are his images of night different from Romeo's images in his "O blessèd, blessèd night" speech in the last scene?*

4. Titan's burning wheels: wheels of the sun god's chariot.

7. osier cage: cage woven of willow branches.

8. baleful: evil or poisonous.

15. mickle: great.

19. strained: turned aside.

20. true birth: true purpose.

22. *What details in the friar's speech casually suggest that these herbs and flowers have qualities that can heal or kill? Where does the friar remind us that good can turn to evil, and evil turn to good?*

23. rind: outer covering.

23. *Romeo enters quietly, unseen by the friar. As the friar talks of the flower he has picked, why might the audience become uneasy about what might happen to Romeo and Juliet?*

24. medicine: medicinal.

25. For . . . part: When the flower is smelled, each part of the body is stimulated.

27. still: always.

30. canker: cankerworm, a larva that feeds on leaves.

31. Benedicite!: Latin for "Bless you!"

33. distemperèd head: troubled mind.

37. unbruisèd: innocent.
unstuffed: untroubled.

40　Therefore thy earliness doth me assure
　　Thou art uproused with some distemp'rature;
　　Or if not so, then here I hit it right—
　　Our Romeo hath not been in bed tonight.

Romeo.
　　That last is true. The sweeter rest was mine.

Friar.
　　God pardon sin! Wast thou with Rosaline?

Romeo.
45　With Rosaline, my ghostly father? No.
　　I have forgot that name and that name's woe.

Friar.
　　That's my good son! But where hast thou been then?

Romeo.
　　I'll tell thee ere thou ask it me again.
　　I have been feasting with mine enemy,
50　Where on a sudden one hath wounded me
　　That's by me wounded. Both our remedies
　　Within thy help and holy physic° lies.
　　I bear no hatred, blessèd man, for, lo,
　　My intercession° likewise steads° my foe.

Friar.
55　Be plain, good son, and homely° in thy drift.
　　Riddling confession finds but riddling shrift.°

Romeo.
　　Then plainly know my heart's dear love is set
　　On the fair daughter of rich Capulet;
　　As mine on hers, so hers is set on mine,
60　And all combined,° save what thou must combine
　　By holy marriage. When and where and how
　　We met, we wooed, and made exchange of vow,
　　I'll tell thee as we pass; but this I pray,
　　That thou consent to marry us today.

Friar.
65　Holy Saint Francis! What a change is here!
　　Is Rosaline, that thou didst love so dear,
　　So soon forsaken? Young men's love then lies
　　Not truly in their hearts, but in their eyes.
　　Jesu Maria! What a deal of brine
70　Hath washed thy sallow cheeks for Rosaline!
　　How much salt water thrown away in waste
　　To season° love, that of it doth not taste!
　　The sun not yet thy signs from heaven clears,
　　Thy old groans ring yet in mine ancient ears.
75　Lo, here upon thy cheek the stain doth sit
　　Of an old tear that is not washed off yet.
　　If e'er thou wast thyself, and these woes thine,
　　Thou and these woes were all for Rosaline.

44. *Does the friar approve? If you were playing the friar, how would you speak to Romeo?*

52. holy physic: the friar's healing power (physic) to make Romeo and Juliet husband and wife.
54. intercession: request. **steads:** helps.
55. homely: simple and straight-forward.
56. shrift: forgiveness (in the religious rite of confession).

56. *As we have seen, the play is basically written in blank verse, but Shakespeare varies his verse forms from time to time. The Prologues are written in sonnet form. The endings of scenes are marked by rhymed couplets. What is the rhyme scheme of this dialogue?*
60. combined: agreed.

65. *In the early part of the play, Shakespeare keeps Romeo's intense love in some kind of perspective by letting us see how others regard him. We have heard Mercutio's sarcastic "The ape is dead." How does Friar Laurence continue with this scolding and ridicule? What actions do you imagine Romeo is engaged in as he listens to the priest?*
72. season: preserve; keep fresh (food was seasoned with salt to keep it from spoiling).

And art thou changed? Pronounce this sentence then:
80   Women may fall when there's no strength in men.
Romeo.
    Thou chid'st me oft for loving Rosaline.
Friar.
    For doting, not for loving, pupil mine.
Romeo.
    And bad'st me bury love.
Friar.   Not in a grave
    To lay one in, another out to have.
Romeo.
85   I pray thee chide me not. Her I love now
    Doth grace° for grace and love for love allow.
    The other did not so.
Friar.   O she knew well
    Thy love did read by rote, that could not spell.°
    But come, young waverer, come go with me.
90   In one respect I'll thy assistant be;
    For this alliance may so happy prove
    To turn your households' rancor to pure love.
Romeo.
    O, let us hence! I stand on° sudden haste.
Friar.
    Wisely and slow. They stumble that run fast.   [*Exeunt.*]

86. grace: favor.
88. Romeo recited words of love without understanding them.
? **92.** *In these times, it was not at all unusual to form alliances and settle disputes by arranging marriages. How does this explain Friar Laurence's decision to help the young couple?*
93. I stand on: I am firm about.
? **94.** *Romeo has gotten what he wants and he dashes offstage. But how do the friar's last words leave us with a sense that danger lies ahead?*

« *For this alliance may so happy prove*
To turn your households' rancor to pure love. »

Scene 4. *A street.*

Enter BENVOLIO *and* MERCUTIO.

Mercutio.
Where the devil should this Romeo be?
Came he not home tonight?
Benvolio.
Not to his father's. I spoke with his man.
Mercutio.
Why, that same pale hardhearted wench, that
   Rosaline,
5   Torments him so that he will sure run mad.
Benvolio.
Tybalt, the kinsman to old Capulet,
Hath sent a letter to his father's house.
Mercutio. A challenge, on my life.
Benvolio. Romeo will answer it.
10   **Mercutio.** Any man that can write may answer a letter.
Benvolio. Nay, he will answer the letter's master, how he
   dares, being dared.
Mercutio. Alas, poor Romeo, he is already dead: stabbed
   with a white wench's black eye; run through the ear
15   with a love song; the very pin° of his heart cleft with
   the blind bow-boy's butt-shaft; and is he a man to
   encounter Tybalt?

"Alas, poor Romeo, he is already dead . . . run through the ear with a love song. . . . "

Benvolio. Why, what is Tybalt?
Mercutio. More than Prince of Cats.° O, he's the coura-
20   geous captain of compliments. He fights as you sing
   pricksong°—keeps time, distance, and proportion; he
   rests his minim rests,° one, two and the third in
   your bosom! The very butcher of a silk button, a
   duelist, a duelist! A gentleman of the very first
25   house,° of the first and second cause.° Ah, the immor-

7. *Now that the play's love story seems to be heading toward a marriage, Shakespeare turns again to the feuding families. Why is Tybalt looking for Romeo?*

15. pin: center (of a target).

19. Prince of Cats: "Tybalt" is the name of a cat in a fable who is known for his slyness.
21. sing pricksong: sing with attention to every note on a printed sheet of music.
22. minim rests: shortest pauses in a bar of music.
25. first house: first rank. **first and second cause:** dueling terms ("first," offense is taken; "second," a challenge is given).

tal passado!° The punto reverso!° The hay!°

Benvolio. The what?

Mercutio. The pox of° such antic, lisping, affecting
fantasticoes°—these new tuners of accent! "By Jesu,
a very good blade! A very tall° man! A very good
whore!" Why, is not this a lamentable thing, grand
sir, that we should be thus afflicted with these
strange flies, these fashionmongers, these pardon-
me's, who stand so much on the new form° that they
cannot sit at ease on the old bench? O, their
bones,° their bones!

30

35

[*Enter* ROMEO.]

Benvolio. Here comes Romeo! Here comes Romeo!

Mercutio. Without his roe,° like a dried herring. O
flesh, flesh, how art thou fishified! Now is he for the
numbers° that Petrarch flowed in. Laura, to his lady,
was a kitchen wench (marry, she had a better love
to berhyme her), Dido° a dowdy, Cleopatra a gypsy,
Helen and Hero hildings° and harlots, Thisbe
a grey eye° or so, but not to the purpose. Signior
Romeo, bonjour! There's a French salutation to your
French slop.° You gave us the counterfeit° fairly
last night.

40

45

Romeo. Good morrow to you both. What counterfeit did
I give you?

Mercutio. The slip, sir, the slip. Can you not conceive?°

50

Romeo. Pardon, good Mercutio. My business was great,
and in such a case as mine a man may strain courtesy.

Mercutio. That's as much as to say, such a case° as yours
constrains a man to bow in the hams.

55

Romeo. Meaning, to curtsy.

Mercutio. Thou hast most kindly hit it.

Romeo. A most courteous exposition.

Mercutio. Nay, I am the very pink of courtesy.

Romeo. Pink for flower.

60

Mercutio. Right.

Romeo. Why, then is my pump° well-flowered.°

Mercutio. Sure wit, follow me this jest now till thou hast
worn out thy pump, that, when the single sole of it is
worn, the jest may remain, after the wearing, solely
singular.

65

Romeo. O single-soled jest, solely singular for the singleness!°

Mercutio. Come between us, good Benvolio! My wits
faint.

70

---

26. **passado:** lunge. **punto
reverso:** backhand stroke. **hay:**
home thrust.

? 26. *Mercutio mocks Tybalt's
dueling style, but what do we
also now know about Tybalt's
ability to fight? What do you
picture Mercutio doing as he talks
of duels? Is he also concerned for
Romeo? How do his actions
change in the next speech as he
mocks people who always want to
wear the latest fashions?*

28. **pox of:** plague on (curse on).

29. **fantasticoes:** dandies; men
who copy French manners and
fashions.

30. **tall:** brave.

34. **new form:** new fashions.

36. **bones:** pun on their use of the
French *bon* ("good").

38. **roe:** pun on *roe,* female deer.
Roe also means "fish eggs," so
Mercutio is also suggesting that love
has made Romeo "gutless."

40. **numbers:** verses. Petrarch was
an Italian poet who wrote verses to
a woman named Laura.

42. **Dido:** queen of Carthage in
the *Aeneid,* who loved Aeneas.
(The women who follow also were
famous lovers in literature: Cleopa-
tra was the queen of Egypt loved by
Antony; Helen of Troy was loved by
Paris; Hero was loved by Leander;
Thisbe was loved by Pyramus.)

43. **hildings:** good-for-nothings.

44. **gray eye:** gleam in the eye.

46. **slop:** loose trousers then
popular in France. **counterfeit:**
slip.

51. **conceive:** understand.

54. **case:** set of clothes.

? 55. *Romeo is being lured by
Mercutio to match wits. How
can you tell that Romeo soon gets
into the spirit of the game and for
the moment forgets his romantic
problems? In the following verbal
duel, the two friends use puns.*

62. **pump:** shoe. **well-flowered:**
pun on "well-floored." Men's shoes
were "pinked," or cut, with decorations.

68. **singleness:** pun on "silliness."

? 70. *What exaggerated action
is Mercutio doing here?*

Romeo. Swits° and spurs, swits and spurs; or I'll cry a match.

Mercutio. Nay, if our wits run the wild-goose chase, I am done; for thou hast more of the wild goose in one of thy wits than, I am sure, I have in my whole five. Was I with you there for the goose?°

Romeo. Thou wast never with me for anything when thou wast not there for the goose.°

Mercutio. I will bite thee by the ear for that jest.

Romeo. Nay, good goose, bite not!

Mercutio. Thy wit is a very bitter sweeting;° it is a most sharp sauce.

Romeo. And is it not, then, well served in to a sweet goose?°

Mercutio. O, here's a wit of cheveril,° that stretches from an inch narrow to an ell broad!°

Romeo. I stretch it out for that word "broad," which, added to the goose, proves thee far and wide a broad° goose.

Mercutio. Why, is not this better now than groaning for love? Now art thou sociable, now art thou Romeo; now art thou what thou art, by art as well as by nature. For this driveling love is like a great natural° that runs lolling up and down to hide his bauble° in a hole.

Benvolio. Stop there, stop there!

Mercutio. Thou desirest me to stop in my tale against the hair.°

Benvolio. Thou wouldst else have made thy tale large.°

Mercutio. O, thou art deceived! I would have made it short; for I was come to the whole depth of my tale, and meant indeed to occupy the argument no longer.

Romeo. Here's goodly gear!°

[*Enter* NURSE *and her man* PETER.]

A sail, a sail!

Mercutio. Two, two! A shirt and a smock.°

Nurse. Peter!

Peter. Anon.

Nurse. My fan, Peter.

Mercutio. Good Peter, to hide her face; for her fan's the fairer face.

Nurse. God ye good morrow, gentlemen.

Mercutio. God ye good-den,° fair gentlewoman.

Nurse. Is it good-den?

Mercutio. 'Tis no less, I tell ye; for the bawdy hand of the dial is now upon the prick of noon.

Nurse. Out upon you! What a man are you!

---

71. **Swits:** switches (a pun on "wits").

76. **Was . . . goose?:** Was I right in calling you a goose?

78. **goose:** here, a woman.

81. **bitter sweeting:** kind of apple.

84. **sweet goose:** sour sauce was considered best for sweet meat.
85. **cheveril:** kid-leather (another reference to fashion).
86. **ell broad:** 45 inches across.

89. **broad:** indecent.

94. **natural:** idiot. **bauble:** literally, trinket or cheap jewel.
? 95. *What does the loyal Mercutio think he has accomplished for Romeo by this game of wits?*
98. **against the hair:** against my inclination.
99. **large:** indecent.

103. **gear:** matter for play and teasing.
? 104. *Having established the fact that Tybalt is looking for Romeo, we now return to the love story, with this comic scene involving the nurse and Peter and the young men. The previous scene might well have seemed to drag if we had not in a sense been promised a confrontation between Romeo and Tybalt. Now the young men laugh openly at the nurse as she and her servant "sail" on stage. What does Romeo's comment suggest about her size?*
105. **A shirt and a smock:** a man (shirt) and a woman (smock).
112. **God ye good-den:** God grant you a good evening.

Romeo. One, gentlewoman, that God hath made, himself to mar.

Nurse. By my troth, it is well said. "For himself to mar," quoth 'a? Gentlemen, can any of you tell me where I may find the young Romeo?

Romeo. I can tell you; but young Romeo will be older when you have found him than he was when you sought him. I am the youngest of that name, for fault of a worse.°

Nurse. You say well.

Mercutio. Yea, is the worst well? Very well took, i' faith! Wisely, wisely.

Nurse. If you be he, sir, I desire some confidence with you.

Benvolio. She will endite° him to some supper.

Mercutio. A bawd, a bawd, a bawd! So ho!

Romeo. What hast thou found?

Mercutio. No hare,° sir; unless a hare, sir, in a Lenten pie,° that is something stale and hoar° ere it be spent.

[*He walks by them and sings.*]

> An old hare hoar,
> And an old hare hoar,
> Is very good meat in Lent;
> But a hare that is hoar
> Is too much for a score
> When it hoars ere it be spent.

Romeo, will you come to your father's? We'll to dinner thither.

Romeo. I will follow you.

Mercutio. Farewell, ancient lady. Farewell (*singing*) "Lady, lady, lady." [*Exeunt* MERCUTIO, BENVOLIO.]

Nurse. I pray you, sir, what saucy merchant was this that was so full of his ropery?°

Romeo. A gentleman, nurse, that loves to hear himself talk and will speak more in a minute than he will stand to in a month.

Nurse. And 'a speak anything against me, I'll take him down, and 'a were lustier than he is, and twenty such Jacks; and if I cannot, I'll find those that shall. Scurvy knave! I am none of his flirt-gills;° I am none of his skainsmates.° And thou must stand by too, and suffer every knave to use me at his pleasure!

Peter. I saw no man use you at his pleasure. If I had, my weapon should quickly have been out, I warrant you. I dare draw as soon as another man, if I see occasion in a

---

125. for fault of a worse: for want of a better.

131. endite: invite. Benvolio mocks the nurse, for she said "confidence" but meant "conference."

132. *Mercutio, who knows nothing of Romeo's plan to marry Juliet, thinks the nurse has come to arrange a secret date between Romeo and her mistress. He mocks and insults the nurse by suggesting that she is a bawd, or "procurer," for Juliet. Mercutio dominates the stage when he's on it. What do you imagine he's doing here?*

134. hare: slang for "morally loose woman."

135. Lenten pie: rabbit pie, eaten sparingly during Lent, so that it is around for a long time and gets stale. **hoar:** gray with mold (the old nurse has gray hair).

142. *Mercutio teases the nurse about being a flirt by singing the chorus from an old song about a "chaste" lady. The nurse is outraged and struggles to keep her fine airs. How does Romeo try to calm her?*

149. ropery: The nurse means "roguery," or vulgar ways.

156. flirt-gills: flirty girls.

157. skainsmates: loose women.

159. *Whom is the nurse talking to here?*

good quarrel, and the law on my side.

Nurse. Now, afore God, I am so vexed that every part
about me quivers. Scurvy knave! Pray you, sir, a word;
and, as I told you, my young lady bid me inquire you
out. What she bid me say, I will keep to myself; but first
let me tell ye, if ye should lead her in a fool's paradise,
as they say, it were a very gross kind of behavior, as
they say; for the gentlewoman is young; and therefore,
if you should deal double with her, truly it were an ill
thing to be offered to any gentlewoman, and very weak
dealing.

Romeo. Nurse, commend me to thy lady and mistress. I
protest unto thee——

Nurse. Good heart, and i' faith I will tell her as much.
Lord, Lord, she will be a joyful woman.

Romeo. What wilt thou tell her, nurse? Thou dost not
mark° me.

Nurse. I will tell her, sir, that you do protest, which, as I
take it, is a gentlemanlike offer.

Romeo.
Bid her devise
Some means to come to shrift this afternoon;
And there she shall at Friar Laurence' cell
Be shrived° and married. Here is for thy pains.

Nurse. No, truly, sir; not a penny.

Romeo. Go to! I say you shall.

Nurse. This afternoon, sir? Well, she shall be there.

Romeo.
And stay, good nurse, behind the abbey wall.
Within this hour my man shall be with thee
And bring thee cords made like a tackled stair,°
Which to the high topgallant° of my joy
Must be my convoy° in the secret night.
Farewell. Be trusty, and I'll quit° thy pains.
Farewell. Commend me to thy mistress.

Nurse.
Now God in heaven bless thee! Hark you, sir.

Romeo.
What say'st thou, my dear nurse?

Nurse.
Is your man secret? Did you ne'er hear say,
Two may keep counsel, putting one away?

Romeo.
Warrant thee my man's as true as steel.

Nurse. Well, sir, my mistress is the sweetest lady.
Lord, Lord! When 'twas a little prating thing—O,
there is a nobleman in town, one Paris, that would
fain lay knife aboard;° but she, good soul, had as

165

170

175

180

185

190

195

200

165. *Which part of this speech is delivered to Mercutio? When does the nurse turn to Romeo? How might her manner change?*

173. *What warning does the nurse give Romeo, and why do you think she does this?*

179. mark: listen to.

185. shrived: forgiven of her sins.

191. tackled stair: rope ladder.
192. topgallant: highest platform on a sailing ship's mast.
193. convoy: means of conveyance.
194. quit: repay.

204. lay knife aboard: take a slice (lay claim to Juliet).

205 lieve see a toad, a very toad, as see him. I anger her
sometimes, and tell her that Paris is the pro-
perer man; but I'll warrant you, when I say so, she
looks as pale as any clout° in the versal° world. Doth
not rosemary and Romeo begin both with a
210 letter?

Romeo. Aye, nurse; what of that? Both with an R.

Nurse. Ah, mocker! That's the dog's name.° R is for
the—no; I know it begins with some other letter;
and she hath the prettiest sententious° of it, of
215 you and rosemary, that it would do you good to
hear it.

Romeo. Commend me to thy lady.

Nurse. Ay, a thousand times. [*Exit* ROMEO.] Peter!

Peter. Anon.

220 **Nurse.** Before, and apace.   [*Exit after* PETER.]

Scene 5. *Capulet's orchard.*

Enter JULIET.

Juliet.
The clock struck nine when I did send the nurse;
In half an hour she promised to return.
Perchance she cannot meet him. That's not so.
O, she is lame! Love's heralds should be thoughts,
5 Which ten times faster glide than the sun's beams
Driving back shadows over low'ring hills.
Therefore do nimble-pinioned doves° draw Love,
And therefore hath the wind-swift Cupid wings.
Now is the sun upon the highmost hill
10 Of this day's journey, and from nine till twelve
Is three long hours; yet she is not come.
Had she affections and warm youthful blood,
She would be as swift in motion as a ball;

My words would bandy her° to my sweet love,
15   And his to me.
       But old folks, many feign as they were dead—
       Unwieldy, slow, heavy, and pale as lead.

[*Enter* NURSE *and* PETER.]

       O God, she comes! O honey nurse, what news?
       Hast thou met with him? Send thy man away.

Nurse.
20   Peter, stay at the gate.   [*Exit* PETER.]

Juliet.
       Now, good sweet nurse—O Lord, why look'st thou sad?
       Though news be sad, yet tell them merrily;
       If good, thou sham'st the music of sweet news
       By playing it to me with so sour a face.

Nurse.
25   I am aweary, give me leave awhile.
       Fie, how my bones ache! What a jaunce° have I!

Juliet.
       I would thou hadst my bones, and I thy news.
       Nay, come, I pray thee speak. Good, good nurse, speak.

Nurse.
       Jesu, what haste! Can you not stay° awhile?
30   Do you not see that I am out of breath?

Juliet.
       How art thou out of breath when thou hast breath
       To say to me that thou art out of breath?
       The excuse that thou dost make in this delay
       Is longer than the tale thou dost excuse.
35   Is thy news good or bad? Answer to that.
       Say either, and I'll stay the circumstance.°
       Let me be satisfied, is't good or bad?

Nurse. Well, you have made a simple° choice; you know
       not how to choose a man. Romeo? No, not he. Though
40   his face be better than any man's, yet his leg excels all
       men's; and for a hand and a foot, and a body, though
       they be not to be talked on, yet they are past compare.
       He is not the flower of courtesy, but, I'll warrant him,
       as gentle as a lamb. Go thy ways, wench; serve God.
45   What, have you dined at home?

Juliet.
       No, no. But all this did I know before.
       What says he of our marriage? What of that?

Nurse.
       Lord, how my head aches! What a head have I!
       It beats as it would fall in twenty pieces.
50   My back a'° t' other side—ah, my back, my back!

14. bandy her: send her back and forth, like a tennis ball.

17. *Juliet either has run on stage or is standing on the balcony. What is her mood as she waits for the nurse's return?*

26. jaunce: tiring journey.

29. stay: wait.

30. *The actress playing the nurse can interpret her actions here in several ways. She could be genuinely weary; she could be teasing Juliet; or she could be fearful about the part she has agreed to play in the elopement. How do you think the nurse should play this scene?*

36. stay the circumstance: wait for the details.

38. simple: foolish.

38. *In comedy, a character sometimes has one peculiarity that always can be counted on for a laugh. You push a button and you get the same response. Such a character is sometimes called a jack-in-the-box. What is the nurse's almost inevitable way of responding when she is asked for information?*

50. a': on.

Beshrew° your heart for sending me about
To catch my death with jauncing up and down!

Juliet.

I' faith, I am sorry that thou art not well.
Sweet, sweet, sweet nurse, tell me, what says my love?

55 **Nurse.** Your love says, like an honest gentleman, and a
courteous, and a kind, and a handsome, and, I warrant,
a virtuous—where is your mother?

Juliet.

Where is my mother? Why, she is within.
Where should she be? How oddly thou repliest!

60 "Your love says, like an honest gentleman,
'Where is your mother?'"

Nurse.   O God's Lady dear!
Are you so hot?° Marry come up, I trow.°
Is this the poultice for my aching bones?
Henceforward do your messages yourself.

Juliet.

65 Here's such a coil!° Come, what says Romeo?

Nurse.

Have you got leave to go to shrift today?

Juliet.

I have.

Nurse.

Then hie you hence to Friar Laurence' cell;
There stays a husband to make you a wife.

70 Now comes the wanton blood up in your cheeks.
They'll be in scarlet straight at any news.
Hie you to church; I must another way,
To fetch a ladder, by the which your love
Must climb a bird's nest soon when it is dark.

75 I am the drudge, and toil in your delight;
But you shall bear the burden soon at night.
Go; I'll to dinner; hie you to the cell.

Juliet.

Hie to high fortune! Honest nurse, farewell. [*Exeunt.*]

---

51. Beshrew: shame on.

52. *What line here indicates that Juliet has tried to humor the nurse by rubbing her back?*

61. *Juliet can play this scene in several ways. Do you imagine she is angry here? Or is she bewildered? Impatient? Or is she mocking the old nurse?*

62. hot: angry. **Marry come up, I trow:** something like, "By the Virgin Mary, come off it, I swear."

65. coil: fuss.

69. *At last, the nurse tells Juliet what she has been waiting for. What do you see Juliet doing as she hears the news?*

78. *Even Juliet puns. What pun does she exit on? What is her mood?*

Scene 6. *Friar Laurence's cell.*

Enter FRIAR LAURENCE *and* ROMEO.

Friar.
So smile the heavens upon this holy act
That afterhours with sorrow chide us not!

Romeo.
Amen, amen! But come what sorrow can,
It cannot countervail° the exchange of joy
5   That one short minute gives me in her sight.
Do thou but close our hands with holy words,
Then love-devouring death do what he dare—
It is enough I may but call her mine.

Friar.
These violent delights have violent ends
10   And in their triumph die, like fire and powder,°
Which, as they kiss, consume. The sweetest honey
Is loathsome in his own deliciousness
And in the taste confounds° the appetite.
Therefore love moderately: long love doth so;
15   Too swift arrives as tardy as too slow.

"*These violent delights have violent ends....*"

[*Enter* JULIET.]

Here comes the lady. O, so light a foot
Will ne'er wear out the everlasting flint.°
A lover may bestride the gossamers°
That idle in the wanton summer air,
20   And yet not fall; so light is vanity.°

Juliet.
Good even to my ghostly confessor.

Friar.
Romeo shall thank thee, daughter, for us both.

Juliet.
As much to him,° else is his thanks too much.

Romeo.
Ah, Juliet, if the measure of thy joy

4. countervail: match or equal.

8. *We are continually prepared for the steps Romeo and Juliet might take if they are separated. What does Romeo say here to remind us again of how desperate their love is?*
10. powder: gunpowder.

13. confounds: destroys.

15. *What warning does the friar give about passionate love? What fear does he express for the future?*

17. flint: stone.
18. gossamers: finest spider threads.

20. vanity: fleeting human love.

23. As much to him: the same to him.

25   Be heaped like mine, and that thy skill be more
        To blazon° it, then sweeten with thy breath
        This neighbor air, and let rich music's tongue
        Unfold the imagined happiness that both
        Receive in either by this dear encounter.

Juliet.

30   Conceit,° more rich in matter than in words,
        Brags of his substance, not of ornament.°
        They are but beggars that can count their worth;
        But my true love is grown to such excess
        I cannot sum up sum of half my wealth.

Friar.

35   Come, come with me, and we will make short work;
        For, by your leaves, you shall not stay alone
        Till holy church incorporate two in one.   *[Exeunt.]*

26. blazon: describe.

? **29.** *What is Romeo asking Juliet to do?*

30. Conceit: genuine understanding.
31. ornament: fancy language.

? **34.** *What is Juliet's response to Romeo's request?*

? **37.** *What do you think the friar's tone is in this last speech? Is there a slight humorous or teasing note here?*

« For, by your leaves, you shall not stay alone Till holy church incorporate two in one. »

No Actresses and No R-Rated Love Scenes

On a visit to Venice in 1608, the English traveler Thomas Coryate recorded his astonishment: "For I saw women act, a thing I never saw before, though I have heard that it hath been sometimes used in London." Coryate was surprised because at the time, in London, boy actors between the ages of about ten and eighteen regularly took the parts of women on stage.

The roots of this custom were bound up with the origins of medieval drama. Centuries earlier, in English cathedrals, stories from the Bible were acted in brief plays. The performers—all male—came from the clergy, and they were assisted by choirboys. It wasn't until 1660 that women were permitted on the English stage—by the express order of King Charles II, whose fondness for the theater (and actresses) was to become a mark of his reign.

Boy actors were divided into two categories. There were members of all-boy companies, like the Children of St. Paul's Cathedral and the Children of the Chapel Royal. These young players enjoyed such popularity (and made so much money for their business managers) that star actors were in great demand. From the records of a 1602 legal case, we know that one schoolboy named Thomas Clifton was actually kidnapped and forced to join the Chapel Children. His father had to sue to get him back.

Other boy actors were apprentices to individual actors in the adult companies. These boys were preparing for a professional career. They took women's parts on stage for several years before and during adolescence. (It was one of these boy actors who took the part of Juliet.) When they were in their late teens, they switched to men's roles.

Some evidence suggests that Elizabethan actors trained their voices to be higher-pitched, for both speaking and singing—so the difference between boys' voices and those of adults might have been less noticeable in Shakespeare's time. In any case, for a part such as Juliet—who is not yet fourteen when she makes her first appearance—costume and makeup for a boy actor could have easily sustained the illusion. Unlike actors and actresses in movies today, the young lovers in Shakespeare's play would have avoided physical contact. The words suggested the intensity of their feelings.

Casting boys as women on the Shakespearean stage had another unexpected twist. Plays with heroines in male disguise were highly popular at the time. Shakespeare wrote five such dramas, including *The Merchant of Venice, As You Like It,* and *Twelfth Night.* In these cases, boys played women who disguised themselves as young men. The mind boggles at the layers of illusion.

Making Meanings Act II

First Thoughts

1. The "balcony scene" (Scene 2) is the most famous love scene in the history of the theater. What lines spoken by Romeo or by Juliet do you think are most important, interesting, or beautiful?

Shaping Interpretations

2. What different feelings do Romeo and Juliet express in the balcony scene? Which character speaks more cautiously about love, and why?

3. Though Act II is a happy act, Shakespeare at times reminds us of the threatening background. He does this by **foreshadowing**—giving clues to what will happen later. Point out lines that foreshadow possible trouble ahead.

4. The nurse is one of Shakespeare's great comic characters. Do you think the nurse is a principled character, a person with a strong sense of right and wrong? Or does she seem to be easily corrupted, someone who will do whatever people want her to do? Find passages to support your answer.

5. The friar agrees to marry Romeo and Juliet because he wants them to be happy, but he also has another **motive**. What is that motive?

6. When the audience knows something that a character does not know, we feel **dramatic irony**. Since we know how the play will end (the Prologue has told us), we feel this irony when we hear the friar's motives. What other moments of dramatic irony did you feel in this act?

7. So far, how do you feel about Friar Laurence's schemes? What else might he have done to help Romeo and Juliet?

Connecting with the Text

8. Does Mercutio's teasing of Romeo remind you of the way friends today tease one another? Do the groups of teenagers in this play (some of them looking for trouble) remind you in any way of the gangs that form today?

9. Romeo's and Juliet's families hate each other, for reasons that we aren't told about. (Maybe the families themselves have forgotten.) What parallels can you think of from real life—what real-life Romeos and Juliets are living in the world today?

Reviewing the Text

a. What plans do Romeo and Juliet make in Scene 2?

b. What fault does Friar Laurence find in Romeo in Scene 3?

c. We hear in Scene 4 that Tybalt is looking for Romeo. Why does he want Romeo?

d. How does Mercutio feel about Tybalt?

e. What part does the nurse play in Romeo and Juliet's schemes?

CHOICES: Building Your Portfolio

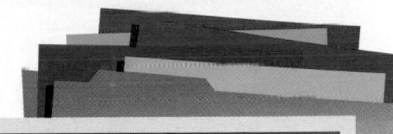

Writer's Notebook

1. Collecting Ideas for an Informative Report

Finding a topic. Using the play as your guide, brainstorm possible topics for the informative report you'll write in the Writer's Workshop on page 870. Try one of the following exercises:

- Romeo and Juliet swear their love in Act II. Free-write about their love and how it reflects Elizabethan customs of courtship and marriage. For instance, girls often married at the age of twelve or thirteen, and marriages were usually arranged by parents.

- Do some research on any of the literary lovers mentioned in the side note for Scene 4, lines 39–44.

Save your notes.

Critical Thinking

2. Cutting Shakespeare

Many directors of Shakespeare's plays cut some of the lines. Franco Zeffirelli, for example, cut about two-thirds of the text for his film version of *Romeo and Juliet*. Imagine that you have been asked to cut Act II, Scene 5, down to twenty lines. How would you do it? Form groups to cut the scene. As you decide what lines to cut and what to keep, think of the director, the actress playing Juliet, and the actress playing the nurse. The director wants to speed up the pace; Juliet and the nurse want to keep the jokes. Work together to decide what to cut, and list your decisions on a chart. In the left-hand column list the lines cut and the reasons for cutting them, and in the right-hand column note any important details you lose by that cut.

LANGUAGE LINK   MINI-LESSON

Style: The Old Problems—Grammar and Vocabulary

Many of Shakespeare's words and expressions are **archaic,** or out of use today, or their meanings have changed. Shakespeare also often omits words. For example, in the Prologue, the speaker says:

> . . . which if you with patient ears attend,
> What here shall miss, our toil shall strive to mend.

The speaker has omitted words here, and he depends on your instinct and ear to provide them. He has also used the word *attend* in a way not commonly used today. Here's how we might say the same thing:

> . . . if you listen patiently,
> We'll try to make clear by our work on stage
> What you've missed from the Prologue.

Try It Out

Rewrite each passage below in the kind of English that is spoken today. Check the side notes for help.

1. Scurvy knave! I am none of his flirt-gills; I am none of his skainsmates.

2. Is your man secret? Did you ne'er hear say, Two may keep counsel, putting one away?

3. . . . but she, good soul, had as lieve see a toad, a very toad, as see him.

ACT III

Scene 1. *A public place.*

Enter MERCUTIO, BENVOLIO, *and* MEN.

Benvolio.
I pray thee, good Mercutio, let's retire.
The day is hot, the Capels° are abroad,
And, if we meet, we shall not 'scape a brawl,
For now, these hot days, is the mad blood stirring.

5   **Mercutio.** Thou art like one of these fellows that,
when he enters the confines of a tavern, claps me
his sword upon the table and says, "God send me no
need of thee!" and by the operation of the second
cup draws him on the drawer,° when indeed there is
10   no need.

Benvolio. Am I like such a fellow?

Mercutio. Come, come, thou art as hot a Jack in thy
mood as any in Italy; and as soon moved to be moody,
and as soon moody to be moved.

15   **Benvolio.** And what to?

Mercutio. Nay, and there were two such, we should have
none shortly, for one would kill the other. Thou!
Why, thou wilt quarrel with a man that hath a hair
more or a hair less in his beard than thou hast.
20   Thou wilt quarrel with a man for cracking nuts, having no other reason but because thou hast hazel
eyes. What eye but such an eye would spy out such a
quarrel? Thy head is as full of quarrels as an egg
is full of meat; and yet thy head hath been beaten
25   as addle° as an egg for quarreling. Thou hast quar-
reled with a man for coughing in the street, because
he hath wakened thy dog that hath lain asleep in the
sun. Didst thou not fall out with a tailor for wearing his new doublet° before Easter? With another
30   for tying his new shoes with old riband? And yet
thou wilt tutor me from quarreling!

Benvolio. And I were so apt to quarrel as thou art, any
man should buy the fee simple of° my life for an hour
and a quarter.

35   **Mercutio.** The fee simple? O simple!°

[*Enter* TYBALT *and others.*]

Benvolio. By my head, here come the Capulets.
Mercutio. By my heel, I care not.

---

2. Capels: Capulets.

? 4. *Romeo's friends enter the stage. Again, Shakespeare "sets the stage" by having the characters tell us what the weather is like. Why does this weather seem to breed trouble?*

9. draws him on the drawer: draws his sword on the waiter (who "draws" the drink).

? 19. *Mercutio mocks Benvolio, who is anything but a troublemaker. (Mercutio is the one who can't seem to resist a quarrel.) If you were playing Benvolio, what would you be doing, as Mercutio goes on and on? If you were playing Mercutio, how would you behave as your comments became more and more exaggerated?*
25. addle: rotten.

29. doublet: jacket.

33. buy the fee simple of: buy insurance on.

35. O simple!: O stupid!

Tybalt.

Follow me close, for I will speak to them.

Gentlemen, good-den. A word with one of you.

Mercutio.

40   And but one word with one of us?

Couple it with something; make it a word and a blow.

Tybalt. You shall find me apt enough to that, sir, and you

will give me occasion.

Mercutio. Could you not take some occasion without

45   giving?

Tybalt. Mercutio, thou consortest with Romeo.

Mercutio. Consort?° What, dost thou make us minstrels?

And thou make minstrels of us, look to hear nothing

but discords. Here's my fiddlestick;° here's that shall

50   make you dance. Zounds,° consort!

Benvolio.

We talk here in the public haunt of men.

Either withdraw unto some private place,

Or reason coldly of your grievances,

Or else depart. Here all eyes gaze on us.

Mercutio.

55   Men's eyes were made to look, and let them gaze.

I will not budge for no man's pleasure, I.

[*Enter* ROMEO.]

Tybalt.

Well, peace be with you, sir. Here comes my man.

Mercutio.

But I'll be hanged, sir, if he wear your livery.°

Marry, go before to field,° he'll be your follower!

60   Your worship in that sense may call him man.

Tybalt.

Romeo, the love I bear thee can afford

No better term than this: thou art a villain.°

Romeo.

Tybalt, the reason that I have to love thee

Doth much excuse the appertaining° rage

65   To such a greeting. Villain am I none.

Therefore farewell. I see thou knowest me not.

Tybalt.

Boy, this shall not excuse the injuries

That thou hast done me; therefore turn and draw.

Romeo.

I do protest I never injured thee,

70   But love thee better than thou canst devise°

Till thou shalt know the reason of my love;

And so, good Capulet, which name I tender°

As dearly as mine own, be satisfied.

47. Consort: Mercutio pretends to think that Tybalt means a *consort,* or group of musicians.
49. fiddlestick: bow for playing violinlike instruments (referring to his sword).
50. Zounds: slang for "by God's wounds."

? *Stage direction: Romeo is returning from his secret marriage—he has no thought about hatred and killing. What would he be doing as he enters? How would he react to the tense situation?*
58. livery: servant's uniform. By "man," Tybalt meant "target"; but Mercutio uses the word to mean "servant."
59. field: dueling field.

62. villain: boor; clumsy, stupid fellow.

64. appertaining: appropriate.

? **68.** *What insult does Tybalt use to make Romeo want to draw his sword?*

70. devise: imagine.

72. tender: value.

? **73.** *Why does Romeo refuse to duel Tybalt?*

Mercutio.

O calm, dishonorable, vile submission!

75 Alla stoccata° carries it away.

[*Draws.*]

Tybalt, you ratcatcher, will you walk?°

Tybalt.

What wouldst thou have with me?

Mercutio. Good King of Cats, nothing but one of your nine lives. That I mean to make bold withal,° and,

80 as you shall use me hereafter, dry-beat° the rest of the eight. Will you pluck your sword out of his pilcher° by the ears? Make haste, lest mine be about your ears ere it be out.

Tybalt. I am for you.

[*Draws.*]

Romeo.

85 Gentle Mercutio, put thy rapier up.

Mercutio. Come, sir, your passado!

[*They fight.*]

Romeo.

Draw, Benvolio; beat down their weapons.
Gentlemen, for shame! Forbear this outrage!
Tybalt, Mercutio, the prince expressly hath

90 Forbid this bandying° in Verona streets.
Hold, Tybalt! Good Mercutio!

[TYBALT *under Romeo's arm thrusts* MERCUTIO *in, and flies.*]

Mercutio.   I am hurt.

A plague a' both houses! I am sped.°
Is he gone and hath nothing?

Benvolio.   What, art thou hurt?

Mercutio.

Ay, ay, a scratch, a scratch. Marry, 'tis enough.

95 Where is my page? Go, villain, fetch a surgeon.

[*Exit* PAGE.]

Romeo.

Courage, man. The hurt cannot be much.

Mercutio. No, 'tis not so deep as a well, nor so wide as a church door; but 'tis enough, 'twill serve. Ask for me tomorrow, and you shall find me a grave man.

100 I am peppered,° I warrant, for this world. A plague a' both your houses! Zounds, a dog, a rat, a mouse, a cat, to scratch a man to death! A braggart, a rogue,

75. Alla stoccata: "at the thrust," a fencing term.

76. walk: make a move.

? **77.** *Mercutio doesn't know of Romeo's marriage to Juliet (a Capulet). Why is Mercutio so outraged? What feeling should Tybalt express (fear? annoyance?) as he asks Mercutio what he wants?*

79. make bold withal: make free with (take away).

80. dry-beat: thrash.

82. pilcher: scabbard (sword holder).

? *Stage direction: The stage direction above simply says "They fight," but how would you—as director—choreograph the action? Would you have Mercutio challenge Tybalt to protect Romeo? Or would you emphasize Mercutio's dislike of Tybalt? The sword-fight can range all over the stage, but where must the three characters be placed when Tybalt stabs Mercutio?*

90. bandying: brawling.
92. sped: wounded.

100. peppered: given a deadly wound ("peppered" food is ready to eat; Mercutio is "ready" to die).

a villain, that fights by the book of arithmetic!° Why
the devil came you between us? I was hurt under your
105 arm.

Romeo.
I thought all for the best.

Mercutio.
Help me into some house, Benvolio,
Or I shall faint. A plague a' both your houses!
They have made worms' meat of me. I have it,
110 And soundly too. Your houses!

[*Exeunt* MERCUTIO *and* BENVOLIO.]

" *A plague a' both your houses!* "

Romeo.
This gentleman, the prince's near ally,°
My very friend, hath got this mortal hurt
In my behalf—my reputation stained
With Tybalt's slander—Tybalt, that an hour
115 Hath been my cousin. O sweet Juliet,
Thy beauty hath made me effeminate
And in my temper soft'ned valor's steel!

[*Enter* BENVOLIO.]

Benvolio.
O Romeo, Romeo, brave Mercutio is dead!
That gallant spirit hath aspired° the clouds,
120 Which too untimely here did scorn the earth.

Romeo.
This day's black fate on more days doth depend;°
This but begins the woe others must end.

[*Enter* TYBALT.]

Benvolio.
Here comes the furious Tybalt back again.

Romeo.
Alive in triumph, and Mercutio slain?
125 Away to heaven respective lenity,
And fire-eyed fury be my conduct now!
Now, Tybalt, take the "villain" back again
That late thou gavest me; for Mercutio's soul
Is but a little way above our heads,
130 Staying for thine to keep him company.
Either thou or I, or both, must go with him.

103. fights by the book of arithmetic: fights according to formal rules for fencing.

106. *How would Romeo say this pathetic line?*

110. *What curse has Mercutio pronounced four times? Some actors playing Mercutio make him seem bitter about his approaching death and hostile to Romeo. Other Mercutios are gallant to the end and extend a hand to Romeo in friendship. How would you play this death speech?*

111. ally: relative. Mercutio was related to Verona's Prince Escalus.

119. aspired: climbed to.

121. depend: hang over.

Stage direction: Does it seem unlikely that Tybalt would return so soon? He must return, of course, so that Romeo can avenge Mercutio. An alternative would have been to have Romeo attack Tybalt as soon as he stabbed Mercutio, but then Shakespeare would have lost Mercutio's great dying speech. How would you stage Tybalt's return so that it seems believable?

Tybalt.
Thou, wretched boy, that didst consort him here,
Shalt with him hence.

Romeo.   This shall determine that.

[*They fight.* TYBALT *falls.*]

Benvolio.
Romeo, away, be gone!

135   The citizens are up, and Tybalt slain.
Stand not amazed. The prince will doom thee death
If thou art taken. Hence, be gone, away!

Romeo.
O, I am fortune's fool!

Benvolio.   Why dost thou stay?

[*Exit* ROMEO.]

[*Enter* CITIZENS.]

Citizen.
Which way ran he that killed Mercutio?

140   Tybalt, that murderer, which way ran he?

Benvolio.
There lies that Tybalt.

Citizen.   Up, sir, go with me.
I charge thee in the prince's name obey.

[*Enter* PRINCE, *old* MONTAGUE, CAPULET, *their* WIVES, *and all.*]

Prince.
Where are the vile beginners of this fray?

Benvolio.
O noble prince, I can discover° all

145   The unlucky manage° of this fatal brawl.
There lies the man, slain by young Romeo,
That slew thy kinsman, brave Mercutio.

Lady Capulet.
Tybalt, my cousin! O my brother's child!
O prince! O cousin! Husband! O, the blood is spilled

150   Of my dear kinsman! Prince, as thou art true,
For blood of ours shed blood of Montague.
O cousin, cousin!

Prince.
Benvolio, who began this bloody fray?

Benvolio.
Tybalt, here slain, whom Romeo's hand did slay.

155   Romeo, that spoke him fair, bid him bethink
How nice° the quarrel was, and urged° withal
Your high displeasure. All this—utterèd
With gentle breath, calm look, knees humbly bowed—

137. *What details in Benvolio's speech tell us what Romeo is doing and how he is feeling after this second death?*

138. *What do you think Romeo means by calling himself "fortune's fool"? What does he realize will now happen to him and Juliet?*

Stage direction: What do you imagine the stage looks like as the prince and his followers enter?

144. discover: reveal.
145. manage: course.

156. nice: trivial. **urged:** mentioned.

160 Could not take truce with the unruly spleen°
Of Tybalt deaf to peace, but that he tilts°
With piercing steel at bold Mercutio's breast;
Who, all as hot, turns deadly point to point,
And, with a martial scorn, with one hand beats
Cold death aside and with the other sends
165 It back to Tybalt, whose dexterity
Retorts it. Romeo he cries aloud,
"Hold, friends! Friends, part!" and swifter than his
    tongue,
His agile arm beats down their fatal points,
And 'twixt them rushes; underneath whose arm
170 An envious° thrust from Tybalt hit the life
Of stout Mercutio, and then Tybalt fled;
But by and by comes back to Romeo,
Who had but newly entertained° revenge,
And to't they go like lightning; for, ere I
175 Could draw to part them, was stout Tybalt slain;
And, as he fell, did Romeo turn and fly.
This is the truth, or let Benvolio die.

Lady Capulet.
He is a kinsman to the Montague;
Affection makes him false, he speaks not true.
180 Some twenty of them fought in this black strife,
And all those twenty could but kill one life.
I beg for justice, which thou, prince, must give.
Romeo slew Tybalt; Romeo must not live.

Prince.
Romeo slew him; he slew Mercutio.
185 Who now the price of his dear blood doth owe?

Montague.
Not Romeo, prince; he was Mercutio's friend;
His fault concludes but what the law should end,
The life of Tybalt.

Prince.   And for that offense
Immediately we do exile him hence.
190 I have an interest in your hate's proceeding,
My blood° for your rude brawls doth lie a-bleeding;
But I'll amerce° you with so strong a fine
That you shall all repent the loss of mine.
I will be deaf to pleading and excuses;
195 Nor tears nor prayers shall purchase out abuses.
Therefore use none. Let Romeo hence in haste,
Else, when he is found, that hour is his last.
Bear hence this body and attend our will.
Mercy but murders, pardoning those that kill.

[*Exit with others.*]

159. **spleen:** anger.
160. **tilts:** thrusts.

170. **envious:** full of enmity or hatred.

173. **entertained:** thought of.

? 177. *Is Benvolio's testimony about events fully accurate?*

? 181. *How does Lady Capulet think Tybalt was killed? Why does she think Benvolio is lying?*

191. **My blood:** that is, Mercutio, his blood relative.
192. **amerce:** punish.

? 199. *The prince has heard arguments from both families and has given judgment in the case. What is Romeo's punishment? Why won't the prince show Romeo mercy?*

The families exit in two separate processions, with their dead. How does this scene contrast with the fighting that has just taken place?

Scene 2. *Capulet's orchard.*

Enter JULIET *alone.*

Juliet.

    Gallop apace, you fiery-footed steeds,°
    Towards Phoebus' lodging! Such a wagoner
    As Phaethon° would whip you to the west
    And bring in cloudy night immediately.
5   Spread thy close curtain, love-performing night,
    That runaways' eyes may wink,° and Romeo
    Leap to these arms untalked of and unseen.
    Lovers can see to do their amorous rites,
    And by their own beauties; or, if love be blind,
10   It best agrees with night. Come, civil° night,
    Thou sober-suited matron all in black,
    And learn me how to lose a winning match,
    Played for a pair of stainless maidenhoods.
    Hood° my unmanned° blood, bating° in my cheeks,
15   With thy black mantle till strange° love grow bold,
    Think true love acted simple modesty.
    Come, night; come, Romeo; come, thou day in night;
    For thou wilt lie upon the wings of night
    Whiter than new snow upon a raven's back.
20   Come, gentle night; come, loving, black-browed night;
    Give me my Romeo; and, when he shall die,
    Take him and cut him out in little stars,
    And he will make the face of heaven so fine
    That all the world will be in love with night
25   And pay no worship to the garish sun.
    O, I have bought the mansion of a love,
    But not possessed it; and though I am sold,
    Not yet enjoyed. So tedious is this day
    As is the night before some festival
30   To an impatient child that hath new robes
    And may not wear them. O, here comes my nurse,

[*Enter* NURSE, *with a ladder of cords.*]

? **Stage direction:** *What do we in the audience know that Juliet at this point still does not know?*
  1. steeds: horses (that pull the sun god Phoebus's chariot across the sky each day).
  3. Phaethon: reckless son of Phoebus, who couldn't hold the horses.
  6. That runaways' eyes may wink: so that the eyes of the sun god's horses may shut.

  10. civil: well-behaved.

  14. Hood: cover. **unmanned:** unmated. **bating:** fluttering.
  15. strange: unfamiliar.

? **24.** *Work in small groups to make a cluster for the word* night. *Include all the associations, images, and synonyms that you can come up with. How do they compare with Juliet's view of night?*
? **26.** *What is the "mansion of a love" Juliet has bought?*
? **31.** *Where does Juliet, in lines of unconscious foreshadowing, make us think of Romeo's death?*

**❝ *O, I have bought the mansion of a love,*
But not possessed it. . . . ❞**

And she brings news; and every tongue that speaks
But Romeo's name speaks heavenly eloquence.
Now, nurse, what news? What hast thou there, the
    cords
That Romeo bid thee fetch?

35 **Nurse.**   Ay, ay, the cords.
Juliet.
    Ay me! What news? Why dost thou wring thy hands?
Nurse.
    Ah, weraday!° He's dead, he's dead, he's dead!
    We are undone, lady, we are undone!
    Alack the day! He's gone, he's killed, he's dead!
Juliet.
    Can heaven be so envious?

40 **Nurse.**   Romeo can,
    Though heaven cannot. O Romeo, Romeo!
    Who ever would have thought it? Romeo!
Juliet.
    What devil art thou that dost torment me thus?
    This torture should be roared in dismal hell.

45   Hath Romeo slain himself? Say thou but "Ay,"
    And that bare vowel "I" shall poison more
    Than the death-darting eye of cockatrice.°
    I am not I, if there be such an "Ay,"
    Or those eyes' shot that make thee answer "Ay."

50   If he be slain, say "Ay"; or if not, "No."
    Brief sounds determine of my weal or woe.
Nurse.
    I saw the wound, I saw it with mine eyes,
    (God save the mark!)° here on his manly breast.
    A piteous corse,° a bloody piteous corse;

55   Pale, pale as ashes, all bedaubed in blood,
    All in gore-blood. I swounded° at the sight.
Juliet.
    O, break, my heart! Poor bankrout,° break at once!
    To prison, eyes; ne'er look on liberty!
    Vile earth,° to earth resign; end motion here,

60   And thou and Romeo press one heavy bier!
Nurse.
    O Tybalt, Tybalt, the best friend I had!
    O courteous Tybalt! Honest gentleman!
    That ever I should live to see thee dead!
Juliet.
    What storm is this that blows so contrary?

65   Is Romeo slaught'red, and is Tybalt dead?
    My dearest cousin, and my dearer lord?
    Then, dreadful trumpet, sound the general doom!
    For who is living, if those two are gone?

---

35. *How does the nurse speak this line?*

37. weraday!: well-a-day! (or alas!)

39. *The nurse rattles on again—but this time, how does she seem to give the wrong news, even as she delays it?*

47. cockatrice: legendary serpent that could kill by a glance.

53. God save the mark!: God forbid!
54. corse: corpse.

56. swounded: swooned (fainted).

57. bankrout: bankrupt.

59. Vile earth: Juliet refers to her own body.
60. *This is one of a series of odd scenes in which we cannot share a character's feelings because we know something that the character does not know. What does Juliet think has happened? How does she foreshadow her own death?*

Nurse.

    Tybalt is gone, and Romeo banishèd;

70   Romeo that killed him, he is banishèd.

Juliet.

    O God! Did Romeo's hand shed Tybalt's blood?

Nurse.

    It did, it did! Alas the day, it did!

Juliet.

    O serpent heart, hid with a flow'ring face!

    Did ever dragon keep so fair a cave?

75   Beautiful tyrant! Fiend angelical!

    Dove-feathered raven! Wolvish-ravening lamb!

    Despisèd substance of divinest show!

    Just opposite to what thou justly seem'st—

    A damnèd saint, an honorable villain!

80   O nature, what hadst thou to do in hell

    When thou didst bower the spirit of a fiend

    In mortal paradise of such sweet flesh?

    Was ever book containing such vile matter

    So fairly bound? O, that deceit should dwell

    In such a gorgeous palace!

85 **Nurse.**   There's no trust,

    No faith, no honesty in men; all perjured,

    All forsworn, all naught, all dissemblers.°

    Ah, where's my man? Give me some aqua vitae.°

    These griefs, these woes, these sorrows make me old.

    Shame come to Romeo!

90 **Juliet.**   Blistered be thy tongue

    For such a wish! He was not born to shame.

    Upon his brow shame is ashamed to sit;

    For 'tis a throne where honor may be crowned

    Sole monarch of the universal earth.

95   O, what a beast was I to chide at him!

Nurse.

    Will you speak well of him that killed your cousin?

Juliet.

    Shall I speak ill of him that is my husband?

    Ah, poor my lord, what tongue shall smooth thy name

    When I, thy three-hours wife, have mangled it?

100   But wherefore, villain, didst thou kill my cousin?

    That villain cousin would have killed my husband.

    Back, foolish tears, back to your native spring!

    Your tributary drops° belong to woe,

    Which you, mistaking, offer up to joy.

105   My husband lives, that Tybalt would have slain;

    And Tybalt's dead, that would have slain my husband.

    All this is comfort; wherefore weep I then?

    Some word there was, worser than Tybalt's death,

70. *Why do you think the nurse waits so long to give Juliet the correct news? Should we feel she is being self-centered here, or is she truly overwhelmed by the news she bears?*

73. *The news that Romeo has killed Tybalt is terrible for Juliet. Try writing stage directions that will help an actress express her horror.*

85. *A moment ago, Juliet thought of Romeo as her very "day in night." Now what does she think of him?*

  87. dissemblers: liars.

  88. aqua vitae: brandy (Latin for "water of life").

90. *What does the nurse think about these events? Where does she think the blame lies? Do you see her being selfish here, or is she wholly concerned for Juliet?*

97. *Why does Juliet turn against her nurse here?*

103. tributary drops: tears poured out in tribute.

That murd'red me. I would forget it fain;° 109. **fain:** willingly.
110 But O, it presses to my memory
Like damnèd guilty deeds to sinners' minds!
"Tybalt is dead, and Romeo—banishèd."
That "banishèd," that one word "banishèd,"
Hath slain ten thousand Tybalts. Tybalt's death
115 Was woe enough, if it had ended there;
Or, if sour woe delights in fellowship
And needly will be ranked with° other griefs, 117. **ranked with:** accompanied by.
Why followed not, when she said "Tybalt's dead,"
Thy father, or thy mother, nay, or both,
120 Which modern° lamentation might have moved?° 120. **modern:** ordinary. **moved:** provoked.
But with a rearward° following Tybalt's death, 121. **rearward:** soldiers at the rear of a troop; here, an additional source of injury and pain after the bad news about Tybalt.
"Romeo is banishèd"—to speak that word
Is father, mother, Tybalt, Romeo, Juliet,
All slain, all dead. "Romeo is banishèd"—

? 124. *Juliet comprehends what has happened. Why does she fix on that one word—banished?*

125 There is no end, no limit, measure, bound,
In that word's death; no words can that woe sound.
Where is my father and my mother, nurse?

? 127. *Juliet pauses before she speaks her last line here. How would you change her tone as she asks the nurse about her father and mother?*

Nurse.
Weeping and wailing over Tybalt's corse.
Will you go to them? I will bring you thither.
Juliet.
130 Wash they his wounds with tears? Mine shall be spent,
When theirs are dry, for Romeo's banishment.
Take up those cords. Poor ropes, you are beguiled,
Both you and I, for Romeo is exiled.
He made you for a highway to my bed;
135 But I, a maid, die maiden-widowèd.
Come, cords; come, nurse. I'll to my wedding bed;
And death, not Romeo, take my maidenhead!
Nurse.
Hie to your chamber. I'll find Romeo
To comfort you. I wot° well where he is.

? 137. *Juliet addresses the rope ladder in this speech. What has she decided to do with the ropes?*
139. **wot:** know.

140 Hark ye, your Romeo will be here at night.
I'll to him; he is hid at Laurence' cell.
Juliet.
O, find him! Give this ring to my true knight
And bid him come to take his last farewell.
[*Exit with* NURSE.]

Scene 3. *Friar Laurence's cell.*

Enter FRIAR LAURENCE.

Friar.
  Romeo, come forth; come forth, thou fearful man.
  Affliction is enamored of thy parts,
  And thou art wedded to calamity.

[*Enter* ROMEO.]

Romeo.
  Father, what news? What is the prince's doom?
5 What sorrow craves acquaintance at my hand
  That I yet know not?

Friar.   Too familiar
  Is my dear son with such sour company.
  I bring thee tidings of the prince's doom.

Romeo.
  What less than doomsday° is the prince's doom?

Friar.
10 A gentler judgment vanished° from his lips—
  Not body's death, but body's banishment.

Romeo.
  Ha, banishment? Be merciful, say "death";
  For exile hath more terror in his look,
  Much more than death. Do not say "banishment."

Friar.
15 Here from Verona art thou banishèd.
  Be patient, for the world is broad and wide.

Romeo.
  There is no world without Verona walls,
  But purgatory, torture, hell itself.
  Hence banishèd is banished from the world,
20 And world's exile is death. Then "banishèd"
  Is death mistermed. Calling death "banishèd,"
  Thou cut'st my head off with a golden ax
  And smilest upon the stroke that murders me.

Friar.
  O deadly sin! O rude unthankfulness!
25 Thy fault our law calls death; but the kind prince,
  Taking thy part, hath rushed aside the law,
  And turned that black word "death" to "banishment."
  This is dear mercy, and thou see'st it not.

3. *When we last saw Romeo he was speaking of himself as "fortune's fool." Now, in the first lines of this scene, how does the friar remind us again that Romeo seems fated for ill fortune?*

9. **doomsday:** my death.

10. **vanished:** escaped.

21. *Romeo, like Juliet, fixes on the word* banished. *What does the word mean to him?*

28. *Why is the friar angry at Romeo?*

Romeo.

     'Tis torture, and not mercy. Heaven is here,

30   Where Juliet lives; and every cat and dog

     And little mouse, every unworthy thing,

     Live here in heaven and may look on her;

     But Romeo may not. More validity,°

     More honorable state, more courtship lives

35   In carrion flies than Romeo. They may seize

     On the white wonder of dear Juliet's hand

     And steal immortal blessing from her lips,

     Who, even in pure and vestal modesty,

     Still blush, as thinking their own kisses sin;

40   But Romeo may not, he is banishèd.

     Flies may do this but I from this must fly;

     They are freemen, but I am banishèd.

     And sayest thou yet that exile is not death?

     Hadst thou no poison mixed, no sharp-ground knife,

45   No sudden mean of death, though ne'er so mean,

     But "banishèd" to kill me—"banishèd"?

     O friar, the damnèd use that word in hell;

     Howling attends it! How hast thou the heart,

     Being a divine, a ghostly confessor,

50   A sin-absolver, and my friend professed,

     To mangle me with that word "banishèd"?

33. validity: value.

" Heaven is here, Where Juliet lives. . . . "

Friar.

     Thou fond° mad man, hear me a little speak.

Romeo.

     O, thou wilt speak again of banishment.

Friar.

     I'll give thee armor to keep off that word;

55   Adversity's sweet milk, philosophy,

     To comfort thee, though thou art banishèd.

Romeo.

     Yet "banishèd"? Hang up philosophy!

     Unless philosophy can make a Juliet,

     Displant a town, reverse a prince's doom,

60   It helps not, it prevails not. Talk no more.

Friar.

     O, then I see that madmen have no ears.

52. fond: foolish.

60. *It may seem that Romeo goes on too much. But it is important that we get the picture of this "fond mad man" in order to understand the action of the play. None of the other characters can understand Romeo's love. They are more levelheaded (perhaps less lucky in love?). How is Romeo's response to banishment like Juliet's?*

Romeo.

How should they, when that wise men have no eyes?

Friar.

Let me dispute with thee of thy estate.°

Romeo.

Thou canst not speak of that thou dost not feel.

65   Wert thou as young as I, Juliet thy love,

An hour but married, Tybalt murderèd,

Doting like me, and like me banishèd,

Then mightst thou speak, then mightst thou tear thy
    hair,

And fall upon the ground, as I do now,

70   Taking the measure of an unmade grave.

[*The* NURSE *knocks.*]

Friar.

Arise, one knocks. Good Romeo, hide thyself.

Romeo.

Not I; unless the breath of heartsick groans

Mistlike infold me from the search of eyes.

[*Knock.*]

Friar.

Hark, how they knock! Who's there? Romeo, arise;

75   Thou wilt be taken.—Stay awhile!—Stand up;

[*Knock.*]

Run to my study.—By and by!—God's will,

What simpleness is this.—I come, I come!

[*Knock.*]

Who knocks so hard? Whence come you? What's your
    will?

[*Enter* NURSE.]

Nurse.

Let me come in, and you shall know my errand.

I come from Lady Juliet.

80   **Friar.**   Welcome then.

Nurse.

O holy friar, O, tell me, holy friar,

Where is my lady's lord, where's Romeo?

Friar.

There on the ground, with his own tears made drunk.

Nurse.

O, he is even in my mistress' case,°

85   Just in her case! O woeful sympathy!

62. *Whom is Romeo talking about?*

63. estate: situation.

70. *How do you think the friar responds to these harsh words?*

71. *There is a great deal of action in this scene while the knocks are heard at the door. What action is the friar engaged in, and what is Romeo doing?*

84. case: condition.

Piteous predicament! Even so lies she,
Blubb'ring and weeping, weeping and blubb'ring.
Stand up, stand up! Stand, and you be a man.
For Juliet's sake, for her sake, rise and stand!
90   Why should you fall into so deep an O?°

Romeo (*rises*). Nurse——
Nurse.
    Ah sir, ah sir! Death's the end of all.
Romeo.
    Spakest thou of Juliet? How is it with her?
    Doth not she think me an old murderer,
95   Now I have stained the childhood of our joy
    With blood removed but little from her own?
    Where is she? And how doth she? And what says
    My concealed lady to our canceled love?
Nurse.
    O, she says nothing, sir, but weeps and weeps;
100   And now falls on her bed, and then starts up,
    And Tybalt calls; and then on Romeo cries,
    And then down falls again.
Romeo.   As if that name,
    Shot from the deadly level° of a gun,
    Did murder her; as that name's cursèd hand
105   Murdered her kinsman. O, tell me, friar, tell me,
    In what vile part of this anatomy
    Doth my name lodge? Tell me, that I may sack°
    The hateful mansion.

[*He offers to stab himself, and* NURSE *snatches the
dagger away.*]

Friar.   Hold thy desperate hand.
    Art thou a man? Thy form cries out thou art;
110   Thy tears are womanish, thy wild acts denote
    The unreasonable fury of a beast.
    Unseemly woman in a seeming man!
    And ill-beseeming beast in seeming both!
    Thou hast amazed me. By my holy order,
115   I thought thy disposition better tempered.
    Hast thou slain Tybalt? Wilt thou slay thyself?
    And slay thy lady that in thy life lives,
    By doing damnèd hate upon thyself?
    Why rail'st thou on thy birth, the heaven, and earth?
120   Since birth and heaven and earth,° all three do meet
    In thee at once; which thou at once wouldst lose.
    Fie, fie, thou sham'st thy shape, thy love, thy wit,
    Which,° like a usurer, abound'st in all,
    And usest none in that true use indeed
125   Which should bedeck° thy shape, thy love, thy wit.

90. O: fit of moaning ("oh, oh, oh").

? **90.** *What action is the nurse engaged in as she speaks these lines?*

103. level: aim.

107. sack: plunder and destroy.

? **108.** *Romeo is disarmed without a struggle, and probably stands broken as the friar, in this long speech, gradually reestablishes control over him. It is important to remember that to the people in this play, suicide was a mortal sin, which damned one to hell forever. Where does the friar angrily remind Romeo of this?*

120. birth and heaven and earth: family origin, soul, and body.

123. Which: who (speaking of Romeo).

125. bedeck: do honor to.

Thy noble shape is but a form of wax,
Digressing from the valor of a man;
Thy dear love sworn but hollow perjury,
Killing that love which thou hast vowed to cherish;
130 Thy wit, that ornament to shape and love,
Misshapen in the conduct° of them both,
Like powder in a skill-less soldier's flask,
Is set afire by thine own ignorance,
And thou dismembered with thine own defense.°
135 What, rouse thee, man! Thy Juliet is alive,
For whose dear sake thou wast but lately dead.
There art thou happy.° Tybalt would kill thee,
But thou slewest Tybalt. There art thou happy.
The law, that threatened death, becomes thy friend
140 And turns it to exile. There art thou happy.
A pack of blessings light upon thy back;
Happiness courts thee in her best array;
But, like a misbehaved and sullen wench,
Thou pouts upon thy fortune and thy love.
145 Take heed, take heed, for such die miserable.
Go get thee to thy love, as was decreed,
Ascend her chamber, hence and comfort her.
But look thou stay not till the watch be set,
For then thou canst not pass to Mantua,
150 Where thou shalt live till we can find a time
To blaze° your marriage, reconcile your friends,
Beg pardon of the prince, and call thee back
With twenty hundred thousand times more joy
Than thou went'st forth in lamentation.
155 Go before, nurse. Commend me to thy lady,
And bid her hasten all the house to bed,
Which heavy sorrow makes them apt unto.
Romeo is coming.

Nurse.
    O Lord, I could have stayed here all the night
160 To hear good counsel. O, what learning is!
My lord, I'll tell my lady you will come.

Romeo.
    Do so, and bid my sweet prepare to chide.

[NURSE *offers to go in and turns again.*]

Nurse.
    Here, sir, a ring she bid me give you, sir.
Hie you, make haste, for it grows very late.   [*Exit.*]

Romeo.
165 How well my comfort is revived by this!

131. conduct: management.

134. And . . . defense: Romeo's own mind (wit), which should protect him, is destroying him.

137. happy: lucky.

151. blaze: announce.

? **154.** *What line in this speech suggests that Romeo has been standing listlessly? Find where the friar first shames Romeo, then appeals to his common sense, then offers him hope.*
? **155.** *The friar turns to the nurse. What are his instructions?*

? **161.** *The nurse's amazement at what she calls the friar's "learning" often brings a laugh from the audience and breaks the tension. Romeo thus far has said nothing. How do you imagine he shows that the friar's speech has brought him back to life?*

Friar.

    Go hence; good night; and here stands all your state:°
    Either be gone before the watch be set,
    Or by the break of day disguised from hence.
    Sojourn in Mantua. I'll find out your man,
170   And he shall signify from time to time
    Every good hap to you that chances here.
    Give me thy hand. 'Tis late. Farewell; good night.

Romeo.

    But that a joy past joy calls out on me,
    It were a grief so brief to part with thee.
175   Farewell.   *[Exeunt.]*

166. state: situation.

? **175.** *In spite of Romeo's and Juliet's anguish, the problem at this point seems to be simple. What plans have been made to resolve the young people's difficulties?*

Scene 4. *A room in Capulet's house.*

Enter old CAPULET, *his wife,* LADY CAPULET, *and* PARIS.

Capulet.

    Things have fallen out, sir, so unluckily
    That we have had no time to move° our daughter.
    Look you, she loved her kinsman Tybalt dearly,
    And so did I. Well, we were born to die.
5   'Tis very late; she'll not come down tonight.
    I promise you, but for your company,
    I would have been abed an hour ago.

Paris.

    These times of woe afford no times to woo.
    Madam, good night. Commend me to your daughter.

Lady Capulet.

10   I will, and know her mind early tomorrow;
    Tonight she's mewed up to her heaviness.°

Capulet.

    Sir Paris, I will make a desperate tender°
    Of my child's love. I think she will be ruled
    In all respects by me; nay more, I doubt it not.
15   Wife, go you to her ere you go to bed;
    Acquaint her here of my son Paris' love
    And bid her (mark you me?) on Wednesday next—
    But soft! What day is this?

Paris.   Monday, my lord.

2. move: persuade (to marry Paris).

? **7.** *Dramatic irony is felt when the audience knows something that the characters on stage do not know. What intense dramatic irony does the audience feel as this scene unfolds? What do we know that the Capulets and Paris are ignorant of?*

11. mewed up to her heaviness: shut away because of her great grief.

12. desperate tender: bold offer.

Capulet.

Monday! Ha, ha! Well, Wednesday is too soon.
20 A' Thursday let it be—a' Thursday, tell her,
She shall be married to this noble earl.
Will you be ready? Do you like this haste?
We'll keep no great ado—a friend or two;
For hark you, Tybalt being slain so late,
25 It may be thought we held him carelessly,
Being our kinsman, if we revel much.
Therefore we'll have some half a dozen friends,
And there an end. But what say you to Thursday?

Paris.

My lord, I would that Thursday were tomorrow.

Capulet.

30 Well, get you gone. A' Thursday be it then.
Go you to Juliet ere you go to bed;
Prepare her, wife, against this wedding day.
Farewell, my lord.—Light to my chamber, ho!
Afore me,° it is so very late
35 That we may call it early by and by.
Good night.   [*Exeunt.*]

? **19.** *Capulet is sometimes played as a foolish old man. Why do you think he wants to get Juliet married as soon as possible? What do you think his mood is here?*

? **32.** *Capulet speaks this line to his wife. Lady Capulet sometimes expresses uneasiness about her husband's plans here. Why would she be uneasy?*
34. Afore me: indeed.
? **36.** *Just as we might feel the situation can be rescued, Shakespeare "raises the stakes" with this short scene. How does this increase our tension in the scene that follows, the wedding-night scene?*

Scene 5. *Capulet's orchard.*

Enter ROMEO *and* JULIET *aloft.*

Juliet.

Wilt thou be gone? It is not yet near day.
It was the nightingale, and not the lark,
That pierced the fearful hollow of thine ear.
Nightly she sings on yond pomegranate tree.
5 Believe me, love, it was the nightingale.

Romeo.

It was the lark, the herald of the morn;
No nightingale. Look, love, what envious streaks
Do lace the severing clouds in yonder east.
Night's candles are burnt out, and jocund day
10 Stands tiptoe on the misty mountaintops.
I must be gone and live, or stay and die.

? *Stage direction:* *This scene was probably played on the upper stage in Shakespeare's time. In movies and modern stage productions, it is often played with varying degrees of frankness in Juliet's bedroom. Perhaps the fact that in Shakespeare's day Juliet was played by a boy dictated the brevity of the scene and the place where it was played. Would any lines not make sense if the scene were played in the bedroom?*

Juliet's first words here alert us to the time: It must be near morning, when Romeo must go to Mantua. We hear the song of a lark, which sings at daybreak. The nightingale, on the other hand, sings at night. Why does Juliet insist she hears the nightingale?

Juliet.
　　Yond light is not daylight; I know it, I.
　　It is some meteor that the sun exhales°
　　To be to thee this night a torchbearer
15　And light thee on thy way to Mantua.
　　Therefore stay yet; thou need'st not to be gone.
Romeo.
　　Let me be taken, let me be put to death.
　　I am content, so thou wilt have it so.
　　I'll say yon gray is not the morning's eye,
20　'Tis but the pale reflex° of Cynthia's brow;°
　　Nor that is not the lark whose notes do beat
　　The vaulty heaven so high above our heads.
　　I have more care to stay than will to go.
　　Come, death, and welcome! Juliet wills it so.
25　How is't, my soul? Let's talk; it is not day.
Juliet.
　　It is, it is! Hie hence, be gone, away!
　　It is the lark that sings so out of tune,
　　Straining harsh discords and unpleasing sharps.
　　Some say the lark makes sweet division;°
30　This doth not so, for she divideth us.
　　Some say the lark and loathèd toad change eyes;°
　　O, now I would they had changed voices too,
　　Since arm from arm that voice doth us affray,°
　　Hunting thee hence with hunt's-up° to the day.
35　O, now be gone! More light and light it grows.
Romeo.
　　More light and light— more dark and dark our woes.

13. exhales: gives off. (It was believed that the sun drew up vapors and ignited them as meteors.)

20. reflex: reflection. **Cynthia's brow:** Cynthia is the moon.

? **26.** *What has Romeo said that makes Juliet suddenly practical and aware of danger?*

29. division: literally, a rapid run of notes, but Juliet is punning on the word's other meaning (separation).
31. A fable to explain why the lark, which sings so beautifully, has ugly eyes, and why the toad, which croaks so harshly, has beautiful ones.
33. affray: frighten.
34. hunt's-up: morning song for hunters.

" *More light and light—more dark and dark our woes.* "

[*Enter* NURSE.]

Nurse. Madam!
Juliet. Nurse?
Nurse.
　　Your lady mother is coming to your chamber.
40　The day is broke; be wary, look about.　　　　[*Exit.*]
Juliet.
　　Then, window, let day in, and let life out.

? **41.** *What is Juliet doing as she speaks these lines?*

«O, think'st thou we shall ever meet again?»

Romeo.
Farewell, farewell! One kiss, and I'll descend.

[*He goes down.*]

Juliet.
Art thou gone so, love-lord, ay husband-friend?
I must hear from thee every day in the hour,
45   For in a minute there are many days.
O, for this count I shall be much in years
Ere I again behold my Romeo!
Romeo.
Farewell!
I will omit no opportunity
50   That may convey my greetings, love, to thee.
Juliet.
O, think'st thou we shall ever meet again?
Romeo.
I doubt it not; and all these woes shall serve
For sweet discourses in our times to come.
Juliet.
O God, I have an ill-divining soul!
55   Methinks I see thee, now thou art so low,
As one dead in the bottom of a tomb.
Either my eyesight fails, or thou look'st pale.
Romeo.
And trust me, love, in my eye so do you.
Dry° sorrow drinks our blood. Adieu, adieu!   [*Exit.*]
Juliet.
60   O Fortune, Fortune! All men call thee fickle.
If thou art fickle, what dost thou with him
That is renowned for faith? Be fickle, Fortune,
For then I hope thou wilt not keep him long
But send him back.

[*Enter Juliet's mother,* LADY CAPULET.]

Lady Capulet.
65   Ho, daughter! Are you up?
Juliet.
Who is't that calls? It is my lady mother.
Is she not down so late,° or up so early?
What unaccustomed cause procures her hither?
Lady Capulet.
Why, how now, Juliet?
Juliet.   Madam, I am not well.
Lady Capulet.
70   Evermore weeping for your cousin's death?
What, wilt thou wash him from his grave with tears?
And if thou couldst, thou couldst not make him live.

43. *Where is Romeo now, as Juliet asks him to communicate with her?*

51. *Remember what the Prologue has told you about what will happen to Romeo and Juliet. How do you feel when you hear Juliet speak this line?*

57. *Friar Laurence might have taken Juliet with Romeo, into exile in Mantua. But we must remember that Juliet is not quite fourteen, and at this point in the story, Friar Laurence thinks the situation can be happily resolved. As the lovers part now, where does Juliet foresee Romeo's doom?*
59. Dry: thirsty (sorrow was thought to drain color from the cheeks).

67. down so late: so late getting to bed.

Therefore have done. Some grief shows much of love;
But much of grief shows still some want of wit.

Juliet.

75 Yet let me weep for such a feeling loss.°

Lady Capulet.

So shall you feel the loss, but not the friend
Which you weep for.

Juliet.   Feeling so the loss,
I cannot choose but ever weep the friend.

Lady Capulet.

Well, girl, thou weep'st not so much for his death
80 As that the villain lives which slaughtered him.

Juliet.

What villain, madam?

Lady Capulet.   That same villain Romeo.

Juliet (*aside*).

Villain and he be many miles asunder—
God pardon him! I do, with all my heart;
And yet no man like he doth grieve my heart.

Lady Capulet.

85 That is because the traitor murderer lives.

Juliet.

Ay, madam, from the reach of these my hands.
Would none but I might venge my cousin's death!

Lady Capulet.

We will have vengeance for it, fear thou not.
Then weep no more. I'll send to one in Mantua,
90 Where that same banished runagate° doth live,
Shall give him such an unaccustomed dram°
That he shall soon keep Tybalt company;
And then I hope thou wilt be satisfied.

Juliet.

Indeed I never shall be satisfied
95 With Romeo till I behold him—dead—
Is my poor heart so for a kinsman vexed.
Madam, if you could find out but a man
To bear a poison, I would temper° it—
That Romeo should, upon receipt thereof,
100 Soon sleep in quiet. O, how my heart abhors
To hear him named and cannot come to him,
To wreak° the love I bore my cousin
Upon his body that hath slaughtered him!

Lady Capulet.

Find thou the means, and I'll find such a man.
105 But now I'll tell thee joyful tidings, girl.

74. *Actresses playing Lady Capulet have interpreted her character in two ways. Some portray her as loving toward Juliet. Others find in her speeches a signal to play her as distant and strong-willed, to contrast with Juliet's helplessness. What do you think Lady Capulet's tone is here, and how would you play the part?*

75. feeling loss: loss so deeply felt.

78. *All Juliet's lines in this scene have double meanings. Whom is she really grieving for?*

90. runagate: fugitive.

91. unaccustomed dram: unexpected drink (of poison).

93. *This is a hard and fearful threat. How does Juliet reply, and with what hidden emotions does she speak her next words? How does she continue to speak with double meanings?*

95. *How should lines 95–96 be said to indicate that Juliet intends* dead *to refer to* heart?

98. temper: mix (she really means "weaken").

102. wreak: avenge (she really means "express").

105. *Has Juliet convinced her mother that she wants Romeo dead?*

"Would none but I
might venge
my cousin's death!"

Juliet.
And joy comes well in such a needy time.
What are they, I beseech your ladyship?

Lady Capulet.
Well, well, thou hast a careful° father, child;
One who, to put thee from thy heaviness,
110 Hath sorted out° a sudden day of joy
That thou expects not nor I looked not for.

Juliet.
Madam, in happy time!° What day is that?

Lady Capulet.
Marry, my child, early next Thursday morn
The gallant, young, and noble gentleman,
115 The County Paris, at Saint Peter's Church,
Shall happily make thee there a joyful bride.

Juliet.
Now by Saint Peter's Church, and Peter too,
He shall not make me there a joyful bride!
I wonder at this haste, that I must wed
120 Ere he that should be husband comes to woo.
I pray you tell my lord and father, madam,
I will not marry yet; and when I do, I swear
It shall be Romeo, whom you know I hate,
Rather than Paris. These are news indeed!

Lady Capulet.
125 Here comes your father. Tell him so yourself,
And see how he will take it at your hands.

[*Enter* CAPULET *and* NURSE.]

Capulet.
When the sun sets the earth doth drizzle dew,
But for the sunset of my brother's son
It rains downright.
130 How now? A conduit,° girl? What, still in tears?
Evermore showering? In one little body
Thou counterfeits a bark,° a sea, a wind:
For still thy eyes, which I may call the sea,
Do ebb and flow with tears; the bark thy body is,
135 Sailing in this salt flood; the winds, thy sighs,
Who, raging with thy tears and they with them,
Without a sudden calm will overset
Thy tempest-tossèd body. How now, wife?
Have you delivered to her our decree?

Lady Capulet.
140 Ay, sir; but she will none, she gives you thanks.
I would the fool were married to her grave!

107. *We know what the "tidings" are, but Juliet doesn't. How would she speak these lines?*
108. careful: full of caring (for Juliet).
110. sorted out: selected.

112. in happy time: at a lucky time.

120. *Juliet becomes sarcastic as she repeats her mother's words. Despite this shocking news, how does Juliet manage to make a reasonable protest to her mother?*

130. conduit: water pipe (Juliet is weeping).

132. counterfeits a bark: imitates a boat.

139. *Lord Capulet, self-satisfied and certain of his scheme, tries to humor and tease the weeping Juliet. Again, what irony do we feel in this scene?*

Capulet.
  Soft! Take me with you,° take me with you, wife.
  How? Will she none? Doth she not give us thanks?
  Is she not proud? Doth she not count her blest,
145 Unworthy as she is, that we have wrought°
  So worthy a gentleman to be her bride?
Juliet.
  Not proud you have, but thankful that you have.
  Proud can I never be of what I hate,
  But thankful even for hate that is meant love.
Capulet.
150 How, how, how, how, chopped-logic?° What is this?
  "Proud"—and "I thank you"—and "I thank you not"—
  And yet "not proud"? Mistress minion° you,
  Thank me no thankings, nor proud me no prouds,
  But fettle° your fine joints 'gainst Thursday next
155 To go with Paris to Saint Peter's Church,
  Or I will drag thee on a hurdle thither.
  Out, you greensickness carrion! Out, you baggage!
  You tallow-face!
Lady Capulet.   Fie, fie! What, are you mad?
Juliet.
  Good father, I beseech you on my knees,
160 Hear me with patience but to speak a word.
Capulet.
  Hang thee, young baggage! Disobedient wretch!
  I tell thee what—get thee to church a' Thursday
  Or never after look me in the face.
  Speak not, reply not, do not answer me!
165 My fingers itch. Wife, we scarce thought us blest
  That God had lent us but this only child;
  But now I see this one is one too much,
  And that we have a curse in having her.
  Out on her, hilding!
Nurse.   God in heaven bless her!
170 You are to blame, my lord, to rate° her so.
Capulet.
  And why, my Lady Wisdom? Hold your tongue,
  Good Prudence. Smatter with your gossips,° go!
Nurse.
  I speak no treason.
Capulet.   O, God-i-god-en!°
Nurse.
  May not one speak?
Capulet.   Peace, you mumbling fool!
175 Utter your gravity o'er a gossip's bowl,
  For here we need it not.
Lady Capulet.   You are too hot.

---

142. Soft! Take me with you:
Wait! Let me understand you.

145. wrought: arranged.

? **149.** *How does Juliet show that she knows her father loves her, even though she hates what he has done for her?*
150. chopped-logic: hair-splitting.
152. minion: badly behaved girl.

154. fettle: make ready.

? **158.** *What insulting names does Capulet call Juliet? What would Capulet's actions be, as he speaks these vicious words to his only daughter? Whom is Juliet's mother talking to, in her next line?*
? **160.** *In the midst of this drama, we have a recognizable domestic scene, a family argument, which might have been played out in any century. What is Juliet doing as she talks to her father here? What does she do during her father's next speech?*

170. rate: berate, scold.

172. Smatter with your gossips: chatter with your gossipy friends.

173. God-i-god-en!: Get on with you! ("God give you good evening.")

Capulet.

God's bread!° It makes me mad.
Day, night; hour, tide, time; work, play;
Alone, in company; still my care hath been

180   To have her matched; and having now provided
A gentleman of noble parentage,
Of fair demesnes, youthful, and nobly trained,
Stuffed, as they say, with honorable parts,
Proportioned as one's thought would wish a man—

185   And then to have a wretched puling° fool,
A whining mammet,° in her fortune's tender,°
To answer "I'll not wed, I cannot love;
I am too young, I pray you pardon me"!
But, and you will not wed, I'll pardon you!°

190   Graze where you will, you shall not house with me.
Look to't, think on't; I do not use to jest.
Thursday is near; lay hand on heart, advise.°
And you be mine, I'll give you to my friend;
And you be not, hang, beg, starve, die in the streets,

195   For, by my soul, I'll ne'er acknowledge thee,
Nor what is mine shall never do thee good.
Trust to't. Bethink you. I'll not be forsworn.°   [*Exit.*]

Juliet.

Is there no pity sitting in the clouds
That sees into the bottom of my grief?

200   O sweet my mother, cast me not away!
Delay this marriage for a month, a week;
Or if you do not, make the bridal bed
In that dim monument where Tybalt lies.

Lady Capulet.

Talk not to me, for I'll not speak a word.

205   Do as thou wilt, for I have done with thee.   [*Exit.*]

Juliet.

O God!—O nurse, how shall this be prevented?
My husband is on earth, my faith in heaven.°
How shall that faith return again to earth
Unless that husband send it me from heaven

210   By leaving earth? Comfort me, counsel me.
Alack, alack, that heaven should practice stratagems
Upon so soft a subject as myself!
What say'st thou? Hast thou not a word of joy?
Some comfort, nurse.

Nurse.   Faith, here it is.

215   Romeo is banished; and all the world to nothing°
That he dares ne'er come back to challenge you;
Or if he do, it needs must be by stealth.
Then, since the case so stands as now it doth,
I think it best you married with the county.

---

177. God's bread!: oath on the sacrament of Communion.

185. puling: whining.
186. mammet: puppet. **in her fortune's tender:** with all her good fortunes.

? **188.** *What does Lord Capulet think are Juliet's reasons for not wanting to marry Paris?*
189. I'll pardon you!: I'll give you permission to go!
192. advise: consider.

197. forsworn: guilty of breaking his vow.

? **197.** *There is usually a moment of stunned silence onstage after Capulet leaves. What exactly will Lord Capulet do if Juliet refuses to marry Paris? In the next speech, how does Juliet appeal to her mother for help?*

207. my faith in heaven: my wedding vow is recorded in heaven.

? **210.** *Romeo and Juliet constantly remind us that they have taken their marriage vows seriously. According to Juliet here, how can these vows be broken?*

215. all the world to nothing: it is a safe bet.

---

220 O, he's a lovely gentleman!
    Romeo's a dishclout° to him. An eagle, madam,
    Hath not so green, so quick, so fair an eye
    As Paris hath. Beshrew° my very heart,
    I think you are happy in this second match,
225 For it excels your first; or if it did not,
    Your first is dead—or 'twere as good he were
    As living here and you no use of him.
Juliet.
    Speak'st thou from thy heart?
Nurse.
    And from my soul too; else beshrew them both.
230 **Juliet.** Amen!
Nurse. What?
Juliet.
    Well, thou hast comforted me marvelous much.
    Go in; and tell my lady I am gone,
    Having displeased my father, to Laurence' cell,
235 To make confession and to be absolved.
Nurse.
    Marry, I will; and this is wisely done.   [*Exit.*]
Juliet.
    Ancient damnation!° O most wicked fiend!
    Is it more sin to wish me thus forsworn,
    Or to dispraise my lord with that same tongue
240 Which she hath praised him with above compare
    So many thousand times? Go, counselor!
    Thou and my bosom henceforth shall be twain.°
    I'll to the friar to know his remedy.
    If all else fail, myself have power to die.   [*Exit.*]

221. dishclout: literally dishcloth; limp and weak.

223. Beshrew: curse.

❓ 227. *What is the nurse's "comfort" and advice for Juliet? Which line in this speech suggests that Juliet has reacted with shock and that the nurse must pause? Did you expect such advice from the nurse?*

❓ 235. *In most productions, the nurse embraces Juliet to comfort her. Now Juliet has made a decision. What do you see Juliet doing as she speaks?*
237. Ancient damnation!: Damned old woman!

242. twain: separate.

❓ 244. *What has Juliet decided about the nurse? We may wonder why Juliet doesn't just tell her parents why she cannot marry Paris. Why do you think she does not take this easy way out? Is she protecting Romeo, or does she feel abandoned by her parents?*

MAKING MEANINGS   ACT III

First Thoughts

1. If you were to assign blame to anyone at this point in the action, who would it be, and why?

Shaping Interpretations

2. Suppose Mercutio had killed Tybalt in the sword fight. How might the action of the play have changed? If he had lived, could Mercutio have persuaded Romeo to act differently? Do you think the old feud would still have erupted again? Explain.

3. Romeo's killing of Tybalt is the **turning point** of the play—the point when something happens that will turn the action toward either a happy ending or a tragic one. What actions does the killing set in motion, with possible tragic consequences?

4. We already know that the play ends in the deaths of Romeo and Juliet. Their willingness to die comes as no surprise to us, because we have been forewarned. Point out the instances in this act where each young person mentions this willingness to die if they are separated.

5. How does the nurse offend Juliet in this act and cease to be her friend? How does this development add to the tragedy of the events that follow?

6. What have the events of this act revealed to you about the **characters** of Romeo and Juliet? Describe how the young lovers are changing. What hard lessons are they learning about life?

7. By the end of Act III, we have reached the highest point of suspense. **Suspense** causes us to ask questions, to wonder anxiously "What will happen next?" Write down the questions you are asking at the end of Act III.

Extending the Text

8. Does the last scene in this act remind you of encounters between parents and their teenage children that you've seen in movies, TV shows, or novels? Do Juliet and her parents remind you of real-life parents and teenagers today? Explain. (If you did the Quickwrite assignment on page 732, check those notes before you answer.)

9. Find some lines from this act that could be spoken today—by children, parents, or counselors.

> ### Reviewing the Text
>
> a. What causes the fatal sword fight between Mercutio and Tybalt? How is Mercutio killed?
>
> b. Why does Romeo kill Tybalt?
>
> c. Now the young lovers are in serious trouble. What does Juliet threaten in Scene 2, after hearing of Romeo's banishment?
>
> d. What is the friar's plan to help them in Scene 3?
>
> e. By the end of Scene 4, a new complication has come up. What plans do Juliet's parents reveal that they have made for her?

CHOICES: Building Your Portfolio

Writer's Notebook

1. Collecting Ideas for an Informative Report

Finding a topic.

Act III is a good place to find a topic for the informative report you'll be writing in the Writer's Workshop on page 870. This act paints a vivid picture of people who have passions just like ours but who live in a society very different from our own. Skim through the act, making notes on one of the following aspects of Renaissance life:

- levels of power, authority, and responsibility assigned to different people: lords, ladies, teenagers, nurses, friars, pages, servants
- ideas of justice, as shown by the prince's instant banishment of Romeo
- relationships between parents and children

Creative Writing

2. Write a Prologue

Did you notice that there was no Prologue for Act III? Yet in this act we have some of the strongest action of the play. Try writing your summary of this act in the form of a sonnet prologue.

Speaking

3. Freeze! Speak!

Work in five groups to create "Living Pictures" of the key action in each scene of Act III. Each actor should choose one character and search the scene for one of that character's most significant lines. Then the actors should arrange themselves in an appropriate opening tableau and freeze. One at a time each character can come to life, say the line, change position and then freeze again. Each group should prepare a short opening and closing statement for the presentation.

VOCABULARY   MINI-LESSON

What's in a Name?

In Act II, Scene 2, Juliet, upset to discover that this handsome young man she has just met is named Montague, delivers these famous lines about the insignificance of names:

> What's in a name? That which we call a rose
> By any other word would smell as sweet.

Names, however, *are* significant in Shakespeare's plays. They are often used to suggest something about a person's character or temperament. Use a dictionary and the side notes to help you answer these questions about three big names in *Romeo and Juliet.*

1. What chemical element is Mercutio named for?
2. What characteristics of this element match Mercutio's character?
3. What does it mean to say that someone is *mercurial* in temperament?
4. Benvolio's name comes from the same Latin words as the adjective *benevolent.* What do these Latin words mean?
5. How does Benvolio's name match his temperament?
6. How is Tybalt like the cat he is named for?
7. If you were renaming these characters for an updated version of the tragedy, what names would you give them?

ACT IV

Scene 1. *Friar Laurence's cell.*

Enter FRIAR LAURENCE *and* COUNT PARIS.

Friar.
   On Thursday, sir? The time is very short.
Paris.
   My father Capulet will have it so,
   And I am nothing slow to slack his haste.
Friar.
   You say you do not know the lady's mind.
5   Uneven° is the course; I like it not.
Paris.
   Immoderately she weeps for Tybalt's death,
   And therefore have I little talked of love;
   For Venus smiles not in a house of tears.
   Now, sir, her father counts it dangerous
10   That she do give her sorrow so much sway,
   And in his wisdom hastes our marriage
   To stop the inundation of her tears,
   Which, too much minded° by herself alone,
   May be put from her by society.
15   Now do you know the reason of this haste.
Friar (*aside*).
   I would I knew not why it should be slowed,—
   Look, sir, here comes the lady toward my cell.

[*Enter* JULIET.]

Paris.
   Happily met, my lady and my wife!
Juliet.
   That may be, sir, when I may be a wife.
Paris.
20   That "may be" must be, love, on Thursday next.
Juliet.
   What must be shall be.
Friar.   That's a certain text.
Paris.
   Come you to make confession to this father?
Juliet.
   To answer that, I should confess to you.
Paris.
   Do not deny to him that you love me.

5. **Uneven:** irregular or unusual.

13. **minded:** thought about.

? **15.** *According to Paris, why is Capulet pushing his daughter to marry so quickly?*

Juliet.

25   I will confess to you that I love him.

Paris.

So will ye, I am sure, that you love me.

Juliet.

If I do so, it will be of more price,
Being spoke behind your back, than to your face.

Paris.

Poor soul, thy face is much abused with tears.

Juliet.

30   The tears have got small victory by that,
For it was bad enough before their spite.°

Paris.

Thou wrong'st it more than tears with that report.

Juliet.

That is no slander, sir, which is a truth;
And what I spake, I spake it to my face.

Paris.

35   Thy face is mine, and thou hast slandered it.

Juliet.

It may be so, for it is not mine own.
Are you at leisure, holy father, now,
Or shall I come to you at evening mass?

Friar.

My leisure serves me, pensive daughter, now.

40   My lord, we must entreat the time alone.

Paris.

God shield° I should disturb devotion!
Juliet, on Thursday early will I rouse ye.
Till then, adieu, and keep this holy kiss.   [*Exit.*]

Juliet.

O, shut the door, and when thou hast done so,

45   Come weep with me—past hope, past care, past help!

Friar.

O Juliet, I already know thy grief;
It strains me past the compass of my wits.
I hear thou must, and nothing may prorogue° it,
On Thursday next be married to this county.

Juliet.

50   Tell me not, friar, that thou hearest of this,
Unless thou tell me how I may prevent it.
If in thy wisdom thou canst give no help,
Do thou but call my resolution wise
And with this knife I'll help it presently.

55   God joined my heart and Romeo's, thou our hands;
And ere this hand, by thee to Romeo's sealed,
Shall be the label° to another deed,°
Or my true heart with treacherous revolt

26. *In this scene, Juliet's action is to keep up appearances and ward off Paris, who presses his attentions on her. She does this by wittily playing with words. We are fascinated by two things here: by what is being done, and by how it is being done. What double meanings does Juliet intend in the exchange with Paris that follows?*

31. spite: injury or damage (to her face).

38. *Juliet must show here that the tension of keeping up this pretense is unbearable. Where do you think she pauses and changes her tone?*

41. God shield: God forbid.

45. *Paris has gone, and Juliet has endured his "holy kiss." Whom is she talking to now?*

48. prorogue: postpone.

54. *What is Juliet holding in her hand? What is she threatening to do?*

57. label: seal. **deed:** contract (of marriage).

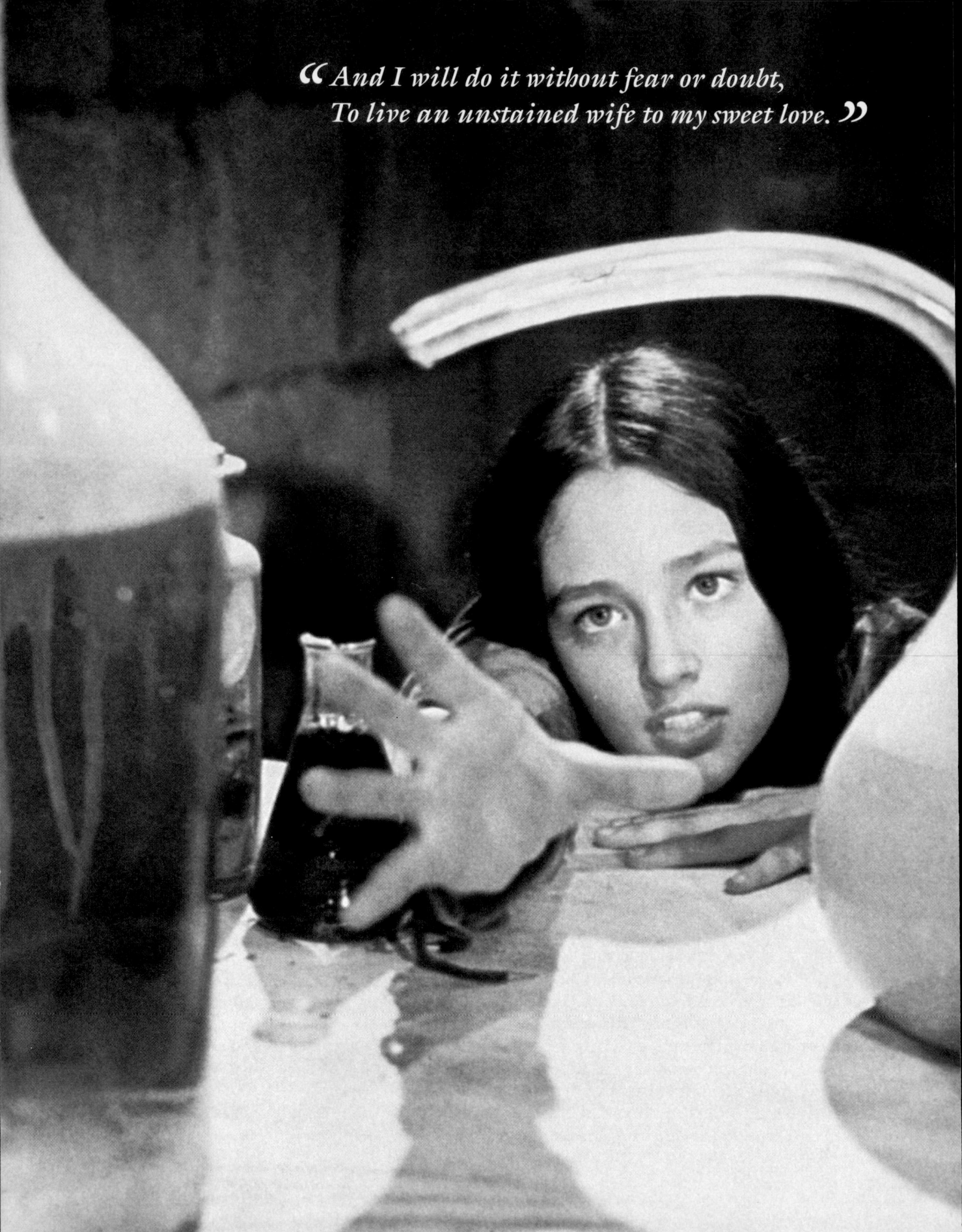

“ *And I will do it without fear or doubt,*
To live an unstained wife to my sweet love. ”

Turn to another, this shall slay them both.
60   Therefore, out of thy long-experienced time,
      Give me some present counsel; or, behold,
      'Twixt my extremes and me this bloody knife
      Shall play the umpire, arbitrating that
      Which the commission° of thy years and art
65   Could to no issue of true honor bring.
      Be not so long to speak. I long to die
      If what thou speak'st speak not of remedy.

Friar.
      Hold, daughter. I do spy a kind of hope,
      Which craves as desperate an execution
70   As that is desperate which we would prevent.
      If, rather than to marry County Paris,
      Thou hast the strength of will to slay thyself,
      Then is it likely thou wilt undertake
      A thing like death to chide away this shame,
75   That cop'st° with death himself to scape from it;
      And, if thou darest, I'll give thee remedy.

Juliet.
      O, bid me leap, rather than marry Paris,
      From off the battlements of any tower,
      Or walk in thievish ways, or bid me lurk
80   Where serpents are; chain me with roaring bears,
      Or hide me nightly in a charnel house,°
      O'ercovered quite with dead men's rattling bones,
      With reeky° shanks and yellow chapless° skulls;
      Or bid me go into a new-made grave
85   And hide me with a dead man in his shroud
      Things that, to hear them told, have made me
          tremble—
      And I will do it without fear or doubt,
      To live an unstained wife to my sweet love.

Friar.
      Hold, then. Go home, be merry, give consent
90   To marry Paris. Wednesday is tomorrow.
      Tomorrow night look that thou lie alone;
      Let not the nurse lie with thee in thy chamber.
      Take thou this vial, being then in bed,
      And this distilling° liquor drink thou off;
95   When presently through all thy veins shall run
      A cold and drowsy humor;° for no pulse
      Shall keep his native° progress, but surcease;°
      No warmth, no breath, shall testify thou livest;
      The roses in thy lips and cheeks shall fade
100   To wanny° ashes, thy eyes' windows fall
      Like death when he shuts up the day of life;
      Each part, deprived of supple government,°

62. *The friar has to put up with a good deal of brandishing of knives and daggers from Romeo and Juliet. Now that the nurse is no longer Juliet's friend, the friar has to be the confidant of both Juliet and Romeo. He must listen with patience to their threats of suicide if they cannot be together. What line in Juliet's speech indicates that she has paused and that the friar, for a time, is silent?*

64. commission: authority.

75. cop'st: negotiates.

77. *What would Juliet's mood be as she delivers this speech? What will she do, rather than marry Paris?*

81. charnel house: house where bones from old graves are kept.

83. reeky: damp, stinking. **chapless:** jawless.

89. *Juliet must pay strict attention to the friar's plan, as must the audience. On what day does the friar tell Juliet to take the potion?*

94. distilling: penetrating.

96. humor: fluid.
97. native: natural. **surcease:** stop.

100. wanny: pale.

102. government: control.

Shall, stiff and stark and cold, appear like death;
And in this borrowed likeness of shrunk death
105 Thou shalt continue two-and-forty hours,
And then awake as from a pleasant sleep.
Now, when the bridegroom in the morning comes
To rouse thee from thy bed, there art thou dead.
Then, as the manner of our country is,
110 In thy best robes uncovered on the bier
Thou shalt be borne to that same ancient vault
Where all the kindred of the Capulets lie.
In the meantime, against° thou shalt awake,
Shall Romeo by my letters know our drift;°
115 And hither shall he come; and he and I
Will watch thy waking, and that very night
Shall Romeo bear thee hence to Mantua.
And this shall free thee from this present shame,
If no inconstant toy° nor womanish fear
120 Abate thy valor in the acting it.

Juliet.
Give me, give me! O, tell not me of fear!

Friar.
Hold! Get you gone, be strong and prosperous
In this resolve. I'll send a friar with speed
To Mantua, with my letters to thy lord.

Juliet.
125 Love give me strength, and strength shall help afford.
Farewell, dear father.   [*Exit with* FRIAR.]

Scene 2. *A hall in Capulet's house.*

Enter father CAPULET, LADY CAPULET, NURSE, *and* SERVING-
MEN, *two or three.*

Capulet.
So many guests invite as here are writ.
                              [*Exit a* SERVINGMAN.]
Sirrah, go hire me twenty cunning° cooks.

Servingman. You shall have none ill, sir; for I'll try if they
can lick their fingers.

Capulet.
5   How canst thou try them so?

Servingman. Marry, sir, 'tis an ill cook that cannot lick
his own fingers. Therefore he that cannot lick his
fingers goes not with me.

---

106. *This may be the most implausible part of the play, but we have been prepared for it. Where have we seen the friar taking care of his herbs and heard him talk of magical potions before? What will happen to Juliet when she takes the drug?*

113. against: before.
114. drift: intentions.

117. *How is Romeo to be told of this plan, and when is he to watch Juliet wake and take her to Mantua?*
119. toy: whim.

122. *What does the friar give Juliet as she exits? What exactly is his plan?*

126. *In some productions, the friar holds Juliet back for just a moment and silently blesses her. Why would this make us more anxious about the outcome of his plan?*

1. *Capulet is sending his servant off to invite guests to Juliet's wedding. How would this comic and busy domestic scene contrast with the previous one?*
2. cunning: skillful.

Capulet. Go, be gone.   [*Exit* SERVINGMAN.]

10   We shall be much unfurnished° for this time.
    What, is my daughter gone to Friar Laurence?
Nurse. Ay, forsooth.
Capulet.
    Well, he may chance to do some good on her.
    A peevish self-willed harlotry it is.

[*Enter* JULIET.]

Nurse.
15   See where she comes from shrift with merry look.
Capulet.
    How now, my headstrong? Where have you been
        gadding?
Juliet.
    Where I have learnt me to repent the sin
    Of disobedient opposition
    To you and your behests, and am enjoined
20   By holy Laurence to fall prostrate here
    To beg your pardon. Pardon, I beseech you!
    Henceforward I am ever ruled by you.
Capulet.
    Send for the county. Go tell him of this.
    I'll have this knot knit up tomorrow morning.
Juliet.
25   I met the youthful lord at Laurence' cell
    And gave him what becomèd° love I might,
    Not stepping o'er the bounds of modesty.
Capulet.
    Why, I am glad on't. This is well. Stand up.
    This is as't should be. Let me see the county.
30   Ay, marry, go, I say, and fetch him hither.
    Now, afore God, this reverend holy friar,
    All our whole city is much bound to him.
Juliet.
    Nurse, will you go with me into my closet,°
    To help me sort such needful ornaments
35   As you think fit to furnish me tomorrow?
Lady Capulet.
    No, not till Thursday. There is time enough.
Capulet.
    Go, nurse, go with her. We'll to church tomorrow.
                        [*Exeunt* JULIET *and* NURSE.]
Lady Capulet.
    We shall be short in our provision.
    'Tis now near night.
Capulet.   Tush, I will stir about,
40   And all things shall be well, I warrant thee, wife.

---

10. unfurnished: unsupplied (without food).

? 14. Harlotry *means a "good-for-nothing," a prostitute. Whom is Capulet referring to as "it"?*

? 15. *Do you think Juliet really has a merry look, or is the nurse trying to cover up?*

? 24. *Why do you think Capulet pushes the marriage up to Wednesday?*

26. becomèd: proper or becoming.

? 28. *According to this speech, what has Juliet been doing since she first addressed her father?*

33. closet: private room.

? 37. *The wedding has been changed to take place on Wednesday. Lady Capulet tries to change her husband's mind, perhaps in consideration of Juliet. But she is not successful. How will this affect the timing of the friar's plans?*

Go thou to Juliet, help to deck up her.
I'll not to bed tonight; let me alone.
I'll play the housewife for this once. What, ho!
They are all forth; well, I will walk myself
45 To County Paris, to prepare up him
Against tomorrow. My heart is wondrous light,
Since this same wayward girl is so reclaimed.

[*Exit with* LADY CAPULET.]

47. *Lord Capulet realizes all the servants are gone. What action is he involved in in this speech? What is his new mood?*

Scene 3. *Juliet's chamber.*

Enter JULIET *and* NURSE.

Juliet.
Ay, those attires are best; but, gentle nurse,
I pray thee leave me to myself tonight;
For I have need of many orisons°
To move the heavens to smile upon my state,
5 Which, well thou knowest, is cross and full of sin.

3. orisons: prayers.

[*Enter* LADY CAPULET.]

Lady Capulet.
What, are you busy, ho? Need you my help?
Juliet.
No, madam; we have culled such necessaries
As are behoveful° for our state° tomorrow.
So please you, let me now be left alone,
10 And let the nurse this night sit up with you;
For I am sure you have your hands full all
In this so sudden business.

6. *Lady Capulet is sometimes played here as loving and gentle with Juliet, perhaps suggesting that she is uneasy about her daughter's change of heart. What emotions should her next speech show?*
8. behoveful: suitable. **state:** ceremonies.

Lady Capulet.   Good night.
Get thee to bed, and rest; for thou hast need.

[*Exeunt* LADY CAPULET *and* NURSE.]

Juliet.
Farewell! God knows when we shall meet again.
15 I have a faint cold fear thrills through my veins
That almost freezes up the heat of life.
I'll call them back again to comfort me.
Nurse!—What should she do here?
My dismal scene I needs must act alone.
20 Come, vial.
What if this mixture do not work at all?

14. *Here is a fine example of the Shakespearean soliloquy, where a character is poised on the edge of action and thinks over its pros and cons. What are the fears and doubts that Juliet must consider before taking the potion?*
Juliet is not standing still as she delivers this speech. What do you think she is doing?

« Romeo, Romeo, Romeo, I drink to thee. »

Shall I be married then tomorrow morning?
No, no! This shall forbid it. Lie thou there.

[*Lays down a dagger.*]

What if it be a poison which the friar
25 Subtly hath ministered to have me dead,
Lest in this marriage he should be dishonored
Because he married me before to Romeo?
I fear it is; and yet methinks it should not,
For he hath still been tried° a holy man.
30 How if, when I am laid into the tomb,
I wake before the time that Romeo
Come to redeem me? There's a fearful point!
Shall I not then be stifled in the vault,
To whose foul mouth no healthsome air breathes in,
35 And there die strangled ere my Romeo comes?
Or, if I live, is it not very like
The horrible conceit of death and night,
Together with the terror of the place—
As in a vault, an ancient receptacle
40 Where for this many hundred years the bones
Of all my buried ancestors are packed;
Where bloody Tybalt, yet but green in earth,°
Lies fest'ring in his shroud; where, as they say,
At some hours in the night spirits resort—
45 Alack, alack, is it not like that I,
So early waking—what with loathsome smells,
And shrieks like mandrakes° torn out of the earth,
That living mortals, hearing them, run mad—
I, if I wake, shall I not be distraught,
50 Environèd with all these hideous fears,
And madly play with my forefathers' joints,
And pluck the mangled Tybalt from his shroud,
And, in this rage, with some great kinsman's bone
As with a club dash out my desp'rate brains?
55 O, look! Methinks I see my cousin's ghost
Seeking out Romeo, that did spit his body
Upon a rapier's point. Stay, Tybalt, stay!
Romeo, Romeo, Romeo, I drink to thee.

[*She falls upon her bed within the curtains.*]

29. still been tried: always been proved.

? **29.** *Audiences always wonder why the friar has not simply told the families of Romeo and Juliet's secret wedding, rather than involve them in such a dangerous plan. How does Juliet explain the friar's actions?*

42. green in earth: newly buried.

47. mandrakes: plants resembling the human body, which were said to grow beneath the gallows and to scream when torn up.

? **54.** *Draw the mental picture you have of the tomb from Juliet's description of it.*

Scene 4. *A hall in Capulet's house.*

Enter LADY CAPULET *and* NURSE.

Lady Capulet.
    Hold, take these keys and fetch more spices, nurse.
Nurse.
    They call for dates and quinces in the pastry.

[*Enter old* CAPULET.]

Capulet.
    Come, stir, stir, stir! The second cock hath crowed,
    The curfew bell hath rung, 'tis three o'clock.
5   Look to the baked meats, good Angelica;
    Spare not for cost.
Nurse.   Go, you cotquean,° go,
    Get you to bed! Faith, you'll be sick tomorrow
    For this night's watching.
Capulet.
    No, not a whit. What, I have watched ere now
10   All night for lesser cause, and ne'er been sick.
Lady Capulet.
    Ay, you have been a mouse hunt° in your time;
    But I will watch you from such watching now.
                [*Exeunt* LADY CAPULET *and* NURSE.]
Capulet.
    A jealous hood,° a jealous hood!

[*Enter three or four* FELLOWS *with spits and logs and
    baskets.*]
                Now, fellow,
    What is there?
First Fellow.
15   Things for the cook, sir; but I know not what.
Capulet.
    Make haste, make haste.   [*Exit* FIRST FELLOW.]
              Sirrah, fetch drier logs.
    Call Peter; he will show thee where they are.
Second Fellow.
    I have a head, sir, that will find out logs°
    And never trouble Peter for the matter.
Capulet.
20   Mass,° and well said; a merry whoreson, ha!
    Thou shalt be loggerhead.°
              [*Exit* SECOND FELLOW, *with the others.*]
              Good faith, 'tis day.

? **1.** *How does this peaceful domestic scene contrast with what has just happened? What is everyone preparing for?*

? **5.** Angelica *is the nurse's name. How does Lord Capulet treat her now, as opposed to how he treated her in Act III, Scene 5? What humor does the nurse add to this scene?*
  6. cotquean: old woman (a man who acts like an old woman).

11. mouse hunt: woman-chaser or night-prowler.
? **12.** *What is Lady Capulet's tone here?*

13. hood: female.

18. I . . . logs: in other words, "I have a wooden head."

20. Mass: mild oath, "by the Mass."
21. loggerhead: blockhead.
? **21.** *Capulet fusses around and has his nose in everything. What actions do you imagine the old man involved in, in this scene?*

The county will be here with music straight,
For so he said he would. (*Play music offstage.*)
                   I hear him near.
Nurse! Wife! What, ho! What, nurse, I say!

[*Enter* NURSE.]

25   Go waken Juliet; go and trim her up.
I'll go and chat with Paris. Hie, make haste,
Make haste! The bridegroom he is come already:
Make haste, I say.   [*Exit.*]

23. *The music is bridal music, for the wedding. What irony would the audience sense on hearing this music and knowing what has happened to Juliet?*

Scene 5. *Juliet's chamber.*

Nurse.
Mistress! What, mistress! Juliet! Fast,° I warrant her, she.
Why, lamb! Why, lady! Fie, you slugabed.
Why, love, I say! Madam; sweetheart! Why, bride!
What, not a word? You take your pennyworths° now;
5   Sleep for a week; for the next night, I warrant,
The County Paris hath set up his rest°
That you shall rest but little. God forgive me!
Marry, and amen. How sound is she asleep!
I needs must wake her. Madam, madam, madam!
10   Ay, let the county take you in your bed;
He'll fright you up, i' faith. Will it not be?

[*Draws aside the curtains.*]

What, dressed, and in your clothes, and down again?
I must needs wake you. Lady! Lady! Lady!
Alas, alas! Help, help! My lady's dead!
15   O weraday that ever I was born!
Some aqua vitae, ho! My lord! My lady!

[*Enter* LADY CAPULET.]

Lady Capulet.
What noise is here?
Nurse.   O lamentable day!
Lady Capulet.
What is the matter?
Nurse.   Look, look! O heavy day!
Lady Capulet.
O me, O me! My child, my only life!

1. Fast: fast asleep.
1. *As the nurse speaks to Juliet and to herself, she is busy arranging clothes, opening windows, and doing things around the room. In what line here does she touch Juliet and discover she is cold?*
4. pennyworths: small naps.
6. set up his rest: become firmly resolved.

20   Revive, look up, or I will die with thee!
      Help, help! Call help.

[*Enter* CAPULET.]

Capulet.
      For shame, bring Juliet forth; her lord is come.
Nurse.
      She's dead, deceased; she's dead, alack the day!
Lady Capulet.
      Alack the day, she's dead, she's dead, she's dead!
Capulet.
25   Ha! Let me see her. Out alas! She's cold,
      Her blood is settled, and her joints are stiff;
      Life and these lips have long been separated.
      Death lies on her like an untimely frost
      Upon the sweetest flower of all the field.

" Death lies on her like an untimely frost Upon the sweetest flower of all the field. "

---

29. *What actions are taking place on stage as the three actors now find Juliet "dead"?*

Nurse.
      O lamentable day!
30 **Lady Capulet.**   O woeful time!
Capulet.
      Death, that hath ta'en her hence to make me wail,
      Ties up my tongue and will not let me speak.

[*Enter* FRIAR LAURENCE *and* PARIS, *with* MUSICIANS.]

Friar.
      Come, is the bride ready to go to church?
Capulet.
      Ready to go, but never to return.
35   O son, the night before thy wedding day
      Hath Death lain with thy wife. There she lies,
      Flower as she was, deflowerèd by him.
      Death is my son-in-law, Death is my heir;
      My daughter he hath wedded. I will die
40   And leave him all. Life, living, all is Death's.
Paris.
      Have I thought, love, to see this morning's face,
      And doth it give me such a sight as this?

Lady Capulet.

　　Accursed, unhappy, wretched, hateful day!
　　Most miserable hour that e'er time saw
45　In lasting labor of his pilgrimage!
　　But one, poor one, one poor and loving child,
　　But one thing to rejoice and solace in,
　　And cruel Death hath catched it from my sight.

Nurse.

　　O woe! O woeful, woeful, woeful day!
50　Most lamentable day, most woeful day
　　That ever ever I did yet behold!
　　O day, O day, O day! O hateful day!
　　Never was seen so black a day as this.
　　O woeful day! O woeful day!

Paris.

55　Beguiled, divorcèd, wrongèd, spited, slain!
　　Most detestable Death, by thee beguiled,
　　By cruel, cruel thee quite overthrown.
　　O love! O life!—not life, but love in death!

Capulet.

　　Despised, distressèd, hated, martyred, killed!
60　Uncomfortable time, why cam'st thou now
　　To murder, murder our solemnity?
　　O child, O child! My soul, and not my child!
　　Dead art thou—alack, my child is dead,
　　And with my child my joys are burièd!

Friar.

65　Peace, ho, for shame! Confusion's cure lives not
　　In these confusions. Heaven and yourself
　　Had part in this fair maid—now heaven hath all,
　　And all the better is it for the maid.
　　Your part in her you could not keep from death,
70　But heaven keeps his part in eternal life.
　　The most you sought was her promotion,
　　For 'twas your heaven she should be advanced;
　　And weep ye now, seeing she is advanced
　　Above the clouds, as high as heaven itself?
75　O, in this love, you love your child so ill
　　That you run mad, seeing that she is well.°
　　She's not well married that lives married long,
　　But she's best married that dies married young.
　　Dry up your tears and stick your rosemary°
80　On this fair corse, and, as the custom is,
　　And in her best array bear her to church;
　　For though fond nature° bids us all lament,
　　Yet nature's tears are reason's merriment.

49. *Here again, as with Juliet's bemoaning Romeo's supposed death in an earlier scene, we have Lord and Lady Capulet and the nurse expressing anguish when we, the audience, know that Juliet is not dead. We listen to them, but we are not moved in the way they are. What words of the Capulets here suggest a loving concern for Juliet that seemed to be missing from earlier scenes? Which character enters and plays dumb about the whole situation?*

58. *In your opinion, what might all these people think caused Juliet's death?*

64. *These expressions of grief are by now sounding mechanical and repetitive. Shakespeare might have written them this way to prevent grief at a false death from gaining our sympathy. How could these lines of the parents, of the nurse, and of Paris also suggest that the speakers' feelings might not be very deep?*

65. *The friar, of course, knows that Juliet is drugged, not dead. His words here suggest that there has been great confusion on stage. What consolation does he offer, and what sharp rebuke does he give the adults?*

76. well: that is, she is in heaven.

79. rosemary: herb that stands for remembrance.
82. fond nature: foolish human nature.

83. *Why does the friar say that reason tells us to be merry about death?*

Capulet.
   All things that we ordainèd festival
85 Turn from their office to black funeral—
   Our instruments to melancholy bells,
   Our wedding cheer to a sad burial feast;
   Our solemn hymns to sullen dirges change;
   Our bridal flowers serve for a buried corse;
90 And all things change them to the contrary.
Friar.
   Sir, go you in; and, madam, go with him;
   And go, Sir Paris. Everyone prepare
   To follow this fair corse unto her grave.
   The heavens do lower° upon you for some ill;
95 Move them no more by crossing their high will.

[*Exeunt, casting rosemary on her and shutting the curtains. The* NURSE *and* MUSICIANS *remain.*]

First Musician.
   Faith, we may put up our pipes and be gone.
Nurse.
   Honest good fellows, ah, put up, put up!
   For well you know this is a pitiful case.   [*Exit.*]
First Musician.
   Ay, by my troth, the case may be amended.

[*Enter* PETER.]

100 **Peter.** Musicians, O, musicians, "Heart's ease,"
   "Heart's ease"! O, and you will have me live, play
   "Heart's ease."
   First Musician. Why "Heart's ease"?
   Peter. O, musicians, because my heart itself plays "My
105 heart is full." O, play me some merry dump° to comfort
   me.
   First Musician. Not a dump we! 'Tis no time to play
   now.
   Peter. You will not then?
110 **First Musician.** No.
   Peter. I will then give it you soundly.
   First Musician. What will you give us?
   Peter. No money, on my faith, but the gleek.° I will give
   you° the minstrel.
115 **First Musician.** Then will I give you the serving-
   creature.
   Peter. Then will I lay the serving-creature's dagger on
   your pate. I will carry° no crotchets. I'll re you, I'll fa
   you. Do you note me?

90. *Does Capulet express any guilt? Is he still self-centered?*

94. lower: frown.

98. *These are the nurse's last lines in the play. True to her character, she jokes as she leaves, though she might do this to cover her grief. The musicians are talking about the cases for their instruments. What "case" is the nurse referring to?*

105. dump: sad tune.

113. gleek: jeer or insult.
114. give you: call you (to be called a minstrel was an insult to a musician).

118. carry: endure.

120 **First Musician.** And you re us and fa us, you note us.

Second Musician. Pray you put up your dagger, and put out your wit. Then have at you with my wit!

Peter. I will dry-beat° you with an iron wit, and put up my iron dagger. Answer me like men.

125   "When griping grief the heart doth wound,
        And doleful dumps the mind oppress,
        Then music with her silver sound"—
     Why "silver sound"? Why "music with her silver sound"?
     What say you, Simon Catling?°

130 **First Musician.** Marry, sir, because silver hath a sweet sound.

Peter. Pretty! What say you, Hugh Rebeck?°

Second Musician. I say "silver sound" because musicians sound for silver.

135 **Peter.** Pretty too! What say you, James Soundpost?°

Third Musician. Faith, I know not what to say.

Peter. O, I cry you mercy,° you are the singer. I will say for you. It is "music with her silver sound" because musicians have no gold for sounding.°

140   "Then music with her silver sound
        With speedy help doth lend redress."   [*Exit.*]

First Musician. What a pestilent knave is this same!

Second Musician. Hang him, Jack! Come, we'll in here, tarry for the mourners, and stay dinner.

                                    [*Exit with others.*]

123. **dry-beat:** beat soundly.

129. **catling:** lute string.

132. **rebeck:** fiddle.

135. **soundpost:** peg on violinlike instrument.

137. **cry you mercy:** beg your pardon.

139. **no gold for sounding:** no money to jingle in their pockets.

? **144.** *Peter, who was always bossed about by the nurse, here has grabbed at the chance to boss the musicians, who are a step below him socially. Meanwhile, the stage behind them is being cleared of bedroom trappings. What actions do you imagine during this exchange of insults? (Note that they all want to stay for dinner.) How does this scene provide relief for us and remind us that ordinary life goes on amid tragedy?*

Shakespeare in the Video Store

Film and television have brought Shakespeare's plays to millions of viewers and confirmed the playwright's position as a world treasure. *Hamlet* has been by far the most popular of his plays, with forty-seven film versions of all or part of the tragedy (as of 1994). The earliest *Hamlet* movie was made in Paris in 1900. This black-and-white silent film had an interesting reversal of the custom of Shakespeare's time, in which boys took women's roles on stage: The role of Hamlet was played by the great Sarah Bernhardt (1844–1923).

For almost a century, film productions of Shakespeare have showcased some of our most distinguished actors: Laurence Olivier, Vanessa Redgrave, Richard Burton, John Gielgud, Katharine Hepburn, Mel Gibson, Glenn Close, Denzel Washington. Between 1978 and 1985, a partnership between the British Broadcasting Corporation (BBC) and Time Warner, Inc., completed the ambitious project of filming all of Shakespeare's plays for television. Now Shakespeare is accessible as never before: A performance of one of his plays is as near as your local video store.

But critics have pointed out drawbacks in the performance of these plays on screen. For example, they argue that film controls our perceptions of the plays and deprives us of the tension we feel when seeing the plays live, in the theater. Film and television productions of Shakespearean comedy are at another disadvantage, since the actors can't respond to the feedback of a live audience. Such feedback is unpredictable, but actors say it's critical in comedy.

Not every Shakespeare movie has had celebrity performers. An outstanding example of a director's success with young unknown actors is Franco Zeffirelli's film *Romeo and Juliet* (1968). A comparison between the film script and the play's text shows the great extent to which the camera does in film what dialogue does onstage: Zeffirelli retained only about a third of Shakespeare's lines. He made other changes as well. Some lines are rearranged within scenes, and a few episodes—for example, the apothecary scene and the death of Paris—are dropped altogether.

The changes in the text of *Romeo and Juliet* are controversial, but most critics have agreed that the fiery, youthful passion of Zeffirelli's film faithfully catches the spirit of Shakespeare's play. The film is stunningly beautiful, in part because of the attractive young actors—Leonard Whiting as Romeo and Olivia Hussey as Juliet—and in part because of the dark beauty of the Italian hill towns Zeffirelli used as a setting for the tragedy. Three decades later, Zeffirelli's film is widely acknowledged to represent Shakespeare on screen at its best.

First Thoughts

1. Why is Juliet so willing to trust the friar's plan? Would you be willing to?

Shaping Interpretations

2. One of the pleasures of watching a play is knowing something that a character on stage does not know. This use of **dramatic irony** makes us feel **suspense**. We wait anxiously to find out what will happen when the characters discover what we already know. Where do you feel dramatic irony in Scenes 2, 3, and 4?

3. What terrible trials does Juliet face in this act? How does she respond to these challenges?

4. What do Juliet's responses tell you about her **character**?

5. Juliet's parents are the **blocking figures** in the play—their plans for Juliet make it seem impossible for the young couple to stay together. Does Shakespeare present the Capulets as bad characters? Or does he help us see them as complex human beings, not as mere stage villains? Explain your feelings.

Reviewing the Text

a. In Scene 1, what does Juliet threaten to do if the friar cannot help her?

b. What is the friar's plan for getting Romeo and Juliet together?

c. In Scene 2, another major problem comes up: What change does Capulet make in the wedding plans?

d. What is the situation in the Capulet house at the end of Act IV?

CHOICES: Building Your Portfolio

Writer's Notebook

1. Collecting Ideas for an Informative Report

Finding a topic. As you search for a topic for the informative report you'll write in the Writer's Workshop on page 870, you might be inspired by issues in the play that remind you of real-life situations today. Racial or ethnic hatreds often divide people and lead to tragedy,

especially for the young and innocent who did not create the antagonisms but were just born into them. You might think of problems in places like Northern Ireland, Eastern Europe, the Middle East— even in the United States, where racial animosities still cause tragedy. Jot down some examples of ethnic or racial or religious animosities you're aware of. Could one of these give you a topic for a report? (Be sure to read the articles on pages 856 and 862.)

Creative Writing

2. Juliet's Thoughts

Write down Juliet's thoughts as you imagine them during this difficult time. (You could write as *I*.) Write about her feelings toward her parents, Romeo, her nurse, Paris, and Friar Laurence. Let Juliet describe her feelings about the drug she is about to take and about her horror of being buried alive.

BECOMING A STRATEGIC READER

Paraphrasing and Context Clues

Paraphrasing means restating a text in your own words. A restatement or paraphrase simplifies a text, but it doesn't necessarily make it shorter. In fact, a paraphrase might be longer than the original passage, and of course it's never as interesting. Paraphrasing is a good way to check on your understanding of the original text. Here is a speech from *Romeo and Juliet* and a paraphrase:

> **Paris.**
> My father Capulet will
>   have it so,
> And I am nothing slow to
>   slack his haste.
>   —Scene 1, lines 2–3

Paraphrase: My father-in-law Capulet wants it like that, and I'm not going to slow him down.

A Checklist for Paraphrasing

✓ Be sure you understand the main idea of the text.
✓ Look up unfamiliar words.
✓ Replace difficult words with simple ones.
✓ Restate figures of speech in your own words, clarifying what's being compared with what.
✓ Try to reproduce the tone or mood of the text. If the text is satiric, the paraphrase should also be satiric.
✓ Be sure your paraphrase has accounted for all details in the original.

Try It Out

Paraphrase each speech below. Be sure to compare your paraphrases in class. It's almost certain that no two paraphrases will be alike.

1. **Paris.**
   Immoderately she weeps for Tybalt's
       death,
   And therefore have I little talked of love;
   For Venus smiles not in a house of tears.
           —Scene 1, lines 6–8

2. **Juliet** (*to the Friar*).
   Be not so long to speak. I long to die
   If what thou speak'st speak not of
       remedy.
               —Scene 1, lines 66–67

3. **Friar Laurence** (*to Juliet*).
   The roses in thy lips and cheeks shall
       fade
   To wanny ashes, thy eyes' windows fall
   Like death when he shuts up the day of
       life. . . .
               —Scene 1, lines 99–101

4. **Juliet** (*holding the poison*).
   O, look! Methinks I see my cousin's
       ghost
   Seeking out Romeo, that did spit his
       body
   Upon a rapier's point. Stay, Tybalt, stay!
               —Scene 3, lines 55–57

ACT V

Scene 1. *Mantua. A street.*

Enter ROMEO.

Romeo.
If I may trust the flattering truth of sleep,
My dreams presage° some joyful news at hand.
My bosom's lord° sits lightly in his throne,
And all this day an unaccustomed spirit
5   Lifts me above the ground with cheerful thoughts.
I dreamt my lady came and found me dead
(Strange dream that gives a dead man leave to think!)
And breathed such life with kisses in my lips
That I revived and was an emperor.
10 Ah me! How sweet is love itself possessed,
When but love's shadows° are so rich in joy!

[*Enter Romeo's man* BALTHASAR, *booted from riding.*]

News from Verona! How now, Balthasar?
Dost thou not bring me letters from the friar?
How doth my lady? Is my father well?
15 How fares my Juliet? That I ask again,
For nothing can be ill if she be well.
Balthasar.
Then she is well, and nothing can be ill.
Her body sleeps in Capel's monument,
And her immortal part with angels lives.
20 I saw her laid low in her kindred's vault
And presently took post° to tell it you.
O, pardon me for bringing these ill news,
Since you did leave it for my office,° sir.
Romeo.
Is it e'en so? Then I defy you, stars!
25 Thou knowest my lodging. Get me ink and paper
And hire post horses. I will hence tonight.
Balthasar.
I do beseech you, sir, have patience.
Your looks are pale and wild and do import
Some misadventure.
Romeo.   Tush, thou art deceived.
30 Leave me and do the thing I bid thee do.
Hast thou no letters to me from the friar?
Balthasar.
No, my good lord.

---

2. presage: foretell.
3. bosom's lord: heart.

11. shadows: dreams.

? **16.** *Some actors playing Romeo reveal in this line that they suspect bad news. What, meanwhile, would Balthasar be doing?*

21. post: post horse (horse kept at an inn and rented by travelers).

23. office: duty.
? **23.** *Balthasar must show that he dreads giving his master the tragic news. What do we know that Balthasar does not know?*

? **26.** *Some actors move away here, or hide their faces in their hands. Romeo could address the stars or fate defiantly or tonelessly, to suggest defeat. What would you say is Romeo's tone here?*

? **29.** *What does Balthasar suggest Romeo looks like, even though he pretends to be calm?*

? **31.** *What letter is Romeo waiting for?*

Romeo.   No matter. Get thee gone.
And hire those horses. I'll be with thee straight.

> [*Exit* BALTHASAR.]

Well, Juliet, I will lie with thee tonight.
35   Let's see for means. O mischief, thou art swift
To enter in the thoughts of desperate men!
I do remember an apothecary,
And hereabouts 'a dwells, which late I noted
In tattered weeds,° with overwhelming° brows,
40   Culling of simples.° Meager were his looks,
Sharp misery had worn him to the bones;
And in his needy shop a tortoise hung,
An alligator stuffed, and other skins
Of ill-shaped fishes; and about his shelves
45   A beggarly account° of empty boxes,
Green earthen pots, bladders, and musty seeds,
Remnants of packthread, and old cakes of roses
Were thinly scattered, to make up a show.
Noting this penury,° to myself I said,
50   "And if a man did need a poison now
Whose sale is present death in Mantua,
Here lives a caitiff° wretch would sell it him."
O, this same thought did but forerun my need,
And this same needy man must sell it me.
55   As I remember, this should be the house.
Being holiday, the beggar's shop is shut.
What, ho! Apothecary!

« O mischief, thou art swift
To enter in the thoughts of desperate men! »

[*Enter* APOTHECARY.]

Apothecary.   Who calls so loud?
Romeo.
Come hither, man. I see that thou art poor.
Hold, there is forty ducats. Let me have
60   A dram of poison, such soon-speeding gear°
As will disperse itself through all the veins
That the life-weary taker may fall dead,
And that the trunk° may be discharged of breath
As violently as hasty powder fired
65   Doth hurry from the fatal cannon's womb.

34. *This line is spoken in a still, quiet moment. After a pause, what does Romeo immediately set out to do? Does he hesitate at all to consider his course of action, or does he plunge into it?*
39. weeds: clothes. **overwhelming:** overhanging.
40. simples: herbs.

45. account: number.

49. penury: poverty.

52. caitiff: miserable.

57. *What actions do you imagine Romeo is engaged in as he delivers this speech about the apothecary?*

60. gear: stuff.

63. trunk: body.

Apothecary.
Such mortal drugs I have; but Mantua's law
Is death to any he that utters° them.

Romeo.
Art thou so bare and full of wretchedness
And fear'st to die? Famine is in thy cheeks,
70   Need and oppression starveth in thy eyes,
Contempt and beggary hangs upon thy back:
The world is not thy friend, nor the world's law;
The world affords no law to make thee rich;
Then be not poor, but break it and take this.

Apothecary.
75   My poverty but not my will consents.

Romeo.
I pay thy poverty and not thy will.

Apothecary.
Put this in any liquid thing you will
And drink it off, and if you had the strength
Of twenty men, it would dispatch you straight.

Romeo.
80   There is thy gold—worse poison to men's souls,
Doing more murder in this loathsome world,
Than these poor compounds that thou mayst not sell.
I sell thee poison; thou has sold me none.
Farewell. Buy food and get thyself in flesh.
85   Come, cordial and not poison, go with me
To Juliet's grave; for there must I use thee.   [*Exeunt.*]

Scene 2. *Friar Laurence's cell.*

Enter FRIAR JOHN.

John.
Holy Franciscan friar, brother, ho!

[*Enter* FRIAR LAURENCE.]

Laurence.
This same should be the voice of Friar John.
Welcome from Mantua. What says Romeo?
Or, if his mind be writ, give me his letter.

John.
5   Going to find a barefoot brother out,
One of our order, to associate° me
Here in this city visiting the sick,
And finding him, the searchers° of the town,
Suspecting that we both were in a house

67. utters: sells.

74. *What argument does Romeo use to persuade the apothecary to break the law?*

79. *What actions do you think have taken place before the apothecary gives Romeo instructions for taking the poison?*

83. *What "poison" has Romeo "sold" the apothecary?*

86. *Why does Romeo call the poison a cordial, which is a kind of medicine that restores the heartbeat?*

3. *In the previous scene, we learned that Romeo had received no letters from the friar. How would the friar's question immediately put questions in the minds of the audience?*

6. associate: accompany.

8. searchers: health officers.

10   Where the infectious pestilence did reign,
        Scaled up the doors, and would not let us forth,
        So that my speed to Mantua there was stayed.
Laurence.
        Who bare my letter, then, to Romeo?
John.
        I could not send it—here it is again—
15   Nor get a messenger to bring it thee,
        So fearful were they of infection.
Laurence.
        Unhappy fortune! By my brotherhood,
        The letter was not nice,° but full of charge,°
        Of dear import; and the neglecting it
20   May do much danger. Friar John, go hence,
        Get me an iron crow and bring it straight
        Unto my cell.
John.   Brother, I'll go and bring it thee.   [*Exit.*]
Laurence.
        Now must I to the monument alone.
        Within this three hours will fair Juliet wake.
25   She will beshrew me much that Romeo
        Hath had no notice of these accidents;°
        But I will write again to Mantua,
        And keep her at my cell till Romeo come—
        Poor living corse, closed in a dead man's tomb!   [*Exit.*]

Scene 3. *A churchyard; in it, a monument belonging to the Capulets.*

Enter PARIS *and his* PAGE *with flowers and scented water.*

Paris.
        Give me thy torch, boy. Hence, and stand aloof.
        Yet put it out, for I would not be seen.
        Under yond yew trees lay thee all along,°
        Holding the ear close to the hollow ground.
5   So shall no foot upon the churchyard tread
        (Being loose, unfirm, with digging up of graves)
        But thou shalt hear it. Whistle then to me,
        As signal that thou hear'st something approach.
        Give me those flowers. Do as I bid thee, go.
Page (*aside*).
10   I am almost afraid to stand alone
        Here in the churchyard; yet I will adventure.°
                                        [*Retires.*]

16. *Another accident! Why was the friar's letter never delivered to Romeo?*

18. nice: trivial. **charge:** importance.

26. accidents: happenings.

29. *If we can accept the "accidents of fate," we have here something like a chase scene. We know, but the friar does not, that Romeo also is on his way to the tomb. Why is it essential that the friar get there first?*

3. all along: at full length (on the ground).

9. *Paris is a surprise. He adds an interesting complication, as well as some action, to this scene. He and his servant, probably wearing dark cloaks, enter on the upper stage. Paris makes his way down alone into the tomb or vault. Why is Paris here?*
11. adventure: risk it.

Paris.
  Sweet flower, with flowers thy bridal bed I strew
      (O woe! thy canopy is dust and stones)
  Which with sweet water nightly I will dew;
15   Or, wanting that, with tears distilled by moans.
  The obsequies° that I for thee will keep
  Nightly shall be to strew thy grave and weep.

[BOY *whistles.*]

  The boy gives warning something doth approach.
  What cursèd foot wanders this way tonight
20 To cross° my obsequies and true love's rite?
  What, with a torch? Muffle° me, night, awhile.
                                        [*Retires.*]

[*Enter* ROMEO *and* BALTHASAR *with a torch, a mattock,
and a crowbar of iron.*]

Romeo.
  Give me that mattock and the wrenching iron.
  Hold, take this letter. Early in the morning
  See thou deliver it to my lord and father.
25 Give me the light. Upon thy life I charge thee,
  Whate'er thou hearest or see'st, stand all aloof
  And do not interrupt me in my course.
  Why I descend into this bed of death
  Is partly to behold my lady's face,
30 But chiefly to take thence from her dead finger
  A precious ring—a ring that I must use
  In dear employment.° Therefore hence, be gone.
  But if thou, jealous,° dost return to pry
  In what I farther shall intend to do,
35 By heaven, I will tear thee joint by joint
  And strew this hungry churchyard with thy limbs.
  The time and my intents are savage-wild,
  More fierce and more inexorable far
  Than empty tigers or the roaring sea.
Balthasar.
40 I will be gone, sir, and not trouble ye.
Romeo.
  So shalt thou show me friendship. Take thou that.
  Live, and be prosperous; and farewell, good fellow.
Balthasar (*aside*).
  For all this same, I'll hide me hereabout.
  His looks I fear, and his intents I doubt.   [*Retires.*]
Romeo.
45 Thou detestable maw,° thou womb of death,
  Gorged with the dearest morsel of the earth,

13. *In Shakespeare's theater, we would see a tomb at the rear of the stage. Juliet's body, in its burial gown, would be placed in this tomb, on top of a raised structure. Tybalt's body would lie nearby. What atmosphere must be suggested in this scene? How would lighting be used on a modern stage to create such an atmosphere?*
16. obsequies: observances or rituals.
20. cross: interrupt.
21. Muffle: hide.

22. *Paris enters with flowers and perfumed water, but Romeo enters with iron tools—a mattock, which is something like a hoe, and a crowbar. Like Paris, Romeo and his servant enter at the upper level. What strange excuse does Romeo give his servant for wanting to descend into the tomb alone?*

32. dear employment: important business.
33. jealous: curious.

39. *Romeo makes sure his servant will not interrupt him. What do the last three lines tell about his state of mind?*

45. maw: mouth.

Thus I enforce thy rotten jaws to open,
And in despite° I'll cram thee with more food.

[ROMEO *opens the tomb.*]

Paris.

This is that banished haughty Montague
50 That murd'red my love's cousin—with which grief
It is supposed the fair creature died
And here is come to do some villainous shame
To the dead bodies. I will apprehend him.
Stop thy unhallowèd toil, vile Montague!
55 Can vengeance be pursued further than death?
Condemnèd villain, I do apprehend thee.
Obey, and go with me; for thou must die.

Romeo.

I must indeed; and therefore came I hither.
Good gentle youth, tempt not a desp'rate man.
60 Fly hence and leave me. Think upon these gone;
Let them affright thee. I beseech thee, youth,
Put not another sin upon my head
By urging me to fury. O, be gone!
By heaven, I love thee better than myself,
65 For I come hither armed against myself.
Stay not, be gone. Live, and hereafter say
A madman's mercy bid thee run away.

Paris.

I do defy thy conjurations°
And apprehend thee for a felon here.

Romeo.

70 Wilt thou provoke me? Then have at thee, boy!

[*They fight.*]

Page.

O Lord, they fight! I will go call the watch.

[*Exit.* PARIS *falls.*]

Paris.

O, I am slain! If thou be merciful,
Open the tomb, lay me with Juliet.   [*Dies.*]

Romeo.

In faith, I will. Let me peruse this face.
75 Mercutio's kinsman, noble County Paris!
What said my man when my betossèd soul
Did not attend° him as we rode? I think
He told me Paris should have married Juliet.
Said he not so, or did I dream it so?
80 Or am I mad, hearing him talk of Juliet,
To think it was so? O, give me thy hand,
One writ with me in sour misfortune's book!

48. **in despite:** to spite you.
48. *Whom or what is Romeo talking to here? What is he doing? What "food" is he going to feed this "mouth"?*

51. *What was believed to be the cause of Juliet's sudden "death"?*

54. *What does Paris do as he speaks this line?*

67. *Romeo doesn't attempt even to fight Paris. How do his words here show calmness and maturity?*
68. **conjurations:** solemn orders.

70. *What has Paris done to provoke Romeo?*

74. *Whatever we thought of Paris before, we understand now that he loved Juliet. What does Romeo do here?*
77. **attend:** pay attention to.

82. *Romeo has spoken of himself as "fortune's fool." Why does he see Paris as another victim?*

I'll bury thee in a triumphant grave.
A grave? O, no, a lanthorn,° slaught'red youth,
85   For here lies Juliet, and her beauty makes
This vault a feasting presence full of light.
Death, lie thou there, by a dead man interred.

[*Lays him in the tomb.*]

How oft when men are at the point of death
Have they been merry! Which their keepers° call
90   A lightning before death. O, how may I
Call this a lightning? O my love, my wife!
Death, that hath sucked the honey of thy breath,
Hath had no power yet upon thy beauty.
Thou art not conquered. Beauty's ensign° yet
95   Is crimson in thy lips and in thy cheeks,
And death's pale flag is not advancèd there.
Tybalt, liest thou there in the bloody sheet?
O, what more favor can I do to thee
Than with that hand that cut thy youth in twain
100   To sunder his that was thine enemy?
Forgive me, cousin! Ah, dear Juliet,
Why art thou yet so fair? Shall I believe
That unsubstantial Death is amorous,
And that the lean abhorrèd monster keeps
105   Thee here in dark to be his paramour?
For fear of that I still will stay with thee
And never from this pallet of dim night
Depart again. Here, here will I remain
With worms that are thy chambermaids. O, here
110   Will I set up my everlasting rest
And shake the yoke of inauspicious stars
From this world-wearied flesh. Eyes, look your last!
Arms, take your last embrace! And, lips, O you
The doors of breath, seal with a righteous kiss
115   A dateless° bargain to engrossing° death!
Come, bitter conduct;° come, unsavory guide!
Thou desperate pilot,° now at once run on
The dashing rocks thy seasick weary bark!
Here's to my love! (*Drinks.*) O true apothecary!
120   Thy drugs are quick. Thus with a kiss I die.

[*Falls.*]

[*Enter* FRIAR LAURENCE, *with lanthorn, crowbar, and
spade.*]

Friar.

Saint Francis be my speed! How oft tonight
Have my old feet stumbled at graves! Who's there?

---

84. lanthorn: a windowed dome.

? 87. *Romeo, dragging Paris's body across the stage, now sees Juliet. What words indicate that he sees the tomb transformed? Who is the "dead man" in line 87?*

89. keepers: jailers.

94. ensign: flag (signal).

? 97. *Romeo turns to see Tybalt's body. Is he angry at his enemy, or does he ask forgiveness?*

? 102. *Where in this speech does Romeo see life in Juliet, reminding us that she is not dead?*

? 108. *Romeo has climbed to Juliet's tomb and lies beside her. What other actions do you see him doing here?*

115. dateless: timeless. **engrossing:** all-encompassing.
116. conduct: guide (the poison).
117. desperate pilot: Romeo himself.

? 120. *Actors playing Romeo interpret this last speech in different ways: Some play him as if he is in a dream; others as if he were mad; others as if he is in full control of himself; others as if he is desperate and out of his mind with grief, desire, and fear. What clues would direct the way you'd interpret Romeo's feelings as he gives his final speech?*

Balthasar.

Here's one, a friend, and one that knows you well.

Friar.

Bliss be upon you! Tell me, good my friend,
125   What torch is yond that vainly lends his light
To grubs and eyeless skulls? As I discern,
It burneth in the Capels' monument.

Balthasar.

It doth so, holy sir; and there's my master,
One that you love.

Friar.   Who is it?

Balthasar.   Romeo.

Friar.

How long hath he been there?

130 **Balthasar.**   Full half an hour.

Friar.

Go with me to the vault.

Balthasar.   I dare not, sir.
My master knows not but I am gone hence,
And fearfully did menace me with death
If I did stay to look on his intents.

Friar.

135   Stay then; I'll go alone. Fear comes upon me.
O, much I fear some ill unthrifty° thing.

? **130.** *What feelings must the friar reveal when he hears that Romeo has gotten to the tomb before he has heard of the plan to drug Juliet?*

136. unthrifty: unlucky.

« Ah, dear Juliet, Why art thou yet so fair? »

Balthasar.
　　As I did sleep under this yew tree here,
　　I dreamt my master and another fought,
　　And that my master slew him.
Friar. 　　　　　　　　　　Romeo!
140　Alack, alack, what blood is this which stains
　　The stony entrance of this sepulcher?
　　What mean these masterless and gory swords
　　To lie discolored by this place of peace?

[*Enters the tomb.*]

　　Romeo! O, pale! Who else? What, Paris too?
145　And steeped in blood? Ah, what an unkind° hour
　　Is guilty of this lamentable chance!
　　The lady stirs.

[JULIET *rises.*]

Juliet.
　　O comfortable° friar! Where is my lord?
　　I do remember well where I should be,
150　And there I am. Where is my Romeo?
Friar.
　　I hear some noise. Lady, come from that nest
　　Of death, contagion, and unnatural sleep.
　　A greater power than we can contradict
　　Hath thwarted our intents. Come, come away.
155　Thy husband in thy bosom there lies dead;
　　And Paris too. Come, I'll dispose of thee
　　Among a sisterhood of holy nuns.
　　Stay not to question, for the watch is coming.
　　Come, go, good Juliet. I dare no longer stay.
Juliet.
160　Go, get thee hence, for I will not away.

　　　　　　　　　　　　　　　　[*Exit* FRIAR.]

　　What's here? A cup, closed in my truelove's hand?
　　Poison, I see, hath been his timeless° end.
　　O churl!° Drunk all, and left no friendly drop
　　To help me after? I will kiss thy lips.
165　Haply some poison yet doth hang on them
　　To make me die with a restorative.

[*Kisses him.*]

　　Thy lips are warm!
Chief Watchman (*within*). Lead, boy. Which way?
Juliet.
　　Yea, noise? Then I'll be brief. O happy° dagger!

[*Snatches Romeo's dagger.*]

141. *Where is the friar as he discovers the bloodstains?*

145. unkind: unnatural.

147. *This short line suggests that the friar rushes to Juliet and waits for her to speak. What must his feelings be?*

148. comfortable: comforting.

152. *For the friar, this is a terrible moment. What is his reaction to the noise he hears?*

159. *What does the friar say will become of Juliet? What is Juliet doing, or refusing to do, as the friar repeatedly tries to move her?*

160. *It is hard to believe that after all his concern for these two young lovers, the friar would become a coward at this moment and leave Juliet to harm herself. How must the friar act here to persuade us that he is frantic and not very sensible?*

162. timeless: untimely.
163. churl: rude fellow (spoken tcasingly).

169. happy: lucky (to be here when she needs it).

« *O happy dagger!*
This is thy sheath; there rust, and let me die. »

170   This is thy sheath; there rust, and let me die.

[*She stabs herself and falls.*]

[*Enter Paris's* BOY *and* WATCH.]

Boy.
    This is the place. There, where the torch doth burn.
Chief Watchman.
    The ground is bloody. Search about the churchyard.
    Go, some of you; whoe'er you find attach.
                          [*Exeunt some of the* WATCH.]
    Pitiful sight! Here lies the county slain;
175   And Juliet bleeding, warm, and newly dead,
    Who here hath lain this two days burièd.
    Go, tell the prince; run to the Capulets;
    Raise up the Montagues; some others search.
                          [*Exeunt others of the* WATCH.]
    We see the ground whereon these woes do lie,
180   But the true ground° of all these piteous woes
    We cannot without circumstance° descry.

[*Enter some of the* WATCH, *with Romeo's man* BALTHASAR.]

Second Watchman.
    Here's Romeo's man. We found him in the churchyard.
Chief Watchman.
    Hold him in safety till the prince come hither.

[*Enter* FRIAR LAURENCE *and another* WATCHMAN.]

Third Watchman.
    Here is a friar that trembles, sighs, and weeps.
185   We took this mattock and this spade from him
    As he was coming from this churchyard's side.
Chief Watchman.
    A great suspicion! Stay the friar too.

[*Enter the* PRINCE *and* ATTENDANTS.]

Prince.
    What misadventure is so early up,
    That calls our person from our morning rest?

[*Enter* CAPULET *and his wife,* LADY CAPULET, *with others.*]

Capulet.
190   What should it be, that is so shrieked abroad?
Lady Capulet.
    O, the people in the street cry "Romeo,"
    Some "Juliet," and some "Paris"; and all run
    With open outcry toward our monument.

Stage direction: *Do you see Juliet in her last moments as being half-crazed, or calm and purposeful, or something else? Do you think this scene can be played only one way? Or can it be played several ways? How would you play the scene?*

180. **ground:** cause.
181. **circumstance:** details.

184. *How do the watchman's words help us picture the state the friar is in?*

193. *As the tomb begins to fill up with people, noises and cries are heard offstage. What does Lady Capulet suggest is being "shrieked abroad" in Verona?*

Prince.
　　What fear is this which startles in your ears?
Chief Watchman.
195　　Sovereign, here lies the County Paris slain;
　　And Romeo dead; and Juliet, dead before,
　　Warm and new killed.
Prince.
　　Search, seek, and know how this foul murder comes.
Chief Watchman.
　　Here is a friar, and slaughtered Romeo's man,
200　　With instruments upon them fit to open
　　These dead men's tombs.
Capulet.
　　O heavens! O wife, look how our daughter bleeds!
　　This dagger hath mista'en, for, lo, his house°
　　Is empty on the back of Montague,
205　　And it missheathèd in my daughter's bosom!
Lady Capulet.
　　O me, this sight of death is as a bell
　　That warns° my old age to a sepulcher.

[*Enter* MONTAGUE *and others.*]

Prince.
　　Come, Montague; for thou art early up
　　To see thy son and heir more early down.
Montague.
210　　Alas, my liege, my wife is dead tonight!
　　Grief of my son's exile hath stopped her breath.
　　What further woe conspires against mine age?
Prince.
　　Look, and thou shalt see.
Montague.
　　O thou untaught! What manners is in this,
215　　To press before thy father to a grave?
Prince.
　　Seal up the mouth of outrage for a while,
　　Till we can clear these ambiguities
　　And know their spring, their head, their true descent;
　　And then will I be general of your woes°
220　　And lead you even to death. Meantime forbear,
　　And let mischance be slave to patience.
　　Bring forth the parties of suspicion.
Friar.
　　I am the greatest, able to do least,
　　Yet most suspected, as the time and place
225　　Doth make against me, of this direful murder;
　　And here I stand, both to impeach and purge°
　　Myself condemnèd and myself excused.

203. **house:** sheath.

207. **warns:** summons.

? **215.** *Whom is Montague talking to here?*

219. **general of your woes:** leader of your mourning.

226. **impeach and purge:** charge and punish.

Prince.

    Then say at once what thou dost know in this.

Friar.

    I will be brief, for my short date of breath°
230 Is not so long as is a tedious tale.
    Romeo, there dead, was husband to that Juliet;
    And she, there dead, that Romeo's faithful wife.
    I married them; and their stolen marriage day
    Was Tybalt's doomsday, whose untimely death
235 Banished the new-made bridegroom from this city;
    For whom, and not for Tybalt, Juliet pined.
    You, to remove that siege of grief from her,
    Betrothed and would have married her perforce
    To County Paris. Then comes she to me
240 And with wild looks bid me devise some mean
    To rid her from this second marriage,
    Or in my cell there would she kill herself.
    Then gave I her (so tutored by my art)
    A sleeping potion; which so took effect
245 As I intended, for it wrought on her
    The form of death. Meantime I writ to Romeo
    That he should hither come as° this dire night
    To help to take her from her borrowed grave,
    Being the time the potion's force should cease.
250 But he which bore my letter, Friar John,
    Was stayed by accident, and yesternight
    Returned my letter back. Then all alone
    At the prefixèd hour of her waking
    Came I to take her from her kindred's vault,
255 Meaning to keep her closely at my cell
    Till I conveniently could send to Romeo.
    But when I came, some minute ere the time
    Of her awakening, here untimely lay
    The noble Paris and true Romeo dead.
260 She wakes; and I entreated her come forth
    And bear this work of heaven with patience;
    But then a noise did scare me from the tomb,
    And she, too desperate, would not go with me,
    But, as it seems, did violence on herself.
265 All this I know, and to the marriage
    Her nurse is privy;° and if aught in this
    Miscarried by my fault, let my old life
    Be sacrificed some hour before his time
    Unto the rigor of severest law.

Prince.

270 We still° have known thee for a holy man.
    Where's Romeo's man? What can he say to this?

---

229. date of breath: term of life.

? **230.** *All of what the friar says here is known by the audience. In some productions, this long speech is cut entirely, but it is important for us to imagine the effect the speech has on the Montagues, the Capulets, and the prince. This is the moment when they discover what we've known all along. Where do you think the friar must pause as the families cry out and weep?*

? **237.** *Whom does the friar mean by "you"?*

247. as: on.

? **261.** *This line expresses the friar's view of life. How would the play have been different if both Romeo and Juliet had been able, from the start, to bear their trials "with patience"? How does this also apply to the adults in the play?*

266. to the marriage . . . privy: The nurse knows about the marriage.

? **269.** *Does the friar accept responsibility for his part in the tragedy? What does he say?*

270. still: always.

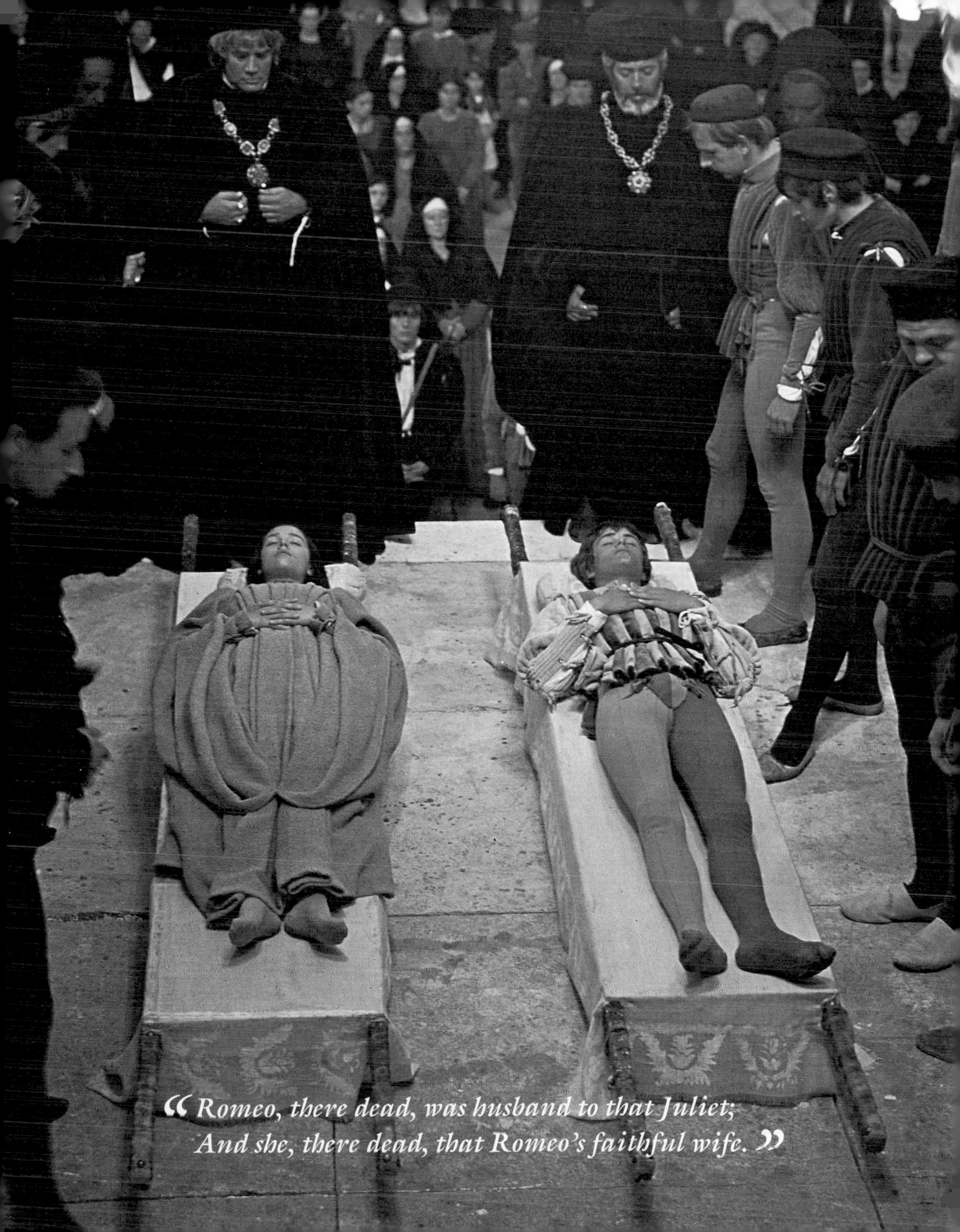

Romeo, there dead, was husband to that Juliet;
And she, there dead, that Romeo's faithful wife.

Balthasar.
I brought my master news of Juliet's death;
And then in post he came from Mantua
To this same place, to this same monument.
275 This letter he early bid me give his father,
And threat'ned me with death, going in the vault,
If I departed not and left him there.
Prince.
Give me the letter. I will look on it.
Where is the county's page that raised the watch?
280 Sirrah, what made your master in this place?
Boy.
He came with flowers to strew his lady's grave;
And bid me stand aloof, and so I did.
Anon comes one with light to ope the tomb;
And by and by my master drew on him;
285 And then I ran away to call the watch.
Prince.
This letter doth make good the friar's words,
Their course of love, the tidings of her death;
And here he writes that he did buy a poison
Of a poor pothecary and therewithal
290 Came to this vault to die and lie with Juliet.
Where be these enemies? Capulet, Montague,
See what a scourge is laid upon your hate,
That heaven finds means to kill your joys with love,
And I, for winking at° your discords too,
295 Have lost a brace° of kinsmen. All are punished.

> **?** **285.** *What would the families be doing as the prince now pauses to read the letter?*

> **294. winking at:** closing his eyes to.
> **295. brace:** pair (Mercutio and Paris).
> **?** **295.** *We have been repeatedly reminded of the role of fate in this tragedy, but the human characters also admit their responsibility. What does the prince admit? Do you think that some people have been punished too harshly and some not severely enough?*

« . . . See what a scourge is laid upon your hate,
That heaven finds means to kill your joys with love. . . . »

Capulet.
O brother Montague, give me thy hand.
This is my daughter's jointure,° for no more
Can I demand.

> **297. jointure:** property passed on to a woman after her husband's death.

Montague.　　　But I can give thee more;
　　　　For I will raise her statue in pure gold,
300　　　That whiles Verona by that name is known,
　　　　There shall no figure at such rate° be set
　　　　As that of true and faithful Juliet.
Capulet.
　　　　As rich shall Romeo's by his lady's lie—
　　　　Poor sacrifices of our enmity!
Prince.
305　　　A glooming peace this morning with it brings.
　　　　　The sun for sorrow will not show his head.
　　　　Go hence, to have more talk of these sad things;
　　　　　Some shall be pardoned, and some punishèd;
　　　　For never was a story of more woe
310　　　Than this of Juliet and her Romeo. [*Exeunt omnes.*]

**❝ . . . For never was a story of more woe
Than this of Juliet and her Romeo. ❞**

---

301. rate: value.

? **304.** *The central focus on stage now is not the families, but the bodies of Romeo and Juliet. Over the bodies of their children, the families join hands. What words of Capulet's admit his part in the tragedy?*

? **310.** *As the actors solemnly file out, the friar is usually the last to exit. Some productions have the fathers leave last. At times, the nurse reappears and makes the final exit. What different effects would be produced by having different characters be the last to leave the stage? Which one would you have exit last?*
　　Finally, only the bodies are left on stage. Can you describe how lighting would be used as the action closes?

"My Very Dear Sarah"

Major Sullivan Ballou

During the American Civil War, 4,500 men were killed, wounded, or captured in a battle in Virginia called Bull Run by the North and Manassas by the South. A week before the battle, an officer in the Union army, Major Sullivan Ballou, wrote the letter opposite to his wife, Sarah, who was in Rhode Island. The love of this couple, like the love of Romeo and Juliet, has survived death and time.

Courtesy of the Atlanta History Center.

Michael J. McAfee Collection.

Nelsonian Institute, Southington, Connecticut.

Before they left their homes for war, soldiers often had photographs taken of themselves and their loved ones. Many of these photographs were carried into battle.

July 14, 1861
Camp Clark, Washington

My very dear Sarah:

The indications are very strong that we shall move in a few days—perhaps tomorrow. Lest I should not be able to write again, I feel impelled to write a few lines that may fall under your eye when I shall be no more. . . .

I have no misgivings about, or lack of confidence in the cause in which I am engaged, and my courage does not halt or falter. I know how strongly American Civilization now leans on the triumph of the Government, and how great a debt we owe to those who went before us through the blood and sufferings of the Revolution. And I am willing—perfectly willing—to lay down all my joys in this life to help maintain this Government and to pay that debt. . . .

Sarah my love for you is deathless, it seems to bind me with mighty cables that nothing but Omnipotence could break; and yet my love of Country comes over me like a strong wind and bears me unresistibly on with all these chains to the battle field.

The memories of the blissful moments I have spent with you come creeping over me, and I feel most gratified to God and to you that I have enjoyed them so long. And hard it is for me to give them up and burn to ashes the hopes of future years, when, God willing, we might still have lived and loved together, and seen our sons grown up to honorable manhood, around us. I have, I know, but few and small claims upon Divine Providence, but something whispers to me—perhaps it is the wafted prayer of my little Edgar, that I shall return to my loved ones unharmed. If I do not my dear Sarah, never forget how much I love you, and when my last breath escapes me on the battle field, it will whisper your name. Forgive my many faults and the many pains I have caused you. How thoughtless and foolish I have often times been! How gladly would I wash out with my tears every little spot upon your happiness. . . .

But, O Sarah! if the dead can come back to this earth and flit unseen around those they loved, I shall always be near you; in the gladdest days and in the darkest nights . . . _always, always,_ and if there be a soft breeze upon your cheek, it shall be my breath, as the cool air fans your throbbing temple, it shall be my spirit passing by. Sarah do not mourn me dead; think I am gone and wait for thee, for we shall meet again. . . .

Major Ballou was killed in the first battle of Bull Run, a week after he wrote this letter.

Romeo and Juliet in Performance

The Royal Opera, London.

Kensington Youth Theater and Employment Skills, Toronto.

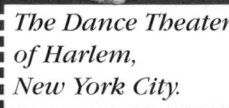
The Dance Theater of Harlem, New York City.

La Scala Opera, Milan.

Düsseldorfer
Schauspielhaus, Düsseldorf.

Itim Theater Ensemble,
Tel Aviv.

Dear Juliet

Any man that can write may answer a letter.

—William Shakespeare
Romeo and Juliet, Act II, Scene 4

LISA BANNON

VERONA, Italy—Fate bequeathed a strange legacy to this small city in northern Italy.

As the setting for Shakespeare's sixteenth-century tragedy *Romeo and Juliet,* Verona inherited the curiosity of literary scholars, a celebrated theatrical tradition, and several hundred thousand tourists a year.

In the bargain, the city also became the star-crossed lovers' capital of the world.

"We don't know how it started exactly," explains Giulio Tamassia, the bespectacled city spokesman for matters relating to Romeo and Juliet. "But one day in the thirties, these letters started arriving unprompted—addressed to Juliet. At a certain point somebody decided Juliet should write back."

Juliet's Address

What began sixty years ago as an occasional correspondence has grown into an industry. This year more than one thousand letters from the lovelorn will arrive in Verona, addressed to Shakespeare's tragic heroine. Many of them land on Mr. Tamassia's desk, with no more address than: Juliet, Italy.

"They tend to be sentimental," says Mr. Tamassia, rifling through stacks of musty airmail in the cramped studio that serves as Juliet's headquarters. Inside big pink folders are thousands of sorrowful letters, break-your-heart tales of love and loss. They come from all over—a teenage girl in Guatemala, a businessman in Boston, a high-school teacher in London. Some but not many are written by students in Shakespearean language. About two percent of letters received are addressed to Romeo, but Juliet replies.

"Writing the letter itself is really the first step toward solving the problem," says Mr. Tamassia, a fifty-nine-year-old retired businessman who wants it known at the outset that he himself is not Juliet. He is more her correspondence secretary.

"People express feelings in the letters that they would never admit to the person they love. Juliet's story inspires them," he says.

A Saudi Version

After much rummaging, he pulls out one of his favorites—describing a modern equivalent of the Montague-Capulet family rivalry.

Hala, an eighteen-year-old Saudi Arabian, wrote in March that she had fallen in love with the only son of her family's mortal enemy. Years ago, in Pakistan, her great-grandfather was responsible for the execution of a man who was using his property for smuggling heroin. From that time on, war was declared between the two families.

Now Hala was in love with a descendant of the executed man. "I am torn between the love for my family, which has made me what I am today, and my love for Omer, the man of my dreams," she wrote.

"Please reply quickly . . . my love, my life and future all depend on your answer."

—from *The Wall Street Journal*

Juliet's balcony, Verona, Italy.

MAKING MEANINGS   ACT V

First Thoughts

1. In your opinion, what really caused the tragedy of Romeo and Juliet? Was it fate or real human errors? Draw a web showing all the people or forces that might be responsible.

Shaping Interpretations

2. What coincidences in Scenes 1 and 2 conspire to wreck the friar's plans? Did any of these coincidences seem unbelievable to you?

3. In which scene of this act did you feel the **dramatic irony** peaked?

4. The **climax** of a play is its most intensely emotional moment, when we know how the conflict will end. In a tragedy it is that moment when we feel overcome with horror, sadness, fear, or regret. The climax of Shakespeare's plays always comes in the final act. When in this act would you say the climax of this play takes place? What were your feelings at this moment?

5. Look back at the prince's speech about love killing the families' joys (Scene 3). It seems ironic that love could kill, but how in this play did love kill joy? In what way is the whole play about the way heaven scourged, or punished, people for hating?

6. What does *Romeo and Juliet* reveal to you about the destructive effects of hatred? In a few sentences state the **theme** of the play as you see it. Be sure to compare your statements of theme in class.

Reviewing the Text

a. What news does Romeo's servant bring him in Scene 1?

b. Why does Romeo buy the poison?

c. Why doesn't Romeo receive the friar's letter explaining the change in plans?

d. What does Romeo find when he enters the tomb?

e. What finally happens to Romeo and then to Juliet?

Extending the Text

7. Read again the comment "Kids these days . . ." on page 732 and review your response in the Quickwrite. Now that you've read the play, what further connections can you see between Romeo and Juliet and their families and people in today's world? What do you think *Romeo and Juliet* has to say to your generation? Be sure to consider the news article on page 856.

Challenging the Text

8. Throughout the eighteenth and nineteenth centuries, *Romeo and Juliet* was often rewritten to have a different ending in which the young lovers do not die but instead live happily ever after. How do you feel about the ending of the play? Would you prefer a happy ending? What changes, if any, would you make in the outcome?

CHOICES: Building Your Portfolio

Writer's Notebook

1. Collecting Ideas for an Informative Report

Narrowing your topic. Look over the ideas you have jotted down in your Writer's Notebook. Is there one you would like to research and explore further in an informative report? Ask yourself these questions before you proceed:

- How can I narrow or focus this topic?

- What do I already know about this topic?

- What would I like to know?

- What resources can I use to find more information?

Most interested in clothing—especially why men's clothes of Shakespeare's time were so much flashier than ours.

I don't know much about topic, but public library has plenty of stuff on fashion.

Most of us love clothes, so I could do a report that would interest my classmates.

Creative Writing

2. A New Ending

Suppose Romeo and Juliet had survived because the friar's schemes worked. Write a scene showing them twenty years later. In their dialogue, make clear what's happened to the Capulets, the friar, the nurse, and Paris. Use stage directions to tell when and where your scene is set.

Creative Writing

3. The Play Today

Work as a group and prepare a plan for how you could update *Romeo and Juliet* so that it takes place in the present-day United States—even in your own community or neighborhood. The chart below shows how Jerome Robbins changed *Romeo and Juliet* to make it into a musical called *West Side Story* (1957). When you finish your rough plan, you might go further and map your scenes. If you're really ambitious, write your own new *Romeo and Juliet*.

	West Side Story	Your Story
Setting	New York 1950s	
Problem	gang war between Jets and Sharks	
Two lovers	Maria and Tony. She is Puerto Rican, he is Polish American	
Authority figure (Prince)	Lieutenant Schrank and Officer Krupke (NYPD)	
Boy's best friend (Benvolio)	Riff	
Girl's best friend (Nurse)	Bernardo's girlfriend, Anita	
Gang leaders	Riff (Jets) Bernardo (Sharks)	
Scenes:		

Critical Thinking/Speaking

4. Characters Endure

Prepare a report for the class in which you tell how the character types presented in *Romeo and Juliet* are found in movies, novels, and TV sitcoms today. Focus on these types:

- beautiful girl
- handsome boyfriend
- socially conscious mother
- grumpy father
- boyfriend approved by the girl's parents
- older woman confidante
- loyal best friend
- hotheaded bully
- dopey guys who follow the gang leader

Creative Writing

5. Family Feud

Write your own original explanation of what might have caused the feud between the Capulets and the Montagues. Tell *when* the hatred started and *why* it started.

Art/Creative Writing

6. Teen Personality Profiles

If Romeo, Juliet, and Mercutio lived today, what might be their preferences in music, clothing, reading, sports, and parties? What future might each one look forward to? Draw a sketch and write a personality profile of each character, as if he or she were living today and attending your school. If you like, do your sketches and profiles as features for a high school yearbook.

Critical Writing

7. Portrait of Juliet

Write a character analysis of Juliet, using the following comment by a critic as your thesis statement. Be sure to use details from the play to support what the critic says about Juliet and how the world treated her.

> Shakespeare's real miracle . . . was Juliet, transformed from an adolescent arrogantly eager to outdo her elders to an appealing child-woman, barely fourteen, who learns to mix courage with her innocence, yet falls victim to a world that only briefly and unintentionally, but fatally, treats her as a plaything.
>
> —J. A. Bryant, Jr.

Critical Thinking/Panel Discussion

8. If Only . . .

Shakespeare doesn't idealize Romeo and Juliet. He is careful to remind us that their love is destructive partly because it fails to see life as it really is. Romeo and Juliet do not act with caution and patience and wisdom. They act on impulse and in haste. And they get bad advice. Form a panel to discuss these questions: (a) What should Romeo and Juliet have done, instead of what they actually did, at three or more points in the play? (b) Could Romeo and Juliet have triumphed—if they'd had good advice? (Be sure to review the webs you made for question 1.) (c) Would Mercutio have helped them had he lived? Before your panel meets, it should agree on a format.

Research/Art

9. Do-It-Yourself Globe Theater

With a group, find library books that show models of the Globe Theater and that describe its unique features in detail. Then work together to make your own model of the Globe. Decide what materials you will use for your model and how you will label and describe its parts. (Commercially printed do-it-yourself cardboard models of the Globe are available in some bookstores. Your group might enjoy working on such a kit.) Display your model in a prominent location in your school.

Figures of Speech

Shakespeare's characters use images and figures of speech so rich and so varied that the play, which has lived now for almost four hundred years, will probably live as long as English continues to be spoken. As you're focusing on Shakespeare's language, you might try to imitate some of his figures of speech.

Similes

The simplest form of figurative language is the **simile,** a clearly stated comparison between two different things. A simile uses a word such as *like* or *as* or *than* in stating its comparison. For example, Romeo, dejected over Rosaline, says of love, "It pricks like thorn." Romeo's simile suggests that love can cause pain, just as a thorn can.

Metaphors

Metaphors omit words such as *like, as,* and *than* and directly equate two different things. When the nurse says of Paris "he's a flower, . . . a very flower," she immediately identifies Paris's good looks with a beautiful blossom. Metaphors may also be **implied**. The prince uses implied metaphors when he angrily accuses the citizens:

> You men, you beasts,
> That quench the fire of
>   your pernicious rage
> With purple fountains
>   issuing from your veins!

The prince compares the anger of the citizens to a fire, and the blood issuing from the wounds to purple water spewing out of fountains.

Personification

Personification is a special kind of metaphor, in which something that is not a person is spoken of as if it were human. When Benvolio says that the sun "peered forth the golden window of the East," he is personifying the sun by saying that it peered, as if it had two eyes.

Puns

Shakespeare's audiences loved **puns,** which are plays on the multiple meanings of words. (Many jokes today are based on puns. Question: "What has four wheels and flies?" Answer: "A garbage truck." This pun is based on two meanings of the word *flies*.) Many of the puns in *Romeo and Juliet* go over our heads today because jokes go out of fashion very quickly and some of Shakespeare's wordplay involves words we don't use today.

Mercutio is the best punster in the play, though Romeo does pretty well in Act II, when he matches wits with his friend. When Mercutio spies Romeo coming down the street, he says Romeo comes "without his roe." *Roe* can refer to a female deer, so if Romeo is without his roe, he's without his girl. *Roe* also refers to fish eggs, so "without his roe" can mean that Romeo's been gutted (we'd say he's "gutless"), as a fish is when its eggs are removed.

Try It Out

Similes

In the following quotations, identify the similes and tell what two things are brought together in each. In what way are the two things alike?

1. Romeo.
O, she doth teach the torches to burn bright!
It seems she hangs upon the cheek of night
As a rich jewel in an Ethiop's ear—
Beauty too rich for use, for earth too dear!
—Act I, Scene 5, lines 46–49

2. Romeo.
Love goes toward love as schoolboys from their books;
But love from love, toward school with heavy looks.
—Act II, Scene 2, lines 157–158

3. Lord Capulet.
Death lies on her like an untimely frost
Upon the sweetest flower of all the field.
—Act IV, Scene 5, lines 28–29

Metaphors

Here are some passages containing metaphors. Pick out each metaphor and identify the two things that it compares.

1. Romeo (to Juliet).
If I profane with my unworthiest hand
This holy shrine, the gentle sin is this:
My lips, two blushing pilgrims, ready stand
To smooth that rough touch with a tender kiss.
—Act I, Scene 5, lines 95–98

2. Romeo (under Juliet's balcony).
But soft! What light through yonder window breaks?
It is the East, and Juliet is the sun!
—Act II, Scene 2, lines 2–3

3. Juliet (to Romeo).
This bud of love, by summer's ripening breath,
May prove a beauteous flower when next we meet.
—Act II, Scene 2, lines 121–122

Personification

Here are some quotations from *Romeo and Juliet* that contain personifications. In each, what nonhuman thing is spoken of as it if were a person? A passage can contain more than one personification.

1. Capulet.
. . . well-appareled April on the heel
Of limping winter treads . . .
—Act I, Scene 2, lines 27–28

2. Chorus.
Now old desire doth in his deathbed lie,
And young affection gapes to be his heir.
—Act II, Chorus, lines 1–2

3. Juliet.
Come, civil night,
Thou sober-suited matron all in black,
And learn me how to lose a winning match. . . .
—Act III, Scene 2, lines 10–12

Puns

Here are three more puns from the play. If you can explain the plays on meaning, you'll have caught the jokes.

1. Mercutio (after he is stabbed).
Ask for me tomorrow, and you shall find me a grave man.
—Act III, Scene 1, lines 98–99

2. Romeo.
Give me a torch. I am not for this ambling.
Being but heavy, I will bear the light.
—Act I, Scene 4, Lines 11–12

3. Romeo.
You have dancing shoes
With nimble soles; I have a soul of lead
So stakes me to the ground I cannot move.
—Act I, Scene 4, lines 14–16

Romeo and Juliet in Bosnia

Bob Herbert

Quickwrite

Think about the title of this editorial and about the photographs that illustrate it. Based on the title and photographs, predict what the story will be about. As you read, continue to take notes on details in the editorial that you might want to talk about later.

If you watch *Frontline* Tuesday night on PBS, you will see the story of two ordinary young people, Bosko Brkic, an Eastern Orthodox Serb, and Admira Ismic, a Muslim, who met at a New Year's Eve party in the mid-1980s, fell in love, tried to pursue the most conventional of dreams, and died together on a hellish bridge in Sarajevo.

The documentary, called "Romeo and Juliet in Sarajevo,"[1] achieves its power by focusing our attention on the thoroughly human individuals caught up in a horror that, from afar, can seem abstract and almost unimaginable. It's one thing to hear about the carnage caused by incessant[2] sniper fire and the steady rain of mortar shells on a city; it's something quite different to actually witness a parent desperately groping for meaning while reminiscing about a lost daughter.

For viewers overwhelmed and desensitized by the relentless reports of mass killings and mass rapes, the shock of "Romeo and Juliet in Sarajevo" is that what we see is so real and utterly familiar. We become riveted by the mundane. Bosko and Admira could be a young couple from anywhere, from Queens, or Tokyo, or Barcelona.

We learn that they graduated from high school in June of 1986 and that both were crazy about movies and music. Admira had a cat named Yellow that she loved, and Bosko liked to play practical jokes.

Admira's father, Zijo, speaking amid clouds of cigarette smoke, says, "Well, I knew from the first day about that relationship and I didn't have anything against it. I thought it was good because her guy was so likable, and after a time I started to love him and didn't regard him any differently than Admira."

Admira's grandmother, Sadika Ismic, was not so sanguine. "Yes, I did have something against it," she says. "I thought, 'He is Serb, she is a Muslim, and how will it work?'"

For Admira and Bosko, of course, love was the answer to everything. While Bosko was away on compulsory military service soon after high school, Admira wrote: "My dear love,

1. **Sarajevo** (sä′rä′ye·vô): capital of Bosnia and Herzegovina, in the former Yugoslavia.
2. **incessant** (in·ses′ənt): never ceasing.

One of the bridges that span the Miljacka River, which runs through the middle of Sarajevo.

Bosko Brkic and Admira Ismic.

Sarajevo at night is the most beautiful thing in the world. I guess I could live somewhere else but only if I must or if I am forced. Just a little beat of time is left until we are together. After that, absolutely nothing can separate us."

Sarajevo at the time was a cosmopolitan city coming off the triumph of the 1984 Winter Olympics. With a population of Serbs, Croats, Muslims, Jews, and others, the city had become a symbol of ethnic and religious tolerance, a place where people were making a serious attempt to live together in peace.

But civilization is an exceedingly fragile enterprise, and it's especially vulnerable to the primal madness of ethnic and religious hatreds. Simple tolerance is nothing in the face of the relentless, pathetic and near-universal need to bolster the esteem of the individual and the group by eradicating the rights, and even the existence, of others.

When the madness descended on Sarajevo, Bosko Brkic faced a cruel dilemma. He could not kill Serbs. And he could not go up into the hills and fire back down on his girlfriend's people. Says his mother, Rada: "He was simply a kid who was not for the war."

Bosko and Admira decided to flee Sarajevo.

To escape, they had to cross a bridge over the Miljacka River in a no man's land between the Serb and Muslim lines. Snipers from both sides overlooked the bridge.

It has not been determined who shot the lovers. They were about two thirds of the way across the bridge when the gunfire erupted. Both sides blame the other. Witnesses said Bosko died instantly. Admira crawled to him. She died a few minutes later. The area in which they were shot was so dangerous that the bodies remained on the bridge, entwined, for six days before being removed.

Only the times and places change. Bosnia today, Rwanda and Burundi tomorrow. Jews versus Arabs, Chinese versus Japanese, blacks versus whites. There are various ostensible reasons for the endless conflicts—ideological differences, border disputes, oil—but dig just a little and you will uncover the ruinous ethnic or religious origins of the clash.

The world stands helpless and sometimes depressed before the madness. Millions upon millions dead, millions more to die. It is not just the curse of our times. It seems to be the curse of all time.

—from *The New York Times*

MEET THE WRITER

On the Scene

Born in Brooklyn, New York, journalist **Bob Herbert** (1945–) earned a Bachelor of Science degree from the State University of New York and has been a reporter ever since. Whether at his first job at *The Star Ledger* in Newark, New Jersey, or on the *NBC Nightly News* or the *Today* show,

Herbert's reporting and commentary on politics, urban affairs, and social trends have been full of valuable information and insights into the stuff communities and nations are made of. He currently covers national and local issues for *The New York Times*. He has taught journalism at Brooklyn College and Columbia University Graduate School of Journalism.

FINDING COMMON GROUND

- You know more about Romeo and Juliet than you do about Bosko and Admira; Shakespeare had an entire play to develop their characters, while Bob Herbert had only a short column to portray what happened on the bridge over the Miljacka. Still, there is something powerful in the simple fact that Bosko and Admira lived while we live, dying only a very short time ago. Perhaps their story, brief as it is, may be more painful for some readers than Shakespeare's tale.

  - Talk over these two stories with a group: Shakespeare's story of Romeo and Juliet and Herbert's story of Bosko and Admira. Which of the two struck you more powerfully? Why? Was it something in the story itself? Did it have something to do with the richness of the language of the play, or with the simplicity and directness of the language of the editorial? Did it have anything to do with time or distance? Or was your response the result of something else?

  - What other observations about the content of the editorial, or about its tone or message, does your group make? Does your group disagree on anything?

  - Assign someone to report to the class on your group's response to the editorial and its relationship to the play. What can you, as a class, agree about? Are there some issues you must agree to disagree on?

READ ON

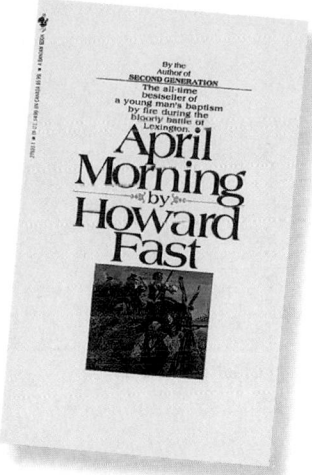

In Love and War

"All's fair in love and war." You've heard that before, but Ruth and Adam might disagree. Howard Fast's novel *April Morning* (Bantam) finds young Adam facing the British soldiers who are marching through town on April 19, 1775. Ruth, the girl who loves him, hears the tragic news—that Adam has not survived the battle. Sound fair? Find out what happens by sundown, April 19, 1775.

New Frontiers

Take two cups of love and mix them into the quickly changing batter of the American frontier—and do it all right around the turn of the century. Willa Cather's classic American love story, *My Ántonia* (Houghton Mifflin), describes the product of this mixture. Find out what happens to two young people in a Nebraska landscape you'll never forget.

Wanda and Friends

It's prom night, and Wanda Hickey is aglow—with sweat. That's according to humorist Jean Shepherd. The short stories in Shepherd's collection *Wanda Hickey's Night of Golden Memories and Other Disasters* (Doubleday) uncover what's awkward, weird, even disastrous about growing up—and all for laughs. Join Wanda and friends—like Ollie Hopnoodle, Josephine Cosnowski, and Daphne Bigelow—and follow Shepherd through romance and murder, and of course, to the Junior Prom.

On the West Side

Romeo and Juliet aren't the only "star-crossed" lovers to walk the stage. Their story has been repeated often—in drama, fiction, and real life. In our own century *West Side Story*'s Tony and Maria have been the most famous couple to re-enact the tragedy of ill-fated love. *West Side Story* is a musical version of the familiar story—set in a neighborhood of New York City. Tragedy follows when love and two different cultures collide. There's a book that contains both plays, *West Side Story* and *Romeo and Juliet* (Laurel-Leaf).

Speaking and Listening Workshop

Stage a scene of *Romeo and Juliet*.

During the run of Romeo and Juliet, *someone wrote and told me that if the dialogue at the ball could be taken in a lighter and* quicker *way, it would better express the manner of a girl of Juliet's age. The same unknown critic pointed out that I was too slow and studied in the balcony scene. She—I think it was a woman—was perfectly right!*

—Ellen Terry,
British actress

STAGING THE PLAY

Romeo and Juliet has been a favorite with directors, actors, set designers, and costumers for centuries. Present a scene of the play with a group of your classmates. (If you're feeling especially Shakespearean, give your "company" a name, such as the King's Women or the Globe Trotters, or, to bring it up to date, the President's Players.)

Getting Started

1. Select a Scene

Some good possibilities include

- the opening fight scene: Act I, Scene 1 (many characters)
- the party at the Capulets, where Romeo and Juliet first meet: Act I, Scene 5 (lots of people, music, dancing, tension)
- the balcony scene: Act II, Scene 2 (two actors only)
- Mercutio and Benvolio teasing Romeo: Act II, Scene 4
- the fight in the square, when Mercutio dies and Romeo kills Tybalt: Act III, Scene 1 (requires good choreography)
- the scene where Lord Capulet threatens to disown Juliet if she doesn't marry Paris: Act III, Scene 5
- the scene when Juliet says goodnight to the nurse and her mother and takes the sleeping potion: Act IV, Scene 3 (requires emotional control)

Whichever scene you choose, include the Prologue as an opener. You might find a choral reading of the Prologue very effective: The speaker speaks as "we." Be sure to watch for commas, periods, and semicolons. These punctuation marks tell you when to pause.

2. Assign Tasks

Here are some of the tasks you'll need to take care of (the very same ones Shakespeare's company had to manage):

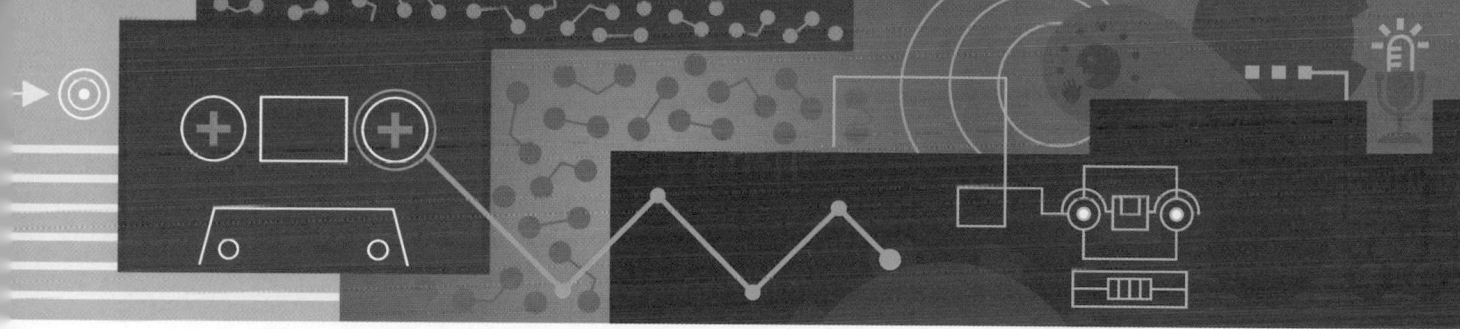

- directing
- lighting
- costuming
- props
- choreography (planning the movement onstage—especially critical in the fight scenes)
- publicity

The balcony scene from *Romeo and Juliet,* performed by the Student Shakespeare Performance Festival, Reno, Nevada.

3. Decide on Your Presentation

Since you are an acting company, you'll want to work as a group to make some of your decisions. Here are some performance possibilities you should consider:

- Assign one role to each group member and act the scene "straight," that is, traditionally, as if you were on a professional stage.

- Create a **tableau,** or frozen moment from the scene. Decide in advance where each character should be situated and what posture, gesture, and facial expression each should have. Once you have created the frozen moment, have a director tap each character in turn, at which point the character can recite his or her most important line in that scene or simply tell, in the language of today, what's going through his or her mind at that moment.

- If you choose a crowd scene, such as the party or the street brawl, some group members can pantomime the action, while the rest of the group does a **choral reading** of the dialogue.

- Record your scene as a **radio drama** using appropriate sound effects. (The fight scene is particularly good for this activity.)

- **Videotape** your scene, trying out different camera shots. Edit your tape to include the best "takes," dub in additional sound effects, and replay the film for an audience.

4. Plan Your Costumes, Props, and Lighting

Costume designers use sketches, paper cutouts, or dressed-up dolls to test different effects. Try to think of pieces of clothing that will convey important aspects of your characters' personalities. Remember you can suggest a lot with types of hats (fancy or plain?), capes, and masks (are they plain or trimmed with feathers, sequins, or lace?). Vests and baggy belted shirts make good costumes for the men. Your costumes and props must be carefully chosen to indicate time and place. You might want to set your performance in the present.

Prepare a list of the props you'll need, such as torches, swords, herbs, and vials (for the "poison"). Appoint one person to collect and keep track of these articles. (Avoid using real swords. The fight scenes are fast, and accidents happen even in professional theaters.)

5. Mark Up Your Scripts

Make copies of your scene to use as a script for each group member. Mark up your scripts as you rehearse, recording decisions you make about how to deliver certain lines, about how actors should make their entrances and exits, about facial expressions and movements and use of voice. These marked-up scripts are called promptbooks.

Romeo enters up right, moves center, stops, exits center right.

Enter Romeo alone.

ROMEO
Can I go forward when my heart is here? *excited*
Turn back, dull earth, and find thy center out. *pause* *say faster*
He withdraws.

enter up right, move center

Enter Benvolio with Mercutio.

BENVOLIO
Romeo, my cousin Romeo, Romeo!

MERCUTIO
He is wise
And, on my life, hath stol'n him home to bed.

searches c.l., then d.l.

BENVOLIO
He ran this way and leapt this orchard wall.
Call, good Mercutio.

MERCUTIO *singsong voice*
Nay, I'll conjure too.
Romeo! Humors! Madman! Passion! Lover! *sighs—making fun*
Appear thou in the likeness of a sigh.
Speak but one rhyme and I am satisfied.
Cry but "Ay me," pronounce but "love" and "dove."

line up arrow in bow, aim at B.

Speak to my gossip Venus one fair word, *quiet*
One nickname for her purblind son and heir,
Young Abraham Cupid, he that shot so trim
When King Cophetua loved the beggar maid.—
He heareth not, he stirreth not, he moveth not. *B. falls*
The ape is dead, and I must conjure him.—
I conjure thee by Rosaline's bright eyes, *M. pretends to be serious*
By her high forehead, and her scarlet lip,
By her fine foot, straight leg, and quivering thigh,

M. moves center, makes shape of woman, B. admires.

Rehearsals: Ironing Out the Problems

1. Read It Through

Many directors have their actors read through a play before they ever try to act it. Sit in a circle or on stage in assigned places and read aloud. If you have trouble understanding a passage, paraphrase it (see page 835). Put the paraphrase in your promptbook.

2. Work on the Poetry: A Tip

If you're having trouble with Shakespeare's language, try writing out your speeches as if they are regular prose. Then read them aloud; you'll soon get the sense of the lines and feel their rhythm. You'll also defuse some of your anxiety about Shakespeare.

3. "How Did I Do?"

Devise some means of evaluating your rehearsals. You might prepare a form that each player can fill out after each rehearsal. You might also assign a group of students to be audience critics, and have them fill out evaluation forms after each rehearsal. Be sure to share your evaluations as a group.

4. Players' Journals

Actors, like writers and artists, often keep journals. Performers find it helpful to keep journals of their acting experience. What has acting taught you about yourselves? About Shakespeare's characters? About language?

5. Remember This

In theater tradition a bad dress rehearsal means a good opening night.

> *I made a terrible flop as Romeo because they said I couldn't speak verse. It was laughable from my point of view. I couldn't speak? I was brought up speaking; I'd been speaking verse ever since I was eight years old. But I didn't sing it, you see, and the fashion was perhaps to sing it.*
>
> —Laurence Olivier,
> British actor

Technology
H E L P

See Writer's Workshop 2
CD-ROM. *Assignment:*
Informative Report.

ASSIGNMENT

**Write a report based
on information you
gather from several
sources.**

AIM

To inform.

AUDIENCE

**Your teacher, class-
mates, school news-
paper. (You choose.)**

EXPOSITORY WRITING

INFORMATIVE REPORT

You read reports of information almost daily: consumer reports, weather reports, news articles, directions, textbooks. When you write an informative report, you gather and arrange facts to help your readers learn or understand something. The more you practice the techniques of gathering information, organizing it, and writing about it, the stronger your writing and thinking skills become.

Prewriting

1. Examine Your Writer's Notebook

Read the notes you wrote as you reflected on *Romeo and Juliet.* Any questions you had about Renaissance life or customs could form the seeds of an infor-mative report. What about the connections you made between the feuding families in the play and the racial, religious, or ethnic groups that are feuding today? Do any of these connections touch on something you'd like to write a report about? If not, you can develop other ideas for a report by trying the exercise that follows.

2. Think Like a Detective

Quickly list a few things that interest you and that you would like to know more about. Then use detective questions—*who, what, where, when, why,* and *how*—to focus your interest. For example, say you're interested in old movies. You might investigate *who* W. C. Fields was, *what* training a stunt person received, *where* your favorite black-and-white movie was shot, *when* the earliest movie car-chase scene appeared, or *how* a particular actor got a start on the screen. Write questions like these under each idea you've listed. Think about how you might answer them in an informative report.

3. Choose a Topic

From your list of topic ideas, choose one that meets all of the following criteria:

- **You are genuinely interested in it.** Your enthusiasm for your topic will generate enthusiasm in your readers as well.

- **You believe it will interest your readers.** You know your classmates' interests and concerns; if you think a topic will appeal to them, you're probably right.

- **You know you can locate several sources of information on the subject.** If your knowledge of your subject comes from a single source, such as a recent magazine article or TV show, brainstorm or talk with friends to find ideas for other sources. Chances are you can't put together a strong report from only one information source.

4. Adjust Your Scope

You must be able to cover your topic thoroughly in a short paper. Check a few resources that deal with your topic. If an hour-long TV show has been devoted to it, if an encyclopedia has a few pages about it, or if whole books have been written about it, your topic is too broad for a short paper. You need to narrow it. If you can find only a few lines of information on your topic, even with a librarian's help, your topic is too narrow. You need to broaden it.

5. Consider Your Readers

As you gather information, keep these questions in mind:

- What do you think your readers already know about your topic?

- What would they probably like to know?

- What background information would help them understand your topic more easily?

6. Gather Material/Get to Know Your Subject

Now you need facts and observations about your topic—the more, the better.

- Start by quickwriting everything you already know about your topic. If you have personal experience with it, write your observations. If others shared your experience, you might interview them and record their observations as well.

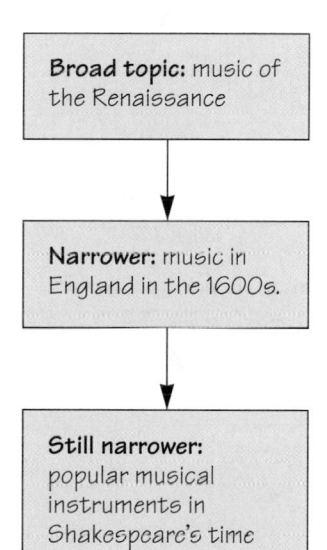

Broad topic: music of the Renaissance

Narrower: music in England in the 1600s.

Still narrower: popular musical instruments in Shakespeare's time

• Explore other sources of information about your topic. You might gather facts from the Internet, museum exhibits, TV documentaries, interviews with experts, magazine and newspaper articles, and other library materials. Write down your facts and sources.

7. Elaborate on Your Information

You might want to use quotations, explore the history of your subject, or tell an anecdote that is relevant. You might even want to supply sketches or maps to elaborate on and support your material.

8. Plan Your Organization

• Your report needs a main point, or **controlling idea**. If you don't already have one in mind, read over your prewriting notes and see what main point they might add up to. You should be able to state it in one clear sentence.

> EXAMPLE   In Shakespeare's time, tunes and even musical instruments were different from those we know today.

• Arrange your information in an order that will help your readers understand it. You might choose **time order** (the

Renaissance Music

Shawm: *double-reed wind instrument, forerunner of the oboe.*
Source: The New Encyclopaedia Britannica, 1995.

Communications Handbook HELP

Taking notes and documenting sources: pages 983-984.

Model

from PARTYING WITH THE BARD

[*Introduction:*]
At the Capulets' party in Act I of Romeo and Juliet, you can be sure the guests weren't dancing to heavy metal. What kind of music were they dancing to? What instruments were used to produce popular music in Shakespeare's time? The music and the instruments were very different from those we know today.

A surprising statement and a question catch readers' interest. States controlling idea.

[*From the body:*]
Any band in Shakespeare's time would have included a lute. This pear-shaped stringed instrument had been popular for centuries. Also popular were the violinlike rebec; the tabor, a small drum; an early version of the trombone; and the shawm, ancestor of the oboe. A band that was really

Specific facts show that the writer knows the subject.

order in which events happened), **spatial order** (the order in which objects are arranged in space), **order of importance,** or **cause-and-effect order**. Or you might make up another organizing principle. The important thing is to choose an order that fits your material. Before you start writing, list your facts and observations in the order you've chosen.

Drafting

1. Start in the Middle

Arrange your prewriting notes in front of you before you start drafting. (If you get bogged down, a glance at them can help you find your direction again.) Then start writing the body of your report. Don't worry yet about an introduction. Just begin putting the main part of your information into words and sentences.

2. Work with Comparisons

Your readers will find your information more specific and much easier to remember if you use comparisons to relate it to things they know.

EXAMPLE   With its pear-shaped body and many strings, a lute looks like a giant, short-necked mandolin.

Try It Out
See if you can think of a comparison that will make each fact easier for your readers to relate to:

1. At 1,454 feet, the Sears Tower is as tall as . . .

2. The average human heart is just under five inches long, about the same size as . . .

with it might also feature the newly invented, portable keyboard called a spinet.

Another new Renaissance instrument was the theorbo, a lute with two sets of strings and an S-curved neck. The theorbo sounded deeper than a lute. With its odd shape and surprising sound, it must have seemed as high-tech as the unusually shaped electric basses in some modern bands. . . .

[*Conclusion:*]
Thanks to new instruments and new musical scales, music was changing fast in Shakespeare's time. The changes must have made music as exciting for the people of the Renaissance as modern music is for us today. Maybe the changes were also irritating to some conservative musicians. After all, rock-and-roll wasn't accepted for a long time.

The conclusion draws parallels between Renaissance music and modern music.

. . . the word processor can concentrate your mind on the craft of writing, revising, and editing—much more powerfully than this has ever been possible, because your words are right in front of you in all their infinite possibility, waiting to be infinitely reshaped. Technology, the great villain, turns out to be your friend. I can't agree with people who say that writing at a terminal will make our writing mechanical, or turn our children into robots. What we write still has to come out of our heads; no machine is going to do that for us.

—William Zinsser

Sentence Workshop HELP

Combining sentences by using appositives: page 876.

Communications Handbook HELP

See Taking Notes and Documenting Sources, page 983.

3. Add an Introduction and a Conclusion

- The first lines of your report should pull your readers in and make them want to read more. You might start with a striking quotation, a surprising statistic, or an apparent contradiction—anything to catch your readers' interest.

- The last lines of your report should focus once more on your controlling idea. You might explore what this idea means to you personally or what its further implications are. One way to give your conclusion a finished feeling might be to refer to the lines that opened your report.

Evaluating and Revising

1. Peer Review

Exchange drafts with a partner. You might use questions like the ones on the next page as you respond to each other's drafts:

Revision Model

	Peer Comments
A band that was really with it	*Do you want to be so informal? It's OK. Just checking.*
might also feature the newly	
invented spinet. ^, portable keyboard called a,	*What's a spinet? Define?*
Another new Renaissance	
instrument was the theorbo, a lute. ^with two sets of strings and an S-curved neck.	*Give me a clear picture of a lute. Different how?*
The theorbo sounded different. With ^deeper than a lute	
its odd shape and surprising sound,	
it must have seemed ~~pretty~~ ^as	*Maybe compare with a modern instrument?*
high-tech. ^as the unusually shaped electric basses in some modern bands.	

- Does the introduction catch your interest? How could it be improved? Is the topic clearly introduced?
- What is the controlling idea?
- Are enough examples or facts cited? Would an anecdote or more description help?

2. Self-Evaluation

If you can, put your report aside for a short time, so it will seem fresh when you read it again. When you're ready, read it as though for the first time. Note places where changes might improve it. Think about your reader's comments and suggestions. Then decide how best to revise your report.

Proofreading

To focus your "proofreading eye," you might find it helpful to go over your revision twice. The first time, look only for errors in grammar or punctuation. The second time, look only for spelling errors. Run your spelling and grammar checkers if you're working on a computer, but remember that they can't tell you if you're using the wrong word (a spelling checker can't tell you when to put an apostrophe in *its*).

Publishing

Use several media to illustrate your report when you present it to your classmates. Depending on your topic, you might add art or photos, an audiotape or a videotape. If you are reporting on a historical period, you might dress in period costume; if you are reporting on another culture, you might bring in samples of its food or say a phrase or two in its language.

Reflecting

Use the following questions to help you reflect on your writing process. If you add your informative report to your portfolio, attach your reflections.

1. Would it have been easier to gather information with a partner? Why or why not?

2. Which of my peer reader's responses were most helpful?

3. What do I like best about my report? Why?

4. What advice would I give to someone just starting this workshop?

■ *Evaluation Criteria*

A good informative report

1. *has an introduction that catches readers' attention*

2. *has a clearly stated controlling idea*

3. *includes facts and observations to illustrate and support the controlling idea*

4. *is organized clearly*

5. *ends by focusing on the controlling idea again*

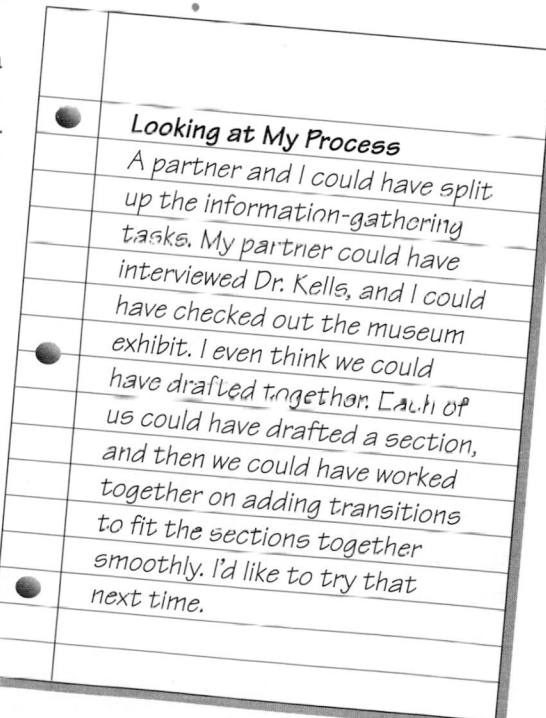

Looking at My Process
A partner and I could have split up the information-gathering tasks. My partner could have interviewed Dr. Kells, and I could have checked out the museum exhibit. I even think we could have drafted together. Each of us could have drafted a section, and then we could have worked together on adding transitions to fit the sections together smoothly. I'd like to try that next time.

Sentence Workshop

Language Handbook H E L P

*See Apposi-
tives, page
1008.*

Technology H E L P

See Language
Workshop
CD-ROM.
*Key word
entry: appos-
itives.*

COMBINING SENTENCES: APPOSITIVES

Here is an awkwardly written paragraph about *Romeo and Juliet*:

> Two families are feuding. The families are the Montagues and Capulets. Romeo falls in love with Juliet. Romeo is a Montague. Juliet is a Capulet.

The paragraph is made up of five very short sentences. Here is one way you can convey the same information in only two sentences.

> Two families, the Montagues and the Capulets, are feuding. Romeo, a Montague, falls in love with Juliet, a Capulet.

These sentences are combined by the use of appositive phrases (which are underscored). Notice that the appositive phrases are set off by commas.

An **appositive** is a noun or pronoun placed beside another noun or pronoun to identify or explain it. Appositives can also be phrases.

When an appositive is a single word and is necessary for the sense of the sentence, it is called **restrictive** and it should not be set off by a comma. Benvolio uses this kind of restrictive appositive in Act II:

> Romeo! My cousin Romeo! Romeo!

If Benvolio had had only one cousin, the appositive would be nonrestrictive and a comma would be necessary:

> My cousin, Romeo!

Writer's Workshop Follow-up: Revision

When you revise your drafts, look for short sentences that simply identify who someone is or what something is. See if this information can be added to another sentence by making it into an appositive. Watch the commas for one-word (or one-title) appositives. Ask yourself if the appositive is necessary for the sense of the sentence. (Omit the appositive to see if the sense of the sentence is clear.)

Try It Out

1. Revise these choppy sentences by combining each pair using an appositive or appositive phrase. Be careful with your commas.

   a. Mercutio is Romeo's friend. He's cynical about love.

   b. Romeo kills Tybalt. Tybalt is Juliet's cousin.

   c. Juliet's father threatens to disown her. Juliet's father is Lord Capulet.

   d. The most famous love scene in drama is the balcony scene. The balcony scene is Act II, Scene 2.

   e. *Romeo and Juliet* was written by William Shakespeare. He is the most famous writer in the world.

2. Be a test-writer. Write five sentences to test your partner on the use of commas to set off one-word appositives.

LEARNING FOR LIFE

Decision Making

Problem

Romeo and Juliet, when faced with horrible choices, made decisions that led to tragedy. In real life the decisions we make also have consequences. How can we learn to make sound decisions?

Project

Analyze and evaluate a decision-making plan, and apply the steps of the plan to a problem, real or imagined.

Preparation

Here is a fairly standard decision-making plan:

1. State all the possible choices that are open to you. If you see only two possible choices, try mixing and matching elements of each, to come up with at least one other possibility.

2. Jot down your thoughts about the possible consequences of each choice, using "If I" statements. ("If I don't try out for the play, I may miss a lot of fun.")

3. What could you gain by making each choice? What could you lose? What's the best thing that could happen if you make each choice? The worst thing?

4. Make a chart of pros and cons for each choice.

5. Imagine someone whose judgment you trust being faced with the same decision. From what you know about the person, what would he or she be likely to do? Why?

6. Weigh the information you've noted on your chart, and make your choice.

Procedure

1. List examples of some choices people must make, based on what you know from literature, the media, or your own experience (use Romeo and Juliet's problem, if you wish). Discuss the ways people approached the problem.

2. Apply one of these problems to the decision-making plan outlined here. What works? What doesn't?

3. Adapt the decision-making plan, adding or omitting steps.

Presentation

Use one of the following formats (or another that your teacher approves).

1. Cartoon Strip

Create a cartoon showing an imaginary character using the decision-making plan. With other students who have chosen this option, display your cartoon in the school media center or lunchroom.

2. Soliloquy

Write a soliloquy (in prose or poetry) for a real or fictional character who is using the plan to make an important decision. Perform your soliloquy in front of the class.

3. Advice Column

Write a letter to an advice columnist as if you are Romeo and Juliet facing your terrible problem. In a second letter, respond as if you are the columnist. Read the advice you give the young couple and discuss it with a group of class-mates. Would following this plan have helped Romeo and Juliet?

Processing

For your portfolio write a brief reflection answering these questions:

• What did you learn from this project?

• What do you think is the strongest feature of the decision-making plan? The weakest? Are there situations where it would not work?

THE EPIC

An epic is an encyclopedia of the manners, customs, and values that bind a whole civilization together.

—W. T. Jewkes

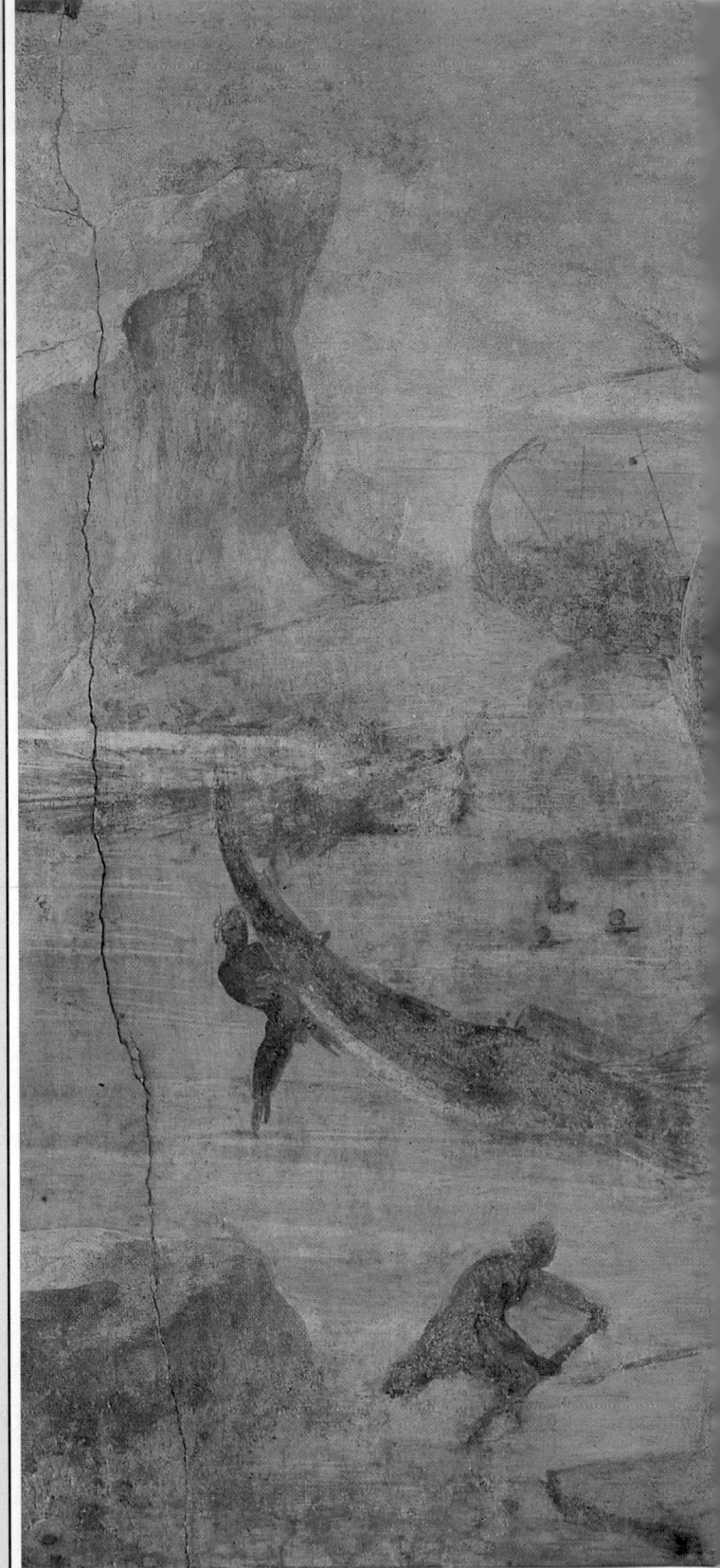

Laestrygonians attacking Odysseus' ships. Roman fresco.

THE ODYSSEY
AN INTRODUCTION *BY* DAVID ADAMS LEEMING

The blind poet Homer (probably made in the 2nd century A.D.). Found near Naples.

Almost three thousand years ago, people who lived in the starkly beautiful part of the world we now call Greece were telling stories about a great war. The person credited with later gathering all these stories together and telling them as one unified epic is a man named Homer (*Homēros,* in Greek). Homer's great war stories are called, in English, the *Iliad* and the *Odyssey.* (In Greek, the *Iliad* is *Ilias* and the *Odyssey* is *Odysseia.*)

Homer's stories probably can be traced to real historical struggles for control of the waterway leading from the Aegean Sea to the Sea of Marmara and the Black Sea. These real battles would have taken place as early as 1200 B.C.—a time that was at least as long ago for Homer's audience as the Pilgrims' landing at Plymouth Rock is for us.

Homer's first epic was the *Iliad,* which tells of a ten-year war fought on the plains outside the walls of a great city called Troy (it was also known as Ilion). The ruins of Troy can still be seen today in western Turkey. In Homer's story the Trojan War was fought between the people of Troy and an alliance of early Greek kings (at this time, each island and area of the Greek mainland had its own king). The *Iliad* tells us that the cause of the war was sexual jealousy: The world's most beautiful woman, Helen, abandoned her Greek husband, King Menelaus, and ran off with a man called Paris, a prince of Troy.

The *Odyssey,* Homer's second epic, is the story of the attempt of one Greek soldier, Odysseus, to get home after the Trojan War. All epic poems in the Western world owe something to the basic patterns established by these two stories.

EPICS AND VALUES

Epics are long narrative poems that tell of the adventures of heroes who in some way embody the values of their civilizations. The Greeks for centuries used the *Iliad* and the *Odyssey* in schools to teach Greek virtues. So it is not surprising that later cultures that admired the Homeric epics created their own epics, imitating Homer's style but conveying their own value systems.

Still, for all the epics written since Homer's time and for all the ones composed before it, when we think of the word *epic* we think primarily of the *Iliad* and the *Odyssey.* Rome's *Aeneid,* France's *Song of Roland,* Italy's *Divine Comedy,* the ancient Sumerian tale of Gilgamesh, India's *Mahabharata* and *Ramayana,* Mali's *Sundiata*—all are great stories in the epic tradition. But to discover the heart of that tradition, we need to examine Homer's epics.

> These real battles would have taken place as early as 1200 B.C.—a time that was at least as long ago for Homer's audience as the Pilgrims' landing at Plymouth Rock is for us.

The *Iliad* is the primary model for the epic of war. The *Odyssey* is the model for the epic of the long journey. The theme of the journey has been basic in Western literature—it is found in fairy tales, in such novels as *The Incredible Journey, Moby-Dick,* and *The Hobbit,* and in such movies as *The Wizard of Oz, Star Wars, The Lion King,* and *Forrest Gump.* Thus, it is the *Odyssey* that has been the more widely read of Homer's two great stories.

THE WAR-STORY BACKGROUND: VIOLENCE AND BRUTALITY

The background for Odysseus' story is found in the *Iliad*—the war epic. The action of the *Iliad* is set in the tenth and final year of the Trojan War. According to the *Iliad,* the Greeks attacked Troy to avenge the insult suffered by Menelaus, king of Sparta, when his wife, Helen, ran off with Paris, a young prince of Troy. The Greek kings banded together under the leadership of Agamemnon, the brother of Menelaus. In a thousand ships, they sailed across the Aegean Sea and encircled the walled city of Troy.

The audience of the *Odyssey* would have known this war story. Listeners would have known that the Greeks were eventually victorious, that they gained entrance to Troy, reduced the city to smoldering ruins, and butchered all the inhabitants, except for those they took as slaves back to Greece. They would have known all about the greatest of the Greek warriors, Achilles, who was to die young in the final year of the war. The audience would probably have heard other epic poems (now lost) that told

The Fall of Troy (1974) by Romare Bearden. Collage and mixed media on board (36" x 48").

of the homecomings of the various Greek heroes who survived the war. They would especially have known about the homecoming of Agamemnon, the leader of the Greek forces, who was murdered by his unfaithful wife when he returned from Troy.

Finally, Homer's listeners might well have been particularly fascinated by another homecoming story—this one about a somewhat unusual hero, known as much for his brain as for his brawn. In fact, many legends had already grown up around this hero, whose name was Odysseus. He was the subject of Homer's new epic, the *Odyssey*.

ODYSSEUS: A HERO IN TROUBLE

In Homer's day heroes were thought of as a special class of aristocrats. They were placed somewhere between the gods and ordinary human beings. Heroes experienced pain and death, but they were always sure of themselves, always "on top of the world."

Odysseus is different. He is a hero in trouble. We can relate to Odysseus because we share with him a sense of being somehow lost in a world of difficult choices. Like Odysseus, we have to cope with unfair authority figures. Like him, we have to work very hard to get what we want.

The *Odyssey* is a story marked by melancholy and a feeling of postwar disillusionment. Odysseus was a great soldier in the war, but his war record is not of interest to the monsters that populate the world of his wanderings. Even the people of his home island, Ithaca, seem to lack respect for him. It is as if society were saying to the returning hero, "You were a great soldier once—or so they say—but times have changed. This is a difficult world, and we have more important things to think about than your record."

In the years before the great war, Odysseus had married the beautiful and ever-faithful Penelope, one of several very strong women in the man's world of the Greek epic. (One critic, Robert Graves, was so impressed by the unusual importance of women and home and hearth in the *Odyssey* that he believed Homer must have been a woman.)

Penelope and Odysseus had one son, Telemachus (tə·lem′ə·kəs). He was still a toddler when Odysseus was called by Agamemnon and Menelaus to join them in the war against Troy. But Odysseus was a homebody. He preferred not to go to war, especially a war fought for an unfaithful woman. Even though he was obligated under a treaty to go, Odysseus tried draft-dodging. It is said that when Agamemnon and Menelaus came to fetch him, he pretended to be insane and acted as if he did not recognize his visitors. Instead of entertaining them, he dressed as a peasant and began plowing a field and sowing it with salt. But the "draft board" was smarter than

The *Odyssey* is a story marked by melancholy and a feeling of postwar disillusionment.

One critic, Robert Graves, was so impressed by the unusual importance of women and home and hearth in the *Odyssey* that he believed Homer must have been a woman.

Odysseus. They threw his baby, Telemachus, in front of his oncoming plow. Odysseus revealed his sanity by quickly turning the plow aside to avoid running over his son.

THE WOODEN-HORSE TRICK

Once in Troy, Odysseus performed extremely well as a soldier and commander. It was he, for example, who thought of the famous wooden-horse trick that would lead to the downfall of Troy. For ten years the Greeks had been fighting the Trojans, but they were fighting outside Troy's massive walls. They had been unable to break through the walls and enter the city. Odysseus' plan was to build an enormous wooden horse and hide a few Greek soldiers inside its hollow belly. After the horse was built, the Greeks pushed it up to the gates of Troy and withdrew their armies, so that their camp appeared to be abandoned. Thinking that the Greeks had given up the fight and that the horse was a peace offering, the Trojans brought the horse into their city. That night, the Greeks hidden inside the wooden body came out, opened the gates of Troy to the whole Greek army, and began the battle that was to win the war.

Trojan Horse (16th century) by Niccolò dell' Abbate.
Galleria Estense, Modena, Italy.

THE ANCIENT WORLD AND OURS

The world of Odysseus was harsh, a world familiar with violence. In a certain sense Odysseus and his men act like pirates on their journey home. They think nothing of entering a town and carrying off all its worldly goods. The "worldly goods" in an ancient city might only have been pots and pans and cattle and sheep. The "palaces" the Greeks raided might have been little more than elaborate mud and stone farmhouses. Yet, in the struggles of Odysseus, Penelope, and Telemachus in their "primitive" society that had little in common with the high Athenian culture that would develop several centuries later, there is something that has a great deal to do with us.

A SEARCH FOR THEIR PLACES IN LIFE

Odysseus and his family are people searching for the right relationships with one another and with the people around them. They want to find their proper places in life. It is this theme that sets the tone for the *Odyssey* and determines the unusual way in which the poem is structured.

Instead of beginning at the beginning with Odysseus' departure from Troy, the story begins with his son, Telemachus. Telemachus is now twenty years old. He is threatened by rude, powerful men

> Odysseus and his family are people searching for the right relationships with one another and with the people around them.

swarming about his own home, pressuring his mother to marry one of them. These men are bent on robbing Telemachus of his inheritance. Telemachus is a young man who needs his father, the one person who can put things right at home.

Meanwhile, we hear that his father is stranded on an island, longing to find a way to get back to his wife, child, and home. It is ten years since Odysseus sailed from Troy, twenty years since he left Ithaca to fight in Troy. While Telemachus is in search of his father, Odysseus is in search of a way out of what we might today call his midlife crisis. He is searching for inner peace, for a way to reestablish a natural balance in his life. The quests of father and son provide a framework for the poem and bring us into it as well—because we all are in search of our real identities, our true selves.

RELATIONSHIPS WITH THE GODS

This brings us to mythic and religious questions in the *Odyssey*. **Myths** are stories that use fantasy to express ideas about life that cannot be expressed easily in realistic terms. Myths are essentially religious because they are concerned with the relationship between human beings and the unknown or spiritual realm.

As you will see, Homer is always concerned with the relationship between humans and gods. Homer is religious: For him, the gods control all things. Athena, the goddess of wisdom, is always at the side of Odysseus. This is appropriate, because Odysseus is known for his mental abilities. Thus, in Homer's stories a god can be an **alter ego,** a reflection of a hero's best or worst qualities. The god who works against Odysseus is Poseidon, the god of the sea, who is known for arrogance and a certain brutishness. Odysseus himself can be violent and cruel, just as Poseidon is.

WHO WAS HOMER?

No one knows for sure who Homer was. The later Greeks believed he was a blind minstrel who came from the island of Chios. Some scholars feel there must have been two Homers; some think he was just a legend. But scholars have also argued about whether a man called Shakespeare ever existed. It is almost as if they were saying that Homer and Shakespeare are too good to be true. On the whole, it seems sensible to take the word of the Greeks themselves. We can at least accept the existence of Homer as a model for a class of wandering bards or minstrels later called rhapsodes.

These **rhapsodes,** or "singers of tales," were the historians and entertainers as well as the myth-makers of their time. There was probably no written history in Homer's day. There were certainly no movies and no television, and there was nothing like a Bible or a

> Odysseus is in search of a way out of what we might today call his midlife crisis.

> Some scholars think Homer was just a legend. But scholars have also argued about whether a man called Shakespeare ever existed. It is almost as if they were saying that Homer and Shakespeare are too good to be true.

book of religious stories. So it was that the minstrels traveled about from community to community singing of recent events or of the doings of heroes, gods, and goddesses. It is as if the author of the Book of Kings in the Bible, the writer of a history of World War II, and a famous pop singer were combined in one person. Homer's people saw no conflict among religion, history, and good fun.

A singer with a lyre (Minoan period). Bronze.

Archaeological Museum, Heraklion, Crete, Greece.

HOW WERE THE EPICS TOLD?

Scholars have found that oral epic poets are still composing today in Eastern Europe and other parts of the world. These scholars suggest that stories like the *Iliad* and the *Odyssey* were originally told aloud by people who could not read and write. The stories were composed orally according to a basic story line. But most of the actual words were improvised—made up on the spot—in a way that fit a particular rhythm or meter. The singers of these stories had to be very talented, and they had to work very hard. They also needed an audience that could listen closely.

We can see from this why there is so much repetition in the Homeric epics. The oral storyteller, in fact, had a store of formulas ready in his memory. He knew formulas for describing the arrival and greeting of guests, the eating of meals, and the taking of baths. He knew formulas for describing the sea (it is always "wine-dark") and for describing Athena (she is always "gray-eyed Athena").

Formulas such as these had another advantage: They gave the

> The oral storyteller, in fact, had a store of formulas ready in his memory. He knew formulas for describing the arrival and greeting of guests, the eating of meals, and the taking of baths.

singer and his audience some breathing time. The audience could relax for a moment and enjoy a familiar and memorable passage, while the singer could think ahead to the next part of his story.

When we think about the audience that listened to these stories, we can also understand the value of the extended comparisons that we call **Homeric** or **heroic similes** today. These similes compare heroic or epic events to simple and easily understandable everyday events—events the audience would recognize instantly. For example, at one point in the *Iliad*, Athena prevents an arrow from striking Menelaus. The singer compares the goddess's actions to an action that every listener would have been familiar with:

> She brushed it away from his skin as lightly as when a mother
> Brushes a fly away from her child who is lying in sweet sleep.

Epic poets such as Homer would come to a city and would go through a part of their repertory while there. A story as long as the *Odyssey* (11,300 lines) could not be told at one sitting. We have to assume that if the singer had only a few days in a town, he would summarize some of his story and sing the rest in detail, in as many sittings as he had time for.

This is exactly what will happen in the selections from the *Odyssey* that are presented here. We'll assume that Homer wants to get his story told to us, but that his time is limited. We'll also assume that the audience, before retiring at the end of each performance, wants to talk about the stories they've just heard. You are now part of that audience.

A LIVE PERFORMANCE

What was it like to hear a live performance of the *Odyssey*? We can guess what it was like because there are many instances in the epic itself in which traveling singers appear and sing their tales. In the court of the Phaeacian king, Alcinous (al·sin′ō·əs), in Book 8, for instance, there is a particularly wonderful singer who must make us wonder if the blind Homer is talking about himself. Let's picture the setting of a performance before we start the story.

Imagine a large hall full of people who are freshly bathed, rubbed with fine oils, and draped in clean tunics. Imagine the smell of meat being cooked over charcoal, the sound of voices. Imagine wine being freely poured, the flickering reflections of the great cooking fires, and the torches that light the room. A certain anticipation hangs in the air. It is said that the blind minstrel Homer is in the city and that he has new stories about that long war in Troy. Will he appear and entertain tonight?

Imagine a large hall full of people who are freshly bathed, rubbed with fine oils, and draped in clean tunics. Imagine the smell of meat being cooked over charcoal, the sound of voices. Imagine wine being freely poured, the flickering reflections of the great cooking fires, and the torches that light the room.

PEOPLE AND PLACES
CHARACTERS IN THE ODYSSEY

The following cast of characters includes only those who take part in the sections of the *Odyssey* included in this book. Note that the Greeks in the *Odyssey* are often referred to as **Achaeans** (ə·kē'ənz) or **Argives** (är'gīvz'). *Achaeans* is the most general term, which also includes the people in Ithaca, the island off the west coast of Greece where Odysseus ruled. The word *Achaeans* is taken from the name of an ancient part of northeastern Greece called Achaea. The name *Argives* usually refers to the Greeks who went to fight at Troy.

Penelope (detail) (1864) by John Roddam Spencer-Stanhope.

THE PEOPLE AND PLACES OF ODYSSEUS' WANDERINGS

Aeaea (ē·ē'ə): home of Circe, the witch-goddess.

Alcinous (al·sin'ō·əs): king of Phaeacia. Odysseus tells the story of his adventures to Alcinous' court.

Calypso (kə·lip'sō): beautiful goddess-nymph who keeps Odysseus on her island for seven years.

Charybdis (kə·rib'dis): female monster who sucks in water three times a day to form a deadly whirlpool. (Thought to be a real whirlpool in the Strait of Messina.)

Cicones (si·kō'nēz): people living on the southwestern coast of Thrace, who battled Odysseus and his men on their journey home.

Circe (sur'sē): witch-goddess who turns Odysseus' men into swine.

Cyclops: See **Polyphemus** below.

Erebus (er'ə·bəs): dark place through which the dead pass before entering Hades.

Eurylochus (yōō·ril'ə·kəs): one of Odysseus' loyal crew.

Lotus Eaters: people who feed Odysseus' men with lotus plants to make them forget Ithaca.

Phaeacia (fē·ā'shə): island kingdom ruled by King Alcinous. The Phaeacians are shipbuilders and traders.

Polyphemus (päl'i·fē'məs): the **Cyclops** (sī'kläps') blinded by Odysseus; the son of the sea god Poseidon. **Cyclopes** (sī·klō'pēz') are a race of brutish one-eyed giants who live solitary lives as shepherds, supposedly on the island now known as Sicily.

Scylla (sil'ə): female monster with six serpent heads, each head having a triple row of fangs. (Thought to be a dangerous rock in the Strait of Messina.)

Circe hands the magic potion to Odysseus (5th century B.C.). Detail from a lekythos, a vase used for oils and ointments.

Athens Museum.

Poseidon (5th century B.C.). Bronze.

Acropolis Museum, Athens.

Athena mourning the death of Achilles at Troy. From a marble stele, or pillar.

Sirens: sea nymphs whose beautiful and mysterious music lures sailors to steer their ships toward the rocks.

Teiresias (tī·rē′sē·əs): famous blind prophet from the city of Thebes. Odysseus meets him in the Land of the Dead.

Thrinakia (thri·nā′kē·ə): land where the sun god Helios keeps his cattle.

THE PEOPLE AT HOME IN ITHACA

Antinous (an·tin′ō·əs): one of Penelope's leading suitors; an arrogant and mean young noble from Ithaca.

Eumaeus (yo͞o·mē′əs): swineherd, one of Odysseus' loyal servants.

Eurycleia (yo͞o·ri·klī′yə): Odysseus' old nurse.

Eurymachus (yo͞o·rim′ə·kəs): suitor of Penelope.

Eurynome (yo͞o·rin′ə·mē): Penelope's housekeeper.

Penelope (pə·nel′ə·pē): Odysseus' faithful wife.

Philoeteus (fi·loi′tē·əs): cowherd, one of Odysseus' loyal servants.

Telemachus (tə·lem′ə·kəs): Odysseus' son.

THE GODS

Apollo (ə·päl′ō): god of poetry, music, prophecy, medicine, and archery.

Athena (ə·thē′nə): favorite daughter of Zeus; the great goddess of wisdom and the arts of war and peace. She favored the Greeks during the Trojan War. She is often called Pallas Athena.

Cronus (krō′nəs): in Greek mythology, a Titan (giant god) who ruled the universe until his son Zeus overthrew him.

Helios (hē′lē·äs′): sun god.

Hephaestus (hē·fes′təs): god of metalworking.

Hermes (hʉr′mēz′): messenger god.

Olympus (ō·lim′pəs): mountain home of the gods.

Poseidon (pō·sī′dən): god of the sea; brother of Zeus. Called Earth Shaker because he is believed to cause earthquakes. Poseidon is an enemy of Odysseus.

Zeus (zyo͞os): the most powerful god, whose home is on Olympus.

THE PERILOUS JOURNEY

WRITING FOCUS: Speculation About Causes or Effects

We've always looked at the horizon and wondered what's out there. Today we have ships probing into the outer regions of the solar system, peering with camera and computer through the clouds of distant planets. Centuries ago, when we believed the earth was flat, we stood on the shore and stared out toward the edge where the ocean dropped off into nothing, and speculated about what we'd find if we sailed that far.

We've always journeyed. We've packed up and moved on, to leave something behind or to find something new. But the journey isn't always out into the unknown—there are also journeys of return, efforts to get home again. . . .

If we are fortunate, if the gods and muses are smiling, about every generation someone comes along to inspire the imagination for the journey each of us takes.

—Bill Moyers

Writer's Notebook

"The journey" is a rich metaphor for life. Think of its many aspects: maps or guides; dangers along the way; chance discoveries; paying for the trip; arriving; returning.

Write briefly about one aspect of your life journey so far. If, for instance, you feel that you've had to work especially hard for something you've accomplished or tried to accomplish, you might write about paying for the ticket—what have you had to do to get there? If you prefer, don't write about your life so far, but about the next several years. Save your notes.

WORK IN PROGRESS

BEFORE YOU READ
THE ODYSSEY

Reading Focus

Heroes at Large

We admire them in movies, TV shows, and the news; in books that range from comics to history texts; on sports teams, in science labs, and in art studios; and, if we look closely, even in our own lives. They're our heroes, and they may be female or male, real or fictional. They set off on the journey that we're all on, deep inside: the quest to discover who we are and what we can do. They encounter challenges, setbacks, and dangers; they make mistakes, lose their way, and find it again. And whether they fail or succeed, they do it on a grand scale, giving us new perspectives on our own lives. As you read these tales of Odysseus' wanderings, notice what he does—and doesn't—have in common with modern heroes.

Quickwrite

What makes a hero? In your Reader's Log, write the names of two or three people, real or fictional, whom you consider heroic. Then take a few minutes to list character traits that you think a hero of any time and place should have. Keep adding to your notes as you read the *Odyssey*.

THE ODYSSEY

HOMER

translated by Robert Fitzgerald

1 Troy	5 Island of Aeolia	9 Circe	13 Thrinakia
2 Cicones	6 Laestrygonians	10 Sirens	14 Calypso
3 Lotus Eaters	7 Circe	11 Charybdis	15 Phaeacia
4 Cyclops	8 Teiresias and the Land of the Dead	12 Scylla	16 Ithaca

TELL THE STORY

Homer opens with an invocation, or prayer, asking the Muse° to help him sing his tale. Notice how the singer gives his listeners hints about how his story is to end.

> Sing in me, Muse, and through me tell the story
> of that man skilled in all ways of contending,°
> the wanderer, harried for years on end,
> after he plundered the stronghold
> on the proud height of Troy.
> 5   He saw the townlands
> and learned the minds of many distant men,
> and weathered many bitter nights and days
> in his deep heart at sea, while he fought only
> to save his life, to bring his shipmates home.
> 10 But not by will nor valor could he save them,
> for their own recklessness destroyed them all—
> children and fools, they killed and feasted on
> the cattle of Lord Helios, the Sun,
> and he who moves all day through heaven
> 15 took from their eyes the dawn of their return.
>
> Of these adventures, Muse, daughter of Zeus,
> tell us in our time, lift the great song again.
> Begin when all the rest who left behind them
> headlong death in battle or at sea
> 20 had long ago returned, while he alone still hungered
> for home and wife. Her ladyship Calypso
> clung to him in her sea-hollowed caves—
> a nymph, immortal and most beautiful,
> who craved him for her own.
>   And when long years and seasons
> 25 wheeling brought around that point of time
> ordained for him to make his passage homeward,
> trials and dangers, even so, attended him
> even in Ithaca, near those he loved.
> Yet all the gods had pitied Lord Odysseus,
> 30 all but Poseidon, raging cold and rough
> against the brave king till he came ashore
> at last on his own land.

(from Book 1)

The Greeks believed that there were nine Muses, daughters of Zeus, the chief god. The Muses inspired people to produce music, poetry, dance, and all the other arts.

2. contending: fighting; dealing with difficulties.

READER'S LOG *Read this prayer to the Muse aloud. (You could read it as a chorus, or you could alternate with single voices.) What does Homer tell you about the hero and about what is going to happen to him? Take notes for your log.*

PART ONE: THE WANDERINGS

"I AM LAERTES' SON...."

The first part of the epic (Books 1–4) tells about Odysseus' son, Telemachus. Telemachus has been searching the Mediterranean world for his father, who had never returned from the ten-year Trojan War. (Today, Odysseus would be listed as missing in action.)

When we first meet Odysseus, in Book 5 of the epic, he is a prisoner of the beautiful goddess Calypso. The old soldier is in despair: He has spent ten years trying to get home. However, even when Calypso finally releases Odysseus, the sea god, Poseidon, refuses to allow him safe passage over the treacherous seas. Odysseus is nearly dead when he is washed up on the island of Scheria, home of the Phaeacians. Welcomed by Alcinous, king of the Phaeacians, Odysseus is a guest at court that evening (Books 6–8).*

To the ancient people of Greece and Asia Minor, all guests were god-sent. They had to be treated with great courtesy before they could be asked to identify themselves and state their business. That night, at the banquet, the stranger who was washed up on the beach is seated in the guest's place of honor. A minstrel, or singer, is called, and the mystery guest gives him a gift of pork, crisp with fat, and requests a song about Troy. In effect, Odysseus is asking for a song about himself.

Odysseus weeps as the minstrel's song reminds him of all his dead companions, who will never see their homes again. Now Odysseus is asked by the king to identify himself. It is here that he begins the story of his journey.

Man with a headband (c. 460–450 B.C.). Bronze.

Now this was the reply Odysseus made:

"I am Laertes' son, Odysseus.

Men hold me

formidable for guile in peace and war:
this fame has gone abroad to the sky's rim.
My home is on the peaked seamark of Ithaca
under Mount Neion's windblown robe of leaves,
in sight of other islands—Doulikhion,
Same, wooded Zakynthos—Ithaca
being most lofty in that coastal sea,
and northwest, while the rest lie east and south.
A rocky isle, but good for a boy's training;

εἴμ' Ὀδυσεὺς Λαερτιάδης,
ὃς πᾶσι δόλοισιν
ἀνθρώποισι μέλω, καί
μευ κλέος οὐρανὸν
ἵκει. ναιετάω δ'
Ἰθάκην εὐδείελον·
ἐν δ' ὄρος αὐτῇ,
Νήριτον εἰνοσίφυλλον
ἀριπρεπές· ἀμφὶ δὲ
νῆσοι πολλαὶ
ναιετάουσι μάλα
σχεδὸν ἀλλήλῃσι,
Δουλίχιόν τε Σάμη
τε καὶ ὑλήεσσα
Ζάκυνθος.

WORDS TO OWN

formidable (fôr′mə·də·bəl) *adj.*: awe-inspiring in excellence; strikingly impressive.

LITERATURE AND ARCHAEOLOGY

Troy: It Casts a Spell

The ancient Greeks and Romans had no doubt that the Trojan War really happened. They believed it took place around 1200 B.C. The Greek historian Thucydides (c. 460–c. 400 B.C.) believed that the causes of the war were really economic and political—he rejected Homer's story of Helen's abduction and the vengeance taken on Troy by the Greeks. By the middle of the nineteenth century, however, most historians had dismissed the Trojan War as a charming legend.

Enter Heinrich Schliemann (1822–1890). Schliemann was a wealthy German merchant who turned archaeologist when he was middle-aged and archaeology was in its infancy. Armed with a well-thumbed copy of Homer's *Iliad,* Schliemann arrived in northwestern Turkey in 1871. A few miles from the Dardanelles, that narrow and windy sea lane that divides Europe from Asia, Schliemann began excavations at a small hill called Hisarlik, perched about a hundred feet above a wide plain.

After five long years, Schliemann made an electrifying discovery. He unearthed gold cups, bracelets, and a spectacular gold headdress. Homer had called Troy "rich in gold," and Schliemann now told the world he had found the treasure of King Priam. (The gold's eventful history was not over. Schliemann

I shall not see on earth a place more dear,
though I have been detained long by Calypso,
loveliest among goddesses, who held me
in her smooth caves, to be her heart's delight,
as Circe of Aeaea, the enchantress,
desired me, and detained me in her hall.
But in my heart I never gave consent.
Where shall a man find sweetness to surpass
his own home and his parents? In far lands
he shall not, though he find a house of gold.

What of my sailing, then, from Troy?
                                    What of those years
of rough adventure, weathered under Zeus?
The wind that carried west from Ilion°
brought me to Ismaros, on the far shore,
a strongpoint on the coast of the Cicones.
I stormed that place and killed the men who fought.

56. Ilion (il′ē·än): another name for Troy.

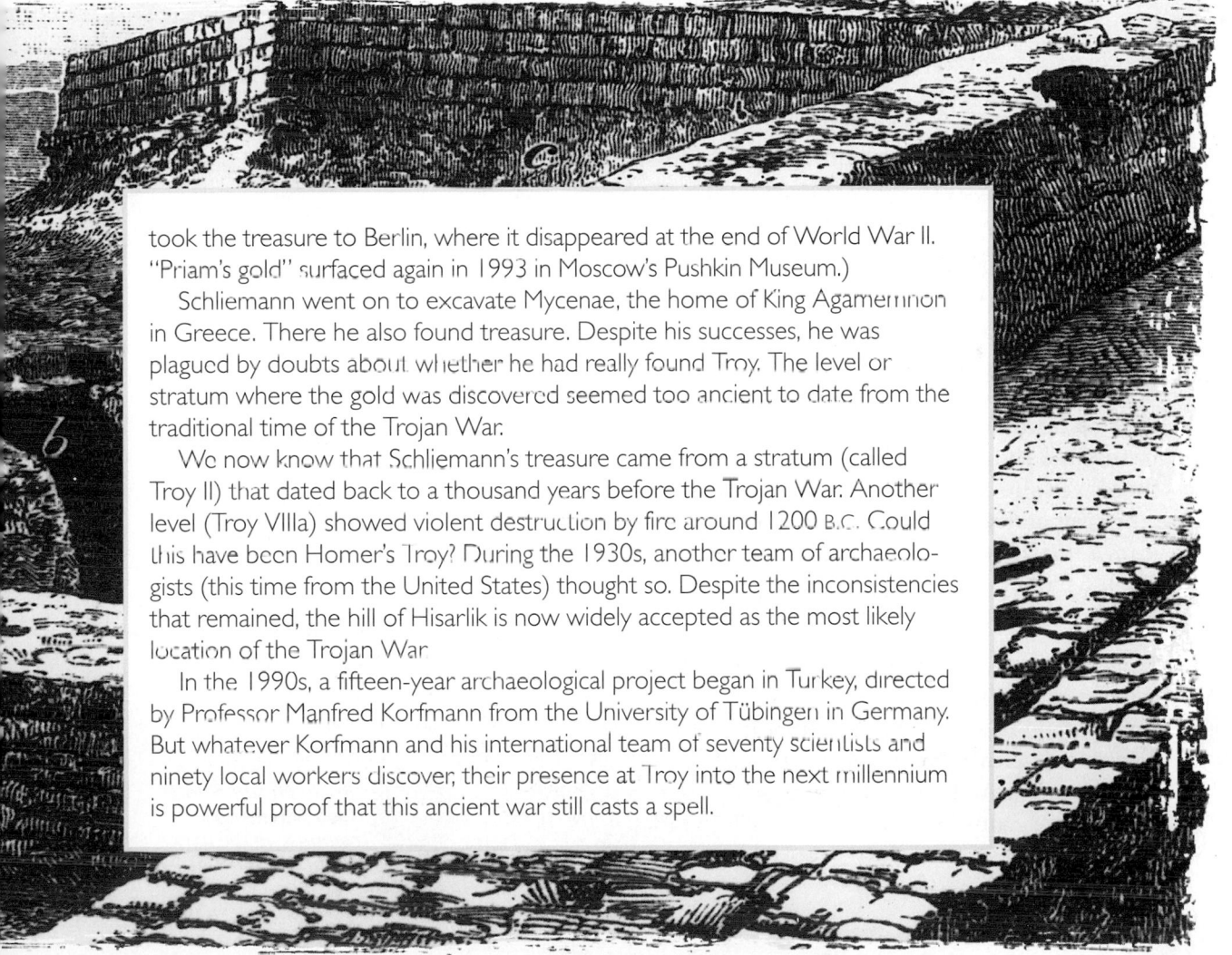

took the treasure to Berlin, where it disappeared at the end of World War II.
"Priam's gold" surfaced again in 1993 in Moscow's Pushkin Museum.)

Schliemann went on to excavate Mycenae, the home of King Agamemnon
in Greece. There he also found treasure. Despite his successes, he was
plagued by doubts about whether he had really found Troy. The level or
stratum where the gold was discovered seemed too ancient to date from the
traditional time of the Trojan War.

We now know that Schliemann's treasure came from a stratum (called
Troy II) that dated back to a thousand years before the Trojan War. Another
level (Troy VIIa) showed violent destruction by fire around 1200 B.C. Could
this have been Homer's Troy? During the 1930s, another team of archaeolo-
gists (this time from the United States) thought so. Despite the inconsistencies
that remained, the hill of Hisarlik is now widely accepted as the most likely
location of the Trojan War.

In the 1990s, a fifteen-year archaeological project began in Turkey, directed
by Professor Manfred Korfmann from the University of Tübingen in Germany.
But whatever Korfmann and his international team of seventy scientists and
ninety local workers discover, their presence at Troy into the next millennium
is powerful proof that this ancient war still casts a spell.

60　Plunder we took, and we enslaved the women,
　　to make division, equal shares to all—
　　but on the spot I told them: 'Back, and quickly!
　　Out to sea again!' My men were mutinous,
　　fools, on stores of wine. Sheep after sheep
65　they butchered by the surf, and shambling cattle,
　　feasting—while fugitives went inland, running
　　to call to arms the main force of Cicones.
　　This was an army, trained to fight on horseback
　　or, where the ground required, on foot. They came
70　with dawn over that terrain like the leaves
　　and blades of spring. So doom appeared to us,
　　dark word of Zeus for us, our evil days.
　　My men stood up and made a fight of it—
　　backed on the ships, with lances kept in play,
75　from bright morning through the blaze of noon
　　holding our beach, although so far outnumbered;
　　but when the sun passed toward unyoking time,
　　then the Achaeans, one by one, gave way.
　　Six benches were left empty in every ship
80　that evening when we pulled away from death.
　　And this new grief we bore with us to sea:
　　our precious lives we had, but not our friends.
　　No ship made sail next day until some shipmate
　　had raised a cry, three times, for each poor ghost
85　unfleshed by the Cicones on that field.

　　Now Zeus the lord of cloud roused in the north
　　a storm against the ships, and driving veils
　　of squall moved down like night on land and sea.
　　The bows went plunging at the gust; sails
90　cracked and lashed out strips in the big wind.
　　We saw death in that fury, dropped the yards,
　　unshipped the oars, and pulled for the nearest lee:
　　then two long days and nights we lay offshore
　　worn out and sick at heart, tasting our grief,
95　until a third Dawn came with ringlets shining.
　　Then we put up our masts, hauled sail, and rested,
　　letting the steersmen and the breeze take over.

　　I might have made it safely home, that time,
　　but as I came round Malea the current
100　took me out to sea, and from the north
　　a fresh gale drove me on, past Cythera.
　　Nine days I drifted on the teeming sea
　　before dangerous high winds."

(from Book 9)

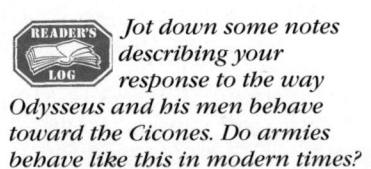
Jot down some notes describing your response to the way Odysseus and his men behave toward the Cicones. Do armies behave like this in modern times?

Like other characters in the Odyssey, *the goddess Calypso has over the years inspired many stories, poems, and songs. Here is how Homer describes Odysseus' feelings about his entrapment by the goddess:*

> The sweet days of his lifetime
> were running out in anguish over his exile,
> for long ago the nymph had ceased to please.
> Though he fought shy of her and her desire,
> he lay with her each night, for she compelled him.
> But when day came he sat on the rocky shore
> and broke his own heart groaning, with eyes wet
> scanning the bare horizon of the sea.

(*from* Book 5)

In the lyrics that follow, a modern songwriter sings once again the story of Odysseus and the lovely Calypso. The singer is Calypso.

Calypso
Suzanne Vega

My name is Calypso
And I have lived alone
I live on an island
And I waken to the dawn
5   A long time ago
I watched him struggle with the sea
I knew that he was drowning
And I brought him into me
Now today
10 Come morning light
He sails away
After one last night
I let him go

My name is Calypso
15 My garden overflows
Thick and wild and hidden
Is the sweetness there that grows
My hair it blows long
As I sing into the wind
20 I tell of nights
Where I could taste the salt on his skin

Salt of the waves
And of tears
And though he pulled away
25 I kept him here for years
I let him go.

My name is Calypso
I have let him go
In the dawn he sails away
30 To be gone forever more
And the waves will take him in again
But he'll know their ways now
I will stand upon the shore
With a clean heart
35 And my song in the wind
The sand will sting my feet
And the sky will burn
It's a lonely time ahead
I do not ask him to return
40 I let him go
I let him go

THE LOTUS EATERS

"Upon the tenth

105   we came to the coastline of the Lotus Eaters,
      who live upon that flower. We landed there
      to take on water. All ships' companies
      mustered° alongside for the midday meal.
      Then I sent out two picked men and a runner
110   to learn what race of men that land sustained.
      They fell in, soon enough, with Lotus Eaters,
      who showed no will to do us harm, only
      offering the sweet Lotus to our friends—
      but those who ate this honeyed plant, the Lotus,
115   never cared to report, nor to return:
      they longed to stay forever, browsing on
      that native bloom, forgetful of their homeland.
      I drove them, all three wailing, to the ships,
      tied them down under their rowing benches,
120   and called the rest: 'All hands aboard;
      come, clear the beach and no one taste
      the Lotus, or you lose your hope of home.'
      Filing in to their places by the rowlocks
      my oarsmen dipped their long oars in the surf,
125   and we moved out again on our seafaring."

(from Book 9)

108. mustered: gathered; assembled.

THE CYCLOPS

In his next adventure Odysseus describes his encounter with the Cyclops named Polyphemus, Poseidon's one-eyed monster son. Polyphemus may well represent the brute forces that any hero must overcome before he can reach home. Now Odysseus must rely on the special intelligence associated with his name. Odysseus is the cleverest of the ancient Greek heroes because his divine guardian is the goddess of wisdom, Athena.

It is Odysseus' famed curiosity that leads him to the Cyclops's cave and that makes him insist on waiting for the barbaric giant.

Odysseus is still speaking to the court of King Alcinous.

      "We lit a fire, burnt an offering,
      and took some cheese to eat; then sat in silence
      around the embers, waiting. When he came
      he had a load of dry boughs on his shoulder
130   to stoke his fire at suppertime. He dumped it
      with a great crash into that hollow cave,
      and we all scattered fast to the far wall.

READER'S LOG *Readers have speculated for years over exactly what it was the sailors ate. With a group, make up your own dialogue to dramatize this scene. Note in your log what you think really happens here.*

Ulysses and His Companions on the Island of the Cyclops by Pellegrino Tibaldi.

Then over the broad cavern floor he ushered
the ewes he meant to milk. He left his rams
135   and he-goats in the yard outside, and swung
high overhead a slab of solid rock
to close the cave. Two dozen four-wheeled wagons,
with heaving wagon teams, could not have stirred
the tonnage of that rock from where he wedged it
140   over the doorsill. Next he took his seat
and milked his bleating ewes. A practiced job
he made of it, giving each ewe her suckling;
thickened his milk, then, into curds and whey,
sieved out the curds to drip in withy baskets,°
145   and poured the whey to stand in bowls
cooling until he drank it for his supper.
When all these chores were done, he poked the fire,
heaping on brushwood. In the glare he saw us.

'Strangers,' he said, 'who are you? And where from?
150   What brings you here by seaways—a fair traffic?
Or are you wandering rogues, who cast your lives
like dice, and <u>ravage</u> other folk by sea?'

We felt a pressure on our hearts, in dread
of that deep rumble and that mighty man.
155   But all the same I spoke up in reply:

'We are from Troy, Achaeans, blown off course
by shifting gales on the Great South Sea;
homeward bound, but taking routes and ways
uncommon; so the will of Zeus would have it.
160   We served under Agamemnon, son of Atreus—
the whole world knows what city
he laid waste, what armies he destroyed.
It was our luck to come here; here we stand,
beholden for your help, or any gifts
165   you give—as custom is to honor strangers.
We would entreat you, great Sir, have a care
for the gods' courtesy; Zeus will avenge
the unoffending guest.'

                                He answered this
from his brute chest, unmoved:

                                'You are a ninny,
170   or else you come from the other end of nowhere,
telling me, mind the gods! We Cyclopes

144. withy baskets: baskets made
from willow twigs.

WORDS TO OWN
ravage (rav′ij) *v.*: destroy violently; ruin.

care not a whistle for your thundering Zeus
or all the gods in bliss; we have more force by far.
I would not let you go for fear of Zeus—
175   you or your friends—unless I had a whim to.
Tell me, where was it, now, you left your ship—
around the point, or down the shore, I wonder?'

He thought he'd find out, but I saw through this,
and answered with a ready lie:

                                     'My ship?

180   Poseidon Lord, who sets the earth atremble,
broke it up on the rocks at your land's end.
A wind from seaward served him, drove us there.
We are survivors, these good men and I.'

Neither reply nor pity came from him,
185   but in one stride he clutched at my companions
and caught two in his hands like squirming puppies
to beat their brains out, spattering the floor.
Then he dismembered them and made his meal,
gaping and crunching like a mountain lion—
190   everything: innards, flesh, and marrow bones.
We cried aloud, lifting our hands to Zeus,

powerless, looking on at this, appalled;
but Cyclops went on filling up his belly
with manflesh and great gulps of whey,
195 then lay down like a mast among his sheep.
My heart beat high now at the chance of action,
and drawing the sharp sword from my hip I went
along his flank to stab him where the midriff
holds the liver. I had touched the spot
200 when sudden fear stayed me: if I killed him
we perished there as well, for we could never
move his ponderous doorway slab aside.
So we were left to groan and wait for morning.

When the young Dawn with fingertips of rose
205 lit up the world, the Cyclops built a fire
and milked his handsome ewes, all in due order,
putting the sucklings to the mothers. Then,
his chores being all dispatched, he caught
another brace of men to make his breakfast,
210 and whisked away his great door slab
to let his sheep go through—but he, behind,
reset the stone as one would cap a quiver.
There was a din of whistling as the Cyclops
rounded his flock to higher ground, then stillness.
215 And now I pondered how to hurt him worst,
if but Athena granted what I prayed for.
Here are the means I thought would serve my turn:

a club, or staff, lay there along the fold—
an olive tree, felled green and left to season
220 for Cyclops' hand. And it was like a mast
a lugger° of twenty oars, broad in the beam—
a deep-seagoing craft—might carry:
so long, so big around, it seemed. Now I
chopped out a six-foot section of this pole
225 and set it down before my men, who scraped it;
and when they had it smooth, I hewed again
to make a stake with pointed end. I held this
in the fire's heart and turned it, toughening it,
then hid it, well back in the cavern, under
230 one of the dung piles in profusion there.
Now came the time to toss for it: who ventured
along with me? Whose hand could bear to thrust
and grind that spike in Cyclops' eye, when mild
sleep had mastered him? As luck would have it,

Odysseus and his men blinding the
Cyclops (530–510 B.C.). Hydria, or
water jar.

Collection Villa Guilia, Rome.

221. lugger: type of sailboat.

WORDS TO OWN
profusion (prō·fyoo′zhən) *n.:* large supply; abundance.

235   the men I would have chosen won the toss—
four strong men, and I made five as captain.

At evening came the shepherd with his flock,
his woolly flock. The rams as well, this time,
entered the cave: by some sheepherding whim—
240   or a god's bidding—none were left outside.
He hefted his great boulder into place
and sat him down to milk the bleating ewes
in proper order, put the lambs to suck,
and swiftly ran through all his evening chores.
245   Then he caught two more men and feasted on them.
My moment was at hand, and I went forward
holding an ivy bowl of my dark drink,
looking up, saying:

                      'Cyclops, try some wine.
Here's liquor to wash down your scraps of men.
250   Taste it, and see the kind of drink we carried
under our planks. I meant it for an offering
if you would help us home. But you are mad,
unbearable, a bloody monster! After this,
will any other traveler come to see you?'

255   He seized and drained the bowl, and it went down
so fiery and smooth he called for more:

'Give me another, thank you kindly. Tell me,
how are you called? I'll make a gift will please you.
Even Cyclopes know the wine grapes grow
260   out of grassland and loam in heaven's rain,
but here's a bit of nectar and ambrosia!'°

Three bowls I brought him, and he poured them down.
I saw the fuddle and flush come over him,
then I sang out in cordial tones:

                          'Cyclops,
265   you ask my honorable name? Remember
the gift you promised me, and I shall tell you.
My name is Nohbdy: mother, father, and friends,
everyone calls me Nohbdy.'

                      And he said:
'Nohbdy's my meat, then, after I eat his friends.
270   Others come first. There's a noble gift, now.'

Even as he spoke, he reeled and tumbled backward,
his great head lolling to one side; and sleep
took him like any creature. Drunk, hiccuping,
he dribbled streams of liquor and bits of men.

261. nectar and ambrosia: drink and food of the gods

275 Now, by the gods, I drove my big hand spike
  deep in the embers, charring it again,
  and cheered my men along with battle talk
  to keep their courage up: no quitting now.
  The pike of olive, green though it had been,
280 reddened and glowed as if about to catch.
  I drew it from the coals and my four fellows
  gave me a hand, lugging it near the Cyclops
  as more than natural force nerved them; straight
  forward they sprinted, lifted it, and rammed it
285 deep in his crater eye, and I leaned on it
  turning it as a shipwright turns a drill
  in planking, having men below to swing
  the two-handled strap that spins it in the groove.
  So with our brand we bored that great eye socket
290 while blood ran out around the red-hot bar.
  Eyelid and lash were seared; the pierced ball
  hissed broiling, and the roots popped.

           In a smithy°

  one sees a white-hot axhead or an adze°
  plunged and wrung in a cold tub, screeching steam—
295 the way they make soft iron hale and hard—
  just so that eyeball hissed around the spike.
  The Cyclops bellowed and the rock roared round him,
  and we fell back in fear. Clawing his face
  he tugged the bloody spike out of his eye,
300 threw it away, and his wild hands went groping;
  then he set up a howl for Cyclopes
  who lived in caves on windy peaks nearby.
  Some heard him; and they came by divers° ways
  to clump around outside and call:

292. smithy: blacksmith's shop, where iron tools are made.
293. adze: tool like an ax but with a longer, curved blade.

303. divers: diverse; various.

Odysseus and three companions blinding Polyphemus (6th century B.C.).
Detail from a Cyrenean cup.

'What ails you,

305 Polyphemus? Why do you cry so sore
in the starry night? You will not let us sleep.
Sure no man's driving off your flock? No man
has tricked you, ruined you?'

Out of the cave

the mammoth Polyphemus roared in answer:

310 'Nohbdy, Nohbdy's tricked me. Nohbdy's ruined me!'

To this rough shout they made a sage reply:

'Ah well, if nobody has played you foul
there in your lonely bed, we are no use in pain
given by great Zeus. Let it be your father,
Poseidon Lord, to whom you pray.'

315   So saying

they trailed away. And I was filled with laughter
to see how like a charm the name deceived them.
Now Cyclops, wheezing as the pain came on him,
fumbled to wrench away the great doorstone

320 and squatted in the breach with arms thrown wide
for any silly beast or man who bolted—
hoping somehow I might be such a fool.
But I kept thinking how to win the game:
death sat there huge; how could we slip away?

325 I drew on all my wits, and ran through tactics,
reasoning as a man will for dear life,
until a trick came—and it pleased me well.
The Cyclops' rams were handsome, fat, with heavy
fleeces, a dark violet.

Three abreast

330 I tied them silently together, twining
cords of willow from the ogre's bed;
then slung a man under each middle one
to ride there safely, shielded left and right.
So three sheep could convey each man. I took

335 the woolliest ram, the choicest of the flock,
and hung myself under his kinky belly,
pulled up tight, with fingers twisted deep
in sheepskin ringlets for an iron grip.
So, breathing hard, we waited until morning.

340 When Dawn spread out her fingertips of rose
the rams began to stir, moving for pasture,

WORDS TO OWN
sage (sāj) *adj.:* wise.

and peals of bleating echoed round the pens
where dams with udders full called for a milking.
Blinded, and sick with pain from his head wound,
345 the master stroked each ram, then let it pass,
but my men riding on the pectoral fleece°
the giant's blind hands blundering never found.
Last of them all my ram, the leader, came,
weighted by wool and me with my meditations.
350 The Cyclops patted him, and then he said:

'Sweet cousin ram, why lag behind the rest
in the night cave? You never linger so,
but graze before them all, and go afar
to crop sweet grass, and take your stately way
355 leading along the streams, until at evening
you run to be the first one in the fold.
Why, now, so far behind? Can you be grieving
over your Master's eye? That carrion rogue°
and his accurst companions burnt it out
360 when he had conquered all my wits with wine.
Nohbdy will not get out alive, I swear.
Oh, had you brain and voice to tell
where he may be now, dodging all my fury!
Bashed by this hand and bashed on this rock wall
365 his brains would strew the floor, and I should have
rest from the outrage Nohbdy worked upon me.'

He sent us into the open, then. Close by,
I dropped and rolled clear of the ram's belly,
going this way and that to untie the men.
370 With many glances back, we rounded up
his fat, stiff-legged sheep to take aboard,
and drove them down to where the good ship lay.
We saw, as we came near, our fellows' faces
shining; then we saw them turn to grief
375 tallying those who had not fled from death.

346. pectoral fleece: wool on an animal's chest.

358. carrion rogue: rotten scoundrel. Carrion is decaying flesh.

Odysseus escaping the cave of Polyphemus under the belly of the ram (c. 510 B.C.). Detail from a krater, a vessel for holding wine.

Badisches Landesmuseum, Karlsruhe, Germany.

I hushed them, jerking head and eyebrows up,
and in a low voice told them: 'Load this herd;
move fast, and put the ship's head toward the breakers.'
They all pitched in at loading, then embarked
380 and struck their oars into the sea. Far out,
as far offshore as shouted words would carry,
I sent a few back to the adversary:

'O Cyclops! Would you feast on my companions?
Puny, am I, in a Caveman's hands?
385 How do you like the beating that we gave you,
you damned cannibal? Eater of guests
under your roof! Zeus and the gods have paid you!'

The blind thing in his doubled fury broke
a hilltop in his hands and heaved it after us.
390 Ahead of our black prow it struck and sank
whelmed in a spuming geyser, a giant wave
that washed the ship stern foremost back to shore.
I got the longest boathook out and stood
fending us off, with furious nods to all
395 to put their backs into a racing stroke—
row, row or perish. So the long oars bent
kicking the foam sternward, making head
until we drew away, and twice as far.
Now when I cupped my hands I heard the crew
in low voices protesting:

400   'Godsake, Captain!
Why bait the beast again? Let him alone!'

'That tidal wave he made on the first throw
all but beached us.'

                                        'All but stove us in!'

'Give him our bearing with your trumpeting,
he'll get the range and lob° a boulder.'   **405. lob:** toss.

405   'Aye
He'll smash our timbers and our heads together!'

I would not heed them in my glorying spirit,
but let my anger flare and yelled:

                                              'Cyclops,
if ever mortal man inquire
410 how you were put to shame and blinded, tell him

- -
WORDS TO OWN
adversary (ad′vər·ser′ē) *n*.: enemy; opponent.
- -

Odysseus, raider of cities, took your eye:
Laertes' son, whose home's on Ithaca!'

At this he gave a mighty sob and rumbled:

'Now comes the weird° upon me, spoken of old.
415   A wizard, grand and wondrous, lived here—Telemus,
a son of Eurymus; great length of days
he had in wizardry among the Cyclopes,
and these things he foretold for time to come:
my great eye lost, and at Odysseus' hands.
420   Always I had in mind some giant, armed
in giant force, would come against me here.
But this, but you—small, pitiful, and twiggy—
you put me down with wine, you blinded me.
Come back, Odysseus, and I'll treat you well,
425   praying the god of earthquake to befriend you—
his son I am, for he by his avowal
fathered me, and, if he will, he may
heal me of this black wound—he and no other
of all the happy gods or mortal men.'

430   Few words I shouted in reply to him:

'If I could take your life I would and take
your time away, and hurl you down to hell!
The god of earthquake could not heal you there!'

At this he stretched his hands out in his darkness
435   toward the sky of stars, and prayed Poseidon:

'O hear me, lord, blue girdler of the islands,
if I am thine indeed, and thou art father:
grant that Odysseus, raider of cities, never
see his home: Laertes' son, I mean,
440   who kept his hall on Ithaca. Should destiny
intend that he shall see his roof again
among his family in his fatherland,
far be that day, and dark the years between.
Let him lose all companions, and return
445   under strange sail to bitter days at home.'"

(*from* Book 9)

Here we will imagine that Homer stops reciting for the night. The listeners would now go off to various corners of the local nobleman's house. The blind poet might take a glass of wine before turning in. The people who heard the poet's stories might ask questions among themselves and look forward to the next evening's installment.

414. weird: fate.

The Cyclops Polyphemus
(2nd century B.C.). Marble.

Read "Welcome: A Religious Duty" on page 909. As you continue the story, trace the ways Homer repeatedly dramatizes the importance of mutual respect between people. Add your own ideas on hospitality today—what are the customs in your family and neighborhood? What about society as a whole?

Welcome: A Religious Duty

Today's visitors to Greece are often struck by the generous hospitality of the people. An ancient tradition lies behind the traveler's welcome in Greece—and it is a tradition that was fundamentally religious before it became a part of social custom.

Zeus, the king of the gods, demanded that strangers be treated graciously. Hosts had a religious duty to welcome strangers, and guests had a responsibility to respect hosts. The tight interconnections and mutual respect in this host-guest relationship are reflected in the fact that the word *xenos* (zē´näs) in ancient Greek can mean both "host" and "guest." The relationship is often symbolized in the *Odyssey* by the presentation of gifts. Alcinous, the king of the Phaeacians, for example, gives Odysseus a magically swift ship to get him home.

What happens when the host-guest relationship is abused or otherwise breaks down? In Homer's epic songs of the Trojan War, the *Iliad* and the *Odyssey*, this happens at least three times. The first occasion caused the war itself: Paris, prince of Troy, ran off with the beautiful Helen from Sparta while he was the guest of Helen's husband, Menelaus. For the Greeks, this insult to *xenia* (hospitality) was at least as serious as Helen's unfaithfulness, and it meant that Zeus would, in the end, allow the Greeks to triumph in the long war.

The second example of violated hospitality has its humorous and ironic side. In the *Odyssey*, the Cyclops is monstrous not only because of his huge size and brutish appearance. He is set apart from civilized beings precisely because of his barbaric outlook on *xenia*. When Odysseus begs the Cyclops for hospitality and warns that Zeus will avenge an injured guest, the Cyclops replies that he and his kind "care not a whistle for . . . Zeus" (line 172). With dark humor, the Cyclops uses the word *xeineion* (Greek for "guest-gift") when he tells Odysseus that he will have the privilege of being eaten last (line 270). The poetic justice of the Cyclops's blinding would not be lost on Homer's Greek audience.

The final example of a breach in the law of hospitality underlies the entire plot structure of the *Odyssey*: Back in Ithaca, the suitors year after year abuse the hospitality of Odysseus— an absent "host"—and threaten to take away his wife. The bloody vengeance that Odysseus takes on these suitors should be understood in the context of their outrageous violation of religious law. The suitors have turned hospitality into a crude mockery. Perhaps it is not accidental that just before the battle Odysseus invokes the host-guest relationship when he quietly gives his son, Telemachus, the signal to fight (lines 923–924):

> "Telemachus, the stranger [*xeinos*]
> you welcomed in your hall has not disgraced you."

The Cyclops in the Ocean

Nikki Giovanni

Moving slowly . . . against time . . . patiently majestic . . .
the cyclops . . . in the ocean . . . meets no Ulysses . . .

Through the night . . . he sighs . . . throbbing against the
shore . . . declaring . . . for the adventure . . .

5 A wall of gray . . . gathered by a slow touch . . . slash and
slither . . . through the waiting screens . . . separating into
nodules . . . making my panes . . . accept the touch . . .

Not content . . . to watch my frightened gaze . . . he clamors
beneath the sash . . . dancing on my sill . . .

10 Certain to die . . . when the sun . . . returns . . .

Tropical Storm Dennis
August 15–18, 1981, Florida

THE WITCH CIRCE

After sailing from the Cyclops's island, Odysseus and his men land on the island of Aeolia. There, the wind king, Aeolus, does Odysseus a favor. He puts all the stormy winds in a bag so that they will not harm the Ithacans. The bull's-hide bag containing the winds is wedged under Odysseus' afterdeck. But during the voyage, the suspicious and curious sailors open the bag, thinking it contains treasure, and the evil winds roar up into hurricanes to threaten the luckless Odysseus again.

After many of his men are killed and eaten by the gigantic cannibals called Laestrygonians, Odysseus' ship lands on Aeaea, the home of the witch Circe. Here, a party of twenty-three men, led by Eurylochus, goes off to explore the island. Odysseus is still telling his story to King Alcinous and his court.

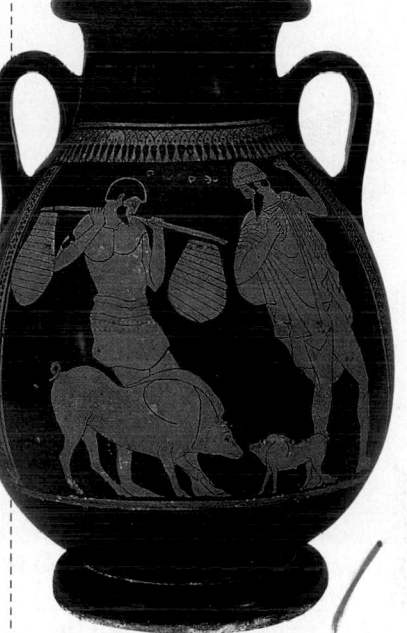

Pigs, swineherd, and Odysseus (470–460 B.C.) by the Pig Painter. Pelike, or jar.

Fitzwilliam Museum, University of Cambridge.

"In the wild wood they found an open glade,
around a smooth stone house—the hall of Circe—
and wolves and mountain lions lay there, mild
in her soft spell, fed on her drug of evil.

450   None would attack—oh, it was strange, I tell you—
but switching their long tails they faced our men
like hounds, who look up when their master comes
with tidbits for them—as he will—from table.
Humbly those wolves and lions with mighty paws

455   fawned on our men—who met their yellow eyes
and feared them.

                   In the entranceway they stayed
to listen there: inside her quiet house
they heard the goddess Circe.

                         Low she sang
in her beguiling voice, while on her loom

460   she wove ambrosial° fabric sheer and bright,
by that craft known to the goddesses of heaven.
No one would speak, until Polites—most
faithful and likable of my officers—said:

'Dear friends, no need for <u>stealth</u>: here's a young weaver

465   singing a pretty song to set the air
atingle on these lawns and paven courts.
Goddess she is, or lady. Shall we greet her?'
So reassured, they all cried out together,
and she came swiftly to the shining doors

460. ambrosial: fit for the gods; divine.

WORDS TO OWN
stealth (stelth) *n.:* secret or sneaky action or behavior.

Circe offers the magic potion to Odysseus. Detail of Greek vase from Thebes.

British Museum, London.

470   to call them in. All but Eurylochus—
    who feared a snare—the innocents went after her.
    On thrones she seated them, and lounging chairs,
    while she prepared a meal of cheese and barley
    and amber honey mixed with Pramnian wine,
475   adding her own vile pinch, to make them lose
    desire or thought of our dear fatherland.
    Scarce had they drunk when she flew after them
    with her long stick and shut them in a pigsty—
    bodies, voices, heads, and bristles, all
480   swinish now, though minds were still unchanged.
    So, squealing, in they went. And Circe tossed them
    acorns, mast,° and cornel berries—fodder
    for hogs who rut and slumber on the earth.

    Down to the ship Eurylochus came running
485   to cry alarm, foul magic doomed his men!
    But working with dry lips to speak a word
    he could not, being so shaken; blinding tears
    welled in his eyes; foreboding filled his heart.
    When we were frantic questioning him, at last
490   we heard the tale: our friends were gone. . . .”

(*from* Book 10)

482. mast: various kinds of nuts
used as food for hogs.

*Note your responses to
this horrible experience.
What have the men
done to deserve being turned into
pigs? How did Circe, too, violate
the laws of hospitality?*

Odysseus leaves the ship and rushes to Circe's hall. The god Hermes stops him to give him a plant that will weaken Circe's power. (Homer calls it a moly; it might have been a kind of garlic.) Protected by the plant's magic, Odysseus resists Circe's sorcery. The witch, realizing she has met her match, frees Odysseus' men. Now Circe, "loveliest of all immortals," persuades Odysseus to stay with her. There Odysseus shares her meat and wine, and she restores his heart. But, after many seasons of feasting and other pleasures, Odysseus and his men beg Circe to help them get home.

She responds to their pleas with the command that Odysseus alone descend to the Land of the Dead, "the cold homes of Death and pale Persephone," queen of the Underworld. There, Odysseus must seek the wisdom of the blind prophet Teiresias.

Odysseus pursuing Circe.
Louvre, Paris.

THE LAND OF THE DEAD

In the Land of the Dead, Odysseus seeks to learn of his destiny. The source of his information is Teiresias, the famous blind prophet from the city of Thebes, whose lack of external sight suggests the presence of true insight. Circe has told Odysseus exactly what rites he must perform to bring Teiresias up from the dead. Odysseus continues his story.

"Then I addressed the blurred and breathless dead,
vowing to slaughter my best heifer for them
before she calved, at home in Ithaca,
and burn the choice bits on the altar fire;
495   as for Teiresias, I swore to sacrifice
a black lamb, handsomest of all our flock.
Thus to assuage the nations of the dead
I pledged these rites, then slashed the lamb and ewe,
letting their black blood stream into the well pit.
500   Now the souls gathered, stirring out of Erebus,°
brides and young men, and men grown old in pain,
and tender girls whose hearts were new to grief;
many were there, too, torn by brazen lanceheads,
battle-slain, bearing still their bloody gear.
505   From every side they came and sought the pit
with rustling cries; and I grew sick with fear.
But presently I gave command to my officers
to flay° those sheep the bronze cut down, and make
burnt offerings of flesh to the gods below—
510   to sovereign Death, to pale Persephone.
Meanwhile I crouched with my drawn sword to keep
the surging phantoms from the bloody pit
till I should know the presence of Teiresias. . . .

Soon from the dark that prince of Thebes came forward
515   bearing a golden staff; and he addressed me:

'Son of Laertes and the gods of old,
Odysseus, master of landways and seaways,
why leave the blazing sun, O man of woe,
to see the cold dead and the joyless region?
520   Stand clear, put up your sword;
let me but taste of blood, I shall speak true.'

At this I stepped aside, and in the scabbard
let my long sword ring home to the pommel silver,
as he bent down to the somber blood. Then spoke
the prince of those with gift of speech:

500. Erebus (er′ə·bəs): dark place under the earth through which the dead passed before entering the Land of the Dead.

508. flay: strip the skin from.

Persephone, queen of the underworld, with her husband, Hades (4th century B.C.).
British Museum, London.

525

'Great captain,

a fair wind and the honey lights of home
are all you seek. But anguish lies ahead;
the god who thunders on the land prepares it,
not to be shaken from your track, implacable,°

530 in rancor for the son whose eye you blinded.
One narrow strait may take you through his blows:
denial of yourself, restraint of shipmates.
When you make landfall on Thrinakia° first
and quit the violet sea, dark on the land

535 you'll find the grazing herds of Helios
by whom all things are seen, all speech is known.
Avoid those kine,° hold fast to your intent,
and hard seafaring brings you all to Ithaca.
But if you raid the beeves, I see destruction

540 for ship and crew. Though you survive alone,
bereft of all companions, lost for years,
under strange sail shall you come home, to find
your own house filled with trouble: insolent men
eating your livestock as they court your lady.

545 Aye, you shall make those men atone in blood!
But after you have dealt out death—in open
combat or by stealth—to all the suitors,
go overland on foot, and take an oar,
until one day you come where men have lived

550 with meat unsalted, never known the sea,
nor seen seagoing ships, with crimson bows
and oars that fledge light hulls for dipping flight.
The spot will soon be plain to you, and I
can tell you how: some passer-by will say,

555 "What winnowing fan° is that upon your shoulder?"
Halt, and implant your smooth oar in the turf
and make fair sacrifice to Lord Poseidon:
a ram, a bull, a great buck boar; turn back,
and carry out pure hecatombs° at home

560 to all wide heaven's lords, the undying gods,
to each in order. Then a seaborne death
soft as this hand of mist will come upon you
when you are wearied out with rich old age,
your countryfolk in blessed peace around you.

565 And all this shall be just as I foretell.'"

(*from* Book 11)

WORDS TO OWN
rancor (raŋ′kər) *n.*: bitter hate; ill will.

529. implacable: unyielding;
merciless.

533. Thrinakia (thri·nā′kē·ə):
island where the sun god Helios
kept his sacred cattle.

537. *Kine* and *beeves* (see line
539) are old terms for "cattle."

555. winnowing fan: device used
to remove the useless dry outer
covering from grain. (These people
would never have seen an oar.)

559. hecatombs: sacrifices of one
hundred cattle at a time to the gods.

*In your log, take notes
on how you might
dramatize this impor-
tant scene in the underworld. How
many actors would you need?
What props would you use? You
might sketch the scene as you
visualize it.*

THE SIRENS; SCYLLA AND CHARYBDIS

Odysseus and his men return to Circe's island, where Circe warns him of the perils that await him—the forces that could prevent him from achieving his destiny. The following passage is in Circe's voice.

"'Listen with care
to this, now, and a god will arm your mind.
Square in your ship's path are Sirens, crying
beauty to bewitch men coasting by;
570   woe to the innocent who hears that sound!
He will not see his lady nor his children
in joy, crowding about him, home from sea;
the Sirens will sing his mind away
on their sweet meadow lolling. There are bones
575   of dead men rotting in a pile beside them
and flayed skins shrivel around the spot.

                    Steer wide;
keep well to seaward; plug your oarsmen's ears
with beeswax kneaded soft; none of the rest
should hear that song.

                 But if you wish to listen,
580   let the men tie you in the lugger, hand
and foot, back to the mast, lashed to the mast,
so you may hear those Harpies'° thrilling voices;
shout as you will, begging to be untied,
your crew must only twist more line around you
585   and keep their stroke up, till the singers fade. . . .'"

The next peril lies between two headlands. Circe continues her warning.

"'. . . That is the den of Scylla, where she yaps
<u>abominably</u>, a newborn whelp's° cry,
though she is huge and monstrous. God or man,
no one could look on her in joy. Her legs—
590   and there are twelve—are like great tentacles,
unjointed, and upon her serpent necks
are borne six heads like nightmares of ferocity,
with triple serried° rows of fangs and deep
gullets of black death. Half her length, she sways

582. Harpies: monsters who are half bird and half woman and are greedy for victims.

587. whelp's: puppy's.

593. serried: crowded together; densely packed.

WORDS TO OWN
abominably (ə·bäm′ə·nə·blē) *adv.*: in an extremely unpleasant or disgusting manner.

----

595 her heads in air, outside her horrid cleft,
hunting the sea around that promontory°
for dolphins, dogfish, or what bigger game
thundering Amphitrite° feeds in thousands.
And no ship's company can claim
600 to have passed her without loss and grief; she takes,
from every ship, one man for every gullet.

The opposite point seems more a tongue of land
you'd touch with a good bowshot, at the narrows.
A great wild fig, a shaggy mass of leaves,
605 grows on it, and Charybdis lurks below
to swallow down the dark sea tide. Three times
from dawn to dusk she spews it up
and sucks it down again three times, a whirling
maelstrom;° if you come upon her then
610 the god who makes earth tremble could not save you.
No, hug the cliff of Scylla, take your ship
through on a racing stroke. Better to mourn
six men than lose them all, and the ship, too. . . .

596. promontory: high land that juts out into a body of water.

598. Amphitrite (am'·fi·trīt'ē): goddess of the sea and wife of Poseidon.

609. maelstrom: large, violent whirlpool.

The Sirens (c. 1875) by Sir Edward Burne-Jones.

Then you will coast Thrinakia, the island
615 where Helios' cattle graze, fine herds, and flocks
of goodly sheep. The herds and flocks are seven,
with fifty beasts in each.

                                    No lambs are dropped,
or calves, and these fat cattle never die. . . .

Now give those kine a wide berth, keep your thoughts
620 intent upon your course for home,
and hard seafaring brings you all to Ithaca.
But if you raid the beeves, I see destruction
for ship and crew.'"

*The Ithacans set off. Odysseus does not reveal Circe's last
prophecy—that he will be the only survivor of their long
journey. Still speaking to Alcinous' court, Odysseus continues
his tale.*

"The crew being now silent before me, I
addressed them, sore at heart:

625   'Dear friends,
more than one man, or two, should know those things
Circe foresaw for us and shared with me,
so let me tell her forecast: then we die
with our eyes open, if we are going to die,
630 or know what death we baffle if we can. Sirens
weaving a haunting song over the sea
we are to shun, she said, and their green shore
all sweet with clover; yet she urged that I
alone should listen to their song. Therefore
635 you are to tie me up, tight as a splint,
erect along the mast, lashed to the mast,
and if I shout and beg to be untied,
take more turns of the rope to muffle me.'

I rather dwelt on this part of the forecast,
640 while our good ship made time, bound outward down
the wind for the strange island of Sirens.
Then all at once the wind fell, and a calm
came over all the sea, as though some power
lulled the swell.

                               The crew were on their feet
645 briskly, to furl the sail, and stow it; then,
each in place, they poised the smooth oar blades
and sent the white foam scudding by. I carved
a massive cake of beeswax into bits
and rolled them in my hands until they softened—

Odysseus and the Sirens
(c. 490 B.C.).

650   no long task, for a burning heat came down
      from Helios, lord of high noon. Going forward
      I carried wax along the line, and laid it
      thick on their ears. They tied me up, then, plumb°
      amidships, back to the mast, lashed to the mast,
655   and took themselves again to rowing. Soon,
      as we came smartly within hailing distance,
      the two Sirens, noting our fast ship
      off their point, made ready, and they sang. . . .

      The lovely voices in ardor appealing over the water
660   made me crave to listen, and I tried to say
      'Untie me!' to the crew, jerking my brows;
      but they bent steady to the oars. Then Perimedes
      got to his feet, he and Eurylochus,
      and passed more line about, to hold me still.
665   So all rowed on, until the Sirens
      dropped under the sea rim, and their singing
      dwindled away.

653. plumb: vertical.

WORDS TO OWN
ardor (är′dər) *n.*: passion; enthusiasm.

My faithful company
rested on their oars now, peeling off
the wax that I had laid thick on their ears;
then set me free.

670   But scarcely had that island
faded in blue air when I saw smoke
and white water, with sound of waves in <u>tumult</u>—
a sound the men heard, and it terrified them.
Oars flew from their hands; the blades went knocking
675 wild alongside till the ship lost way,
with no oar blades to drive her through the water.

Well, I walked up and down from bow to stern,
trying to put heart into them, standing over
every oarsman, saying gently,

                              'Friends,
680 have we never been in danger before this?
More fearsome, is it now, than when the Cyclops
penned us in his cave? What power he had!
Did I not keep my nerve, and use my wits
to find a way out for us?

                         Now I say
685 by hook or crook this peril too shall be
something that we remember.

                     Heads up, lads!
We must obey the orders as I give them.
Get the oar shafts in your hands, and lie back
hard on your benches; hit these breaking seas.
690 Zeus help us pull away before we founder.

You at the tiller, listen, and take in
all that I say—the rudders are your duty;
keep her out of the combers° and the smoke;
steer for that headland; watch the drift, or we
695 fetch up in the smother,° and you drown us.'

That was all, and it brought them round to action.
But as I sent them on toward Scylla, I
told them nothing, as they could do nothing.
They would have dropped their oars again, in panic,
700 to roll for cover under the decking. Circe's
bidding against arms had slipped my mind,
so I tied on my cuirass° and took up
two heavy spears, then made my way along
to the foredeck—thinking to see her first from there,

Scylla. Greek bronze.
National Archaeological Museum, Athens.

693. combers: large waves.

695. smother: commotion; violent action or disorder.

702. cuirass (kwi·ras′): armor for the breast and back.

WORDS TO OWN
tumult (tōō′mult′) *n*.: commotion; uproar; confusion.

705   the monster of the gray rock, harboring
torment for my friends. I strained my eyes
upon that cliffside veiled in cloud, but nowhere
could I catch sight of her.

                          And all this time,
in travail,° sobbing, gaining on the current,
710   we rowed into the strait—Scylla to port
and on our starboard beam Charybdis, dire
gorge° of the salt sea tide. By heaven! when she
vomited, all the sea was like a caldron
seething over intense fire, when the mixture
suddenly heaves and rises.
715   The shot spume
soared to the landside heights, and fell like rain.

But when she swallowed the sea water down
we saw the funnel of the maelstrom, heard
the rock bellowing all around, and dark
720   sand raged on the bottom far below.
My men all blanched° against the gloom, our eyes
were fixed upon that yawning mouth in fear
of being devoured.
                      Then Scylla made her strike,
whisking six of my best men from the ship.

725   I happened to glance aft at ship and oarsmen
and caught sight of their arms and legs, dangling
high overhead. Voices came down to me
in anguish, calling my name for the last time.

A man surf-casting on a point of rock
730   for bass or mackerel, whipping his long rod
to drop the sinker and the bait far out,
will hook a fish and rip it from the surface
to dangle wriggling through the air;
                               so these
were borne aloft in spasms toward the cliff.

735   She ate them as they shrieked there, in her den,
in the dire grapple,° reaching still for me—
and deathly pity ran me through
at that sight—far the worst I ever suffered
questing the passes of the strange sea.
                          We rowed on.
740   The Rocks were now behind; Charybdis, too,
and Scylla dropped astern.
                    Then we were coasting
the noble island of the god, where grazed
those cattle with wide brows, and bounteous flocks
of Helios, lord of noon, who rides high heaven.

709. travail: hard, exhausting work or effort; tiring labor.

712. gorge: throat and jaws of a greedy, all-devouring being.

721. blanched: grew pale.

736. dire grapple: terrible struggle.

745   From the black ship, far still at sea, I heard
     the lowing of the cattle winding home
     and sheep bleating; and heard, too, in my heart
     the words of blind Teiresias of Thebes
     and Circe of Aeaea: both forbade me
750   the island of the world's delight, the Sun. . . ."

(from Book 12)

 *Suppose you wanted to write a script dramatizing this famous part of the* Odyssey—*the crew's struggle against the Sirens and against Scylla and Charybdis. Who would be your main characters? How would you use music and visuals—especially in the Sirens scene? Write down your ideas about a dramatic presentation.*

The Companions of Ulysses Slaying the Cattle of the Sun God Helios (16th century) by Pellegrino Tibaldi.

Because they are dying of starvation, Odysseus' men disobey his orders and eat the sacred cattle of the sun god, Helios. When they set sail again, they are punished by death—a thunderbolt from Zeus destroys their boat and all the men drown. Only Odysseus survives. Exhausted and nearly drowned, he makes his way to Calypso's island, where he becomes her prisoner.

Odysseus has brought us up to date. He can now rest and enjoy the comforts of Alcinous' court—but not for long. Ahead lies his most difficult task—reclaiming his own kingdom.

At this moment of suspense, Homer might have put aside his harp until the next night.

MAKING MEANINGS   PART ONE

First Thoughts

1. If you were one of Odysseus' ship-mates, how would you feel about him? Is he foolhardy or a reliable leader? Do you all agree?

Shaping Interpretations

2. The *Odyssey* was used as part of Greek children's education for centuries after the poem was written down. How could the adventure with the Lotus Eaters teach them about the tempta-tion to forget their troubles by dropping out of school or society?

3. How does Odysseus describe the Cyclopes' way of life? In what ways could their customs be seen as exactly the opposite of what a truly human community should be? (Be sure to think about the significance of the cannibalism.)

4. "Nobody" in Greek is *oudeis,* which sounds like *Odysseus.* How does Odysseus show that one of his greatest powers is his skill with language?

5. What could you learn about the deceptive nature of beauty from the Circe episode?

Reviewing the Text

a. Describe the internal conflict Odysseus' men face among the Lotus Eaters.

b. Describe three strategies that Odysseus uses to outwit the Cyclops Polyphemus. What curse at the end of the adventure foreshadows trouble for Odysseus?

c. Explain how Circe's powers affect Odysseus' crew.

d. Summarize what Odysseus learns about his future from the prophet Teiresias.

e. Describe how Odysseus survives the Sirens and Scylla and Charybdis.

Extending the Text

6. So far, from what you've observed of Odysseus, how would you describe what the Greeks valued in a hero? Do we value these same characteristics today?

7. The tale of Odysseus versus the Cyclops has parallels in other stories told throughout the ages. Fill in a chart like the one opposite, comparing this story with another that you have read.

	Odyssey	Other Story
A normal-sized person vs. a giant		
Intelligence vs. brute strength		
A surprise victory		

Challenging the Text

8. How many of the monsters or threats to Odysseus in this part of the epic are female? What do you think of the way women are portrayed in the story so far?

CHOICES: Building Your Portfolio

Writer's Notebook

1. Collecting Ideas for a Speculation About Causes or Effects

Finding a topic. By now you may have noticed several ways in which Homer's heroes differ from ours. For the Writer's Workshop on page 958, you might want to focus on the causes of this changing idea of the hero. First, identify some differences between Odysseus and modern heroes—both fictional and real. Then, note changes in technology, values, or both that might have caused our ideas about heroes to change over the three thousand years since the *Odyssey* was written. Save your notes.

(work in progress logo)

Difference
Modern heroes aren't as good at talking as Odysseus was.

Possible Cause
With all our books, TV, etc., we're bombarded by media messages. Maybe we don't value language skills in anyone anymore.

Creative Writing

2. In the Cave

Choose one of the characters trapped in the Cyclops's cave—perhaps one of Odysseus' men, who might get eaten for breakfast—and keep a diary of the events that occur from that character's point of view. What are the character's thoughts about what he is seeing and feeling?

Creative Writing/Art

3. It's Alive!

Homer describes a whirlpool and a dangerous rock as living monsters: Scylla and Charybdis. The whirlpool and the rock are **personified:** They are, in reality, inanimate (nonliving), but the poet describes them as if they have life. In the modern poem on page 910, Nikki Giovanni personifies a tropical storm as a Cyclops. Write a paragraph (or draw a cartoon) personifying some other violent force of nature. Use details that suggest that the force is a monster with destructive intentions. You might describe (or draw) a volcano, an earthquake, a blizzard, or a flood. Show how the monster looks and sounds, what it hunts for, and what it does with its prey.

Creative Writing/ Performance

4. Make It Real

Choose one of Odysseus' perilous encounters and dramatize it. (You might already have some notes in your log about dramatizing the story.) With classmates, write a script, creating dialogue to show action and to reveal character. Then assign roles and rehearse them. Use music and scenery as you wish. Videotape your performance so your teacher can show next year's class the *Odyssey Live.*

Creative Writing

5. Life as a Journey

Before you started the *Odyssey,* you should have taken some notes on life as a journey (see page 889). Refer to those notes now and describe a meaningful "journey" or quest in your own life. It may be a journey you have already completed or one just begun. Try to identify the following: What was it that "called" you? Who were or will be your helpers? What tests, trials, or ordeals did you face or do you expect to face? What did you learn as a result of your journey, or what do you expect to learn?

LANGUAGE LINK

Handbook of Literary Terms
H E L P

See Figure of Speech.

Style: Figures of Speech—Homeric Similes

In a **figure of speech,** a writer compares one thing to something else, something quite different from it in all but a few important ways. For example, Homer compares the army of the Cicones to "the leaves and blades of spring" (lines 70–71). He is saying that enemy soldiers suddenly appeared everywhere, as green grass and leaves do in spring. The comparison is surprising because a fierce army seems very different from the tender leaves and grass of spring.

The **Homeric simile** is an extended comparison between something that the audience cannot have seen (such as Odysseus boring out the Cyclops's eye) and something ordinary that they would have been familiar with (such as a shipbuilder drilling a plank; see lines 285–290 on page 904).

Try It Out

1. Re-read lines 729–734 on page 921. Explain how this Homeric simile brings the audience into the story by comparing a strange, unfamiliar occurrence with something familiar.

2. Make up three Homeric similes of your own, in which you compare something strange or unfamiliar with something ordinary and familiar. You might consider describing something like the following:

   - a space launch
   - the surface of the moon
   - something you see through a microscope

VOCABULARY   HOW TO OWN A WORD

WORD BANK
formidable
ravage
profusion
sage
adversary
stealth
rancor
abominably
ardor
tumult

Map It

Work with a partner to create a semantic map for each word in the Word Bank. Make up questions about each word and provide your own answers. A sample map is done for *formidable*. Be sure to compare your maps in class.

Who is formidable in the *Odyssey*?		Do I want to be called formidable?
• Odysseus • Cyclops • the gods	**formidable**	• Yes, I'd like to be formidable as a center forward.
What have I seen that is formidable?		What is not formidable?
• Josh on football field • Emma in math class • volcano		• ant • baby • peaceful pond

PART TWO: COMING HOME

In Book 13, Odysseus, laden with gifts, is returned in secret to Ithaca in one of the magically swift Phaeacian ships. In Ithaca, Athena appears to the hero. Because his home is full of enemies, she advises him to proceed disguised as a beggar. This new hero of the postwar age must succeed not only by physical power but also by intelligence.

In Book 14, Odysseus, in his beggar's disguise, finds his way to the hut of his old and trusty swineherd, Eumaeus. Eumaeus is the very image of faithfulness in a servant—a quality much admired by Homer's society. The introduction of the so-called servant class as important actors is unusual in epic poetry, and it indicates Homer's originality. Odysseus is politely entertained by Eumaeus, but the king remains disguised from his old servant.

In Book 15, Athena appears to Odysseus' son, Telemachus, who has been searching for his father. She advises him to return to Ithaca. His home—the Palace of Odysseus—is overrun with his mother's suitors. These arrogant men have taken over Odysseus' house. They are partying with money from the son's inheritance and are demanding that his mother, Penelope, take one of them as a husband. Athena warns Telemachus that the suitors plan to ambush him. Telemachus boards a ship for home, lands secretly on Ithaca, and heads toward the cottage of the swineherd.

In Book 16, father and son are at last reunited. "I am that father whom your boyhood lacked," the old soldier tells his weeping son.

Return of Odysseus (5th century B.C., first half).
Relief, believed to be from the island of Melos. Terra cotta.
The Metropolitan Museum of Art, New York, Fletcher Fund, 1930 (30.11.9).

THE BEGGAR AND THE FAITHFUL DOG

Telemachus returns to the family compound and is greeted tearfully by his mother and his old nurse, Eurycleia. A sooth-sayer has told his mother, Penelope, that Odysseus is alive and is already in Ithaca. But Telemachus does not report that he has already seen his father. The suspense builds as Odysseus, once again disguised as a beggar, finally returns to his home accompanied only by the swineherd. He has been away for twenty years. Only one creature recognizes him.

While he spoke

    an old hound, lying near, pricked up his ears
    and lifted up his muzzle. This was Argos,
    trained as a puppy by Odysseus,
755   but never taken on a hunt before
    his master sailed for Troy. The young men, afterward,
    hunted wild goats with him, and hare, and deer,
    but he had grown old in his master's absence.
    Treated as rubbish now, he lay at last
760   upon a mass of dung before the gates—
    manure of mules and cows, piled there until
    field hands could spread it on the king's estate.
    Abandoned there, and half destroyed with flies,
    old Argos lay.

But when he knew he heard

765   Odysseus' voice nearby, he did his best
    to wag his tail, nose down, with flattened ears,
    having no strength to move nearer his master.
    And the man looked away,
    wiping a salt tear from his cheek; but he
770   hid this from Eumaeus. Then he said:

    "I marvel that they leave this hound to lie
    here on the dung pile;
    he would have been a fine dog, from the look of him,
    though I can't say as to his power and speed
775   when he was young. You find the same good build
    in house dogs, table dogs landowners keep
    all for style."

And you replied, Eumaeus:

    "A hunter owned him—but the man is dead
    in some far place. If this old hound could show
780   the form he had when Lord Odysseus left him,
    going to Troy, you'd see him swift and strong.
    He never shrank from any savage thing
    he'd brought to bay in the deep woods; on the scent
    no other dog kept up with him. Now misery

Odysseus is recognized by Eurycleia (1st century A.D.).

785   has him in leash. His owner died abroad,
    and here the women slaves will take no care of him.
    You know how servants are: without a master
    they have no will to labor, or excel.
    For Zeus who views the wide world takes away
790   half the manhood of a man, that day
    he goes into captivity and slavery."

    Eumaeus crossed the court and went straight forward
    into the megaron° among the suitors;
    but death and darkness in that instant closed
795   the eyes of Argos, who had seen his master,
    Odysseus, after twenty years.

(*from* Book 17)

793. megaron: great hall or central room.

 Here again we hear about people who mock the sacred laws of respect and hospitality. We find that the suitors and servants in Odysseus' home have mistreated his old hound, Argos. Make some notes about the ways we treat animals today. What does this reveal about our values?

In the hall, the "beggar" is taunted by the evil suitors, but Penelope supports him. She has learned that the ragged stranger claims to have news of her husband. Unaware of who the beggar is, she invites him to visit her later in the night to talk about Odysseus.

In Book 18, Penelope appears among the suitors and reproaches Telemachus for allowing the stranger to be abused. She certainly must have warmed her husband's heart by doing this and by singing the praises of her lost Odysseus.

In Book 19, the suitors depart for the night and Odysseus and Telemachus discuss their strategy. The clever hero goes as appointed to Penelope with the idea of testing her and her maids. (Some of the maids have not been loyal to the household and have even slept with the suitors.) The faithful wife receives her disguised husband. We can imagine the tension Homer's audience must have felt. Would Odysseus be recognized?

The "beggar" spins a yarn about his origins, pretending that he has met Odysseus on his travels. He cannot resist praising the lost hero, and he does so successfully enough to bring tears to Penelope's eyes. We can be sure that this does not displease the beggar.

The story-telling beggar reveals that he has heard that Odysseus is alive and is even now sailing for home. Penelope calls for the old nurse and asks her to wash the guest's feet—a sign of respect and honor. As Eurycleia does so, she recognizes Odysseus from a scar on his leg.

Quickly Odysseus swears her to secrecy. Meanwhile, Athena has cast a spell on Penelope so that she has taken no notice of this recognition scene. Penelope adds to the suspense by deciding on a test for the suitors on the next day. Without realizing it, she has now given Odysseus a way to defeat the men who threaten his wife and kingdom.

In Book 20, Odysseus, brooding over the shameless behavior of the maidservants and the suitors, longs to destroy his enemies but fears the revenge of their friends. Athena reassures him. Odysseus is told that the suitors will die.

Odysseus is recognized by Eurycleia.
Detail from a skyphos, a drinking cup.
Museo Archeologico, Chiusi, Italy.

Telemachus and Penelope (c. 1509) by Bernadino Pínturícchio.

Penelope to Ulysses

Penelope, distressed by the demands of her suitors that she marry one of them, thinks of a way to trick them. She sets up her weaving in the hall, saying to the suitors that she is weaving a shroud (a cloth used to wrap a body for burial) for Odysseus and promising that she will choose a husband when she has completed the work. "So every day I wove on the great loom, but every night by torchlight I unwove it. . . ." With this simple trick she is able to deceive her suitors for three years.

Like a spider committing suicide
each night I unweave the web of my day.
I have no peace.
About me the insistent buzz of flies   5
drones louder every day.
I am starving.
I watch them, always, unblinking stare.
All my dwindling will
I use in not moving, not trying, unweaving.   10
I pull in my empty nets
eating myself, waiting.

—Meredith Schwartz
Highland Park School
Highland Park, New Jersey

THE TEST OF THE GREAT BOW

In Book 21, Penelope, like many unwilling princesses of myth, fairy tale, and legend, proposes an impossible task for those who wish to marry her. By so doing, she causes the bloody events that lead to the restoration of her husband. The test involves stringing Odysseus' huge bow, an impossible feat for anyone except Odysseus himself. Odysseus had left his bow home in Ithaca twenty years earlier.

Odysseus slaying the suitors (detail) (c. 440 B.C.) by the Penelope Painter. Attic red-figured skyphos, or drinking cup, from Tarquinii.

Now the queen reached the storeroom door and halted.
Here was an oaken sill, cut long ago
and sanded clean and bedded true. Foursquare
800   the doorjambs and the shining doors were set
by the careful builder. Penelope untied the strap
around the curving handle, pushed her hook
into the slit, aimed at the bolts inside,
and shot them back. Then came a rasping sound
805   as those bright doors the key had sprung gave way—
a bellow like a bull's vaunt° in a meadow—
followed by her light footfall entering
over the plank floor. Herb-scented robes
lay there in chests, but the lady's milk-white arms
810   went up to lift the bow down from a peg
in its own polished bow case.

                      Now Penelope
sank down, holding the weapon on her knees,
and drew her husband's great bow out, and sobbed
and bit her lip and let the salt tears flow.
815   Then back she went to face the crowded hall
tremendous bow in hand, and on her shoulder hung
the quiver spiked with coughing death. Behind, her
maids bore a basket full of ax heads, bronze
and iron implements for the master's game.
820   Thus in her beauty she approached the suitors,
and near a pillar of the solid roof
she paused, her shining veil across her cheeks,
her maids on either hand and still,
then spoke to the banqueters:

                            "My lords, hear me:
825   suitors indeed, you recommended this house
to feast and drink in, day and night, my husband
being long gone, long out of mind. You found
no justification for yourselves—none
except your lust to marry me. Stand up, then:
830   we now declare a contest for that prize.
Here is my lord Odysseus' hunting bow.
Bend and string it if you can. Who sends an arrow

806. vaunt: boast.

through iron ax-helve sockets,° twelve in line?
I join my life with his, and leave this place, my home,
835   my rich and beautiful bridal house, forever
to be remembered, though I dream it only."

*Many of the suitors boldly try the bow, but not a man can even
bend it enough to string it.*

Two men had meanwhile left the hall:
swineherd and cowherd, in companionship,
one downcast as the other. But Odysseus
840   followed them outdoors, outside the court,
and coming up said gently:

"You, herdsman,
and you, too, swineherd, I could say a thing to you,
or should I keep it dark?

No, no; speak,
my heart tells me. Would you be men enough
845   to stand by Odysseus if he came back?
Suppose he dropped out of a clear sky, as I did?
Suppose some god should bring him?
Would you bear arms for him, or for the suitors?"

The cowherd said:

"Ah, let the master come!
850   Father Zeus, grant our old wish! Some courier°
guide him back! Then judge what stuff is in me
and how I manage arms!"

Likewise Eumaeus
fell to praying all heaven for his return,
so that Odysseus, sure at least of these,
told them:

855   "I am at home, for I am he.
I bore adversities, but in the twentieth year
I am ashore in my own land. I find
the two of you, alone among my people,
longed for my coming. Prayers I never heard
860   except your own that I might come again.
So now what is in store for you I'll tell you:
If Zeus brings down the suitors by my hand
I promise marriages to both, and cattle,

833. An ax helve is an ax handle; a socket is a hollow piece lined with iron at the end of the handle. Shooting an arrow through a line of ax-helve sockets would be a task possible only to a hero like Superman or Odysseus.

850. courier: guide or messenger.

WORDS TO OWN
adversities (ad·vur′sə·tēz) *n.*: great misfortunes; hardships.

and houses built near mine. And you shall be
865   brothers-in-arms of my Telemachus.
       Here, let me show you something else, a sign
       that I am he, that you can trust me, look:
       this old scar from the tusk wound that I got
       boar hunting on Parnassus——"
                                        Shifting his rags
870   he bared the long gash. Both men looked, and knew
       and threw their arms around the old soldier, weeping,
       kissing his head and shoulders. He as well
       took each man's head and hands to kiss, then said—
       to cut it short, else they might weep till dark—

875   "Break off, no more of this.
       Anyone at the door could see and tell them.
       Drift back in, but separately at intervals
       after me.
                                Now listen to your orders:
       when the time comes, those gentlemen, to a man,
880   will be dead against giving me bow or quiver.
       Defy them. Eumaeus, bring the bow
       and put it in my hands there at the door.
       Tell the women to lock their own door tight.
       Tell them if someone hears the shock of arms
885   or groans of men, in hall or court, not one
       must show her face, but keep still at her weaving.
       Philoeteus, run to the outer gate and lock it.
       Throw the crossbar and lash it."

*Now Odysseus, still in his beggar's clothes, asks to try the bow.
The suitors refuse to allow a mere beggar to try where they
have failed, but Penelope insists that the stranger be given his
chance. The suspense is very great—by this act, Penelope has
accepted her husband as a suitor.*

*Eumaeus, the swineherd, hands Odysseus the bow and tells
the nurse to retire with Penelope and the maids to the family
chambers (the harem) and to bolt the doors. Odysseus had
earlier told Telemachus to remove the suitors' weapons from
the great hall. Now he takes the bow.*

                                And Odysseus took his time,
890   turning the bow, tapping it, every inch,
       for borings that termites might have made
       while the master of the weapon was abroad.
       The suitors were now watching him, and some
       jested among themselves:

                                   "A bow lover!"

"Dealer in old bows!"

895   "Maybe he has one like it
at home!"

                     "Or has an itch to make one for himself."

"See how he handles it, the sly old buzzard!"

And one _disdainful_ suitor added this:

"May his fortune grow an inch for every inch he bends it!"

900   But the man skilled in all ways of contending,
        satisfied by the great bow's look and heft,
        like a musician, like a harper, when
        with quiet hand upon his instrument
        he draws between his thumb and forefinger

WORDS TO OWN
disdainful (dis·dān′fəl) _adj._: scornful; contemptuous.

Odysseus slaying the suitors (c. 440 B.C.) by the Penelope Painter. Attic red-figured skyphos, or drinking cup, from Tarquinii.

Antikensammlung Staatliche Museen zu Berlin Preussischer Kulturbesitz.

905   a sweet new string upon a peg: so effortlessly
Odysseus in one motion strung the bow.
Then slid his right hand down the cord and plucked it,
so the taut gut vibrating hummed and sang
a swallow's note.

                    In the hushed hall it smote the suitors
910   and all their faces changed. Then Zeus thundered
overhead, one loud crack for a sign.
And Odysseus laughed within him that the son
of crooked-minded Cronus° had flung that omen down.
He picked one ready arrow from his table
915   where it lay bare: the rest were waiting still
in the quiver for the young men's turn to come.
He nocked° it, let it rest across the handgrip,
and drew the string and grooved butt of the arrow,
aiming from where he sat upon the stool.

                        Now flashed
920   arrow from twanging bow clean as a whistle
through every socket ring, and grazed not one,
to thud with heavy brazen head beyond.

                    Then quietly
Odysseus said:

                "Telemachus, the stranger
you welcomed in your hall has not disgraced you.
925   I did not miss, neither did I take all day
stringing the bow. My hand and eye are sound,
not so contemptible as the young men say.
The hour has come to cook their lordships' mutton—
supper by daylight. Other amusements later,
930   with song and harping that <u>adorn</u> a feast."

He dropped his eyes and nodded, and the prince
Telemachus, true son of King Odysseus,
belted his sword on, clapped hand to his spear,
and with a clink and glitter of keen bronze
935   stood by his chair, in the forefront near his father.

                    (from Book 21)

913. Cronus: father of Zeus, called crooked-minded because of his schemes to destroy his children.

917. nocked: fitted to the bowstring.

This scene and the next one are well worth staging. In your Reader's Log make notes about how you visualize these scenes. Where are various characters placed? How are they reacting? It might help to draw a picture of the Great Hall and indicate where various actions take place.

WORDS TO OWN
adorn (ə·dôrn′) *v.*: add beauty to; decorate.

An Ancient Gesture

Edna St. Vincent Millay

Penelope at Her Loom (1480–1483) from the series "The Story of Virtuous Women." Wool; tapestry weave.

I thought, as I wiped my eyes on the corner of my apron:
Penelope did this too.
And more than once: you can't keep weaving all day
And undoing it all through the night;
5   Your arms get tired, and the back of your neck gets tight;
And along towards morning, when you think it will never be light,
And your husband has been gone, and you don't know where, for years,
Suddenly you burst into tears;
There is simply nothing else to do.

10   And I thought, as I wiped my eyes on the corner of my apron:
This is an ancient gesture, authentic, antique,
In the very best tradition, classic, Greek;
Ulysses did this too.
But only as a gesture,—a gesture which implied
15   To the assembled throng that he was much too moved to speak.
He learned it from Penelope . . .
Penelope, who really cried.

DEATH AT THE PALACE

The climax of the story is here, in Book 22. Odysseus is ready to reclaim his rightful kingdom. But first he must deal with more than a hundred young and hostile suitors. The first one he turns to is Antinous. All through the story, Antinous has been the meanest of the suitors and their ringleader. He hit Odysseus with a stool when the hero appeared in the hall as a beggar, and he ridiculed the disguised king by calling him a bleary vagabond, a pest, and a tramp.

Now shrugging off his rags the wiliest fighter of the
    islands
leapt and stood on the broad door sill, his own bow in
    his hand.
He poured out at his feet a rain of arrows from the quiver
and spoke to the crowd:

        "So much for that. Your clean-cut game is over.
940   Now watch me hit a target that no man has hit before,
if I can make this shot. Help me, Apollo."°

He drew to his fist the cruel head of an arrow for
    Antinous
just as the young man leaned to lift his beautiful drinking
    cup,
embossed, two-handled, golden: the cup was in his
    fingers,
945   the wine was even at his lips, and did he dream of death?
How could he? In that <u>revelry</u> amid his throng of friends
who would imagine a single foe—though a strong foe
    indeed—
could dare to bring death's pain on him and darkness on
    his eyes?
Odysseus' arrow hit him under the chin
950   and punched up to the feathers through his throat.

Backward and down he went, letting the wine cup fall
from his shocked hand. Like pipes his nostrils jetted
crimson runnels,° a river of mortal red,
and one last kick upset his table
955   knocking the bread and meat to soak in dusty blood.
Now as they craned to see their champion where he lay
the suitors jostled in uproar down the hall,
everyone on his feet. Wildly they turned and scanned

WORDS TO OWN
revelry (rev′əl·rē) *n.:* merrymaking; festivity.

 *As you read this action scene, imagine it as a film. After you finish reading, draw the scene in your notebook, placing the characters Odysseus, Alcinous, the faithful servant, and Telemachus. Make a list of the props you would need if you were filming the battle.*

941. Odysseus prays to Apollo because this particular day is one of the god's feast days. Apollo is also the god of archery.

953. runnels: streams.

the walls in the long room for arms; but not a shield,
not a good ashen spear was there for a man to take and
        throw.
960   All they could do was yell in outrage at Odysseus:

"Foul! to shoot at a man! That was your last shot!"

"Your own throat will be slit for this!"

                                  "Our finest lad is down!
You killed the best on Ithaca."

                         "Buzzards will tear your eyes out!"

For they imagined as they wished—that it was a wild
965   shot,
an unintended killing—fools, not to comprehend
they were already in the grip of death.
But glaring under his brows Odysseus answered:

"You yellow dogs, you thought I'd never make it
home from the land of Troy. You took my house to
970   plunder,
twisted my maids to serve your beds. You dared
bid for my wife while I was still alive.
Contempt was all you had for the gods who rule wide
        heaven,
contempt for what men say of you hereafter.
975   Your last hour has come. You die in blood."

As they all took this in, sickly green fear
pulled at their entrails,° and their eyes flickered
looking for some hatch or hideaway from death.
Eurymachus° alone could speak. He said:

980   "If you are Odysseus of Ithaca come back,
all that you say these men have done is true.
Rash actions, many here, more in the countryside.
But here he lies, the man who caused them all.
Antinous was the ringleader, he whipped us on
985   to do these things. He cared less for a marriage
than for the power Cronion° has denied him
as king of Ithaca. For that
he tried to trap your son and would have killed him.
He is dead now and has his portion. Spare
990   your own people. As for ourselves, we'll make
restitution of wine and meat consumed,

977. **entrails:** guts.

979. **Eurymachus:**
(yoo·rim′ə·kəs).

986. **Cronion:** another name for
Zeus, meaning "son of Cronus."

WORDS TO OWN
restitution (res′tə·too′shən) *n.*: compensation; repayment.

and add, each one, a tithe of twenty oxen
with gifts of bronze and gold to warm your heart.
Meanwhile we cannot blame you for your anger."

995   Odysseus <u>glowered</u> under his black brows
and said:

           "Not for the whole treasure of your fathers,
all you enjoy, lands, flocks, or any gold
put up by others, would I hold my hand.
There will be killing till the score is paid.
1000   You forced yourselves upon this house. Fight your way out,
or run for it, if you think you'll escape death.
I doubt one man of you skins by." . . .

*Telemachus joins his father in the fight. They are helped by the
swineherd and cowherd. Now the suitors, trapped in the hall
without weapons, are struck right and left by arrows, and
many of them lie dying on the floor.*

    At this moment that unmanning thundercloud,
the aegis, Athena's shield,
took form aloft in the great hall.
1005   And the suitors mad with fear
at her great sign stampeded like stung cattle by a river
when the dread shimmering gadfly strikes in summer,
in the flowering season, in the long-drawn days.
After them the attackers wheeled, as terrible as falcons
from eyries° in the mountains veering over and diving
1010   down
with talons wide unsheathed on flights of birds,
who cower down the sky in chutes and bursts along the
     valley—
but the pouncing falcons grip their prey, no frantic wing
     avails,
and farmers love to watch those beakèd hunters.
1015   So these now fell upon the suitors in that hall,
turning, turning to strike and strike again,
while torn men moaned at death, and blood ran smoking
over the whole floor.

                        (*from* Book 22)

 *What does this bloody
scene add to the epic's
theme about the value
of hospitality and about what
happens to people who mock
divine laws?*

1010. **eyries** (er'ēz): nests built in high places.

- -

WORDS TO OWN
glowered (glou'ərd) *v*.: glared; stared angrily.

- -

Ulysses Slaying the Suitors (1802) by Henry Fuseli.

Kunsthaus Zurich, Zurich, Switzerland.

ODYSSEUS AND PENELOPE

Odysseus now calls forth the maids who have betrayed his household by associating with the suitors. He orders them to clean up the house and dispose of the dead. Telemachus then "pays" them by hanging them in the courtyard.

Eurycleia runs to Penelope to announce the return of Odysseus and the defeat of the suitors. The faithful wife—the perfect mate for the wily Odysseus—suspects a trick from the gods and decides to test this stranger who claims to be her husband.

Make notes on Penelope as you read this scene. What must she be thinking? Write her thoughts in the form of a journal entry or internal dialogue.

Crossing the doorsill she sat down at once
1020   in firelight, against the nearest wall,
across the room from the lord Odysseus.

                                          There

leaning against a pillar, sat the man
and never lifted up his eyes, but only waited
for what his wife would say when she had seen him.
1025   And she, for a long time, sat deathly still
in wonderment—for sometimes as she gazed
she found him—yes, clearly—like her husband,
but sometimes blood and rags were all she saw.
Telemachus' voice came to her ears:

                                     "Mother,

1030   cruel mother, do you feel nothing,
drawing yourself apart this way from Father?
Will you not sit with him and talk and question him?
What other woman could remain so cold?
Who shuns her lord, and he come back to her
1035   from wars and wandering, after twenty years?
Your heart is hard as flint and never changes!"

Penelope answered:

                         "I am stunned, child.
I cannot speak to him. I cannot question him.
I cannot keep my eyes upon his face.
1040   If really he is Odysseus, truly home,
beyond all doubt we two shall know each other
better than you or anyone. There are
secret signs we know, we two."

                               A smile

came now to the lips of the patient hero, Odysseus,
1045   who turned to Telemachus and said:

"Peace: let your mother test me at her leisure.
Before long she will see and know me best.
These tatters, dirt—all that I'm caked with now—
make her look hard at me and doubt me still. . . ."

Odysseus orders Telemachus, the swineherd, and the cowherd to bathe and put on fresh clothing.

1050   Greathearted Odysseus, home at last,
        was being bathed now by Eurynome
        and rubbed with golden oil, and clothed again
        in a fresh tunic and a cloak. Athena
        lent him beauty, head to foot. She made him
1055   taller, and massive, too, with crisping hair
        in curls like petals of wild hyacinth
        but all red-golden. Think of gold infused
        on silver by a craftsman, whose fine art
        Hephaestus° taught him, or Athena: one
1060   whose work moves to delight: just so she <u>lavished</u>
        beauty over Odysseus' head and shoulders.
        He sat then in the same chair by the pillar,
        facing his silent wife, and said:

                                    "Strange woman,
        the immortals of Olympus made you hard,
1065   harder than any. Who else in the world
        would keep <u>aloof</u> as you do from her husband
        if he returned to her from years of trouble,
        cast on his own land in the twentieth year?

        Nurse, make up a bed for me to sleep on.
        Her heart is iron in her breast."
1070   Penelope

        spoke to Odysseus now. She said:

                                    "Strange man,
        if man you are . . . This is no pride on my part
        nor scorn for you—not even wonder, merely.
        I know so well how you—how he—appeared
1075   boarding the ship for Troy. But all the same . . .

        Make up his bed for him, Eurycleia.
        Place it outside the bedchamber my lord
        built with his own hands. Pile the big bed
        with fleeces, rugs, and sheets of purest linen.

1080   With this she tried him to the breaking point,
        and he turned on her in a flash, raging:

        "Woman, by heaven you've stung me now!
        Who dared to move my bed?

1059. Hephaestus (hē·fes′təs): god of metalworking.

Penelope (detail) (1864) by John Roddam Spencer-Stanhope.

WORDS TO OWN

lavished (lav′isht) *v.*: gave generously.
aloof (ə·lo͞of′) *adj.*: at a distance; unfriendly.

No builder had the skill for that—unless
1085 a god came down to turn the trick. No mortal
in his best days could budge it with a crowbar.
There is our pact and pledge, our secret sign,
built into that bed—my handiwork
and no one else's!

                                        An old trunk of olive
1090 grew like a pillar on the building plot,
and I laid out our bedroom round that tree,
lined up the stone walls, built the walls and roof,
gave it a doorway and smooth-fitting doors.
Then I lopped off the silvery leaves and branches,
1095 hewed and shaped the stump from the roots up
into a bedpost, drilled it, let it serve
as model for the rest, I planed them all,
inlaid them all with silver, gold, and ivory,
and stretched a bed between—a <u>pliant</u> web
of oxhide thongs dyed crimson.
1100   There's our sign!
I know no more. Could someone else's hand
have sawn that trunk and dragged the frame away?"

Their secret! as she heard it told, her knees
grew <u>tremulous</u> and weak, her heart failed her.
1105 With eyes brimming tears she ran to him,
throwing her arms around his neck, and kissed him,
murmuring:
                        "Do not rage at me, Odysseus!
No one ever matched your caution! Think
what difficulty the gods gave: they denied us
1110 life together in our prime and flowering years,
kept us from crossing into age together.
Forgive me, don't be angry. I could not
welcome you with love on sight! I armed myself
long ago against the frauds of men,
1115 impostors who might come—and all those many
whose underhanded ways bring evil on! . . .
But here and now, what sign could be so clear
as this of our own bed?
No other man has ever laid eyes on it—
1120 only my own slave, Actoris, that my father

- -

WORDS TO OWN
pliant (plī′ənt) *adj*.: flexible.
tremulous (trem′yo͞o·ləs) *adj*.: trembling; shaking.

- -

sent with me as a gift—she kept our door.
You make my stiff heart know that I am yours."

Now from his breast into his eyes the ache
of longing mounted, and he wept at last,
1125 his dear wife, clear and faithful, in his arms,
longed for
       as the sun-warmed earth is longed for by a swimmer
spent in rough water where his ship went down
under Poseidon's blows, gale winds and tons of sea.
Few men can keep alive through a big surf
1130 to crawl, clotted with brine, on kindly beaches
in joy, in joy, knowing the abyss behind:
and so she too rejoiced, her gaze upon her husband,
her white arms round him pressed, as though forever.

(from Book 23)

Penelope and Her Suitors (1912) by J. W. Waterhouse.

Ithaca

C. P. Cavafy

translated from Greek by Edmund Keeley and Philip Sherrard

When you set out for Ithaca,
pray that your road's a long one,
full of adventure, full of discovery.
Laistrygonians, Cyclops,
5   angry Poseidon—don't be scared of them:
you won't find things like that on your way
as long as your thoughts are exalted,
as long as a rare excitement
stirs your spirit and your body.
10   Laistrygonians, Cyclops,
wild Poseidon—you won't encounter them
unless you bring them along inside you,
unless your soul raises them up in front of you.

Pray that your road's a long one.
15   May there be many a summer morning when—
full of gratitude, full of joy—
you come into harbors seen for the first time;
may you stop at Phoenician trading centers
and buy fine things,
20   mother-of-pearl and coral, amber and ebony,
sensual perfumes of every kind,
as many sensual perfumes as you can;
may you visit numerous Egyptian cities
to fill yourself with learning from the wise.

25   Keep Ithaca always in mind.
Arriving there is what you're destined for.
But don't hurry the journey at all.
Better if it goes on for years
so you're old by the time you reach the island,
30   wealthy with all you've gained on the way,
not expecting Ithaca to make you rich.
Ithaca gave you the marvelous journey.
Without her you wouldn't have set out.
She hasn't anything else to give.

35   And if you find her poor, Ithaca won't have fooled you.
Wise as you'll have become, and so experienced,
you'll have understood by then what an Ithaca means.

The Sea Call

Nikos Kazantzakis
translated from Greek by Kimon Friar

When Odysseus met Teiresias in the Under-world, the prophet told him that he would reach home but would then take yet another journey to a land where people live who know nothing of the sea. (See pages 914–915.) In this excerpt from a modern sequel to the Odyssey *by the twentieth-century Greek poet Nikos Kazantzakis, Odysseus has returned to Ithaca. Sitting by the hearth with his family, his eyes alight with excitement, he relates his adventures. But then . . .*

Odysseus sealed his bitter lips and spoke no more,
but watched the glowering fire fade, the withering flames,
the ash that spread like powder on the dying coals,
then turned, glanced at his wife, gazed on his son and father,
5 and suddenly shook with fear and sighed, for now he knew
that even his native land was a sweet mask of Death.
Like a wild beast snared in a net, his eyes rolled round
and tumbled down his deep eye-sockets, green and bloodshot.
His tribal palace seemed a narrow shepherd's pen,
10 his wife a small and wrinkled old housekeeping crone,
his son an eighty-year-old drudge who, trembling, weighed
with care to find what's just, unjust, dishonest, honest,
as though all life were prudence, as though fire were just,
and logic the highest good of eagle-mounting man!
15 The heart-embattled athlete laughed, dashed to his feet,
and his home's sweetness, suddenly, his longed-for land,
the twelve gods, ancient virtue by his honored hearth,
his son—all seemed opposed now to his high descent.
The fire dwindled and died away, and the four heads
20 and his son's smooth-skinned calves with tender softness glowed
till in the trembling hush Penelope's wan cries
broke in despair like water flowing down a wall.
Her son dashed and stood upright by his mother's throne,
touched gently with a mute compassion her white arm,
25 then gazed upon his father in the dim light, and shuddered,
for in the last resplendence of the falling fire
he could discern the unmoving eyes flash yellow, blue,
and crimson, though the dark had swallowed the wild body.
With silent strides Odysseus then shot back the bolt,
30 passed lightly through the courtyard and sped down the street.
Some saw him take the graveyard's zigzag mountain path,
some saw him leap on rocks that edged the savage shore,
some visionaries saw him in the dead of night
swimming and talking secretly with the sea-demons,
35 but only a small boy saw him in a lonely dream
sit crouched and weeping by the dark sea's foaming edge.

MAKING MEANINGS PART TWO

First Thoughts

1. Do you think Odysseus has changed since his earlier adventures with the Cicones? Explain your responses to Odysseus as a hero.

Shaping Interpretations

2. In showing us how Odysseus' old dog is kept, what is Homer telling us about conditions in Ithaca?

3. It is rare in ancient epics for heroes to have much to do with ordinary people, but in the *Odyssey* servants play important roles. How does Odysseus treat Eumaeus and the cowherd? What values might Homer be trying to teach through that treatment?

4. What characteristics of Odysseus and Penelope's marriage bed suggest the strength and endurance of their love?

Reviewing the Text

a. Describe Argos's condition when Odysseus sees him.

b. What is the test of the bow, and how has Penelope said she will reward the winner of the contest?

c. Just before trying the bow, Odysseus reveals himself to two people. Who are they? Why does he confide in them?

d. List at least five images or events from Odysseus' battle with the suitors.

e. How does Penelope test Odysseus after the battle?

Connecting with the Text

5. The *Odyssey* is many centuries old. Do you think the feelings and needs shown by the people in the *Odyssey* are still important to people today? Which experiences or people in this story did you most identify with?

Extending the Text

6. Do you know of any other stories, movies, or TV shows in which the hero (male or female) appears in a disguise? What do these heroes often learn while they are in disguise?

7. Suppose Odysseus were a modern general who fought a war for ten years and was missing for another ten years. What emotional problems might he (or she) face after that ordeal? What changes might he (or she) find in the home and family after twenty years?

8. In "Ithaca" (page 946), a modern Greek poet reflects on the *Odyssey*. Explain what you think "arriving in Ithaca" could mean for all of us.

Challenging the Text

9. Do you think Odysseus' revenge on the suitors and maids is excessive or too brutal? Explore this question from Odysseus' viewpoint (remember he was the rightful king) and from your own modern viewpoint.

CHOICES: Building Your Portfolio

Writer's Notebook

1. Collecting Ideas for a Speculation About Causes or Effects

Finding a topic. The *Odyssey* is full of ideas you might use in an essay speculating on the possible causes of something, or on the possible effects of something (see the Writer's Workshop on page 958). Think of various episodes, themes, feelings, and characters you've met in these stories from the epic. What causes or effects could you speculate, or guess, about? Brainstorm your ideas in a cluster diagram like the one below.

effects of war on families (Odysseus' family)

how a parent's absence affects a child (Telemachus)

effects

how lack of leadership affects a nation (Ithaca)

how our values involving hospitality affect our behavior

Creative Writing

2. Prophetic Puzzler

Homer's audiences would have known who Teiresias was and would have realized that his prophecies always came true. In Part One, lines 546–565 (page 915), Teiresias prophesies that Odysseus will make a strange journey. Several writers after Homer have tried to imagine exactly what Teiresias' mysterious prophecy means. (For part of one writer's extension of the story, see Nikos Kazantzakis' "The Sea Call" on page 947.) Write your own extension of Odysseus' story based on this prophecy. Tell what Odysseus does, where he goes, and what happens after he takes over his kingdom again. Be sure to include all the details contained in the prophecy.

Creative Writing

3. And Now— the Movie

Write a proposal suggesting ways for the *Odyssey* to be made into a movie that's set in the present. Imagine that the readers of the proposal will be the producers of the movie.

Explain how you would modernize the epic. Use the following chart to organize your ideas.

1200 B.C.	Today
Trojan War as background.	
Hero is soldier who fought in war.	
Travels around Mediterranean and down to Underworld.	
Uses ships with oars and sails.	
Meets Lotus Eaters, Sirens, Cyclops, Scylla and Charybdis.	
Is tempted by Calypso and Circe.	
Fortune hunters at home hound his wife.	
Dog lives on garbage heap.	
Son is insulted.	
Gods affect the action.	

Creative Writing

4. Her Odyssey

Write a story plan for an *Odyssey* with a woman as the voyaging hero. (For example, what if Penelope, rather than Odysseus, had been the

voyager?) You may set your story in any time and place, from Odysseus' Greece to your present hometown to a distant galaxy in the future. As you plan your characters, plot, and action, consider the following:

- occupation of the heroine
- reasons for being away from home
- situation at home
- trials of her journey home
- how she deals with people opposed to her
- how her family responds to her return

Critical Writing
5. Timeless Messages

A work of literature cannot be important to us unless it speaks to us and to our lives. In one or more paragraphs, discuss at least four ways in which the *Odyssey* speaks to you today. You might consider how it says something about these values:

- courtesy and respect for all classes of people
- courage, trust, and discipline
- community and law
- home and family
- obedience to the divine world

Be sure to review your Reader's Log for ideas.

Critical Thinking/ Speaking
6. Speak Your Mind

Use the following quotation as the basis for a brief talk on the *Odyssey*. Cite specific passages from the epic that you think support the ideas in the quotation. If you disagree with the quotation, cite specific passages from the epic to support your own opinion, which you should make clear in your opening statement.

> . . . what has made Homer for three thousand years the greatest poet in the world is his *naturalness*. We love each other as in Homer. We hate each other as in Homer. We are perpetually being interfered with as in Homer by change and fate and necessity, by invisible influences for good, and by invisible influences for evil. . . .
> —John Cowper Powys

Creative Writing
7. Another Viewpoint

Present one of the epic's episodes through the eyes of another character. (Be sure to check your Reader's Logs for ideas.) Write in journal form or in the form of a poem. (See the poems about Penelope on pages 931 and 937.)

Performance
8. Tell the Story . . .

Since the *Odyssey* was meant to be performed, select a portion of the epic to present as a play or as a dramatic reading. (Derek Walcott, a Nobel Prize–winning poet from St. Lucia, in the West Indies, wrote a play based on the *Odyssey*. His storyteller is a blind singer called Billy Blue. His Cyclops calls himself The Eye.) Be sure to refer to the Reader's Log notes you took as you read the epic. Work with a group to decide the form your presentation will take, the episode you'll focus on, and props and costumes you'll need. Where will you set the story?

Art
9. Can You Picture . . . ?

Illustrate your favorite character from the *Odyssey*. You might draw or paint a portrait, assemble a collage of images clipped from magazines, or take photographs. Try to reveal your character's personality through objects he or she is holding or working with; or through images in the background.

LANGUAGE LINK

**Handbook
of Literary
Terms
H E L P**

See Epithet.

Style: Epithets

An **epithet** is an adjective or phrase used to characterize someone. *Catherine the Great, baby boomers, The Refrigerator*—these epithets are used to characterize an empress, a generation, and a football player. Homer uses many epithets as formulas to characterize places and people. When Penelope is referred to as "faithful Penelope," we are instantly reminded of her outstanding character trait.

A Famous Epithet Mystery

One of Homer's most famous epithets is the formula description "the wine-dark sea." Since wine is red or white or yellowish, and the sea is none of these hues, the description is puzzling. Some say that the ancient Greeks diluted their wine with water and that the alkali in the water changed the color of the wine from red to blue. Others think the sea was covered with red algae. Still others suggest that the Greeks were colorblind. But Robert Fitzgerald, the great translator of the *Odyssey*, thought about the question when he was sailing in the Aegean Sea:

"The contrast of the bare arid baked land against the sea gave the sea such a richness of hue that I felt as though we were sailing through a bowl of dye. The depth of hue of the water was like the depth of hue of a good red wine."

Try It Out

1. Odysseus is called "<u>versatile</u> Odysseus," "<u>wily</u> Odysseus," "the <u>strategist</u>," and "the <u>noble and enduring</u> man." What does each underlined word mean?

2. Telemachus is called "<u>clear-headed</u> Telemachus." How would you define *clear-headed*? What is its opposite?

3. Dawn is described as "<u>rosy-fingered</u>." What does this epithet help you see?

Make up your own epithets for these characters in the *Odyssey*: Odysseus, Cyclops, Circe, Argos, Penelope, the suitors. Then make up epithets for at least three characters that are popular on TV or in the news today (sports stars? singers?).

VOCABULARY HOW TO OWN A WORD

WORD BANK

adversities
disdainful
adorn
revelry
restitution
glowered
lavished
aloof
pliant
tremulous

Synonyms

Synonyms are words with similar meanings—like *large* and *big*, *subtract* and *deduct*, or *beast* and *monster*. You have to use synonyms with care. Synonyms do not always mean exactly the same thing. Use a diagram like the one here to map synonyms for each word in the Word Bank. Do the synonyms work when you substitute them in the original sentence in the text?

adversities

| **SYNONYMS** |
| misfortunes, afflictions, difficulties, troubles |

| **ORIGINAL SENTENCE** | **RESPONSE TO SUBSTITUTIONS** |
| "I bore adversities. . . ." | *Adversities* suggests intense troubles. *Afflictions* could work. The other words are too mild to describe what Odysseus suffered. They could refer to problems as minor as troubles with your hair. |

A Dialogue with the Text

As you read this epic, picture the situation—the scenes of great destruction, the danger, the desperation of Aeneas as he tries to save his family from the burning city. Keep a record of your responses. Does the epic remind you of any journeys taken by refugees in today's world?

Background

The following episode is from the *Aeneid,* the Roman epic written in the first century B.C. by the poet Virgil. Like the *Odyssey,* it tells of the fall of Troy, but it follows a Trojan warrior who flees his city and travels far to find a new home. In one sense Aeneas is a refugee—as so many people are today.

Aeneas is more than just a soldier—he is a Trojan prince, son of a man named Anchises and the goddess Venus. As this episode opens, his home, Troy, is in flames. The Greeks have murdered the old Trojan king Priam. All of Aeneas's men have been killed. As a husband and father, Aeneas is desperate and in his fury tries to return to the fight.

Aeneas is telling his own story.

from the # Aeneid

Virgil
translated by Rolfe Humphries

The Flight of Aeneas from Troy (18th century) by Carle Van Loo.
Louvre, Paris.

"Let me go back to the Greeks, renew the battle,
We shall not all of us die unavenged."
Sword at my side, I was on the point of going,
Working the left arm into the shield. Creusa
5 Clung to me on the threshold, held my feet,
And made me see my little son:—"Dear husband,
If you are bent on dying, take us with you,
But if you think there is any hope in fighting,
And you should know, stay and defend the house!
10 To whom are we abandoned, your father and son,
And I, once called your wife?" She filled the house
With moaning outcry. And then something happened,
A wonderful portent. Over Iulus' head,
Between our hands and faces, there appeared
15 A blaze of gentle light; a tongue of flame,
Harmless and innocent, was playing over
The softness of his hair, around his temples.
We were afraid, we did our best to quench it
With our own hands, or water, but my father
20 Raised joyous eyes to heaven, and prayed aloud:—
"Almighty Jupiter, if any prayer
Of ours has power to move you, look upon us,
Grant only this, if we have ever deserved it,
Grant us a sign, and ratify the omen!"
25 He had hardly spoken, when thunder on the left
Resounded, and a shooting star from heaven
Drew a long trail of light across the shadows.
We saw it cross above the house, and vanish
In the woods of Ida, a wake of gleaming light
30 Where it had sped, and a trail of sulphurous odor.
This was a victory: my father rose
In worship of the gods and the holy star,
Crying: "I follow, son, wherever you lead;
There is no delay, not now; Gods of my fathers,
35 Preserve my house, my grandson; yours the omen,
And Troy is in your keeping. O my son,
I yield, I am ready to follow." But the fire
Came louder over the walls, the flames rolled nearer
Their burning tide. "Climb to my shoulders, father,
40 It will be no burden, so we are together,
Meeting a common danger or salvation.
Iulus, take my hand; Creusa, follow
A little way behind. Listen, you servants!
You will find, when you leave the city, an old temple
45 That once belonged to Ceres;° it has been tended
For many years with the worship of our fathers.
There's a little hill there, and a cypress tree;

The Family

Aeneas (i·nē′əs): prince of Troy.
Creusa (krē·yōō′sə): his wife.
Iulus (yōōl′əs): their young son.
Anchises (an·kī′sēz′): Aeneas's old father.

45. Ceres (sir′ēz′): goddess of agriculture, known for her benevolence to humans. In Greek mythology she is called Demeter.

And that's where we shall meet, one way or another.
And one thing more: you, father, are to carry
50 The holy objects and the gods of the household,
My hands are foul with battle and blood, I could not
Touch them without pollution."

                                    I bent down
And over my neck and shoulders spread the cover
Of a tawny lion-skin, took up my burden;
55 Little Iulus held my hand, and trotted,
As best he could, beside me; Creusa followed.
We went on through the shadows. I had been
Brave, so I thought, before, in the rain of weapons
And the cloud of massing Greeks. But now I trembled
60 At every breath of air, shook at a whisper,
Fearful for both my burden and companion.
        I was near the gates, and thinking we had made it,
But there was a sound, the tramp of marching feet,
And many of them, it seemed; my father, peering
Through the thick gloom, cried out:—"Son, they are
65   coming!
Flee, flee! I see their shields, their gleaming bronze."
Something or other took my senses from me
In that confusion. I turned aside from the path,
I do not know what happened then. Creusa
70 Was lost; she had missed the road, or halted, weary,
For a brief rest. I do not know what happened,
She was not seen again; I had not looked back,
Nor even thought about her, till we came
To Ceres' hallowed home. The count was perfect,
75 Only one missing there, the wife and mother.
Whom did I not accuse, of gods and mortals,
Then in my frenzy? What worse thing had happened
In the city overthrown? I left Anchises,
My son, my household gods, to my companions,
80 In a hiding place in the valley; and I went back
Into the city again, wearing my armor,
Ready, still one more time, for any danger.
I found the walls again, the gate's dark portals,
I followed my own footsteps back, but terror,
85 Terror and silence were all I found. I went
On to my house. She might, just might, have gone there.
Only the Greeks were there, and fire devouring
The very pinnacles. I tried Priam's° palace;
In the empty courtyards Phoenix° and Ulysses
90 Guarded the spoils piled up at Juno's altar.
They had Trojan treasure there, loot from the altars,
Great drinking-bowls of gold, and stolen garments,

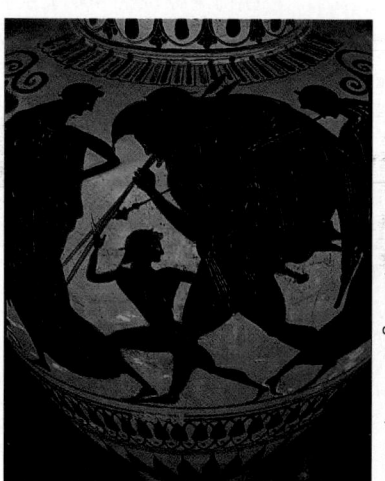

Aeneas carrying his father, Anchises, while young Iulus runs ahead (c. 520 B.C.). Detail from an amphora, or vase.

88. Priam (prī′əm): king of Troy.
89. Phoenix: a Greek who was the tutor of Achilles, enemy of the Trojans.

And human beings. A line of boys and women
Stood trembling there.
95 I took the risk of crying through the shadows,
Over and over, "Creusa!" I kept calling,
"Creusa!" and "Creusa!" but no answer.
No sense, no limit, to my endless rushing
All through the town; and then at last I saw her,
100 Or thought I did, her shadow a little taller
Than I remembered. And she spoke to me
Beside myself with terror:—"O dear husband,
What good is all this frantic grief? The gods
Have willed it so, Creusa may not join you
105 Out of this city; Jupiter denies it.
Long exile lies ahead, and vast sea-reaches
The ships must furrow, till you come to land
Far in the West; rich fields are there, and a river
Flowing with gentle current; its name is Tiber.°
110 And happy days await you there, a kingdom,
A royal wife.° Banish the tears of sorrow
Over Creusa lost. I shall never see
The arrogant houses of the Myrmidons,°
Nor be a slave to any Grecian woman;
115 I am a Dardan° woman; I am the wife
Of Venus' son; it is Cybele° who keeps me
Here on these shores. And now farewell, and love
Our son." I wept, there was more to say; she left me,
Vanishing into empty air. Three times
120 I reached out toward her, and three times her image
Fled like the breath of a wind or a dream on wings.
The night was over; I went back to my comrades,
                    I was surprised to find so many more
Had joined us, ready for exile, pitiful people,
125 Mothers, and men, and children, streaming in
From everywhere, looking for me to lead them
Wherever I would. Over the hills of Ida
The morning-star was rising; in the town
The Danaans held the gates, and help was hopeless.
130 I gave it up, I lifted up my father,
Together we sought the hills.

109. Tiber (tī′bər): river that flows through Rome.

111. royal wife: Aeneas later marries Lavinia, daughter of the king of Latium, and together they are the founders of Roman civilization.

113. Myrmidons (mur′mə·däns′): Greek soldiers who fought with the hero Achilles. The Greeks took many of the surviving Trojans back to Greece as slaves. Another name for the Greeks is Danaans (dan′ə·ənz) (see line 129).

115. Dardan: Trojan. Dardanus was the founder of Troy.

116. Cybele (sib′ə·lē): nature goddess, often called the Great Mother.

Bosnian Serb refugees flee Croatia, 1995.

Rome's National Poet

Virgil (70 B.C.–19 B.C.), or Publius Vergilius Maro as he was known in his lifetime, was born into a lower-class, rural family. It was poetry that brought him fame and dignity in the very highest circles of Roman society. In fact, Virgil came to be regarded as the national poet of Rome and the voice of Rome's greatness. Virgil's works were taught in Roman schools because they could easily

Virgil (detail). Roman mosaic.
Musée Nationale du Bardo, Le Bardo, Tunisia.

be adapted to the study of literature, religion, history, and politics.

The *Aeneid* was Virgil's masterwork, an epic that gave Rome a heroic past and a great destiny. Virgil deliberately modeled his epic on Homer's *Iliad* and *Odyssey*. But where Odysseus returns to a small island kingdom, Aeneas founds the great civilization of Rome. The light that is dancing around his little son's head in this part of the epic is a sign from heaven that Aeneas's descendants are divinely favored.

FINDING COMMON GROUND

- And so Aeneas set out as a refugee, on the perilous journey that was to lead to the founding of Rome, the greatest city of its era. What modern-day perilous journeys were you reminded of when you read this excerpt from the *Aeneid*? Consider the great migrations of the twentieth century and the homelessness that has been created by war and famine.

1. Meet in a small group to discuss the quests made in the twentieth century—perilous journeys undertaken by immigrants and refugees to find a new peaceful life for themselves and for their children.

2. Members of your group should do research to find at least one book or one film about a modern-day refugee experience. Read the book (or view the film) and discuss ways in which the experience described there is like and unlike Aeneas's experience.

3. Convene as a class and share your notes on the books and films you have chosen. How pervasive do you think the perilous journey is as a theme in modern literature and film?

READ ON

Another Odyssey at Sea

You've read adventure fiction, and you've seen action movies, but *Kon-Tiki* (Pocket/Simon & Schuster) is a real-life adventure story. Thor Heyerdahl journeyed 4,300 nautical miles across the Pacific Ocean—on a log raft. Read this now-classic tale (it has been translated into sixty-five languages) of Heyerdahl's journey and relive the perils that threatened the Kon-Tiki crew: encounters with strange "monsters," leaks in the raft, and life-and-death struggles with a treacherous sea.

A Space Odyssey

It was a routine journey—the fifth time U.S. astronauts had set out for the moon. But on April 13, 1970, Jim Lovell, Fred Haise, and Jack Swigert felt a strange explosion in their spacecraft. The lights dimmed, and the air got thinner. The three astronauts abandoned ship—for a tiny lunar module with room and supplies for only two. *Apollo 13* (Pocket), co-written by Jim Lovell himself (along with Jeffrey Kluger), tells the story of the epic journey. In 1995, the book was made into a successful movie starring Tom Hanks.

An American Odyssey

How far is too far when it comes to survival? You may know that the Donner party was a group migrating to California over one hundred years ago. It was just a few months from winter and the treacherous Sierra Nevada mountains lay between them and their new homes. George R. Stewart's *Ordeal by Hunger* (Houghton Mifflin) is a compelling, terrifying, and human account of the most horrifying of America's pioneer odysseys.

Odysseys at the Movies

A New Kind of Hero: Follow an unusual hero on a journey through recent American history in *Forrest Gump* (1994).

A Modern Epic: Harrison Ford brings the heroism and adventure of the old epics to the modern screen in *Indiana Jones and the Temple of Doom* (1984).

Writer's Workshop

Technology HELP

See Writer's Workshop 2 CD-ROM. *Assignment: Cause and Effect.*

ASSIGNMENT

Write an essay specu-lating about the causes or the effects of a trend, a situation, or an event. The topic can come from something you've observed firsthand, or from something in the news, or from a piece of literature you've read. Be sure to support your speculations with convincing evidence.

AIM

To inform; to persuade.

AUDIENCE

Your teacher and class-mates; your family; readers of the school newspaper; readers of your local newspaper. (You decide.)

EXPOSITORY WRITING

SPECULATION ABOUT CAUSES OR EFFECTS

Speculation calls for "what if" and "why" thinking. To **speculate,** you weigh possibilities, choosing the one that seems most reasonable to you.

You speculate about causes and effects in many ways each day, from trying to understand the cause of a friend's upset to imagining the effects of choosing one school over another. The ability to speculate helps a lawyer imagine how a surprise witness might affect the jury. It helps a naturalist figure out the causes of the growth of the mosquito population. It helps a coach figure out how new strategies will affect a game. Speculation lets people think about causes and anticipate effects. It calls for creative thinking as well as careful reasoning.

In this workshop you will speculate about the causes or the effects of a situation, an event, or a trend. You won't report on causes or effects that are already known. Instead, you'll choose a situation, event, or trend whose causes or effects are uncertain, and you'll present your own ideas about them.

Prewriting

1. Find a Topic

The main thing about a topic is this: It must be something you feel passionate about or are very interested in. We all write best about things we care about.

a. **Look through your Writer's Notebook.** Re-read your notebook, looking for entries that might give you topics for this workshop. For example, as you read the *Odyssey,* did you take notes on any broad contemporary topics that interested you? What speculations can you make about their causes or the ways they are affecting life today?

b. **Open up: Look around you.** What is happening in school or in your community or country that interests you? Here is a list showing a writer's brainstorming to find a topic in the life around him:

The history
of the written
word is rich and time
Once upon a time
Page 1

Causes:

- of new conservative mood in the United States
- of increased litter in neighborhood
- of team's string of losses this year
- of poor school spirit
- of prejudice
- of gangs

Effects:

- of the ways we feel about strangers or people who are different
- of poor reading skills
- of closing of playground
- of gene therapy
- of computers
- of censorship

c. **Think about other literature you've read.** Here at the right is a notebook entry by someone looking for a topic based on *The Miracle Worker*. Notice the "what if" thinking: What if something had happened differently? (What if the text had ended differently?)

Causes	Effects
of Helen's violent behavior	on Annie if she had been fired
of problems between Keller and James	of Annie's work with Helen
of Annie's terrors	of situation in the Keller family if Annie had not been successful

d. **Focus on fads.** What are your favorite—and least favorite—fads or trends? On your own or with classmates, brainstorm lists showing what's "in" right now in areas such as slang, clothing, food, music, and recreation. Then scan the lists for items you love—or hate. You might speculate about reasons for the popularity of a certain fad. You might try to figure out how a trend got started, or you might try to predict how it will affect people's lives over the next few years.

2. Find Supporting Details

Once you've chosen your topic, brainstorm possible causes or effects related to it. Stretch your imagination and list all the possibilities that occur to you. Don't worry about logic or even

■ **Strategies for Supporting Speculations**

- *cite historical facts*
- *cite literary examples*
- *cite statistics*
- *tell personal anecdotes*
- *deal with conflicting arguments*

repetition—just write. Then look over your ideas. Choose strong ones that make the most sense, and find evidence that supports these causes or effects. This evidence may come from your own experiences or from information you've gathered from reliable sources. Here is a list of details gathered to support the writer's speculation about the effects of gene therapy (the deliberate alteration of genes to prevent diseases or defects):

Effect 1: Many common diseases will be cured or prevented.
Support: Newspaper says scientists can already cure some diseases in animals by altering genes.

Effect 2: People will want to "design" babies with popular traits.
Support: Many people want plastic surgery just to be more attractive. They'd probably use gene therapy the same way.

Effect 3: New generations will be weaker.
Support: Overbred animals are weak and disease-prone.

Model

My speculation focuses on Odysseus and what happens to him when he settles in at home. Home isn't the same, of course, and neither is he. What might his life be like after his return? I think it might be better than ever and that Odysseus will be a changed man—for the better.

Topic is made clear.

First, Odysseus, the family man, will probably appreciate his wife and son more than ever. Telemachus fights the suitors bravely. That will make Odysseus proud. Penelope shows how faithful she is by holding off the suitors. Odysseus always loved her—he left Circe and Calypso for her. Now he must admire her even more.

The writer indicates the order of the speculations by using transitional words like "first," "second." Details from the epic provide the basis for each speculation. More solid examples from epic to back up the speculation.

Second, Odysseus learns a great deal from all his sufferings. He learns the value of his civilizing beliefs by observing the destructive, brutish Cyclops who does not share Greek values. He learns self-discipline in his adventure with the sirens. He learns the value of loyalty from his faithful servants and even from his old dog. All of these experiences will make him

3. Consider Your Audience

Ask yourself what your readers probably know about your topic. (That's right—now you're speculating about your readers!) Then note information that your readers might need, such as background information or definitions of key terms.

Drafting
1. Make It Clear: State Your Topic

Start by describing the situation, event, or trend you are going to talk about. Write down any ideas you have. Provide details and background that will help your readers feel comfortable with your topic.

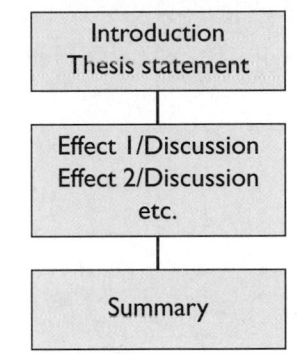

■ *Need a framework?*

Introduction
Thesis statement

Effect 1/Discussion
Effect 2/Discussion
etc.

Summary

different from the way he was before he left home. And they can't help but make him a better father, husband, and ruler.

Finally, Odysseus learns something about the gods and their power. When he sees his men plucked off his ship and drowned, or eaten by the Cyclops, he must realize that human beings have little power over their own fates. The gods pull the strings. No man could live through what Odysseus lives through and still be arrogantly sure of his power to control his own destiny.

Some writers, I know, take seriously the prophecy that Odysseus will die in a foreign place, and so they imagine that he got restless at home and wanted more adventure. I disagree. I think the effects of his perilous journey could only have made him more compassionate as a father, husband, and ruler. I think that writers who like to imagine a restless Odysseus are just being very modern, making Odysseus like some suburban husband who can't resolve his midlife crisis. I think there is no question that Odysseus solved his.

The most important effect is cited last.

A strong statement supporting the speculation.

A strong conclusion that sums up the writer's main point.

2. State Your Speculations

Write your ideas about the causes of your topic or its effects. Put your speculations in an appropriate order. Some writers present possible causes or results in time order; others prefer to open with the least important detail and end with a bang—with the most important.

Evaluating and Revising
1. Peer Review

Trade drafts with a partner. Make notes about the parts of your partner's essay that seem strongest. Write questions and suggestions that might help the writer. Be sure to comment on the essay's persuasiveness: Is the writer convincing?

Revision Model

	Peer Comments
My speculation focuses on Odysseus and what happens to him when he settles in at home. ~~When Odysseus finally gets home,~~ ∧	Make your topic clearer. Not sure what it is.
and ∧ home isn't the same. ~~Of course,~~ ∧	
neither is he. What might his life be I think it might be better than ever and that Odysseus will be a changed man—for the better. like after his return? ∧	I don't know what your speculation is. Tell me. Transitions would help indicate your main points.
First, Odysseus, the family man, will ∧	
probably appreciate his wife and	
son more than ever.	

2. Self-Evaluation

Think about your peer reviewer's questions and suggestions. If a reader is confused about your topic, you might describe it in more detail or include more background information. If a reader disagrees with your speculations, you might add more evidence or recheck your reasoning. One technique for strengthening your speculation is to add a paragraph acknowledging the disagreement and responding to it.

■ Evaluation Criteria

A good essay speculating about causes or effects

1. *clearly answers at least one of these questions: Why did it happen? and What are the results?*

2. *clearly states and describes the topic: an event, a situation, a trend, a possibility*

3. *presents the writer's ideas about possible causes of the situation or possible effects*

4. *supports the writer's speculations with convincing evidence*

5. *organizes the evidence so the content is clear to readers*

6. *shows careful reasoning*

Proofreading

You may miss errors if you're reading your essay for the third or fourth time in a row. Try setting it aside for a while before you proofread. Then, to focus your attention, use a sheet of clean paper to block out all the lines below the line you're examining.

Publishing

You may wish to submit your essay to the editors of your school newspaper or local newspaper if this is the audience you had in mind as you wrote. If you wrote for your teacher, classmates, or family, work with friends to make a visual aid to accompany your essay. For example, you could create a poster, a diorama, or a political cartoon.

Reflecting

If you want to add this essay to your portfolio, date the final version and attach your prewriting notes and earlier drafts. Then think about your experiences with your essay. Write your reflections, including your responses to the following questions.

1. Did anything surprise me as I worked on my essay?

2. Which part of the writing process was easiest (or hardest) for me in this workshop, and what made it easy (or hard)?

3. Which parts of my final draft do I consider strongest? Why?

Sentence Workshop
H E L P

Avoiding wordiness:
page 964.

Linoleum block by Nadya Barabanov, a student at the Riverdale Country School, Bronx, New York.

Reprinted by permission of Nadya Barabanov.

At first, I hated this assignment. I thought it would be boring. But I didn't expect to have all these ideas about Odysseus when he returned. I started out thinking about how he would just appreciate his family, but then I got into the character and what I think the epic is really all about. Usually I like prewriting best, but this time prewriting was hardest for me. I didn't get any new ideas until I started drafting. I also had an excellent peer reviewer. I think all my examples are good. I like my last paragraph best. I think I refuted those other ideas about Odysseus pretty well.

Sentence Workshop

**Language
Handbook
H E L P**

*See Sentence
Structure,
page 1010.*

**Technology
H E L P**

See Language
Workshop
CD-ROM.
*Key word
entry:
wordiness.*

REVISING SENTENCES: AVOIDING WORDINESS

Good writers never use more words than are necessary to get the message across. Read the two sentences below. Notice how the unnecessary words make the first one hard to follow.

WORDY   The first part of the long epic, consisting of Books 1, 2, 3, and 4, gives us an introduction to the character called Odysseus, the leader of a band of Greeks who fought against their common enemy in the Trojan War.

CONCISE   The first four books of the epic introduce Odysseus, the leader of a band of Greek veterans of the Trojan War.

Here are some tips for creating sentences that aren't wordy.

- Don't use two or three words to say something that can be expressed in one word.

- Don't use fancy, difficult words where plain, simple ones will express the same idea.

- Don't repeat words or ideas unless it is absolutely necessary.

- Avoid saying things like "owing to the fact that" (just say "since" or "because") and "the question as to whether" (just say "whether").

Try It Out

Revise the following wordy sentences by eliminating unnecessary or repetitive words.

1. The *Odyssey* opens with Odysseus' son, Telemachus, searching every corner of the then-known world, which encompassed all the countries bordering on the coast of the Mediterranean Sea, for his long-lost father who had been absent away from home for ten long years.

2. One of Odysseus' most memorable encounters is his unforgettable meeting with the Cyclops, the deformed monster with one eye, by the name of Polyphemus.

3. The wandering Odysseus is waylaid in his seemingly endless journey home by the powerful charms of the persuasive Circe, who tempts him with the delights of sensual pleasures.

4. Odysseus does not inform his crew of men that Circe has foretold that in the future he alone will live to return alive to his homeland, Ithaca, the place where his wife Penelope awaits his coming.

5. Owing to the fact that the suitors swarmed over his home as well as his wife, Odysseus was a man who was cautious.

Writer's Workshop Follow-up: Revision

Read a draft of your speculation essay to a partner. Ask your partner to note wordy or repetitive passages. Review the essay yourself to see if you can streamline your writing by eliminating unnecessary words.

LEARNING FOR LIFE

Looking at Heroes

Problem

Odysseus was a hero of his time, and he embodied the characteristics his society valued. Each year we get lists of the most admired men and women. In some cases these "heroes" are also good role models—but in other cases they're not. What qualities should a person possess to serve as a role model for young people?

Project

Identify a real person, or describe an imaginary one, who qualifies as a good role model.

Preparation

1. With a group of classmates, brainstorm to develop a list of the qualities a role model should have. You may not need to look any further than your own household: Think of a parent or guardian, an older sibling, or another family member. Then move outward, considering people from your neighborhood, school, place of worship, community, state, and nation. Your group may also want to consider characters in stories, poems, and essays you've read.

2. Work together to list the criteria a role model should meet. Be specific. For example, if one criterion is service to others, is it enough that the service is performed, or must it be done willingly, without a concern for self?

Procedure

1. First decide whether you will focus on a real person or describe an imaginary character. If you choose a real person, take notes on what you already know about him or her. (If you need more information, consider interviewing the person or finding library sources that will give you more background.)

2. Decide what audience you'd like to share your ideas with. This can help you to choose the format you'll use and to adapt your ideas to their needs and interests.

Presentation

Use one of the following formats (or another that your teacher approves).

1. Collage

Create a collage that suggests the person's qualities. Combine a variety of materials and objects—drawings, photographs, scraps of material, words, or anything you find meaningful. Give your collage a catchy title. Exhibit your work at the next open house or meeting of the parent-teacher organization.

2. Personality Profile

Write a one-page profile of the person, using headings such as these: Name, Home, Occupation, Hobbies, Latest Accomplishment, and Goals. If possible, include a statement by the person. Post your profile in the classroom, and if it is about a real person, give him or her a copy.

3. Personal Essay

Write a personal essay expressing your views on why young people need role models and where they can find them. Submit your essay to the community or school newspaper or to a magazine that accepts student writing. (Your media specialist can help you find a suitable magazine.)

Processing

What did you learn about your own values by doing this project? What was most difficult for you? most rewarding? Write a reflection for your portfolio that includes answers to these questions.

HANDBOOK OF LITERARY TERMS

For more information about a topic, turn to the page(s) in this book that are indicated on a separate line at the end of the entry. For example, to learn more about *Autobiography,* turn to page 355.

On another line are cross-references to entries in this Handbook that provide closely related information. For instance, at the end of *Diction* is a cross-reference to *Connotation, Style, Tone.*

ALLITERATION   Repetition of the same consonant sounds in words that are close together in a poem, or repetition of consonant sounds that are very similar. In this example, the sounds "fl," "t," "n," and "w," are repeated in line I and the "s" sound is repeated in line 2:

> Open here I flung the shutter, when with
>   many a flirt and flutter,
> In there stepped a stately Raven of the saintly
>   days of yore.

> —Edgar Allan Poe, from "The Raven"

See page 560.

ALLUSION   Reference to a statement, a person, a place, or an event from literature, history, religion, myth, politics, sports, science, or pop culture. In calling one of his stories "The Gift of the Magi" (see page 202), O. Henry used an allusion to the wise men from the East called the Magi, who presented the Christ child with the first Christmas gifts.

ARGUMENT   Special form of persuasion that uses reason to try to convince a reader or listener to think or act in a certain way. Like all persuasive writing, argument is aimed at winning people to the writer's point of view, but argument uses only facts and logical reasoning to achieve its purpose. (Other persuasive writing may use different methods, including an unashamed appeal to the emotions.) Debate societies use arguments to win points. Good arguments are also sometimes found in editorials and magazine articles.

See also *Persuasion.*

ASIDE   Words that are spoken by a character in a play to the audience or to another character but that are not supposed to be overheard by the others onstage. Stage directions usually tell when a speech is an aside. For example, there are two asides in the opening scene of *Romeo and Juliet* on page 737. Sampson speaks to Gregory in an aside, and Gregory responds to him in another aside, as they pick a fight with the servants of the house of Montague. Sampson and Gregory hear each other's asides, and so do we in the audience, but Montague's servants do not.

See page 768.

ASSONANCE   Repetition of similar vowel sounds that are followed by different consonant sounds, especially in words that are close together in a poem. The words *base* and *fade* and the words *young* and *love* are examples of assonance. The lines that follow are especially musical because of assonance:

> Seeing the snowman standing all alone
> In dusk and cold is more than he can bear.
> The small boy weeps to hear the wind prepare
> A night of gnashings and enormous moan.

> —Richard Wilbur,
>   from "Boy at the Window"

See also *Alliteration, Onomatopoeia, Rhyme.*

"I think I'll wait for the next elevator."

Drawing by Chas. Addams; © 1988 The New Yorker Magazine, Inc.

AUTOBIOGRAPHY An account of the writer's own life. An example of a book-length autobiography is *I Know Why the Caged Bird Sings* by Maya Angelou (an extract is on page 357). Abraham Lincoln's "Not Much of Me" on page 348 is an example of a short autobiographical essay.

See page 355.

BALLAD Song that tells a story. Folk ballads are composed by unknown singers and are passed on from generation to generation by word of mouth before they are written down. **Literary ballads,** on the other hand, are composed by known individuals and are written down in imitation of the old folk ballads. "Ballad of Birmingham" by Dudley Randall (page 383) is a modern literary ballad. Ballads usually tell sensational stories of tragedy or adventure, using simple language with a great deal of repetition. They also usually have regular rhythm and rhyme patterns, which make them easy to memorize.

BIOGRAPHY An account of a person's life, written or told by another person. A classic American biography is Carl Sandburg's life of Abraham Lincoln in several volumes. Today, biographies are written about movie stars, TV personalities, politicians, sports figures, self-made millionaires, even underworld figures. Biographies are among the most popular forms of contemporary literature. "Annie" (page 710) is an excerpt from Joseph P. Lash's biography of Helen Keller and her teacher Annie Sullivan.

See page 355.

BLANK VERSE Poetry written in unrhymed iambic pentameter. *Blank* means the poetry is not rhymed. *Iambic pentameter* means that each line contains five iambs, or metrical feet that consist of an unstressed syllable followed by a stressed syllable (⌣ ´). Blank verse is the most important poetic form in English epic and dramatic poetry. It is the major verse line used in William Shakespeare's plays. Here, for example, are two lines of blank verse from *Romeo and Juliet*.

⌣ ´ ⌣ ´ ⌣ ´ ⌣ ´ ⌣ ´
It was the nightingale, and not the lark,

⌣ ´ ⌣ ´ ⌣ ´ ⌣ ´ ⌣ ´
That pierced the fearful hollow of thine ear.

—William Shakespeare,
from *Romeo and Juliet*

See pages 740–741.
See also *Iambic Pentameter, Meter*.

CHARACTER Person in a story, poem, or play. Sometimes, as in George Orwell's novel *Animal Farm*, animals are characters. In myths the characters are divinities or heroes who have superhuman powers, such as Poseidon and Athena and Odysseus in the *Odyssey* (page 891). But most often a character is an ordinary human being, as is the grandmother in Toni Cade Bambara's "Blues Ain't No Mockin Bird" (page 266).

The process of revealing the personality of a character in a story is called **characterization.** A writer can reveal a character by

1. letting us hear the character speak
2. describing how the character looks and dresses
3. letting us listen to the character's inner thoughts and feelings
4. revealing what other people in the story think or say about the character
5. showing us what the character does—how he or she acts
6. telling us directly what the character's personality is like: cruel, kind, sneaky, brave, and so on

The first five ways of revealing a character are known as **indirect characterization**. When a writer uses indirect characterization, we have to use our own judgment to decide what a character is like, based on the evidence the writer gives us. But when a writer uses the sixth method, known as **direct characterization,** we don't have to decide for ourselves; we are told directly what kind of person the character is.

Characters can be classified as static or dynamic. A **static character** is one who does not change much in the course of a story. By contrast, a **dynamic character** changes as a result of the story's events.

Characters can also be classified as flat or round. A **flat character** has only one or two traits, and these can be described in a few words. In other words, a flat character has no depth, like a flat piece of cardboard. A **round character,** like a real person, has many different character traits, which sometimes contradict one another.

The fears or conflicts or needs that drive a character are called **motivation.** A character can be motivated by many factors, such as vengeance, fear, greed, love, even boredom.

See pages 130–131, 627–629.

CONFLICT   Struggle or clash between opposing characters or between opposing forces. In an **external conflict,** a character struggles against an outside force. This outside force might be another character, or society as a whole, or something in nature. "The Most Dangerous Game" by Richard Connell (page 13) is about the external conflict between the evil General Zaroff and the hunter Rainsford. By contrast, an **internal conflict** takes place entirely within a character's own mind. An internal conflict is a struggle between opposing needs or desires or emotions within a single person. In James Hurst's "The Scarlet Ibis" (page 315), the young narrator struggles with an internal conflict—between love for his brother and hatred of his brother's disabilities. Many works, especially longer ones, contain both internal and external conflicts, and an external conflict often leads to internal problems.

See pages 32–33, 626–627.

CONNOTATION   All the meanings, associations, or emotions that a word suggests. For example, *skinny* and *slender* both have the same literal definition— "thin." But their connotations are completely different. If you call someone skinny, you are saying something unflattering. If you call someone slender, you are paying him or her a compliment. The British philosopher Bertrand Russell once gave a classic example of the different connotations of words: "I am firm. You are obstinate. He is a pigheaded fool." Connotations, or the suggestive power of certain words, play an important role in creating **mood.**

See page 451.

COUPLET   Two consecutive lines of poetry that rhyme. Alexander Pope wrote this sarcastic couplet for a dog's collar (Kew is a place in England):

I am his Highness' dog at Kew;
Pray tell me, Sir, whose dog are you?

—Alexander Pope

Couplets work nicely for humor and satire because the punch line comes so quickly. However, they are most often used to express a completed thought. Shakespeare uses a couplet to give a sense of closure to each act of *Romeo and Juliet* (page 735).

See page 740.

DESCRIPTION   Type of writing intended to create a mood or emotion or to re-create a person, a place, a thing, an event, or an experience. Description is one of the four major techniques used in writing. (The others are **narration, exposition,** and **persuasion**.) Description works by creating images that appeal to the senses of sight, smell, taste, hearing, or touch. Writers use description in all forms of fiction, nonfiction, and poetry.

On the riverfront some of the houses was sticking out over the bank, and they was bowed and bent, and about ready to tumble in. The people had moved out of them. The bank was caved away under one corner of some others, and that corner was hanging over. People lived in them yet, but it was dangersome, because sometimes a strip of land as wide as a house caves in at a time. Sometimes a belt of land a quarter of a mile deep will start in and cave along and cave along till it all caves into the river in one summer. Such a town as that has to be always moving back, and back, and back, because the river's always gnawing at it.

—Mark Twain,
from *Huckleberry Finn*

See page 452.

DIALECT   Way of speaking that is characteristic of a particular region or of a particular group of people. Dialects may have a distinct vocabulary, pronunciation system, and grammar. In a sense, we all speak dialects; but one dialect usually becomes dominant in a country or culture and becomes accepted as the standard way of speaking. In the United States, for example, the formal written language Is known as Standard English. (This is what you usually hear spoken by TV newscasters on the national channels.) Writers often imitate dialects that are heard in particular regions or that reveal a person's economic or social class, in order to give a story "local color," the sense of being authentic to a place or people. For example, Toni Cade Bambara's "Blues Ain't No Mockin Bird" (page 266) is written in a black dialect of the rural South. The model of description on page 969 is written in a Missouri dialect spoken by the main character, Huck Finn.

See page 277.

DICTION A writer's or speaker's choice of words. People use different types of words depending on the audience they're addressing, the subject they're discussing, and the effect or mood they're trying to produce. For example, slang words that would be suitable in a casual conversation with a friend ("This song is *awesome*") would be unsuitable in a formal essay. Similarly, the language in a scientific report about the moon would be different from the language in a poem about the moon.

Diction is an essential element of a writer's **style**. Some writers use simple, down-to-earth, or even slang words (*house, home, digs*); others use ornate, official-sounding, or even flowery language (*domicile, residence, abode*). The **connotations** of words are an important aspect of diction.

See page 211.
See also *Connotation, Tone*.

DRAMA Story that is written to be acted for an audience. The action of a drama is usually driven by a character who wants something very much and who takes steps to get it. The elements of a dramatic plot are **exposition, complications, climax,** and **resolution**.

See pages 626–630.

EPIC Long story told in elevated language (usually poetry), which relates the great deeds of a larger-than-life hero who embodies the values of a particular society. Most epics include elements of myth, legend, folk tale, and history. Their tone is serious and their language is grand. Most epic heroes undertake quests to achieve something of tremendous value to themselves or their people. Often the hero's quest is set in both Heaven and Hell. Homer's *Iliad* and *Odyssey* (see page 891) are the best-known epics in Western civilization. The great epic of ancient Rome is Virgil's *Aeneid* (see page 952), which, like the *Iliad* and *Odyssey*, is based on events that happened during and immediately after the Trojan War.

The English-speaking people have two major epics. *Beowulf* is about a hero who saves a people from two monsters who threaten the stability of their kingdom. *Paradise Lost*, written by John Milton in the seventeenth century, is an epic that retells the Biblical story of the creation and fall of the human race. The great Spanish national epic is the story of a knight called *El Cid;* Mali's epic is called *Sundiata;* India's is *Mahabharata,* and Japan's is *The Tales of the Heike*.

See pages 880–886.

EPITHET Adjective or descriptive phrase that is regularly used to characterize a person, place, or thing. We speak of "Honest Abe," for example, and "America the Beautiful."

Homer created so many epithets in his *Iliad* and *Odyssey* that his name is permanently associated with a type of epithet. The **Homeric epithet** in most English translations consists of a compound adjective that is regularly used to modify a particular noun. Three famous examples are "*wine-dark* sea," "*rosy-fingered* dawn," "the *gray-eyed* goddess Athena."

See page 951.

ESSAY Short piece of nonfiction that examines a single subject from a limited point of view. Most essays can be categorized as either **personal** or **formal**. (Personal essays are also called **informal** or **familiar** essays.)

The **personal essay** is the type of essay included in the nonfiction collections of this book. It generally reveals a great deal about the writer's personality and tastes. Its tone is often conversational, sometimes even humorous, and there may be no attempt to be objective. In fact, in a personal essay we are interested in the writer's feelings and responses to an experience.

The **formal essay** is usually serious, objective, and impersonal in tone. Its purpose is to inform its readers about some topic of interest or to convince them to accept the writer's views. The statements in a formal essay should be supported by facts and logic.

See page 399.

EXPOSITION Type of writing that explains, gives information, defines, or clarifies an idea.

Exposition is one of the four major techniques used in writing. (The others are **narration, description,** and **persuasion.**) We find exposition in news articles, in histories, in biographies (and even in cookbook recipes). In fact, each entry in this Handbook of Literary Terms is an example of exposition.

Exposition is also the term for that part of a plot that gives information about the characters and their problems or conflicts.

See page 452.
See also *Plot.*

FABLE Very brief story in prose or verse that teaches a moral, or a practical lesson about how to get along in life.

The characters of most fables are animals that behave and speak like human beings. Some of the oldest fables come from China. If you know any of the Greek fables of Aesop, you'll recognize the clever fox in this Chinese fable.

The Tiger Behind the Fox

A tiger caught a fox. The fox said, "You wouldn't dare eat *me*! The gods in Heaven have made me the leader of all animals. It would be a violation of the gods' mandate for you to make a meal of me. If you doubt it, let me walk in front, and you follow to see if any animal dares stand his ground." The tiger consented and went with the fox, nose to heels. Every animal that saw them fled. Amazed, and agreeing that the fox was leader of all the animals, the tiger went on his way.

—Chan Kuo Ts'e

See page 244.

FIGURE OF SPEECH Word or phrase that describes one thing in terms of another and is not meant to be understood on a literal level.

Figures of speech always involve some sort of imaginative comparison between seemingly unlike things.

Some 250 different types of figures of speech have been identified. The most common are the **simile** ("I wandered lonely as a cloud"), the **metaphor** ("Fame is a bee"), and **personification** ("The wind stood up and gave a shout").

See pages 520–521.
See also *Metaphor, Personification, Simile.*

FLASHBACK Scene in a movie, play, short story, novel, or narrative poem that interrupts the present action of the plot to "flash" backward and tell what happened at an earlier time.

That is, a flashback breaks the normal time sequence of events in the narrative, usually to give the readers or viewers some background information that helps them make sense of the story. Much of the *Odyssey* (page 891) is told in the form of a flashback, as Odysseus describes his previous adventures to the Phaeacian court of King Alcinous. Flashbacks are extremely common storytelling devices in movies. In fact, the word *flashback* comes from film criticism and it has spread to the rest of literature.

See page 686.

FOIL Character who is used as a contrast to another character.

The cynical, sophisticated Mercutio is used as a foil to the romantic, naive Romeo. A writer uses a foil to accentuate and clarify the distinct qualities of two characters. The word *foil* is also used for a thin sheet of shiny metal that is placed beneath a gem to intensify its brilliance. A character who is a foil, like the metal behind the gem, sets off or intensifies the qualities of another character.

See page 762.

FORESHADOWING The use of clues to hint at events that will occur later in the plot.

Foreshadowing is used to build up suspense and sometimes anxiety in the reader or viewer. In a drama, the gun found in a bureau drawer in Act I is likely to foreshadow violence later in the play. In "The Cask of

Amontillado" (page 233) Poe uses foreshadowing skillfully. For example, when Montresor produces a trowel from beneath his cloak, he is foreshadowing the means he will use to murder his enemy. When later he begins to build a wall around Fortunato, we remember that trowel.

See page 46.

FREE VERSE **Poetry that does not have a regular meter or rhyme scheme.** Poets writing in free verse try to capture the natural rhythms of ordinary speech. To create its music, free verse may use **internal rhyme, alliteration, onomatopoeia, refrain,** and **parallel structure**. For an example of a poem written in free verse, read "When I Heard the Learn'd Astronomer" (page 496).

See page 555.

IAMBIC PENTAMETER **Line of poetry that contains five iambs.** An **iamb** is a metrical foot, or unit of measure, consisting of an unstressed syllable followed by a stressed syllable ($\smile$ $\prime$). *Pentameter* comes from the Greek *penta* ("five") and *meter* ("measure"). Here is one iamb: *arise*. Here is a line measuring five iambs:

> But soft! What light through yonder window breaks?
>
> —William Shakespeare,
> from *Romeo and Juliet*

Iambic pentameter is by far the most common verse line in English poetry.

See pages 740–741.
See also *Blank Verse, Meter, Rhythm.*

IMAGERY **Language that appeals to the senses.** Most images are visual—that is, they create pictures in the reader's mind by appealing to the sense of sight. Images can also appeal to the senses of sound, touch, taste, or smell, or even to several senses at once. While imagery is an element in all types of writing, it is especially important in poetry. The following lines contain images that make us see, hear, and even smell what the speaker experiences as he travels to meet someone he loves.

> Then a mile of warm sea-scented beach;
> Three fields to cross till a farm appears;
> A tap at the pane, the quick sharp scratch
> And blue spurt of a lighted match . . .
>
> —Robert Browning,
> from "Meeting at Night"

See pages 492–493.

INVERSION **Reversal of the normal word order of a sentence.** The elements of a standard English sentence are subject, verb, and complement, and in most sentences this is the order in which they appear. (*Ray rowed the boat.*) In most sentences, adjectives precede the words they modify (*silky blouse,* not *blouse silky*). Writers use inversion to gain emphasis and variety. They may also use it for more technical reasons—to create end-rhymes or to accommodate a given meter. In a statement about Ulysses S. Grant and Robert E. Lee, historian Bruce Catton wrote, "Daring and resourcefulness they had too. . . ." Catton inverted the order of the sentence so that the important words (*daring* and *resourcefulness*) came first.

IRONY **Contrast or discrepancy between expectation and reality—between what is said and what is really meant, between what is expected to happen and what really does happen, or between what appears to be true and what is really true.**

In **verbal irony,** a writer or speaker says one thing but really means something completely different. If you call a clumsy basketball player "the new Michael Jordan," you are using verbal irony. The murderer in Edgar Allan Poe's "The Cask of Amontillado" is using verbal irony when he says to his unsuspecting victim, ". . . your health is precious" (page 235).

Situational irony occurs when there is a contrast between what would seem appropriate and what really happens, or when what we expect to happen is in fact quite contradictory to what really does take place.

Dramatic irony occurs when the audience or the reader knows something important that a character in a play or story does not know. In *Romeo and Juliet,* for example, we know, but Romeo does *not,* that when he finds Juliet in the tomb, she is drugged, not dead. Thus we feel a terrible sense of dramatic irony as we watch Romeo kill himself upon discovering her body.

See pages 212–213.

LYRIC POETRY Poetry that does not tell a story but is aimed only at expressing a speaker's emotions or thoughts. Most lyrics are short, and they usually imply, rather than directly state, a single strong emotion. The term *lyric* comes from the Greek. In ancient Greece, lyric poems were recited to the accompaniment of a stringed instrument called a lyre. Today poets still try to make their lyrics "sing," but they rely only on the musical effects they create with words (such as **rhyme, rhythm,** and **onomatopoeia**).

See also *Sonnet.*

METAPHOR Figure of speech that makes a comparison between two unlike things, in which one thing becomes another thing without the use of the words *like, as, than,* or *resembles.* The poet Robert Burns's famous comparison "O my love is like a red, red rose" is a simile. If he had written "O my love *is* a red, red rose" or "O my love bursts into bloom," he would have been using a metaphor.

Notice that the comparison in the second metaphor is implied, or suggested, rather than directly stated as it is in the first metaphor. An **implied metaphor** does not tell us directly that one thing *is* something else. Instead, it uses words that suggest what the nature of the comparison is. The phrase "bursts into bloom" implies that the feeling of love is like a developing flower.

An **extended metaphor** is a metaphor that is extended, or developed, over several lines of writing or even throughout an entire poem. In the following poem, the soul is identified with an oyster in its shell. The metaphor is extended for several lines, until we arrive at another metaphor: The poet's art is identified with a precious pearl. (*Hermetic* means "tightly sealed.")

Art

I would like to think
that someday I could open

the hermetic oyster
where my soul sleeps.
Sprinkle on it
the bitter juice of the afternoon.
Eat it
and find a pearl in my mouth.

—Hjalmar Flax

A **dead metaphor** is a metaphor that has been used so often that we no longer realize it is a figure of speech—we simply skip over the metaphorical connection it makes. Examples of dead metaphors are *the roof of the mouth, the eye of the storm, the heart of the matter,* and *the arm of a chair.*

A **mixed metaphor** is the inconsistent mixture of two or more metaphors. Mixed metaphors are a common problem in bad writing, and they are often unintentionally funny. You are using a mixed metaphor if you say "Put it on the back burner and let it germinate" or "That's a very hard blow to swallow" or "Let's set sail and get this show on the road."

See page 521.
See also *Figure of Speech, Personification, Simile.*

METER A generally regular pattern of stressed and unstressed syllables in poetry. When we want to indicate the metrical pattern of a poem, we mark the stressed syllables with the symbol (ˊ) and the unstressed syllables with the symbol (˘). Indicating the metrical pattern of a poem in this way is called **scanning** the poem, or **scansion** (skanˈ·shən). Notice the pattern of stressed and unstressed syllables in the first four lines of this poem:

Slowly, silently, now the moon

Walks the night in her silver shoon;

This way, and that, she peers, and sees

Silver fruit upon silver trees. . . .

—Walter de la Mare, from "Silver"

See pages 554–555.

NARRATION **Type of writing or speaking that tells about a series of related events.** Narration is one of the four major techniques used in writing. (The others are **description, exposition,** and **persuasion.**) Narration can be any length, from a brief paragraph to an entire book. It is most often found in short stories, novels, epics, and ballads. But narration is also used in any piece of nonfiction that relates a series of events that tell "what happened"—such as a biography, essay, news story—even a scientific analysis or a report of a business meeting.

See page 452.
See also *Point of View.*

NONFICTION **Prose writing that deals with real people, things, events, and places.** The most popular forms of nonfiction are **biography** and **autobiography.** Other examples of nonfiction include essays, newspaper stories, magazine articles, historical writing, scientific reports, and even personal diaries and letters.

See page 342.

NOVEL **Long fictional story that is normally somewhere between one hundred and five hundred book pages long and uses the elements of storytelling: plot, character, setting, theme, and point of view.** Modern writers often do away with one or more of the novel's traditional elements. Some novels today are basically character studies, with only the barest, stripped-down story lines.

ONOMATOPOEIA (ăn′ō·mat′ō·pē′ə) **Use of a word whose sound imitates or suggests its meaning.** Onomatopoeia is so natural to us that we begin using it instinctively as children. *Crackle, pop, fizz, click, zoom,* and *chirp* are examples of onomatopoeia. Onomatopoeia is an important element in the music of poetry.

And in the hush of waters was the sound
Of pebbles, rolling round;
Forever rolling, with a hollow sound:

And bubbling seaweeds, as the waters go,
Swish to and fro
Their long cold tentacles of slimy gray. . . .

—James Stevens, from "The Shell"

See page 560.
See also *Alliteration, Assonance.*

PARALLELISM **Repetition of words, phrases, or sentences that have the same grammatical structure or that state a similar idea.** Parallelism, or **parallel structure,** helps make lines rhythmic and memorable and heightens their emotional effect:

It was the best of times, it was the worst of times, it was the age of wisdom, it was the age of foolishness, it was the epoch of belief, it was the epoch of incredulity, it was the season of Light, it was the season of Darkness, it was the spring of hope, it was the winter of despair, we had everything before us, we had nothing before us, we were all going direct to Heaven, we were all going direct the other way. . . .

—Charles Dickens, from *A Tale of Two Cities*

See pages 467, 722.

PERSONIFICATION **Special kind of metaphor in which a nonhuman thing or quality is talked about as if it were human.** Here are a few lines in which poetry itself is personified—that is, it is described as behaving and feeling the way people do:

This poetry gets bored of being alone,
it wants to go outdoors to chew on the
    winds,
to fill its commas with the keels of
    rowboats. . . .

—Hugo Margenat, from "Living Poetry"

See page 521.
See also *Figure of Speech, Metaphor.*

PERSUASION **Type of writing that is aimed at convincing the reader or listener to think or act in a certain way.** Examples of persuasive writing are found in newspaper editorials, in speeches, and in many essays and articles. Persuasion can use language that appeals to the emotions, or it can use logic to appeal to reason. When persuasive writing appeals to reason and not to the emotions, it is called **argument**.

See pages 452–453.
See also *Argument*.

PLOT **Series of related events that make up a story or drama.** Plot is "what happens" in a story, novel, or play. The following graphic is called a story map. When the details are filled in, the map will show the bare bones of a story's plot.

Story Map

Basic situation:	
Setting:	
Main character:	
His/Her problem:	
Main events/ Complications:	
Climax:	
Resolution:	

The **climax** of the plot is that exciting or tense moment, usually toward the end of the story, when we realize what the outcome of the conflict will be. The **resolution** is the moment when all the problems are resolved one way or another and the story is closed.

See pages 32–33, 626–630.

POETRY **Type of rhythmic, compressed language that uses figures of speech and imagery to appeal to the reader's emotions and imagination.** The major forms of poetry are the **lyric,** the **epic,** and the **ballad.** Beyond this, poetry is difficult to define, though many readers feel it is easy to recognize. The poet Wallace Stevens, for example, once described poetry as "a search for the inexplicable."

See page 488.

POINT OF VIEW **Vantage point from which the writer tells the story. In broad terms, there are three possible points of view: omniscient, first-person, and third-person limited.**

In the **omniscient** (or "all-knowing") **point of view,** the person telling the story knows everything there is to know about the characters and their problems. This all-knowing narrator can tell us about the past, the present, and the future of all the characters. He or she can even tell us what the characters are thinking. The narrator can also tell us what is happening in other places. In the omniscient point of view, the narrator is not in the story at all. In fact, the omniscient narrator is like a god telling the story.

In the **first-person point of view,** one of the characters is actually the narrator telling the story, using the pronoun *I*. We get to know this narrator very well, but we can know only what this person knows, and we can observe only what this person observes. All of our information about the events in the story must come from this one person.

In the **third-person limited point of view,** the narrator, who plays no part in the story, zooms in on the thoughts and feelings of just one character. With this point of view, we feel we are observing the action through the eyes and with the feelings of this one character.

See page 218–219.

PUN **A play on the multiple meanings of a word, or on two words that sound alike but have different meanings.** Most often puns are used for their humorous effects; they are used in jokes all the time. ("What has four wheels and flies?" Answer: "A garbage truck.") Shakespeare was one of the great punsters of all time. The servants in *Romeo and Juliet* make crude puns as they clown around at the start of the play. Later, Romeo and his friend Mercutio trade wits in a series of more sophisticated puns. Since word meanings change so quickly, some of Shakespeare's puns are barely understandable to us today, just as puns popular today may be puzzling to people a hundred years from now.

Puns are also common in poetry. The nineteenth-century poet on the next page uses the double meaning of *lie* for humorous effect:

O dream eyes
They tell sweet lies of Paradise;
And in those eyes the lovelight lies
And lies—and lies—and lies!

—Anita Owen

See page 524.

"Does the doctor make mouse calls?"

Drawing by Bernard Schoenbaum; © 1991 The New Yorker Magazine, Inc.

REFRAIN A repeated word, phrase, line, or group of lines. Though refrains are usually associated with songs and poems, they are also used in speeches and other forms of literature. Refrains are most often used to build rhythms, but they may also provide commentary or build suspense.

See page 571.

RHYME Repetition of accented vowel sounds and all sounds following them, in words that are close together in a poem. *Choice* and *voice* are rhymes, as are *tingle* and *jingle*.

End-rhymes are rhymes at the ends of lines. In this poem, the words *defense/tense, know/go,* and *Spain/Maine* are end-rhymes.

Old Mary

My last defense
Is the present tense.
It little hurts me now to know

I shall not go
Cathedral-hunting in Spain
Nor cherrying in Michigan or Maine.

—Gwendolyn Brooks

Internal rhymes are rhymes in the middle of a line. This line has an internal rhyme (*dreary* rhymes with *weary*):

Once upon a midnight dreary, while I
pondered, weak and weary

—Edgar Allan Poe, from "The Raven"

When two words are alike in some sound but do not rhyme exactly, they are called **approximate rhymes** (or **near rhymes,** or **slant rhymes**). In Brooks's poem on this page, she uses approximate rhyme with the words *now* and *know*.

The pattern of rhymes in a poem is called a **rhyme scheme**. The rhyme scheme of a stanza or poem is indicated by the use of a different letter of the alphabet for each rhyme. For example, the rhyme scheme of Brooks's poem is *aabbcc*.

See pages 559–560.

RHYTHM Musical quality in language produced by repetition. Rhythm occurs naturally in all forms of spoken and written language. The most obvious kind of rhythm is produced by **meter,** the regular repetition of stressed and unstressed syllables found in some poetry. But writers can also create rhythm by using rhymes, by repeating words and phrases, and even by repeating whole lines or sentences. This stanza by Walt Whitman is written in free verse and so does not follow a metrical pattern. Yet the lines are rhythmical because of Whitman's repeated use of certain sentence structures, words, and sounds.

Give me the splendid silent sun with all his
beams full-dazzling,
Give me juicy autumnal fruit ripe and red
from the orchard,
Give me a field where the unmowed grass
grows,

Give me an arbor, give me the trellised grape,
Give me fresh corn and wheat, give me
    serene-moving animals teaching content,
Give me nights perfectly quiet as on high
    plateaus west of the Mississippi, and I
    looking up at the stars. . . .

—Walt Whitman, from "Give Me the
Splendid Silent Sun"

See pages 554–555.
See also *Meter*.

SATIRE **Type of writing that ridicules something—a person, a group of people, humanity at large, an attitude or failing, a social institution—in order to reveal a weakness.** Most satires are an attempt to convince us of a point of view or to persuade us to follow a course of action. They do this by pointing out how the opposite point of view or action is ridiculous or laughable. Some satires ridicule other works of literature. "The Princess and the Tin Box" (page 244) by James Thurber satirizes fables and fairy tales. Thurber is not trying to get us to stop reading fables or fairy tales. He is just poking fun at some of the standard characters and plots of such stories.

See page 132.

SETTING **The time and place of a story or play.** Most often the setting of a narrative is established early in the story. For example, in the fourth paragraph of "The Cask of Amontillado" (page 233), Edgar Allan Poe tells his readers, "It was about dusk, one evening during the supreme madness of the carnival season. . . ." Setting often contributes to a story's emotional effect. In "The Cask of Amontillado" the descriptions of the gloomy Montresor palace, with its damp catacombs full of bones, help create the story's mood of horror. Setting can also contribute to the conflict in a story, as the harsh environment does in Dorothy Johnson's "A Man Called Horse" (page 167). Setting can also be used to reveal character, as it does in "A Christmas Memory" (page 145).

See page 164.

SHORT STORY **Short, concentrated, fictional prose narrative.** Some say Edgar Allan Poe was the first short-story writer. He was also one of the first to attempt to define the short story. He said "unity of ef-fect" was crucial, meaning that a short story ought to concentrate on a single purpose. Short stories are usually built on a plot that consists of these "bare bones": the **basic situation** or **exposition, complications, climax,** and **resolution.** Years ago, most short stories were notable for their strong plots. Today's short-story writers tend to be more interested in character.

See page 2.

SIMILE **Figure of speech that makes a comparison between two unlike things, using a word such as *like, as, resembles, or than*.** William Shakespeare, in one of his famous sonnets, uses a simile with an ironic twist, comparing two things that are *not* alike.

My mistress' eyes are nothing like the sun

We would expect a love poem to compare the light in a lover's eyes to the bright sun. But instead, Shakespeare puts a twist into a common comparison—in order to make a point about the extravagant similes found in most love poems of his day.

See pages 520–521, 886, 925.
See also *Figure of Speech, Metaphor*.

SOLILOQUY **An unusually long speech in which a character who is on stage alone expresses his or her thoughts aloud.** The soliloquy is a very old dramatic convention, in which the audience is supposedly overhearing the private thoughts of the character. Perhaps the most famous soliloquy is the "To be or not to be" speech in Shakespeare's play *Hamlet*. There are also several soliloquies in *Romeo and Juliet*, including Friar Laurence's soliloquy at the opening of Act II, Scene 3 (page 774); Juliet's at the end of Act IV, Scene 3 (page 824); and Romeo's in Act V, Scene 3 (page 841).

SONNET **Fourteen-line lyric poem that is usually written in iambic pentameter and that has one of several rhyme schemes.** The oldest kind of sonnet is called the **Italian sonnet,** or **Petrarchan sonnet,** after the fourteenth-century Italian poet Petrarch. The first eight lines, or **octet,** of the Italian sonnet pose a question or problem about love or some other subject. The concluding six lines, or **sestet,** are a response to the octet. The octet has the rhyme scheme *abba abba;* the sestet has the rhyme scheme *cde cde.*

Another important sonnet form, widely used by William Shakespeare, is called the **Shakespearean sonnet**. It has three four-line units, or **quatrains,** followed by a concluding two-line unit, or **couplet**. The most common rhyme scheme for the Shakespearean sonnet is *abab cdcd efef gg.*

See pages 735, 764.

SPEAKER **The voice that is talking to us in a poem.** Sometimes the speaker is identical with the poet, but often the speaker and the poet are not the same. The poet may be speaking as child, a woman, a man, a whole people, an animal, or even an object. For example, the speaker in "The Lesson of the Moth" by Don Marquis (page 140) is a cockroach.

See page 526.

STANZA **Group of consecutive lines in a poem that form a single unit.** A stanza in a poem is something like a paragraph in prose: It often expresses a unit of thought. A stanza may consist of one line, or two, three, four, or any other number of lines. The word *stanza* is Italian for "stopping place" or "place to rest." Emily Dickinson's poem "I Never Saw a Moor" (page 522) consists of two four-line stanzas, or **quatrains,** each one expressing a unit of thought.

STEREOTYPE **Fixed idea or conception of a character that does not allow for any individuality.** Stereotypes are often based on racial, social, religious, sexist, or ethnic prejudices. Some common stereotypes are the ideas that all football players are dumb, that all New Yorkers are rude, that all Texans are rich. Stereotypes are often used in comedies for laughs.

SUSPENSE **The uncertainty or anxiety we feel about what is going to happen next in a story.** In "The Most Dangerous Game" (page 13) our curiosity is aroused at once when we hear about Ship-Trap Island and sailors' fear of it. When Rainsford lands on that very island and is hunted by the sinister General Zaroff, suspense keeps us on the edge of our seats. We wonder: Will Rainsford be another victim who is hunted down and killed by the evil and weird Zaroff?

See page 76.
See also *Plot.*

SYMBOL **A person, a place, a thing, or an event that stands for itself and for something beyond itself as well.** For example, a scale has a real existence as an instrument for measuring weights but it also is used as a symbol of justice. Other familiar symbols are the cross that symbolizes the Christian religion, the six-pointed star that symbolizes the Jewish religion, and the bald eagle that symbolizes the United States. These are symbols that most people know, but in literature writers sometimes create new symbols that can only be understood from their context. One of the great symbols in literature is Herman Melville's great white whale, used as a symbol of the mystery of evil in the novel *Moby-Dick.*

See page 314.

THEME **The central idea of a work of literature.** A theme is not the same as a subject. The subject of a work can usually be expressed in a word or two: love, childhood, death. The theme is the idea the writer wishes to reveal *about* that subject. The theme is something that can be expressed in at least one complete sentence. For example, one theme of *Romeo and Juliet* might be stated as: Love is more powerful than family loyalty. Theme is not usually stated directly in a work of literature. Most often, the reader has to think about all the elements of the work and use them to make an inference, or educated guess, about what its theme is.

See page 264–265.

TONE **The attitude a writer takes toward the audience, a subject, or a character.** Tone is conveyed through the writer's choice of words and details. For example, Truman Capote's "A Christmas Memory" (page 145) is affectionate and nostalgic in tone. Charles Kuralt's "Misspelling" (page 468) is humorous and lightly mocking in tone.

See pages 586–587.
See also *Diction.*

TRAGEDY **Play, novel, or other narrative that depicts serious and important events in which the main character comes to an unhappy end.** In a tragedy the main character is usually dignified and courageous. This person's downfall may be caused by a character flaw, or it may result from forces beyond human control. The tragic hero or heroine usually wins some self-knowledge and wisdom, even though he or she suffers defeat, perhaps even death.

COMMUNICATIONS HANDBOOK

READING STRATEGIES

Whether you're reading for pleasure or for information, you can become a more effective reader by practicing these five strategies.

1. USING PRIOR KNOWLEDGE

Good readers use their past experiences and knowledge as they read, especially when they read nonfiction. For example, if you are reading "Choice: A Tribute to Dr. Martin Luther King, Jr." (page 367) and you already know something about Dr. Martin Luther King, Jr., you'll use that information as you read. Before you read a nonfiction selection, try making a KWL chart like this one:

K	W	L
What I already **know**	What I **want** to know	What I **learned**

Applying the Strategy

Choose a nonfiction selection from Collections 5–7. Either alone or with a partner, copy the KWL chart above and fill in the first two columns. After you've read the selection, complete the last column (What I learned). Then go back to the first column. Is any of the information you listed there inaccurate? If so, correct it.

2. FORMING OPINIONS

You have lots of opinions, so you're already used to making up your own mind about things. Whether you realize it or not, you're forming opinions as you read. For example, when reading fiction, you may think a character is someone you'd like for a friend or someone you're glad you don't have to meet. When reading nonfiction, you form opinions about whether the writer's views agree with your own and whether they seem logical and reasonable.

Remember that opinions are different from facts. A **fact** is a statement that can be proved true or false. "There are about 200,000 known kinds of flowers" is a statement of fact. An **opinion** is a judgment or belief that *can't* be proved true or false. For example, "Roses are the prettiest flowers" is an opinion. A **valid opinion** is an opinion that is supported with strong evidence. "Flowers are prized for their beauty" is a valid opinion. Get in the habit of supplying evidence to back up your opinions when you form them.

Applying the Strategy

Choose a selection from Collection 7. Before you read, write your opinion (supported by as many facts as you can supply) on an issue related to the selection you've chosen: the treatment of American Indians, the rights of the disabled, the homeless, or standardized spelling. Use your Reader's Log to record your opinions. After you've read the selection, review your initial opinions. Have they changed as a result of your reading? Compare your opinion-forming process with that of a partner or a group.

3. PREVIEWING THE TEXT AND MAKING PREDICTIONS

Before you read, **preview** the text by looking at the illustrations, chapter titles, headings and so on. A preview will help you determine what type of text it is (fiction or nonfiction), how quickly you should plan to read it, and whether you want to take notes as you read.

Good readers are flexible. As they read, they guess ahead (make **predictions**), adjust their predictions when they get new information, and make new predictions. This process makes reading fun, somewhat like solving a puzzle.

You probably do more predicting as you read than you realize. Try plotting your predictions in a chart like the one on the next page. Keep reading to see if your predictions are right or if they need to be adjusted.

Overall prediction: This selection is about

_____ .

Prediction 1: _____

   Prediction was correct: _____

   Prediction needs adjustment: _____

Prediction 2: _____

   Prediction was correct: _____

   Prediction needs adjustment: _____

   _____

etc.

Applying the Strategy

Select a story from Collections 1–4. Preview the story by looking at the title and illustrations. Then make some predictions. What do you think the story will be about? As you read, write down your predictions about what will happen next. Make adjustments to your predictions as necessary. When you've finished the story, compare your predictions with those of a partner.

4. MAKING INFERENCES

An **inference** is a guess based on evidence. For example, in "Thank You, M'am" Langston Hughes describes a woman's actions after she is mugged: "The large woman simply turned around and kicked him right square in his blue-jeaned sitter." From this one action you can infer, or guess, a lot about the woman. The inferences you make when reading literature are based on what the writer chooses to tell you. Here are some inferences you are often asked to make and some of the clues you can use to make them:

- **Inferences about character:** Look at a character's speech, appearance, thoughts, actions; look at what other characters say and think about the character.

- **Inferences about tone (writer's attitude):** Look at the writer's choice of words and details.

- **Inferences about theme:** Look at key passages; look at how the main character changes or what he or she has learned.

Applying the Strategy

Choose one story from Collections 1–4. In a chart like the following one, record any inferences you make and the evidence you base them on. For each inference, circle the strongest evidence that leads you to that inference.

Inference 1:
Evidence:
Inference 2:
Evidence:
etc.

5. REVIEWING THE TEXT

When you finish reading a selection, think about what it means. You'll use different strategies for reviewing different kinds of text. Try **paraphrasing** a poem, using your own words to express every idea, line by line. For example, here is a paraphrase of Robert Frost's "Fire and Ice." (The poem appears on page 541.)

Paraphrase of "Fire and Ice"
According to the speaker, some people say the world will end in fire, while others say it will end in ice. From the speaker's experience with desire, he agrees with those who say the world will end in fire. However, if the world had to end twice, the speaker's experience with hate tells him that ice would also be enough to cause the world to end.

For a short story, make a story map that summarizes important elements in the story.

Story Map

Basic situation:
Setting:
Main character:
His/Her problem:
Main events/ Complications:
Climax:
Resolution:

For a work of nonfiction, complete a chart like this one for each of the writer's main ideas:

Main idea:
Supporting detail:
Supporting detail:
etc.

Applying the Strategy

With a partner, choose a poem from Collections 8–11 or a nonfiction piece from Collections 5–7. After you re-read the text, write a paraphrase of the poem or complete the main-idea chart shown opposite for a nonfiction selection. Compare your paraphrase or chart with your partner's. Do you agree or disagree? If you disagree, find evidence in the text to support your view of the text.

STRATEGIES FOR WRITING A RESEARCH PAPER

When you write a research paper, you discover the facts and the ideas and views of others about a specific topic and then draw a conclusion. A formal research paper presents information from several sources and identifies those sources.

STEPS IN WRITING A RESEARCH PAPER

Writing a research paper is a sizable task that usually requires several weeks of work. The following overview breaks down the assignment into a series of steps that will help you organize your sources and notes.

Prewriting

1. Choose a specific topic that interests you. Make sure you can find information about your topic in several different sources.
2. Develop a list of research questions—things you'd like to know about your topic.
3. Find possible sources of information, and evaluate each one to make sure it's relevant to your specific topic, reliable, and recent (unless your topic is a historical one). Make a source card (see page 983) for each source you use.
4. Develop an early plan—a rough outline that will help you focus your research.
5. Use separate note cards to take notes from each source. Summarize main points in your own words

and record quotations exactly. Keep careful track of your sources.
6. Write a thesis statement expressing the main idea of your report and indicating what you plan to cover.
7. Prepare a working outline that arranges your main ideas and quotations in a logical order. Arrange your note cards into stacks according to the working outline.

Writing the First Draft

1. The draft of your paper should have an introduction, a body, and a conclusion. Your thesis statement should appear in the introduction.
2. Include short quotations to show the weight and authority of your research. Quotations also provide variety and interest.
3. Document the source of all original opinions or theories, facts and statistics, and quotations that you use. (See Parenthetical Citations, page 984.)

Evaluating and Revising

1. Make sure you have included your thesis statement and supported it with information from three or more sources.
2. Check to see that your information is accurately documented. Then prepare your Works Cited list (see pages 984 and 985).
3. Read through your paper to see that your ideas are clear and easy to follow and that your paper reads smoothly.

Proofreading and Publishing

1. Check your paper for errors in spelling, grammar, usage, and punctuation.
2. Make sure your documentation follows the format your teacher requires.
3. Find a way to share your paper with others.

USING THE LIBRARY OR MEDIA CENTER

The best place to start your research is in the library or media center. To find books on your topic, you can use the library's **catalog**. This may be a **card catalog,** a series of file cabinets with drawers containing alphabetically arranged cards for all the books in the library. Each book has a title card and an author card; nonfiction books also have subject cards. "See" or "see also" cards direct you to additional subjects.

Many libraries use a computerized **on-line catalog**. To use it, you type an author, title, or subject at a computer workstation. An on-line catalog tells which branches have the book you are looking for and whether the book has been checked out or is in the library.

Reference Materials

A special section is devoted to **reference materials** that you can use in the library but not check out. Here you'll find encyclopedias, general biographical reference books, atlases, almanacs, books of quotations, and books of synonyms.

Some libraries have access to **electronic databases** (huge quantities of data, or information, stored in a computer or on a disc) through on-line services or through the **Internet**. You'll need to use a computer to read these databases, which are constantly being updated. Ask your librarian whether such databases are available and how to use them.

Periodicals

The *Readers' Guide to Periodical Literature* indexes articles in more than 100 magazines. Paperback editions are printed throughout the year and compiled into a single volume for each year. In the *Readers' Guide* you'll find articles listed alphabetically by author and by subject.

Magazines and newspapers are also indexed on computers. InfoTrac, for example, is a computerized index of general-interest magazines published from 1985 to the present. Some computerized indexes provide an **abstract** (brief summary of key ideas) for each article. Sometimes the actual text can be read on the computer and printed out.

Back issues of newspaper and magazine articles may be stored on **microfilm** (a reel of film) or **microfiche** (a sheet of film). These contain greatly reduced photographs of each page, which can be read when you use a projector that enlarges the images on a screen.

USING COMMUNITY RESOURCES

You can call or visit local offices of state and federal government agencies to get up-to-date information on many topics. You can also find information by contacting local museums, businesses, newspaper offices, television and radio stations, colleges and universities.

Conducting an Interview

You can probably find people in your community who are experts on some aspect of your topic. If you are planning to interview someone, be sure to speak to your teacher and to a parent or guardian about your plans.

Before the Interview   When you call to make an appointment, be courteous and businesslike. Explain who you are, what your paper is about, and how much time you would like. Draft six to ten questions that will elicit more than "yes" or "no" answers. Dress appropriately, and be prompt.

During the Interview   Take notes or ask permission to tape-record the interview. Listen carefully and give the person time to answer each question fully. Respect the person's opinion even if you disagree. If you're not sure you've understood something, ask follow-up questions. At the end of the interview, thank the person for his or her help and ask for permission to quote the person.

After the Interview   While you remember the interview clearly, write note cards or a summary of the information. Be sure to send a thank-you letter to the person you interviewed.

TAKING NOTES AND DOCUMENTING SOURCES

In your research paper you will need to document all your sources so your readers will know where you found the information. Keep complete and accurate records of each source as you take notes. Be especially careful to avoid **plagiarism** (using another writer's words or ideas without giving the writer credit).

Preparing Source Cards

For each source that you consult, prepare a 3" x 5" source card. To see the kind of information that you need to record, look at the sample source card below and the Works Cited list on page 985.

1. Assign each source a number and write it in the upper right-hand corner. Later, when you're taking notes, it will save time to write a source number instead of the author and title.
2. Record full publication information. Double-check names, title, page numbers, and publication date.
3. Note the call number or location of the source.

Sample Source Card

> 3
>
> Krutch, Joseph Wood. "Poe, Edgar Allan." Encyclopedia Americana. 1994 ed.

Taking Notes

Here are some tips for taking notes.

1. Use a 4" x 6" card or a half-sheet of paper for each source and item of information.
2. Write a key word or phrase in the upper left-hand corner and the source-card number in the upper right-hand corner.
3. As you take notes, you can quote, summarize, or paraphrase the material. Place the page number(s) of the source in the lower right-hand corner.
   - **Quote** only when it is important to know the author's exact words. Copy the source material word for word, including punctuation, and enclose it in quotation marks.
   - **Summarize** when you need to remember only the main idea. Read or listen to the material first. Then write the note in your own words.
   - **Paraphrase** when you need to remember detailed information. Restate the material using your own words and sentence structure.

Sample Note Card

> Poe's dark imagination   2
>
> - turned to his imagination to escape harshness of life
> - dark side to his genius
> - central body of his work "a tissue of nightmares"
>
>   p. 19

Using Quotations

Short quotations add interest and authority to your paper. Follow these guidelines to work quotations smoothly into your paper. (Note: The examples show parenthetical citations, which are written as a number in parentheses following the quotation. See page 984.)

GUIDELINES FOR USING QUOTATIONS

- **A quotation that is an incomplete sentence:** Include it within your own sentence, and enclose the quoted material in quotation marks.

  EXAMPLE   According to Vincent Buranelli, Poe is "the most complex personality in the entire gallery of American authors" (19).

- **A quotation of four or fewer lines:** Introduce a short quotation in your own words, and enclose it in quotation marks. Make the quotation part of the text; do not set it off.

  EXAMPLE   Floyd Stovall notes that "Poe's poems, like his tales, are notable for their original conceptions and for the technical perfection of their execution" (xv).

[Continued on next page]

[Continued from page 983]

GUIDELINES FOR USING QUOTATIONS

- **A long quotation:** Set off a longer quotation (of four or more lines) in an indented "block." Indent each line ten spaces from the left margin. Introduce the quotation in your own words, followed by a colon or sometimes by a period. Do *not* use quotation marks.

Documenting Sources

You will need to give credit to your sources throughout your paper as well as in a Works Cited list at the end of the paper. It is not necessary to document information that can be found easily in several general reference sources.

Parenthetical Citations   A **parenthetical citation** in the body of the paper is an abbreviated reference to an entry in the Works Cited list. Parenthetical citations are enclosed in parentheses and include just the author's last name and a page number. (Often your sentence will make clear which work you are referring to by stating the author's name or the author and title, as in the example below. In such cases you need to include only the page number.) Follow these guidelines for placing parenthetical citations:

1. Place the citation as close as possible to the material it documents. If possible, place it at the end of a sentence.
2. Place the citation outside the end quotation mark but before the end punctuation mark.

> EXAMPLE   In her book Edgar Allan Poe Bettina Knapp says that Poe's "inner emotions were encompassed in the mood he created, in the music of the words" (46).

List of Works Cited   The **Works Cited** list appears at the end of your report. (You may title the list a **Bibliography** if all the works listed are print sources.) The Works Cited list contains full information for every source that you credit in your paper.

The chart on page 985 lists sample citations in the Modern Language Association of America (MLA) style for different types of sources.

GUIDELINES FOR THE WORKS CITED LIST

- On a separate piece of paper, center the words *Works Cited* (or *Bibliography*).

- Alphabetize the sources by the last names of the authors. If no author is given for a source, alphabetize by the first word in the title (ignoring *A, An,* and *The*).

- If you use two or more sources by the same author, write the author's full name in the first entry only. For all succeeding entries, put three dashes where the author's name should be, followed by a period and then the rest of the source information.

  EXAMPLE

  Poe, Edgar Allan. "The Cask of Amontillado." The Collected Tales and Poems of Edgar Allan Poe. New York: Modern Library, 1992.
  – – –. "The Raven." The Collected Tales and Poems of Edgar Allan Poe. New York: Modern Library, 1992.

- Double-space the entries on the list, beginning each entry at the left margin. If an entry is longer than one line, indent all additional lines five spaces.

WRITING WITH A COMPUTER

A computer is an extremely useful tool when you research information and when you write essays, reports, and letters.

Researching with a Computer

If the computer you're using has a modem, you can access **databases, electronic magazines and encyclopedias,** and other reference works through on-line services. In *Grolier's Academic American Encyclopedia* on CompuServe, for instance, when you type a key word or phrase and hit the search command, an encyclopedia article (which you can print for later use) appears on your screen.

CD-ROM   If you use a computer with **CD-ROM capability,** sound and images are added to the text.

SAMPLE ENTRIES FOR THE LIST OF WORKS CITED

STANDARD REFERENCE WORKS

Encyclopedia	Krutch, Joseph Wood. "Poe, Edgar Allan." Encyclopedia Americana. 1994 ed.
Biographical Reference Book	"Poe, Edgar Allan." Merriam-Webster's Biographical Dictionary. 1995 ed.

BOOKS

Book with One Author	Meyers, Jeffrey. Edgar Allan Poe. New York: Scribners, 1992.
Book with Two or More Authors	Ober, Warren U., Paul S. Burtness, and William R. Seat, Jr. The Enigma of Poe. Boston: Heath, 1960.
Book with One Editor	Tate, Allen, ed. The Complete Poetry and Selected Criticism of Edgar Allan Poe. New York: New American Library, 1981.
Book with Two or More Editors	O'Neill, Edward H., and Arthur Hobson Quinn, eds. The Complete Poems and Stories of Edgar Allan Poe. New York: Knopf, 1946.

SELECTIONS WITHIN BOOKS

Selection from Book of Works by One Author	Buranelli, Vincent. "The Problem of Poe." Edgar Allan Poe. Boston: Twayne, 1977.
Selection from Book of Works by Several Authors	Kissling, Dorothy, and Arthur E. Nethercot. "The Poet of Ravens and Lost Ladies." Muse Anthology of Modern Poetry. New York: Straub, 1938.
Selection from Book of Works with an Editor	Poe, Edgar Allan. "The Cask of Amontillado." The Collected Tales and Poems of Edgar Allan Poe. New York: Modern Library, 1992.

ARTICLES FROM MAGAZINES, NEWSPAPERS, AND JOURNALS

Magazine Article	Gould, S. J. "Poe's Greatest Hit." Natural History July 1993: 10+.
Newspaper Article	O'Donnell, M. "The Tell-Tale Tube." New York Times Magazine 9 Apr. 1995: 92.

OTHER SOURCES

Telephone Interview	Morales, Betty. Telephone interview. 21 Feb. 1995.
Sound Recording	Poe, Edgar Allan. Tales of Mystery and Horror. Perf. Christopher Lee. Listen for Pleasure, 1981.
Radio or TV Program	Nightline. WABC, New York. 12 Dec. 1994.
Film, Filmstrip, or Videotape	"The Cask of Amontillado." Video recording. Prod. Films for the Humanities, 1988.

When you look up Shakespeare's *The Tragedy of Romeo and Juliet* in a CD-ROM encyclopedia, for instance, you'll probably find video clips of performances of some of its famous speeches.

The Internet   Through on-line services, local providers, and many public libraries, you can gain access to the **Internet,** a vast, worldwide network of information. You'll need some help getting started, but once you learn to "surf the Net," you can find information about practically anything. Using the Internet, you can read and print out information as well as send messages and participate in special-interest discussion groups. (Note: On-line services and providers usually charge according to the amount of time you use the service, so keep an eye on the clock.)

Word Processing

A computer can save you time and effort at every step in the writing process.

Prewriting   When you **brainstorm** or **freewrite,** try turning down the brightness of your computer screen. Then you won't be distracted by seeing what you type. When you run out of ideas, you can turn up the brightness control and look at what you've written. You can also use the computer to jot down questions, take notes, and do a rough outline. If you print a copy of the material you created during prewriting, you can decide which ideas to use and how best to organize them.

Drafting   It's easy to make changes as you write. You can use the cut-and-paste feature to copy or move words, sentences, and paragraphs. To insert new material, move the cursor to where you want the insertion, and just type whatever you want to add.

Evaluating and Revising   With a computer you can print copies of your draft to share with peer editors. You can also edit directly on the computer screen as you re-read the text. Many writers prefer to revise on "hard copy" (a paper printout), making changes in pencil that they later transfer onto the computer document.

Here are some common proofreading symbols you can use as you edit your draft:

PROOFREADING SYMBOLS		
SYMBOL	**EXAMPLE**	**MEANING**
≡	Fifty-first street	Capitalize lower-case letter.
/	Jerry's Aunt	Lowercase capital letter.
∧	the capital ⁀of Ohio	Insert.
ℰ	Where's the the key?	Delete.
⌢⌣	a close friend ship	Close up space.
∿	thier	Change the order of the letters.
¶	¶ "Hi," he said.	Begin new paragraph.
⊙	Stay well ⊙	Add period.
∧	Of course, you may be wrong.	Add comma.

Special Tools   Most word-processing programs have three useful tools you can apply before you print your final copy. A **spelling checker** zooms through the document and stops at any word that looks like a spelling mistake. A **grammar checker** alerts you to incomplete sentences and other mistakes in grammar, usage, and punctuation. A **thesaurus** suggests possible synonyms for any word you highlight, and it can help you if you're trying to find a substitute for a word you've used frequently.

Perfect Form   You don't have to know how to type to create a perfect paper. Just hit the appropriate keys, read and revise the text, fix any mistakes, and hit the print command. Your final version comes out of the printer without smudges, correction fluid, or crossed-out words. If your teacher requires double spacing and wide margins, no problem—you can adjust your paper's format in an instant.

STUDY SKILLS

USING A DICTIONARY

When you look up a word in a dictionary, you will find helpful information about how that word is used.

1. **Entry word.** The entry word shows how the word is spelled and divided into syllables. It may also show capitalization and alternate spellings. If more than one spelling is given, the first spelling is the preferred one.

2. **Pronunciation.** Accent marks and phonetic spellings or diacritical marks (special symbols placed above the letters) show how the entry word is pronounced. A pronunciation guide usually appears on every other page.

3. **Part-of-speech labels.** These labels tell how the entry word is used in a sentence. When a word can be used as more than one part of speech, definitions are grouped by part of speech. The sample entry gives three definitions for *indulge* as a transitive verb and one for it as an intransitive verb.

4. **Other forms.** Forms may be given for plural nouns, principal parts of verbs, and comparative forms of adjectives and adverbs.

5. **Etymology.** The etymology (et′ə·mäl′ə·jē) traces a word's origin and history. The etymology for *indulge* tells us that the word comes from the Latin word *indulgere,* which probably comes from the prefix *in* added to the Greek base word *dolichos* and the Gothic base word *tulgus.*

6. **Examples.** Phrases or sentences show how the entry word is used.

7. **Definitions.** If a word has more than one meaning, the separate meanings are numbered or lettered.

8. **Special usage labels.** These labels identify special meanings or special uses of the word. In the sample entry the label *Archaic* indicates an outdated meaning of the word.

9. **Related word forms.** Other forms of the entry word are listed. Usually these are created by the addition of suffixes or prefixes.

10. **Synonyms and antonyms.** Synonyms (words that have the same meaning) and **antonyms** (words with opposite meaning) are listed at the end of some word entries. To find additional synonyms and antonyms, use a **thesaurus**.

A SAMPLE ENTRY

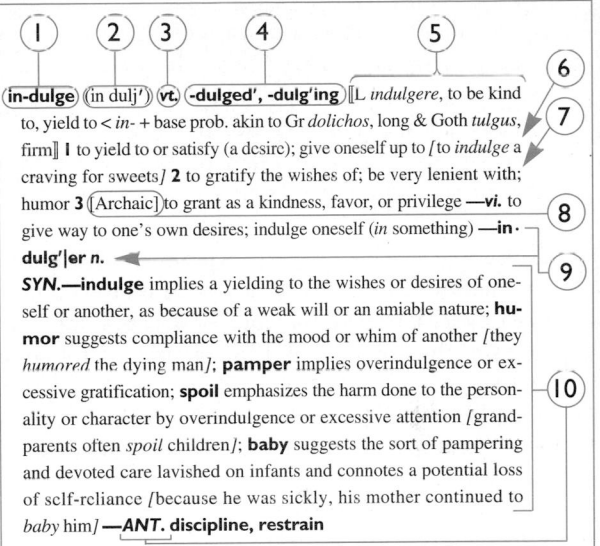

in-dulge (in dulj′) **vt.** **-dulged′, -dulg′ing** [L *indulgere,* to be kind to, yield to < *in-* + base prob. akin to Gr *dolichos*, long & Goth *tulgus,* firm] **1** to yield to or satisfy (a desire); give oneself up to [to *indulge* a craving for sweets] **2** to gratify the wishes of; be very lenient with; humor **3** [Archaic] to grant as a kindness, favor, or privilege —**vi.** to give way to one's own desires; indulge oneself (*in* something) —**in·dulg′er** *n.*

SYN.—indulge implies a yielding to the wishes or desires of oneself or another, as because of a weak will or an amiable nature; **humor** suggests compliance with the mood or whim of another [they *humored* the dying man]; **pamper** implies overindulgence or excessive gratification; **spoil** emphasizes the harm done to the personality or character by overindulgence or excessive attention [grandparents often *spoil* children]; **baby** suggests the sort of pampering and devoted care lavished on infants and connotes a potential loss of self-reliance [because he was sickly, his mother continued to *baby* him] —**ANT. discipline, restrain**

©1994 Webster's New World Dictionary of American English, Third College Edition.

READING MAPS, CHARTS, AND GRAPHS

Types of Maps

Physical maps illustrate the natural landscape of an area, using shading and colors to show landforms and elevation. The map of part of New Mexico on page 400 is a physical map. **Political maps** show political units such as states and nations. They usually include national borders, capitals, and other major cities. The map on page 988, which shows some of the Southern states mentioned in Collections 5 and 6, is a political map. **Special-purpose maps** present specific information such as the routes of explorers or the outcome of an election. The map you drew of Ship-Trap Island (see page 30) is a special-purpose map.

How to Read a Map

1. **Determine the focus of the map.** The map's title and labels tell you its focus—its subject and the geographical area it covers.
2. **Study the map legend.** The **legend,** or **key,** explains any special symbols, lines, colors, and shadings used in the map.
3. **Check directions and distances.** Maps often include a **compass rose,** or **directional indicator,** showing north, south, east, and west. If there is no compass rose, assume that north is at the top, west is to the left, and so on. Many maps also include a scale to help you relate distances on the map to actual distances.
4. **Be aware of the larger context of the area.** The **absolute location** of any place on the earth is given by its **latitude** (number of degrees north or south of the equator) and **longitude** (number of degrees east or west of the prime meridian). Some maps also have **locator maps,** which show the area of focus in relation to surrounding areas or to the entire world.

Types of Charts

Flowcharts show a sequence of events or the steps in a process. Cause-and-effect relationships are often shown by flowcharts like the one on page 417. **Time** lines list historical events according to their chronological order (the order in which they happened). **Tables** use columns to present data, such as statistics, in categories that are easy to understand and compare. You can find a table on page 858.

Types of Graphs

Line graphs generally show changes in quantity over time. Dots showing the quantity at each point in time are connected to create a line. **Bar graphs** are usually used to compare quantities within categories. **Pie graphs,** or **circle graphs,** like the one on page 311, show proportions by dividing a circle into different-sized sections like slices of a pie.

How to Read a Chart or Graph

1. **Read the title** to find out the subject and purpose of the chart or graph.
2. **Read the headings and labels** to determine the type of information that is presented.
3. **Analyze the details.** Read numbers carefully. Note increases or decreases in quantities. Look for the direction or order of events, trends, relationships, and changes in the data.

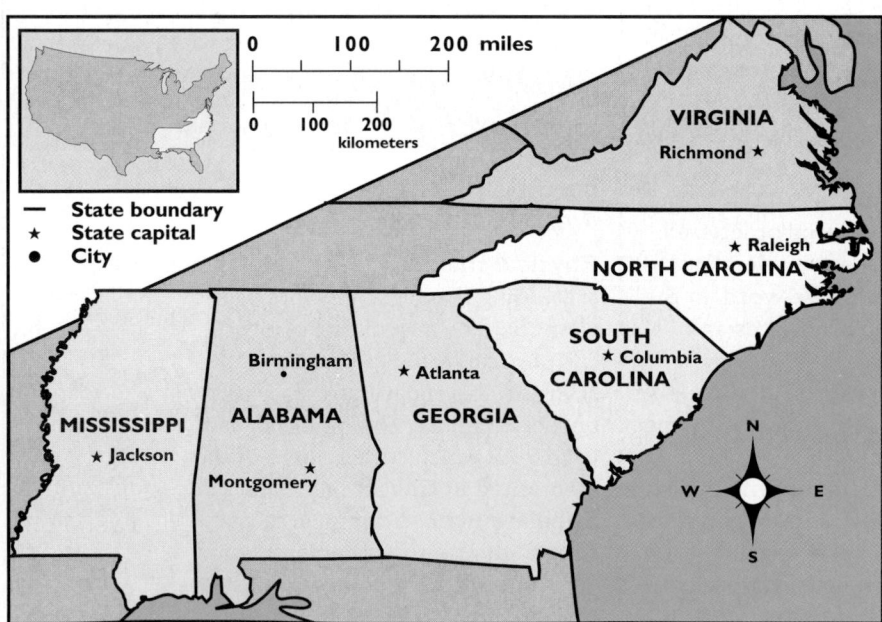

WRITING BUSINESS LETTERS

The ability to write clear and effective letters, memos, and résumés can help you greatly, whatever career you choose. Follow these guidelines whenever you write a business letter:

1. **Use formal, standard English.** The tone of your letter should be polite and respectful.

2. **Be clear.** Explain your purpose clearly. Include all the necessary information, but be as brief as possible.

3. **Use correct form.** Type, print, or write your letter neatly on white 8 1/2" x 11" paper. Follow **modified block form** (shown below) or **block form** (each part of the letter—including the heading, closing, and signature—starts at the left margin).

A Sample Business Letter (Modified Block Form)

1050 Ocean Parkway, Apt. 25A
Brooklyn, New York 11213
January 10, 1996

Thomas M. Ross, Esq.
Assistant District Attorney
Kings County District Attorney's Office
Municipal Building
210 Joralemon Street
Brooklyn, New York 11201

Dear Mr. Ross:

Abraham Lincoln High School is planning a "Law and Order Day" on March 26. We are inviting speakers from law enforcement and the criminal justice system. I am chairperson of the speakers' committee.

We would be honored if you would speak that day on an issue related to the prosecution of criminal cases.

You can reach me at my home address above. My phone number is 718–555–8306. We would be most grateful for your participation.

Sincerely yours,

Carla Ruiz

Carla Ruiz

Heading
Your street address
Your city, state, and ZIP code
Date you write the letter

Inside Address
Name, title, and address of person you are writing to. Use a title (*Mr., Ms., Mrs., Dr., Esq.,* etc.) with the person's name, and put his or her business title after the name.

Salutation (greeting)
Use *Dear* and the person's name or business title, followed by a colon.

Body
The body of the letter contains your message. If the body is longer than one paragraph, leave a blank line between paragraphs.

Closing
Yours truly, Sincerely, or *Sincerely yours,* followed by a comma.

Signature
Type or print your name, leaving space for your signature. Sign your name in ink.

STRATEGIES FOR TAKING TESTS

At the beginning of a test, **scan** the test quickly to count the number of items. Then decide how to budget your time. Here are some specific strategies for answering five common kinds of test questions.

Multiple-choice questions ask you to select a correct answer from a number of possible choices.

EXAMPLE **1. Onomatopoeia** is
  A the repetition of the same consonant sound in several words
  B the use of words that almost rhyme
  C the use of words that sound like what they mean
  D the use of a regular rhythm in poetry

HOW TO ANSWER MULTIPLE-CHOICE ITEMS

- Read the opening question or statement carefully. Make sure you understand the question or statement before examining the choices.

- Look for **qualifiers,** such as *not* or *always,* which might help you eliminate some choices.

- Read all the choices before selecting an answer. Eliminate choices you know are incorrect.

- Think carefully about the remaining choices and select the one that makes the most sense to you.

True/false questions require you to decide whether a statement is true or false.

EXAMPLE **1.** T F In a short story the **denouement** comes just before the climax.

HOW TO ANSWER TRUE/FALSE ITEMS

- Read the statement carefully. If any part of the statement is false, the whole statement is false.

- Check for qualifiers (words that limit a statement), such as *always* or *never.* A statement is true only if it is always true; there can be no exceptions.

Matching questions require you to match items in one list with items in a second list.

EXAMPLE **Directions:** Match each item in the left-hand column with its definition in the right-hand column.
  ____**1.** alliteration   **A** a comparison between two unlike things
  ____**2.** metaphor   **B** repeated vowel sounds
  ____**3.** assonance   **C** repeated consonant sounds

HOW TO ANSWER MATCHING ITEMS

- Read the directions carefully. Some items might not be used, and some items might be used more than once.

- Scan the columns. First, match items you know. Then match items you are less sure about.

- Complete the rest of the matching. Make the best guess you can for the items that remain.

Analogy questions require you to recognize the relationship between a pair of words and then identify another pair of words that have a similar relationship.

EXAMPLE **Directions:** Select the best pair of words to complete the analogy.
  CARROT: VEGETABLE : :
  A flower: tree   **C** rose: flower
  B sentence: paragraph   **D** pea: green

HOW TO ANSWER ANALOGY ITEMS

- Identify the relationship in the first pair of words. (In the example a *carrot* is a kind of *vegetable.*)

- Express the analogy in a statement or question. For example, "A *carrot* is a kind of *vegetable.* In what other pair of items is the first item 'a kind of' the second item?"

- Select the pair of words that have the same relationship as the first pair. (A *rose* is a kind of *flower.*)

Essay questions ask you to think critically about material you have learned and to express your understanding in an organized way. You are expected to write one paragraph or more for your answer.

The first chart below gives tips for answering essay questions. The second chart lists typical verbs in essay questions and defines the task called for by each verb. Sample questions are included.

HOW TO ANSWER ESSAY QUESTIONS

- Scan the questions quickly. If you have a choice of questions, decide which ones you can answer best. Plan how much time you can spend on each answer to stay on schedule.
- Find the key verbs (see chart) and note how much evidence you are asked to give.
- Make notes or a simple outline on scratch paper, organize your ideas logically, and write a thesis statement expressing your main idea.
- Revise as you write to tighten and clarify.
- Proofread to correct any mistakes in spelling, mechanics, and usage.

ESSAY TEST QUESTIONS

KEY VERB	TASK	SAMPLE QUESTION
analyze	Take something apart to see how it works.	Analyze the character of Zaroff in "The Most Dangerous Game."
argue	Take a stand on an issue, and give reasons supporting your opinion.	Argue a case for or against standardized English spellings.
compare/contrast	Discuss likenesses/differences.	Compare and contrast Helen and Annie in *The Miracle Worker*.
define	Give specific details that make something unique.	Define the term *metaphor* and give an example.
demonstrate (*also* illustrate, present, show)	Provide examples to support a point.	Demonstrate O. Henry's use of irony in "The Gift of the Magi."
describe	Give a picture in words.	Describe the setting of "The Sniper."
discuss	Examine in detail.	Discuss how du Maurier builds suspense in "The Birds."
explain	Give reasons.	Explain why Odysseus began his travels.
identify	Point out specific persons, places, things, or characteristics.	Identify two main themes in Shakespeare's *The Tragedy of Romeo and Juliet*.
interpret	Give the meaning or significance of something.	Interpret the symbolism of the ibis in "The Scarlet Ibis."
list (*also* outline, trace)	Give all steps in order or all details about a subject.	List important events regarding rights of the disabled.
summarize	Give a brief overview of the main points.	Summarize the plot of Poe's "The Cask of Amontillado."

STRATEGIES FOR SPEAKING AND DEBATING

GIVING A SPEECH

Choose a topic that interests you and that you think will interest your audience. As you plan your speech, keep in mind your purpose (to inform, to persuade, or to entertain), the occasion for your speech, and what your audience might already know about your topic.

Follow essentially the same process you would use for writing a paper. Draft a thesis statement that expresses your main idea. Then make a rough outline of your main points and supporting details. On separate note cards, write each main point along with its supporting details. Number the cards in the order in which you'll present your information. Make separate cards for material you plan to read word for word, such as quotations or statistics.

GUIDELINES FOR DELIVERING A SPEECH

- **Stand confidently.** Look interested and use natural gestures.
- **Speak clearly.** Speak loudly enough for the back row to hear every word. Pronounce your words carefully.
- **Make eye contact with your audience.**
- **Vary your voice.** To emphasize important ideas and to keep your voice from being monotonous, vary your **volume** (loudness), **stress** (emphasis of words or phrases), **pitch** (rise and fall of your voice), and **rate** (speed at which you talk).

DEBATING

A **formal debate** is a speaking contest in which two teams argue opposite sides of an issue. The debate focuses on a **proposition,** a statement that recommends a specific policy or action. The **affirmative team** argues in support of the proposition; the **negative team** opposes it.

To prepare for a debate, plan your **argument,** or **case,** to persuade your specific audience. You'll need two or three strong **reasons** (statements of why the proposition should or should not be enacted) as well as evidence to support each reason. **Evidence** can include facts, statistics, examples, anecdotes (brief true stories), analogies (comparisons), and quotations from experts.

Carefully prepare strong support for your own case, but spend almost as much time preparing evidence to **refute,** or disprove, the arguments you expect your opponents to make.

GUIDELINES FOR DEBATERS

- State your opinion clearly at the beginning of your speech and restate it at the end.
- Support your opinion with strong reasons and evidence.
- Express your ideas as clearly as you can.
- Give your listeners a "road map" so they know what to expect. For example, at the beginning tell them that you'll discuss three reasons, and then use the word *first, second,* or *third* to introduce each reason as you come to it.
- Make eye contact with your audience.
- Speak and act confidently.

COOPERATIVE LEARNING

In many of your classes you work in groups to complete a project or to solve a problem. The first step for the group is to analyze the project or problem, breaking it down into tasks that can be assigned to individuals. In an effective group each member takes an active part, cooperates with other members, and listens respectfully. After you complete a cooperative activity, take some time to reflect as a group on how well the group functioned.

1 THE PARTS OF SPEECH

PART OF SPEECH	DEFINITION	EXAMPLES
NOUN	Names person, place, thing, or idea	captain, swimmers, Maria Tallchief, team, Stratford-on-Avon, stories, "The Scarlet Ibis," justice, honesty
PRONOUN	Takes place of one or more nouns	
Personal	Refers to one(s) speaking (first person), spoken to (second person), spoken about (third person)	I, me, my, mine, we, us, our, ours you, your, yours he, him, his, she, her, hers, it, its, they, them, their, theirs
Reflexive	Refers to subject and directs action of verb back to subject	myself, ourselves, yourself, yourselves, himself, herself, itself, themselves
Intensive	Refers to and emphasizes noun or another pronoun	(See Reflexive.)
Demonstrative	Refers to specific one(s) of group	this, that, these, those
Interrogative	Introduces question	what, which, who, whom, whose
Relative	Introduces subordinate clause and refers to noun or pronoun outside clause	that, which, who, whom, whose
Indefinite	Refers to one(s) not specifically named	all, any, anyone, both, each, either, everybody, many, none, nothing
ADJECTIVE	Modifies noun or pronoun by telling *what kind, which one, how many,* or *how much*	**an old, flea-bitten** dog, **a Sioux** custom, **that** one, **the twelve red** roses, **more** water
VERB	Shows action or state of being	
Action	Expresses physical or mental activity	paint, jump, write, know, imagine
Linking	Connects subject with word identifying or describing it	appear, be, seem, become, feel, look, smell, sound, taste
Helping	Combines with another verb to form a verb phrase	be, have, may, can, shall, will, would
ADVERB	Modifies verb, adjective, or adverb by telling *how, when, where,* or *to what extent*	drives **carefully, quite** dangerous, **shortly afterward,** arrived **there late**
PREPOSITION	Relates noun or pronoun to another word	across, between, into, near, of, on, with, aside from, instead of, next to
CONJUNCTION	Joins words or word groups	
Coordinating	Joins words or word groups used in same way	and, but, for, nor, or, so, yet

(continued)

PART OF SPEECH		DEFINITION	EXAMPLES
Correlative		Joins words or word groups used in same way	both . . . and, either . . . or, neither . . . nor, not only . . . but (also)
Subordinating		Begins subordinate clause and connects it to independent clause	as though, because, if, since, so that, than, when, where, while
INTERJECTION		Expresses emotion	hey, oops, ouch, wow

Determining Parts of Speech

The way a word is used in a sentence determines the word's part of speech.

EXAMPLES

The fine feathers of young birds are called **down.** [noun]

She wore a **down** vest. [adjective]

Did the tackle **down** the ball in the end zone? [verb]

Her poster fell **down.** [adverb]

My cousin lives **down** the street from my school. [preposition]

Let's get a drink of **water.** [noun]

Did you **water** the plants? [verb]

Most **water** sports offer good exercise. [adjective]

He promised us **that** he would meet us after the game. [conjunction]

That CD didn't cost much. [adjective]

I never said **that.** [pronoun]

Avoiding Overused Adverbs

The adverbs *really, too, so,* and *very* are often overused. To keep your writing lively, replace those inexact, overused words with more specific adverbs such as *completely, definitely, entirely, especially, extremely, generally, largely, mainly, mostly, particularly, rather,* and *unusually.*

Try It Out

For each of the following sentences, replace the italicized adverb with a more specific adverb.

1. Elie Wiesel's speech was *very* direct.
2. It *really* focused on personal responsibility.
3. People accept injustice *too* easily.
4. One person's actions can be *very* important.
5. The worst part was to be *so* forgotten.

2 AGREEMENT

AGREEMENT OF SUBJECT AND VERB

2a. A verb should always agree with its subject in number. Singular subjects take singular verbs. Plural subjects take plural verbs.

SINGULAR **She searches** for Mme. Forestier's necklace.

PLURAL **They search** for Mme. Forestier's necklace.

SINGULAR Miss Lottie's flower **garden was destroyed.**

PLURAL Miss Lottie's **marigolds were destroyed.**

COMPUTER NOTE

Some word-processing programs can identify problems in subject-verb agreement. If you have access to such a program, you can use it to help you search for errors when you are proofreading your writing. If you are not sure whether a problem identified by the word processor is truly an error, look it up in this section of the Language Handbook.

 For information about identifying subjects and verbs, see pages 1011–1012.

2b. **The number of the subject is not changed by a phrase following the subject.**

SINGULAR   The **sign** near the glass doors **explains** the theme of the exhibit.

PLURAL   Several **paintings** by Emilio Sánchez **were hanging** in the gallery.

SINGULAR   **Romeo**, together with Benvolio and Mercutio, **goes** to Lord Capulet's party.

PLURAL   The **combs** made of pure tortoise shell **were** expensive.

☞ For information about kinds of phrases, see Part 6: Phrases.

The number of the subject is not changed by a negative construction following the subject.

EXAMPLE

A **human being,** not a tiger nor any other animal, **becomes** the prey hunted by General Zaroff in "The Most Dangerous Game."

2c. **The following indefinite pronouns are singular: *anybody, anyone, anything, each, either, everybody, everyone, everything, neither, nobody, no one, nothing, one, somebody, someone, something.***

EXAMPLES

Each of the poems about farm workers **was written** by Gary Soto.

Has anyone else in your study group **read** all of *The Miracle Worker?*

2d. **The following indefinite pronouns are plural: *both, few, many, several.***

EXAMPLES

Both of the poems about the San Joaquin Valley **were written** by Gary Soto.

Have many in your study group **read** *The Miracle Worker?*

2e. **The indefinite pronouns *all, any, most, none,* and *some* are singular when they refer to singular words and are plural when they refer to plural words.**

SINGULAR   **Some** of the show **is** funny.

PLURAL   **Some** of the skits and other acts **are** funny.

SINGULAR   **All** of the house **looks** clean.

PLURAL   **All** of the houses **look** clean.

2f. **A *compound subject,* which is two or more subjects that have the same verb, may be singular, plural, or either.**

(1) Subjects joined by *and* usually take a plural verb.

EXAMPLE

Both **Leslie Marmon Silko** and **Mari Evans are** poets.

A compound subject that names only one person or thing takes a singular verb.

EXAMPLES

My **pen pal and best friend is** my cousin.

Macaroni and cheese makes a good side dish.

(2) Singular subjects joined by *or* or *nor* take a singular verb.

EXAMPLES

Either the **principal** or the **coach has** to approve it.

Neither **Della** nor **Jim was** disappointed.

(3) When a singular subject and a plural subject are joined by *or* or *nor,* the verb agrees with the subject nearer the verb.

EXAMPLES

Neither the losers nor the **winner was** happy with the outcome of the match.

Neither the winner nor the **losers were** happy with the outcome of the match.

 NOTE   If such a construction sounds awkward, revise the sentence to give each part of the subject its own verb.

EXAMPLE

The **losers were** not happy with the outcome of the match, and neither **was** the **winner.**

 For more information about subjects, see pages 1011–1012.

2g. **Don't and doesn't must agree with their subjects.**

With the subjects *I* and *you* and with plural subjects, use *don't (do not).*

EXAMPLES

I **don't** know.

You **don't** seem happy.

Some people **don't** care.

With other subjects, use *doesn't (does not).*

EXAMPLES

He **doesn't** drive.

Donna **doesn't** work.

It **doesn't** have one.

2h. A collective noun takes a singular verb when the noun refers to the group as a unit and takes a plural verb when the noun refers to the individual parts or members of the group.

A *collective noun* is singular in form but names a group of persons or things.

SINGULAR The class **has** elected its officers.
[class = a unit]

PLURAL The class **have** completed their projects on *Romeo and Juliet*.
[class = individual students]

Collective Nouns

army	club	group	public
assembly	committee	herd	squad
audience	couple	jury	staff
band	crew	majority	swarm
cast	crowd	number	team
chorus	family	pack	troop
class	flock	pair	wildlife

2i. A verb agrees with its subject, not with its predicate nominative.

SINGULAR The main **attraction is** the marching bands.

PLURAL The marching **bands are** the main attraction.

2j. A verb agrees with its subject even when the verb precedes the subject, as in sentences beginning with *here* or *there* and in questions.

SINGULAR Here **is** [*or* here's] my **drawing** of the Cyclops.

PLURAL Here **are** my **drawings** of the Cyclops.

SINGULAR When in the program **does** the **skater perform** her triple axel?

PLURAL When in the program **do** the **fans start** clapping to the music?

NOTE Contractions such as *here's, there's,* and *where's* should be used only with subjects that are singular in meaning.

2k. An expression of an amount (a length of time, a statistic, or a fraction, for example) is singular when the amount is thought of as a unit or when it refers to a singular word and is plural when the amount is thought of as many parts or when it refers to a plural word.

SINGULAR **Twenty dollars is** the amount Della receives for her hair. [Twenty dollars is the single amount Della receives.]

PLURAL **Twenty dollars were stuck together**. [Twenty individual dollars were stuck together.]

SINGULAR **Three fourths** of the class **has seen** *Romeo and Juliet*. [*Three fourths* refers to *class*, a singular word.]

PLURAL **Three fourths** of the students **have seen** *Romeo and Juliet*. [*Three fourths* refers to *students*, a plural word.]

2l. The title of a creative work (such as a book, song, film, or painting) or the name of an organization, a country, or a city (even if it is plural in form) takes a singular verb.

EXAMPLES
"**Marigolds**" **is** a story by Eugenia W. Collier.
Friends of the Earth was founded in 1969.
The Netherlands has thousands of canals.

2m. A few nouns, although plural in form, take singular verbs.

EXAMPLE
The **news** of the nominee for the Supreme Court **was** a surprise to many observers.

Some nouns that end in *–s* take a plural verb even though they refer to a single item.

EXAMPLES
The **scissors need** to be sharpened.
Were these **pants** on sale?
The **pliers are** next to the wrench.

AGREEMENT OF PRONOUN AND ANTECEDENT

A pronoun usually refers to a noun or another pronoun. The word that a pronoun refers to is called its *antecedent*.

2n. A pronoun agrees with its antecedent in number and gender. Singular pronouns refer to singular antecedents. A few personal pronouns indicate gender: feminine, masculine, or neuter. Plural pronouns refer to plural antecedents. No plural pronouns indicate gender.

MASCULINE	he	him	his	himself
FEMININE	she	her	hers	herself
NEUTER	it	it	its	itself

EXAMPLES

Juliet stabs **herself.** [singular, feminine]

General Zaroff thinks that Rainsford has escaped **him.** [singular, masculine]

After eating the Lotus plant, the **men** did not want to return to **their** homeland. [plural]

2o. A singular pronoun is used to refer to *anybody, anyone, anything, each, either, everybody, everyone, everything, neither, nobody, no one, nothing, one, somebody, someone,* or *something.* The gender of any of these pronouns is determined by a word in the phrase following the pronoun.

EXAMPLES

Each of the **boys** held some pebbles in **his** hand.

Everyone on the **girls'** tennis team won **her** match.

When the antecedent could be either masculine or feminine, use both the masculine and the feminine pronoun forms connected by *or.*

EXAMPLE

Everybody should choose **his or her** friends carefully.

Avoiding the *His or Her* Construction

When an antecedent could be either masculine or feminine, you can avoid the *his or her* construction by using plural nouns and pronouns. You can also change the possessive *his or her* to an article (*a, an, the*) or eliminate it altogether.

ORIGINAL

A person should choose his or her friends carefully.

REVISED

People should choose **their** friends carefully.

A person should choose **a** friend carefully.

People should choose friends carefully.

Try It Out

Revise each of the following sentences to eliminate the *his or her* construction.

1. Each person had to hide his or her talents.
2. Could anyone take off his or her handicap bag?
3. Everybody had to be equal to his or her neighbor.
4. Did Harrison or the dancer realize his or her fate?
5. Neither he nor she wore his or her handicaps.

2p. A singular pronoun is used to refer to two or more singular antecedents joined by *or* or *nor.*

EXAMPLES

Paula or Janet will present **her** interpretation of Denise Levertov's "The Secret."

Neither **Richard nor Bob** has read **his** report on Ray Bradbury.

If a sentence sounds awkward when the antecedents are of different genders, revise it.

AWKWARD   Either Ben or Maya will read his or her report on O. Henry.

REVISED   Either **Ben** will read **his** report on O. Henry, or **Maya** will read **hers.**

2q. A plural pronoun is used to refer to two or more antecedents joined by *and.*

EXAMPLES

Romeo and Juliet marry despite the feud between **their** families.

Doodle and his **brother** spent much time with each other; **they** became very close.

2r. The number of a relative pronoun (*who, whom, whose, which,* or *that*) depends on the number of its antecedent.

EXAMPLES

Aretha is one **friend who** always **keeps her** word. [*Who* refers to the singular noun *friend.* Therefore, the singular forms *keeps* and *her* are used to agree with *who.*]

Many who volunteer find **their** experiences rewarding. [*Who* refers to the plural pronoun *many.* Therefore, the plural forms *volunteer* and *their* are used to agree with *who.*]

For more about relative pronouns in adjective clauses, see page 1009.

3 USING VERBS

THE PRINCIPAL PARTS OF VERBS

3a. The four principal parts of a verb are the *base form*, the *present participle*, the *past*, and the *past participle*. These principal parts are used to form all the different verb tenses.

3b. A *regular verb* forms its past and past participle by adding *–d* or *–ed* to the base form.

3c. An *irregular verb* forms its past and past participle in some other way than by adding *–d* or *–ed* to the base form.

COMMON REGULAR VERBS			
BASE FORM	**PRESENT PARTICIPLE**	**PAST**	**PAST PARTICIPLE**
ask	(is) asking	asked	(have) asked
attack	(is) attacking	attacked	(have) attacked
raise	(is) raising	raised	(have) raised
plan	(is) planning	planned	(have) planned
try	(is) trying	tried	(have) tried

COMMON IRREGULAR VERBS			
BASE FORM	**PRESENT PARTICIPLE**	**PAST**	**PAST PARTICIPLE**
be	(is) being	was, were	(have) been
begin	(is) beginning	began	(have) begun
bring	(is) bringing	brought	(have) brought
burst	(is) bursting	burst	(have) burst
drink	(is) drinking	drank	(have) drunk
drive	(is) driving	drove	(have) driven
eat	(is) eating	ate	(have) eaten
fall	(is) falling	fell	(have) fallen
find	(is) finding	found	(have) found
freeze	(is) freezing	froze	(have) frozen
go	(is) going	went	(have) gone
keep	(is) keeping	kept	(have) kept
lay	(is) laying	laid	(have) laid
lead	(is) leading	led	(have) led
lie	(is) lying	lay	(have) lain
ride	(is) riding	rode	(have) ridden
rise	(is) rising	rose	(have) risen
set	(is) setting	set	(have) set
shake	(is) shaking	shook	(have) shaken
sing	(is) singing	sang	(have) sung
sit	(is) sitting	sat	(have) sat
steal	(is) stealing	stole	(have) stolen
swim	(is) swimming	swam	(have) swum
tear	(is) tearing	tore	(have) torn

NOTE The examples in the chart at the left include *is* and *have* in parentheses to show that helping verbs (forms of *be* and *have*) are used with the present participle and past participle forms.

Drop the final silent *e* in the base form of a verb when adding *–ing* and *–ed* to form the present participle and past participle.

PRESENT PARTICIPLES
share + –ing = shar**ing**
dive + –ing = div**ing**

PAST PARTICIPLES
raise + –ed = rais**ed**
receive + –ed = receiv**ed**

EXCEPTIONS
dye + –ing = dy**eing**
singe + –ing = sing**eing**

 For more about correct spelling when adding suffixes to words, see page 1033.

NOTE If you are not sure about the principal parts of a verb, look in a dictionary. Entries for irregular verbs give the principal parts. If no principal parts are listed, the verb is a regular verb.

TENSE

3d. The *tense* of a verb indicates the time of the action or the state of being expressed by the verb. Every English verb has six tenses: *present, past, future, present perfect, past perfect,* and *future perfect.* The tenses are formed from the verb's principal parts.

(1) The *present tense* is used mainly to express an action or a state of being that is occurring now.

EXAMPLES
Mrs. Haynes **leads** the choir.
Alonzo and she **walk** to school every day.

The present tense is also used

- to show a customary or habitual action or state of being
- to express a general truth—something that is always true
- to make historical events seem current (such use is called the **historical present**)
- to discuss a literary work (such use is called the **literary present**)
- to express future time

EXAMPLES
Every November she **bakes** fruitcakes for her friends. [customary action]
The sun **sets** in the west. [general truth]
In 1905, Albert Einstein **proposes** his theory of relativity. [historical present]
Maya Angelou's *I Know Why the Caged Bird Sings* **tells** the story of her childhood. [literary present]
Finals **begin** next week. [future time]

(2) The *past tense* is used to express an action or a state of being that occurred in the past but that is not occurring now.

EXAMPLES
Jim **gave** Della a set of combs.
The children **annoyed** Miss Lottie.

A past action or state of being can also be shown with the verb *used to* followed by the base form.

EXAMPLE
We **used to live** in Chicago.

(3) The *future tense* (formed with *will* or *shall* and the verb's base form) is used to express an action or a state of being that will occur.

EXAMPLES
I **shall play** the part of Romeo.
They **will arrive** soon.

A future action or state of being can also be shown in other ways.

EXAMPLES
They **are going to win.**
We **leave** for the theater **in an hour.**

(4) The *present perfect tense* (formed with *have* or *has* and the verb's past participle) is used to express an action or a state of being that occurred at some indefinite time in the past.

EXAMPLES
Doodle **has learned** how to walk.
We **have read** the *Odyssey.*

The present perfect tense is also used to express an action or a state of being that began in the past and continues into the present.

EXAMPLE
We **have lived** in the same house for nine years.

(5) The *past perfect tense* (formed with *had* and the verb's past participle) is used to express an action or a state of being that was completed in the past before some other past action or event.

EXAMPLES
Lizabeth regretted what she **had done.** [The doing occurred before the regretting.]
When you called, I **had** already **eaten** supper. [The eating occurred before the calling.]

(6) The *future perfect tense* (formed with *will have* or *shall have* and the verb's past participle) is used to express an action or a state of being that will be completed in the future before some other future occurrence.

EXAMPLES
By the time Mom returns, I **will have done** my chores. [The doing will be completed before the returning.]
He **will have finished** his Hebrew lessons before his bar mitzvah. [The finishing will be completed before the bar mitzvah.]

Each of the six verb tenses has an additional form called the *progressive form.* The progressive form expresses a continuing action or state of being. It consists of the appropriate tense of *be* plus the verb's present participle. For the perfect tenses, the progressive form also includes one or more helping verbs.

Present Progressive	am, are, is giving
Past Progressive	was, were giving
Future Progressive	will (shall) be giving
Present Perfect Progressive	has, have been giving
Past Perfect Progressive	had been giving
Future Perfect Progressive	will (shall) have been giving

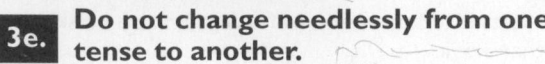

3e. Do not change needlessly from one tense to another.

INCONSISTENT   Jim sold his watch and buys Della a set of combs. [change from past to present tense]

CONSISTENT   Jim **sold** his watch and **bought** Della a set of combs. [past tense]

Using Appropriate Verb Tenses

Using different verb tenses is often necessary to show the order of events that occur at different times.

NONSTANDARD   I regretted that I chose such a broad topic.

STANDARD   I **regretted** that I **had chosen** such a broad topic. [Since the action of choosing was completed before the action of regretting, the verb should be *had chosen*, not *chose*.]

Try It Out ✏

For each of the following sentences, change the verb tenses to show the order of events that occur at different times. If a sentence is correct, write *C*.

1. Before he went away, they spent much time together.
2. When they gathered enough nuts, they go shopping.
3. By the time the moon rises tonight, they will finish.
4. She told ghost stories and was superstitious.
5. He was grateful for all they shared during the past year.

ACTIVE AND PASSIVE VOICE

3f. A verb in the *active voice* expresses an action done by its subject. A verb in the *passive voice* expresses an action received by its subject.

A verb in the passive voice is always a verb phrase that includes a form of *be* and the main verb's past participle.

ACTIVE VOICE   Rainsford **surprised** General Zaroff. [The subject, *Rainsford*, performs the action.]

PASSIVE VOICE   General Zaroff **was surprised** by Rainsford. [The subject, *General Zaroff*, receives the action.]

ACTIVE VOICE   William Gibson **wrote** *The Miracle Worker*.

PASSIVE VOICE   *The Miracle Worker* **was written** by William Gibson.

3g. Use the passive voice sparingly.

The passive voice is not any less correct than the active voice, but it is less direct, less forceful, and less concise. As a result, a sentence written in the passive voice can often be wordy and can sound awkward or weak.

AWKWARD PASSIVE   Mme. Forestier's necklace was borrowed by Mme. Loisel.

ACTIVE   Mme. Loisel **borrowed** Mme. Forestier's necklace.

The passive voice is useful, however, in certain situations:

1. when you do not know the performer of the action

EXAMPLE
The Globe Theater **was built** in 1599.

2. when you do not want to reveal the performer of the action

EXAMPLE
Unfounded accusations **were made** against the candidate.

3. when you want to emphasize the receiver of the action

EXAMPLE
Abraham Lincoln **was elected** president of the United States in 1860.

COMPUTER NOTE   Some software programs can identify and highlight passive voice verbs. If you use such a program, keep in mind that it can't tell why you used the passive voice. If you did so for one of the reasons listed under 3g above, you may want to leave the verb in the passive voice.

4 USING PRONOUNS

CASE

Case is the form that a noun or pronoun takes to indicate its use in a sentence. In English, there are three cases: *nominative, objective,* and *possessive.* Most personal pronouns have a different form for each case.

NOTE The form of a noun is the same for both the nominative and the objective case. For the possessive case, however, a noun changes its form, usually by adding an apostrophe and an s to singular nouns and only an apostrophe to plural nouns.

NOMINATIVE	The **sniper** fired his rifle.
OBJECTIVE	Someone shot the **sniper.**
POSSESSIVE	Who was the **sniper's** enemy?

The Nominative Case

4a. A subject of a verb is in the nominative case.

EXAMPLES
She was glad that **they** were elected. [*She* is the subject of *was; they* is the subject of *were elected.*]
Is **Della** or **he** disappointed? [*Della* and *he* are the compound subject of *is.*]

4b. A predicate nominative is in the nominative case.

A *predicate nominative* follows a linking verb and explains or identifies the subject of the verb.

EXAMPLES
The woman who borrows the necklace is **she.** [*She* follows *is* and identifies the subject *woman.*]
The main characters are **he** and his **brother** Doodle. [*He* and *brother* follow *are* and identify the subject *characters.*]

NOTE Expressions such as *It's me, That's him,* and *Could it be her?* are informal usage. Avoid such expressions in formal speaking and writing.

The Objective Case

4c. A direct object of a verb is in the objective case.

A *direct object* follows an action verb and tells *whom* or *what.*

EXAMPLES
Lizabeth destroyed **them.** [*Them* tells *what* Lizabeth destroyed.]
Friar Laurence helps **her** and **him.** [*Her* and *him* tell *whom* Friar Laurence helps.]

PERSONAL PRONOUNS			
SINGULAR			
	NOMINATIVE	**OBJECTIVE**	**POSSESSIVE**
FIRST PERSON	I	me	my, mine
SECOND PERSON	you	you	your, yours
THIRD PERSON	he, she, it	him, her, it	his, her, hers, its
PLURAL			
	NOMINATIVE	**OBJECTIVE**	**POSSESSIVE**
FIRST PERSON	we	us	our, ours
SECOND PERSON	you	you	your, yours
THIRD PERSON	they	them	their, theirs

NOTE Notice in the chart at the left that *you* and *it* are the only personal pronouns that have the same form in both the nominative case and the objective case.

☞ For more information on possessive personal pronouns, see page 1029.

4d. An indirect object of a verb is in the objective case.

An *indirect object* comes before a direct object and tells *to whom* or *to what* or *for whom* or *for what*.

EXAMPLES

Buddy gave **her** a kite. [*Her* tells *to whom* Buddy gave a kite.]

Molly made **him** and **me** a tape. [*Him* and *me* tell *for whom* Molly made a tape.]

4e. An object of a preposition is in the objective case.

An *object of a preposition* comes at the end of a phrase that begins with a preposition.

EXAMPLES

Mme. Loisel borrows a necklace from **her**.
This gift is for **him** and **her**.

SPECIAL PRONOUN PROBLEMS

4f. The pronoun *who* (*whoever*) is in the nominative case. The pronoun *whom* (*whomever*) is in the objective case.

NOMINATIVE   **Who** wrote *Black Boy*? [*Who* is the subject of *wrote*.]

OBJECTIVE   From **whom** did Mme. Loisel borrow the necklace? [*Whom* is the object of the preposition *from*.]

When choosing between *who* and *whom* in a subordinate clause, be sure to base your choice on how the pronoun functions in the subordinate clause.

EXAMPLES

The sniper learned **who** his enemy had been. [*Who* is the predicate nominative identifying the subject *enemy*.]

The sniper learned the identity of the man **whom** he had shot. [*Whom* is the direct object of *had shot*.]

NOTE In spoken English, the use of *whom* is becoming less common. In fact, when speaking, you may correctly begin any question with *who*. In written English, however, you should distinguish between *who* and *whom*.

INFORMAL	**Who** did you see at the mall?
FORMAL	**Whom** did you see at the mall?
INFORMAL	**Who** did you go skating with?
FORMAL	With **whom** did you go skating?

Using *Whom* in Formal Situations

Frequently, *whom* is left out of subordinate clauses.

EXAMPLE

The person [**whom**] I have always admired most is Dr. Margaret Mead. [*Whom* is understood to be the direct object of *admired*.]

Leaving out *whom* in such cases tends to make writing sound more informal. In formal situations, it is generally better to include *whom*.

Try It Out

For each of the following sentences, insert *whom* where appropriate. Make any other changes needed for the sentence to sound correct in a formal situation.

1. The girl they admired was reading.
2. Do you know boys like the ones he speaks of?
3. They talked about the woman each of them would marry.
4. The field of carpentry appealed to the boy that kind of work was easy for.
5. The other boy Gary Soto wrote of said that he would go to school.

4g. An appositive is in the same case as the noun or pronoun to which it refers.

An *appositive* is a noun or pronoun placed next to another noun or pronoun to identify or explain it.

EXAMPLES

In the story, the main characters, **Doodle and he,** are brothers. [The appositive, *Doodle and he,* is in the nominative case because it identifies the subject, *characters*.]

Miss Lottie did not say a word to either of the children, **Lizabeth or him.** [The appositive, *Lizabeth or him,* is in the objective case because it identifies an object of a preposition, *children*.]

Sometimes the pronouns *we* and *us* are used with noun appositives.

EXAMPLES

We cast members have a dress rehearsal tonight. [The pronoun *we* is in the nominative case because it is the subject of *have*.]

The principal praised **us** members of the Ecology Club. [The pronoun *us* is in the objective case because it is the direct object of *praised*.]

4h. A pronoun following *than* or *as* in an incomplete construction is in the same case as it would be if the construction were completed.

Notice how the meaning of each of the following sentences is determined by the pronoun form in the incomplete construction.

EXAMPLES
I wrote you more often than **he** [wrote you].
I wrote you more often than [I wrote] **him.**

Did you help Ada as much as **I** [helped Ada]?
Did you help Ada as much as [you helped] **me**?

Clear Pronoun Reference

4i. A pronoun should refer clearly to its antecedent.

An *antecedent* is the word a pronoun stands for.

(1) Avoid an *ambiguous reference,* which occurs when a pronoun can refer to either one of two antecedents.

AMBIGUOUS	Miss Lottie saw Lizabeth when she was in the garden. [Who was in the garden, Miss Lottie or Lizabeth?]
CLEAR	When **Miss Lottie** was in the garden, **she** saw Lizabeth.
CLEAR	When **Lizabeth** was in the garden, Miss Lottie saw **her.**

(2) Avoid a *general reference,* which occurs when a pronoun refers to a general idea rather than to a specific antecedent.

GENERAL	Rainsford had escaped. This annoyed General Zaroff. [*This* has no specific antecedent.]
CLEAR	That Rainsford had escaped annoyed General Zaroff.

(3) Avoid a *weak reference,* which occurs when a pronoun refers to an implied antecedent.

WEAK	Ralph enjoys writing poetry, but he never shows them to anyone else. [*Them* most likely refers to the unstated plural noun *poems,* but the writer has used the singular noun *poetry* instead.]
CLEAR	Ralph enjoys writing poetry, but he never shows his poems to anyone else.

(4) Avoid using an *indefinite reference,* which occurs when the pronoun *you, it,* or *they* refers to no particular person or thing.

INDEFINITE	In the owner's manual, they explain how to program the VCR. [*They* has no antecedent.]
CLEAR	The owner's manual explains how to program the VCR.

 NOTE The indefinite use of *it* is acceptable in familiar expressions such as *It is snowing, It seems as though . . . ,* and *It's late.*

5 USING MODIFIERS

WHAT IS A MODIFIER?

A *modifier* is a word or group of words that limits the meaning of another word or group of words. The two kinds of modifiers are *adjectives* and *adverbs.* An **adjective** limits the meaning of a noun or a pronoun. An **adverb** limits the meaning of a verb, an adjective, or another adverb.

Adjective or Adverb?

Although many adverbs end in *–ly,* many others do not. Furthermore, not all words with the *–ly* ending are adverbs. Some adjectives also end in *–ly.* Therefore, you can't tell whether a word is an adjective or adverb simply by looking for the *–ly* ending.

ADVERBS NOT ENDING IN –LY	arrive **soon**	sit **here**
	not angry	run **loose**
	walk **home**	**very** hot
ADJECTIVES ENDING IN –LY	**daily** diet	**holy** place
	curly hair	**silly** joke

In addition, some words can be used as either adjectives or adverbs.

ADJECTIVES	ADVERBS
He is an **only** child.	She has **only** one sister.
I have an **early** class.	I get up **early.**
Tina has a **fast** bicycle.	The baby is **fast** asleep.
We caught the **last** bus.	We left **last.**

COMPARISON OF MODIFIERS

5a. The forms of modifiers change to show comparison.

The three degrees of comparison are *positive, comparative,* and *superlative.*

Regular Comparison

(1) Most one-syllable modifiers form the comparative and superlative degrees by adding *–er* and *–est.*

POSITIVE	COMPARATIVE	SUPERLATIVE
deep	deeper	deepest
gentle	gentler	gentlest
careful	more careful	most careful
slowly	more slowly	most slowly
significantly	more significantly	most significantly
fresh	less fresh	least fresh
common	less common	least common

(2) Some two-syllable modifiers form the comparative and superlative degrees by adding *–er* and *–est.* Other two-syllable modifiers form the comparative and superlative degrees by using *more* and *most.*

(3) Modifiers of more than two syllables form the comparative and superlative degrees by using *more* and *most.*

(4) All modifiers, no matter how many syllables they have, show decreasing degrees of comparison by using *less* and *least.*

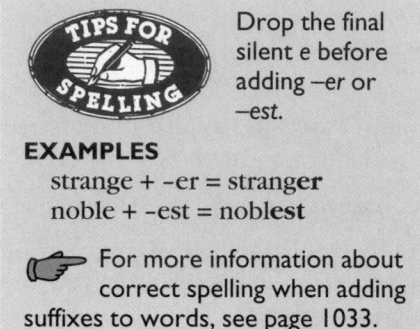 **TIPS FOR SPELLING**

Drop the final silent e before adding *–er* or *–est.*

EXAMPLES
strange + –er = strang**er**
noble + –est = nobl**est**

☞ For more information about correct spelling when adding suffixes to words, see page 1033.

Irregular Comparison

(5) Some modifiers form the comparative and superlative degrees in other ways.

POSITIVE	COMPARATIVE	SUPERLATIVE
bad	worse	worst
good/well	better	best
little	less	least
many/much	more	most

NOTE Do not add *–er, –est, more,* or *most* to irregular comparative and superlative forms. Use *worse,* not *worser* or *more worse,* and *best,* not *bestest.*

☞ For information about using *good* and *well,* see page 1036; for information about using *bad* and *badly,* see page 1035.

Use of Comparative and Superlative Forms

5b. Use the comparative degree when comparing two things. Use the superlative degree when comparing more than two.

COMPARATIVE Rainsford was **more resourceful** than Zaroff had expected him to be.

SUPERLATIVE "The Most Dangerous Game" is one of the **most suspenseful** stories I have ever read.

5c. Include the word *other* or *else* when comparing one thing with others in the same group.

ILLOGICAL Ruth is more agile than any member of her gymnastics team. [Ruth is a member of her team. Logically, she cannot be more agile than herself.]

LOGICAL Ruth is more agile than any **other** member of her gymnastics team.

ILLOGICAL Carlos ran faster than everyone. [*Everyone* includes Carlos. Logically, he cannot run faster than himself.]

LOGICAL Carlos ran faster than everyone **else.**

5d. Avoid a *double comparison*—the use of both *–er* and *more* (or *less*) or both *–est* and *most* (or *least*) to modify the same word.

EXAMPLES
William Sydney Porter, **better** [*not* more better] known as O. Henry, wrote "The Gift of the Magi."
This is the **cheapest** [*not* most cheapest] bicycle in the store.

5e. Avoid comparing items that cannot logically be compared.

ILLOGICAL The average temperature in Dallas is higher than Spokane. [illogical comparison between a temperature and a city]

LOGICAL The average temperature in Dallas is higher than **the average temperature in** Spokane.

ILLOGICAL A coral snake's venom is more dangerous than a rattlesnake. [illogical comparison between a snake's venom and a snake]

LOGICAL A coral snake's venom is more dangerous than a **rattlesnake's** [*or* **rattlesnake's venom**].

State both parts of an incomplete comparison if there is any chance of misunderstanding.

UNCLEAR I visited her more than Elise.
CLEAR I visited her more than **I visited** Elise.
CLEAR I visited her more than Elise **visited her.**

PLACEMENT OF MODIFIERS

5f. Avoid using a *dangling modifier*—a modifying word or word group that does not sensibly modify any word or word group in the same sentence.

DANGLING Working together, our goal can be attained within a few months.
CLEAR Working together, we can attain our goal within a few months.
CLEAR We can attain our goal within a few months by working together.

You may correct a dangling modifier

- by adding a word or words that the dangling modifier can sensibly modify
- by adding a word or words to the dangling modifier
- by rewording the sentence

DANGLING Peering over the parapet, an armored car was seen. [Who or what was peering over the parapet?]
CLEAR Peering over the parapet, the **sniper** saw an armored car.

DANGLING To understand Denise Levertov's poetry, some knowledge of figurative language is necessary. [Who needs to know figurative language?]
CLEAR To understand Denise Levertov's poetry, the **reader** needs some knowledge of figurative language.

DANGLING While burying the scarlet ibis, a hymn is sung. [Who or what is burying the scarlet ibis?]
CLEAR While burying the scarlet ibis, **Doodle** sings a hymn.

NOTE A sentence may appear to have a dangling modifier when *you* is the understood subject. In such cases, the modifier is not dangling; it modifies the understood subject.

EXAMPLE
To find the correct spelling, [**you**] look up the word in a dictionary.

For more information about understood subjects, see 8g (4) on page 1012.

5g. Avoid using a *misplaced modifier*—a modifying word or word group that sounds awkward or unclear because it seems to modify the wrong word or word group.

To correct a misplaced modifier, place the modifier as near as possible to the word or word group you intend it to modify.

MISPLACED Doodle reveals to his family that he has learned to walk on his sixth birthday. [Does Doodle reveal or does he learn on his sixth birthday?]
CLEAR **On his sixth birthday,** Doodle reveals to his family that he has learned to walk.

MISPLACED Born eight weeks ago, we adopted one of the puppies. [Were we or the puppies born eight weeks ago?]
CLEAR We adopted one of the puppies **born eight weeks ago.**

For more information on phrase and clause modifiers, see Part 6: Phrases and Part 7: Clauses.

6 PHRASES

6a. **A *phrase* is a group of related words that is used as a single part of speech and that does not contain both a verb and its subject.**

EXAMPLES
has been sitting [verb phrase; no subject]
about you and me [prepositional phrase; no subject or verb]

 If a group of words has both a subject and a verb, it is called a clause. For more information, see Part 7: Clauses.

PREPOSITIONAL PHRASES

6b. **A *prepositional phrase* begins with a preposition and ends with a noun or pronoun that is called the *object of the preposition*. A prepositional phrase may also contain modifiers of the object of the preposition.**

EXAMPLES
The sniper ran **across the street.** [The noun *street* is the object of the preposition *across*.]
In front of him was Fortunato. [The pronoun *him* is the object of the compound preposition *in front of*.]
Kyoko called **to Nancy and me.** [Both *Nancy* and *me* are objects of the preposition *to*.]

(1) A prepositional phrase that modifies a noun or pronoun is called an **adjective phrase.**

An adjective phrase tells *what kind* or *which one*.

EXAMPLES
Lizabeth destroyed Miss Lottie's garden **of marigolds.** [*Of marigolds* modifies the noun *garden*, telling *what kind*.]
All **of them** watched Doodle bury the scarlet ibis. [*Of them* modifies the pronoun *all*, telling *which ones*.]

An adjective phrase always follows the word it modifies. That word may be the object of another preposition.

EXAMPLE
"Poison" is the title **of a story by Roald Dahl.** [*Of a story* modifies the noun *title. By Roald Dahl* modifies the noun *story*, the object of the preposition *of*.]

More than one adjective phrase may modify the same noun or pronoun.

EXAMPLE
The bottle **of vitamins on the shelf** is almost empty. [*Of vitamins* and *on the shelf* modify the noun *bottle*.]

(2) A prepositional phrase that modifies a verb, an adjective, or an adverb is called an **adverb phrase.**

An adverb phrase tells *when, where, how, why,* or *to what extent.*

EXAMPLES
By his sixth birthday Doodle could walk. [*By his sixth birthday* modifies *could walk*, telling *when*.]
Had a snake crawled **under the sheet**? [*Under the sheet* modifies *had crawled*, telling *where*.]
She answered **with a smile.** [*With a smile* modifies *answered*, telling *how*.]
Everyone remained quiet **because of the snake.** [*Because of the snake* modifies *quiet*, telling *why*.]
Is the water warm enough **for swimming**? [*For swimming* modifies *enough*, telling *to what extent*.]

An adverb phrase may come either before or after the word or word group it modifies.

EXAMPLES
For Christmas, Buddy gave her a kite.
Buddy gave her a kite **for Christmas.**

More than one adverb phrase may modify the same word or group of words.

EXAMPLE
In November she and Buddy bake fruitcakes **for their friends.** [*In November* tells *when* they bake the fruitcakes, and *for their friends* tells *why* they bake them.]

 For more information about placement of modifying phrases, see page 1005.

VERBALS AND VERBAL PHRASES

A *verbal* is a form of a verb used as a noun, an adjective, or an adverb. A *verbal phrase* consists of a verbal and its modifiers and complements. The three kinds of verbals are *participles, gerunds,* and *infinitives.*

Participles and Participial Phrases

6c. A *participle* is a verb form that can be used as an adjective. A *participial phrase* consists of a participle and all the words related to the participle.

(1) *Present participles* end in *–ing*.

EXAMPLES

Doodle collapsed in the **pouring** rain. [The present participle *pouring* modifies the noun *rain.*]

Lying quietly in his bed, Harry told Timber about the snake. [The participial phrase *lying quietly in his bed* modifies the noun *Harry.* Both the adverb *quietly* and the adverb phrase *in his bed* modify the present participle *lying.*]

(2) Most *past participles* end in *–d* or *–ed*. Others are irregularly formed.

EXAMPLES

Lizabeth sat in the **ruined** garden and cried. [The past participle *ruined* modifies the noun *garden.*]

The speaker, **known for her strong support of recycling,** was loudly applauded. [The participial phrase *known for her strong support of recycling* modifies the noun *speaker.* The adverb phrase *for her strong support* modifies the past participle *known.* The adjective phrase *of recycling* modifies *support.*]

Do not confuse a participle used as an adjective with a participle used as part of a verb phrase.

ADJECTIVE	Fortunato, **struggling** to free himself, begged Montresor to unchain him.
VERB PHRASE	Fortunato, who **was struggling** to free himself, begged Montresor to unchain him.

For more information about participles, see page 998. For more about the placement of participial phrases, see page 1005.

Gerunds and Gerund Phrases

6d. A *gerund* is a verb form ending in *–ing* that is used as a noun. A *gerund phrase* consists of a gerund and all the words related to the gerund.

EXAMPLES

Violently destroying the marigolds was Lizabeth's last act of childhood. [The gerund phrase is the subject of *was.* The adverb *violently* modifies the gerund *destroying,* and *marigolds* is the direct object of *destroying.*]

They enjoy **making fruitcakes together.** [The gerund phrase is the direct object of *enjoy. Fruitcakes* is the direct object of the gerund *making,* and the adverb *together* modifies *making.*]

His job is **giving the customers their menus.** [The gerund phrase is the predicate nominative explaining the subject *job. Customers* is the indirect object and *menus* is the direct object of the gerund *giving.*]

Rainsford escaped from Zaroff by **leaping into the sea.** [The gerund phrase is the object of the preposition *by.* The adverb phrase *into the sea* modifies the gerund *leaping.*]

Do not confuse a gerund with a present participle used as an adjective or as part of a verb phrase.

EXAMPLE

Following the basketball coach's advice, she was **planning** to go on with her **training.** [*Following* is a present participle modifying *she. Planning* is part of the verb phrase *was planning. Training* is a gerund used as the object of the preposition *with.*]

 NOTE When preceding a gerund, a noun or pronoun should be in the possessive form.

EXAMPLES

Pedro's constant practicing improved **his** playing.

Infinitives and Infinitive Phrases

6e. An *infinitive* is a verb form, usually preceded by *to*, that can be used as a noun, an adjective, or an adverb. An *infinitive phrase* consists of an infinitive and all the words related to the infinitive.

NOUN	**To proofread your writing carefully** is important. [The infinitive phrase is the subject of *is. Writing* is the direct object of the infinitive, *to proofread,* and the adverb *carefully* modifies *to proofread.*] Why did she finally decide **to buy that video**? [The infinitive phrase is the direct object of *decide. Video* is the direct object of the infinitive *to buy.*] Zaroff's plan was **to hunt Rainsford.** [The infinitive phrase is the predicate nominative identifying the subject *plan. Rainsford* is the direct object of the infinitive *to hunt.*]

ADJECTIVE	Friar Laurence's plan **to help Romeo and Juliet** failed. [The infinitive phrase modifies the noun *plan*. *Romeo* and *Juliet* are the direct objects of the infinitive *to help*.]
ADVERB	Fortunato was eager **to taste the amontillado.** [The infinitive phrase modifies the adjective *eager*. *Amontillado* is the direct object of the infinitive *to taste*.]

Sometimes the *to* of the infinitive is omitted.

EXAMPLE
Mother said that you should go [to] get a warmer jacket.

NOTE Do not confuse an infinitive with a prepositional phrase that begins with *to*. An infinitive is a verb form. A prepositional phrase ends with a noun or pronoun.

EXAMPLE
Doodle and he went **to the creek** [prepositional phrase] **to swim.** [infinitive]

6f. An infinitive may have a subject, in which case it forms an *infinitive clause.*

EXAMPLE
Juliet trusted Friar Laurence and asked **him to help her.** [The infinitive clause is the direct object of *asked*. *Him* is the subject of the infinitive *to help*. *Her* is the direct object of *to help*.]

Notice in this example that a pronoun that functions as the subject of an infinitive clause takes the objective form.

Avoiding Split Infinitives
A *split infinitive* is created when a word is placed between the *to* and the verb in an infinitive. Although split infinitives are commonly used in informal speaking and writing, you should avoid using them in formal situations.

SPLIT	It's wise to always have some money in savings.
REVISED	It's wise always **to have** some money in savings.
REVISED	It's wise **to have** some money in savings always.
REVISED	It's always wise **to have** some money in savings.

Try It Out ✎
Revise each of the following sentences to eliminate the split infinitive.
1. His fate was to never be able to see.
2. He wants people to just treat him as an equal.
3. To successfully graduate with honors takes much effort.
4. Yet, he couldn't get anyone to even hire him.
5. Laws require businesses to also hire people with disabilities.

APPOSITIVES AND APPOSITIVE PHRASES

6g. An *appositive* is a noun or a pronoun placed beside another noun or pronoun to identify it or explain it. An *appositive phrase* consists of an appositive and its modifiers.

EXAMPLES
Kurt Vonnegut wrote the story **"Harrison Bergeron."** [The appositive *"Harrison Bergeron"* identifies the noun *story*.]

In the movie, Anne Bancroft played the role of Annie Sullivan, **Helen's teacher.** [The appositive phrase *Helen's teacher* explains the noun *Annie Sullivan*.]

Odysseus blinded Cyclops, **the one-eyed giant.** [The appositive phrase *the one-eyed giant* explains the noun *Cyclops*.]

An appositive phrase usually follows the noun or pronoun it refers to. For emphasis, however, it may come at the beginning of a sentence.

EXAMPLE
A noble leader of his people, Chief Joseph spoke with quiet dignity.

Appositives and appositive phrases are usually set off by commas. However, if the appositive is closely related to the preceding noun or pronoun, it should not be set off by commas.

EXAMPLES
My brother **Richard** goes to college. [The writer has more than one brother, and the appositive identifies which brother goes to college. Because this information is essential to the meaning of the sentence, it is not set off by commas.]

My brother, **Richard,** goes to college. [The writer has only one brother; therefore, the appositive is not necessary to identify him. Because the information is nonessential, it is set off by commas.]

7 CLAUSES

7a. A *clause* is a group of words that contains a verb and its subject and that is used as part of a sentence.

KINDS OF CLAUSES

7b. An *independent (or main) clause* expresses a complete thought and can stand by itself as a sentence.

EXAMPLES
Della gives Jim a watch chain, and **Jim gives Della a set of combs.**
When I wrote my report on William Shakespeare, **I quoted from *Romeo and Juliet, Hamlet,* and *Macbeth.***

7c. A *subordinate (or dependent) clause* does not express a complete thought and cannot stand alone.

SUBORDINATE CLAUSES
whom you know
because I told him the truth
what the show is about

SENTENCES
Will the player **whom you know** autograph our baseball gloves?
Because I told him the truth, Dad wasn't too angry about the broken window.
Stephanie wants to know **what the show is about.**

7d. An *adjective clause* is a subordinate clause that modifies a noun or pronoun.

An adjective clause, which always follows the word it modifies, usually begins with a *relative pronoun,* such as *who, whom, whose, which,* or *that.* Besides introducing an adjective clause, a relative pronoun has its own function within the clause.

EXAMPLES
In "The Gift of the Magi," Della and Jim, **who are deeply in love,** make sacrifices to buy gifts for each other. [The adjective clause modifies *Della* and *Jim. Who* is the subject of *are.*]
Not all the stories **that Edgar Allan Poe wrote** deal with horror or terror. [The adjective clause modifies *stories. That* is the direct object of *wrote.*]

I read about Sequoyah, **whose invention of an alphabet aided other Cherokees.** [The adjective clause modifies *Sequoyah. Whose* modifies *invention.*]

A relative pronoun is sometimes left out of an adjective clause.

EXAMPLES
Was *The Miracle Worker* the first play [that] **William Gibson wrote**?
The mechanic [whom] **you recommended** fixed my stepfather's motorcycle.

Occasionally, an adjective clause begins with the *relative adverb* *where* or *when.*

EXAMPLES
We visited the town **where Shakespeare was born.**
Summer is the season **when I feel happiest.**

Revising for Sentence Variety

Although short sentences can be effective, it's a good idea to alternate between shorter sentences and longer ones. To change choppy sentences into smoother writing, revise them into adjective clauses that express the same ideas.

CHOPPY	Mary Cassatt was an American painter. I enjoy her works. She was an Impressionist.
SMOOTH	I enjoy the works of Mary Cassatt, who was an American Impressionist painter.

Try It Out

Use adjective clauses to combine each of the following pairs of short, choppy sentences.

1. Many people do not have homes. They wander the cities.
2. Ann appears in this article. She is one of these homeless people.
3. At one time, Ann had lived in a house. It had yellow siding.
4. Now she has only a coat. The coat is dirty and creased.
5. People like Ann need help, not labels. Their lives are hard.

7e. An *adverb clause* is a subordinate clause that modifies a verb, an adjective, or an adverb.

An adverb clause, which may come before or after the word it modifies, tells *how, when, where, why, to what extent* (*how much*), or *under what condition.* An adverb clause begins with a **subordinating conjunction,** such as *although, because, if, so that,* or *when.*

EXAMPLES
Because we students did so well in the discussion of *Romeo and Juliet*, our teacher did not assign any homework. [The adverb clause modifies *did assign,* telling *why.*]
I wrote a poem about war **after I read "The Sniper."** [The adverb clause modifies *wrote,* telling *when.*]
If Harry moves, he may disturb the sleeping snake. [The adverb clause modifies *may disturb,* telling *under what condition.*]
His pitching arm is stronger today **than it ever was.** [The adverb clause modifies *stronger,* telling *to what extent.*]
He can run faster **than Doodle can.** [The adverb clause modifies *faster,* telling *how much.*]

7f. A *noun clause* is a subordinate clause used as a subject, a complement (predicate nominative, direct object,

or indirect object), or an object of a preposition.

The words commonly used to begin noun clauses include *that, what, whether, who,* and *why.*

SUBJECT	**What Odysseus did** was clever.
PREDICATE NOMINATIVE	The captains are **who pick the players for their teams.**
DIRECT OBJECT	The sniper discovered **that his brother was the enemy.**
INDIRECT OBJECT	The clerk should tell **whoever calls** the sale prices.
OBJECT OF PREPOSITION	He knew the price of **whatever they requested.**

The word that introduces a noun clause may or may not have a function within the noun clause.

EXAMPLES
Lizabeth regretted **what she had done.** [*What* is the direct object of *had done.*]
Mme. Loisel learned **that the necklace was fake.** [*That* has no function in the clause.]

Sometimes the word that introduces a noun clause is not stated, but its meaning is understood.

EXAMPLE
His mother said [that] **he could go to the concert.**

8 SENTENCE STRUCTURE

SENTENCE OR SENTENCE FRAGMENT?

8a. A *sentence* is a group of words that contains a subject and a verb and that expresses a complete thought.

A sentence should begin with a capital letter and end with a period, a question mark, or an exclamation point. A group of words that looks like a sentence but does not make sense by itself is called a **sentence fragment.**

FRAGMENT	Romeo banished from Verona?
SENTENCE	Why was Romeo banished from Verona?
FRAGMENT	What a clever plan!
SENTENCE	What a clever plan he had!

FRAGMENT	When the Montagues and the Capulets learned of the deaths of Romeo and Juliet.
SENTENCE	When the Montagues and the Capulets learned of the deaths of Romeo and Juliet, they ended their feud.

COMPUTER NOTE

Many style-checking software programs can identify sentence fragments. If you have access to such a program, use it to help you evaluate your writing. Then, revise each fragment to make sure that all your sentences express complete thoughts.

SUBJECT AND PREDICATE

8b. **A sentence consists of two parts: the subject and the predicate. The *subject* tells *whom* or *what* the sentence is about. The *predicate* tells something about the subject.**

In the following examples, all the words labeled *subject* make up the **complete subject,** and all the words labeled *predicate* make up the **complete predicate.**

SUBJECT	PREDICATE
Tybalt	was Juliet's cousin.

SUBJECT	PREDICATE
Two of Prince Escalus's kinsmen	died.

SUBJECT	PREDICATE
The setting of the play	is fourteenth-century Italy.

PREDICATE	SUBJECT	PREDICATE
Why did	Juliet	take the sleeping potion?

The Simple Subject

8c. **The *simple subject* is the main word or group of words that tells *whom* or *what* the sentence is about.**

EXAMPLES
An **excerpt** from Richard Wright's *Black Boy* appears in this book. [The complete subject is *an excerpt from Richard Wright's* Black Boy.]
The talented **Georgia O'Keeffe** is known for her paintings of huge flowers. [The complete subject is *the talented Georgia O'Keeffe.*]

The Simple Predicate

8d. **The *simple predicate,* or *verb,* is the main word or group of words that tells something about the subject.**

A simple predicate may be a single word or a **verb phrase** (a verb with one or more helping verbs).

EXAMPLES
Montresor **led** Fortunato to the catacombs. [The complete predicate is *led Fortunato to the catacombs.*]
Did Mme. Loisel **find** the necklace? [The complete predicate is *did find the necklace.*]

NOTE In this book, the term *subject* refers to the simple subject, and the term *verb* refers to the simple predicate unless otherwise indicated.

The Compound Subject and the Compound Verb

8e. **A *compound subject* consists of two or more subjects that are joined by a conjunction—usually *and* or *or*—and that have the same verb.**

EXAMPLES
Does **Rainsford** or **Zaroff** win the game?
Romeo, Benvolio, and **Mercutio** attend the Capulets' party.

8f. **A *compound verb* consists of two or more verbs that are joined by a conjunction—usually *and, but,* or *or*—and that have the same subject.**

EXAMPLES
Della **sold** her hair and **bought** Jim a watch chain.
Timber **looked** for the snake but **did** not **find** it.

Finding the Subject of a Sentence

8g. **To find the subject of a sentence, ask "Who?" or "What?" before the verb.**

EXAMPLE
The price of those videos seems high. [What seems high? The price seems high. *Price* is the subject.]

(1) The subject of a sentence is never in a prepositional phrase.

EXAMPLES
Her **garden** of marigolds was ruined. [What was ruined? *Garden* was ruined. *Marigolds* is the object of the preposition *of.*]
On the rooftop crouched the **sniper.** [Who crouched? *Sniper* crouched. *Rooftop* is the object of the preposition *on.*]

(2) The subject of a sentence expressing a question usually follows the verb or a part of the verb phrase. Turning the question into a statement may help you find the subject.

QUESTION	Did **she** give Buddy a kite?
STATEMENT	**She** did give Buddy a kite.

QUESTION	Is the *Odyssey* an epic?
STATEMENT	The *Odyssey* is an epic.

(3) The word *there* or *here* is never the subject of a sentence.

EXAMPLES
There are your **keys.** [What are there? *Keys* are.]
Here is your **pencil.** [What is here? *Pencil* is.]

(4) The subject of a sentence expressing a command or request is always understood to be *you*, although *you* may not appear in the sentence.

EXAMPLE
[You] Listen carefully to his question. [Who is to listen? *You* is understood.]

The subject of a command or request is *you* even when the sentence contains a **noun of direct address,** a word naming the one or ones spoken to.

EXAMPLE
Ellen, [you] please read the part of Juliet.

COMPLEMENTS

8h. A *complement* is a word or group of words that completes the meaning of a verb.

Three kinds of complements are the *subject complement,* the *direct object,* and the *indirect object.*

The Subject Complement

8i. A *subject complement* is a word or word group that completes the meaning of a linking verb and that identifies or modifies the subject.

The two types of subject complements are the *predicate nominative* and the *predicate adjective.*

(1) A *predicate nominative* is a noun or pronoun that follows a linking verb and that renames or identifies the subject of the verb.

EXAMPLES
"The Most Dangerous Game" is an exciting **story.** [The noun *story* identifies the subject *"The Most Dangerous Game."*]
The only people in line were **they.** [The pronoun *they* renames the subject *people.*]
The main characters are **Helen Keller** and **Annie Sullivan.** [The nouns *Helen Keller* and *Annie Sullivan* identify the subject *characters.*]

(2) A *predicate adjective* is an adjective that follows a linking verb and that modifies the subject of the verb.

EXAMPLES
The necklace was **inexpensive.** [The adjective *inexpensive* modifies the subject *necklace.*]
Miss Lottie looked **sad.** [The adjective *sad* modifies the subject *Miss Lottie.*]
The corn tastes **sweet** and **buttery.** [The adjectives *sweet* and *buttery* modify the subject *corn.*]

The Direct Object and the Indirect Object

8j. A *direct object* is a noun or pronoun that receives the action of a verb or that shows the result of the action. It tells *whom* or *what* after a transitive verb.

EXAMPLES
The sniper killed his own **brother.** [killed whom? brother]
Jim sold his gold **watch.** [sold what? watch]
Shakespeare wrote not only great **plays** but also beautiful **sonnets.** [wrote what? plays and sonnets]

8k. An *indirect object* is a noun or pronoun that precedes the direct object and that usually tells *to whom* or *for whom* (or *to what* or *for what*) the action of the verb is done.

EXAMPLES
Sheila read the **children** a story by Truman Capote. [read to whom? children]
Frank gave the **Red Cross** a donation. [gave to what? Red Cross]
She made her **neighbors** and other **friends** fruitcakes for Christmas. [made for whom? neighbors and friends]

NOTE A complement may precede the subject and the verb.

DIRECT OBJECT	What a good **friend** Buddy has!
PREDICATE ADJECTIVE	How **happy** Della and Jim are!

CLASSIFYING SENTENCES ACCORDING TO PURPOSE

8l. Sentences may be classified as *declarative, imperative, interrogative,* or *exclamatory.*

(1) A *declarative sentence* makes a statement. It is followed by a period.

EXAMPLES
One of my favorite stories is "Thank You, M'am."
Jonathan, the CD-ROM you ordered a while back has finally arrived.
It's raining.

(2) An *imperative sentence* makes a request or gives a command. It is usually followed by a period. A very strong command, however, is followed by an exclamation point.

EXAMPLES
Please open your books to page 3. [request]
Be careful of the undertow. [mild command]
Stop! [strong command]

NOTE In a command or a request, the understood subject is *you*.

(3) An *interrogative sentence* asks a question. It is followed by a question mark.

EXAMPLES
Did Friar Laurence's plan fail?
What did Romeo do when he found Juliet lying there so still and pale?

(4) An *exclamatory sentence* expresses strong feeling. It is followed by an exclamation point.

EXAMPLES
What a mess we're in now!
The battery is dead!

CLASSIFYING SENTENCES ACCORDING TO STRUCTURE

8m. **Sentences may be classified as *simple*, *compound*, *complex*, or *compound-complex*.**

(1) A *simple sentence* has one independent clause and no subordinate clauses.

EXAMPLE
Frankenstein and *Dracula* were both written during the nineteenth century.

(2) A *compound sentence* has two or more independent clauses but no subordinate clauses.

EXAMPLES
Rita wanted to see an adventure film, **but** Carlos preferred a comedy. [two independent clauses joined by a comma and the coordinating conjunction *but*]
Harriet Tubman was a leader of the Underground Railroad; she rescued more than three hundred people. [two independent clauses joined by a semicolon]
Romeo killed Tybalt, Juliet's cousin; **as a result,** Romeo was banished from Verona. [two independent clauses joined by a semicolon and the transitional expression *as a result*]

(3) A *complex sentence* has one independent clause and at least one subordinate clause.

EXAMPLES
Romeo let Juliet declare her love for him before he spoke to her. [The independent clause is *Romeo let Juliet declare her love for him.* The subordinate clause is *before he spoke to her.*]
On Shakespeare's gravestone is an inscription that places a curse on anyone who moves his bones. [The independent clause is *on Shakespeare's gravestone is an inscription.* The subordinate clauses are *that places a curse on anyone* and *who moves his bones.*]

(4) A *compound-complex sentence* contains two or more independent clauses and at least one subordinate clause.

EXAMPLE
William Golding received the Nobel Prize in 1983; his best-known novel is *Lord of the Flies,* which he published in 1954. [The independent clauses are *William Golding received the Nobel Prize in 1983* and *his best-known novel is* Lord of the Flies. The subordinate clause is *which he published in 1954.*]

  For more on clauses, see Part 7: Clauses.

Varying Sentence Structure

Paragraphs in which all the sentences have the same structure can make for monotonous reading. To help keep your readers interested, evaluate your writing to see whether you've used a variety of sentence structures. If you have not, use revising techniques—add, cut, replace, and reorder—to vary the structure of your sentences.

Try It Out

The following paragraph is composed of simple sentences. Revise the paragraph, using a variety of sentence structures.

   [1] In "Independence," Cathy and Sharon did not want to stay home during the summer. [2] They wanted to do something and to go somewhere. [3] Anywhere would do. [4] The sisters wanted a taste of independence. [5] Cathy found an advertisement. [6] It triggered their imaginations. [7] They applied for the job in the ad. [8] Both of them got it. [9] However, working as maids did not meet their expectations. [10] A few weeks later, they called their parents for a ride home.

9 WRITING COMPLETE SENTENCES

SENTENCE FRAGMENTS

9a. Avoid using a *sentence fragment*— a part of a sentence that has been punctuated as if it were a complete sentence.

You may correct a sentence fragment in one of two ways.

1. Add words that will make the thought complete.

FRAGMENT Shortly after his birth, was baptized in a small church in Stratford. [The verb *was* has no subject. Who was baptized?]

SENTENCE Shortly after his birth, **Shakespeare was baptized** in a small church in Stratford.

FRAGMENT Odysseus a great hero of the Greeks. [The verb is missing. What about Odysseus?]

SENTENCE Odysseus **became** a great hero of the Greeks.

FRAGMENT For the well-known balcony scene in *Romeo and Juliet*. [The subject and the verb are missing. What about the balcony scene?]

SENTENCE **The actors are preparing** for the well-known balcony scene in *Romeo and Juliet*.

2. Attach the fragment to the sentence that comes before or after it.

FRAGMENT One of my favorite stories by Edgar Allan Poe is "X-ing a Paragrab." A comic tale of a feud between two newspaper editors.

SENTENCE One of my favorite stories by Edgar Allan Poe is "X-ing a Paragrab," **a comic tale of a feud between two newspaper editors.** [appositive phrase]

FRAGMENT When she takes off her coat. Mme. Loisel discovers that she is no longer wearing the necklace.

SENTENCE **When she takes off her coat,** Mme. Loisel discovers that she is no longer wearing the necklace. [subordinate clause]

FRAGMENT Odysseus figured out a way for his men and him. To escape from the Cyclops.

SENTENCE Odysseus figured out a way for his men and him **to escape from the Cyclops.** [infinitive phrase]

☞ For more information about sentence fragments, see page 1010.

RUN-ON SENTENCES

9b. Avoid using a *run-on sentence*—two or more complete sentences that run together as if they were one complete sentence.

There are two kinds of run-on sentences.

● A *fused sentence* has no punctuation between the complete sentences.
● A *comma splice* has only a comma between the complete sentences.

FUSED SENTENCE Della sold her hair to buy Jim a chain for his watch Jim sold his watch to buy Della combs for her hair.

COMMA SPLICE Della sold her hair to buy Jim a chain for his watch, Jim sold his watch to buy Della combs for her hair.

You may correct a run-on sentence in one of five ways.

1. Make two sentences.

REVISED Della sold her hair to buy Jim a chain for his watch. Jim sold his watch to buy Della combs for her hair.

2. Use a comma and a *coordinating conjunction*— *and, but, or, yet, for, so,* or *nor.*

REVISED Della sold her hair to buy Jim a chain for his watch, **and** Jim sold his watch to buy Della combs for her hair.

3. Use a semicolon.

REVISED Della sold her hair to buy Jim a chain for his watch; Jim sold his watch to buy Della combs for her hair.

4. Use a semicolon and a *conjunctive adverb,* such as *therefore, instead, meanwhile, still, also,* or *however.* Follow a conjunctive adverb with a comma.

REVISED   Della sold her hair to buy Jim a chain for his watch**; however,** Jim sold his watch to buy Della combs for her hair.

5. Change one of the complete thoughts into a subordinate clause.

REVISED   Della sold her hair to buy Jim a chain for his watch **while** Jim sold his watch to buy Della combs for her hair.

 For more information about combining sentences, see rules 10a–10e on pages 1015–1016.

 **COMPUTER NOTE**   Style-checking software can help you evaluate your writing for the use of clear, complete sentences. Many such programs can identify and highlight sentence fragments. You can also use the "Search" command offered by computer programs to identify sentences in which you've used a comma and a coordinating conjunction—one search for each different conjunction and the comma in front of it. These searches can help you check to make sure that the ideas you've combined in a compound sentence are complete and are closely related and equally important.

 **Identifying Run-on Sentences**

One way to spot run-on sentences is to read your writing aloud. A natural, distinct pause in your speech often means that you need to separate sentences in some way. You can also check for run-ons by identifying subjects and verbs. Checking for clauses will help you find where one complete thought ends and another begins.

RUN-ON   The family thought that Doodle would die they built him a coffin.

REVISED   **Because** the family thought that Doodle would die**,** they built him a coffin.

REVISED   The family thought that Doodle would die**, so** they built him a coffin.

REVISED   The family thought that Doodle would die**; consequently,** they built him a coffin.

Try It Out

Revise each of the following run-on sentences.

1. Doodle and his brother had an active fantasy world, they created stories and imaginary plans.
2. Doodle was afraid of being left behind, he cried when his brother started to leave.
3. Brother taught Doodle to walk Brother was ashamed of Doodle.
4. Doodle didn't think that he could walk after much help and practice, he did.
5. He could walk perhaps he could run.

WRITING EFFECTIVE SENTENCES

10

SENTENCE COMBINING

10a. Combine related sentences by taking a key word (or by using another form of the word) from one sentence and inserting it into another.

ORIGINAL   Edgar Allan Poe led a short life. His life was tragic.

COMBINED   Edgar Allan Poe led a short, **tragic** life.

ORIGINAL   Edgar Allan Poe wrote strange stories. He wrote stories of suspense.

COMBINED   Edgar Allan Poe wrote strange, **suspenseful** stories.

 When you change the form of a key word, you often need to add an ending that makes the word an adjective or an adverb. Usually this ending is *–ed, –ing,* or *–ly.*

10b. Combine related sentences by taking (or creating) a phrase from one sentence and inserting it into another.

ORIGINAL *A Fire in My Hands* is a collection of poems. The poems were written by Gary Soto.

COMBINED *A Fire in My Hands* is a collection of poems **by Gary Soto.** [prepositional phrase]

ORIGINAL Romeo kills Tybalt. Tybalt is Juliet's cousin.

COMBINED Romeo kills Tybalt, **Juliet's cousin.** [appositive phrase]

10c. Combine related sentences by using a coordinating conjunction (*and, but, or,* or *nor*) to make a compound subject, a compound verb, or both.

ORIGINAL After lunch Doodle went to Horsehead Landing. His brother went, too.

COMBINED After lunch **Doodle and** his **brother** went to Horsehead Landing. [compound subject]

ORIGINAL Ernesto Galarza's family immigrated to the United States. They eventually settled in Sacramento, California.

COMBINED Ernesto Galarza's family **immigrated** to the United States **and** eventually **settled** in Sacramento, California. [compound verb]

Using Compound Subjects and Compound Verbs

When you combine sentences by using compound subjects and compound verbs, make sure that your new subjects and verbs agree in number.

ORIGINAL Della has little money. Jim also doesn't have much.

COMBINED **Della and Jim have** little money. [The compound subject *Della and Jim* takes the plural verb *have.*]

Try It Out ✎

Combine each of the following pairs of sentences into one sentence that has a compound subject or a compound verb.

1. Mrs. Johnson's husband moved to Oklahoma. He studied religion.
2. The cotton gin would not hire her. Neither would the lumber mill.
3. She didn't want to become a servant. She saw another possibility.
4. The cotton gin workers walked to her stand and bought lunch. The lumber workers also walked to her stand and bought lunch there.
5. In time, syrup was sold at the store. Canned goods were, too.

10d. Combine related sentences by creating a compound sentence.

You can form a compound sentence by linking two or more independent clauses with a comma and a coordinating conjunction, a semicolon, or a semicolon and a conjunctive adverb.

ORIGINAL Buddy makes his friend a kite. She makes him one, too.

COMBINED Buddy makes his friend a kite**, and** she makes him one, too. [comma and coordinating conjunction]

COMBINED Buddy makes his friend a kite**;** she makes him one, too. [semicolon]

COMBINED Buddy makes his friend a kite**; meanwhile,** she makes him one, too. [semicolon and conjunctive adverb]

10e. Combine related sentences by creating a complex sentence.

You can form a complex sentence by joining one independent clause with one or more subordinate clauses (adjective clause, adverb clause, or noun clause).

ORIGINAL Gwendolyn Brooks often writes about Chicago. She has won a Pulitzer Prize for her poetry.

COMBINED Gwendolyn Brooks, **who has won a Pulitzer Prize for her poetry,** often writes about Chicago. [adjective clause]

ORIGINAL Zaroff turned on the light. He saw Rainsford.

COMBINED **When Zaroff turned on the light,** he saw Rainsford. [adverb clause]

ORIGINAL The snake in "Poison" is just an illusion on Harry's part. Many readers think this.

COMBINED Many readers think **that the snake in "Poison" is just an illusion on Harry's part.** [noun clause]

For more information about compound and complex sentences, see page 1013.

Varying Sentence Structures

 In your writing, try to use a mix of simple, compound, complex, and compound-complex sentences.

EXAMPLE

As the music and the thump of the drums grew louder, the people lined up along the street. [complex] Finally, with a blast of brass, the high school band rounded the corner. [simple] First came the drum major; setting the tempo with her baton, she proudly raised her feet as high as possible. [compound] Behind her, leading the parade of colorful floats, the musicians marched in their bright purple-and-red jackets. [simple sentence]

Try It Out

The following paragraph is composed of simple sentences. Revise the paragraph, using varied sentence structures.

[1] The boy had known hunger before. [2] This hunger was different. [3] It could not be satisfied by just a few bites. [4] It gnawed at his insides and made him weak. [5] His mother got a job. [6] She sent him to the store for groceries. [7] Some boys took his money. [8] She gave him more money and sent him again. [9] Again, the boys took his money. [10] His mother gave him a stick this time and told him to fight.

IMPROVING SENTENCE STYLE

10f. Use the same grammatical form (*parallel structure*) to express equal ideas.

NOT PARALLEL	Buddy and she liked baking fruit-cakes and to fly kites. [gerund phrase paired with infinitive phrase]
PARALLEL	Buddy and she liked **baking fruitcakes** and **flying kites**. [gerund phrase paired with gerund phrase]
PARALLEL	Buddy and she liked **to bake fruitcakes** and **to fly kites**. [infinitive phrase paired with infinitive phrase]

NOT PARALLEL	Harry received help from not only Timber but also from Ganderbai. [noun paired with prepositional phrase]
PARALLEL	Harry received help from not only **Timber** but also **Ganderbai**. [noun paired with noun]
PARALLEL	Harry received help not only **from Timber** but also **from Ganderbai**. [prepositional phrase paired with prepositional phrase]

10g. Avoid using stringy sentences—sentences that have too many independent clauses strung together with coordinating conjunctions like *and* or *but*.

You may revise a stringy sentence in one of two ways.

1. Break the sentence into two or more sentences.
2. Turn some of the independent clauses into subordinate clauses or into phrases.

STRINGY	The fire alarm rang, and everyone started to file out of school, but then our principal came down the hall, and he said that the bell was a mistake, and we went back to our classes.
REVISED	The fire alarm bell rang, and everyone started to file out of school. Then our principal came down the hall to say that the bell was a mistake. We went back to our classes
REVISED	When the fire alarm bell rang, everyone started to file out of school. Then our principal came down the hall. He said that the bell was a mistake, and we went back to our classes.

 For more information about phrases, see Part 6: Phrases. For more about clauses, see Part 7: Clauses.

COMPUTER NOTE Whenever you revise your writing on a computer, you can use functions such as "Copy," "Cut," and "Move" to experiment with your sentences. Try a variety of sentence beginnings and structures. Then, decide which ones work best with the other sentences in a particular paragraph.

10h. Avoid using unnecessary words.

Here are three tips for avoiding wordiness.

1. Don't use more words than you need to use.
2. Don't use difficult words where simple ones will do.
3. Don't repeat yourself unless it's absolutely necessary.

WORDY Fortunato is a wine connoisseur who has much knowledge of and great appreciation for fine wines.

REVISED Fortunato is a connoisseur of fine wines.

WORDY In the event that they were able to find the missing necklace belonging to Mme. Forestier by the last day of the month of February, the Loisels could return the other necklace.

REVISED If they could find Mme. Forestier's necklace by the end of February, the Loisels could return the other necklace.

10i. Use a variety of sentence beginnings.

The basic structure of an English sentence is a subject followed by a verb. The following examples show how you can revise sentences to avoid beginning with the subject every time. Notice that a comma follows the introductory word, phrase, or clause in each revision.

SUBJECT FIRST	Della excitedly opened her present.
ADVERB FIRST	**Excitedly,** Della opened her present.
SUBJECT FIRST	You must study to make good grades.
INFINITIVE PHRASE FIRST	**To make good grades,** you must study.
SUBJECT FIRST	Romeo fell in love with Juliet as soon as he saw her.
ADVERB CLAUSE FIRST	**As soon as Romeo saw Juliet,** he fell in love with her.

11 CAPITALIZATION

11a. Capitalize the first word in every sentence.

EXAMPLES
The two boys in "The Talk" discuss their plans.
Stop!

(1) Capitalize the first word of a direct quotation.

EXAMPLE
Maria asked me, "Have you written your report on Gary Soto?"

(2) Traditionally, the first word of a line of poetry is capitalized.

EXAMPLES
Two roads diverged in a wood, and I—
I took the one less traveled by,
And that has made all the difference.
                    —Robert Frost, "The Road Not Taken"

NOTE Some writers do not follow these practices. When you are quoting, use capital letters exactly as they are used in the source of the quotation.

 For more information about using capital letters in quotations, see pages 1026–1027.

11b. Capitalize the first word both in the salutation and in the closing of a letter.

EXAMPLES
To Whom It May Concern:
Dear Ann,   Dear Sir:
Sincerely,   Yours truly,

11c. Capitalize the pronoun *I* and the interjection *O*.

EXAMPLES
Mom says that **I** can go this weekend.
Who says "Romeo can, / Though heaven cannot.
    O Romeo, Romeo"?

11d. Capitalize proper nouns and proper adjectives.

A **common noun** is a general name for a person, a place, a thing, or an idea. A **proper noun** names a particular person, place, thing, or idea. A **proper adjective** is formed from a proper noun.

Proper nouns and proper adjectives are always capitalized. Common nouns are not capitalized unless they begin a sentence, begin a direct quotation, or are part of a title.

COMMON NOUNS	PROPER NOUNS	PROPER ADJECTIVES
poet	Homer	Homeric simile
planet	Mars	Martian landscape

In proper nouns that have more than one word, do *not* capitalize articles (*a, an, the*), prepositions of fewer than five letters (such as *at, for,* and *with*), coordinating conjunctions (*and, but, for, nor, or, so, yet*), or the sign of the infinitive (*to*) unless they are the first word of the proper noun.

EXAMPLES
American Society **f**or **t**he Prevention **o**f Cruelty **t**o Animals
National Campers **a**nd Hikers Association
"Writing **a** Paragraph **t**o Inform"

(1) Capitalize the names of persons and animals.

PERSONS Sandra Cisneros Langston Hughes
ANIMALS Old Yeller Brer Rabbit

(2) Capitalize geographical names.

TYPE OF NAME	EXAMPLES	
Towns and Cities	San Francisco	St. Charles
Counties, Townships, and Parishes	Hayes Township Union Parish	Kane County Manhattan
States and Territories	Florida Guam	North Carolina Northwest Territory
Countries	Canada	United States of America
Continents	Africa	North America
Islands	Long Island	Isle of Palms
Mountains	Rocky Mountains	Mount McKinley
Other Land Forms and Features	Cape Hatteras Kalahari Desert	Niagara Falls Mammoth Cave
Bodies of Water	Pacific Ocean Cross Creek	Gulf of Mexico Blue Springs
Parks	Yellowstone National Park Cleburne State Recreation Area	
Regions	the North New England	the Middle West the Great Plains
Roads, Streets, and Highways	Route 66 Gibbs Drive	Pennsylvania Turnpike Thirty-first Street

TIPS FOR SPELLING

For names with more than one word, capitalization may vary. Always check the spelling of such a name with the person whose name it is, or look in a reference source.

EXAMPLES
Kees van Dongen Henry Van Dyke

Abbreviations such as *Ms., Mr., Dr.,* and *Gen.* should always be capitalized.

EXAMPLES
Mr. James Thurber Dr. Mary McLeod Bethune

Capitalize the abbreviations *Jr.* and *Sr.* after a name, and set them off with commas.

EXAMPLE
In 1975, Gen. Daniel James, Jr., became the first African American four-star general in the U.S. Air Force.

NOTE Words such as *north, west,* and *southeast* are not capitalized when they indicate direction.

EXAMPLES
north of town
traveling southeast

NOTE In a hyphenated number, the second word begins with a small letter.

EXAMPLE
Thirty-first Street

NOTE Words like *city, river, street,* and *park* are capitalized only when they are part of a name.

EXAMPLES
go to the park
go to Central Park

across the river
across the Pecos River

(3) Capitalize the names of organizations, teams, business firms, institutions, buildings and other structures, and government bodies.

TYPE OF NAME	EXAMPLES
Organizations	United Nations National Basketball Association
Teams	Tampa Bay Buccaneers Minnesota Twins
Business Firms	Quaker Oats Company Aluminum Company of America
Institutions	United States Naval Academy Bethune-Cookman College
Buildings and Other Structures	Apollo Theater Taj Mahal Golden Gate Bridge
Government Bodies	Federal Bureau of Investigation House of Representatives

NOTE Capitalize words such as *democratic* or *republican* only when they refer to a specific political party.

EXAMPLES
The new leaders promised **d**emocratic reforms.
The **D**emocratic candidates for mayor held a rally.

The word *party* in the name of a political party may be capitalized or not.

EXAMPLE
Federalist **P**arty *or* **p**arty

(4) Capitalize the names of historical events and periods, special events, holidays, and other calendar items.

TYPE OF NAME	EXAMPLES
Historical Events and Periods	French Revolution Middle Ages Boston Tea Party Mesozoic Era
Special Events	Interscholastic Debate Tournament Kansas State Fair
Holidays and Calendar Items	Labor Day Saturday December Fourth of July National Book Week

NOTE Do not capitalize the name of a season unless it is being personified or used in the name of a special event.

EXAMPLES
I'm on the committee for the **W**inter Carnival.
Soon **A**utumn will begin painting the leaves in bright colors.

(5) Capitalize the names of ships, trains, aircraft, spacecraft, monuments, awards, planets, and other particular places, things, or events.

TYPE OF NAME	EXAMPLES
Ships and Trains	*Mayflower* *Silver Meteor*
Aircraft and Spacecraft	*Spirit of St. Louis* Lockheed **C-5A G**alaxy *Pioneer 10* Hubble Space Telescope
Monuments and Memorials	Washington Monument Statue of Liberty Vietnam Veterans Memorial
Awards	Pulitzer Prize Congressional Medal of Honor Stanley Cup Key Club Achievement Award
Planets, Stars, and Constellations	Mercury Dog Star Ursa Major Pluto Big Dipper Rigel

NOTE The word *earth* is not capitalized unless it is used along with the names of other heavenly bodies that are capitalized. The words *sun* and *moon* are not capitalized.

EXAMPLES
The **m**oon is a satellite of the **e**arth.
Venus is closer to Earth than Mars is.

(6) Capitalize the names of nationalities, races, and peoples.

EXAMPLES
Greek   African Americans   Hispanic   Cherokee

(7) Capitalize the brand names of business products but not the common nouns that follow the names.

EXAMPLES
Chevrolet van   Teflon pan

11e. Do *not* capitalize the names of school subjects, except for languages or course names followed by a number.

EXAMPLES
algebra   English   Typing I

11f. Capitalize titles.

(1) Capitalize the title of a person when it comes before the person's name.

EXAMPLES
President Clinton   Mr. Vonnegut

Usually, do not capitalize a title that is used alone or following a person's name, especially if the title is preceded by *a* or *the*.

EXAMPLE
Cleopatra reigned as the queen of Egypt between 51 and 30 B.C.

When a title is used alone in direct address, it is usually capitalized.

EXAMPLE
I think, Senator, that the issue is critical.

(2) Capitalize words showing family relationship when used with a person's name but *not* when preceded by a possessive.

EXAMPLES
Aunt Clara   my mother
Harold's grandmother

(3) Capitalize the first and last words and all important words in titles of books, periodicals, poems, stories, essays, speeches, plays, historical documents, movies, radio and television programs, works of art, musical compositions, and cartoons.

TYPE OF TITLE	EXAMPLES
Books	*The Pearl* *I Know Why the Caged Bird Sings*
Periodicals	*The Atlantic Monthly* *Field and Stream*
Poems	"The Road Not Taken" "The Girl Who Loved the Sky"
Stories	"The Cask of Amontillado" "The Most Dangerous Game"
Essays and Speeches	"The Death of a Tree" "Work and What It's Worth"
Plays	*The Miracle Worker* *The Phantom of the Opera*
Historical Documents	Declaration of Independence Emancipation Proclamation
Movies	*Dances with Wolves* *Stand and Deliver*
Radio and Television Programs	*All Things Considered* *Nova* *Star Trek: The Next Generation*
Works of Art	*American Gothic* *The Thinker*
Musical Compositions	"The Tennessee Waltz" "The Flight of the Bumblebee"
Cartoons	*Calvin and Hobbes* *The Neighborhood*

NOTE Unimportant words in a title are articles (*a, an, the*), prepositions of fewer than five letters (such as *for* and *from*), and coordinating conjunctions (*and, but, so, nor, or, yet, for*).

NOTE The words *a, an,* and *the* written before a title are capitalized only when they are part of the official title. The official title of a book is found on the title page. The official title of a newspaper or a periodical is found on the masthead, which is usually on the editorial page.

EXAMPLES
The Autobiography of
    Malcolm X
the *Austin American-Statesman*
A Tale of Two Cities

☞ For information about when to use italics for titles, see page 1026. For information about when to use quotation marks for titles, see page 1028.

(4) Capitalize the names of religions and their followers, holy days and celebrations, holy writings, and specific deities.

TYPE OF NAME	EXAMPLES	
Religions and Followers	Judaism Taoism	Quaker Muslim
Holy Days and Celebrations	Passover Ramadan	Good Friday Lent
Holy Writings	Bible Koran	Upanishads Genesis
Specific Deities	Allah Brahma Zeus	

COMPUTER NOTE   Some software programs can identify errors in capitalization. However, even the most complete programs may not include all the terms you need. In addition, the program may be based on rules that vary from the ones you've been given to follow. If your software allows it, modify the capitalization of words already in the program, and add terms that you use frequently.

12 PUNCTUATION

END MARKS

Sentences

End marks—periods, question marks, and exclamation points—are used to indicate the purpose of a sentence.

 For a discussion of how sentences are classified according to purpose, see pages 1012–1013. For information on using quotation marks with end marks, see page 1027.

12a. A statement (or declarative sentence) is followed by a period.

EXAMPLE
Dorothy M. Johnson wrote "A Man Called Horse."

12b. A question (or interrogative sentence) is followed by a question mark.

EXAMPLE
Did Penelope recognize Odysseus?

 NOTE Be sure to distinguish between a declarative sentence that contains an indirect question and an interrogative sentence, which asks a direct question.

INDIRECT QUESTION	He asked me **what was worrying her.** [declarative]
DIRECT QUESTION	What is worrying her? [interrogative]

A direct question may have the same word order as a declarative sentence. Since it *is* a question, however, it is followed by a question mark.

EXAMPLES
A cat can see color?   The plane was late?

12c. An exclamation is followed by an exclamation point.

EXAMPLE
Wow! What a great play *The Miracle Worker* is!

12d. A command or request (or imperative sentence) is followed by either a period or an exclamation point.

A mild command or an imperative sentence that makes a request is followed by a period. An imperative sentence that shows strong feeling is followed by an exclamation point.

EXAMPLES
Please be quiet. [request]
Turn off your radio. [mild command]
Be quiet! [strong command]

Sometimes a command or request is stated in the form of a question. Because of its purpose, however, the sentence is really an imperative sentence and should be followed by a period or an exclamation point.

EXAMPLES
Could you please send me twenty-five copies.
Will you stop that!

Abbreviations

12e. An abbreviation is usually followed by a period.

TYPES OF ABBREVIATIONS	EXAMPLES
Personal Names	A. E. Housman Eugenia W. Collier
Organizations and Companies	Assn.　Co.　Inc. Ltd.　Corp.
Titles Used with Names	Mr.　Mrs.　Jr.　Dr.
Times of Day	A.M.　P.M.
Years	B.C. (written after the date) A.D. (written before the date)
Addresses	Ave.　St.　Blvd.　Pkwy.
States	Calif.　Mass.　Tex.　N. Dak.

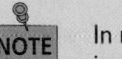

NOTE Two-letter state abbreviations without periods are used only when the ZIP Code is included. Each letter of the abbreviation is capitalized, and no comma separates the abbreviation from the ZIP Code.

EXAMPLE

Cincinnati, OH 45233

NOTE In most cases, an abbreviation is capitalized only if the words it stands for are capitalized. If you are unsure whether to capitalize an abbreviation or to use periods with it, look in a recent dictionary.

If a statement ends with an abbreviation, do not use an additional period as an end mark. However, do add a question mark or an exclamation point if the sentence should have one.

EXAMPLES

Mrs. Tavares will be arriving at 3 P.M.

Can you go to meet her at 3 P.M.?

Abbreviations for government agencies and international organizations and some other frequently used abbreviations are written without periods. Abbreviations for most units of measurement are commonly written without periods, especially in science books.

EXAMPLES

CD, VCR, FM, IRS, TV, UFO

cm, kg, lb, ml

NOTE Include a period with the abbreviation for *inch* (*in.*) so that it will not be confused with *in*, the word.

COMMAS

12f. Use commas to separate items in a series.

EXAMPLES

Odysseus slays Antinous, Eurymachus, and Penelope's other suitors.

We can meet before school, at lunch, or after school.

(1) If all items in a series are joined by *and* or *or*, do not use commas to separate them.

EXAMPLE

The names of the characters in "Poison" are Harry **and** Timber **and** Dr. Ganderbai.

Some words—such as *bread and butter, rod and reel,* and *law and order*—are used in pairs and may be considered one item in a series.

EXAMPLE

My favorite breakfast is milk, **biscuits and gravy,** and fruit.

(2) Independent clauses in a series are generally separated by semicolons. Short independent clauses, however, may be separated by commas.

EXAMPLE

The sky darkened, branches swayed, the cold deepened, and snow fell.

12g. Use commas to separate two or more adjectives preceding a noun.

EXAMPLE

Montresor leads Fortunato to the dark, cold vaults below the palazzo.

When the last adjective in a series is thought of as part of the noun, the comma before the adjective is omitted.

EXAMPLE

The Loisels bought an expensive **diamond necklace.**

12h. Use commas before *and, but, or, nor, for, so,* and *yet* when they join independent clauses.

EXAMPLE
General Zaroff was confident he would kill Rainsford, **but** the hunt did not go as the general had planned.

12i. Use commas to set off nonessential clauses and nonessential participial phrases.

A *nonessential* (or *nonrestrictive*) clause or participial phrase adds information that is not needed to understand the main idea in the sentence.

| NONESSENTIAL CLAUSE | Langston Hughes, **who was a key figure in the Harlem Renaissance,** often used the rhythms of jazz and blues in his poetry. |

Omitting the adjective clause in this example would not change the main idea of the sentence: *Langston Hughes often used the rhythms of jazz and blues in his poetry.*

An *essential* (or *restrictive*) clause or phrase provides information that is needed to understand the sentence, and commas are *not* used.

| ESSENTIAL PHRASE | Actors **missing more than two rehearsals** will be replaced. |

Omitting the participial phrase above would affect the meaning of the sentence, because the phrase tells *which actors.*

12j. Use commas after certain introductory elements.

(1) Use a comma after a word such as *next, yes,* or *no* as well as after an introductory interjection such as *why, well,* or *oops.*

EXAMPLES
Yes, I've read "Salvador Late or Early."
Ah, there's nothing like cold water on a hot day!

(2) Use a comma after an introductory participial phrase.

EXAMPLE
Having passed Penelope's last test, Odysseus reclaims his home and his kingdom.

(3) Use a comma after the last of two or more introductory prepositional phrases.

EXAMPLE
Of all of his novels, Charles Dickens liked *David Copperfield* best.

(4) Use a comma after an introductory adverb clause.

EXAMPLE
Until he meets Juliet, Romeo is madly in love with Rosaline.

12k. Use commas to set off elements that interrupt a sentence.

EXAMPLES
Dr. Ganderbai, **in fact,** worked very hard.
The storm, **the worst this winter,** raged for days.

(1) Appositives and appositive phrases are usually set off by commas.

EXAMPLE
My sister gave me a copy of *Gorilla, My Love,* **Toni Cade Bambara's first collection of stories.**

NOTE An appositive that tells which one(s) of two or more is a *restrictive appositive* and should not be set off by commas.

EXAMPLE
The television special is about Graham Greene the British writer, not Graham Greene the Canadian actor.

(2) Words used in direct address are set off by commas.

EXAMPLE
Linda, please read the part of Juliet.

(3) Parenthetical expressions are set off by commas.

Parenthetical expressions are side remarks that add minor information or that relate ideas to each other.

EXAMPLE
He was not angry and, **on the contrary,** was actually glad that you told him about the error.

A contrasting expression introduced by *not* or *yet* is parenthetical and is set off by commas.

EXAMPLE
It is the spirit of the giver, **not the cost of the gift,** that counts.

12l. Use commas in certain conventional situations.

(1) Use a comma to separate items in dates and in addresses (except between a two-letter state abbreviation and a ZIP Code).

EXAMPLES
My family moved to Oakland, California, on Wednesday, December 5, 1990.
On December 5, 1990, our address became 25 Peralta Road, Oakland, CA 94611.

(2) Use a comma after the salutation of a friendly letter and after the closing of any letter.

EXAMPLES
Dear Ms. Chen,   Yours truly,

(3) Use a comma to set off an abbreviation such as *Jr.*, *Sr.*, or *M.D.*, including after the abbreviation unless it ends the sentence.

EXAMPLE
Dr. Martin Luther King, Jr., delivered that speech.

SEMICOLONS

12m. Use a semicolon between independent clauses if they are not joined by *and, but, or, nor, for, so,* or *yet.*

EXAMPLE
I enjoyed reading *The Miracle Worker;* it tells what Helen Keller's youth was like.

12n. Use a semicolon between independent clauses joined by a conjunctive adverb—such as *however, therefore,* and *furthermore*—or a transitional expression—such as *for instance, in fact,* and *that is.*

EXAMPLES
Sherlock Holmes is a fictional character; **however,** many people are convinced that he actually did exist.
My parents are strict; **for example,** I can watch TV only on weekends.

Notice in the two examples above that a comma always follows a conjunctive adverb or a transitional expression that joins independent clauses.

12o. Use a semicolon (rather than a comma) before a coordinating conjunction to join independent clauses that contain commas.

EXAMPLE
Doodle's mother, father, and brother went back inside the house; **but** Doodle remained outside to bury the scarlet ibis.

12p. Use a semicolon between items in a series if the items contain commas.

EXAMPLE
I have postcards from Paris, France; Rome, Italy; Lisbon, Portugal; and London, England.

COLONS

12q. Use a colon to mean "note what follows."

(1) In some cases a colon is used before a list of items, especially after the expressions *the following* and *as follows.*

EXAMPLE
The reading list includes the following titles: "The Gift," "The Sniper," and "The Necklace."

Do not use a colon before a list that follows a verb or a preposition.

INCORRECT   The list of literary terms includes: *conflict, climax,* and *resolution.*
CORRECT   The list of literary terms includes *conflict, climax,* and *resolution.*

INCORRECT   In the past five years, my family has lived in: Texas, Oregon, Ohio, and Florida.
CORRECT   In the past five years, my family has lived in Texas, Oregon, Ohio, and Florida.

(2) Use a colon before a long, formal statement or a long quotation.

EXAMPLE
O. Henry had this to say about Della and Jim: "But in a last word to the wise of these days, let it be said that of all who give gifts, these two were the wisest."

12r. Use a colon in certain conventional situations.

(1) Use a colon between the hour and the minute.

EXAMPLES
9:30 P.M.   8:00 A.M.

(2) Use a colon after the salutation of a business letter.

EXAMPLES
Dear Ms. González: Dear Sir or Madam:
To Whom It May Concern:

(3) Use a colon between chapter and verse in referring to passages from the Bible.

EXAMPLES
Esther 3:5   Exodus 1:6–14

(4) Use a colon between a title and a subtitle.

EXAMPLE
"Shakespeare and His Theater: A Perfect Match"

13 PUNCTUATION

ITALICS

When writing or typing, indicate italics by underlining. If your composition were to be printed, the typesetter would set the underlined words in italics. For example, if you typed the sentence

Alice Walker wrote The Color Purple.

it would be printed like this:

Alice Walker wrote *The Color Purple.*

COMPUTER NOTE If you use a computer, you can probably set words in italics yourself. Most word-processing software and many printers are capable of producing italic type.

13a. **Use underlining (italics) for titles of books, plays, films, periodicals, works of art, recordings, long musical works, television series, trains, ships, aircraft, and spacecraft.**

TYPE OF TITLE	EXAMPLES	
Books	*Black Boy*	*Odyssey*
Plays	*The Miracle Worker* *Romeo and Juliet*	
Films	*The Lion King*	*Jurassic Park*
Periodicals	*Seventeen*	*USA Today*

NOTE The articles *a, an,* and *the* written before a title are italicized only when they are part of the official title. The official title of a book appears on the title page. The official title of a newspaper or periodical appears on the masthead, which is usually found on the editorial page.

EXAMPLE
We subscribe to ***The*** *Wall Street Journal* and **the** *Austin American-Statesman.*

TYPE OF TITLE	EXAMPLES
Works of Art	*Death of Cleopatra* *Mona Lisa*
Recordings	*Music Box* *Two Worlds, One Heart*
Long Musical Works	*The Magic Flute* *Rhapsody in Blue*
Television Series	*60 Minutes* *The Simpsons*
Trains and Ships	*Orient Express* *U.S.S. Nimitz*
Aircraft and Spacecraft	*Spirit of St. Louis* *Apollo 13*

 For examples of titles that should be placed in quotation marks rather than be italicized, see page 1028.

13b. **Use underlining (italics) for words, letters, and figures referred to as such and for foreign words not yet a part of English vocabulary.**

EXAMPLES
The word *excellent* has two *l*'s.
The *3* on that license plate looks like an *8.*
The *corrido* is a fast-paced ballad.

QUOTATION MARKS

13c. **Use quotation marks to enclose a *direct quotation*—a person's exact words.**

EXAMPLES
She asked, "How much does the necklace cost?"
"The Loisels pay thirty-six thousand francs," answered Lamont.

Do not use quotation marks for indirect quotations.

DIRECT QUOTATION	Stephanie said, "I'm going to plant some marigolds." [the speaker's exact words]
INDIRECT QUOTATION	Stephanie said that she was going to plant some marigolds. [not the speaker's exact words]

An interrupting expression is not a part of a quotation and should never be inside quotation marks.

EXAMPLE

"Let's fly our kites," Jennifer suggested, "before the breeze dies down."

When two or more sentences by the same speaker are quoted together, use one set of quotation marks.

EXAMPLE

Brennan said, "I'm making a fruitcake. Do you like fruitcake?"

 **A direct quotation begins with a capital letter.**

EXAMPLES

Mrs. Perez asked, "**W**ho is Mercutio?"
Charles answered, "**O**ne of Romeo's friends."
[Although this quotation is not a sentence, it is Charles's complete remark.]

 If a direct quotation is obviously a fragment of the original quotation, it should begin with a lowercase letter.

EXAMPLE

To Romeo, Juliet is like "**a** wingèd messenger of heaven."

 When a quoted sentence is divided into two parts by an interrupting expression, the second part begins with a lowercase letter.

EXAMPLE

"I wish," she said, "**t**hat we went to the same school."

If the second part of a quotation is a new sentence, a period (not a comma) follows the interrupting expression, and the second part begins with a capital letter.

EXAMPLE

"I requested an interview," the reporter said**.** "**S**he told me she was too busy."

 When used with quotation marks, other marks of punctuation are placed according to the following rules.

(1) A comma or a period is always placed inside the closing quotation marks.

EXAMPLES

"I haven't seen the film version of *Romeo and Juliet***,**" remarked Jeannette, "but I understand it's excellent**.**"

(2) A semicolon or a colon is always placed outside the closing quotation marks.

EXAMPLES

My mom's favorite poem is Maya Angelou's "Woman Work"**;** in fact, I can recite it.
Find examples of the following figures of speech in "I Wandered Lonely as a Cloud"**:** simile, personification, and alliteration.

(3) A question mark or an exclamation point is placed inside the closing quotation marks if the quotation is a question or an exclamation; otherwise, it is placed outside.

EXAMPLES

"Where does Romeo first meet Juliet**?**" asked Mr. Suarez.
"Help me, please**!**" she exclaimed.
Which of the characters says "Parting is such sweet sorrow"**?**
It is *not* an insult to be called a "bookworm"**!**

 When you write dialogue (a conversation), begin a new paragraph every time the speaker changes.

EXAMPLE

The gait of my friend was unsteady, and the bells upon his cap jingled as he strode.
"The pipe," said he.
"It is farther on," said I; "but observe the white web-work which gleams from these cavern walls."
—Edgar Allan Poe, "The Cask of Amontillado"

 When a quoted passage consists of more than one paragraph, put quotation marks at the beginning of each paragraph and at the end of only the last paragraph.

EXAMPLE

"At nine o'clock this morning," read the news story, "someone entered the Millford Bank by the back entrance, broke through two thick steel doors guarding the bank's vault, and escaped with sixteen bars of gold.

"No arrests have yet been made, but state and local police are confident the case will be solved within a few days.

"FBI agents are due to arrive on the scene later today."

 Use single quotation marks to enclose a quotation within a quotation.

EXAMPLE

"Do you agree with O. Henry that Della and Jim 'were the wisest'?" asked Greg.

13j. **Use quotation marks to enclose titles of articles, short stories, essays, poems, songs, individual episodes of TV shows, and chapters and other parts of books and periodicals.**

 For examples of titles that should be italicized rather than enclosed in quotation marks, see page 1026.

TYPE OF TITLE	EXAMPLES
Articles	"Computers in the Classroom" "Returning from Space"
Short Stories	"Thank You, M'am" "The Princess and the Tin Box"
Essays	"How to Name a Dog" "The Death of a Tree"
Poems	"The Secret" "Fire and Ice" "who are you,little i"
Songs	"Circle of Life" "Lean on Me"
TV Episodes	"Farewell, Friends" "The Surprise Party"
Chapters and Other Parts of Books and Periodicals	"Life in the First Settlements" "The Talk of the Town" "Laughter, the Best Medicine"

 NOTE Neither italics nor quotation marks are used for the titles of major religious texts or for the titles of legal or historical documents.

RELIGIOUS TEXTS
New Testament   Koran   Rig-Veda

LEGAL AND HISTORICAL DOCUMENTS
Declaration of Independence
Code of Hammurabi

EXCEPTION
Names of court cases are usually italicized.

EXAMPLE
Brown v. *Board of Education of Topeka*

Using Italics for Emphasis

Occasionally, writers will use italics (underlining) to emphasize a particular word or phrase. This technique can be especially effective in written dialogue. The italic type helps to show how the sentence is spoken by the character. Read the following sentences aloud. Notice that by italicizing different words, the writer can alter the meaning of the sentence.

EXAMPLES

"Are you *certain* that she said to be here at nine o'clock?" asked Suzanne. [Are you certain, not just guessing?]

"Are you certain that *she* said to be here at nine o'clock?" asked Suzanne. [Did she say so, or did someone else?]

"Are you certain that she said to be here at *nine* o'clock?" asked Suzanne. [Did she say nine o'clock, or was it eight?]

Although italicizing (underlining) words for emphasis is a handy technique, it should not be overused, because it can quickly lose its effectiveness.

Try It Out

Revise the following dialogue by adding commas, end marks, quotation marks, and paragraph breaks where necessary. In addition, underline words you think the speakers would emphasize.

[1] You know what really bothers me about a lot of stories? said Kyle. [2] What? inquired Erin. [3] I can never—well, not never, but often I can't—figure out if a story is fiction or if it really happened, he explained. [4] Yeah she nodded I know what you mean. That reminds me of the story A Man Called Horse. Did it really happen or not? [5] I don't know he answered When I saw the movie, I thought it did, but now I'm not so sure. [6] Erin added, It's the same with stories that don't give the narrator's name. [7] I always wonder whether the narrator is the writer or not. [8] Yes, and the more I like the story, the more I wonder! Kyle agreed. [9] Erin replied Hey let's check the book out again and see if we can find out if Horse was a real person or not. [10] As they read the notes and comments about the story, Kyle said with surprise Wow it says here that Dorothy Johnson also wrote the story The Man Who Shot Liberty Valance!

APOSTROPHES

Possessive Case

The *possessive case* of a noun or pronoun shows ownership or relationship.

OWNERSHIP **Mme. Forestier's** necklace
RELATIONSHIP **Buddy's** friend

14a. To form the possessive case of a singular noun, add an apostrophe and an *s*.

EXAMPLES
Miss Lottie's marigolds   a bus's wheel

> **NOTE** For a proper name ending in *s*, add only an apostrophe if adding 's would make the name awkward to pronounce.
>
> **EXAMPLES**
> West Indies' island   Mrs. Saunders' class

14b. To form the possessive case of a plural noun ending in *s*, add only the apostrophe. To form the possessive case of a plural noun that does not end in *s*, add an apostrophe and an *s*.

EXAMPLES
birds' feathers   Capulets' party
children's shoes   deer's food

TIPS FOR SPELLING

Do not use an apostrophe to form the *plural* of a noun. Remember: An apostrophe shows ownership or relationship.

PLURAL   Doodle and he are **brothers**.
POSSESSIVE   The **brothers'** relationship is special.

14c. Possessive personal pronouns—*my, mine, your, yours, his, her, hers, its, our, ours, their,* and *theirs*—do not require an apostrophe.

EXAMPLES
This is **our** plant.
This plant is **ours**.

14d. Indefinite pronouns—such as *everybody* and *neither*—in the possessive case require an apostrophe and an *s*.

EXAMPLES
nobody's wish   another's viewpoint

14e. In compound words, names of organizations and businesses, and word groups showing joint possession, only the last word is possessive in form.

EXAMPLES
brother-in-**law's** gift   City **Garage's** tow trucks
United **Fund's** drive   Della and **Jim's** home

14f. When two or more persons possess something individually, each of their names is possessive in form.

EXAMPLE
Poe's and **Dahl's** stories

Contractions

14g. Use an apostrophe to show where letters, words, or numerals have been omitted in a contraction.

EXAMPLES
let us . . . . **let's**   you are . . . . . . **you're**
1991 . . . . **'91**   of the clock . . . **o'clock**

Ordinarily, the word *not* is shortened to –*n't* and added to a verb with no change to the verb's spelling.

EXAMPLES
are not . . . . . . **aren't**   has not . . . . . **hasn't**
EXCEPTIONS
will not . . . . . . **won't**   cannot . . . .**can't**

Do not confuse contractions with possessive pronouns.

CONTRACTIONS	PRONOUNS
Who's [Who is] at bat?	**Whose** bat is that?
It's [It is] roaring.	Listen to **its** roar.
You're [You are] late.	**Your** friend is late.
There's [There is] a kite.	That kite is **theirs**.
They're [They are] here.	**Their** bus is here.

Plurals

14h. **Use an apostrophe and an *s* to form the plurals of all lowercase letters, some capital letters, and some words that are referred to as words.**

EXAMPLES
Grandma always tells me to mind my *p*'s and *q*'s.
Those *U*'s look like *V*'s. [Without an apostrophe, the plural of *U* would spell *Us*. An apostrophe and an *s* are used to form the plural of *V* to make the style consistent.]
His *hi*'s are always cheerful. [Without an apostrophe, the plural would spell the word *his*.]

Using Apostrophes

In your reading you may have noticed that some writers do not use apostrophes to form the plurals of numbers, capital letters, symbols, and words used as words.

EXAMPLE
Their music was popular in the **1970s.**

However, using an apostrophe is never wrong. Therefore, it is best always to use the apostrophe.

Try It Out

For each of the following sentences, add an apostrophe wherever it is needed.

1. As in your studies are great, but Bs are good, too.
2. If you use *its*, make sure that they clearly refer to specific words.
3. Try not to include *I*s in the opening paragraph of a business letter.
4. The *10*s in this chart indicate the highest scores.
5. These *his*s should be *theirs*s.

HYPHENS

14i. **Use a hyphen to divide a word at the end of a line.**

EXAMPLE
"The Most Dangerous Game" is a very suspense-ful story.

When you divide a word at the end of a line, keep in mind the following rules.

(1) Do not divide one-syllable words.

(2) Divide a word only between syllables.

EXAMPLES
fi-an-cé   wor-thy

 NOTE If you need to divide a word and are not sure about its syllables, look it up in a current dictionary.

(3) Words with double consonants may usually be divided between those two consonants.

EXAMPLES
rib-bon   man-ners
EXCEPTION
Words that end in double consonants followed by a suffix are divided before the suffix.
fall-ing   will-ing

(4) Usually, a word with a prefix or a suffix may be divided between the prefix or suffix and the base word (or root).

EXAMPLES
pro-gressive   govern-ment

(5) Divide an already hyphenated word only at a hyphen.

EXAMPLES
man-of-war   daughter-in-law

(6) Do not divide a word so that one letter stands alone.

14j. **Use a hyphen with compound numbers from *twenty-one* to *ninety-nine* and with fractions used as adjectives.**

EXAMPLES
twenty-four chairs
one-half cup [*One-half* is an adjective.]
one half of the money [*Half* is a noun.]

14k. **Use a hyphen with the suffix –*elect* and with all prefixes before a proper noun or proper adjective.**

EXAMPLES
president-elect   pre-Revolutionary

14l. **Hyphenate a compound adjective that precedes the noun it modifies.**

EXAMPLES
a well-written book   a world-famous skier

Do not use a hyphen if one of the modifiers is an adverb that ends in –*ly*.

EXAMPLE
a **bitterly cold** day

NOTE Some compound adjectives are always hyphenated, whether they precede or follow the nouns they modify.

EXAMPLE
an up-to-date dictionary
a dictionary that is up-to-date

If you're not sure whether a compound adjective should be hyphenated, check a recent dictionary.

DASHES

14m. Use a dash to indicate an abrupt break in thought or speech or an unfinished statement or question.

EXAMPLE
Judy—Ms. Lane, I mean—will be your new coach.

14n. Use a dash to mean *namely, that is, in other words,* and similar expressions that introduce an explanation.

EXAMPLES
Dr. Ganderbai considered using an anesthetic—ether or chloroform. [namely]
William Sydney Porter—O. Henry—is my favorite writer. [that is]

NOTE When you type or input your writing on a word processor, you may indicate a dash by using two hyphens. (Do not leave a space before, between, or after the hyphens.) If you are using a computer, you may also find a dash available in your word processing software. When you write by hand, use an unbroken line about as long as two hyphens.

PARENTHESES

14o. Use parentheses to enclose material that is not considered of major importance in a sentence.

EXAMPLES
Richard Wright (1908–1960) wrote *Black Boy*.
Aunt Constance (Mother's aunt and my great-aunt) will meet us at the airport.

Capitalize and use end punctuation for parenthetical matter that stands alone as a sentence. Do not capitalize and use end punctuation for parenthetical matter contained within a sentence.

EXAMPLES
Complete the form. (Please print or type.)
The protagonist (the author did not give him a name) is a sniper.

15 SPELLING

UNDERSTANDING WORD STRUCTURE

Many English words are made up of roots and affixes (prefixes and suffixes). The **root** of a word is the part that carries the word's core meaning. A **prefix** is one or more than one letter or syllable added to the beginning of a word to create a new word with a different meaning. A **suffix** is one or more than one letter or syllable added to the end of a word to create a new word with a different meaning. Learning how to spell commonly used word parts and how to combine them can help you spell thousands of words.

COMMONLY USED ROOTS		
ROOTS	**MEANINGS**	**EXAMPLES**
–aud–, –audit–	hear	audible, auditorium
–bene–	well, good	benefit, benevolent
–chron–	time	chronological, synchronize
–cycl–	circle, wheel	cyclone, bicycle
–dem–	people	democracy, epidemic

(continued)

COMMONLY USED ROOTS (continued)

ROOTS	MEANINGS	EXAMPLES
–gen–	birth, kind, origin	generate, generic, generous
–graph–	write, writing	autograph, geography
–hydr–	water	hydrant, hydrate
–log–, –logue–	study, word	logic, mythology, dialogue
–micr–	small	microbe, microscope
–morph–	form	metamorphosis, polymorph
–phil–	like, love	philanthropic, philosophy
–phon–	sound	phonograph, euphony
–port–	carry, bear	export, important
–psych–	mind	psychology, psychosomatic
–verse–, –vert–	turn	reverse, convert
–vid–, –vis–	see	television, evident

COMMONLY USED PREFIXES

PREFIXES	MEANINGS	EXAMPLES
anti–	against, opposing	antipathy, antithesis
bi–	two	bimonthly, bisect
contra–	against	contradict, contrast
de–	away, off, down	defect, desert, decline
dis–	away, off, opposing	dismount, dissent
hemi–	half	hemisphere, hemicycle
hyper–	excessive, over	hyperactive, hypertension
inter–	between, among	intercede, international
mis–	badly, not, wrongly	misfire, misspell
over–	above, excessive	oversee, overdo
post–	after, following	postpone, postscript
re–	back, backward, again	revoke, reflect, reforest
tra–, trans–	across, beyond	traffic, transport
un–	not, reverse of	untrue, unfold

COMMONLY USED SUFFIXES

SUFFIXES	MEANINGS	EXAMPLES
–able	able, likely	capable, changeable
–cy	state, condition	accuracy, normalcy
–er	doer, native of	baker, westerner
–ful	full of, marked by	thankful, masterful
–ic	dealing with, caused by, person or thing showing	classic, choleric, heretic
–ion	action, result, state	union, fusion, dominion
–ish	suggesting, like	smallish, childish
–ist	doer, believer	monopolist, capitalist
–ly	like, characteristic of	friendly, cowardly
–ness	quality, state	softness, shortness
–or	doer, office, action	director, juror, error
–ous	marked by, given to	religious, furious
–tion	action, condition	selection, relation
–tude	quality, state	fortitude, multitude

SPELLING RULES

ie and ei

15a. **Write *ie* when the sound is long *e*, except after *c*.**

EXAMPLES
ach**ie**ve ch**ie**f n**ie**ce c**ei**ling dec**ei**t rec**ei**ve
EXCEPTIONS
either l**ei**sure n**ei**ther s**ei**ze w**ei**rd prot**ei**n

15b. **Write *ei* when the sound is not long *e*.**

EXAMPLES
for**ei**gn forf**ei**t h**ei**ght h**ei**r r**ei**gn w**ei**gh
EXCEPTIONS
anc**ie**nt consc**ie**nce fr**ie**nd misch**ie**f v**ie**w

–cede, –ceed, and –sede

15c. **The only English word ending in *–sede* is *supersede*. The only words ending in *–ceed* are *exceed*, *proceed*, and *succeed*. Most other words with this sound end in *–cede*.**

EXAMPLES
ac**cede** inter**cede** re**cede**
con**cede** pre**cede** se**cede**

Adding Prefixes

15d. **When adding a prefix, do not change the spelling of the original word.**

EXAMPLES
im + mortal = **im**mortal   mis + step = **mis**step
re + elect = **re**elect   over + run = **over**run

Adding Suffixes

15e. **When adding the suffix *–ness* or *–ly*, do not change the spelling of the original word.**

EXAMPLES
fair + ness = fair**ness**   sure + ly = sure**ly**
EXCEPTIONS
For most words ending in *y*, change the *y* to *i* before adding *–ness* or *–ly*:
empty—empt**iness**   easy—eas**ily**

However, most one-syllable words ending in *y* follow rule 15e.

EXAMPLES
dry + ness = dry**ness**   sly + ly = sly**ly**

15f. **Drop the final silent *e* before a suffix beginning with a vowel.**

EXAMPLES
hope + ing = hop**ing**   strange + est = strang**est**
EXCEPTIONS
Keep the final silent *e*

- in words ending in *ce* or *ge* before a suffix that begins with *a* or *o*: knowledg**eable**, outrag**eous**
- in *dye* and in *singe*, before *–ing*: dy**eing**, sing**eing**
- in *mile* before *–age*: mil**eage**

15g. **Keep the final silent *e* before a suffix beginning with a consonant.**

EXAMPLES
nine + ty = nine**ty**   entire + ly = entire**ly**
EXCEPTIONS
nine + th = nin**th**   awe + ful = aw**ful**
judge + ment = judg**ment**
argue + ment = argu**ment**

15h. **For words ending in *y* preceded by a consonant, change the *y* to *i* before any suffix that does not begin with *i*.**

EXAMPLES
fifty + eth = fift**ieth**   mystery + ous = myster**ious**

15i. **For words ending in *y* preceded by a vowel, simply add the suffix.**

EXAMPLES
joy + ful = joy**ful**   boy + hood = boy**hood**
EXCEPTIONS
day + ly = da**ily**   pay + ed = pa**id**
say + ed = sa**id**   lay + ed = la**id**

15j. **Double the final consonant before a suffix that begins with a vowel if the word *both* (1) has only one syllable or has the accent on the last syllable *and* (2) ends in a single consonant preceded by a single vowel.**

EXAMPLES
drop + ing = dro**pping**
occur + ence = occu**rrence**
strum + ed = stru**mmed**
thin + er = thi**nner**

NOTE   The final consonant in some words may or may not be doubled. Both spellings are equally correct.

EXAMPLES
travel + er = trave**ler** *or* trave**ller**
shovel + ed = shove**led** *or* shove**lled**

Forming Plurals of Nouns

15k. To form the plurals of most English nouns, add –s.

EXAMPLES
boats   houses   nickels   Lincolns

15l. To form the plurals of other nouns, follow these rules.

(1) For nouns ending in s, x, z, ch, or sh, add –es.

EXAMPLES
glasses   boxes   waltzes   beaches   Bushes

(2) For nouns ending in y preceded by a consonant, change the y to i and add –es.

EXAMPLES
armies   babies   skies   mysteries
EXCEPTION
For proper nouns, add –s: Hardys

(3) For nouns ending in y preceded by a vowel, add –s.

EXAMPLES
joys   keys   Momadays

(4) For some nouns ending in f or fe, add –s. For others, change the f or fe to v and add –es.

EXAMPLES
beliefs   roofs   safes   giraffes
calves   wives   leaves   shelves
EXCEPTION
For proper nouns, add –s: Radcliffs, Rolfes

(5) For nouns ending in o preceded by a vowel, add –s.

EXAMPLES
radios   patios   Sotos   stereos

(6) For nouns ending in o preceded by a consonant, add –es.

EXAMPLES
echoes   heroes   vetoes   tomatoes
EXCEPTIONS
For some common nouns ending in o preceded by a consonant, especially musical terms, and for proper nouns, add only –s: tacos, pianos, Sotos

(7) The plurals of a few nouns are formed in irregular ways.

EXAMPLES
children   feet   men   teeth   mice

(8) For a few nouns, the singular and the plural forms are the same.

SINGULAR AND PLURAL
deer   Japanese   Navajo   sheep   trout   series

(9) For a compound noun written as one word, form the plural of only the last word of the compound.

EXAMPLES
iceboxes   blackberries   businesspeople

(10) For a compound noun that is hyphenated or written as separate words, form the plural of the noun that is modified.

EXAMPLES
sisters-in-law   runners-up   music boxes

(11) For some nouns borrowed from other languages, the plurals are formed as in the original languages.

EXAMPLES
crisis—crises   phenomenon—phenomena

A few nouns borrowed from other languages have two plural forms.

EXAMPLES
appendix—appendices or appendixes
formula—formulas or formulae

(12) For numerals, symbols, most capital letters, and words used as words, add an –s or both an apostrophe and an –s.

EXAMPLES
6—6s or 6's   R—Rs or R's
&—&s or &'s   and—ands or and's

To prevent confusion, always use an apostrophe and an –s to form the plurals of lowercase letters, certain capital letters, and some words used as words.

EXAMPLES
Your *i*'s look like *e*'s. [Without an apostrophe, the plural of *i* would like *is*.]
Ramón got all **A's** last semester. [Without an apostrophe, the plural of A would look like *As*.]
Her ***and so*'s** began to get tiresome. [Without the apostrophe, the plural of *so* would look like *sos*.]

COMPUTER NOTE   Spell-checking software can help you proofread your writing. Even the best spelling checkers aren't foolproof, however. Some accept British and archaic spellings, and most do not identify words that are spelled correctly but are used incorrectly (such as *affect* for *effect*). Always double-check your writing to make sure that your spelling is error free.

The Glossary of Usage is an alphabetical list of words, expressions, and special terms with definitions, explanations, and examples. Some examples have usage labels. *Standard* or *formal* usages are appropriate in serious writing and speaking, such as in compositions and in speeches. *Informal* words and expressions are standard English usages generally appropriate in conversation and in everyday writing such as in personal letters. *Nonstandard* usages do not follow the guidelines of standard English.

---

accept, except   *Accept* is a verb that means "receive." *Except* may be either a verb or a preposition. As a verb, *except* means "leave out." As a preposition, *except* means "excluding."

EXAMPLES
We **accept** your apology.
All children under age three will be **excepted** from the fee. [verb]
Everyone **except** Bob and me has seen the exhibit. [preposition]

advice, advise   *Advice* is a noun meaning "suggestion about what to do." *Advise* is a verb meaning "offer a suggestion; recommend."

EXAMPLES
He gave me some excellent **advice.**
She **advised** me to finish high school.

affect, effect   *Affect* is a verb meaning "influence." As a verb, *effect* means "accomplish." As a noun, *effect* means "result (of an action)."

EXAMPLES
What he said did not **affect** my decision.
The mayor has **effected** many changes during her administration. [verb]
What **effect** will the new factory have on the environment? [noun]

ain't   Avoid using this word in formal speaking and in all writing other than dialogue; it is nonstandard English.

all together, altogether   *All together* means "everyone or everything in the same place." *Altogether* is an adverb meaning "entirely."

EXAMPLES
When we were **all together,** we voted.
He was **altogether** wrong.

a lot   Do not write the expression *a lot* as one word.

EXAMPLE
In addition to short stories, Edgar Allan Poe also wrote **a lot** [*not* alot] of poetry.

among   See **between, among.**

and etc.   The abbreviation for the Latin phrase *et cetera,* meaning "and other things" is *etc.* Thus, do not use *and* with *etc.*

EXAMPLE
My younger sister collects stickers, bottle caps, string, **etc.** [*not* and etc.]

anyways, anywheres   Use these words (and others like them, such as *everywheres, somewheres,* and *nowheres*) without the final *s.*

EXAMPLES
I have to baby-sit tonight **anyway** [*not* anyways].
The Loisels could not find the necklace **anywhere** [*not* anywheres].

as   See **like, as.**

as if   See **like, as if.**

at   Do not use *at* after *where.*

NONSTANDARD   Where was Romeo at?
   STANDARD   **Where** was Romeo?

bad, badly   *Bad* is an adjective. *Badly* is an adverb. In standard English, only *bad* should follow a linking verb, such as *feel, look, sound, taste,* or *smell,* or forms of the verb *be.*

EXAMPLE
The fruitcake doesn't taste **bad** [*not* badly].

being as, being that   Use *since* or *because* instead of these expressions.

EXAMPLE
Because [*not* being as] President Clinton admired Maya Angelou's writing, he invited her to write a poem for his inauguration.

beside, besides   *Beside* is a preposition that means "by the side of" or "next to." As a preposition, *besides* means "in addition to" or "other than." As an adverb, *besides* means "moreover."

EXAMPLES
His rifle lay **beside** him.
Who **besides** Timber tried to help? [preposition]
I don't want to go; **besides,** it's snowing. [adverb]

between, among Use *between* when you are referring to two things at a time, even though they may be part of a group consisting of more than two.

EXAMPLES

There was a feud **between** the Montagues and the Capulets.

The manager could not decide which of the four players to select, because there was not much difference **between** them. [Although there are more than two players, each one is being compared with the others separately.]

Use *among* when referring to a group rather than to separate individuals.

EXAMPLE

We were able to collect only ten dollars **among** the four of us.

bust, busted Avoid using these words as verbs. Use a form of either *burst* or *break,* depending on the meaning.

EXAMPLES

The balloon **burst** [*not* busted] loudly.

The firefighters **broke** [*not* busted] a window.

consul, council, counsel *Consul* is a noun meaning "representative of a foreign country." *Council* is a noun meaning "group called together to accomplish a job." As a noun, *counsel* means "advice." As a verb, it means "give advice."

EXAMPLES

The French **consul** outlined his government's plan.

The city **council** will debate the issue.

I'm grateful for your **counsel.** [noun]

Did the doctor **counsel** her to get more rest? [verb]

could of See **of.**

discover, invent *Discover* means "be the first to find, see, or learn about something that already exists." *Invent* means "be the first to do or make something."

EXAMPLES

Marguerite Perey **discovered** the element francium.

The zipper was **invented** in 1893.

double negative A double negative is the use of two negative words when one is enough. Avoid using double negatives.

Common Negative Words

barely	never	no one	not (–n't)
hardly	no	nowhere	nothing
neither	nobody	none	scarcely

NONSTANDARD	I had not read none of Emily Dickinson's poems.
STANDARD	I **had not read any** of Emily Dickinson's poems.
STANDARD	I **had read none** of Emily Dickinson's poems.

| NONSTANDARD | Doodle couldn't hardly walk. |
| STANDARD | Doodle **could hardly** walk. |

double subject See **he, she, it, they.**

effect See **affect, effect.**

etc. See **and etc.**

everywheres See **anyways, anywheres.**

except See **accept, except.**

fewer, less *Fewer* tells "how many"; it is used with plural nouns. *Less* tells "how much"; it is used with singular nouns.

EXAMPLES

There are **fewer** gypsy moths this year than there were last year.

Reading the *Odyssey* took **less** time than we had thought.

good, well *Good* is an adjective. *Well* may be used as an adjective or an adverb. Never use *good* to modify a verb; instead, use *well* as an adverb meaning "capably" or "satisfactorily."

EXAMPLE

Sandra Cisneros writes **well** [*not* good].

As an adjective, *well* means "healthy" or "satisfactory in appearance or condition."

EXAMPLES

Lying in his bed, Harry did not look **well.**

Friar Laurence thought that all would be **well** with the Montagues and the Capulets.

NOTE *Feel good* and *feel well* mean different things. *Feel good* means "feel happy or pleased." *Feel well* means "feel healthy."

EXAMPLES

The news made her feel **good.**

I didn't feel **well,** so I went home.

had ought, hadn't ought Unlike other verbs, *ought* is not used with *had.*

EXAMPLES

I think Doodle's brother **ought** [*not* had ought] to be more patient; he **ought not** [*not* hadn't ought] to push Doodle so hard.

hardly See **double negative.**

he, she, it, they Do not use an unnecessary pronoun after the subject of a verb. This error is called the *double subject*.

| NONSTANDARD | Miss Lottie she likes to grow marigolds. |
| STANDARD | Miss Lottie likes to grow marigolds. |

hisself, theirselves In formal situations, do not use these words for *himself* and *themselves*.

EXAMPLE
Romeo unburdens **himself** [*not* hisself] to Friar Laurence.

imply, infer *Imply* means "suggest indirectly." *Infer* means "interpret" or "draw a conclusion (from a remark or an action)."

EXAMPLES
Doug **implied** that he will vote for me.
From Doug's remark, I **inferred** that he will vote for me.

inside of See **of.**

invent See **discover, invent.**

it See **he, she, it, they.**

its, it's *Its* is the possessive form of *it*. *It's* is the contraction of *it is* or *it has*.

EXAMPLES
The bird stopped **its** singing.
It's [it is] an easy problem.
It's [it has] been raining since noon.

kind of, sort of In formal situations, avoid using these terms to mean *somewhat* or *rather*.

| INFORMAL | Zaroff was kind of surprised to see that Rainsford was still alive. |
| FORMAL | Zaroff was **somewhat** [*or* **rather**] surprised to see that Rainsford was still alive. |

kind of a, sort of a Avoid using *a* after *kind of* and *sort of* in formal situations.

| INFORMAL | What kind of a snake was it? |
| FORMAL | What **kind of** snake was it? |

kind(s), sort(s), type(s) Use *this* or *that* with the singular form of each of these nouns. Use *these* or *those* with the plural form.

EXAMPLES
I like **this kind** of jeans better than any of **those** other **kinds.**

lay See **lie, lay.**

learn, teach *Learn* means "acquire knowledge." *Teach* means "instruct" or "show how."

EXAMPLES
Doodle **learns** to walk.
His brother **teaches** him to walk.

leave, let *Leave* means "go away" or "depart from." *Let* means "allow" or "permit." Avoid using *leave* for *let*.

EXAMPLE
Let [*not* leave] her speak if she insists.

less See **fewer, less.**

let See **leave, let.**

lie, lay The verb *lie* means "rest" or "stay, recline, or remain in a certain position." *Lie* never takes an object. Its principal parts are *lie, lying, lay, lain*. The verb *lay* means "put (something) in a place." Its principal parts are *lay, laying, laid, laid*. *Lay* usually takes an object.

EXAMPLES
Is there a real snake **lying** on Harry's stomach? [no object]
He **laid** her gift on the table. [Gift is the object of *laid*.]

like, as In formal English, use *like* to introduce a prepositional phrase, and use *as* to introduce a subordinate clause.

EXAMPLES
Does Juliet look **like** Rosaline? [The preposition *like* introduces the phrase *like Rosaline*.]
Juliet does **as** Friar Laurence suggests. [The subordinating conjunction *as* introduces the clause *as Friar Laurence suggests*.]

like, as if In formal situations, *like* should not be used for the compound conjunction *as if* or *as though*.

EXAMPLE
Juliet looks **as though** [*not* like] she is alive.

might of, must of See **of.**

moral, morale As an adjective, *moral* means "good; virtuous." As a noun, it means "lesson of conduct." *Morale* is a noun meaning "spirit; mental condition."

EXAMPLES
In Pearl Buck's short story "The Old Demon," Mrs. Wang's **moral** values compel her to help the Japanese pilot. [adjective]
James Thurber's fables end with **morals** quite unlike the ones in traditional fairy tales. [noun]
The employees' **morale** is high.

nowheres See **anyways, anywheres.**

of *Of* is a preposition. Do not use *of* in place of *have* after verbs such as *could, should, would, ought (to), might,* and *must.* Also, do not use *had of* for *had.*

NONSTANDARD	You would of enjoyed our production of *The Miracle Worker.*
STANDARD	You **would have** [*or* **would've**] enjoyed our production of *The Miracle Worker.*
NONSTANDARD	If I had of known it was your birthday, I would of given you a card.
STANDARD	If I **had** known it was your birthday, I **would have** given you a card.

Also, do not use *of* after other prepositions such as *inside, off,* or *outside.*

EXAMPLES

The sniper's enemy fell **off** [*not* off of] the roof.

The sleeping Juliet is carried **inside** [*not* inside of] the Capulets' tomb.

off of See **of.**

ought See **had ought, hadn't ought.**

ought to of See **of.**

peace, piece *Peace* means "calmness; absence of war or strife." *Piece* means "part of something."

EXAMPLES

After the long war, **peace** was welcome.

Do you have a **piece** of paper I can borrow?

principal, principle As a noun, *principal* means "the head of a school." As an adjective, it means "main or most important." *Principle* is a noun meaning "a rule of conduct" or "a general truth."

EXAMPLES

Ted had a long talk with the **principal.** [noun]

Winning is not our **principal** goal. [adjective]

My friends have high **principles.**

I don't know the **principles** of physics.

rise, raise The verb *rise* means "go up" or "get up." *Rise* never takes an object. Its principal parts are *rise, rising, rose, risen.* The verb *raise* means "cause (something) to rise" or "lift up." *Raise* usually takes an object. Its principal parts are *raise, raising, raised, raised.*

EXAMPLES

Everyone **rose** when the judge entered the room. [no object]

The sniper **raised** his revolver and fired. [*Revolver* is the object of *raised.*]

scarcely See **double negative.**

set See **sit, set.**

she See **he, she, it, they.**

should of See **of.**

sit, set The verb *sit* means "rest in an upright, seated position." *Sit* almost never takes an object. Its principal parts are *sit, sitting, sat, sat.* The verb *set* means "put (something) in a place." *Set* usually takes an object. Its principal parts are *set, setting, set, set.*

EXAMPLES

The campers were **sitting** around the fire. [no object]

Ganderbai **set** the bag on a chair. [*Bag* is the object of *set.*]

some, somewhat In formal situations, do not use *some* to mean "to some extent" or "slightly." Instead, use *somewhat.*

| INFORMAL | My spelling has now improved some. |
| FORMAL | My spelling has now improved **somewhat.** |

somewheres See **anyways, anywheres.**

sort(s) See **kind(s), sort(s), type(s)** and **kind of a, sort of a.**

sort of See **kind of, sort of.**

teach See **learn, teach.**

than, then *Than* is a conjunction used in comparisons. *Then* is an adverb meaning "at that time" or "next."

EXAMPLES

This box is heavier **than** that one.

Did the sniper know **then** who his enemy was?

First, I read *Romeo and Juliet;* **then,** I watched the film version.

that See **who, which, that.**

their, there, they're *Their* is a possessive form of *they.* As an adverb, *there* means "at that place." *There* is also used to begin a sentence. *They're* is the contraction of *they are.*

EXAMPLES

Their daughter, Juliet, was in love with a Montague.

Harry Pope lay **there** quietly.

There is a conflict between Odysseus and the Cyclops.

They're throwing pebbles at Miss Lottie's flowers.

theirs, there's   *Theirs* is a possessive form of the pronoun *they*. *There's* is the contraction of *there is*.

EXAMPLES
Our team was ready to play, and so was **theirs**.
There's a sniper on the rooftop.

theirselves   See **hisself, theirselves**.

them   *Them* should not be used as an adjective. Use *those*.

EXAMPLE
Their unselfish love is symbolized by **those** [*not* them] gifts.

then   See **than, then**.

there   See **their, there, they're**.

there's   See **theirs, there's**.

they   See **he, she, it, they**.

they're   See **their, there, they're**.

this, that, these, those   See **kind(s), sort(s), type(s)**.

try and   Use *try to*, not *try and*.

EXAMPLE
Timber and Ganderbai **try to** [*not* try and] keep Harry calm.

type(s)   See **kind(s), sort(s), type(s)**.

unless   See **without, unless**.

way, ways   Use *way*, not *ways*, in referring to a distance.

EXAMPLE
Odysseus traveled quite a long **way** [*not* ways] to get back home.

well   See **good, well**.

what   Use *that*, not *what*, to introduce an adjective clause.

EXAMPLE
The poem **that** [*not* what] I wrote about was Naomi Shihab Nye's "Daily."

when, where   Do not use *when* or *where* to begin a definition.

NONSTANDARD	A "bomb" in football is when a backfielder throws a long pass.
STANDARD	A "bomb" in football is a long pass thrown by a backfielder.

Also, do not use *where* or *when* for *that*.

EXAMPLE
I read in this book **that** [*not* where] Robert Frost won the Pulitzer Prize four times.

where ... at   See **at**.

who, which, that   *Who* refers to persons only; *which* refers to things only; *that* may refer to either persons or things.

EXAMPLES
Isn't Walt Whitman the poet **who** [*or* that] wrote *Leaves of Grass*? [person]
They decided to replace Mme. Forestier's necklace, **which** they did not know was fake. [thing]
The necklace **that** the Loisels bought cost thirty-six thousand francs. [thing]

who's, whose   *Who's* is the contraction of *who is* or *who has*. *Whose* is the possessive form of *who*.

EXAMPLES
Who's [who is] the narrator of "A Christmas Memory"?
Who's [who has] been helping Helen?
Whose autobiography is titled *Black Boy*?

without, unless   Do not use the preposition *without* in place of the conjunction *unless*.

EXAMPLE
I will not be able to sing **unless** [*not* without] my cold gets better.

would of   See **of**.

your, you're   *Your* is a possessive form of *you*. *You're* is the contraction of *you are*.

EXAMPLES
What is **your** opinion of General Zaroff?
You're [you are] my best friend.

GLOSSARY

The glossary below is an alphabetical list of some of the words found in the selections in this book. Use this glossary just as you use a dictionary—to find out the meanings of unfamiliar words. (Some technical, foreign, and more obscure words in this book are not listed here but instead are defined in footnotes.)

Many words in the English language have more than one meaning. This glossary gives the meanings that apply to the words as they are used in the selections in this book. For some of these words, an additional meaning is given and the separate meanings are numbered. Words closely related in form and meaning are usually listed together in one entry (for instance, *prosper* and *prosperous*), and the definition is given for the first form.

The following abbreviations are used:

adj.	adjective
adv.	adverb
n.	noun
v.	verb

Each word's pronunciation is given in parentheses. A guide to the pronunciation symbols appears at the bottom of each right-hand glossary page.

For more information about the words in this glossary, or for information about words not listed here, consult a dictionary.

abatement (ə·bāt′mənt) *n.*: lessening; reduction.

abominable (ə·bäm′ə·nə·bəl) *adj.*: extremely unpleasant or disgusting. **—abominably** *adv.*

abscond (ab·skänd′) *v.*: go away hastily and secretly.

abyss (ə·bis′) *n.*: 1. deep hole in the earth. 2. something beyond understanding or measurement.

accost (ə·kôst′) *v.*: approach and speak to, especially in an intrusive way.

accumulate (ə·kyoom′yoo·lāt′) *v.*: pile up; collect.

adorn (ə·dôrn′) *v.*: add beauty to; decorate.

adversary (ad′vər·ser′ē) *n.*: enemy; opponent.

adversity (ad·vur′sə·tē) *n.*: misfortune; hardship.

affable (af′ə·bəl) *adj.*: pleasant and friendly.

affront (ə·frunt′) *n.*: insult.

aghast (ə·gast′) *adj.*: horrified.

agility (ə·jil′ə·tē) *n.*: quickness of movement.

agitation (aj′ə·tā′shən) *n.*: stirring up disturbance or excitement.

aloof (ə·loof′) *adj.*: distant; unfriendly.

amendment (ə·mend′mənt) *n.*: change; revision.

amenities (ə·men′ə·tēz) *n.*: comforts and conveniences.

anonymous (ə·nän′ə·məs) *adj.*: with no name; not easily distinguished from others.

anthem (an′thəm) *n.*: religious song; song of praise.

aperture (ap′ər·chər) *n.*: 1. opening; gap. 2. opening through which light passes in a camera or telescope.

apparition (ap′ə·rish′ən) *n.*: strange, ghostlike figure.

appellation (ap′ə·lā′shən) *n.*: name; title.

appraisal (ə·prāz′əl) *n.*: evaluation; sizing up.

apprehensive (ap′rē·hen′siv) *adj.*: fearful; uneasy.

arbitrary (är′bə·trer′ē) *adj.*: not fixed by rules.

ardent (ärd′′nt) *adj.*: eager.

ardor (är′dər) *n.*: passion; enthusiasm.

asperity (ə·sper′ə·tē) *n.*: sharpness of temper.

assiduous (ə·sij′oo·əs) *adj.*: industrious; careful and hard-working. **—assiduously** *adv.*

atonement (ə·tōn′mənt) *n.*: something done to make up for wrong deeds.

attribute (a′trə·byoot′) *n.*: quality; typical way of behaving.

baffle (baf′əl) *v.*: confuse.

bedeck (bē·dek′) *v.*: decorate.

beguile (bē·gīl′) *v.*: charm or delight, often in order to deceive. **—beguiling** *v.* used as *adj.*

benediction (ben′ə·dik′shən) *n.*: blessing.

benign (bi·nīn′) *adj.*: good-natured; harmless.

billow (bil′ō) *v.*: rise or swell like a wave.

bounteous (boun′tē·əs) *adj.*: plentiful.

brandish (bran′dish) *v.*: wave in a threatening way.

bravado (brə·vä′dō) *n.*: pretense of courage or confidence.

brazen (brā′zən) *adj.*: 1. made of brass. 2. bold; showing no shame.

buoyancy (boi′ən·sē) *n.*: 1. ability to keep something afloat. 2. cheerfulness.

burnish (bur′nish) *v.*: make shiny; polish.

callous (kal′əs) *adj.*: unfeeling; insensitive.

caper (kā′pər) *v.*: jump about playfully.

caricature (kar′i·kə·chər) *n.*: exaggerated portrait.

carnage (kär′nij) *n.*: slaughter.

cavort (kə·vôrt′) *v.*: leap about.

clamor (klam′ər) *n.*: 1. loud outcry. 2. noisy disturbance.

clarity (klar′ə·tē) *n.*: clearness.

commence (kə·mens′) *v.*: begin.

compel (kəm·pel′) *v.*: force.

compromise (käm′prə·mīz′) *v.*: 1. give up something to receive something one desires; settle for less than one wants. 2. adjust conflicting viewpoints.

compunction (kəm·puŋk′shən) *n.*: feeling of guilt and regret.

condone (kən·dōn′) *v.*: approve of; forgive.

conformity (kən·fôrm′ə·tē) *n.*: behavior that follows the usual customs.

connoisseurship (kän′ə·sur′ship) *n.*: expert knowledge.

consolation (kän′sə·lā′shən) *n.*: thing that comforts.

consternation (kän′stər·nā′shən) *n.*: fear; bewilderment.

consummate (kən·sum′it) *adj.*: 1. complete or perfect. 2. very skillful. —**consummately** *adv.*

contaminate (kən·tam′ə·nāt′) *v.*: pollute; poison. —**contaminating** *v.* used as *adj.*

contemptuous (kən·temp′choo·əs) *adj.*: scornful.

contrition (kən·trish′ən) *n.*: deep feelings of guilt and repentance.

contrive (kən·trīv′) *v.*: 1. think up; devise. 2. manage cleverly.

converse (kän′vurs) *adj.*: opposite. —**conversely** *adv.*

coordinate (kō·ôr′də·nāt′) *v.*: adjust so that the various parts or people work smoothly together.

covet (kuv′it) *v.*: 1. long for. 2. envy. —**coveted** *v.* used as *adj.*

cower (kou′ər) *v.*: draw back or crouch in fear and helplessness.

customary (kus′tə·mer′ē) *adj.*: usual; established by custom.

decree (dē·krē′) *v.*: 1. give an official order. 2. command or decide beforehand.

deferential (def′ər·en′shəl) *adj.*: showing polite respect.

deft *adj.*: skillful in a quick, sure, and easy way.

deplorable (dē·plôr′ə·bəl) *adj.*: regrettable; very bad.

depreciate (dē·prē′shē·āt′) *v.*: 1. belittle. 2. lower the value of.

desolation (des′ə·lā′shən) *n.*: 1. loneliness. 2. ruin.

desperado (des′pər·ä′dō) *n.*: bold outlaw.

detractor (dē·trak′tər) *n.*: one who makes something seem less important or less valuable.

deviation (dē′vē·ā′shən) *n.*: change from usual behavior.

devoid (di·void′) *adj.*: empty.

dilapidated (də·lap′ə·dāt′id) *adj.*: shabby; falling apart.

diligent (dil′ə·jənt) *adj.*: careful and hard-working.

disarming (dis·ärm′iŋ) *adj.*: removing or lessening suspicions or fears.

discern (di·zurn′) *v.*: see; detect by looking carefully.

disconsolate (dis·kän′sə·lit) *adj.*: very unhappy.

disdainful (dis·dān′fəl) *adj.*: scornful; contemptuous.

disillusion (dis′i·loo′zhən) *v.*: disappoint; make feel bitter. —**disillusioning** *v.* used as *adj.*

disperse (di·spurs′) *v.*: break up; scatter. —**dispersing** *v.* used as *adj.*

dispirited (di·spir′it·id) *adj.*: depressed; discouraged.

disposition (dis′pə·zish′ən) *n.*: usual frame of mind; personality or temperament.

dispossession (dis′pə·zesh′ən) *n.*: taking away of one's possessions.

diverting (də·vurt′iŋ) *adj.*: amusing; entertaining.

docile (däs′əl) *adj.*: easy to manage; submissive.

doggedness (dôg′id·nis) *n.*: stubbornness; persistence.

droll (drōl) *adj.*: amusing in an odd way.

earnest (ur′nist) *adj.*: serious; sincere. —**earnestly** *adv.*

ecstatic (ek·stat′ik) *adj.*: filled with delight.

elated (ē·lāt′id) *v.* used as *adj.*: very happy.

elude (ē·lood′) *v.*: get away from.

embark (em·bärk′) *v.*: 1. go aboard. 2. begin a journey.

embody (em·bäd′ē) *v.*: make real, give form to, or include.

emit (ē·mit′) *v.*: send out.

endeavor (en·dev′ər) *v.*: try.

enfeeble (en·fē′bəl) *v.*: weaken, usually by old age or illness. —**enfeebled** *v.* used as *adj.*

at, āte, cär; ten, ēve; is, īce; gō, hôrn, look, tool; oil, out; up, fur; ə *for unstressed vowels, as* a *in* ago, u *in* focus; ′ *as in* Latin (lat′′n); chin; she; zh *as in* azure (azh′ər); thin, *the*; ŋ *as in* ring (riŋ)

enthrall (en·thrôl′) v.: fascinate; hold as if in a spell.

enthusiasm (en·thōo′zē·az′əm) n.: eager interest.

enunciate (ē·nun′sē·āt′) v.: pronounce clearly.

envelop (en·vel′əp) v.: conceal; wrap; surround. —**enveloped** v. used as adj.

ephemeral (e·fem′ər·əl) adj.: short-lived; passing quickly.

euphoria (yōo·fôr′ē·ə) n.: feeling of vigor or well-being.

exasperate (eg·zas′pər·āt′) v.: annoy greatly.

exhilarate (eg·zil′ə·rāt′) v.: gladden; excite.

exorbitant (eg·zôr′bi·tənt) adj.: much too high in price or amount.

exotic (eg·zät′ik) adj.: fascinating; strangely beautiful; foreign.

expedient (ek·spē′dē·ənt) n.: 1. means; resource. 2. device used in an emergency.

expenditure (ek·spen′di·chər) n.: payment for expenses.

falter (fôl′tər) v.: hesitate; be unsteady.

fanatic (fə·nat′ik) n.: person with extreme beliefs.

fathom (fath′əm) n.: unit for measuring the depth of the ocean.

feigned (fānd) adj.: pretended or faked.

feisty (fīs′tē) adj.: high-spirited; lively.

ferocity (fə·räs′ə·tē) n.: fierceness.

festoon (fes·tōon′) v.: decorate.

flank (flaŋk) v.: be at the side of.

forestall (fôr·stôl′) v.: prevent by acting ahead of time.

formidable (fôr′mə·də·bəl) adj.: awe-inspiring in excellence; strikingly impressive.

founder (foun′dər) v.: fill with water and sink.

frenzied (fren′zēd) adj.: wild and frantic.

fretful (fret′fəl) adj.: irritable and discontented.

frivolous (friv′ə·ləs) adj.: silly; not as serious as the occasion requires.

furtive (fur′tiv) adj.: stealthy, as if to avoid being seen or heard. —**furtively** adv.

futile (fyōot′′l) adj.: pointless.

gallant (gal′ənt) adj.: graciously polite. —**gallantly** adv.

gambol (gam′bəl) v.: skip about.

gangly (gaŋ′glē) adj.: loose and awkward; more commonly spelled **gangling**.

garish (gar′ish) adj.: too bright; showy.

gesticulation (jes·tik′yōo·lā′shən) n.: movement of hands or arms to express a thought or feeling

glower (glou′ər) v.: glare; stare angrily.

goad (gōd) v.: drive; push into action.

grimace (gri·mās′) n.: twisting of the face because of pain or distress.

haversack (hav′ər·sak′) n.: canvas shoulder bag.

heifer (hef′ər) n.: young cow.

hindrance (hin′drəns) n.: obstacle; thing that restrains or prevents an activity.

imminent (im′ə·nənt) adj.: about to happen.

immobile (im·mō′bəl) adj.: not moving.

immolation (im′ə·lā′shən) n.: destruction.

impassive (im·pas′iv) adj.: showing no emotion. —**impassively** adv.

impediment (im·ped′ə·mənt) n.: defect that makes doing something difficult.

imperative (im·per′ə·tiv) adj.: extremely important; urgent.

imperious (im·pir′ē·əs) adj.: arrogant; expecting others to obey one's orders.

impertinent (im·purt′′n·ənt) adj.: shamelessly disrespectful; rude.

implicit (im·plis′it) adj.: absolute; unquestioning; implied or suggested but not expressed in words.

implore (im·plôr′) v.: plead. —**imploringly** adv.

impose (im·pōz′) **upon** v.: take advantage of.

imposture (im·päs′chər) n.: deception.

impotent (im′pə·tənt) adj.: powerless; helpless.

impoverish (im·päv′ər·ish) v.: make poor. —**impoverished** v. used as adj.

imprudent (im·prōod′′nt) adj.: unwise.

impudent (im′pyōo·dənt) adj.: shamelessly disrespectful; rude. —**impudence** n.

impunity (im·pyōo′ni·tē) n.: freedom from punishment.

inarticulate (in′är·tik′yōo·lit) adj.: not expressed clearly enough to be understood.

inaugurate (in·ô′gyoo·rāt′) v.: formally begin.

incessant (in·ses′ənt) adj.: constant; continual. —**incessantly** adv.

incite (in·sīt′) v.: stir up.

incredulous (in·krej′oo·ləs) adj.: unwilling to believe or unable to believe.

indolent (in′də·lənt) adj.: lazy; idle. —**indolently** adv.

indomitable (in·däm′i·tə·bəl) adj.: unconquerable; not easily discouraged or defeated.

inexorable (in·eks′ə·rə·bəl) adj.: unyielding; immovable; unchangeable.

inexplicable (in·eks′pli·kə·bəl) *adj.:* unexplainable; without apparent reason. —**inexplicably** *adv.*

infallibility (in·fal′ə·bil′ə·tē) *n.:* inability to make a mistake.

infatuated (in·fach′o͞o·āt′id) *adj.:* carried away by shallow or foolish love.

insolent (in′sə·lənt) *adj.:* boldly disrespectful.

instigate (in′stə·gāt′) *v.:* give rise to; provoke or urge on to some action.

interminable (in·tur′mi·nə·bəl) *adj.:* endless. —**interminably** *adv.*

intermittent (in′tər·mit′′nt) *adj.:* occurring from time to time. —**intermittently** *adv.*

intersect (in′tər·sekt′) *v.:* cross each other.

intimate (in′tə·māt′) *v.:* hint.

intimidate (in·tim′ə·dāt′) *v.:* frighten.

intolerable (in·täl′ər·ə·bəl) *adj.:* unbearable; too painful or severe to be endured.

intone (in·tōn′) *v.:* say or recite in a dull, unchanging tone.

intravenous (in′trə·vē′nəs) *adj.:* directly into a vein. —**intravenously** *adv.*

intrepid (in·trep′id) *adj.:* fearless; brave.

intricate (in′tri·kit) *adj.:* complicated; elaborately detailed.

invalid (in′və·lid) *adj.:* having a long-term illness.

invariable (in·ver′ē·ə·bəl) *adj.:* without exception. —**invariably** *adv.*

irascible (i·ras′ə·bəl) *adj.:* irritable; easily angered.

jostle (jäs′əl) *v.:* bump or shove.

keel (kēl) *v.:* 1. fall over. 2. capsize.

lacerate (las′ər·āt′) *v.:* tear.

lavish (lav′ish) *v.:* give generously.

leer (lir) *v.:* look sideways in an unpleasant way. —**leering** *v.* used as *adj.*

legacy (leg′ə·sē) *n.:* 1. money or property left to someone in a will. 2. something handed down from an ancestor or from the past.

literal (lit′ər·əl) *adj.:* actual. —**literally** *adv.*

loam (lōm) *n.:* rich, dark soil.

lore (lôr) *n.:* knowledge that is passed from person to person, often without being written down.

luxuriant (lug·zhoor′ē·ənt) *adj.:* thick; growing in great abundance.

malicious (mə·lish′əs) *adj.:* spiteful.

mandate (man′dāt′) *v.:* require; formally order.

maneuver (mə·no͞o′vər) *n.:* skillful movement.

mar (mär) *v.:* spoil; make less attractive.

mediate (mē′dē·āt′) *v.:* settle a dispute or argument by bringing the opposing sides together.

migrate (mī′grāt′) *v.:* move from one place to another.

mingle (miŋ′gəl) *v.:* mix.

mirage (mi·räzh′) *n.:* scene or object that looks real but isn't actually there.

misconception (mis′kən·sep′shən) *n.:* false idea.

misgiving (mis′giv′iŋ) *n.:* doubt; uneasy feeling.

mockery (mäk′ər·ē) *n.:* imitation, often to make fun of someone or something.

monosyllabic (män′ō·si·lab′ik) *adj.:* one-syllable.

monotony (mə·nät′′n·ē) *n.:* 1. lack of variation. 2. tiresome sameness.

morose (mə·rōs′) *adj.:* gloomy. —**morosely** *adv.*

mottled (mät′′ld) *adj.:* spotted.

murmur (mur′mər) *v.:* speak softly.

nimble (nim′bəl) *adj.:* moving quickly and lightly.

noncommittal (nän′kə·mit′′l) *adj.:* not admitting or committing to any particular purpose or point of view.

oasis (ō·ā′sis) *n.:* fertile place; place or thing offering welcome relief.

obstinate (äb′stə·nət) *adj.:* stubborn; persistent. —**obstinately** *adv.*

obstruction (əb·struk′shən) *n.:* blockage; hindrance.

omen (ō′mən) *n.:* sign; thing or happening believed to foretell an event.

ominous (äm′ə·nəs) *adj.:* suspicious; threatening; suggesting future problems. —**ominously** *adv.*

opiate (ō′pē·it) *n.:* anything that tends to soothe or calm someone; medicine containing opium or a related drug used to relieve pain.

oppressive (ə·pres′iv) *adj.:* heavy; hard to endure.

---

at, āte, cär; ten, ēve; is, īce; gō, hôrn, look, to͞ol; oil, out; up, fur; ə *for unstressed vowels, as* a *in* ago, u *in* focus; ′ *as in* Latin (lat′′n); chin; she; zh *as in* azure (azh′ər); thin, *the;* ŋ *as in* ring (riŋ)

---

pageant (paj′ənt) *n.:* 1. elaborate parade. 2. drama celebrating a historic or religious event.

palate (pal′ət) *n.:* sense of taste.

palpable (pal′pə·bəl) *adj.:* easily felt or touched.

paraphernalia (par′ə·fər·nāl′yə) *n.:* equipment; gear.

paroxysm (par′əks·iz′əm) *n.:* 1. sudden outburst; spasm. 2. fit of laughter, rage, or sneezing.

pauper (pô′pər) *n.:* very poor person.

peril (per′əl) *n.:* danger.

perplexed (pər·plekst′) *adj.:* puzzled.

perverse (pər·vʉrs′) *adj.:* rebellious; stubbornly disobedient.

petitioner (pə·tish′ən·ər) *n.:* person seeking favors.

pious (pī′əs) *adj.:* 1. showing religious devotion. 2. seemingly virtuous.

piteous (pit′ē·əs) *adj.:* arousing pity or compassion. **—piteously** *adv.*

placid (plas′id) *adj.:* undisturbed; calm; tranquil; untroubled.

pliant (plī′ənt) *adj.:* flexible; adaptable.

plod (pläd) *v.:* trudge; walk heavily.

poignant (poin′yənt) *adj.:* sad; emotionally moving. **—poignantly** *adv.*

ponderous (pän′dər·əs) *adj.:* 1. very heavy. 2. dull.

potent (pōt′′nt) *adj.:* 1. powerful. 2. convincing; influential.

precarious (prē·ker′ē·əs) *adj.:* unsteady; unstable; unsure. **—precariously** *adv.*

preclude (prē·klo͞od′) *v.:* make impossible in advance; prevent.

pretext (prē′tekst′) *n.:* excuse.

privation (prī·vā′shən) *n.:* 1. hardship. 2. lack of something needed for a happy, healthy life.

procession (prō·sesh′ən) *n.:* parade.

proffer (präf′ər) *v.:* offer.

profusion (prō·fyo͞o′zhən) *n.:* large supply; abundance.

prolong (prō·lôŋ′) *v.:* make longer; extend. **—prolonged** *v.* used as *adj.*

proposition (präp′ə·zish′ən) *n.:* suggestion; plan.

prosaic (prō·zā′ik) *adj.:* ordinary.

pummel (pum′əl) *v.:* hit repeatedly.

querulous (kwer′yo͞o·ləs) *adj.:* complaining.

quizzical (kwiz′i·kəl) *adj.:* questioning. **—quizzically** *adv.*

rancid (ran′sid) *adj.:* spoiled; tasting or smelling bad.

rancor (raŋ′kər) *n.:* bitterness; resentment; ill will.

ravage (rav′ij) *v.:* destroy violently; ruin.

realm (relm) *n.:* kingdom.

recoil (ri·koil′) *v.:* move backward, as if in horror. **—recoiling** *v.* used as *adj.*

recollect (rek′ə·lekt′) *v.:* remember.

recount (ri·kount′) *v.:* describe in detail; narrate.

reiterate (rē·it′ə·rāt′) *v.:* repeat.

relinquish (ri·liŋ′kwish) *v.:* surrender.

remonstrance (ri·män′strəns) *n.:* protest.

replica (rep′li·kə) *n.:* model or copy.

repose (ri·pōz′) *n.:* rest.

resound (ri·zound′) *v.:* make a loud echo.

restitution (res′tə·to͞o′shən) *n.:* compensation; repayment.

restive (res′tiv) *adj.:* restless; unsettled.

restriction (ri·strik′shən) *n.:* 1. rule. 2. limitation.

resurrection (rez′ə·rek′shən) *n.:* coming or bringing back to life.

retaliate (ri·tal′ē·āt′) *v.:* cause an injury or wrong in response to one that has been caused.

retribution (re′trə·byo͞o′shən) *n.:* punishment; revenge.

revelry (rev′əl·rē) *n.:* merrymaking; festivity; noisy, lively celebration.

revert (ri·vʉrt′) *v.:* go back, as to a former state.

ruse (ro͞oz) *n.:* trick.

ruthless (ro͞oth′lis) *adj.:* without pity.

sacrilegious (sak′rə·lij′əs) *adj.:* disrespectful of religion.

sage (sāj) *adj.:* wise.

scalpel (skal′pəl) *n.:* knife used by surgeons.

scanty (skan′tē) *adj.:* small; only just enough.

scruples (skro͞o′pəlz) *n.:* feelings of doubt or guilt about a suggested action.

scrutinize (skro͞ot′′n·īz′) *v.:* look at carefully.

scrutiny (skro͞ot′′n·ē) *n.:* close inspection.

sensibility (sen′sə·bil′ə·tē) *n.:* capacity for being emotionally responsive.

serum (sir′əm) *n.:* 1. fluid used in medical treatment. 2. clear, yellowish fluid that is part of blood.

servile (sʉr′vəl) *adj.:* humbly submissive; like a slave.

sever (sev′ər) *v.:* separate; break or cut off.

siege (sēj) *n.:* stubborn, continued effort to win or control something.

silhouette (sil′o͞o·et′) *v.:* show as a dark shape against a light background.

simultaneous (sī′məl·tā′nē·əs) *adj.:* happening at the same time. **—simultaneously** *adv.*

sloop (slo͞op) *n.:* type of sailing ship.

sojourn (sō′jʉrn) *v.:* 1. stay briefly. 2. live temporarily.

solace (säl′is) *n.*: comfort; easing of grief.

solemnity (sə·lem′nə·tē) *n.*: seriousness.

solicitous (sə·lis′ə·təs) *adj.*: showing concern. —**solicitously** *adv.*

solicitude (sə·lis′ə·tōod′) *n.*: concern.

somber (säm′bər) *adj.*: 1. solemn; dull. 2. depressed.

sprawl (sprôl) *v.*: spread out in relaxed position.

squalor (skwäl′ər) *n.*: filth or shabbiness.

squander (skwän′dər) *v.*: waste.

staccato (stə·kät′ō) *adj.*: consisting of short, sharp sounds.

stamina (stam′ə·nə) *n.*: ability to keep going.

starboard (stär′bərd) *adj.*: on the right-hand side of a ship.

stealth (stelth) *n.*: secret or sneaky action or behavior.

stifle (stī′fəl) *v.*: hold back; prevent from being expressed.

stifling (stī′fliŋ) *adj.*: 1. making breathing difficult; suffocating. 2. too close and confining.

stolid (stäl′id) *adj.*: 1. showing no emotion. 2. unexcitable.

stronghold (strôŋ′hōld′) *n.*: place that is strongly built for protection from enemies.

stupefy (stōo′pə·fī′) *v.*: 1. paralyze; make numb. 2. amaze; bewilder. —**stupefying** *v.* used as *adj.*

stupor (stōo′pər) *n.*: dull or half-conscious state of mind.

suave (swäv) *adj.*: gracious and confident; smoothly polite.

subservient (səb·sur′vē·ənt) *adj.*: submissive; showing too great a willingness to serve or obey.

succession (sək·sesh′ən) *n.*: series.

suffuse (sə·fyōoz′) *v.*: spread over or through.

sullen (sul′ən) *adj.*: gloomy.

surmount (sər·mount′) *v.*: be at the top of.

sustenance (sus′tə·nəns) *n.*: 1. nourishment; food. 2. support.

symmetry (sim′ə·trē) *n.*: balanced arrangement.

synchronize (siŋ′krə·nīz′) *v.*: cause to occur at the same rate or time.

synonymous (si·nän′ə·məs) *adj.*: similar in meaning.

tangible (tan′jə·bəl) *adj.*: able to be touched.

taunt (tônt) *v.*: 1. jeer. 2. mock; reproach.

tawdry (tô′drē) *adj.*: cheap and flashy; sleazy.

temperance (tem′pər·əns) *n.*: 1. self-restraint. 2. moderation in drinking alcohol.

tentative (ten′tə·tiv) *adj.*: hesitant; uncertain. —**tentatively** *adv.*

terse (turs) *adj.*: using few words. —**tersely** *adv.*

thoroughbred (thur′ō·bred′) *adj.*: carefully bred, or raised, for a special purpose. The term is often used to describe animals such as racehorses.

tremulous (trem′yōo·ləs) *adj.*: trembling; shaking.

trepidation (trep′ə·dā′shən) *n.*: fearful uncertainty.

tress (tres) *n.*: lock of hair.

truant (trōo′ənt) *adj.*: 1. staying away from school. 2. idle. 3. straying.

tumult (tōo′mult′) *n.*: commotion; uproar; confusion.

uncanny (un·kan′ē) *adj.*: eerily remarkable.

undertow (un′dər·tō′) *n.*: current of water that moves beneath and in a different direction from the surface water.

unencumbered (un·en·kum′bərd) *adj.*: 1. not blocked or cluttered. 2. free to act.

unperturbed (un·pər·turbd′) *adj.*: untroubled; not upset.

unwieldy (un·wēl′dē) *adj.*: awkward; difficult to handle.

veranda (və·ran′də) *n.*: open porch along the outside of a building.

verification (ver′ə·fi·kā′shən) *n.*: proof of accuracy or truth.

verve (vurv) *n.*: liveliness.

vexation (veks·ā′shən) *n.*: annoyance.

vigilant (vij′ə·lənt) *adj.*: 1. alert for danger or trouble. 2. watchful.

virile (vir′əl) *adj.*: strong.

vitality (vī·tal′ə·tē) *n.*: energy.

vivacious (vī·vā′shəs) *adj.*: very lively.

voluminous (və·lōom′ə·nəs) *adj.*: large and bulky.

wince (wins) *v.*: move back slightly, as if in pain.

wither (with′ər) *v.*: dry up; lose freshness.

wrench (rench) *v.*: twist sharply.

zealous (zel′əs) *adj.*: enthusiastic and thorough.

---

at, āte, cär; ten, ēve; is, īce; gō, hôrn, look, tōol; oil, out; up, fur; ə *for unstressed vowels, as* a *in* ago, u *in* focus; ′ *as in* Latin (lat′'n); chin; she; zh *as in* azure (azh′ər); thin, *the*; ŋ *as in* ring (riŋ)

ACKNOWLEDGMENTS

For permission to reprint copyrighted material, grateful acknowledgment is made to the following sources:

American Library Association: Newbery Medal that appears on the jacket cover of *Roll of Thunder, Hear My Cry* by Mildred D. Taylor.

Arte Público Press: "Hate" from *Mainstream Ethics* by Tato Laviera. Copyright © 1988 by Tato Laviera. Published by Arte Público Press—University of Houston, Houston, TX, 1988. "Extranjera legal" (translation of "Legal Alien") by Pat Mora, translated by Nicolás Kanellos. Copyright © 1997 by Nicolás Kanellos. "Legal Alien" from *Chants* by Pat Mora. Copyright © 1984 by Pat Mora. Published by Arte Público Press—University of Houston, Houston, TX, 1984.

Asian American Voices: Untitled essay by Li-Young Lee from *Chinese American Poetry: An Anthology,* edited by L. Ling-chi Wang and Henry Yiheng Zhao. Copyright © 1991 by L. Ling-chi Wang and Henry Yiheng Zhao.

Atheneum Publishers, an imprint of Macmillan Publishing Company: *The Miracle Worker* by William Gibson. Copyright © 1956, 1957 by William Gibson; copyright © 1959, 1969 by Tamarack Productions, Ltd., and George S. Klein and Leo Garel as trustees under three separate deeds of trust; copyright renewed © 1977 by William Gibson. No performance of any kind may be given without permission in writing from the author's agent, Samuel French, Inc., 45 West 25th Street, New York, 10010.

Ballantine Books, a division of Random House, Inc.: Jacket cover from *Dave Barry's Greatest Hits* by Dave Barry, cover photograph by Bill Wax. Copyright © 1988 by Dave Barry. Jacket cover from *Family—The Ties That Bind . . . and Gag!* by Erma Bombeck. Copyright © 1987 by Erma Bombeck. Jacket cover from *Sweet Summer: Growing Up with and Without My Dad* by Bebe Moore Campbell. Copyright © 1989 by Bebe Moore Campbell. Jacket cover from *Homecoming* by Cynthia Voigt. Copyright © 1981 by Cynthia Voigt. Jacket cover from *The Time Machine/The War of the Worlds* by H. G. Wells. Cover copyright © by Ballantine Books, a division of Random House, Inc.

Howard A. Balsam: "Driver's Ed?" by Howard A. Balsam from *Pegasus,* Literary-Arts Publication, vol. XVII, 1990. Copyright © 1990 by Howard A. Balsam. Published by Half Hollow Hills High School East, Dix Hills, NY.

Karma Bene Bambara: Adapted from "What It Is I Think I Am Doing Anyhow" by Toni Cade Bambara from *The Writer on Her Work,* edited by Janet Sternburg. Published by W. W. Norton & Co., Inc., 1980.

Bantam Books, a division of Bantam Doubleday Dell Publishing Group, Inc.: Jacket cover from *Bradbury Classic Stories 1* by Ray Bradbury, cover art by Barclay Shaw. Cover art copyright © 1990 by Barclay Shaw. Jacket cover from *April Morning* by Howard Fast. Copyright © 1961 by Howard Fast.

Elizabeth Barnett, Literary Executor: "An Ancient Gesture" from *Collected Poems* by Edna St. Vincent Millay. Copyright © 1954, 1982 by Norma Millay Ellis. Published by HarperCollins Publishers, Inc.

Susan Bergholz Literary Services, New York: From "My English" by Julia Alvarez. Copyright © 1989 by Julia Alvarez. First published in the "Proceedings of the Ollantay Center Conference." "Snow" from *How the Garcia Girls Lost Their Accents* by Julia Alvarez. Copyright © 1991 by Julia Alvarez. Published by Plume, an imprint of New American Library, a division of Penguin Books USA Inc. First published in hardcover by Algonquin Books of Chapel Hill. "A Conversation with Sandra Cisneros." Copyright © 1997 by Sandra Cisneros. "Those Who Don't" from *The House on Mango Street* by Sandra Cisneros. Copyright © 1984 by Sandra Cisneros. Published in the United States by Vintage Books, a division of Random House, Inc., New York; and in hardcover by Alfred A. Knopf, a division of Random House, Inc., New York, in 1994. "Salvador Late or Early" from *Woman Hollering Creek* by Sandra Cisneros. Copyright © 1991 by Sandra Cisneros. Published in the United States by Vintage Books, a division of Random House, Inc., New York. Originally published in hardcover by Random House, Inc., New York, in 1991.

Yogi Berra: Comment "It ain't over till it's over" by Yogi Berra, 1973.

Black Sparrow Press: "Prologue" from *Counting Myself Lucky: Selected Poems 1963–1992* by Edward Field. Copyright © 1992 by Edward Field.

BOA Editions, Ltd., 92 Park Ave., Brockport, NY 14420: "this morning" from *good woman: poems and a memoir 1969–1980* by Lucille Clifton. Copyright © 1987 by Lucille Clifton. "The Gift" from *Rose* by Li-Young Lee. Copyright © 1986 by Li-Young Lee.

Brandt & Brandt Literary Agents, Inc.: "The Most Dangerous Game" by Richard Connell. Copyright 1924 by Richard Connell; copyright renewed © 1952 by Louise Fox Connell.

George Braziller, Inc.: "Fork" from *Dismantling the Silence* by Charles Simic. Copyright © 1971 by Charles Simic.

Broadside Press: "Ballad of Birmingham" by Dudley Randall. Published by Third World Press.

Gwendolyn Brooks: "Old Mary" and from "We Real Cool" from *Blacks* by Gwendolyn Brooks. Copyright © 1991 by Gwendolyn Brooks. Published by Third World Press, Chicago.

Ashaki M. Brown: "Tick Tock" by Ashaki M. Brown from *Pegasus,* 1991. Copyright © 1991 by Ashaki M. Brown. Published by Brookwood High School, Snellville, Georgia.

Almerina Buzzati, c/o Agenzia Letteraria Internazionale: "The Colomber" from *Restless Nights: Selected Stories of Dino Buzzati,* translated by Lawrence Venuti. Originally published in *Il Colombre;* copyright © 1966 by Arnoldo Mondadori Editore.

Gladys Cardiff: "Combing" from *To Frighten a Storm* by Gladys Cardiff. Copyright © 1976 by Gladys Cardiff. Comment on "Combing" by Gladys Cardiff. Copyright © 1997 by Gladys Cardiff.

Eugenia W. Collier: Comment on "Marigolds" by Eugenia W. Collier. Copyright © 1992 by Eugenia W. Collier. "Marigolds" by Eugenia W. Collier from *Negro Digest,* November 1969. Copyright © 1969 by Johnson Publishing Company, Inc. Slightly adapted.

Columbia University Press: English translations of "Art" by Hjalmar Flax and from "Living Poetry" by Hugo Margenat from *Inventing a Word: An Anthology of Twentieth-Century Puerto Rican Poetry,* edited by Julio Marzán. Copyright © 1980 by Columbia University Press.

Don Congdon Associates, Inc.: "The Gift" by Ray Bradbury. Copyright © 1952 and renewed © 1980 by Ray Bradbury.

The Crisis Publishing Company, Inc.: From "Fanniedell Peeples: A Volunteer of Love" by Denise Crittendon from *The Crisis,* vol. 101, no. 5, July 1994. Copyright © 1994 by The Crisis Publishing Company, Inc.

Crown Publishers, Inc.: From *The Diary of Latoya Hunter* by Latoya Hunter. Copyright © 1992 by Latoya Hunter.

Roald Dahl Nominee Ltd. and Penguin Books Ltd.: Jacket cover from *Boy* by Roald Dahl. Copyright © 1984 by Roald Dahl.

Delacorte Press/Seymour Lawrence, a division of Bantam Doubleday Dell Publishing Group, Inc.: From "The Making of Annie Sullivan" (retitled: "Annie") from *Helen and Teacher* by Joseph P. Lash. Copyright © 1980 by Joseph P. Lash. "Harrison Bergeron" from *Welcome to the Monkey House* by Kurt Vonnegut, Jr. Copyright © 1961 by Kurt Vonnegut, Jr.

Dell Books, a division of Bantam Doubleday Dell Publishing Group, Inc.: Jacket cover from *Stranger with My Face* by Lois Duncan. Copyright © 1981 by Lois Duncan. Jacket cover from *Karen* by Marie Killilea. Copyright 1952 and renewed © 1980 by Marie Killilea. Jacket cover from *Romeo and Juliet/West Side Story.* Copyright © 1965 by Dell Publishing Co., Inc.

Doubleday, a division of Bantam Doubleday Dell Publishing Group, Inc.: "The Birds" from *Kiss Me Again Stranger* by Daphne du Maurier. Copyright 1952 by Daphne du Maurier. From *Anne Frank: The Diary of a Young Girl* by Anne Frank. Copyright 1952 by Otto H. Frank. "The Road Block" ("Get out of the road") by Chora from *An Introduction to Haiku* by Harold G. Henderson. Copyright © 1958 by Harold G. Henderson. "The Lesson of the Moth" from *Archy and Mehitabel* by Don Marquis. Copyright 1927 by Doubleday, a division of Bantam, Doubleday, Dell Publishing Group, Inc. Quotes by Naomi Shihab Nye and Sharon Olds from *The Language of Life: A Festival of Poets* by Bill Moyers. Copyright © 1995 by Public Affairs Television, Inc., and David Grubin Productions, Inc. Quote by Bill Moyers from *The Power of Myth* by Joseph Campbell with Bill Moyers. Copyright © 1988 by Apostrophe S Productions, Inc., and Alfred van der Marck Editions, Inc., for itself and the estate of Joseph Campbell. Jacket cover from *Wanda Hickey's Night of Golden Memories and Other Disasters* by Jean Shepherd. Copyright © 1971 by Jean Shepherd. From *Conversations with Isaac Bashevis Singer* by Isaac Bashevis Singer and Richard Burgin. Copyright © 1978, 1980, 1985 by Isaac Bashevis Singer and Richard Burgin.

Stephen Dunn and David Weiss: Response by Stephen Dunn from "Spending More Time on the Turtle's Back," an interview with Stephen Dunn by David Weiss, from *Seneca Review*, vol. XIV, no. 2, 1984. Copyright © 1984 by Hobart & William Smith Colleges, Geneva, NY.

Dutton Signet, a division of Penguin Books USA Inc.: Adapted footnotes and excerpt by J. A. Bryant, Jr., from *Romeo and Juliet* by William Shakespeare, edited by J. A. Bryant, Jr., Copyright © 1964, 1986, and renewed © 1992 by J. A. Bryant, Jr. Jacket cover from *Frankenstein* by Mary Shelley. Cover copyright © by Dutton Signet.

Anita Endrezze: "The Girl Who Loved the Sky" from *At the Helm of Twilight* by Anita Endrezze. Copyright © 1988 by Anita Endrezze. Published by Broken Moon Press, 1992. Comment on "The Girl Who Loved the Sky" by Anita Endrezze. Copyright © 1997 by Anita Endrezze.

Mari Evans: "If There Be Sorrow" from *I Am a Black Woman* by Mari Evans. Copyright © 1970 by Mari Evans. Published by William Morrow & Co.

Farrar, Straus & Giroux, Inc.: "Filling Station" from *The Complete Poems 1927–1979* by Elizabeth Bishop. Copyright © 1979, 1983 by Alice Helen Methfessel. Jacket design and "Prologue" from *In My Place* by Charlayne Hunter-Gault. Copyright © 1992 by Charlayne Hunter-Gault. Jacket design and "The Washwoman" from *A Day of Pleasure* by Isaac Bashevis Singer. Copyright © 1969 by Isaac Bashevis Singer; Jacket photograph copyright © 1969, 1979, 1983 by Roman Vishniac. "The Puppy" from *Stories and Prose Poems* by Alexander Solzhenitsyn, translated by Michael Glenny. Translation copyright © 1971 by Michael Glenny.

Ellis J. Freedman: From "Ishmael Reed" from *Conversations with Writers II*, Vol. 3. Copyright © 1978 Gale Research Company. "Beware: Do Not Read This Poem" from *New and Collected Poems* by Ishmael Reed. Copyright © 1970 by Ishmael Reed. Originally appeared in *Scholastic Voice*.

Gale Research Inc.: Adapted quote by Judith Ortiz Cofer from "Judith Ortiz Cofer" from *Contemporary Authors: New Revision Series*, vol. 32, edited by James G. Lesniak. Copyright © 1991 by Gale Research Inc. Quotes by Cynthia Rylant from "Cynthia Rylant" from *Something About the Author*, vol. 50, edited by Anne Commire. Copyright © 1988 by Gale Research Inc. Quote by Ruth Sasaki from "R. A. Sasaki" from *Contemporary Authors*, vol. 136, edited by Susan M. Trosky. Copyright © 1992 by Gale Research Inc.

Frances Goldin on behalf of Essex Hemphill: "American Hero" from *Ceremonies: Prose and Poetry* by Essex Hemphill. Copyright © 1992 by Essex Hemphill.

Graywolf Press, Saint Paul, MN: "Independence" from *The Loom and Other Stories* by R. A. Sasaki. Copyright © 1991 by R. A. Sasaki.

Grove Press, Inc.: Quote by Denise Levertov from "Statements on Poetics" from *The New American Poetry*, edited by Donald M. Allen. Copyright © 1959 by Denise Levertov.

Alicia Pax Guevara: "A Vietnam Remembrance" by Alicia Guevara from *The Muse*, vol. 1, May 1993. Published by Marymount School, New York, NY.

Harcourt Brace & Company: From "East Coker" from *Four Quartets* by T. S. Eliot. Copyright 1943 by T. S. Eliot; copyright renewed © 1971 by Esme Valerie Eliot. Quote by W. T. Jewkes from *Man the Voyager* by W. T. Jewkes and Northrop Frye. Copyright © 1974 by Harcourt Brace & Company. "The Necklace" from *Adventures in Reading*, Laureate Edition. Copyright © 1963 by Harcourt Brace & Company; copyright renewed © 1991 by Deborah Jean Lodge, Alice Lodge, Jeanne M. Shutes, Jessica Sand, Lydia Winderman, Florence F. Potell, and Mary Rives Bowman. From "Tentative (First Model) Definitions of Poetry" from *Good Morning, America* by Carl Sandburg. Copyright 1928 and renewed © 1956 by Carl Sandburg. Jacket cover from *Harvest Poems 1910–1960* by Carl Sandburg. Copyright © 1958, 1960 by Carl Sandburg; copyright renewed © 1986, 1988 by Margaret Sandburg. Jacket cover and "Choice: A Tribute to Dr. Martin Luther King, Jr." and from "To the Editor of *Ms.* Magazine" from *In Search of Our Mothers' Gardens: Womanist Prose* by Alice Walker, cover design by Joy Chu, cover photograph by Mark London. Copyright © 1983 by Alice Walker; cover photograph copyright © 1991 by Masterson Productions. "Women" from *Revolutionary Petunias & Other Poems* by Alice Walker. Copyright © 1970 by Alice Walker. "Running, 1933" from *Walking to Sleep: New Poems and Translations* by Richard Wilbur. Copyright © 1968 by Richard Wilbur. Four lines of poetry

by Anita Owen from "Wits, Wags & Literary Weasels" from *The Literary Life and Other Curiosities* by Robert Hendrickson.

HarperCollins Publishers, Inc.: From "I Saw a Wonderful Thing" from *Pilgrim at Tinker Creek* by Annie Dillard. Copyright © 1974 by Annie Dillard. "Americans All" from *Paper Trail* by Michael Dorris. Copyright © 1994 by Michael Dorris. Jacket cover from *The Land I Lost: Adventures of a Boy in Vietnam* by Huynh Quang Nhuong. Text copyright © 1982 by Huynh Quang Nhuong; illustrations copyright © 1982 by Vo-Dinh Mai. Jacket cover from *El Bronx Remembered: A Novella and Stories* by Nicholasa Mohr. Cover illustration copyright © by Joanie Schwarz; cover copyright © 1993 by HarperCollins Publishers. Jacket cover from *A Tree Grows in Brooklyn* by Betty Smith, cover design by Suzanne Noli. Cover illustration © 1992 by Barry Marcus. Jacket cover from *The Other Side of the Mountain* by E. G. Valens, cover photo by Burk Uzzle, cover design by Diana Coe. Copyright © 1966, 1988 by E. G. Valens; photographs copyright © 1966, 1988 by Burk Uzzle. Excerpt and quote from *Black Boy* by Richard Wright. Copyright 1937, 1942, 1944, 1945 by Richard Wright; copyright renewed © 1973 by Ellen Wright. Jacket cover from *American Dragons* by Laurence Yep. Jacket art copyright © 1993 by Kam Mak; jacket copyright © 1993 by HarperCollins Publishers.

Thor Heyerdahl: Jacket cover from *Kon-Tiki* by Thor Heyerdahl, translated by F. H. Lyon. Copyright 1950 by Thor Heyerdahl.

Henry Holt and Company, Inc.: From "The Black Cottage," "Dust of Snow", and "Fire and Ice" from *The Poetry of Robert Frost,* edited by Edward Connery Lathem. Copyright 1951 by Robert Frost; copyright 1923, © 1969 by Henry Holt and Co., Inc. Jacket cover from *You Come Too* by Robert Frost, cover wood engraving by Thomas W. Nason. Copyright 1936, 1942, 1944, 1951, © 1956, 1958, 1962 by Robert Frost; copyright © 1964, 1967, 1970, 1975 by Lesley Frost Ballantine; copyright © 1959 by Henry Holt and Co., Inc. From "The Figure a Poem Makes" from *Selected Prose of Robert Frost*, edited by Hyde Cox and Edward Connery Lathem. Copyright 1946 by Robert Frost; copyright 1939, © 1967 by Henry Holt and Company, Inc. Jacket cover from *Talking to the Sun: An Illustrated Anthology of Poems for Young People* by Kenneth Koch and Kate Farrell. Compilation, introduction, and comments copyright © 1985 by Kenneth Koch and Kate Farrell.

Houghton Mifflin Company: Jacket cover from *The Autobiography of a Face* by Lucy Grealy. Copyright © 1994 by Lucy Grealy; jacket photograph © 1994 by Alen MacWeeney. All rights reserved. Jacket cover from *Ordeal by Hunger: The Story of the Donner Party* by George R. Stewart, cover illustration by Harvey T. Dunn, cover design by Michaela Sullivan. Copyright 1936, © 1960 and renewed © 1963 by George R. Stewart; copyright renewed © 1988 by Theodosia B. Stewart. All rights reserved. Jacket cover from *The Hobbit* by J.R.R. Tolkien. Copyright © 1966 by J.R.R. Tolkien. All rights reserved.

Houghton Mifflin Company/Seymour Lawrence: "All Watched Over by Machines of Loving Grace" from *The Pill Versus the Springhill Mine Disaster* by Richard Brautigan. Copyright © 1965 by Richard Brautigan. All rights reserved.

Houston Chronicle: Adapted from "Eyeglasses for the Mind," an interview with Stephen King, by George Christian from *Houston Chronicle*, September 30, 1979. Copyright © 1979 by Houston Chronicle.

Phillip Whittington Hughes: "So Much Better Back Then" by Whit Hughes from *Earthwinds 1993*, vol. XXII. Copyright © 1993 by Whit Hughes. Published by Jackson Preparatory School, Jackson, Mississippi.

James R. Hurst: "The Scarlet Ibis" by James R. Hurst from *The Atlantic Monthly*, July 1960. Copyright © 1960 by The Atlantic Monthly.

INTERVIEW Inc.: Quote by Sandra Cisneros from "Why Write Now?" from *INTERVIEW*, vol. XXI, no. 5, May 1991. Copyright © 1991 by INTERVIEW. *INTERVIEW* Magazine is published by Brandt Publications.

Alfred A. Knopf, Inc.: "Poison" from *Someone Like You* by Roald Dahl. Copyright © 1950 by Roald Dahl. "Dream Deferred" ("Harlem") from *The Panther and the Lash* by Langston Hughes. Copyright © 1951 by Langston Hughes.

Charles Kuralt: Quote by Charles Kuralt from an article by Arthur Ungar from *The Christian Science Monitor*.

Lescher & Lescher, Ltd., on behalf of Paula Fox: From *A Servant's Tale* by Paula Fox. Copyright © 1994 by Paula Fox.

Lescher & Lescher, Ltd., on behalf of the Estate of Isaac Bashevis Singer: Quote by Isaac Bashevis Singer from "Singer: 'Every Encounter Is to Me a Potential Story' " by Edith Gold from *Authors in the*

News, vol. 2, edited by Barbara Nykoruk. Originally appeared in *Miami Herald*, March 7, 1976.

Little, Brown and Company: From "The Porcupine" from *Verses from 1929 On* by Ogden Nash.

Liveright Publishing Corporation: "in Just-" and "who are you,little i" from *Complete Poems, 1904–1962* by E. E. Cummings, edited by George J. Firmage. Copyright © 1923, 1925, 1926, 1931, 1935, 1938, 1939, 1940, 1944, 1945, 1946, 1947, 1948, 1949, 1950, 1951, 1952, 1953, 1954, 1955, 1956, 1957, 1958, 1959, 1960, 1961, 1962 by E. E. Cummings. Copyright © 1961, 1963, 1966, 1967, 1968 by Marion Morehouse Cummings. Copyright © 1963, 1972, 1973, 1974, 1975, 1976, 1977, 1978, 1979, 1980, 1981, 1982, 1983, 1984, 1985, 1986, 1987, 1988, 1989, 1990, 1991 by the Trustees for the E. E. Cummings Trust. From "A Poet's Advice to Students" from *A Miscellany Revised* by E. E. Cummings, edited by George James Firmage. Copyright 1955 by E. E. Cummings; copyright © 1965 by Marion Morehouse Cummings; copyright © 1958, 1965 by George James Firmage; copyright renewed © 1993 by Marion Morehouse Cummings and George James Firmage.

Wing Tek Lum: "But It Was" from *Expounding the Doubtful Point* by Wing Tek Lum. Copyright © 1987 by Wing Tek Lum.

Gretchen R. Lund: "Photo Album" by Gretchen Lund from *Dead Center Literary Magazine*, vol. XVII, 1991. Copyright © 1991 by Gretchen Lund. Published by Highland Park High School, Highland Park, NJ.

Macmillan Reference USA, a Division of Simon & Schuster: From *Webster's New World Dictionary*, Third College Edition. Copyright © 1988, 1991, 1994 by Simon & Schuster, Inc.

McIntosh and Otis, Inc.: "A Man Called Horse" by Dorothy M. Johnson. Copyright © 1949 and renewed © 1977 by Dorothy M. Johnson.

Merlyn's Pen, Inc.: "Coward" by Drake Bennett from *Merlyn's Pen*, February/March 1993. Copyright © 1993 by Merlyn's Pen, Inc. First appeared in *Merlyn's Pen: The National Magazine of Student Writing*.

N. Scott Momaday: From *The Names: A Memoir* by N. Scott Momaday. Copyright © 1976 by N. Scott Momaday. "Riding Is an Exercise of the Mind" from *The Strange and True Story of My Life with Billy the Kid* by N. Scott Momaday. Copyright © 1985 by N. Scott Momaday.

John Morgan: "Waiting for the Beep" by John Morgan from *Pegasus*, vol. XVIII, 1991. Copyright © 1991 by John Morgan. Published by Half Hollow Hills High School East, Dix Hills, NY.

William Morrow & Company, Inc.: "The World Is Not a Pleasant Place to Be" from *My House* by Nikki Giovanni. Copyright © 1972 by Nikki Giovanni. "The Cyclops in the Ocean" from *Those Who Ride the Night Winds* by Nikki Giovanni. Copyright © 1983 by Nikki Giovanni. "Kidnap Poem" from *The Women and the Men* by Nikki Giovanni. Copyright © 1970, 1974, 1975 by Nikki Giovanni.

New Directions Publishing Corporation: "The Secret" from *Poems 1960–1967* by Denise Levertov. Copyright © 1966 by Denise Levertov.

The New York Times Company: "Darkness at Noon" by Harold Krents from *The New York Times*, May 5, 1978. Copyright © 1978 by The New York Times Company. From "The Private World of Truman Capote" (Part 1), an interview by Anne Taylor Fleming, from *The New York Times Magazine*, July 9, 1978. Copyright © 1978 by The New York Times Company. From "Looking Back at 'The Miracle Worker' on TV" by William Gibson from *The New York Times*, October 14, 1979. Copyright © 1979 by The New York Times Company. From "Public & Private; Enough Bookshelves" by Anna Quindlen from *The New York Times*, August 7, 1991. Copyright © 1991 by The New York Times Company. From "Langston Hughes on the IRT" by Joe Sexton from *The New York Times*, March 2, 1994. Copyright © 1994 by The New York Times Company. From "In America; Romeo and Juliet in Bosnia" by Bob Herbert from *The New York Times*, May 8, 1994. Copyright © 1994 by The New York Times Company. From "Solzhenitsyn Looks Home, to Russia" by Sara Rimer from *The New York Times*, May 26, 1994. Copyright © 1994 by The New York Times Company. From "After the Beats: A New Generation Raises Its Voice in Poetry" by Diana Jean Schemo from *The New York Times*, September 26, 1994. Copyright © 1994 by The New York Times Company. "While We're Young" by Gregg Easterbrook from *The New York Times*, December 23, 1994. Copyright © 1994 by The New York Times Company. "An Open Mind" by Nicole A. Plumail from *The New York Times*, March 25, 1995. Copyright © 1995 by The New York Times Company. From "Sunday View; Perfectly Tuned Actors Hit a High Note" by Margo Jefferson from "Arts & Leisure" from *The New York Times*, April 23, 1995. Copyright © 1995 by The New York Times Company.

The New Yorker: "The Seven Ages of Man" cartoon by S. Harris from *The New Yorker*, April 11, 1994. Copyright © 1994 by Sidney Harris.

W. W. Norton & Company, Inc.: "The Sacred" from *Between Angels* by Stephen Dunn. Copyright © 1989 by Stephen Dunn. Jacket cover from *Shackleton's Boat Journey* by F. A. Worsley, cover design by Tim Gaydos. Copyright © 1977 by W. W. Norton & Company, Inc.

Naomi Shihab Nye: "Daily" and from "Famous" from *Hugging the Jukebox* by Naomi Shihab Nye. Copyright © 1982 by Naomi Shihab Nye.

Harold Ober Associates Incorporated: "Thank You M'am" from *The Langston Hughes Reader*. Copyright © 1958 by Langston Hughes; copyright renewed © 1986 by George Houston Bass.

Harold Ober Associates Incorporated and Yale Collection of American Literature, The Beinecke Rare Book and Manuscript Library, Yale University: Quotations from "Draft Ideas," December 3, 1964, by Langston Hughes, as published in *The Life of Langston Hughes, Vol. II: 1941–1967—I Dream a World* by Arnold Rampersad. Copyright © 1988 by Arnold Rampersad. Manuscript in the James Weldon Johnson Collection, Beinecke Rare Book and Manuscript Library.

Brooke Olson and Voices of Youth: Educational Goals Study Group: From "My Room" by Brooke Olson from *Voices of Youth*, September/October 1993. Copyright © 1993 by Voices of Youth: Educational Goals Study Group.

Orchard Books, New York: From *But I'll Be Back Again* by Cynthia Rylant. Copyright © 1989 by Cynthia Rylant.

Pantheon Books, a division of Random House, Inc.: "How Poetry Comes to Me" from *No Nature: New and Selected Poems* by Gary Snyder. Copyright © 1992 by Gary Snyder.

Penguin Books Ltd: "Silent, but . . ." by Tsuboi Shigeji (p. 191) from *The Penguin Book of Japanese Verse*, translated by Geoffrey Bownas and Anthony Thwaite. Translation copyright © 1964 by Geoffrey Bownas and Anthony Thwaite. Published by Penguin Books, 1964.

Persea Books, Inc.: Jacket cover from *America Street*, edited by Anne Mazer, cover design by REM Studio, Inc. Copyright © 1993 by Anne Mazer. Cover painting *The Block II* by Romare Bearden, 1972, courtesy of ACA Galleries, New York, NY.

Peters Fraser & Dunlop Group Ltd.: "The Sniper" from *The Martyr* by Liam O'Flaherty. Published by Jonathan Cape Ltd.

Prentice Hall, a division of Simon & Schuster, Inc.: From *Three Genres: The Writing of Poetry, Fiction and Drama*, Second Edition, by Stephen Minot. Copyright © 1965, 1971 by Prentice Hall, Inc.

Prentice Hall, Upper Saddle River, New Jersey: From *The Aeneid* by Virgil, translated by Rolfe Humphries. Copyright 1951 by Charles Scribner's Sons.

Princeton University Press: "Ithaca" from *Selected Poems by C. P. Cavafy*, translated by Edmund Keeley and Philip Sherrard. Translation copyright © 1975 by Edmund Keeley and Philip Sherrard. Revised edition, 1992.

Publishers Weekly: From "Michael Dorris," an interview by Dulcy Brainard, from *Publishers Weekly*, vol. 236, no. 5, August 4, 1989. Copyright © 1989 by Publishers Weekly.

Puffin Books, a division of Penguin Books USA Inc.: Jacket cover from *Woodsong* by Gary Paulsen, cover by Neil Waldman. Cover illustration copyright © 1991 by Neil Waldman. Jacket cover from *Roll of Thunder, Hear My Cry* by Mildred D. Taylor, Puffin cover illustration by Max Ginsburg. Cover illustration copyright © 1991 by Max Ginsburg.

The Putnam Publishing Group: "Misspelling" from *On the Road with Charles Kuralt* by Charles Kuralt. Copyright © 1985 by CBS Inc.

Random House, Inc.: "The Round Walls of Home" from *A Natural History of the Senses* by Diane Ackerman. Copyright © 1990 by Diane Ackerman. From Chapter 5 (Retitled: "When I Lay My Burden Down") from *I Know Why the Caged Bird Sings* by Maya Angelou. Copyright © 1969 by Maya Angelou. Slightly adapted. From "On the Pulse of Morning" from *On the Pulse of Morning* by Maya Angelou. Copyright © 1993 by Maya Angelou. "New Directions" from *Wouldn't Take Nothing for My Journey Now* by Maya Angelou. Copyright © 1993 by Maya Angelou. From *Days of Grace* by Arthur Ashe and Arnold Rampersad. Copyright © 1993 by Jeanne Moutoussamy-Ashe and Arnold Rampersad. "Blues Ain't No Mockin Bird" from *Gorilla, My Love* by Toni Cade Bambara. Copyright © 1971 by Toni Cade Bambara. "A Christmas Memory" and excerpt from *A Christmas Memory* by Truman Capote. Copyright © 1956 by Truman Capote. "Poem" from *Mainland* by Victor Hernandez Cruz. Copyright © 1973 by Victor Hernandez Cruz. "Homeless" from *Living Out Loud* by Anna

Quindlen. Copyright © 1987 by Anna Quindlen.

Rembar & Curtis on behalf of Louise Erdrich: From "What My Mother Taught Me: Nests" by Louise Erdrich from *Ladies' Home Journal,* vol. 110, May 1993. Copyright © 1993 by Louise Erdrich.

Lois Rosenthal: From "Writing as Breathing" by Nikki Giovanni from *Writer's Digest,* February 1989. Copyright © 1989 by Nikki Giovanni.

St. Martin's Press, Inc., New York, NY: Quotes by Diane Ackerman from *Contemporary Poets,* Fourth Edition, edited by James Vinson and D. L. Kirkpatrick. Copyright © 1985 by St. James Press. Excerpt (Retitled: "Haven't I Made a Difference!") from *All Things Bright and Beautiful* by James Herriot. Copyright © 1973, 1974 by James Herriot. From "The Books I Almost Never Wrote" (Introduction) from *The Best of James Herriot: Favourite Memories of a Country Vet* by James Herriot. Introduction copyright © 1976, 1977 by James Herriot; copyright © 1982 by The Reader's Digest Association, Inc. Published simultaneously by the Reader's Digest Association and St. Martin's Press, Inc., New York.

Layne Sakwa and Voices of Youth: Educational Goals Study Group: From "A House Is Not a Home" by Layne Sakwa from *Voices of Youth,* September/October 1993. Copyright © 1993 by Voices of Youth: Educational Goals Study Group.

Meredith Anne Schwartz: "Penelope to Ulysses" by Meredith Schwartz from *Dead Center Literary Magazine,* 1992. Copyright © 1992 by Meredith Anne Schwartz. Published by Highland Park High School, Highland Park, New Jersey.

Louise H. Sclove: "Motto for a Doghouse" from *Lyric Laughter* by Arthur Guiterman.

Simon & Schuster, Inc.: From *Parting the Waters* (Retitled: "The Story Behind the Ballad") by Taylor Branch. Copyright © 1988 by Taylor Branch. "Forgive My Guilt" from *Selected Poems* by Robert P. Tristram Coffin. Copyright © 1946 and renewed © 1974 by Robert P. Tristram Coffin. A Macmillan Publication. "The Sea Call" from *The Odyssey: A Modern Sequel* by Nikos Kazantzakis, translated by Kimon Friar. Copyright © 1958 and renewed © 1986 by Simon & Schuster, Inc. From *Shakespeare Set Free: Teaching Romeo and Juliet, Macbeth, and A Midsummer Night's Dream* by The Folger Shakespeare Library, edited by Peggy O'Brien. Copyright © 1993 by The Folger Shakespeare Library.

Dorothy Stafford: "Fifteen" from *Stories That Could Be True* by William Stafford. Copyright © 1964 by William E. Stafford.

Gloria Steinem: Quote by Alice Walker from "Do You Know This Woman? She Knows You: A Profile of Alice Walker" by Gloria Steinem from *Ms.* magazine, June 1982. Copyright © 1982 by Ms. Foundation for Education and Communication, Inc.

The Literary Estate of May Swenson: Comment from "Southbound on the Freeway" from *The Complete Poems to Solve* by May Swenson. Published by Macmillan in 1993. "Southbound on the Freeway" by May Swenson. Copyright © 1963 and renewed © 1991 by May Swenson.

Bob Tester: "Local Review: 'Babe,' the pig, is a blast" by Bob Tester from *Great Falls Tribune,* September 9, 1995. Copyright © 1995 by Bob Tester.

Rosemary A. Thurber: "The Princess and the Tin Box" from *The Beast in Me and Other Animals* by James Thurber. Copyright 1948 by James Thurber; copyright renewed © 1976 by Helen Thurber and Rosemary A. Thurber. Published by Harcourt Brace & Company. "My Fifty Years with James Thurber" from *The Thurber Carnival* by James Thurber. Copyright © 1945 by James Thurber; copyright renewed © 1973 by Helen Thurber and Rosemary A. Thurber. Published by HarperCollins.

Mai Trang: "Childhood" by Mai Trang from *Rites of Passage: A Literary Magazine,* 1991–92. Copyright © 1992 by Mai Trang. Published by Thomas Jefferson High School, Portland, OR.

Charles E. Tuttle Co., Inc., 77 Central Street, Boston, MA: "The old pond" by Matsuo Bashō, "A morning glory" by Chiyo, and "A dragonfly!" by Kobayashi Issa from *Zen Art for Meditation* by Stewart W. Holmes and Chimoyo Horioka. Copyright in Japan © 1973 by Charles E. Tuttle Co., Inc. All rights reserved.

United Press International, Inc.: From "Hundreds of Birds Invade Home in California" by United Press International from *The New York Times,* May 5, 1983. Copyright © 1983 by United Press International, Inc.

The University of Georgia Press: "American History" from *The Latin Deli* by Judith Ortiz Cofer. Copyright © 1993 by Judith Ortiz Cofer. Slightly adapted.

University of Nebraska Press: "Claiming Breath" and untitled poem from *Claiming Breath* by Diane Glancy. Copyright © 1992 by the University of Nebraska Press. Quote by N. Scott Momaday from *Ancestral Voice: Conversations with N. Scott Momaday* by Charles L. Woodard. Copyright © 1989 by the University of Nebraska Press.

The University of North Carolina Press: "Ain't I a Woman?" by Sojourner Truth, adapted by Erlene Stetson, from *Sojourner Truth: God's Faithful Pilgrim* by Arthur Huff Fauset. Copyright © 1938 by The University of North Carolina Press.

University Press of New England: "The Bagel" from *Rescue the Dead* by David Ignatow. Copyright © 1968 by David Ignatow. Published by Wesleyan University Press. "The Talk" from *A Summer Life* by Gary Soto. Copyright © 1990 by University Press of New England.

Suzanne Vega: Lyrics from "Calypso" from *Solitude Standing* by Suzanne Vega. Copyright © 1978 by Suzanne Vega.

Viking Penguin, a division of Penguin Books USA Inc.: Jacket cover from *Not That You Asked* by Andrew A. Rooney, cover design by Melissa Jacoby, cover photograph by Benno Friedman. Cover photograph copyright © 1989 by Random House, Inc. Jacket cover from *Travels with Charley* by John Steinbeck. Copyright © 1961, 1962 by The Curtis Publishing Co.; copyright © 1962 by John Steinbeck; copyright renewed © 1990 by Elaine Steinbeck, Thom Steinbeck, and John Steinbeck IV.

Vintage Books, a division of Random House, Inc.: Jacket cover from *My Ántonia* by Willa Cather, cover illustration by Sally Mara Sturman, cover design by Susan Mitchell. Cover copyright © by Vintage Books, a division of Random House, Inc. From the *Odyssey* by Homer, translated by Robert Fitzgerald. Copyright © 1961, 1963 by Robert Fitzgerald; copyright renewed © 1989 by Benedict R. C. Fitzgerald.

The Wall Street Journal: From "Juliet of Verona Gets a Lot of Letters from the Lovelorn" by Lisa Bannon from *The Wall Street Journal,* November 10, 1992. Copyright © 1992 by Dow Jones & Company, Inc. All rights reserved worldwide.

Warner Books, Inc.: Jacket cover from *To Kill a Mockingbird* by Harper Lee. Copyright © 1960 by Harper Lee; cover copyright © 1987 by Warner Books.

Robynn Waterstrat and Young Voices Magazine, subscriptions, guidelines, and sample copies, P.O. Box 2321, Olympia, WA 98507, (206) 943–3711: "The Orca" by Robynn Waterstrat from *Young Voices,* May/June 1993. Copyright © 1993 by Robynn Waterstrat.

The Waterways Project of Ten Penny Players, Inc.: "In the Dark" by Leeann Watkins from *Streams* [4].

James Welch: "The Man from Washington" from *Riding the Earthboy 40* by James Welch. Copyright © 1971 by James Welch.

Halley Wheeless and Voices of Youth: Educational Goals Study Group: "A Chance Meeting" by Halley Wheeless from *Voices of Youth Magazine,* September/October 1993. Copyright © 1993 by Voices of Youth: Educational Goals Study Group.

Kate Wilkinson and Voices of Youth: Educational Goals Study Group: From "Para Mi Emilio, Señor" by Kate Wilkinson from *Voices of Youth,* April/May 1993. Copyright © 1993 by Voices of Youth: Educational Goals Study Group.

Elizabeth Wong: "The Struggle to Be an All-American Girl" by Elizabeth Wong.

William K. Zinsser: From "Rewriting and Word Processing" and from "Simplicity" from *On Writing Well,* Fifth Edition, by William K. Zinsser. Copyright © 1976, 1980, 1985, 1988, 1990, 1994 by William K. Zinsser.

Zondervan Publishing House, a division of HarperCollins Publishers: Jacket cover from *Quiet Strength* by Rosa Parks with Gregory J. Reed, cover design by John M. Lucas. Copyright © 1994 by Rosa Parks.

"The Loophole of Retreat" from *Incidents in the Life of a Slave Girl* by Harriet A. Jacobs has been slightly adapted.

PICTURE CREDITS

viii, (top) The Journey (1991) © Mel Rosas/courtesy Maxwell David-son Gallery, New York, (bottom) courtesy of the National Museum of the American Indian, Smithsonian Institution (17/8027); ix, (left) Mom Alice (1944) by William Johnson, The Howard University Gallery of Art, Washington, D.C., (right) © Muky Munkacsi, courtesy Frank Perry; x, (top left) © Gianfranco Gorgoni/Woodfin Camp & Associates, (bottom left) Oregon Historical Society (OrHi62660), (right) Gee's Bend (1947) by Jacob Lawrence, Evansville Museum of Arts and Science, Evansville, Indiana; xi, (left) © David Young-Wolff/Tony Stone Images, (right) © Dave Wilhelm/The Stock Mar-ket; xii, (left) Washing a Dish (1986) by Candida Alvarez, photo by Manu Sassoonian, courtesy June Kelly Gallery, New York, (right) © Charles Moore/Black Star; xiii, (left) America Hurrah, New York, (top right) Corbis-Bettmann, (bottom right) © Gregory Heisler/The Image Bank; xiv, (top) Dialogue of Two Poets Disguised as Birds (1988) by Alfredo Castasguised as Birdsu Sassoonian, courtesy June Kelly Gallery, New York, (right) © Charles MooreA Magician Turn-ing Paper into Cranes (detail) (1819) from the Manga (a book of hu-morous sketches), vol. 10, by Katsushika Hokusai, The Metropolitan Museum of Art, New York, Rogers Fund, 1931 (JIB 81.10); xv, (left) First Steps (19th century), after Millet by Vincent van Gogh, The Metropolitan Museum of Art, New York, gift of George N. and Helen M. Richard, 1964 (64.165.2), photograph by Malcolm Varon, (right) Highway Patrol (1986) by James Doolin, courtesy of Koplin Gallery, Santa Monica, CA; xvi, (left) © David Young Wolff/Tony Stone Images, (right) Iroquois bone comb, Herbert Bigford, Sr., collection, Longyear Museum of Anthropology, Colgate University, Hamilton, NY; xvii, (left) Lewis Archibald/Everett Collection, (right) Theatre Virginia, Richmond; xviii, (top) Romeo and Juliet for Circle in the Square, New York, 1977, directed by Theodore Mann, designed by Ming Cho Lee, photo courtesy of Ming Cho Lee, (middle) Everett Collection, (bottom) © 1980 Jack Vartoogian; xix, (top) Scala/Art Resource, New York, (middle) Badisches Landesmuseum, Karlsruhe, Germany, (bottom) © Farrell Grehan/Photo Researchers, Inc.; xx, (top) Penelope (detail) (1864) by John Roddam Spencer-Stanhope, The De Morgan Foundation/The Bridgeman Art Library, London, (bottom) Return of Odysseus (5th century B.C., first half), The Metropolitan Museum of Art, Fletcher Fund, 1930 (30.11.9); 2, AP/Wide World Photos; 4, © Adam Woolfitt/Woodfin Camp & As-sociates, (left) © Charles Traub; 4–5, © Louis H. Jawitz/The Image Bank; 6–10, © Karen Daher/Gamma Liaison; 11, © Larry Mayer/Gamma Liaison; 25, © Kaz Mori/The Image Bank; 28, courtesy Brandt & Brandt Literary Agents, Inc.; 34–35, © Jacana/The Image Bank; 36, © Dan Hummel/The Image Bank; 37, © Steve Wylymz/Comstock; 38, © Steve Wylymz/Comstock; 40, © Harold Sund/The Image Bank; 40–41, © James Stevenson/Photo Researchers, Inc.; 42–43, © David Weintraub/Photo Researchers, Inc.; 71, © Topham/The Image Works; 72, © Michael Venture/Bruce Coleman, Inc.; 74, Photofest; 85, © Nancy Crampton; 86, © Tom McHugh/The National Audubon Society Collection/Photo Researchers, Inc.; 90–91, © Steve Dunwell/The Image Bank; 99, © Charles S. Collier; 100, © Robert Bull; 104–109, (background) Memphis and Shelby County Room, Memphis/Shelby County Public Library and Informa-tion Center; 106, © Costa Manos/Magnum Photos, Inc.; 109, Corbis-Bettmann; 111, (top) Houghton Mifflin © 1966, (bottom) Max Gins-burg © 1991 by Max Ginsburg; 119, © Sue Klemens/Stock Boston, Inc.; 125, © Henri Cartier-Bresson/Magnum Photos, Inc.; 126, © Scott Thode; 132–133, photography by David Allison, New York; 139, © Leonard Freed/Magnum Photos, Inc.; 148, © Murray Al-cosser/The Image Bank; 154, © Nancy Crampton; 156, (left) © Muky, courtesy Frank Perry, (right) © Muky, courtesy Frank Perry; 157, (left) Photofest; 158, (left) Photofest, (right) © Muky, courtesy Frank Perry; 159, (left) © Muky, courtesy Frank Perry, (right) Photofest; 160, FPG International; 164, © G. K. & Vicki Hart/The Image Bank; 170, photo © Dave Heald; 178, Montana Historical Society, Helena; 182–185, (background) © Mike Mazzaschi/Stock Boston, Inc.; 182, © Luis Castaneda/The Image Bank; 184, AP/Wide World Photos; 186, © Marcel Isy-Schwart/The Image Bank; 191, The Jewish Museum/Art Resource, New York; 192, © Nancy Crampton; 193, (top left) © 1991 by Neil Waldman, (bottom left) Alen Mac Weeney © 1994, (top right) Warner © 1987, (bottom right) © 1992 Charlayne Hunter-Gault; 201, © de Cossy/The Image Bank; 207, Corbis-Bettmann; 208, © Mike Yamashita/Woodfin Camp & Associates; 214–216, (background) Phototone; 214–215, © Nuridsany et Peren-nou/Science Source/Photo Researchers, Inc.; 215, © Terry Vine/Tony

Stone Images; 216, courtesy Algonquin Books; 220, Monica Steven-son; 223, Corbis-Bettmann; 228, Brown Brothers; 232–233, © Fran-cisco Hidalgo/The Image Bank; 234–239, (background) © David Hamilton/The Image Bank; 234, © Catherine Ursillo/Photo Re-searchers, Inc.; 236, Scala/Art Resource, New York; 237, © RB stu-dio/The Stock Market; 239, © Gianfranco Gorgoni/Woodfin Camp & Associates; 240, (background) © Francisco Hidalgo/The Image Bank; 240, Corbis-Bettmann; 244, Corbis-Bettmann; 245, © Guy Marche/FPG International; 247, © Henri Cartier-Bresson/Magnum Photos, Inc.; 249, (top) © by Dutton Signet, (middle) © by Ballantine Books, (bottom) Barclay Shaw © 1990; 257, © Tim Davis/Photo Re-searchers, Inc.; 258–259, © Gary Cralle/The Image Bank; 260, (back-ground) © Gary Cralle/The Image Bank, © Marc Romanelli/The Image Bank; 261, © Kenneth Johansson/Outline Press; 267, National Museum of American Art, Washington, D.C./Art Resource, New York; 269, © Garry Gray/The Image Bank; 274, Annie Valva; 278–279, © Mark Lewis/Gamma Liaison; 281, © Elisa Leonelli/Tony Stone Images; 282–283, © Stephen Frisch/Stock Boston, Inc.; 284, © David Young-Wolff/Tony Stone Images; 285, courtesy Susan Sasaki; 288, © David Nunuk/The National Audubon Society Collection/ Photo Researchers, Inc.; 297, Arte Publico Press, University of Hous-ton; 298, © Rusing Photography; 302–308, (background) © Michael Melford/The Image Bank; 302–303, Oregon Historical Society, #OrHi62660; 303, Oregon Historical Society, #OrHi36112; 306, © Richard Erdoes; 308, photo courtesy of the Newberry Library Archives, The Newberry Library; 309, photographer, L. A. Huffman, Montana Historical Society, Helena; 310, photo courtesy of the De-troit Institute of Arts, Detroit, © Dirk Bakker, photographer; 312, photographer, L. A. Huffman, Montana Historical Society, Helena; 314, FPG International; 314–315, © Erich Hartmann/Magnum Photos, Inc.; 318–319, © Eastcott/Momatiuk/Woodfin Camp & Associates; 323, © Margarette Mead/The Image Bank; 324, Giraudon/Art Re-source, New York; 326, © Deborah Gilbert/The Image Bank; 328–329, © Karen Kasmauski/Woodfin Camp & Associates; 331, (top left) REM studio © 1993 by Anne Mazur, (bottom left) © 1989 by Ballantine, (top right) cover design by Suzanne Noli, cover illustra-tion © 1992 by Barry Marcus, (bottom right) jacket art © 1993 by Kam Mak, jacket © 1993 by HarperCollins; 340–341, © Dave Wil-helm/The Stock Market; 342, (top) © Ruben Guzman, courtesy Knopf Publishers; 344–345, © Geoffrey Gove/The Image Bank; 347, © H. Jawitz/The Image Bank; 348–349, Louis A. Warren Lincoln Li-brary and Museum, Fort Wayne, Indiana; 349, Illinois State Historical Library; 350, Library of Congress; 352, Louis A. Warren Lincoln Li-brary and Museum, Fort Wayne, Indiana; 356–357, © William Strode/Woodfin Camp & Associates; 361, © Nancy Crampton; 362, © Mike Mazzaschi/Stock Boston, Inc.; 364, Library of Congress; 366, © Charles Moore/Black Star; 369, © Richard Howard; 370, (top) © Penni Gladstone/Outline Press, (bottom) © Ernst Haas/Magnum Pho-tos, Inc.; 373, Library of Congress; 376, photograph, Manu Sassoon-ian; 378, M. L. Marinelli; 379, The Bridgeman Art Library, London; 384, photo courtesy of Broadside Press, Detroit, Michigan; 385, (top left) © 1958, 1980 by Marie Killilea, (bottom left) © 1984 by Roald Dahl, (top right) jacket photograph © 1969, 1979, 1983 by Roman Vishniac, (bottom right) cover illustration © 1993 by Joanie Schwarz; 393, © L. George/H. Armstrong Roberts; 396, Orchard Books; 400–401, © Marcia Keegan/The Stock Market; 403, © Nancy Cramp-ton; 406–407, © Peter Miller 1989/The Image Bank; 409, © Bullaty Lomeo/The Image Bank; 410–411, © Adam Woolfitt/Woodfin Camp & Associates; 413, © Steve Proehl/The Image Bank; 415, © Barry Lewis 1994/Network/Matrix; 416, © Peter Beck 1993/The Stock Market; 418, © P. Royer/H. Armstrong Roberts; 420–421, NASA; 422, © Nancy Crampton; 422–423, © K. Iwasaki/The Stock Market; 426, The Schomburg Center for Research in Black Culture, The New York Public Library, Astor, Lenox and Tilden Foundations; 426–427, Library of Congress; 430, The Schomburg Center for Research in Black Culture, The New York Public Library, Astor, Lenox and Tilden Foundations; 434–435, © Beverly Sedan/The Image Bank; 436, © Joanna Eldredge Morrissey/W. W. Norton; 437, (top) © 1981 by Cynthia Voight, (middle) © 1961, 1962 by the Curtis Publishing Group, (bottom) illustration © 1982 by Vo-Dihn Mai; 445, Athena Blackorby; 446–447, © John Smart; 447, National Portrait Gallery, Washington, D.C./Art Resource, New York; 448, Corbis-Bettmann; 448–449, © John Smart; 455, © Patti McConville/The Image Bank; 457, Harvard Law Art Collection, photographer, Gwendolyn Stewart Brooks; 461, America Hurrah, New York City; 463, © Joyce Ravid/Onyx; 464, © Bob Daemmrich/The Image Works; 465, Amer-

INDEX OF SKILLS

Literary Terms

Reading and Critical Thinking

Vocabulary and Spelling

380, 386-391
Narrowing a topic 858, 871
Newspaper article 44, 339
Note taking 11, 46, 88, 120, 194, 201, 217, 328, 339, 347, 353, 364, 373, 386, 404, 418, 438, 466, 485, 508, 519, 529, 535, 539, 556, 566, 583, 585, 597, 605, 609, 631, 687, 708, 716, 720, 723, 817, 936, 942, 962, 965, 983
Objective criteria 332-335
Observational essay 128, 142, 162, 180, 187, 194-199, 424
Occasion 438
Onomatopoeia collection 575
Opinion 288, 418, 466
Oral history 339, 609
Order of importance 479, 873
Organization
  block method 616
  cause-and-effect order 873
  chronological order 44, 113, 872-873
  flashback 44, 113
  order of importance 479, 873
  point-by-point method 616
  spatial order 873
  time order 872-873
Paragraph 88, 210, 276, 326, 418, 459, 498, 513, 529, 545, 609, 708, 924, 950
Paraphrase 539, 835
Peer review (peer editing) 116, 198-199, 254, 336-337, 390, 442, 481-482, 484, 720, 874-875, 962
Personal essay 965
Personality profile 859, 965
Personification 508, 575, 924
Persuasive writing 263, 276, 288, 300, 312, 326, 332-337, 450, 458, 466, 472, 478-483, 924, 958-963
Pet story 418
Photo essay 723
Place description 373, 398, 472
Poem, evaluation of a 545
Poetry writing 44, 128, 162, 187, 276, 330, 498, 508, 513, 529, 535, 539, 545, 550-552, 563, 569, 575, 597, 600, 605
Point of view 230, 242, 250-251, 312, 326, 364
Portfolio building 30, 44, 74, 88, 102, 112-117, 118, 128, 142, 162, 180, 187, 194-199, 200, 210, 217, 230, 242, 250-255,

256, 263, 276, 288, 300, 312, 326, 332-337, 338, 353, 364, 373, 380, 386-391, 392, 398, 404, 418, 424, 432, 438-443, 444, 450, 458, 466, 472, 478-483, 484, 498, 508, 513, 516-518, 529, 535, 539, 545, 550-552, 558, 563, 569, 575, 578, 582-584, 597, 600, 605, 609, 614-619, 620, 661, 687, 708-709, 716-721, 722, 763, 789, 817, 834, 858-859, 866-869, 870-875, 876, 924, 949-950, 958-963, 964
Prewriting 112-113, 194-195, 250-251, 332-335, 386-387, 438-439, 478-479, 550-551, 614-616, 716-717, 870-873, 958-961, 981
Problem solution 187, 339, 466, 485, 621, 723, 877, 965
Prologue 817
Promptbook 868
Proofreading 75, 89, 116, 199, 200, 231, 254-255, 256, 289, 337, 354, 391, 425, 433, 443, 473, 483, 618, 720, 875, 963
Proposal for TV special 263
Prose poem 597
Public service announcement 723
Publishing 116, 199, 254, 337, 391, 443, 483, 618, 720, 875, 963
Quatrain 552
Quickwrite 46, 76, 90, 120, 132, 182, 202, 214, 220, 232, 244, 258, 266, 278, 290, 302, 328, 348, 356, 375, 387, 434, 454, 468, 474, 494, 496, 499, 502, 504, 509, 514, 522, 524, 526, 530, 533, 536, 540, 542, 556, 561, 564, 566, 570, 572, 576, 579, 588, 590, 598, 601, 606, 610, 732, 862, 871, 890
Reflecting 116, 117, 187, 199, 255, 337, 339, 389, 391, 443, 483, 485, 515, 549, 584, 618-619, 621, 720, 875, 877, 963, 965
Reflective essay 398, 404, 418, 424, 432, 438-443
Report 44, 88, 180, 187, 217, 242, 276, 300, 312, 609, 763, 789, 817, 834, 858, 859, 870-875, 981-984
Revising 31, 45, 75, 116-117, 118, 129, 181, 198-199, 200, 211, 254, 255, 256, 289, 301, 326,

327, 336-337, 338, 390, 392, 405, 441-442, 444, 467, 481-483, 484, 618, 619, 620, 720, 721, 722, 789, 874-875, 876, 962, 964, 981, 986, 997, 1000, 1002, 1008, 1009, 1013, 1015, 1017, 1028
Rhyme 552
Rhymed couplet 552
Road poem 605
Scene 288, 708, 858
Script 558, 563, 575, 578, 584, 924
Self-evaluation 116, 199, 337, 441-442, 482-483, 720, 875, 962
Sensory details 162, 194-195, 386
Sequel 30, 210, 230, 708, 858, 949
Setting 74, 180, 195, 263
Short short story 210, 217, 230, 242, 250-255
Simile 529, 925
Society column 763
Soliloquy 877
Song 330
Sound devices 569, 575
Spatial order 873
Speculation about causes or effects 924, 949, 958-963
Speech 44, 242, 450, 606
Sports reporting 575
Story 242, 364, 949
Story map 44, 210
Storyboard 288
Style 31, 45, 103, 129, 163, 181, 211, 243, 277, 301, 313, 327, 365, 374, 405, 419, 451, 459, 467, 789, 925, 951
Summary 276
Supporting evidence 333, 479
Symbol 687, 717
Theme, writing about 288, 708
Thesis statement 450, 478, 479, 616, 717
Thought connections 438-439
Time capsule 210
Time line 353
Tips for spelling 998, 1004, 1015, 1019
Tips for writers 89, 103, 994, 997, 1000, 1002, 1008, 1009, 1013, 1015, 1016, 1017, 1028, 1030
Title, writing about a 276
Tone 335, 380
Topic, choosing a 112, 194, 250, 332, 386, 438, 478, 550-551, 614-615, 716-717, 870-871, 958-959
Transitional expressions 618

Crossing the Curriculum

INDEX OF ART

Fine Art

INDEX OF AUTHORS AND TITLES

Page numbers in italic type refer to the pages on which author biographies appear.

Index of Student Authors